Family Factbook

Reference books published by Marquis Academic Media

Annual Register of Grant Support
Consumer Protection Directory
Directory of Publishing Opportunities
Directory of Registered Lobbyists and Lobbyist Legislation
Environmental Protection Directory
Family Factbook
Grantsmanship: Money and How To Get It
NASA Factbook
NIH Factbook
NSF Factbook
Sourcebook of Equal Educational Opportunity
Sourcebook on Aging
Sourcebook on Food and Nutrition
Standard Education Almanac
Standard Medical Almanac
Yearbook of Adult and Continuing Education
Yearbook of Higher Education
Yearbook of Special Education
Worldwide Directory of Computer Companies
Worldwide Directory of Federal Libraries

Family Factbook®

First edition

Consulting editor:

Dr. Helena Znaniecki Lopata
Center for the Comparative Study of Social Roles
Loyola University of Chicago

Marquis Academic Media
Marquis Who's Who, Inc.
200 East Ohio Street
Chicago, Illinois 60611

Library of Congress Card Number 78-50451
International Standard Book Number 0-8379-4601-8
Product Code Number 031067

Manufactured in the United States of America.

Contents

Preface : xi

Part one. Family (general) : 1

Family (general)

Results of Social Change: Social Institutions-Community-Family : 3
Helena Znaniecki Lopata

Interpersonal Relationships and Changing Perspectives on the Family : 9
Nona Glazer-Malbin

Family Time and Historical Time : 25
Tamara K. Hareven

Statistics

Households, by Race of Head, and Population per Household: 1930 to 1976 : 38

Households, Families, Subfamilies, Married Couples, and Unrelated Individuals: 1950 to 1976 : 38

Households, by Number of Persons: 1950 to 1976 : 39

Households, Families, and Individuals—Projections: 1977 to 1990 : 39

Households—States: 1950 to 1975 : 40

Households and Families, by Type of Head: 1960 to 1976 : 41

Households, by Selected Characteristics of Head: 1968 to 1976 : 41

Families, by Characteristics: 1960 to 1976 : 42

Families Not Headed by a Husband and Wife: 1960 to 1976 : 42

Households, Families, Subfamilies, Married Couples, and Unrelated Individuals: 1790 to 1970 : 43

Annual Estimates of the Population, by Age: 1900 to 1970 : 44

Median Age of the Population, by Race, Sex, and Nativity: 1790 to 1970 : 45
U.S. Bureau of the Census

Part two. Adults : 47

Men's and women's roles

The Work-Family Role System : 49
Joseph H. Pleck

Changes in Family Roles, Socialization, and Sex Differences : 59
Lois Wladis Hoffman

Wives and mothers

Marital Status and Family : 73
Arlene Kaplan Daniels

Legal Status of the Homemaker in the Fifty States : 78
Editors of the World Almanac

Housework: A Review Essay : 87
Nona Glazer-Malbin

Motherhood, Family Planning, and Child Care : 94
Barbara Everitt Bryant
Family Life Cycle Events : 101
Paul C. Glick and Arthur J. Norton

Fathers
Fathers : 106
Carlfred Broderick
Single-parent Fatherhood: An Emerging Family Life Style : 113
Dennis K. Orthner, Terry Brown, and Dennis Ferguson

Parents
Parent and Family Life Education : 122
Douglas B. Bailey and Robert L. Lindamood
Programs for Parents of Infants and Young Children : 125
The Education Commission of the States Early Childhood Project
Female Family Heads—Characteristics, by Race: 1960 to 1976 : 130
U.S. Bureau of the Census

Marriage
Process in Marriage: Power, Negotiation, and Conflict : 131
Letha Scanzoni and John Scanzoni
Marriage: Focus on Change (with a new section, Divorce in the United States) : 175
Elizabeth Wright
Marrying, Divorcing, and Living Together in the U. S. Today : 188
Paul C. Glick and Arthur J. Norton
Marital Status of the Population, by Sex: 1940 to 1976 : 199
Marital Status of the Black Population: 1960 to 1976 : 199
Marital Status of the Spanish-Origin Population: 1970 to 1976 : 200
Marital Status of the Population, by Sex and Age: 1976 : 200
Number, Timing, and Duration of Marriages and Divorces in the United States: June 1975 : 201
U.S. Bureau of the Census

Mid-life transition
Mid-life Transition and Contextual Change : 212
Phyllis Handelman

Widowhood
Widowhood: Social Norms and Social Integration : 217
Helena Znaniecki Lopata

Part three. Children : 227

Children (general)
Current Status and Future Prospects for the Nation's Children and Their Families : 229
John H. Meier
The Need for States to Provide Services to Parents with Young Children : 243
The Education Commission of the States Early Childhood Project
Title XX: Social Services in Your State: A Child Advocate's Handbook for Action : 246
Children's Defense Fund of the Washington Research Project, Inc.

Child development
Baby Carriers in Bolivia and Sweden : 270
Kamala Ditella and John Lind
The Kibbutz as a Social Experiment and as a Child-Rearing Laboratory : 272
Benjamin Beit-Hallahmi and Albert I. Rabin
Longitudinal IQ Outcomes of the Mother-Child Home Program : 282
John Madden, Phyllis Levenstein, and Sidney Levenstein
A Pilot with a Difference : 292
Elizabeth Urrows and Henry Urrows
Father Caretaking Characteristics and Their Influence on Infant-Father Interaction : 295
Milton Kotelchuck

Television and Free Time : 301
Marie Winn Miller

Day care

Serving Prechool Children : 321
Donald J. Cohen, in collaboration with Ada S. Brandegee

Family Day Care: An Education and Support System Model Developed by Cooperative Extension of New York State : 351
Natalie D. Crowe and Barbara A. Pine

National Summary of Type of Day Care : 359
U.S. Department of HEW, Office of Human Development

Child abuse

The Diagnostic Process and Treatment Programs : 368
Ray E. Helfer

American Humane Association Publishes Highlights of National Study of Child Neglect and Abuse Reporting for 1975 : 375
Vincent De Francis

Working with Abusive Parents : 378
An Interview with Jolly K. by Judith Reed

HEW News, Monday, January 7, 1977 : 381
Administration for Children, Youth and Families

Child Abuse and Neglect: The Alcohol Connection : 382
Margaret Hindman

Adolescents

Early Adolescents: Neglected, Misunderstood, Miseducated : 387
Karl N. Stauber

Programs for Adolescents : 390
The Education Commission of the States Early Childhood Project

Group Foster Homes : 393
Dodie Butler, with Joe Reiner, and Bill Treanor

Statistics

Day Care Arrangements of Children 3 to 13 Years Old, by Selected Characteristics: 1974 and 1975 : 408
Persons under 18 Years Old, by Presence of Parents and Whether Living with Mother Only, by Marital Status of Mother: 1968 to 1976 : 409
Percent Distribution of Families, by Number of Own Children under 18 Years old: 1950 to 1976 : 409
Child Adoptions—Selected States and Puerto Rico: 1970 and 1975 : 409
Child Adoptions, by Type: 1952 to 1971 : 410
Orphans, by Type: 1955 to 1976 : 410
Juveniles Held in Custody, by Type of Facility—Summary: 1974 and 1975 : 410
Children's Cases Disposed of by Juvenile Courts: 1960 to 1974 : 411
Juvenile Court-Cases Handled: 1940 to 1970 : 411
Persons in Custody in Training Schools for Juvenile Delinquents and in Detention Homes: 1950, 1960, and 1970 : 411
U.S. Bureau of the Census

Part four. Health : 413

Health (general)

Persons with a Usual Place of Medical Care : 415
Usual Place of Medical Care : 416
Persons with Barriers to Medical Care : 419
Contraceptive Use by Currently Married Women 15-44 Years : 421
Life Expectancy at Specified Ages : 423
Death Rates : 424
Persons Exercising Regularly and Type of Exercise : 425
Obesity among Persons Aged 20-74 Years Based on Triceps Skinfold Measurements : 425
Venereal Disease Cases, According to Type : 426
Consumption of Alcohol by Persons 18 Years of Age and Over : 428

Smoking Status of Persons 21 Years of Age and Over : 429
Consumer Products with the Highest Product Hazard Index Scores : 430
U.S. Department of HEW, Public Health Service, Health Resources Administration
Helping People at Home in Sweden and the Netherlands : 432
Alfred J. Kahn and Sheila B. Kamerman
Family Therapy in Alcoholism : 447
Margaret Hindman

Childbirth

Births to Date and Lifetime Births Expected per 1,000 Women by Race and Marital Status: June 1976 : 454
Children Ever Born Born per 1,000 Women by Race and Marital Status, and Percent Childless for Women Ever Married: 1960 to 1976 : 455
Fertility Rate and Birth Rate, by Age of Mother, by Race: 1940 to 1970 : 456
Birth Rate, by Race, by Live-Birth Order: 1940 to 1970 : 457
Median Interval between Births, by Race: 1930 to 1969 : 458
U.S. Bureau of the Census
Choices in Childbirth—The Nurse-Midwifery Service at San Francisco General Hospital : 459
Judith Goldschmidt and Rosemary Mann

Children

Height of Children and Youths at Selected Percentiles, According to Sex and Age: United States : 462
Weight of Children and Youths at Selected Percentiles, According to Sex and Age: United States : 463
Self-assessed Drinking Levels of Junior and Senior High School Students, According to Marijuana Use, Use of Hard Drugs, and School Grades: United States, Spring 1974 : 464
Current Cigarette Smoking among Persons 12-18 Years of Age, According to Sex and Age: United States, Selected Years 1968-74 : 465
U.S. Department of HEW, Public Health Service, Health Resources Administration
What Difference Does Health Care Make in the Lives of Children? : 466
Major Federal Programs Which Finance or Provide Health Services for Children and Expectant Mothers : 471
Children's Defense Fund of the Washington Research Project, Inc.

Part five. Work and income : 475

Work and income

The Working Family in Crisis: Who is Listening? : 477
Nancy Seifer
Money Income and Poverty Status of Families and Persons in the U.S.: 1975 and 1974 Revisions : 488
Familes and Unrelated Individuals by Total Money Income in 1975 : 489
Selected Characteristics of All Families—Number of Families, Median Income, Mean Income, and Standard Errors, by Race of Head and Spanish Origin of Head: 1975, 1974 (Revised), and 1974 : 490
Selected Characteristics for Families with Heads Working Year Round Full Time—Number of Families, Median Income, Mean Income, and Standard Errors, by Race of Head and Spanish Origin of Head: 1975, 1974 (Revised), and 1974 : 493
Family Income in 1947, 1950, 1955, 1960, 1965, and 1967 to 1975—Families by Total Money Income, by race of Head : 496
Family Income in 1947, 1950, 1955, 1960, 1965, and 1967 to 1975—Families by Total Money Income in Constant Dollars, by Race of Head : 497
Age of Head—Families and Unrelated Individuals by Total Money Income: 1975 and 1974 (Revised) : 498
Selected Characteristics of All Persons 14 Years Old and Over—Number with Income, Median Income, Mean Income, and Standard Errors, by Sex: 1975, 1974 (Revised), and 1974 : 499
Selected Characteristics of Persons 14 Years Old and Over Working Year Round Full Time—Number with Income, Median Income, Mean Income, and Standard Errors, by Sex: 1975, 1974 (Revised), and 1974 : 501

Work Experience and Total Money Earnings—Civilians 14 Years Old and Over, by Sex: 1975, 1974 (Revised), and 1974 : 503
Residence, Race, Sex, Age, and Educational Attainment of Head—Households by Total Money Income: 1975, 1974 (Revised), and 1974 : 505
Persons Below the Poverty Level by Family Status, Sex of Head, Race, and Spanish Origin: 1966, 1969, 1971, and 1973 to 1975 : 508
Selected Characteristics of Families Below the Poverty Level by Sex and Race of Head: 1975, 1974 (Revised), and 1974 : 510
Employee-Benefit Plans—Summary: 1960 to 1975 : 516
Protection Against Short-term Sickness Income Loss: 1950 to 1975 : 517
U.S. Bureau of the Census
The Life Work of Women : 518
Market Opinion Research, National Commission on the Observance of International Women's Year
Women Who Head Families: A Socioeconomic Analysis : 527
Beverly Johnson McEaddy

Part six. Housing : 535

Housing

Rent or Buy? Evaluating Alternatives in the Shelter Market : 537
U.S. Department of Labor, Bureau of Labor Statistics
Women and Housing: A Report on Sex Discrimination in Five American Cities : 566
National Council of Negro Women, Inc.
Equal Opportunity in Housing: A Manual for Corporate Employers : 590
Westchester Residential Opportunities, Inc.
Home Mortgage Lending and Solar Energy : 601
Division of Energy, Building Technology and Standards, U.S. Department of HUD
Construction Materials—Indexes of Wholesale Prices: 1970 to 1976 : 616
Percent of New Privately-Owned One-Family Houses with Various Characteristics: 1970 to 1976 : 616
U.S. Bureau of the Census
General Housing Characteristics : 617
Standard Metropolitan Statistical Areas: 1970 (Map) : 618
Characteristics of the Housing Inventory: 1975 and 1970 : 620
Financial Characteristics of the Housing Inventory: 1975 and 1970 : 629
Selected Housing Characteristics for Mobile Homes and Trailers: 1975 : 633
Selected Housing Characteristics for New Construction Units: 1975 : 638
Characteristics of Housing Units with Black Household Head: 1975 and 1970 : 646
Financial Characteristics of Housing Units with Black Household Head: 1975 and 1970 : 654
Characteristics of Housing Units with Household Head of Spanish Origin: 1975 and 1970 : 658
Financial Characteristics of Housing Units with Household Head of Spanish Origin: 1975 and 1970 : 666
U.S. Department of Commerce, U.S. Bureau of the Census, and U.S. Department of HUD

Part seven. Index : 671

Preface

Family Factbook, first edition, has attempted to provide interesting and useful materials in areas which relate to the family. There are six sections and a subject index. All of the sections include text as well as statistics, with more lengthy statistics sections appearing in "Part Five: Work and Income" and "Part Six: Housing." Credit lines giving the sources of material will be found at the end of each selection from a given publication. These sources, and the references at the end of many of the selections, may be of use to persons who wish to pursue a subject further.

The focus of *Family Factbook* is the family in the United States. However, one article in "Part Four: Health" and two in "Part Three: Children" describe practices in other countries. In "Part One: Family (General)," the first article, "Results of Social Change: Social Institutions-Community-Family" describes family life in Europe as well as in the United States.

"Part One: Family (General)" begins with three articles by sociologists which give some historical perspective on the family, how the individuals in the family influence it and are influenced by it, and various forms the family has taken and can take. These articles are followed by tables from the Bureau of the Census which provide statistics on households in the United States.

"Part Two: Adults" includes articles on men's and women's roles, parenting, negotiation in marriage, mid-life transition, and widowhood. Most of the statistics in this section are at the end of the sub-section on marriage.

"Part Three: Children" opens with three articles which describe how government programs serve children and how interested persons and organizations can participate in formulating new programs. Child development, day care, child abuse, and adolescents are the other topics included, with some general statistics at the end of the section.

"Part Four: Health" contains several tables from *Health, United States, 1976-1977,* a publication of the National Center for Health Services Research and the National Center for Health Statistics. Text materials include an article on the importance of good health care for children, another on the nurse-midwifery service at San Francisco General Hospital, a third on home helps in Sweden and the Netherlands, and a fourth on family therapy in alcoholism.

"Part Five: Work and Income" begins with a look at the problems working class families face. An extensive section of statistics on family income follows, and the last two items in this section both treat the subject of working women.

"Part Six: Housing" has four text selections which include information needed to make a choice between renting or owning, the availability of mortgage loans for solar housing, a report on discrimination against women seeking housing, and a manual which explains how corporations have aided minority employees in finding housing. The remainder of Part Six consists of tables prepared by the Bureau of the Census and the U.S. Department of Housing and Urban Development giving information on housing in the United States.

We wish to express our sincere appreciation to Dr. Helena Lopata, Professor of Sociology and Director of the Center for the Comparative Study of Social Roles at Loyola University of Chicago. Dr. Lopata referred us to several of the people whose work you will find in this book. She and the people she recommended were a pleasure to work with in addition to providing articles of great value.

In an effort to provide a reference tool that will be of optimum value to its audience, Marquis Academic Media, a division of Marquis Who's Who, Inc., invites reactions to the contents, organization, and scope of *Family Factbook.*

Part one:
Family (general)

Family (general)

RESULTS OF SOCIAL CHANGE: SOCIAL INSTITUTIONS—COMMUNITY—FAMILY

by Dr. Helena Znaniecki Lopata

American society is in the early stages of a very dramatic revolution in the world of work and in its relation to the rest of human life. The foundation for this revolution lies in the development of a relatively stabilized, urbanized, industrialized—or post-industrial as it is now called—middle-class population and culture.[1] Its seeds were the movement of the 1960s which questioned traditional views of the family, of work and of our whole value system with its strong emphasis on the economic institution. The youth movement may not have directly revolutionalized the "establishment," but it did raise the questions and its now adult participants, as well as the youth of the 1970s are not as heavily committed to hard work in pursuit of making money and to upward mobility as were the immigrants and the following two or more generations which bought the Protestant work ethic, with its Puritanical rigidity and saw obvious rewards pulling them out of the ghetto to the "good life." The seeds of the new revolution are also in the pre-Friedan movement of women out of the isolated home once the children started or finished grade or high school into their own competence building schooling and/or paid employment. Betty Friedan's (1963) *Feminine Mystique,* preceded by Simone de Beauvoir's (1953) *The Second Sex* and the less known Richard LaPierre's (1959) *The Freudian Ethic* opened fully the questioning of the logic and consequences of the way our society had developed. The feminist movement is having effects way beyond its membership. Recent change inducing submovements of a variety of forms, including both men's and women's consciousness raising groups, encounter groups, assertiveness training programs, "flexible careers" employment agencies, and so forth, supported by a mushrooming of literature in the form of books, periodicals and pamphlets are the small plants growing out of these seeds. So is the refusal of many men to be geographically transferred at stages of life which they deem bad for the family, or to be transferred at any stage. The mushrooming divorce rate can also be seen as a revolutionary symptom, as people get out of traditional marriages which stifled them personally being as yet sufficiently unsophisticated and bewildered by all the *freedom from* constraints to be able to creatively change that marriage instead of trying with a new mate to establish a more fulfilling relation (Fromm 1941). The plants of the new social changes are still young, and they have to offset centuries of prior changes which thrust Europe and America out of pre-industrial societal systems to its present condition. In order to understand what is happening now, we must examine the previous systems and the past changes.

Dr. Helena Znaniecki Lopata is Professor of Sociology and Director, Center for the Comparative Study of Social Roles, Loyola University of Chicago.

Pre-Industrial Europe

Philippe Aries (1963), in his charming *Centuries of Childhood,* points out that life prior to the 18th century, at least in Western Europe, was very public. There were no tight lines demarking the family from the rest of the home or the community. In the village, social interaction, work, leisure and political arrangements were made in the road as people went from one small plot to another, to church or just out of the homes. Everyone interacted with a variety of others, regardless of age or sex and the work groups consisted of mixed members, with a division of labor by age and by sex but with cooperative units being formed by need. The Nobel prize winning *The Peasants* by Ladislas Reymont (1925) also describes such a public life in a Polish village, with non-family residents living in many of the homes. The same was true, even to a greater extent, in the manor homes. These traditionally contained children of other families serving as servants, tutors, scribes, other servants, etc., and the large common room served many functions with people coming in and going out at all times of day and even night. Folding tables were brought out at meal time, folding beds at night. People were born and died in such rooms. Edward Shorter (1975) finds life in the towns of England or France also very public. Laslett and Wall (1965) enumerate all the people living in a baker's homeshop combination, and many of the new historians show both men and women working and interacting in shops and streets. Women were members of guilds, according to Ann Oakley (1974), and widows inherited the businesses of their husband, with whom they had worked before, and managed them with the help of different kinds of workers. Mothers did not rear their children, or at least did not do so alone. Among the upper classes in France, for example, mothers even sent babies to wet nurses in villages and few people invested much attention or affection in young children because of the high death rate (Shorter, 1975). Children as young as seven years of age were sent as servants to other homes, returning only at about age 14. Multiple child rearers existed at all levels of the whole society, with differences in socialization methods by class. Marriage was embedded in a network of relations and was not considered the primary or affectionate bond (Shorter, 1975).

Early paid labor came in the form of cottage industries, with capitalists farming out raw material to village homes where the wife and children processed it into a finished product, sometimes with the help of the men. When factories evolved with the introduction of steam and large scale machinery, all members of the family left the home to work in them, often moving the home nearby (Oakley, 1974). By then the family had been privatized, the household structure changed into one of many specialized rooms, the servants of the top classes cut off in their quarters and visitors admitted only at special "visiting hours." Wars of centralization developed nation states in Europe and the breakdown of the power of manor lords facilitated the creation of a nationalistically motivated mass education system. Aries (1963) claims that childhood as a concept and a set of relations to adults emerged only after the creation of the school system. In any case, boys, and later girls, were taken from the home and schooled into a literate national culture. The youth learned skills necessary for marketing themselves to employers and thus freed themselves of the power of the patriarchal family line. Simultaneously, and the new historians disagree as to the major factor causing this change, restrictive or so-called protective legislation started moving women out of the factory and into the home to take care of the children who were not yet in, or who came home from, school. These historians do agree, however, that women lost many rights following the removal of production from the home and their removal from the productive sphere of life outside of the home. This loss was particularly strong in societies focusing on the Protestant Ethic, which judged work for pay as more valuable than other effort and economic success as warranting even harmful adjustment by all other institutions. By making the focal institution of society the economic one, Western Europe and especially the United States developed societies of abundance for most of their members, but at a cost to many other aspects of their lives. The older generation was justifiably left behind geographically and culturally during social mobility. Siblings moved in different directions in the social system. Friendship was pushed aside or converted into a more social companionship which was not allowed to interfere with the man's work and career. Religion was modified so as not to interfere with the business world and life became increasingly segmentalized with separate value and personality packages. Puritanism insured that leisure time was spent in "recreation" of energy for the work day and "Seriousness of purpose was heightened by strong religious feeling; the average man locked himself in his office and his wife in his home (Dulles, 1965: 98)." Even the middle class home lost its place as a center of societal life, the returning husband and children wanting peace, not excitement. Not surprisingly, the role of housewife lost the stature it had in the previous world.

The nuclear family was freed from control by older generations and siblings of the male family of orientation but simultaneously it became boxed into a highly interdependent small unit lacking automatic external support systems. If the man has to go out of the home to make the money by which the home and the family are maintained, and servants no longer exist as an available set of supports because people can get better pay working in other occupations, then someone has to stay home to take care of the small children. That someone became the wife-mother, isolated from societal life in all but the upper classes by her 24 hour-a-day vigil and held responsible for all consequences of her socialization of the children. The burden of total emotional and social support all day long between the mother and the children is reportedly dysfunctional to the mental health of either, as psychologists and sociologists have been saying for years (Bernard, 1974).

The stage of intensive childrearing is, however, short and by midlife the American woman faces 30 years of healthy and energetic life with no major function, especially during the 15-16 years when even the husband is gone by death and possibly even before that through divorce. In the meantime the husband has had to make a life-constraining decision as to what occupation he will plunge into and he must continue working there, with one or two shifts in his career, until he dies or retires. As Fromm (1947) pointed out, the marketing mentality of American society even deprives him of some of the pleasure in retirement, since his worth as a man is measured by what he is worth to employers and now he is worth nothing.

By the late 1950s American society had settled down, having absorbed millions of immigrants who accepted the basic value system, with however, tremendous intergenerational struggles as these socialized into a different type of world of the village or the ethnic community fought with their children wanting to "make it" the American way. An elaborate ideology and value system justified our whole way of life as "natural" with the help of neo-Freudians such as Helene Deutsch (1944). Women were supposed to contently stay at home, and not be involved seriously in the life outside of it. Voluntary associations and volunteer work were allowed, but only if such activities did not interfere with the flow of life at home. Men were taught to put all their efforts into their jobs, accepting any demands made upon them as an inevitable consequence of a system which paid them for any sacrifices so that they could own homes, cars, and well fed and well clothed families. In order to so function they were taught to always protect themselves from others and to be strong, never showing physical or emotional weakness.

Social Roles of Americans, Now and the Future

I started studying American urban women in the years between 1956 and 1966 because of an awareness of the tremendous gap between what I observed as a foreigner and a sociologist and what I was reading about the family in this country. Having come from Poland directly to Champaign-Urbana for schooling through most of high school and an MA and then to the University of Chicago for a PhD, I was startled in finding women whom I met when we finally settled in a suburb of Chicago who were entirely different from those I had been reading about in American books and periodicals. These were the years of *The Generation of Vipers* (Wylie, 1946), *The Lonely Crowd* (Riesman, 1950), *The Organization Man* (1956), and *Modern Woman: The Lost Sex* (Lundberg and Farnham, 1947). However, although the behavior of young Chicago area women displayed competence and creativity, their self-definitions were not positive. "I'm just a housewife," was the most frequently heard answer to occupational questions. At the same time, they did not feel right in wanting to go back to work, accepting the idea that wives and mothers should stay home. The double-bind effect of living in a society which trained them to be competent and then put them in a role defined as not requiring competence, while forbidding other roles, took an enormous toll on these women. The society simply did not understand the social forces which made life for them so difficult in three stages: when they suddenly left social roles outside of the home and found themselves within it alone with a small infant, when they were left with an "empty nest" for varying amounts of time when only half way thru life with no new direction, and when they became widowed.

In spite of a complete lack of societal supports and understanding, American women started in the 1960's to create their own solutions to these problems. Coffee-clatches provided opportunities for the sharing of solutions, much in the same way "brain-storming" sessions accomplish it for people in other occupations or work groups. Sharing child care and housewifering activities became common place. Spock's (1956) book, and those by other experts provided greater feelings of competence in the role of mother than provided by many pediatricians. New sub-cultures were developing in the suburbs and inner city which lessened the heavy pressure of traditional norms. And, gradually, wives and mothers were slipping out of the back door of the house, going to school and even to work. The movement has grown considerably since the 1960's, aided by the feminist movement and particularly by the door opening book, *The Feminine Mystique* (Friedan, 1963), which caught the women's imagination more than any other book analyzing the ideology rigidifying their lives had been able to do. Although few women are members of the divergent branches of the feminist movement, the influence on them and on men has undoubtedly loosened the mold of the past and will provide the impetus for the future revolutionary changes.

In the meantime, some of the hidden hostility between men and women in American society, so apparent to visitors and new members, surfaced. The middle class, middle aged man, working hard to earn more money while fearing that his death is around the corner deeply resented the initial stages and the more vocal branches of the feminist movement which labeled him the oppressor. The movement has mainly shifted focus to the system within which both men and women are functioning, trying to change its inflexible demands and discriminatory policies. Men have for the most part not joined forces with the women, being still fearful of their own careers and reputations to a degree making them unwilling to challenge the system in spite of the benefits which could come not just to their wives but to them from changes in it. It will take an unmeasurable amount of time before the fears instilled into boys will weaken sufficiently to permit them to go through the painful reexamination of values and goals when they reach adulthood, or at any time for that matter, which women are now undertaking. It may také another generation of boys growing up with less sexist socialization by self-examining mothers before women and men become willing to join forces to push for a greater balance and flexibility in the life course, and for a change of values serving as guides for involvement in social roles. As yet, men's sensitivity groups are appearing mainly on campuses, while the business world is, not surprisingly, more focused on encounter groups and assertiveness training.

Thus, the change in the feminist movement, and Betty Friedan (1976) is one of the spokeswomen and leaders of this movement, is a realization by the women that the system must be changed through cooperative effort in order to free life into a variety of time segments, worked through teamships. People who are reexamining the relation between work and other social roles, and reexamining the rhythm of occupational engagement are coming up with a variety of solutions to the current problems of both men and women. There is no economically unsolvable reason for work and other roles to be organized the way they currently are in America. Two people can hold a single job more efficiently than can one in a majority of occupations, whether the team be composed of a husband and wife or two persons with similar training who do not want to work fulltime for other reasons but can not afford part-time pay. Abbott Laboratories has a position of chemist which is being very satisfactorily filled by two people. Gustafus Adolphus college has split an academic job in like manner and librarianship positions would appear to be a natural for this.

Flexibility can be introduced differently in many stages of the life course. For example, if a couple decides to share a life together they can plan the most efficient set of role complexes possible. If both can not continue school, the man can probably drop out with a higher income from a job than can the woman, who can then continue to be trained for a better paying and more satisfying occupation than held by most women. The child bearing and rearing stage does not have to be entered by a couple in their teens or young twenties, when it is more logical for the couple to invest in further training, a start at a career and saving money for their parenting years. Careers do not have to have a steady line, in fact, much of the recent research shows that most people do not have them anyway, for a variety of unplanned reasons (Lopata and Norr, 1975). Upon the birth of a child the couple can alternate parenting, both taking 2-person jobs, or handling a traditional two-person single job, held by the mother or the father. There is a variety of ways parenting and jobs can be combined in early years of a child's life. In addition, these years when a child is small comprise a very short segment of a person's life and other social roles can be pushed into the background because of the importance of the parental role for both the mother and the father. The isolated household is also dysfunctional, if not harmful, at that time, so joint households or across threshhold cooperative ventures can be initiated without tying people down to such arrangements for decades.

The next stage of the life course can involve both partners and the children in a variety of social role complexes, depending not on tradition or happenstance, but on planning with long-range goals and values in mind. Some couples may opt for a heavy concentration of effort on the career of one member, others may find ways of comfortably containing dual career arrangements with high levels of concentration and commitment, while a third type of dyad may distribute their efforts more evenly among several roles, enjoying friendships, leisure-time pursuits, contribution to voluntary organizations upon which communities are dependent, parenting, etc. at several stages of the life course.

Higher education has become much more flexible and responsive to a variety of people in the past few years and you see all kinds of students in your libraries. The area of societal activity which is only now beginning to open up occasional and exceptional flexibilities is the economic one and it is here that basic value and activity patterns must shift in the future as people change their willingness to sacrifice other aspects of their selves and social roles for the job and the money it pays. The organization of work in current time slots and occupational packages, with the constant emphasis on the career line, varied as it is within different occupations, has rigidified life to an extent with which people are decreasingly satisfied. We are now experiencing not only a "revolt of the client" but a revolt of the professional and other occupation holders (Haug, 1975, 1976; Haug and Sussman, 1969a, 1969b). There is consistent evidence that increasingly competent human beings are, and will be, making demands on the system to change and become more flexible. Organized protests are being supplemented by the less visible one as in the patient referral system and the changing patient-doctor relations created in one-to-one interaction (Friedson, 1973).

Summary

There have been dramatic changes in the lives of Europeans and Americans in the last few centuries. Some of these are judged by most observers as generally beneficial in that they have increased health and longevity, opened up a variety of resources to a variety of people and created economically abundant societies. Some of the social roles and relations of these people have suffered, however, from the strong emphasis on the economic institution and the insistance that other institutions adjust to its demands and from the rigidification of work engagement and schedules. The relatively isolated nuclear family, the high pressured male breadwinner, the underutilized abilities of women for a major part of their life cycle, these consequences of the way our societies, and particularly America, have developed are costs which many people are no longer willing to pay. Various indicators of change are apparent on the American scene and they are apt to grow rapidly in the near future, pushing on the world of work to become more flexible and more evenly balanced in its power to control life with the other social roles of its participants, and all those people who are now discouraged from participating. Changes in interpersonal relations are in greater evidence in America than are changes in the way people are engaged in the large bureaucratic organizations, particularly in those where most men, half of the women and those close to them are now economically dependent.

FOOTNOTE

1. Of course, there are still large segments of this population which, because of discrimination or recency of arrival are still lower-class, not fully urbanized and without sophisticated occupational skills but they form a lower proportion of the total than true of, for example, the turn of the century.

REFERENCES

Aries, Philippe.
1965 *Centuries of Childhood.* New York: Vintage Books.

Bernard, Jessie.
1975 *Future of Motherhood.* New York: Penguin Books.

de Beauvoir, Simone.
1953 *The Second Sex.* New York: Alfred Knopf.

Deutsch, Helene.
1944 *The Psychology of Women.* New York: Grune and Stratton.

Dulles, Foster Rhea.
1965 *A History of Recreation: America Learns to Play.* New York: Appleton Century Crofts.

Friedan, Betty.
1963 *The Feminine Mystique.* New York: Norton.
1976 Speech at the Conference on Women in Midlife Crises at Cornell University, October 28-31.

Freidson, Eliot.
1973 *The Professions and Their Prospects.* Beverly Hills, Calif.: Sage Publications.

Fromm, Erich.
1941 *Escape from Freedom.* New York: Farrar and Rinehart.
1947 *Man for Himself.* New York: Rinehart and Company.

Haug, Marie R.
1975 "The deprofessionalization of everyone?" *Sociological Focus* 8: 197-213.
1976 "The erosion of professional authority: a cross-cultural inquiry in the case of the physicians." *Health and Society* (Winter): 83-106.

Haug, Marie R. and Marvis B. Sussman.
1969a "Professional autonomy and the revolt of the client." *Social Problems* 17: 153-161.
1969b "Professionalism and the public." *Sociological Inquiry* 39: 57-64.

La Pierre, Richard.
1959 *The Freudian Ethic.* New York: Duell, Sloan and Pierce.

Laslett, Peter and Richard Wall.
1965 *Household and Family in Past Time.* Cambridge: University Press.

Lopata, Helena Z. and Kathleen Norr.
1975 "Changing Commitments of Women to Work and Family Roles." Proposal for study, Social Security Administration.

Lundberg, Ferdinand and M.F. Farnham.
1947 *Modern Women, The Lost Sex.* New York: Harper & Row, Publishers, Inc.

Oakley, Ann.
1974 *The Housewife, Past and Present.* New York: Pantheon Books.

Reymont, Ladislas.
1925 *The Peasants: Fall, Winter, Spring, Summer.* 4 vols. New York: Knopf.

Reisman, David et. al.
1950 *The Lonely Crowd.* New Haven and London: Yale University Press.

Shorter, Edward.
1975 *The Making of the Modern Family.* New York: Basic Books.

Spock, Benjamin.
1956 *Baby and Child Care.* New York: Pocket Books.

Whyte, William H. Jr.
1956 *The Organization Man.* New York: Simon and Schuster.

Wylie, Philip.
1946 *Generation of Vipers.* New York: Rinehart and Company.

Another paper by Dr. Lopata may be found at the end of the ADULT section titled "Widowhood: Social Norms and Social Integration."

"Results of Social Change: Social Institutions-Community-Family," by Dr. Helena Znaniecki Lopata. Paper presented to the Allerton Park Institute 22, "Changing Times" on November 16, 1976 at Champaign, Illinois. Reprinted with permission.

Interpersonal Relationships And Changing Perspectives On The Family

Nona Glazer-Malbin

While acknowledging our mutual affection by publicly assuming the relationship of husband and wife, yet in justice to ourselves and a great principle, we deem it a duty to declare that this act on our part implies no sanction of, nor promise of voluntary obedience to such of the present laws of marriage, as refuse to recognize the wife as an independent, rational being, while they confer upon the husband an injurious and unnatural superiority, investing him with legal powers which no honorable man would exercise, and which no man should possess.

Henry B. Blackwell and Lucy Stone
Worcester Spy, 1855

Protests against family relationships in the United States are not new as the document drawn up by Henry Blackwell and Lucy Stone upon their marriage in 1855 shows. Freedom to remake the interpersonal relationship between people is, however, both magnificient and frightening. At once, the array of possible new relationships tempts, while we realize, however dimly, that the cost is a loss of the comfort of knowing *what* is expected, with *whom*, and for *how* long. Our freedom has expanded far beyond mate selection or the recognition of the independent legal status of the wife. A series of complex choices face us: we may ask, for example, with whom shall we live, in what domestic arrangement, shall we have children, with which sex shall we live, and perhaps, most basic, is it necessary to live with another person in order to raise children and to live a generally satisfying life?

This chapter is an introduction to a volume of articles which discuss some of the current family styles available to contemporary Americans. Sociologists and social psychologists focus their attention on interpersonal relationships in the family though not without often using the familiar concepts of social organization to aid understanding. Interpersonal relationships between women and men, men and men, and women and women in the family are examined in a variety of contexts which depart often from the traditional notion of what a family is: these include relationships between women and men among the married and the cohabiting; between a widow and her couple friends; between women and men in a commune; between women as friends and as lovers; between men as friends; between women and men where sexuality is the main bond; and finally, between geographically separated kin.

The discussion which follows considers: (1) the concept of interpersonal relationships; (2) the contrast between the institutional and companionate family style, and the differing interpersonal relationships of the two styles; (3) some social sources of the current attempts to remake the family; (4) historical and contemporary alternatives to the traditional American family; and (5) the challenges of the alternatives to the premises of the traditional family form.

INTERPERSONAL RELATIONSHIPS

Each of us straddles two social worlds. First, there is the world of large scale *social organization*—the rules and regulations of factory, office, school, church, and so on, the dos and don'ts of social roles. Second, there is the world of *interpersonal relationships*—the ways we interact with other people as we follow those rules and regulations or violate them. The interpersonal world connects the individual, on the one side, and the society, on the other. Within the framework of societal rules, in love, marriage, and friendship, in medical and legal consultation, in the orchestra, the store, and on the assembly bench, for example, each of us works out interpersonal relationships with those with whom we interact.

Types of Interpersonal Relationships

Interpersonal relationships have one of four main concerns: self-confirmation, personal change, instrumental gain, and emotional expression.[1] *Self-confirming relationships* are those in which we gain a sense of who we are and how worthy we are. The process of developing and maintaining an identity as a woman, a man, a "good provider," a "bad boy," or whatever is an important aspect of the interpersonal relationship between, for example, parent and child as well as between wife and husband. *Personal change* is illustrated in social relationships which lead to a change in self-perception. These relationships include that between parent and child in socialization, between teacher and student in education, between therapist and convict in a prison's rehabilitation program as well as in relationships such as seduction, "conning," and voluntary therapy, as between Don Juan and his fancy, the con man and his mark, the psychiatrist and the analysand.[2] *Instrumental relationships* include work relationships mainly, friendly and antagonistic, in which the relationships are carried on for the production of goods or services. Examples include the assembly line worker and her peers, the office manager and the typists, the cabdriver and her fare, the nurse and his aide. Finally, there are social relationships in which *emotional expression* is basic. In love, in marriage, and in friendship, the expression of feeling is supposed to be the basis of the relationship between lovers, between wife and husband, between confidants, be they two women, two men, or a woman and a man.

All social relationships include a blend of these four purposes. For example, self-confirmation may take precedent in a specific relationship but there will also very likely be evidence of personal change, a task, and the expression of feelings. Similarly, even in a relationship whose main concern is the joint production of a service, such as between two window-cleaners, other dimensions are present: the window-cleaners are likely to be interested in confirming their identities as "good workers" and sharing their annoyance about an uncooperative customer. The extent to which one or the other of these four purposes is the primary function of the relationship can be found by seeing what happens to the relationship which no longer includes a given function. For example, if a child feels too controlled by the parent, she may alter the interpersonal relationship in order to establish an independent sense of self. If a woman ceases to feel that she can "be herself" with her spouse, she may end the relationship provided marriage is not the exclusive setting in which the instrumental function can be carried out. If the primary orientation of the marriage relationship is the fulfillment of instrumental goals, then regardless of how dissatisfying the expressive dimension of the interpersonal relationship is, the woman may remain in the marriage.

THE FAMILY

William Goode coined the charming phrase "the classical family of Western nostalgia" to warn against romanticizing grandma's family into a happy group of three generations, working harmoniously together on the family farm, and enjoying relationships with kin and neighbor.[3] And he cautions against exaggerating the nineteenth-century family, from the opposite perspective, into a stolid, domineering husband, the cowed wife, and quietly submissive, repressed children. Goode's warnings are apt. Hence, my comparisons of the institutional- and companionate-oriented families are not of the "bad" family of the past with the "good" family of the present, or vice versa. Not only does the present family face considerable problems, but it is difficult to reconstruct how people actually experienced interpersonal relationships in the traditional family. Novels and diaries are one source of information, but the stories which they tell are quite varied. The important point is that whether the personal anguish was great or small, the women and men who lived in the institutional family had few alternatives since family life was important, often crucial to survival.

The Institutional Family

Interpersonal relationships in the typical American family—if there is a typical family—are characterized by an uneasy and often ambiguous blend of the four focuses. Contrasting the major focus of the institutional- and companionate-oriented families will both show how the two types differ and illustrate the blend. The institutional family is oriented toward survival, the accomplishment of tasks having to do with production, reproduction, socialization of the young, sexuality, and other functions. In agrarian United States, the family lived together and family members worked together to produce goods and perform services. Children were born and raised without much reliance on people outside the household though neighbors, kin, and the church did have an influence. Rarely, it is likely, did a Tevye ask his wife: "Do you love me?" as a way of making or breaking a marriage. What women and men did was marry and stay married, regardless of the level of personal emotional (and sexual) satisfaction. (Self-confirmation was probably gained from carrying out the responsibilities inherent in being a "good wife" and a "good husband.") Closely tied family members were the result of the extreme difficulty of surviving outside a family. Survival, not happiness; duty, not pleasure; sustenance, not personal growth were keystones of family solidarity regardless of how much women and men might have hungered for romance, passion, and everlasting love. It is true that single men could live alone and, in fact, were often forced to live alone by the lopsided sex ratio resulting from the vast numbers of men and the relatively few women who came to the United States or who moved westward. But, for most people and especially for women, family life was the usual and desirable living style. This did not necessarily mean marriage for women, but it meant remaining in the household of birth or attaching oneself to the household of kin.

Industrialization had an enormous impact on the family.[4] Husband, wife, and children ceased to work side by side in productive activities. Men and children left the household for wage work on farms and in factories, leaving women behind in "woman's place" as she gradually assumed nearly total responsibility for household chores as well as often doing work in the home for pay. While homemaking became a full-time occupation, ironically, many activities which had once been carried on virtually only at home were becoming the function of institutions outside the family.

The distinction between the institutional and the companionate family is one of emphasis. It is evident that women and men have some considerable interest in finding love, affection, and companionship in the institutional family, and that they try to fulfill a variety of needs quite aside from love, affection, and companionship in the companionate family.

The Companionate Family

Before turning to the companionate-oriented family, I would like to note the distinction between the extended and the conjugal family. In the *extended family*, the nuclear unit (husband, wife, their offspring) is embedded in a large and active kin network which may include several older as well as younger generations and which extends bilaterally to include the siblings of each generation, their spouses, and offspring. Economic cooperation and mutual social and emotional support is expected among the kin. Since lineage is important, relatives play an important part in each other's lives, including mate selection. In the *conjugal system*, the dominant contemporary pattern in America, kin are much less important even though they still have a role. Members of a nuclear unit consider themselves to be kin of the immediately contingent generations mainly: to their parents and grandparents, and bilaterally, to their own siblings and their own children's spouses and offspring. This kinship group may be a major source of support—financial, emotional, social—but friends as well as formal institutions such as village groups, government agencies, and private companies play a role unknown in the era of the extended family. Formal institutions may be so important that spouses may give relatively little emotional and financial support to their own parents, and in turn, expect little support from their grown children, though the children may continue to expect a variety of kinds of support from their parents.

The change from the institutional to the companionate family follows upon technological changes and the organization of an urban-industrial society. According to Ogburn, technological change gradually decreases the functions which the family performs for its members. Production moves to factory and office, religion to the church, the care of the sick to hospitals, education to the schools, and so on.[5] Recently, the "Pill" as well as changes in mores have made sexuality easily available to women outside of marriage; there are strong demands for daycare for children, and a small proportion of nonmarrieds have or adopt children.

The institutional-oriented family brings a woman and a man together primarily on the basis of their interdependence and their abilities to perform certain complementary functions. If love, companionship, sexual satisfaction, mutual respect, and happiness are found in marriage, then it is as a bonus rather than as a marital right. The decreased importance of the family as a provider of certain basics as well as the increasing impersonality of society and a growing demand for personal happiness change the emphasis in marriage toward companionship. Bureaucratization, rapid social change, geographical mobility, and impersonality make the family more and more of a haven, a solace in mass society.

Interpersonal Relationships in the Family

Contrasting the *formal* and *personal* social relationships[6] will clarify further distinctions between the institutional and companionate family. In the institutional family, *formal* social relationships predominate. There are fairly clear obligations and rights attached to the social role *wife* and the social role *husband*, and the persons who fill these roles are guided in their interaction with each other mainly by the constraints of the roles. Personal elements enter into their interaction as the idiosyncracies of each, their strengths and weaknesses of character, special talents, inner and outer resources, and so on are taken into account. But, basically, social interaction is constrained by role expectations.

In the companionate family, *personal* social relationships predominate and constrain the interaction between the woman and the man to a considerably greater degree than in the institutional family. A personal relationship is one in which knowledge about each other—needs, tastes, capacities, resources, background characteristics, and the like—is the main constraint on social interaction. The knowledge each spouse uses is highly individualistic: about Mary, rather than about women or wives, and about John, rather than about men or husbands, though categorical information is used, too.

Some part of the interpersonal tension in marriage—and this is an observation, not a plea for greater clarity—can be attributed to the inherent ambiguity in expressively oriented relationships as to what constitutes the appropriate blend of formal and personal social relationships. The problem in marriage may be exaggerated because of sex role stereotypes. Hence, at one moment, John treats Mary as "wife" when she may want to be treated as Mary, and Mary treats

John as "John" just when he would prefer to be treated as "husband." For example, John wants Mary to cook because "wives cook," while Mary wants her mate to recognize that she hates cooking and would like him to prepare meals. Yet John may be willing to suppress his enjoyment of cooking to play the *formal* role of husband and man.

THE SEARCH FOR NEW FAMILY FORMS

The Background

The last decade, and especially the last five years, has seen an enormous amount of concern about interpersonal relationships as well as about the nature of the family. In this section, I will consider some of the social sources of these interests in bettering the quality of daily existence by improving relationships with spouses, lovers, friends, off spring, colleagues, and neighbors. If the attention of the 1960s was riveted on changing the social order, then the attention of the 1970s seems riveted on finding solutions through increasing interpersonal competencies. A wide variety of activities, such as Esalen, group marathons, transactional analysis, and Gestalt therapy which have roots in the 1960s, are attempts to reorganize the world at the personal and interpersonal levels rather than at the level of social organization.

Mass Society. That the United States is becoming increasingly impersonal is almost a truism. Urbanization, bureaucratization, the continued concentration of wealth and power, high rates of geographical mobility, and the sheer size of social units (communities, work groups, church groups, and other organizations) contribute to feelings of alienation. Alienation—a sense of powerlessness, meaninglessness, anomie—has its roots in a variety of social situations including an absence of commitment to values, conformity to norms, a perception that one's social role is depriving, and a threat to the self.[7] Solace may be sought in satisfying interpersonal relationships which, while not changing the sources of alienation, may be seen—correctly or not—as making the experience more tolerable.

The family is seen as a major institution which has the potential for countering the sense of alienation so widely experienced in contemporary American society. Talcott Parsons even suggests that the American family bears a special burden for providing emotional sustenance because of its social and geographic isolation and because of transitory friendships encouraged by geographical and social mobility.[8] In Parson's analysis, the organization of the economy demands geographical mobility and small, isolated units which can experience upward and downward mobility easily. Furthermore, the taboos against intense same-sex or cross-sex relationships which might compete with the marital bond place a further burden on the spouses. Especially important in the idea that the family may be a counter to the problems of mass society is the wife's role as socio-emotional leader and her special task of continuing the socialization of her husband and their children. From a symbolic interactionist perspective, Peter Berger and Hansfried Kellner see marriage as a place in which *nomos* building takes place, that is, a place in which people can develop a new reality and find a sense of being in control of their social world which then counters the anomic surroundings.[9] Marriage is a social context within which a new and apparently satisfying self may be constructed. The family becomes a haven from the alienation of the outside world of politics and work, though the new reality may provide better for the man than for the woman whose "work" and "haven" are often both within the marriage.

Sex Equality. One source of alienation from which the woman has no haven in marriage—the nature of women's roles—needs further examination. The growing similarity between women and men and the ideology of equality which flourished so in the 1960s certainly have an influence on the interest in interpersonal relationships and the attempts to reinvent the "family." Regardless of how far the reality of egalitarianism is from the ideal, women and men have become more like each other as women have entered into the "man's world" by working outside the home, by running for political office, by heading households, by gaining higher education, and other activities. And, men have become more like women as their work has altered toward more concern with people (for example, high school and grade school teaching, social work, and other service occupations). Moreover, the 1972 Census report shows that the proportion of men entering white-collar jobs and service work has continued to increase as the proportion in blue-collar work has declined. Both sexes have become somewhat more alike from experiencing coeducation, especially in the high school years. The pool of common activities creates a basis for easier communication. Both sexes' belief that men and women are so unlike that they cannot understand each other has been lessened as the women's movement pounds away, emphasizing the similarities between the sexes.

From Objects to People. A lessening involvement with control over the material world (as exemplified in the labor force changes noted above) has opened up a new frontier: people. One might even say that after coping to some degree with the material world, Americans now seem to believe that they are ready for the "luxury" of concern about human relations. (And the concern is not simply to improve economic production, which was the 1920s version of interest in human relations.) In *The Lonely Crowd*, a brilliant post-World War II analysis of changing American character, David Riesman proclaims the development of the other-directed character type for whom "their contemporaries are the source of direction" in contrast to the driving internalized standards about hard work, honesty, and justice which the inner-directed hold.[10] In a sense, this signals a far greater concern than ever before with the interpersonal relationships between people, even though for a variety of reasons sociologists were neglecting social relationships for larger problems of social organization.

Riesman characterizes the change from inner-directed to other-directed as a shift "from morals to morale," for where once the question was "Is it right?" the question became "Will others think it okay?" It is, I believe, a short step from a concern with the reactions of others to a concern with the feelings of the self. I suggest that an updated portrait of the other-directed is needed, perhaps, using labels which would capture and contrast the preoccupation with moral "oughts" with a preoccupation with feelings. The portrait would include not simply blind response to the perceived expectations and needs of others but a sensitivity and response to one's own feelings and the acceptance of these feelings as legitimate guides to action.

The Failure of Politics. The protest movements of the 1960s are germane to understanding the new family forms. American society experiences periodic swings between two disparate approaches to grappling with alienation, loneliness, and rootlessness. First, there are attempts to change the social conditions of life, and second, there are attempts to change interpersonal and intrapersonal conditions. Attempts to change social conditions which predate the 1960s include the social reform movements of the late nineteenth century, populism in both the nineteenth and twentieth centuries, the socialist and communist movements which captured imaginations in the 1930s, as well as the welfare policies of the New Deal.

Interspersed between such attempts to change the basic structure of society have been efforts to change human misery and to alter the human condition by changing individuals. In this century, a scientific base for the philosophical predilection of Americans for an individualistic approach appears in the work of Freud and his followers as well as his detractors. Under the influence of psychiatry and psychology, a wide variety of individualistic therapies flourish. Even social conflict, between workers and managers, between citizens and government, between students and teachers, and others, has sometimes been "explained" as results of personal pathology.

The social movements of the 1960s had an array of goals ranging from the withdrawal of American ground troops from Indochina through the implementation of the Supreme Court decision on school desegration to the basic reorganization of American economic and political institutions. Among people in the counterculture, there were women and men who "protested" against the materialism of the American system by living a life style which deemphasized "things" and instead emphasized loving, caring, sharing, and "doing your own thing." However successful or unsuccessful the life styles were and however well or poorly conceived much of the political activity of the antiwar, antiracism, and anticapitalism movements may have been, we are left with two legacies. The first is the variety of alternative life styles that was brought to public attention by the activities of members of the counterculture; the second is a disillusionment with political action à la the styles of demonstrations, marches, mass organization, and so on as a means of changing the quality of life in the United States within or outside of the system. Overwhelmed by the power of government and big business, split by internal factions, and infiltrated by government agent provocateurs, many activists turned away from direct political action as a technique of social change and instead changed their own life styles as a kind of political act. Others, simply disillusioned with political action, sought an alternative to the establishment life style or endeavored to live their political beliefs out at a personal level. And, it appears that the Establishment find alternative life styles far less threatening than political action.

The Women's Movement. The women's movement has played a particularly important role in the movement toward new life styles and the growing sensitivity to interpersonal relationships. What began as a challenge to the interpersonal relationships between movement women and men,[11] led to increasing sensitivity and anger among women in a wide variety of social situations about the interpersonal relationships between women as well as between women and men. (The women's movement is, of course, not limited to a concern with interpersonal relationships; Betty Friedan's "problem that has no name," job discrimination, legal rights, the putdown of women in the mass media, and so on are among the other problems to which the movement addresses itself.) The movement not only makes interpersonal relationships between people a concern but incorporates a specific ideology of sisterhood (see Chapter 8) into the organization of the "women's liberation" section of the movement. The ideology includes an emphasis on conducting human social relationships in which individuals are treated as ends rather than means and in which the expression of respect and care is more central than the pursuit of efficiency.

The Conjugal Family. If nothing else indicates the dissatisfaction of women and men with the current family, the high divorce rate does. Despite fluctuations (for example, the excessively high rate in 1946), the general trend continues toward a higher and higher rate. That divorce is more socially acceptable, too, is evident in the trend toward allowing the dissolution of marriage on grounds of irreconcilable differences, a considerable contrast with the old grounds which sometimes made a demonstration (real or phony) of adultery mandatory for a divorce decree to be granted. Finally, the increasing experimentation with alternatives to traditional, monogamous marriage demonstrates the dissatisfaction of people—older people as well as married, noncollege as well as college people. Rural and urban communes, marriage contracts, cohabitation, swinging, family networks, serial monogamy, homosexual pairing, group marriages, and divorce itself, of course, are among the new life styles tasted, discarded, and kept by people groping for new, more satisfactory ways of living.

Contemporary conjugal family life appears burdened by a number of demands: (1) the emotional, social, and sexual exclusivity which is a basic characteristic of the conjugal pair may ask the impossible of individuals trained to flee from intimacy and conditioned to protect their autonomy by fending off closeness. Even under ideal conditions (for example, those where individuals are socialized to meet the intrapersonal demands of close relationships), probably no one individual can meet all of the needs of another. (2) The expectations of women and men have expanded from marital satisfaction which depends on rather solid, extrinsic rewards such as a clean house, a well-prepared meal, overt respect, good earnings, to a desire for ephemeral, intrinsic satisfactions such as happiness, personal growth, sexual satisfaction, closeness, and the like. (3) The compensatory function of the family has expanded. The emotional repercussions of the fear of atomic wars and the "end of civilization as we know it," the fear of city streets (day and night), the intimations of a depression in the 1970s which will make the 1930s seem to be a "Truman Recession," and the daily involvement in dreary, boring, unrewarding work are all to be compensated for by marital and family happiness. Not only is the family supposed, therefore, to satisfy emotional and social needs which arise simply from our being human, or at least, from contemporary views of what human needs are, but the marital pair has now also been asked to take on the stupendous job of compensating for "a world they never made." Impossible, yes— and hence, another reason for the search for new family forms.

THE SEARCH FOR NEW FAMILY FORMS

The search for new family forms and the renconstruction of the family are not new. Americans have been objecting to the traditional family form by constructing new ones for hundreds of years. The Moravian community, present in colonial America, attempted to deflect the involvement of individuals in small family units by making child rearing a joint responsibility and by organizing its members into choirs within which individuals ate, worked, slept, and prayed. Even though the intent was to focus people's attention on religious rather than secular interests, the Moravians did offer an alternative to traditional family life.[12] Religious communities such as the Amish and Mennonites also organize their lives around small, tight-knit communities which share the responsibilities of the nuclear family. The Mormons developed polygamy, a slightly different alternative family form, established multiple-households, engaged in cooperative economic activities, and sought a territory in which they could be isolated from non-Mormon persecutors and free to follow their religious doctrine. The Oneida community is probably most in tune with modern attempts to reshape the family. The community was founded in upstate New York in 1848 and continued until about 1880. Welded together by shared religious beliefs, it practiced economic communism, group marriage, scientific breeding and espoused sexual equality.[13] These communities seem to thrive because of dedication to a shared religious doctrine, a shared territory or residence, and isolation from nonmembers—and probably, the ability to depend, when necessary, upon a surrounding community to provide what the communities could not—protection against intruders, markets for products, supplies of goods not produced by the community. A family form outside the United States which has been quite provocative because it has survived for over fifty years is the Israeli kibbutz. Economic communism, professional child care, an ideology of sex equality, isolation from major population centers, and a dedication to the military protection of the nation characterize social organization within the kibbutz.[14]

Reinventing the Family

What is the family? . . . the family appears as a natural object but is actually a cultural creation. There is nothing inevitable about the form or role of the family. It is the function of

> *ideology to present these given social types as aspects of Nature itself. . . . The apparently natural condition can be made to appear more attractive than the arduous advance of human beings toward culture.*[15]

The impetus for inventing new family forms and new styles of interpersonal relationships comes not only from the social sources discussed earlier, but from the gradual realization, as Mitchell notes, that the family is a cultural creation. Social scientists have struggled with the questions "What is the family?" and "Is the family universal?" The answers depend on the meaning of *family.* Melford Spiro, after arguing that the family is not universal in view of the success of the Israeli kibbutz, later suggests that the kibbutz would satisfy a definition of marriage such as: "any socially sanctioned relationship between non-sanguineally-related cohabiting adults of opposite sex which satisfied felt needs—mutual, symmetrical, or complementary."[16] Spiro's definition drops only the usual criterion of shared economic activity. Donald Ball suggests what is to me the most useful definition, an even more inclusive one than Spiro's, defining the family as "any cohabiting domestic relationship which is (or has been) sexually consequential, i.e., gratification for members or the production of offspring" thereby eliminating the criterion of opposite sex partners.[17] Other family sociologists would include as cohabitors those people who do not have a sexually consequential relationship.[18] I suppose it would be possible to eliminate even the characteristic of a domestically consequential relationship to be able to include couples who may have separate residences but who have emotional and sexual relationships (for example, Simone de Beauvoir and Jean-Paul Sartre), but these seem marginal cases in which activities are segregated for various reasons. These modified definitions are attempts to recognize the new family forms with their emphasis on companionship rather than institutional functions that have been adopted during the past decade.

In concluding this chapter, I will consider the challenges implied by the reinvention of family forms, looking at the areas of privatization, including property, sexuality, socialization, and sex equality. The new family forms include rural and urban communes, group marriage, "open marriage," family networks, swinging, homosexual pairings, marriage contracts, and cohabitation, many of which are considered in the articles which follow. While I indicate below that particular new family forms adhere to social values, behaviors, relationships, and other practices which challenge old assumptions, it should be understood that each family form does not necessarily include or practice every new life style. For example, sexual exclusiveness is likely to be rejected in communes, but some communes do adhere to exclusivity, and even in communes in which many members do not, some members probably will. This kind of variation on a theme is undoubtedly true for each family form.

Privatization. The contemporary American family is made up of a highly private set of social relationships. As Philippe Ariés has noted, however, this was not always the case. The eighteenth-century family "began to hold society at a distance, to push it back beyond a steadily extending zone of private life,"[19] gradually excluding servants, clients, and friends from intensive participation in the daily life of the family. Suburban life in the United States and life in the large apartment complexes of our cities epitomize the private life of the family; in the former, the world is shut out in the isolation of the house while outdoor life centers in the backyard, away from public eyes. In the latter, the conventions so isolate people from each other that one family may not even know the name of its neighbors, upstairs and down, as well as on the same floor.

To the extent that new life styles bring together people on the basis of friendship, love, affection, or even convenience rather than by ties of blood or marriage, these styles are a challenge to century-old beliefs, customs, and expectations. This deprivatizing appears to be characteristic, to some extent, of all of the new life styles, but especially so in communes, group marriages, family networks, cohabitation, and same-sex pairings. The implications are that living arrangements become a matter of personal choice, fairly changeable, rather than a commitment to an unselected bond (consanguineal) or a long-discarded choice (conjugal). There is no doubt that this arrangement will have problems, especially that of providing stability for achieving long-range goals or providing emotional and social stability in twosomes as well as perhaps for children. But it also means that incompatibility between mates, between children, and between parents and children does not have to be tolerated.

Socialization. The task of socializing children and the continued socialization of adults—whether or not such socialization tasks are formally shared or not—is no longer a burden on one or two individuals, but becomes shared. Each person may now experience multiple styles of intimacy and learn multiple patterns of interpersonal styles, even though biological parents may have the major responsibility.

Property. Family units such as communes and group marriage are challenges to the notions of individualized consumption of consumer goods—a washing machine for each house, a lawn mower for each lawn, a family room for each American castle. Any extensive pattern of sharing residences, goods, and services would have a vast repercussion on the American economy. That result is less likely than the possibility that the participants in such a family will have less need for money. Therefore, they may select to do less wage work than is usual in our society and to devote time to other kinds of activities or have a good deal more discretionary income available for luxury goods—stereos, travel, and the like. The chances are, given the present composition of communes, that it will more likely be the first than the second. In any case, these new families challenge the basic assumption in American middle-class families that it is necessary to have private space and private consumer goods available as well as the notion that earnings must be shared only with family members.

Sexuality. Two aspects of sexuality are challenged by the new family forms: (a) sexual exclusiveness, and (b) heterosexual orientations. Certainly, sexual exclusivity has been considered a basis of virtually all Western family systems (the main exception being the

Mormon family). The violation of monogamy, especially by the woman, has usually been considered grounds for dissolving the marriage. Hence, such activities as swinging, group marriage, or intimate friendships offer a considerable alternative to the conventional family system. Just as the deprivatizing of the family offers group members some alternative close relationships, so the discarding of sexual exclusiveness as a basic premise of relationships opens up opportunities for variety, experimentation, and personal growth. Whether Americans who have been socialized to the conventional practices of monogamy can accept nonexclusiveness is another question, for there are indications that jealousy can be a considerable problem. Heterosexuality as the only legitimate basis for a stable social relationship has also been challenged by the attempts of homosexuals to gain legal rights, to cease to have their sexual orientation considered pathological, and to argue for marriage on the same basis as heterosexuals. The most important aspect of the current movement for homosexual rights is that it may lead to the possibility of greater stability in same-sex relationships, for it is difficult to know what role the laws against homosexuals have played in encouraging their often-noted, fairly unstable relationships. The recognition of homosexuality as an alternative, nonpathological orientation also opens up new opportunities for closeness and variations in sexual expression.

Sex Equality. "Open marriage" and marriage contracts appear to be the only life styles that incorporate sex equality, though swinging, to the extent that it discards the double sexuality standard, may also be included. Whether or not group marriages, communes, family networks, or cohabitation are characterized by much sex equality appears to depend on the specific group. Some communes, for example, are characterized by highly segregated sex roles while others adhere to sex equality. Sex equality, therefore, seems a character quite apart from any particular life style. The marriage contract offers the clearest challenge to traditional sex roles, since by this device all of the traditional roles which men and women play can be examined systematically and accepted or rejected.

Commitment Period. Unlike conventional marriage, none of the living styles I have been discussing assumes a lifetime commitment, although a contract marriage, since it occurs within the framework of legal marriage, may be an exception. Otherwise, the relationships are for as long as the participants are satisfied. As I noted when discussing the antiprivatization aspect of the new family styles, the openness of the period of commitment is not without problems.

Negotiation. The basis of commitment itself constitutes an important challenge to the family whose organization and function have been controlled to a considerable degree by legal institutions. The law regulates who may form a family (according to age, sex, degree of kinship, marital status, and so forth), family roles (economic, sexual, housekeeping responsibilities), and grounds for dissolution and rights after dissolution (economic, parenting). The informal or extralegal commitments which women and men make to each other in the new family forms have an ambiguous legal status—for example, marriage contracts are not yet enforceable in law insofar as the relational items are concerned and are not anyway, unless formal legal procedures are followed; or a state may recognize the children of a consensual unit for purposes of Workmen's Compensation yet not legally recognize the mother of the children. The absence of control by legal institutions extends the areas which are subject to negotiation in a social relationship to an enormous degree and challenges the right of the state to intervene in the relationship except in the broadest possible ways.

CONCLUSIONS

The wit and energy of most women and men in the United States no longer need be directed with great intensity toward sheer physical survival. Both sexes, moreover, see the possibility of satisfying lives outside the boundary of traditional marriage, and the government has withdrawn from supporting institutional reform while often harassing those who do. In this context, many Americans have focused their attempts to improve the quality of life on improving interpersonal relationships, especially between friends, between lovers, and between kin.

Without detracting from the contributions which the new interpersonal styles make to individual satisfaction, growth and development, and even to changing social organization, I want to suggest several questions which confront us.

First, what is the relationship between the interpersonal behavior of individuals and social organization? Basically, the question is whether or not the private islands people create—communes, egalitarian relationships between women and men, "living together," gay pairings, and so on—can flourish successfully without institutional supports. For example, are egalitarian relations between the sexes possible when sexism persists in the economic and political institutions and in daily experiences of women and men; will not each sex be pushed back toward traditional roles unless institutions and experiences change? Can urban communes succeed where cities establish ordinances governing the number and legal relationships between persons sharing household? (In the spring of 1974, for example, the Portland, Oregon, City Council passed an ordinance which defines family so as to restrict the number of adults and children in a household. Section 33.12.310 of the Code of the City of Portland includes this definition: "*Family* means one person or two or more persons related by blood, marriage, legal adoption or guardianship plus not more than four additional persons excluding servants, all living together as a single housekeeping unit in a dwelling unit.") Or can couple cohabitation survive the legal and financial problems which effect credit, health insurance, Workmen's Compensation, and so forth? Sociological data strongly suggest that it is difficult for interpersonal relationships to be drastically altered and/or to remain so when the institutions in society are incompatible with them.[20]

Second, how important is it for the emotional well-being of the individual to have an interpersonal relationship of *primacy* in which each member of the dyad is the "most important" person to the other? (I call this *primacy* in contrast to monogamy, for probably the relationship does not have to be exclusive; primacy would include all or some of the following dimensions—emotional, sexual, intellectual.) Family theorists have commented at length on the dangers of too much dependence on the part of one or both persons in a relationship, especially on the difficulties of expecting another to meet all of one's needs. Little attention has been given to the problem of primacy, although O'Neill and O'Neill seem to suggest in discussing "open marriage" that just such a primacy in the marriage relationship serves as a foundation for conducting nonthreatening, extramarital sexual, emotional, and intellectual relationships.

Finally, what are the sociological and social psychological consequences of separating dimensions of interpersonal relationships, particularly separating sexuality from emotional dimensions? For example, it is often suggested that the sexes differ in their sexuality because women, unlike men, presumably, have a far greater need to interweave sexual with emotional feelings. Sometimes this difference is explained as a basic biological difference (men have a stronger sex drive than women), and sometimes as rooted in culture (women are taught that strong positive emotional feelings are a prerequisite to legitimate sexual expression). But, the difference has been explained from a perspective of justifying the greater sexual freedom of men or of "allowing" women the same sexual freedom as men. Turning the question around, we might ask if men have less satisfactory sexual experiences than they otherwise might because they separate sexuality (presumably they are taught to do so) from other aspects of interpersonal relationships. The array of life styles are a "natural laboratory" from which we may be able to find information for answering these and other questions.

Additional questions about interpersonal styles are raised or implied in the articles which follow, and the reader will no doubt have many other questions.

NOTES

1. Warren G. Bennis, Edgar H. Schein, Fred I. Steele, and David E. Berlew, *Interpersonal Dynamics* (Homewood, Ill.: Dorsey Press, 1968), pp. 8–9.
2. Ibid., pp. 337–38.
3. William J. Goode, *World Revolution and Family Patterns* (New York: The Free Press, 1970), pp. 7–10. See E. T. Pryor, Jr., "Rhode Island Family Structure: 1875–1960" in *Household and Family in Past Time,* Peter Laslett, ed. (London: Cambridge University Press, 1972), pp. 571–89, for an historical analysis of the question of family size and structure.
4. Ivy Pinchbeck, *Women Workers and the Industrial Revolution, 1750–1850* (London: George Routledge and Sons, Ltd. 1930); Robert W. Smuts, *Women and Work in America* (New York: Columbia University Press, 1959).
5. William F. Ogburn and Clark Tibbitts, "The Family and Its Functions," Report of the President's Research Committee, *Recent Social Trends in the United States* (New York: McGraw-Hill Book Co. 1934), pp. 661–708.
6. George J. McCall, "The Social Organization of Relationships," in George J. McCall, et al., *Social Relationships* (Chicago: Aldine Publishing Co., 1970), pp. 5–6.
7. Marvin B. Scott, "The Social Sources of Alienation," in *The New Sociology: Essays in Honor of C. Wright Mills,* Irving L. Horowitz, ed.

(New York: Oxford University Press, 1956), pp. 241–46.
8. Talcott Parsons. "The Kinship System of Contemporary United States," in *Essays in Sociological Theory* (New York: The Free Press, 1964).
9. Peter L. Berger and Hansfried Kellner, "Marriage and the Construction of Reality," in *Woman in a Man-Made World,* Nona Glazer-Malbin and Helen Y. Waehrer, eds. (Chicago: Rand McNally, 1972) p. 174.
10. David Riesman, *The Lonely Crowd* (New Haven: Yale University Press, 1961).
11. See Jo Freeman, "The Origins of the Women's Movement," *American Journal of Sociology,* 78 (January, 1973): 30–49; Catharine Stimpson, " 'Thy Neighbor's Wife, Thy Neighbor's Servants': Women's Liberation and Black Civil Rights," in *Woman in Sexist Society: Studies in Power and Powerlessness,* Vivian Gornick and Barbara K. Moran, eds. (New York: Basic Books, 1971) 622–57.
12. Gillian Lindt Gollin, "Family Surrogates in Colonial America: The Moravian Experiment," *Journal of Marriage and the Family,* 31 (November, 1969): 650–58.
13. William M. Kephart, "Experimental Family Organization: An Historico-Cultural Report on the Oneida Community," *Journal of Marriage and the Family,* 25 (August, 1963): 261–71.
14. Yonina Talmon, *Family and Community in the Kibbutz* (Cambridge, Mass.: Harvard University Press, 1972).
15. Juliet Mitchell, "Women: The Longest Revolution," *New Left Review* (December, 1966): p. 11.
16. Melford Spiro, "Is the Family Universal?" *American Anthropologist,* 56 (October, 1954): 839–46. Addendum in Norman Bell and Ezra Vogel, eds., *A Modern Introduction to the Family* (New York: The Free Press, 1968).
17. Donald W. Ball, "The Family as a Sociological Problem: Conceptualization of the Taken-for-Granted as a Prologue to Social Problems Analysis," *Social Problems,* 19 (1972): 302.
18. Eleanor Macklin's study of cohabitation includes persons who share a residence but are not engaged in sexual relationships: "Heterosexual Cohabitation Among Unmarried College Students," *The Family Coordinator* (October, 1972): pp. 463–71.
19. Philippe Ariés, *Centuries of Childhood* (New York: Vintage Books, 1962), pp. 390–403.
20. See Yonina Talmon, "Differentiation and Elite Formation," in *Family and Community in the Kibbutz* (Cambridge, Mass.: Harvard University Press, 1972).

Another paper by Dr. Glazer may be found as the fifth item in the ADULTS section, titled "Housework: A Review Essay."

Family Time and Historical Time

TAMARA K. HAREVEN

HISTORY IS OFTEN INVOKED TO SHOW "how we got where we are." While historical research can perform that function, it can also perform two others: it can offer a comparative perspective on the present, and it can suggest models for future change. The first of these functions is a new task more frequently performed by cross-cultural studies of "primitive" societies—that is, to compare current conditions, modes of behavior, and values with those in past societies. Such a comparative perspective does not necessarily carry built-in explanations of development and change, but it provides a vantage point from which to see both the unique and the common features of current behavior and problems, illuminating such questions as whether the family is "in trouble" or "going out of existence," and whether the crises currently experienced in American society are really "unprecedented." Through this comparison of present and past, historical analysis can point to major continuities and discontinuities in family development. A relatively new field, the history of the family has tantalized historians and scholars in other disciplines precisely because the data it addresses can illuminate issues such as these. The questions asked by family historians have much in common with those raised by sociologists, psychologists, anthropologists, and economists. The contribution of historians lies in the change-over-time perspective which informs their questioning and in the social and cultural context specific to the different time periods under investigation.[1]

Historical studies about the family share with the "new social history" an interest in studying whole populations rather than simply the "great" individuals or elites within them. By delving into census records, birth, marriage, and death records, private diaries, public documents, medical and educational treatises, and family letters, historians have begun to reconstruct the family patterns of large numbers of anonymous individuals. The history of the family has thus served to reintroduce human intimacy into historical research and, at the same time, to generate a realistic view of the complexities of historical change.[2] An understanding of how individuals and families have responded to historical changes and, at the same time, what their roles were in affecting such changes can considerably broaden our understanding of the process of change itself.

As the field has developed, historians have expanded their inquiry from an earlier preoccupation with the classifications of household and family structure to a broad range of subjects, encompassing marriage and sexual behavior, child-rearing, and relations among kin. In trying to understand the role of the family and its internal dynamics in the past, historians are gradually moving from a concentration on the family itself to an exploration of its interaction with other social processes and institutions. Studies examining the role of the family in migration or the interaction between the family and the industrial process have begun to advance new views about past family behavior.[3]

Particularly important has been a revision of the traditional notion that the family broke down under the impact of industrialization and urbanization.

Rather than continuing to view the family as a passive agent, historical studies have revealed that the role of the family was in fact that of an active agent, fostering social change and facilitating the adaptation of its members to new social and economic conditions. The family not only did not break down under the impact of urbanization and industrialization; under certain circumstances, it actually helped to foster those changes.[4] Reacting against earlier studies of family change, especially those advanced by "modernization" theory, students of the family have been able to show that families did not "modernize" automatically in response to sweeping changes in the larger society. Rural families who migrated into urban areas and working-class families already in the cities held on to their traditions, protected their members from drastic dislocations, and prevented family breakdown. Nonetheless, families did act as agents of change, socializing and preparing their members for new ways of life, facilitating their adaptation to industrial work and to living in large complex urban communities.

These findings have refined some basic conceptions about the adaptations of different groups to changing social conditions and have offered insights into how the *process* of change functions in different levels of society. Particularly important has been the realization that family behavior was paced differently among different social groups, that people could be "modern" at work and "traditional" at home, and that the family exercised the power of initiative and choice in accepting new ways of life. Even in industrial society, traditional patterns have persisted among families of different cultural and ethnic groups, contradicting established notions that individuals and institutions uniformly shed their traditional customs as the larger society becomes "modernized."[5]

This dynamic approach to family behavior also views the family as a constantly changing entity, as its members move through life. Social scientists have often studied the family as a monolithic institution. In reality, the family is in constant flux. It is the scene of interaction between various fluid individual lives. Individual transitions into and out of different family roles, such as leaving home, getting married, setting up an independent household, commencement of parenthood, or—at the other end of the cycle—widowhood are interrelated with changes in the family as a collective unit.

How did individuals time their transitions into and out of various family roles, and how were these patterns of timing related to the family as a collective unit? At issue here is the synchronization of several concepts of time—individual time, family time, and historical time.

This essay examines some aspects of their interaction over the past two centuries in the United States.

Family Time and Historical Time

Most activities in modern life are governed by specific and often rigidly enforced schedules, whether they result from personal relationships or other kinds of social communication. Being early, late, or on time, juggling complicated schedules, and fulfilling a series of conflicting roles within time slots have been essential characteristics of modern society, the product of urban, industrial living. Timing has also become a central feature in the scheduling of family events and the transitions of individuals into different family roles. One of the most fascinating problems is that of the synchronizing of all the different "time clocks" that govern both the movement of individuals and families through life and larger patterns of societal change. Historical time is generally defined as a linear chronological movement of changes in a society over decades or centuries, while individual lifetime is measured according to age. But age and chronology both need social contexts to be meaningful. Social age is different from chronological age: in certain societies, a twelve-year-old is an adolescent; in others, he is already an adult; in certain societies, a person of fifty is middle aged; in others, he is old. How were typical lives "timed" in the past, and how did these life-course patterns fit into their economic, institutional, and demographic setting?

The understanding of "time" patterns along the life course provides an insight into one of the least understood aspects of family behavior—namely, the process of decision making within the family. Since we know that the structure of the family has persisted in its nuclear form over the past two centuries, examinations of how families time their behavior can reveal the important areas in which the major changes in family behavior have taken place.[6]

The concept of "family time" designates the timing of events such as marriage, birth of a child, leaving home, and the transition of individuals into different roles as the family moves through its life course. Timing has often been a major source of conflict and pressure in the family, since "individual time" and "family time" are not always in harmony. For example, the decision to leave home, to marry, or to form one's own family could not in the past be timed strictly in accordance with individual preferences, depending instead on the decisions and needs of the family as a collective unit and on institutional supports. Research has only just begun to sketch some of the basic patterns of the timing of family transitions and to link them with "historical time"—that is, with changing social conditions.

The social values governing timing have also changed under different historical circumstances. For example, the age at which a young man is considered a "drop-out" or a woman an "old maid" varies in different societies and periods. What constitutes a violation of "normal" sequences in the timing of family events also varies among different societies. For example, teenage marriage is under some circumstances, but not under others, considered an act of deviance, and motherhood preceding marriage is considered a violation of social norms in most societies.

Historical changes have impinged upon the timing of family events by providing the institutional or social conditions under which such transitions can be implemented or impeded. It would have been impossible, for instance, to enforce societal requirements for school attendance if public schools had not been readily available; similarly, it would have been difficult to impose compulsory retirement without institutionalized social security or old-age pensions. Institutions of social welfare and social control and public welfare programs have taken over many of the welfare functions previously performed by the family. Under historical conditions where most of the educational, economic, and welfare functions are concentrated in the family, the timing of transitions within the family was more significant than in modern society. In addition to institutional buttresses, a variety of social and economic developments have affected individual and family timetables. Wars and depressions have drastically altered patterns of family timing. Even on a smaller scale, however, such events as migration or the shutdown of a factory, while they do not affect the entire society, can have an important impact on timing for the families involved. Without denying the importance of large-scale transformations, viewing social change from the perspective of the family offers a considerable refinement of our understanding of the interaction between it and individual and family behavior. Migration, for example, could have a greater impact than war upon the behavior of a particular family, despite the larger societal implications of the war.[7]

One of the recurring themes in American history is that of the variation in norms by ethnic cultures within the larger society. "Irish family time" differed in certain respects from "French-Canadian family time," while both differed from native-American family time. These variations result from discrepancies and conflicts between the traditions and practices of different cultural groups and those of the dominant culture. Irish immigrants in late-nineteenth-century Massachusetts, for example, married later than French Canadians or native Americans. Native Americans married earlier and commenced childbearing earlier than Irish immigrants, but they also stopped childbearing earlier, while Irish families had larger numbers of children spread over a longer time period.[8]

A focus on timing enables us to see the point at which family members converge or diverge at different stages of their individual development and how such patterns relate to the collective experience of the family at different points of its development.[9] Even the use of the word "children" within the family is ambiguous, because, in families with large numbers of children encompassing a broad age distribution, an older child will be in an entirely different position within the family vis-à-vis adults and siblings than either the younger ones or those in the middle. As the age configuration of children within the family changes, the status of each child in the family becomes different as well; for example, after the oldest child leaves home, the next child becomes the "oldest" and takes on a new status.

The distinctions are important because individuals fulfill a multiplicity of roles. They can simultaneously be members of their family of origin and their family of procreation. After forming his own family, an individual maintains some ties with his family of origin, but also forms a new allegiance with that of the spouse. The complexity of affiliations casts an individual into various overlapping and, at times, conflicting family roles, which continue to vary at different stations along the life course. Some roles become more active, others recede in importance. A son becomes a father; later, after his own children become independent and his parents have reached the age of needing assistance, he becomes a son again, sometimes even more intensively. The various familial roles held by individuals could come into competition or conflict under different historical conditions, particularly during migration or unemployment, for example.

As Talcott Parsons has pointed out, the kinship system of the United States is loosely structured so that most forms of assistance among kin are informal and voluntary.[10] While the mutual obligations of husbands and wives or parents and children are clearly sanctioned and defined, relationships with extended kin are not. But under different historical and personal circumstances the interaction of individuals both with other members of the nuclear family and with extended kin can vary considerably, because the individual's position in his own family and his relationship to other family members and to more distant kin are entwined with the family's development as a collective unit.

Historical Differences in the Timing of Family Transitions

One widely held myth about the past is that the timing of family transitions was once more orderly and stable than it is today. The complexity that governs family life today and the variations in family roles and in transitions into them are frequently contrasted to this more placid past. The historical record, however, frequently reveals precisely the opposite condition. Patterns of family timing in the past were often more complex, more diverse, and less orderly than they are today: voluntary and involuntary demographic changes that have come about since the late nineteenth century have in fact paradoxically resulted in greater uniformity in the timing of transitions along the life course, despite greater societal complexity. The growing uniformity in timing has been accompanied by a shift from involuntary to voluntary factors affecting the timing of family events.[11] The increase in life expectancy, the decline in fertility, and an earlier marriage age have, for example, greatly increased the chances for temporal overlap in the lives of family members. Families are now able to go through a life course much less subject to sudden change than that experienced by the majority of the population in the nineteenth century.

The "typical" family cycle of modern American families includes early marriage and early commencement of childbearing, but a small number of children. Between 1810 and 1930 the birth rate declined from an average of 8 children per mother to slightly less than 3. Families following this type of family cycle experience a compact period of parenthood in the middle years of life, then an extended period, encompassing one-third of their adult life, without children; and finally often a period of solitary living following the death of a spouse, most frequently of the husband.[12]

This type of cycle has important implications for the composition of the family and for relationships within it in current society: husbands and wives are spending a relatively longer lifetime together, they invest a shorter segment of their lives in child-rearing, and they more commonly survive to grand-parenthood. This sequence has been uniform for the majority of the population since the beginning of the twentieth century. In contrast to past times, most families see their children through to adulthood with both parents still alive. As Peter Uhlenberg points out:

> The normal family cycle for women, a sequence of leaving home, marriage, family formation, child-rearing, launching and survival at age 50 with the first marriage still intact, unless broken by divorce, has not been the dominant pattern of family timing before the early twentieth century.[13]

Prior to 1900, only about 40 per cent of the female population in the United States experienced this ideal family cycle. The remainder either never married, never reached marriageable age, died before childbirth, or were widowed while their offspring were still young children.[14]

In the nineteenth century, the combination of a later age at marriage and higher fertility provided little opportunity for a family to experience an empty-nest stage. Prior to the decline in mortality among the young at the beginning of the twentieth century, marriage was frequently broken by the death of a spouse before the end of the child-rearing period. Even when fathers survived the child-rearing years, they rarely lived beyond the marriage of their second child. As a result of higher fertility, children were spread over a wider age range; frequently the youngest child was just entering school as the oldest was preparing for marriage. The combination of later marriage, higher fertility, and widely spaced childbearing resulted in a different timing of family transitions. Individuals became parents later, but carried child-rearing responsibilities almost until the end of their lives. Consequently the lives of parents overlapped with those of their children for shorter periods than they do in current society.

Under the demographic conditions of the nineteenth century, higher mortality and higher fertility, functions within the family were less specifically tied to age, and members of different age groups were consequently not so completely segregated by the tasks they were required to fulfill. The spread of children over a larger age spectrum within the family had important implications for family relationships as well as for their preparation for adult roles. Children were accustomed to growing up with larger numbers of siblings and were exposed to a greater variety of models from which to choose than they would have been in a small nuclear family. Older children often took charge of their younger siblings. Sisters, in particular, carried a major share of the responsibility for raising the youngest siblings and frequently acted as surrogate mother if the mother worked outside the home, or if she had died. The smaller age overlap between children and their parents was also significant: the oldest child was the one most likely to overlap with its father in adulthood; the youngest child, the least likely to do so. The oldest children were most likely to embark on an independent career before the parents reached old-age dependency; the youngest children were most likely to carry responsibilities for parental support, and to overlap in adulthood with a widowed mother. The oldest child had the greatest chance to overlap with grandparents, the youngest child the least. Late-marrying children were most likely to be responsible for the support of a widowed mother, while early-marrying children depended on their parents' household space after marriage.[15] One can better grasp the implications of these differences in age at marriage, number of children, assigned tasks, and generational overlap when one takes into consideration the uncertainties and the economic precariousness that characterized the period; these made the orderly sequence of progression along stages of the family cycle, which sociologists have observed in the contemporary American population, impossible for the nineteenth-century family.

Another comparison between what is considered the "normal" family cycle today and its many variants in the nineteenth century reverses one more stereotype about the past—namely that American society has been experiencing breakdown and diversification in family organization. In reality, the major transitions in family roles have been characterized by greater stability and conformity, because of the greater opportunity for generational continuities. The opportunity for a meaningful period of overlap in the lives of grandparents and grandchildren is a twentieth-century phenomenon, a surprising fact that runs counter to the popular myth of a family solidarity in the past that was based on three-generational ties.

The relative significance of transition into family roles also differed in the nineteenth century. In the nineteenth century, when conception was likely to take place very shortly after marriage, the major transition in a woman's life was represented by marriage itself. But, as the interval between marriage and first pregnancy has increased in modern society, the transition to parenthood has become more significant than the transition to marriage. Family limitation has also had an impact on the timing of marriage. Since marriage no longer inevitably leads to parenthood, postponing marriage is no longer needed to delay it. On the other end of the life course, transitions *out* of parental roles are much more critical today than they were in the past when parental or surrogate-parental roles encompassed practically the entire adult life span.[16] Completion of parental roles today involves changes in residence, in work, and eventually, perhaps, removal into institutions or retirement communities.

Some familial transitions are also more easily reversible today than they were in the past. Marriages can now be ended by divorce, while, prior to the middle of the nineteenth century, they were more likely to be ended by the death of a spouse.

The overall historical pattern of family behavior has thus been marked by a shift from involuntary to voluntary forces controlling the timing of family events. It has also been characterized by greater rigidity and uniformity in the timing of the passage from one family role to another. In their comparison of such transitions in nineteenth-century Philadelphia with the present, Modell, Furstenburg, and Hershberg conclude that transitions into adult roles (departure from the family of origin, marriage, and the establishment of a household) follow a more ordered sequence and are accomplished over a shorter time period in a young person's life today than they were in the nineteenth century. Such transitions to familial roles also coincide today with transitions into occupational roles: "Transitions are today more contingent, more integrated because they are constrained by a set of formal institutions. 'Timely' action to nineteenth-century families consisted of helpful response in times of trouble; in the twentieth century, timeliness connotes adherence to a schedule."[17]

Life-Course Transitions and Family Strategies

What factors guided these transitions and moves into different family roles, what constituted continuities and discontinuities in such transitions, and how did they affect family behavior? Historical research has only barely begun to address these questions. Seemingly "disorderly" patterns in the timing of transitions in the nineteenth century were the result of the special role which the family fulfilled in the society and the prevailing view of its role and organization. The family was a corporate body operating as a collective unit, and the functions of the members within it were defined on that basis.

In modern society, we are accustomed to think of most family and work-career decisions as having been made by individuals. Even marriage is perceived as an individual decision, as an act resulting in independence from one's parents. But until recently these apparently individual transitions were treated as *family* moves and were, therefore, synchronized with other family needs and strategies. Marriage was not seen so much as a union between two freely acting individuals as an alliance between two families. The decision to marry, the choice of spouse, and the timing of the event all depended on calculations relating to the transmission of property, the finding of a job and housing, the support of aging parents, and to a wide variety of other family needs; it was not merely an impulse of romantic love. Collective family decisions took precedence over individual preferences. The careers of individuals were directed by the "familistic" ideology which remained powerful to the end of the nineteenth century, and which persisted in the lives of certain social groups into the twentieth century.

In Western society today, the major burdens of family relationships are emotional, while, in the nineteenth century, they were heavily weighted toward economic needs and tasks. Nor was this situation limited to the rural and urban working classes; the upper class as well maintained a corporate view and organization of family relationships. Family members were valued not only for the way they related to each other and for the degree of emotional satisfaction and nurturing they offered, but also for the contributions they could make to fulfilling familial obligations and maintaining continuity and stability in the family's daily existence. Family and kin were particularly valued for providing assistance during periods of crisis and need, with the understanding that their help could be reciprocated in the future.[18]

Relationships between husbands and wives, parents and children, distant kin, and even family members and strangers were based on socially sanctioned mutual obligations that transcended personal affection and sentiment. Parents raised and supported their children with the dual expectations that the children would start to work as soon as they were able and that they would ultimately support the parents in old age. This "instrumental" view of family relationships has survived the industrial revolution, and it persists in the lives of working-class and rural families today. But in the absence of institutionalized public welfare, such instrumental exchanges between family members in the nineteenth century were essential for survival. They formed the backbone of familial relationships, providing continuity from one generation to the next.[19]

Although the obligations that family members had for each other were not contractually defined, they rested on established social norms, and families had their own methods for enforcing them and for ensuring that the younger members in particular would not put their own interest before that of the family as a collective unit. In rural society, these sanctions were based on the inheritance of land, control of which offered aging parents the necessary leverage for securing old-age support from their sons. In industrial society, sanctions were less formal and were enforced mainly by the need for reciprocity dictated by the insecurities of urban life. Mutual assistance from more distant kin was more apt to entail routine help on a daily basis, such as exchanges of tools, child care, loans, temporary sharing of housing space, and support during crisis situations, such as childbirth, illness, or death. Structured and long-range exchanges across the life course generally involved only close kin—parents and children or siblings to each other.

One of the underlying goals of such reciprocal relationships was the maintenance of familial self-sufficiency. Families preferred to rely on each other for assistance rather than on strangers, even if the strangers were nearer. Individuals were expected to postpone or sacrifice their personal advancement if it jeopardized the family's autonomy as a unit, because the autonomy of the household was felt to be the foundation of family self-sufficiency. Regardless of class, occupation, or ethnic background, most American households in the nineteenth century were nuclear, as they are today, reflecting society's commitment to this autonomy. Families shared their household space with other kin only as a last resort, during periods of housing shortage or severe economic constraint.[20] Co-residence of married children with their parents was generally temporary. Young couples, particularly at the stage of family formation, strove to establish independent households; older couples, as they moved into their later years of life, tried to hold on to the independent household they had. If households became extended, it was usually only late in life. In most situations, even widows tried to maintain their own household by taking in strangers as tenants, rather than live in other people's houses.[21] Autonomy of the household should not be confused, however, with the notion of privacy as we have become accustomed to it. When people had to share their household space they did not hesitate to do so. Households functioned like accordions, expanding and contracting in accordance with changing family needs and external conditions.

Families generally tended to prefer the co-residence of strangers to relatives—at least the boarders or lodgers in most households far outnumbered the kin. We do not know why, and can only surmise that taking in boarders or lodgers represented a clearly defined economic relationship, restricted to a certain period, while sharing one's household with kin could result in a greater and longer-range infringement of the household space as well as in family conflicts. Reciprocity in family relationships was thus more heavily weighted toward exchanging resources and services than toward sharing living space.[22]

Mutual obligations and needs within the family imposed serious pressures on the timing of family transitions, and obviously caused trouble when individual preferences came into conflict with the family's collective timetable. Children had to leave school and start work early to support their younger siblings; sons and daughters often had to postpone marriage, or never marry, to support their aging parents. Individual wishes to leave home or to marry were frequently frustrated in the effort to sustain the family of origin. The types of tensions and pressures arising from such situations were only rarely recorded, and therefore cannot be easily retrieved, but the conflict and frustration individuals experienced when their own plans had to give way to family needs do seep through occasionally, particularly in oral history records. Judging from these occasional statements, family members often reconciled or escaped tensions by drastic moves such as leaving home or migrating. If they did so, they opened up new opportunities for employment and marriage and provided at least temporary escape from family pressures. But marriage or migration rarely broke the magic circle of obligations to kin forever; it extended across the life course.

How conflicts within families were resolved and how the distribution of resources was equalized are still questions in need of exploration. That they existed is itself of importance, however: the emphasis in this essay on the viability of instrumental relationships should not produce a new set of clichés for idealizing the past; rather it should highlight the flexibility in the organization of the household and in the allocation of tasks within the family which served to meet the mutual obligations of family members and to confront the uncertainties of their lives.

Historical Implications

What are the implications of these differences in the timing of individual transitions for the understanding of historical changes in the family generally? Slow and uneven transitions of individuals out of the family of origin and into independent adult roles were the result of a more continuous integration within the family of origin. This meant a greater continuity in the obligations of young people to their parents, which reached more deeply into their own adulthood and often overlapped with their own parental responsibilities. It also entailed a prolonged apprenticeship for future family roles which individuals carried out in their families of origin and, therefore, a less abrupt transition when they did marry and become parents. Closer integration within the family of origin offered greater opportunity for exchange along the life course. In the past, long-term familial obligations were imperative because of mortality, migration, and economic constraints under which the majority of the population functioned. Prior to the "affluent" society and the assumption of important familial functions by the welfare state, the family had mainly itself to rely on to meet its economic needs, to stave off dependency, and to cope with insecurities and disasters. Mutual help by family members was essential for survival. The modern notion of independent autonomous careers, linearly directed toward individual success and an almost exclusive investment in one's conjugal family, is dissonant with conceptions of family obligations in the past. Under earlier conditions when work careers were erratic and unpredictable, the insecurities of the market dictated a tight integration and an interchangeability of the tasks and functions of different family members. When occupational opportunities favored young women, a daughter was sent to work, and when they favored young men, a son was sent. When husbands and wives both found work outside the home, they shared household tasks as well; if only one could find work, the other carried the major burden of domestic responsibilities. This integration of individuals into the family's economic effort is characteristic primarily of rural society, but it also carried over into industrial society in the lives of the working class.[23]

Individualistic patterns of family behavior first appeared in the nineteenth century among the urban middle class, and with them came patterns of segregation in family roles. Middle-class families were the first to follow a clear timing sequence for their children's entry into, and exit from, school, and to promulgate an orderly career pattern that led from choosing an occupation to leaving the parental household, marrying, and forming the new family. Orderly progression along the life course and structured transitions from one stage to the next were related to the "discovery" of childhood and, subsequently, adolescence as distinct stages of life. The segregation of age groups in accordance with their functions also occurred first among middle-class families. The emergence of the private, child-centered family consciously separating itself from the outside world brought about major redefinitions of traditional family roles and functions. This new family type placed emphasis on the family as a center for nurture and affection rather than as a corporate unit. Their wages no longer needed, women and children in the middle class were exempted from the labor force. Wives were expected instead to be the custodians of the family and to protect the home as a refuge from the world of work, and children, although expected to help with household tasks, were freed from serious work responsibilities until their late teens.[24]

Members of middle-class, native-American families were the first to marry younger, to control fertility, and to space their children more closely. In their behavior, as well as in their mentality, they began to approximate the middle-class-family type which has become so common in the twentieth century. Working-class and first-generation immigrant families, on the other hand, continued to hold on to traditional views of family roles, functions, and patterns of timing, at least in the first generation. The various ethnic groups and the working class thus lagged behind the middle class in adopting this new timing and in role segregation among ages. The influx of new groups from rural and small-town backgrounds continued to infuse pre-modern patterns of timing into an increasingly homogenizing society. As state institutions gradually took over the functions of welfare, education, and social control that had previously lodged in the family, there was greater conformity in timing. The gradual introduction of age-related requirements, such as compulsory school attendance, child-labor legislation, and mandatory retirement have all combined to impose more rigid patterns of timing in the larger society and, in the process, have also caused greater uniformity in the timing of family behavior.

Modern American society thus presents a paradox: while, on the one hand, involuntary factors affecting timing of family roles have declined and, on the other hand, voluntary means of manipulating timing, in postponing or reversing transitions, and in juggling a variety of roles have increased, the resulting "liberalization" of timing patterns has been accompanied by a greater rigidity and uniformity in timing of family transitions in modern society than had been experienced in the past. The increase in uniformity in family time has coincided with a growing diversity both in career and opportunity choices and in familial and non-familial arrangements. The broadening opportunity structure, increasing affluence, and a diffusion of obligations previously contained within the family were expected to lead to more flexible timing.

Changes in timing, however, do not always coincide with the availability of opportunity. One of the important sources of historical unrest, as revealed, for example, in the women's movement, has been the incongruity between the norms of timing and the availability of opportunities within the society to conform to those norms. During certain historical periods, individuals who desired to follow the newly established norms were not able to do so because the opportunity was not available. For example, women reached marital age, but were unable to marry because of the imbalance in sex ratios. Young men came of age for the commencement of their first job only to find that there was no job available. This disjuncture between timing and opportunity could also take the opposite form—under certain conditions, changes in the opportunity structure could alter timing patterns, but rigid familial traditions and ideology could prevent individuals from responding to them. In the late nineteenth century, for example, demographic and occupational factors combined to offer optimal conditions for the entry of married women into the labor force, but traditional patterns of timing and ideological constraints prevented middle-class women from taking advantage of these opportunities.[25]

The homogenization and growing conformity in family behavior have not been sufficiently matched by corresponding ideological and attitudinal changes. Demographic stability has been accompanied by psychological and internal conflict within the family. The increased chance for stability in the family as a result of diminishing involuntary disruptions (e.g., decline in mortality) has been counteracted by rising voluntary ones (e.g., increasing divorce rates). What does this suggest? Are families not capable of functioning in a stable and consistent way, as the norms articulated in the larger society expect them to? Or is the family unable to tolerate the demographic stability it has finally achieved?

Stability and conformity, particularly in an affluent society, have led to a greater concentration on the emotional content and function of the family. In periods when the family's economic stability was at stake, emotional gratification had less importance than had instrumental relationships. Parents burdened with the worry of raising numerous children had less time and energy to question personal relationships under conditions of high mortality and economic insecurity. Continuity and survival took precedence over intimacy. By contrast, the emphasis on privacy that characterizes the modern nuclear family has increased isolation and has forced husbands and wives and parents and children to fall back on their own emotional resources within the family, thus eliminating the opportunity for diversity in interaction between kin and strangers that existed in nineteenth-century families.

The decline in instrumental family relationships and the related emergence of privatism as the major ideological base of the family in society have tended to reinforce role segregation along age and sex lines. The modern, private, nuclear family has been frequently characterized as representing progress toward a more rational and equalized family existence. Sociologist William Goode, for example, has linked progress toward sex-role equality to the emergence of the "modern" conjugal family.[26] The historical experience actually shows that the increase in role segregation among family members (a direct product of nuclear-family isolation) has tended to diminish the opportunity for equality within the family. It also shows that sex and age segregations in family roles have been inventions of the past century rather than permanent features of family behavior. Motherhood as a full-time vocation has emerged only since the middle of the nineteenth century. Ironically, its glorification as a lifelong pursuit for women began to emerge at a time when demographic and social factors were significantly reducing the total proportion of a woman's life actually needed for it.[27] The time invested in various family functions and roles over the life course and their significance are still governed by nineteenth-century anachronisms, and are not in harmony with modern demographic and social realities. One major task families face today is bridging that gap.

Advocates of change have invoked historical precedent to reinforce arguments for reform, while custodians of tradition have invoked it to prove that we are threatened by social breakdown. Throughout American history, the family has been seen as the linchpin of the social order and stable governance. When larger societal processes are reflected in the family they have always been viewed with great anxiety. From the early settlers in Plymouth to modern reformers and social scientists, the fear of the breakdown of the family has haunted American society. Every generation seems to be witnessing difficulties and to be predicting the family's collapse. Social science has provided theoretical formulations for these historical anxieties; the breakdown of traditional family patterns under the impact of social change and modernization has been the standard sociological explanation for the "crisis" of the contemporary family.

The discovery of complexity in family behavior in the past, particularly in the area of timing, can provide a new perspective on the problems families face in contemporary society. The model of family behavior which emerges from the past is one of diversity and flexibility, a kind of controlled disorder that varied in accordance with pressing social and economic needs. The complexities, conflicts in roles, and variations imposed on individuals in modern society require an even greater diversity and malleability. If nothing else, history offers proof that families are able to display variety and diversity in their organization and timing and to contain conflicts between the needs of individuals and the collective demands of the family under changing historical conditions.

The family has never been a utopian retreat from the world, except in the imagination of social reformers and social scientists. Some of the major problems besetting family life today emanate from the heavy demands placed upon it by individuals in society who require that it be a haven of nurture and a retreat from the outside world. The modern family's growing discomfort suggests the need for expansion and diversity in what we expect from it and in its adaptation to new social conditions with diverse timing schedules and a multiplicity of roles for its members, rather than for seeking refuge in a non-existent past.

References

[1]On the development of the field, see Tamara K. Hareven, "The History of the Family as an Interdisciplinary Field," *Journal of Interdisciplinary History*, 2 (Autumn, 1971), pp. 399-414. Recent research in the field can be found in the new *Journal of Family History, Studies in Family, Kinship, and Demography*.

[2]See, for example, John Demos, *A Little Commonwealth: Family Life in Plymouth Colony* (New York, 1970); Philip Greven, *Four Generations: Population, Land, and Family in Colonial Andover, Massachusetts* (Ithaca, New York, 1970); Philippe Ariès, *Centuries of Childhood*, trans. Robert Baldick (New York, 1962); Peter Laslett and Richard Wall, eds., *Household and Family in Past Time* (Cambridge, 1972).

[3]The important pioneering work in this area is Neil Smelser, *Social Change in the Industrial Revolution* (Chicago, 1959). More recent works include Michael Anderson, *Family Structure in Nineteenth-Century Lancashire* (Cambridge, 1971); Virginia Y. McLaughlin, "Patterns of Work and Family Organization: Buffalo's Italians," *Journal of Interdisciplinary History*, 2 (Autumn, 1971), pp. 299-314; Tamara K. Hareven, "Family Time and Industrial Time," *Journal of Urban History*, 1 (May, 1975), pp. 365-89.

[4]William Goode, *World Revolution and Family Patterns* (New York, 1963).

[5]William Goode, "The Theory and Measurement of Family Change," in *Indicators of Social Change: Concepts and Measurements*, ed. Eleanor B. Sheldon and Wilbert Moore (New York, 1968), pp. 295-348; Tamara K. Hareven, "Modernization and Family History," *Signs*, 2 (Autumn, 1976), pp. 190-206.

[6]*Ibid.*

[7]An important theoretical formulation of the life course as it changes over time is Glen Elder, "Family History and the Life Course," in Tamara K. Hareven, ed., *The Family Cycle and the Life Course in Historical Perspective* (forthcoming); John Modell, Frank Furstenberg, and Theodore Hershberg, "Social Change and Transitions to Adulthood in Historical Perspective," *Journal of Family History*, 1 (Autumn, 1976), pp. 7-32.

[8]Tamara K. Hareven and Maris Vinovskis, "Marital Fertility, Ethnicity, and Occupation in Urban Families: An Analysis of South Boston and the South End in 1880," *Journal of Social History*, 3 (Spring, 1975), pp. 69-93; Hareven, "Family Time" (cited above, note 3); Howard Chudacoff, "Newlyweds and Familial Extension: First Stages of the Family Cycle in Providence, R.I., 1864-1880," forthcoming in Tamara K. Hareven and Maris Vinovskis, eds., *Demographic Processes and Family Organization in Nineteenth-Century American Society*.

[9]Elder (cited above, note 7).

[10]Talcott Parsons, "The Kinship System of the Contemporary United States," *American Anthropologist*, 45 (January-March, 1943), pp. 22-38.

[11]Peter Uhlenberg, "Cohort Variations in Family Life Cycle Experiences of U.S. Females," *Journal of Marriage and the Family*, 36 (May, 1974), pp. 284-92.

[12]Paul Glick, "The Family Cycle," *American Sociological Review*, 12 (April, 1947), pp. 164-74; "The Life Cycle of the Family," *Marriage and Family Living*, 18 (February, 1955), pp. 3-9.

[13]Uhlenberg (cited above, note 11).

[14]*Idem*, "Changing Configurations of the Life Course," in Tamara K. Hareven, ed. (cited above, note 7).

[15]*Ibid.*

[16]Alice Rossi, "Transition to Parenthood," *Journal of Marriage and the Family*, 30 (February, 1968), pp. 26-40.

[17]Modell, Furstenberg, and Hershberg (cited above, note 6).

[18]Anderson (cited above, note 3).

[19]*Ibid.*; and Tamara K. Hareven, "The Dynamics of Kin in American Industrial Communities" (forthcoming).

[20]The prevalence of nuclear households has been confirmed by historical demographers for both Europe and the United States and for both the pre-industrial period and the nineteenth century. See Laslett and Wall (cited above, note 2), and Tamara K. Hareven, ed., *Family and Kin in American Urban Communities, 1780-1920* (New York, 1977).

[21]John Modell and Tamara K. Hareven, "Urbanization and the Malleable Household: An Examination of Boarding and Lodging in American Families," *Journal of Marriage and the Family*, 35 (August, 1973), pp. 467-79; Howard Chudacoff and Tamara K. Hareven, "The Later Years of Life and the Family Cycle" (forthcoming).

[22]Modell and Hareven, "Urbanization and the Malleable Household" (cited above, note 21).

[23]Hareven, "Family Time and Industrial Time" (cited above, note 3).

[24]Richard Sennett, *Families Against the City* (Cambridge, Mass., 1970); Barbara Welter, "The Cult of True Womanhood: 1820-1860," *American Quarterly*, 18 (October, 1966), pp. 151-74; Kirk Jeffrey, "Family History: The Middle-Class American Family in the Urban Context" (Ph.D. dissertation, Stanford University, 1972); Mary Ryan, "American Society and the Cult of Domesticity" (Ph.D. dissertation, University of California at Santa Barbara, 1972).

[25]Robert Smuts, *Women and Work in America* (New York, 1971), Daniel Scott Smith, "Family Limitation, Sexual Control, and Domestic Feminism in Victorian America," in Mary Hartman and Lois W. Banner, eds., *Clio's Consciousness Raised* (New York, 1974), pp. 119-37.

[26]Goode (cited above, note 4).

[27]Rossi (cited above, note 16).

"Family Time and Historical Time," by Tamara K. Hareven. Daedalus, Vol. 106, No. 2 (Spring 1977)

Statistics

Households, by Race of Head, and Population per Household: 1930 to 1976

[Prior to 1960, excludes Alaska and Hawaii. Data for **1930–1970** are for census dates; see table 1 for population. For definition of household, see text, p. 3. See also *Historical Statistics, Colonial Times to 1970*, series A 288, A 304, and A 320–322]

ITEM	1930 (Apr.)	1940 (Apr.)	1950 (Apr.)	1960 (Apr.)	1970 (Apr.)	1973 (Mar.)	1974 (Mar.)	1975 (Mar.)	1976 (Mar.)
All households_______1,000__	**29,905**	**34,949**	**42,857**	**53,021**	**63,450**	**68,251**	**69,859**	**71,120**	**72,867**
Average annual change since prior year shown_1,000__	[1] 542	504	791	1,016	1,043	[2] 1,646	[2] 1,636	[2] 1,560	[2] 1,592
Percent [3]______________________	2.02	1.56	2.06	2.15	1.80	2.50	2.46	2.32	2.34
Population per household [4]_______	4.11	3.77	3.52	3.38	3.20	3.07	3.02	2.99	2.94
White households__________1,000__	26,983	31,680	[5] 39,044	47,868	56,529	60,618	61,965	62,945	64,392
Percent of total________________	90.2	90.6	91.2	90.3	89.1	88.8	88.7	88.5	88.4
Black households__________1,000__	2,804	3,142	[5] 3,633	5,153	6,180	6,809	7,040	7,262	7,489
Other-race households_____1,000__	118	127	[5] 149		741	824	854	913	986

[1] Average change from 1920. [2] Average annual change since 1970.
[3] Computed using the formula for continuous compounding.
[4] Obtained by dividing total population by number of households; hence, not strictly average size of household because total population includes members of group quarters.
[5] Occupied housing units from U.S. Census of Housing reports.

Source: U.S. Bureau of the Census, 1930, 1950, and 1970 census reports, and *Current Population Reports*, series P-20, forthcoming report, and earlier issues.

Households, Families, Subfamilies, Married Couples, and Unrelated Individuals: 1950 to 1976

[**In thousands, except as indicated.** As of **March,** except as noted. Prior to 1960, excludes Alaska and Hawaii. Based on Current Population Survey; includes members of Armed Forces living off post or with their families on post, but excludes all other members of Armed Forces; see text, p. 1. Minus sign (−) denotes decrease. For definition of terms, see text, p. 3. See also *Historical Statistics, Colonial Times to 1970*, series A 288–319]

TYPE OF UNIT	1950	1955 [1]	1960	1965 [2]	1970 [2]	1974	1975	1976	PERCENT CHANGE	
									1960–1970	1970–1976
Households______________	**43,554**	**47,874**	**52,799**	**57,436**	**63,401**	**69,859**	**71,120**	**72,867**	**20.1**	**14.9**
Primary families_______	38,838	41,732	44,905	47,838	51,456	54,917	55,563	56,056	14.6	8.9
Primary individuals___	4,716	6,142	7,895	9,598	11,945	14,942	15,557	16,811	51.3	40.7
Avg. size of household___	3.37	3.33	3.33	3.29	3.14	2.97	2.94	2.89	(X)	(X)
Families________________	**39,303**	**41,951**	**45,111**	**47,956**	**51,586**	**55,053**	**55,712**	**56,245**	**14.4**	**9.0**
Husband-wife________	34,440	36,378	39,329	41,749	44,755	46,812	46,971	47,318	13.8	5.7
Other male head_____	1,184	1,339	1,275	1,181	1,239	1,438	1,499	1,444	−2.8	16.5
Female head_________	3,679	4,234	4,507	5,026	5,591	6,804	7,242	7,482	24.1	33.8
Primary families_______	38,838	41,732	44,905	47,838	51,456	54,917	55,563	56,056	14.6	8.9
Husband-wife________	34,075	36,251	39,254	41,689	44,728	46,787	46,951	47,297	13.9	5.7
Other male head_____	1,169	1,328	1,228	1,167	1,228	1,421	1,485	1,424	–	16.0
Female head_________	3,594	4,153	4,422	4,982	5,500	6,709	7,127	7,335	24.4	33.4
Secondary families_____	465	219	207	118	130	137	149	189	−37.2	45.4
Husband-wife________	365	127	75	60	27	25	20	22	−64.0	(B)
Other male head_____	15	11	47	14	11	17	14	20	(B)	(B)
Female head_________	85	81	85	44	91	95	115	147	7.1	61.5
Avg. size of family_______	3.54	3.59	3.67	3.70	3.58	3.44	3.42	3.39	(X)	(X)
Subfamilies_____________	**2,402**	**1,973**	**1,514**	**1,293**	**1,150**	**1,178**	**1,349**	**1,190**	**−24.0**	**3.5**
Husband-wife__________	1,651	1,178	871	729	617	512	576	547	−29.2	−11.3
Other male head_______	113	69	115	72	48	63	69	52	−58.3	8.3
Female head___________	638	726	528	492	484	602	705	591	−8.3	22.1
Married couples__________	**36,091**	**37,556**	**40,200**	**42,478**	**45,373**	**47,324**	**47,547**	**47,866**	**12.9**	**5.5**
With own household___	34,075	36,251	39,254	41,689	44,728	46,787	46,951	47,297	13.9	5.7
Without own household	2,016	1,305	946	789	645	537	596	569	−31.8	−11.8
Percent without_____	5.6	3.5	2.4	1.9	1.4	1.1	1.3	1.2	(X)	(X)
Unrelated individuals____	**9,136**	**9,891**	**11,092**	**12,333**	**14,988**	**18,587**	**19,100**	**20,509**	**35.1**	**36.8**
Primary individuals___	4,716	6,142	7,895	9,598	11,945	14,942	15,557	16,811	51.3	40.7
Male_______________	1,668	2,059	2,716	3,277	4,063	5,654	5,912	6,548	49.6	61.2
Female_____________	3,048	4,083	5,179	6,321	7,882	9,288	9,645	10,263	52.2	30.2
Secondary individuals_	4,420	3,749	3,198	2,735	3,043	3,646	3,543	3,698	−4.8	21.5
Male_______________	2,541	2,128	1,746	1,432	1,631	2,059	2,087	1,965	−6.6	20.5
Female_____________	1,879	1,621	1,451	1,303	1,412	1,586	1,456	1,733	−2.7	22.7

– Represents zero. B Percent not shown; base less than 75,000. X Not applicable.
[1] As of April. [2] Data revised using population controls based on the 1970 census, therefore, figures do not agree with tables 57 and 59. The latter use population controls based on the 1960 census. These data were not revised by race or other characteristics.

Source: U.S. Bureau of the Census, *Current Population Reports*, series P-20, No. 296, and earlier issues.

HOUSEHOLDS, BY NUMBER OF PERSONS: 1950 TO 1976

[**In millions, except percent.** As of **March.** See headnote, table 56. See also *Historical Statistics, Colonial Times to 1970,* series A 335–349]

SIZE OF HOUSEHOLD	1950 [1] [2]	1955 [2]	1960 [2]	1965 [2]	1970 [2]	1971 [2]	1972	1973	1974	1975	1976
Total	**43.5**	**47.8**	**52.6**	**57.3**	**62.9**	**64.4**	**66.7**	**68.3**	**69.9**	**71.1**	**72.9**
1 person	4.7	5.2	6.9	8.6	10.7	11.4	12.2	12.6	13.4	13.9	15.0
Male	1.8	1.7	2.3	2.9	3.5	3.8	4.1	4.4	4.7	4.9	5.4
Female	3.0	3.5	4.6	5.7	7.2	7.6	8.1	8.2	8.6	9.0	9.6
2 persons	12.5	13.6	14.6	16.1	18.1	18.8	19.5	20.6	21.5	21.8	22.3
3 persons	9.8	9.7	9.9	10.2	10.9	11.0	11.5	11.8	11.9	12.4	12.5
4 persons	7.7	9.1	9.3	9.2	9.9	10.0	10.7	10.7	10.9	11.1	11.4
5 persons	4.4	5.3	6.1	6.3	6.5	6.6	6.4	6.4	6.5	6.4	6.3
6 persons	2.2	2.6	3.0	3.3	3.5	3.4	3.4	3.2	3.1	3.1	3.0
7 or more	2.1	2.3	2.9	3.5	3.2	3.2	3.0	2.8	2.7	2.5	2.4
Percent of total:											
1 person	10.9	10.9	13.1	15.0	17.0	17.7	18.3	18.5	19.1	19.6	20.6
2 persons	28.8	28.5	27.8	28.1	28.8	29.2	29.2	30.2	30.8	30.6	30.6
3 persons	22.6	20.4	18.9	17.9	17.3	17.1	17.3	17.3	17.1	17.4	17.2
4 persons	17.8	18.9	17.6	16.1	15.8	15.5	16.0	15.7	15.6	15.6	15.7
5 persons	10.0	11.1	11.5	11.0	10.4	10.3	9.6	9.4	9.3	9.0	8.6
6 persons	5.1	5.4	5.7	5.8	5.6	5.3	5.1	4.8	4.4	4.3	4.1
7 or more	4.9	4.9	5.4	6.1	5.1	5.0	4.5	4.1	3.8	3.5	3.2

[1] Covers related persons only; therefore, not strictly comparable with later years. [2] See footnote 2, table 56.

Source: U.S. Bureau of the Census, *Current Population Reports,* series P-20, forthcoming report and earlier issues.

HOUSEHOLDS, FAMILIES, AND INDIVIDUALS—PROJECTIONS: 1977 TO 1990

[**In thousands.** As of **July 1.** Includes members of the Armed Forces living off post or with their families on post, but excludes all other members of the Armed Forces. See text, p. 3, for definitions of households and families. Series B assumes that the trends in marital status and household proportions observed over the period 1960 to 1974 will continue to 1990. Series A and Series C are based on weighted averages of the Series B proportions and the 1974 observed proportions. Series K assumes that the levels of proportions observed in 1974 will continue to 1990. For additional explanation, see source]

YEAR AND SERIES	HOUSEHOLDS								All families	Unrelated individuals [1]
	Total	Primary families				Primary individuals				
		Total	Husband-wife	Other male head	Female head	Male	Female			
1977:										
Series A	74,952	58,130	49,379	1,491	7,260	6,468	10,355		58,222	20,075
Series B	74,681	58,091	49,384	1,489	7,218	6,353	10,237		58,187	19,911
Series C	74,136	58,013	44,395	1,484	7,134	6,121	10,001		58,117	19,586
Series K	73,863	57,975	49,401	1,482	7,092	6,006	9,883		58,082	19,425
1980:										
Series A	79,953	61,230	51,806	1,566	7,858	7,331	11,393		61,312	21,853
Series B	79,356	61,144	51,825	1,561	7,758	7,076	11,135		61,234	21,477
Series C	78,159	60,974	51,864	1,550	7,560	6,565	10,620		61,080	20,735
Series K	77,560	60,891	51,885	1,543	7,463	6,309	10,361		61,004	20,368
1985:										
Series A	88,456	66,380	55,715	1,723	8,942	8,932	13,144		66,440	24,877
Series B	87,188	66,181	55,757	1,713	8,711	8,395	12,612		66,255	24,054
Series C	84,655	65,791	55,845	1,686	8,260	7,320	11,545		65,894	22,437
Series K	83,391	65,599	55,891	1,668	8,040	6,783	11,010		65,718	21,645
1990:										
Series A	96,318	70,909	59,033	1,893	9,983	10,541	14,868		70,943	27,712
Series B	94,270	70,551	59,073	1,877	9,601	9,688	14,032		70,606	26,389
Series C	90,185	69,850	59,163	1,830	8,857	7,981	12,354		69,947	23,788
Series K	88,144	69,502	59,209	1,798	8,495	7,129	11,513		69,622	22,514

[1] Includes primary individuals, shown separately, and secondary individuals (14 years old and over), not shown separately; see text, p. 3.

Source: U.S. Bureau of the Census, *Current Population Reports,* series P-25, No. 607.

HOUSEHOLDS—STATES: 1950 TO 1975

[**1950** through **1970**, as of **April 1; 1975**, estimated as of **July 1**. For definition of household, see text, p. 3]

STATE	TOTAL HOUSEHOLDS: Number (1,000)			TOTAL HOUSEHOLDS: Percent change		TOTAL HOUSEHOLDS: Average annual percent change [1]			HUSBAND-WIFE HOUSEHOLDS (1,000)		
	1960	1970	1975, prel.	1960–1970	1970–1975	1950–1960	1960–1970	1970–1975	1960	1970	1975, prel.
U.S.	**53,021**	**63,450**	**71,537**	**19.7**	**12.7**	**2.1**	**1.8**	**2.3**	**39,210**	**44,062**	**47,200**
Regions:											
Northeast	13,521	15,482	16,730	14.5	8.1	1.8	1.4	1.5	9,829	10,487	10,793
North Central	15,377	17,537	19,157	14.0	9.2	1.7	1.3	1.7	11,593	12,451	12,971
South	15,503	19,259	22,442	24.2	16.5	2.0	2.2	2.9	11,595	13,573	15,047
West	8,619	11,172	13,208	29.6	18.2	3.4	2.6	3.2	6,193	7,551	8,389
N.E.	**3,116**	**3,645**	**4,029**	**17.0**	**10.5**	**1.7**	**1.6**	**1.9**	**2,277**	**2,511**	**2,656**
Maine	280	303	345	8.2	13.9	1.0	.8	2.5	209	215	236
N.H.	180	225	266	25.0	17.9	1.5	2.2	3.1	134	162	184
Vt.	111	132	152	18.9	14.7	.7	1.7	2.6	82	93	103
Mass.	1,535	1,760	1,936	14.7	10.0	1.6	1.4	1.8	1,096	1,176	1,236
R.I.	257	292	307	13.6	5.1	1.3	1.3	.9	186	200	201
Conn.	753	933	1,024	23.9	9.7	2.8	2.1	1.8	571	665	697
M.A.	**10,405**	**11,837**	**12,701**	**13.8**	**7.3**	**1.9**	**1.3**	**1.3**	**7,552**	**7,976**	**8,137**
N.Y.	5,248	5,914	6,313	12.7	6.8	1.9	1.2	1.2	3,690	3,838	3,871
N.J.	1,806	2,218	2,408	22.8	8.5	2.7	2.1	1.6	1,374	1,573	1,632
Pa.	3,351	3,705	3,980	10.6	7.4	1.4	1.0	1.4	2,487	2,565	2,634
E.N.C.	**10,710**	**12,382**	**13,498**	**15.6**	**9.0**	**1.9**	**1.5**	**1.6**	**8,107**	**8,804**	**9,142**
Ohio	2,852	3,289	3,554	15.3	8.0	2.1	1.4	1.5	2,178	2,354	2,428
Ind.	1,388	1,609	1,755	15.9	9.1	1.7	1.5	1.7	1,068	1,174	1,225
Ill.	3,085	3,502	3,745	13.5	6.9	1.8	1.3	1.3	2,254	2,405	2,436
Mich.	2,239	2,653	2,947	18.5	11.1	2.2	1.7	2.0	1,730	1,915	2,023
Wis.	1,146	1,329	1,497	16.0	12.6	1.7	1.5	2.3	877	956	1,030
W.N.C.	**4,668**	**5,155**	**5,660**	**10.4**	**9.8**	**1.2**	**1.0**	**1.8**	**3,486**	**3,647**	**3,830**
Minn.	992	1,154	1,292	16.3	12.0	1.6	1.5	2.2	742	821	877
Iowa	841	896	978	6.5	9.1	.7	.6	1.7	638	645	676
Mo.	1,360	1,521	1,649	11.8	8.4	1.3	1.1	1.5	987	1,050	1,087
N. Dak.	173	182	202	5.2	11.0	.7	.5	2.0	133	132	141
S. Dak.	195	201	222	3.1	10.5	.6	.3	1.9	148	144	153
Nebr.	433	474	528	9.5	11.4	.9	.9	2.1	327	335	357
Kans.	673	727	790	8.0	8.6	1.4	.8	1.6	511	520	540
S.A.	**7,268**	**9,439**	**11,205**	**29.9**	**18.7**	**2.7**	**2.6**	**3.3**	**5,410**	**6,595**	**7,438**
Del.	129	165	187	27.9	13.7	3.5	2.5	2.4	98	118	127
Md.	863	1,175	1,324	36.2	12.7	3.0	3.1	2.3	661	833	891
Dist. of Col.	252	263	280	4.4	6.7	1.2	.4	1.2	131	113	108
Va.	1,074	1,391	1,592	29.5	14.5	2.4	2.6	2.6	814	997	1,085
W. Va.	521	547	604	5.0	10.4	(Z)	.5	1.9	394	389	414
N.C.	1,205	1,510	1,743	25.3	15.4	1.9	2.2	2.7	933	1,098	1,209
S.C.	604	734	863	21.5	17.5	1.6	1.9	3.1	451	522	583
Ga.	1,070	1,369	1,572	27.9	14.8	1.8	2.5	2.6	803	964	1,049
Fla.	1,550	2,285	3,039	47.4	33.0	6.3	3.9	5.4	1,125	1,561	1,972
E.S.C.	**3,307**	**3,868**	**4,367**	**17.0**	**12.9**	**1.0**	**1.6**	**2.3**	**2,507**	**2,763**	**2,986**
Ky.	852	984	1,102	15.5	12.0	.9	1.4	2.2	651	710	766
Tenn.	1,003	1,213	1,383	20.9	14.0	1.4	1.9	2.5	768	874	951
Ala.	884	1,034	1,162	17.0	12.4	1.2	1.6	2.2	669	737	792
Miss.	568	637	719	12.1	13.0	.2	1.1	2.3	419	442	477
W.S.C.	**4,928**	**5,952**	**6,870**	**20.8**	**15.4**	**1.8**	**1.9**	**2.7**	**3,679**	**4,215**	**4,623**
Ark.	524	615	717	17.4	16.5	(Z)	1.6	2.9	392	438	491
La.	892	1,052	1,183	17.9	12.4	2.1	1.7	2.2	649	725	774
Okla.	735	851	959	15.8	12.7	1.0	1.5	2.3	540	596	640
Tex.	2,778	3,434	4,011	23.6	16.8	2.4	2.1	3.0	2,098	2,456	2,718
Mt.	**1,976**	**2,518**	**3,158**	**27.4**	**25.4**	**3.1**	**2.4**	**4.3**	**1,489**	**1,805**	**2,143**
Mont.	202	217	253	7.4	16.3	1.4	.7	2.9	147	152	169
Idaho	194	219	266	12.9	21.6	1.4	1.2	3.7	151	163	190
Wyo.	99	105	126	6.1	20.0	1.6	.6	3.5	75	76	88
Colo.	529	691	859	30.6	24.4	3.0	2.7	4.2	390	484	569
N. Mex.	251	289	358	15.1	23.6	3.5	1.4	4.0	195	209	243
Ariz.	367	539	730	46.9	35.4	5.6	3.8	5.8	276	386	495
Utah	242	298	358	23.1	20.1	2.5	2.1	3.5	190	226	259
Nev.	92	160	209	73.9	30.5	6.0	5.5	5.1	65	109	131
Pac.	**6,644**	**8,654**	**10,050**	**30.3**	**16.1**	**3.5**	**2.6**	**2.8**	**4,704**	**5,746**	**6,245**
Wash.	894	1,106	1,248	23.7	12.9	1.9	2.1	2.3	648	768	817
Oreg.	558	692	819	24.0	18.4	1.5	2.2	3.2	413	486	546
Calif.	4,981	6,574	7,639	32.0	16.2	4.0	2.8	2.9	3,488	4,284	4,645
Alaska	57	79	97	38.6	23.0	6.1	3.3	3.9	43	60	69
Hawaii	153	203	246	32.7	21.2	3.1	2.8	3.7	112	148	168

Z Less than .05 percent. [1] Computed using the formula for continuous compounding.

Source: U.S. Bureau of the Census, *Current Population Reports*, series P–25, No. 623, and earlier issues.

HOUSEHOLDS AND FAMILIES, BY TYPE OF HEAD: 1960 TO 1976

[As of **March.** See headnote, table 56. See also *Historical Statistics, Colonial Times to 1970*, series A 292–295 and A 320–334]

TYPE OF HEAD	NUMBER (1,000)					PERCENT				
	1960	1965 [1]	1970 [1]	1975	1976	1960	1965 [1]	1970 [1]	1975	1976
Households, total	**52,799**	**57,251**	**62,874**	**71,120**	**72,867**	(X)	(X)	(X)	(X)	(X)
White	**47,665**	**51,441**	**56,248**	**62,945**	**64,392**	**100.0**	**100.0**	**100.0**	**100.0**	**100.0**
Husband-wife	36,175	38,132	40,781	42,951	43,295	76.2	74.1	72.5	68.2	67.2
Other male head	3,365	3,839	4,367	6,295	6,720	6.8	7.5	7.8	10.0	10.4
Female head	8,125	9,470	11,099	13,700	14,377	17.0	18.4	19.7	21.8	22.3
Black and other	**5,134**	**5,808**	**6,626**	**8,175**	**8,475**	**100.0**	**100.0**	**100.0**	**100.0**	**100.0**
Husband-wife	3,079	3,455	3,627	4,000	4,002	60.3	59.5	54.7	48.9	47.2
Other male head	579	599	813	1,103	1,252	11.0	10.3	12.3	13.5	14.8
Female head	1,476	1,754	2,187	3,073	3,221	28.7	30.2	33.0	37.6	38.0
Families, total	**45,111**	**47,836**	**51,237**	**55,712**	**56,245**	(X)	(X)	(X)	(X)	(X)
White	**40,869**	**43,081**	**46,022**	**49,451**	**49,873**	**100.0**	**100.0**	**100.0**	**100.0**	**100.0**
Husband-wife	36,212	38,171	40,802	42,969	43,311	88.7	88.6	88.7	86.9	86.8
Other male head	1,100	1,028	1,036	1,270	1,182	2.6	2.4	2.3	2.6	2.4
Female head	3,557	3,882	4,185	5,212	5,380	8.7	9.0	9.1	10.5	10.8
Black and other	**4,242**	**4,752**	**5,215**	**6,262**	**6,372**	**100.0**	**100.0**	**100.0**	**100.0**	**100.0**
Husband-wife	3,117	3,474	3,634	4,002	4,007	73.6	73.1	69.7	63.9	62.9
Other male head	175	153	185	230	262	4.0	3.2	3.5	3.7	4.1
Female head	950	1,125	1,395	2,030	2,102	22.4	23.7	26.7	32.4	33.0

X Not applicable. [1] See footnote 2, table 56.

Source: U.S. Bureau of the Census, *Current Population Reports*, series P–20, Nos. 153, 218, 276, 291, and forthcoming report.

HOUSEHOLDS, BY SELECTED CHARACTERISTICS OF HEAD: 1968 TO 1976

ITEM	1968	1969	1970	1971	1972	1973	1974	1975	1976
Total mil	**60.8**	**62.2**	**63.4**	**64.8**	**66.7**	**68.3**	**69.9**	**71.1**	**72.9**
PERCENT DISTRIBUTION									
Male	79.6	79.2	78.9	78.2	77.8	77.4	77.1	76.4	75.8
Female	20.4	20.8	21.1	21.8	22.2	22.6	22.9	23.6	24.2
White	89.6	89.6	89.5	89.4	89.2	88.8	88.7	88.5	88.4
Black and other	10.4	10.4	10.5	10.6	10.8	11.2	11.3	11.5	11.6
Age of head:									
14–24 years	6.3	6.6	6.8	7.3	7.8	8.0	8.4	8.2	8.1
25–34 years	17.5	18.3	18.5	18.4	19.2	19.9	20.5	21.0	21.3
35–44 years	19.7	19.0	18.6	18.2	17.3	17.2	16.8	16.7	16.8
45–54 years	19.8	19.7	19.5	19.4	19.1	18.8	18.5	18.2	17.6
55–64 years	17.1	17.1	17.1	17.0	16.7	16.4	16.0	15.9	16.0
65 years and over	19.5	19.4	19.5	19.6	19.9	19.7	19.9	20.1	20.3
Educational attainment:									
Less than 8 years	16.1	15.5	14.6	14.0	13.5	12.9	12.4	12.1	11.5
8 years	14.1	13.5	13.2	12.8	12.2	11.6	11.0	10.3	9.7
1–3 years high school	17.3	16.7	16.7	16.4	16.5	16.1	15.7	15.3	15.3
4 years high school	29.5	30.6	31.0	31.3	32.0	32.6	32.7	33.0	33.1
1–3 years college	10.5	10.9	11.4	11.8	11.9	12.4	13.1	13.6	14.0
4 years college or more	12.5	12.7	13.1	13.6	13.9	14.3	15.1	15.7	16.4

Source: U.S. Bureau of the Census, *Current Population Reports*, series P–60, No. 103, and earlier issues.

FAMILIES, BY CHARACTERISTICS: 1960 TO 1976

[As of **March.** Based on Current Population Survey; includes members of the Armed Forces living off post or with families on post, but excludes other of the Armed Forces; see text, p. 1. For definition of families, see text, p. 3]

CHARACTERISTIC	ALL FAMILIES		MALE HEAD: Married, wife present		MALE HEAD: Other marital status		FEMALE HEAD		FAMILIES OF OTHER THAN WHITE PERSONS	
	Number (1,000)	Percent	Number (1,000)	Percent	Number (1,000)	Percent	Number (1,000)	Percent	Number (1,000)	Percent
1960	45,111	100.0	39,329	100.0	1,275	100.0	4,507	100.0	(NA)	(NA)
1965	47,956	100.0	41,749	100.0	1,181	100.0	5,026	100.0	(NA)	(NA)
1970	51,586	100.0	44,755	100.0	1,239	100.0	5,591	100.0	5,324	100.0
1974	55,053	100.0	46,812	100.0	1,438	100.0	6,804	100.0	6,134	100.0
1975	55,712	100.0	46,971	100.0	1,499	100.0	7,242	100.0	6,262	100.0
1976										
Total	**56,245**	**100.0**	**47,318**	**100.0**	**1,444**	**100.0**	**7,482**	**100.0**	**6,372**	**100.0**
White	49,873	88.7	43,311	91.5	1,182	81.9	5,380	71.9	(X)	(X)
Black and other	6,372	11.3	4,007	8.5	262	18.1	2,102	28.1	6,372	100.0
Size of family:										
2 persons	21,280	37.8	17,037	36.0	890	61.6	3,354	44.8	1,948	30.6
3 persons	12,252	21.8	9,858	20.8	336	23.2	2,058	27.5	1,387	21.8
4 persons	11,276	20.0	10,122	21.4	120	8.3	1,033	13.8	1,229	19.3
5 persons	6,171	11.0	5,688	12.0	58	4.0	425	5.7	684	10.7
6 persons	2,969	5.3	2,649	5.6	19	1.3	302	4.0	492	7.7
7 or more persons	2,296	4.1	1,965	4.2	22	1.5	310	4.1	631	9.9
Own children under age 18:										
None	26,067	46.3	22,208	46.9	998	69.1	2,861	38.2	2,408	37.8
1	11,100	19.7	8,928	18.9	270	18.7	1,902	25.4	1,423	22.3
2	10,279	18.3	8,762	18.5	110	7.6	1,407	18.8	1,080	16.9
3	5,243	9.3	4,463	9.4	40	2.8	740	9.9	689	10.8
4 or more	3,555	6.3	2,957	6.2	27	1.9	572	7.6	771	12.1
Own children under age 6:										
None	42,818	76.1	35,680	75.4	1,379	95.5	5,759	77.0	4,484	70.4
1	9,360	16.6	8,041	17.0	53	3.7	1,266	16.9	1,303	20.4
2	3,460	6.2	3,077	6.5	11	.8	373	5.0	460	7.2
3 or more	606	1.1	520	1.1	2	.1	84	1.1	123	1.9

NA Not available. X Not applicable.

Source: U.S. Bureau of the Census, *Current Population Reports*, series P-20, Nos. 276, 291, 296, and forthcoming report.

FAMILIES NOT HEADED BY A HUSBAND AND WIFE: 1960 TO 1976

[**In thousands, except percent.** As of **March.** Persons 18 years old and over, except as noted. See headnote, table 63]

CHARACTERISTIC	Total, 1960 [1]	Total, 1970	Total, 1975	1976: Total	1976: Age of head (in years): 18–24	25–34	35–44	45–54	55–64	65 or older
Number of family units	**5,727**	**6,778**	**8,717**	8,906	**825**	**1,955**	**1,866**	**1,627**	**1,210**	**1,423**
Percent distribution	(X)	(X)	(X)	100.0	9.3	22.0	21.0	18.3	13.6	16.0
Male head	**1,233**	**1,211**	**1,489**	**1,440**	**100**	**187**	**267**	**348**	**240**	**298**
Married, wife absent	166	200	318	232	8	47	55	68	41	13
Widowed	465	414	386	387	2	5	18	79	86	197
Divorced	115	180	340	386	5	57	141	118	50	15
Single	487	416	445	435	85	78	53	83	63	73
Female head	**4,494**	**5,567**	**7,228**	**7,466**	**725**	**1,768**	**1,599**	**1,279**	**970**	**1,125**
Married, husband absent	1,099	1,321	1,642	1,770	226	603	490	284	125	42
Widowed	2,325	2,389	2,560	2,373	10	77	243	487	614	942
Divorced	694	1,258	2,108	2,360	161	823	759	431	150	36
Single	376	599	918	963	328	265	107	77	81	105
PERCENT BY MARITAL STATUS										
Male head	**100.0**	**100.0**	**100.0**	**100.0**	**100.0**	**100.0**	**100.0**	**100.0**	**100.0**	**100.0**
Married, wife absent	13.5	16.5	21.4	16.1	8.0	25.1	20.6	19.5	17.1	4.4
Widowed	37.7	34.2	25.9	26.9	2.0	2.7	6.7	22.7	35.8	66.1
Divorced	9.3	14.9	22.8	26.8	5.0	30.5	52.8	33.9	20.8	5.0
Single	39.5	34.4	29.9	30.2	85.0	41.7	19.9	23.9	26.3	24.5
Female head	**100.0**	**100.0**	**100.0**	**100.0**	**100.0**	**100.0**	**100.0**	**100.0**	**100.0**	**100.0**
Married, husband absent	24.5	23.7	22.7	23.7	31.2	34.1	30.6	22.2	12.9	3.7
Widowed	51.7	42.9	35.4	31.8	1.4	4.4	15.2	38.1	63.3	83.7
Divorced	15.4	22.6	29.2	31.6	22.2	46.5	47.5	33.7	15.5	3.2
Single	8.4	10.8	12.7	12.9	45.2	15.0	6.7	6.0	8.4	9.3

X Not applicable. [1] Persons 14 years old and over.

Source: U.S. Bureau of the Census, *Current Population Reports*, series P–20, No. 306, and earlier issues.

U.S. Bureau of the Census, Statistical Abstract of the United States: 1977 (98th edition) Washington, D.C., 1977.

Series A 288–319. Households, Families, Subfamilies, Married Couples, and Unrelated Individuals: 1790 to 1970

[In thousands, except average size. As of March, except as noted]

Year	Households				Families												
									Primary families				Secondary families				
	Total	Primary families	Primary individuals	Average size	Total	Husband-wife	Other male head	Female head	Total	Husband-wife	Other male head	Female head	Total	Husband-wife	Other male head	Female head	Average size
	288	289	290	291	292	293	294	295	296	297	298	299	300	301	302	303	304
1970	63,401	51,456	11,945	3.14	51,586	44,755	1,239	5,591	51,456	44,728	1,228	5,500	130	27	11	91	3.58
1969	62,214	50,729	11,485	3.16	50,823	44,110	1,232	5,481	50,729	44,086	1,221	5,422	94	24	11	59	3.60
1968	60,813	50,012	10,801	3.20	50,111	43,530	1,211	5,370	50,012	43,507	1,195	5,310	99	23	16	60	3.63
1967	59,236	49,086	10,150	3.26	49,214	42,805	1,203	5,206	49,086	42,743	1,190	5,153	128	62	13	53	3.67
1966	58,406	48,399	10,007	3.27	48,509	42,312	1,178	5,019	48,399	42,263	1,163	4,973	110	49	15	46	3.69
1965	57,436	47,838	9,598	3.29	47,956	41,749	1,181	5,026	47,838	41,689	1,167	4,982	118	60	14	44	3.70
1964	56,149	47,381	8,768	3.33	47,540	41,395	1,245	4,900	47,381	41,341	1,204	4,836	159	54	41	64	3.70
1963	55,270	46,872	8,398	3.33	47,059	40,975	1,333	4,751	46,872	40,888	1,295	4,689	187	87	38	62	3.68
1962	54,764	46,262	8,502	3.31	46,418	40,470	1,296	4,652	46,262	40,404	1,268	4,590	156	66	28	62	3.67
1961	53,557	45,383	8,174	3.34	45,539	39,678	1,222	4,639	45,383	39,620	1,199	4,564	156	58	23	75	3.70
1960*	52,799	44,905	7,895	3.33	45,111	39,329	1,275	4,507	44,905	39,254	1,228	4,422	207	75	47	85	3.67
1959	51,435	43,971	7,464	3.34	44,232	38,574	1,319	4,339	43,971	38,410	1,285	4,276	261	164	33	63	3.65
1958	50,474	43,426	7,047	3.34	43,696	38,056	1,324	4,315	43,426	37,911	1,278	4,237	269	145	46	78	3.64
1957	49,673	43,262	6,411	3.33	43,497	37,856	1,263	4,378	43,262	37,718	1,241	4,304	235	138	22	75	3.60
1956	48,902	42,593	6,309	3.32	42,889	37,204	1,440	4,245	42,593	37,047	1,408	4,138	296	157	32	107	3.58
1955 [1]	47,874	41,732	6,142	3.33	41,951	36,378	1,339	4,234	41,732	36,251	1,328	4,153	219	127	11	81	3.59
1950	43,554	38,838	4,716	3.37	39,303	34,440	1,184	3,679	38,838	34,075	1,169	3,594	465	365	15	85	3.54
1947 [1]	39,107	34,964	4,143	(NA)	35,794	31,211	1,186	3,397	34,964	30,612	1,129	3,223	830	599	57	174	(NA)
1940 [1]	34,949	31,491	3,458	3.67	32,166	26,971	1,579	3,616	31,491	26,571	1,510	3,410	675	400	69	206	3.76

Year	Households		Year	Households		Year	Households		Year	Households		Year	Households	
	Total	Average size		Total	Average size		Total	Average size		Total	Average size		Total	Average size
	288	291		288	291		288	291		288	291		288	291
1930 [1]	29,905	4.11	1910 [2]	20,256	4.54	1890 [2]	12,690	4.93	1870 [1]	7,579	5.09	1850 [1]	3,598	5.55
1920 [2]	24,352	4.34	1900	15,964	4.76	1880 [1]	9,946	5.04	1860 [1]	5,211	5.28	1790 [1]	558	5.79

Year	Subfamilies				Married couples				Unrelated individuals						
							Without own household			Primary individuals			Secondary individuals		
	Total	Husband-wife	Other male head	Female head	Total	With own household	Total	Percent	Total	Total	Male	Female	Total	Male	Female
	305	306	307	308	309	310	311	312	313	314	315	316	317	318	319
1970	1,150	617	48	484	45,373	44,728	645	1.4	14,988	11,945	4,063	7,882	3,043	1,631	1,412
1969	1,168	603	66	499	44,713	44,086	627	1.4	14,154	11,485	3,890	7,595	2,669	1,415	1,254
1968	1,225	661	80	484	44,191	43,507	684	1.5	13,425	10,801	3,658	7,143	2,624	1,294	1,330
1967	1,292	679	91	522	43,484	42,743	741	1.7	12,725	10,150	3,419	6,731	2,575	1,286	1,289
1966	1,383	721	92	570	43,033	42,263	770	1.8	12,558	10,007	3,299	6,708	2,551	1,350	1,201
1965	1,293	729	72	492	42,478	41,689	789	1.9	12,333	9,598	3,277	6,321	2,735	1,432	1,303
1964	1,343	742	83	518	42,137	41,341	796	1.9	11,433	8,768	2,965	5,803	2,665	1,428	1,237
1963	1,375	786	87	502	41,761	40,888	873	2.1	11,330	8,398	2,838	5,560	2,932	1,561	1,371
1962	1,407	815	82	510	41,285	40,404	881	2.1	11,563	8,502	2,932	5,570	3,061	1,654	1,407
1961	1,532	903	78	551	40,581	39,620	961	2.4	11,231	8,174	2,779	5,395	3,057	1,548	1,509
1960*	1,514	871	115	528	40,200	39,254	946	2.4	11,092	7,895	2,716	5,179	3,198	1,746	1,451
1959	1,630	943	103	584	39,518	38,410	1,108	2.8	11,062	7,464	2,449	5,015	3,598	2,077	1,520
1958	1,730	1,068	75	587	39,124	37,911	1,213	3.1	10,568	7,047	2,329	4,718	3,520	1,987	1,534
1957	1,804	1,091	97	615	38,947	37,718	1,229	3.2	9,901	6,411	2,038	4,374	3,489	2,057	1,432
1956	1,825	1,106	120	600	38,310	37,047	1,263	3.3	10,019	6,309	2,058	4,250	3,710	2,187	1,523
1955 [1]	1,973	1,178	69	726	37,556	36,251	1,305	3.5	9,891	6,142	2,059	4,083	3,749	2,128	1,621
1950	2,402	1,651	113	638	36,091	34,075	2,016	5.6	9,136	4,716	1,668	3,048	4,420	2,541	1,879
1947 [1]	3,123	2,332	83	708	33,543	30,612	2,931	8.7	8,491	4,143	1,388	2,755	4,348	2,464	1,884
1946 [2]	(NA)	(NA)	(NA)	(NA)	31,550	28,850	2,700	8.6	(NA)	(NA)	(NA)	(NA)	(NA)	(NA)	(NA)
1945 [3]	(NA)	(NA)	(NA)	(NA)	28,200	26,835	1,365	4.8	(NA)	(NA)	(NA)	(NA)	(NA)	(NA)	(NA)
1940 [1]	2,062	1,546	52	464	28,517	26,571	1,946	6.8	9,277	3,458	1,599	1,859	5,819	3,343	2,476
1930 [1]	------	------	------	------	25,174	23,649	1,525	6.1	------	------	------	------	------	------	------
1910 [2]	------	------	------	------	17,175	16,250	925	5.4	------	------	------	------	------	------	------

* Denotes first year for which figures include Alaska and Hawaii.
NA Not available.
[1] As of April.
[2] As of June.
[3] As of September.

Series A 29–42. Annual Estimates of the Population, by Age: 1900 to 1970

[**In thousands.** As of July 1. 1900–1939, resident population; 1940–1970, total population, including Armed Forces overseas. 1960–1970, preliminary; for description of estimates, see text for series A 6–8]

Year	Total	Age group (in years): Under 5	5–14	15–24	25–34	35–44	45–54	55–64	65 and over	Selected cumulative age groups (in years): 14 and over	16 and over	18 and over	21 and over	62 and over
	29	30	31	32	33	34	35	36	37	38	39	40	41	42
1970	204,879	17,156	40,733	36,496	25,293	23,142	23,310	18,664	20,085	151,087	142,949	135,177	124,024	25,050
1969	202,677	17,376	40,884	35,236	24,681	23,383	23,047	18,390	19,680	148,465	140,462	132,905	122,019	24,552
1968	200,706	17,913	40,772	34,090	23,990	23,731	22,758	18,088	19,365	145,988	138,171	130,815	120,098	24,073
1967	198,712	18,563	40,496	33,196	23,156	24,038	22,440	17,752	19,071	143,520	135,905	128,785	117,823	23,625
1966	196,560	19,208	40,051	32,012	22,725	24,276	22,125	17,408	18,755	141,069	133,651	126,665	116,523	23,184
1965	194,303	19,824	39,426	30,773	22,465	24,447	21,839	17,077	18,451	138,726	131,542	124,572	115,198	22,800
1964	191,889	20,165	38,783	29,519	22,396	24,562	21,580	16,758	18,127	136,480	129,427	122,206	113,844	22,426
1963	189,242	20,342	38,124	28,223	22,410	24,584	21,346	16,436	17,778	134,322	127,275	120,822	112,274	22,039
1962	186,538	20,469	37,435	26,909	22,494	24,519	21,124	16,131	17,457	132,172	124,864	119,412	111,063	21,682
1961	183,691	20,522	37,031	25,242	22,692	24,392	20,875	15,847	17,089	129,952	123,404	117,900	109,926	21,277
1960	180,671	20,341	35,735	24,576	22,919	24,221	20,578	15,625	16,675	127,365	121,835	116,146	108,856	20,836
1959*	177,830	20,175	34,564	23,988	23,169	24,023	20,262	15,401	16,248	125,888	120,287	114,780	107,824	20,402
1959	177,073	20,055	34,390	23,890	23,062	23,917	20,189	15,357	16,213	125,411	119,837	114,356	107,425	20,356
1958	174,141	19,768	33,322	23,162	23,430	23,693	19,857	15,139	15,771	123,875	118,108	113,139	106,394	19,895
1957	171,274	19,379	32,515	22,311	23,737	23,496	19,513	14,973	15,353	122,365	116,790	112,108	105,517	19,459
1956	168,221	18,895	31,423	21,869	24,015	23,160	19,143	14,815	14,902	120,531	115,489	110,956	104,500	18,962
1955	165,275	18,467	30,248	21,667	24,175	22,818	18,824	14,586	14,489	119,011	114,276	109,803	103,436	18,455
1954	162,391	17,962	29,092	21,641	24,233	22,571	18,501	14,350	14,040	117,662	113,088	108,739	102,459	17,899
1953	159,565	17,548	27,880	21,658	24,233	22,359	18,171	14,135	13,582	116,430	111,922	107,673	101,445	17,354
1952	156,954	17,228	26,656	21,796	24,197	22,109	17,881	13,918	13,169	115,333	110,957	106,683	100,446	16,874
1951	154,287	17,252	25,055	22,018	24,085	21,833	17,623	13,654	12,768	114,141	109,878	105,678	99,250	16,384
1950	151,684	16,331	24,477	22,260	23,932	21,557	17,400	13,364	12,362	113,031	108,753	104,624	97,998	15,886
1949	149,188	15,607	23,770	22,570	23,729	21,187	17,260	13,145	11,921	111,947	107,729	103,445	96,684	15,386
1948	146,631	14,919	23,089	22,866	23,494	20,794	17,107	12,824	11,538	110,722	106,503	102,066	95,265	14,925
1947	144,126	14,406	22,257	23,122	23,236	20,421	16,970	12,528	11,185	109,602	105,252	100,724	93,871	14,498
1946	141,389	13,244	21,844	23,382	22,954	20,073	16,820	12,244	10,828	108,520	104,042	99,501	92,595	14,068
1945	139,928	12,979	21,599	23,705	22,734	19,787	16,642	11,988	10,494	107,623	103,042	98,372	91,326	13,662
1944	138,397	12,524	21,573	23,999	22,511	19,505	16,419	11,719	10,147	106,627	101,924	97,153	89,976	13,233
1943	136,739	12,016	21,699	24,065	22,194	19,226	16,199	11,472	9,867	105,404	100,630	95,836	88,592	12,871
1942	134,860	11,301	21,823	24,093	21,911	18,950	15,976	11,220	9,584	104,132	99,328	94,489	87,151	12,499
1941	133,402	10,850	22,089	24,074	21,691	18,692	15,759	10,959	9,288	102,878	98,036	93,136	85,766	12,115
1940	132,122	10,579	22,363	24,033	21,446	18,422	15,555	10,694	9,031	101,607	96,732	91,763	84,429	11,781
1939	130,880	10,418	22,701	23,819	21,176	18,178	15,336	10,487	8,764	100,209	95,283	90,311	83,104	11,467
1938	129,825	10,176	23,146	23,655	20,953	18,001	15,077	10,310	8,508	98,981	94,018	89,073	81,978	11,163
1937	128,825	10,009	23,564	23,487	20,723	17,866	14,785	10,132	8,258	97,734	92,754	87,876	80,867	10,854
1936	128,053	10,044	23,942	23,309	20,505	17,783	14,495	9,949	8,027	96,575	91,594	86,791	79,825	10,553
1935	127,250	10,170	24,213	23,130	20,275	17,712	14,208	9,739	7,804	95,350	90,435	85,698	78,751	10,256
1934	126,374	10,331	24,402	22,963	20,022	17,640	13,933	9,502	7,582	94,079	89,247	84,553	77,619	9,961
1933	125,579	10,612	24,531	22,820	19,750	17,569	13,684	9,249	7,363	92,838	88,070	83,393	76,482	9,680
1932	124,840	10,903	24,614	22,716	19,484	17,504	13,481	8,992	7,147	91,699	86,968	82,295	75,411	9,411
1931	124,040	11,179	24,629	22,617	19,242	17,412	13,296	8,735	6,928	90,598	85,877	81,209	74,358	9,144
1930	123,077	11,372	24,631	22,487	19,039	17,270	13,096	8,477	6,705	89,439	84,722	80,069	73,256	8,867
1929	121,767	11,734	24,470	22,151	18,941	16,921	12,761	8,315	6,474	87,902	83,233	78,619	71,897	8,576
1928	120,509	11,978	24,320	21,811	18,953	16,540	12,430	8,178	6,299	86,536	81,898	77,325	70,701	8,328
1927	119,035	12,111	24,152	21,430	18,948	16,172	12,092	8,003	6,127	85,071	80,489	75,978	69,472	8,076
1926	117,397	12,189	23,906	21,037	18,867	15,847	11,786	7,805	5,960	83,575	79,050	74,619	68,244	7,840
1925	115,829	12,316	23,614	20,691	18,720	15,576	11,521	7,605	5,786	82,149	77,677	73,324	67,068	7,615
1924	114,109	12,269	23,358	20,314	18,557	15,337	11,278	7,387	5,609	80,704	76,297	72,035	65,914	7,399
1923	111,947	12,119	23,089	19,798	18,231	15,066	11,068	7,165	5,411	78,915	74,606	70,461	64,518	7,184
1922	110,049	12,031	22,788	19,402	17,924	14,823	10,899	6,951	5,231	77,362	73,144	69,102	63,297	6,998
1921	108,538	11,879	22,515	19,140	17,747	14,665	10,721	6,791	5,080	76,233	72,102	68,154	62,446	6,847
1920	106,461	11,631	22,158	18,821	17,416	14,382	10,505	6,619	4,929	74,708	70,683	66,839	61,235	6,663
1919	104,514	11,536	21,849	18,465	16,912	14,008	10,402	6,456	4,886	73,144	69,170	65,407	59,911	6,577
1918	103,208	11,606	21,732	18,071	16,445	13,879	10,293	6,356	4,826	71,886	67,899	64,092	58,670	6,490
1917	103,268	11,527	21,369	18,836	16,913	13,647	10,068	6,194	4,714	72,361	68,425	64,646	59,030	6,332
1916	101,961	11,442	21,008	18,872	16,776	13,388	9,846	6,026	4,603	71,476	67,579	63,811	58,176	6,176
1915	100,546	11,347	20,660	18,844	16,580	13,130	9,618	5,866	4,501	70,482	66,623	62,863	57,224	6,029
1914	99,111	11,244	20,316	18,796	16,370	12,875	9,398	5,711	4,401	69,470	65,652	61,907	56,272	5,887
1913	97,225	11,082	19,904	18,649	16,070	12,562	9,135	5,542	4,281	68,127	64,364	60,650	55,048	5,719
1912	95,335	10,915	19,503	18,477	15,772	12,252	8,875	5,372	4,169	66,775	63,068	59,387	53,828	5,562
1911	93,863	10,796	19,214	18,355	15,530	12,003	8,657	5,234	4,074	65,688	62,022	58,369	52,839	5,427
1910	92,407	10,671	18,950	18,212	15,274	11,759	8,454	5,101	3,986	64,598	60,974	57,346	51,852	5,301
1909	90,490	10,509	18,670	17,871	14,923	11,471	8,204	4,964	3,878	63,093	59,531	55,970	50,579	5,155
1908	88,710	10,364	18,440	17,526	14,585	11,202	7,974	4,840	3,779	61,659	58,157	54,660	49,375	5,021
1907	87,008	10,220	18,240	17,184	14,257	10,945	7,755	4,724	3,684	60,275	56,828	53,397	48,216	4,894
1906	85,450	10,092	18,067	16,864	13,952	10,705	7,554	4,621	3,595	58,993	55,595	52,224	47,142	4,778
1905	83,822	9,944	17,888	16,526	13,631	10,461	7,350	4,517	3,505	57,668	54,322	51,014	46,036	4,658
1904	82,166	9,791	17,697	16,178	13,315	10,211	7,150	4,410	3,414	56,331	53,035	49,792	44,919	4,541
1903	80,632	9,645	17,524	15,858	13,019	9,974	6,964	4,313	3,335	55,094	51,848	48,661	43,886	4,436
1902	79,163	9,502	17,360	15,555	12,737	9,745	6,788	4,220	3,256	53,911	50,710	47,578	42,896	4,333
1901	77,584	9,336	17,158	15,242	12,442	9,504	6,606	4,122	3,174	52,676	49,523	46,448	41,862	4,229
1900	76,094	9,181	16,966	14,951	12,161	9,273	6,437	4,026	3,099	51,511	48,403	45,379	40,879	4,130

* Denotes first year for which figures include Alaska and Hawaii.

Series A 143–157. Median Age of the Population, by Race, Sex, and Nativity: 1790 to 1970

Year	All races			White			Negro			Other races			Foreign-born white		
	Total	Male	Female	Total	Male	Female	Total	Male	Female	Total	Male	Female	Total	Male	Female
	143	**144**	**145**	**146**	**147**	**148**	**149**	**150**	**151**	**152**	**153**	**154**	**155**	**156**	**157**
1970	28.1	26.8	29.3	28.9	27.6	30.2	22.4	21.0	23.6	24.7	24.4	24.9	54.6	54.5	54.7
1960 *	29.5	28.7	30.3	30.3	29.4	31.1	23.5	22.3	24.5	24.3	25.2	23.2	57.7	58.4	57.1
1960	29.6	28.7	30.4	30.3	29.5	31.2	23.5	22.3	24.5	24.5	25.5	23.4	57.7	58.2	57.2
1950	30.2	29.9	30.5	30.8	30.4	31.1	26.1	25.8	26.4	24.5	26.9	21.8	56.1	59.0	55.5
1940	29.0	29.1	29.0	29.5	29.5	29.5	25.3	25.3	25.3	24.1	27.6	19.9	51.0	51.4	50.5
1930	26.5	26.7	26.2	26.9	27.1	26.6	23.5	23.7	23.3	23.3	25.9	18.6	43.9	44.1	43.7
1920	25.3	25.8	24.7	25.6	26.1	25.1	22.3	22.8	22.0	26.1	30.4	20.5	40.0	40.1	39.9
1910	24.1	24.6	23.5	24.5	24.9	23.9	20.8	21.0	20.7	26.5	29.2	19.8	37.2	36.9	37.6
1900	22.9	23.3	22.4	23.4	23.8	22.9	19.5	19.5	19.5	27.3	30.9	20.3	38.5	38.8	38.1
1890	22.0	22.3	21.6	22.5	22.9	22.1	18.1	17.9	18.3	28.9	33.2	27.2	37.1	37.1	37.0
1880	20.9	21.2	20.7	21.4	21.6	21.1	(NA)	(NA)	(NA)	(NA)	(NA)	(NA)	38.3	38.5	38.0
1870	20.2	20.2	20.1	20.4	20.6	20.3	18.3	17.8	18.8	28.1	29.1	23.0	34.6	35.3	33.9
1860	19.4	19.8	19.1	19.7	20.1	19.3	17.5	17.5	17.5	26.1	27.5	20.5	------	------	------
1850	18.9	19.2	18.6	19.2	19.5	18.8	17.4	17.3	17.4	------	------	------	------	------	------
1840	17.8	17.9	17.8	17.9	18.0	17.8	17.6	17.5	17.6	------	------	------	------	------	------
1830	17.2	17.2	17.3	17.3	17.2	17.3	17.2	17.1	17.3	------	------	------	------	------	------
1820	16.7	16.6	16.8	16.6	16.5	16.6	17.2	17.1	17.4	------	------	------	------	------	------
1810	------	------	------	16.0	15.9	16.1	------	------	------	------	------	------	------	------	------
1800	------	------	------	16.0	15.7	16.3	------	------	------	------	------	------	------	------	------
1790	------	------	------	------	(1)	------	------	------	------	------	------	------	------	------	------

* Denotes first year for which figures include Alaska and Hawaii.
NA Not available.

[1] Median falls in the open-ended age group, 16 years and over, which includes 50.3 percent of the white male population.

U.S. Bureau of the Census, Historical Statistics of the United States, Colonial Times to 1970, Bicentennial Edition, Part 1. Washington, D.C., 1975

Part two : Adults

Men's and women's roles

The Work-Family Role System

by Joseph H. Pleck

The male work role, the female work role, the female family role, and the male family role, are conceptually analyzed as components of the work-family role system. The links among these roles are examined. I then analyze two kinds of structural "buffers" in the linkages among these roles, specifically, sex-segregated labor markets for both paid work and family tasks, and asymmetrically permeable boundaries between work and family roles for each sex. Finally, several issues in the future development of a less sex-segregated work-family role system are considered.

The study of work and the study of the family have traditionally constituted separate sub-disciplines in sociology. Rapoport and Rapoport (1965) and Kanter (1976), among others, have aptly stressed the need for greater examination of work and family roles in relation to each other. Such joint consideration is necessary to describe how individuals' functioning in either of these spheres is affected by their involvement in the other. Further, the current examination of sex roles brings added impetus to the analysis of work-family interrelationships. A major part of what is usually meant by change in "sex roles" is specifically change in the traditional allocation of work and family roles between men and women. Traditional sex role norms prescribed the specialization of work and family responsibilities by sex, but a new option for each sex to integrate roles in both work and the family is now emerging.

This paper analyzes some aspects of what I term the "work-family role system." The work-family role system is composed of the male work role, the female work role, the female family role, and the male family role. Each of these roles may be fully actualized, or may be only partly actualized or latent, as is often the case with the female work role and the male family role. The analysis of these four roles as a system provides a useful way of organizing research about the relations among these roles, and suggests new relations to be examined. It also makes possible some inferences about the dynamics of future changes in women's and men's roles in work and the family.

*Revised version of a paper given at the 1975 Annual Meeting of the American Sociological Association. I would like to thank Arlie Hochschild, Jeylan Mortimer, and Elizabeth Pleck for their comments on earlier drafts.

Analyzing men's and women's work and family roles as components of a role system involves specifying how each role articulates with the others to which it is linked, and how variations in the nature of each role, or whether the role is actualized at all, affects the others. For example, to describe the link between the female work and the female family roles, we consider how the extent of the female work role (ranging from no paid work at all, to the most demanding and highest status full time work) both affects and is affected by the extent of the female family role. These links can be considered at two conceptual levels. They can be analyzed at the level of the individual couple, e.g., the relation between wives' employment status and wives' role performance in the family. Each link can also be considered at the aggregate or macrosocial level, e.g., the relation between married women's labor force participation rate and married women's level of household work and childcare (expressed, for example, in mean hours per day).

FIGURE 1

The Work-Family Role System

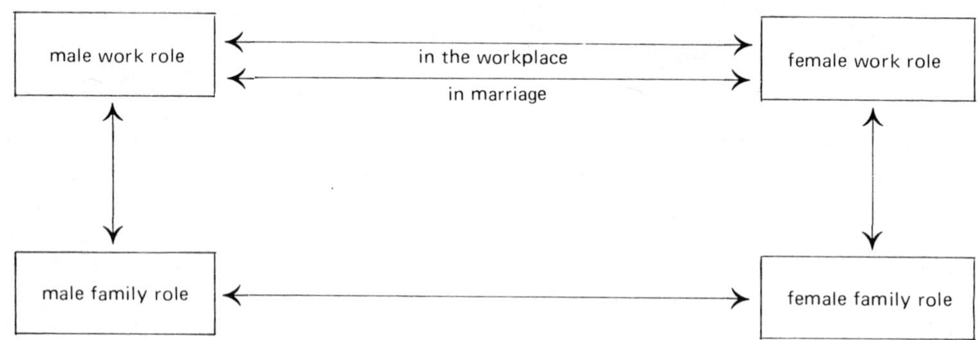

FEMALE WORK AND FAMILY ROLES

Let us start with the link between the female work and female family roles, and move clockwise around the figure. Research on the effects of married female employment on the family (see Hoffman and Nye, 1974; Howell, 1973a, 1973b) contains much information relevant to this link. The three major topics in this research have been the effects of wives' employment on children's psychological well-being, marital satisfaction and happiness, and marital power. The consensus today appears to be that when other variables are controlled, wives' employment has no clear positive or negative effect on children's well-being, and when freely chosen, has no negative effect on marital happiness and satisfaction. Most reviews (cf. Bahr, 1974) conclude that wives' employment is associated with some increase in wives' marital power (primarily assessed by wives' reports of how the couple would make various hypothetical decisions). However, Safilios-Rothschild (1970) has questioned the support for this and other aspects of the "resource" theory of marital power.

The most important aspect of married females' employment in the present analysis is simply its effect on the level of wives' performance of family roles. Blood and Wolfe's (1960) examination of the relation between household division of labor and wives' employment indicated that when wives held paid jobs, they reported doing a lower proportion of the work performed by the couple on eight household tasks (not including childcare). Several analyses of time budget data (Walker, 1969; Meissner, et. al., 1975; Robinson, Juster, and Stafford, 1976) have likewise shown, predictably enough, that wives holding paid jobs outside the family spend less time performing family tasks than wives not so employed. In Walker's data, for example, wives' average time in family tasks was 8.1 hours per day when not employed and declined, through several intermediate categories of part-time employment, to 4.8 hours per day when the wife was employed thirty or more hours per week.

Two observations should be made about this inverse relationship between wives' performance of work roles and family roles. First, it is not clear as yet whether the composition of wives' family role performance changes when they hold paid work. The various time budget analyses do not indicate a consistent reduction in wives' family work disproportionately greater in some categories than others. But the categories for family tasks used in these analyses may be too broad. Second, it should be emphasized that the overall reduction in employed wives' time in family work is not fully commensurate to their increased time in paid employment. The total burden of work and family roles combined is substantially greater for the employed than the non-employed wife.

FEMALE AND MALE FAMILY ROLES

The first and most obvious feature of the articulation between females' and males' family roles is that women and men generally perform different family tasks.[1] That is, there is a marital division of family labor. There is no single accepted way of quantifying how far family tasks are segregated by sex, and any quantitative index would be strongly dependent on which tasks were selected for study, and how narrowly or broadly each was defined. In an analysis of eight household tasks (not including childcare) in a 1955 Detroit sample, Blood and Wolfe (1960) found that six were performed predominately by one or the other spouse, and only two were performed relatively equally by both spouses. Duncan et al. (1974), replicating these items in a similarly drawn Detroit sample in 1971, concluded the general principle that household tasks should be segregated by sex had been maintained with only slight adjustments on particular tasks since the earlier study.

Ideological support for the traditional division of family labor by sex remains quite strong. Robinson, Yerby, Feiweger, and Somerick (1976) note that in their national sample of married women in 1965-66, only nineteen percent responded "yes" to the question, "Do you wish your husband would give you more help with the household chores?" Repeating the question in a 1973 national survey, the percentage of agreement rose only four points to twenty-three percent. The increase in the percentage of wives wanting more help from their husbands in household work was considerably greater in certain subgroups, however. There was, for example, an increase of twenty-three percent for black women, and twenty percent for women who graduated from college. The increase in these groups may presage a challenge to the traditional division of household labor which will become more widespread in the future.

A second important feature of the link between male and female family roles concerns simply the relation between the overall levels of each. Though no direct analyses of this relation have been located, it can be inferred from the relation between males' family role performance and wives' employment status, since the latter is associated with variations in females' family role performance. Walker's (1970) time budget data indicate that, on average, there is *no* variation in husbands' mean time in family roles (about 1.6 hours per day) associated with their wives' employment status. That is, husbands contribute about the same time to family tasks whether their wives are employed (and doing an average of 4.8 hours of family work per day), or are not employed (and doing an average of 1.8 hours of family work per day). Other time budget studies (Meissner et al., 1975; Robinson, Juster, and Stafford, 1976) confirm Walker's general findings. In Walker's data, husbands' family time does increase slightly, to 2.1 hours per day, when their wives are employed if a child under two is present, but otherwise the independence of husbands' family time from wives' employment status holds true when age and number of children are controlled.

Blood and Wolfe (1960: 62-68) and later studies using their methods (see Bahr, 1974), however, find an increase in the proportion of household work performed by husbands, when their wives are employed. At least two factors may account for the discrepancy between Blood and Wolfe's and the time budget findings. First, Blood and Wolfe's measure sampled only a few household tasks, and expressly excluded childcare. It may be that the particular tasks Blood and Wolfe sampled are ones in which husbands do increase their participation when their wives are employed, but this explanation seems unlikely. The time budget

[1] Glazer-Malbin (1976) provides a useful analysis of current theoretical approaches to household work.

analyses do not indicate any change in the composition of husbands' unvarying family time according to wives' employment status, though the categories of family tasks used in these analyses may be too broad. In small-sample British and American studies, Oakley (1970) and Lein et al. (1974) suggest that husbands of working wives are more likely to increase their participation in childcare than in other household work. But if so, then it is quite paradoxical that Blood and Wolfe's measure, which does not include childcare, shows an increase in husbands' family role performance in response to wives' employment, while the time budget measures, which do include childcare, do not indicate such an increase.

A more likely account for the discrepancy is that the time budget data concern each spouse's contribution to family work in absolute terms, while Blood and Wolfe's measure indicates only the relative division of labor between husband and wife. If the husband's absolute time in family tasks remains constant when his wife is employed, and if his wife spends less time in family work, the husband's *relative* share of family work increases. Thus, Blood and Wolfe's results and the time budget data are not inconsistent.

The two most significant features of the relation between husbands' and wives' family role performance are, then, that family tasks are strongly segregated by sex, and that husbands' time in family tasks does not vary in response to the changes in wives' family work resulting from wives' paid employment. Note that the time budget data indicating that husbands do not increase their family role performance when their wives are employed are cross-sectional rather than longitudinal in nature. It is possible that longitudinal analysis might find changes in husbands' level of family work as their wives enter the labor force, leave it during childbearing, and then re-enter it, in the family life cycle pattern so frequent today. Further, although there is no average increase in husbands' family time when their wives have paid jobs, this average lack of response many conceal subgroups of husbands who do take on a significantly greater family role. If so, there must be subgroups of husbands who actually decrease their family role when their wives work. More needs to be known about the determinants of individual variation in husbands' family role performance, and in their responsiveness to their wives' paid employment.

MALE FAMILY AND WORK ROLES

The effect of the male work role on the family is receiving increasing attention. Scanzoni (1970) notes that functionalist theory emphasizes how the family is linked to the larger society through the husband-father's occupational role, and how this extrafamilial link affects family relationships. A number of studies and reviews (Aberle and Naegele, 1952; Dyer, 1956, 1965; Miller and Swanson, 1958; Scanzoni, 1965, 1970; Aldous, 1966; Gronseth, 1971, 1972; Pearlin, 1974) have considered how characteristics of the male's occupational role (especially his occupational status) affect the family and particularly the socialization of children.

The most obvious and direct effect of the male occupational role on the family, however, has so far received little analytical attention: the restricting effect of the male occupational role on men's family role. Again using time budget and division of labor measures, data from Walker (1974) and Blood and Wolfe (1960) indicate that role performance in work and family are inversely related to each other for husbands as they are for wives.

While the extent of the husband's family role co-varies with the extent of his work role, variation in the extent of the husband's family role occurs around a low baseline *not* accounted for by the demands of his work role. Rather, men's family role varies within the limits imposed by the traditional division of family labor by sex. Though both men's and women's family roles vary according to their employment status, fully employed men still do only a fraction of the family work that fully employed women do—about one-third, according to Walker's data. To put it another way, though employment status has a significant main effect on family work, sex has a stronger effect and accounts for much more of the variance in an individual's time in family work than does his or her employment status.

Thus, it would be misleading to state that men's role work is the primary determinant of the limited family role men typically hold at present. It would be more accurate to say that the objective demands of the male work role are now a latent and secondary constraint, but will emerge as the primary constraint on men's family role if and when ideological support for the traditional division of family labor by sex is weakened. Until then, reduction in the demands of the male work role (for example, shortening the workweek) may not lead to much of an increase in males' family role, as compared to increases in overtime work, the holding of two jobs, and leisure.

Several other aspects of the relation between male work and family roles can be considered. When the methods and assumptions traditionally used in the analysis of married females' employment and its relation to the family are applied to married men, it becomes apparent that many important questions have not yet been asked. For example, economic literature on the "labor supply response" (Mincer, 1962; Cain, 1966) uses slightly different analytic models for husbands and wives. Wives are assumed to allocate time among paid market work, "home market" work (i.e., housework and childcare), and leisure. The parallel analytical equations for men, however, omit "home market" work and include as dependent variables only paid market work and leisure. That is, men's actual participation in family roles is analytically invisible. Such analytical formulations reflect an assumption that men's contribution to family roles is unvarying and of little conceptual significance.[2] For another example, maternal employment has long, and incorrectly, been thought to harm children psychologically. Despite decades of clinical stereotypes about psychologically absent or "weak, passive" fathers, it was rarely asked whether or how *paternal* employment might harm children.

There has been considerable research on the effects of husbands' occupational status and, to a lesser extent, other occupational characteristics, on marital satisfaction and marital power (see Scanzoni, 1970). Of particular note are two recent studies on the effects of a previously overlooked aspect of men's occupational role: the overall salience of men's occupational role in comparison to their family role as a source of satisfaction. Bailyn (1971) classified husbands as oriented primarily to work or to the family, according to their self-rating of which gave them more satisfaction. In marriages where wives held paid employment and valued it positively, marital satisfaction was high if the husband was family-oriented, but markedly low if the husband was work-oriented. Husband's orientation was not associated with marital satisfaction, however, in other marriages. Rapoport et al. (1974), classifying husbands in the same way, found that both husbands and wives reported greater enjoyment of everyday activities with their spouses if the husband was family-oriented than if he was not. Interestingly, both studies noted that husbands' orientation to work or family appeared to have a stronger effect on marital variables than did wives' orientation.

MALE AND FEMALE WORK ROLES

There are two distinct contexts in which male and female work roles articulate with each other: in work environments themselves, and in marriage. In the workplace, the most significant feature of the articulation of male and female work roles is the high degree of occupational segregation by sex (Waldman and McEaddy, 1974; Blaxall and Reagan, 1976), with females concentrated in lower-paying, lower status occupations. Within this overall occupational segregation, two dominant patterns for the articulation of male and female work roles can be distinguished. In the older pattern, typical in much blue-collar employment, women and men work in entirely separate settings, and do not generally interact with each other in their work roles. Females are completely excluded from male workplaces. Males are not completely excluded from female workplaces, since women work under the authority and control of male employers. However, this control is largely administered through a cadre of female supervisors, thus greatly minimizing male-female contact.

A major source of this pattern of occupational segregation historically has been men's desire to exclude women in order to keep their own wages up (Hartmann, 1976). This

---

[2] The present analysis, it should be noted, omits consideration of children's family role performance. Walker and Gauger (1973) found that children aged 12-17 contribute an average of slightly over an hour a day to family tasks.

pattern may derive from non-economic sources as well. Caplow (1954) proposed that a fundamental norm that women and men should not interact with each other except in romantic and kinship relationships underlies this sex-segregation of the workplace. Caplow speculatively argued that a major psychological source of this norm is that aggression toward females is severely punished in male childhood socialization, and is therefore highly anxiety-provoking to males. Since interaction with work partners inevitably entails some degree of competition and aggression, Caplow argues, interacting with women in the workplace makes men anxious. We can also note similarities between these traditional norms prescribing complete segregation of male and female work roles and what anthropologists term "pollution ideology" (Douglas, 1970). According to pollution ideology, if certain categories of social objects (e.g., menstrual blood) are not segregated or handled in special ways, the order of the world is disturbed and catastrophe will result. In similar fashion, many miners and seamen in the past have resisted the introduction of women as co-workers because they superstitiously believed that women would be a "jinx" or "bad luck" bringing on mining disasters and shipwrecks.

The more recent pattern for the articulation of male and female work roles, whose ideal type is the modern office, is the integration of women into mixed-sex workplaces, but in roles that are segregated from and clearly subordinate to men's. Thus, women and men do not compete for the same jobs, and do not have to interact with each other as peers. In this pattern, the potential for interacting with members of the other sex, particularly if unmarried, has almost attained the status of a fringe benefit. The shift from the first pattern of work organization to the second has not received sufficient attention. Several studies have examined how certain previously male occupations became female ones (Prather, 1972; Davies, 1974), but that these occupational shifts transformed previously all-male work environments into mixed-sex ones has not been adequately analyzed as yet.

The second context for the articulation of male and female work roles is marriage. The critical factor affecting this link is primarily psychological in nature, based on men's investment in their performance of the paid breadwinner role as uniquely validating their masculinity. Yankelovich (1974: 44-45) has suggested that for the large majority of men whose jobs are not inherently psychologically satisfying, daily work is made worthwhile by pride in hard work. The sacrifices made to provide for their families' needs validate them as men. Wives working thus takes away a major source of these men's identity, and is psychologically threatening.

Two dominant patterns for the articulation between male and female roles in marriage are apparent, corresponding to the two patterns noted in the workplace. In the more traditional pattern, husbands cannot tolerate their wives taking or holding any paid employment. Supporting this pattern, in many workplaces married women were ineligible for employment, and single women were dismissed if they married. In the more recent pattern, husbands can accept their wives' employment as long as it does not come too close to, or worse surpass, their own in prestige, earnings, or psychological commitment. The segregation of women in lower paying, lower status occupations helps insure that this limit is not breached. Further, husbands' acceptance of their wives' work in this pattern is conditional on their wives' continuing to meet their traditional family responsibilities.

Taking an overview of the workplace and marriage, the second pattern for the articulation of male and female work roles in each is not necessarily more equitable or less restrictive to women than the first. The emergence of the second pattern was, however, inevitable as the married female labor force has expanded over the course of this century. The question now is whether a third pattern can emerge on a widespread scale in which wives can have work roles of equal or greater status than their husbands' (Rapoport and Rapoport, 1971), and in which female workers can interact with male workers as equals in the workplace.

STRUCTURAL "BUFFERS" IN THE WORK-FAMILY ROLE SYSTEM

What are the more general characteristics of the links in the work-family role system? How do these links affect whether change in one role does or does not lead to accommodating change in the other roles to which it is linked? We consider here two structural "buffers" in the links among these roles, limiting how much change in one role affects the others.

The first kind of buffer is *sex-segregated market mechanisms* for both paid work and family work. A sex-segregated, dual market for paid work means that women and men do not compete for the same jobs. As a result, changes in the level of female employment occur neither at the expense nor to the benefit of male employment. Further, since women are segregated into not only different but inferior jobs, women will rarely have jobs of equal or greater status than men's, psychologically threatening their husbands or co-workers. In these ways, the dual market for paid work insulates the male work role from the changes in the female work role that have occurred so far in our society.

Household work and childcare can likewise be conceptualized as allocated by a sex-segregated, dual market mechanism. This market mechanism is supported by ideology concerning the appropriate household activities of the two sexes as well as by differential training in family tasks. The result is that the husband's family role is generally unresponsive to changes in the wife's family role. If a wife's employment requires her to reduce the level of her family role performance, the husband is unlikely to increase his. He may perceive that family work needs doing, but he will not perceive the kind of work that needs to be done as appropriate or suitable to him. The dual market for household work and childcare thus has insulated men's family role from the changes in the female family role resulting so far from paid employment.

The second kind of structural buffer in the work-family role system is *asymmetrically permeable boundaries between work and family roles* for both men and women. For women, the demands of the family role are permitted to intrude into the work role more than vice versa. Though working mothers try to devise schedules to accommodate the demands of both roles, if an emergency or irregularity arises requiring a choice between the two, the family will often take priority. For example, when there is a crisis for a child in school, it is the child's working mother rather than working father who will be called to take responsibility. This vulnerability of the female work role to family demands is an important part of negative stereotypes about women workers. It is also a major source of stress for women on the job, since the sex role norm that women take responsibility for the family conflicts with the norms of the job role.

For husbands, the work-family role boundary is likewise asymmetrically permeable, but in the other direction. Many husbands literally "take work home" with them or need to use family time simply to recuperate from the stresses they face in their work role. Husbands are expected to manage their families so that their family responsibilities do not interfere with their work efficiency, and so that families will make any adjustments necessary to accommodate the demands of husbands' work roles.

CHANGE IN THE WORK-FAMILY ROLE SYSTEM

As is well known, over the course of this century there has been a major increase in married women's rate of labor force participation (Oppenheimer, 1970). Married women's increased employment has induced a partially accommodating reduction in women's family role, but as yet almost no increase in husbands' family role, as indicated by the time budget data considered earlier. In consequence, employed wives face considerable problems of strain and exhaustion in both their work and family roles. As Rapoport and Rapoport (1972) have formulated it, there is a psychosocial lag between the changes occurring for women in the macrosocial world of work and changes in the microsocial world of the family. In their analysis, this psychosocial lag generates transitional problems of adjustment, but these will be resolved as the family "catches up" to changes in the workplace. Young and Willmott (1973) have likewise argued that the family is becoming more "symmetrical," that is, evolving toward a pattern where each marital partner has a significant role in both paid work and in the family. The analysis of the work-family role system developed here makes possible a more specific consideration of the issues these social changes will involve.

First, it is clear that one of the most pressing changes needed in the work-family role system is an end to the traditional norms prescribing the sex-segregated and unequal division of household work and childcare. As noted earlier, however, if and when these norms break down, the demands of the male work role will emerge as the crucial constraint on how much men can increase their family role. Expansion of the scope of the male family role without accommodating changes in the male work role will lead to role strain in men similar to the strains now faced by working wives. While this distribution of strain throughout the role system will be more equitable than the current one, it will continue to be a source of instability. Husbands who are committed to equal sharing of household work and childcare will find that the demands of their jobs make this quite difficult, and that a diversion of their energy from work into the family will penalize them in the competition for job advancement. The idea of paternity leave—admittedly only beginning to be raised in labor negotiations, and not widely taken advantage of in the few palces where it has been implemented—is perhaps the first indication of the kind of workplace practices needed to legitimate a shift of husbands' energies from work to the family.

A second potential future change in the work-family role system is the breakdown of occupational sex segregation. Recent progress toward reducing occupational segregation, when it has been evident at all, has been dishearteningly slow (Waldman and McEaddy, 1974; Blaxall and Reagan, 1976). If occupational segregation is significantly reduced, major adjustments will be required in men's self-conceptions as primary family breadwinners and in the norms governing male-female interaction on the job. In addition, women holding higher-status jobs may give added impetus to the desegregation of family work and the enlargement of the male family role. First, women holding higher-status jobs may require that women's boundary between their work and family roles become more like men's, that is, their work role will more often need to take priority over their family role, and they will be able to do less family work. Second, women holding jobs more equal in status to their husbands' will give greater legitimation to the demand for a more equal sharing of family work. Contrary to these two effects, however, the increased income provided by women's holding higher-status jobs may make it more possible for families to purchase goods and services to compensate for the reduction in women's family role than is possible now where women are in relatively low-paying jobs. If these goods and services are available, purchasing them may be less stressful than trying to increase men's family role.

Third, if the sex segregation of both family work and paid work is significantly reduced, a fundamental change in the nature of the work role may be necessary, not just for men but for both sexes. As the paid work role has evolved in modern society, it has come to call for full time, continuous work from the end of one's education to retirement, desire to actualize one's potential to the fullest, and subordination of other roles to work. This conception of the work role has been, in effect, the male model of the work role. Women, because of the family responsibilities traditionally assigned to them, have had considerable difficulty fitting themselves to this male model of work. To a large extent, it has been possible for men in modern society to work according to this model precisely because women have subordinated their own potential work role and accepted such an extensive role in the family. In doing so, wives take on the family responsibilities that husbands might otherwise have to fill, and in additional emotionally, and often practically, support their husbands in their work role.[3]

In the past, it has been possible for families to function, though not without strain, with one marital partner, the husband, performing according to this male work model. Families have also been able to function, though with even more strain, with one partner conforming to the male work model and with the other partner in a less demanding job role. Though it is stressful, especially for the wife, this kind of two-job family is on the verge of being the statistically dominant pattern (Hayghe, 1976). However, it does not seem possible for large numbers of families to function with *both* partners following the traditional male work model. Such a pattern could become widespread only if fertility dropped significantly further or if household work and childcare services became inexpensive, widely available,

[3] Mortimer et al. (1976) have drawn attention to the extent to which wives can directly contribute to their husbands' work as an alternative to holding paid work of their own, a further indication of the demanding nature of the male work role.

and socially accepted on a scale hitherto unknown.[4] In the absence of such developments, greater equality in the sharing of work and family roles by women and men will ultimately require the development of a new model of the work role and a new model for the boundary between work and the family which gives higher priority to family needs.

REFERENCES

Aberle, David and Kaspar Naegele
1952 "Middle-class fathers' occupational role and attitudes toward children." American Journal of Orthopsychiatry 22: 366-378.

Aldous, Joan
1969 "Occupational characteristics and males' role performance in the family." Journal of Marriage and the Family 31: 707-712.

Bahr, Stephen
1974 "Effects on power and division of labor in the family." Pp. 167-185 in Lois W. Hoffman and F. Ivan Nye (eds.), Working Mothers. San Francisco: Jossey-Bass.

Bailyn, Lotte
1971 "Career and family orientations of husbands and wives in relation to marital happiness." Human Relations 23: 97-113.

Blaxall, Martha and Barbara B. Reagan (eds.)
1976 "Women and the Workplace: The Implications of Occupational Segregation." Signs 1(3, Pt. 2): entire.

Blood, Robert O. and Donald Wolfe
1960 Husbands and Wives. New York: Free Press.

Cain, Glann
1966 Married Women in the Labor Force: An Economic Analysis. Chicago: University of Chicago.

Caplow, Theodore
1954 The Sociology of Work. Minneapolis: University of Minnesota.

Davies, Marjorie
1974 "Women's place is at the typewriter: the feminization of the clerical labor force." Radical America 8(4): 1-37.

Douglas, Mary
1970 Purity and Danger: An Analysis of Concepts of Pollution and Taboo. Baltimore: Penguin Books.

Dyer, William
1956 "The interlocking of work and family social systems among lower occupational families." Social Forces 34: 230-233.
1965 "Family reactions to the father's job." Pp. 86-91 in Arthur Shostak and William Gomberg (eds.), Blue-Collar World. Englewood Cliffs, N.J.: Prentice-Hall.

Duncan, Otis D., Howard Schuman, and Beverly Duncan
1974 Social Change in a Metropolitan Community. New York: Russell Sage.

Glazer-Malbin, Nona
1976 "Housework." Signs 1:905-922.

Gronseth, Erik
1971 "The husband-provider role: a critical appraisal." Pp. 11-31 in Andree Michel (ed.), Family Issues of Employed Women in Europe and America. Leiden: E. J. Brill.
1972 "The breadwinner trap." Pp. 175-191 in Louise Kapp Howe (ed.), The Future of the Family. New York: Simon and Schuster.

Hayghe, Howard
1976 "Families and the rise of working wives: an overview." Monthly Labor Review 99(5): 12-19.

Hartmann, Heidi
1976 "Capitalism, patriarchy, and job segregation by sex." Signs 1(3, Pt. 2): 137-170.

Hoffman, Lois W. and F. Ivan Nye (eds.)
1974 Working Mothers. San Francisco: Jossey-Bass.

Howell, Mary
1973a Employed mothers and their families (I). Pediatrics 52: 252-263.
1973b "Effects of maternal employment on the child (II). Pediatrics 52:327-343.

Kanter, Rosabeth
1976 Work and Family in America: A Critical Review and Research Agenda. Social Science Frontiers Monograph Series. New York: Russell Sage.

Lein, Laura, Maureen Durham, Michael Pratt, Michael Schudson, Robert Thomas and Heather Weiss
1974 Final Report: Work and Family Life. National Institute of Education Project No. 3-3094. Cambridge, Mass.: Center for the Study of Public Policy.

Meissner, Martin, Elizabeth Humphreys, Scott Meis, and William Scheu
1975 "No exit for wives: sexual division of labor and the cumulation of household demands." Canadian Review of Sociology and Anthropology 12: 424-439.

[4] Safilios-Rothschild (1976) has analyzed in a somewhat different way the structural changes that may occur to accommodate families in which both parents have high status jobs.

Miller, Daniel R. and Guy E. Swanson
1958 The Changing American Parent. New York: Wiley.
Mincer, Jacob
1962 "Labor force participation of married women." Pp. 63-97 in National Bureau of Economic Research (ed.), Aspects of Labor Economics. Princeton: Princeton University.
Mortimer, Jeylan, Richard Hall, and Reuben Hill
1976 "Husbands' occupational attributes as constraints on wives' employment." Paper given at the Annual Meeting of the American Sociological Association.
Oakley, Ann
1972 "Are husbands good housewives?" New Society 112: 377-379.
Oppenheimer, Valerie K.
1970 The Female Labor Force in the United States. Population Monograph Series No. 3. Berkeley: University of California.
Pearlin, Leonard I.
1974 Class Context and Family Relations. Boston: Little, Brown.
Prather, Jane
1971 "When the girls move in: a sociological analysis of the feminization of the bank teller's job." Journal of Marriage and the Family 33: 777-782.
Rapoport, Robert and Rhona Rapoport
1965 "Work and family in modern society." American Sociological Review 30: 381-394.
Rapoport, Rhona and Robert Rapoport
1971 Dual-career Families. Baltimore: Penguin Books.
1972 "The working woman and the enabling role of the husband." Paper given at the XIIth International Family Research Seminar, International Sociological Association, Moscow.
Rapoport, Rhona, Robert Rapoport, and Victor Thiessen.
1974 "Couple symmetry and enjoyment." Journal of Marriage and the family 36: 588-591.
Robinson, John, Thomas Juster, and Frank Stafford
1976 American's Use of Time. Ann Arbor, Mich.: Institute for Social Research.
Robinson, John, Janet Yerby, Margaret Feiweger, and Nancy Sommerick
1976 "Time use as an indicator of sex role territoriality." Unpublished paper.
Safilios-Rothschild, Constantina
1970 "The study of family power structure: a review 1960-1969." Journal of Marriage and the Family 32: 539-552.
1976 "Dual linkages between the occupational and family systems: a macrosociological analysis." Signs 1(3, Pt. 2): 51-60.
Scanzoni, John
1965 "Resolution of occupational-conjugal role conflict in clergy marriages." Journal of Marriage and the Family 27: 396-402.
1970 Opportunity and the Family. New York: Free Press.
Waldman, Eleanor and Barbara McEaddy
1974 "Where women work: an analysis by industry and occupation." Monthly Labor Review 95 (5): 3-13.
Walker, Kathryn E.
1969 "Time spent in household work by homemakers." Family Economics Review 3:5-6.
1970 "Time spent by husbands in household work." Family Economics Review 4: 8-11.
1974 Unpublished data.
Walker, Kathryn E. and William Gauger
1973 "Time and its dollar value in household work." Family Economics Review 7: 8-13.
Yankelovich, Daniel
1974 "The meaning of work." Pp. 19-48 in J. M. Rosow (ed.), The Worker and the Job. Englewood Cliffs, N.J.: Prentice-Hall.
Young, Michael and Peter Willmott.
1973 The Symmetrical Family. New York: Pantheon.

Changes in Family Roles, Socialization, and Sex Differences

LOIS WLADIS HOFFMAN

ABSTRACT: *Sex differences in socialization experiences reflect adult role expectations that females will be mothers and males will be workers. However, because of smaller family size, longer life expectancy, and higher employment rates for women, motherhood has come to occupy less of a woman's adult life, and work has come to occupy more. As awareness of these social changes increases, the sex-linked differences in socialization may be expected to diminish, with the result that sex differences in behavior will also eventually diminish. The research literature supporting this thesis is reviewed. This includes findings bearing on (a) the change in the woman's role, (b) sex differences in socialization and behavior that appear to reflect traditional sex role expectations, and (c) the direct effects of maternal employment on sex differences in children.*

The focus of this article is on changes in the family roles of women—and also of men—and the effects of these changes on the child's socialization experiences. There are two changes that I will concentrate on: First, motherhood—childbearing and child rearing—has come to occupy a smaller proportion of the American woman's adult life; and second, a closely related change, the employment of women, especially maternal employment, has become increasingly common. Both of these events have significance for the socialization experience, particularly that of girls, and are likely to contribute to a decrease in the differences between the sexes.

The first of these changes, the fact that women are spending a smaller proportion of their lives in mothering activities, is extremely significant. The reproductive role has been a major factor in determining the status of women in society. This is an important point, because as we move into a situation where there is greater control over fertility and a smaller portion of a woman's life is given over to reproductive functions, we may find that many things taken as given—many sex differences, specifically—are not given but are only derived from the fact that women were often *and unpredictably* pregnant.

In almost all societies there are similar sex differences in temperament and division of labor. While the degree of aggressiveness may vary from one society to another, the men in most societies are likely to be more aggressive than the women. Similarly, most societies view women as nurturant, cooperative, expressive of emotions, and tender (D'Andrade, 1974; Whiting & Edwards, 1974). Women are more likely to be assigned the tasks that are in or near the home. Thus, women may make important economic contributions to the society if their tasks can be carried out relatively near the house, as in gardening or gathering, the cottage industries, crafts, or piecework at home (Blumberg, Note 1). But they are not the hunters or warriors. Neither have they been likely to take up those occupations that require a constant commitment to work, for their pattern has been to leave the labor force for pregnancy and child care (Oppenheimer, 1975). If property is inherited through the male line, there is usually a double standard of sexual morality—chastity being more required of women. These similarities across cultures and over time have led many to conclude that sex differences must be biologically based and unchangeable.

I would like to suggest that they are biologically based but not unchangeable. They are based on the fact that women are the childbearers and, until recently, spent much of their lives pregnant, nursing, or caring for children. But in the United States today this is no longer the case. This change has resulted primarily from three converging factors—smaller family size, longer life expec-

---

This article was the opening address to the annual meeting of the National Council on Family Relations, New York City, October 20, 1976.

Some of the research reported here was supported by Grant HD08287 from the National Institute of Child Health and Human Development.

Requests for reprints should be sent to Lois Wladis Hoffman, Department of Psychology, University of Michigan, Ann Arbor, Michigan 48109.

tancy, and higher employment rates for women throughout the life cycle.

Smaller Families, Longer Lives, and Higher Employment Rates for Women

The decrease in family size has been attributed to a number of factors. Some of these, such as the current economic recession and the salience of the concern with overpopulation, may be only temporary influences. Others, however, seem to be more permanent. Very important are the improved methods of birth control and their wide acceptance. Just 15 years ago, the pill, contraceptive sterilization, and the IUD, the most effective contraceptive measures, were used by only a very small proportion of couples or were nonexistent, but by 1973 about 50% of the married couples of reproductive age were using one of these methods. If the relatively effective diaphragm and condom are added, this figure rises to over 60%. Rapid acceptance of the new methods has led Westoff (1976) to estimate that "by the end of the 1970's, almost all married couples at risk of unintended pregnancy will be using contraception, and almost all contraceptors will be protected by the most effective medical methods" (p. 57).

With effective contraception so widely practiced and the increased availability of legal abortion, the birth of a child is far more likely to be planned, timed, and predictable. Widespread use of contraceptives has made premarital sex more available to women and thus may have facilitated the current later age of marriage. Because it has increased the likelihood of the first child's being planned, it has contributed to the present tendency to postpone the birth of the first child. Marrying at an older age and postponing the birth of the first child tend to decrease the total number of children that a couple will have. Furthermore, confidence about contraception affects even desired family size, since to some extent the number of children desired is enhanced to match the number expected (Hoffman & Hoffman, 1973). It is largely as a result of the increased control over fertility, then, that we now find American women marrying later, having children later, and having fewer children.

In addition, the increased acceptance and expectation of female employment tend to reduce the number of children wanted. So too does the recent increase in the proportion of women pursuing higher education (Hoffman, 1974).

Whether or not the birth rate will remain at its present low level is difficult to predict, but there is clearly an increase in the number of couples in the United States who expect to have only two children. In 1960, 25% of the married women under 40 expected to have two children (Whelpton, Campbell, & Patterson, 1966); in 1974, 43% had this expectation (U.S. Bureau of the Census, 1975a). And the percentage expecting to have more than four children shows a steady and impressive decline.

Another important factor that has led to women's spending a smaller proportion of their adult life in mothering is increased longevity. The average life expectancy for women in 1974 (computed from live births) was almost 76 years. In 1950, it was 71; in 1920, it was under 55 (U.S. Bureau of the Census, 1976a). Very simply then, there are many years of living left after the child-rearing years. When we add to the decreased family size and the increased life expectancy the fact that mothers are also likely to be wage earners, even while their children are young, it is clear that mothering now occupies only a small portion of the adult years.

In discussing the decline of motherhood as a pervasive aspect of a woman's life, I have avoided mentioning social changes that may be transitory or comparatively trivial. For example, I have read any number of articles recently that have heralded the new trend toward voluntary childlessness. The problem in assessing this view lies in deciding when a trend is really a trend. In national-sample studies of married women under 40, carried out between 1955 and 1965, between 1% and 2% of the women interviewed wanted no children (Ryder & Westoff, 1971; Whelpton et al., 1966). In a study I carried out in 1975 with a comparable sample (Hoffman, 1975, in press), 5.8% of the women (and 4.4% of the men) indicated they wanted no children. This is an increase, of course, but it is still not a very large percentage of the population. Furthermore, it was obtained during a period of economic recession, and estimates based on the Indianapolis study of women who were in their childbearing years during the depression of the 1930s indicate that intended childlessness was even higher then than it is now (Whelpton et al., 1966). Furthermore, *actual* childlessness has decreased since the 1930s, reflecting in part the decrease in involuntary childlessness through fertility impairments (Freedman,

Whelpton, & Campbell, 1959; U.S. Bureau of the Census, 1975b).

These figures may seem startling to those of us who talk mainly to college students. Two independent 1972 studies of undergraduate women, in California and in Ann Arbor, found that 10% of them wanted no children (Hoffman, 1974). This is higher than the national figures and higher than previous data for college women, but the women were not yet married and it is difficult to know how permanent these views are.

So, I'm not sure yet whether the childless family is a trend. And similarly, there are other possible trends that might be described as contributing to a decrease in the predominance of the mother role —the high divorce rates, lower marriage rates, increased acceptance of sex without marriage, and the whole package sometimes called "alternative life-styles." But the trends cited earlier—smaller families and longer lives—are more clearly permanent changes resulting from medical–technological advance, and these two are enough. If a woman starting in her twenties has two children and if she has them 3 years apart, in 8 years the youngest will be in school; in 21 years both children will have completed high school. She is only in her forties then with many healthy years ahead. And even during the child-rearing years, as I will discuss more fully later, most women are not exclusively involved in the mother role. Maternal employment rates have reached an unprecedented high. Over the life span, many women already are spending more of their lives in employment than in mothering.

Adult Roles and Socialization

Why is this so important? Because this new pattern portends a whole new set of changes in sex roles and sex differences. Adult sex roles are converging, and therefore sex differences among children and future generations of adults can be expected to diminish. The socialization process tends—though often in an imperfect way—to mold the child to fit the adult role he or she will occupy. Much of the socialization experience of girls across cultures is geared toward motherhood, and if motherhood is no longer the major role of women in society, then the socialization process can be expected to change. If the adult roles of men and women converge, sex-based differences in child-rearing patterns will diminish. Sex differences in personality—including social orientations and cognitive styles—are in large measure a function of different socialization experiences; thus, as differences in the socialization of children diminish, so too will personality differences.

I shall now discuss what the differences between males and females are at present and then take up the corresponding differences in the socialization experiences of children of each sex. I hope to show in this way that sex differences do reflect socialization differences and also that the socialization experiences reflect the traditional adult role expectations that girls will be mothers and boys will be breadwinners.

Sex Differences

The task of identifying which sex differences do in fact exist and what differences there are in the socialization process is difficult at best because of the complexities of the data. If we were to summarize, for example, all of the studies on sex differences in dependency behavior, we would have to deal with many different kinds of dependency and many different measures of each kind. Do we mean by *dependency* relying on other persons as a means of coping rather than making a direct attack on the problem? Do we mean being easily influenced by others, and if so, do we mean being influenced by adults or by peers? Do we mean how far an 11-month-old will move from his or her mother if placed next to her in a strange room? These distinctions are important, because assessing sex differences from the findings of many different studies requires that we deal with clear, homogeneous concepts. One sex may be more dependent in one sense and less dependent in another. Furthermore, if we were to combine the findings across studies, we would have to consider the age of the subjects, for some sex differences may not be manifest until later ages. In addition, the quality of the study must be considered; thus, a study finding no sex differences might reflect a valid fact or it might reflect insensitive measures, a poor design, or a small N.

But added to the complexities of the task itself are the political overtones and passions that this topic generates. An earlier view held that there were such extreme differences between the sexes that one sex was not fit to carry out the role typically assigned to the other. Perhaps as a reaction to this, recent views tend to stress the *lack* of differences between the sexes.

In a recent review of the literature on psychological sex differences, for example, Maccoby and Jacklin (1974) primarily stress the lack of empirical evidence for differences in personality traits and abilities between the sexes. Among the few sex differences they feel are substantiated are differences in aggressiveness, male superiority in visual–spatial ability and mathematical skills, and female superiority in verbal skills. On the other hand, an excellent critical review of their book by Block (1976), as well as new data that have come out since the book was published, seems to indicate that while the differences between the sexes are only central tendencies with considerable overlap, there is empirical support for the existence of many other sex differences. Females seem to have more pronounced affiliative needs, and the affiliative motive more often influences their behavior in a variety of situations (Hoffman, 1972). They have less confidence in their ability to perform many tasks and are more likely to seek the help and reassurance of others, and they are more compliant with adults, at least at the younger ages at which compliance has been studied (Block, 1976; Fagot, Note 2). Research on sex differences in empathy have been reviewed by M. Hoffman (1977): In every study considered—16 in all—girls were found to be more empathetic. There are also differences in the achievement orientations of girls—particularly as they reach adolescence. Though no less achievement-oriented than males, females appear to be more attuned to the negative consequences of academic and occupational success, and this reflects the realities of their situation (Mednick, Tangri, & Hoffman, 1975; Romer, 1975). That is, for women—particularly during the adolescent and college years when heterosexual relations are particularly salient—the rewards of high academic and occupational success are uncertain and their costs—often in the form of affiliative loss—are real. Furthermore, for women, the alternative satisfactions of marriage and motherhood are available, and these are often seen as incompatible with career achievement. Thus, if we compare the sexes on sheer desire for achievement, they are not different, but when we compare them on sustained, anxiety-free, goal-directed behavior, we find differences that favor the males. In recent years, these differences may have diminished. For example, the percentage of college and graduate degrees going to women has, since 1960, made an upturn, although it is still below that for men (Hoffman, 1974).

It is probably too crude, but it would not be inaccurate, to generalize from the findings and say that females in the United States tend to be less aggressive, more affiliative-oriented or nurturing, more empathic, less independent in their coping style, and less motivationally pitched toward outside-the-home occupations. These characteristics, I think, reflect a socialization process—similar across cultures—which assumes that women will spend most of their adult life engaged in mothering. It is not a conscious, planned socialization, but a socialization that has evolved. In part, it reflects the direct teaching of the child—the parents encouraging those traits that their own experience has led them to believe will be helpful when the child is an adult. If occupational pursuits are deemed important, the parents seek to develop those characteristics that seem occupationally relevant. If being a wife and a mother are the salient goals, interpersonal skills may be stressed more. In part, the socialization also involves the parents' simply responding to the child in terms of the stereotypes of society, which they have themselves internalized and which reflect adult social roles.

Differences in Socialization Experiences of Boys and Girls

Let us now turn to some of the research on sex differences in socialization experiences of boys and girls so we can see how these experiences reflect the role expectations of society and affect sex differences. Gauging sex differences in socialization patterns requires a variety of research techniques to obtain a full picture. In some cases, subjects can be interviewed directly. For example, parents might be questioned about their interactions or the different goals they have for sons and daughters (Block, 1976). But some of the differences are more subtle, and the parents may not be aware that the sex of the child is affecting their behavior toward the child. Thus, the infant labeled female seems fragile, sweet, and pink to the new mother, and she may not know that she is responding differently to her daughter than she would if the child had been labeled male. Or when the father watches the toddler careening precariously on the top of the jungle gym, the extra involvement in the male child's physical prowess and daring may be enough to enable the father to keep from expressing the anxiety he feels for the child's safety. So in addition to verbal reports, behavioral observations are an important means of gathering data. Observations of parents, even of those with newborn infants, confirm that there are differences in the way both parents behave toward sons and daughters (Moss, 1967; Parke & O'Leary, 1976; Rebelsky & Hanks, 1971; Thoman, Leiderman, & Olson, 1972). Nor should this be surprising. Sex is the first fact announced at birth and a salient concern throughout pregnancy.

PREFERENCE FOR BOYS

In fact, sex differences in socialization, or at least the foundation for these differences, might be seen as existing prior to the child's birth. There is, for example, a preference for male children in most countries throughout the world. The United States, while not as extreme as some other countries, also shows this pattern, as documented in the 1975 national-sample study referred to earlier (Hoffman, 1975). In this study, over 1,500 married women under 40 (a representative sample from the 48 contiguous states) and one fourth of their husbands were interviewed. Though most respondents wanted children of each sex, the preference was clearly for boys. This was documented by a number of different questions. Perhaps the best single measure of sex preference is the Coombs scale, in which the respondent is given a series of choices about the sexes she would prefer if she had three children (Coombs, Coombs, & McClelland, 1975). A consistent pattern of choosing more males than females indicates a male preference. In this sample, almost twice as many preferred boys as preferred girls. This pattern was more pronounced among the men: Between three and four times as many men preferred boys to girls.

Responses to the interview questions were consistent with a behavioral pattern revealed in this study and in other studies in the United States—that couples are more likely to continue to have children if they have only girls. They will have more children than they originally planned to in order to try for a boy.

All respondents, whether they preferred boys or girls, were asked why they would want to have each sex. It is interesting to note that the most common reasons women gave for wanting boys were to please their husbands, to carry on the family name (the husband's family name, of course), and to be a companion to the husband. The most common reasons women gave for wanting a girl were to have a companion and that it would be "fun to dress her and fuss with her hair." Other answers included that the child would be more like the mother, that girls are easier to raise and more obedient, that girls could help with and learn about housework and caring for the other children, that girls stay closer to their parents than boys, and that girls are cuter, sweeter, or not as mean. No unisex here.

Thus, the male enters the world, even today in the United States, as the preferred sex, and the basis for the value of each sex is different.[1] In view of this, it is not surprising to learn that boys and girls are treated differently by their parents. I will not try to give a complete review of the research on sex differences in socialization, but instead I will present a kind of sampler of the studies—just enough to give a picture of the nature of the differences and to illustrate the different research approaches.

PERCEPTION OF GIRLS AS MORE VULNERABLE

Let us first consider studies of the newborn, where behavioral observation of parent–child interaction has revealed interesting patterns. Some of the differences in the ways parents interact with male and female infants may indeed be a response to the different stimuli each sex presents. For example, some research seems to indicate that male neonates fuss more and sleep less (Moss, 1967; Sander, Note 3). Several studies have indicated that females are more tactilely sensitive (Bell & Costello, 1964; Bell, Weller, & Waldrop, 1971; Weller & Bell, 1965). Some of the differences in parental handling, however, seem to stem more from the cultural stereotypes about what little boys and little girls are supposd to be like. For example, one pervasive finding is that mothers and fathers seek to elicit gross motor behavior more in their sons than in their daughters—that is, they play more roughly and vigorously with infant boys (Moss, 1967; Yarrow, Rubenstein, & Pedersen, Note 4). One might say that this is because baby boys are sturdier, but they are not. Indeed, female neonates are actually more physiologically

[1] Research carried out in India (Poffenberger & Poffenberger, 1973) and in Asia (Arnold et al., 1975) indicates that the preference for boys is more extreme there than in the United States. While the reasons given in the United States are also given in India and Asia, the value of boys as workers and contributors to the family income is stressed in both of these other areas, while neither boys nor girls are seen as economic assets in the United States.

mature and more resistant to disease and injury (Garai & Scheinfeld, 1968). The differences in handling boy and girl newborns, then, seem to stem at least in part from cultural stereotypes about males and females. In any case, there does appear to be an assumption that girls are more fragile, and it extends beyond infancy. There is evidence that parents of 9- and 27-month-old babies are more apprehensive about their daughters' physical well-being (Minton, Kagan, & Levine, 1971; Pedersen & Robson, 1969). And in the national-sample study described earlier, it was found that parents reported that girls were more of a worry than boys, and the worries about girls had to do with a greater assumed vulnerability. I might add here that the specific vulnerability most often cited by mothers was premarital pregnancy—a concern that might be expected to diminish with the improved birth control methods and legalized abortion.

ENCOURAGEMENT OF BOYS' INDEPENDENT EXPLORATIONS

In addition to the rougher handling of boy babies and the assumed vulnerability of girls, there is more encouragement by parents of boys for independent moving about and independent exploration of the environment. For example, Fagot (Note 2) found that parents of toddlers were more likely to encourage daughters and discourage sons from following them around the house. In another study, mothers of 4-year-olds were asked at what age they thought parents should expect or permit certain behaviors by their children, such as crossing the street alone, using a sharp scissors without adult supervision, and being allowed to play away from home for long periods without first telling their parents where they would be. The mothers of boys gave younger ages than the mothers of girls (Callard, 1964). Here again, there does not seem to be a basis for this expectation outside of the concept of sex roles. Boys are not more advanced in the necessary skills, and if anything, they are more impulsive and less mature.

In another study, this time of elementary-school-aged children (Saegert & Hart, 1976), it was found that boys were allowed by parents to roam over a wider area of the community without special permission. And in a study in the Detroit area conducted in 1953 and replicated in 1971, running errands was expected of boys earlier than of girls—although this difference was not found for less expansive tasks such as getting dressed or putting away toys or clothes (Duncan, Schuman, & Duncan, 1973).

Such patterns—in which autonomy and independence of this sort are encouraged more in boys than in girls—can be extremely important in the development of sex differences, even though they may originate only in cultural stereotypes. I do not think the daughter is trained in dependency so much as she is deprived of the training in independence that her brother receives. It is the boy who is seen as having to earn a living outside the home among strangers, and as such, he must have encouragement in independently coping with the environment. The boy's experience in these independent explorations, which girls lack, very likely has considerable importance in the development of independent coping styles, a sense of competence, and even specific skills.

TOYS

Another source of difference in socialization patterns comes from the kinds of toys given to children. The toys for girls are the playthings of the mother role—dolls, dishes, miniature household appliances—while boys are given toys that represent the world of work—trucks, tools, and building equipment. Although the sex typing of playthings may have diminished, the general pattern still holds, as demonstrated in recent parent-interview and home-observation studies, as well as in experimental investigations of adults interacting with infants introduced as male or female (Fagot, 1974; Fein, Johnson, Kosson, Stork, & Wasserman, 1975; Rheingold & Cook, 1975; Seavey, Katz, & Zalk, 1975). An interesting new line of research is providing evidence that sex-typed toys may have more pervasive effects than that of simply teaching sex roles. For example, in a study by Rosenfeld (Note 5), such toys were presented to children in Grades 1 to 3, and the children were asked to "think of the strangest, most exciting, and most interesting way you can for changing this toy so that boys and girls will have more fun playing with it." Both boys and girls responded with more varied approaches for improving the masculine toys, which suggests that these toys had more potential for inventive use. Additional advantages of masculine toys—particularly building materials—for developing the very skills in which boys are found to excel have been suggested by the results of other studies (Connor, in press; Saegert & Hart,

1976). I know of no research that considers which kinds of play activities involve more verbal communication, and it may be that girls have the advantage here. There is, incidentally, some research suggesting that, at least in the middle class, mothers talk directly to infant girls more than to infant boys.

CHILDREN'S LITERATURE

Children's literature, of course, has been analyzed to show the portrayal of sex-typed activities and traits on the part of both the child and adult characters (Weitzman, 1972). The percentage of mothers depicted in children's readers as staying home all day far exceeds the actual percentage in the real world of 1977. Males are portrayed as more instrumental, more active, and less expressive. Furthermore, in one study just completed, children's picture books published before 1963, between 1963 and 1965, and after 1965 were compared, and it was found that sex role stereotyping had not decreased since the advent of the women's movement (St. Peter, Note 6). One of the ways children learn their sex roles is by accumulating a picture of the behaviors and traits ascribed to their sex in books and other media. Thus literature and, of course, TV programs that perpetuate the traditional roles tend to socialize the child in this direction (Sternglanz & Serbin, 1974).

HOUSEHOLD TASKS

Also relevant is research on the household tasks assigned to boys and girls. In general, girls are assigned the tasks traditionally carried out by the mother in the house—dishes, beds, dusting; boys are assigned the tasks typically carried out by the father. Particularly interesting are the data assessing change over time. A study in the Detroit area carried out in 1971 repeated questions on this topic that had been asked in 1953 (Duncan, Schuman, & Duncan, 1973). There was, as one would expect, a shift from sex-specific assignments. For example, in 1953, 65% of the mothers interviewed said that only boys should be asked to shovel walks and to wash the car. In 1971, 50% said only boys should shovel, and 31% said only boys should wash the car. In 1953, 66% said only girls should dust, and 52% said that only girls should make beds. These figures dropped to 62% and 29% in 1971. The important thing to note here is that there are still substantial sex differences in the assignment of household tasks to children, although these differences are evident in a smaller proportion of the population than previously.

PRESSURES FOR ACHIEVEMENT

Pressures for achievement are considered next. The research indicates that although boys and girls are both encouraged to do well in school, some important sex differences in achievement pressures may exist. In a study of preschoolers carried out by Block, Block, and Harrington (Note 7), parents were put in a teaching situation with their children, and their behavior was observed. An important finding was that sex-differentiated behavior was noted more in fathers than in mothers. The fathers of boys were more concerned with the child's achievement and emphasized the cognitive aspects of the teaching situation, while the fathers of girls appeared to be more attuned to the interpersonal aspects of the situation and were less concerned with performance. There are a number of interesting implications of this study. The authors suggested that cognitive achievement may be a less salient socialization domain for mothers, relative to fathers. They also made the interesting suggestion that the prevalent view of mothers as primarily responsible for child rearing may have obscured the fact that fathers may be more important in certain areas. Related to this was their additional suggestion that the failure to study father–child interaction may have led to an underestimation of sex differences in achievement pressures and skill training.

In another study by Block (in press), parents were asked to describe various interactions with one of their children. Both mothers and fathers who were describing interactions with sons emphasized achievement and competition to a greater extent than did parents describing their interactions with daughters.

Similar findings have been obtained in studies that ask parents what their goals are for their children. For example, in the 1975 national survey already mentioned (Hoffman, 1975), parents were first asked the following question:

> We are interested in the qualities or characteristics that people like to see in their children when they grow up. First, what kind of person would you want your son to become?

After they answered, they were asked,

Now, what kind of person would you want your daughter to become?

These were open-ended questions; respondents could answer in any way they wished. The answers have been analyzed for all subjects who had at least one child, including in all 1,259 mothers and 356 fathers. Of the fathers, 21% answered in terms of career or occupational success when asked about sons, while 14% gave this kind of answer for daughters. Mothers also gave this kind of answer more often when asked about sons than when asked about daughters, although the difference was less pronounced.

Another answer the parents gave more often when asked about sons was that they wanted them to be hardworking and ambitious. Twice as many parents advanced this as a goal for sons than for daughters. Other traits desired more often in sons included being intelligent or highly educated, honest or responsible, independent or self-reliant, and aggressive or strong-willed. Qualities more often desired in daughters included being kind or unselfish, loving, attractive or well-mannered, having a good marriage, and being a good parent.

In another pair of questions, the parents were asked whether they would be most satisfied if their son (or daughter) when grown were happily married, a good parent, successful and respected in work, or financially well-off. The most common choice for both sons and daughters was happily married. "Successful and respected in work," however, was a far more common goal for sons than for daughters.

Actually, the amount of sex role socialization that goes on is probably underestimated by direct questions such as the ones used in this national study. In 1974, one of my students interviewed a group of mothers who were professional women on the faculty of the University of Michigan (Banker, Note 8). The women were asked about differences in their general goals for sons and daughters; most answered indicating that they would not differentiate but would hold the same goals for either sex. However, each woman was also asked questions about her specific goals for one of her children. The findings were interesting. Despite their expressed equalitarian ideology, the mothers who discussed sons had higher academic and occupational goals in mind for them and indicated that they would be more disappointed if these goals were not achieved than did the mothers who discussed daughters.

CONTROL OF EMOTION

So far, I have discussed differences in the socialization experience that might make girls feel more vulnerable, less confident in their independent abilities to cope and explore, short-changed with respect to certain kinds of cognitive learning experiences, and less pressured to achieve in competitive and occupational spheres. But how do girls fare with respect to emotional expression? Though there is not a great deal of empirical evidence here, the data available suggest, not surprisingly, that both mothers and fathers encourage their sons more than their daughters to *control* the expression of affect (Block, in press). This may be particularly true with respect to warmth, physical closeness, and crying. Parental acceptance of aggressive behavior seems to vary depending on who the target is. Block (in press), for example, found fathers less tolerant of aggression directed toward themselves by sons than by daughters. Aggression toward peers, however, may be more tolerated in sons.

INSTRUMENTAL VERSUS EXPRESSIVE

The distinction made by Parsons that the male in the family fulfills the instrumental function and the female fulfills the expressive–affective function has been much criticized, and the terms are probably too general to have real value. Nevertheless, parents seem, even today, to be socializing their sons for the occupational role—instrumental in that limited sense—and their daughters for the mother role—expressive in that limited sense. The problem is that this distinction may not fit the new adult roles.[2] The role of the woman has clearly changed, with the mother role occupying less and the wage-earner role occupying more of her adult life. Both of these changes have significance for the man's role too, with corresponding adjustments beginning to appear in the form of a more active fathering role and a decreased emphasis on the breadwinner role.[3] The discrep-

---

[2] Bernard (1975) has pointed out that the female's socialization may not be appropriate preparation for modern motherhood either.

[3] Increase in the man's role as parent can be expected from the press of the woman's dual role of mother and wage earner. Decrease in the man's breadwinner role can be expected partly because that role is increasingly being shared with his wife, partly as an adjustment in the form of shorter work hours that also increase the number of jobs, and partly because of other changes in

ancy between these new adult role requirements and the existing socialization practices creates a force for change. Thus, to return to my original theme, sex differences in socialization practices, and the differences between males and females that result, can be expected to diminish as the lack of coordination between the new family roles and the traditional socialization patterns becomes more apparent.

Increased Employment of Women

Since a considerable portion of this article has been devoted to the significance of the decreased predominance of the mother role for women, I now want to turn to the parallel trend, the increased predominance of the employment role. At this time, 38.8 million women in the United States are in the labor force ("Women Entering Job Force," 1976). At every stage in the life cycle, women are more likely than in previous years to be employed. The increased participation of women in the labor force is another trend that is not a transitory phenomenon, and there is every reason to assume that it will continue. Technological advances have streamlined housekeeping and cooking to the point that the housewife role is not a full-time job and does not seem an essential or adequate contribution as a sole commitment. Motherhood has been one way of augmenting this role, and the increase in desired family size in the 1940s and 1950s was seen by some as a reaction to the diminished importance of the housewife role. At best, however, motherhood is a stopgap solution. The youngest child eventually starts school no matter how long mothering is stretched out. The wife's working is a natural and inevitable outcome of technological advance, limited family size, and increased health and longevity. Several studies (e.g., Hoffman & Nye, 1974) indicate that the full-time housewife whose children are all in school is generally low in self-esteem and high in psychological symptoms. And this generalization is based not only on the overstudied middle class but also on national-sample data. Bringing home a paycheck is a tangible contribution—a meaningful symbol of competence. Home production can rarely match mass production in economy so long as one is aware that the housewife's time has potential monetary value.

The prevalence of female employment underscores the previous point that the adult role for females has shifted and that women will be spending more time as wage earners than as mothers. But maternal employment itself also has effects on the family and particularly on socialization patterns and sex differences.

The increase in maternal employment in the United States is well known. Of women with school-aged children and husbands present, the percentage who are employed passed the 50% mark in 1972 and has been steadily climbing at each reading since. The 1972 rate was about double the 1948 rate. Employment rates for mothers of preschoolers almost tripled during that same period, and currently over 36% of the mothers of preschool children—with husbands present—are employed.[4] These figures are even higher when one considers female-headed households. The 1972 data show that 62% of the divorcées with preschool children are employed. And, of course, the population of female-headed households is increasing (Hoffman & Nye, 1974).

Maternal Employment and Sex Differences

With respect to the effects of maternal employment on sex differences, there is a considerable body of research comparing families with employed mothers and those with nonemployed mothers, as well as reports from women about changes that occurred when they entered or left the labor force. As I have stressed elsewhere, the studies that compare families with working and nonworking mothers to ascertain the effects of employment require careful matching, lest the differences, or the lack of differences, observed turn out to be merely a function of selective factors (Hoffman & Nye, 1974). Statistically speaking, women are

---

society that have affected men's achievement orientation. I have discussed the decrease in the man's breadwinner role elsewhere (Hoffman, 1972, 1973, 1977; Hoffman & Nye, 1974).

---

[4] According to 1975 census figures (U.S. Bureau of the Census, 1976b), 51% of the blacks with preschoolers and husbands present were employed, as were 35% of the whites with similar families. For women with school-aged children only and husbands present, 61% of the blacks and 52% of the whites were employed. According to national-sample data collected in 1975 (Hoffman, 1975), 43% of the mothers of preschoolers—with husbands present—were employed, and 59% of the mothers of school-age children (all races) were employed. In the latter study, all mothers were under 40.

more likely to be working if they are mothers without husbands, if their husbands' incomes are low, and if the women are educated, have fewer children, have no preschool children, live in areas where jobs are available, and are black. The husbands of employed women are generally more favorable to female employment than are the husbands of nonemployed women. The employed mothers are more likely to have other adults living in the home and are more likely to have been married more than once. In general, these are characteristics that make employment either more necessary or more feasible. These differences, which are selective factors, are important to consider in attempts to demonstrate the effects of maternal employment, and failure to consider such factors can obscure differences as well as suggest spurious effects.

For example, one effect of maternal employment is that the division of tasks within the house is affected and the husband helps more with the housework. The result is not an equal division of labor; the wife still maintains the larger share, but a reallocation of tasks, with the husband taking on some of the tasks conventionally defined as feminine (particularly when the children are young), has been demonstrated across social classes and by means of different research designs (Hoffman, in press; Hoffman & Nye, 1974). Time-use data have sometimes been used to refute this effect. But since nonworking women have larger families and family size is rarely accounted for in these studies, the data are usually not directly applicable. Where family size and age of children are controlled, however, the working–nonworking differences do appear (Robinson, in press; Walker & Gauger, 1973).[5] The research findings, on the whole, show that the husbands of working women help more in household tasks—including child care—than the husbands of nonworking women. This fact has significance for sex differences in several ways. First, it is itself a diminution of sex differences. In the working-mother family, the pattern of the father as breadwinner and the mother as the exclusive performer of certain household tasks and parent functions is weakened. Second, the models of sex roles that the parents present for the child are less stereotypically traditional, and consequently, the child's concept of what males and females are is less differentiated.

For example, the children of working mothers do describe a less traditional household division of labor between their parents. In addition, in studies in 1961 and 1974, elementary-school-aged daughters of working mothers were more likely than the daughters of nonworking mothers to say that *both* men and women typically engage in a wide variety of specified adult activities—inside and outside the house (Hartley, 1961; Miller, 1975). They saw women as less restricted to their homes and more active in the world. In a national-sample study of adolescents, the daughters of working mothers scored lower on an index of traditional femininity. In a study of college students' attitudes, the sons and daughters of working mothers were less stereotyped in their perceptions of males and females. Daughters of working mothers saw women as more competent and effective than did the daughters of nonworking mothers; sons of working mothers saw men as warmer and more expressive than did the sons of nonworking mothers. In addition, many studies have shown that the children of working mothers are more likely to approve of maternal employment and that the adolescent daughters are more likely to be already employed and to plan to work when they become mothers (Hoffman & Nye, 1974).

The finding that daughters of working women see women as more competent has been borne out in other studies. For example, in an interesting study by Baruch (1972), college women were administered a measure in which they were asked to judge the quality of a number of journal articles. Half of the articles were given female names as authors and half were given male names. Previous research had indicated that college women tend to attach a lower value to the articles attributed to women authors. Baruch found that the daughters of employed women were significantly different from the daughters of full-time housewives in that they did not downgrade the articles attributed to women, while the daughters of full-time housewives did. Thus, the daughters of working mothers were less likely to assume lower competence on the part of women authors.

[5] The Robinson (in press) time-use data showed that husbands of working women helped more with housework and had more total child contact but did not have more primary child contact. The Walker and Gauger (1973) data indicated that the husband's time in housework was not increased when there was only one child, and that it increased most when there were preschool children. Other data, however, showed that the husbands of employed women did more housework even when there was only one child (Hoffman, in press) and also that husbands helped more with child care as well as housework (Hoffman, 1958).

We might expect that if the daughters of working mothers view women as more competent, they are themselves more confident and have higher academic and career aspirations. There is some evidence for this, although it is confined to college-educated samples. A number of studies have found that college women who are career oriented or planning less conventionally feminine careers are more likely to be the daughters of working than nonworking women. Similarly, several studies have found that highly educated professional women were more likely to have had working mothers (Hoffman & Nye, 1974). Possibly, the counterpart to this among less-educated, blue-collar groups is the tendency for daughters of working mothers to plan to work themselves.

There is also some evidence that the daughters of working mothers are more independent and autonomous. This finding, which has been obtained with both young children and adolescents, may result in part because the working mother provides a more independent role model. It may also reflect the fact that working mothers are more apt than nonworking mothers to stress independence training. By and large, the evidence supports the idea that working mothers encourage independence in their children, although under certain conditions—when the children are young and the mother feels guilty about working—this is not the case. With older children, however, the findings are more straightforward. To the nonworking mother, the move from protector and nurturer to independence trainer, which is required as the child moves toward adolescence, is often very difficult. For the working mother, on the other hand, the child's growing independence eases the strain of the dual roles of worker and mother. Furthermore, the psychological threat of becoming less essential to the child is lessened by the alternative role and source of self-worth. In any case, the evidence based on mothers of preadolescent and adolescent children and on noncollege mothers of younger children does suggest that working mothers stress independence training to a greater extent than nonworking mothers. This is particularly relevant for daughters, since as I have noted, they are often handicapped by overprotection and insufficient encouragement of independence. The effect of maternal employment on independence also has significance for achievement patterns, since encouragement of independence relates to high achievement motivation, competence, and achievement behavior in both males and females.

The Father's Role in Child Care

One other aspect of maternal employment that I want to consider is the father's role in the working-mother family. I have already indicated that fathers play a more active part in child rearing when the mother is employed. Furthermore, it is reasonable to expect that the father's role in child rearing will increase even more as maternal employment, especially for mothers of preschool children, becomes more prevalent and acceptable. Less rigid sex roles in general should lead to increased father participation, for the dual role of worker and mother involves considerable strain, and the more equal sharing of child rearing is a natural solution so long as the traditional sex role prescriptions are relaxed.

But what will be the effect of the increased participation of fathers in child rearing on the socialization of the child, particularly with respect to sex differences—the focus of this article? On the one hand, the father is often seen as the independence trainer for both boys and girls. Since the mother has typically been the primary caretaker during the child's early years, the father's role in weaning the child from this early dependency is seen as very important. Furthermore, research suggests that the father may be more important than the mother in fostering achievement motivation (Block, Block, & Harrington, Note 7). Studies have also shown that high-achieving women often have backgrounds that include close relationships with fathers who encouraged them in independence strivings and achievement behavior. These considerations may lead one to conclude that the father's increased participation in child rearing will facilitate the development of independence and achievement in girls as well as boys, possibly lessening the sex differences that still seem to exist.

On the other hand, there is evidence that the father, to a greater degree than the mother, treats sons and daughters differently. This has been found in behavioral observations (Lamb & Lamb, 1976), in the extent to which parents describe infants in sex-typed terms (Fagot, 1974; Rubin, Provenzano, & Luria, 1974), and in the amount of sex differentiation in child-rearing goals, as indicated earlier. From these data, one might conclude that the more active the father is in parenting, the greater the differences that will develop between boys and girls.[6]

However, there is still another possibility: As fathers become more broadly active in nurturance and child rearing, some of the differences between parents that now exist may disappear. To some extent, the existing difference in mothers' and fathers' behavior may itself be a function of their differential involvement. In addition, during this period of social change in women's roles, mothers and fathers may have different expectations about adult roles. In almost all the research—based on national samples as well as select groups—men have proven more traditional in their sex-role attitudes than women. But it has also been found that the husbands of working women are less traditional than the husbands of nonworking women (Hoffman & Nye, 1974). While this last difference may be in part a selective factor, it also seems to be an effect of having a working wife. To use an obvious example, a man becomes more aware of sex discrimination in pay scales when his own family income is diminished by the policy. Thus, the experience of actively caring for the children, combined with the experience of living with a working wife, may affect the father's child-rearing behavior and his assumptions of what the adult roles are for which he is socializing his children. Under these conditions, the father may not differentiate sons from daughters as much as he does at present. It is difficult to extrapolate from the present data to the future situation.[7]

Conclusions

The general thrust of the evidence, however, is that maternal employment, like the decrease in the proportion of time women spend in mothering, functions to narrow the differences in the socialization experiences of boys and girls and thus can be expected to lead to a decrease in sex differences. But social trends are not instantly effective, particularly with respect to child-rearing patterns. Even when parents finally realize it is a new world, their child-rearing behavior is only partly responsive to the new world's demands; and it continues to be influenced by the style of parenting that their parents used. Thus in 1977 we are still finding sex differences and we are still finding sex-based differences in socialization patterns.

In anticipating changes in sex role socialization, I have focused on women's increased participation in employment and decreased preoccupation with mothering. The resulting shift in socialization seems to be toward more independence training and occupational orientation for girls. But if this shift also involves an increase in the competitiveness and aggressiveness of girls, the question may be raised as to whether either sex will receive encouragement for nurturance, warmth, and expressiveness. The problem is that the shift in the role of women toward work is more clearly documented than the shift in the role of men toward parenting. There is some evidence that as wives come increasingly to share the breadwinner role, husbands are under less pressure to be breadwinners. Husbands of working wives, for example, are less likely to be moonlighters, and they spend more time in leisure pursuits (Robinson, Yerby, Feiweger, & Somerich, Note 9). So, it is tempting to predict that as men become more involved in the parent role and feel less pressure to achieve occupationally, new child-rearing practices will allow both boys and girls to develop the positive emotions of warmth and empathy. At the present time, however, this prediction does not yet have a really solid base.

To summarize, the traditional family roles reflect the fact that women are the childbearers. Technological–medical advances, however, have altered the significance of this fact. At present, a woman spends more of her life working than mothering. The father's traditional breadwinner role is shared with his wife, and he in turn may participate in more of the child-rearing functions than previously. Although socialization patterns still reflect traditional role expectations, shifts more in keeping with the new adult role requirements are already beginning. At present there are differences between males and females, and these, at least to some extent, reflect the traditional, sex-differentiated socialization patterns. Thus, these sex differences may be expected to diminish—some even to disappear—as socialization practices accommodate to the reality of the new adult roles. Fewer children, longer life, and working mothers—none of which are new, but all

---

[6] It is possible (but the problem has not been adequately researched) that the father functions at present to increase sex differences in some areas but to decrease them in others.

[7] Johnson (1975) also suggests that the devaluing of females results in part because the primary nurturer is a woman and this view helps the male break that primary tie and establish his masculinity. If the primary nurturer were also a man, the motive for devaluing femininity would be eliminated.

of which are now pervasive, normative, and I think here to stay—add up to new family roles, new socialization patterns, and a decrease in the differences between the sexes.

REFERENCE NOTES

1. Blumberg, R. L. *Structural factors affecting women's status: A cross cultural paradigm.* Paper presented at the meeting of the International Sociological Association, Toronto, Canada, 1974.
2. Fagot, B. I. *Sex determined reinforcing contingencies in toddler children.* Paper presented at the meeting of the Society for Research in Child Development, New Orleans, 1971.
3. Sander, L. *Twenty-four-hour distributions of sleeping and waking over the first month of life in different infant caretaking systems.* Paper presented at the meeting of the Society for Research in Child Development, Philadelphia, 1973.
4. Yarrow, L. J., Rubenstein, J. L., & Pedersen, F. A. *Dimensions of early stimulation: Differential effects on infant development.* Paper presented at the meeting of the Society for Research in Child Development, Minneapolis, 1971.
5. Rosenfeld, E. F. *The relationship of sex-typed toys to the development of competency and sex-role identification in children.* Paper presented at the meeting of the Society for Research in Child Development, Denver, 1975.
6. St. Peter, S. *Jack went up the hill but where was Jill?* Paper presented at the meeting of the Society for Research in Child Development, New Orleans, 1977.
7. Block, J. H., Block, J., & Harrington, D. M. *The relationship of parental teaching strategies to ego-resiliency in preschool children.* Paper presented at the meeting of the Western Psychological Association, San Francisco, 1974.
8. Banker, J. *Attitudes and parental role orientations of married professional women and the self-concept of their children.* Unpublished manuscript, University of Michigan, 1974.
9. Robinson, J. P., Yerby, J., Feiweger, M., & Somerich, N. *Time use as an indicator of sex role territoriality.* Unpublished manuscript, Cleveland State University, March 1976.

REFERENCES

Arnold, R., Bulatao, R., Buripakdi, C., Ching, B. J., Fawcett, J. T., Iritani, T., Lee, S. J., & Wu, T. S. *The value of children; Introduction and comparative analysis* (Vol. 1). Honolulu, Hawaii: East-West Population Institute, 1975.

Baruch, G. K. Maternal influences upon college women's attitudes toward women and work. *Developmental Psychology,* 1972, *6,* 32–37.

Bell, R. G., & Costello, N. S. Three tests for sex differences in tactile sensitivity in the new born. *Biologica Neonatorium,* 1964, *7,* 335–347.

Bell, R. G., Weller, G. M., & Waldrop, M. F. New born and preschooler: Organization of behavior and relations between periods. *Monographs of the Society for Research in Child Development,* 1971, *36*(1 and 2, Serial No. 142).

Bernard, J. Adolescence and socialization for motherhood. In S. E. Dragastin & G. H. Elder (Eds.), *Adolescence in the life cycle; Psychological change and social context.* Washington, D.C.: Hemisphere, 1975.

Block, J. H. Issues, problems, and pitfalls in assessing sex differences. *Merrill-Palmer Quarterly,* 1976, *22,* 283–308.

Block, J. H. Another look at sex differentiation in the socialization behaviors of mothers and fathers. In F. Denmark & J. Sherman (Eds.), *Psychology of women: Future directions of research.* New York: Psychological Dimensions, in press.

Callard, E. *Achievement motive in the four year old and its relationship to achievement expectancies of the mother.* Unpublished doctoral dissertation, University of Michigan, 1964.

Connor, J. Behaviorally based masculine and feminine activity preference scales for preschoolers: Correlates with other classroom behaviors and cognitive tests. *Child Development,* in press.

Coombs, C. H., Coombs, L. C., & McClelland, G. H. Preference scales for number and sex of children. *Population Studies,* 1975, *29,* 273–298.

D'Andrade, R. G. Sex differences and cultural institutions. In R. A. LeVine (Ed.), *Culture and personality: Contemporary readings.* Chicago: Aldine, 1974.

Duncan, D., Schuman, H., & Duncan, B. *Social change in a metropolitan community.* New York: Russell Sage, 1973.

Fagot, B. I. Sex differences in toddler's behavior and parental reaction. *Developmental Psychology,* 1974, *10,* 554–558.

Fein, G., Johnson, D., Kosson, N., Stork, L., & Wasserman, L. Sex stereotypes and preferences in the toy choices of 20-month-old boys and girls. *Developmental Psychology,* 1975, *11,* 527–528.

Freedman, R., Whelpton, P. K., & Campbell, A. A. *Family planning, sterility, and population growth.* New York: McGraw-Hill, 1959.

Garai, J. E., & Scheinfeld, A. Sex differences in mental and behavioral traits. *Genetic Psychology Monographs,* 1968, *77,* 169–299.

Hartley, R. C. What aspects of child behavior should be studied in relation to maternal employment? In A. E. Siegel (Ed.), *Research issues related to the effects of maternal employment on children.* University Park: Pennsylvania State University, Social Science Research Center, 1961.

Hoffman, L. W. Effects of the employment of mothers on parental power relations and the division of household tasks (Doctoral dissertation, University of Michigan, 1958). *Dissertation Abstracts,* 1958, *19,* 2179. (University Microfilms No. 58-3675)

Hoffman, L. W. Early childhood experiences and women's achievement motives. *Journal of Social Issues,* 1972, *28,* 129–155.

Hoffman, L. W. The professional woman as mother. In R. B. Kundsin (Ed.), *A conference on successful women in the sciences.* New York: New York Academy of Sciences, 1973.

Hoffman, L. W. The employment of women, education and fertility. *Merrill-Palmer Quarterly,* 1974, *20,* 99–119.

Hoffman, L. W. The value of children to parents and the decrease in family size. *Proceedings of the American Philosophical Society,* 1975, *119,* 430–438.

Hoffman, L. W. Fear of success in 1965 and 1974: A follow-up study. *Journal of Consulting and Clinical Psychology,* 1977, *45,* 310–321.

Hoffman, L. W. Effects of the first child on the woman's

role. In W. B. Miller & L. F. Newman (Eds.), *The first child and family formation.* Chapel Hill, N.C.: Carolina Population Center, in press.

Hoffman, L. W., & Hoffman, M. L. The value of children to parents. In J. T. Fawcett (Ed.), *Psychological perspectives on fertility.* New York: Basic Books, 1973.

Hoffman, L. W., & Nye, F. I. *Working mothers.* San Francisco: Jossey-Bass, 1974.

Hoffman, M. L. Social and personality development. *Annual Review of Psychology,* 1977, *28,* 295–321.

Johnson, M. M. Fathers, mothers and sex typing. *Sociological Review,* 1975, *45,* 15–26.

Lamb, M. E., & Lamb, J. E. The nature and importance of the father–infant relationship. *The Family Coordinator,* 1976, *25,* 379–385.

Maccoby, E. E., & Jacklin, C. N. *Psychology of sex differences.* Stanford, Calif.: Stanford University Press, 1974.

Mednick, M. S., Tangri, S. S., & Hoffman, L. W. (Eds.). *Women and achievement: Social and motivational analyses.* Washington, D.C.: Hemisphere, 1975.

Miller, S. M. Effects of maternal employment on sex-role perception, interests, and self-esteem in kindergarten girls. *Developmental Psychology,* 1975, *11,* 405–406.

Minton, D., Kagan, J., & Levine, J. A. Maternal control and obedience in the two-year-old. *Child Development,* 1971, *42,* 1873–1894.

Moss, H. A. Sex, age, and state as determinants of mother–infant interaction. *Merrill-Palmer Quarterly,* 1967, *13,* 19–36.

Oppenheimer, V. K. The sex labeling of jobs. In M. Mednick, S. Tangria, & L. W. Hoffman (Eds.), *Women and achievement: Social and motivational analyses.* Washington, D.C.: Hemisphere, 1975.

Parke, R. D., & O'Leary, S. E. Family interaction in the newborn period: Some findings, some observations, and some unresolved issues. In K. Riegel & J. Meacham (Eds.), *The developing individual in a changing world.* Vol. II: *Social and environmental issues.* The Hague, Netherlands: Mouton, 1976.

Pedersen, F. A., & Robson, K. S. Father participation in infancy. *American Journal of Orthopsychiatry,* 1969, *39,* 466–472.

Poffenberger, T., & Poffenberger, S. B. The social psychology of fertility behavior in a village in India. In J. T. Fawcett (Ed.), *Psychological perspectives on population.* New York: Basic Books, 1973.

Rebelsky, F., & Hanks, C. Fathers' verbal interaction with infants in the first three months of life. *Child Development,* 1971, *42,* 63–68.

Rheingold, H. L., & Cook, K. V. The contents of boys' and girls' rooms as an index of parents' behavior. *Child Development,* 1975, *46,* 459–463.

Robinson, J. P. *How Americans use time: A sociological perspective.* New York: Praeger, in press.

Romer, N. The motive to avoid success and its effect on performance in school-age males and females. *Developmental Psychology,* 1975, *11,* 689–699.

Rubin, J. A., Provenzano, F. J., & Luria, A. The eye of the beholder: Parents' views on sex of newborns. *American Journal of Orthopsychiatry,* 1974, *44,* 512–519.

Ryder, N. D., & Westoff, C. F. *Reproduction in the United States 1965.* Princeton, N.J.: Princeton University Press, 1971.

Saegert, S., & Hart, R. The development of sex differences in the environmental competence of children. In P. Burnett (Ed.), *Women in society.* Chicago: Maaroufa Press, 1976.

Seavey, C. A., Katz, P. A., & Zalk, S. R. Baby X: The effect of gender labels on adult responses to infants. *Sex Roles,* 1975, *1,* 103–110.

Sternglanz, S. H., & Serbin, L. H. Sex role stereotyping in children's television programs. *Developmental Psychology,* 1974, *10,* 710–715.

Thoman, E. B., Leiderman, P. H., & Olson, J. P. Neonate-mother interaction during breast feeding. *Developmental Psychology,* 1972, *6,* 110–118.

U.S. Bureau of the Census. *Fertility expectations of American women: June 1974* (Current population reports, Series P-20, No. 277). Washington, D.C.: U.S. Government Printing Office, February 1975. (a)

U.S. Bureau of the Census. *Statistical abstract of the United States: 1975* (96th ed.). Washington, D.C.: U.S. Government Printing Office, 1975. (b)

U.S. Bureau of the Census. *Statistical abstract of the United States: 1976* (97th ed.). Washington, D.C.: U.S. Government Printing Office, 1976. (a)

U.S. Bureau of the Census. *A statistical portrait of women in the United States* (Current population reports, Series P-23, No. 58). Washington, D.C.: U.S. Government Printing Office, 1976. (b)

Walker, K. E., & Gauger, W. H. Time and its dollar value in household work. *Family Economics Review,* Fall 1973, pp. 8–13.

Weitzman, L. J. Sex-role socialization in picture books for preschool children. *American Journal of Sociology,* 1972, *77,* 1125–1150.

Weller, G. M., & Bell, R. Q. Basal skin conductance and neonatal state. *Child Development,* 1965, *36,* 647–657.

Westoff, C. F. Trends in contraceptive practice: 1965–1973. *Family Planning Perspectives,* 1976, *8,* 54–57.

Whelpton, P. K., Campbell, A. A., & Patterson, J. E. *Fertility and family planning in the United States.* Princeton, N.J.: Princeton University Press, 1966.

Whiting, B., & Edwards, C. P. A cross-cultural analysis of sex differences in the behavior of children aged three through eleven. In R. A. Levine (Ed.), *Culture and personality: Contemporary readings.* Chicago: Aldine, 1974.

Women entering job force at "extraordinary" pace. *New York Times,* September 12, 1976, p. 1.

Wives and mothers

MARITAL STATUS AND FAMILY

by Arlene Kaplan Daniels

Although women bear and nurse the children, their role in childrearing is to some degree a product of sociocultural and technological (as well as biological) factors and thus is susceptible to change (Rosaldo and Lamphere, 1974). Moreover, the twin beliefs that a woman's place is in the home and that her basic functions are those of wife and mother are oversimplified (ignoring differences in the life styles and problems of women at different socioeconomic levels) and incomplete (overlooking the unmarried, the divorced, the widowed, as well as the woman who must function as a single parent). Serious questions are coming from all sides—radicals and conservatives, religious leaders and revolutionaries, feminists and traditionalists—about the viability of the family and about its future. Not all the forecasts are gloomy. What new forms of, or adaptations to, family life are emerging? And how are these new forms influencing and being influenced by the changing roles of women? (Bernard, 1971a, 1972, 1974; Epstein, 1971; Holmstrom, 1972; Howe, 1972; Lipman-Blumen, 1974, forthcoming; Lopata. 1971; Weil, 1971.) This section considers (1) the family in socioeconomic context, (2) marriage, including some of its new forms, (3) divorce, (4) singlehood, and (5) parenting.

The Family in Socioeconomic Context

A closer look at the connections between the overall economic structure, the family, and women's position in our society is needed. How are relations between husbands and wives and between parents and children affected by a particular society's views on ownership of property, production of goods, and rights to those goods? For instance, would having extra goods affect the division of labor between men and women? Would it affect the way in which children are treated? Some evidence suggests that, in American society, money and goods are used to influence children and to buy their affection (Aries, 1962; Bettelheim, 1969; Bronfenbrenner and Condry, 1970). To what extent is this true at various socioeconomic levels?

Individual family analysis across various sectors of the population is also needed (Astin, 1969; Ginzberg et al., 1966; Komarovsky, 1962; Safilios-Rothschild, 1974). Catherine Bodard Silver (CUNY, Brooklyn) believes that there are many differences, depending on social class, in how women spend their time at work and at leisure. Are there differences by race as well? We might postulate, for instance, that black women spend more time in church-related activities whereas white women are more active in charitable and health drives. What are the differences, by social class and race, in leisure activities directed chiefly at entertainment (e.g., watching television, reading, going to movies, socializing with friends)? To what extent does educational level override race and socioeconomic background?

The issues involved in budget management might also be studied, and the findings that emerge compared with data already collected in France—for instance, by Andrée Michel (Centre National de la Recherche Scientifique, Paris).

Various aspects of family life in this nation have been studied in some detail (e.g., Bernard, 1972; Blood and Wolfe, 1960; Fuchs, 1972), with particular emphasis on the woman's function, whether as working wife/mother (Callahan, 1971; Nye and Hoffman, 1963; Rapoport and Rapoport, 1971) or as homemaker exclusively (Gavron, 1966; Lopata, 1971; Tindal, 1971). However excellent, many of these studies have, for instance, samples such as upper-middle-class white families or families from a restricted geographical area and thus need extension and replication with other groups. Moreover, times change rapidly, so many of these studies may need updating.

Women at the Poverty Level. Considerable statistical information on the demography, income, and employment of women at the poverty level and on welfare is available, much of it from government sources (e.g., U.S. Commission on Civil Rights, 1974b). But we need to know more about how various public assistance programs, most notably Aid to Families with Dependent Children (AFDC), affect the family. Legal researchers should address themselves to investigating agency compliance with existing laws against sex discrimination with particular attention to the problems of poor women. Are the regulations for monitoring agency compliance adequate? What informal bureaucratic pressures impede the implementation of antidiscrimination laws? Do agency employees tend to organize their work so as to please their superiors (and minimize cost to themselves) at the expense of service to clients? Some existing studies suggest that the AFDC regulations forbidding aid when a man is in residence have unfavorable consequences for family life and female independence (Wilensky and Lebeaux, 1958). Can pilot projects, with built-in evaluation requirements, be established to weigh the efficiency and practicability of alternative programs? What indicators of cost effectiveness can be applied to innovative programs so as to reassure budget-conscious county, state, and federal administrators? (See U.S. Joint Economic Committee, Congress, 1968.)

Working-Class Women. The working class in America is often regarded as conservative socially and politically. Is this an oversimplification? To what extent do working class families reflect traditional values in such matters as marriage, sex roles within the family, and child-rearing? Lillian Rubin (the Wright Institute, Berkeley, California) has pointed out that working-class wives often choose to stay at home and raise their children and thus are unaware of many women's liberation issues. Considering the outside jobs available to them, these women may find the task of homemaker infinitely preferable. Studies are needed to document and explain this choice from the point of view of the women. For instance, how do they see their work and family roles? Do various ethnic groups among the blue collars (e.g., Polish-American, Irish-American) differ in their views on these issues? Even simple attitude studies would provide more information than is now available. As a first step, an updating of Komarovsky's *Blue-Collar Marriage* (1964) would be helpful. (See also Beer, 1957; Klein, 1965; Ladner, 1971; Rubin, forthcoming.)

Middle-Class Women. Paradoxically, though much of the literature from the women's movement deals, at least implicitly, with the middle-class woman—her image, values, and exploited status—studies of specific sectors of the population tend to focus on the extremes: the poverty-level woman or the professional woman. Yet most of the women in the country belong to the middle class and, if they work, are employed in ordinary white-collar jobs such as secretary or salesclerk. We need to know more about these women as a group and, in particular, about how they may have changed in recent years. Does the prototypal suburban housewife delineated in the literature still exist? What are her attitudes toward her marriage, her family, herself? To what extent has she been influenced by the women's movement? How does she spend her time, particularly after her children are in school: working on a full- or part-time basis? continuing her education? doing volunteer work?

We might want to examine the recent phenomenon of fugitive children—largely from upper-middle-class families—from the standpoint of these women. What role, if any, does the woman play in creating the teenage runaway? What are her responses to the crisis of running away?

Women in High-Status Occupations. We know much about professionalization but little about its interpersonal consequences. What stresses and strains is the dual-career family subject to, both in husband-wife relations (especially in situations where the wife earns more than the husband) and in relations between parents and children? What information can research give to young married couples embarking on careers (with particular life styles attached) so as to ease interpersonal tensions? Intensive longitudinal studies of couples belonging to a variety of family patterns are required to answer such questions. If early retirement for professionals becomes commonplace, how will family life be affected? How are the children affected by having a mother who achieves in her profession? (See Astin, 1969; Bernard, 1966; Epstein, 1971; Etzioni, 1969;

Garland and Poloma, 1971; Holmstrom, 1972; Lopata, 1971; Papanek, 1973; Rapoport and Rapoport, 1971; Rossi, 1973d; Simon et al., 1967; Theodore, 1971.)

Minority Women. Race and ethnicity cut across socioeconomic lines to a considerable extent and merit separate treatment. Various studies examine marriage and family life among blacks (e.g., Bernard, 1966; Frazier, 1951; Staples, 1971), but more extensive treatment of other racial/ethnic groups—e.g., Chicanos, American Indians, Puerto Ricans, Orientals—is needed. What special stresses is the family subjected to in each of these groups? How far are the stresses a function of economic factors? One might speculate, for instance, that the family retains a strength among Spanish speaking minorities because of the influence of the Roman Catholic church. But what of American Indians, who have also come under that influence? For each of the subgroups, is the tendency with respect to sex roles in marriage toward the traditional, the egalitarian, or some other form? How do child-rearing practices compare with those of the middle-class white? What image do women in these groups have of themselves—as family members and as workers (U.S. Commission on Civil Rights, 1974a)?

Marriage

The Judeo- Christian ideal of marriage as a commitment that involves both permanence and exclusivity has in recent decades come to seem more the exception than the rule. Divorce rates continue to rise. As early as 1929, Bertrand Russell argued that a true and rationally based marriage permitted outside sexual relations; since then extramarital affairs have become commonplace if not socially approved. More recently, new forms of marriage—in the sense of more or less stable commitments between or among human beings—have received serious attention. For instance, group marriage-involving anything from a ménage-â-trois to a free-love pattern among members of a commune—has been proposed as a sensible and meaningful alternative (Constantine and Constantine, 1973). Just how widespread and how workable is this form of marriage? Veysey (1974) suggests that our national emphasis on individualism and freedom of self-expression is too strong for enduring group commitments to communal life. Bernard (1972) maintains that most group marriages, while giving lip service to egalitarianism, in actuality are sexist. Case studies of such multilateral marriages might provide further evidence.

Returning to more conventional arrangements, we may ask whether the trend toward companionate, or "shared-role," marriages is a strong one in our society. Under what conditions do such marriages succeed or fail? What are the divisions of responsibility for housework and child care? What are the formal and informal decision-making processes? How satisfied is each partner with the egalitarian marriage? Again, in-depth longitudinal studies are required to answer such questions (Cuber, 1966; Fullerton, 1972; Giele, 1971; Hower, 1972; Lopata, 1971; Poloma and Garland, 1971; Scanzoni, 1972).

Divorce

Divorce, while obviously related to the topics of marriage and of singlehood, warrants separate consideration because it is complicated by political and emotional issues and because it involves complex legal questions. Here is an area where legal researchers and social scientists can collaborate in designing and pursuing studies (Weitzman et al., 1974). Many states have enacted, or are considerating, no-fault divorce. Further changes in divorce laws, affecting property settlements, may be expected after passage of the Equal Rights Amendment. But will these changes result in a more equitable situation? Even under existing law, we do not know enough about how closely actual practice follows formal regulations. What is the relation between social patterns and the law?

Nor do we know much about the emotional impact of divorce on the men and women involved. Pioneer work on how divorce and legal separation are managed has been undertaken by Goode (1956), Bohannon (1970), and Weiss (forthcoming). What support networks are available to each partner after divorce? Only after their common—and distinct—problems are identified can the most equitable types of divorce settlements be formulated.

Beyond the effect of divorce laws on divorce rates—which is what lawyers study—how does divorce affect the structure of the family? We need specific data on the following questions:

(1) Do current laws really favor women in divorce, particularly with respect to property settlement?
(2) If so, will no-fault divorce put women at a disadvantage?
(3) In establishing new divorce legislation, will the courts create custom or legitimize a fait accompli?
(4) To what extent are requirements for child support actually met?
(5) What factors account for noncompliance with family support decrees by some fathers?

Efforts to achieve equity through no-fault divorce may only perpetuate existing inequities in the society. If no-fault divorce is to be truly equitable, property laws may have to change. Richard Criswell (Vanderbilt Law School) is now studying this problem.

Singlehood

Closely connected with divorce is the plight of the single parent, who is often a divorced woman (though, of course, the unmarried mother who raises her child also belongs in this category). What support systems exist to aid the single mother not only in the practical but also in the emotional aspects of bringing up a child by herself? For example, the lower-class single mother may have friendship groups to support her when family and paid services are unavailable. In addition, the black community may accept single parenthood more readily than the white community. How do these differences—and others related to socioeconomic level and race—relate to the kinds of problems faced by single parents and the responses they make? *MOMMA*, a newspaper and a single parents' organization in Los Angeles, is designed to help the single mother. What other formal organizations exist? One approach to looking at these problems is suggested by the work of Nancy Stoller Shaw (University of California at Santa Cruz), who has studied sex roles and specialization in child care settings. Can this research be applied to women in other situations?

The single woman without dependents—whether she is someone who has never married, a divorced woman, or a widow—also merits study. Margaret Adams (forthcoming) writes about the stresses that single people experience because of their deviance in a married society and about the compensatory supports available to them. For instance, the terms *old maid* and *spinster* are both highly derogatory and almost invariably coupled with *neurotic*, although statistical evidence indicates that, relative to other groups, never-married women rank high in mental health. What is the status and image of never-married women today? Are there differences in the degree to which they are accepted by different racial/ethnic groups and at different socioeconomic levels? Have attitudes toward them changed recently, and if so, what factors contributed to the change? What range of alternatives in life styles is available to them? For instance, we might hypothesize that the woman who does not marry is "excused" this deviance if, when young, she shows strong commitment to a professional career and, when older, she is highly successful in that career. Other topics that merit investigation include:

(1) the needs and emotional reactions of recently divorced women;
(2) the situation of divorced mothers who do not (as was once customary) take custody of the children, and the effects of this arrangement upon the children;
(3) the supports available to single women from such sources as feminist groups and counseling centers;
(4) the achievement orientation of never-married women;
(5) suicide rates among single women;
(6) the role models that strengthen unmarried mothers who keep their children;
(7) the problems faced by young widows; and
(8) the problems faced by older widows (problems complicated by the plight of the aged generally in our society).

Finally, how do single women, of whichever category, apportion their time; do they have fewer problems than, say, working wives in arranging their schedules? (See O'Brien, 1973; Taves, 1968.)

Parenting

Child rearing involves many complicated questions. What do children really need at various stages of their lives? For example, it would seem that they do not require attention from the same mother figure all day long; research is needed to test this possibility.

We know very little about parenting, as opposed to either mothering or fathering. Boocock (1973), Bourne (1971), Roby (1973), and Rowe (1972) have discussed research and social policy in establishing day care centers, and their work points directions that future research might take.

From Philip Wylie to Philip Roth, the dangers to children of excessive mothering have been denounced. More empirically, Pauline Bart (1970) and Jessie Bernard (1974) have discussed some of its deleterious effects on mothers. We need to know more about maternal *over*-preoccupation. Among what groups of women is it most common? For example, welfare mothers may provide examples of women whose chief activity is the care of children under difficult circumstances, isolated from any alternative activity that might give them a sense of purpose and self-esteem (Eddington, 1973). Similarly, nonworking wives of the middle class, conditioned to believe in the supremacy of motherhood, may overdo it. What happens to the children in such circumstances? Just as important, what happens to the mother, particularly after the children are grown?

The father's influence in child care needs investigation. What aspects of child care do fathers take upon themselves? Are there differences—by race, socioeconomic level, and educational level—in the attitudes and actual behavior of fathers toward their children? For instance, we might speculate that blue-collar husbands have less to do with child care on the grounds that it is woman's work. Or it may be that the professional, career-oriented male tends to neglect his children. But what will empirical investigation show?

Recent emphasis upon greater egalitarianism in child care—with mothers and fathers taking equal responsibility—raises the question of how far expressed attitudes coincide with actual practice. What happens to children reared in truly egalitarian fashion, with boys and girls treated in the same way? Can the "new" species of egalitarian children be studied systematically?

More generally, parenting raises other questions about the process of socialization (Chafetz, 1974; Chodorow, 1974; Hochschild, 1973a; Hoffman, 1972; Sells, 1972). Does early socialization affect the child's idea of what a woman is and what she does? Studies that compare the attitudes of children in homes where women do and do not work would be helpful in answering this question (Lipman-Blumen, 1972; Nye and Hoffman, 1963). How do communal patterns of child rearing affect socialization? Cross-cultural studies are particularly useful here (Berger et al., 1971, 1974; Bettelheim, 1969; Spiro, 1958). Investigation of these issues would demonstrate the importance of two kinds of research, one emphasizing identification and understanding of past inequities, and the other providing more viable models for the future (Bart, 1971; Giele, 1971, 1972a, 1972b).

A Survey of Research Concerns on Women's Issues, by Arlene Kaplan Daniels, 1975, Project on the Status and Education of Women of the Association of American Colleges, the National Science Foundation.

LEGAL STATUS OF HOMEMAKERS

Little has been written to inform the homemaker of her legal rights in marriage, divorce, and widowhood; therefore, the National Commission on the Observance of International Women's Year Committee on Homemakers, chaired by former Congresswoman Martha Griffiths, sponsored a series of papers to explore the status of homemakers in each state from the viewpoint of the woman not employed outside the home. These informational papers point to little known aspects of domestic relations law and emphasize laws and judicial precedents that fail to give proper recognition to the value of the homemaker and the welfare of children.

The following chart extracts from the homemaker papers parts of the state laws that are of special interest, and those which are either grossly unfair to homemakers or unique to a particular state. The material offered is of general interest and should not be used by researchers writing precise legal papers. It may not reflect changes in family law made in recent months. The chart was prepared by Sheryl Swed and reviewed by Roxanne Barton Conlin.

Copies of the legal status of the homemaker papers for each state are available for $1.25 each from: Superintendent of Documents, U.S. Government Printing Office, Washington, D.C. 20402.

ALABAMA

RIGHTS: Women may marry with their parents' consent at age 14 and at age 18 without it. Men are not allowed to marry until age 17 with parental consent or at 19 without it. Alabama requires a woman to take her husband's name upon marriage. If a woman has written a will before marriage, it is automatically revoked after her marriage without regard to her wishes. This law does not apply to husbands. A man who finds his wife in the act of adultery with another man and immediately kills her is not guilty of murder, (punishable by death or life imprisonment) but of manslaughter only, (punishable by one to ten years imprisonment). There is no such defense for a woman who murders her husband under similar circumstances.

PROPERTY: The only state that requires a husband give his wife permission to sell her own separate real estate. He must actually sign the deed with his wife as if he owned it.

INHERITANCE: If a husband dies without a will, the widow must divide the personal property of the husband with the children equally. Children are entitled to inherit real estate from their father even ahead of their mother.

RAPE: It is not a crime for a man to force sexual intercourse on his wife, even if not living together or if one has filed for a divorce.

ALASKA

SUPPORT: It is estimated that fewer than 50% of the women in Alaska who are supposed to be receiving child support are actually receiving it. A married homemaker has no civil right to a share of the family's income short of seeking to end the marriage by divorce or putting her husband in jail. Courts refuse to intervene in an ongoing marriage to assure that the wife and children are provided with the necessities of life. The wife must depend on her husband's good faith and sense of responsibility.

PROPERTY: A wife is free to buy, sell, or lease her separate real property without interference from her husband. Both spouses are personally and solely liable for their own separate debts incurred either before or during marriage.

ABUSE: If a wife beater is arrested, he is likely to be released quickly on $25 bond. The sentence for a convicted wife beater is usually a fine of $25–$50 which may be suspended. Separate reporting of wife beating is not required; thus data is limited. The average total time spent by police on each wife-beating complaint is 17 minutes.

INHERITANCE: If a husband dies without a will, the wife receives the first $50,000 of the estate but only ½ of the remainder if there are children or parents of the husband.

ARIZONA

SUPPORT: Because of the refusal of the courts to interfere in a continuing marriage, the homemaker dependent on her husband's earnings has no access to them except through her husband's sense of fairness. Arizona permits courts to award support beyond the age of 18 for mentally or physically disabled children. Court ordered child support payments may not be retroactively decreased.

PROPERTY: Either spouse separately may acquire, manage, control or dispose of community property or bind the community. A wife has all the legal power over community property that her husband has.

DISSOLUTION/DIVORCE: The only ground for dissolution is the allegation that the marriage is "irretrievably broken." Essentially a divorce may be obtained at the will of one of the spouses.

INHERITANCE: All of a couple's property, whether separate or community, goes to the survivor if a will has not been written. A wife is protected even if her spouse decides to write a will giving all his property away, since half of the community is hers, and he cannot will her half away.

RAPE: Rape is not a crime when perpetrated by a husband on a wife even if the parties are separated or one has filed for a divorce.

ARKANSAS

PROPERTY: The homestead right is the husband's, not the wife's and the husband can choose and abandon a homestead at will without the wife's consent. Once the homestead is abandoned by the will of the husband, it can be sold by him without his wife's consent. The law presumes that all personal property, such as money, household furnishing and the like, belong to the husband. In order to protect her personal property from sale by her husband without her consent or attachment by his creditors, a married woman must file a schedule of her separate property with the county recorder. If she does not, the burden is on her to prove that she bought the property out of her separate funds. No such burden is ever placed on the husband.

DISSOLUTION/DIVORCE: The property division allowed depends on fault and does not take into account a spouse's contribution as homemaker.

INHERITANCE: If a husband dies without leaving descendants, and has been married at least three years preceding his death, then all property goes to widow. If he is not survived by descendants and has been married less than three years, his widow receives one-half of all his property plus statutory allowances and homestead rights. If the husband is survived by descendants, then regardless of the length of the marriage, the widow receives only statutory allowances, homestead rights, and dower, and all remaining property is divided among the descendants.

CALIFORNIA

SUPPORT: The right to support depends on *need* rather than *sex*. 75% of all welfare recipients are women. Women receiving assistance must register for employment when youngest child is 6.

PROPERTY: Community property — Since 1975 both spouses have had an equal power of management and control over community property.

ABUSE: Wife and child beating are covered under the same section of the penal code; statistics are compiled jointly. Charges of abuse are generally not brought because local authorities view incidents as personal matters.

DISSOLUTION/DIVORCE: In a divorce situation community property is divided equally. However, the husband's earning power or capacity is not viewed as a property asset of the community and is never divided equally. Both spouses are eligible for alimony and have an equal right to custody of the children and an equal duty to support them.

INHERITANCE: If there is no will, all of the community property goes to surviving spouse and at least ⅓ of the separate property goes to surviving spouse.

RAPE: A husband cannot be charged with raping his wife even if they are separated and awaiting divorce.

COLORADO

LEGAL RIGHTS: Women may sue or be sued in regard to their property, person or reputation. They may carry on their own business and their earnings are their sole property. A married woman has the same right to sue for loss of consortium as her husband.

SUPPORT: Both spouses are liable for the reasonable and necessary expenses of the family and both are equally liable for the support of children. Any purchases made by husband or wife which are for use of family and which are appropriate to their station in life may be charged to both the husband and the wife or to either separately. Child support continues as a duty after the death of the person owing that support and may be handled by maintaining life insurance on the person owing support.

ABUSE: Assault and battery by a husband is a crime but no real remedy is available to Colorado's wives. Law enforcement officials are not anxious to intervene in "domestic squabbles"; few shelters are available to battered wives seeking protection.

DISSOLUTION/DIVORCE: All property acquired during marriage, no matter whose name it is placed in, is subject to division by the court. A Colorado statute requires the court to consider the contribution of a homemaker in dividing marital property. The law provides for the appointment of an attorney for the child in custody cases.

RAPE: A husband may be charged with rape if the spouses are living apart.

CONNECTICUT

SUPPORT: Husband and wife are jointly responsible for family expenses.

PROPERTY: "Common law" property system: whatever income you earn and whatever property you accumulate during marriage is yours and your spouse has no control over it.

ABUSE: Husbands and wives can be arrested for assaulting their spouses, for threatening them, or for recklessly endangering their life or health. However, the police do not want to be involved in "domestic squabbles."

DIVORCE: Has a partial no-fault system where a divorce is granted if the marriage has irretrievably broken down or if the parties have been living apart for 18 months and there is no chance of reconciliation. The law now does not require that the court consider the value of the homemaker's work in awarding alimony and in dividing marital property. The law permits a judge to assign to either the husband or wife all or any part of the estate of the other. Financial security for a child is playing an increasingly important role in courts' decisions to award custody.

INHERITANCE: If the husabnd or wife dies without a will, the surviving spouse is entitled to the first $50,000 of the estate plus one-half of the remainder.

RAPE: A wife has no legal protection against sexual assault or rape by her husband even if she is separated from him and has filed for divorce.

DELAWARE

PROPERTY: A man and wife may enter into an agreement before marriage to determine what rights each shall have in the other's estate.

ABUSE: Assaults between spouses are referred to the family court which may hear only third degree assault, that is the least degree of assault, no matter how extensive the injuries inflicted. Thus the charge and punishment against a wife beater are lessened.

DISSOLUTION/DIVORCE: The unwillingness of one party to be divorced is not grounds for denial of the petition. There is no authority by statute or under case law to award permanent alimony. In making a division of marital property the court is obligated to consider the contributions of a homemaker. The duty to support minor children rests equally upon both parents and the non-monetary contribution made by the custodial parent is to be considered in equating the amount to be contributed by the noncustodial parent. Where a man is simultaneously liable for the support of more than one dependent, a statutory scheme for determining priority among dependents exists.

INHERITANCE: A woman who has been given a small portion or none of her husband's estate may refuse the inheritance and receive one-third of the estate, or $20,000, whichever is less.

DISTRICT OF COLUMBIA

SUPPORT: Unless a woman is willing to end her marriage, she has no enforceable means of requiring her husband to support her.

ABUSE: A married woman may not sue her husband for physically abusing her.

DISSOLUTION/DIVORCE: A divorce may be granted where the parties have been voluntarily separated for 6 months or where they have been separated for one year even though one spouse may not have consented to the separation. Unless the parties have made a valid agreement concerning their respective property rights acquired during marriage, the court may distribute as it deems just all property acquired during the marriage (other than by gift, bequest, etc.), whether the property is held in the name of both parties or one. While a wife may lose alimony as a result of her misconduct, the courts specifically reject using alimony to penalize a man for his misconduct.

INHERITANCE: If a husband dies without a will, the widow will inherit the whole estate only if there are virtually no living relatives, including brothers, sisters, nieces, nephews, parents, children or grandchildren.

RAPE: Consent to marital relations cannot be retracted while the marriage is legally intact, even though the parties are living separate and apart even if one has filed for divorce.

FLORIDA

LEGAL RIGHTS: A wife has the right to sue a person who has injured her husband for loss of her husband's companionship, affection, and consortium, including sexual relations.

PROPERTY: A full-time homemaker can be effectively prevented from securing any part of the property acquired during marriage if her wage-earning husband places all property in his name.

ABUSE: If a woman files an action for dissolution of marriage she may secure a mutual restraining order to keep her husband from molesting her; however, enforcement of the order is difficult. Authorities see wife abuse as a "domestic dispute."

DISSOLUTION/DIVORCE: Under a no-fault dissolution, the court may consider the adultery of the spouse seeking alimony, which is usually the wife, although court interpretation of this law is not consistent. Although alimony is given in only a small percentage of cases, rehabilitative alimony is available to assist a divorced person thorugh vocational or therapeutic training or retraining. The dissolution statute does not specifically require the courts to consider the economic contribution of the homemaker to the marriage.

INHERITANCE: If a husband dies without a will, the wife takes the entire estate only if the husband left no surviving lineal descendants, that is children or grandchildren.

GEORGIA

SUPPORT: A wife can bring no legal action to enforce support unless she separates from husband.

PROPERTY: Separate property state. The house occupied by the family belongs only to husband, even if wife is the wage earner, and makes the payments. A child is, by law, under the control of his/her father who has the sole right to his or her services and the proceeds of his or her labor when the parents are living together.

ABUSE: Abuse may be prosecuted as a simple battery or aggravated battery. However, police officials have been reluctant to become involved in these cases.

DISSOLUTION/DIVORCE: Upon separation of husband and wife, the obligation to pay alimony and child support falls only upon husband. Although husband is legally obligated to provide support for family during marriage, if his wife provides for the needs of herself and children, upon divorce she may be forced to continue to be self-supporting.

INHERITANCE: If there is no will, upon the death of husband without children, the wife is sole heir and takes all his estate. If there are children in the marriage, the wife and each child take equal shares, except that in no event will the wife take less than a 1/5 share.

RAPE: Wives are not protected against forcible sexual acts of their husbands. Sexual intercourse is deemed a right until marriage is dissolved. Refusal of sexual relations may be grounds for divorce for desertion.

HAWAII

LEGAL RIGHTS: A married woman by statute in Hawaii is not liable for her husband's debts. Law establishes a parent-child relationship regardless of the marital status of the parents. Unmarried parents are permitted to file the names of both parents on a child's birth certificate, thereby in effect legitimizing the child.

SUPPORT: A wife is liable for the support of her children where the husband is unable or absent and her property and earnings can be taken to provide for them.

PROPERTY: Common law property state where property belongs solely to the person whose name is on the title.

ABUSE: Permits a wife to charge her husband with assault. However, if a woman is injured by her husband and incurs medical expenses, loss of wages and other damages, she cannot sue him for those expenses.

DISSOLUTION/DIVORCE: "No-fault" state. All that is required is proof that "the marriage is irretrievably broken." In contested divorces, the court has the discretion to divide all the marital property, regardless of its source or characterization.

INHERITANCE: If a man dies and leaves a will which excludes his wife, or which gives her only a small share of his estate, she has the right to elect to take against the will and receive one-third of his net estate.

IDAHO

LEGAL RIGHTS: A wife or husband may sue each other in Idaho for injuries either intentionally or negligently caused.

SUPPORT: In general, courts refuse to interfere in an on-going marriage to insure support. As long as the parties live together, the wife is entitled to only what the husband chooses to give her or what she herself earns.

PROPERTY: All property or income acquired after marriage, except inheritances and gifts, belong to the husband and wife equally, regardless of who earns it, and each spouse has an undivided half interest in everything. Since 1974 both husband and wife have had the right to manage and control the community property.

DISSOLUTION/DIVORCE: Where a husband seeks a divorce from his wife or where divorce is granted on a "no-fault" ground, no alimony of any kind is awarded.

INHERITANCE: When a married person dies, the surviving spouse is entitled to one-half of the property and money acquired by the couple during the period of their marriage. Therefore, only half the community property may be disposed of in a will or is subject to inheritance taxes. If a spouse dies without a will, Idaho law provides that the half of the community property of the deceased spouse passes to the survivor.

RAPE: It is possible for a wife to charge her husband with rape if she has filed for divorce or separation or if she has not lived with her husband for six months.

ILLINOIS

SUPPORT: The courts refuse to intervene in an on-going marriage to allocate family resources. Both spouses are equally liable for family expenses and either may be sued separately by a creditor for those debts.

PROPERTY: Common law property system under which property acquired during a marriage belongs to whoever holds the title.

DISSOLUTION/DIVORCE: One of the few remaining states without no-fault divorce. In making an award of alimony the court is not required to take into account the value of a homemaker's unpaid labor. A wife who is "at fault" will not get alimony except under special circumstances. However, in making an award of alimony, the court may not consider a husband's misconduct. No statutory standards governing the disposition of marital property. The law does permit conveyance of property held solely in the name of one spouse to the other spouse, in the court's discretion.

INHERITANCE: If a man dies without a will, his widow will get all the estate if there are no children and one-third of the estate if there are children, with the remaining two-thirds going to them.

RAPE: Illinois law defines rape as sexual intercourse with a woman who is not the wife of the perpetrator, forcibly and against her will.

INDIANA

LEGAL RIGHTS: A homemaker's domicile does not necessarily have to be the same as her husband's.

PROPERTY: A wife has no power to prevent a husband from disposing of his real and personal property: he may do so without her consent and without her knowledge.

ABUSE: A homemaker cannot recover medical expenses or other damages from her husband for injuries caused by his physical abuse.

DISSOLUTION/DIVORCE: The most frequently used statutory ground for dissolution of marriage is the no-fault "irretrievable breakdown of marriage." No provision for on-going spousal support after a dissolution. The effects of the combination of no-fault divorce and no alimony are disastrous for a homemaker. In dividing property, the court must consider the contribution of a spouse as homemaker.

INHERITANCE: Neither spouse may completely disinherit the other. If the surviving spouse is a second or other subsequent spouse and did not have children by the deceased, then the surviving spouse shall take only a life estate in one-third of the real estate of the decedent and the remaining interest shall vest at once in the children of the decedent's former marriage.

RAPE: A man cannot be charged with sexually abusing his wife even when the parties are not living together or where one has filed for a divorce.

IOWA

SUPPORT: Both spouses are liable for the reasonable and necessary expenses of the family and for the support of the children. Any purchases that either the husband or wife make which are for the use of the family and which are appropriate for their station in life may be charged to both the husband and wife or to either separately. Nothing requires a creditor to seek payment first from the husband and then from the wife.

ABUSE: Figures from a recent survey indicate nearly one of four married women are beaten by their husbands. A wife may charge husband with assault which carries a penalty up to 30 days in jail or a fine of $100 or both.

DISSOLUTION/DIVORCE: **Iowa law prevents either spouse from removing the other from the homestead until after divorce is granted. In 90% of divorce cases that come before the Iowa courts, no alimony is awarded. In 1973, 73% of all child support payments were between $10 and $20 per week; in 20% of the cases involving children, no child support of any kind was allowed.**

INHERITANCE: If a deceased spouse leaves a will, surviving spouse may decide to take what is granted by its terms or may take a ⅓ interest in all the real estate, all personal property of the family, and ⅓ of the other personal property.

RAPE: A husband may be charged with raping his wife if he injures her or threatens her with a weapon even if they are living together.

KANSAS

SUPPORT: A person has a duty to support spouse and can be criminally charged if s/he does not. Duty is based upon ability to support and is limited to necessary items only. No legal tools are in place to enforce support.

PROPERTY: A married woman may sell and convey real and personal property or contract regarding her property in the same manner and extent as a married man.

ABUSE: Women may press criminal charges but probably will face lack of cooperation from legal officials who do not want to interfere in "domestic disturbances."

DISSOLUTION/DIVORCE: During a divorce proceeding, all real and personal property is under control of divorce court. If a woman has co-signed on a debt with her husband, she is still liable even if husband has been ordered to pay the debt.

INHERITANCE: A man may not disinherit his wife. She will receive at least ½ of her husband's property despite terms of will. If divorced prior to death, alimony and child-support awards do not extend past death and cannot be claimed against the estate.

RAPE: No legal protection to a woman against sexual assault by husband,even if she is separated or in the divorce process.

KENTUCKY

LEGAL RIGHTS: A married woman may sue her husband for negligent acts he may commit against her. Children born to a man and woman who are married must be given the surname of the father, even though both husband and wife want to name the child with the mother's surname.

SUPPORT: A husband is not responsible for the wife's debts before or after marriage, except to the extent he received property from the wife as a result of the marriage. The husband is legally required to furnish only the wife's "necessaries" during marriage.

DISSOLUTION/DIVORCE: Under a new divorce law, courts must consider the economic contribution of the wife, including domestic services, in a division of property. However, up to now the wife's role as a homemaker has not been as highly valued as that of the breadwinner. The general rule of thumb is that the wife gets approximately one-third of jointly held property if she has been a homemaker and up to a maximum of one-half if she has been a wage-earning participant in the accumulation of the property.

RAPE: Although the law does not specifically exempt a husband from being charged with rape of his wife, there is a possibility that a husband cannot be found guilty of committing this offense against his wife.

LOUISIANA

SUPPORT: A wife may file a criminal neglect of the family charge for nonsupport but such cases require that the husband provide *no* money for six weeks in order to show intentional neglect.

PROPERTY: A husband has the power to sell and mortgage community property including home without consent or knowledge of wife. Creditors may seize both husband's and wife's interest in community property when the husband defaults on a debt. Community property system contemplates equal share for husband and wife of all that is earned and accumulated during the marriage. However, law says that husband has "total control and charge of all community affairs and all property belonging thereto." Earnings are included in community and are subject to husband's control.

DISSOLUTION/DIVORCE: Alimony is not granted on the basis of past services of wife or length of marriage but on present need and ability to pay of husband. To receive alimony wife must prove separation was not her fault, that she needs support and that husband can pay; but in no case can wife receive more than ⅓ of husband's income.

INHERITANCE: A wife is not heir to husband's half of community unless he writes a will to this effect. Wife cannot receive husband's half of community if husband has children or living parents since they are forced heirs and must receive a share in his estate regardless of provisions in the will.

MAINE

PROPERTY: If a husband and wife jointly run a business the profits are the property of the husband. Although the law recognizes the married woman's right to hold and manage property, the courts have demonstrated a readiness to find that the husband is his wife's agent for management of her property. If a husband earns most of the income, that income, and any family assets purchased with it will be the husband's property. Because a married woman's contribution to the family partnership economy is in services rather than money, the law does not recognize the real value of her contribution.

DISSOLUTION/DIVORCE: A wife may receive a lump sum payment in lieu of alimony. When dividing marital property, the court is required to consider the contribution made by the homemaker.

INHERITANCE: If a husband leaves no will, the share of the widow in the husband's estate (after payment of funeral costs, debts, taxes and estate administration costs) will range from something more than 33⅓% to 100%, the exact percentage depending on a complex of factors involving size of the estate, existence of children or close relatives, and the nature of the property left.

MARYLAND

LEGAL RIGHTS: One spouse cannot sue the other for such civil offenses as intentional or negligent infliction of emotional distress, slander, libel, or assault and battery.

PROPERTY: There is no Maryland law that imposes an obligation on a husband to permit his wife to share in the control of family resources. Courts and administrative agencies generally assume ownership of marital property by the husband in the absence of proof of ownership by the wife. A wife has no claim on property in the husband's name, even the family home or personal property, unless she has made a financial contribution which the court chooses to recognize. Maryland courts have not recognized the performance of a wife's duties as a contribution to the marriage.

ABUSE: While it is possible in Maryland to have one's husband prosecuted under criminal law for assault and battery, in practice this remedy accomplishes little. When a husband is prosecuted and found guilty, often the result is merely unsupervised probation. Rarely is a husband incarcerated or offered counseling.

DISSOLUTION/DIVORCE: In granting alimony, the court will consider the wife's conduct even though the divorce itself is based on non-fault grounds.

INHERITANCE: If there is no will, or where there is a will and wife renounces it, a wife will inherit the entire estate only if there are no surviving children, parent or brother or sister of the deceased.

MASSACHUSETTS

PROPERTY RIGHTS: Retains a form of property ownership known as a tenancy by the entireties, which is available only to a husband and wife. The property is owned jointly by both spouses, but only the husband has the right to manage and control it and to receive any profits from it.

WIFE ABUSE: A woman may sue her husband if he injures her intentionally or negligently and may recover her medical expenses and other damages from him.

DIVORCE/DISSOLUTION: No such thing as a "legal" separation. Massachusetts has both no-fault and traditional fault grounds for divorce, such as adultery and desertion. By statute, the right to custody of children is equal in the absence of parental misconduct and the welfare and happiness of the children is the determinate. Child support payments may be awarded even beyond the age of majority, which is 18, up to the age of 21. The court is not required to consider the contribution of a homemaker to the acquisition of marital property.

INHERITANCE: Neither spouse may totally disinherit the other. A surviving spouse will receive at least one-third of the real and personal property of the deceased spouse.

RAPE: A man cannot be charged with the rape of his wife, even if he and his wife are separated and she has filed for divorce.

MICHIGAN

SUPPORT: Theoretically a husband is bound to furnish his wife a home and other needs to the extent of his ability and in return a wife owes her husband her services as a homemaker. However, courts will not interfere in an on-going marriage to insure support.

PROPERTY: Contracts and promissory notes between spouses are void under Michigan law and unenforceable.

ABUSE: Under the Criminal Compensation Act, if a husband causes his wife injury, she may sue him for damages. Under the Criminal Compensation Act, she is ineligible for any payment except for medical expenses.

DISSOLUTION/DIVORCE: There is one no-fault ground for divorce. It is nearly impossible for one spouse to prevent the other from getting a divorce if he or she wants it. No-fault divorce was enacted without providing economic protections for the homemaker. The court may divide the parties' property; however, there are no standards for such division and there is no requirement that the court recognize homemaking as a contribution.

INHERITANCE: If a husband dies without a will, the widow takes from one-third to all of his real and personal estate depending on whether there are children or other relatives.

RAPE: A woman can charge her husband with sexual assault if they are living apart and one of them has filed for divorce.

MINNESOTA

LEGAL RIGHTS: A woman may sue her husband for damages if he negligently injures her. A woman may seek damages for loss of consortium, that is loss of companionship, services, and sex due to injuries inflicted upon the spouse.

SUPPORT: Within the context of the marriage the wife has no legal right to support beyond that which her husband is willing to voluntarily provide for her. Husband and wife are both liable whether jointly or separately for all necessary goods and services furnished to and used by the family.

ABUSE: Assault and battery is a crime; however, the police respond slowly and indifferently to calls involving "domestic quarrels."

DISSOLUTION/DIVORCE: Joint property of the parties is divided as the court shall determine to be just, with wide discretion granted the court. The court may award up to one-half the value of a spouse's separate property to the other. Courts are not required to recognize the value of the services provided by the homemaker when dividing marital property.

INHERITANCE: The law will not presume joint ownership with survivor's rights unless this is specifically stated in the deed to the property.

RAPE: A husband may be charged with rape only if the parties are living apart and one of them has filed for a divorce or for separate maintenance.

MISSISSIPPI

LEGAL RIGHTS: Even though a woman works eight hours a day for six days a week and earns twice as much as her husband, she cannot be considered the head of the household under the law. A wife and husband may sue each other in certain circumstances, but the law prohibits them from suing each other for personal wrongs, such as assault and a battery or negligence.

SUPPORT: In order to require a husband to support his wife and family, a wife must separate from her husband and engage in legal action. Courts will not interfere in an ongoing marriage as a matter of policy.

PROPERTY: The law requires the signature of both spouses in any conveyance of the homestead.

ABUSE: Even though it is technically a crime for a man to beat his wife, law enforcement officials tend not to treat it as a serious matter.

DISSOLUTION/DIVORCE: In determining whether alimony and/or division of the property is necessary after the marriage ends, State courts are not required to consider the contribution made by the homemaker to the family and the community. There is no absolute right to alimony in Mississippi.

INHERITANCE: If a husband dies without leaving a will and does not have any children or descendants of children, the wife is entitled to his entire estate after all debts are paid. If he leaves children or descendants of children, a wife is entitled to a share equal to each child's part of his estate.

MISSOURI

LEGAL RIGHTS: When a wife engages in activities which earn money but which are performed in the home or in conjunction with her husband, she may find that those earnings are not considered hers but are her husband's as a matter of legal right.

SUPPORT: Although the husband has a legal duty to support his wife, it is an obligation defined and controlled solely by him and not enforceable by the wife. If the husband is the only wage earner, the wife has no claim on his wages or assets during the marriage.

DISSOLUTION/DIVORCE: Any property acquired by either spouse during the marriage other than gift or inheritance to one sponse, no matter in whose name it is titled, is subject to being divided between the two spouses as the court deems just. Courts are to consider the contribution of each spouse to the acquisition of the marital property, including the contribution of a spouse as homemaker, when dividing property.

INHERITANCE: If there is no will and no children, parents or siblings of the deceased spouse, the survivor will inherit all of the property. If there are children or grandchildren, the surviving spouse inherits half while the other half of the estate is dividied among these others.

RAPE: Although a husband may force intercourse, due to the marital relationship, this cannot be defined as the crime of rape.

MONTANA

SUPPORT: Both the husband and wife have a duty to support each other. The noncompensated services of a spouse acting as homemaker are specifically included in the definition of support.

ABUSE: A wife who is assaulted by her husband may not sue him civilly, and husbands and wives may not sue each other for any intentional or negligent injury.

DISSOLUTION: The court may apportion all the property of either party regardless of when and how it was acquired and regardless of marital fault. In apportioning the property the court is required to consider, among other things, the contribution of a spouse as homemaker or as wage earner to the family unit. No law requiring full financial disclosure under oath by both parties to a divorce.

RAPE: Montana law exempts from the definition of rape all forcible intercourse between husband and wife even if the spouses are no longer living together.

PREGNANCY: A pregnant woman cannot be required to terminate her employment because of her pregnancy. She must be allowed to take reasonable leave of absence for her pregnancy and childbirth. The law requires that disability caused by pregnancy and childbirth must be treated the same as any other disability in any policy of disability or leave benefits or the like maintained by an employer.

NEBRASKA

SUPPORT: A wife has a legal right only to what her husband chooses to give her. If it is insufficient to meet her needs, or her children's needs, her only legal recourse is divorce.

PROPERTY: A creditor must sue a husband first before he attempts to collect a debt for necessities from a wife. A married woman may contract with her husband, but not for domestic services. Domestic services are considered to be a duty of the wife and she therefore cannot legally be compensated by her husband for their performance, except by a "gift" from him.

ABUSE: Although a great number of wives report that they are beaten by their husbands and although a man can be criminally charged if he beats his wife, no cases have been found where a wife has filed a complaint against her husband for assaulting or threatening her.

INHERITANCE: A widow is entitled to a share of her husband's property if he dies without a will or he makes a will which excludes her.

DISSOLUTION/DIVORCE: In dividing marital property, the court is obliged to consider the history of the contributions to the marriage by each party, including contributions to the care and education of the children and interruption of personal careers and educational opportunities. The court may not modify or cancel already accrued alimony amounts that are in arrears.

NEVADA

SUPPORT: The husband is supposed to support the wife with necessaries but there is no legal machinery in the state to force him to do so except to file a complaint in court for separate maintenance or to file for a divorce.

PROPERTY: A wife has equal management and control of the community property with her husband. The law recognizes written agreements between a husband and a wife as to the nature of their property.

ABUSE: It is not police policy to arrest a wife abuser unless the battering is enough to charge the husband with a felony, i.e., assault with a deadly weapon.

DISSOLUTION/DIVORCE: Nevada has three no-fault grounds for divorce: incompatibility, separation without cohabitation for one year, and defendant's insanity for two years. The court has jurisdiction over community property but none over separate property of the husband or wife, except that the court may set aside separate property of one or the other to assure payment of court ordered child support or alimony.

INHERITANCE: A husband and wife may each will away his or her half of the community property to anyone. The other half belongs to the surviving spouse and is not subject to administration in the deceased spouse's estate. The separate property of any person may be willed to anyone. A decedent may even disinherit spouse or children.

NEW HAMPSHIRE

LEGAL RIGHTS: If a woman lives with a man to whom she is not legally married for a period of three years, during which time they acknowledged each other as husband and wife and are generally reputed as such, she shall be deemed legally married upon the death of the man involved and entitled to inherit, assert homestead claims and receive social security payments to the same extent as any other surviving spouse.

SUPPORT: A court can order a husband to provide "suitable support" for his wife and/or children, but there are no cases recorded where action was brought when the husband and wife were living together.

PROPERTY: Any property, real or personal, that a wife accumulates prior to marriage remains hers during marriage unless she voluntarily transfers title to her husband. Any personal property a wife earns, acquires, or inherits during marriage is exclusively hers free from any interference or control by her husband. If a wife co-signs on her husband's obligations and he defaults, the loan company can proceed against the wife whether or not they first seek to collect from the husband.

ABUSE: Penalties for wife beating or simple assault range from a verbal warning to a small fine.

DISSOLUTION/DIVORCE: Law does not require the court to consider the contribution of a spouse as a homemaker in dividing marital property. The trial judge exercises almost absolute discretion in making financial awards and property settlements.

NEW JERSEY

SUPPORT: Traditionally courts have been hesitant to intervene in an on-going marriage to assure that a wife is being provided adequate support.

ABUSE: A wife who has been physically abused by her husband can file a complaint against him in the municipal court which is then registered as an assault and battery, depending upon the degree of the injury. There is no statistical breakdown in court reports for assault and battery against a spouse.

DISSOLUTION/DIVORCE: Real and personal property owned by a couple is divided by the court upon a judgment of divorce or separation. When making an equitable distribution of property the court is not required to recognize the economic value of the services of a homemaker. During the 1973-1974 term in N.J., 19,628 divorces were decreed.

INHERITANCE: If a husband dies without a will and the family residence is in his name alone, title to the house descends to the children. In a case where a husband deliberately makes a will which excludes his wife, she is entitled only to her dower interest which is a one-half life estate in the real property of the husband. That means that while she may occupy the property, or collect and use the profits, she may not sell it or otherwise dispose of it without the consent of other heirs and distribution to them.

NEW MEXICO

INHERITANCE: In 1973 the New Mexico legislature voted to allow wives in the state to will their halves of the community property to anyone they choose, just as their husbands could. However, the legislature specifically provided that this law would only apply to wills made after July 1, 1973.

PROPERTY: Community property acquired primarily through the earnings of either the husband or wife after marriage, including all increases in the value of those earnings as well as any property purchased with either the husband's or wife's earnings, belongs to both marriage partners. However, if a husband puts his paycheck into his own account, the wife would have no way of helping to manage this part of the community property.

ABUSE: The City Attorney's Office in Albuquerque has an official policy of not prosecuting any complaint by a wife who is still living with her husband. There are no shelters for abused women in New Mexico.

DISSOLUTION/DIVORCE: New Mexico law does not prevent a husband from transferring part of the community property to someone else when a divorce is pending. In a division of community property at divorce, the earning capacity of the husband, which has often been developed at the expense of the wife's own earnings and career potential, is not considered. A woman has no legal interest in the retirement rights of her husband unless those rights have "vested" before the divorce. This is so even though part of his salary, which is legally community property, went into a retirement fund.

NEW YORK

SUPPORT: A husband has a legal duty to provide his wife and children with necessaries. Ordinarily this duty may not be enforced while the parties are living together. Parents have a duty to support their children until they are 21.

PROPERTY: What a husband has purchased with his money and put in his name alone, is his.

ABUSE: A divorce is not automatically granted in all cases of wife beating: evidence of a pattern of violence or a concerted course of conduct by the husband against the wife must be shown.

DISSOLUTION/DIVORCE: Housewives' services are not given monetary value in a division of property. A new law requires both parties in a divorce action to disclose all of their assets.

INHERITANCE: Through large debts, trust funds, life insurance, and gifts or savings bonds to other people, a husband may decrease the amount of a wife's inheritance to almost nothing. When a person dies without a will, law distributes the estate among the surviving relatives. A wife with no children would get $25,000, plus one-half of the residue, with the remainder going to the husband's father and mother. A wife with one child would take $2,000, plus one-half of the residue, with the remainder going to the child.

RAPE: A husband cannot be convicted of raping his wife, even when they are not living together.

NORTH CAROLINA

SUPPORT: A recent study indicated that 47% of all court-ordered support payments are not met by husbands.

PROPERTY: When real property is owned jointly, the wife is usually not entitled to manage or control the property. The husband is entitled to full possession, control and use of the estate, and to the rents and profits arising therefrom to the exclusion of the wife during their marriage of property held in tenancy of the entirety. The domestic services of a wife, while living with her husband, are presumed to be gratuitous, and the performance of labor and work beyond the scope of her usual household and marital duties, in the absence of a special contract, is also presumed to be gratuitous.

INHERITANCE: It may be possible for a husband to disinherit his wife or limit the inheritance passing. A husband may provide for his widow in such a way as to deprive her of control of her inheritance by willing his property to a trustee who is directed to invest the property and pay the income from these investments to the widow.

RAPE: A husband is legally incapable of raping his wife or assaulting her with intent to commit rape, even while they are separated and/or in the process of getting a divorce.

NORTH DAKOTA

SUPPORT: A husband must support wife by his property or labor, but he alone decides in what manner and to what extent he will provide support. A wife must support husband by separate property if he is too ill to support himself and has no funds to do so. No ability to sue for support in on-going marriage. Both husband and wife are liable for family debts which are for food, clothing, shelter, fuel and education for the minor children.

PROPERTY: Separate property state. If property is in husband's name, wife has no rights to it. A wife's contribution to the family unit as a homemaker is not recognized by the law. A married woman has the same rights in making contracts and owning property as if she were single.

ABUSE: A wife may bring assault charges; however, many times such cases are not taken seriously by law enforcement officials. There are very few places where a woman may seek protection.

DISSOLUTION/DIVORCE: Most divorce actions are brought on the grounds of irreconcilable differences. There is little a wife can do under "no fault" law to prevent husband from divorcing her.

INHERITANCE: If husband has a will, wife may take what is given in the will or ⅓ of the total estate. If there is no will she will get the entire estate only if there are no children or husband's parents.

OHIO

SUPPORT: The level of support a husband is required to maintain for his wife is totally discretionary with him.

PROPERTY: Upon marriage, the rights of the spouses merge and each must obtain the other spouse's signature to sell any real estate during the time the marriage exists, regardless of whether the property was individually owned before the marriage took place. The law permits a husband to act as his wife's agent in transactions involving her separately held real estate and she is personally liable for expenses incurred.

ABUSE: There are no Ohio statistics on the problem of the battered or sexually abused wife and there seems to be reluctance by the authorities to discuss the matter.

DIVORCE: Under a modified no-fault statute, a divorce may be granted if the parties live apart for two years. In determining whether to award alimony and in what amount, the court is required to consider the contribution of a spouse as homemaker.

INHERITANCE: Upon marriage each spouse relinquishes the right to disinherit the other and must leave the other spouse at least one-half of her or his estate if there are no children or only one child.

RAPE: The statutes cover the rape of a wife by her husband when the parties are legally separated or one has filed for separation or divorce.

OKLAHOMA

LEGAL RIGHTS: Either spouse may sue the other for any damages suffered from negligent or intentional harm. A wife may enter into contracts with others and her husband. Any labor a wife performs for her husband is presumed to be gratuitous, even when it is outside ordinary household duties.

SUPPORT: A husband must support his wife but there is no practical means for enforcing the law. Courts refuse to intervene in an on-going marriage. A homemaker has the "right" only to what her husband chooses to give her. If purchases are not necessities a wife is liable for separate debts before and after marriage.

PROPERTY: Oklahoma is a common law state with separate property. A wife has no interest in property acquired by her husband in his name.

DISSOLUTION/DIVORCE: Oklahoma pioneered joint or split custody of children. Oklahoma has twelve fault grounds for divorce, including incompatibility which is the most frequent ground used.

INHERITANCE: If the husband dies without leaving a will and has been married only once and has only one child, the wife and child each receive half of the estate according to a statutory formula.

RAPE: A man may not be charged with raping his wife even when they are not living together or are in the process of getting a divorce.

OREGON

LEGAL RIGHTS: Oregon law refuses to recognize common law marriages and provides no jurisdiction for domestic relations judges to hear matters in dispute between persons who are living together without formal ceremony.

SUPPORT: For practical purposes, a wife's right to support from her husband is unenforcible except upon separation or dissolution of the marriage.

ABUSE: Police departments view domestic quarrels skeptically and hesitate even to appear on the scene unless a divorce proceeding has begun and a restraining order has been secured.

DISSOLUTION/DIVORCE: If a party has paid support for a former spouse for more than ten years under a court decree, and if the former spouse has not made reasonable effort to become financially self-supporting, the party paying support may ask the court to set aside the portion of the decree which allows support for the former spouse.

INHERITANCE: If a husband dies without a will, with surviving children and a wife, his wife receives one-half of his estate. If she survives him and there are no children, she is granted all of the net estate.

RAPE: It is not possible for a man to commit the crime of rape upon his wife.

PENNSYLVANIA

PROPERTY: Married couples may own property under "tenancies by the entirety" where both parties own the entire property, and neither can rent, sell, mortgage, or otherwise dispose of it without the other's consent. When one party dies the other automatically owns the whole. A wife is not entitled to an accounting of assets held in tenancies by the entirety which are controlled and managed by her husband.

ABUSE: A wife who has been beaten by her husband cannot sue him for the medical expenses she incurs in treating her injuries. She is ineligible for assistance under Crime Victim's Compensation Act.

DISSOLUTION/DIVORCE: Pennsylvania divorce laws are the worst in the nation for homemakers: there is no permanent alimony and no real property division. There are no "no-fault" grounds for divorce.

INHERITANCE: If a husband dies without a will, his widow is entitled to a proportion of his separate estate and automatically becomes the sole owner of entireties properties. The surviving spouse inherits the entire estate only if there are no surviving children, parents, siblings, nieces, nephews, grandparents, uncles and aunts.

RAPE: A wife who is the victim of sexual assault by her husband can charge him with a crime if they are living in the same residence but are legally separated by agreement or court order.

RHODE ISLAND

SUPPORT: There is not a single reported case in R.I. in which any court ordered a husband to pay any amount to a wife or child for support when the parties were still living together and were not also seeking a divorce or separation. As a matter of public policy, the courts will not involve themselves in disputes within ongoing marriages. A homemaker's security depends solely on her husband's sense of commitment and good will and not on the law.

DISSOLUTION/DIVORCE: In 1974 there were 11,009 children whose mothers had to go to court to obtain support from their fathers. Although the legislature has established irreconcilable differences as a no-fault ground for divorce, the law requires the court to consider fault in determining awards of alimony and child custody.

INHERITANCE: If a husband leaves a spouse and children and has no will, the wife would receive ½ of the husband's personal property and the children would get the other half. The wife would have a life estate (that is, use of the property until her death) in his real estate and the children would inherit the remaining interest. If a husband leaves a will which excludes his wife, she may elect to take ⅓ of the real property for life only.

SOUTH CAROLINA

LEGAL RIGHTS: A wife who is injured by her husband can sue him in civil court for the damages he causes her. Wife has obligation to be tolerant, within reason, of the husband's shortcomings.

SUPPORT: Any able-bodied man must support his wife and minor children by providing a place to live at the location of his choosing, food and some clothing. The husband is not required to pay for anything else as long as they reside together.

PROPERTY: Common law property state. Property is owned by whomever holds the title, whether that property is acquired before or after marriage.

ABUSE: If a woman flees home because of abuse and files for divorce, she must prove that the physical cruelty endangered her life and also that she did not "provoke" the conduct of which she complains.

DISSOLUTION/DIVORCE: A woman is absolutely precluded from receiving alimony if she is found guilty of adultery. Alimony may not be used to punish an errant husband.

INHERITANCE: A married man can't will more than ¼ of his property to his mistress or illegitimate children, if he has a wife living and legitimate children. A woman forfeits her dower rights (to own for her life ⅓ of all the real estate her husband acquired during the marriage) by her misconduct, and also forfeits the estate part she would receive if there were no will. There is no similar provision requiring the forfeiture of a man's right to wife's property.

SOUTH DAKOTA

LEGAL RIGHTS: A husband and wife cannot contract with each other to alter the legal relations that are spelled out by statute.

SUPPORT: Unless a wife wants to file for separate maintenance or divorce, her right to support during marriage is limited to what her husband chooses to give her. A wife is responsible for the support of her "infirm" husband but she is not liable for his debts contracted prior to or during marriage out of her separate earnings or separate property.

DISSOLUTION/DIVORCE: Not a no-fault state. When a divorce is granted for the fault of either party, the court may make an equitable division of all the property, whether the title to the property is in the name of the husband or the wife. Marriage and divorce between reservation Indians may be governed by individual Tribal Codes.

INHERITANCE: South Dakota is one of the few states which allows either spouse to completely disinherit the other spouse. There is no "forced share." Since 1953 S.D. has presumed that husbands and wives have made equal contributions towards the acquisition of joint tenancy property and therefore taxes only one/half of the property upon the death of either.

TENNESSEE

PROPERTY: There is no legal principle by which family income from whatever source can be regarded as equally owned by both partners. At present, a wife cannot enforce a right to one-half of the marital assets, nor does she have any legal recourse if her husband uses marital assets held in his name without her permission, or even without her knowledge. The services of a homemaker have always been assumed to be "gratuitous."

ABUSE: A wife has no legal remedy in damages for physical injury at the hands of her husband. Facilities to shelter abused women have been virtually nonexistent although a few private efforts are beginning.

DISSOLUTION/DIVORCE: Divorce courts have so much discretion that awards and even decisions fluctuate almost with the temperment of the judges. Statute on child support is not sex-specific and a wife can be ordered to pay. If alimony is involved only a husband will be affected. There is no specific provision compelling strict financial disclosure by parties to a divorce action.

TEXAS

SUPPORT: Husband has duty to support wife. Wife has duty to support husband if he is unable to support himself. However, courts will not interfere in an on-going marriage to enforce support.

PROPERTY: Community property state. Each person manages own separate property and own earnings.

ABUSE: Police are "reluctant to interfere in family disputes." "Substantial physical injury" is necessary for any conviction.

DISSOLUTION/DIVORCE: Each person manages own earnings. Thus a homemaker who makes no salary may have no management rights in family money. In a divorce settlement a spouse is not entitled to future earnings of other spouse. No permanent alimony or maintenance provision. Retirement benefits may be awarded to a wife in a divorce settlement if and when received by the husband. If a woman has co-signed on a debt with her husband, she is still liable to the creditor even if the husband has been ordered to pay the debt in a divorce decree.

INHERITANCE: If there is no will, portions of estate go to childen and widow.

RAPE: A husband cannot be found guilty of raping his wife.

UTAH

SUPPORT: The expenses of the family and the education of the children are the responsibility of both husband and wife. A married woman's obligation to support her husband in times of need is terminated upon divorce, but a woman separated from her husband pending divorce could find herself liable for his support.

ABUSE: Laws against assault are systematically not enforced when violated in a family context.

DISSOLUTION/DIVORCE: The "fault" concept of divorce is maintained. The courts are not required to consider the wife's contribution as a homemaker in making a division of debts and marital property. The wife is presumed to be the most fit person to have custody of young children.

INHERITANCE: If a husband does not leave a will, the widow will receive all of the property only if there are no lineal descendants, and no parents, siblings, nieces or nephews, or grandnieces or grandnephews.

RAPE: A married woman cannot sue her husband for rape, even where the parties are separated and one of them has filed for divorce.

CREDIT: Arbitrary decisions based on sex and marital status are being used to deny credit to women. Many businesses refuse to grant a woman credit in her own name, even if she never assumed her husband's surname in marriage. These practices are illegal.

VERMONT

LEGAL RIGHTS: Vermont permits a woman to enforce contracts with her husband, but not for her services as a homemaker. Vermont allows legal actions by one spouse against the other.

PROPERTY: Property acquired during marriage belongs to the spouse who has title. However, a deed for real property to a married woman must explicitly exclude her husband, or the property is not her sole property. When couples own their property jointly, the husband has the right to purchase goods and services for the upkeep of the jointly held property, even without the wife's consent or knowledge.

DISSOLUTION/DIVORCE: If a husband is granted a divorce because of the wife's adultery, her own separate property may be given to her husband. The husband is entitled to his, no matter how adulterous. Disclosure of real and personal property cannot be compelled for property division or for child support allocation but only when alimony is considered. When support is ordered to be paid for a wife, the court may appoint a trustee and require all payments to be paid through that person. No similar provision exists to prevent a husband from having full and free access to money awarded to him.

INHERITANCE: A court may prevent a woman from breaking her husband's will; however, the court has no right to make this kind of a determination if the surviving spouse is male.

VIRGINIA

SUPPORT: The principal that a husband has a "natural and legal duty" to support his wife is enunciated only in cases where there has been a breakdown of the marital relationship and the parties are not living together.

PROPERTY: Common-law property state. Each party owns and controls own earnings and property. However, an exception to the law presumes the husband is the owner of all property. Therefore a wife's property may be taken to pay for her husband's debts, while a husband's property cannot be taken to pay his wife's debts. The presumption is that whatever the wife owns she received because of something furnished by her husband.

ABUSE: A wife does not have the right to sue her husband for damages resulting from his physical attack on her.

DISSOLUTION/DIVORCE: The court cannot divide a couple's property upon divorce, which therefore necessitates a second legal action for partition. A new law requires that the courts consider the value of a homemaker's unpaid labor in setting alimony.

INHERITANCE: If a husband leaves a will, a wife in Va. can choose to take what she is granted by its terms or she may "break the will" and take what she would have received if he had died without a will which is a one-third life estate in the real property.

RAPE: A husband cannot be convicted of the crime of rape if he forces his sexual attentions on a wife even when they are living separately.

WASHINGTON STATE

PROPERTY: Community property state: each spouse has a one-half ownership interest in the community property. Both spouses have the power to manage the community property.

DISSOLUTION/DIVORCE: The basis for a dissolution of marriage is that the marriage be "irretrievably broken." The court will divide property only when the parties do not agree on the disposition of it. If a child has not completed her or his education or is incompetent, the court may order child support beyond the age of majority (age 18). Even though a dissolution decree divides the debts between the parties, creditors are not bound by it and can collect from either spouse.

INHERITANCE: Neither spouse may devise or bequeath by will more than his or her one-half of the community property, but each may dispose of separate property in any ways he chooses. If a spouse dies without a will, the surviving spouse receives the decedent's share of the community estate. Distribution of the separate estate depends on whether the decedent is survived by children, parents, or brothers and sisters.

RAPE: A man may not be charged with raping his wife even if the parties are separated or one of them has filed for a dissolution.

WEST VIRGINIA

LEGAL RIGHTS: In spite of a statute which states that earnings of a married woman belong to her, the courts have decided that when a wife earns money working in her husband's business, those earnings belong to the husband.

SUPPORT: The homemaker whose husband earns an income and simply refuses to share it has little recourse unless she wishes to divorce him or to charge him with a crime. Creditors have the right to proceed against either husband or wife when a debt is contracted for family purposes.

PROPERTY: If title to property is in the husband's name only, and the couple divorces, the wife has no claim to any part of it. A woman who does not work outside the home and who has no separate estate, has no right to assets accumulated during the marriage in her husband's name.

DISSOLUTION/DIVORCE: The courts cannot take property owned by one spouse and give it to the other in a divorce proceeding.

INHERITANCE: If a person dies without making a will, any interest in real estate he or she has will pass to his or her children and their descendants. If there are no children, or descendants of children, *only then* does the real estate pass to the wife or the husband. A surviving spouse, be it a man or a woman, is entitled to dower, that is a life estate in one-third of all real estate of the deceased.

WISCONSIN

LEGAL RIGHTS: Although a married woman may own and control her own earnings, her husband has control of earnings "from labor performed for her husband, or in his employ or payable by him."

PROPERTY: Separate property state where property acquired by either spouse during marriage belongs to the one who acquires it, that is, the one who pays for it. If the husband is the only spouse earning money, all property acquired during the marriage is paid for and owned by him. The law does not recognize the value of the homemaker's contribution.

ABUSE: Wife beating may be a misdemeanor or a felony carrying fines and jail terms. However, the district attorney and judges may treat cases superficially.

DIVORCE: Still requires proof of "fault" for divorce, the "no-fault" grounds being limited to cases of voluntary separation for a year or the mental illness of one spouse. Alimony, child support and property division are set at the discretion of the trial court.

INHERITANCE: If a husband leaves no will, the wife is the sole heir and receives everything if there are no children.

RAPE: It is a crime for a man to rape his wife if they are living apart and an action for annulment, legal separation, or divorce has begun.

WYOMING

SUPPORT: A husband and wife are both liable jointly and separately for the necessary expenses of the family and for the costs of educating the children. A creditor may sue either the wife or husband or both to collect debts.

DISSOLUTION/DIVORCE: Although statutes provide a plaintiff with 11 grounds, the most commonly used ground is "irreconcilable difference." Courts do not generally award alimony. Though the statute does not require it, courts presume that a mother is best able to care for young children.

INHERITANCE: A widow cannot be divested of her husband's total estate. If the deceased spouse deprived the living spouse of more than half the estate in a will, the living spouse may elect to take half the estate. If a spouse does not leave a will, the surviving spouse is entitled to the entire estate only if there are no lineal descendants, parents, brothers, sisters, nieces or nephews. If a deceased husband was in debt at death, creditors have the right to sell a homestead worth more than $6,000 and divide the excess over $6,000.

RAPE: Because it is not unlawful for a man to have carnal knowledge of his wife, either forcibly or not, a man can never be convicted of raping his wife, even if they are not living together or have started divorce proceedings.

HOUSEWORK:

A REVIEW ESSAY

Nona Glazer

The invisibility of women in scholarship has drawn a good deal of commentary in recent years, but hardly anywhere has the sociological acumen failed as embarrassingly as in its inability to recognize women's work—housework—as work. In *The Sociology of Housework*, Ann Oakley (1975) summarizes the underlying sociological axioms that support the invisibility of women's work:

1. Women belong in the family, while men belong "at work."
2. Therefore, men work, while women do not work.
3. Therefore, housework is not a form of work.

I would add several complementary axioms to these:

4. Monetary and social rights belong to those who work—to those who are economically productive.
5. Women do not work but are parasitic.
6. Therefore, women are not entitled to the same social and economic rights as men.

Ignoring woman's work provides a rationale for her second-class status both inside and outside the home. Recent scholarship, compatible to varying degrees with a feminist concern, has begun to center on a discernible set of issues, each of which I shall consider.

Beginning in the mid-1950s with the Blood and Wolfe studies of the husband-wife relationship, sociologists have usually studied housework because of a concern with the possible relation between the wife's working outside the home and the marital division of labor. The main theoretical perspective that has been used to explain the division of labor—the wife's responsibility for "traditional" feminine tasks and the husband's responsibility for "traditional" masculine tasks—is an assumed rational imperative (based on the biological differences between the sexes). Hence, Blood and Wolfe (1960:48) write:

> To a considerable extent, the idea of shared work is incompatible with the most efficient division of labor. Much of the progress of our modern economy rests upon the increasing specialization of its division of labor.

The questionable theoretical framework is complemented by methodological difficulties of sampling, of the definitions of housework, and of measurement.

The findings of such studies are frequently interpreted as indicating a shift toward greater participation by husbands in household tasks over the last decades. This shift has occurred, it is said, in response to the wife's being in the labor force. However, other studies suggest that the shift has been greatly exaggerated, with the husbands of employed wives doing very little housework compared with that of their wives. Indeed, the husbands of employed wives do about the same amount of housework as the husbands of nonemployed wives.

THE MONETARY VALUE OF HOUSEWORK

Only the low status of women and the disparagement of housework can explain why economists have found it so difficult to calculate the contribution of housework to economic well-being. Although Marxian economists have a theoretical reason, neoclassical or institutional economists, for whom housework has economic utility, have no such justification for failing to estimate the monetary value of housework.

Economists finally began to calculate the estimated monetary value of housework because of male demands. A number of court suits over the loss of wives' services prompted American economists finally to overcome the so-called weighty problems of gathering data on the time women spend doing housework and to calculate the estimated monetary value of their work. (Of course these same economists had overlooked for nearly forty years the time-budget studies done in the 1920s.)

There are a variety of methods for estimating the monetary value of the work of the American housewife. Pyun (1969) combines two approaches: an opportunity approach, which uses estimates of the housewife's possible earnings in the labor force, given her educational attainment, and a market cost approach, which considers the cost of hiring her substitute(s). Consider a hypothetical white woman who dies at the age of forty-one. At the time of her death, she was the mother of three, a full-time homemaker, and the holder of a degree from an eastern liberal arts college. Pyun estimates that it would cost $82,640 to replace her services for the next eleven years, until the age when she would have completed her child-rearing responsibilities. Economists also use the market cost approach alone, and utilize varying wage bases for estimating replacement costs. Even if the housewife's value is based on low-paid, low-status occupations such as dishwasher, cook, or charwoman, her replacement value is higher ($4,705 for 1972) than if her work is considered simply the equivalent of a domestic worker ($3,935 for 1972). If higher status, better paid occupations—e.g., interior decorator, nursery school teacher, caterer—are considered to be the marketplace equivalents of her work, then her replacement cost can rise as high as $13,364 for 1973 (Galbraith, 1973:33).

The models used in the computation of costs (e.g., the cost of a woman's leaving the labor force to care for a child) have been criticized for being aggregate choice models. Galbraith considers an aggregate choice model of limited use since it avoids consideration of the impact of the individual choice by collapsing all family members into the category "household." In this model, the cost of a woman's foregoing employment to do housework is seen as affecting only her family rather than as having a potential effect on her, too. For example, her willingness to remain out of the labor force may lessen her future employability (for instance, a licensed nurse forfeits her right to practice in the State of Oregon after five years of not being employed.)

THE INEVITABILITY OF DOMESTICITY

The analysis of cross-cultural data is relevant to the question of whether or not women are inevitably domestic, responsible for housework as well as child care and excluded from power and authority. Beginning with the statements of Judith K. Brown (1970; 1973) about women and Sharlotte N. Williams (1971) about primates, anthropologists question increasingly the universal domestication theme. Peggy Sanday (1974:-192) contrasts women's roles and women's status in twelve quite different societies. In some of the societies women's status in the public domain is high, while in others it is low. Sanday's research points up the fact that there are societies in which women have attained high status in the public domain.

Ester Boserup (1970) has attacked the myth of inevitable domesticity by her examination of women's economic role in African societies. The power of African women was eroded by the presence of Europeans acting on the basis of their own cultural myths about "women's place," which excluded women from significant participation in and control of the political economy. Ernestine Friedl (1975) reviews the position of women in hunting and gathering societies and in horticultural societies. Friedl concludes that childbearing and child rearing are accommodated *to* women's role in the public economy (not vice versa), that it is not women's contribution to subsistence but her control over the products of her work that is crucial for her political and personal power.

There are two especially useful discussions of women's domesticity in industrial society: Martin and Voorhies (1975) examine women in a variety of technological levels of society; Oakley (1974) investigates women's status in industrial society. Both studies dispel the myth that since Adam and Eve women have been confined to the household except for minor aberrations. "Women's place is in the home" is a relatively new proscription, a by-product of the transfer of production for the market from the home to the factory.

HOUSEWORK AND SOCIAL ROLES: THE HOUSEWIFE

Helena Z. Lopata (1971) provides us with the first comprehensive study of American housewives as occupants of social roles. She treats seriously and at length the varied experiences of women in the city and suburbs around Chicago during a decade that began in the 1950s. Lopata studies housework as an aspect of the housewife role, which she examines over the life cycle, rather than as a static role. How women gain the necessary knowledge to be a homemaker; who assists the housewife with her jobs (family members as well as commercial workers); the frequency with which jobs involve interaction with others in the community; the division of labor in the marital relationship; women's perceptions about being a housewife and doing housework—these are among Lopata's topics. She suggests that the role of the housewife in the United States is similar to that of a lower-class European housewife: she is a drudge and a menial rather than, as in the European aristocratic style, a manager, a coordinator, a hostess of soirees, and a participant in the mainstream of the life of the society.

A somewhat contrasting view of the housewife and housework emerges from Ann Oakley's (1975) study of housework. As far as I know hers is the only full-fledged sociological study of housework and is a companion volume to her *Woman's Work*. The contrast between the creativity and innovativeness that characterize the women Lopata studies and the dissatisfaction with housework that Oakley found in the British sample is dependent on the distinction between doing *housework* and being a *housewife.* Oakley finds that women are dissatisfied with the first and yet satisfied with the second. Oakley limits her study, insofar as possible, to women's reactions to *housework* as work. She discovers the fragmentation, monotony, and isolation that women dislike about housework. She examines children's influences insofar as these interfere with doing housework, since the demands of being a good mother may contradict the demands of being a good housekeeper.

HOUSEWORK AND THE POLITICAL ECONOMY

An Institutional Analysis. John Kenneth Galbraith (1973) sees women as exploited, as, in his words, "crypto-servants." His interpretation of women's social position is an interesting departure from conventional economics because he is concerned with the *ease of consumption* rather than with the problem of choice among goods and services. The problem of choice in the neoclassical model assumes that consumption itself is problem-free, but Galbraith believes that rising standards of consumption are attractive only if the consumers themselves do not have to expend much time and energy preparing the goods for final consumption. Whether or not modern economies, rather than the special character of capitalism, have forced women into this menial role is open to argument; it is also open to future events. The only major attempts to relieve women of private responsibility for housework that have met with some success appear to be in situations of privation (e.g., the People's Republic of China, the early years of the kibbutzim movement) or in some of the short-lived communes that have sprung up in the United States. Most of the communes in the United States have been characterized by a division of labor by sex that assigns "inside" labor to women and "outside" labor (farmwork, construction, etc.) to men. An exception to this may be some of the contemporary secular communes whose members are committed to the ideology of sex equality and whose structure, according to Rosabeth Moss Kanter (1975), supports new conceptions of gender roles.

A Radical Analysis. Marxian analyses approach the question of women and housework by examining capitalism, an approach that led initially to the conclusion that women would cease to be oppressed with the advent of socialism. Given the dreary picture of the European socialist societies, where women have not been relieved of housework responsibilities, many Marxians now recognize that factors other than the organization of the economy need to be considered. Juliet Mitchell notes that four structures—socialization of children, reproduction, and sexuality as well as production—must be understood to grasp women's condition in modern society. Women "produce" children in the home "in a sad mimicry" of how their husbands produce commodities in their work outside the home, but Mitchell does not examine housework itself. Housework itself is considered in Margaret Benston's analysis.[1] She uses the concepts of "exchange-value" and "use-value" to explain how women's exclusion from commodity production (or her minimal participation through intermittent employment in low-paying jobs) and the continued private nature of housework are the bases of the housewife's inferior position.

---

1. Part Two of Woman in a Man-Made World contains articles by Juliet Mitchell and by Margaret Benston.

Mariarosa Dalla Costa (1972) sees the condition of women's work in the home as isolating them from the experience of social labor, from contacts with other women doing the same work, and from knowledge about the world outside of family responsibilities. In addition, women benefit only partially from modern capitalism; for example, while we tend to see the modern kitchen as the best of modern technology (especially in the United States), it is not the best that is available given our technical sophistication. Dalla Costa sees women's housework as *productive* labor in that it reproduces labor. This includes, especially, bearing and rearing children but also involves helping men to prepare for another day of work. At the same time, the economic dependency of women (and children) locks men into wage labor. Seeing as she does the problems facing workers under capitalism (boring work, low wages, cyclical unemployment), Dalla Costa does not believe that entering the labor force will emancipate working-class women. Nor does she see paying housewives as likely to change women's status—on the contrary, it would freeze them into the home, into doing "woman's work."

Some Marxians, such as Wally Secombe (1974), object to describing the activities of housewives as *productive labor*, reserving this term for a particular aspect of the theory of capitalism. According to Marxian theory, *production* in capitalism means the creation of surplus value. The workers sell their labor power to the capitalist, who pays them a wage sufficient for survival but less than the value their labor has added to the product. In other words, the workers' labor is only partially compensated for. The portion that is not compensated for is called *surplus value*. According to Marx, the capitalist's appropriation of this surplus value is *exploitation*. Using this analysis, it can be reasoned that the housewife is not exploited (another technical term) because her goods, although they have use-value, do not enter the commodity market but instead are consumed in the home. However, the housewife is oppressed. She is oppressed by her economic dependency on her husband, whose health and well-being as well as goodwill are crucial to her own well-being. She is oppressed by being isolated from other women like herself because of her home duties, by having to perform work that she and others see as trivial, and by being seen by herself and others as "parasitic" since her housework brings her no money.

Secombe objects to seeing housework as productive labor for several reasons. First, the housewife does not relate to either the means of production or the means of exchange, which she did in the precapitalist world. While labor in the home may add value (to the commodities being consumed), the value does not enter the marketplace because the housewife does not create *surplus* value. Thus, service that does not produce surplus value is not considered economically productive—which is the reason the Eastern European socialist countries exclude even the market costs of services from the GNP. I am not convinced that this is a reasonable view of work in the labor force—that services cannot be considered an equivalent of commodities—nor am I convinced that the direct control by the capitalist of a worker's time is somehow more real than the indirect control by the capitalist of the activity of women in the household. If the labor of the domestic worker is necessary for production and necessary for the reproduction of labor (i.e., for bearing and rearing children and for preparing men to work each day for wages), then the capitalist's criterion of a monetary value seems irrelevant.

Whether or not the radical analysts agree on the exact meaning of housework under capitalism, they agree that the housewife works for the maintenance of capitalism rather than simply being a worker for her family. This is important: if housework is seen as being for the family only, then we study the housewife and suggest research questions and social policy that focus on the husband-wife relationships, which is what has been done. The answer to the question, "Who must pay for housework?" is easy: "The husband!" Thus, it has been suggested by various critics of contemporary women's position that a wife is entitled to half of her husband's wages or, alternatively, that husbands pay wives for housework on some hourly or weekly basis. Husbands (and children) are seen as the beneficiaries of the domestic work of wives, a view that privatizes the family, turning each family into a small-scale production unit. This view supports the conventional division of labor between the sexes by implying that it is the husband who exploits his wife if he demands that she be responsible for housework (and fails to share work in the home with her to any substantial degree regardless of her status in the labor force). The wife's assuming responsibility for the housework is "in exchange" for the husband's assuming responsibility for the financial support of her and their children.

Many American sociologists do see the husband and wife as a complementary unit. The marital relationship is then examined using concepts such as balance and exchange. The division of labor *for* the marital couple becomes an issue of balancing the man's activities against the woman's activities, the man's interests against the woman's interests, and so on. If, in contrast, we conceptualize women's work as supporting capitalism (considering it either as labor or as "productive" labor), we pose a different set of questions about the family. Our analysis shifts from exploring the relationships between husband and wife, in the home, to asking how their relationships to institutions outside the home affect husband-wife relationships. We deprivatize the family in our research. As sociologists we appear to believe that the family is isolated from society, somewhat in the same way that ideology leads family members to see themselves as constructing a private world away from the turmoil of modern industrial-urban life. In the broadest sense, then, a Marxian analysis means developing a "sociology" of the family (relatively neglected for the past several decades) as a complement to the "social psychology" of the family.

CONSTRUCTING THEORY: HOUSEWORK AND A SOCIOLOGY FOR WOMEN

I want to end this review with a brief reference to Dorothy E. Smith's critique of a sociology *of* women, and her model for a sociology *for* women.[2] A sociology *for* women begins by inquiring into how the everyday world is experienced by women, as described by women, rather than attempting to squeeze women's experiences into preexisting rational-administrative models of the world. The subsequent steps involve connecting the everyday world, as seen by women, to the larger social context of the political economy. A sociology for women would connect the world that women experience as housewives (as well as wives and mothers) to the less immediately apprehended world that shapes their everyday experiences. We may then succeed in connecting personal troubles to public issues.

2. Part One of Woman in a Man-Made World contains the article by Dorothy E. Smith.

REFERENCES

Blood, Robert O., Jr., and Donald M. Wolfe.
1960 Husbands and Wives: The Dynamics of Married Living. New York: Free Press.

Boserup, Ester.
1970 Woman's Role in Economic Development. London: George Allen and Unwin.

Brown, Judith K.
1971 "A note on the division of labor by sex." American Anthropologist 73:805–806.
1973 "Leisure, busywork and housekeeping." Anthropos 68(5):881–888.

Dalla Costa, Mariarosa.
1972 "Women and the subversion of community." Radical America 6(January-February):67–102.

Friedl, Ernestine.
1975 Women and Men: An Anthropologist's View. New York: Holt, Rinehart and Winston.

Galbraith, John Kenneth.
1973 Economics and the Public Purpose. Boston: Houghton-Mifflin.

Gilman, Charlotte Perkins.
1972 The Home, Its Work and Influence. Urbana: University of Illinois Press. First published in 1903.

Lopata, Helena Z.
1971 Occupation: Housewife. New York: Oxford University Press.

Martin, M. Kay, and Barbara Voorhies.
1975 Female of the Species. New York: Columbia University Press.

Oakley, Ann.
1974 Woman's Work: A History of the Housewife. New York: Pantheon Books.
1975 The Sociology of Housework. New York: Pantheon Books.

Pyun, Chong Soo.
1969 "The monetary value of a housewife: An economic analysis for use in litigation." American Journal of Economics and Sociology 28(July):271–284. Reprinted in Nona Glazer-Malbin and Helen Y. Waehrer (eds.), Woman in a Man-Made World. First Edition. Chicago: Rand McNally, 1972.

Sanday, Peggy R.
1974 "Female status in the public domain," in Michelle Zimbalist Rosaldo and Louise Lamphere (eds.), Woman, Culture and Society. Stanford, Calif.: Stanford University Press.

Secombe, Wally.
1974 "The housewife and her labour under capitalism." New Left Review 83(January-February):3–24.

Vanek, Joann.
1974 "Time spent in housework." Scientific American 231(November):14, 116–120.

Williams, Sharlotte Neely.
1971 "The limitations of the male/female activity distinction among primates: An extension of Judith K. Brown's 'A note on the division of labor by sex.' " American Anthropologist 73:805–806.

The essay appears in this form in Woman in a Man-Made World, 2nd edition (1977, Rand McNally, Chicago). Excerpted and revised from Nona Glazer-Malbin's "Housework," in Signs: Journal of Women in Culture and Society 1 (Summer 1976)

Motherhood, Family Planning, and Child Care

Barbara Everitt Bryant

The National Commission on the Observance of International Women's Year, 1975, was appointed by the President of the United States to study barriers to women's equality and to make recommendations designed to end those barriers. The United Nations designated 1975 as International Women's Year.

One of the many activities undertaken by the National Commission was to contract with Market Opinion Research for a national survey of women: assessing women's attitudes and opinions, recording their current activities, looking at the patterns of their lives, and asking about their views of the future.

This book is an analysis of that survey, which was based on interviews from a geographically stratified probability sample of 1,522 adult women in the United States. Interviews were made in August and September 1975.

What They Believe

Who are the *Traditional Outlook women?* They believe in the kind of marriage in which the husband provides the major financial support and the wife takes most of the responsibility for the home and children. Traditional Outlook women may indeed hold jobs outside the home, but those who work feel their jobs are secondary to those of their husbands; that the achievements of husbands are more important than the achievements of wives.

The Traditional Outlook woman thinks that mothers who stay home can do a better job of providing a secure environment for their children than mothers employed outside the home can provide. Most of these women oppose efforts to change or strengthen women's status in society today.

Balancing Outlook women, caught in the middle, want some things to change and others to remain as they are. Some in this group simply don't know whether they favor or oppose present moves toward change.

Expanding Outlook women know they want change. They favor all that is happening tò improve women's status. They want lives which offer options of home, marriage, and careers outside the home in all possible combinations. They are not rejecting the homemaker role but want to combine it with employment, whether they are married or single. If married, they view marriage as a relationship in which responsibilities are shared, with both partners responsible for financial support and child and home care.

While most women, including those in the other two categories, feel capable of handling their own and their families' financial affairs, Expanding Outlook women have greater confidence than others in their ability to do so.

One difference in the views of Expanding Outlook women versus Traditional Outlook women is the way they perceive educational and career counseling opportunities available to girls. Expanding Outlook women perceive the opportunities for girls in these areas as very unequal to those given boys.

Traditional and some Balancing Outlook women say they think girls have the same chance as boys for education and for occupational and vocational counseling. (Overall there *is* more agreement that educational opportunities are equal than that occupational or vocational counseling is nondiscriminatory.)

Motherhood

Nearly three-fourths of adult women have had a baby, but only 43 percent have minor children (17 or under) living in their households now. The rest have sons and daughters who are grown.

One-fifth of women (21 percent) have preschool children at home now.

One-third of all mothers have had two children; 16 percent have had five or more; and 3 percent have had nine or more.

Three percent of women are natural mothers who also have an adopted, step, or foster minor child in their household now. One percent of women never had a child of their own but have an adopted, step, or foster minor child at home now (table 4-1).

Younger mothers with preschool children are slightly less apt to hold the Traditional Outlook, while older mothers, whose children have grown, are far more likely to have a Traditional Outlook (figure 4-1).

Women who have never had children—and a large number of this group are young singles—are more apt to have Expanding Outlook views.

Half of all three types of mothers—Expanding, Balancing, or Traditional Outlook—agree that the ideal lifestyle would include staying home while children are small.

Family Planning

Virtually all women feel that the decision about when to have children should be made jointly by the man and the woman. However, only one-third planned the timing of all their pregnancies; one-third planned some of their pregnancies; and one-third had all their children unplanned.

The proportion of planned pregnancies varies by race (figure 4-3) and rises with education (figure 4-2) and income. Younger women are planning their pregnancies more than older women did (figure 4-4).

Three-fourths of unplanned pregnancies occurred because the woman was not using any birth control method; one-fourth occurred because a method failed or because the method was not used properly.

TABLE 4-1

NUMBER OF CHILDREN

Have given birth to a child			73%
Number of children among those who have given birth:			
One child	20%		
Two children	32		
Three children	20		
Four children	12		
Five children	7		
Six children	4		
Seven children	1		
Eight children	1		
Nine or more children	3		
	100		
Have given birth to a child and also have adopted/step/foster minor child now		3%	
Have never given birth to a child			27%
Never given birth but have adopted/step/foster minor child now		1%	
			100

Forty-three percent of women in the main child-bearing years (18-44) are presently using some form of birth control. One-fourth of all adult women practice birth control. This proportion is similar among groups of never-marrieds, currently-marrieds, and divorced and separated. Usage varies most with age (figure 4-5).

Only 5 percent of those not practicing birth control claim they want to.

Child Care

Women who work and have young children are heavily dependent on the traditional forms of child care: babysitters, husbands, and their own mothers.

Formal child-care facilities and services—day-care centers and nursery schools—are in relatively low usage, in part because they are unavailable or have schedules unsuited to the needs of working mothers. Therefore, working mothers who can afford them turn to babysitters, while others work out schedules with husbands, mothers, and older sons and daughters.

One-fifth of women have preschool children at home. One-third of this group use child care on a regular basis, including women who are not working but who use babysitters and nursery schools for personal or child-education reasons.

Forty-three percent of women have children under 18 at home, but only 7 percent of them use afterschool or vacation child care (table 4-2).

As shown in table 2-8 (p. 18), 21 percent of adult women are not employed now, but they expect to return to employment outside the home. To seek paid employment now, or to obtain additional education and job training, nearly half of these women would need afterschool and vacation child care.

Nearly two-thirds of all women agree that the government should assist in providing child care on an ability-to-pay basis. There are age and race differences on this issue. But whether women plan to use child care or not, there is substantial majority agreement that the option of government-assisted child care on an ability-to-pay basis should be available to mothers (table 4-3).

TABLE 4-2

USE AND TYPE OF CHILD CARE

	Preschool for Women With Children Age 5 and Younger	*After School for Women With Children 0-17*
Child care on regular basis		
Yes	32%	7%
No/not stated	68	93
	100	100
What type of child care is that? (some multiple answers)		
Baby sitter	44	46
Relative:		
Husband/parent	22	23
Son/daughter 14 years or over	7	14
Son/daughter under 14	1	...
Private nursery school	14	8
State-subsidized day care	7	2
Family day care	2	2
Exchange babysitting	3	2
Friend	5	2
Nonlicensed facility or person [1]	...	2
Other	4	6

[1] Many other child-care sources are probably unlicensed.

TABLE 4-3

AGREEMENT/DISAGREEMENT: "THE GOVERNMENT SHOULD ASSIST IN PROVIDING CHILD CARE ON AN ABILITY-TO-PAY BASIS FOR THOSE WHO NEED CHILD CARE"

		AGE		
	All Women	*Under 35*	*35-54*	*55 and Over*
Agree	73%	82%	67%	67%
Disagree	19	14	23	21
No opinion	8	4	10	12
	100	100	100	100

	RACE		
	White	*Black*	*Spanish American*
Agree	71%	85%	82%
Disagree	20	10	13
No opinion	9	5	5
	100	100	100

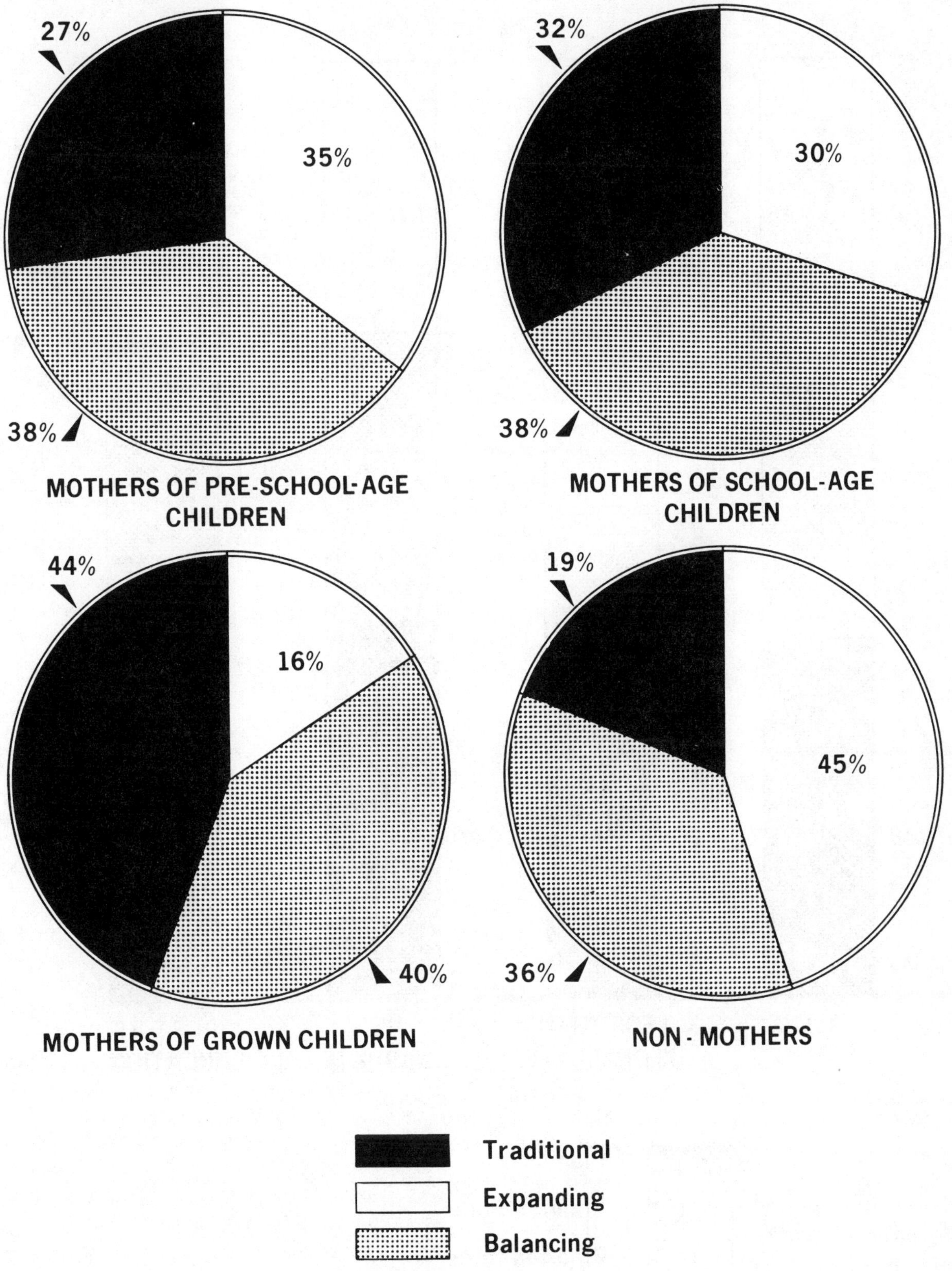

FIGURE 4-1 OUTLOOK OF WOMEN'S ROLES BY MOTHERHOOD

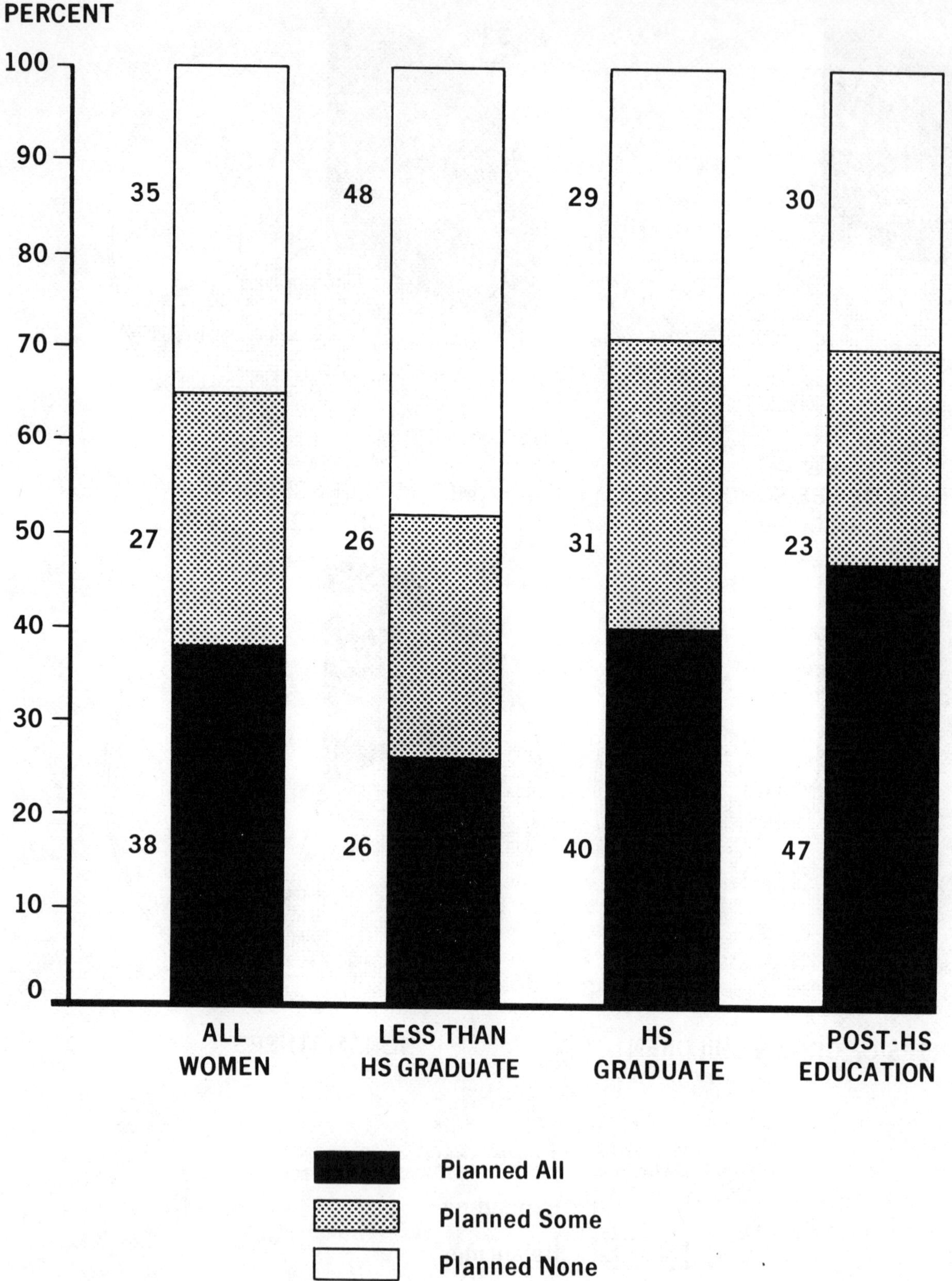

FIGURE 4-2 PLANNED PREGNANCIES BY EDUCATION LEVEL

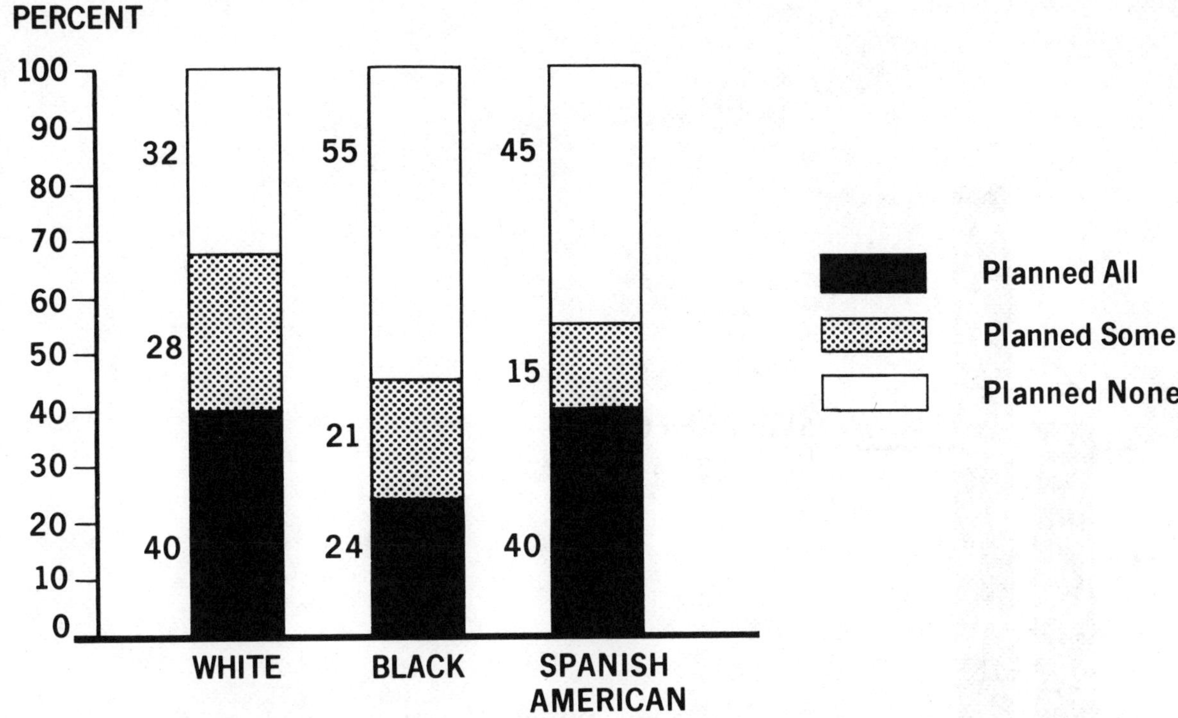

FIGURE 4-3 PLANNED PREGNANCIES BY RACE

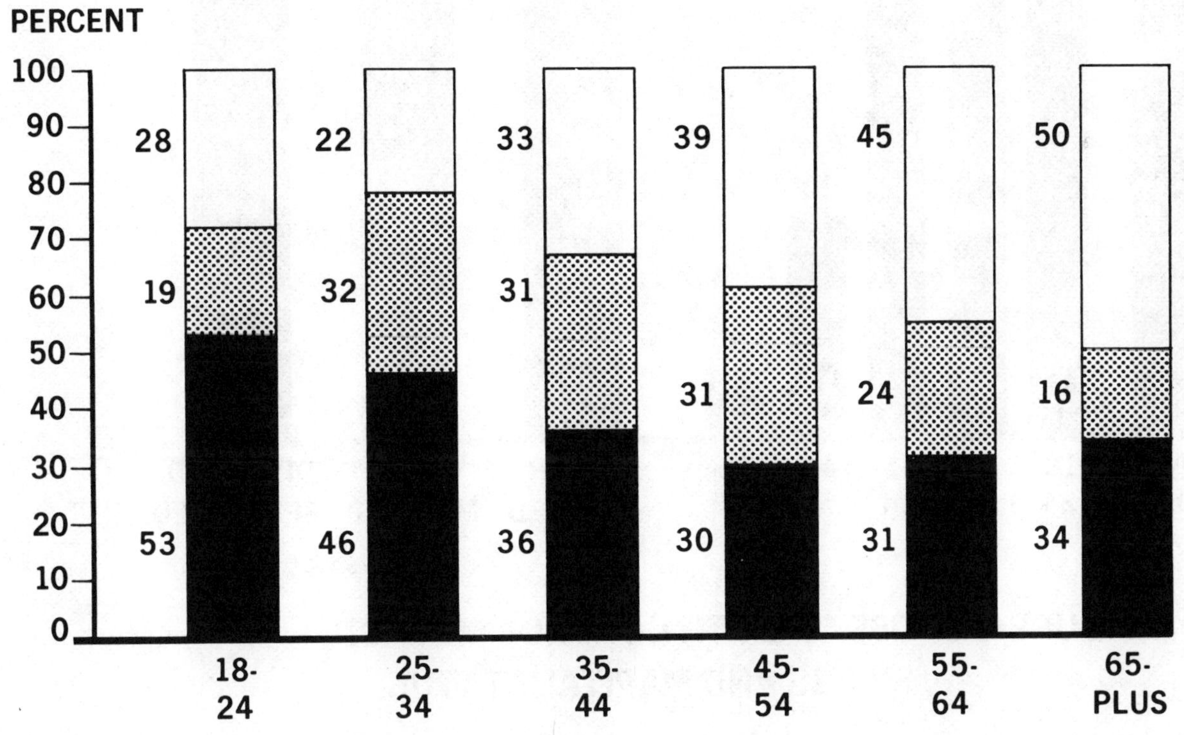

FIGURE 4-4 PLANNED PREGNANCIES BY AGE

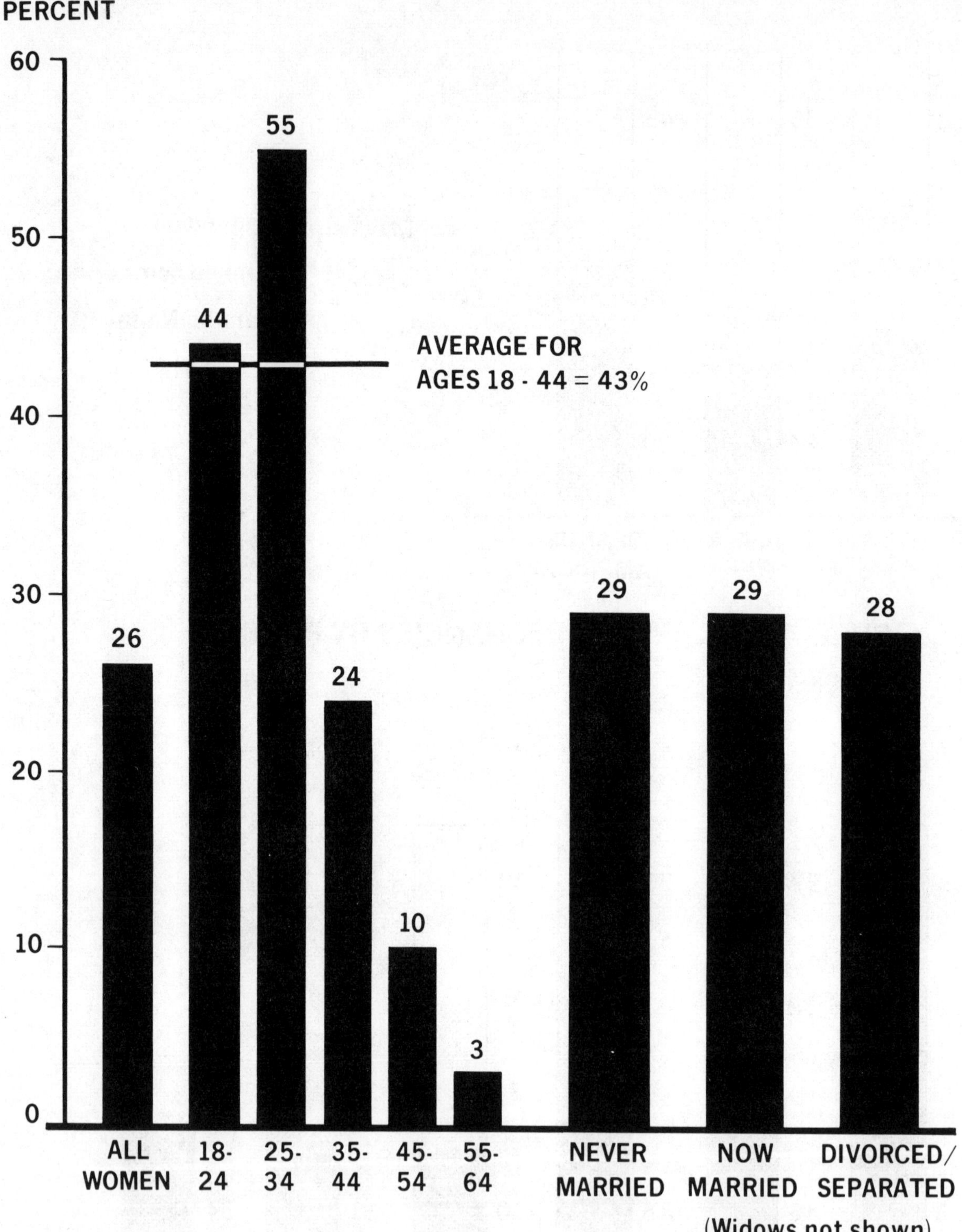

FIGURE 4-5 USE OF BIRTH CONTROL METHOD BY AGE AND MARITAL STATUS

American Women Today & Tomorrow, Market Opinion Research, 1977, National Commission on the Observance of International Women's Year (GPO Stock No. 052-003-00249-3)

Family Life Cycle Events

Paul C. Glick and Arthur J. Norton

Changing trends in marriage, divorce, childbearing, and mortality have affected the family life cycle of even the most "typical" of families. Most Americans, however, still play out their lives in some version of the traditional family life cycle.

Family life cycle for "typical" mothers

A recent updating of changes in the family life cycle for typical mothers over the last 80 years is presented in Figure 5. The figure is limited to married women who had borne at least one child, because they represent the most usual family pattern. Through the years, the proportion of women who have never married has varied from 9 percent during the early part of the 20th century to only about half that level a couple of decades ago; it may return to 7 percent for those now of the most marriageable ages. The proportion of married women who have remained childless has varied from about 20 percent for those who married in the 1920s to only a projected 4 to 6 or 7 percent for those who married in the 1960s and 1970s.

A look at Figure 5 reveals the following trends.

The median age for women at first marriage has varied from an early level of 20.0 years in the familistic 1950s to 21.4 years in the first decade of the 20th century and during the Great Depression of the 1930s, slightly later than the 21.2 years of today. The average mother has borne her first child about 1.3 to 2.1 years after marriage.

The median age for mothers at the birth of their last child has moved generally downward, from 33 years in the early 1900s to an expected 30 years for those now in the midst of family formation. In tandem with this, the line for mothers' median age at marriage of the last child slopes down from 55 years in the early 1900s to 52 years. These family life cycle events relating to the last child

Figure 5. Median Age of Typical Mothers at Selected Points in the Family Life Cycle

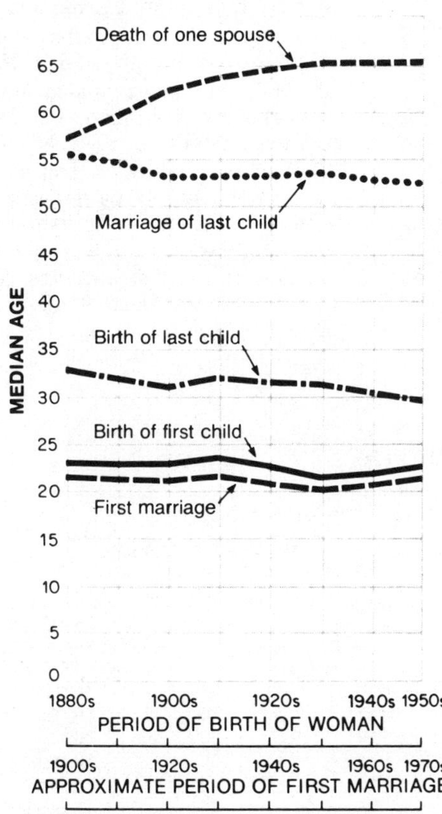

Source: Paul C. Glick, "Updating the Life Cycle of the Family," *Journal of Marriage and the Family,* Vol. 39, No. 1 (February 1977) Figure 1, p. 7. Copyrighted 1977 by the National Council on Family Relations. Reprinted by permission.

reflect a decline in childbearing from 3.9 children per mother in the early 1900s to an expected 2.5 per mother for those now having their children. Primarily because women are having fewer children, the period of childbearing has been compressed to about seven years (beginning at age 23 and ending at 30) for today's typical mother, as compared with ten years (from age 23 to 33) for the mother of the early 1900s.

The most impressive and probably the most significant feature of Figure 5 is the greatly elongated period between marriage of the last child and the death of one spouse, an expansion of 11 years. The declining birth rate accounts for three of these 11 additional "empty nest" years, and the increasing joint survival rate for the husband and wife accounts for the other eight. Along with the approximately two years of "child-free" married life before the first child arrives, a typical couple now entering marriage may expect to live together as a two-person family for a total of about 13 years. This adds up to nearly a third of the average 44 years of married life ahead at the time of marriage. The empty nest years are not spent entirely bereft of children, however. According to one survey, three-fourths of parents 65 years old and over live within an hour's distance from their nearest child.[6]

With the recent upsurge in divorce and premarital births, it is evident that an increasing proportion of people do not experience the family life cycle of the socalled typical mother and father. Nonetheless, a majority of couples do experience various approximations of that cycle.

Premaritally-conceived births

In the June 1975 Current Population Survey, information was recorded for ever-married women on the date of first marriage and the birth dates of their first three and last two children. Table 10 presents the proportion of first births after several intervals of time since these women's first marriage. Actually 9 percent of first children born in the early 1970s were reported as born before the woman had married (8.5 percent of white and 58 percent of black children). About 85 percent of women with premarital births marry eventually, according to data from the 1970 census.[7]

Besides this 9 percent, another 24 percent were born less than 9 months after first marriage. Thus, a maximum of about 33 percent, or one-third, of all first births during the early 1970s were premaritally conceived. (Putting the cut-off point at eight months after marriage reduces the proportion by only two percentage points.)

One-half of all first births during the early 1970s had occurred by the time women had been 27 months married, including premarital births. For women first married in the decade from 1955 to 1964, the corresponding interval was only about half as long, 15 months, but for those married between 1930 and 1944, it was nearly as long as now—24 to 26 months. This pattern is consistent with the general observation that the lower the birth rate the longer the interval between births, and vice versa. The last column of Table 9 and knowledge of recent birth trends indicate that child-

Table 10. Timing of First Births

(Cumulative percent of women ever married whose first child was born during successive intervals since first marriage: U.S., 1975)

Year of woman's first marriage	Percent with first child born before first marriage	Months after first marriage before first child was born			Percent remaining childless
		Up to 8 months	12 months	One half by—	
1930-1934	5	13	27	26 mo.	16
1935-1939	4	13	27	25 mo.	16
1940-1944	5	11	26	24 mo.	12
1945-1949	6	14	33	20 mo.	10
1950-1954	6	17	35	18 mo.	8
1955-1959	8	22	42	15 mo.	8
1960-1964	8	25	44	15 mo.	7
1965-1969	8	25	40	18 mo.	na
1970-1974[a]	9	24	32	27 mo.	na

Source: U.S. Bureau of the Census, *Current Population Reports,* Series P-20, No. 288, "Fertility History and Prospects of American Women: June 1975," Table 9.

[a]Data adjusted for the part of the cohort that had not reached the stated interval since first marriage.

Table 11. Timing of Births to Remarried Women: U.S., 1975 and 1971

(Children born before first marriage, during first marriage, between marriages, and after start of second marriage; for women aged 30-39 in currently intact second marriage after divorce)

Years of school completed, and family income	Children ever born per 1,000 women: All women aged 30-39 in intact second marriages — Rate	Percent	Before start of first marriage	During first marriage	Between end of first and start of second marriage	After start of second marriage
1975, total	2,778	–	107	1,530	298	843
Percent	–	100.0	3.9	55.1	10.7	30.3
Years of school completed						
0-11 years	3,467	100.0	5.1	52.8	12.1	30.0
12 years	2,523	100.0	2.8	56.3	10.0	30.8
13 years or more	2,108	100.0	2.8	58.7	8.5	30.1
Wives in own household, total	2,780	100.0	3.8	55.1	10.8	30.3
Family income:						
Under $10,000	3,461	100.0	5.6	49.9	13.6	30.9
$10,000 or more	2,539	100.0	2.6	58.0	9.4	30.0
1971, total	3,169	–	121	1,735	236	1,078
Percent	–	100.0	3.8	54.7	7.4	34.0

Sources: U.S. Bureau of the Census, *Current Population Reports,* Series P-20, No. 263, "Fertility Histories and Birth Expectations of American Women: June 1971," Table 59; and unpublished *Current Population Survey* data.

lessness also tends to vary inversely with the level of lifetime childbearing.

Children born between marriages

One-tenth of remarried women's children are born between marriages.

This inference is drawn from the fertility experience of more than a million women near the end of their childbearing period at the time of the June 1975 Current Population Survey. Stated more specifically, women then in their thirties who were in an intact second marriage reported that 11 percent of their children to date were born between the end of their first marriage and the start of their second marriage (Table 11). Those "born between the first and second marriage" presumably do not include children who were born *before* their mother's second marriage while she was still separated, because her first marriage had not really ended yet; they also exclude children who were conceived between marriages but born after the mother had remarried. The 11 percent may also be affected somewhat by the exclusion of children who will be born *later* in the woman's second marriage. The corresponding 1970 proportion of children born between the first and second marriages (with the same measurement limitations) was 7 percent, somewhat below the figure for 1975.[8]

The remarried women had borne three-fifths of their children before the end of their first marriage. Presumably, most of these children are now living with a stepfather, that is, their mother's second husband. As expected, the chances that these children were born during, rather than before, their mother's first marriage were greater as the mother's education and family income increased.

Pregnancy outcomes

Information was assembled from several sources for Tables 12, which attempts to approximate the distribution of all pregnancies occurring in the United States from 1970 to 1975 among categories of live births and fetal deaths. The table shows a continuous decline in the proportion of pregnancies resulting in legitimate births, from 59 percent in 1970 to 51 percent in 1975, and a small increase in illegitimate births, from 7.0 percent to 8.5 percent. Total numbers of pregnancies fluctuated within a narrower range than most persons may have expected, in view of the known decline in the birth rate.

The most striking change in the early 1970s occurred in the number and proportion of pregnancies terminated by legal abortions. Even before the Supreme Court's legalization of abortion on request for the nation as a whole in January 1973, legally performed abor-

Table 12. Pregnancy Outcomes: U.S., 1970-1975

(Pregnancies resulting in legitimate and illegitimate live births, legal and illegal induced abortions, and spontaneous abortions)

Year	Total preg-nancies	Live births		Fetal deaths		
				Induced abortions		Spontaneous abortions and still-births
		Legitimate	Illegitimate	Legal	Illegal	
			Number (in thousands)			
1970	5,682	3,332	399	193	530	1,228
1971	5,462	3,155	401	480	250	1,176
1972	5,060	2,855	403	587	130	1,085
1973	4,998	2,730	407	745	54	1,062
1974	5,156	2,742	418	899	12	1,085
1975	5,288	2,692	448	1,034	10	1,100
			Percent			
1970	100.0	58.6	7.0	3.4	9.3	21.6
1971	100.0	57.8	7.3	8.8	4.6	21.5
1972	100.0	56.4	8.0	11.6	2.6	21.4
1973	100.0	54.6	8.1	14.9	1.1	21.2
1974	100.0	53.2	8.1	17.4	0.2	21.0
1975	100.0	51.0	8.5	19.6	0.2	20.8

Sources: Live births; U.S. National Center for Health Statistics, *Monthly Vital Statistics Report, Advance Report, Final Natality Statistics, 1975*, Vol. 25, No. 10 Supplement, Tables 1 and 12, and *1974*, Vol. 24, No. 11 Supplement 2, Table 11, and *Vital Statistics of the United States, 1973*, Vol. 1, *Natality*, Tables 1-1 and 1-29. Legal abortions: Ellen Sullivan, Christopher Tietze, and Joy G. Dryfoos, "Legal Abortion in the United States, 1975-1976," *Family Planning Perspectives*, Vol. 9, No. 3 (May/June 1977) pp. 116-129, especially p. 121. Illegal abortions: Estimated by method described by Willard Cates, Jr., and Roger W. Rochat, "Illegal Abortions in the United States: 1972-1974," *Family Planning Perspectives*, Vol. 8, No. 2 (March/April 1976) pp. 86-92, especially p. 92. Spontaneous abortions and stillbirths: on advice of Christopher Tietze, assumed to be 30 percent as numerous as live births plus 15 percent as numerous as induced abortions.

tions had risen sharply and estimated numbers of illegal abortions had fallen at close to the same rate. By 1975 legal abortions were estimated at over a million—five times the number in 1970. Meanwhile, illegal abortions fell from an estimated 530,000 to some 10,000 only. Close to 20 percent of pregnant women in 1975 evidently preferred an induced abortion to bearing an unwanted child. Presumably effective means of preventing unwanted *conceptions* will become more universally used in the future, so that fewer women will be faced with the difficult choice between abortion and unwanted childbirth.

The estimates of spontaneous abortions and stillbirths shown in Table 12 are subject to considerable error. They are probably more likely to be too high than too low. If the true numbers are only two-thirds as large as those in the table, such pregnancies would constitute an even smaller minority than about one-fifth. In any event, only a small proportion of spontaneous abortions are preventable by medical intervention.

Expected lifetime births and the total fertility rate

The "average number of children per family" depends on how one defines children. Recent changes in two frequently used lifetime measures of children born per woman are charted in Figure 6, and the number of children currently present in the household (or family) is discussed in a later section.

Two decades ago, the total fertility rate was higher than the average number of lifetime births expected, but now the total fertility rate is the lower measure. Trends in the total fertility rate indicate that women would have 3.6 children in their lifetime if they experienced at each year of age the birth rate of women of that age in the year 1960, but only 1.8 children—half as many—if they experienced the birth rates of 1976. The total fertility rate is a "period" rate for a given year, transformed by a ratio estimating procedure into a lifetime rate.

By contrast, the trend line for the number of lifetime births expected shows that women would have 3.1 children if they actually bore the number expected by wives who were 18 to 24 years old in 1960, but 2.1—only two-thirds as many—if they had the corresponding number expected in 1976. Called a "cohort" rate, this expected number of lifetime births is projected from data

Figure 6. Total Fertility Rate and Lifetime Births Expected by Wives Aged 18-24: U.S., 1960-1976

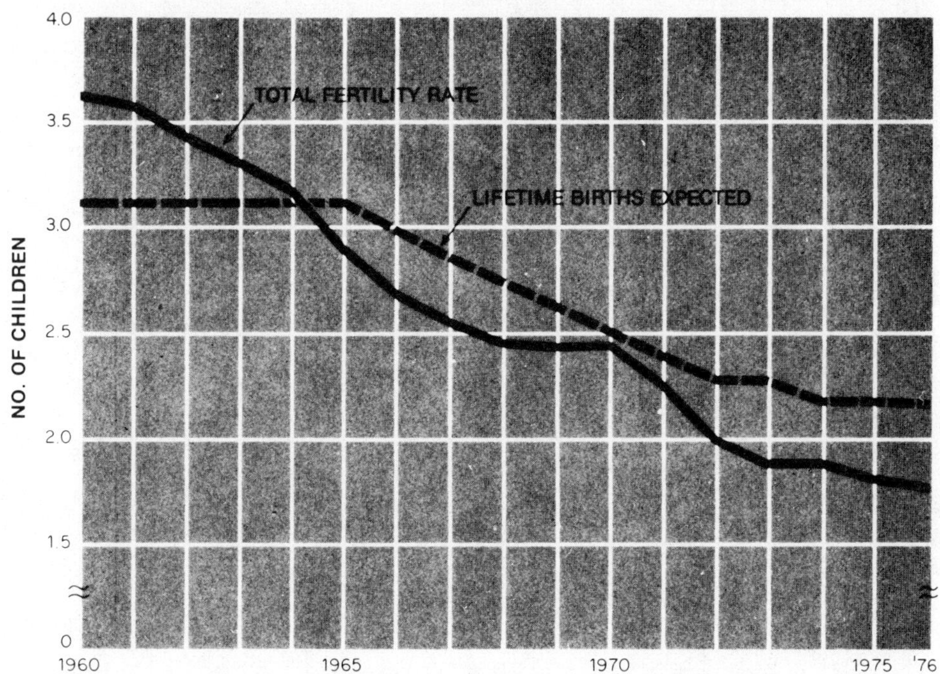

Source: U.S. Bureau of the Census, *Current Population Reports*, Series P-20, No. 308, "Fertility of American Women: June 1976," Table A.

collected annually in the Current Population Survey from married women aged 18 to 24. It includes children already born, plus additional children expected.

Depending on the measure adopted, then, the lifetime number of births per woman in the U.S. is now only half or only two-thirds what it was in the baby boom period. Most demographers would probably say that the number of births expected is a more realistic measure. No age group (cohort) of women for many decades past has actually borne a lifetime average of 3.6 children, the total fertility rate for 1960. At the same time, the chances are good that the average number of lifetime births for young women now entering their childbearing period will not be as low as 1.8, the total fertility rate for 1976.

The 2.1 figure is based on data for wives, whereas the 1.8 figure is based on data for all women. But even if the 2.1 children expected by young *wives* in 1976 were adjusted to apply to *all* women, it would still be about 2.0 children per woman. Significantly, the average number of children expected by *single* women aged 18 to 24 who were interviewed in the June 1976 Current Population Survey was 1.9. But women aged 18 to 24 who are still single include a disproportionate number who will marry at a relatively late age and have fewer children than women who marry earlier.

For today's mother of only two children, family life is very different from what it was for the typical mother of four children in the early 20th century.

6. Epstein, Lenore A. and Janet H. Murray, *The Aged Population of the United States: The 1963 Social Security Survey of the Aged,* Research Report No. 19, U.S. Social Security Administration (1967) p. 164.
7. Grabill, Wilson H., "Premarital Fertility," *Current Population Reports,* Series P-23, No. 63, U.S. Bureau of the Census (1976) p. 11.
8. For additional information on this subject, see Ronald R. Rindfuss and Larry L. Bumpass, "Fertility During Marital Disruption," *Journal of Marriage and the Family,* Vol. 39, No. 3 (August 1977) pp. 517-528. These authors report on page 518 that "about a quarter of the remarried women in the 1970 National Fertility Study report a birth during a period of marital disruption."

Excerpts from Marrying, Divorcing, and Living Together in the U.S. Today, by Paul C. Glick and Arthur J. Norton. Vol. 32, No. 5 (October 1977) of the Population Bulletin. Courtesy of the Population Reference Bureau, Inc. Washington, D.C.

Additional excerpts from this booklet may be found in the Marriage section of this Part II-ADULTS chapter.

Fathers

FATHERS

by Carlfred B. Broderick

This paper is about fathers. The data to be cited are from an as yet unpublished study done under the direction of Rosemary Erickson of the Western Behavioral Science Institute of La Jolla, Calif. My own relationship to the project was as a rather active consultant. While the data are, therefore, in a sense borrowed, I must assume responsibility for the analyses and especially the interpretations reported here.

My purpose in presenting these materials on fathers is two fold. First, of course, it is hoped that some further perspective might be gained on the range of paternal styles. But secondly, it is hoped that through the lens of these data an enlarged perspective on ourselves—on those of us who study and serve families—may be achieved. For it is my view that our expectations as professionals are often quite unrealistic and inappropriate. We study a relatively narrow band of variables and yet we are dissatisfied to explain only 25% of the variance. We administer to the needs of families enmeshed in a complex social system with a handful of primitive therapeutic tools and yet we are chagrined that we help only 75% of those who come to us and complain that only a small, particular, non-representative group come to us at all. We bemoan the lack of sound family policy and our inability to influence government yet we couldn't agree on what to do with it if the entire navigation of the ship of state were turned over to us.

Often we feel that to justify our existence we ought to be able to stamp out unwanted pregnancy, V.D., and interfamily violence, to delay young marriages and reduce divorce, to increase personal growth and freedom and, it goes without saying, to do all this while pulling down a top salary at a respectable university or agency while appearing from time to time on national television.

In this paper it is my goal to examine and evaluate our professional objectives through an analysis of the roles of fathers and what the profession could reasonably hope to do for them or about them.

Types of Fathers

It is conventional when discussing the paternal role to begin with a lament on how little work has been done on fathers and fathering compared to the attention given mothers and mothering. In fact, just ten years ago Brenton's (1966) highly quotable observation that in the socialization literature "every day is Mother's Day" was fully defensible. During the intervening decade things have

*This is an edited version of the Presidential address delivered to the National Council of Family Relations in their meeting in New York, October 24, 1976.

**Carlfred B. Broderick is Professor, Department of Sociology, University of Southern California, Los Angeles, CA 90007.

improved considerably, however. In 1968 Benson's book, *Fatherhood,* abstracted materials on the paternal role from over 600 sources and in 1974 Lynn's book, *The Father: His Role in Child Development,* cited over 700 sources. The oversized October 1976 issue of the *Family Coordinator* was devoted entirely to fathers and each of the recent NCFR annual meetings has included the presentation of papers on this topic.

Despite this upsurge of interest in fathers, however, there are still some areas where Brenton's observation remains applicable. The U.S. census is a particularly good example.

Do you want to know how many women are living with their own children and compare them to women living with children not related to them by blood? The data are readily available in the census. Do you need figures on how many children women have by each age and by the end of their fertile period? No problem; it is all there. Is it important to be able to compare the fertility rates of women from different ethnic or racial backgrounds? The figures fairly leap out at you. But if you want to ask these same questions about fathers, be prepared for a disappointment. There is simply nothing there. Granted that it is not difficult to figure out why it is easier to ask questions and get answers on maternity than on paternity, still one is left with almost no direct information on the distribution of fathers among even the most obvious categories.

In view of this information vacuum, the findings of a survey of representative households in San Diego County may be of general rather than merely regional interest. These data were generated by the survey phase of the WBSI study referred to earlier. Their country-wide sample turned up 1,700 households with dependent children. In each of these households the child nearest to 14 years of age was selected as the reference for determining relationships and the following distribution was observed:

- 75% lived with both natural parents
- 15% lived with their mother in a fatherless household
- 9% lived with their mother and a stepfather
- 1% lived with their father in a motherless household

In a second phase, this same study selected 106 stepfather families and a group of 84 natural families matched on demographic variables. In these 190 families the father or step-father, the mother and the child nearest 14 years of age were interviewed in depth. Selective data from these interviews were then submitted to factor analysis. Four strong groupings of variables emerged which seemed to define four different styles of fathering.

Style 1: The Autocrat

Fathers high on this factor describe themselves as demanding of achievement and organization. Their children describe them as controlling and punative. At the risk of perpetuating an unfortunate stereotype, we must report that this style was more common among step-fathers than among natural fathers. Moreover, the autocratic father himself is likely to have come from a broken home. Another way of describing this style is to say that fathers who adopt it attempt to control their children through unilateral power assertions. The children of these fathers (in this study clustering around a mode of 14 years of age) responded by avoiding them as much as possible. More than any other group of children in the study, they found their social involvement outside their families among their peers. They were always among the troublemakers at school and apparently internalized the anti-social power-assertive style which their fathers modeled.

Style 2: The Patriarch

Fathers high on this factor govern their families from a strong moral-religious base. Church membership and commitment are the father's focal concerns. Both the children and wives in these families agree that the final say in matters concerning the child rests with the father. This is likely to be a large family and the patriarch himself is likely also to have grown up in a large family. His occupation is liable to be blue collar and his background "ethnic."

His children tend not to do very well academically but this may very well be a function of other aspects of their ethnicity than their fathers' parenting style. In contrast to the children of autocratic fathers, they do not exhibit a high degree of antisocial behavior. Quite possibly this reflects the strong support and legitimacy which the subculture provides for their fathers' authority. The fact that his domination is rationalized and socially justified rather than viewed as hedonically derived is probably crucial. Very probably this father's behavior is, in fact, more under the supervision and control of his community. It is not only more legitimated but more lawbound.

Style 3: The Detached Provider

Fathers high on this factor agree with their wives that punitive interventions in their children's lives are to be avoided. Indeed, children in these families report very little contact with their fathers of any kind, punitive or otherwise. When they do spend time with their fathers it is likely to be in the context of a weekend outing or a family vacation. Typically, this father has a good upper-middle class job, a good income, and a good education. He reports himself to be quite concerned about the intellectual and cultural life of his family. Not too surprisingly, his children tend to do well in school. It appears that these fathers avoid the use of direct power confrontations and it may be inferred that they and their wives govern as the rule bound administrators of family policies.

Style 4: The Expressive Leader

Fathers high on this factor are described by their children and their wives as being warm and involved in the family. They, themselves, report frequent contact with their children and a major concern for family harmony and cohesiveness. They rate themselves good fathers. Among their children, both morale and school achievement are high. This style occurs relatively infrequently among step-fathers. Power confrontations almost never occur in these families. It is not even accurate to describe them as rule bound. Rather, relationships appear to be governed by principles affirming the importance of each person's point of view and the need for give and take in the interest of harmony.

Elsewhere (Broderick, 1975) I have suggested that these various styles of family interaction are analogous to Lawrence Kohlberg's (1964) three levels of moral reasoning. At the most primitive level moral reasoning is based on hedonistic principles. In our view this corresponds closely to the unilateral power impositions of the autocrat whose main concerns are focused upon his own needs above anyone elses. At the next level is the morality of conventional role conformity. In our view this comprehends both the traditional patriarchal style and the more modern detached provider style. Both are based on the principle of government by law rather than by personal impulse. Finally, Kohlberg's third level—the morality of self accepted moral principles—seems to correspond to the style of the expressive leader.

Now then, I have sketched four fathering styles and implied a fifth—the Absent Father Style—an important category which I am seeking a grant to study more fully. It is all very well to hiss the villainous Autocrats and cheer the warm and wonderful Expressive Leaders but assuming for the moment the validity of the typology, what further response is our profession capable of? If we grant that fathering is an important element in child outcome and that good fathering is better than bad fathering, what have we to offer to improve the general level of fathering in our society? For the remainder of this paper I should like to address that question.

The Social Determinants of Fathering Style

Marital Instability

Without question the major social determinant of fathering style is the stability of the father's marriage. Relatively little is known about the range of categories involved in the Absent Fathering style. Fathers, who through separation, divorce, or desertion do not live with their children, still affect the child's socialization through their absence as well as through the quality of whatever interaction with the child they may manage. We do know that as a group children with absent fathers (and no replacement) are disadvantaged in several ways.

We know more about the consequences of remarriage, of acquiring a step-father. It has already been noted that an undue number of step-fathers fall into the autocratic category and that the children of autocrats do poorly in school and in life, being prone to delinquency, dropping out of school and other unhappy life experiences. The WBSI study, however, reveals that the children of autocratic step-fathers exhibit fewer of these problems than the children of autocratic natural fathers. Kenneth Buhr (1974), in a separate analysis of some of the WBSI data, found that in step-father families the mother was likely to intervene between the child and the male parental figure. She was liable to attempt to insulate or compensate to a greater degree than in natural parent families. The fact that step-children, taken as a group, did as well as natural children in school, among their friends and in their own self esteem, seems to bear witness to the effectiveness of these mothers' compensatory efforts.

Thus, reconstituted families not only tend to be more effective socializing agents than one parent families, they tend to be more effective than natural parent families in which the father is an autocrat. Further, the advantage does not lie in the better behavior of the surrogate fathers but in the greater effectiveness of these remarried mothers. It is as though she felt constrained in the natural parent situation to keep out of the father-child conflicts based on some norm supporting the father's right to tyrannize his own child. In the reconstituted situation it appears that she feels freed of any such constraint and perhaps even defines her role as mediator between her husband and her children.

Thus, in some cases divorce and remarriage seem to result in benefit to the child. Yet, in the common case, it is surely conducive to better father-child relations to preserve the original family unit. Probably no other social change could result in as much improvement in father-child relations as reversing the trend toward more frequent divorce involving children. What contributions might we, as professionals, make to accomplish this reversal?

To answer, we might look at the classic model of marital stability outlined by Levinger (1965). He noted that four elements are involved in preserving marital stability: (a) a lack of viable alternatives to the marriage, (b) social barriers, that is, negative religious and social sanctions against divorce giving it higher social cost, (c) pragmatic bonds based on joint investments and the division of labor and (d) affectional bonds.

Let us examine each of these in turn to see where our intervention as professionals might be effective. First, the issue of alternatives. To begin with, would any of us wish to reduce the alternatives to marriage which have so recently become available to women especially? Would we reduce her career opportunities? Her access to government programs of support? I suspect that if she or he is to stay married, few of us would want it to be because there were no other choices. For that matter, if we felt otherwise, what skill or influence do we have or could we have to reverse the social changes which have resulted in those increased alternatives?

Second is the question of social barriers. Do we really want to increase the legal, social and religious costs of divorce? Could we if we wished to?

In 1960 Carle Zimmerman and Lucias Cervantez came out with a remarkable book. Entitled *Successful American Families,* it reported an unparalleled study of thousands of American families in eight major metropolitan centers across the nation. Yet most professionals in the field have never heard of the book and it appears on the shelves of few scholars. Why? Because the authors found that *successful* families (*i.e.,* those who avoided divorce, delinquency and other shameful failures) achieved their success partly through excluding unsuccessful families from their friendship network. The conclusion followed inevitably: if you would be successful—shun the failures. Keep the children of divorce away from your kids. Don't invite divorced families into your home and don't visit theirs.

It does not take much imagination to picture the uproar that this conclusion provoked in the year which brought John F. Kennedy into the White House. The volume was pilloried by professional and social critics alike. It became a rare book before its time. Yet the prescription is sociologically sound and would probably work. It is one of the few approaches that might have a chance of actually reversing the trend toward divorce. We reject it not because it is impractical but because it outrages our sense of social equity, or humanity. So probably we could not whip up much enthusiasm for increasing the social cost of divorce by shunning those who fail.

What about increasing pragmatic bonds, making men and women more dependent upon each other because of large families or a sharp division of labor along sex lines? I doubt we could generate a groundswell for those values at this point in our history.

That leaves increasing affectional bonds as the only remaining point at which family professionals might make a contribution to familial stability. After all, the researchers, educators and therapists among us have developed and evaluated various techniques for improving communication skills and other elements required for intimacy. Unhappily, it has not been demonstrated that these skills are as related to achieving stability as they are to achieving some elusive style of intimacy which we value. I would go so far as to suggest that we know almost nothing about teaching couples to commit well, to hang in when they are upset. On the contrary, we teach them not to put up with any garbage, to be assertive in demanding their own needs be met. We do not teach sacrifice or devotion to duty or any of the things which are related on the face of it to marital *stability* and much that is related to personal growth and achieving a full range of options and, in short, to marital instability.

Well, so much for our turning the rising divorce rate around. What other elements in society account for variation in fathers' style of interaction with their children?

Location in the Informal Social Network

In considering fathering styles we noted that one of the crucial differences between capricious power assertion and legitimate authority was the degree of connection of the family with a larger social network. Studies of child abuse show that the parents who neglect or abuse children are likely to be socially isolated parents. They are not in constant interaction with friends and relatives who might teach them what to expect from a child and how to treat a child. Those of us who work with such fathers (and mothers) find time after time that they have no concept of the developmental facts of life. If they yell at a crying 6-month-old baby to *shut up* and the baby continues to cry, they interpret it as defiance and conclude that the child must be taught a lesson, must be taught to *mind.* There is no one in their social world to tell them, "Hey, the kid's only 6 months old, she doesn't understand what you're talking about." "Don't worry, she'll understand when I get through with her." "Look, you just don't hit a 6-month-old like that—get hold of yourself." That exchange doesn't happen in most cases. There is no process of adult socialization and social control to reeducate and constrain these frustrated parents.

At the Estes Park meetings of NCFR, one physician who works with these parents reported a case where a mother (but it could have been a father) brought her 2½-year-old to the interview with her because she couldn't get a baby sitter. She was there because her 9-month-old baby had suffered 7 or 8 green-stick fractures at her hand. As the doctor invited her in from the waiting room, she told her 2½-year-old to wait for mommy and not to move out of her chair for the next 45 minutes. The doctor insisted that the little girl come in also. When she did she immediately noticed that the ash tray was full, emptied it in the waste basket and took a kleenex from a box on his desk to wipe it out with. When he commented on how unusual a performance this was, the mother said, "Oh, yes. She's mommy's little helper. She does almost all the house work." You see, she had no one to tell her that 2½-year-olds are too young to vacuum and wash dishes and do all the rest, so she proceeded to train her, using whatever training techniques were necessary. Can you imagine what those might be? But no one was in and out of her home on a regular basis to tell her, "Are you crazy? She's only 2½!"

The loose, spider web network of kin and friends so well described by Zimmerman and Sussman and Bott and Willmott and Young and all the rest, is the social matrix of the family. Parents and children succeed or fail in their roles partly as a function of whether they receive support and also control from the network. If that fragil fabric is torn, it is similar to what happens if the fabric of the of the ecological system is torn. It has consequences out of all proportion to the original violation.

While I was in Australia recently I discovered that in one of the states there, the government had responded heroically to the great influx of immigrants by building more housing units in a shorter time to meet their needs than any other agency ever had. They were proud of their response to the housing needs of these immigrants. They were appalled however when the suicide rate and mental illness and child abuse rates skyrocketed in these projects. For they had built miles upon miles of houses—good houses, well designed to accommodate these families —but with no parks, no stores, no pubs, no churches, no public buildings, no public transportation, no public space in the schools, no social agencies, no opportunities to meet. As one mother lamented, "We don't even have any place to meet to complain about no place to meet."

Unintentionally, they had created an environment that was diabolically effective at insulating families—at destroying the social ecology which keeps fathers and mothers and children on track.

While I was there they determined to set up a regular meeting of governmental department heads to evaluate the impact on families of their various projects and policies. That puts them a step ahead of our own nation.

But the point of all this is that as family researchers and policy advisors and educators and therapists concerned with, for one thing, how fathers behave toward their children, we need to consider the protection of the informal social network without which fathers fail. I am not sure we have ever perceived that as a central goal of the profession. I recommend we reconsider.

Availability of Adequate Fathering Models

One final issue that our own data have suggested as a crucial determinant of fathering style is the models available to fathers. We have noted that autocratic fathers may be the sons of autocratic fathers. Child abusers were most often abused themselves as children. Presumably the same patterns hold for the more effective styles. But one's own father is not the only model which influences fathering style.

Viktor Gekas (Note 1) has recently reviewed the impressive amount of evidence that fathering style is modeled partly on the style of interaction a man experiences in his daily occupation. Men who are themselves dominated by arbitrary employers or supervisors tend to take that as their model at home. Similarly, if they experience a respectful collegueship at work, it is easy to carry that pattern of interaction into the home. I suppose it is not surprising that how a man spends most of his waking hours should have some impact on his parenting style. But what do family scholars do with this observation? After all, what do we know about unionization, bureaucratization, decentralization and the other facets of the work world? That's the domain of another set of specialists. If changes in fathering depends upon developing better models in the work setting—do we have any idea of what to do to effect such changes?

Relatively little work has been done on intentional modeling in therapy or in group work although most people-changers hope to influence fathers in this way. Bernard Gurney and his colleagues at Penn State have worked specifically with mothers in providing them training and modeling opportunities in their "filial therapy" program but so far as I know they have not tackled fathers.

I suspect that most educators and therapists underestimate the power of modeling because we are so in to trying to change people by other forms of teaching. I remember on one occasion I got a telephone call from a former student whom I had done some counseling with early in my career. Now, ten years later she had married and had been to a whole roster of therapists, none of whom had helped her. She was sure that I could be of help. Would I let her fly out to work with me for a couple of intensive weeks. The temptation was enormous because I had *learned* so much in those 10 years. I had received training and clinical supervision and I had all those hours of additional experience. Despite everyone's advice not to touch it, I had her come for 10 days with the agreement that her husband approved and that she would accept a referral to a colleague back in her home community. She came and we worked every evening for three or four hours in some of the most intense therapy I had ever experienced. We went into layers that would have made Freud sit up and take notice. Meanwhile, since she had nothing to do all day every day, my wife was kind enough to have her come over to the house and be part of our family during the daylight hours.

After she had returned home and seen the therapist I referred her to for a couple of sessions he wrote me a "thank you for the referral" note. He complimented me on all I had accomplished and then, with a regretable lack of tact added, "I hope you won't be offended, however, if I tell you that she got a great deal more from your wife than from her sessions with you." You see, the woman had grown up in a chaotic, conflicted household and had established a chaotic, conflicted household of her own and had never seen an orderly, affectionate family operate. But for ten days she had watched an expert and that was what she took home with her. The therapist was so impressed with her improvement that he set up a program of "foster homes" for adult women from that type of background. He reported to me that it worked well but he quickly ran out of "model families" who were willing to be on display in that fashion.

At least it was a noble experiment. So far as I know no one has suggested a foster home for fathers who don't know how to be fathers. I suppose that would be even harder to manage but perhaps we at least might acknowledge the need for more powerful approaches than we now use.

Conclusion

At the beginning I indicated that this paper would put forth a perspective on the profession through the analysis of fathering and what we could do as a profession to improve it. Let me summarize my view by saying that we can only go one of two ways without deceiving ourselves.

First, and perhaps this is the more profitable route, we can increase in modesty. We can acknowledge that we deal with only a tiny portion of the important determinants of fathers' (and others') behavior, that we lack the knowledge, the skill and the power to reach very deeply into the matter. Divorce rates, social networks, occupational experiences and most other major social forces operate at an entirely different level than we know or can influence. Let us, if we follow this route take pride in an honorable profession which can deal successfully with 25% of the variance, with 75% of the problems of the small number of people who come to us. We do not have to do everything but we can make a contribution to life that is positive and real though undeniably modest.

I am not even sure there is a second route. If there is it involves addressing the larger issues even though they seem overwhelming —somehow finding out enough about divorce and work and social networks and fathers and ourselves and our government and economic institutions to put it all together a little differently. That is utopian. That is grandiose.

But for me, it comes down to this: we ought to claim less or do more—for fathers, for families, for ourselves.

REFERENCE NOTE

1. Gekas, V. *Assessing theories of social class and socialization.* Paper presented at the annual meeting of the National Council on Family Relations, New York City, October, 1976.

REFERENCES

Benson, L. *Fatherhood: A sociological perspective.* Brentan, NY: Random House, 1968.

Benton, M. *The American male.* New York: Coward-McCann, 1966.

Broderick, C.B. Power in the goverance of families. In D. Olsen & R. Cormwell (Eds.), *Power in families.* New York: Sage, 1975.

Buhr, K. Stress, marital interaction and personal competance in natural parent and step-father families. Unpublished doctoral dissertation, University of Southern California, 1974.

Kohlberg, L. Development of moral character and moral ideology. In M.L. Hoffman & L. W. Hoffman (Eds.), *Review of Child Development Research* (Vol. 1). New York: Russell Sage, 1964.

Levinger, G. Marital cohesiveness and dissolution: An integrative review. *Journal of Marriage and the Family,* 1965, **27**, 19-28.

Lynn, D. B. *The father: His role in child development.* Monterey, Calif.: Brooks/Cole, 1974.

Zimmerman, C.C, & Cervantez, L. *Successful American families.* New York: Pageant, 1960.

Single-parent Fatherhood: An Emerging Family Life Style*

DENNIS K. ORTHNER, TERRY BROWN, AND DENNIS FERGUSON**

This paper examines the growing phenomenon of fathers being primary parents due to widowhood, divorce, separation, or adoption. Changes in mortality rates, legal custody arrangements, and adoption procedures are analyzed as primary factors in altering the composition of single-parent fathers in the population. Interviews with 20 single-parent fathers consider the successes and strains they experience in childrearing, in using compensatory services, and in their own adult life style. Recommendations for supportive services and programs needed by these fathers are presented.

Fatherhood is receiving increased attention in the popular and professional literature. This seemingly new discovery that paternity and parenthood are reconcilable has been hailed by some as an important answer to the perceived decline in family stability. Nevertheless, this developing concern over fatherhood almost universally lies within the context of his role as a supplementary, or at best, complementary, parent. The status of primary parent is in little jeopardy of being dislodged from the mother, even if she shares in the provider responsibility for the household (Poloma & Garland, 1971; Holmstrom, 1972).

But in nearly a half-million families in the United States, the father is the primary parent because there is no mother present in the household. These men represent a growing dimension of both fatherhood and parenthood—the single parent father. Suggestions that single parenthood may be a pathological environment for childbearing are not new nor do they appear to have declined markedly. The concern in most cases, however, has been discussed and analyzed in terms of single mothers. The focus of the present paper is on the situation of the single parent father, some of the reasons why this phenomenon is growing, the strengths and stresses he faces, and the kinds of resources he needs to successfully meet his personal and parental responsibilities.

By definition, a single parent family consists of one parent and dependent children living in the same household. The resident parent may be single due to widowhood, divorce, separation, non-marriage, and more recently, single parent adoption. In the United States, there are over 4.5 million families with children under 18 headed by a single parent (U.S. Census Bureau, 1975). Approximately 90 percent of these families are headed by women and 10 percent are headed by men. These figures do not include those single parents who live with a relative or someone else who may be the head of the household. In general, fathers appear to represent a minority of single parents but this may be changing.

Factors Changing Single-Parent Fatherhood

There are several different means by which a male may receive exclusive cus-

*Data were collected under a grant from the North Carolina Department of Human Resources and Title IV-A, Special Projects, U.S. Social Security Administration. Appreciation is expressed for the sponsorship of the North Carolina Training Center for Infant-Toddler Care, Department of Child Development and Family Relations, University of North Carolina at Greensboro.

**Dennis K. Orthner is Assistant Professor; Terry Brown and Dennis Ferguson are graduate students in the Department of Child Development and Family Relations, University of North Carolina at Greensboro, Greensboro, N.C. 27412.

tody over minor children—death of his spouse, court designated custody of his children, and adoption. Each of these factors is undergoing considerable change and may result in a different pattern of single-parent fatherhood emerging.

Maternal Mortality

Over history, it has not been unusual for either men or women to be single parents. But prior to the twentieth century, the major cause of single-parenthood was the death of the marital partner. Because of the combination of a higher average age at marriage and a longer childbearing period with a higher adult mortality rate, many mothers and fathers were forced to rear their children without the other parent. While mortality rates were generally lower for women, men were not spared the combination of widowerhood and parenthood.

One of the most critical periods in the adult life cycle for women used to be the childbearing years. A casual glance at tombstones in old cemeteries reveals that many women died in childbirth, leaving the remaining children to their husbands. As recently as 1935, the maternal mortality rate was 58 deaths per 10,000 live births, which compares to today's rate of approximately 2.5 deaths per 10,000 births (U.S. Bureau of Census, 1975). Rapid advances in medical technology, improved methods of contraception, and more widespread access to prenatal medical attention and nutrition have largely accounted for this decline in maternal mortality. A by-product of these innovations has been a decline in the proportion of fathers who become single parents because of the deaths of their wives.

Custody Arrangements

The most significant influence on the recent acceptance of single parent fatherhood has been a change in the legal custody arrangements for minor children. Prior to 1960, very few fathers were awarded custody of their children and then, only in unusual circumstances. Fathers rarely contested the assumption of mother custody and if they did, the courts demanded that they prove the mother "unfit" for parenthood. Also, the backlog of divorce settlements rarely allowed a judge the luxury of carefully selecting between the two parental alternatives. This kind of social and legal process probably led Goode to make the following conclusion from his study of divorced women:

> There are many factors to make us believe that the father actually does approve of the custody arrangement that gives care of the child to the mother. Most of these factors may be classified under the headings of (a) the social role of the father; (b) male skills; and (c) allocation of time to occupation . . . These factors operate to make husband custody neither easy nor very desirable (to husbands) in our time. Consequently, we are inclined to believe our respondents when four out of five claim that their husbands agreed to the custodial arrangements, which almost always gave the custody to the wife (1956, 312-313).

It has been suggested by some persons in and outside the legal profession that certain "presumptions" may ease the strain of child custody contests. One such opinion that has received considerable attention was rendered by Ellsworth and Levy and prepared for the National Conference of Commissioners on Uniform State Laws:

> A uniform divorce act should contain a presumption that the mother is the appropriate custodian—at least for young children, and probably for children of any age . . . Since wives will, under most circumstances, be awarded custody regardless of the statutory standard, and since it seems wise to discourage traumatic custody contests whenever possible to do so, the act should discourage those few husbands who wish to contest by establishing a presumption that the wife is entitled to custody (1970, 202-203).

In contrast to these rather traditional perspectives, which may be valid in many cases, fathers who legitimately feel they have a right to custody of their children are beginning to get their day in court. No-fault divorce legislation, which has passed in some form in at least 41 states (Rosenberg & Mendelsohn, 1975) often includes increased rights to negotiation for children on the part of fathers. A provision in the statutes of Colorado was designed to give both fathers and mothers equal rights to their children after divorce (Ellsworth & Levy, 1970). The spirit of these new regulations is summed up well in the report of the California Governor's Commission on the Family:

> We believe that the Court should make a custody disposition which as nearly as possible meets the needs of the child, and that it should be able to do so with minimum harm to all parties involved . . . The role of the women in today's society is substantially different from what it was when the preference [for the mother] was formulated; and we agree with the Assembly Committee on Judiciary that in a substantial number of cases, the preference prevents the father from asserting his custodial right and leads to a result incompatible with

the child's best interest (California Assembly Reports, 1966, 154-161).

The new roles of women are also having their effect on fatherhood. The wife-mother "drop-out" or desertion phenomenon is beginning to be noted in the popular literature. Women are demanding more opportunities in the world outside the home and many are placing more emphasis on these goals than on parenthood. In light of this, the courts are now giving more favorable attention to fathers receiving exclusive child custody if their partner rejects the child, even if they are not married (Schlesinger, 1966). In Illinois, a state-statute had held that unmarried fathers were unfit to have custody of their children. However, in the case of Stanley vs. Illinois, the U.S. Supreme Court held that this law was unconstitutional, breaking further ground for the rights of single-parent fathers.

There is some evidence that these legal and social changes are beginning to be seen in the single-parent statistics. While the proportion of men who were granted legal custody of their children during the 1950's was about 10 percent (Goode, 1956), it now appears that men are increasing this percentage. Between 1965 and 1972, a period of rapidly rising divorce rates, the number of independent divorced and separated mothers heading households increased by 58 percent but the number of divorced and separated fathers heading households alone increased by 71 percent over that period ("Rising Problems of Single-parents", 1973). This difference in rate of increase means that by 1972, over 13 percent of the single parent households resulting from divorce or separation were headed by fathers. By comparison, the number of single-parent households that resulted from spouse mortality only increased from 1965 to 1972 eight percent for fathers and three percent for mothers, comparable to the rise in the size of the overall population. Undoubtedly, divorce and separation are rapidly replacing death as the major cause of single-parenthood, even among fathers.

Single-Parent Adoption

At the present time, adoption is only a minor factor in single-parent fatherhood. With the decline in the birthrate and rise in abortions, demand for adoptable children by intact families, the preferred choice of the agencies, far exceeds the supply. Nevertheless, regulations are changing and the number of single adoptive parents is increasing. Between 1968 and 1974, there were 50 recorded in New York City but this is only indicative of a nationwide trend ("Single Adoptive Parents Unite", 1974). Typically, single persons can only adopt children who are hard-to-place, i.e., those who are older, mixed racially, or handicapped (Kadushin, 1970). Male single parents, who make up only a small minority of these adoptions, are almost routinely limited to male children.

Characteristics of Single-Parent Fathers

There is surprisingly little information in the literature on the life-style of single-parent fathers. In an attempt to partially remedy this situation, lengthy semi-structured interviews were conducted with 20 of these fathers from the Greensboro, North Carolina area. The fathers were studied as part of a larger investigation of the overall situation of male and female single-parents. The sample is not considered to be necessarily representative of all single-parent fathers, but because of a deliberate attempt to locate fathers from different socioeconomic backgrounds, we do have some idea of the breadth of the experiences they represent. Each of the fathers studied has custody of the children who are living with him. Preschool children between the ages of 18 months and five years are found in 10 of the households, while the remaining 10 have school-age children between the ages of six and 17 years. Nine of the men are living with one child, nine with two children, and two with three children. The youngest father is 25 years of age and the oldest is 64, while the average age of the fathers is 37 years.

The fathers in this study represent a variety of reasons for single-parenthood, with the exception of single-parent adoption. Only three of the men are widowers which supports the decline of female mortality as a factor in single-parenthood. Fifteen of the fathers in the sample have their children as a result of divorce or separation. A highly unusual phenomenon is the situation of the never married father, yet two of our respondents fall into this category.

It is not too surprising to find that the average social status level of the single-parent fathers is above the norm. For a man to get custody of minor children, he has to demonstrate a degree of resource availability that will be respected by the courts, his peers, and perhaps his former spouse. Twelve of the men we interviewed are in professional or managerial positions, another is in sales. There are only five blue-collar men in the sample and the remaining two included a student and a previous manager who is unemployed. Sixteen of the fathers had some post-high school education; 13 held college degrees and nine had advanced or professional degrees. Their average annual income exceeded $18,000. Concerted but comparatively unsuccessful attempts to locate lower income single parent fathers suggests that their frequency is lower in the population and that they may remarry faster than those men with higher incomes.

Even though these fathers appear to have the resources that will enable them to be competent fathers, a majority of the 15 divorced or separated fathers received custody because their former wives did not want or were unable to care for the children. It is difficult to tell if this is the pattern nationally but in this sample, fathers reported getting the children because of desertion, mental illness, drug and alcohol abuse, or general instability of their wives. Many of the men, in short, received custody of their children on the basis of spouse allocation rather than adjudication.

Adult Life Style

Almost all of the fathers interviewed reported an active social life. Without a spouse in the house, this is a primary means by which single parents are able to derive adult companionship. While half of the men restricted most of their activities to their children, female friends, or themselves, the other half indicated a substantial amount of interest in activities with their male friends. It might be anticipated that male friends of the single-parent fathers would also be single but there was no indication that acquaintances were limited to other singles. In fact, while female single-parents are sometimes given derisive labels such as "wife snatcher" or "she devil" (Burgess, 1970), single fathers do not appear to feel these same negative images. Perhaps, by being male, they are perceived as having the traditional freedom for initiating social contact with women and are not considered to be as threatening to intact marriages as women who more passively attract a male suitor.

An important part of the life-style of single-parent fathers is dating. All but one of the fathers reported some recent dating activity and most of the men considered themselves to be "dating around" rather than seeing one person exclusively. This was somewhat surprising since, on the average, these fathers had been single parents for almost three years. We had anticipated some desire to remarry, if for no other reason than just to alleviate their parental strain. But, contrary to our expectations, these fathers considered themselves to be quite satisfied with their life-style and in no hurry to once again marry. Only half of the sample considered marriage in their future plans with the remainder unsure of marriage and presently committed to remaining single.

Sex is one area of their adult social life that generated some concern on the part of the fathers. One-third of them indicated rather frequent sexual contacts and others may have been less inclined to discuss this. Part of their sensitivity emerged when they were asked about their attitudes on cohabitation. Over two-thirds of the fathers viewed this as totally unacceptable for themselves and in direct contradiction to their parental responsibility to be sexually discrete. The majority felt that "living together" is an acceptable means for other persons to test their relationship prior to marriage but they could not see themselves so involved. In addition to the felt need for sexual discretion, the fathers commonly rejected cohabitation on the grounds that it would "lack permanence" and that "children need someone they can count on."

Parental Responsibilities and Attitudes

The professional literature commonly states that a two-parent environment does not automatically insure good childrearing and conversely, a one parent family does not mean an inadequate childrearing situation (e.g., Hill, 1968; Nye, 1957). The majority of the interviewed single-parent fathers have come to believe this and, defensively, they state that one parent is often better than two *if* the two cannot live together happily. Most seem to feel, nevertheless, that the best situation for the child is a stable two parent relationship.

The efficacy of daughters being reared by their fathers has frequently been questioned. The courts have traditionally looked askance at this and rarely in a contested case do judges grant a father custody of a girl. The fathers we interviewed were somewhat split on the issue of whether boys and girls should be brought up the same or differently; 12 felt they should be reared the same and eight, differently. But the fathers who had daughters were more likely to note the need for differences in socialization. Two of the fathers had daughters who were going through puberty at the time and they expressed considerable dismay about having to give them "proper" sex education. This should not be taken to mean that these fathers felt less competent in rearing daughters. Many mothers, in fact, share the same concerns. The fathers in question considered problems such as this to be situational, not continual and, overall, they felt they were quite successful in rearing their daughters.

The majority of the problems in adjusting to single parenthood come from harmonizing parental and adult roles and responsibilities. In many ways, the feelings of these fathers are similar to those expressed by many working mothers who also have to reconcile their adult and primary parent roles. Common problems mentioned by the fathers are lack of patience and time for their children, making decisions alone, and having to be away from their children more than they want to be. The fathers generally felt they demanded more independence in their children than other parents might.

An interesting change in attitude about parenting seems to have taken place in many of the fathers, particularly among those who had previously held more traditional role expectations. Since becoming single parents, these fathers became much more appreciative of the responsibilities of being the primary parent. In particular, they had become less discipline oriented, more concerned about the adequacy of day care, more interested in education, and more protective of their children. One case was particularly striking. A father of a preschool child was the president of a small textile firm. He had never been very concerned about the child care responsibilities of his female employees; he took it for granted that plenty of facilities were available. But when he became a single parent, he too faced the plight of finding adequate day care. Now he is thinking in terms of operating a professionally run day care center at his plant as a benefit for his employees.

Parent-Child Relationship

It is difficult to tell what the "real" relationship is between two or more persons when only one person is queried. But it is strikingly evident that the fathers we interviewed feel they have good parent-child rapport. All of them report a relationship with their children which is "close" and "affectionate." Two-thirds of the fathers feel that their children are having family experiences similar to those of most other children their age.

The desire to compensate for being the only parent by giving as much time as possible to their children was a common theme. The list of recent activities they participated in included, everything from camping trips to regular attendance at local plays. All but two of the fathers reported that at times they even take their children along on dates. This gives their children some idea of the kind of woman they enjoy being with and serves to approximate, for an afternoon or an evening at least, something like an intact family.

The Use of Role Compensating Services

The single parent father's situation is such that he requires special services rendered from a variety of sources. His needs are special since a single parent, by virtue of his situation, must somehow compensate for the roles lost or shared with a marital partner. Areas from which this compensation may come include child care arrangements, government assistance, single parent organizations, domestic help, and kinship networks.

Child Care Arrangements

Single parent fathers are usually employed and rarely do they receive alimony or child support. Since all but one of our fathers were employed, this necessitated establishing some kind of care arrangements for their children during working hours.

The most commonly used arrangement by fathers of preschool children involved day care centers or nursery schools. Only one child was cared for by a relative, in this case, the father's sister. Another father placed his child in a half-day nursery school program, with a live-in nanny for afternoon care. These arrangements are consistent with the finding that most of our fathers preferred group care to at home care by a friend, relative, or nanny. A majority felt that the teaching program was the most important criterion in selecting a child care arrangement; safety and security came second. When asked if they preferred male or female caregivers, or both equally, the answers were evenly split between preferring both equally and preferring female caregivers.

For most of the fathers, child care has not presented a major problem to their employment. When they were asked if child care problems had interfered with their work, 88 percent said no. In one case, however, a father did lose his job because of his new parental responsibilities. Because of interruptions in his work schedule to see teachers periodically, take the child to a physician, or other such responsibilities, he began to get unfavorable evaluations and, in a tight economy, was fired.

One half of the fathers in the sample had children of school age. After-school care for these children varied from fulltime housekeeper, female relative, or older sibling to no supervision at all. Those with children over the age of nine provided no supervision for the period between the end of a school day and the end of the father's working day.

Caregiving services utilized by single parent fathers, other than during working hours, were minimal. With the exception of dating, most of the fathers reported taking their children shopping, on short errands, and visiting friends. Only four fathers reported taking their children on evening dates or to club meetings. Child care for those situations was arranged with babysitters, friends, relatives, or older siblings.

Government Assistance

There are a variety of governmental assistance programs that can help subsidize the income of single-parents. These include such things as food stamps, child care scholarships, social security, G. I. Bill, public housing, Aid-to-Families of Dependent Children (AFDC), and so on. Programs such as AFDC, however, are much more likely to go to single-parent mothers than fathers, according to local and state sources. Again, the higher average income of most of these fathers does not make them as dependent on public support but part of the reason is also the matter of demonstrating their independence and competence as parents; sometimes this is required if they are to maintain custody of their children.

This independence was particularly evident in the sample of fathers we interviewed. One-third received some form of public assistance, including social security, G. I. Bill, and food stamps, but rarely was this tied to their being a single-parent. Funds which some might have received in the form of child care subsidies of AFDC were not requested. When asked if they felt the government should help them financially because they were single parents, a majority of the fathers responded negatively. Of the seven who answered affirmatively, five specified tax breaks as the area in which the government should provide assistance. One respondent mentioned that any school experiences through college should be tax deductible.

Single-Parent Organizations

There are several different types of organizations which serve the needs of single parent fathers. Recreational and dating opportunities are the primary draw of the singles and solo parent clubs that abound in this and other areas. Informational programs on single parenthood are run by the Family Life Council and other community and religious agencies. Parents Without Partners, which had just been organized locally prior to our investigation, attempts to provide for both the informational and social needs of single-parents.

The question of the effectiveness of these organizations in meeting the needs of single parent fathers drew mixed reactions. Half of the fathers had attended meetings of some singles oriented group and half of these found them therapeutic and emotionally supportive. Organizations such as Parents Without Partners were considered to be especially beneficial and informative. One problem that is evident, however, is the lack of supportive organizations for the lower income single-parents. Many of the men who do not participate do not go because they find babysitting money hard to come by or they are uncomfortable in the "status-seeking" (which might be called independence-assertiveness") that goes on in most of these organizations.

The sex ratio in singles organizations also has its advantages and disadvantages for the single-parent father. Since women far outnumber men, the men find it easy to meet a variety of women. But at the same time, the men find themselves uncomfortable being in the minority and "being chased" by their more aggressive counterparts. One father expressed his feelings this way: "I'll never go to another one of those meetings. All those women want is a father for their children and they'll do anything to get me!" This is not a unique reaction and this "fear of being trapped" kept several of the non-participants away.

Household Services

It may be assumed that the single parent, especially the single parent father, would seek help in doing household duties. However, three-fourths of the fathers reported no help with house work. Of those receiving help, only one had a full-time housekeeper. The remaining employers of housekeepers had this service on a part-time basis only.

Since a majority of the fathers reported receiving no help with the housework, one might suspect the fathers encourage their children to do household chores. When asked if their children ever help out at home, most fathers said they did. The preschool children were usually responsible for picking up their toys, and the older children helped with the preparation of meals. In essence, the older the child, the more help he provided around the house.

Kinship Support

Parents of single parents were found to be generally supportive, providing emotional assurance, child care, financial and housekeeping assistance. Two-thirds of the fathers reported that their parents supported them with one or more of the aforementioned functions (the parents of four of the interviewed fathers were deceased). The majority have contact with their parents weekly or more than weekly; only two reported having no contact with parents who were living. Relatives were commonly used for child care during periods when the father needed time to adjust to new situations; sometimes this lasted for several months. When family problems arise, the majority of fathers contact their relatives, especially their parents. The next most consulted group consists of friends, then professional counselors. One father reported that he also discussed problems with his minister.

Conclusion

It is difficult to generalize from the limited data we have presented to all single-parent fathers, but the issues that have been raised and the results considered appear to be representative of the concerns these fathers express. We have tried to go beyond most research on fatherhood and actually ask the fathers themselves about their lifestyles, their problems and successes. We also tried to avoid using only a clinical population that might have biased our results toward a pathology of parenthood. In general, we feel that each of these fathers represents a different, unique situation with an underlying thread of commonality.

If there is one most impressive conclusion we can make from our interviews with single-parent fathers, it is this: these fathers feel quite capable and successful in their ability to be the primary parent of their children. The confidence they express and the satisfaction they seem to derive in fatherhood is very difficult to deny. We had anticipated a significant problem with role strain and adjustment to being the primary parent but we found little evidence that this is a major handicap. All of the fathers experienced some problems but these were not unlike the difficulties experienced in most families. The sense of pride in being able to cope with the challenge of parenthood and seeing their children mature under their guidance is a major compensating force.

Single-parent fathers appear to be taking advantage of the trend toward allowing men to be more nurturing. Some of them received custody because they felt they were more nurturing than their wives, and others were allocated their children because their wives felt less capable of being a nurturing parent. Hopefully, the notion that fathers are the instrumental leaders of the family while mothers control the expressive roles (Parsons & Bales, 1955) has been laid to rest. Most of the fathers expressed some concern over their ability to be a nurturing parent; they wanted to know if they spent enough time reading and playing with their children, if they were understanding things at the child's level, and if they should get more involved in their children's education. But these concerns are similar to those of most parents and, overall, the single-parent fathers felt quite comfortable in their expressive roles.

Some recent attempts to examine fatherhood have suggested that single-parent fathers may tend to over-use "mother substitutes" (Biller & Meredith, 1975; Weiss, 1975) to the detriment of the child. We did not find this to be the pattern at all. Day care was almost universally used but evening and weekend time was quite carefully allocated to their children. There were exceptions to this at times, but these were exceptions, not the rule.

In those areas where the single-parent fathers do indicate strain, solutions could be forthcoming if some of the following recommendations are considered:

1. *Day care facilities that extend services into the evenings.* Several of the fathers found that they sometimes had to work late and the hours of most day care centers put them into uncomfortable dilemmas in their jobs. Other fathers would have liked knowing that there were facilities for taking care of their children in the evenings when they had spur-of-the-moment opportunities to go out for dinner or something else. Locating a babysitter at the last minute is a commonly repeated problem.
2. *Child care facilities in shopping centers.* This is an extension of the first recommendation. With small children, shopping can be very burdensome and for single-parents particularly, having child care available at the shopping center would shorten the time required and make the experience less frustrating for all concerned.
3. *Organizing of babysitting cooperatives.* Most fathers do not know how to operate a babysitting cooperative and many might be interested in its cost-saving advantages. Several of the fathers expressed a desire for this kind of service.
4. *Transportation of children to and from day care centers.* It is often difficult for a working parent to transport children from school to an after-school child care center. There are other times when, because of location of the work situation, a father would prefer to have a child returned home from the child care center to the care of an older sibling or someone else until he arrives.
5. *Classes on single-parenthood.* Most of the fathers expressed considerable dismay over their lack of preparation for parenthood. Rarely did they have the time to learn what to expect from their children. They had depended on their wives for that. Lack of information raised their anxiety and some orientation course would have been helpful. The seminars on this subject that are presented in the local community are very well attended but they need to be made available to even more persons, particularly fathers with lower incomes.
6. "*Big sisters.*" A counterpart to "Big brother" type organization is needed for those fathers who are rearing daughters. In many cases, these are arranged informally and it is probably easier for fathers to find adult female companions for the daughters than for mothers to find male companions for their sons. But not all fathers find it easy to locate women who really want to help their daughters instead of finding a husband.

These recommendations are not exclusive to single-parent fathers. Most of them also apply to single-parent mothers and other persons as well. Leadership in implementing these and other suggestions might fruitfully be undertaken by local Family Life Councils, churches, community agencies, and single-parent organizations.

Single-parent fathers, themselves, seem to have demonstrated the willingness and ability to competently handle parenthood. If the support and resources they need can be garnered, there is every reason to believe that they can and will rear responsible children. There is little doubt that the number of single-parent fathers will grow, because of their own demands and the gradual shifting of responsibilities in the family. Now is the time to develop the programs and leadership to help fathers better adapt to their changing roles and relationships.

REFERENCES

Biller, H. & Meredith, D. *Father power*. New York: Anchor Press/Doubleday, 1975.

Burgess, J. The single-parent family: A social and sociological problem. *Family Coordinator*, 1970, **19**, 137-144.

California assembly reports, 1963-1965. Sacramento, California State Assembly, 1966.

Ellsworth, P. & Levy, R. Legislative reform and child support adjudication. *Law and Society Review*, 1970, **4**, 166-225.

Goode, W. *After divorce*. New York: Free Press, 1956.

Hill, R. Social stresses on the family. In M. Sussman (Ed.), *Sourcebook in marriage and the family*, (3rd ed.). Boston: Houghton, 1968.

Holmstrom, L. *The two-career family*. Cambridge, Mass.: Schenkman, 1972.

Kadushin, A. Single-parent adoptions: An overview: Some relevant research. *Social Science Review*, 1970, **44**, 263-274.

Nye, I. Child adjustment in broken and unhappy homes. *Marriage and Family Living*, 1965, **27**, 333-343.

Parsons, T. & Bales, R. *Family, socialization, and interaction process*. New York: Free Press, 1955.

Poloma, M. & Garland, T. The married professional woman: A study in the tolerance of domestication. *Journal of Marriage and Family*, 1971, **33**, 531-540.

Rising problems of single-parents. *U.S. News and World Reports*, July 16, 1973, 32-35.

Rosenberg, B., & Mendelsohn, E. Legal status of women in the council of state governments. In *The book of the states*, 1974. (Available from the U.S. Women's Bureau)

Schlesinger, B. The one-parent family: An overview. *Family Coordinator*, 1966, **15**, 133-138.

Single adoptive parents unite. *New York Times*, July 22, 1974, 24.

U.S. Census Bureau. Washington, D.C.: Government Printing Office, 1975.

Weiss, R. *Marital separation*. New York: Basic Books, 1975.

Parents

Parent and Family Life Education

The Parent and Family Life Education staff in Columbus, Ohio, developed two approaches for teaching parents to be parents.

by Douglas B. Bailey
Robert L. Lindamood

Family life education programs for parents are more likely to meet the needs and expectations of program participants when the participants themselves help to plan, implement and evaluate these programs. With the foregoing opinion as their fundamental viewpoint, the Parent and Family Life Education (P&FLE) staff at Franklin County Children Services (FCCS), a social service agency covering the greater Columbus, Ohio, metropolitan area, embarked upon a parent education project intended to "help children by first helping their parents to improve their child rearing skills." This article describes the two basic program development methods used in the FCCS project.

Douglas B. Bailey is director of the Parent and Family Life Education Department, Franklin County Children Services in Grove City, Ohio. Robert L. Lindamood is director of the Community Services Division, Franklin County Children Services.

The first method uses as its basic approach, the development of programs by local planning committees from specific geographical target areas. The basic approach of the second method is the construction of predesigned programs for parents who are FCCS clients.

In the approach that uses local planning committees from designated geographical areas, six target areas within Franklin County were selected at the outset of the project. They included

- an elementary school attendance area in a suburban, middle class neighborhood;
- a school district for a village and surrounding rural area;
- an elementary school attendance area in a predominantly white, low income, Appalachian section of Columbus;
- a junior high school attendance area in a blue collar, lower middle income section of Columbus;
- a settlement house service area in a low income Columbus neighborhood with a racially-varied population; and
- a Columbus low income housing project in a predominantly black neighborhood.

These suburban, rural, and urban areas were selected to determine whether or not the same program development model (based on the use of local planning committees) could function effectively in vastly different types of communities and neighborhoods. In five of the six target areas the planning committee method of program development proved to be successful. Although planning committees did succeed in launching programs in the low income housing project, this target area had to be dropped because local residents were unwilling to enroll in *groups* as such—educational, political, social, etc.—and the P&FLE Department was not authorized to attempt other educational alternatives besides the group approach.

The planning committee in a target area consists of parents who want to enroll in a parent education program and who are willing to help in planning and implementing this program. The planning committee works directly with a P&FLE staff person and has various functions to perform in regard to program planning, implementation, and evaluation.

The committee's responsibilities in program planning include selecting the program topic, deciding what questions and concerns that topic will cover, assisting the P&FLE staff person in deciding upon a family life specialist to be invited to be the program instructor, deciding upon the number of program sessions to be scheduled, selecting the program dates and meeting place, assigning committee members to take charge of various practical details and arrangements, and evaluating.

Program implementation tasks include making publicity posters, encouraging friends and neighbors to attend the program, and making follow-up phone calls to program participants who are absent from a session. Also in the middle income target areas, these tasks include furnishing refreshments and providing a volunteer babysitting service for children of program participants at the meeting place where the program is being held. In the low income target areas, the P&FLE Department provides the refreshments and hires a paid babysitter.

Program evaluation is a vital function of the planning committee. Along with the usual evaluation task of providing feedback after the conclusion of a program, the committee's most important job is to issue weekly feedback to the P&FLE staff throughout the duration of the program, so that the program's learning activities can be continually monitored and revised whenever changes are indicated.

The P&FLE staff person assigned to a target area follows a regular cycle in getting a program launched. This cycle begins at a program's final session when the staff person recruits a new planning committee for the next program and surveys the program participants to receive their suggestions for future program topics. The staff person meets with the new planning committee to review the topic survey results, select a topic, and decide upon an instructor to conduct the program. Then the staff person hires an instructor who is a qualified family life specialist from a community agency, local school system, or educational institution. This instructor and the staff person meet with the planning committee to work out the final details for the program.

The P&FLE staff person arranges for a meeting place where the program will be held, and commits the program publicity tasks to the FCCS media relations specialist who prepares news articles and school fliers for children to take home. The instructor and the P&FLE staff person keep in close contact throughout the program and work together to evaluate each participant's progress and the program's overall effectiveness. The staff person attends only the final session of a middle income target area program. However, the staff person either attends and helps to facilitate all sessions at a low income target area program, *or* has a social work student (in field placement with the agency) serve as observer and teacher aid at all program sessions.

"The first method uses as its approach, the development of programs by local planning committees from specific geographical areas."

Program topics generally are selected from a survey list of 45 topics by planning committee members and other parents enrolled in programs. These topics encompass the three broad areas of family relationships, home economics, and community concerns that affect the family unit. However, often the planning committee's chosen topic is a combination of two or three topics on the list. Also, planning committees frequently come up with original topics not mentioned on the list. Some typical target area programs have included titles such as Family Communication Skills; Your Child—A Responsible, Unique Individual; Parents Are People; How to Stretch Your Dollar; and Your Children and the Public Schools.

A second and different approach to program development was adopted in order to launch programs specifically for parents who are FCCS clients. Pre-designed programs are developed for clients, only because it has not been possible to work out arrangements within the agency so that the planning committee approach could be used. In order to make topic selection simpler for caseworkers to handle so they may refer clients to programs, the list of 45 topics was condensed to five topics representing the three broad subject areas mentioned above and including building parents' self-esteem, parent-child communication, basic homemaker skills such as food preparation, and problem solving and planning skills to help a client take advantage of community resources (i.e., adult education, job training, settlement house program, etc.) The parent-child communication topic was subdivided to include separate programs for parents of preschoolers, parents of elementary school age children and junior high youth, and parents of junior high and senior high teenagers. The initial sets of client programs were designed and conducted generally by instructors who already had proven themselves to be effective as instructors for the P&FLE Department's target area programs. The format of programs has been continually revised as necessary.

The P&FLE staff person assigned to a client program must be able to line up an instructor who is highly adept at relating to clients' characteristic strengths, limitations, and feelings. As in the case of the majority of the low income target area programs, the staff person must personally attend and monitor any client program which has a format that is largely experimental, tentative, and unproven. Although social work students are being assigned the prime responsibility to assist the instructors in client programs that have proven themselves, the staff person, nevertheless, must carefully supervise the work of the student.

In consulting with caseworkers about their clients, the staff person must make sure that the caseworker has sufficiently screened the client's needs before referring the client to a particular program. Also, he must be aware of various educational resources in the community to which caseworkers can refer clients. Furthermore, he must be able to suggest to the caseworker a developmental sequence of programs suited to a particular client's interests and goals. In order to receive clients' input and feedback, the staff person must converse with clients at program sessions and must also make periodic telephone calls or visits to clients in their homes. During the course of a program, the staff person keeps case managers and caseworkers informed regarding their clients' progress and any problems related to their clients' attendance and participation. The effective implementation of client programs is very much dependent upon the P&FLE staff persons being able to integrate the expertise of the instructor, the service objectives of the agency, and the client's motivations and concerns.

In comparing the merits of the P&FLE Department's two methods of program development, both the target area program model and the client program model can produce high quality programs and require about the same amount of effort on the part of P&FLE staff. The critical factor in the task of program implementation is the extent to which effective publicity and recruitment channels are available. The suburban and rural target area programs generally have made their attendance goals with the aid of news publicity in the local community weekly newspapers and program announcement fliers sent home to parents from the public schools. However, the urban low income target areas have not made their attendance quotas. There are no local neighborhood newspapers in these urban areas and publicity fliers have very little impact. Further efforts of planning committee members to recruit other parents in the low income target areas have had limited effectiveness. It now appears that the recruitment task in these areas will need additional personnel who would visit the homes of low income residents, provide family life information and instruction to individual parents in their homes, and eventually persuade these parents to form an educational group in their neighborhood.

In contrast to the low income target areas which must depend upon "neighbors recruiting neighbors," the client programs have the advantage of an available "professional recruiter," namely the agency caseworker who personally recruits the client. The client programs do a better job than the suburban, rural and urban target area programs in reaching the parent who strongly resists enrolling in any type of educational or group activity.

The primary advantage of the target area programs in comparison with the client programs is that the planning committee approach gives the majority of program participants a strong sense of "ownership" and incentive to continue enrolling. Client programs may also produce enthusiastic participants who continue to enroll in programs over a period of time. However, there are always those client participants compelled to attend programs because "my caseworker sent me" or "so that the agency (hopefully) will return my kids from the foster home, if I do what they tell me to do." This attitude definitely hampers clients' ability to gain insight about themselves and their parental responsibilities. Instructors, nevertheless, do a remarkable job of helping clients (who often resent the caseworker's authority) to deal constructively with their hostile feelings and become genuinely interested in learning how to improve their parental competence. Although various bureaucratic hurdles have made it difficult to include the planning committee approach in the system for launching client programs, this feature would be highly desirable as a means of strengthening a client's sense of "ownership" and personal responsibility for learning. The planning committee approach as a component of client program development could be one step in the direction of helping clients overcome the sense of dependency imposed by the welfare system.

After nearly three years, P&FLE program instructors, community residents, agency clients, case mangers, and caseworkers are convinced that the department is directed rightly in its overall approach to family life education for Franklin County parents.

"Parent and Family Life Education," by Douglas B. Bailey and Robert L. Lindamood, Lifelong Learning: The Adult Years, October 1977 (Vol. 1, No. 2) Adult Education Association of the USA. Washington, D.C.

Programs for Parents of Infants and Young Children

Parent education has become a component of an increasing number of educational, medical and social service programs directed toward the welfare of very young children. This emphasis recognizes the parents' role as the major educators of their preschool children and offers them new skills and knowledge to further the development of their children through their natural daily activities and relations. In addition, many programs teach parents how to impart basic skills to their child, how to recognize early psychological and physical difficulties and, where necessary, how to provide remedial help for any recognized deficiency, supplementing professional aid.

Because programs for educating parents can be offered in a wide range of settings and for several different purposes, it is not possible to establish a single set of criteria regarding their quality. However, two guidelines should be kept in mind. On the one hand, programs developed for parents by professionals in any field cannot be implemented successfully without serious input by the parents whom the program is to serve. On the other hand, while addressing the expressed needs of parents, the programs must be founded on a firm base of professional information and skills. A balance must be achieved between respect for the autonomy and private goals of the family and the value of the professional instruments and knowledge that can enhance the capabilities of the family in rearing its children.

The emphasis in parenting programs should not rest on imparting information but in teaching skills. For example, it is not enough to simply tell parents that it is better to speak to their children in full sentences; they should be shown ways of talking and playing with the child, criteria for selecting toys appropriate to the child's age and interests, and skills in reading to a child or telling a story. Parents need to know not only that play is the child's way of learning but also how, realistically, they can provide opportunities for exploration and discovery, for manipulation and for identification of the various elements of the environment.

Parent education programs have been useful components in a variety of institutional settings such as schools, hospitals, clinics and day care centers. In addition, a number of home-based programs, primarily for remedial purposes, have been developed and are beginning to be disseminated under the auspices of school systems, medical programs and state agencies. Less formal approaches such as drop-in centers and toy libraries have sprung up as independent projects or as adjuncts to larger programs. Two other approaches to education for parenthood are worthy of note: parent-implemented programs and the use of public media. Moreover, there are several model federal programs that offer comprehensive services to young children by working through the parents and the home setting.

Descriptions of such programs and settings are offered below as concrete examples of approaches states might sponsor or encourage.

1. *School-related parent education programs.* School-related parent education programs have long been offered under such traditional auspices as adult education and the Parent-Teachers Association. Most of these programs provide information on improved housekeeping, better money management, preparation of more nutritional meals and sewing. Many classes also include some instruction in child development and child management. The expectation is the same in both cases—that, with greater knowledge, parents will be able to better provide for the child's physical, social and emotional well-being. While such programs have had a loyal though limited following, little is known about their effect upon parent behavior.

Recently, new curricula for this type of program have been developed that focus specifically on improving certain skills of the parents. Mothers learn new songs and games to play with their children, and they learn to make educational games and toys from inexpensive household objects, such as counting books made from magazine pictures and sorting and matching activities using miscellaneous household items and an egg carton for a sorting tray. The emphasis on applied skills—things parents can do—rather than on general information appears to be effective in enhancing the interaction between parent and child.

a. *Family-oriented programs.* A far more extensive program has been developed by a school district in St. Cloud, Minnesota. Under the Family Oriented Structured Preschool Activity program, any parent with a child between ages 2 and 5 may come to a center for a six-day orientation course of specific activities and materials for at-home learning. At the same time, the child is evaluated for skills in five areas. After the orientation week the parent is given an activity kit designed by staff members to enhance the child's abilities in any areas where he appeared weak. Enrichment kits are available for children whose abilities are exceptional. Parents can return weekly for conferences with staff members and every six weeks for group sessions with staff and other parents. The program is open without cost to parents of any social or economic group.[2]

b. *A comprehensive approach—the BEEP program.* An ambitious program that uses the schools as the sponsoring institution is the Brookline (Massachusetts) Early Education Project (BEEP). A combination center-home visitor program sponsored by the Brookline public schools in conjunction with Children's Hospital in Boston and the Preschool Project of the Harvard Graduate School of Education, BEEP offers a comprehensive approach to diagnostic and educational services for very young children and their parents, from the prenatal period until school entrance. By offering an unusual opportunity for pediatricians and educators to work together, BEEP can provide an array of services to families from a wide range of backgrounds. Heavy emphasis is placed on diagnostic services so that no child progresses through the preschool years with an undetected educational or physical handicap. For most parents, these services provide reassurance about their child's health, as well as extensive information about growth and development. For parents whose children need extra help, a referral system ensures that once a handicap or potential deficiency is identified, parents can locate specialized medical care and can obtain follow-up services at once.

The aim of the BEEP education program is to provide resources for parents in their role as the child's first teacher. The program is founded on research that indicates that parents are an underused resource who, with training and guidance, can do much more than expected to educate and protect the health of their children. Each family is assigned a teacher on whom it can call for information and help. There are home visits and scheduled seminars. Parents can drop in at the center any time with their children to explore materials about early childhood, borrow books, pamphlets and toys; view films and videotapes on child development topics and other aspects of childhood; and learn about other recreational, educational or medical resources for young children in the Boston area.[3]

2. *Parent education in a medical setting.* A medical clinic, a maternity ward in a hospital or a well-baby or sick-baby clinic is an opportune setting for making initial contact with a parent before, during or shortly after the birth of the infant. Through the use of nurses, social workers and multimedia technology such as videotape or film strips, instruction can be given regarding pregnancy, nutrition, childbirth, the importance of the parental role and the process of infant and child development. Follow-up services through home visits can be arranged through the Visiting Nurses Association and other social services.

The Comprehensive Pediatric Care Center in Baltimore, for example, employs an interdisciplinary staff of physicians, nurses, nurses aides, social workers, a dental assistant and a community health aide. A major component of the program is the Parents' Club, which

[2] For more information, contact School District 742, 13th Avenue and 7th Street South, St. Cloud, Minn.

[3] For more information, contact Mr. Donald Pierson, Director, Brookline Early Education Project, 40 Centre St., Brookline, Mass. 02146.

helped to establish a morning recreation program for neighborhood preschoolers and turned the clinic waiting room into a supervised play center where parents and children can discover new toys and new ways of playing together and relating to each other.

Counseling services regarding child care and family problems, as well as health care, are available through the clinic's professional staff. The Parents' Club allows parents to meet together to discuss problems and share experiences and provides the means for parents to be involved in determining the kind of health care they and their children receive.[4]

San Francisco General Hospital operates a program especially for 16- to 21-year-old girls who are pregnant. It provides counseling about pregnancy, nutrition, child development, birth control and family planning. The program is coordinated with other city services, such as education and social service, to provide a comprehensive program for young parents.

The major obstacle to providing a parent education program through a medical setting is frequently lack of knowledge on the part of pediatricians, gynecologists and other physicians about child growth and development, about nutrition and about the problems faced by new parents. Counseling techniques and affective aspects of patient care are not standard components of a medical education. Greater involvement of pediatric nurses, nurses aides and social workers would serve to alleviate this difficulty.[5]

3. *Parent education in day care settings.*
Less structured forms of parent education can be offered through day care centers. Parents should be encouraged to discuss the development of their child with the center professionals and should be permitted to observe or participate in the program. A day care center can be used in the same way as a school setting for instruction in child development and methods of discipline and in the use of specific skills, such as songs and games to enhance parent-child interaction.

4. *Home-based programs with a remedial purpose.*
Home-based parent training programs have been in existence on a small scale for a number of years, usually under the auspices of university research projects. Many are now being replicated with favorable results by a variety of public and private agencies, including family service agencies, public health programs and school systems.

The purpose of these programs is to enhance the cognitive development of young children from deprived environments by improving the ways in which his parents talk and play with him. Some, like the Home Visitors Program of the Georgia Department of Human Resources, have broader child development goals that include the cognitive. The key to the success of such efforts seems to be the emphasis placed on the parent as the child's primary educator and the active involvement of the parent in the education of his child.

Better known programs of this type include the Demonstration and Research Center for Early Education (DARCEE) at George Peabody College in Nashville, Tennessee; the Florida Parent Educator Program at the University of Florida; the Perry Preschool Project at the High/Scope Educational Research Foundation in Ypsilanti, Michigan; and the Mother-Child Program of the Verbal Interaction Project in Freeport, New York.

The Tennessee Department of Public Health in Applachian, Tennessee, has worked closely with DARCEE to develop and implement a training program for teams of nurses, social workers and home educators in a comprehensive program for families with young children. The Michigan Department of Education has adopted the parent education component of the High/Scope preschool program to help prepare preschool children for successful entry into the education system. In Pittsfield, Massachusetts, the school system has incorporated the Verbal Interaction Project as the first component in an educational support system that moves from infant education to Head Start to elementary school and Follow Through.

5. *Smaller, less structured program approaches.*
A number of relatively simple support services can be remarkably useful to parents. Drop-in

---

[4]Eugene Langellotto, "Involving Parents in a Children's Clinic," *Children*, November-December 1971. For more information, contact the Baltimore City Health Department, the Baltimore City Department of Social Services and the Greater Baltimore Medical Center.

[5]For more information, contact the San Francisco General Hospital and the Office of the Superintendent, San Francisco Unified School District, 135 Van Ness Ave., San Francisco, Calif.

centers where a parent can chat informally with other parents and find out about other professional services can do a great deal to ease the sense of isolation that afflicts so many parents.

Another program, which could be coupled with a program like the above or used alone, is a toy-lending library. Here, parents learn how to use a game or toy or puzzle to help their child develop a skill, learn a concept or solve a problem. They may then take the toy home for a week and try it with their own children. After the course, parents may continue to borrow toys and games from the library as often as they wish.

Toy libraries may be staffed almost exclusively by parents. With the help of a skillful kindergarten teacher or Head Start instructor, parents can learn to operate such a program after a week of special training and some assistance during the first couple of course sequences. In addition to former parent participants, volunteers can be trained in the same training program as parents and employed with equal success as aides, home visitors or toy demonstrators. The use of volunteers, of course, can cut program costs substantially.

Many parent education programs, in fact, may generate new staff from their participants. Parents who have been through a parent education course can, with two to four weeks of additional training, learn to pass on to other parents the new skills they have learned regarding toy making, health and safety, playing with the child and observing the child's growth and development. Often a parent can communicate more easily with another parent than can a teacher or other professional. Parents with such interests could be encouraged to recycle their knowledge by becoming classroom aides, home visitors or toy demonstrators. They should be paid for such work, but their salaries would be only about half that of professionals doing the same work.

6. *Parent-implemented programs.*
One model that states might well explore for practical suggestions or guidelines is the parent education program, which for years has characterized many parent-cooperative nursery schools, play groups and centers. Parents typically work with professionals in the classrooms, have meetings to discuss child development and bring in experts to enhance their own and the professionals' learning. Cooperatives have tended to demonstrate (1) that participation offers the young parent of a first child an opportunity to end the isolation of caring for one child at home, as well as the opportunity to observe what other children of the same age are doing in the program and to learn how other mothers deal with problems similar to theirs; (2) that what is learned affects how later children will be reared; and (3) that this experience often leads to parents becoming community leaders when all their children are in school.

The parent-cooperative programs have evolved into a national organization—the American Council of Parent Cooperatives—comprising state and regional councils affiliated internationally through Parent Cooperative Preschools International.

Because parents must pay fees, "parent co-ops" tend to be a middle-class option. Some have developed arrangements with state agencies to accommodate a broader socioeconomic spectrum, but states need to take greater initiative in this direction. A few cooperatives, like the Greeley (Colorado) Parent-Child Center, are operated with great success by poverty-level families despite the constant struggle for public funding. States should consider ways to encourage this type of self-help parent-child educational and support service with small grants for start-up funds. State agencies could also work with parent-sponsored programs to open more co-ops to parents from lower-income levels.[6]

An example of a parent-implemented program sponsored by a state agency is the Regional Intervention Program (RIP) of the Tennessee State Department of Mental Health. The purpose of this program is to teach parents effective techniques for preventing or overcoming emotional and behavioral problems in their young children. Parents participate in an orientation course on child management, taught by parents who are graduates of the RIP program. Only six staff members are professional, and most services are provided by parents. Since each mother pays for her training by guaranteeing to work for the program for six months, RIP has become a self-perpetuating parent-implemented system. The program also provides comprehensive social services that range from routine parent-

[6] Stanley Kruger, Education for Parenthood Project, U.S. Office of Education, Room 2181, 400 Maryland Ave. SW, Washington, D.C. 20013.

to-parent emotional support for all parents to finding food, clothing, housing or jobs for individuals who need them.

7. *Media technology.*
States should consider expanding the use of television and radio for parent education. Funds should be provided to promote short public service announcements, repeated frequently, as well as longer programs produced in cooperation with public television and radio broadcasting and with local network affiliations. The Children's Television Workshop encourages this kind of use of local time in conjunction with their programs of "Sesame Street," "The Electric Company" and "Feeling Good."

Use of major media, of course, can serve to reach a large audience with information about the role of the parent in child development. Perhaps equally important, the media can help to impart to parenting a significance and status it presently lacks. To this end, public service announcements and filmed programs must be of high professional quality.

Filmed television shows can also be used by state and local parent and child programs as a supplement to other teaching approaches and as a tool to promote discussion in group meetings. Cable television could be used extensively to broadcast more specifically focused programs to individual communities.

8. *Model federal programs.*
Several federal programs address comprehensive services to poverty-level parents who have children under age 3, the usual enrollment age for Head Start programs. In contrast to Head Start, these programs concentrate on reaching the child through, not outside of, the parents and the home setting. Among the most prominent of these programs are the following:

a. *Parent and child centers* provide a variety of programs designed to stimulate the development of infants and toddlers from very deprived environments, along with a range of services to parents, especially mothers. These services include health care for parents and children, social services, day care, parent education programs, family management classes, job skills and opportunities for parents to participate as staff assistants and on policy advisory committees. Home visitor programs are directed toward improving child-rearing practices by providing information, demonstrating activities and giving temporary relief from isolation and loneliness.

b. *The child and family resource program* provides integrated delivery of services to children and families on an individualized basis, using existing Head Start programs as a nucleus and expanding services to additional families through a system of formal and informal linkages to community resources. Services cover the same range as Head Start—health, nutrition, mental health, education and social welfare—but are available to families with children from the prenatal period to 8 years of age.

c. *Home Start* has been described as helping parents do, or learn to do, the same kind of things for their children, in their own homes, that Head Start staff do for children attending Head Start Centers. The programs rely principally on home visitors who visit parents on a weekly basis, bringing them materials and ideas for playing with and teaching their children.

Television programs like "Sesame Street" and "Captain Kangaroo" as well as parent meetings, help supplement the work of the home visitor.

As in Head Start, Home Start draws on comprehensive community resources in the health, education and social service areas and helps parents learn to find and use these resources.

These federal programs lie entirely outside the state service systems, of course, but like Head Start before them, they provide enormous amounts of research and evaluation data, as well as working models of techniques and mechanisms for enhancing the parents' roles in providing for the education and welfare of their children.

Two other excerpts from The Role of the Family in Child Development: Implications for State Policies and Programs will be found as the second and eighteenth items in the CHILDREN section.

Excerpted from The Role of the Family in Child Development: Implications for State Policies and Programs; The fifteenth report of The Education Commission of the States Early Childhood Project (December 1975). Denver, Colorado. Reprinted with permission.

FEMALE FAMILY HEADS—CHARACTERISTICS, BY RACE: 1960 TO 1976

[As of **March** of year shown, except **1960** as of **April**]

ITEM	1960	1970	1976	ITEM	1960	1970	1976
WHITE				BLACK			
Female family heads, total..1,000..	3,306	4,185	5,380	**Female family heads, total..1,000..**	890	1,349	2,004
Median age.......years..	52.2	50.4	44.7	Median age.......years..	43.8	41.3	37.7
Marital status:				Marital status:			
Single.......percent..	11.8	9.2	9.1	Single.......percent..	10.8	16.2	23.0
Married, spouse absent.percent..	17.6	18.5	19.8	Married, spouse absent.percent..	37.4	39.7	33.7
Separated.......percent..	9.6	11.4	15.2	Separated.......percent..	30.2	33.8	30.0
Other.......percent..	7.9	7.2	4.6	Other.......percent..	7.2	5.9	3.7
Widowed.......percent..	52.5	47.0	34.9	Widowed.......percent..	40.2	29.9	24.0
Divorced.......percent..	18.1	25.3	36.2	Divorced.......percent..	11.6	14.2	19.3
Presence of children under 18 yr:				Presence of children under 18 yr:			
No own children.......percent..	57.8	52.0	41.7	No own children.......percent..	44.4	33.5	28.4
With own children.......percent..	42.2	48.0	58.3	With own children.......percent..	55.6	66.6	71.6
1 child.......percent..	19.2	18.8	25.4	1 child.......percent..	16.9	19.1	25.7
2 children.......percent..	12.0	15.0	19.5	2 children.......percent..	12.8	14.4	17.1
3 children.......percent..	6.1	7.8	8.3	3 children.......percent..	9.4	12.5	14.2
4 or more children.......percent..	5.0	6.4	5.1	4 or more children.......percent..	16.5	20.6	14.6
Mean number of children.......	.85	1.00	1.09	Mean number of children.......	1.57	1.96	1.71
Total children under 18 years old in families.......mil..	54.5	58.5	54.1	Total children under 18 years old in families.......mil..	8.4	9.3	9.4..
Living with:				Living with:			
Both parents.......percent..	91.9	88.1	85.7	Both parents.......percent..	69.2	58.7	50.1
Mother only.......percent..	6.2	8.6	11.9	Mother only.......percent..	20.6	30.8	40.5

Source: U.S. Bureau of the Census, *Current Population Reports*, series P-23, No. 50, and series P-20, No. 306 and forthcoming report.

U.S. Bureau of the Census, Statistical Abstract of the United States: 1977 (98th edition) Washington, D.C., 1977.

Marriage

PROGRESS IN MARRIAGE:
Power, Negotiation, and Conflict

BY LETHA SCANZONI AND JOHN SCANZONI

An experienced secretary and bookkeeper saw no reason that she shouldn't go back to work now that her children were in school. Her husband said no. Explaining the problem to a newspaper advice columnist, the woman wrote: "My husband said if I want to work outside the home I should work for him. (He owns a small retail business.) I don't want to work for him because he refuses to pay me. He says: 'You don't need any money of your own. If you want something, ask me and I'll give you the money for it.' (In the past when I've asked for money he has had to know where every dime is going.) He enjoys having me ask him for money. It makes him feel important."[1]

Persons who assert that marriage can stand on love alone are suggesting an imbalanced precarious posture. Marriage requires two legs—love and justice. Aristotle defined justice as simply "the good of others."[2] And Robert Seidenberg, a psychiatrist, points out: "Love without justice is a yoke, which more often than not, not only enslaves but strangulates the human spirit."[3] The wife in the letter quoted feels that she is being treated unfairly by her husband; she defines her situation as one of injustice, no matter what her husband may say about feelings of love for her.

However, if this wife presses for her rights and insists on furthering her own interests even though they are in opposition to her husband's interests, she is aware that a situation of conflict will develop. Negotiation will be necessary so that a satisfactory settlement can be reached and the relationship continued.

The issue of *power* also comes into play. The wife's power is limited by her dependence on her husband for resources. Aware of this, the husband refuses to allow her any discretionary income of her own even if she were to earn it in his place of business ("he refuses to pay me"). Instead he wants her to ask for any small amount as she needs it, thus keeping both himself and his wife alert to her dependence upon him and his power over her ("He enjoys having me ask him for money. It makes him feel important."). Further evidence of his power is the husband's demand for an accounting of how each dime is spent when he does give his wife money; there is a very real tie between his total control of the resources and his power in the marriage in general.

"Process in Marriage: Power, Negotiation and Conflict," (Ch. 8) in Men, Women, and Change: A Sociology of Marriage and Family by Letha Scanzoni and John Scanzoni (McGraw-Hill: New York)

The wife senses that as long as she is utterly dependent upon her husband for material resources, his power over her will be great and she will find it necessary to go along with his wishes while submerging her own interests. Yet she seems to realize that if she can obtain resources of her own (the principle of alternate rewards as discussed in Chapter 4), her power will be increased and her husband's decreased.

POWER IN THE HUSBAND-WIFE RELATIONSHIP

Many persons have the mistaken notion that issues such as justice, negotiation, conflict and power have no place in discussions of marriage. Such issues are thought to be appropriate when it comes to discussing political affairs or labor-management disputes but not when it comes to discussing the husband-wife relationship. Yet marriage is a social system and involves social processes no less than is true of the relationships between two parties negotiating business interests or two nations trying to work out a trade agreement.

What Is Power?

The word *power* derives from the Latin *potere,* which means "to be able." Power includes the ideas of ability and control. In this sense, "I can" is the essence of power. I can do something rather than being at the mercy of other forces. I can produce an effect on something or someone else. Thus, we speak of how science has increased the ability of humans to control the environment, to have power over nature, and so on.

As psychologist David Winter points out, the behavioral scientist is concerned specifically with social power, that is, "when one or more persons have an effect on the behavior or emotions of another *person* or persons. . . . Power over things is of interest in this context only insofar as it leads to social power."[4] Furthermore, says Winter, such power means that there is intention behind it, that one's effect on others is not merely accidental. "To say that someone has the ability or can produce an effect strongly suggests that he can do something when, how, and in the way that he wants to do it." This is true even if such intentions are unconscious or denied. Winter's definition sums up the usual meaning of power as it is spoken of by psychologists, sociologists, and political scientists: "Social power is the ability or capacity of [one person or group] to produce (consciously or unconsciously) intended effects on the behavior or emotions of another person [or group] . . ."[5]

How Sociologists Measure Marital Power

We saw in Chapter 1 that selecting concepts, measuring them, and examining their interrelationships are all involved in sociological theory building. To explain the why of social behavior, we must first understand something of the what and the how. *Concepts* are notions or ideas; and in order to find out how concepts are operating in social relationships, sociologists devise ways of measuring them. For example, we have seen that the *sociological measurements* of social class (a concept) usually involve education, income, and occupational status. Each of these three items is also a concept in itself, which in turn must be measured. Education is measured by years of formal schooling, and income is measured in terms of dollars. One way that occupational status has been measured has involved the devising of a scale or index which takes into account the evaluations of large numbers of people who have been asked to rate various occupations as to their relative prestige. For instance, most people have rated a surgeon higher than a truckdriver, a schoolteacher higher than a supermarket clerk, and so on.

The concept of marital power has posed problems for sociologists, both in terms of defining it and measuring it. In fact, a great deal of controversy has raged over this subject in recent years as various sociologists who study the family have disagreed among themselves.[6] The problem in defining marital power has occurred because some sociologists use the term synonymously with other terms, such as authority, decision making, or influence, while other sociologists make distinctions between the various terms.

Sociologist Constantina Safilios-Rothschild makes the criticism that too many studies have examined only husband-wife *decision making* in measuring marital power while failing to pay enough attention to what goes on behind the scenes, such as "the patterns of tension and conflict management, or the type of prevailing division of labor." She suggests that the total configuration of these behavioral patterns must be examined and not one aspect alone if power is to be understood. In Safilios-Rothschild's thinking, family power structure should be thought of in terms of three components: *authority* (who is considered to have the legitimate right to have the most say, according to prevailing cultural and social norms), *decision-making* (who makes the decisions, how often, and so on), and *influence* (less obvious maneuvering; the degree to which a spouse is able to impose his or her point of view through various subtle or not-so-subtle pressures even though the other spouse initially opposed that point of view.)[7]

Another problem pointed out by some sociologists is that there may be various levels to familial power structure. Which level is being explored? Are we concerned with who makes particular decisions, or who decides that this person may make those decisions, or even beyond that, who determines who will decide which spouse will make the decision?[8] The picture begins to look like the proverbial "house that Jack built"! In other words, suppose a husband and wife reach an impasse on a certain decision. Finally, just to get the matter settled so that the couple can go on with other things, one of them says to the other, "*You* decide. Since we can't make up our minds, I'll turn the matter over to you and I'll abide by your decision." The spouse who gets to make the decision may seem at first glance to be the one with the greater power; after all it is his or her wishes that will be carried out. However, as Safilios-Rothschild points out, "the one spouse may relegate one or more decisions to the other spouse because he finds these decisions relatively unimportant and very time-consuming." The "relegating" spouse in such cases has considerably more power than the one who might appear to make the decisions, because the relegating spouse "can orchestrate the power structure in the family according to his preferences and wishes."[9]

Survey method of studying power Sociologists study power in marriage by using two basic methods: *asking* or *watching and listening.* The "asking" method is sometimes called the survey method or the reputational method. A sample of husbands or wives (or both) is drawn, and questions are asked about the balance of power in their marriage. Sometimes a sample of children is drawn to find out which parent the children think has the greater power in the family. Variables such as social status, stage of the life cycle, and other factors are also introduced in an effort to find patterns that may aid in understanding marital power better. Questions used in the survey method may have to do with decision making or with the handling of conflicts. Or a key question might be as direct as this: "Who is the real boss in your marriage?" A question used in several studies including our own research is this one: "When you disagree about [particular items the respondent has listed as areas of disagreement in his or her marriage], who usually gets his way, you or your spouse?" The spouse with the higher score of "winning out" in disagreements is considered to have the greater power.

One frequently used method of measuring marital power has been to ask respondents who makes the final decisions in each of a number of areas. The list might include matters like the choice of work for either spouse, vacation decisions, what kind of car to buy, and so on. Blood and Wolfe utilized this method in their pioneering Detroit study of husband-wife relationships.[10] Yet, their approach to the issue of power has been criticized because each of the eight items they listed was given equal weight. In other words, when they tabulated the final results to find out a person's power score, decisions about the weekly food budget were treated as being just as important as the choice of the husband's job or the purchase of a house.

The problem of measuring power is further complicated by a lack of consistency in the kinds of questions asked even when marital power is thought of only in terms of decision making. Blood and Wolfe singled out eight areas of household decision making; and while some studies have duplicated these, other studies have utilized lists containing other items. Thus, it is difficult to compare studies.[11]

Another problem in connection with the survey approach relates to the respondents who are being queried. Some studies have focused on wives only, whereas other studies have sought to find out husbands' perception of decision-making power. There are also studies in which *both* husbands and wives are asked their perceptions of power within their marriages, and in addition there are studies in which children are asked to tell whom they perceive to have the greater power in their respective families. Comparison of various studies again becomes a problem, because it has been amply demonstrated that different members of the family may perceive the power structure differently.[12]

In addition to the problems clustering around the kinds of questions that are asked and the persons who are asked them, there remains the more basic problem of limiting measurements of power to the matter of decision making alone. Some sociologists suggest that rather than focusing on the *outcome* of decision making, it might prove more fruitful to concentrate on the *process* by which decisions are arrived at.[13] But how can sociologists study the processes of decision making that go on within family units? This brings us to the second commonly used method for investigating marital power.

Observational-experimental method of studying power Whereas the survey method is built around asking, the observational-experimental method is built around watching and listening. Laboratory situations are set up so that couples may be observed while they settle disagreements and make decisions. The sessions are usually tape-recorded and later evaluated by a panel of judges who code the observed behavior according to a specified rating scale. (For example, they might keep a record of who made the most interruptions in a family discussion, who made the greater number of suggestions in a husband-wife dialogue about some disagreement, and so on.)

Game techniques may also be utilized so that a couple is faced with decision making in simulated situations.[14] Sometimes a series of short stories are used as stimuli so that the husband and wife must come to an agreement about hypothetical problem situations and find ways to resolve conflicts. Their interactions are observed in an effort to see who exercises the greater power, who is most persuasive, or who gets his or her way.[15]

There are, of course, problems with the observational-experimental method just as there are with the survey method. Some critics point out that couples or families who know they are being watched may not act naturally and may present a picture somewhat different than they would in actual decision-making situations in their day-to-day living, thus creating an "onstage" effect. But other researchers have answered such criticisms with evidence that much accurate information about family interaction has been gained from observational methods. Two sociologists attempted to compare the two methods by using both on the same random sample of 211 families in metropolitan Toronto. One interesting finding was that "the questionnaire measures showed husband dominance to prevail, while the observational measures showed a balance between the spouses."[16]

Sociologist David Heer draws attention to a crucial problem common to both methods of researching marital power, namely, the fact that a person who has the greater power in one area of marital decision making may have a much smaller degree of power in another area. It is not easy to find ways to ascertain and measure power since "power is not unidimensional."[17] Heer's statement is but one more indication of the difficulties surrounding research on power in marriage. Sociologists speak of these as *methodological* problems, since they relate to methods of conceptualizing, gathering necessary data, and measuring findings. But an awareness of these problems should not mean that we despair of any understanding at all of marital power. While there are many things that sociologists do not know about this concept, there are many other things they do know. And it is on the basis of information already in that we can proceed to build theory and seek explanations about the part power plays in the marital process.

How Power Is Obtained and Maintained

A basic principle in sociology links power with resources. That is, the more resources a person, group, or nation possesses, the greater is the power held with relation to others who desire such resources. For example, suppose a country we'll call "Plentyland" has resources which another country ("Scarceland") lacks and desperately needs (oil, wheat, certain raw materials necessary for manufacturing, or other goods). Plentyland will then have a considerable amount of power over Scarceland and can force Scarceland to act in certain ways, either through threats of withholding the needed materials or through promises to increase such goods, provide better economic deals, and so on. If Scarceland's resources offered in exchange are not so essential to Plentyland as Plentyland's resources are to Scarceland, it follows that Scarceland is much more dependent upon Plentyland than is Plentyland on Scarceland. Therefore, Plentyland has the greater power and may be expected to exercise considerable influence and control over Scarceland.

But can resource theory be applied to *marital* power? Once again a certain amount of controversy has raged among sociologists.[18] Safilios-Rothschild questions limiting the concept of resources to assets that will almost without question be found in greater abundance among *husbands* in traditional marriages (for example, education, income, occupational status), while other kinds of resources are ignored. "Does not the wife have at her disposal other 'resources' tangible and intangible which she can (and does) contribute or withdraw at will and thus 'control' even the most occupationally successful husband?" asks Safilios-Rothschild. As examples of such control of resources, she names food preparation (poorly prepared or the husband's favorite dish), sloppy versus neat housekeeping, sexual enthusiasm or frigidity, the control of the home atmosphere and hospitality (or the lack of it) through pleasant or sour moods, and so on.[19]

In spite of her criticisms of resource theory, Safilios-Rothschild is herself speaking in terms of rewards, costs, and punishments. She does not appear to deny the basic sociological principle linking power with the ability to grant or withhold valued resources. Rather, her hesitancy seems to be associated with a reluctance to limit resources to an economic base.

However, in modern industrial societies, it is productive work in the marketplace that counts in terms of social worth. The work of women in the home is not assigned the same value as the work of men which is converted into dollars. "In a society in which money determines value, women are a group who work outside the money economy," writes Margaret Benston. She goes on to point out that household work when performed by a wife is not considered to be worth money, and since it isn't, society considers it valueless and not even real work at all. This in turn leads to the conclusion that "women themselves, who do this valueless work, can hardly be expected to be worth as much as men, who work for money."[20]

In commenting upon Benston's statement, sociologist Dair Gillespie emphasizes a point we have made throughout this book: Power is linked with one's degree of involvement in the economic-opportunity system. She writes: "Thus it is clear that for a wife to gain even a modicum of power in the marital relationship, she must gain it from external sources, i.e., she must participate in the work force, her education must be superior to that of her husband, and her participation in organizations must excel his."[21]

Blood and Wolfe utilized the personal-resource theory to explain their findings on marital power in the Detroit study. After seeing that a husband's degree of decision-making power was related to his education, income, and occupational status, these researchers concluded that "the higher the husband's social status, the greater his power." In other words, as the husband brings increasing amounts of resources into the marriage, his wife is increasingly willing to defer to his wishes and consider him to have the right to have his way in decisions. There was also evidence that the wife who brings educational and occupational achievements to the marriage has a greater share in the marital balance of power because of these resources.[22]

A number of sociologists have criticized the interpretations of Blood and Wolfe, pointing out that even the findings of the Detroit study did not consistently fit with resource theory, because low blue-collar husbands had more power than high blue-collar husbands—just the opposite of the relationship between resources and power at other status levels. Also, when different areas of decision making were measured by other sociologists, the findings did not always fit so neatly with the Blood and Wolfe explanation.[23]

Three sociologists who conducted a large study among husbands and wives in Los Angeles found that some of their findings clearly supported the resource theory of marital power as set forth by Blood and Wolfe, but other of their findings did not.[24] Nevertheless, Centers, Raven, and Rodrigues do not toss out the notion that control of valued resources plays an important part in husband-wife power relations. They feel it is but one factor among several others. They call attention to personality factors, cultural factors (especially the influence of norms in the couple's culture or subculture about how much power husband or wife should have), and "role patterning" (the way the domain of authority varies by prevailing societal sex roles; in both their study and the Detroit study, wives had more to say about the choice of food for example, and husbands had more power in choices about the husband's job).

They also agree with Heer's suggestion that the *relative competence* and *relative involvement* of the spouses in specific decision-making areas must also be taken into account in examining family power. Certain decisions might require skills which one spouse possesses to a greater degree than the other. For example, in a particular marriage, the wife might decide on the color to paint the living room and the furnishings to buy because of her interest and abilities in interior decorating; the husband might make the decision about when to purchase new tires for the car since he may be the more knowledgeable in auto maintenance. Also, the spouse who is more involved in or concerned with a specific matter might be expected to be the one to make the final decision on that matter.

Modifications of resource theory Several sociologists who see merit in resource theory as an explanation of marital power and yet are aware of certain weaknesses have suggested revisions or modifications. Heer suggests a theory of exchange which takes into account *alternatives* to resources provided by one's spouse.[25] In Blood and Wolfe's interpretation, the emphasis had been on a comparison of the respective resources brought by each spouse into the marriage; and the conclusion had been that the more resources either one has in comparison to those of the other, the greater will be his or her power. Heer adds another comparison: What is the value of the resources provided by the spouse in comparison to resources available to that person outside the marriage? In other words, would the man or woman be better off married to someone else or not married at all? For example, if a wife thought the alternatives were better elsewhere, she might be less willing to defer to a dominating husband, thereby diminishing his power. The wife in such a case may be willing to risk terminating the relationship because she considers the cost of losing the husband less punishing than submitting to his control.

Heer's modification of resource theory fits with a point we have made repeatedly: a person's power over another diminishes as the second person finds that other sources of rewards are available. Sociologist Willard Waller's "principle of least interest" is also relevant.[26] According to this principle, the person who is the less interested in keeping a relationship going has the greater power. The one to whom a relationship matters the most and who feels the greater need is more willing to defer to the other in order to preserve the relationship. When preservation of the relationship ceases to matter so much, the other party loses power.

In comparing cross-cultural studies, sociologist Hyman Rodman also found some difficulties in explaining marital power solely in resource terms and therefore suggested another modification.[27] Rodman found that in France and in the United States it was true that the higher the husband's education, income, and occupational status, the greater his power in marriage; but just the opposite was found to be true in Greece and Yugoslavia. Husbands with the highest educational levels in these countries had the lowest marital-power scores. How can this be explained?

Rodman proposes a "theory of resources in cultural context" in which he sees the distribution of power in marriage as resulting from the interaction of two factors. One is the comparative resources of the husband and wife, and the other is the prevailing social norm about marital power in a particular culture or subculture. In other words, if a culture expects husbands to have the greater power in marriage, this norm can have a profound effect upon marital power in spite of the comparative resources of the husband and wife. On the other hand, if a culture favors a more equalitarian view of marriage, power is not automatically assumed and taken for granted as an inherent right of the male. Rather, any power one has must be earned, and this is where resources come in.

Rodman views the United States and France as being more flexible with regard to the distribution of power in marriage and more favorable to equalitarian ideology; therefore power is not something that is already "there" for males. Power comes instead from resources; it must be earned. Thus the higher power of higher-status husbands in advanced, industrialized countries is not surprising. On the other hand, in developing nations with strong patriarchal traditions where social norms support the husband's right to dominate, the social classes more likely to embrace modern, egalitarian marriage ideals are those who have had opportunities for advanced education. Thus, in Greece and Yugoslavia, more highly educated, higher-status husbands have been more willing than lower-status husbands to grant wives more power, with a resulting decrease in power for themselves.

In looking at this cross-national data and Rodman's explanations, we are not by any means suggesting that higher-status Yugoslavian and Greek marriages within a strongly patriarchal society are somehow more equalitarian than higher-status marriages in the United States or other advanced, industrialized nations. Rather, the comparisons were concerned with degrees of authority *within* the respective countries under study in an effort to see how social status and power were linked in a particular cultural setting.

We have already seen how the option to work (especially when it is exercised) increases a wife's marital power. And we may recall the example of West African tribes in which wives exercised high degrees of power because of their economic holdings. Similarly, women in Iran with high education and professional skills are treated and paid equally to men and have a high degree of power in their marriages. It may be that in rapidly developing countries, even if there has been a patriarchal tradition in the past, the need for competent leaders and workers is so great that discriminatory employment practices based upon sex are not given the chance to develop.

All of this brings us back to the resource theory once more. Elements of it are there even when we examine Yugoslavian and Greek data. In a 1966 study, two Yugoslavian sociologists found that in their country women who are employed gain in marital power.[28] And Safilios-Rothschild also found this to be true in her study of wives in Athens. In spite of her misgivings about resource theory, she has written that there is some evidence for its holding true for Greek women more than Greek men. When a wife is employed and especially when her occupational accomplishments are higher than those of her husband, her power in the family tends to be increased, "because the possessed resources prove her abilities in such a way that even the traditional-minded males have to accept her competence."[29]

A recognition of the part that beliefs and cultural norms play in marital power, as in Rodman's modification of resource theory, need not be seen as contradicting resource theory but rather as something that interacts with it and aids in an understanding of how power is distributed. Norms lend legitimacy to power; they do not create power.

It cannot be overstressed that power springs from resources. "Haves" possess more power than "have-nots" in a society. Norms are created to lend support to the possession of power and to show that it is "right" for those who hold power to do so. Thus, the norm that husbands should be more dominant in marriage than wives ultimately goes back to the fact that males have traditionally had greater access to the economic-opportunity system and therefore have had greater resources. Husbands *have* had greater power in marriage, and therefore behavioral expectations (or norms) have developed to support their right to this greater power. In turn, one's degree of acceptance of these norms can have an effect on marital power, along with one's resources as compared to those of the spouse. As women gain greater resources, and with these resources greater marital power, we may expect norms to develop sanctioning wives' rights to such power just as they have supported husbands' rights in the past.

Power: Legitimate and Nonlegitimate

If the following two hypothetical statements by wives were heard, the observer would immediately be struck by both a similarity and a difference with respect to their comments on their husbands.

Joyce: My husband and I make most decisions together. We talk things over and then decide what to do. But he decides the really important things—particularly if we disagree. For example, he wanted to take a trip to Florida for our vacation and I wanted to visit relatives instead. Needless to say, he won! And I feel he had a right to. After all, he works hard all year to provide our family with a good standard of living. He deserves to decide how to use his time off work and what kind of vacation to take. I feel the same about major expenditures. He earns the money after all! Why shouldn't he be the one to decide how it's spent?

Martha: My husband bought this house trailer we're living in. He didn't even ask what I thought about it—just got it and moved us in. And now he can't even keep up the payments. He's never earned a decent living in all the years we've been married. You can tell that by just looking around our shabby place! But he sure acts like a king around here. "Get me a beer, Martha!" "I need clean socks. You'd better make sure you get to the Laundromat more often. What kind of a wife are you?" Yet he won't buy me a washing machine, and he takes the car every day so that I have to try to find neighbors who'll drive me to the Laundromat. And Pete is always telling me what I can't do, always bossing me around. Like the other night, my friend Judy called and wanted me to go to one of those parties in someone's house where they sell kitchen things, but Pete said, "No, you're not going! I don't want you to." And that was that. But it doesn't seem fair.

In comparing the two statements, we notice first of all that both wives indicate that their husbands hold greater power in marriage than they themselves do. But second, we notice that one wife feels this is right and fair while the other does not. The key factor here is involvement in the economic-opportunity system.

Joyce's husband has rewarded his family with status and material benefits; thus she feels he has the right to the greater power in the marriage. Martha's husband, on the other hand, has not provided such resources and therefore she resents the way he seizes power in the marriage and tries to control her life. Unconsciously, she is acknowledging that he hasn't earned the right to have authority over her. He has failed in what sociologist George Homans has called "the most important single factor in making a man a leader," namely, "the ability to provide rare and valued rewards for his followers."[30]

Joyce feels that her husband's power in their marriage is legitimate. Martha feels that the power her husband exercises is not legitimate. This distinction is an important one which turned up in our Indianapolis study of marriages, and it throws light on many of the problems that have emerged in studies of marital power.

Some sociologists have sought to clarify the two kinds of influence and control over others by distinguishing between the terms *authority* and *power.* Authority is viewed as legitimate, power as nonlegitimate. Sociologist Walter Buckley, for example, defines *authority* as "the direction or control of the behavior of others for the promotion of collective goals, based on some ascertainable form of their knowledgeable consent. Authority thus implies informed, voluntary compliance."[31]

In contrast, *power,* according to Buckley, is "control or influence over the actions of others to promote one's goals without their consent, against their 'will,' or without their knowledge or understanding." He points out that by the term *consent* he means something deeper than "mere acquiescence or overt compliance." Persons may give in to the wishes of another person who holds sway over them, but their submission need not mean they are actually consenting to such an exercise of power ("He has no right to tell me to do this, but I'd better do it anyway!").

Other sociologists used the terms *authority* and *power* somewhat interchangeably as in ordinary, everyday speech. Thus, they may speak of "authority relations in marriage" or "the balance of power in marriage" as being synonymous. Or what one sociologist calls the "mean power score" of a marriage partner might be termed the "mean authority score" by another sociologist. Goode has even spoken of "negative authority," which he defines as "the right to prevent others from doing what they want."[32] Since lack of consent is involved, such a definition comes close to Buckley's definition of power.

There appears to be a problem in terminology, because in normal usage the word *authority* includes the notion of power. It therefore becomes awkward to perch "power" and "authority" on two ends of a pole as opposites. Yet, the concepts involved are valid. There is a difference between control or influence over others that is deemed legitimate and involves knowledgeable consent and, on the other hand, control or influence that is not considered legitimate and which is exercised apart from the consent of the governed. But both cases involve power as defined earlier. In both instances, there is demonstrated an ability or capacity to produce intended effects on another person's (or group's) behavior or emotions. Thus, we suggest Figure 8-1 as an attempt to clarify the distinction.

Power may be exercised in a way that is legitimate (by being earned and consented to) or in a way that is nonlegitimate (by being seized and not consented to). Legitimate power, as a process involving bargaining and negotiation, moves toward *authority*—an institutionalized state. A position of authority involves a recognition of the right of a person or group to be in charge, to rule, to have control, to make decisions, to influence and direct the behavior of others. Conversely, nonlegitimate power moves in an opposite direction toward *domination.* Domination includes the idea of lording it over others against their will (the word derives from the Latin *dominus,* meaning "master, lord, owner, despot").

From the standpoint of exchange theory, we might say that nonlegitimate power is viewed by those under it as being undeserved because it was taken without having been earned and without providing sufficient rewards for the

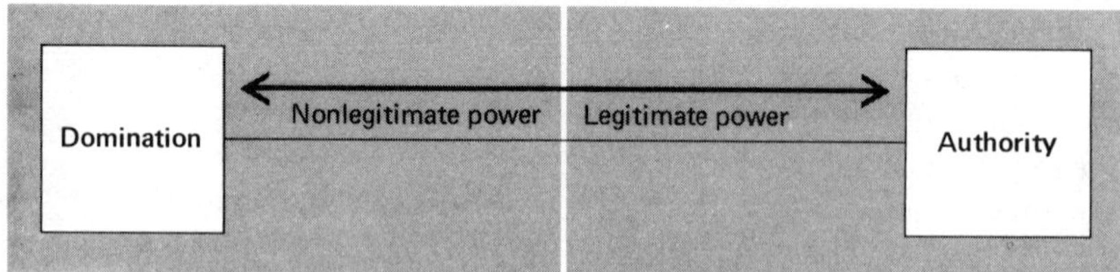

Figure 8-1 A continuum of power.

leader's followers. It is thus seen in terms of net loss (giving up one's own desires against one's will for the sake of giving in to the desires of another). In contrast, legitimate power is viewed by those who submit to it as having been earned and deserved by the one who holds the power. Therefore it is seen in terms of net profit (the rewards provided outweigh the costs of submitting to the will of another).

Nonlegitimate power tends to rely on coercion, threats, and punishment; whereas legitimate power relies on "friendly persuasion" and the provision of benefits. We might compare the distinction to the old problem of motivating the peddler's horse. The peddler might get his wagon moving again by either applying a stick to the animal from behind or by holding a carrot on a string out front to lure the animal onward. Legitimate power tends to emphasize the "carrot approach," while nonlegitimate power puts the emphasis upon the stick.

In the Indianapolis study, we found that it is an oversimplification merely to state without qualification that with greater status comes greater husband power—unless we take into account the *kind* of power. Actually, the study showed that lower-status husbands tended to exercise more power in their marriages than did higher-status husbands. Men with less education, income, and occupational prestige tended to resolve conflicts unilaterally, carrying out their own wishes rather than paying attention to their wives' desires. Furthermore, they were less interested in working with their wives in making decisions about matters of spouse disagreement. In the processes of conflict resolution, wives were permitted little participation as compared to the situation in upper-status homes.

We saw earlier that Blood and Wolfe had also found that husbands in the lowest status group had more power than husbands in the next category (high-blue-collar) which broke the consistency of the pattern that had otherwise shown that husband power rises with social status.[33] Their only attempt at an explanation was to comment that the group of lowest-status men with high power scores were presumably older men who were carrying on a pre–World War I patriarchal ideology which held that a husband should be the boss.

Komarovsky, too, found in her sample of fifty-eight blue-collar marriages that the lower-blue-collar husbands had greater marital power than the higher-blue-collar husbands (skilled workers). She suggests that educational differences might account for this finding. The less-educated couples tended to have more patriarchal attitudes, with masculine dominance viewed as the norm. The better-educated couples (high school graduates) tended to have more equalitarian ideals. Furthermore, the wives in these marriages expected and demanded more of their marriages. Often they were better educated than their husbands, since the relatively high earnings of skilled workers make it possible for such blue-collar men to "marry upward." In some cases, men had even learned their skilled trades as a result of having married high school graduates who had encouraged them to enlarge their achievement aspirations. However, as Komarovsky notes, upper-blue-collar husbands, by marrying better-educated women, "lose the degree of power enjoyed by the semi-skilled over their less-educated wives."[34]

Education is a resource wives may bring into a marriage, and again it is evident that resources bring greater power. The wife's educational resources and the husband's economic resources in skilled-worker marriages bring about more of a balance of power than in lower-blue-collar marriages. In upper-blue-collar families, decisions are more likely to be talked over and resolved jointly. This contrasts with the husband's unilateral decision making and conflict resolution in lower-blue-collar families.

Beliefs and practices In our own study, we measured both what respondents said they *believed* and what they said they *did* with regard to marital power. We found that beliefs do make a difference and that there was no support for Blood and Wolfe's contention that patriarchal traditions are no longer operative. Respondents were assigned a "male authority ideology" score based upon their replies to two questions read separately at different stages of the interview. The items were these: (1) "The wife should have equal authority with the husband in making decisions." (2) "The husband should be the head of the home." Structured responses (which made coding and assigning a score possible) were "strongly agree, agree, disagree, strongly disagree."[35]

Among wives, it was found that the higher the social status (based on husband's education, occupation, and income), the more patriarchal were wives' beliefs. With increasing levels of social status, there appeared to be an increasing acceptance of traditional views regarding a husband's right to leadership within the marriage. Conversely, our research showed that the lower the level of social status, the less likely were wives to accept patriarchal beliefs. Lower-status wives rejected traditional notions of masculine authority and leaned toward modern equalitarian ideals. Husbands, for their part, were found at all status levels to believe that the husband should be the dominant person in the marital relationship.

The concepts of legitimate and nonlegitimate power fit nicely here. Husbands evidently feel they have the right to greater power in marriage. Lower-status husbands lean heavily on traditional norms which have given the male the final say as "head of the house." Higher-status husbands have both the traditional norms and economic achievement to support their claim to power. Wives seem to view matters somewhat differently. If husband power appears to be earned (by economic achievement and resources brought to the marriage), wives are willing to grant the right to power *ideologically* as well (by expressing a belief in traditional patriarchal ideals). Thus, with rising status, there comes a willingness on the part of wives to view husband power as *right,* legitimate, earned on the basis of rewards provided. Joyce, in our earlier illustration, is a wife who looks at the matter in this way.

However, lower-status wives are less willing to grant power to husbands ideologically, since the husbands have not earned such power economically, even though the husbands tend to feel that the patriarchal belief system in itself should be enough to assure their greater power in the marriage. The hypothetical Martha in our illustration demonstrated such a marital situation. The husband feels the wife should defer to him simply because he is a man; the wife feels he doesn't deserve such deference since he has been so unsuccessful in the economic-opportunity system. Any power he takes is considered by her to be nonlegitimate and therefore *domination.* The higher-status wife, in contrast, sees her husband's greater power as legitimate and thus *authority.*

The same distinction between domination and authority emerged in our research as we focused on actual practice as well as on beliefs. The method of measurement used was based upon conflict resolution rather than routinized household decision making (which, as we have seen, poses many problems in drawing conclusions from the data). We reasoned that a more realistic picture of marital power emerges if we examine matters considered important by a couple and over which there is disagreement, and then endeavor to find out which spouse has the final say in resolving the conflict.

In a nutshell, our findings were these: The lower the social status of the husband, the more frequent is his settling of issues unilaterally ("We will do what I say! And that's that!"), and the less he tends to share decisions with his wife ("Let's talk it over and try to find an answer that suits us both"). Conversely, the higher the status of the husband, the less unilateral is his power, and the more he is likely to share decisions with his wife. Rather than saying, "I have the last word by virtue of tradition and economic success," the higher-status husband is more likely to display an attitude that says, "Maybe we can come to a compromise," or "I don't want to make the final decision by myself; let's work on it together."

Thus, although as social status increases both husbands and wives believe the husband should have the greater power in marriage, in actual conflict resolution there is greater participation by both spouses than in lower-status marriages. Less frustrated in the occupational realm and more secure in the power they hold (because it is earned and thus considered legitimate in the eyes of their wives), higher-status husbands are willing to act in a way that is more or less equalitarian, even when contested issues are being discussed. Lower-status husbands, on the other hand, may hang on tightly to every shred of marital power that tradition has granted them since they have no power elsewhere, not having achieved in the economic system and thus lacking the resources that bring power. They therefore *take* power even though in their wives' eyes they have not earned it. In such marriages, in spite of the equalitarian ideals of the wives, husbands tend to make unilateral decisions in areas of disagreement. They are less apt to permit or encourage the participation of their wives in making such decisions, and this lack of shared power is resented by the wives.

In both cases (higher status and lower status), husbands hold the power. But how wives see that power is different. Higher-status wives tend to see it as right and proper; lower-status wives do not. Higher-status wives get to share in husbands' power; lower-status wives do not. In a certain sense, we might see here a distinction in types of power that has been made in psychoanalytic theory. Freud, Adler, and Horney all took pains to show a difference in *positive power* which originates in strength and *negative power* which originates in weakness.[36] As viewed by lower-status wives, the domination of their husbands is negative power.

It must be kept in mind that we are speaking here of marriages in the traditional sense in which the husband is the chief provider or only provider. Research on equal-partner marriages in which each spouse is equally committed to a career and equally a provider of economic resources might be expected to show a considerable change in the marital power picture. Hints of this were found in the Indianapolis data with regard to wife employment. We found, as have other researchers, that a wife's employment is associated with greater power in her marriage—both in terms of her beliefs (more favorable to equality than to patriarchy) and her actual behavior (she tends to make more decisions alone rather than sharing them jointly with her husband).[37]

NEGOTIATION

In marriage, as in any relationship between intimates (friends, lovers, parents and children, siblings), there is an ongoing give-and-take.[38] The power structure plays an important part in this exchange, but simply knowing who has the greater influence does not totally explain the exchange itself. Who gives what, and why? Who takes what, and why? Who gains? Who loses? What kinds of processes occur in making decisions, solving problems, resolving disagreements, working out compromises, developing plans, and so on?

Probably the best word to describe these kinds of social exchanges is *negotiation.* Negotiation may be defined as arranging the terms of a contract, transaction, or agreement through talking matters over and working things out. The word has its roots in the Latin *negotior* which refers to doing business or trading. The husband-wife relationship involves negotiation in that there generally is mutual discussion and an arrangement of terms of agreement concerning areas of married life. How will the spouses divide up household chores? How will they make decisions about whether or not to have children? How will they decide on leisure, friends, visits to relatives, and other aspects of social life? What kind of house or car should they buy? How can they arrange their sex life so that it will be satisfactory to both of them?

In arriving at terms of agreement, the husband and wife do not necessarily settle a particular issue once and for all. As circumstances change or as desires of one or the other change, various matters may need to be renegotiated. Again, the idea of process enters the picture. Marriage involves an *ongoing* series of exchanges—in other words, continuous negotiation and renegotiation. Even a relationship that over the years seems to have settled into very routinized ways of doing things often is caught unawares by new circumstances and faces the issue of renegotiation. Time brings changes. The children grow into different stages and require new kinds of guidance or have different needs than earlier. One spouse's health may fail, necessitating a renegotiation on how the household will be run or how the income will be produced. The retirement period of life may jolt a couple into seeing areas of their marriage needing reexamination and calling for efforts toward change.

The Latin origin of the term *negotiation* fits well with what goes on in such husband-wife interchanges. In a very real sense, it is a matter of "doing business" through a series of trade-offs. The tit-for-tat might not be conscious in every case. Nevertheless, an exchange is taking place that entails both rewards and costs. "I did that for him, so he should do that for me." "If I gave up a big chunk of my day off to help her out, I don't see why she can't give up some time to bake pies for the guys coming over to play cards tonight—even if she doesn't like my friends!" "Of course, I'm going to hear my wife's speech at the PTA tonight. She always cheers me on when I do things like that; why shouldn't I encourage her, too?" "George got a big raise! Now we can take that trip we've been dreaming about! I'm going to do something special tonight. I asked my mother to take the children overnight, and George and I can have a special evening together making plans—and making love. I'll cook his favorite meal and maybe we'll even eat by candlelight!" "Well, it seems to me that if a wife works at a job all day, she shouldn't have to come home and do all the housework, too. That's why I try to help Sue with the dishes and cleaning and stuff."

Statements such as these illustrate how rewards and costs shape everyday marital life. The husband who gave up much of his day off to help his wife (costs) expects her to likewise give up time for him (costs again) in order to reward him as he rewarded her. The husband who has been rewarded with his wife's encouragement and approval is willing to take the time (costs, the extent of which depends on how else he might have used that particular block of time) in order to provide her likewise with encouragement and approval by listening to her speech. The wife who is delighted by the increased rewards of her husband's raise tries to find a way to reward him in turn; she chooses to go the "expressive" route by planning a romantic evening. The husband who is rewarded by his wife's monetary earnings accepts the costs of added participation in household chores to reward his wife with more free time.

Case Study

A hypothetical couple named Bob and Julie illustrate how marital negotiation works. Their case seems particularly apt because it combines elements of both traditional marriage (in that Bob is the chief provider) and modern, equalitarian ideals (in that Julie has a job which gives her a greater degree of power than would be likely otherwise). In terms of the four main kinds of marital structures, we would say that Bob and Julie come closest to the senior partner–junior partner arrangement.

Let's assume that Bob and Julie have been married about six months. Without necessarily thinking in terms of bargaining, the two have negotiated with one another as to how their marriage should be structured in terms of rights, duties, and options. Bob was already established as a real estate agent at the time of their marriage, and they have mutually agreed that Julie will teach elementary school for two or three years before they think about having children. Household chores are divided between them. Bob straightens up the apartment and does the laundry. Julie takes care of the meal planning, shopping, and cooking. Additional arrangements have been worked out for other areas of marriage, both in the expressive and instrumental realms. Birth-control methods, use of leisure time, budgeting, visiting relatives, personal habits—these and more have all been subjects of negotiation.

Implicit in such a set of marital negotiations is the question of legitimate power or authority. Bob and Julie have agreed to pattern their marriage so that Bob is the chief provider, which means that he has certain fixed, fully structured rights and duties which are inherent in the breadwinner role. Julie shares in breadwinning, but her commitment to work is less than Bob's. It is understood and agreed upon by both husband and wife that the main support of the family will be Bob's responsibility. He is the senior partner.

Bob's position gives him the stronger leverage in decision-making processes and conflict resolution within the marriage. Thus, when Julie suggested Bob's doing the cooking several evenings a week, since her own schedule seemed pressured with commuting and extracurricular school activities, Bob rejected the suggestion. "Sure, my hours are more flexible than yours," he said, "but still my work requires me to be on call constantly. If a prospective customer wants to look at a house, I've got to be free at *their* convenience, not mine. I can't be tied down with cooking! But I'll tell you what I will do. I can help you out by doing the shopping, and that will give you some extra free time on Saturdays. You'll still have to plan the meals and make out the list so I'll know what to buy; but I'm willing to save you the time and energy that you'd have to spend on picking up the stuff. How's that for a compromise?"

As we have seen, the person in an exchange relationship who has the greater resources to offer tends to have more legitimate authority. Therefore, that person tends to shape or influence decision making in his or her favor. If, for example, Julie were the full-time support of her husband while he completed college, she might have considerably more authority than in her present situation. Or if she were not employed at all, she would have less.

As matters now stand, however, Bob has more legitimate power than Julie does. This is true not only because of his greater financial resources, but also because of the chief provider role he fills. His job is looked upon by both him and his wife as being more important than hers. He can always argue that whatever might interfere with his career will be punishing or costly to both of them. Sociologist William Goode has pointed out that upper-status men obtain many rights and have a high degree of power because they can always claim that family demands must not interfere with their work. Such a man, writes Goode, "takes preference as a professional, not as a family head or as a male; nevertheless, the precedence is his. By contrast, lower-class men demand deference as *men,* as heads of families."[39]

So long as Julie accepts the senior partner–junior partner structural arrangement and values the rewards Bob supplies her, she will tend to recognize as legitimate Bob's authority. "After all," she says, "*someone* has to have the final say if we can't agree on something. Somebody has to be the last court of appeals. We feel it's only right that it should be Bob. Even though we like to think of each other as equals, and we certainly talk everything over, there's still a sense in which Bob is sort of 'in charge' of the marriage. He has the main responsibility to provide for us. My income comes in handy, but it's his that we always depend on. Mine might stop someday because we'll probably have children and I'll quit work. But Bob can't do that. He has to shoulder the greater load, so I guess he deserves to have the greater power."

Bob and Julie are maintaining a relationship in which each considers the exchange to be profitable. They are providing benefits to one another (at cost to each individually), but in return they are receiving certain rewards. They are maintaining an ongoing situation of *maximum joint profit,* to use the term from economics. The situation is comparable to that in which a single buyer of a certain commodity and a single seller of that commodity enter into bargaining. Maximum profit for each is the goal. Psychologist Sidney Siegel and economist Lawrence Fouraker have pointed out that such a situation "appeals to the mutual interests of the participants, and would seem to call for harmonious cooperation between them." But at the same time, "the interests of the participants are exactly in opposition, and acrimonious competition would seem to be the behavior norm." If these two opposing factors (cooperation and competition) can be made to work together in the decision-making process, it becomes possible for the two parties in the negotiations to be forced into a contract which is in their *mutual* interest.[40] Each individual and the relationship as a whole benefit. Both buyer and seller are satisfied that profit has been maximum for each. At the same time, the transaction sets up a bond between the bargainers and a climate conducive to doing further business together.

In the ongoing exchanges of Bob and Julie, the greater authority of Bob as senior partner and chief provider has been acceptable to Julie. The "costs" of her deferring to him in certain decisions and stalemates are considered to be fewer than the rewards she receives from him; therefore she is satisfied with her margin of profit in the relationship. Bob too feels that his rewards from the marriage are high. The offers and counteroffers of their various negotiations have resulted in a situation of maximum joint profit.

However, at any point in these exchanges, one or the other partner may come to define the distribution of rewards and costs as being unfair. Homans calls such a perception of inequity "the problem of *distributive justice*."[41] In other words, has the distribution of rewards and costs between the persons been just and equitable? Rewards should be comparable to investments for person A relative to person B if the bargain they have struck is to be considered fair by each.

To illustrate, let's assume that there comes a time when Bob's sales have fallen off and his commissions are down. Julie's salary has remained constant and her income is now higher than Bob's. Yet, she is continuing to do the cooking and finds it a real hardship in view of her tight schedule—especially now that she is helping the fifth graders put out a school newspaper and is staying an extra hour after school. Bob, in contrast, has more free time on his hands than ever and is almost always back at their apartment long before she arrives home. Julie has begun to resent his unwillingness to prepare the evening meal. She feels that she is providing many rewards to him at the same time that she is incurring costs which she considers unacceptable (the necessity of rushing home to cook after an exhausting day of teaching), while in her opinion, Bob isn't bearing sufficient costs. She feels he "has it a lot easier" than she. Her schedule is fixed while his is flexible, he is home more hours than she is, he is providing less income now than she does. In view of all this, his refusal to cook seems unjust. Julie begins to negotiate, making clear her feelings about the matter. Since there has been a shift in the relative resources of this husband and wife over time, the gap in their relative authority is much less.

In order for the situation to change and the problem to be resolved, Julie and Bob will have to have some honest discussions. Earlier, we saw the important role that empathy plays in marriage. Being able to listen to, understand, share with, and enter into the feelings of the other person is important in any close relationship—and particularly so in the daily interaction of a husband and wife. Thus, social psychologist Philip Brickman makes the important point that in the process of bargaining over a particular issue so that a situation will be changed, "a prerequisite . . . is the ability of the parties in the situation to communicate with one another about their various alternatives and intentions." At the same time, he stresses that problems of communication should not be considered the *cause* of the need for renegotiation or the cause of conflict.[42] The prime cause of a bargainer's desire to change situational profits is a sense of inequity rather than a lack of communication. But communication is essential if renegotiation is to take place. An inability to communicate could only worsen the difficulties and delay the solution.

Going back to Bob and Julie, we find that as soon as the sense of unfairness crystallizes in her own mind, Julie brings up the matter again to Bob. She makes a suggestion to alleviate the unfairness (Bob should cook), and in view of their changed circumstances and her better bargaining situation, Bob is more open to her proposal than previously. Julie has not let her resentment smolder but has acted immediately. After time spent in negotiation, the couple arrive at a new exchange in which Bob agrees to do the cooking—with certain qualifications. He will cook for a three-month trial period to find out how costly it will be to him and also to find out how things go with his job situation. But for the time being at least, Julie has persuaded him that it is only fair for him to take on this household duty. Bob accepts the legitimacy of Julie's request, and both persons begin to maintain their new, renegotiated sets of costs and rewards. Both have established what has been variously called "balance" or "equilibrium,"[43] and there is a sense of "distributive justice." Once again, both parties feel that current exchanges are operating for maximum joint profit and mutual gain.

The process of negotiating and renegotiating exchanges in marriage is illustrated as a series of steps in Figure 8-2. Bob and Julie's story focuses on just one area of renegotiation, but such renegotiations may take place in many other areas as well—often concurrently. For example, in the area of sex relations, one spouse might suggest having intercourse more frequently or trying new positions and techniques, and this matter could be renegotiated. For another couple, leisure time and companionship might be issues requiring renegotiation as one spouse complains of the other's absorption in occupational interests.

Written contracts All of the ongoing exchanges between a husband and wife are interconnected. And altering one exchange is bound to have certain effects on other exchanges as well. These complex webs, plus changing conditions both internal and external to a marriage relationship, point up the difficulty of written marriage contracts. While it is sometimes proposed that spelling out negotiated bargains about who does what and when can serve to make the bargaining process explicit, written contracts have a major drawback. That drawback is the complexity that would be required in order for an agreement to be drawn up which adequately covered all the possibilities that might emerge in a marriage. A contract would have to be complex because marriage itself is complex. To spell out all projected negotiations and renegotiations at the beginning of marriage would likely mean writing something as intricate and detailed as any meticulous legal document. Even then as new situations would arise, there would have to be constant amendments (and negotiations about making the amendments!). A couple might find such a contract cumbersome to implement and burdensome to alter.

A major theorist in sociology, Emile Durkheim noted decades ago that much of the force even of legal contracts lies with the noncontractual rules that surround them.[44] It simply isn't possible to write everything into a contract. In social exchange, trust is essential[45]—just as "good faith" is highly important in ongoing exchanges between buyers and sellers in the business world.[46] Persons must *believe* that others will fulfill their obligations—that they will do what is fair and just by them. And in a dyad (two-person relationship) such as marriage, many behaviors must be left relatively unspecified with the understanding—implicit or explicit—that each person is seeking the best interests of both (maximum joint profit).

Apart from such confidence that others will reciprocate, it is exceedingly difficult for stable, ongoing social relations to exist.[47] However, trust cannot be written into a contract. It develops because two parties strongly value the rewards that each supplies to the other. These rewards may be tangible or intangible, extrinsic or intrinsic, but in either case they mean much to the parties involved. Neither person wants to risk losing them, and therefore, each puts forth an effort to act toward the other in good faith.

CONFLICT AND ITS MANAGEMENT

Let's move back to Bob and Julie. Something new is happening in their ongoing exchanges as we rejoin them. Their situation is no longer one of negotiation, but rather one of *conflict.* It started when Bob decided they should buy a new car. Julie insisted they couldn't afford it and there was no use even thinking about it. Bob now feels a sense of "distributive injustice." He feels that his investment in the relationship is not producing desired payoffs.

Bob seeks to renegotiate the matter, and communication is established quickly; but in the bargaining that follows, it becomes clear that Bob's authority in this particular matter is less than his wife's. Real estate sales have continued to be low and Bob's earnings have remained less than Julie's for several months. There is no assurance that matters will change in the near future. If the couple were to buy a new car, Julie's larger income would be the main resource to make the monthly payments.

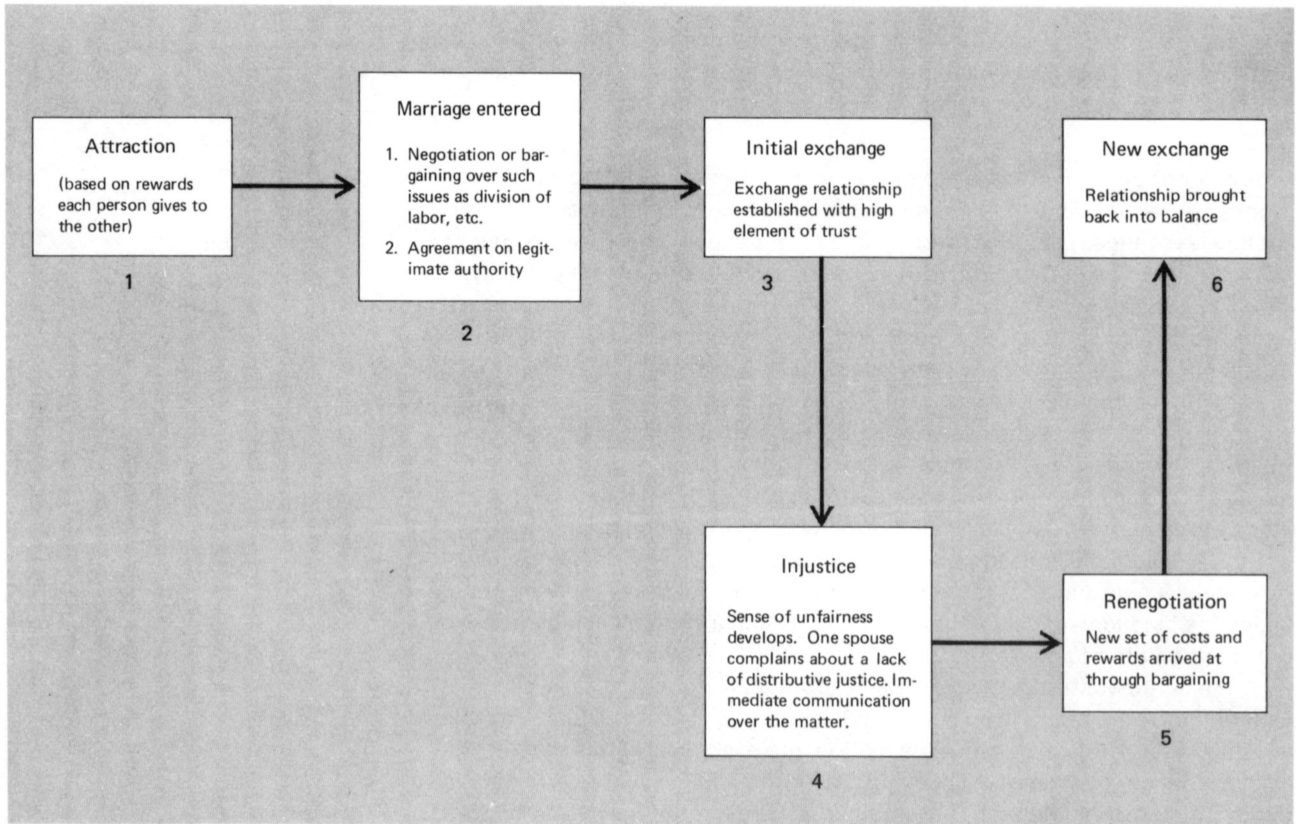

Figure 8-2 Marital negotiation and renegotiation.

At a certain point in the negotiations between Bob and Julie, conflict emerges. Social conflict may be defined as *a struggle over limited resources and/or incompatible goals so that it appears that the more one party gets, the less the other party can have.*[48]

The struggle concerns *limited* resources, because if the resources were infinite there would not be the problem of dividing them up so that all parties would feel they had enough. Farmers in an area with abundant rainfall are unlikely to engage in conflict over water supplies. But in an area where water is scarce, two farmers are likely to engage in conflict when one finds the other has dammed the creek to hoard the scanty water supply for his own farm needs. Two children who race for the one remaining swing in the playground are also likely to engage in conflict because the resources are limited ("I got here first!" "No, I did! It's mine!"); but on another day when all the swings are empty, they will each take one and play together amiably.

Similarly, *incompatible goals* may be the basis of conflict. If one person wants to go one way and the other person wants to go in the opposite direction, they cannot walk together and simultaneously reach both goals. One can yield to the other so that they pursue one of the goals, or they might take a third goal as a compromise. Or they might go their separate ways with each pursuing his or her own goal. In a marriage, for example, one spouse might desire a large family while the other desires maximum freedom from anything that would tie them down. One person sees marriage in terms of child-centeredness and wants at least four children; the other person sees marriage in terms of couple-centeredness and wants no children. Their goals are clearly incompatible. Another illustration might be that of a spouse who is deeply involved in social issues and wants a simple life-style with much of their income given to humanitarian causes, but the other spouse wishes to live lavishly. Again, the two goals are incompatible, and conflict is likely to emerge.

The key word in the definition, however, is *struggle*. Whenever one party *resists* the claims of another, they are then engaged in conflict.[49] Resistance, contention, or struggle occurs when counteroffers are refused outright or no modifications are suggested. The negotiations have reached a seeming dead end; they can evidently proceed no further. However, one or both parties continue to press their claims, and one or both keep resisting because they believe that it is *not* in their best interests to accept the claims of the other. Each perceives that it would be too costly to do so. In the case of Bob and Julie, Julie feels the financial cost. Their material resources are limited at this particular time. Her aim is to put as much money as possible into regular savings rather than spending it. Bob's goal, on the other hand, is to have a new car. He not only feels that the reward of the car is being denied him but that his status and authority are being undercut as well—a loss that is costly to him.

During the process of conflict, communication may continue in the sense that both parties press their claims and each completely understands and accurately perceives what the other wants. Clear communication in itself, however, is no guarantee that conflict will cease. Henry Kissinger is quoted as saying that "a diplomat believes that an international conflict derives from misunderstanding. Therefore he seeks a verbal formula to overcome it. The statesman believes that conflict derives from a difference of interest and confrontation positions. Therefore he tries to change the realities on the ground."[50]

Since, as psychologist Morton Deutsch notes, the same principles that apply to international and intergroup conflict may also apply to interpersonal conflict as well,[51] they are applicable to the marital situation. Here the point is that marital "diplomacy" (seeking to resolve the conflict through talking things over and clearing up alleged misunderstandings) is neither as significant nor as important to conflict resolution as is "statesmanship" (changing the situation so that grievances and inequities are removed in a manner satisfactory to both sides).

This is not to say that communication plays no part in situations of conflict. Conflict often tends to be associated with garbled communication or with a breakdown of communication. There is a variety of data from the laboratory and from investigations of wars showing that misperceptions, miscalculations, and misinterpretations can seriously affect conflict.[52] Many Americans became deeply concerned about the seriousness of the cold war between the United States and the Soviet Union when Premier Khrushchev made the statement: "We will bury you." They interpreted it to mean that the Soviets planned to destroy the United States. However, Khrushchev was simply using a Russian phrase that means, "We will outlive you."[53] In other words, the thought was something like, "Our nation will outlast yours. We'll be around long after you."

Misperceptions especially can affect the resolution of conflict. In the case of Bob and Julie, Bob might be saying that he wants *any* new car, whereas Julie may be understanding him to insist on a luxury car—since this is what he has always spoken of in the past. Bob might be understanding Julie to say she wouldn't even consider *any* new car under *any* circumstances, whereas Julie's resistance has mainly been buttressed against the idea of an expensive, luxury car that she is persuaded lies beyond their means. Somehow these two persons have failed to convey their own feelings and to hear what the other is saying. By attributing to one another motives and intentions that are not there at all, they have hindered effective communication.

Sometimes communication is simply broken off at some point during the conflict process. The parties concerned may decide they have nothing more to say to one another, and attempts to negotiate are given up. However, silence itself may become a form of communication. Social scientists T. C. Schelling and M. H. Halperin note that "failure to deny rumors, refusal to answer questions, attempts to take emphasis away from certain issues, all tend to communicate something."[54]

Whether or not verbal communication exists, and whether or not it is garbled, one or both parties may move toward trying to settle the conflict. In the case of our hypothetical couple, Julie seeks to resolve it by fiat—by giving an order or issuing a directive. Her pronouncement is, "No, we're not going to get a new car for you at this particular time." By using her authority based on their relative incomes, she attempts to end the conflict by simply refusing Bob's wishes outright.

However, at any point in the conflict process, legitimate authority can be transformed into nonlegitimate power. When one person or group makes demands on the other that seem excessive, the party on whom the demands are being made tends to develop a sense of exploitation.[55] Demands become "excessive" when they are not justified by sufficient levels of rewards. In our illustration, the wife makes a demand ("Forget about the car"), but the husband considers it excessive. Bob doesn't feel that Julie is offering any reward that would justify her demand or that would somehow "make up" for the sacrifice that would be required on his part by giving up his wishes for the new car. Second, Bob still thinks of himself as chief provider deserving to exercise the greater power in the marriage. He considers his current financial setbacks to be merely temporary, and he doesn't feel that his wife has the right to be as arbitrary as he feels she is.

When demands become excessive in the eyes of persons who are nevertheless forced to comply with them, such persons feel they are being coerced into situations they would not choose for themselves. These situations are regarded as painful, punishing, and costly. The power being exercised over them is no longer viewed as right or legitimate authority; rather it is seen as raw, nonlegitimate power. An example of such a conflict situation occurred in the 1974 feud between members of the National Football League Players Association (NFLPA) and the team owners. Players demanded numerous changes in the way summer training camps and exhibition schedules were being conducted. Life in the training camps was austere and uncomfortable. Rigid restrictions governed virtually every aspect of the men's lives. Curfews kept the players confined to the camp after a certain hour. Lights-out rules and bed checks demanded that they be in bed when they were ordered to be, and guards made regular rounds to make sure everyone was asleep. There were rules against using alcohol, wearing mod clothes, and dating local women (with heavy fines for those who failed to comply). Not surprisingly, the football players began to call such regulations "leash laws" and insisted that they be eliminated. Some men, resentful of being told how to run their lives and of being penned up in what they regarded as a kind of detention camp, were willing to give up football. Others engaged in all-out conflict in the form of a strike. They felt the power of the owners was nonlegitimate because of demands the players considered excessive. "It's the owners' way of showing their power and maintaining their monopoly of all decision making," the NFLPA executive director was quoted as saying. He went on to say that whereas that kind of control had worked in the past, it would not work any longer.[56] On the other side, the team owners felt that their power was legitimate, and that since they paid the bills they had every right to tell the players what they may or may not do.

One consequence of nonlegitimate power is that the trust we spoke of earlier can become corroded. Parties who feel exploited may begin to doubt that the other party is really concerned for their best interests. Instead, the other person appears to be unduly selfish and more concerned with profit for himself than with maximum joint profit. This became a common gripe among the football players. They felt underpaid and complained that the owners had worked out a system in which the men were working almost for nothing during the preseason months of practice and exhibition games. The owners appeared to care only about lining their own pockets. Similarly, this breakdown of trust was beginning to occur between Bob and Julie. Bob resented her telling him they could not purchase the car, and he began to wonder if she was hoarding her earnings selfishly toward her own goals rather than caring about him.

By trying to settle the conflict through simply giving an order, Julie was seeking to reestablish the kind of exchange relationship that existed prior to the conflict. She wanted the conflict to "be over with." Thus, she took advantage of her present position of power based on control of the resources. But to Bob, that power seemed nonlegitimate. He is unwilling to let the conflict end in such a manner. He wants the conflict to be *resolved*, not merely *regulated*.

Any relationship based on nonlegitimate power is potentially unstable and can easily become unbalanced or even unglued. Persons who feel exploited want to change the status quo and thus are apt to resist and struggle in the face of what they consider unfair demands and insufficient rewards. Therefore, Bob simply refuses to accept his wife's decision and persuades her to reopen communication. "The conflict is *not* settled," Bob declares, convincing Julie that they should engage in renegotiation. This time he is able to strike a bargain with her. While it is true that originally he had set his heart on a particular luxury model, he had begun thinking matters over and became increasingly willing to settle for a less expensive car—even a sub-compact. Julie concedes that with careful budgeting they can try to afford a car of this kind. They decide to visit various automobile showrooms and will choose a car together.

The conflict has been resolved satisfactorily in the sense that the original injustice has been removed along with the sense that nonlegitimate power is being exercised. Feelings of exploitation are also gone, and the sense of trust is restored. The struggle over authority and allocation of material resources is ended in that each party feels not only that his (her) own aims have been achieved, but also perceives that the other feels the same way. The renegotiation has led to a new exchange relationship in which the relative authority of each party is deemed legitimate, and the costs and rewards experienced by each are considered fair. In other words, a new balance of genuine mutual profit has been accomplished. (See Figure 8-3.)

Something else has likely been taking place in the relationship of Bob and Julie—though not necessarily in a rational manner or consciously. Persons or groups in any social situation are continually making "comparison levels for alternatives."[57] Comparisons are made between the current profit level (rewards minus costs) and what profit levels might exist in other potentially available situations. Persons are more likely to remain in their present situation if they define the rewards offered there as being greater than those elsewhere. In the case of Bob and Julie, their renegotiation and conflict resolution have reinforced their sense of overall profit so that the situation in which they find themselves seems more desirable than any alternative one. They have no desire to end the relationship.

Inevitability of Conflict

Up until recently, sociologists tended to view social conflict as "bad." In terms of the structure-functionalist approach, conflict was thought to disrupt and tear apart social systems. Conflict within the institution of marriage was thought to have only negative consequences and was to be avoided at all costs.

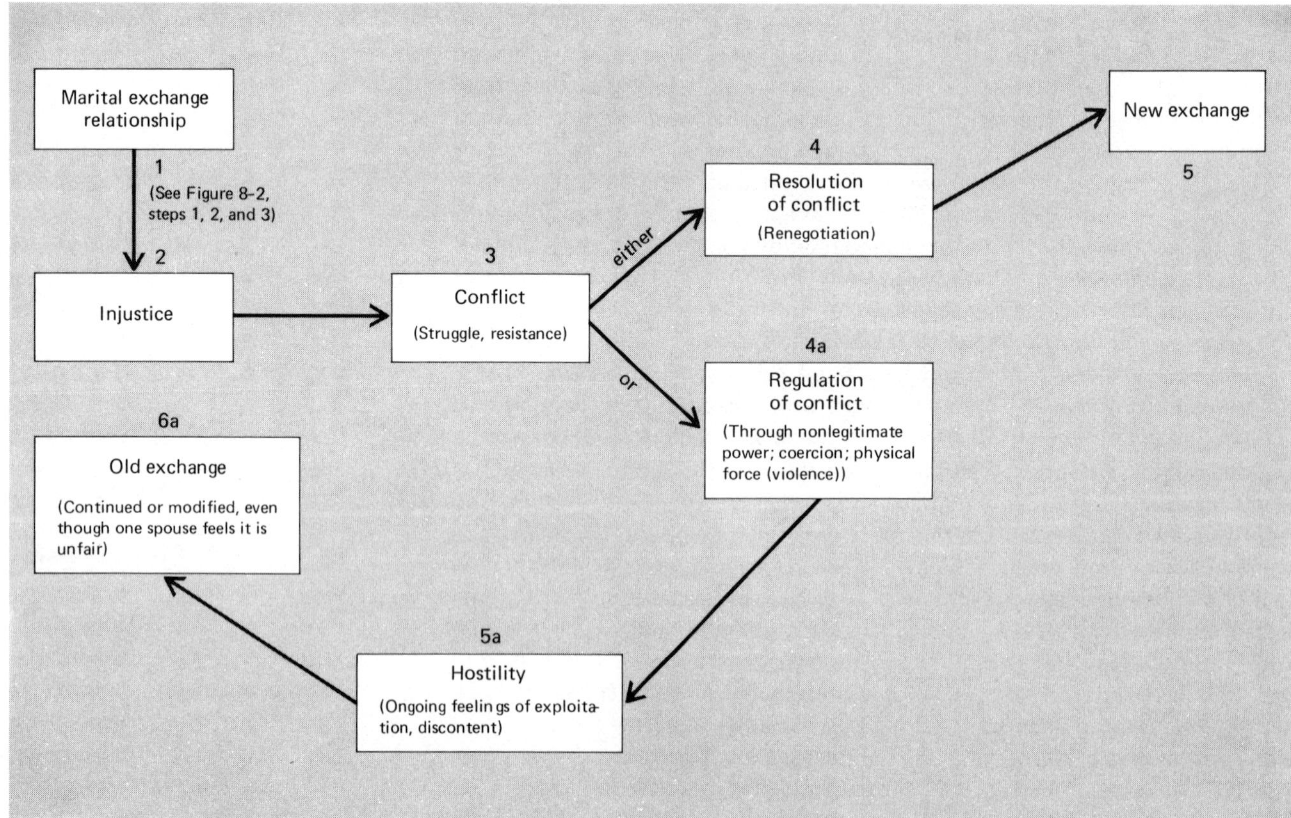

Figure 8-3 Directions in which marital conflict may move: resolution or regulation.

Currently, the overwhelming weight of evidence suggests that conflict is an inevitable part of any ongoing social relationship—including marriage. Given the processes of social exchange and given the likelihood that all parties involved are seeking to maximize rewards and minimize costs, a certain amount of conflict on occasion is to be expected. There are bound to be occasions of struggling over incompatible goals or resisting the profit seeking of others because of the costs to oneself.

Given its inevitability, the issue becomes not how to avoid conflict but how to resolve it. Increasingly, social scientists agree that conflict may often strengthen the bonds of a social relationship and make it more rewarding.[58] Conflict, when satisfactorily resolved, removes injustice and punishments. The end result of conflict can be such that maximum joint profit is greater than it was before. "Opposition," says sociologist Peter Blau, "is a regenerative force that introjects new vitality into a social structure. . . ."[59] The new bargains that grow out of the conflict mean that numerous aspects of the total relationship can be revised, altered, and made more rewarding than if resistance and struggle had not occurred.

This "regenerative" process can be viewed not only from the micro perspective, such as the husband-wife unit; it can also be viewed on the macro level, where nations contend with one another or groups within society dispute with one another (for example, labor and management). Historically, the feminist movement has meant social conflict between women and men. Females have sought to increase their share of scarce resources (material rewards, education, prestige, power) inevitably at the expense of male dominance and control. The struggle of blacks against whites has been of the same type. When a minority group presses for a greater share of rewards disproportionately enjoyed by a majority group, there is conflict. During the conflict, there is likely to be suffering (costs) on both sides; but when the conflict is resolved satisfactorily, both sides are likely to benefit and experience maximum joint profit.

Looking back over the past two centuries, virtually all social scientists would conclude that the conflicts between blacks and whites and between males and females have indeed been "regenerative" or "healthy" for Western societies. American society is probably stronger and more stable than it would have been had not resistances occurred. And it is not only that these minority groups are becoming better off. It may be assumed that men and whites in general are also better off as a result of gains made by women and blacks. Although it has been costly to males and whites in terms of traditional rewards (privileged position, unchallenged economic advantages, greater power, and so on), new rewards have been emerging as compensation. For example, society benefits through a greater utilization of talents when certain persons aren't blocked from achievement because of race or sex. Freedom from racial or sex-role stereotypes may enable persons to be themselves and relate as human beings with much in common to unite them rather than stressing differences that separate. Husbands might find that they are emancipated from many pressures as wives come to share the economic load. And wives may prove to be more interesting companions as well.

However, Coser raises the question: "If conflict unites, what tears apart?"[60] In saying that conflict has the potential of being cohesive (holding social groups together and bringing benefits), we are not denying that conflict also has the potential of being divisive (tearing groups apart, breaking up relationships). Conflicts can bring about the dissolution of business partnerships, entertainment teams, alliances between nations, friendships, and marriages. If a husband and wife, for example, try to resolve conflicts by continually resorting to nonlegitimate power, feelings of exploitation, discontent, and distrust may be generated. The partner who feels exploited might eventually leave the relationship. As we saw earlier, there is some indication that working-class husbands try to resolve conflicts through exercising power that their wives do not recognize as legitimate, since the husbands have fewer resources and give their wives fewer economic-status benefits than is true of middle-class husbands. This may be one reason why divorce rates are higher among working-class marriages than among middle-class marriages. Conflicts tend not to be resolved in ways that are regenerative but rather in ways that are disruptive.

Areas of Conflict in Marriage

What kinds of issues are involved in conflicts between husbands and wives? In our study of Indianapolis marriages, we asked each respondent to name in rank order the four things the respondent and spouse disagreed about most often. The question was open ended; that is, there was no list read of areas of potential conflict in marriages. Thirty-eight percent of the respondents said that the major area of contention in their marriages was money (producing it and spending it); 19 percent cited issues connected with children, 10 percent indicated problems over friends, and 3 percent said problems over kin. Twenty-one percent were placed in a category called "miscellaneous" since they indicated problems common only to a few families, problems too individualized to warrant a special category for each one; and 9 percent of the respondents reported nothing.[61]

Among areas of disagreement placed in the miscellaneous category were issues sometimes called "tremendous trifles" (matters pertaining to personal habits, preferences, and manners of conducting day-to-day living). Slightly more than one-fifth of our respondents cited some such issue as the major area of disagreement. Examples were decisions about colors to paint the home interior, concerns about punctuality, disagreements over the thermostat setting, and so on. Such matters can become highly significant in a husband-wife conflict, particularly when one feels the other is exercising nonlegitimate power and taking unfair advantage.

Although many people think that sexual problems are the major cause of husband-wife disagreements, the number of respondents who mentioned sex as their number one contention area was too few to warrant listing sex as a separate category. The seven-tenths of 1 percent who did name sex were included under "miscellaneous." Blood and Wolfe, in their Detroit study, also found that only a very small percentage of their respondents (less than one-half of 1 percent) specified sexual conflict as their major trouble area.[62] Perhaps folklore, movies, the popular press, and reports of case studies by marriage counselors and sex counselors have combined to present an exaggerated picture of the part sexual disagreements play in marital conflict and dissolution.

On the other hand, Blood and Wolfe may have a point in saying that there may be an *underreporting* of sex problems as the major area of disagreement. These researchers suggest that persons might be shy and hesitant to name this area of marriage, since sex is generally considered to be a personal and private matter. Yet, the social climate regarding sexual matters has become increasingly open. More than a decade has passed since the Blood and Wolfe findings; and while it is possible that the shyness-privacy explanation may have been a factor in the low reporting of sexual conflict in their study, it would seem to be less valid as an explanation of the low percentage in more recent research. For example, our own latest study indicates that only 1.4 percent of husbands and wives consider sex to be their major area of disagreement.[63] While there is no denying serious conflicts over sex in some marriages, the weight of evidence shows that among marriages in general there are disagreement areas of far more concern to the couples involved. Money and children continue to be the main issues over which there is husband-wife conflict.

Table 8-A compares the findings of Blood and Wolfe with those of our Indianapolis study and also with our more recent study in which 3,096 husbands and wives in ten major northern metropolitan areas were interviewed.[64] In this latest research effort, nearly 33 percent reported money matters as the major area of marital disagreement, and 18.6 percent specified child-related matters. Each remaining category shows a lower percentage than either of these.

Economic matters Given the interrelationship of the family with the economic-opportunity system, it is not surprising that issues relating to money and jobs are so important to husband and wives. Self-worth is intricately bound up with achievement and acquisitiveness in a modern industrial society, and husbands and wives are apt to have great concern about whether or not they are living up to personal and societal expectations. Their concern might sometimes take the form of disagreements over occupational matters (the *production* aspect of the economic side of marriage) or over matters of expenditure (the *consumption* aspect). The couple might disagree about the wife's career aspirations or about the husband's working overtime or moonlighting on a second job, or about changing jobs. They might have conflicts about how much they should pay for new furniture, about how far to go into debt, about a spouse's extravagance (or conversely, a spouse's miserliness and hoarding), about having a joint checking account, about savings, investments, credit cards, and a myriad of other matters.

TABLE 8-A MAJOR CONFLICT AREAS IN MARRIAGE (PERCENT OF RESPONDENTS REPORTING EACH AREA)

Chief Disagreement	*Blood and Wolfe, 1960*	*Scanzoni, 1970*	*Scanzoni, 1975*
Money-related matters (producing and spending)	24%	38%	33%
Child-related matters (e.g., discipline and number)	16	19	19
Friend-related matters		10	1
Kin-related matters	6	3	3
Companionship, leisure, recreation (kind, quality, and quantity)	16		8
Activities disapproved by spouse (problem drinking, gambling, extramarital affairs, etc.)	14		3
Roles, household division of labor	4		3
Miscellaneous (all else, including religion, politics, sex, communication in marriage, "tremendous trifles," etc.)	3	21	13
"Nothing" reported, "Nothing specific," not ascertained	17	9	17
Total	100%	100%	100%
Number	(731)	(916)	(3,096)

Source: Adapted from Blood and Wolfe, 1960, p. 241; Scanzoni, 1970, p. 157; Scanzoni, unpublished data from the study described in 1975b.

Disagreements over children Since children require a considerable investment on the part of parents, they constitute another area of great importance and potential husband-wife disagreement. Emotionally and financially, as well as in terms of time and energy, parents are spending a great deal on children. In spite of these costs, parents also may view children as sources of rewards. Husbands and wives may disagree about the best way to ensure that the rewards of children will exceed the costs. To one spouse, the very idea of having children in the first place might appear to be too costly; while to the other spouse, "starting a family" may be a cherished goal. Similarly, there may be conflict about the spacing of children or the number desired. In one situation, a father continued to pressure his wife to "try one more time for a boy" after they had eight daughters. The wife balked at the suggestion.

Child-related marital conflicts are not only centered around having children (if, when, and how many) but also about how to rear them. One spouse might be strict, while the other is lenient; the result is often severe disagreement about matters of nurture and discipline. Clashes about techniques of securing obedience from small children, or about how much allowance to give the elementary schoolchild, or about how much freedom to grant adolescents are not uncommon as husbands and wives share the task of parenting.

Conflicts in marriage, whether about money or children or anything else, may be settled amiably through negotiation, or they may lead to a breakup of the marital relationship. Sometimes, however, they explode into actual violence—a possibility that has often been overlooked by researchers, perhaps because of the "touchiness" and unpleasantness of the subject and the common belief that violence only occurs on occasion in "abnormal" families.[65]

Violence in Marriage

One June day in 1974, an Indiana minister and his wife went for a drive. The trip ended tragically. When their bodies were found one week apart floating in the Wabash River, law officers theorized that an assailant must have slain the couple and stolen their car. Later, however, the automobile was found submerged at the point where it had been driven 200 feet into a stream. After an extensive investigation, a coroner's jury concluded that the plunge into the water had been deliberate and that the minister planned to kill his wife and possibly himself. The charge of homocide was definite, although there was some doubt about the suicide attempt in view of evidence that the minister had tried to escape but had been trapped when his shoe caught on something in the car. In its study, the jury learned that the couple, both in their mid-thirties and married only six months, had been having severe marital difficulties.

This case may seem as bizarre as it is tragic. Yet, according to the National Commission on the Causes and Prevention of Violence, what appear to be automobile "accidents" have not infrequently been found to have been intentional acts of murder and suicide.[66] Not only is the family car sometimes the murder weapon itself; it also serves as the setting for many murders in which other weapons are used—such as in the case of a woman depressed over her forty-fifth birthday who asked her husband to go for a drive with her and then, as he slid behind the steering wheel, shot him and then herself. Other common settings for family murders are the kitchen (a central location for interaction between family members and often the site of arguments) and the bedroom (where husband and wife are closed off in privacy with one another at the end of the day, providing an occasion where built-up tensions and hostilities may suddenly erupt).[67]

According to official FBI statistics, murders within the family accounted for about one-fourth of all murder offenses during 1972. In over half of these family killings, one spouse killed the other spouse. The victims in these husband-wife murders were almost evenly divided with regard to sex and race. Wives were victims in 52 percent of the incidents, and husbands were victims in 48 percent. Blacks were victims in 52 percent of spouse killings, whites in 47 percent, and other races accounted for the remaining 1 percent.

Spouse killings in 1972 accounted for 12.5 percent of all murders. In nearly 3 percent of all homocide offenses, parents killed their children. And 9 percent of murder incidents involved other kinds of in-family killings.[68] Family homicide is a gruesome reality in which husbands kill wives, wives kill husbands, parents kill children, children kill parents, brothers and sisters kill one another, people kill in-laws and grandparents, and so on. Viewed this way, the family looks more like a bloodstained battlefield than a peaceful haven of love and tenderness.

Most families, of course, are not broken up by the murder of one family member by another family member. Yet, many other kinds of violence may be far more common than is generally realized. Until recently, sociologists have given little attention to family violence, and research has been scanty. We simply do not know the actual incidence of physical force or the threat of physical force between spouses. Similarly, even though the problem of the "battered child syndrome" has been more publicized, there are no statistics on the actual number of children who are physically abused by their parents—although officially reported cases run between six and ten thousand per year.[69] Furthermore, exactly what constitutes *abuse* in the case of children is somewhat more difficult to determine, since societal norms permit parents to use physical force (such as spankings) in disciplining their offspring. No laws exist against employing such means of correction.

Up until late in the last century, the situation was similar in the case of wives. Wife beating was considered to be a husband's right, supported by laws affirming such chastisement as a means of enforcing "domestic discipline." Although husbands have lost the right to beat their wives, social scientists who have examined legal history conclude that the change came about not because of new laws but rather because of socioeconomic changes in the population.[70] As educational and occupational opportunities opened for women, and as women took greater steps toward equality (by pressing for the vote, for example), the owner-property pattern of marriage which permitted husbands to use physical force came to be viewed as less desirable. Legislation against wife beating reflected these structural changes.

This is not to say that wife beating (or husband beating, for that matter) no longer occurs. According to a national sample survey conducted for the Violence Commission, more than one-fifth of the respondents said they approved of spouse slapping under certain conditions.[71] How many husbands and wives actually do resort to hitting each other is not known with certainty. One legal researcher has pointed out that more police calls are made for family fights than for any other kind of criminal incident.[72] Calls for police intervention in domestic disturbances are not popular with policemen because such work can be very dangerous. Irate husbands and wives sometimes turn and vent their rage on the police, throwing bottles or furniture or even using knives and guns. In 1972, more policemen were assaulted while responding to the category of "disturbance calls" (primarily family quarrels, man with a gun, and the like) than in responding to any other kind of calls. Twenty-seven percent of assaults on police officers occurred under such circumstances. In that same year, of the 112 policemen killed, 15 (or 13.5 percent) died as a result of responding to disturbance calls.[73]

The exact amount of husband-wife violence is not known with certainty because so little research has focused on the subject. Some researchers have endeavored to find some answers through interviews with applicants for divorce. In one such study, 17 percent of those interviewed spontaneously mentioned physical abuse as a reason for the deterioration of their marriage and a major factor in initiating divorce action.[74]

In another study, George Levinger examined records of 600 applicants for divorce in the greater Cleveland area, where, by order of the court, divorce applicants with children under fourteen years of age were required to meet with experienced marriage counselors. In analyzing the counselors' interview records, Levinger found that physical abuse was a complaint in more than one-third of the cases, with wives complaining far more than husbands of being physically hurt by the spouse. Nearly 37 percent of the women applying for divorce voiced such a complaint, compared to 3.3 percent of husbands. Social-class differences were also found. Among middle-class couples in Levinger's sample, 22.8 percent of wives and 2.9 percent of husbands complained of being physically abused by the marital partner. Among working-class and lower-class couples, 40.1 percent of wives reported that their husbands hurt them physically, and 3.5 percent of husbands complained of physical abuse by their wives.[75] While such figures may provide some rough idea of the extent of physical violence in marriages that end in divorce, they do not furnish us with data on marriages in general. Thus, generalizations from these figures should be avoided.

Since violence has often been regarded as almost exclusively a phenomenon of the lower socioeconomic strata of society, the extent to which it occurs in middle-class marriages may strike many as surprising. While it is true that more violence occurs in lower-class marriages than occurs at higher levels, there is nevertheless evidence that a considerable amount of physical abuse does occur among middle-class couples. Slightly more than one out of five middle-class wives in Levinger's study of divorce applicants reported violence, as compared to two out of five working-class and lower-class wives.

Murray Straus is a sociologist who has devoted much attention and exploratory study to the issue of violence in marriage. In one study, 385 university students filled out questionnaires indicating whether or not their parents were known to have used or threatened physical force during the last year in which the student lived at home. Sixteen percent of the students indicated that one or the other parent had *threatened* to hit or throw something at the spouse, or had actually done so, or had pushed, grabbed, or shoved the other during a disagreement.[76] However, as Straus cautions, "An obvious limitation of this data is that it describes only unbroken families with a child in college, which is far from representative of the population as a whole. . . . Consequently, a description of the amount of violence between family members based on this data is likely to be an underestimate." Also, the information tells us only about a single year of a couple's married life, and it may be incomplete inasmuch as parents might be hesitant to engage in violence in the presence of their children—even though they might resort to it in private.

Another sociologist, Richard Gelles, in a series of depth interviews with eighty couples, found that in more than half of these marriages at least one instance of husband-wife physical force had occurred at some time.[77] Furthermore, he and other researchers make the point that it is erroneous to consider physical violence (whether between spouses or parents and children) as simply "an abnormality—something which involves sick families."

However, as Murray Straus and his colleague Suzanne Steinmetz write, "The fact that almost all family violence, including everyday beating, slapping, kicking and throwing things, is carried out by normal everyday Americans rather than deranged persons should not lead us to think of violence as being desirable or even acceptable."[78] Rather, they suggest asking *why* so many families resort to violence. Gelles emphasizes that psychological explanations in which "mental illness" is viewed as the major reason for physical abuse are inadequate in themselves. There needs also to be an examination of social situational factors such as childhood socialization patterns, socioeconomic status, community or subcultural values regarding violence, structural stress (unemployment, excess children, and so on), and an awareness of immediate precipitating situations that bring on acts of violence in some families.[79]

Why violence occurs To understand violence, we may want to recall our definition of conflict as a struggle over limited resources and/or incompatible goals in which it appears that one person or group will have its way at the expense of the other party or group. Conflict need not and often does not result in violence. However, in some situations persons may resort to violence because it may seem there is no other way out. Sociologist William Goode points out that when persons begin to feel a continuing imbalance between investments and payoffs in the daily exchanges of family life they may engage in conflict over this imbalance. For various reasons, they may feel they cannot take one of the other roads usually open in such a situation—escape, submission, or righting the balance. As a result, the conflict "can escalate to the point of violence because no simpler or easier resolution emerges."[80]

In some marriage and family situations, one of the other routes may be chosen. Some persons decide that escape is the answer; thus, the child runs away from home or a spouse deserts the family or files for divorce. In other cases, submission (though given grudgingly and with resentment) might appear to be the only way to "keep the peace." Yielding to the demands of a domineering spouse, for example, may seem easier to the other spouse than bringing injustices out into the open and engaging in conflict. Goode's third alternative, righting the balance, would seem the most desirable way to handle what one or the other spouse feels are imbalances in the husband-wife exchange. This is the renegotiation process we spoke of earlier as exemplified in the way Bob and Julie handled their conflict over the new car. Articles and books have been written to help couples approach the problem of conflict in this way and to fight "creatively," "fairly," and "properly"—in other words, to fight constructively rather than destructively.[81] As sociologist Jetse Sprey has written, "The successful management of conflict requires the ability to negotiate, bargain, and cooperate: a range of behavioral skills."[82] However, some persons fail to develop such behavioral skills and seek a solution to dissension by either escaping or submitting to the wishes and demands of the other person even if they seem unfair. Or out of desperation, either party in a conflict may resort to the fourth alternative mentioned by Goode—actual violence.

It should not be assumed that the *absence* of conflict as we have defined it (in the sense of struggle) suggests a more satisfactory or solidary husband-wife relationship. Seething resentments and hostilities may underlie an outwardly calm marital life. In the example of our hypothetical couple, suppose that neither had expressed feelings of injustice. Julie might have kept to herself (or shared with some relatives or women friends) her feelings that Bob was acting unfairly by not doing the cooking. Resentments could have piled up, but to avoid conflict she would not have voiced her complaints to Bob. Instead, she might have acted increasingly distant and cool toward him. As it was, she was able to bring up the matter and work with Bob toward a constructive solution though negotiation—even before an actual conflict emerged in which each would have struggled for his or her own way. The couple did engage in actual conflict over the car Bob wanted, but again they were able to resolve it since they didn't try to bury the problem but instead were willing to renegotiate after Bob pressed for what he felt was fairness.

Why the family may be a setting for violence Suppression of perceived injustice in order "not to rock the boat" or to be "selfless" or "altruistic" can generate strong feelings which could explode at some unexpected time. Several observations of sociologist Lewis Coser are worth noting in this regard. He points out that "there is more occasion for the rise of hostile feelings in primary than in secondary groups."[83] Primary groups are composed of persons having a close relationship to one another in which, as much as possible, the total range of roles and the complete personality of each is known to the other. The family is probably the most obvious example of such a group. Secondary relationships, on the other hand, involve persons who know and relate to one another segmentally; they share only certain aspects of their lives and see one another only in specific roles. A patient may know a doctor only in the role of physician and know nothing of the physician's role as spouse, parent, church or club member, friend, and so on. The patient and physician are involved in one another's lives only on a secondary level; the physician's relationship with his or her spouse, children, and closest friends, however, is on a primary level. Areas of one's personality and interests which are not disclosed in a secondary relationship are revealed and out in the open in a primary one, such as the family. "If you could see him at home, you'd know what he's really like," is a common bit of folk wisdom.

Coser emphasizes that since primary relations tend to involve the total personality, feelings of intimacy are strengthened. Sharing all aspects of life makes people feel close to each other. Paradoxically, however, such intimacy has the potential of breeding hate as well as love. This happens because persons in close contact are bound to "rub one another the wrong way" on occasion. But since conflict is usually considered "bad" and disruptive for primary relationships, deliberate efforts are made to avoid it. The desire to engage in conflict is suppressed out of concern for affectionate sentiments, peace, and group cohesiveness. However, suppression of conflicts often means that an accumulation of hostilities is occurring, and any eruption of these feelings is likely to have great intensity both because persons in primary relations are so totally involved in one another's lives and also because the hostile feelings have grown to huge proportions by not having been allowed expression earlier.[84]

An outburst in which spouses furiously unleash their gathering storms of hostilities is not likely to solve problems or help their situation. Hostilities and conflict are not one and the same. In the words of Coser, "Whereas conflict necessarily changes the previous terms of the relationship of the participants, mere hostility has no such necessary effects and may leave the terms of the relationship unchanged."[85] To renegotiate, bargain, or engage in actual conflict is like the safety valve on a boiler.[86] "Letting off steam" keeps the entire mechanism from exploding.

When husbands and wives keep hostilities and resentments to themselves, sudden convulsions might occur at any time in the form of devastating, heated verbal exchanges or actual physical violence. Often *both* verbal aggression and physical violence take place. Straus conducted a study to test the hypothesis that verbal aggression is a substitute for physical aggression. The results showed just the opposite: "The more verbal expression of aggression, the more physical aggression."[87] In using the term *verbal aggression,* Straus is not referring to settling an argument through rational discussion, negotiating, and talking over and working through disagreements. Rather, he focused on such aggressive tactics as yelling and insulting the spouse, calling the spouse derogative names, sulking and refusing to talk (the "silent treatment" can be very aggressive), and angrily stomping out of the room.

Types of violence John O'Brien, a social researcher who has given attention to violence in divorce-prone families, defines violence as "any behavior which threatens or causes physical damage to an object or person." Examples of family violence in the divorce records he examined included wife beating, child beating, threats with a gun, extreme sadomasochism in sex relations, and the starving of the spouse's pet cats.[88] Some sociologists suggest that a distinction should be made between two types of violence. Steinmetz and Straus, for example, speak of violence in which physical force is used to cause pain or injury as an end in itself in contrast to violence in which "pain or injury or physical restraint" is used "as a punishment to induce the other person to carry out some act."[89]

Perhaps we could think of the distinction in terms of what we might call "explosive" violence and "coercive" violence. The child who throws a temper tantrum, the wife who suddenly begins pounding her husband's chest when he tries to smoothe over a disagreement by making sexual overtures when she wants to talk, the husband who kicks over a chair in a fit of rage all may be expressing *explosive* violence. They feel angry and frustrated and feel some need to "get it out of their system" through striking out. *Coercive* violence, in contrast, is goal-oriented and is directed toward accomplishing a task, namely to persuade someone to do or not to do something, or to punish the person, or in some other way to exercise control through physical force. The parent who shakes the child in order to extract the truth when lying is suspected is an example of coercive physical force. "You'd better tell me the truth or I'm just going to shake it out of you!" The husband who reacts to finding his wife in bed with another man by beating them both black and blue is another example of coercive violence (though no doubt combining "explosive" elements as well). "There, that'll show you both! That'll teach you never to do anything like that again, you no-good whore!"

Physical violence is not likely to be conducive to satisfactory social relationships of any sort. Persons in marital situations where violence occurs frequently or where it is intense are likely to want to leave those situations. Since violence may occur because of pent-up hostilities and through *suppressing* desires to struggle for change through renegotiation attempts, it is possible that marital dissolution may come about even though a social conflict situation has not occurred. In fact, social conflict satisfactorily handled might even strengthen the relationship and prevent dissolution or violence.

On the other hand, social conflict may also lead to violence—particularly when nonlegitimate power is used in an attempt to resolve the conflict. One or the other partner may try to force the other into doing something against the person's wishes. The coercion may be verbal and involve threats of rewards withheld or certain nonphysical punishments, or it may be actual physical aggression on the part of the person trying to control the other. The husband blocks the door and snatches away the car keys, yelling at his wife, "I said I don't want you to go!" Conversely, the person who is attempting to resist the coercion may resort to violence. The wife kicks her husband, scratches his arm with her fingernails in an attempt to get back the car keys, and tries to push him away from the doorway as she shouts, "Let me go, you bully!"

Socioeconomic status and violence We have already seen that husbands who are blocked from success in the economic-opportunity system are likely to attempt to resolve disagreements through exercising power that their wives consider nonlegitimate. There is also some evidence that violence is one of the ways this nonlegitimate power may be exercised in marriage.

A husband might turn to brute force as a means of dominating his wife if it seems the only way he can persuade her to comply with his wishes. As one blue-collar wife told Komarovsky, "Women got to figure men out, on account of men are stronger and when they sock you, they could hurt you." Another wife told of a time her husband pulled off a banister and ripped up three steps in a fit of anger toward her—which caused her to stop and think of what might happen if that physical strength were applied *directly* toward her.[90] Thus, according to Komarovsky, "the threat of violence is another ground of masculine power," particularly at lower socioeconomic levels. In her sample of blue-collar marriages, Komarovsky found that 27 percent of husbands with less than twelve years of education and 33 percent of wives with less than twelve years of education reported that conflicts were handled through violent quarreling, with occasional beating and breaking things. Among the high school graduates in her sample, 17 percent of the husbands and 4 percent of the wives reported such violence in marital quarreling.[91]

O'Brien likewise reports evidence of a connection between violence and a family's relationship to the economic-opportunity structure.[92] O'Brien's sample of 150 divorce applicants included 24 percent upper middle class, 29 percent lower middle class, and 47 percent working class. In one out of six families, violence had occurred to such an extent that it was considered a major reason for initiating divorce.

O'Brien separated the 25 cases of families spontaneously reporting violence from the 125 cases where violence had not been reported as a reason for divorce. He found evidence that physical force on the part of the husband-father was commonly linked with underachievement in the breadwinner role. (See Table 8-B.) Since his sample did not include families with husbands chronically unemployed, the lower class was not represented. Otherwise even more evidence of violence would likely have shown up. The greater incidence of violence characterizing underclass families in ghetto areas says O'Brien, "reflects, not a subcultural disposition toward violence, but rather a greater incidence of men in the father/husband role who fail to have the achievement capacities normally associated with this role."

But why should men become violent with their wives and children because they as husbands and fathers haven't been achievers in the economic-opportunity system? Some men may react aggressively out of a sense of frustration at being blocked from the rewards which achievement in that system would have brought them. Unable to attack the system directly or the forces which they feel hold them back from its benefits, such men turn their attacks upon their families. Their reaction is what we have described as explosive violence.

On the other hand, it is quite possible that coercive violence takes place as well as explosive violence in homes where the husband has not achieved at a high level. Lacking legitimate authority earned by his accomplishments in the realm of work, such a husband may nonetheless feel that he has the right to domineer over his wife. He accepts an ideology of male supremacy, even if his wife views his power as nonlegitimate and does not submit to it unquestioningly or happily. If there is no other means of getting his way, such a husband may try physical force. One behavioral scientist says that the husband's perception of a failure to be in control underlies his violent outbursts.[93] In the thinking of such a husband, not to be "in control" of his wife and children is not to be fully a man.

Goode points out that social systems contain four major elements by which persons may move others to carry out their wishes: (1) money or other material resources, (2) prestige or respect (such as commanded by a person in a position to which others look up), (3) winsomeness (likeability, attractiveness, friendship, love), and (4) force or the threat of force.[94] In other words, we are back to the "carrot and stick" analogy. Persons may get their way either through rewards or punishments meted out to those whom they wish to control. Husbands who lack

TABLE 8-B COMPARISON OF ACHIEVEMENT STATUS OF HUSBANDS IN VIOLENCE AND NONVIOLENCE SUBGROUPS OF UNSTABLE FAMILIES

	Prevalence in:	
Achievement Status of Husband	*Violence Subgroup (Number = 25)*	*Nonviolence Subgroup (Number = 125)*
Husband was seriously dissatisfied with his job	44%	27%
Husband started but failed to complete either high school or college	44	18
Husband's income was the source of serious and constant conflict	84	24
Husband's educational achievement was less than his wife's	56	14
Husband's occupational status was lower than that of his father-in-law (wife's marital mobility downward)	37	28

Source: O'Brien, 1971, p. 695.

positive resources with which to reward their wives are likely to find it more difficult to extract submission or compliance from them. Thus, they turn to the one resource that appears to remain to them—physical force.

O'Brien has taken ideas from conflict theory as it applies to the larger society and has shown how these same ideas may be applied to the family. He points out that those in a superior position in a social system may hold such a position because of an *ascribed* status—a status they have not earned but have been granted by virtue of their membership in some social category (whites in a white-dominant society, males over females, feudal lords over peasants, and so on). In such a social system, those in an inferior position may accept and support the arrangement, believing that the group in the superior position has the right to rule because of its advantaged skills and resources. However, says O'Brien, "One of the most common situations leading to a rejection of the legitimacy of those in high status is when their achieved status fails to measure up to their ascribed status."[95] If the superior group is not able to back up its privileged position with a display of adequate resources, or if it fails to distribute such resources fairly to those over whom it holds power, a conflict situation emerges which may erupt in violence.[96] Perceiving a threat to the legitimacy of its superior position, the dominant group may resort to coercive action (violence) against the subordinate group that has dared to challenge its supremacy. Applying these ideas to the family, O'Brien concludes that "one should find that violence is most common in those families where the classically 'dominant' member (male-adult-husband) fails to possess the superior skills, talents or resources on which his preferred superior status is supposed to be legitimately based."

Another reason for more violence at lower socioeconomic levels may relate to childhood gender-role socialization in which boys are encouraged to develop what Jackson Toby has termed "*compulsive* masculinity," with an exaggerated emphasis on roughness and toughness as a sign of manhood. Toby suggests that boys at such levels, having grown up with little opportunity to understand, appreciate, and wield *symbolic* power (such as the power of a physician or business executive), may look on violence as "the most appropriate way to protect one's honor, to show courage, or to conceal fear, especially fear of revealing weakness."[97]

Types of Conflict

Although, as we have seen, violence is one way to resolve conflicts, it is by no means the only way. In order to understand other directions in which conflict may move, it helps to look at three ways of categorizing conflict.

Zero-sum and mixed-motive conflict In a bullfighting contest, either the matador or the bull will win—not both. The goal of the game is to conquer the opponent. Social conflict may also be of this type and is sometimes called zero-sum; the contesting parties expect to have either all or nothing. An assassin stalks and kills his victim; the United States Congress impeaches the President and removes him from office; one nation gains a military victory and forces another nation to surrender unconditionally. Persons or groups on the losing end gain no apparent benefits. The winning party or group takes home "all the marbles," and the game is over. Zero-sum conflict is resolved in the majority of instances by extraordinary coercion or else actual violence.

However, there is another type of conflict insofar as objectives are concerned. Rather than a "winner take all" approach, there occurs a "mixed-motive situation." This kind of conflict is far more frequent in social interaction than is the zero-sum type. In mixed-motive conflict, the contesting parties also want to gain benefits at the other's expense, but they do not wish to totally crush or destroy the other. It is in the interests of both, their maximum joint profit, to continue the relationship—if they are able. The term *mixed motive* is used, writes social psychologist Philip Brickman, "since each party may be partly motivated by a desire to cooperate around the common interests in the relationship and partly motivated by a desire to compete for the more favorable share of those resources which must be divided up."[98]

In the past several decades, wars have come to be fought in ways that suggest mixed-motive rather than zero-sum conflict. The Korean war and the Vietnam war are both examples of no-win struggles. Thus, they are sometimes spoken of as "police actions," "limited warfare," or efforts at "containment," rather than as calls to conquer and divide the spoils. In such conflicts, a nation desires to gain its objectives without destroying the other nation. Being unwilling for the total destruction that atomic warfare would bring, world powers since World War II have contended with one another in mixed-motive fashion.

In our story of Bob and Julie's negotiations over the new car, the conflict was mixed-motive. Each wanted to gain at the expense of the other, but neither wanted to wipe the other out in zero-sum fashion. Each saw value in maintaining their relationship and wanted to cooperate on the basis of all they held in common, even though their competing interests were pulling in different directions. Bob was not ready to insist on a new car to the point of breaking up the marriage, nor was Julie ready to resist to this point. Thus, they had to deal with mixed motives: competition and cooperation.

Personality-based and situational conflict Another hypothetical couple, the Wilsons, sought a counselor's help because of severe conflicts in their marriage. Ted Wilson complained that his wife neglected household chores to read or watch television. "And she's always nagging me to give her time off from taking care of the kids. What kind of woman is she if she can't stand taking care of her own children and can't keep the house decently clean? Something's wrong with her!" At this point, Betty Wilson broke in: "He's always saying something's wrong with me! Why doesn't he ever look at himself? The first thing he says when he comes in the door each evening is, 'What's for dinner?' or 'Don't you have anything cooked *yet*?' He's only affectionate if he wants sex. He only cares about himself. He won't even baby-sit so that I can take some evening-school courses."

Viewing the Wilsons' problem solely as a *personality-based* conflict, the counselor told Betty she should accept her wife-mother role and "adjust to her womanhood" rather than fight against it. She should stop rebelling against her responsibilities as a homemaker and should leave her husband free to pursue his occupational interests. Her interests should be secondary to those of Ted and the children. Ted, for his part, must learn to be more understanding. "Show Betty more affection and consideration," the counselor advised.

The Wilsons went home, tried out the counselor's advice, and found it didn't work. After a few more months of conflict, they visited a different counselor.

To the second counselor, the Wilsons' case was one of *situational* conflict. Resolution of such conflict lies in changing the situation rather than trying to change the people to fit the situation. The Wilsons were helped first to see what lay at the root of their problem. Betty felt frustrated in her homemaker role not out of malice or laziness but because she felt blocked from finishing college. She watched programs on public television and read books constantly to keep stretching her mind beyond what she felt housekeeping would allow. The counselor helped the couple see that trying to force Betty to "adjust" or "adapt" wasn't the answer. What they needed to do was to negotiate and find ways to make it possible for her to continue her education.

The Wilsons worked out a plan for sharing household chores and child care, and both the negotiation process and the sharing has strengthened their relationship. Watching his wife's accomplishments and happiness, Ted has a new appreciation and respect for her and finds himself being much more affectionate now that the old hostilities are gone. Betty is so grateful for Ted's willingness to finance her education as well as his sharing child care and home responsibilities that she feels a new love for him. And even housework isn't the same old drudgery that it was in the days of her sulking and resentment. The Wilsons are finding that the changed situation is removing their old complaints about each other.

When sociologists speak of social conflict, they are primarily concerned with conflict of the situational type. There is no denying that personality-based conflicts exist, and there is no denying that personality factors may play a part in certain aspects of situational conflict. However, it helps to make a distinction between fighting that is an end in itself (such as giving vent to tensions and aggressions) and fighting that has a goal in view (settling a disagreement, coming to a decision, changing a structural situation).

Coser refers to persons who act belligerently out of an apparent "need" to fight, hate, and release hostilities. They are always ready to battle, and the "enemy" is not so important to them as is the act of fighting. This is conflict for its own sake. However, it is a serious but common error to try to explain social conflict solely in terms of tension release. *Structural* factors account for much if not most social conflict. Coser cites the example of a worker engaged in strike activity in order to effect changes, such as higher wages, fringe benefits, better working conditions, and so on, and shows how such a man's conflict differs from that of another worker who simply hates the boss because he is an authority figure and reminds him of his father. The first worker's conflict with management is situational; the second man's is personality-based.[99]

Similarly, marital conflicts may have either a situational or personality base; but perhaps far more than is generally realized, such conflicts stem from factors relating to situations which spouses could seek to remedy, instead of simply complaining about one or the other's "unpleasant personality" or how hard it is to get along with him or her. Resolving social conflict over incompatible goals or limited resources is not a matter of "adapting" or "adjustment;" rather it calls for *change.*

Basic and nonbasic conflict It is one thing to engage in conflict within agreed-upon rules of a game; it is quite another to have a conflict about the rules. The first kind of conflict is *nonbasic.* When the rules themselves are called into question and contested, the conflict is clearly *basic.*

When Congress passes a bill and the President vetoes it, Congress may or may not override the veto. But the whole sequence of events is a struggle within the rules set down by the Constitution. That sort of conflict is routine nonbasic conflict. However, what happens when Congress overrides a President's veto and instructs the executive branch to spend money for sewers and roads, only to have the President impound the funds? When that actually happened during the Nixon administration, the conflicts were resolved by court decisions ordering Nixon to use the funds. Again, the rules provided by the Constitution were able to resolve the resistance and struggle.

But at another point in the Nixon administration, journalists were talking about a "constitutional crisis" in which the President was ordered by the courts to release certain papers and tapes which be claimed were covered by "executive privilege." A "crisis" could occur if Nixon did not back down. Would the court use physical coercion to enforce its will? Yet, how could it proceed against the head of the Armed Forces and of the Justice Department? As it turned out, Nixon complied with the basic rule of political conflict that the courts have ultimate legitimate authority in such matters and thus the last word. Had he acted in any other way, it would have been seen as a gross use of raw nonlegitimate power.

Principles involved in conflict-resolution processes at the macro level also may be applied at the micro level. In other words, the same principles that apply to struggles between executive, courts, and Congress apply as well to marital conflict. To illustrate, let's return once again to our story of Bob and Julie. We saw how they resolved their conflict over a new car by renegotiating within the existing rules or role norms which characterize their kind of marriage arrangement. However, at another point, Bob is offered a job in another locale—a position he considers much more challenging and financially rewarding than his current job. But an exciting opportunity has also come up for Julie in their present location. She has been invited to develop and direct a special-education program in the local schools, while at the same time pursuing a master's degree at a nearby university. The stage is set for conflict over their different goals.

Under the rules or norms of a senior partner–junior partner marriage, Bob would expect Julie to forgo her opportunities in special education and move with him, since his role has been defined as chief provider. As such, his occupational demands necessarily take precedence over most other family demands. Another norm characterizing traditional marriage arrangements has been the expectation that marriage will mean children. It is virtually taken for granted that the union of a husband and wife should produce children at some point in order that the gratifications of the father and mother roles may be experienced.

To complicate Bob and Julie's situation further, Bob has started to talk about having a child soon. He feels that his new position will make it possible to manage the economic costs of a baby and suggests that it's time to have one. Julie need not continue working, Bob says, since he will be able to support a family totally if he takes the new job. Thus, still acting under the "rules of the game" for the kind of marriage Bob and Julie have been maintaining, Bob begins to negotiate a new exchange with his wife. He believes that the rules furnish him with legitimate authority to ask her to move with him and to undertake motherhood soon after.

Julie, however, has other ideas. Having always leaned toward modern, equalitarian sex-role norms, she is now beginning to ask questions about the senior partner–junior partner arrangement. The opportunity of a career in developing and administering special-education programs seems challenging. Bob's requests therefore strike her as unjust. She feels that her costs will rise and her rewards drop substantially if she goes along with her husband. She begins to struggle and resist. Conflict has emerged.

Julie bargains, saying she is willing for Bob to move and for them to commute alternately on weekends. Through her conflict and in her specific negotiating process, she is in effect beginning to challenge the norms that govern the senior partner–junior partner arrangement. Open communication was established as negotiations began, but as the conflict progresses certain deep issues begin to move to the fore. Should Julie have children or should she remain voluntarily childless? Should their marriage continue to be based on role specialization, or should they shift patterns to one based on role interchangeability so that Julie would be considered an equal partner in a dual-career arrangement?

These conflicts are clearly basic in that they involve contention over what the rules of the game should be. The game (marriage) will be very different if fundamental rules are changed. Rules governing American football are very different from those governing European football—a game which is more like soccer than football. In politics, the rules in the United States say that the President shall not use force to resist the courts or Congress. But in many countries today generals and presidents openly use military force to get their way when parliaments or courts cross them. These are two very different political games.

The earlier conflict of Bob and Julie over the purchase of a new automobile was nonbasic. We saw that even nonbasic conflict is likely to bring about situational changes. This is doubly so for basic conflict. But in addition, basic conflict has the potential for serious system disruption. For any social system, basic conflict can mean instability or even total collapse. For instance, if an American President could persuade a general to mobilize troops to resist a congressional order to remove him from office, there would occur the most serious and devastating disruption of American democracy in two centuries. Or if two companies were to experience basic conflict over the rules of their buyer-seller relationship, they might simply terminate the association. Such a breaking off of the relationship would not be so likely to occur over nonbasic conflict, which is more easily negotiable.

In marriage, basic conflict may take place over several core issues. Earlier, we saw that marriage has both an expressive side (love, empathy, companionship, displaying affection) and an instrumental side (economic functions, household tasks, and so on). Both in the personal realm and the practical realm of marriage, basic conflict may occur. Marriage was defined as a relationship in which there is both sexual and economic interdependence between two persons, and thus social norms for the marital relationship include the expectation that the husband and wife will have sexual intercourse with one another and will share their material wealth. Basic conflict may occur over either of these norms.

For example, a distressed middle-aged woman wrote to a newspaper advice columnist with the following story: She and her husband were both in their second marriages, and for six years they had found together what she described as a happiness neither had dreamed possible. Almost nightly, they had sexual relations which both enjoyed immensely. Then the husband joined a religious cult and changed his attitudes entirely. The wife wrote: "He said he could no longer kiss me, or touch me, or sleep in the same bed with me because if he did he could not enter the kingdom of heaven because he would be committing adultery since we had both been married before!" After eight months of living this way, the wife was seeking help[100] because the conflict was of the most basic sort.

How basic conflict may occur over economic sharing is illustrated in the later life of novelist Leo Tolstoy and his wife the Countess Tolstoy. Tolstoy had become obsessed with a concern for nonmaterialistic values and a desire to share his royalties and other wealth with those who were poor. His wife considered him selfish and neglectful of his own family. Why should he give away *their* money to strangers? Didn't she deserve some reward for all her years of hard work in caring for their home and rearing the children? For Tolstoy to give away his royalties appeared to his wife as a breaking of the fundamental rules of the game as they applied to economic provision and sharing. The *consumption* of resources for survival and for status is a basic issue in marriage just as is economic *production.*

As we have seen, each of the four ways marriage may be structured also has rules about which partner is the unique or chief provider. The issue of whether or not to have children is also basic—particularly where marriage has been viewed in traditional terms. At the same time, there may occur *nonbasic* conflicts within the same general areas that have been discussed (sex, the provider role, the consumption of resources, and the issue of children). Such secondary conflicts may center around the hours the husband or wife is working, how to discipline the children, how often and with what techniques should sex relations take place, or how to keep expenditures within the budget. But underlying each of these secondary conflicts is an assumption that there is agreement as to the four basic core issues (i.e., that there will be sexual intercourse, that the provider role has been acknowledged to be the primary responsibility of one or both partners, that parenthood will be undertaken or avoided voluntarily, and that consumption and life-style will be of a certain kind). To the degree that such basic consensus exists, struggles which are less central can more satisfactorily be resolved.

In the case of Bob and Julie, Julie's objective is to resolve their basic conflict in such a way that she will become an equal partner with her husband, with her career and interests considered just as important as his. She is also increasingly open to the possibility of remaining childless and avoiding the mother role entirely. This is a very different "game" or arrangement than the couple had before when Julie seemed content to be a junior partner and planned to work only a few years before settling down to have a family. Yet it is precisely those former rules and that earlier game which Bob wants. Since each spouse wants to play a different game with a different set of rules, how can they resolve their mutual struggles and resistances? How can they hold their relationship together and avoid separation or divorce?

Some persons might argue that if the husband could somehow retain final authority, as was traditionally the case, then basic conflicts such as these could be resolved. The husband could simply declare, "This is what we will do," and the issue would be settled. However, that argument overlooks the twin questions of justice and accountability. Husbands have generally tended to resolve conflicts in ways they thought best, with "best" meaning ways that seemed favorable to themselves simply because they were considered to have the final authority. Again it seems appropriate to echo John Stuart Mill's argument of a century ago that there is no inherent structural reason that one partner in a voluntary association such as a business partnership should allow the other to be the final authority.

Moreover, traditionally husbands had authority but no accountability, much as did preparliamentary monarchs. But today even a President who says the "buck stops here" is accountable for the exercise of nonlegitimate power. He is accountable to Congress who can impeach him, the courts who can reverse him, or to voters who can turn him out of office. Thus, in marriage, an appeal to some ultimate authority based on gender whose decisions cannot be disputed, modified, or rejected, or who could not be removed from his position of authority is simply not considered fair or wise in modern society. What Lord Acton said about political power applies as well to the notion of the male (or female) as absolute final arbiter in marriage. "Power corrupts, but absolute power corrupts absolutely."

There are several alternative modes of conflict resolution that Bob and Julie can pursue. Assuming reasonable communication and willingness to negotiate, Bob can agree to a bargain in which the rules are indeed changed. Julie would then become an equal partner with her husband in the sense that each would be equally committed to a career, with the career interests of each given equal priority. As for the matter of starting a family, neither having children nor childlessness is requisite to the equal-partner marriage arrangement; decisions about children are somewhat more optional here than in the other marital patterns (owner-property, head-complement, and senior partner–junior partner). Thus, Bob may try to negotiate with Julie about having a child. If they do decide to have one, issues such as timing and child care become additional matters for negotiation. How extensively should they rely on nursery and day-care facilities? How responsible will Bob be for child care?

Besides bargaining for a child, Bob may also aim negotiation toward persuading Julie to move with him. Let us assume she can find educational and career opportunities in the new locale comparable to those in the old. When Julie agrees to pursue these opportunities rather than her original plans, a new exchange is established in which both spouses experience maximum joint profit. Julie has a new game; she is now an equal partner. At the same time, she has conceded to move and also to have a child—both however under conditions that she does not consider excessively costly or punishing. Bob, for his part, has gained the benefits he wanted (the move and the child), but he agrees to a new game based on role interchangeability in which he is now merely a co-provider and in which Julie possesses as much authority and autonomy as he does.

However, the story could have a different ending. Upon facing their basic conflict, Bob and Julie may simply decide on another mode of resolution—ending the marriage. The key is whether or not Bob is willing for the basic changes in the rules for which Julie is pressing. In other words, is he willing for a new game? If he is not, it is difficult to see what meaningful concessions Julie can make, given her objectives. They are resisting each other over very basic issues; and since both perceive that so much is at stake, no significant negotiations or bargaining can take place. The couple may therefore decide that it is in the best interests of both of them simply to separate and file for divorce. (See Figure 8-4.) Each compares the level of alternatives (rewards and costs) within the marriage with alternatives outside it. Each concludes that the latter alternatives are more desirable or "profitable" (fewer costs, greater rewards) than those in their present situation. And so they leave it.

Collective Conflict

The conflict of Bob and Julie may at first appear to be simply a case of two individuals in conflict, and indeed that is possible. On the other hand, what is happening in the lives of Bob and Julie may reflect on the micro level what is also going on at the macro level of society. Throughout this book, we have focused on processes of social organization at the closeup or individual level *within the context of larger social forces.* Perhaps a better understanding of the individual conflict of Bob and Julie will be gained if we look at what is undoubtedly the most significant of these larger social forces affecting male-female relationships today, namely, the revival of feminism.

A high-priority objective of the women's movement is to raise the consciousness of women as a whole as to their interests vis-à-vis those of men. Feminist leaders encourage collective legal, political, and economic action (in other words, struggle or conflict) in order to enhance women's interests. Sociologist Peter Blau's description of the formation of any protest movement seems fitting. He writes:

> Collective disapproval of power engenders opposition. People who share the experience of being exploited by the unfair demands of those in positions of power, and by the insufficient rewards they receive for their contributions, are likely to communicate their feelings of anger, frustration, and aggression to each other. . . . The social support the oppressed give each other in the course of discussing their common grievances and feelings of hostility justifies and reinforces their aggressive opposition against those in power. It is out of such shared discontent that opposition ideologies and movements develop. . . .[101]

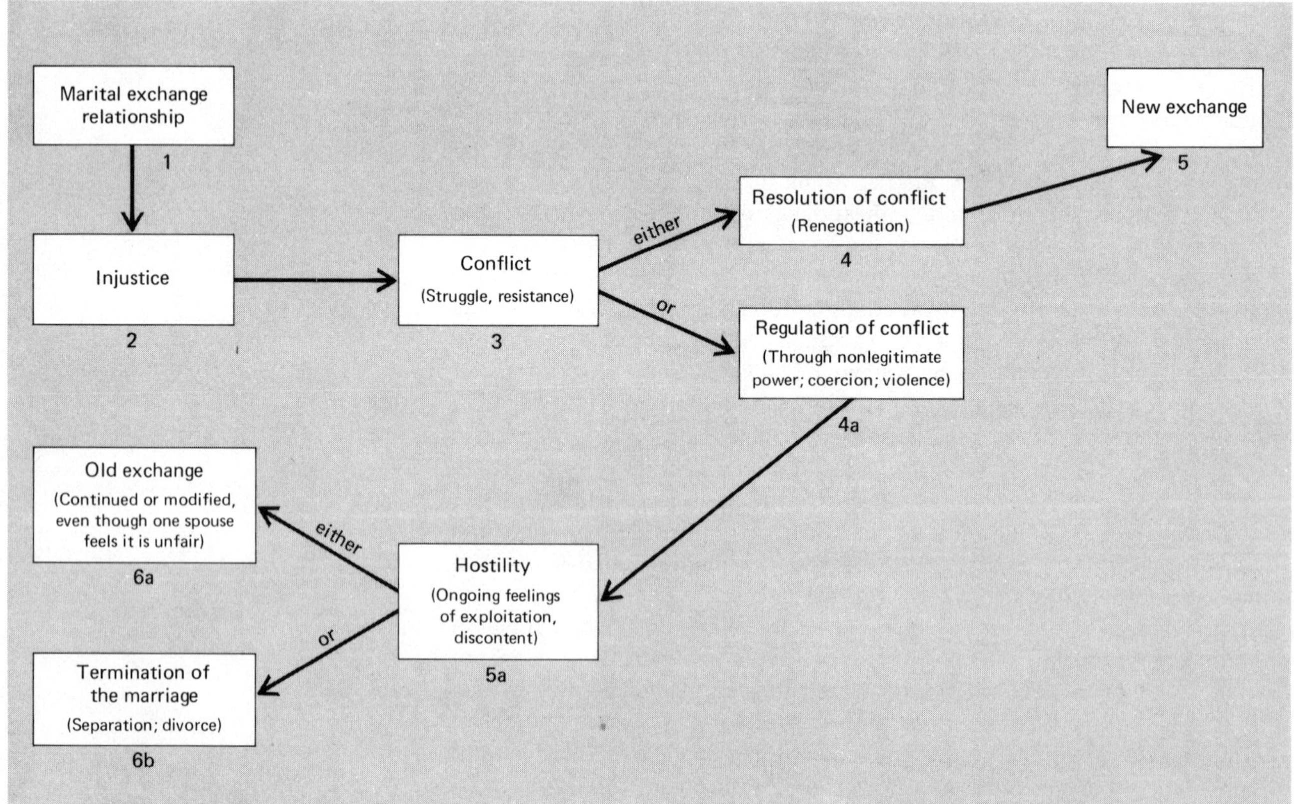

Figure 8-4 Three possible outcomes of marital conflict: resolution, regulation, or termination of the marriage (to be compared with Figure 8.3).

The collective opposition embodied in the women's movement does not mean that every individual female is in actual conflict with every individual male. But it does mean that in the future we may expect that increasing numbers of married women will become more aware of and sensitive to the issue of distributive justice in terms of male-female interests. Consequently, it is possible that increasing numbers of wives who began marriage in the status of either complement or junior partner may later define those situations as not sufficiently rewarding. Through bargaining, negotiation, and basic conflict, they may seek to change the rules of their marital relationship after having been married for a certain time period.

Thus, even though certain bargains may be struck at the outset of marriage, causing the husband to perceive that he is entering a relatively traditional arrangement, current and future conditions of modern society are such that even the basic rules of the relationship may subsequently be challenged. In some instances, husbands may be willing for and may even encourage these kinds of "radical" shifts in the game. In other instances, husbands may be unwilling to make the basic changes for which their wives are pressing; and for a while such situations might contribute to continuing increases in rates of divorce. In time, however, as more males grow up learning less traditional roles for both sexes, divorces resulting from such basic clashes should begin to taper off.

NOTES

1 Bloomington-Bedford Sunday Herald Times, "Dear Abby," June 9, 1974.
2 Aristotle, "The Nicomachean Ethics," quoted in Blau, 1964, p. 199.
3 Seidenberg, 1970, p. 304; see also Niebuhr, 1957.
4 Winter, 1973, p. 4.
5 Winter, 1973, p. 5.
6 Rodman, 1967, Buric and Zecevic, 1967; Safilios-Rothschild, 1967; Michel, 1967; Hallenbeck, 1966; Safilios-Rothschild, 1970; Herr, 1963; Centers, Raven, and Rodrigues, 1971; Liu, Hutchison, and Hong, 1973; Turk and Bell, 1972; Rodman, 1972; Olson and Rabunsky, 1972; Sprey, 1972; Bahr, 1972.
7 Safilios-Rothschild, 1970.
8 Ryder, 1970; Komarovsky, 1962; Safilios-Rothschild, 1969, 1970.
9 Safilios-Rothschild, 1970, p. 540.
10 Blood and Wolfe, 1960.
11 Safilios-Rothschild, 1970.
12 See Turk and Bell, 1972; Scanzoni, 1965; Safilios-Rothschild, 1969; Brown and Rutter, 1966; Hess and Torney, 1962.
13 Olson and Rabunsky, 1972.
14 Greenblat, Stein, and Washburne, 1974.
15 See summaries in Turk and Bell, 1972; Liu, Hutchison, and Hong, 1973.
16 Turk and Bell, 1972, p. 220.
17 Heer, 1963
18 Safilios-Rothschild, 1970; Rodman, 1967, 1972.
19 Safilios-Rothschild, 1970, p. 548.
20 Benston, 1969, pp. 3–4.
21 Gillespie, 1971, p. 457.
22 Blood and Wolfe, 1960.
23 Safilios-Rothschild, 1969, 1970; Centers, Raven, and Rodrigues, 1971; Rodman, 1967, 1972.
24 Centers, Raven and Rodrigues, 1971.
25 Heer, 1963.
26 Waller, 1951, pp. 190–192.
27 Rodman, 1967, 1972.
28 Buric and Zecevic, 1967.
29 Safilios-Rothschild, 1967.
30 Homans, 1961, p. 287.
31 Buckley, 1967, p. 186.
32 Goode, 1964, p. 75.
33 Blood and Wolfe, 1960, pp. 30–33.
34 Komarovsky, 1962, pp. 225–229.
35 Scanzoni, 1970, p. 151.
36 See summary in Winter, 1973, p. 157.

37 Scanzoni, 1970, pp. 159–162; Heer, 1958; Blood and Wolfe, 1960.
38 Davis, 1973, chap. 5; also Lederer and Jackson, 1968, for their concept of *quid pro quo* or "something for something."
39 Goode, 1963, pp. 21–22.
40 Siegel and Fouraker, 1960, pp. 1, 9.
41 Homans, 1961, p. 74.
42 Brickman, 1974, pp. 27, 228.
43 Alexander and Simpson, 1971.
44 Durkheim, 1893.
45 Blau, 1964; Fox, 1974; for a somewhat different perspective on personal marriage contracts, see Weitzman, 1974, pp. 1249–1258.
46 Kelley and Schenitzki, 1972, pp. 304, 306; Siegel and Fouraker, 1960, p. 20.
47 Blau, 1964, p. 99.
48 This definition is based on a combination of Coser, 1956, p. 8; Kriesberg, 1973, p. 17; and Brickman, 1974, p. 1.
49 Kriesberg, 1973, p. 4.
50 As quoted in *Time,* Vol. 103, No. 13 (April 1, 1974), p. 26.
51 Deutsch, 1971, p. 54.
52 Kelley and Stahelski, 1970; White, 1966.
53 Klineberg, 1964, p. 153, as quoted in Brickman, 1974, p. 153.
54 Schelling and Halperin, 1961, p. 8, as quoted in Brickman, 1974, p. 153.
55 Blau, 1964, p. 22.
56 Quoted in Al Stump, "Another Oppressed Minority Is Heard From," *TV Guide,* vol. 22, no. 30 (July 27, 1974), pp. 32–35.
57 Thibaut and Kelley, 1959, pp. 21–23.
58 Blau, 1964; Coser, 1956.
59 Blau, 1964, p. 301.
60 Coser, 1956, p. 73.
61 Scanzoni, 1970, pp. 157–158.
62 Blood and Wolfe, 1960, pp. 243–244.
63 Scanzoni, 1975b.
64 Scanzoni, 1975b.
65 O'Brien, 1971, p. 692.
66 Mulvihill, Tumin, and Curtis, 1969, app. 10.
67 Steinmetz and Straus, 1974, pp. 39 and 93.
68 FBI Uniform Crime Reports, 1973.
69 Gil, 1971.
70 Calvert, 1974.
71 Stark and McEvoy, 1970.
72 Parnas, 1967.
73 FBI Uniform Crime Reports, 1973.
74 O'Brien, 1971.
75 Levinger, 1966.
76 Straus, 1974.
77 Gelles, 1973a.
78 Steinmetz and Straus, 1973.
79 Gelles, 1973b.
80 Goode, 1971.
81 See for example Bach and Wyden, 1968.
82 Sprey, 1971.
83 Coser, 1956, p. 62.
84 Coser, 1956, pp. 63–63. 79.
85 Coser, 1956, p. 40.
86 Blau, 1964, p. 304.
87 Straus, 1974.
88 O'Brien, 1971.
89 Steinmetz and Straus, 1974, p. 4.
90 Komarovsky, 1962, p. 227.
91 Komarovsky, 1962, p. 363.
92 O'Brien, 1971.
93 Whitehurst, 1974, p. 76.
94 Goode, 1971, p. 624.
95 O'Brien, 1971.
96 Grimshaw, 1970.
97 Toby, 1966.
98 Brickman, 1974.
99 Coser, 1956, p. 50.
100 Bloomington (Ind.) Herald-Telephone, "Dear Abby," Mar. 16, 1973.
101 Blau, 1964, p. 23.

BIBLIOGRAPHY*

Alexander, C. Norman, Jr., and Richard Simpson
1971 "Balance theory and distributive justice." Pp. 69–80 in Herman Turk and Richard Simpson (eds.), *Institutions and Social Exchange.* Indianapolis: Bobbs-Merrill.

Bach, G. and P. Wyden
1968 *The Intimate Enemy.* New York: Morrow.

Bahr, Stephen J.
1972 "Comment on 'the study of family power structure: a review 1960–1969.'" *Journal of Marriage and the Family* 34:239–243.

Benston, Margaret
1969 "The political economy of women's liberation." *Monthly Rev.* (September):3–4.

Blau, Peter
1964 *Exchange and Power in Social Life.* New York: Wiley.

Blood, Robert O., Jr., and Donald M. Wolfe
1960 *Husbands and Wives.* New York: Free Press.

Brickman, Phillip (ed.)
1974 *Social Conflict.* Lexington, Mass.: Heath.

Brown, George and Michael Rutter
1966 "The measurement of family activities and relationships." *Human Relations* 19:241–263.

Buckley, Walter
1967 *Sociology and Modern Systems Theory.* Englewood Cliffs, N.J.: Prentice-Hall.

Buric, O. and A. Zelevic
1967 "Family authority, marital satisfaction and the social network in Yugoslavia." *Journal of Marriage and the Family* 29:325–336.

Calvert, Robert
1974 "Criminal and civil liability in husband-wife assault." Pp. 88–91 in Steinmetz and Straus, 1974.

Centers, R., B. Raven, and A. Rodrigues
1971 "Conjugal power structure: a re-examination." *American Sociological Review* 36:264–278.

Coser, Lewis A.
1956 *The Functions of Social Conflict.* New York: Free Press.

Davis, Murray S.
1973 *Intimate Relations.* New York: Free Press.

Deutsch, Morton
1971 "Conflict and its resolution." Pp. 36–57 in C. G. Smith (ed.), *Conflict Resolution.* Notre Dame, Ind.: Notre Dame Univ. Press.

Durkheim, Emile
1893 *The Division of Labor in Society.* Translated by George Simpson. New York: Free Press edition, 1933.

Federal Bureau of Investigation
1973 *Uniform Crime Reports, 1972.* Washington, D.C.: U.S. Government Printing Office.

Fox, Alan
1974 *Beyond Contract: Work, Power and Trust Relations.* London: Faber and Faber.

Gelles, Richard
1973a "An exploratory study of intra-family violence." Unpublished Ph.D. dissertation, University of New Hampshire, Durham, N.H.

1973b "Child abuse as psychopathology: a sociological critique and reformulation." *American Journal of Orthopsychiatry* 43:611–621. (Reprinted in Steinmetz and Straus, 1974.)

Gil, David G.
1971 "Violence against children." *Journal of Marriage and the Family* 33:637–657.

Gillespie, Dair L.
1971 "Who has the power? The marital struggle." *Journal of Marriage and the Family* 33:445–458.

Goode, William J.
1963 *World Revolution and Family Patterns.* New York: Free Press.
1964 *The Family.* Englewood Cliffs, N.J.: Prentice-Hall.
1971 "Force and violence in the family." *Journal of Marriage and the Family* 33:624–636.

Greenblat, Cathy, Peter Stein, and Norman Washburne
1974 *The Marriage Game: Understanding Marital Decision Making.* New York: Random House.

Grimshaw, Allen D.
1970 "Interpreting collective violence: an argument for the importance of social structure." *Annals* 391 (September):9–20.

Hallenbeck, Phyllis
1966 "An analysis of power dynamics in marriage." *Journal of Marriage and the Family* 28:200–203.

Heer, David
1958 "Dominance and the working wife." *Social Forces* 36:341–347.
1963 "The measurement and bases of family power: an overview." *Journal of Marriage and the Family* 25:133–139.

Hess, Robert and Judith Torney
1962 "Religion, age and sex in children's perceptions of family authority." *Child Development* 33:781–789.

Homans, George C.
1961 *Social Behavior: Its Elementary Forms.* New York: Harcourt, Brace, and World.

Kelley, Harold and Anthony Stahelski
1970 "Social interaction basis of cooperators' and competitors' beliefs about others." *Journal of Personality and Social Psychology* 16:66–91.

Kelley, H. H. and D. P. Schenitzki
1972 "Bargaining." In C. G. McClintock (ed.), *Experimental Social Psychology.* New York: Holt.

Klineberg, O.
1964 *The Human Dimension in International Relations.* New York: Holt.

Komarovsky, Mirra
1962 *Blue-Collar Marriage.* New York: Random House.

*These items were excerpted from the full, 15 page bibliography of Men, Women, and Change.

Kriesberg, Louis
1973 *The Sociology of Social Conflicts.* Englewood Cliffs, N.J.: Prentice-Hall.

Lederer, W. J. and D. D. Jackson
1968 *The Mirages of Marriage.* New York: Norton.

Levinger, George
1966 "Physical abuse among applicants for divorce," an excerpt from "Source of marital satisfaction among applicants for divorce," *American Journal of Orthopsychiatry* 36 (October). as reprinted in Steinmetz and Straus, 1974, pp. 85–88.

Liu, William T., I. W. Hutchinson, and L. K. Hong
1973 "Conjugal power and decision making: a methodological note on cross-cultural study of the family." *American Journal of Sociology* 79:84–98.

Michel, Andree
1967 "Comparative data concerning the interaction in French and American families." *Journal of Marriage and the Family* 29:337–344.

Mulvihill, J. J., M. M. Tumin, and L. A. Curtis
1969 *Crimes of Violence.* Staff Report to the National Commission on the Causes and Prevention of Violence. Washington, D.C.: U.S. Government Printing Office.

Niebuhr, Reinhold
1957 *Love and Justice.* Edited by D. B. Robertson. Cleveland: World.

O'Brien, John
1971 "Violence in divorce-prone families." *Journal of Marriage and the Family* 33:692–698.

Olson, D. and C. Rabunsky
1972 "Validity of four measures of family power." *Journal of Marriage and the Family* 34:224–234.

Parnas, Raymond
1967 "The police response to the domestic disturbance." *Wisconsin Law Review* 914 (Fall):914–960.

Rodman, Hyman
1967 "Marital power in France, Greece, Yugoslavia, and the United States: a cross-national discussion." *Journal of Marriage and the Family* 29:320–324.
1972 "Marital power and the theory of resources in cultural context." *Journal of Comparative Family Studies* 3:50–67.

Ryder, Robert G.
1970 "Dimensions of early marriage." *Family Process* 9 (March):51–68.

Safilios-Rothschild, Constantina
1967 "A comparison of power structure and marital satisfaction in urban Greek and French families." *Journal of Marriage and the Family* 29:345–352.
1969 "Family sociology or wives' family sociology? A cross-cultural examination of decision making." *Journal of Marriage and the Family* 31:290–301.
1970 "The study of family power structure: a review 1960–1969." *Journal of Marriage and the Family* 32:539–552.

Scanzoni, John
1965 "A note on the sufficiency of wife responses in family research." *Pacific Sociological Review* (Fall):109–115.
1970 *Opportunity and the Family.* New York: Free Press.
1975b *Sex Roles, Life Styles, and Childbearing: Changing Patterns in Marriage and Family.* New York: Free Press.

Schelling, T. C. and M. H. Halperin
1961 *Strategy and Arms Control.* New York: Twentieth Century Fund.

Seidenberg, Robert
1970 *Marriage Between Equals.* First published as *Marriage in Life and Literature.* New York: Philosophical Library. Doubleday, Anchor Press edition, 1973.

Siegel, Sidney and Lawrence Fouraker
1960 *Bargaining and Group Decision Making.* New York: McGraw-Hill.

Sprey, Jetse
1971 "On the management of conflict in families." *Journal of Marriage and the Family* 33:722–732.
1972 "Family power structure: a critical comment." *Journal of Marriage and the Family* 34:235–238.

Stark, Rodney and James McEvoy
1970 "Middle class violence." *Psychology Today* 4 (November):52–65.

Steinmetz, Suzanne and Murray Straus
1974 (eds.), *Violence in the Family.* New York: Dodd, Mead.

Straus, Murray
1974 "Leveling, civility, and violence in the family." *Journal of Marriage and the Family* 36:13–29.

Thibaut, J. W. and H. H. Kelley
1959 *The Social Psychology of Groups.* New York: Wiley.

Toby, Jackson
1966 "Violence and the masculine ideal: some qualitative data." Pp. 20–27 in Marvin Wolfgang (ed.), *Patterns of Violence: The Annals of the American Academy of Political and Social Science* 364 (March).

Turk, J. L. and N. W. Bell
1972 "Measuring power in families." *Journal of Marriage and the Family* 34:215–223.

Waller, Willard
1951 *The Family.* Revised by Reuben Hill. New York: Dryden Press. (Original edition published in 1938.)

Weitzman, Lenore
1974 "Legal regulation of marriage: tradition and change." *California Law Review* 62 (July–September):1169–1288.

White, Ralph
1966 "Misperception as a cause of two world wars." *Journal of Social Issues* 22:1–19.

Whitehurst, Robert
1974 "Violence in husband-wife interaction." Pp. 75–82 in Steinmetz and Straus, 1974.

Winter, David
1973 *The Power Motive.* New York: Free Press.

MARRIAGE:
FOCUS ON CHANGE

by Elizabeth Wright

A summary of current attitudes towards marriage and the family in several countries with an annotated bibliography of readings.

--by Elizabeth K. Wright

The purpose of this paper is to present the findings of a varied group of authors who are currently writing on the subject of marriage. Two special aspects will be explored: problems of discrimination in law and custom affecting marriage today; and the changing structure of marriage with predictions for the future.

Women's Rights Within Marriage -- An International Perspective

As part of its mandate to support economic and social progress, the United Nations, through UNESCO and the Commission on the Status of Women, is addressing the world-wide problem of ending discrimination against women. In a working paper, the following rights for married as well as unmarried women have been proposed:

- Equal rights to maintain nationality though married to an alien;
- Equal rights to acquire, administer, inherit, and dispose of property;
- Equal rights in the law;
- Equal rights to movement of persons and residence;
- Equal right to choose a name;
- Freedom to leave a country including one's own;
- Equal rights to enter into marriage, to choose or refuse a spouse;
- Equal rights during marriage and at its dissolution, and in matters pertaining to children;
- The forbidding of child marriage and betrothal of children.

In addition, in education and employment the following rights are sought, and in each case the phrase "including married women" is used: equal rights to receive vocational training, to work, to choose a profession, to professional and vocational advancement, to equal pay and equal fringe benefits, to receive family allowances. Measures are also proposed to prevent dismissal from employment due to marriage or maternity, to provide paid maternity leave with job security after such leave, and to provide supporting social services to parents, including child care facilities.

Some of these rights are already established in the United States. Many still need a concerted effort. Two of the most troublesome areas lie in property law, which tends to favor men, and in equal rights during marriage and at its dissolution. The housewife's efforts do not entitle her to social security in her own name. Her legal right to support--or a fair share in the family income--can generally be enforced only through action for separation or divorce. The right of a woman to choose her own name in marriage and to define her legal place of residence are not generally recognized. For working women, there are almost no provisions for paid maternity leave, and social services and child care are inadequate. Although we now have sweeping laws against discrimination, in most cases long standing practices have not changed.

What is the status of equality for women, especially married women, in other countries and where does the United States lag behind? The countries where equality for women has been most fully recognized through laws giving them equal status in marriage, divorce, name, domicile, property, and child support are those of Eastern Europe. Women in Russia, for instance, rose from chattel status to full legal equality following the 1918 revolution. Similarly, other communist countries have followed Marxist doctrine on full equality for all citizens, recognizing the need for women to share in the economic process in order that the productive potential of the state might be fully realized. Though in Russia attitudes toward divorce, abortion, and child support have shifted with the perceived needs of the central government, basic rights to name, domicile, employment, property, separation, divorce, and abortion that are still being sought by women in other countries have remained unchanged.

Though equality is the basic policy in these countries, in actuality some problems also found in the West remain. Women in the USSR still bear the chief burden of housework, shopping, and child care; grandparents are in demand for child care, for nurseries and day care centers are not universally available and children occasionally fall ill. Husbands help, but equality in the home is not the rule. Soviet literature admits that the load of the Soviet wife who is both mother and worker is heavy indeed, and that in practice, equality has not been reached. The fact that women hold a disproportionate number of low paid jobs is a related point. While far more heavily represented in all professions (traditionally considered male), including the technological, women are not equally represented at the highest levels in either industry or politics. In the latter case it is explained that political activity is largely unpaid after-hours work. Major responsibility for home duties effectively excludes women from climbing the ladder of party structure. So despite the official position on equality, the fact that women are child-bearers and traditional tenders of home and children continues to mitigate against sexual equality as an actual fact.

Among non-communist countries, Sweden has the most favorable laws and policies on married women. Not only is there equality in law, but supportive social services--such as child care facilities, child allowances, and leave for child-rearing--are widely available. Recently, when a leading sociologist suggested the best pattern for women would be an initial career experience, followed by several years leave for rearing children, then resumption of career, there was widespread criticism from professional women who feared loss of career skills and advancement opportunities. The prevailing trend for women is continuance of a career, at least part time, while raising a family and sharing home burdens equally with men.

In other Western European countries, Asia, and Africa, progress toward equality in marriage varies considerably, but everywhere industrialization is inexorably pulling women into the mainstream of the productive process, and as a parallel effect, bringing movement toward independence and equal treatment under the law. The impression is strong that there is more recognition in many foreign countries that women are needed in the productive process outside the home, that their entry into the world of work should be facilitated, with the result that there is less emphasis on their traditional role than in the United States. But change is occurring here and will continue, not only in response to the women's movement, though that is certainly a factor, but also in response to these world-wide trends.

A Finnish representative to a United Nations conference made the following analysis. Fearing that a proposed article "might be interpreted as implying that it is not possible to achieve equality between men and women while preserving the unity and harmony of the family," the speaker noted that

> From an historical point of view, women's emancipation and the industrialization of countries are parallel processes. Industrialization makes it possible to transfer part of the work that earlier was performed at home into large industrial production units. The role of domestic work and the importance of the family as a productive unit has been decreased. The employment of women has been transferred outside their home. In the same historical process, birth rates tended to decrease in economically advanced countries, the educational level of both women and men rose and vocational training became more common. It also became necessary for governments to make effort in their social policies in order to transfer child-care and other traditional functions of the family partially to society. This trend has also caused an increase in the number of divorce cases, as women's independence, in respect of earning a living, makes divorce possible in practice. While it might appear that women's emancipation would risk a loosening in family ties, these phenomena are interrelated only as parallel results of industrialization. Along with economic independence for women the relations and understanding

> between the spouses has become more important than before. It is therefore inopportune to connect the unity and harmony of the family with women's emancipation, and further, the responsibility for unity and harmony in the family should lie equally with both men and women.

Changing Structure of Marriage in the United States

In the United States the factors most widely mentioned as causal in changing marriage are greater sexual permissiveness, easy divorce, working wives, smaller families due to "the pill" and legalized abortion, and the alleged decline of family and home influence. What is the actual situation? Are marriage and the family threatened? Up to 1973 the statistical evidence (allowing for increased population) indicated more marriages, younger marriages, fewer children, more divorces (greatest among those who married young and in low-income groups), more second marriages especially of divorced. Marriage had, up to this time, not been dying but increasing. A recent (January, 1975) United Press International story, however, suggests a change. A check of 22 cities and states showed more than 54% of marriage licence bureaus reporting a decrease in the number of licences issued in 1973 and in 1974. The decrease is variously attributed to the women's movement, the uncertain future, and the recession. The figures are too new and few to be called a trend.

Surveys show that more couples are living together without marriage, especially among the young as a form of courtship. Such relationships should not be seen as promiscuous since faithfulness tends to be the pattern. Most pairs eventually marry, especially if they want children. Legally, it is disadvantageous to bring up children out of wedlock, though some do so, and today more unwed mothers bring up their children rather than give them up for adoption. There is less pressure on married women to have children, with a consequent lowering of the birth rate. The steady increase in divorce and re-marriage has led to discussions of "serial monogamy" as the current form of marriage in the United States. However, one author points out that while many persons have been married twice, relatively few have been married more than twice, and concludes that second marriages are often successful and lasting. A related fact may be that marriages among the very young have the highest divorce rate.

College-educated, middle-class professionals often begin trends which are followed later by the general population. Among these it is becoming more common to live together without marriage if a previous marriage has failed, especially if children are not involved. This trend is noted both in the relatively young and with middle-aged couples, but is not yet statistically significant for the entire population. However, it helps explain the previously described sudden drop in marriages in some areas. The temper of the times has been described as fostering a movement toward self-realization and emphasis on the individual, bringing with it greater independence between spouses.

Traditional marriage in which the man supports the family and the wife does the housework and raises the children is still the norm in the United States. It is probably the most approved pattern, still desired and expected by many young women. Most young women work before marriage, from choice or necessity, and often continue until children are born. Many continue after childbearing, but there is still some prejudice against this course, as opposed to general acceptance if a wife gives up her work. However, most studies show no harm to children of working mothers, and many two career families feel their children gain in independence and responsibility. Women are living longer and increasingly turn to the job market after children are older, either to find a new career or resume one previously pursued. For those who do not, the nuclear family and the increasing independence of children make transition difficult for those older women who were entirely home-centered. It is said that the modern woman spends as much time on housework as her predecessors who were without mechanical aids, and that this proliferation of homekeeping duties arises as much from a lack of useful function in the society as from necessity. Some fill the gap with useful volunteer work; others simplify their home duties and take on a second paid career.

Even conventional marriage has varied patterns. One form of traditional marriage has been referred to as the "two-person career," in which the husband holds the position but the wife is expected to perform duties in connection with that career, even though she is unpaid. The most conspicuous example is the Presidency of the United States, but it is also true for the wives of diplomats, politicians, most upper-echelon government officials, business executives, university presidents, and clergymen. Usually the duties entail entertaining for the husband and freeing him from minor household duties and irritations. The wife is expected to be a behind-the-scenes helper and expediter, available at any time for a subsidiary role. For some fortunate women, this is a role they enjoy and handle well, finding great satisfaction in knowing that they are involved in their husband's success. But for others it can be frustrating. Business management has recently noted that the geographically mobile executive characteristic of American business may find satisfaction in success and in his business contacts, while his transplanted wife may have a breakdown when a community tie that gave interest and prestige to her life is cut off by a transfer. A diplomat's wife, whose principal job was to arrange dinners, shopping, informal meetings, and other activities, for persons attending international conferences where her husband played an important role, complained more or less jokingly, "All I do is arrange affairs for my husband to meet with other women." In her situation, some of the officials attending the meetings were women, but wives were never included. Most of these wives are capable and talented, but not only do the duties expected of them preclude a separate career, but they must expect to move frequently to radically new situations. One such wife when asked if the foreign service wife's role should be recognized by being paid replied, "Eventually, I believe this should happen. But right now I think that recognition in the form of academic credit could be given to wives who master a new environment, a new language, and substantially assist their husbands in representing their country." At any rate, more recognition or more options seem indicated.

An increasing number of couples, though still comparatively few, have what can be called the two-career marriage, in which both wife and husband have serious, continuing occupations whether they have children or not. Conventional opinion and the lack of social services in support of the career wife still make this a difficult course to pursue. Several surveys have been made of successful professional two-career marriages, mostly in the academic professions. Most have not included the professional women who did not marry, or those whose marriages failed. What does appear from these surveys, both in England and in the United States, is that true equality is hard to attain. Mobility in occupations presents difficulties. Rules against nepotism hamper the couple, especially if both partners work in the same field. When a new job offer beckons, who is to make the sacrifice? Two serious deterrents are the lack of good child-care facilities and the lack of opportunity in most professions for part-time work. Often, though not always, it is the wife who sacrifices her career; often she still assumes major home responsibility. The formulas for success in such marriages depend, as might be expected, on individual variations and compromises. Most husbands in these surveys of successful two-career marriages were interested in and supportive of their wives' careers, even in some cases moving and finding a new job to enable a wife to advance. Some wives worked part time for a while,or took a year or more off to care for children. Some expressed pleasure at the variety of their lives as compared to those of most men.

As for home responsibilities, they were either shared rather completely, minimized and made more efficient, or if possible, help was hired. Social life tended to be with similar couples and to be informal and less frequent than in traditional marriages. Some felt little in common with housewives or felt that housewives tended to be hostile. In the case of these well educated and successful couples the satisfactions outweighed the very real difficulties.

Future Prospects for Marriage

What changes in marriage and family pattern can we expect in the future? Most of the predictions which follow are based on the patterns we have described and presuppose a stable economy. A worldwide recession or depression could profoundly affect these trends, and probably not in favor of equality and independence for women. With this caveat, this is how most experts see marriage and family relationships developing.

The factor for change most agreed upon is the emphasis on individual self-realization. As girls and women are educated to seek independent roles, and as unisex standards gain, women's freedom and responsibility will increase. An autonomous rather than a dependent

relationship is expected to prevail in marriage and in family relationships. Marriage will be more like friendship with the emphasis on a close relationship, not necessarily a permanent one.

There will be greater diversity in forms of marriage and greater tolerance for varied patterns. The single life, living with another without legal marriage, unisex standards in sexual relationships, homosexual unions, group marriage, communal living, marriage contracts for limited periods, easier divorce, serial relationships--all will be more accepted.

Momogamous legal marriage will remain the most popular form of adult relationship. Some sociologists predict that a common pattern will be living together for the young, marriage in the child-bearing years, and serial relationships for the middle-aged. Others suggest polygyny, the marriage of one man with several women, because of the preponderance of women in an increasing older population. It will probably not become institutionalized because of opposition in law and custom. There will continue to be more women in the work force. Both divorce and remarriage are expected to increase.

What about children of these marriages of the future? There will be fewer born. The decision to have children will be carefully considered with less social disapproval of childlessness. Possibly a license and special preparation for parenthood may be required. Child-rearing will be more equally shared. More mothers will continue to work outside the home, and there will be more supportive services in the form of child care and maternity leave. Part-time opportunities and flexible schedules will be more common. Some sociologists feel that children will turn more to peers and siblings for social standards, and with the emphasis on self-fulfillment, the generation gap will increase. With easier divorce the reconstituted family with parents bringing up children from several unions will become common.

The emphasis on individual self-fulfillment and sex equality which all seem to agree are dominant factors bringing about change in marriage will, some believe, bring more happiness and more satisfactory relationships to both men and women. All agree that marriage, though its forms may vary, will endure.

In a study called Women and Success, The Anatomy of Achievement, Iolanda B. Low comments, "We can all agree that many more women can be called successful if we use a more open-ended definition of success. We can encompass all those who have an inner sense of their own identity and worth as persons or self-esteem as women---without reference to money or career accomplishment. Society needs more of these 'successful' women, free in their choice of roles (including the domestic ones), flexible to the needs around them, freed of guilt feeling and expenditure of negative energy." Under such a definition many life styles are possible.

SELECTED BIBLIOGRAPHY

1. Bernard, Jessie. The Future of Marriage. World, 1972. Also Bantam. Introduces the concept of "his marriage" and "her marriage" with discussions of past, present and future marriage. Well documented and readable. The author's more recent book, The Future of Motherhood is also of interest.

2. Carter, Hugh and Glick, Paul C. Marriage and Divorce. A social and economic study. Harvard, 1970. (American Public Health Ass'n Vital and Health Statistics Monographs). Comprehensive statistical analysis.

3. Citizen's Advisory Council on the Status of Women. U.S. Department of Labor. 1968. Report of the Task Force on Family Law and Policy. Recommendations leading toward economic partnership in marriage and more equitable laws concerning property and children.

4. Duberman, Lucile. Marriage and Its Alternatives. Praeger, 1974. Designed as a short treatise for beginning students of sociology, it includes interesting summaries of past sociologic theory, current status of marriage and predictions for the future. Readable, comprehensive, especially recommended.

5. Fogarty, Michael P., Rapoport, Phona & Rapoport, Robert N. Sex, Career and Family. Sage Publ. (Allen & Unwin) 1971. How and why women are successful and how to create conditions which will enable more women to enter the productive process. Part of the underlying research has been published by the Rapoports in Dual Career Families, Penguin, 1971, which gives detailed case histories of several British couples.

6. Holmstrom, Lynda. The Two-Career Family. Schenkman, 1972. A study of twenty two-career families in the Boston-Amherst area and a few couples of similar educational background where the wife had given up her career for marriage.

7. Howe, Louise Kapp, ed. The Future of the Family. Simon & Schuster, 1972. An anthology of stimulating selections from different countries, classes of society and ethnic groups, fiction and non-fiction.

8. Kundsin, Ruth B. Women and Success: The Anatomy of Achievement. Morrow, 1974. Life experiences of successful career women, followed by an examination of family attitudes and relationships that produce such women, plus a discussion of the professional woman as mother.

9. O'Neill, Nena and George. Open Marriage; A New Life Style for Couples. M. Evans, 1972. The persuasive thesis of these authors, husband and wife anthropologists, is that traditional marriage narrows friendships and activities to those mutually enjoyed, that a more independent relationship broadens and enriches marriage. In popular parlance "open marriage" has come to imply sexual variety, but the authors approach this aspect with considerable caution.

10. Polòna, Margaret M., & Garland, T. Neal. The Dual Profession Family. Business & Professional Women's Foundation, 1971. Still another study, this time of 53 couples where the wife was a doctor, lawyer or educa-

tor. Spouse relationships seem more traditional than in similar surveys.

11. St. George, George. Our Soviet Sister. Luce, 1973. The Soviet woman from the Revolution to the present. Interesting for comparison with our own laws and attitudes.

12. Seidenberg, Robert. Corporate Wives--Corporate Casualties? AMACON, 1973. The problems for wives and for marriages arising from executive mobility.

13. UNESCO. Commission on the Status of Women. Consideration of Proposals Concerning a New Instrument of International Law to Eliminate Discrimination Against Women. Working Paper. (EKN.6/573/Nov. 1973) General discussion by commission members from many countries plus a draft convention submitted by the Philippine delegation.

14. UNESCO. Commission on the Status of Women. (E/CN.6/584.11/20/73) Legal Capacity of Married Women: Capacity to Engage in Independent Work.

15. Weitzman, Lenore J. "Legal Regulation of Marriage: Tradition and Change," California Law Review, Vol. 62, no. 4, July-September 1974.

DIVORCE IN THE UNITED STATES

A 1976 report of the U. S. Census Bureau thus summarizes the changes occurring in marriage and divorce.

"Trends in the rate of first marriage, divorce, and remarriage of women since the early 20th century reflect patterns of change in the economic and social conditions in the United States. Each ... was at a relatively low point during the depression years of the 1930's, gradually climbing to a peak in the immediate post World War II period, and then declining throughout the 1950's. While the rate of first marriages continued to drop during the 1960's and into the 1970's, the rates of divorce and remarriage began an upturn around 1960 and increased dramatically from 1960 to 1970. Since 1970 the divorce rate has continued to climb, but the rate of remarriage has levelled off and may actually be declining somewhat. Some probable correlates of these recent trends include liberalization of divorce laws, growing societal acceptance of divorce and remaining single, and implicitly, a reduction in the economic cost of divorce. Also, the broadening educational and work experience of women has contributed to increased economic and social independence which, in the short run at least, may contribute to marital dissolution. At the same time that the rate of divorce has been increasing, women and men have, on the average, been remaining single longer. ...

"The net effect of recent trends in marriage and divorce is a growing proportion of women who are single or divorced and have not remarried. ... As the number of divorced women has increased, the number of female-headed families has also risen... 13% of all families and approximately a 73% increase since 1960.

Another section of the same report points out that though the number of women working full time increased substantially from 1960 to 1974, the female median income remained in 1974 about 57% of the median for comparable men. The income of the increasing number of female-headed families has not risen as much as that of male-headed families between 1970 and 1974, and the number of female-headed families below the poverty level increased, with this increase occurring exclusively among families with children under 18. Thus the "growing societal and economic independence of women" mentioned in the quotation above would seem to be severely limited. The need for an examination of the problems of divorced women and their children is obvious.

Contrary to popular myth, few divorced women are awarded alimony--14% in a recent survey, and of these less than half were receiving it regularly. In divided families the father supplies, on the average, less than half of the support of children.

Women are generally disadvantaged upon divorce because they are disadvantaged in marriage. Except in the few community property states women do not share equally in property acquired during marriage and most of these few do not provide for joint management of such property. A wife may be liable for inheritance taxes when her husband would not in similar circumstances, and pension and social security rights are often lost on divorce. The wife's contribution as a homemaker to marriage is not regularly recognized in divorce settlements, nor is the economic disadvantage she suffers by remaining out of the employment market during prime years. So great are the problems of the growing number of divorced and widowed older women that special relief is being sought in the form of "displaced homemaker" bills in the states and the U. S. Congress.

The publication in 1970 of the Uniform Marriage and Divorce Act greatly stimulated the enactment of no-fault divorce. In 1974, only 5 states retained fault grounds only, while 13 states had no-fault or irretrievable breakdown as the only grounds, and the rest had added some form of no-fault procedure. Unfortunately the economic safeguards and property division provisions suggested in the Act have seldom been adopted as well, with the consequent loss of some of the economic leverage for women in financial settlements.

The Homemakers Committee of the National Commission on the Observance of International Women's Year has set as a goal equal partnership of men and women in marriage and to that end has made these recommendations:

> Eliminate gift and inheritance taxes between spouses.
>
> Cover the homemaker in her own right under Social Security.
>
> Adopt as a minimum the economic protections of the Uniform Marriage and Divorce Act of 1973, and in addition consider requiring disclosure of assets, and support of children who are attending school until age 26.

The Committee also recommends that state laws contain a statement of intent such as introduced in Wisconsin as follows:

"It is the intent of the legislature that a spouse who has been handicapped socially or economically by his or her contributions to a marriage shall be compensated for such contributions at the termination of the marriage, insofar as this is possible, and may be reeducated where necessary to permit the spouse to become self-supporting at a standard of living reasonably comparable to that enjoyed during the marriage. It is further the intent of the legislature that the standard of living of any minor children of the parties be maintained at a reasonable level, so that insofar as is possible the children will not suffer economic hardship."

The Committee also raises questions for further study that are of interest to women's groups on property division and on enforcement of maintenance and child support awards. The Homemaker Committee is in the process of publishing separate leaflets on the legal status of the homemaker for each state which should be very useful.

Local and state women's groups can take two approaches to the problems of divorce: first, by studying local family law provisions, formulating and urging needed reforms and monitoring legislative action; and second, by surveying and supplementing current community resources for legal, economic and emotional support for women during and after the process of separation and divorce. The following bibliography is designed to help in both approaches.

BIBLIOGRAPHY--DIVORCE IN THE UNITED STATES

Background for Reform

1. Uniform Marriage and Divorce Act. 1970, 1973. With prefatory notes and comments. National Conference of Commissioners on Uniform State Laws.

The basic document for a discussion of divorce reform and the basis for many recent changes in state laws. In general the act provides for dissolution of marriage if irretrievably broken, for maintenance only if need is shown, for custody to be determined according to the best interests of the child. It encourages joint petitions and amicable voluntary settlements.

2. A Statistical Portrait of Women in the U.S., 1976. U. S. Bureau of the Census. U. S. Government Printing Office, Washington, DC 20402. $2.10.

A valuable collection of all census statistics on women during the 20th century. See especially sections on marital and family status, fertility, income and poverty status.

3. "To Form a More Perfect Union." Justice for American Women. Report of the National Commission on the Observance of International Women's Year, 1976. U. S. Government Printing Office, Washington, DC 20402. $5.20.

An excellent source of material on women's issues. See especially sections on the homemaker, children, the future and recommendations of the Homemaker and Child Development Committees.

4. Legal Status of Women in ___________. A leaflet for each state is available from the Homemakers Committee, IWY Commission, Department of State, Washington, DC, 20520. One copy free upon request. Additional copies may be obtained from U.S. Government Printing Office, Washington, DC, 20402.

5. Family Law Quarterly. Published by the Family Law Section of the American Bar Association. Available in law libraries.

Many pertinent articles. For instance see Summer, '74. "Anatomy of a Family Code: How to Get a New Code on the Books" and Summer, '75. "Dissolution of the Family Under Swedish Law".

6. Journal of Social Issues, Winter, 1976. Available in public libraries.

This issue consists entirely of articles on marital dissolution, several of interest.

7. Citizen's Advisory Countil on the Status of Women, U.S. Department of Labor, Washington DC 20210, has published the following pamphlets. Single copies are usually free.

Report of the Task Force on Family Law & Policy, 1968.

The Equal Rights Amendment and Alimony and Child Support Laws.

Contribution of Homemakers and Protection of Children in Divorce Law and Practice.

Women in ________________. 1974, 1975, etc. Issued yearly. A leaflet for each state is available upon request from the above address.

8. WEAL and WEAL Fund have available:

The Equal Rights Amendment by Marguerite Rawalt. 50¢

Decade for Women (condensed version of World Plan of Action). 50¢

Survival and Support

1. Women's Survival Manual. A Feminist Handbook on Separation and Divorce. by Women in Transition, Inc. 1972 Scribner. $12.95, $6.95 paper or try public library.

A much praised pratical work compiled by a Philadelphia women's group. Useful as a model for other groups.

A less expensive and very good model if such a guide for your area is not already available is:

2. Survival Directory for Women: 1975. A Resource Guide for Separation and Divorce in the Washington Area. by Molly B. Tinsley and Linda S. Ulfelder. Dryad Press, P. O. Box 1650, Washington, DC 20013. $2.

Both of these give names, addresses and advice for legal help, employment, financial aid, cheap food and rent, counselling, day care, women's support groups and for most of the problems faced by women suddenly on their own.

3. Creative Divorce. A New Opportunity for Personal Growth. by Mel Krantzler. Evans, 1973.

Your public library will have this along with dozens of other books of advice, from the legal and emotional points of view. This is fairly upbeat as the title indicates, is written by a divorce counsellor who has been divorced himself, and seems sensitive to both women's and men's problems.

Marrying, Divorcing, and Living Together in the U.S. Today

By **Paul C. Glick**
and **Arthur J. Norton**

The authors of this Bulletin *are leading authorities on the statistics of marriage, divorce, and the family in the United States.*

Paul Glick is Senior Demographer in the Population Division of the U.S. Bureau of the Census. Among his numerous contributions to research in the family field are the monographs, American Families *(1957), and* Marriage and Divorce: A Social and Economic Study *(with Hugh Carter), first published in 1970 and updated in 1976.*

Arthur Norton is Chief of the Census Bureau's Marriage and Family Statistics Branch and has major responsibility for the Bureau's publication program in this area. His articles on marriage and family-related topics have appeared in several professional journals and monographs.

The authors and editor of this Bulletin *are grateful for the thoughtful comments of Conrad Taeuber, Director of the Center for Population Research, The Kennedy Institute for the Study of Human Reproduction and Bioethics, Georgetown University.*

To judge from the media, the America of the late 1970s has come a long way from the early marrying, familistic era which spawned the baby boom of the 1950s. Divorce statistics are featured in the evening telecasts; Sunday supplements dwell on unwed motherhood; and "living together" makes the cover of a national newsweekly. The traditional family life cycle circumscribed by marriage and childbearing, it would seem, is going out of style.

As indicated by the statistics presented in this *Bulletin*, each of these concerns has some base in reality. Forty percent of all marriages among young women now in their late twenties may end in divorce, if these women repeat the recent experience of their older sisters. Both first marriage and remarriage rates are declining. Close to two million unrelated men and women not married to each other are currently sharing living quarters; 15 million adults live alone; and only 67 percent of children under 18 live with their own, once-married parents. About one in three births are conceived premaritally; one-tenth of remarried women's children are born between marriages; and only half of all pregnancies result in legitimate live births.

These changed demographic patterns undoubtedly reflect changes in basic social attitudes toward conformity with traditional behavior—changes which now permit a greater choice in lifestyles and more flexibility in the development of individual potentialities. The "typical" American family of the future may indeed vary from that of the past. But marriage and childbearing are in no danger of extinction. Some two of every three first marriages taking place today are expected to last "until death do them part," and young women queried in Census Bureau surveys expect to have an average two children.

Marriage and Married People

International comparisons of marriage and divorce

The United States has had one of the highest marriage rates—and the highest divorce rate—among the world's industrialized countries during recent years. This country's marriage rate reached a peak of 11.0 per 1,000 population in 1972—well above the rate for any other large country—but has declined in each subsequent year. In 1976, when the U.S. rate was 9.9, other countries with high marriage rates included the U.S.S.R. (10.1), Egypt (10.0 in 1975), Canada (8.7 in 1975), Israel (8.5), Australia (8.1), and Japan (7.8).[1] In most of these countries the rate for 1976 was lower than in one of the recent years. Through May 1977, the U.S. marriage rate remained steady at 9.9 per 1,000

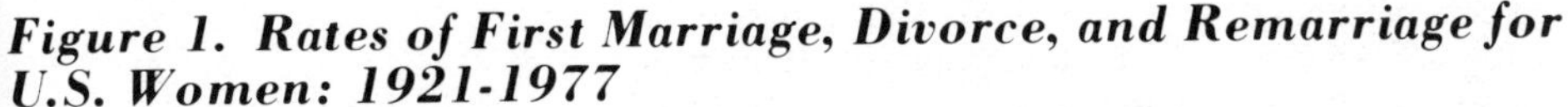

Figure 1. Rates of First Marriage, Divorce, and Remarriage for U.S. Women: 1921-1977

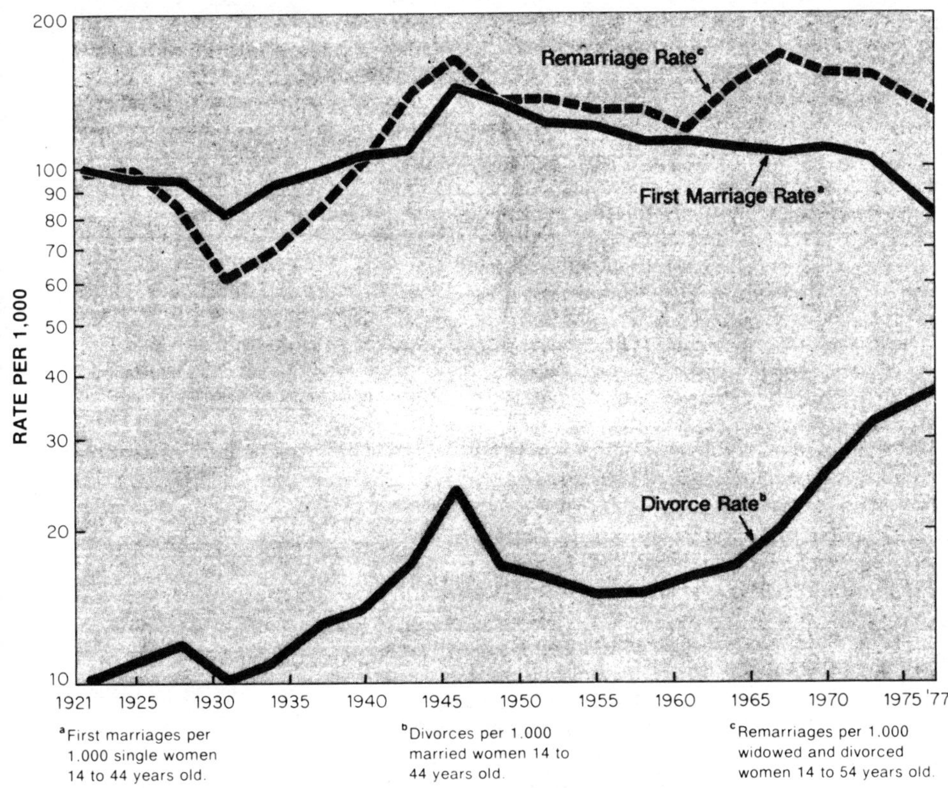

Sources: Adapted with permission from Hugh Carter and Paul C. Glick, *Marriage and Divorce: A Social and Economic Study*, Rev. ed. (Cambridge, Mass.: Harvard University Press, 1976) Figure 13.1, p. 394; with computations added for 1975-1977.

population.[2] Very likely the world economic climate has a considerable bearing on the marriage rate in industrialized countries.

One reason for the high U.S. marriage rate is the fact that the U.S. divorce rate is also high and that most divorced persons (four of every five) remarry, thus swelling the total number of marriages in any given year. Another probable contributing factor—at least until recently—is the historic expansion of the U.S. job market, which has no doubt tended to instill optimism in young adults about their ability to enter marriage and to obtain relatively secure employment at an early adult age.

The U.S. divorce rate has consistently far exceeded that of any other country, but the gap has been narrowing. Between 1965 and 1976, the country's divorce rate doubled from 2.5 to 5.0 per 1,000 population. However, as of May 1977 it had stayed at 5.0 during all but one of the 12 preceding months. Among other countries with relatively high divorce rates in 1976 were Australia (4.3), the U.S.S.R. (3.4), Sweden (2.7), Denmark (2.5), Canada (2.2 in 1975), Finland (2.1), and Egypt (2.0). A majority of the industralized countries registered higher divorce rates in the most recent year for which data are available than in the preceding year. An exception was Sweden, where the rate declined from a peak of 3.3 in 1974 to 2.7 in 1976. Reasons for country differences in divorce rates vary considerably, no doubt, but a factor that appears to transcend national boundaries is that the earlier the typical age at marriage the greater the likelihood of divorce.

Longtime trends in U.S. marriage and divorce

An understanding of longtime trends in U.S. marriage and divorce is provided by an examination of changes in first marriage rates and remarriage rates, as shown in Figure 1. After a low point during the Depression of the 1930s, both marriage rates rose to a peak after World War II, as did also the divorce rate. The remarriage rate was near an all-time high; many marriages that failed during the war were followed by divorce and remarriage. For a decade after these postwar peaks, the two marriage rates and the divorce rate fell in unison, but then began to take divergent paths.

Reasons for the high divorce rate

The divorce rate turned up again in the late 1950s and has mounted rapidly ever since.

The 1960s and early 1970s saw a prolonged war in Vietnam, followed by an often difficult readjustment to a peacetime economy and postwar family living. The upsurge in divorce has also coincided with several other rapid social changes. Along with the improvement in the status of ethnic minorities came the reinvigoration of the women's movement and more liberal attitudes toward personal behavior among most religious denominations. Along with increasing use of effective birth control methods came more delay in marriage and more years of independent living between departure from the parental home and marriage. And along with these changes came an increasing tolerance of divorce to end unsatisfactory marriages. The declining birth rate meant that young married women were having few if any children to complicate a return to "singlehood" if the decision was made to do so. Under these conditions, more and more couples were deciding to go through at least a mild crisis (divorce) in order that each partner might make another and hopefully more successful start in life through remarriage to someone else—in the light of past experience during the first marriage.[3]

Delay in first marriage and remarriage

The annual first marriage rate has declined almost continuously for two decades. Postponement of marriage has been especially great among women in their early twenties. The proportion of women still single at ages 20 to 24 has gone up by one-half since 1960, from 28 percent to 43 percent.

The decline in first marriage rates can be explained by many of the same factors which worked to increase the divorce rate.

During the Vietnam War, increasing numbers of young men postponed marriage because of active military service while others enrolled in college as a means of delaying induction into the armed forces. Meantime, increasing numbers of young single women continued their education and obtained experience in the labor market. Thus many more women than ever before were exposed to a taste of independent self-maintenance and an attractive option to early marriage and preoccupation with child care.

For women during this period, embarking upon matrimony was further complicated by a "marriage squeeze;" the number of women reaching the usual ages at which women first marry (18 to 24) exceeded by 5 to 10 percent the number of men aged 20 to 26—the usual ages for men at first marriage. This phenomenon was a consequence of the postwar baby boom, coupled with the tendency for first-time grooms to be two or three years older than their brides. As the baby boom rose to its peak (in 1957), the number of girls born each year outstripped the number of boys born two to three years earlier.

Another legacy of the baby boom continues to have a marked effect on the first marriage rate. In the past decade, employers have found it impossible to hire the swollen number of young applicants flooding into the job market and the competition for available jobs has become increasingly stiff. Thus, undoubtedly unoptimistic about being able to establish a home and provide for a family, many young people have been postponing entry into first marriage. And yet, while delaying marriage, an increasing number of women have been bearing children out of marriage. From only 5 percent of all births in 1960, premarital births went up to 14 percent in 1975 (7 percent for white births and 49 percent for black births).

The trend in remarriage was sharply upward throughout most of the 1960s while the divorce rate was also rising. But during the early 1970s the divorce rate continued to rise, while the remarriage rate reached a peak, leveled off, and then moved markedly downward (Figure 1). Moreover, after many years of gradual decline, the first marriage rate plunged downward after 1972. The following rates are for men, but the patterns are similar for women.

		Remarriage rate	
Year	First marriage rate	After divorce	After widowhood
1972	70	229	41
1975	56	190	40
3-year decline	20%	17%	2.5%

These impressive changes may be explained, to an unknown extent, by the economic recession of the mid-1970s. Obviously a very substantial number of persons who would have married under other circumstances have decided not to do so during these last few years. Some are feeling the financial pinch of having to maintain two residences while they are divorced, and others are opting for the lifestyle of singlehood instead of marriage.

The rates presented above show that divorced men are three times as likely to remarry as never-married men are to enter first marriage. Evidently, divorced men strongly prefer being married, albeit with a different partner. As would be expected, the much older widowed men are far less likely to remarry than the much younger divorced men.

First marriage rates are far lower than remarriage rates, yet the *vast majority of marriages* still occur among those who have not been previously married (Figure 2). Back in 1960, fully 81 percent of men's marriages were their first. This proportion edged down gradually to 77 percent in 1972. Then in just three years, by 1975, the proportion of all marriages that were first marriages dropped 5 percentage points—more than in the preceding 12 years—to only 72 percent. Meantime, the ground lost by first marriages was made up almost entirely by remarriages after divorce; they moved up 5 percentage points from 14 percent of all marriages in 1960 to 19 percent in 1972 and then shot up another 5 points to 24 percent in 1975. As a consequence, remarriages after divorce accounted for nearly one-fourth of men's marriages in 1975 compared to less than one-seventh in 1960.

Perspective on the changing marriage patterns may be gained by relating them to the time when persons born during the baby boom of the late 1940s and the 1950s approached the customary age to marry. Persons who were born about 20 years before the 1972 peak of marriages entered life close to the middle of the high-birthrate period, which lasted from late 1945 until 1961. By the mid-1970s, the impact of the post-World War II bulge in births on the marriage market had passed its crest and was beginning to subside. Then, as single persons increasingly postponed first marriage, divorced persons followed suit and have been increasingly postponing remarriage—partly because they, like single persons, have been facing stiff competition for jobs.

Figure 2. Marriages for Men by Previous Marital Status: U.S., 1960-1975

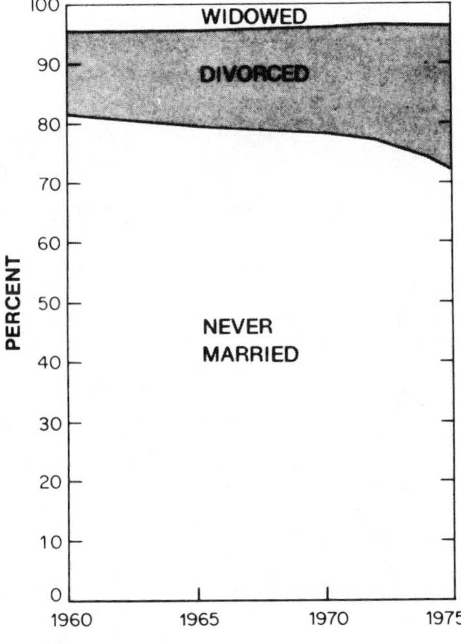

Sources: Various reports of the U.S. National Center for Health Statistics.

Time spent in and out of marriage

How much time do people spend in and out of marriage? One way to estimate this is to compare the median ages at first marriage, divorce, remarriage, and redivorce. These are shown in Figure 3 (next page), based on replies to questions asked in the Census Bureau's Current Population Survey for June 1975.*

A better way to measure the median length of time between changes in marital status is to determine the relevant interval for each person and then find the midpoint of the distribution. Results obtained in this way are presented in the following exhibit for 1967 and 1975, based on comparable Census Bureau Surveys.

Divorce after first marriage is evidently now occurring about a half year to a year sooner than a decade ago—down from close to eight to around seven years—for those who obtain a divorce.

*The Current Population Survey is a monthly sample survey of approximately 47,000 households interviewed across the United States. Although the survey's primary purpose is to obtain monthly labor force statistics, supplementary questions provide current demographic data on the civilian noninstitutional population between the decennial censuses.

Median number of years between—	Men 1967	Men 1975	Women 1967	Women 1975
First marriage and divorce	7.7	6.7	7.9	7.3
Divorce and remarriage	3.1	3.1	3.4	3.2
Remarriage and redivorce	6.2	5.0	7.6	5.5

Half of those who remarry after divorce still do so within three years. Those who obtain a second divorce after they have remarried tend to do so a year and a half to two years sooner than it took them to obtain their initial divorce—about 5.3 years versus 7.0 years (for men and women combined). Moreover, recent redivorces appear to be occurring about a year and a half sooner after remarriage than a decade or so ago.

The upshot is that young adults have been entering first marriage later and shortening the intervals not only between marriage and divorce but also between remarriage and redivorce. Thus, marital events are being compressed into a shorter span of years.

Although 1975 data show that four of every five divorced persons had remarried by middle age, the sharp decline (or delay) in remarriage since 1972 suggests that this proportion may decline in the near future. Even though a large majority of divorced persons remarry, many others do not. Among the consequences is an accumulation of divorced persons who have not remarried. For persons 35 to 54 years old, the proportion of persons currently divorced went up by one-third between 1970 and 1975 (from 4.6 percent to 6.2 percent). During the same period, the proportion "ever-divorced" rose about one-sixth (from 16.9 percent to 19.7 percent). Because the remarriage rate is still quite high, the proportion ever-divorced continues to be three to four times the level of the proportion currently divorced.

Marital stability and educational level

Because marital status is very highly correlated with age, and because marital patterns are undergoing considerable change, the data in Table 1 on continuous first marriage by number of school years completed are limited to persons 35 to 54 years old. These persons are old enough to include most of those who will ever divorce, and yet young enough to have been affected considerably by the upsurge in divorce since 1960.

Persons who have not graduated from high school (i.e., with less than 12 years of schooling) have consistently fallen short of the overall average percentage of married persons in this age bracket who are still in their first marriage. For

Figure 3. Median Age at Marital Events for U.S. Men and Women Born 1900-1959

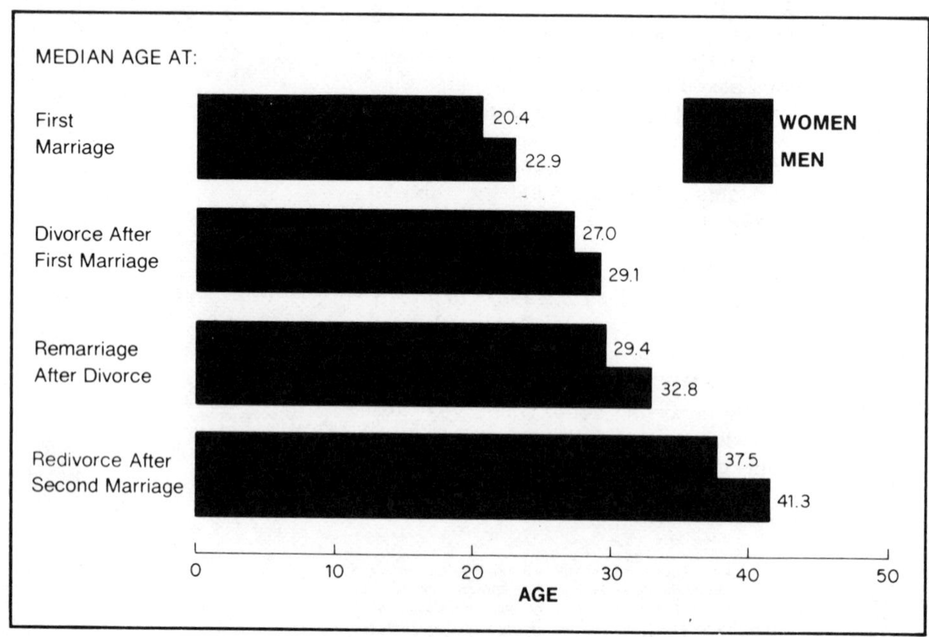

Source: U.S. Bureau of the Census, *Current Population Reports*, Series P-20, No. 297, "Number, Timing, and Duration of Marriages and Divorces in the United States: June 1975," Table H.

Table 1. Percent of Persons Aged 35-54 in Intact First Marriages, by Education: U.S., 1960 and 1975

Years of school completed	Percent married once, spouse present: Men 35-54, 1960	1975	Women 35-54, 1960	1975	Percent change 1960-1975[a]: Men	Women
Total	72.8	72.5	67.4	66.0	0.2	2.3
0-11 years	67.6	64.6	62.5	57.1	-44.9	-44.3
12 years	74.6	72.2	69.8	66.4	42.6	48.7
13 or more	78.3	76.8	69.3	70.4	66.0	49.2
13-15 years	75.5	72.1	70.8	69.1	41.5	27.3
16 years	81.3	78.6	73.0	77.3	86.1	65.8
17 or more	80.2	81.8	54.8	63.4	86.4	136.1

Sources: U.S. Bureau of the Census, *Current Population Reports*, Series P-20, No. 312, "Marriage, Divorce, Widowhood, and Remarriage by Family Characteristics: June 1975," Tables F and 3; and *Census of Population: 1960*, Vol. II, 4D, *Marital Status*, Table 4.

[a] In terms of the number of married persons with spouse present.

instance, in 1975, when 73 percent of all men of this age were still married to a first spouse, the average for men who stopped short of high school graduation was 65 percent. By contrast, in both 1960 and 1975, college graduates were above the general averages. Marital stability is greatest for men who have graduated from college or who have gone on to graduate school. Women differ in that those who have gone on to graduate school (17 or more years of completed schooling) record below-average marital stability. Thus, for men the relationship between socioeconomic status (whether measured by education or income) and marital stability is consistently positive. For women, however, an exception occurs among the highly educated. The reasons vary from woman to woman but probably include such factors as the many more options for career development which these women have, which often conflict with harmonious marriage, and, sometimes, personality traits that reduce their prospects for both entering and remaining in marriage.

Changes since 1960 in the number of persons aged 35 to 54 with stable first marriages have been uneven. Only about half as many such persons now as a decade and a half ago have not graduated from high school; this results from both a general increase in educational attainment and a decline in marital stability.

Despite their low marriage proportions, women with graduate school training recorded an outstanding rate of increase between 1960 and 1975 in the number who entered and remained in an initial marriage until they were in or near middle age (136 percent). This reflects both an exceptionally great increase in the number of women aged 35 to 54 who have pursued their education beyond an undergraduate degree (from 461,000 in 1960 up to twice as many, 938,000, in 1975) and the marked improvement in their marital stability (from 55 percent still in a first marriage in 1960 up to 63 percent in 1975). Evidently far more capable women are being encouraged to prepare for highly responsible positions and a growing proportion are successfully combining a professional or administrative career and marriage. It is also possible that men are more ready to accept highly educated women as wives (or vice versa), or more willing to see them add to their college credentials after marriage. The women's movement may now be beginning to affect men too, and thus their acceptance of more egalitarian marriages.

Changes in the stability of marriage that will take place during the next decade or two among those now aged 20 to 40 cannot be predicted with much precision. But if present trends persist, the consequences for women in their forties might include: an increase from the present 4 percent single to 6 or 8 percent single; an increase from the present 8 percent to 10 or 12 percent divorced; and a complementary decrease from about two-thirds of women with first marriages continuing into their forties as at present down closer to 60 percent. But the proportion of middle-years adults with a high educational level should continue to rise, and this will have a far-reaching impact on the nature of this age group's social, economic, and cultural activities.

Divorce and Divorced People

In several following sections, attention is focused primarily on characteristics of persons who are divorced or who are more likely than others to do so. Ordinarily these persons pass through a transitional stage of separation, but many separated couples are eventually reconciled, while others continue indefinitely in a state of legal or informal separation.

To separate and/or to divorce?

In 1976 the number of "separated" persons in the United States was only about half as large as the number of divorced persons (3.8 million versus 7.2 million). A million more women than men report themselves as separated (2.4 million versus 1.4 million), evidently because many never-married mothers claim to be separated or because some separated men living with nonrelatives were reported as single in the Current Population Survey for March of that year. The largest proportions of men reported as currently separated (3 percent) or divorced (6 percent) were found among those 40 to 44 years old. Among women the corresponding peak was at age 35 to 39 (5 percent separated and 9 percent divorced).

During recent years, the number of divorced persons has increased more rapidly than the number of separated persons. This suggests that more of those with serious marital conflicts are resolving them through a divorce decree which they can now afford to obtain—or is more easily obtainable—and which frees them for possible remarriage to a (hopefully) more suitable partner. Those who remain separated tend to include a disproportionately larger number of men with a relatively small amount of education and income. (Separation is sometimes referred to as "the poor man's divorce.") Black adults are somewhat more likely to be divorced than white adults and much more likely to be separated (with six times the white proportion of separated persons in 1976).

Early and late marriages are less stable

Teenage marriages are twice as likely to end in divorce as marriages that occur in the twenties (Figure 4). Among women who entered first marriage three to five years before the 1970 census, 11 percent of those married in their teens had divorced before the census date, compared with 5 percent of those who married in their twenties. Similarly, among women who first married six to ten years before the census, 18 percent of the teenage marriages versus 9 percent of the marriages in the twenties had ended in divorce.

Surveys show that women who remarry after divorce are about two years younger at first marriage, on the average, than those of comparable current age still living with their first husband.

Figure 4. Percent of Women Divorced Within 3 to 5 and 6 to 10 Years After First Marriage: U.S., 1970

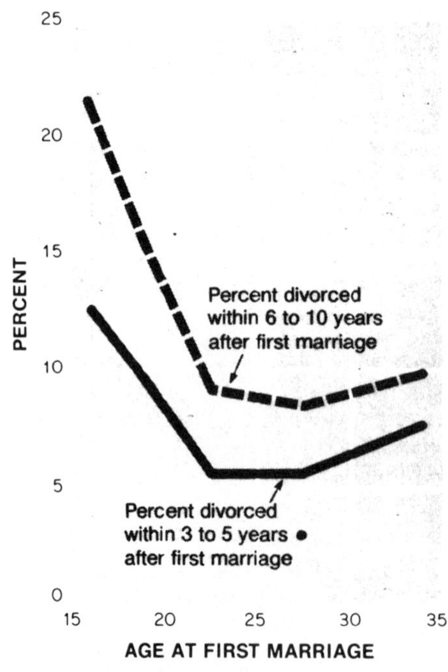

Source: U.S. Bureau of the Census, *Census of Population: 1970*, 4D, *Age at First Marriage*, Table 4.

These findings are undoubtedly associated with the relatively large amount of marital instability among women who are premaritally pregnant. They are probably also associated with a general tendency for those who marry and/or become pregnant at a young age to be less mature and self-disciplined than those who marry later.

On the other hand, Figure 4 shows that women who marry for the first time after the age of 30 also tend to have less stable marriages than those who marry in their twenties. According to the 1970 census, "older" brides were close to half again as likely to end their first marriage within three to five years as those with an intermediate age at marriage. This no doubt reflects the relatively large proportion of women with graduate school training among older brides, who are known to have a high divorce rate. Still others may have been women who had not found a marital partner until they had presumably developed habits of independent living that created special stresses in marriage. The statistics, however, also imply that late marriage is less likely than early marriage to be followed by divorce.

The same pattern applies to men as well as to women, except that the optimum age range for stable first marriages among men is 25 to 29 years. This is the period when most of the men who are college graduates become married.

Divorce up most for college men

Table 6 shows the changing relation since 1960 between the proportion currently divorced and level of education for men and women aged 35 to 54. Most of those who will ever divorce have done so by this time in life. At each level of college education shown, the proportion of men who were divorced at the time of the 1975 survey was at least twice as high as in 1960. For all college levels combined (13 completed school years or more), the proportion divorced in 1975 was exactly the same as the average for all men of the same age (4.6 percent). Back in 1960, college men had a significantly lower proportion divorced than the average (2.2 percent versus 2.8 percent).

One reason for the higher proportion of divorced college men in 1975 was the high level of divorce among men with incomplete college education—5.6 percent of ai! such men aged 35 to 54—well above the figure for any other education level shown for men. By contrast, men with four or more years of college still had clearly the lowest divorce level of all in 1975 (4.0 percent). Like men in higher income brackets, these men not only have a strong tendency to stay married, but also tend to remarry sooner than other men if they do become divorced. However, the divorce level for college men as a whole (including those with less than four years of college) has gone up fastest and has thus converged with the level for other men.

A noteworthy change in women's current divorce level is the below-average (but still large) increase for those with 17 or more years of education. Evidently the divorce level for these women is tending to converge with that for other women because of a slower rise in their tendency to divorce.

Downward mobility and marital instability

Findings from a special 1973 survey offer another perspective on marital instability.[5] As seen in Table 7, they show that the proportion of men aged 35 to 54 who were *not* in intact first marriages at the time was half again as large for those with *less* education than *either* parent (36 percent) as for men with *more* education than *either* parent (23 percent). These findings provide a measure that is consistent with the expected relationship: downward social mobility tends to increase the chances

Table 6. Percent Currently Divorced Among Persons Aged 35-54, by Educational Level: U.S., 1960 and 1975

Years of school completed	Percent currently divorced				Ratio of % in 1975 to that in 1960	
	Men 35-54		Women 35-54			
	1960	1975	1960	1975	Men	Women
Total	2.8	4.6	4.0	7.8	1.64	1.95
0-11 years	3.1	5.0	4.0	7.8	1.61	1.95
12 years	2.6	4.3	3.8	7.4	1.65	1.95
13 or more	2.2	4.6	4.3	8.5	2.09	1.98
13-15 years	2.8	5.6	4.5	9.2	2.00	2.04
16 years	1.8	4.0	3.4	6.5	2.22	1.91
17 or more	1.6	4.0	5.2	9.4	2.50	1.80

Sources: U.S. Bureau of the Census, *Current Population Reports*, Series P-20, No. 312, "Marriage, Divorce, Widowhood, and Remarriage by Family Characteristics: June 1975," Tables C, D, and 3; and *Census of Population: 1960*, Vol. II, 4D, *Marital Status*, Table 4.

Table 7. Percent of Men Aged 35-54 Who Were Not in an Intact First Marriage, by Educational Level of the Man and His Parents: U.S., 1973

	Percent of men *not* in an intact first marriage			
		Man's versus his mother's educational level		
Man's versus his father's educational level[a]	All men aged 35-54	Man has more education	Man has same amount	Man has less education
All men aged 35-54	24.7	22.9	26.4	32.6
Man has more education	23.4	23.0	25.4	27.5
Man has same amount	25.9	21.6	26.1	32.9
Man has less education	33.4	25.7	34.4	35.7

Source: U.S. Bureau of the Census, tabulation of data from the "Study of Occupational Change in a Generation" conducted in March 1973 for David L. Featherman and Robert M. Hauser of the University of Wisconsin, with funding from the National Science Foundation.

[a]Educational level is measured in terms of five groups of years of school completed: 0-7, 8-11, 12, 13-15, and 16 and over.

that a man will not marry or, if he does, that he will not stay married.

The evidence suggests further that having *less* education than either parent increases the son's chances of marital instability (or of never marrying) to a greater extent than having *more* education increases the son's chances of having a stable first marriage. Men with the same amount of education as both parents had about 26 chances out of 100 of *not* being in an intact first marriage. By comparison, those with more education had 23 chances—or *three fewer*—whereas those with less education had 36 chances—or *ten more*—of not being in an intact first marriage.

The survey revealed that over half (56 percent) of the 35- to 54-year-old men had more education than either of their parents; 19 percent had the same amount; and only 3 percent had less education than either parent and in this sense were downwardly mobile. The remaining 22 percent had some other combination of broad educational levels for the father, the son, and the mother.

Regardless of the measure applied, the results indicate that upward mobility is associated with more marital stability and downward mobility is associated with less. Thus, 82 percent of the men college graduates whose parents were both also college graduates were in stable first marriages. By comparison, 72 percent of the men who, together with their parents, had no high school education were likewise in stable unions after first marriage. In addition, the study showed that men with at least five more years of school than their father had a smaller proportion separated or divorced than men with no more education than their father (4 percent versus 6 percent).

Chances of divorce for today's young women

Data from the Census Bureau's Current Population Survey for June 1975 provide a basis for projecting the likelihood of eventual divorce for persons currently in their late twenties. It is assumed that the future divorce experience of these young adults will mirror that of older adults in recent years. According to these projections, about 38 percent of women now in their late twenties may end their first marriage in divorce. Of the three-quarters who will later remarry, about 44 percent may redivorce. In other words, approximately 40 percent of all current and potential marriages among young women now in their late twenties may eventually end in divorce. (The corresponding projections for men yield results several percentage points lower, but since women are more often the respondents in these household surveys, the information for them is probably more complete in this respect than that for men.)

The hypothesis was tested that projections of eventual divorce would vary according to the educational level of the person. The results are presented in Table 8. They show that for both young adult men and women (in their late twenties) the chances for ending the first marriage in divorce were highest for those with incomplete college education. For example, half (49 percent) of the women who had completed one to three years of college were projected as likely to end their first marriage in divorce, as compared with "only" three-

Table 8. Likelihood of Divorce for Persons Born 1945-1949 by Educational Level: U.S., 1975

Years of school completed	Percent of persons whose first marriage had ended in divorce by 1975		Percent of persons whose first marriage may eventually end in divorce	
	Men	Women	Men	Women
All ever-married persons born 1945-1949	13	17	34	38
0-11 years	15	24	34	44
12 years	15	17	36	37
13-15 years	15	19	42	49
16 years	8	8	29	29
17 or more	8	9	30	33

Source: U.S. Bureau of the Census, *Current Population Reports*, Series P-20, No. 312, "Marriage, Divorce, Widowhood, and Remarriage by Family Characteristics: June 1975," Table H.

tenths (29 percent) of those with exactly four years of college. These findings, along with many others, suggest that the same configuration of personal, social, and economic circumstances that tend to be associated with reaching a terminal educational level tend also to be associated with relatively stable marriage.

Perspectives on remarriage

The 1975 survey data confirm that most divorces occur before women reach age 30 and among women with fewer than three children; and that remarriage tends to occur relatively soon after divorce if at all (Table 9, page 20). Two of every three women whose first marriage had ended in divorce (65 percent) had become "single again" before they had passed their twenties, and two of every three of the remainder before they had passed their thirties. Of those with a divorce before 30, very few (13 percent) had borne more than two children before divorce, but half (54 percent) had borne one or two children; the other third (33 percent) had borne none.

Fully 80 percent of the women who were young (under 30) and childless at

Table 9. Characteristics of Divorced Women: U.S., 1975

(Women whose first marriage ended in divorce, by age at divorce, number of children born before divorce, duration of divorce, and whether remarried)

Age at divorce and number of children born before divorce	All women with first marriage ended in divorce		Percent remarried by survey date	Median years divorced[a]		
					At survey date	
	Number	Percent		Total	Divorced	Remarried
Total aged 14-75 with fewer than 6 children born before divorce	9,068	100.0	66.0	3.6	4.7	3.2
Aged 14-29 at divorce	5,845	64.5	76.3	3.1	3.4	3.1
No children	1,932		79.6	2.9	2.6	2.9
1 child	1,947		75.0	3.1	3.6	3.0
2 children	1,233		74.9	3.1	3.4	3.0
3-5 children	732		73.6	4.0	5.2	3.8
Aged 30-39 at divorce	2,202	24.3	56.2	4.5	5.8	3.8
Aged 40-75 at divorce	1,021	11.3	28.1	5.5	6.5	2.9

Source: U.S. Bureau of the Census, *Current Population Reports*, Series P-20, No. 312, "Marriage, Divorce, Widowhood, and Remarriage by Family Characteristics: June 1975," Tables I, J, and K.

[a]Number of years between divorce and survey date for those still divorced; number of years between divorce and second marriage for those remarried.

the time of divorce had remarried by the survey date. By way of comparison, only 66 percent of *all* women (regardless of age and number of children) had remarried after their first marriage ended in divorce. The young childless divorcees who were still divorced at the survey date had the shortest average duration of divorce (2.6 years)—only half the duration for young divorcees with three to five children.

---

1. Marriage and divorce rates for selected foreign countries were provided by the United Nations Statistical Office.
2. Marriage and divorce rates for the United States for the year ending in May 1977 are from the U.S. National Center for Health Statistics, *Monthly Vital Statistics Report,* Vol. 26, No. 5, "Births, Marriages, Divorces, and Deaths for May 1977," p. 1.
3. For additional discussion of the factors underlying the increase in divorce, see Samuel H. Preston and John McDonald, "The Incidence of Divorce Within Cohorts of Marriages Contracted Since the Civil War," paper presented at the annual meeting of the Population Association of America, St. Louis, Missouri, April 21-23, 1977.
5. These results are based on data from a survey conducted by the Bureau of the Census for Robert M. Hauser and David L. Featherman to study "Occupational Changes in a Generation." For more information about the survey, see these two authors' article, "White-Nonwhite Differentials in Occupational Mobility Among Men in the United States, 1962-1972," *Demography,* Vol. 11, No. 2 (May 1974) pp. 247-265.

This material has not been excerpted in its entirety.

Excerpts from Marrying, Divorcing, and Living Together in the U.S. Today, by Paul C. Glick and Arthur J. Norton. Vol. 32, No. 5 (October 1977) of the Population Bulletin. Courtesy of the Population Reference Bureau, Inc. Washington, D.C.

Marital Status of the Population, by Sex: 1940 to 1976

[1940–1960, persons 14 years old and over; thereafter, 18 and over. As of **March**, except as noted. Prior to 1960, excludes Alaska and Hawaii. Beginning 1950, excludes Armed Forces except those living off post or with their families on post. See *Historical Statistics, Colonial Times to 1970*, series A 160–171, for decennial data]

Sex and marital status	1940 [1]	1950	1960	1965	1970	1973	1974	1975	1976
Total 1,000	**101,103**	**111,732**	**125,457**	**121,780**	**132,507**	**138,038**	**140,618**	**143,214**	**145,784**
Single 1,000	31,529	25,461	27,651	18,169	21,443	22,865	23,915	25,105	26,171
Married 1,000	60,282	74,860	84,406	89,159	94,999	98,159	99,080	99,666	100,615
Widowed 1,000	7,844	9,263	10,551	10,943	11,784	11,775	11,669	11,921	11,812
Divorced 1,000	1,447	2,148	2,850	3,506	4,282	5,238	5,955	6,523	7,186
Percent of total	**100.0**	**100.0**	**100.0**	**100.0**	**100.0**	**100.0**	**100.0**	**100.0**	**100.0**
Single	31.2	22.8	22.0	14.9	16.2	16.6	17.0	17.5	18.0
Married	59.6	67.0	67.3	73.2	71.7	71.1	70.5	69.6	69.0
Widowed	7.8	8.3	8.4	9.0	8.9	8.5	8.3	8.3	8.1
Divorced	1.4	1.9	2.3	2.9	3.2	3.8	4.2	4.6	4.9
Males, total 1,000	**50,554**	**54,762**	**60,582**	**58,027**	**62,513**	**65,248**	**66,589**	**67,869**	**69,058**
Single 1,000	17,593	14,322	15,356	10,261	11,838	12,737	13,360	14,098	14,656
Married 1,000	30,192	37,227	41,831	44,206	47,058	48,623	49,044	49,409	49,826
Widowed 1,000	2,144	2,296	2,253	2,129	2,051	1,924	1,855	1,817	1,793
Divorced 1,000	624	917	1,145	1,429	1,567	1,963	2,331	2,545	2,783
Percent of total	**100.0**	**100.0**	**100.0**	**100.0**	**100.0**	**100.0**	**100.0**	**100.0**	**100.0**
Single	34.8	26.2	25.3	17.7	18.9	19.5	20.1	20.8	21.2
Married	59.7	68.0	69.1	76.2	75.3	74.5	73.7	72.8	72.2
Widowed	4.2	4.2	3.7	3.7	3.3	2.9	2.8	2.7	2.6
Divorced	1.2	1.7	1.9	2.5	2.5	3.0	3.5	3.7	4.0
Standardized for age: [2]									
Single	30.7	26.2	25.3	16.4	16.5	15.7	16.2	16.6	16.7
Married	62.6	67.4	69.1	77.5	77.6	78.0	77.1	76.6	76.2
Widowed	5.4	4.7	3.7	3.6	3.3	3.1	2.9	2.8	2.7
Divorced	1.3	1.7	1.9	2.5	2.6	3.2	3.7	4.0	4.3
Females, total . 1,000	**50,549**	**56,970**	**64,875**	**63,753**	**69,994**	**72,790**	**74,029**	**75,345**	**76,726**
Single 1,000	13,936	11,139	12,295	7,908	9,605	10,128	10,555	11,007	11,515
Married 1,000	30,090	37,633	42,575	44,953	47,941	49,536	50,036	50,257	50,789
Widowed 1,000	5,700	6,967	8,298	8,814	9,733	9,851	9,814	10,104	10,019
Divorced 1,000	823	1,231	1,705	2,077	2,715	3,275	3,624	3,978	4,403
Percent of total	**100.0**	**100.0**	**100.0**	**100.0**	**100.0**	**100.0**	**100.0**	**100.0**	**100.0**
Single	27.6	19.6	19.0	12.4	13.7	13.9	14.3	14.6	15.0
Married	59.5	66.1	65.6	70.5	68.5	68.1	67.6	66.7	66.2
Widowed	11.3	12.2	12.8	13.8	13.9	13.5	13.3	13.4	13.1
Divorced	1.6	2.2	2.6	3.3	3.9	4.5	4.9	5.3	5.7
Standardized for age: [2]									
Single	24.2	20.0	19.0	11.6	12.1	11.9	12.2	12.4	12.6
Married	59.3	63.9	65.6	71.8	70.8	70.4	70.0	69.2	68.9
Widowed	14.8	14.0	12.8	13.3	13.0	13.0	12.7	12.8	12.4
Divorced	1.6	2.1	2.6	3.3	4.1	4.8	5.2	5.6	6.1

[1] As of April. [2] 1960 age distribution used as standard. Figures show percent distribution with effects of changes in age distribution removed.

Source: U.S. Bureau of the Census, *U.S. Census of Population: 1950*, vol. II, part 1, and *Current Population Reports*, series P–20, Nos. 144, 255, 271, and 306.

Marital Status of the Black Population: 1960 to 1976

[1960 and 1965, persons 14 years old and over; thereafter, 18 and over. **1960** as of **April**; based on 25-percent sample; other years as of **March** and based on Current Population Survey, which includes members of Armed Forces living off post or with their families on post but excludes all other members of Armed Forces. See text, p. 1]

Sex and year	Number of persons (1,000)					Percent distribution				
	Total	Single	Married	Widowed	Divorced	Total	Single	Married	Widowed	Divorced
MALE										
1960	5,713	1,692	3,619	264	139	100.0	29.6	63.3	4.6	2.4
1965	6,211	1,980	3,795	245	191	100.0	31.9	61.1	3.9	3.1
1970	5,898	1,435	3,944	307	212	100.0	24.3	66.9	5.2	3.6
1973	6,115	1,699	3,829	335	252	100.0	27.8	62.6	5.5	4.1
1974	6,284	1,712	3,959	308	305	100.0	27.2	63.0	4.9	4.9
1975	6,368	1,733	3,990	319	327	100.0	27.2	62.7	5.0	5.1
1976	6,560	1,861	4,042	271	386	100.0	28.4	61.6	4.1	5.9
FEMALE										
1960	6,375	1,386	3,842	910	237	100.0	21.7	60.3	14.3	3.7
1965	7,062	1,621	4,201	949	291	100.0	23.0	59.5	13.4	4.1
1970	7,074	1,233	4,366	1,120	355	100.0	17.4	61.7	15.8	5.0
1973	7,514	1,522	4,295	1,210	486	100.0	20.3	57.2	16.1	6.5
1974	7,702	1,556	4,429	1,209	508	100.0	20.2	57.5	15.7	6.6
1975	7,894	1,716	4,383	1,202	593	100.0	21.7	55.5	15.2	7.5
1976	8,108	1,882	4,416	1,181	631	100.0	23.2	54.5	14.6	7.8

Source: U.S. Bureau of the Census, *U.S. Census of Population, 1960, Nonwhite Population by Race*, PC(2)1C; and *Current Population Reports*, series P–20, Nos. 155, 255, 271, and 306.

Marital Status of the Spanish-Origin Population: 1970 to 1976

[Persons 14 years old and over. **1970** as of **April**; other years as of **March** and based on Current Population Survey, which includes members of Armed Forces living off post or with their families on post but excludes all other members of Armed Forces. See text, p. 1]

SEX AND YEAR	NUMBER OF PERSONS (1,000)					PERCENT DISTRIBUTION				
	Total	Single	Married	Widowed	Divorced	Total	Single	Married	Widowed	Divorced
TOTAL										
1970	5,872	1,718	3,666	287	201	100.0	29.3	62.4	4.9	3.4
1971	5,606	1,614	3,599	230	163	100.0	28.8	64.2	4.1	2.9
1972	5,765	1,668	3,687	234	176	100.0	28.9	64.0	4.1	3.1
1973	6,631	1,952	4,217	280	184	100.0	29.4	63.6	4.2	2.8
1974	6,857	2,079	4,300	261	218	100.0	30.3	62.7	3.8	3.2
1975	7,264	2,293	4,378	298	296	100.0	31.6	60.3	4.1	4.1
1976	7,192	2,203	4,358	297	335	100.0	30.6	60.6	4.1	4.7
MALE										
1970	2,838	914	1,801	56	67	100.0	32.2	63.5	2.0	2.3
1971	2,679	841	1,748	47	44	100.0	31.4	65.2	1.7	1.6
1972	2,751	890	1,790	37	34	100.0	32.4	65.0	1.4	1.2
1973	3,171	1,056	2,040	43	33	100.0	33.3	64.3	1.4	1.0
1974	3,282	1,120	2,058	41	63	100.0	34.1	62.7	1.2	1.9
1975	3,520	1,277	2,103	42	98	100.0	36.3	59.7	1.2	2.8
1976	3,415	1,197	2,065	55	99	100.0	35.0	60.5	1.6	2.9
FEMALE										
1970	3,033	804	1,864	231	134	100.0	26.5	61.5	7.6	4.4
1971	2,927	773	1,851	183	119	100.0	26.4	63.3	6.3	4.1
1972	3,014	778	1,897	197	142	100.0	25.8	63.0	6.5	4.7
1973	3,460	896	2,177	237	151	100.0	25.9	62.9	6.8	4.4
1974	3,575	959	2,242	220	155	100.0	26.8	62.7	6.2	4.3
1975	3,744	1,016	2,275	256	198	100.0	27.1	60.8	6.8	5.3
1976	3,777	1,006	2,293	242	236	100.0	26.6	60.7	6.4	6.3

Source: U.S. Bureau of the Census, *U.S. Census of Population, 1970, Persons of Spanish Origin,* PC(2)1C and *Current Population Reports,* series P-20, No. 306, and earlier issues.

Marital Status of the Population, by Sex and Age: 1976

[**In thousands of persons 18 years old and over, except percent.** As of **March.** Based on Current Population Survey, which includes members of Armed Forces living off post or with their families on post, but excludes all other members of the Armed Forces. See text, p. 1. See *Historical Statistics, Colonial Times to 1970,* series A 160–171, for decennial census data]

SEX AND AGE	Total	Single	Married	Widowed	Divorced	PERCENT DISTRIBUTION				
						Total	Single	Married	Widowed	Divorced
Male	**69,058**	**14,656**	**49,826**	**1,793**	**2,783**	**100.0**	**21.2**	**72.2**	**2.6**	**4.0**
18-19 years	3,959	3,638	313	–	7	100.0	91.8	7.9	–	.2
20-24 years	9,197	5,711	3,319	5	162	100.0	62.1	36.1	.1	1.8
25-29 years	8,465	2,111	6,004	6	344	100.0	24.9	70.9	.1	4.1
30-34 years	6,801	833	5,572	5	391	100.0	12.2	81.9	.1	5.7
35-44 years	11,107	808	9,662	37	601	100.0	7.3	87.0	.3	5.4
45-54 years	11,296	634	9,908	169	584	100.0	5.6	87.7	1.5	5.2
55-64 years	9,320	526	8,002	344	448	100.0	5.6	85.9	3.7	4.8
65-74 years	5,944	250	4,979	528	187	100.0	4.2	83.8	8.9	3.1
75 years and over	2,969	145	2,067	699	58	100.0	4.9	69.6	23.5	2.0
Female	**76,726**	**11,515**	**50,789**	**10,019**	**4,403**	**100.0**	**15.0**	**66.2**	**13.1**	**5.7**
18-19 years	4,166	3,261	876	1	27	100.0	78.3	21.0	(Z)	.6
20-24 years	9,614	4,099	5,159	14	341	100.0	42.6	53.7	.1	3.5
25-29 years	8,754	1,296	6,775	39	644	100.0	14.8	77.4	.4	7.4
30-34 years	7,128	502	5,955	71	599	100.0	7.0	83.5	1.0	8.4
35-44 years	11,712	551	9,862	294	1,006	100.0	4.7	84.2	2.5	8.6
45-54 years	12,156	537	9,880	876	862	100.0	4.4	81.3	7.2	7.1
55-64 years	10,447	513	7,374	1,992	567	100.0	4.9	70.6	19.1	5.4
65-74 years	7,778	457	3,785	3,266	270	100.0	5.9	48.7	42.0	3.5
75 years and over	4,971	299	1,120	3,465	86	100.0	6.0	22.5	69.7	1.7

– Represents zero. Z Less than .05 percent.

Source: U.S. Bureau of the Census, *Current Population Reports,* series P-20, No. 306.

U.S. Bureau of the Census, Statistical Abstract of the United States: 1977 (98th edition) Washington, D.C., 1977.

Number, Timing, and Duration of Marriages and Divorces in the United States: June 1975

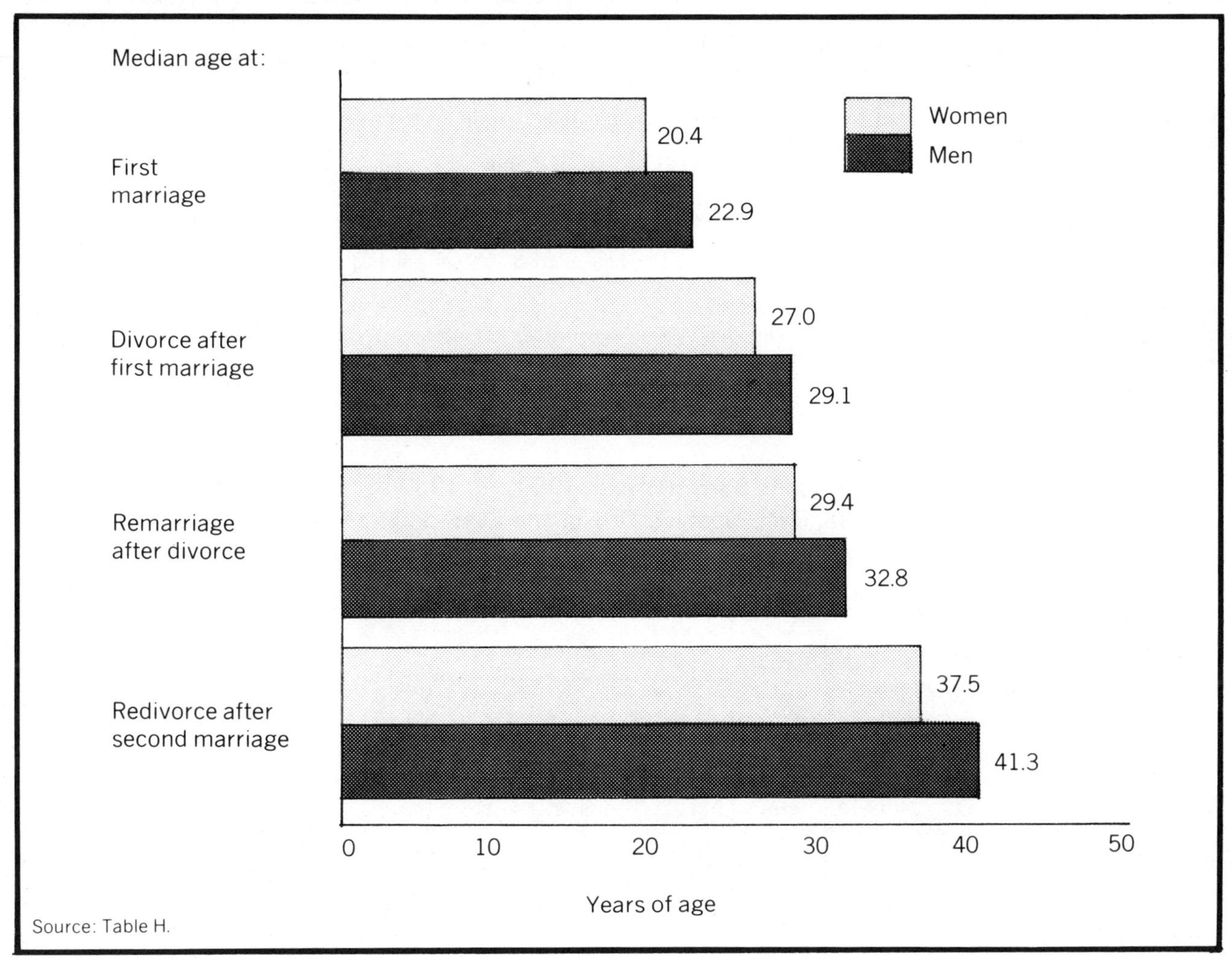

INTRODUCTION

This report presents results of a study of the marital history of men and women that was conducted in June 1975 by the Bureau of the Census. The analysis covers the number of times adults born since 1900 have married, their ages at marriage and divorce, and the number of years between marriage and divorce and between divorce and remarriage. The June 1975 survey also included questions about the fertility history of women; the first report on this subject has been published.[1] Earlier studies of marital history were made in 1971 and 1967.[2]

---

[1] Series P-20, No. 288, "Fertility History and Prospects of American Women: June 1975."

[2] Series P-20, No. 239, "Marriage, Divorce, and Remarriage by Year of Birth: June 1971"; and Series P-20, No. 223, "Social and Economic Variations in Marriage, Divorce, and Remarriage: 1967." Both of these reports are out of print.

Those who use this report are cautioned that the findings for some of the subgroups require careful interpretation. Thus, most of the discussion centers around comparative analyses of data by period of birth, and the findings for the youngest groups are based on persons with somewhat limited marital experience; moreover, those for the oldest groups are based on persons who made most of their changes in marital status several years before the recent upsurge in the divorce rate occurred. Consequently, the results that are featured in the analysis are generally for those persons who are currently in their intermediate years (30 to 60 years of age). Also, since the respondents were often reporting on marital events that had occurred several years earlier, the findings may be affected to some extent by errors of memory. However, the results from successive surveys on retrospective reporting of marital events are sufficiently consistent to support the belief that the reporting is reasonably reliable.

The statistics presented in this report are based on sample data and are therefore subject to sampling variability as well as other sources of error. For a further discussion of the sampling variability see the section on "Reliability of the Estimates."

NUMBER OF MARRIAGES AND DIVORCES

Few persons marry more than twice. About 3 percent of all persons 40 to 75 years old who have ever married have married more than twice, according to the results of the June 1975 survey (table A and table 1). However, according to the National Center for Health Statistics, the divorce rate has more than doubled in the last dozen years, from 2.3 per 1,000 population in 1963 to 4.8 in 1975, and (as will be shown below) the proportion of divorced persons who remarry is quite high. Accordingly, it should not be surprising if the proportion who marry more than twice may also increase correspondingly at the older ages by the time those now in their late twenties reach their sixties.

All but about 4 percent of the women and 5 percent of the men in their middle years have married. This applies to persons born between 1920 and 1934, who were in their forties or early fifties at the survey date in 1975. Of those in their forties who had married, 83 percent had married only once, 15 percent had married twice, and 2 percent three or more times (table 1). At the younger ages, the great majority of the marital dissolutions are by divorce, but as age advances an increasing proportion occur by widowhood.

Table A. Percent Distribution of Persons Born Between 1900 and 1959 by Number of Times Married, Year of Birth, Race, Spanish Origin, and Sex: June 1975

Race, Spanish origin, and year of birth	Men					Women				
	Total (percent)	Single in 1975	Ever married in 1975: times married			Total (percent)	Single in 1975	Ever married in 1975: times married		
			Once	Twice	3 or more times			Once	Twice	3 or more times
Total born in 1900 to 1959	100.0	26.1	62.5	9.8	1.5	100.0	20.6	67.0	10.8	1.7
White	100.0	25.2	63.7	9.7	1.5	100.0	19.5	68.1	10.7	1.7
Black	100.0	33.3	53.2	11.7	1.8	100.0	29.0	57.7	11.8	1.5
Other races	100.0	35.3	58.3	6.1	0.3	100.0	23.3	69.4	6.6	0.8
Spanish origin[1]	100.0	29.9	61.1	8.2	0.8	100.0	23.5	66.2	9.3	1.0
Born in--										
1955 to 1959	100.0	93.9	6.0	0.1	-	100.0	83.9	15.9	0.2	-
1950 to 1954	100.0	54.7	43.5	1.7	0.1	100.0	37.6	58.9	3.3	0.2
1945 to 1949	100.0	20.0	73.2	6.3	0.5	100.0	12.8	77.8	8.8	0.6
1940 to 1944	100.0	9.7	78.6	10.6	1.1	100.0	6.9	80.0	11.7	1.4
1935 to 1939	100.0	6.5	77.8	13.9	1.7	100.0	4.5	79.6	13.8	2.1
1930 to 1934	100.0	5.0	80.4	12.6	2.0	100.0	4.2	79.4	13.9	2.5
1925 to 1929	100.0	5.1	78.9	13.6	2.4	100.0	4.1	78.2	15.4	2.3
1920 to 1924	100.0	5.2	77.5	14.6	2.7	100.0	4.2	78.1	15.2	2.5
1915 to 1919	100.0	5.4	77.4	14.5	2.7	100.0	4.8	77.0	15.1	3.1
1910 to 1914	100.0	4.7	75.0	17.8	2.6	100.0	6.1	74.2	20.7	2.9
1905 to 1909	100.0	5.2	74.3	16.9	3.6	100.0	5.9	73.7	17.4	3.0
1900 to 1904	100.0	4.7	71.5	20.5	3.2	100.0	7.3	73.8	15.2	3.7

\- Represents zero.

[1]Persons of Spanish origin may be of any race.

Table 1. YEAR OF BIRTH BY CURRENT MARITAL STATUS, WHETHER (AND HOW) THE FIRST MARRIAGE ENDED, NUMBER OF TIMES MARRIED, RACE, SPANISH ORIGIN, AND SEX, FOR PERSONS WHO WERE BORN BETWEEN JANUARY 1900 AND DECEMBER 1959: SURVEY DATE JUNE 1975

(In thousands)

Number of times married, current marital status, and how first marriage ended	Total born, 1900 to 1959	Year of birth (age 15 to 75 in June 1975)											
		1955 to 1959	1950 to 1954	1945 to 1949	1940 to 1944	1935 to 1939	1930 to 1934	1925 to 1929	1920 to 1924	1915 to 1919	1910 to 1914	1905 to 1909	1900 to 1904
ALL RACES													
Men	69,672	10,011	8,520	7,908	6,471	5,405	5,300	5,699	5,637	4,858	4,149	3,426	2,289
Single (at survey date)	18,219	9,403	4,663	1,579	630	354	265	293	291	262	193	178	108
Married once	43,577	604	3,709	5,786	5,089	4,207	4,259	4,495	4,371	3,762	3,111	2,546	1,637
Married (except separated)	39,962	577	3,418	5,290	4,722	3,903	3,968	4,188	4,033	3,472	2,810	2,229	1,353
Separated	921	12	117	189	109	72	74	93	85	58	57	36	20
Divorced	1,800	15	168	301	246	221	202	172	168	117	95	65	31
Widowed	893	-	5	6	12	11	15	42	85	116	150	217	233
Married twice	6,841	3	144	500	684	752	669	777	822	704	737	580	470
Married:													
Divorced after first marriage	4,967	3	129	448	626	648	550	606	589	485	408	287	188
Widowed after first marriage	1,086	-	-	8	11	46	44	87	127	120	226	211	205
Separated:													
Divorced after first marriage	147	-	12	16	9	20	18	19	21	16	11	2	3
Widowed after first marriage	36	-	-	2	-	-	-	8	4	4	5	7	7
Divorced:													
Divorced after first marriage	374	-	3	23	38	36	49	46	60	50	36	22	12
Widowed after first marriage	56	-	-	3	-	2	2	9	3	8	8	11	9
Widowed:													
Divorced after first marriage	92	-	-	-	-	-	6	3	14	15	18	16	20
Widowed after first marriage	84	-	-	-	-	-	-	-	4	6	25	24	25
Married three or more times	1,034	-	4	43	68	92	106	134	153	131	107	122	74
Married:													
Divorced after first marriage	753	-	4	35	62	84	91	96	102	109	73	68	28
Widowed after first marriage	95	-	-	1	2	1	4	5	13	10	9	22	28
Separated:													
Divorced after first marriage	39	-	-	3	3	-	2	7	15	-	3	4	2
Widowed after first marriage	5	-	-	-	-	-	2	-	-	-	2	2	-
Divorced:													
Divorced after first marriage	92	-	-	3	2	7	6	24	17	3	13	14	3
Widowed after first marriage	23	-	-	-	-	-	1	-	3	5	1	3	9
Widowed:													
Divorced after first marriage	17	-	-	-	-	-	-	2	-	5	3	6	2
Widowed after first marriage	10	-	-	-	-	-	-	-	2	-	3	3	3
Women	76,302	10,275	9,276	8,334	6,906	5,870	5,805	6,046	6,070	5,357	4,924	4,300	3,139
Single (at survey date)	15,695	8,622	3,486	1,063	475	264	243	249	254	258	302	252	228
Married once	51,110	1,630	5,462	6,480	5,525	4,670	4,611	4,726	4,741	4,126	3,652	3,169	2,318
Married (except separated)	40,782	1,511	4,806	5,620	4,734	4,039	3,940	3,924	3,910	3,147	2,424	1,766	962
Separated	1,721	70	290	327	279	185	161	127	85	73	71	33	20
Divorced	3,246	47	339	495	454	367	346	370	278	204	138	126	82
Widowed	5,361	1	28	38	59	80	164	305	468	701	1,019	1,244	1,254
Married twice	8,213	23	310	737	809	812	805	934	923	807	825	750	477
Married:													
Divorced after first marriage	4,591	18	262	609	612	601	526	549	482	346	293	204	89
Widowed after first marriage	1,457	-	14	33	57	72	118	173	212	226	229	213	110
Separated:													
Divorced after first marriage	281	2	17	30	28	48	32	45	39	19	10	11	-
Widowed after first marriage	80	-	-	3	9	3	9	14	6	10	11	9	4
Divorced:													
Divorced after first marriage	613	4	15	58	90	67	77	100	54	58	47	34	10
Widowed after first marriage	146	-	-	3	6	5	10	16	29	26	28	17	6
Widowed:													
Divorced after first marriage	632	-	2	2	6	11	25	35	77	81	130	141	124
Widowed after first marriage	415	-	-	-	-	6	7	3	24	41	78	122	133
Married three or more times	1,284	-	18	54	97	125	145	138	153	166	145	129	115
Married:													
Divorced after first marriage	670	-	16	38	64	85	102	77	87	70	64	34	33
Widowed after first marriage	163	-	-	3	7	13	5	13	21	30	21	24	24
Separated:													
Divorced after first marriage	47	-	-	6	5	3	6	8	5	8	2	2	2
Widowed after first marriage	19	-	-	-	2	-	2	-	6	2	3	2	3
Divorced:													
Divorced after first marriage	170	-	-	6	17	18	26	29	20	23	14	9	6
Widowed after first marriage	26	-	2	-	-	-	3	5	5	2	3	4	2
Widowed:													
Divorced after first marriage	147	-	-	-	-	3	2	5	6	29	35	41	26
Widowed after first marriage	42	-	-	-	2	2	-	1	3	2	3	12	18
WHITE													
Men	61,777	8,587	7,460	6,996	5,749	4,803	4,704	5,073	5,080	4,408	3,748	3,088	2,079
Single (at survey date)	15,570	8,037	4,025	1,301	521	289	233	249	252	238	175	157	93
Married once	39,328	547	3,293	5,217	4,546	3,773	3,780	4,070	3,977	3,444	2,844	2,322	1,514
Married (except separated)	36,429	522	3,045	4,804	4,256	3,524	3,565	3,838	3,716	3,215	2,614	2,067	1,261
Separated	585	11	95	138	60	51	39	53	46	31	32	17	11
Divorced	1,559	14	148	270	220	189	161	150	145	102	80	54	25
Widowed	755	-	5	4	10	10	13	29	70	96	117	184	216

Table 1. YEAR OF BIRTH BY CURRENT MARITAL STATUS, WHETHER (AND HOW) THE FIRST MARRIAGE ENDED, NUMBER OF TIMES MARRIED, RACE, SPANISH ORIGIN, AND SEX, FOR PERSONS WHO WERE BORN BETWEEN JANUARY 1900 AND DECEMBER 1959: SURVEY DATE JUNE 1975—Continued

(In thousands)

Number of times married, current marital status, and how first marriage ended	Total born, 1900 to 1959	Year of birth (age 15 to 75 in June 1975)											
		1955 to 1959	1950 to 1954	1945 to 1949	1940 to 1944	1935 to 1939	1930 to 1934	1925 to 1929	1920 to 1924	1915 to 1919	1910 to 1914	1905 to 1909	1900 to 1904
WHITE--Continued													
Men--Continued													
Married twice	5,971	3	138	436	613	657	594	641	720	612	634	509	413
Married:													
Divorced after first marriage	4,384	3	127	396	559	576	493	510	525	424	366	244	159
Widowed after first marriage	968	-	-	8	11	36	42	70	115	111	192	193	191
Separated:													
Divorced after first marriage	99	-	8	11	8	15	11	12	13	8	11	2	2
Widowed after first marriage	17	-	-	2	-	-	-	-	2	1	2	5	6
Divorced:													
Divorced after first marriage	329	-	3	18	35	28	43	40	51	48	32	17	12
Widowed after first marriage	47	-	-	1	-	2	2	7	3	6	7	11	8
Widowed:													
Divorced after first marriage	66	-	-	-	-	-	3	3	6	10	14	16	15
Widowed after first marriage	61	-	-	-	-	-	-	-	3	4	12	21	22
Married three or more times	909	-	4	42	68	84	98	114	132	114	94	100	60
Married:													
Divorced after first marriage	683	-	4	35	62	78	86	87	88	97	65	58	24
Widowed after first marriage	77	-	-	-	2	1	2	3	11	8	9	20	21
Separated:													
Divorced after first marriage	26	-	-	3	3	-	-	5	11	-	1	-	2
Widowed after first marriage	2	-	-	-	-	-	2	-	-	-	-	-	-
Divorced:													
Divorced after first marriage	79	-	-	3	2	4	6	18	16	2	13	12	3
Widowed after first marriage	20	-	-	-	-	-	1	-	3	3	1	3	7
Widowed:													
Divorced after first marriage	13	-	-	-	-	-	-	2	-	5	2	3	2
Widowed after first marriage	9	-	-	-	-	-	-	-	2	-	3	3	2
Women	66,790	8,732	7,941	7,220	5,965	5,078	5,055	5,326	5,446	4,844	4,421	3,881	2,881
Single (at survey date)	13,001	7,256	2,789	812	361	192	206	216	219	227	279	228	216
Married once	45,486	1,453	4,848	5,669	4,785	4,063	4,042	4,184	4,304	3,770	3,311	2,902	2,155
Married (except separated)	37,158	1,347	4,340	5,021	4,265	3,625	3,585	3,572	3,633	2,968	2,238	1,661	903
Separated	970	64	196	193	126	90	71	63	54	38	38	20	17
Divorced	2,713	40	291	430	363	302	268	304	234	180	116	111	74
Widowed	4,645	1	21	25	31	45	117	246	383	585	920	1,111	1,161
Married twice	7,150	23	286	685	727	707	677	799	786	696	701	645	418
Married:													
Divorced after first marriage	4,110	18	245	569	571	535	459	479	426	294	253	188	73
Widowed after first marriage	1,303	-	11	31	45	63	101	147	190	210	215	188	103
Separated:													
Divorced after first marriage	180	2	16	27	17	32	21	29	14	11	6	6	-
Widowed after first marriage	47	-	-	1	3	-	5	11	5	9	4	4	4
Divorced:													
Divorced after first marriage	535	4	13	54	80	58	65	90	47	53	37	26	8
Widowed after first marriage	129	-	-	2	6	5	7	13	25	23	26	17	6
Widowed:													
Divorced after first marriage	495	-	2	2	6	9	18	28	55	58	100	112	106
Widowed after first marriage	351	-	-	-	-	4	2	3	23	38	59	104	118
Married three or more times	1,152	-	18	54	92	116	130	126	138	150	130	105	92
Married:													
Divorced after first marriage	612	-	16	38	61	77	92	69	77	63	59	32	27
Widowed after first marriage	152	-	-	3	7	13	3	13	21	29	20	22	20
Separated:													
Divorced after first marriage	40	-	-	6	3	3	6	8	3	6	-	2	2
Widowed after first marriage	19	-	-	-	2	-	2	-	6	2	3	2	3
Divorced:													
Divorced after first marriage	160	-	-	6	17	18	22	27	20	20	14	9	5
Widowed after first marriage	21	-	2	-	-	-	3	3	5	2	3	2	1
Widowed:													
Divorced after first marriage	117	-	-	-	-	3	2	5	4	27	28	29	20
Widowed after first marriage	32	-	-	-	2	2	-	1	2	2	3	8	13
BLACK													
Men	6,905	1,276	928	774	612	522	517	546	489	400	374	292	174
Single (at survey date)	2,300	1,226	544	229	82	56	30	40	30	23	16	17	6
Married once	3,672	50	379	491	465	368	408	357	342	278	249	183	104
Married (except separated)	2,981	47	337	409	390	314	331	288	268	220	180	121	79
Separated	329	1	22	49	49	21	34	39	39	24	23	19	8
Divorced	226	2	21	31	24	31	40	17	19	14	14	11	1
Widowed	136	-	-	2	2	2	2	13	15	20	31	32	16
Married twice	810	-	6	53	65	90	71	131	97	83	96	70	49
Married:													
Divorced after first marriage	539	-	2	44	61	71	55	94	59	51	35	43	25
Widowed after first marriage	108	-	-	-	-	8	2	14	12	9	35	18	11
Separated:													
Divorced after first marriage	45	-	4	5	2	5	5	8	7	8	-	-	2
Widowed after first marriage	19	-	-	-	-	-	-	8	2	2	4	2	2
Divorced:													
Divorced after first marriage	41	-	-	2	2	7	6	6	8	2	4	4	-
Widowed after first marriage	8	-	-	2	-	-	-	2	-	2	1	-	1
Widowed:													
Divorced after first marriage	26	-	-	-	-	-	3	-	7	6	4	-	5
Widowed after first marriage	23	-	-	-	-	-	-	-	1	2	13	4	4

Table 1. YEAR OF BIRTH BY CURRENT MARITAL STATUS, WHETHER (AND HOW) THE FIRST MARRIAGE ENDED, NUMBER OF TIMES MARRIED, RACE, SPANISH ORIGIN, AND SEX, FOR PERSONS WHO WERE BORN BETWEEN JANUARY 1900 AND DECEMBER 1959: SURVEY DATE JUNE 1975—Continued

(In thousands)

Number of times married, current marital status, and how first marriage ended	Total born, 1900 to 1959	Year of birth (age 15 to 75 in June 1975)											
		1955 to 1959	1950 to 1954	1945 to 1949	1940 to 1944	1935 to 1939	1930 to 1934	1925 to 1929	1920 to 1924	1915 to 1919	1910 to 1914	1905 to 1909	1900 to 1904
BLACK--Continued													
Married three or more times	122	-	-	1	-	8	9	18	21	16	13	22	14
Married:													
Divorced after first marriage	67	-	-	-	-	5	5	7	14	12	8	10	5
Widowed after first marriage	18	-	-	1	-	-	2	2	2	2	-	2	7
Separated:													
Divorced after first marriage	13	-	-	-	-	-	2	2	4	-	2	4	-
Widowed after first marriage	3	-	-	-	-	-	-	-	-	-	2	2	-
Divorced:													
Divorced after first marriage	12	-	-	-	-	2	-	6	2	-	-	2	-
Widowed after first marriage	3	-	-	-	-	-	-	-	-	2	-	-	2
Widowed:													
Divorced after first marriage	4	-	-	-	-	-	-	-	-	-	1	3	-
Widowed after first marriage	1	-	-	-	-	-	-	-	-	-	-	-	1
Women	8,356	1,395	1,168	931	790	680	652	631	555	475	45[illegible]	39[illegible]	234
Single (at survey date)	2,424	1,247	613	219	102	67	32	29	30	26	23	2[illegible]	12
Married once	4,822	148	536	663	614	512	491	470	385	324	295	243	142
Married (except separated)	2,954	135	400	464	358	336	288	289	233	155	149	93	54
Separated	722	5	88	125	149	90	90	64	29	35	32	13	1
Divorced	488	8	41	62	82	52	73	62	41	25	22	14	6
Widowed	658	-	7	12	25	34	41	55	81	109	91	124	80
Married twice	987	-	19	49	70	96	119	121	125	109	119	103	57
Married:													
Divorced after first marriage	443	-	14	40	34	58	63	64	48	51	40	16	15
Widowed after first marriage	138	-	1	-	9	9	16	25	17	15	14	24	7
Separated:													
Divorced after first marriage	94	-	2	4	10	16	8	13	25	8	4	5	-
Widowed after first marriage	32	-	-	1	6	3	4	3	1	1	6	5	-
Divorced:													
Divorced after first marriage	70	-	2	3	10	7	11	6	7	5	9	7	3
Widowed after first marriage	17	-	-	1	-	-	3	3	4	3	2	-	-
Widowed:													
Divorced after first marriage	136	-	-	-	-	1	7	7	22	23	30	29	17
Widowed after first marriage	57	-	-	-	-	2	5	-	1	3	14	17	15
Married three or more times	123	-	-	-	5	5	10	11	15	16	15	24	23
Married:													
Divorced after first marriage	53	-	-	-	3	5	8	8	10	7	5	2	6
Widowed after first marriage	11	-	-	-	-	-	2	-	-	2	1	2	4
Separated:													
Divorced after first marriage	7	-	-	-	2	-	-	-	2	2	2	-	-
Widowed after first marriage	-	-	-	-	-	-	-	-	-	-	-	-	-
Divorced:													
Divorced after first marriage	6	-	-	-	-	-	-	2	-	3	-	-	1
Widowed after first marriage	5	-	-	-	-	-	-	2	-	-	-	2	1
Widowed:													
Divorced after first marriage	30	-	-	-	-	-	-	-	1	3	7	13	6
Widowed after first marriage	11	-	-	-	-	-	-	-	2	-	-	5	4
SPANISH ORIGIN													
Men	3,089	541	443	426	338	278	295	215	165	137	121	74	54
Single (at survey date)	893	494	213	75	37	24	15	10	2	8	10	3	3
Married once	1,903	47	226	329	264	212	239	177	138	94	82	54	40
Married (except separated)	1,762	47	210	299	252	201	220	168	122	91	73	46	32
Separated	57	-	8	17	5	3	8	2	5	2	5	2	-
Divorced	59	-	9	11	6	6	10	4	5	-	3	5	-
Widowed	25	-	-	1	-	2	-	3	7	1	2	2	8
Married twice	268	-	3	23	34	40	37	27	22	30	28	15	10
Married:													
Divorced after first marriage	208	-	3	21	30	37	32	19	17	24	15	6	3
Widowed after first marriage	42	-	-	2	-	1	5	5	2	6	6	8	5
Separated:													
Divorced after first marriage	3	-	-	-	-	2	-	-	-	-	2	-	-
Widowed after first marriage	-	-	-	-	-	-	-	-	-	-	-	-	-
Divorced:													
Divorced after first marriage	7	-	-	-	4	-	-	-	3	-	-	-	-
Widowed after first marriage	3	-	-	-	-	-	-	2	-	-	1	-	-
Widowed:													
Divorced after first marriage	1	-	-	-	-	-	-	-	-	-	-	-	1
Widowed after first marriage	3	-	-	-	-	-	-	-	-	-	3	-	-
Married three or more times	25	-	-	-	3	3	5	2	4	5	1	2	2
Married:													
Divorced after first marriage	24	-	-	-	3	3	5	2	4	5	-	2	2
Widowed after first marriage	-	-	-	-	-	-	-	-	-	-	-	-	-
Separated:													
Divorced after first marriage	-	-	-	-	-	-	-	-	-	-	-	-	-
Widowed after first marriage	-	-	-	-	-	-	-	-	-	-	-	-	-
Divorced:													
Divorced after first marriage	1	-	-	-	-	-	-	-	-	-	1	-	-
Widowed after first marriage	-	-	-	-	-	-	-	-	-	-	-	-	-
Widowed:													
Divorced after first marriage	-	-	-	-	-	-	-	-	-	-	-	-	-
Widowed after first marriage	-	-	-	-	-	-	-	-	-	-	-	-	-

Table 1. YEAR OF BIRTH BY CURRENT MARITAL STATUS, WHETHER (AND HOW) THE FIRST MARRIAGE ENDED, NUMBER OF TIMES MARRIED, RACE, SPANISH ORIGIN, AND SEX, FOR PERSONS WHO WERE BORN BETWEEN JANUARY 1900 AND DECEMBER 1959: SURVEY DATE JUNE 1975—Continued

(In thousands)

Number of times married, current marital status, and how first marriage ended	Total born, 1900 to 1959	Year of birth (age 15 to 75 in June 1975)											
		1955 to 1959	1950 to 1954	1945 to 1949	1940 to 1944	1935 to 1939	1930 to 1934	1925 to 1929	1920 to 1924	1915 to 1919	1910 to 1914	1905 to 1909	1900 to 1904
SPANISH ORIGIN--Continued													
Women--Continued													
Women	3,506	593	500	480	382	370	285	241	226	151	106	103	71
Single (at survey date)	829	472	165	77	32	12	15	14	16	6	6	10	3
Married once	2,329	121	317	368	305	286	223	185	180	121	91	73	60
Married (except separated)	1,832	104	271	309	260	235	184	146	136	82	47	34	24
Separated	184	13	30	30	21	25	18	6	13	11	10	3	5
Divorced	148	3	16	26	22	16	17	16	9	7	9	7	-
Widowed	166	-	-	3	2	10	5	17	23	21	25	29	32
Married twice	315	-	17	35	42	67	34	39	28	21	9	17	6
Married:													
Divorced after first marriage	211	-	11	27	37	50	21	25	16	14	3	8	-
Widowed after first marriage	40	-	3	3	•2	5	5	3	4	1	2	8	5
Separated:													
Divorced after first marriage	30	-	3	3	2	9	2	8	-	3	-	-	-
Widowed after first marriage	-	-	-	-	-	-	-	-	-	-	-	-	-
Divorced:													
Divorced after first marriage	14	-	-	2	2	2	5	-	2	-	3	-	-
Widowed after first marriage	5	-	-	-	-	-	2	2	2	-	-	-	-
Widowed:													
Divorced after first marriage	9	-	-	-	-	-	-	-	3	3	-	1	1
Widowed after first marriage	6	-	-	-	-	1	-	2	2	-	1	-	-
Married three or more times	33	-	-	-	3	5	13	3	2	3	-	3	1
Married:													
Divorced after first marriage	14	-	-	-	2	3	6	-	-	2	-	2	-
Widowed after first marriage	1	-	-	-	-	-	-	-	-	-	-	-	1
Separated:													
Divorced after first marriage	3	-	-	-	-	-	-	3	-	-	-	-	-
Widowed after first marriage	2	-	-	-	2	-	-	-	-	-	-	-	-
Divorced:													
Divorced after first marriage	10	-	-	-	-	-	7	-	2	-	-	1	-
Widowed after first marriage	-	-	-	-	-	-	-	-	-	-	-	-	-
Widowed:													
Divorced after first marriage	2	-	-	-	-	-	-	-	-	2	-	-	-
Widowed after first marriage	2	-	-	-	-	2	-	-	-	-	-	-	-

- Represents zero.

White adults were more likely than Black adults to have been married only once. Thus, 64 percent of the White men as compared with 53 percent of the Black men born between 1900 and 1959 had been married once (table A). For women, the corresponding proportions married once were 68 percent for Whites and 58 percent for Blacks. The difference is attributable in part to the greater delay in marriage among Blacks. However, a part of the difference is attributable to the larger proportion of Blacks who reported that they had been married more than once.

Persons who were reported as currently married at the time of the survey in 1975 were the least likely to have ever been remarried. Only 15 percent of those born since 1900 who had ever married had been remarried by the survey date (table B). Divorced and separated persons reported a considerably larger proportion of second or subsequent marriages than did married persons (23 percent and 20 percent versus 15 percent, respectively). These findings support the general conclusion that persons (mostly below old age) who had remarried after one marriage had been dissolved were more likely than persons still in their first marriage to have been experiencing serious marital difficulties at (or before) the survey date.

Older cohort experience indicates that four of every five divorced persons may eventually remarry. Among persons who had reached the age range of 50 to 75 years in 1975, five of every six men and three of every four women whose first marriage ended in divorce had remarried (table C and table 1). Thus, divorce after first marriage is generally not the final marital step but only one of the steps in a transition between first marriage and second marriage, with divorced men being 5 to 10 percentage points more likely than divorced women to eventually remarry.

Widowed persons, age for age, are less likely than divorced persons to remarry. Only one-half of the persons in their early fifties in 1975 had remarried after their first marriage ended in widowhood, as compared with about four-fifths of those of a comparable age whose first marriage had ended in divorce (table C and table 1). The proportion of widowers of this age who had remarried was about 25 percentage points above that of widows (65 versus 40 percent). As a partial consequence, the number of widowers in their early fifties (241,000) was only about one-third as great as the number of widows (774,000). Among persons in their early seventies the number of widowed persons who had remarried (586,000) was not different from the number of divorced persons who had remarried (548,000); however, the proportion of widowed persons in this age group who had remarried (28 percent) was only one-third as great as the proportion of divorced persons of similar age who had remarried (83 percent).

Table B. Persons Ever Married Born Between 1900 and 1959 by Number of Times Married, Marital Status, and Sex: June 1975

(Numbers in thousands)

Sex and marital status	Persons born between 1900 and 1959				
	Total	Percent by number of times married			
		Total	Once	Twice	Three or more
Both sexes, ever married	112,060	(X)	94,687	15,054	2,318
Percent	(X)	100.0	84.5	13.4	2.1
Married	97,822	100.0	85.2	12.9	1.8
Not separated	94,526	100.0	85.4	12.8	1.8
Separated	3,296	100.0	80.2	16.5	3.3
Divorced	6,546	100.0	77.1	18.2	4.8
Widowed	7,693	100.0	81.3	15.9	2.8
Men, ever married	51,453	(X)	43,577	6,841	1,034
Percent	(X)	100.0	84.7	13.3	2.0
Married	48,011	100.0	85.2	13.0	1.9
Not separated	46,863	100.0	85.3	12.9	1.8
Separated	1,148	100.0	80.3	16.0	3.8
Divorced	2,345	100.0	76.8	18.3	4.9
Widowed	1,096	100.0	81.5	16.1	2.5
Women, ever married	60,607	(X)	51,110	8,213	1,284
Percent	(X)	100.0	84.3	13.6	2.1
Married	49,811	100.0	85.3	12.9	1.8
Not separated	47,663	100.0	85.6	12.7	1.7
Separated	2,148	100.0	80.1	16.8	3.1
Divorced	4,201	100.0	77.3	18.1	4.7
Widowed	6,597	100.0	81.3	15.9	2.9

X Not applicable.

A greater amount of divorce has occurred among the young despite their shorter period of marriage. For instance, women in their late thirties were half again as likely to have been divorced as women in their early seventies even though the younger women had been married (and thus subject to the possibility of divorce) for a far shorter period of time than the older women (about 15 to 20 years, on the average, versus 50 to 55 years). More specifically, 22 percent of the women ever married who were born in 1935 to 1939 were "known to have been divorced" (after their first marriage and/or their latest marriage) as compared with only 13 percent of those born in 1900 to 1904 (table D and table 1).

Most of those who are known to have been divorced report only one divorce. This can be illustrated with data in table D for women ever married in their late thirties (who were born in 1935 to 1939). Of these women, 75 percent were reported as having been married once and never divorced or widowed; 22 percent as having been divorced—20 percent once (after their first or latest marriage but not both) and 2 percent at least twice (after both their first and latest marriages); and the remaining 3 percent as having been widowed but not divorced. Close to nine-tenths of the reported divorces occurred after the first marriage; this finding applies to virtually all of the ethnic groups shown in table D and to all of the periods of birth except the two youngest who were born as recently as the 1950's.

A few adults report having been both divorced and widowed. For all women born between 1900 and 1959, 2 percent were in this category, but the corresponding proportions increased with age (table 1). Thus, the proportion of women who had been both divorced and widowed was only 1 percent for those in their early forties, whereas it was 5 percent for those in their early seventies. Among women in their early forties, 21 percent had been divorced as compared with 6 percent who had been widowed. By contrast, among those in their late sixties, 40 percent had been widowed whereas 15 percent had been divorced.

Table C. Percent Remarried After First Marriage Ended in Divorce or in Widowhood, for Persons Born in Selected Periods Between 1900 and 1944 by Sex: June 1975

(Numbers in thousands)

Year of birth and sex	Divorced after first marriage				Widowed after first marriage			
	Total		Not remarried	Remarried	Total		Not remarried	Remarried
	Number	Percent			Number	Percent		
BOTH SEXES								
Born in--								
1940 to 1944..............	2,262	100.0	30.9	69.1	167	100.0	42.5	57.5
1930 to 1934..............	2,066	100.0	26.5	73.5	386	100.0	46.4	53.6
1920 to 1924..............	2,034	100.0	21.9	78.1	1,015	100.0	54.5	45.5
1910 to 1914..............	1,393	100.0	16.7	83.3	1,824	100.0	64.1	35.9
1900 to 1904..............	661	100.0	17.1	82.9	2,073	100.0	71.7	28.3
MALE								
Born in--								
1940 to 1944..............	986	100.0	24.9	75.1	25	(B)	(B)	(B)
1930 to 1934..............	924	100.0	21.9	78.1	68	(B)	(B)	(B)
1920 to 1924..............	986	100.0	17.0	83.0	241	100.0	35.3	64.7
1910 to 1914..............	660	100.0	14.4	85.6	429	100.0	35.0	65.0
1900 to 1904..............	289	100.0	10.7	89.3	519	100.0	44.9	55.1
FEMALE								
Born in--								
1940 to 1944..............	1,276	100.0	35.6	64.4	142	100.0	41.5	58.5
1930 to 1934..............	1,142	100.0	30.3	69.7	318	100.0	51.6	48.4
1920 to 1924..............	1,048	100.0	26.5	73.5	774	100.0	60.5	39.5
1910 to 1914..............	733	100.0	18.8	81.2	1,395	100.0	73.0	27.0
1900 to 1904..............	372	100.0	22.0	78.0	1,554	100.0	80.7	19.3

B Base less than 75,000.

PROPORTION OF MARRIAGES THAT END IN DIVORCE

More divorces occur at young ages. Evidence that an increasing proportion of first marriages end in divorce at a relatively young age is provided by the underscored numbers in table E, which was derived from table 3. The underscored numbers refer to the proportion of persons whose first marriage had ended in divorce by the time they were in their upper twenties. Thus, only 4.5 percent of the married men who were born in 1900 to 1904 had ended their first marriage by 1930 to 1934 when they were about 25 to 34 years old. The corresponding proportions increased steadily to 7.9 percent for those born in 1915 to 1919, to 10.4 percent for those born in 1930 to 1934, and to 13.1 percent for those born in 1945 to 1949.

These data show that about three times as large a proportion of the youngest group as of the oldest group had ended their first marriage before the age of 35 years. For women, the corresponding results for the two youngest groups (13.1 percent and 17.1 percent, respectively) were somewhat higher than those for men; this difference arises because women marry when they are two or three years younger than men, on the average, and therefore have been subject to divorce for a longer number of years than men by the time when they reach their upper twenties.

Likewise, divorces after the second marriage have been occuring at increasingly younger ages (tables F and 4). As the underscored numbers in table F imply, about four times as large a proportion of men in their early forties in 1975 as compared with those of similar age in 1945 had ended their second marriage in redivorce (8.0 percent versus 1.8 percent). For women the contrast appears to be even greater (11.3 percent versus 1.8 percent), but because the data are based on a sample and involve "retrospective" reporting on earlier events, the difference is attributable to sampling variability or to incomplete reporting or misreporting.

One-third of recent first marriages may end in divorce. Additional evidence from the survey in June 1975 that the divorce experience of young adults had already far exceeded that of older adults when they had been of comparable age is presented in the first column of table G. Close to 19 percent of several birth cohorts under 50 years old (born since 1925) had ended their first marriage in divorce by the survey date, as compared with

Table D. Percent Distribution of Women Ever Married Who Were Born Between 1900 and 1959 by Whether Known to Have Been Divorced or Widowed, Year of Birth, Number of Times Married, and Race: June 1975

Race, Spanish origin, and year of birth	Total women ever married (percent)	Never divorced or widowed by 1975	Known to have been divorced				Known to have been widowed but not divorced[3]
			Total	Divorced after--			
				First marriage only[1]	First and latest marriage	Latest marriage only[2]	
Total born in 1900 to 1959.	100.0	70.1	17.4	15.9	1.3	0.3	12.4
White........................	100.0	70.9	16.9	15.4	1.3	0.3	12.2
Black........................	100.0	62.0	22.7	21.1	1.3	0.4	15.3
Other races..................	100.0	78.9	12.2	10.8	1.4	-	9.1
Spanish origin[4].............	100.0	75.2	16.6	15.6	0.9	0.2	8.1
Born in--							
1955 to 1959...............	100.0	95.6	4.3	4.1	0.2	-	0.1
1950 to 1954...............	100.0	88.0	11.2	10.9	0.3	(Z)	0.7
1945 to 1949...............	100.0	81.8	17.2	16.2	0.9	(Z)	1.1
1940 to 1944...............	100.0	78.0	19.9	18.2	1.7	0.1	2.1
1935 to 1939...............	100.0	75.3	21.5	19.9	1.5	0.1	3.1
1930 to 1934...............	100.0	73.7	20.8	18.7	1.9	0.2	5.5
1925 to 1929...............	100.0	69.9	21.4	18.8	2.2	0.4	8.8
1920 to 1924...............	100.0	68.7	18.6	16.7	1.3	0.6	12.7
1915 to 1919...............	100.0	63.1	17.0	14.8	1.6	0.5	19.8
1910 to 1914...............	100.0	54.0	16.5	14.5	1.3	0.7	29.5
1905 to 1909...............	100.0	44.4	15.4	13.8	1.1	0.5	40.2
1900 to 1904...............	100.0	33.7	13.1	12.2	0.5	0.3	53.1

- Represents zero.
Z Less than 0.05 percent.
[1]Divorced after their first marriage but not after their latest, if ever remarried.
[2]Divorced after their latest marriage but not after their first marriage.
[3]Widowed after their first and/or latest marriage but not divorced after either marriage.
[4]Persons of Spanish origin may be of any race.

Table E. Percent of Persons Ever Married Whose First Marriage Ended in Divorce by Specified Calendar Years, for Persons of Selected Years of Birth by Sex: June 1975

Year of divorce after first marriage	Men ever married born in--				Women ever married born in--			
	1945 to 1949	1930 to 1934	1915 to 1919	1900 to 1904	1945 to 1949	1930 to 1934	1915 to 1919	1900 to 1904
Percent whose first marriage ended in divorce by--								
Mid-1975.........................	13.1	18.4	17.4	13.3	17.1	20.5	16.4	12.8
1970.............................	5.1	15.4	16.5	13.0	8.1	17.4	15.9	12.6
1965.............................	0.4	11.3	15.3	13.0	1.2	13.9	14.8	12.6
1960 to 1964.....................	0.2	10.4	15.1	12.7	0.7	13.1	14.5	12.6
1955 to 1959.....................	(X)	6.2	13.6	12.4	(X)	8.2	13.2	12.2
1950 to 1954.....................	(X)	1.6	10.6	11.7	(X)	3.6	11.5	11.8
1945 to 1949.....................	(X)	0.1	7.9	10.6	(X)	0.5	8.6	11.3
1940 to 1944.....................	(X)	(X)	3.9	8.3	(X)	(X)	6.1	10.0
1935 to 1939.....................	(X)	(X)	0.7	6.9	(X)	(X)	2.3	8.1
1930 to 1934.....................	(X)	(X)	(Z)	4.5	(X)	(X)	0.5	6.5

X Not applicable.
Z Less than 0.05 percent.

Table F. Percent of Persons Married Twice Whose Second Marriage Ended in Redivorce by Specified Calendar Years, for Persons of Selected Years of Birth by Sex: June 1975

Year of redivorce after second marriage	Men married twice born in--				Women married twice born in--			
	1945 to 1949	1930 to 1934	1915 to 1919	1900 to 1904	1945 to 1949	1930 to 1934	1915 to 1919	1900 to 1904
Percent whose second marriage ended in redivorce by-								
Mid-1975	4.9	8.0	9.2	6.3	8.4	11.3	11.1	4.5
1970	0.4	2.4	3.9	4.5	0.3	6.4	9.5	3.6
1965	-	0.5	3.2	4.0	-	2.0	6.0	3.6
1960	-	0.5	2.8	3.6	-	1.8	5.2	3.6
1955	(X)	-	2.5	2.7	(X)	0.3	2.6	3.1
1950	(X)	-	1.8	2.7	(X)	0.3	1.0	2.7
1945	(X)	-	0.4	1.8	(X)	-	0.2	1.8
1940	(X)	(X)	-	0.9	(X)	(X)	-	0.4
1935	(X)	(X)	-	-	(X)	(X)	-	-
1930	(X)	(X)	-	-	(X)	(X)	-	-

- Represents zero.
X Not applicable.

only 13 percent for the oldest group (persons in their early seventies). Moreover, the young adults will surely increase considerably their proportion of first marriages that end in divorce by the time they reach their seventies.

Consequently, a projection technique was used to estimate the proportion of first marriages of young adults that may end in divorce by the time when these persons reach old age. The results are given in the second column of table G. These results were derived from tables E and 3 by using the survey findings on added divorce experience between calendar year 1969 and calendar year 1974 for successively older 5-year birth cohorts to estimate the approximate amount of successive 5-year increments in divorce that the younger groups may experience by the time they reach their early seventies.[3]

The projections imply that about one-third of the married persons between 25 and 35 years old in 1975 may eventually end their first marriage in divorce, including those who have already done so. This level is between two and three times as high as the estimated 13 percent for persons in their early seventies, very few more of whom will end their first marriage in divorce after 1975. The large difference between these two levels of divorce is one of the measures of the increasing propensity for more young adults to legally terminate their first marriage through a divorce proceeding.

A word of caution is in order regarding the interpretation of these findings. They are based on the stated assumption about future increments of divorce, which in turn were based on sample data that are subject to sampling variability and to errors of reporting. However, the close consistency observed between the same types of results from the 1975 and 1971 surveys provides a basis for accepting the projected general levels of eventual divorce after first marriage as reasonable prospects for persons now about 30 years old.

A higher proportion of recent second marriages may end in redivorce. Although, as the third column of table G shows, no more than about 10 percent of the second marriages for men in any given cohort and 15 percent of the second marriages among women in any given cohort for those in their thirties to sixties had already ended in redivorce by the survey date in June 1975, surely a much larger proportion of those in the younger part of this age range will eventually become redivorced. The approximate level to which the proportion is likely to rise was estimated by the same type of projection technique as that described in the preceding section. The results appear in the final column of table G.

The projections imply that about four-tenths of the persons in their late twenties and early thirties who had entered their second marriage (after their first marriage had ended in divorce) may expect eventually to have their second marriage also end in divorce, including those who have already done so. This level is several times as high as the estimated level for persons now in their sixties or early seventies.

The anticipated large increase may reflect, among other things, the growing proportion of adults who have been through the experience of divorce once at a relatively early age; these persons have more remaining years in which to experience divorce for a second time than those who are one or more decades older. Moreover, as suggested above, many (but by no means all) of those who have been divorced once evidently resist becoming divorced for a second time by a lesser amount than persons of similar age in their first marriage resist becoming divorced for the first time. Perhaps persons who become divorced at a relatively young age tend to have personal and social characteristics that are somewhat different from those of persons who never become divorced.

[3] For a fuller statement of this projection method, see Paul C. Glick and Arthur J. Norton, "Perspectives on the Recent Upturn in Divorce and Remarriage," **Demography**, Vol. 10, No. 3, pp. 301-14, especially the appendix.

Table G. Percent of Ever-married Persons Whose First Marriage May Eventually End in Divorce and Whose Second Marriage May Eventually End in Redivorce, by Year of Birth and Sex: June 1975

Year of birth and sex	Percent of ever-married persons whose first marriage--		Percent of persons married twice whose second marriage--	
	Had ended in divorce by 1975	May eventually end in divorce[1]	Had ended in redivorce by 1975	May eventually end in redivorce[1]
MEN				
1945 to 1949	13	34	5	35
1940 to 1944	17	31	6	32
1935 to 1939	20	29	5	28
1930 to 1934	18	24	8	24
1925 to 1929	18	22	7	20
1920 to 1924	18	20	9	18
1915 to 1919	17	18	9	13
1910 to 1914	17	17	7	9
1905 to 1909	15	15	7	8
1900 to 1904	13	13	6	6
WOMEN				
1945 to 1949	17	38	8	44
1940 to 1944	20	34	12	40
1935 to 1939	21	31	10	31
1930 to 1934	21	26	11	26
1925 to 1929	21	24	14	23
1920 to 1924	18	20	8	15
1915 to 1919	16	17	11	16
1910 to 1914	16	16	10	12
1905 to 1909	15	15	9	9
1900 to 1904	13	13	5	5

[1]If their future divorce experience is similar to that of persons in older age groups between 1969 and 1974.

The foregoing discussion of the proportions of persons whose marriages may end in divorce is based on a "cohort" or lifetime analysis. However, the projected proportions are somewhat smaller than others that were prepared a few years ago at the Bureau of the Census on the basis of a different methodology and different source material.[4] The earlier estimates were based on "period" data on the number of divorces reported in vital statistics for the year 1970 classified by duration of marriage, and on estimates of first marriages and remarriages based on a combination of census data and vital statistics. Those estimates showed that 37.0 percent of first marriages may end in divorce and that 58.5 percent of the remarriages may end in divorce if the 1970 level of divorce should continue for a lifetime. Demographers usually prefer the use of the cohort approach rather than the period approach in making estimates such as those presented here, but the required data for the application of the cohort method have not been available until recently. However, even the cohort method seems likely to show in the next few years that the lifetime chances of redivorce will approach closer to one-half of the twice-married persons.

[4]Paul C. Glick, "Dissolution of Marriage by Divorce and Its Demographic Consequences," **International Population Conference,** Liege 1973, Vol. 2, pp. 69-79, 1973. See especially table 5.

Excerpts from U.S. Bureau of the Census, Current Population Reports, Series P-20, No. 297 "Number, Timing, and Duration of Marriages and Divorces in the United States: June 1975." U.S. Government Printing Office, Washington, D.C., 1976.

Mid-life transition

MID-LIFE TRANSITION AND CONTEXTUAL CHANGE

by Phyllis Handelman

The recognition of mid-life as a stage of significance in the life course is only now being fully established. Interest in the various stages of development has been successive, first infancy and early childhood, then adolescence followed by an era of concern with the elderly. During the time that the infant and adolescent were being so thoroughly researched the behavior of the mid-life adult had not changed sufficiently to be an area of concern. The concern with adults at mid-life came about with the recognition that there is both change and continuity taking place during this period of the life span. Adults, in American culture have traditionally been viewed as the custodians of the society, responsible and stable. The concept of changing behavior could not have been accepted while the adult was seen as someone who was capable of coping, guiding and transmitting values. The behavior attributed to adults was couched in words such as control, achievement, success and stability, all terms indicating both a sense of fulfillment as well as satisfaction.

A few writers in the thirties took recognition of the changes that occur in adults during their mid-years. Jung (1933) and Buhler (1933) both saw adulthood as a period of complex phases in the life course. However, significant study or examination of this stage of development did not take place until much later. It was only after changed adult behavior was recognized that interest intensified. The 'eight stages' of adulthood were not defined until Erikson's classic work was published (1950), only five years following the conclusion of World War II.

The literature that has addressed itself to a concern with mid-life has basically been divided in two areas; the first has emphasized the psychological aspects of growth and development of the adult in our society; the second has focused on the adult's perception of himself in relation to the social structure. In order to further clarify these different approaches the first will be identified as the socio-psychological and the second as the socio-cultural. The socio-psychological perspective has looked at the adult in terms of the individual's capacity for self-examination, reevaluation, adaptation and coping mechanisms. The socio-cultural examination of the mid-life adult has considered the cohort and the historical period and sees the culture as being the determining factor in adult perception. Some authors have treated these two approaches as mutually exclusive. Rather they should be considered as two valid approaches that are mutually supportive or additive.

A third dimension has been added to this stage of the life course and that is the concept of mid-life 'crisis.' Mid-life crisis has been interpreted as a series of experiential phenomenon or major events that are negative in nature coming together somewhere between the years 35 to 55. These years, plus the social circumstances that the adult may be found in, do include the possibilities of simultaneously experiencing aging parents, adolescent children, and changed or declining sexual interests.

The term 'crisis' is value laden and must be understood when defining changes that occur from within the individual as well as around the individual. The term can imply a turning point, an emotionally significant event or a decisive moment. To Jaques (1965) the term implies a coming to grips with the realization that half of one's life is over.

Changing the perspective from 'crisis' to transitions allows the experiences of the mid-life period to be seen as a series of transforming events that take place in a sequential pattern. Mid-life transition allows for a broader conceptual framework as well as the interjection of the concept of developmental growth (Levinson, 1974).

Biological growth and maturation are a natural part of infancy, childhood, adolescence and adulthood. In much the same way psychological, social and cultural growth are expected to continue to and through adulthood. What is considered normal growth is largely the result of biological development as well as age appropriate behavior (Neugarten and Datan, 1973). Growth does imply change even when it follows a normative sequence, and major changes appear to take place during the years under consideration. Changes that have been most frequently noted by observers of this stage in the life course include the following:

Endocrinal changes that result in overt physical change.

Realization that life goals may have been reached and that a state of achievement exists, or possibly there has been a hiatus in attaining one's goals.

Development of a need to redefine one's personal life as well as social life (essentially a reappraisal of oneself in relationship to others).

The acceptance of one's chronological age and the confrontation with death (Jaques, 1965).

A period of stagnation vs. growth may set in (Erikson, 1950).

A decline in the competitive spirit (Guttman, 1967).

A sense of capitulation setting in as opposed to mastery (Neugarten, 1973).

Resurgence of "The Dream" (Levinson, 1974).

A change in perspective by the individual. Future orientation is replaced by concern with short range plans (Sarason, 1977).

The types of changes noted above are socio-personal as well as socio-psychological in content. While the events are transpiring in the individual the general experience tends to be shared by those in the same class and culture.

A brief review of some of the major writing on adult development (in this instance limited to mid-life) indicates that social-psychological growth, self-awareness, and crisis have been concerns that cover several dimensions.

As early as 1933 Carl Jung was writing on the various stages of the life course. He noted that both childhood and old age were distinctly different from adulthood, or what we now call mid-life. He felt that both the beginning and the end of the life course were free of conscious problems while the period of adulthood was not. For Jung a 'grown-up' was an individual who could have some questions about himself and function without necessarily being in a state of harmony. However, he felt that this phase of life would be less painful:

> If these persons had filled up the beaker of life earlier and emptied it to the lees, they would feel quite differently about everything now; had they kept nothing back, all that wanted to catch fire would have been consumed and the quiet of old age would be welcome to them (Jung, 1933, p. 110).

He felt that as the individual approached mid-life certain changes would appear, a change in character, new interests, and sometimes rigidity. If the individual attempted to recapture a lost youth the risk of lost discretion might be encountered. Jung refuted the idea that changes are due to the fear of death; rather he felt they are initiated from within the psyche. He went full cycle back to the endocrinal change concept and noted that the reversal of masculine-feminine traits had a profound effect on the adult's interpretation of his environment.

Charlotte Buhler (1933 & 1968) concluded that the biological life cycle was reflected in attitude toward life generally. At the time of her earlier writing, the theories of structure and processes in relationship to personality had not yet fully emerged. However, she did find that in the first part of life, "Wishes prevail which indicate striving for self-development and self-improvement. At around age 40 self assessments take place which often lead to redirection of one's life (1968, p. 333)." She notes information on physical and mental abilities are sometimes conflicting. The general trend seems to be until a person is about 20 his abilities in all areas grow, with physical prime being reached between 20 and 35, and mental prime being reached between 20 and 45, and with decline setting in between 45 and 50.

Erik Erikson (1950) first revealed his concept of the "eight stages" of man in *Childhood and Society*. This theory was essentially an eight stage breakdown of the interplay of successive life stages. Growth was seen as a continuous process, neither stabilized nor completed when the individual reached physical maturity. To Erikson, the last three stages of development are the important periods for the adult. The young adult is concerned with establishing "intimacy vs. isolation" and the older adult has finally accepted his life as something that had to be, a stage defined as "ego integrity vs. despair." However, it is only when man reaches the seventh stage or second phase of adulthood, that of maturity, that he is concerned with the mid-life experience. It is in this period when the mature adult faces the problem of "generativity vs. stagnation." When this stage is successful the individual is shown to be primarily interested in establishing and guiding the next generation. If this stage is unsuccessful, stagnation sets in and a regressive need for pseudo intimacy develops as well as interpersonal impoverishment.

Elliott Jaques (1965) has used the term 'mid-life crisis' to define that period of life, around 35 years, as the point where the realization that half of one's life is over settles in. It is his belief that a crisis is precipitated by this realization. Jaques examines the lives of creative men and concludes that one of three experiences takes place at this time: the creative individual may stop functioning or may actually die; a creative ability may be first realized; or, a major change in the creative work may be seen. The major differences in the content and mode of work for the personalities that he studied was in going from a lyrical quality to one of tragic and philosophical content.

Daniel Levinson (1974) looks at adult males in terms of "life-structure" which comprises the actor's personal and social system. The individual actor's "life structure" is unique to him but operates within the social system. Levinson's theory of psychosocial development is based on a study of "developmental periods" or stages. The years 40 to 60 he labels middle adulthood, but allows for several years on either side. He is interested in developing hypotheses concerning relatively universal genotypic age-linked, adult developmental periods within which variations occur. Levinson examines quite carefully various stages of the adult life cycle in men. The stage labeled "Becoming One's Own Man" or BOOM is the period of interest to this review (although to do justice to Levinson the whole adult period should be considered). This period occurs in the middle to late thirties and is the connecting link to the mid-life transition. Levinson notes that, "A key element in this period is the feeling that no matter what he has accomplished to date, he is not sufficiently his own man. He feels overly dependent upon and constrained by persons or groups who have authority over him or who, for various reasons, exert great influence upon him" (1974, p. 251). At this juncture the sense of constraint and oppression may occur not only in work but also in marriage and other relationships. Levinson notes that many professional men have mentors during this period, a phenomenon that he considers key. He feels that those who do not have a mentor suffer developmental impairments and face greater problems at mid-life. The mentor is respected by the mentee, he represents wisdom, authority, care, sponsorship, and he is the one who bestows his blessings on the younger man. In the later part of the 30's the relationship with the mentor ends and the mentee now incorporates some of these qualities. He is then able to become a mentor himself. This step involves giving up childhood, realizing that one is an adult with a significant position and recognition of one's self as a competent individual. If this period has been a good experience then the transition to mid-life is smooth. If the event is negative or fails to take place then the individual is found wanting.

The transition to mid-life takes place whether or not the individual is properly prepared and willing to accept this phase of life. At mid-life the actor must determine if he has gained an "inner sense from living within a particular structure and found what he wants for himself." It is a period of determining "what it is I really want." If the individual has not "made it" in his own eyes, a crisis does not necessarily occur. However, if he has to modify or change his structure Levinson feels he is then experiencing a crisis. The experiences that may lead to a crisis but which are definitely transitions are: the sense of body decline and the realization of mortality; the sense of aging; the realization for males, that one has some feminine characteristics and that they are not all bad, and the flowering of fantasies about various women, maternal as well as young erotic types. Essentially, he feels that the self is experiencing change and in a sense is reawakened.

The socio-cultural approach combining cohort and historical perspectives places the individual within a social structure and views him in relationship to that structure.

As early as 1928 Mannheim was concerned with the problem of 'location' of the individual in society. Mannheim felt that the social and cultural outlook of an individual was strongly affected by the historical position of his cohort. He felt that each cohort shared social identities and social realities. It was the shared social and historical experiences he felt, that would shape their lives and understanding of the world. He noted, that since each generation would educate the next, the expectation was that values and perceptions of the world would be transmitted. However, he felt that cohorts would have greater influence on each other than the preceding or later generations. Shared social identities and similar modes of expression led to closer relationships with cohort members. He repeatedly emphasized that age was the key variable and more than any other characteristic served to locate the individual in the social structure.

Bernice Neugarten (1968) and her associates have looked at the life cycle in regard to values held, personality characteristics, definitions and expectations at various ages, and attitude toward death. They have been concerned with relating personality change to chronological age. In some of their studies they found age to be a key personality factor yet in others they found that the position in the life course was measured in terms of "body, career, and family" (1968, p. 94). There has been a great deal of interest by these researchers on how to measure the change that they know occurs. They found that one of the most significant conceptual perspectives by those at mid-life, is that time is evaluated in terms of time left to live. The examination of time from that perspective might be considered a crisis or may be the beginning of a transition to the next phase of the life course.

Lowenthal, Thurner and Chiriboga (1975) conducted a study where adults at 'mid-life' referred to a parent group about to experience the empty nest syndrome. They were interested in the transitions that people face when preparing for role and status change. All of the subjects interviewed were facing either 'incremental' transitions (role gains) or 'decremental' transitions (role loss). They found women at mid-life who were facing the post parental period to be in the most critical state. Women whose identity was tied into child rearing faced the greatest difficulties. However, those who had clear objectives, and those who viewed the empty nest as an opportunity for self-renewal faced mid-life with a healthy outlook. Their interviews with middle-aged men revealed a concern with being able to work until retirement so that they might enjoy a comfortable post-retirement period.

Maas and Kuypers (1974) carried out extensive interviews with elderly persons to determine if the earlier and later stages of adulthood are related. The study examined four dimensions of life style; interaction, involvement, satisfaction, and perception of change. They concluded that those persons who had worked, who had been involved in activities outside the home, and who led a full life in early adulthood were more satisfied at the latter end of the life cycle. Essentially they came to the same conclusions that Jung had come to some 40 years earlier.

This rather abbreviated review leads to two issues that should be examined if 'mid-life' with its attendant transitions is to be viewed as a particular stage in the life cycle. First is the problem of universality. The studies to date have not been extensive enough to determine if the problems faced at this stage are experienced the same way by various classes and cultures. Transitions may very well be taking place in all persons who are at mid-life, however they may be manifested in different ways.

Secondly, since World War II the American social structure has undergone significant contextual change. The concept of contextual change refers to the changes that have occurred in the interrelated areas of the political, economic, historic, and social conditions. Mead (1970) referred to these changes in terms of the significant continuities and discontinuities in a culture. Schooler (1972, p. 299) notes that today's adults were reared in, "Complex multifaceted environments that resulted in high levels of intellectual functioning, a rejection of external constraints and a subjectivism stressing concern for the quality of one's inner life." Turner (1976) refers to a shift in cultural emphasis over the past several decades manifested by value orientation going from "institution to impulse." He indicates that this has led to a desire to seek inner or personal truth rather than accepting what the culture has determined as good.

World War II is viewed as a pivotal point for contextual change. The War created a set of conditions that included the demise of the extended family and the rise of the nuclear one. Increasing numbers of women left the domestic environment for work in the labor force, divorce rates began their climb, higher education became available to more people in the post war years, and government services increased. The technological and scientific advancement that flourished during the War developed new industries and created a mobile population. The political picture shifted dramatically in the 1950's; the Korean War, McCarthyism and the growing Civil Rights Movement offered change in a way that was unfamiliar. The 1960's found America involved in a war that frequently pitted father against son ideologically, a Youth Revolution that saw the rise of flower children, sexual freedom, and a drug culture (Slater, 1970).

In the 1970's the Women's Movement first created challenge and then change. The set of changed mores that came with this period challenged the value system as well as tempted the tastes of the parent generation. These events as well as countless others not only threatened the authority and leadership given to mid-life adults but also made them consciously think about what it was they had missed and what it was they wanted. Quite possibly it was the questioning and doubting by those young adults that made the mid-life adult question and encounter change.

In concluding one might suggest that the experiences of those at mid-life cannot simply be viewed as the result of either a development and psychological progression or as the end product of the changed social structure but preferably as the result of the interaction between the two. Additionally the concept of 'crisis' must be examined for its universality as well as for its positive and negative content. A new awareness is frequently the by-product of change and transition.

Buhler, Charlotte
The Human Course of Life as a Psychological Problem. Leipzig: S. Hirzel, 1933

Buhler, Charlotte and Massrik, Fred
The Course of Human Life. New York: Springer Publishing Co., 1968

Erikson, Erik H.
Childhood and Society. New York: W.W. Norton, 1950

Guttman, David
"Aging Among the Highland Maya." *Journal of Personality and Social Psychology,* Vol. 7, 1967

Jaques, Elliott
"Death and the Mid-Life Crisis." *International Journal of Psychoanalysis,* Vol. 46, 1965

Jung, C.G.
Modern Man In Search of a Soul. New York: Harcourt, Brace and World, 1933

Levinson, Daniel, Darrow, C.M., Klein, E.B., Levinson, M., and McKee, B.
"The Psychosocial Development of Men in Early Adulthood and Mid-Life Transition" in Ricks, D., Thomas, H., and Roff, M. (eds.) *Life History Research in Psychopathology.* Minneapolis: University of Minnesota Press, 1974

Lowenthal, M.F., Thurner, M., and Chiriboga, D.
Four Stages of Life. San Francisco: Jossey-Bass Books, 1975

Maas, H. and Kuypers, J.A.
From Thirty to Seventy. San Francisco: Jossey-Bass Books, 1974

Mannheim, R.
"The Problems of Generations" in *Essays in the Sociology of Knowledge.* London: Routledge, Kegan, Paul (ed, 1952) 1928

Mead, Margaret
Culture and Commitment. New York: Basic Books, 1970

Neugarten, Bernice
Middle Age and Aging. Chicago: University of Chicago Press, 1973

Neugarten, Bernice and Datan, N.
"Sociological Perspectives of the Life Cycle" in Baltes, P. and Schaie, K. (eds.) *Life Span Developmental Psychology: Personality and Socialization.* New York: Academic Press, 1973

Sarason, Seymour
Work, Aging, and Social Change. New York: Free Press, 1977

Schooler, Carmi
"Social Antecedents of Adult Psychological Functioning." *American Journal of Sociology,* Vol. 78, 1972

Slater, Philip
The Pursuit of Loneliness. Boston: Beacon Press, 1970

Turner, Ralph
"The Real Self: From Institution to Impulse." *American Journal of Sociology,* Vol. 81, 1976

Widowhood

WIDOWHOOD: SOCIAL NORMS AND SOCIAL INTEGRATION

by Dr. Helena Znaniecki Lopata

The relation of the individual to the social units of which she or he is a member, including the society at large, have changed considerably in recent centuries, changes which have been accelerated in recent decades in Europe and America, as well as in many other parts of the world. These revolutionary modifications in the relation between an individual and larger social units are evident in the variations in the social integration of the widowed, particularly of widowed women. Several sets of factors affect the social integration and life styles of persons whose spouse died, including the norms and social structure of the society and the community in which they live, their manner of integration prior to the death and personal resources. In addition, throughout human history, age and sex identities have strongly influenced the social roles and relations available to, or enforced upon, the widowed. Most of human history has been spent in patriarchal, patrilineal and patrilocal family systems, with a definite division of labor by age and sex, although the content of the work performed by each category of member has varied considerably (D'Andrade, 1966; Scanzoni and Scanzoni, 1976). In all cases, the social roles performed by one person are deeply interwoven with those of other people, always with members of the family and often with persons and groups outside of this unit. In addition, most societies of the world have been, until recent times, interested in high reproduction rates, insuring continued birth of new members as long as biologically or socially possible on the part of the parents. Birth as well as child care and socialization have generally been deemed best when occurring in a family unit consisting as a minimum of a father and a mother, married to each other. Elaborate norms cover situations in which the birth occurs in the absence of a social father, or when dependent children are deprived of a parent in one manner or another. Generally speaking, the life circumstances of widowers have been historically different from those of widows. In fact, there is little anthropological literature about the situation of widowers, beyond descriptions of norms for remarriage, while there is much more written about widows, with a wide range of variations in life style ranging from suicide, through lifelong chastity, to remarriage or freedom of choice of future (Lopata, 1972, 1973a; Bock and Webber, 1972; Harvey and Bahr, 1974; Ropp, 1976; Sarasvati, 1888). One reason for this lack of anthropological attention seems to be the ease with which deceased wives are replaced in patriarchal societies in which the man continues his support network throughout his life. Such societies allow remarriage to the widower more often than to the widow and control her selection of a mate if she is allowed a new one, especially if the deceased had already fathered children with her. In such family systems, the children are affiliated with the father's line, which would make it difficult for everyone if she had children connected with two family lines. The husband's line has the right and the obligation to care for the children and the widow after his death and the survivors usually do not have the right to move away from its control (Bohannan, 1963). It is not difficult to hypothesize that the weakening of rights over each nuclear unit by the male line will result in greater variations in social integration for both widowers and widows.

This paper is devoted to the examination of the social systems and norms influencing the social integration of widows and, to a lesser extent, of widowers, who are beyond the age in which the communities in which they live are interested in their continued procreating contributions. At least in the case of women, biological changes prevent continued child bearing after menopause, although the child rearing activities can continue until her children reach independence or in other kinds of mothering relations. The norms and social structure of the society and community do not stop affecting the roles and role clusters available to men and women past the age when they are expected to make their major contribution to the system, or at least past their peak level of contribution. Many societies of the past, and some at the present time, enforce a definite role of widow upon the no longer reproducing woman whose spouse has died, signified by distinctive clothing,

Dr. Helena Znaniecki Lopata is Professor of Sociology and Director, Center for the Comparative Study of Social Roles, Loyola University of Chicago although there does not seem to be an equivalent role for widowers. Whether or not the widow can inherit from her deceased spouse, the absence or the presence of inherited property and its size, as well as methods by which the widowed can support themselves are basic consequences of the social structure. Patriarchal societies often do not allow the widow to inherit from her husband so that she must maintain herself through other means, or be automatically included in the family unit which does inherit the property. Although there are many cases reported in fictional and historical literature of widows maintaining themselves in villages or towns through exchanges with neighbors of specialized production or services, and although elderly widows are frequently given a great deal of freedom (Cowgill and Holmes, 1972), the most frequent system has been for the son who inherits his father's land, home and other property to acquire the obligation to care for his widowed mother. The elderly woman then continues to live in or near the house in which she lived as a wife and contributes in a variety of ways to its maintenance as a member of the family. Her status changes considerably if she turns over household management to the son's wife and her duties and rights are modified, but she retains membership in the unit. Of course, there have been many situations in countries such as traditional India, in which the widow does not lose power over the household even if her son inherits property rights, the daughter-in-law becoming more like a servant to her than the new mistress of the house (Ross, 1961; Lopata, 1972). The elderly widower retains rights to his property in spite of the death of the wife in patriarchal societies in any but exceptional cases. He gives up these rights only if retirement is institutionalized so that he must turn over the property to the eldest, or another son, in which case he becomes as dependent as is the widow who is no longer the manager of a house. If he retains the headship of his household, he usually must find a woman, a new wife or daughter-in-law, an unmarried daughter or a servant to help manage it.

Widowhood in Modern Societies

Various changes in the relation of family members to each other and of the family as a unit to other social units have occurred all over the world in recent times, but particularly in Europe and America, sometimes preceding but mainly following upheavals in the larger social structures (Shorter, 1973, 1975; Aries, 1965). The family became privatized and restricted in other forms of sociability as early as the 18th century, according to Philippe Aries (1965). At about the same time childhood was converted into an important stage of life and motherhood became an emotionally charged relation with the major responsibility for care of the offspring. Mass education and the organization of work into paid jobs in large organizations outside of the home freed the man from control by his family of orientation, enabling him to set up his own household with the help of a mutually selected wife and to maintain it independently from his parents and siblings (Shorter, 1973, 1975; Laslett and Wall, 1972; Laslett, 1971). The shifting of the whole value and normative systems of European and American countries away from those based on religion to the economic institution, accompanying the Protestant Reformation, provided justification for the freeing of the nuclear family from kinship control. It simultaneously deprived these units from consistent and automatic economic, service and social supports from the extended family.

Although work for pay preceded the Industrial Revolution, changes it introduced by the removal of production from the home and its surrounding territory dramatically changed family life. At first all but the very young or very old family members left home to work for pay, however, "protective" legislation during the middle 1800s in England and more or less at similar times in other parts of Europe and America gradually removed the child and the woman from this world (Oakley, 1975). The apprenticeship and child exchange systems also vanished and children became age graded through school. Women not only left paying jobs at marriage or at least at the birth of children, but were removed from guilds, restricted to a limited number of sex-segregated occupations and severely discouraged from "serious" involvement in the life of the society away from home in any but charitable activity, simultaneously losing many rights held in the past (Aries, 1965; Oakley, 1975). The contributions women made to the establishment and maintenance of a home, involving secondary production in the conversion of goods for household consumption became devalued and not counted as a contribution to the income of the breadwinner. The economic systems of Western European and American societies view the worker as a one person unit, even in situations in which it takes two people to enable the one to function in a job outside of a home. These dramatic changes depriving women who are in the roles of wife and mother of a share in economic production and service activities paid for by large organizations in the form of wages or salaries, have had many side effects on their lives. The restriction of involvement is expected to last not only in the active stages of family roles, but from the time they enter such roles for the rest of their lives. This means that they became economically dependent upon the wages of their husbands, upon what they are able to save from these wages when the husband is working full-time, or upon some system of survivor benefits the work organization or the society sets up to support them after his death. Widowers, in turn, had to replace a deceased wife in order to have the household and children taken care of while they are at jobs and because of trained incapacity in the home. Of course, recent decades of European and American societal histories are witnessing a change in this joint pattern, as women return to the labor force after children become relatively independent of them, and as the number of women who are heads of households increases in great numbers. However, many of the living older widows followed the life course outlined above, typical of the early 20th century work-home sequence. Future generations of widows will be able to draw upon their own resources much more than are many present older widows who have been caught in a squeeze, traditional family support systems having been removed, although they were socialized to be dependent upon such systems. It is difficult to determine how the lives of widowers will change in the future, aside from increasing ease of men maintaining a home.

There are, however, various paths the life courses of European and American women and men have taken, due to the changes and the widening of choices, depending on the society, the community and the personal resources available to each one. The resulting situation of the widows and the widowers can be outlined briefly as follows:

1. The rural widow in American society is often unable to maintain her farm, because of the dispersal of children and its isolation from a community, and thus tends to sell it and settle in a nearby town (Pihlblad and Rosencranz, 1968; Pihlblad and Adams, 1972). The rural widower is more apt to stay on his land, but to be socially isolated (Berardo, 1967, 1968). The rural European widow or widower can often retain his or her life style with not as many changes because of the presence of the village neighbors and family still in the household (Shanas et.al., 1968). Some of the farming in Europe has become so feminized, anyway, due to the involvement of men in nearby or even distant industry, that only health problems prevent a widow from continuing to maintain herself (Turowski and Szwengrub, 1976; Tryfan, 1976). Many mothers migrate to the cities upon reaching widowhood to help take care of the children and households of their children (Lobodzinska, 1974).
2. In urban centers in situations where the family is not dispersed and where there is a housing shortage, as in Poland and Yugoslavia, the older widow or widower frequently has one or more relatives living with her or him, with variations in household headship. For example, a woman who has an apartment in Zagreb while still married is apt to retain it in widowhood and to share it, often with a young relative from a village or town lacking more than primary education who comes to the city for schooling. There are housing-food exchanges, as well as service supports going both ways (Lopata, 1974). The London "mum" is reportedly involved in complex support systems across separate but near-by households with her daughters (Bott, 1957; Young and Wilmott, 1957; Wilmott and Young, 1960).
3. In many European countries in which it is necessary for both parents to bring in income from employment, older widows take care of the grandchildren and help with housekeeping (Lobodzinska, 1974; Piotrowski, 1963). They thus have automatically involving support systems. Widowers are less often involved in such exchanges, but in societies which went through World War II there is such a shortage of men, that they tend to rapidly remarry.
4. Widows and widowers who are of an age and sufficient experience and expertise to hold down a full- or part-time job, often do so (Steinhart, 1976a, 1976b; Lopata, 1977; Marris, 1958). In fact, the higher the education the greater the probability that the woman worked even before widowhood (U.S. Department of Labor, 1975; Rapoport and Rapoport, 1976; Oakley, 1974).
5. There are many urban areas in Europe, and even in more mobile parts of America, with stable neighborhoods and extensive neighboring (Lopata, 1971, 1973; Gans, 1962; Suttles, 1968). Of course, smaller communities are even more noted for such interaction (Pihlblad and Rosencranz, 1968; Pihlblad and Adams, 1972). Such areas provide a milieu favorable to social integration, as are housing arrangements guaranteeing interaction.
6. There are some "cosmopolitan" men and women, who utilize the resources of the society and the larger community to build complex social life spaces and support systems during marriage and to rebuild them after the death of the spouse and the period of grief work is over (Lopata, 1973a, 1973b, 1977). These people tend to have a background of urbanization and education extending more than one generation, but the modern schooling system and opportunities for upward mobility are sufficient to develop skills and personal resources for such living in even one generation.
7. Finally, there are, at least in American society, widows and widowers who are socially isolated or living within very narrow or other restricted social life spaces (Berardo, 1967, 1968; Lopata, 1973a, 1973b, 1977).

Widows in an American City: A Case Study

There are over ten million widows in the United States, but less than two million widowers, a fact which reflects sex differences in life style more probably than biological survival strengths and weaknesses, although the distinctions are not as yet scientifically separated. In any case, the ratio of five widows to one widower helps explain the different ratios of remarriage between the widows and the widowers. In addition, there are many differences in life style of men and women in this society which are reflected in the variation between the sexes when the spouse dies. As mentioned before, the few studies which have included widowers find them faced with social isolation and home management problems. *U. S. News and World Report* (1974) documents a high rate of death among widowers, two and a half higher than among widows, due to suicide, automobile accidents, poor dietary and drinking habits. Widowers have high ratios, compared to married men and widows, of other indices of personal disorganization (see also Berardo, 1970; Bernard, 1973). Harvey and Bahr (1974) attribute these problems to social isolation due, as mentioned before, to a specialization of tasks within the modern family in which social contact is maintained through the wife. They find the trend even in other societies besides America.

Results from a recent study of 1,169 widows of all ages who are former or current beneficiaries of social security and who reside in metropolitan Chicago, U.S.A. exemplify the trends in support systems and life styles of women who become husbandless due to the death of the spouse.[1] Four different support systems were examined through an intensive personal interview: economic, service, social and emotional. In all, the women were asked to name up to three people who contribute to, or are beneficiary of, 65 separate supports for a total of 195 "chances" for people to appear in the systems. A support is identified in this study as any object or action which the giver or receiver, or both define as necessary or contributive to the maintenance of a style of life (Lopata, 1974). The economic supports beyond the regular sources of income include gifts of money, and payment or help in the payment of rent or mortgage, food, clothing, or other bills such as those incurred in a hospital or on a vacation. Both the in-flow and the out-flow of such supports as well as of the service supports were elicited. The service system includes transportation, minor house repairs, and help with housekeeping, shopping, yard work, child care, car care, care during illness, making decisions and legal aid. The social supports include the sharing of the following social activities: going to public places such as movie theaters, visiting, entertaining, having lunch, going to church, playing sports, cards and other games, traveling out of town, celebrating holidays and engaging in any other activity mentioned by the respondent. The emotional system consists of two parts; the first contains relational sentiments including feeling close to, enjoying being with, telling problems to, being comforted when depressed, being made to feel important, being angry with, and turning to in times of crisis. The "feeling states" of this support include the feelings of being respected, useful, independent, accepted, self-sufficient and secure. Both segments of the emotional system were obtained both for "the year before your husband's illness or accident which finally caused his death" and for the current time. In each case we asked who provided that support, tracing the person to the resource network and separating sets, as when the respondent lists "Janet and Tom" as suppliers of a specific support.

Detailed analyses of the support systems of Chicago area widows are available elsewhere, and will be forth coming in the future; the main point being made here is that many of these women, particularly the older ones, are very limited in the people they are able to involve in their support systems, in the activities in which they are engaged, and in their use of societal resources.[2] They do not have a sufficiently urbanized and schooled background to provide them with personal resources with which to engage in society, even before the husband's death, let alone now, while the traditional support resources of extended family and community are often unavailable to them. The group as a whole uses only one-fourth of the opportunities to list some one in the different supports, and the less educated and urbanized women are heavily dependent upon their children or parents, in the few cases where the family of orientation is still living and well. Parents and siblings are simply absent from the support systems of most of these women, because they are no longer living, because they are located in another country or another state, or because they have not been in active contact. This last-named situation is particularly true of siblings, who are not contributive in the day by day life of the widows and who do not even appear in a frequency of more than 10 percent in the emotional supports. Thus, lack of involvement in economic, service and social supports carries over into a lack of feelings of being close to, or comforted by, a brother or sister. The same is true of all other relatives besides children and parents. Friends appear in the social supports but much less frequently in the service and emotional systems, and mainly in the lives of the financially better off and more educated women. For example, although 58 percent of the widows who play sports, cards or other games do so with friends, such associates do not enter most of the emotional supports. Friends are listed in one of three places in only 19 percent of the cases as people who make the widow feel important, and in 16 percent of the listings as one of the people she most enjoys being with. Elsewhere the percentages are smaller. Thus, the relation seems emotionally weak since sharing social activities does not translate itself to emotional feelings of closeness in the lives of many women.

The Chicago area widows also underuse societal

resources. Only half of them belong to voluntary associations and a quarter work for pay outside of the home. People outside of the family-friendship network seldom appear in any of the four systems, and this statement applies to co-members of associations, co-workers, church or other societally developed helping groups or professionals. Ministers, priests and rabbis are conspicuous in their absence not only from current supports, but at the time the husband was ill, immediately after his death and while the widow was trying to develop a new life. In fact, if mentioned at all, such religious personnel are apt to be described as not helpful when needed. Few of these women use lawyers or banks, mainly because they are not of an income or life style that requires such help or brings such professionals into the range of resources. Ten percent of the women list no income, and two-fifths of the remaining are living on a family income falling below the Social Security Administration's cutoff low or poverty level. White women suffered more of a drop in widowhood than did the blacks, because so many of the latter were already near the poverty line when the husband was living. Three-quarters of these women were widowed when less than 65 years of age and their husband had been working at a full-time job before the fatal illness or accident. Now most of the widows are dependent upon social security. The best off economically are those who have more than one earner in the family, particularly if it includes a new husband, or if they are working themselves. Only the younger ones are able to work, if they are not caring for small children and if they have sufficient training to get a job.

In spite of the fact that so many of the respondents are living close to the poverty line, very few are involved in an exchange of economic supports. Income does influence the in-flow and out-flow of help but only at the extremes, and there is a sizable proportion of women who do not have any economic help from others although they are poor. The widows are not heavily involved in service supports. Ninety-six percent have no help with child care or do not need it, and only 21 percent are helping others in this way. Not surprisingly in view of role specialization and their personal life styles, 81 percent do not receive and 99 percent do not give legal aid, 87 percent do not get and 100 percent do not give help with car care, 68 percent do not receive and 96 percent do not help with yard work. In addition, 77 percent do not have assistance with housekeeping and 88 percent do not give it, 61 percent do not get and 87 percent do not give help with shopping, 57 percent do not obtain and 98 percent do not undertake minor household repairs. Forty-five percent do not receive transportation and 82 percent do not transport others, mainly because they do not have an automobile. The most frequent help received by the widow and offered by her is care during illness, 56 percent experiencing an in-flow and 36 percent engaging in an out-flow of this support. In fact, this set of respondents considers itself to be a recipient more often than a giver of service supports, although many are independent of these. One reason for the low frequency of reference to service exchanges is the tendency of the widows not to consider activities which form the normal flow of work and life as "help." Thus, a remarried widow or one with children living at home does not consider herself as helping them by shopping or housekeeping. Such an activity is considered "help" only if it is formally organized as an exchange of duties and rights or if it occurs across household thresholds. This is a traditional view of the role of the housewife (see Lopata, 1971). Half of the widows are now living alone, reflecting a trend all over the world which has accompanied social and economic independence of women, and it is interesting to note the self-sufficiency of these women and the infrequency of across household assistance, in spite of the claims of some sociologists that the "modified extended family" is a viable provider of a variety of service and social supports (see Shanas and Streib, 1965; Litwak, 1965; Sussman, 1965).

Although the social activities included in that support system were obtained from extensive exploratory interviewing, many of the Chicago area widows state that they do not engage in them, with the exception of celebrating holidays. Only eight percent of the respondents do not celebrate holidays at all, but 58 percent never engage in sports, cards, or other games and 51 percent never go to public places such as movie houses. Visiting seems to have a different meaning than does entertaining, since only 21 percent never visit, while 40 percent do not entertain. Over one-third do not share lunch with someone else, 40 percent never travel out of town and an additional 21 percent go alone. Only a fourth never go to church, but an additional third goes alone. Activities other than those included in the system are rarely mentioned.

In looking at the positive aspects of the support systems we find that the late husband was a major contributor to the emotional supports the year before his fatal illness or accident, either because of the actual closeness of the relation, or because of husband idealization, a process which many widows undertake even to the point of sanctification.[3] His involvement was not even, the likelihood of his being listed first being much higher than is a second or third place listing. He is most apt to be mentioned as the person the widow most enjoyed being with, who made her feel important and secure (about 75 percent of first listings). Interestingly, from the point of view of symbolic interactionism, 40 percent of the respondents feel that they obtained their feelings of independence and sufficiency from the late husband, while between 39 and 42 gave the expected answer of "myself." Few women list the husband as the person who most often made them angry, but then half of them would not admit anger at anyone.

The children appear as the second most frequent providers of emotional supports to the widow the year before the late husband's illness or accident, with some references to co-workers and employers as providers of the feeling of being respected and club co-members as contributors to the feeling of being accepted (11 percent each). The children take over the emotional support system of the present time, with some dispersal of reference to friends and other people or groups. The self takes over as the primary source of the feelings of independence and self-sufficiency, as well as security. The few women who have remarried and remained in that relation focus heavily on the new husband, to an extent even higher than on the late husband as the person who comforts them when they are depressed and the one to whom they tell their problems. He is also the one to whom they would turn in times of crises more so than all the widows remember their late husband. Of course, the remarrieds are younger than the population as a whole.

Children are definitely the major suppliers of service supports, with some input by persons and groups outside of the family-friend network. The few widows who provide services scatter their recipients among a whole variety of people, being involved in a complex support network. Contributions to social supports vary by activity. Holidays are celebrated mainly with children and "other relatives" outside of parents and which usually means grandchildren. Friends are people with whom one goes to public places, visits, entertains, shares lunch and plays sports, cards and games. Women travel and go to church alone but generally meet others at the destination.

All in all, a generational history of urbanization and relatively long schooling produces definite results in the support systems of widowed women in an American city Women whose father and mother had more schooling, in a city and especially in a northern American city, rather than in the American south or in other countries, married more educated men, set up more middle class households and developed more complex support systems and social life spaces of roles and relations while he was still living. The more education a woman has and the more middle class a life style she and her husband develop when he is still living, the more disorganized her life becomes with his death, but the more resources she has to re-build the support system and life space once the period of grief is over (Lopata, 1973a). Most of the older Chicago area widows, and some of the younger ones, have been very disadvantaged in life, living peripherally to the urban society, minimally engaged during marriage and even less so at the present time.

Summary and Conclusion

The study of widows of all ages who are former or current recipients of social security and who reside in metropolitan Chicago, U.S.A., documents the trends in the support systems and life styles of women who become husbandless due to the death of the spouse in a rapidly changing society. Urbanization, industrialization, societal complexity and large size, combined with mass education, the lengthening of the life span of many people, especially women and similar changes have created societies requiring voluntaristic and flexible forms of social engagement throughout the life course. The older widows in the Chicago area exemplify more than one generation of women unable to take advantage of the resources of the modern urban environment in which they are living because they lack the personal resources necessary to convert other resources into support systems and social roles. They were socialized into ascribed social roles limited to the family and the immediate neighborhood, into traditional "feminine" passivity vis-a-vis the world outside of their own territory. Some of these women gained the education and skills necessary for functioning in the society providing resources for voluntaristic engagement, but most did not, depending either on their adult children or old friends made in unchanging neighborhoods for their support systems or living very restricted lives. American urban society has changed rapidly in recent decades, so that lives disorganized by such an event as the death of a husband, the moving away of friends, or own transplantation, produces step by step disengagement because of the lack of ability to find new relations and new social roles for re-engagement. The same is true of many widowers who had depended upon their wives and their work for social contact, so that loss of both creates social isolation.

The cases in which widows or widowers are able to re-engage after the previous network is disrupted by many transitional events are always ones in which the survivor has the self-confidence, skills and sophistication in the use of societal resources to obtain occupational training, find a new job, join an organization, make friends, move to a neighborhood with people in a similar life situation who are willing to interact, modify old friendships, etc. All these voluntaristic actions require a complex sequence of steps often frightening to traditional women and men reared in fatalistic and self-effacing lower class cultures (Scanzoni and Scanzoni, 1976; Cohn, 1973; Komarovsky, 1967; Berger, 1970; Gans, 1962). Future generations of Americans, particularly of American women, better educated than those of the past, more urbanized, more assertive and confident of their independent identities, directly or indirectly influenced by the current movements re-examining human values, more experienced in engagement in social roles outside of the home, more flexibly oriented toward changes in their life course, and more able to utilize effectively opportunities for movement in and out of social relations and social roles will be less restricted in widowhood, as they will have been earlier in life. In the meantime, modern societies can hopefully develop local social networks assisting their members in the transitions between one form of social engagement and another, when events disorganize past support systems. Such neighborhood networks can serve as connecting links between societal members who can not change their whole personalities and approaches to the world but who become socially isolated because of the lack of personal resources. Such networks can utilize already existing resources and social groups to provide assistance during acute problem periods and can continue contact as the person going through the transition experiences all the processes of change in life style and support systems. Each of the modern European and American societies already have resources which could be utilized in building these neighborhood networks. These resources are being used by the more sophisticated members but not by those who need them most. The resources are the professionals and agencies who provide information and services, voluntary organizations, mutual help groups, churches and synagogues. Research focused on the Chicago area widows shows that those most needing the help of these resources do not get them. The existing helping persons and groups are failing these women, at the time during the husband's fatal illness, immediately after his death, when the widow is trying to build a new life, and when she stabilizes herself in a life style and support system, extensive or restricted as those may be. The professionals, agencies and voluntary associations are too often focused on providing services only to those people who have the personal resources to search them out. The more passive and needful, the non-confident and inarticulate person whom our societies socialized to be so because they were structured for large and passive lower classes and for non-assertive women, especially outside of the home, simply do not benefit from these societal resources, while the push at economic development of these societies has deprived them of traditional support systems.

FOOTNOTES

1. The study of the support systems of widows in urbanized areas was funded through a contract with the Social Security Administration (SSA - 71 - 3411). Many thanks go to Dr. Henry Brehm, Chief of Research Grants and Contracts in the Office of Research and Statistics, Social Security Administration; Dr. Adam Kurzynowski of the Szkola Glowna Planowania i Statystyki, Warsaw, Poland and his consultant Professor Jerzy Piotrowski; Dr. Nada Smolic Krkovic of the Institute of Social Work in Zagreb, Yugoslavia and her consultants, and to everyone at the Center for the Comparative Study of Social Roles. Parts of the study are being reproduced in Cairo, Egypt under the direction of Dr. Nawal Nadim and in Tehran, Iran by the team headed by Dr. Jacqueline Touba. The Chicago area study consists of five samples, drawn in different ratios by the Social Security Administration statisticians from records of women receiving widow's benefits in old age, mothers of dependent children, "lump sum" beneficiaries, former beneficiaries whose children have reached adult status and former widows who have remarried. The interviews, when weighted in accordance to sample ratios, represent a population of 82,085 widows.
2. The final report to the Social Security Administration was finished early spring, 1977. The references list some of the products of the study and the contributions of the extended family, friendships, and the sanctification scale which are currently being examined in detail. A non-statistically presented book, *Women as Widows,* is being written under contract with Elsevier Publishing Company.
3. The sanctification scale was a result of the tendency of women to so idealize their late husband and relational aspects of the marriage as to make analyses of life as it actually was before his death impossible. The scale has two components, a semantic differential set of husband's traits and a set of statements eliciting degree of agreement. The final statement of that set states "My husband had no irritating habits." Anyone interested in forthcoming analyses can write to the Center for the Comparative Study of Social Roles for them.

REFERENCES

Aries, Philippe.
1965 *Centuries of Childhood.* New York: Vintage Books.

Atchley, Robert C.
1975 "Dimensions of Widowhood in Later Life." *The Gerontologist.* 15, No. 2 (April): 176-178.

Berardo, Felix.
1967 "Social Adaptation to Widowhood Among a Rural-Urban Aged Population." Agricultural Experiment Station Bulletin 689 (December): Washington State University.

1968 "Widowhood Status in the United States: Perspective on a Neglected Aspect of the Family Life-Cycle." *The Family Coordinator*. 17 (July): 191-203.

1970 "Survivorship and Social Isolation: The Case of the Aged Widower." *The Family Coordinator*. 1 (January): 11-25.

Berger, Peter L.
1970 with Hansfried Kellner. "Marriage and the Construction of Reality." in Hans Dreitzel (ed.), *Recent Sociology # 2*. London: Collier-Macmillan: 50-73.

Bernard, Jessie.
1973 *The Future of Marriage*. New York: Bantam Books.

Bock, E. Wilber and Irving L. Webber.
1972 "Suicide Among the Elderly: Isolating Widowhood and Mitigating Alternatives." *Journal of Marriage and the Family*. 34, 1 (February).

Bohannan, Paul J.
1963 *Social Anthropology*. New York: Holt, Rinehart and Winston.

Bott, E.
1957 *Family and Social Network*. London: Tavistock.

Cohn, Ann Rochelle.
1973 "Influences of Selected Characteristics on Widows' Attitudes Towards Self and Others." M.S. thesis, Department of Psychology, Illinois Institute of Technology.

Cowgill, Donald and Lowell Holmes. (eds.)
1972 *Aging and Modernization*. New York: Appleton-Century-Crofts.

D'Andrade, Roy G.
1966 "Sex Differences and Cultural Institutions." in Eleanor E. Maccoby, (ed.) *The Development of Sex Differences*. Stanford, California: Stanford University Press: 174-204.

Gans, Herbert.
1962 *The Urban Villagers*. New York: The Free Press of Macmillan.

Harvey, Carol D. and Howard M. Bahr.
1974 "Widowhood, Morale and Affiliation." *Journal of Marriage and the Family*. Vol. 36, 1 (February): 97-106.

Komarovsky, Mirra.
1967 *Blue-Collar Marriage*. New York: Random House.

Laslett, Peter.
1971 *The World We Have Lost*. New York: Charles Scribner's Sons, second edition.

Laslett, Peter and Richard Wall.
1972 *Household and Family in Past Time*. Cambridge: Cambridge University Press.

Litwak, Eugene.
1965 "Extending Kin Relations in an Industrial Democratic Society." in Ethel Shanas and Gordon Streib (eds.) *Social Structures and the Family: Generational Relations*. Englewood Cliffs, New Jersey: Prentice-Hall, Inc.

Lobodzinska, Barbara.
1974 *Rodzina w Polsce*. Warszawa: Wydawnictwo Interpress.

Lopata, Helena Znaniecki.
1971 *Occupation Housewife*. New York: Oxford University Press.

1972 "Role Changes in Widowhood: A World Perspective." in Donald Cowgill and Lowell Holmes (eds.) *Aging and Modernization*. New York: Appleton-Century-Crofts.

1973a *Widowhood in an American City*. Cambridge, Mass.: Schenkman Publishing Company, General Learning Press.

1973b "The Effect of Schooling on Social Contacts of Urban Women." *American Journal of Sociology*. Vol. 79, No. 3 (November): 604-619.

1974 "Support Systems Involving Widows: USA." A research Proposal for the Social Security Administration.

1975 "Contributions of the Extended Family to Support Systems of Chicago Area Widows." presented at the International Congress of Gerontology in June 1975.

1977 "Support Systems Involving Widows in a Metropolitan Area of the United States." Report to the Social Security Administration.

Marris, Peter.
1958 *Widows and Their Families*. London: Routledge and Kegan Paul, Ltd.

Oakley, Ann.
1975 *Woman's Work*. New York: Vintage Books.

Pihlblad, Terance and Howard Rosencranz.
1968 *Old People in the Small Town*. Columbia, Missouri: University of Missouri Press.

Pihlblad, Terance and D. L. Adams.
1972 "Widowhood, Social Participation and Life Satisfaction." *Aging and Human Development*. 3: 323-330.

Piotrowski, Jerzy.
1963 *Praca Zawodowa Kobiety a Rodzina.* Warszawa: Ksiazka i Wiedza.

Rapoport, Rhona and Robert N. Rapoport.
1976 "Dual-Worker Families." in *Dual-Career Families.* New York: Harper & Row; London: Martin Robertson, second edition.

Ropp, Paul S.
1976 "The Seeds of Change: Reflections on the Condition of Women in the Early and Mid Ch'ing." *Signs: Journal of Women in Culture and Society.* V. 1: 5-23.

Rosow, Irving.
1967 *The Social Integration of the Aged.* New York: The Free Press of Macmillan.

Ross, Arlene.
1961 *The Hindu Family in its Urban Setting.* Toronto: The University of Toronto Press.

Sarasvati, Pundita R.
1888 *The High-Caste Hindu Woman.* Philadelphia: The James B. Rodgers Printing Co.

Scanzoni, Letha and John Scanzoni.
1976 *Men, Women and Social Change: A Sociology of Marriage and the Family.* New York: McGraw-Hill Book Co.

Shanas, Ethel and Gordon Streib. (eds.)
1965 *Social Structure and the Family: Generational Relations.* Englewood Cliffs, New Jersey: Prentice-Hall, Inc.

Shanas, Ethel, P. Townsend, D. Wedderburn, H. Friss, P. Milhos and J. Stehouwer.
1968 *Old People in Three Industrial Societies.* New York: Atherton.

Shorter, Edward.
1973 *The History of Work in the West: An Overview.* New York: Harper & Row: chapter 1, 1-33.
1975 *The Making of the Modern Family.* New York: Basic Books.

Steinhart, Frank.
1975a "The Social Correlates of Working Widows." Paper presented at the Annual Midwest Sociological Society Meetings, Chicago (April).
1975b "Labor Force Participation as a Resource for Support Systems." Chapter for Helena Z. Lopata's preliminary report of Support Systems Involving Widows in American Urban Areas to the Social Security Administration.

Sussman, Marvin.
1965 "Relationships of Adult Children with Their Parents in the United States." in Ethel Shanas and Gordon Streib (eds.) *Social Structure and the Family: Generational Relations.* Englewood Cliffs, New Jersey: Prentice-Hall, Inc.

Suttles, Gerold D.
1968 *The Social Order of the Slum: Ethnicity and Territory in the Inner City.* Chicago: University of Chicago Press.

Tryfan, Barbara.
1976 "Changes in the Situation of Country Women in Poland." in Jan Turowski and Lili Maria Szwengrub (ed.) *Rural Social Change in Poland.* Wroclaw: The Polish Academy of Sciences Press: 305-323.

Turowski, Jan and Lili Maria Szwengrub.
1976 *Rural Social Change in Poland.* Wroclaw: The Polish Academy of Sciences Press.

U.S. Department of Labor.
1975 *Handbook on Women Workers.* Washington, D.C.: U.S. Government Printing Office.

U.S. News and World Report.
1974 "The Plight of America's Two Million Widowers." 15 (April): 59-60.

Wilmott, Peter and Michael Young.
1960 *Family and Class in a London Suburb.* London: Routledge and Kegan Paul, Ltd.

Young, Michael and Peter Wilmott.
1957 *Family and Kinship in East London.* New York: The Free Press of Macmillan.

"Widowhood: Social Norms and Social Integration," by Helena Znaniecki Lopata. Unpublished paper presented at the Institut de la Vie World Conference: "Aging: A Challenge for Science and Social Policy." April 24-30, 1977. Reprinted with permission.

Part three : Children

Children (general)

Current Status and Future Prospects for the Nation's Children and Their Families

(Address given November 13, 1976, at the 50th Annual Convention of the National Association for the Education of Young Children held in Anaheim, California)

by John H. Meier*

Introductory Acknowledgements

It is always a pleasure to see and meet with my many friends and colleagues who have contributed so much to the growth and development of NAEYC. You have all heard and read about NAEYC's evolution as the nation's largest single nongovernmental organization concerned with early childhood education. It is second in magnitude only to the U.S. Office of Child Development's Bureau of Head Start. The heartwarming chronicle of some of the highlights of NAEYC's evolution from a committee of 25 to a vital membership of 28,500 persons is eloquent testimony to its professional value. Professor Emeritus Stolz's cogent and entertaining remarks during the opening evening's reception epitomize the humane qualities of this organization's history and promise. Her renaissance approach to age-old problems in early childhood education is rare and refreshing, inspiring us all to better educate the whole young child in the future. Bruce Gardner's presidency is now history and Bud Spodek's presidency is full of promise. May I take this opportunity to publicly extend my congratulations and best personal and professional wishes to each of these leaders and friends and to each of you as they and you continue to be among the most articulate advocates for children's inalienable rights, including life, liberty, and the pursuit of happiness. It seems appropriate that NAEYC's 50th Birthday Anniversary be held in Disneyland, defined as the world's biggest man trap built by a mouse, since it does show what can be done for children and the child in each of us. In keeping with this year's convention theme, I have been reflecting on how federal programs have in the past and promise in the future to enrich the lives of young children and their families, increase their liberty to more fully realize their optimum growth and development potential and to enjoy happiness in the pursuit of such a quality of life.

Some Observations and Suggestions

I would like to suggest that inasmuch as there is an Older American's Act

---

Editor's note: In a phone conversation with Dr. Meier, he expressed his pleasure that the following events have occurred since he gave this address: As a result of longitudinal studies showing the effectiveness of early intervention programs, Congress approved a $150,000,000 increase in funding for the expansion and general improvement of the Head Start Program. The Office of Child Development has been renamed the Administration of Children, Youth and Families. Funding for youth and children is now coordinated within this one agency. Dr. Meier and his staff emphasized the importance of the family in children's lives, and therefore feel special satisfaction in seeing more focus on the family now.

Dr. Meier was Director of the U.S. Office of Child Development and Chief of the Children's Bureau in the Department of Health, Education, and Welfare from 1975 to 1977. He is now Director at Children's Village (for abused and neglected children and their families) in Beaumont, California.

even moreso should there be a Younger American's Act. Moreover, whereas there will be a spokesperson for the elderly in the White House even moreso should there be a spokesperson for children in the White House. Although the senior citizens could be aptly represented by Ms. Lillian, the junior citizens in this Country cannot rely on Amy, despite her charm and access to power, to adequately represent their cause. And this difference simply underscores the fact that children cannot satisfactorily serve themselves, since they have neither a vote nor a sufficiently persuasive command of the language nor the national resources to guarantee that their needs will be given equitable and appropriate attention. A cabinet level Department for Children and Their Families may ultimately be the best way to get it all together.

Eloquent testimony to this inferior status of children, who many still believe should be seen and not heard, is the fact that less than 7% of the federal budget is spent on children and youth who constitute about 40% of our population and 100% of our future. Children are the most important and delicate natural resources we have... and remember, when today's children become tomorrow's voters and have to decide about our old age provisions, they will little note nor long remember what is said here but they will remember what we do or fail to do during the next few years in their behalf. Of course, I'm not suggesting that everything we do should be motivated by enlightened and, in this case, far-sighted self-interest. I am simply stating that this Nation cannot afford to be myopic any longer about our children and their families made up of us, "we the people," lest we squander our most precious resource and reap another generation of alienated, disgruntled, delinquent and ultimately self-destructive citizens. In my keynote speech to the NAEYC group two years ago, I addressed some of these issues, much as did John Goodlad two nights ago here. We must all work together to put our collective resources, talents, and energies where our rhetoric has been. With some few noteworthy exceptions, the recommendations forthcoming from the past 7 White House Conferences on Children sound like broken records, dispelling the popular and consoling myth that America is a child-centered society. We simply have taken precious little action on the many high-sounding recommendations from such conferences. The Environmental Protection Agency does environmental impact studies and there is now interest in family impact studies -- I submit that we need child impact studies to forecast the probable impact of any new legislation on children and their families.

During the National bicentennial year and NAEYC's semi-centennial year, we have all been engaged in reflecting over the past and if the past is indeed prologue the future looks a bit bleak. It reminds me of a bumper sticker I saw here in California several years ago which read, "Jesus is coming and boy is he mad!" However, if we can realize the hopes aroused by the promises of the incoming administration, the future looks much brighter. Let me repeat to you some salient words heard at the Children's Bureau's National Conference on Child Abuse and Neglect held in Atlanta last January, words spoken by one of this country's outstanding champions of children and their families, the then Senator and now Vice-President elect, Walter Mondale:

"You are a group that has proven its commitment to children and families. In working to prevent child abuse and neglect (or, I would parenthetically insert, working to improve child development and early childhood education) we must not lose sight of the still-extensive agenda that must be addressed if future Americans are to grow up healthy, well-educated, and economically secure. We must not forget that some 10 million children still live in poverty; that a quarter of a million children are born each year with birth defects, many of which could be prevented; and, that nearly two million school-age children are not even enrolled in school, according to the recent study by the Children's Defense Funds.

One rather cynical observer, who studies the seven White House Conferences on Children that have been held in this century, said:

'In the sweep of seven decades, the image conveyed is one of children, smaller than everyone else, lighter in physical weight and political clout, easily picked up and blown wherever the minds of economic, political, and social movements were heading.'

The challenge to those of us who are committed to ending child abuse and neglect is to prove that observation wrong, to prove that we are not simply indulging in a social fad, to prove that we indeed share the goal articulated by one participant in a White House Conference on Children -- that 'what the best and wisest parent wants for his own child, that must the community want for all of its children'."

I would submit that the Office of Child Development should play the lead role in stimulating communities to provide what is best for all of their children and their families. One effective mechanism for OCD's exercising considerable leadership leverage would be a series of grants to states for the support of state offices of child development, contingent upon the submission of a satisfactory state plan for improving the development, coordination, and maintenance of services to needy children and their families.

My First Days (Daze) At the Office of Child Development

This occasion gives me an opportunity to report to you the progress we have made at the Office of Child Development during my first year as director of this lead agency for children in the Federal government.

One of our staff recently observed that I am the epitome of upward mobility from trout rancher, builder and volunteer fireman in rural Colorado, to parent, to elementary and secondary school teacher, to school psychologist, to cofounder of a residential school for emotionally disturbed boys, to university professor, to cofounder of the New Nursery School in Greeley, to trainer and technical assistant for Head Start, Title I (ESEA), Follow-Through, and POC's, to child clinical/development psychologist, to Director of the John F. Kennedy Child Development Center for children with developmental and learning disabilities to National Director of the Office of Child Development and Chief of the U.S. Children's Bureau. Sometimes, when reviewing this odyssey, I wonder which way is up since I recall the satisfying days as a teacher when observable and immediate results were forthcoming from interacting effectively with a few children or youth.

At my swearing in more than one year ago I quoted a line from Robert Frost's poem, "Stopping by Woods on a Snowy Evening," which I fondly remember his reciting to us as students at Dartmouth College. A person pauses on a journey through the enchanting snow-covered woods to admire their beauty and says:

> The woods are lovely, dark and deep.
> But I have promises to keep,
> And miles to go before I sleep,
> And miles to go before I sleep.

Little did I suspect how many thousands of miles and many sleepless nights I was committing myself to as a visitor to and advocate for numerous domestic and foreign programs for children -- blowing in, blowing off, and blowing out -- around the world.

And all of this only to contract more promises and enjoy less sleep -- I now feel an even more pervasive and goading restlessness, in light of my increased exposure to all that must be done for our Nation's children and their families.

I have frequently spoken of the child and family advocacy role of OCD and that the "O" in OCD stood for optimum child development for all the Nation's children. Many knowledgeable and seasoned members of the press were sympathetically impressed but traditionally skeptical of my or anyone's ability to make many significant changes in the system. I took the job to learn about the system, hopefully to dispel some of my own cynicism about the bureaucracy, and most importantly to introduce some salutory changes in programs for children and their families, drawing upon my past 15 years of training and experience in child development and early childhood education.

I was attracted to directing the Children's Bureau in light of its illustrious history of child advocacy over the more than sixty years of its existence. Besides, a sort of patriotic fervor beckoned me to serve the Nation during its 200th anniversary; I can't deny some rescue phantasy and cockeyed optimism which motivates many of us behavioral and social scientists to constantly try to change things for the better. I was generally deeply impressed by the many senior senators I paid courtesy calls to, in preparation for their confirmation of me as Chief of the Children's Bureau; these men had given a great deal to our Country and perhaps I too could make some modest contribution.

Of course I'd been forewarned about the red tape involved in getting anything done in the bureaucracy, which was defined as a mammoth mechanism for converting creative energy into solid waste, located on about 16 square miles within the District of Columbia and surrounded by reality. I had decided that the marble halls of government couldn't be any more isolated from reality than the ivy-covered ivory towers of academia I had been living in during much of my adult life. As the song lyrics go, "Where wise men (people) fear to tread, fools rush in." It has been likened by some newcomers to the bureaucracy as being given a brand new beautiful automobile without a steering wheel, brakes, or accelerator -- and jumping aboard to guide it while it was moving at full (albeit not terribly swift) speed.

I knew I was taking on a major responsibility for directing an Office responsible for orchestrating nearly 500 federal virtuosi, scattered across the country in 10 regional offices as well as within headquarters, all responsible for administering nearly $500 million each year, the bulk of which was directly and favorably affecting the lives of nearly 350,000 impoverished Head Start children and their families and more than 50,000 Head Start staff members.

Looking Back over the First Year at OCD

I have now somehow survived about 450 days in the bureaucratic/political hub of the United States and would like to share briefly with you some of my perspective of the current status of and future prospects for the nation's children and their families.

Shortly after assuming this responsibility, I became privy to the incredibly complex and interwoven interpersonal, inter-office, inter-agency, interstate and international dynamics which interact in many of the policy formulation and decision-making processes. And the key actors are not playing for peanuts, if you'll pardon the pun. They're scheming to protect and build their respective empires -- and the competition for turf is keen and relentless.

Besides the many well-wishers among my colleagues and other friends of children's causes, there were many bearers of bad and often ill-founded news. I was warned that Head Start was to be phased out, shifted to the Office of Education, or bloc-granted to the States at any moment -- a perennially recurring wish from several rumor mongers envious of Head Start's many enviable successes.

One of the greatest Head Start successes has been in its parent involvement component. When public schools allow parents to participate in the hiring and firing of principals and teachers, they will have made a giant stride toward more meaningful parent involvement. It is gratifying to note that many public schools are encouraging greater parent participation in their children's schooling -- a favorable change in attitude due in large part, I daresay, to the influence and evaluation studies of Head Start and Follow-Through programs. At least part of the washout effect seems to be due to a sort of regression to the mean performance in many mediocre public school programs.

I'm pleased to announce that before the end of this year OCD will release a monograph, authored by Julie Richmond and Ed Zigler, old friends of young children, recounting many of the other unparalleled successes of Head Start during its First Decade; they include mention of the emergence of a "sleeper effect" whereby the "washout effect" seems to be attenuated with the passage of more time. Even the New York Times recently ran an article linking impressive reading gains by elementary school children with Head Start and other compensatory early intervention programs the children had previously attended.

This is in addition to much other rich longitudinal data we are now mining to yield lodestones showing the efficacy of early intervention programs. Some of the gems being discovered are like the following:

In Ira Gordon's program 30% of the matched controls were in special education by fifth grade whereas only 1% of the experimentals were referred -- a dollar saving which would easily pay for several such programs, not to mention the prevention of human waste and suffering. That is why Glen Nimnicht and I started the New Nursery School in Greeley, Colorado. A disproportionate number of children from Spanish-speaking homes were being placed in special education whereas with the systematic intervention of the New Nursery School experience these previously "Six Hour Retarded Children" were able to be mainstreamed and to cope successfully with the public schools. Of course many critics of the public schools offer persuasive arguments for changing the schools to better accommodate the culturally different child but until that happens, it is important to enable today's children to function successfully in today's society.

Rick Heber's Milwaukee Project is now being replicated by Jim Gallagher and is yielding similar results; moreover, the experimental children from the Milwaukee Project are continuing to do extraordinarily well in elementary school whereas their controls have continued to decline to borderline and lower levels of mental retardation and special education function. The Brookline Early Education Project is providing extensive data on various degrees of intensity and duration of intervention procedures and promises to be quite instructive regarding optimum matches for individualizing experiences for children in need of enrichment to compensate for deprived home environments and experiences.

OCD has recently funded a number of the Nation's outstanding child development and early childhood education leaders to collaborate in a major data-gathering effort to cumulate the longitudinal findings of their several studies. Irv Lazar is spear-heading this project, which is coordinated through the Education Commission of the States, and is presently pooling data from the ongoing longitudinal studies of Kuno Beller, Bettye Caldwell, Cynthia and Martin Deutsch, Ira Gordon, Susan Gray, Ronald Lally, Sylvia Levenstein, Frank Palmer, Dave Weikart, Ed Zigler and others. Sounds like a familiar litany, doesn't it? Lazar reports that at this preliminary state he is most pleased with the favorable data, which by such pooling will allow conclusions to be drawn based upon as many as 3000 experimental subjects in some parameters. It is most gratifying to know that Ed Zigler, the first Director of OCD, is compiling a major book about Head Start, further chronicling the growth and development of this super societal effort in behalf of impoverished children and their families. Moreover, there is a rich and expanding literature on Head Start and analogous programs spurred on by their presence and achievements. We are now aware of over 600 studies on Head Start alone, many of which report very favorable findings. Abstracts of these studies, including doctoral dissertations, are kept at George Washington University under an OCD contract to maintain an information clearinghouse on child and family development and early childhood education. Educational Testing Service is also warehousing a great deal of data which Virginia Shipman and others are currently analyzing.

The introduction and debugging of the Head Start Performance Standards, a Management Information System, and the Child Development Associate credentialling system all augur well for a reasonably fail-safe, high quality national early childhood education and child and family development program capable of massive expansion in the event that a national commitment and concomitant resources are made available. We are getting our act together and it promises to be dramatic indeed.

I was warned that the Children's Bureau was dead, having been eviscerated, emasculated, and generally incapacitated during the past few years. As Mark Twain vigorously observed that stories of his death were exaggerated, likewise for the Children's Bureau -- contrary to various rumors, the Children's Bureau is alive and well. Although our efforts regarding child abuse and neglect, foster care, and adoption have been the most visible, there are numerous other exciting endeavors underway. It is conceivable and certainly organizationally and programmatically desirable that several of the Bureau's previous programs, such as the Title IVB Child Welfare authority and the Maternal and Child Health Division, be returned to OCD. For maximum coherence and coordination, several other programs (or at least the parts relevant to children and their families) should be placed in OCD.

In order to complete OCD's internal reorganization, I moved our Day Care Division into the Children's Bureau, where it is receiving a great deal of attention and promises a high yield of policy-relevant information, including useful insights on the controversial stipulations of the Federal Interagency Day Care Requirements. Speaking of Day Care, I was warned that even mentioning Day Care would be the Kiss of Death. Last Spring OCD received up to 5000 letters per week which had been written to the President in angry opposition to unfounded rumors that the Feds were proposing to take over the Nation's children, tantamount to the allegations that a previously proposed national day care bill smacked of "sovietization." Since one prime sponsor, Senator Mondale, was receiving up to 7000 vicious letters a day, it was clear that people cared about day care. This prompted me and others to further investigate the underlying societal and familial factors contributing to a kind of free-floating paranoia and hostility toward anything aimed at the faltering family.

Some Societal and Familial Factors Leading to a Focus on the Family

Our investigation of a variety of sources, including several studies completed or ongoing under OCD auspices, revealed the following representative list of salient factors:

- 33% of mothers with preschool children work outside their home at least part-time.
- 7.5 million children are in day care,

over 90% of which is in unlicensed homes, many of which reportedly are of only custodial quality, at best.

-40% of marriages end in divorce, 80% of teenage marriages end in divorce within 5 years and many divorced mothers do not remarry.

-In 1960, 5% of births were out of wedlock, in 1976 - 12%; in 1976 - 51% (of 9700) births in Washington, D.C. were to unwed, often teenage mothers.

-600,000 children each year are born to teens with a significantly increased risk of birth defects.

-For each 1 million teenage pregnancies: 400,000 are aborted, 300,000 are born to unwed mothers; 300,000 of the mothers enter forced and unstable marriages (80% of which dissolve within 5 years).

-In 1910, 40% of the U.S. population lived in an urban setting; in 1976, 75% of population lives in urban home environments many of which are expanding ghettos.

-In 1900, 50% of the Boston households had extended families (i.e. 2 parents, children, and at least one other relative); In 1970 only 4% had extended families.

-Presently, nearly 400,000 children are in foster care and 100,000 are in institutions (50% of whom are mentally retarded -- much of which can be prevented).

-The average American family moves 14 times; 20% of the U.S. population moves each year.

-The average child by the age of 16 spends more time watching TV than in school -- during age 5 to 15 years, the average child sees 13,000 killings, not to mention other violence on TV, including many "cartoons."

-1 million youth run away from home each year.

-Suicide is the second leading cause of death for youths 15-24 years of age.

-5% of our teens have an alcohol drinking problem.

-The number of youth arrested for murder, robbery, rape, and assault has gone up 254% since 1960 (though the absolute number is not huge, yet).

-Unemployment is the prime reason for family deterioration, yet 18% of 2-parent families had non-working fathers and 42% of single parent families with children under 6 had a mother who couldn't get employment.

-When unemployment reached the 20% level in Flint, Michigan, suicide among unemployed auto workers went up 30 times; alcoholism, drug abuse and child abuse soared.

-The variable most frequently related to child abuse is father's unemployment.

-Admissions to mental hospitals soar as a direct result of unemployment.

An Ongoing Model of Family-Centered Intervention

The evidence to date indicates that the family is the most effective and economical means for fostering the development of the child. Active participation of family members is critical to the success of any intervention program. Ideally, intervention begins in preparation for parenthood and in providing an adequate cultural milieu for nourishment of the newborn infant. Large-scale Parent-Child Development Centers (OCD's PCDCs and PCCs) established as rational experiments have clearly demonstrated the value of parental training in the first years of life followed by preschool group experiences in which parent and child continue to work closely together. Highly significant results have been obtained not only for disadvantaged black families but also for middle-class white families, Spanish-speaking Mexican-Americans, and other ethnic groups. A closer look at one of OCD's research-oriented Parent-Child Development Center (PCDCs) for Spanish-speaking Mexican-American children in Houston illustrates the way in which this type of educational-social intervention improves the functioning of children and their families.

In the Houston model program, social intervention consists of working closely with both the mother and father of very young children. Beginning at the age of 12 months, frequent home visits by a bilingual worker introduce the mother (and hopefully the father, too) to a number of techniques for intellectual stimulation of the child. The mother is coached in her communication with the child in order to promote intellectual and personality growth and development while maintaining strong affectional bonds. Mothers and fathers meet regularly several times a month in the evening to discuss their family problems, to share their ideas and to seek advice. The family is dealt with as a whole and the techniques are carefully adapted to the cultural values and milieu in which the family lives. Consequently, the parents are enthusiastic and most cooperative.

When the child is two years old, mother and child attend a special nursery four mornings a week where parent-child relations continue to be stressed at the same time that the child is introduced to social interactions with other children in a controlled and stimulating but playful environment. Videotape recordings of mother-child interactions are played back for the mother so that she can see where she is facilitating or inhibiting desired behavior in the child. Periodic contacts with the family are maintained after the child is three years old in preparation for entering school. Ideally, the child graduates into a preschool program like Head Start in order to maintain and further develop his growing and developing interests and abilities.

A model program of this type, incorporating the best techniques from earlier experiments, is expensive, particularly when carried out as an experiment with a great deal of research and evaluation accompanying the program. However, the essentials of such a family development program can be achieved without a great financial investment by using volunteers and the heavy involvement of parents.

Nevertheless, one can rightly ask whether or not the benefits from such a program, or reasonably approximate variations on the theme, are worth the costs. The final answers to this important question are not all yet available at this time. However, early returns from extensive evaluative research over the past five years indicate the following few representative findings and trends when the experimental families receiving the program are compared to similar families who do not participate:

1) Parent (primarily mother) benefits: Changes in parents' child-rearing behaviors, skills values and attitudes vary somewhat among models, but are significant in all three programs. The program effects on participating parents are especially notable because they are congruent with the whole body of research and theory dealing with the relation of parent (primarily mother) characteristics that are causally linked with high early and sustained levels of child development. Statistically significant differences between participating and randomly assigned control mothers provide evidence that participating mothers are:

   - More sensitive to children's social, emotional and intellectual developmental needs.
   - More accepting of their children.
   - More affectionate and warmer, using less punishment and more praise.
   - More aware of causes of child distress, more skillful in allaying distress and comforting children.
   - More aware of the range of individual differences among children, placing less value on stereotypic expectations for children.
   - Use more, and more complex, language with child, encouraging child verbalization more.
   - Reason more with children placing less emphasis on authority as shaper of desired behaviors, praising child initiatives more and encouraging exploratory behaviors more.

-Feel less restricted and/or intimidated by child-rearing and homemaking tasks; find children more interesting and enjoyable.
-Pursue own educational development more.
-Use community agencies more, and more skillfully, to meet family's and children's needs.

2) Child benefits
Both pre-post and experimental-control group comparisons show the following statistically and (what's more important) really favorable program impact on participating children:

a) Intellectual-Language

-Greater attentiveness, awareness and response to new and discrepant experiences in first year, followed by more exploratory behaviors in second and third years.
-Greater readiness for, and skills in dealing with problem-solving situations.
-Greater vocalization in early months, more and more complex language skills achieved earlier in second and third years.
-Significantly higher general cognitive development as measured by Bayley Scales of Mental Development at about twenty months, and by the Stanford-Binet Test of Intelligence at 36 months. Most importantly, these short term effects are retained or extended at 48 months, while the children in the matched control group gradually fall further behind.

b) Social-emotional Development

-Earlier and stronger attachment to mothers, followed by earlier and stronger explorativeness, greater capacity to relate to strangers in second and third years.
-Interactions first with mother, and later with others are richer in texture, in vocalization, touching, smiling, proximity-seeking to share discoveries; more eye contact and verbalization from distances, etc.
-More and richer play behaviors and fantasy, shared first with mothers and then with other adults.

As the PCDC concept is further refined and programs are running smoothly, impacts on mothers' child rearing concepts and skills emerge earlier and stronger, and developmental differences between experimental and control infants emerge earlier and stronger and promise to endure longer.

Reports on the longitudinal effectiveness of similar programs elsewhere indicate that the children of trained parents or parent surrogates (primarily mothers) have excelled in general development and school achievement, compared to children growing up in comparable homes where the mothers do not receive training. The gains resulting from such intervention programs are largest and most likely to endure when substantial changes occur in the entire environment (or what Urie Bronfenbrenner calls the ecology) of the child as well as in the quality of the mother-child interaction alone. When adequate health care, nutrition, housing, and general support of the family as a child-rearing system are not provided, the gains tend to fade once the intervention program is discontinued.

I am delighted to announce that the first wave of replication of OCD's PCDC's is progressing smoothly, thanks to the support of the Eli Lilly Endowment and the coordination of Bank Street College. Moreover, several large states and other foundations have expressed sincere interest in participating in subsequent replication waves. Hence, the future augurs well for this modest exemplary effort, but more is required given the magnitude of need. In this regard, I have attempted to distill the highest proof ingredients from a number of OCD and other programs to produce a powerful mixed portion which will be served throughout the country with whatever adaptations may be necessary for local tastes and, perhaps, tolerances.

Recommendation for Neighborhood Family Development Centers

The following skeletal items outline the salient features of a proposed network of omnibus Neighborhood Family Development Centers (NFDCs) with which all families might affiliate in a variety of ways for a variety of reasons:

-For fiscal/administrative agents, use existing mechanisms: 1) in State Offices of Child Development or their counterparts, 2) in appropriate agencies located in each of 3,300 counties, and/or 3) in streamlined Community Action Agencies.

The designation of a lead agency would depend on the organization/reorganization of each given State and/or local bureaucracy (e.g. one NFDC could be located in each county and possibly have satellite service stations (SSS) for outreach and serving large geographic or very heavily populated areas).

-Build NFDCs on aforementioned early intervention service, training and research bases plus any new germane findings (e.g. collaboration with the Bureau of Education for Handicapped's First Chance Network has been salutory for both OCD & BEH).

-Build on Head Start network by elaborating upon OCD's Parent Child Centers, Parent-Child Development Centers, Comprehensive Family Resource Projects Home Starts, etc.

A conference was held in October, 1976 to introduce further coherence among OCD's in-house programs for infants and toddlers before venturing beyond. The White House mini-conferences on infancy last summer (1976) underscored the need for programs for prenatal through 6 year-old children and their families. I suggested that 1977 be declared the Year of the Family.

The Office of Education's Follow-Through Program, the Western half of which I helped launch several years ago in Greeley, Colorado, is a logical vertical upward extension of Head Start to ensure a smoother articulation into elementary school for Head Start graduates, much as OCD's Project Developmental Continuity is doing. The NFDC concept proposes at least to include the horizontal and vertical downward expansion of Head Start.

-Health must be regarded as more than a freedom from disease. Rapid advances in medical technology promise to require less of our physician's time for curing, freeing more of their time for caring and prevention.

Emphasis on prevention through well-baby (prenatal included) maternal and infant care, adequate nutrition, accident prevention, and elimination of child abuse and neglect. Use pediatric associates and/or other physician extenders for developmental screening to identify children at risk of later delays and go beyond Social Rehabilitation Services current Early Periodic Screening Diagnosis and Treatment (EPSDT) practices which raise many expectations but rarely include the "T", treatment.

Health maintenance program included -- for example, rates for polio and measles shots now falling behind, especially in poverty areas where only 60% of the children are now being immunized and rubella epidemics are now recurring in the U.S. even while we're debating the necessity of swine flu shots.

-Exceptional Children, including gifted and talented, must be identified early and enabled to realize their full

potential -- "right hemisphere" abilities (non-verbal functions like art, music, and so forth) should receive attention and nurturance, too.
Individualized prescription for handicapping conditions be based on and tracked by each child's own developmental profile -- the NFDC monitors each child's progress.

-Family Liaison Person -- These persons work out of the NFDC like a county extension agent only they are trained in family maintenance techniques and have child caregiving competencies (home visitor or lay therapist types); ultimately there should be a Child Development Associate credential for such child caregivers who could work in a variety of settings. There are now 663 credentialled CDAs and we expect 3000 by 1978 for center-based Head Start and day care-settings.

-Parenting Skill Development -- OCD's Education for Parenthood program may eventuate in parenting proficiency certification. During the past several years just before coming to OCD I tried a pilot effort of training Department of Agriculture county extension agents in doing developmental screening of children in remote farm and ranch homes in six western states. It's remarkable how much more is known about animal husbandry and even midwifery than about child rearing.

-Family Support -- A recently completed study by the National Academy of Sciences commissioned by OCD recommends a guaranteed minimum income for families (which may include vouchers for child care to give parents the flexibility of choosing among several alternative caregiving options for their children). The NFDC itself would provide and/or coordinate a variety of options ranging from full-year full-day programs to multiple lesser variations on the theme in both center and home settings.

-Resource Access Center -- the NFDC serves as a materials and information exchange center as part of a national computerized network. The referral and tracking of children, including those eligible for foster care and adoption would be provided. The NFDC would function as a clearinghouse for a variety of individualized curricula and latest research findings, possibly electronically linked to an international secretariat/clearinghouse being established in Paris.

-Community Activity Center -- The NFDC is the hub of many related activities:
Volunteer services -- opportunity for Boy/Girl Scouts, 4H, VISTA, etc. to serve and advance family development as well as learning parenting skills (perhaps for merit badges or other appropriate awards).

After-School day-care and recreational program since aforementioned factors characterizing today's families show a need for day-care for a large age range of children. Moreover, some provision should be made for drop-in emergency health and child-care services 24 hours per day, 7 days per week for those unbearably stressful times when children often become the innocent victims.

The elderly would be encouraged to assist in caregiving and to participate in games, handicrafts and to act as grandparent-surrogates in new extended families, where parenting instruction can be given and received congenially and part of the generation gap may be bridged.

The neighborhood's youth would be encouraged to give one year of their teens for human services -- NFDC Teeny Boppers Brigade.

-Application of government and university findings -- NFDCs would serve as living laboratories for studying a variety of approaches to strengthening the family, however it is defined. What are the developmental milestones in becoming and being a parent/grandparent? What are a family's developmental stages, when is it normal, when is it in trouble?
NFDC would serve as a reality base for generating and updating national

policy for children and families (all OCD grants are terminated with policy implication papers (PIPS), which inform next modification of dynamic NFDCs).

-The NFDC's are a basis for modifying or at least supplementing a child and family's total ecology. I would hope that it would lead to neighborhood planning, indeed city planning, according to Doxiadis's Ekistics theory, i.e. humanizing the environment and making technology more responsive to human needs instead of the other way around.

-The NFDC prototype and other exemplary models would serve as international centers for visiting scholars and dignitaries, as seen in the USSR pavillion of achievement. Besides visiting the Russian showplaces, I recently attended the opening of the Children's Museum built by Eli Lilly Foundation in Indianapolis, which contains not only examples of our children's best art, ballet, puppets, music, etc. but also contains one of OCD's replicated PCDCs -- a living museum piece of great contemporary significance, showing some of the best in the state of the art.

NFDC Cost Calculations

OCD now has nearly 12 years of experience in funding and operating Head Start programs located throughout the U.S. and trust territories. A doubling of the Head Start budget, to allow some horizontal but largely vertical downward extension of many of its existing centers would require an additional $500 million. This increase would enable a variety of programs to be delivered to approximately 1 million impoverished children and their families, about 25% of those now eligible for Head Start participation. Although Head Start has been on a survival, no-growth budget for several years now, it has been refining its delivery system with each passing year and a doubling of its size as a first step during 1977 toward a national network of NFDCs would be a reasonable beginning with minimal waste and maximum impact on the target children and their families.

The full development and operation of a national network of Neighborhood Family Development Centers would be more costly and would have to be budgeted in light of decisions regarding geographic size and location of each catchment area, eligibility for services, sliding fee considerations, and many related management considerations having fiscal implications. The experience of Neighborhood Health Centers, Community Mental Health Centers; County Extensions Offices, etc. is instructive in such budgeting. OCD stands ready, willing and able to begin the necessarily more detailed planning and implementing of the NFDC Network when the required legislation is passed. We continue to argue the cliche that these relative ounces of prevention promise to far outweigh the pounds of later attempted cures, such as prisons, drug-abuse programs, runaway youth programs, and so on, ad nauseum.

Revised Forward Plan for OCD

A Forward Plan should represent the delineation of an agency's best current thinking projected onto a sort of master blueprint for the next five years. OCD's present Forward Plan is severely limited, since it was based on a no-growth, static level of funding with no new initiatives allowed. For the record, as is often said during various hearings, it is important to note that within OCD we had several good and new projects for which we prepared skeleton plans ready to be fleshed out if Administration policies and commitments changed. The preceding NFDC example is a case in point.

Regrettably, the entire Neighborhood Family Development Center notion was rejected at higher levels (OHD) and was purged from OCD's Forward Plan. This OCD Director's dream became a bureaucratic nightmare. In fact, no imaginative nor innovative initiatives were approved for inclusion in OCD's proposed next five years of effort. The strictly status quo mentality characterized by a number of the long range "planners," many of whom represent the penultimate of the Peter Principle, stifled all further brainstorming, since it was clearly an exercise in futility.

What was instituted several years ago as a means of keeping the HEW Secretary informed about major program operations, the Operational Planning System (OPS), had become the tail wagging the dog -- the means become an end in itself. Planning became a means of preventing change by a process which deteriorated to a chronic paralysis of analysis.

If some of the planners OCD had to contend with were confronted with a four-legged ape's ever standing erect, they would have cited all the reasons why it wasn't anatomically feasible and asked all the hard questions about cost/benefits in terms of training, bruises from falling, and back discomfort. They would typically and dogmatically demand hard data on the benefits of walking upright before it had been tried. It has been stated that bureaucrats make inadequate lovers because they always want to do feasibility studies first and by then the mood or opportunity has passed. I prefer the more contemporary definition of planning as an improvisation on a general sense of direction, which would far more likely enable man to stand, walk, dance, run a mile in less than 4 minutes and use his newly-freed forefeet to make and use tools and technology to further master his environment.

A compromise to establishing one or more pilot Neighborhood Family Development Centers was a proposition for horizontal and downward vertical extension of Head Start to accommodate more of the presently unserved eligible poverty children, birth through school age, since less than 15% are presently in programs. However, this was repeatedly rejected due to fiscal restraints consistent with prevailing Administration policies and commitments, which we honored. However, we were also often rebuffed by the same planners because of our weak rationale although there was far more justification for our proposed expansion than there ever was for kindergarten!

Thus, OCD's Forward Thrust emerged from the planning and high level clearance process as a Side Step at best but more like a Backward Lurch, at which time I submitted my resignation for want of anything stimulating to manage except some possibly worthwhile tinkering with existing programs always needing refinement. Nonetheless, I was persuaded to hang on for the full cycle -- whatever that is.

I'm in full agreement with and supportive of careful planning for good management and the OPS process is very useful in driving systematically and accountably toward major goals and objectives. The tragedy here is that the unimaginative and repressive use of the planning process resulted in a regressive OCD Forward Plan which in turn dictated OCD's R & D planning and efforts, which becomes concomitantly narrow and sterile. The traditional visionary and advocacy initiatives of the Children's Bureau have been reduced to myopic and tunnel-visioned foster care and adoption services. Admittedly, these represent important rifle shots when only limited resources are available but they do not address the broad-gauged shot-gun targets requiring more scattered and yet patterned thrusts if the kaleidoscopic concerns of children and their families are to be included in the Children's Bureau shooting range.

If we are permitted to more fully plan and ultimately implement some of our exciting new ideas, I am sure it will take considerable time and effort. I thought you might be interested in hearing the various steps a new idea must go through and, if you apply these to the Child Development Associate credentialling idea and its implementation, you can more fully appreciate the following ten steps in the

Evolution of Reaction to a New Idea

1) Indignant Rejection
2) Reasoned Objection
3) Qualified Opposition
4) Tentative Acceptance
5) Qualified Endorsement
6) Judicious Modification
7) Cautious Adoption
8) Impassioned Espousal
9) Proud Parenthood
10) Dogmatic Propagation

APHA Journal 55:1436, 1965

Many have called for new national policies placing families and children first among our priorities. Few, if any, have expressed this plea as well as my friend Nick Hobbs, who stated the following in an address on mental health, families, and children:

> We need to rekindle the caring spirit in America. To nurture altruistic impulse. To restore civility. To rediscover self in the service of others. To encourage fidelity to family. To honor those who fulfill the difficult role of parent, of father and mother. We need a revived national ethos that cherishes communities, families, and children, out of respect for our heritage and in the service of a noble national tomorrow (Hobbs, May 3, 1976, University of Texas at Austin).

I would humbly submit that getting on with the Neighborhood Family Development Center network is a pragmatic beginning toward brighter prospects for this Nation's children and their families.

<u>My Future Plans</u>

To dispel some other rumors running rife during these tumultuous transition days, I'd like to state that for the past 64 years there has been a tradition for the Chief of the Children's Bureau to remain through changes in administration (with one exception). The Office of Child Development, on the other hand was created by executive order and is subject to elimination by one fell swoop of a pen. Children and families are a non-partisan issue requiring poly-partisan and broad-based concern and support. It is standard protocol for all Presidential appointees, whether appointed for political or professional reasons, to submit their resignation for the incoming administration to accept or not. Now that I have learned the system, survived the traditional culture-shock experienced by non-political appointees entering government for the first time, and have a definite sense of direction not only from within but also from NAEYC members and other child and family advocates. I would be pleased to stay in this two-hatted position or its reorganized counterpart if asked to do so. Regardless of where I am or OCD/CB may be next year at this time, with your good counsel and collaboration and the supportive attitude of the incoming Administration, I daresay that we'll all be able to continue to advance the cause of children and their families in the more promising future. Godspeed to you in your efforts and thank you for coming and staying!

Credits:

Some of the facts and ideas contained in this address were drawn from papers produced by U. Bronfenbrenner, J. Califano, N. Hobbs, W. Holtzman, C. H. Kempe, F. Palmer, J. Richmond, V. Seitz, E. Zigler, Children's Defense Fund, Child Welfare League of America, National Council of Organizations for Children and Youth (now Coalition for Children & Youth), National Academy of Sciences, National Science Foundation, Social Research Group at George Washington University, and various members of OCD staff (who are exceptionally competent and dedicated bureaucrats).

Address given November 13, 1976 at the 50th Annual Convention of the National Association for the Education of Young Children, held in Anaheim, California. Reprinted with Dr. Meier's permission.

THE NEED FOR STATES TO PROVIDE SERVICES TO PARENTS WITH YOUNG CHILDREN

Two assumptions have pervaded American attitudes toward families and child-rearing: (1) that the ability to raise children wisely is a natural talent possessed by most parents and (2) that child-rearing is always a joyful, positive experience. Partly as a result of these beliefs, no coherent policy of continuous family service has been developed in this country. Yet there is growing evidence that neither of these assumptions is entirely true. While raising children is one of the most rewarding of human experiences, with many joyful moments, it is also one of the most demanding.

Data gathered during the last two decades indicate that, for most couples, child-rearing is a seriously stressful experience—economically, emotionally and psychologically. For example, a study of 46 couples done by E. E. LeMasters, professor of Social Work and Sociology at the University of Wisconsin, reported a "general disenchantment with the parental role" expressed by many of these young parents after the birth of their first child. The couples were college-educated and in middle-class occupations, and most of them not only wanted but planned for the child. None were having unusual economic, psychological, emotional or physical difficulties. Yet 83 percent of this group declared they had experienced "severe crisis" in adjusting to the effects of the newborn on their lives. "Practically nothing in school or out of school got (these couples) ready to be fathers and mothers—*husbands* and *wives*, yes, but not *parents*," declared LeMasters in the conclusion to his study.[1]

The responsibilities and skills required in caring for young children too often take young parents by surprise. Guiding the development of a young child from helpless infant to mature adult is a complex and unrelenting task, and the pleasures of having children can be overshadowed by feelings of inadequacy, insecurity concerning child-rearing methods and lack of outside resources for advice, support, help and temporary relief from the continuous responsibilities of parenthood.

Furthermore, children are expensive. A recent study by the Commission on Population Growth and the American Future estimated that the cost of raising one child in the U.S. to age 18 is $34,464. This figure climbs to $98,361 if one adds a college education and an estimate of the wages the mother lost by taking care of the child instead of holding a paying job. The study concludes: "Having a child will not only mean giving up one life style for another, but also potentially giving up one standard of living for another."[2]

In light of this reality, the participation of mothers in the labor force has almost doubled—from 22 percent in 1950 to 42 percent in 1970. By 1980 working mothers of preschool children alone are expected to increase by over 1.5 million.[3]

For single parents or wives of low-income husbands, the ability to stay at home and care for children is a luxury not available except at the expense of public assistance. The following table indicates the distribution of family income nationally as of 1969. These figures include the income of working mothers. This is an important fact because a two-parent family in which the father earns $10,000 and the mother does not work has very different child-rearing needs from those of a family in

[1] E. E. Le Masters, "The Crisis in Parenthood," in *Sourcebook in Marriage and Family*, Marvin B. Sussman, ed. (New York: Houghton-Mifflin, 1968).

[2] Sarane Spense Boocock, "The Status of the Child and Alternative Structures for Child Care Systems," speech presented at the annual meeting of the American Educational Research Association, April 18, 1974.

[3] U.S. Senate Committee on Finance, *Child Care: Data and Materials* (Washington, D.C.: U.S. Government Printing Office, 1971).

which the father earns $6,000 and the mother $4,000.

1970 Selected Statistics Related to Distribution of U.S. Family Income[4]

Total U.S. Population	203.2 million
Children 0-5	17.0 million (8 percent of total)
Children 5-19	58.3 million (28 percent of total)
Number of families	51.3 million

1969 Income	*Percent of families*
$0 – 3,999	15.2
$4000 – 5999	10.8
$6000 – 9999	26.7
$10,000 – 14,999	26.6
$15,000 – 24,999	16.0

The stresses of child-rearing, coupled with lack of knowledge about child development and the parental role, prevent many parents from adequately meeting their children's needs. This situation was documented by a variety of statistics compiled for the 1970 White House Conference on Children:

> One-fourth of American children suffer from some degree of malnutrition; 50 percent of children under age 6 have substandard levels of vitamin A; 40 percent of children under age 2 have low values of vitamin C; and 50 percent of children under 2 have insufficient iron in their diets.
>
> Almost one-half the population under age 19 has not been adequately immunized against diphtheria-pertussis-tetanus. Fewer than 75 percent of persons in the same age group have been immunized against rubeola. The percentage of children ages 1 through 4 who are fully immunized against poliomyelitis has fallen from a high of 87.6 percent in 1964 to 67.7 percent in 1969.
>
> Fifteen thousand children under age 15 die each year from accidents; another 19 million are injured severely enough to need medical care. Most accidents involving children take place in the home.[5]

In addition, an estimated 35 percent of apparently normal children display behavioral difficulties by the age of 4.[6] And, perhaps most devastating of all, it is estimated that more than 60,000 children are victims of serious child abuse each year.[7]

The problem for many families is that supportive resources tend to be unavailable until family breakdown is complete. Then help comes too often in the form of crisis service, emergency wards, police and the courts. We know that very young children are especially responsive to preventive and corrective treatment, and that nearly one-third of later crippling conditions could be eliminated by treatment in the preschool years.

We also know that children with serious handicaps can often learn to manage their lives and to master tasks if help is given early. Yet the educational and medical systems do not track most of these children during the critical period between birth and the school entrance age, and no other system has been developed sufficiently to fill this gap. For example, of the 4 to 4.5 million preschool children whose mothers work, only about three percent have found places in licensed day care homes or centers. The majority of children are left in the care of neighbors, friends or relatives, and many are left entirely alone during the work day.[8]

Even when services for young children are available, individual programs tend to disregard the family as a unit and deal only with the child—medically, educationally or socially—as an isolated individual. In recent years, many public officials have recognized the need to provide comprehensive services to meet the developmental needs of young children. Often, however, fundamentally sound child development or child health services have not given full weight to the child's family situation or background. The resulting lack of continuity between program and home may prevent such programs from fully achieving their stated objectives for the child. Moreover, placing an expert between the

---

[4] Adapted from *Issues in the Design of a Delivery System for Day Care and Child Development Services to Children and Their Families*, Joan M. Bergstrom, Gwen Morgan, Wheelock College, for the Day Care and Child Development Council of America, Inc., May 1975, p. 7.

[5] White House Conference on Children, *Profiles of Children* (Washington, D.C.: U.S. Government Printing Office, 1970).

[6] Joint Commission on Mental Health of Children, *Crisis in Child Mental Health: Challenge for the 1970's* (New York: Harper and Row, 1970).

[7] Early Childhood Project, *Child Abuse and Neglect: Model Legislation for the States*, Report No. 71 (Denver, Colo: Education Commission of the States, 1975).

[8] U.S. Senate Committee on Finance, *op. cit.*

parent and child in order to further a child's development can have the unintended effects of weakening the parent's confidence in his or her own child-rearing abilities, encouraging abdication to the expert the responsibility for the child.

The present arrangement of independent resources through hospitals, community health, welfare services and the schools is highly fragmented and fails for the most part to deliver significant aid to children and their families. Family needs are varied and interrelated. Integrated, coordinated services addressed to the family as a unit are required to meet these needs. States should develop a comprehensive coordinated service system applicable at state and local levels, available to families from all socioeconomic strata. Existing agencies and services should be examined and new structures considered to determine how best to establish a single-entry-access agency through which parents can obtain the full range of services applicable to their individual needs. Continuing services need to be readily accessible to all families long before serious difficulties are evident. Emphasis should be on identifying the need for assistance and providing such assistance early enough in the child's development for optimum benefit, and on supporting the family *as a unit.*

Two other excerpts from The Role of the Family in Child Development: Implications for State Policies and Programs can be found in this book. One is the eighteenth item in this CHILDREN section and one is Item 10 in the ADULTS section.

Excerpted from The Role of the Family in Child Development: Implications for State Policies and Programs, The fifteenth report of The Education Commission of the States Early Childhood Project (December 1975). Denver, Colorado. Reprinted with permission.

TITLE XX: SOCIAL SERVICES IN YOUR STATE
A CHILD ADVOCATE'S HANDBOOK FOR ACTION

INTRODUCTION

Title XX of the Social Security Act, which became effective on October 1, 1975, provides money to your state for a broad range of social services programs. Those programs may include such services as child day care, homemaker services, services to the handicapped, protective services, legal services, senior citizens programs, and information and referral. Each state is allotted a share of $2.5 billion in federal funds, which can be used to pay 75 percent of the costs of social services included in that state's Comprehensive Annual Services Plan. To get the federal money, the state must raise the other 25 percent, through state appropriations or through donations from public or private agencies.

The federal government does not tell your state how to spend its Title XX money. It does prohibit use of Title XX funds for major medical or subsistence (i.e. room and board) costs, sets maximum limits on eligibility, and requires certain administrative and record-keeping procedures. But within these broad guidelines, the state is free to define its own services, to determine who will receive them, and to contract with service providers--including local community groups.

Title XX is not a totally new program. It replaces the social services programs previously authorized under Titles IV-A and VI of the Social Security Act. The $2.5 billion was available to states under these sections of the law and, in fact, a number of states were already spending their share of the national ceiling before Title XX became effective.

What is new about Title XX is the requirement that your state undertake an open public planning process. This gives you a chance to find out what the state is doing with your social services dollars and to organize so that children and families get their fair share. If your state is already spending all of its Title XX funds, this may mean working to shift priorities within the plan. If you have unspent federal funds, you may have to concentrate on finding the money to pay the state's 25 percent matching share.

The emphasis in Title XX is on community-based services. Whether or not your community groups can get these funds, and whether you can serve children with the greatest need, will depend on what the plan says. The Children's Defense Fund has prepared this Handbook to help you influence that plan.

PART I: THE PLANNING PROCESS

Before it can receive Title XX funds, your state must prepare a Comprehensive Annual Services Program Plan (CASP). This plan must contain specific information about the types of services the state will fund, eligibility, fee schedules, geographic areas where services will be offered, sources of the state's matching funds, and the administration of the program. Federal law requires that this planning process be an open one, and that the public have the opportunity to participate in it.

There are several key stages in the planning process where you should be involved. You should not wait until the plan is published to try to change it. That may be too late.

A. THE PRE-PUBLICATION PHASE

No later than 90 days before the start of a new program year, your state must publish a proposed plan for public comment. However, by that time, the most important decisions about the social services program already may have been made. It may be much easier to influence the plan before it is published than to try to change it during the comment period.

1. The Needs Assessment - In developing its plan, your state must consider the needs of all residents and all geographic areas of the state. This assessment is to take place before a proposed plan is published.

The federal government does not say how the needs assessment is to be done. In many states, in the first year it was an informal collection of information rather than a careful analysis and documentation of what services were needed, what was available, and where the gaps existed. For example, some states simply circulated questionnaires and asked interested citizens to check which services they thought were most important in their community. In other places, public meetings were held. Still another form of "assessment" was to ask various state agencies to identify needs. Obviously, the results of such random assessments depend directly upon the ability of specific interest groups to weight the process in their favor. Thus, if child care advocates fill out the most questionnaires, or have the largest attendance at public meetings, then the assessment will show child care to be a high priority need.

Some states are beginning to develop more systematic methods for assessing needs. Particularly where this is the case, the needs assessment will have significant influence on the proposed plan. Whatever the process, this is a critical stage for child advocates to make certain that the state agency has strong documentation of the needs for children's services and that those needs are given full attention in the development of the proposed plan.

2. Raising the Non-Federal Share - To get federal Title XX funds, your state must have one dollar for every three dollars it claims. If this matching money is not available, then it will not make much difference what services are included in the plan or how high the eligibility levels are set.

One source of matching money is state appropriations. The process and the timing for appropriating state funds differ from state to state. Generally, at the beginning of a new session of the state legislature, the Governor submits a budget which includes whatever money he/she wants appropriated for social services. Responsibility for acting on the budget is assigned to one or more committees in each house and ultimately, the entire legislature votes on the level of state funding for the program.

Advocates must make certain that the budget which the Governor submits is adequate to meet the needs for children's services and that the budget which the legislature ultimately approves includes all of those funds. Many legislatures will complete action on the budget before the proposed social services plan is published. You must know when and how the appropriations process works in your state.

Not all matching funds come from state appropriations. States may use -- and some require -- county and local funds. Some states accept private donated funds -- from United Way or other community fund-raising activities. At the same time you are trying to influence the state plan, you should be attempting to raise local or private matching funds, and should make certain that the state agency will accept such funds as part of the non-federal share. (Obviously, this is not necessary if you are certain that the state appropriation is high enough to meet the entire matching requirement.)

Again, even if the state plan finally includes the children's services you need in your community or allows the expansion of those services, if you do not have the matching money and cannot get it from the state, the plan may not mean very much. Further, the state agency may refuse to include such services in the plan unless it is clear that the matching money is available.

B. PUBLICATION OF THE PROPOSED PLAN AND THE PUBLIC COMMENT PERIOD

Your state's proposed plan must be published at least 90 days before the new program year begins. Some states start their new program year on July 1 -- which means their proposed plans must be published by April 2. In other states the program year begins on October 1, so there the proposed plans must be published by July 2. (Appendix A shows the beginning of the program year in each state. However, some states have indicated they may change their program year; you should check with your state agency to make certain the date is still the same as it appears in this Handbook.)

You have a right to see your state's plan. At a minimum, federal law requires that your state do the following.

On April 2 or July 2 (depending on your state's program year), a display ad must appear in the newspaper of widest circulation in your area, and in foreign language newspapers if that is appropriate. This ad will tell you:

-- where and how to comment on the proposed plan,

-- the toll-free number to call for a free detailed summary of the plan,

-- the address of a local public office (for example, the post office or the court house) where you can get the summary, and

-- the address of the local public office where you can look at the complete plan and can purchase it at a reasonable cost.

(If you miss the ad, you can get all of this information by contacting the State office listed in Appendix C, or you may be able to get it at the local welfare office. Most public libraries keep back issues of newspapers -- you can also check there.)

You also have a right to submit to your state agency written comments on the plan, for at least 45 days after it is published. All of the comments which the state receives must be made available for public inspection.

Although public hearings are not required by federal law, in the first year many states did hold such hearings in order to receive citizen reactions to the plan. You should insist on such hearings, with wide advance notice to the public, and should make certain that children's interests are adequately represented whenever these hearings occur.

Remember, both the quality and the quantity of the comments, submitted in writing and presented at public hearings, will have an impact on the final plan. They should be specific, and they should come from a variety of interested persons -- consumers, providers, and concerned citizens. Copies of your comments and testimony should be sent to other influential people in your community and state; for example, the governor, your state legislators, your Congressperson or Senator, your local newspaper, the regional office of HEW. They can help you get the changes you seek.

C. AFTER THE FINAL PLAN IS PUBLISHED

Following the 45-day comment period and before the beginning of the new program year, the state must publish its final plan, using the same procedures (display advertisements, toll-free telephone numbers, distribution through local public offices) as for the proposed plan. The state agency must explain any changes that were made, and must summarize the public comments it received.

Your job is not over once the final plan is published. On the contrary, this is perhaps the most critical time for aggressive advocacy on behalf of children.

1. Monitoring the Plan - It is up to you to find out how the plan is working -- whether the state is actually providing the services described in the plan, and what kinds of problems are developing. This is essential to assure that families in your area receive the services to which they are entitled and that community institutions have an opportunity to provide those services. It is also crucial that you know how the current plan is working in order to work for improvements, either through amendments to the existing plan or through changes in the plans for next year.

2. Amending the Final Plan - The state may make changes in the plan even after it is published in final form. To do this, the state agency must publish a proposed amendment and follow the same public procedure as it did when it published the proposed plan in the first place -- except that the period for public comment is 30 days. The state must go through this formal amending process in order to make any substantial changes -- for example, to provide a new service, to change eligibility, to create a fee schedule, to expand a service into a new geographic area.

Amendments can be made at any time during the program year. If you did not get everything you wanted in the final plan, then you should work to amend the plan -- using the evidence you can collect through monitoring to support your arguments. In addition, you should watch for amendments proposed by others, and be prepared to comment on them if they will affect children's services.

PART II: WHAT TO LOOK FOR IN YOUR STATE'S SOCIAL SERVICES PROGRAM

This section of the Handbook is divided according to the major issues which will affect the delivery of services to children. It suggests questions for you to ask about your own state's program; you will think of others. You can get some answers by looking at the plan, but to get a complete picture of what is actually happening, you will need to talk to the state agency, to providers, and to recipients of services.

A. THE FUNDS

(See Appendix A for figures on your state's allotment and its planned expenditures for the first program year.)

1. Is your state planning to use its full allotment of federal funds? If not, why not?

2. Did your state actually use all of the federal money it estimated it would use in this year's plan? If not, why not?

3. Does your state plan to spend any more for social services in the coming year? the same? less?

4. Where is your state getting its matching money now?

   (a) From state appropriations? How much? Did the state agency get as much as it requested from the state legislature?

   (b) From county or local funds? How much?

   (c) From private contributions? If so, from what sources?

5. Will there be any change in the source of matching in the coming year?

6. Is the state having difficulty raising its matching share? If so, has it explored all possibilities? Is there any surplus in the state treasury? Is the state willing to use private donated funds?

7. Are Title XX funds fairly distributed within the state? Are areas with the greatest need (e.g. concentration of low-income families, lack of current services) getting the largest share?

B. ELIGIBILITY

1. How much money can a family have and still get services? What does the percentage of median income mean in actual dollars? (See Appendix A for your state's median income. Eligibility can be set at any point up to 115 percent of that figure.)

2. Are there any eligibility requirements in addition to income?

3. Do these income (and other) limits exclude any children and families who are presently receiving services?

4. Do these limits exclude children and families who need services? If so, how would you change them?

5. How does eligibility for children's services (for example, child care) compare with eligibility for other services? Is it fair?

6. Who determines eligibility? Is the process efficient? If not, how can it be improved?

   (a) Has the state delegated eligibility determinations to providers of services?

   (b) Are the forms as simple as they can be? Is the state asking for more information than the absolute minimum necessary to determine eligibility? (Federal regulations permit the state to use a simple self-declaration method, without elaborate documentation or verification of income.)

7. Is the state providing information and referral services and protective services for children without regard to income? Do protective services include such things as child care?

C. FEES

1. Is there a fee schedule for services? for children's services specifically?

2. How do fees for children's services compare with fees for other services? Are they fair?

3. At what income level does the state start charging fees? Is that too low? too high? (The state must charge a fee if income exceeds 80 percent of the median.)

4. How much will the fees be? Will the state be charging families more than they can afford to pay?

5. Do the fees take into account family size?

6. Is there a maximum total fee for a family receiving more than one service?

7. Will the fee schedule discourage families from using services?

8. Is there any danger that use of a fee schedule might operate to shift services away from the poorest families for whom the state must pay the entire bill?

D. SERVICES

1. What services for children and families are provided for your community?

2. Are these the services which are most needed?

3. Are there any needed services which are missing from the plan? Are they available to families in other parts of the state?

4. Does the plan describe the services well enough to understand exactly what will be provided in your

area? Does it tell how many people will be served? Who will be eligible? Whether there will be fees charged? Who will provide the services?

5. Will the plan allow expansion of services in your area or does it only include those services which are already there?

6. Does the state provide any technical assistance to community groups who are trying to provide services?

E. ADVISORY COMMITTEES

1. Does your state have an advisory committee on social services?

2. Who is on the committee? How are they selected? How many are child advocates? parents? community representatives?

3. How often does the committee meet? Are its meetings open to the public? Are minutes of the meetings available?

F. CHILD DAY CARE SERVICES

This section suggests additional questions to ask about child care specifically. They could be modified for other children's services which you might want to examine in more detail. (See Appendix B for details on child care taken from the states' first year plans.)

1. Are there special eligibility conditions for child care in addition to income limits? (For example, must both parents work? Can students qualify? Is it limited to single-parent households?)

2. Is child care available only to let parents work, or can it be provided for other purposes? (For example, for retarded or handicapped children, in circumstances of family stress, as a protective service to prevent neglect or abuse.)

3. How much is being spent on child care in your state? How much is being spent per child? (You can get a

very rough idea of this by dividing the total dollars being spent by the number of children being served.) Is this per child expenditure adequate to assure quality care?

4. What is the level of reimbursement a child care provider receives? (This is usually a payment per child per day.) Does it vary from place to place within the state? Is it adequate to pay for good care? Are providers receiving their payments from the state on time?

5. Where are services being provided? In centers? In family day care homes?

6. Are the child care facilities licensed? Are federal child care standards being met? What is the ratio of staff to children?

7. Are child care services meeting particular family needs; for example, for infant or school-age care? for night-time care?

8. Are the subsidized facilities distributed within your community and state so that they are available where the need is?

PART III: STRATEGIES FOR INFLUENCING YOUR STATE'S TITLE XX PROGRAM

A. GET YOUR FACTS TOGETHER

1. Do Your Own Needs Assessment - Put together specific, detailed evidence about the needs for children's services in your community, geographic area, and/or state. Interview child care operators to find out about waiting lists. Conduct a survey of parents to find out what kind of services they need and want, and what kinds of problems they have in finding those services (e.g. none available, too expensive, not eligible). Do a survey of agencies providing services for children to find out where they are, what they are offering, and what is missing. Evaluate the quality of care children are receiving. Analyze Census Bureau data, talk to manpower agencies, interview employers, to determine how many working mothers there are who need child care services.

2. Analyze the Current Title XX Plan - Identify the strengths and weaknesses of the current state plan. Decide which provisions you need to change, and which ones you may have to fight to retain. Find out whether the state is actually providing the services described in the plan.

3. Develop Your Priorities for Action - Decide which problems need the most attention first. For example, is it most important to expand eligibility? to install (or get rid of) a fee schedule? to change policies on use of private matching funds? to raise reimbursement rates for child care? to provide additional services? Prepare specific recommendations for the state agency, using the evidence you gathered in your needs assessment to support your arguments.

B. GET YOUR FRIENDS TOGETHER

This is not a job you can do by yourself. There are probably lots of individuals and groups who will help, if you find out who they are and get them together.

1. Locate All of Your Potential Allies - For example, if your issue is child care, begin with other child care programs in the state. Be sure to involve parents -- they are your most important resource. Other groups which have a direct stake in child care -- like women's organizations and labor unions -- are natural allies, as are the churches and other organizations traditionally concerned with human services. You will probably find also that many of your concerns about the state plan are shared by groups interested in other services, like the aged or the handicapped. Elected officials and other public figures can be particularly helpful in getting access to the state agency and in generating publicity.

Get a name for your coalition -- it helps the state agency and the press keep track of who you are and what you are doing.

2. Set Up a Communications System - Once you have located all of your allies, you have to be able to keep them informed. And you must be able to mobilize them to action on short notice -- when there are letters to write, comments to file, meetings or hearings to attend, rallies or marches to organize. If the group is large and spread around the state, it might be practical to set up a network of key individuals whom you can contact and who, in turn, can get in touch with the rest of the people in their own parts of the state. You may find it useful to start a simple newsletter.

C. GET THE MEDIA INVOLVED

Your local newspaper, radio and television station are always looking for news stories. Get them to write or talk about your activities, and get them to do their own stories about the effect of Title XX on programs, children and families in your community. Invite reporters to your meetings. Get television cameras into your child care centers. Take advantage of local "talk shows" to discuss Title XX.

D. GET A COMMITMENT FROM THE STATE AGENCY TO INCLUDE YOU IN THE TITLE XX PROCESS

If you are going to influence what the state agency is doing, you have to know what is going on. Set up a meeting with a top official in the state agency and get a commitment to include you in the process at every stage. Demand invitations to planning sessions, direct participation in the needs assessment, advance notice of public meetings and hearings and, especially, formal membership on any planning or advisory committees. Your own representatives in the state legislature and other elected officials can be especially helpful here. You should ask them for their support.

The calendar on the following pages suggests a timetable for your activities. If you have not already done so, get started today.

PART IV: EXAMPLES OF EFFECTIVE CHILD ADVOCACY

A. KANSAS

The Kansas experience demonstrates the importance of (1) early involvement in the state's planning process, (2) a statewide network of child advocates, (3) direct efforts to raise local matching funds, and (4) cooperation with agencies interested in other types of social services.

The Wichita Child Day Care Association, an established non-profit organization, serves as an umbrella for the delivery of child care services in that city and maintains a network of child advocates around the state. That network includes child care operators, parents and interested organizations such as women's groups and churches.

When Title XX became law in January 1975, the Association went to the state agency, through its representatives in the

A TITLE XX CALENDAR FOR CHILD ADVOCATES

*(Note: This calendar is based on a Title XX program year beginning July 1. If your state's year begins on October 1, change the months accordingly. October becomes January, April 2 is July 2, etc.)

	OCTOBER	NOVEMBER	DECEMBER	JANUARY	FEBRUARY	MARCH
APPROPRIATIONS	State budget is prepared. Title XX agency submits recommendations to Governor for appropriations for state matching funds for coming fiscal year.		Governor's office completes work on budget for coming fiscal year.	Governor submits budget to state legislature. Legislature holds hearings on budget; votes on appropriations for coming fiscal year. (Exact timing will vary from state to state)		
PLANNING PROCESS	Preliminary work begins on needs assessment for coming program year.			Needs assessment in process. Title XX agency begins drafting new Title XX plan for coming program year.		
ADVOCATES ACTION	Start your own needs assessment. Meet with state agency to discuss its needs assessment; get a timetable for their assessment. Meet with Title XX agency to discuss budget recommendations. Submit your own estimates of appropriations needed.		Submit your needs assessment to the state agency. Meet with Governor's office to support (or to urge increases in) the Title XX agency's budget recommendations.	Meet with state agency to get your recommendations into the proposed plan, and to discuss the planning process. Get dates and places for hearings Submit evidence to state legislature about need for appropriations for Title XX matching. Meet with your own legislators. Testify at hearings on the budget If state appropriations will not be adequate to cover matching requirements, start raising other funds from local and county officials and from private sources.	Write to all legislators in support of the Title XX appropriations.	

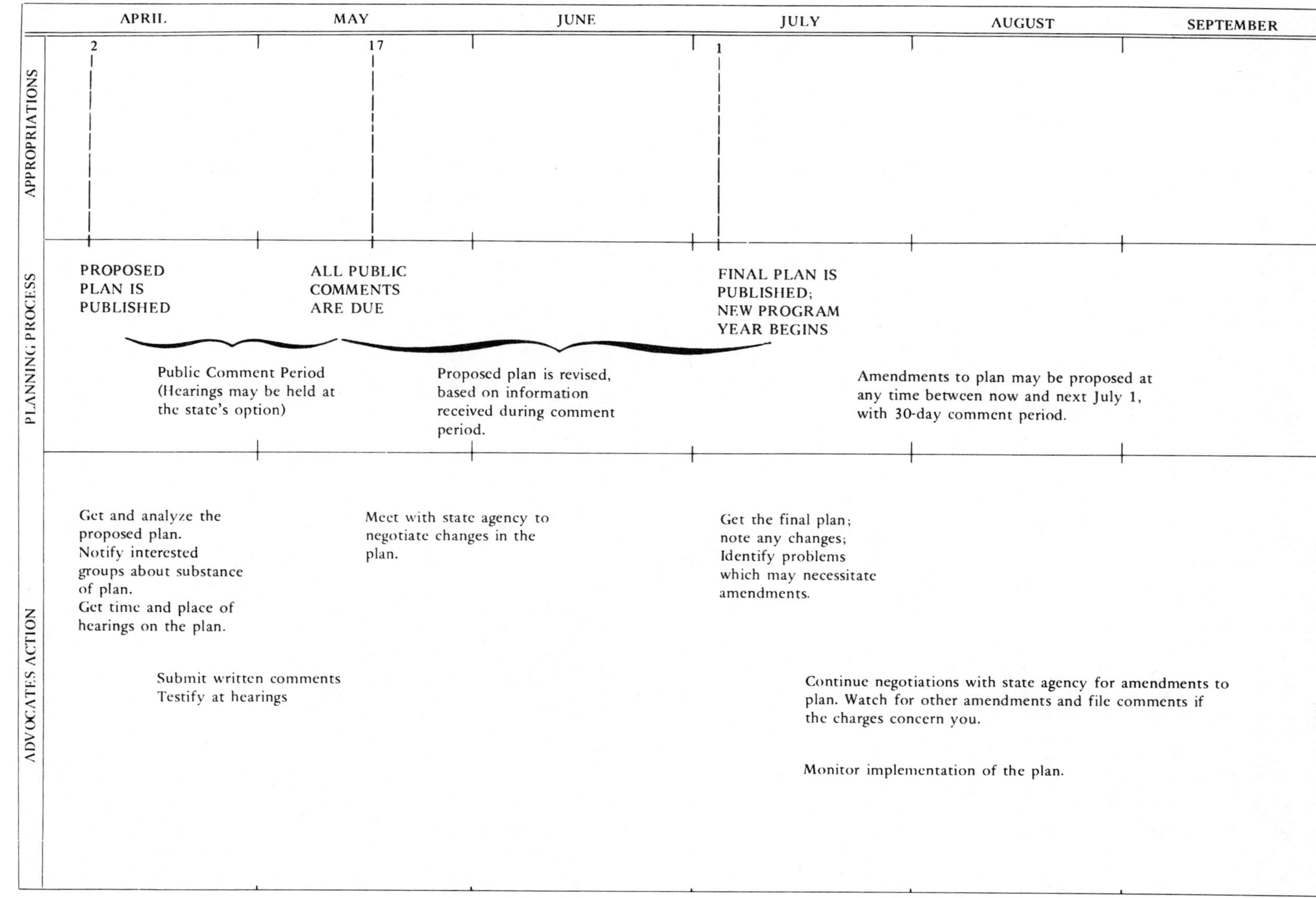
APRIL
MAY
JUNE
JULY
AUGUST
SEPTEMBER
APPROPRIATIONS
2
17
1
PLANNING PROCESS
PROPOSED PLAN IS PUBLISHED
ALL PUBLIC COMMENTS ARE DUE
FINAL PLAN IS PUBLISHED; NEW PROGRAM YEAR BEGINS
Public Comment Period (Hearings may be held at the state's option)
Proposed plan is revised, based on information received during comment period.
Amendments to plan may be proposed at any time between now and next July 1, with 30-day comment period.
ADVOCATES ACTION
Get and analyze the proposed plan. Notify interested groups about substance of plan. Get time and place of hearings on the plan.
Meet with state agency to negotiate changes in the plan.
Get the final plan; note any changes; Identify problems which may necessitate amendments.
Submit written comments
Testify at hearings
Continue negotiations with state agency for amendments to plan. Watch for other amendments and file comments if the charges concern you.
Monitor implementation of the plan.

legislature, and demanded a role in the state's planning process from the outset. The agency agreed, and the Wichita group used its access to maximize involvement of child advocates across the state. Thus, when the state agency invited the Association to an early planning session, more than 50 advocates from all parts of the state appeared. When the agency announced it would hold 36 hearings across the state as part of its prepublication needs assessment, the network was used to publicize the hearings and to organize participation. In some areas, child advocates were the only people to attend. As a result, the state concluded that child care was one of the services which people in Kansas needed most.

After publishing the proposed plan, the state agency scheduled three hearings at the state capitol. Child care providers, parents, and other advocates participated in all of those hearings, from beginning to end. The success of these activities is evidenced in the final Title XX plan in Kansas, which includes $11.9 million for child care and extends services to more families through the use of a fee schedule at higher income levels. Child advocates are working now to raise reimbursement rates.

In addition to this statewide mobilization, the Wichita Association was at work in its own county, raising local matching funds for child care and developing a coordinated approach to the state plan. To avoid competition for limited funds, the Association turned to the Community Planning Council of the United Fund. The Planning Council agreed to hold a series of meetings at which all service agencies and interested groups worked together to develop priorities for services in the county, drawing together facts and statistics to support those services. From that process came a multiple services proposal for the county, which was submitted to the state agency; much of it was incorporated into the state plan.

In response to the overwhelming interest shown throughout the state, once the first plan was finalized, the state agency created a task force to develop a five-year plan for child care. That task force included 15 individuals from the network, including two from the Wichita Association. That long-range plan has been completed and will form the basis for adjustments to the Title XX program in the coming years.

For further information, contact:

Wichita Child Day Care Association
216 East Second Street
Wichita, Kansas 67202
316/265-0871

B. TEXAS

In Texas, efforts by child advocates to influence Title XX began well before the federal law was enacted. Child care providers contracting with the state agency under the old Title IV-A system had already organized an association to deal with the federal law and the Texas Department of Public Welfare. In addition, a statewide mobilization known as Child Care '76 was underway, to increase the visibility of child care as a public issue.

Closely watching the progress of the proposed Title XX legislation at the federal level, these groups went to work in the state legislature and the state agency to assure that Texas would be ready to implement the new law. By the time Title XX took effect in October 1975, state legislation had been passed to deal with issues like pre-payments to providers and audit systems. What is more, child advocates had achieved statewide recognition for their knowledge of Title XX. They were in a strong position to claim full representation on the state's Advisory Committee on Social Services, and were included on each of nine Task Forces set up by the state agency to examine various aspects of Title XX and to prepare the state's plan for social services.

The influence of child advocates was reflected in the proposed plan, in the percentage of funds allotted for child care, the decision to prevent refinancing of state expenditures for services, and the expansion of eligibility from an originally proposed level of less than 40 percent up to a finally agreed level of 60 percent of the state's median income.

Once the proposed plan had been published, advocates used the public comment period to focus on what they had identified as the single largest remaining problem with the plan -- the fee schedule, which failed to give adequate consideration to the wide variations in living costs throughout a state as big and diverse as Texas. The short-term effect of those efforts was to eliminate all fee schedules for the first program year. They are working now to devise a flexible fee schedule which will meet federal requirements.

Since publication of the first year's final plan, child care providers formed a coalition with other services providers, particularly with family planning and senior citizens groups, to work on Title XX issues in the state and to influence federal policies on issues such as eligibility determination.

Child advocates attribute their success in Texas to two factors: first, a sophisticated communications system which linked providers, parents, and individuals and groups broadly representative of the community; and second, serious homework on Title XX issues and developments in Washington, which have made child advocates the most informed participants in the state's planning process. In the words of one leader of the effort, the Title XX planning period was a "time of confusion" and "child care groups controlled the confusion."

For further information, contact:

Child Care 76
818 East Fifty-third
Austin, Texas 78751
512/451-7361

C. ILLINOIS

In Illinois, leadership on Title XX came from a non-profit community-based child advocacy group, the Day Care Crisis Council of Chicago. The Crisis Council includes child care providers, staff, and parents, and a range of women's organizations, civic, neighborhood and church groups, which represent a cross section of the entire community.

The Illinois advocacy effort was characterized by early involvement; persistence, even after the final plan had been published; development of specific proposals as alternatives to the state plan; effective publicity; and mobilization of broad support from all parts of the state, including among others the director of the state's Office of Child Development, the State Advisory Committee on Day Care, and members of Congress and the state legislature. Demands for changes in the plan went not just to the state Title XX agency, but to the Governor as well.

At the outset, the Council insisted on public hearings as part of the state's needs assessment process and then, a second set of hearings once the proposed plan had been published. Attention at these hearings focused on eligibility for child care. The proposed plan would have limited child care to purposes directly related to employment or training. The Crisis Council developed its own five categories of eligibility for both single and two-parent families -- protective services in cases of actual or potential child abuse, services necessary for the parents to maintain employment, services necessary because of retardation or medical or psychological needs of the child, services to allow parents to enroll in training or to seek employment and for students, and preventive services to avoid family stress. That proposal was circulated statewide. Virtually every witness at the hearings spoke in favor of it and the State Day Care Advisory Committee endorsed it. The final plan included the five classifications developed by the Council.

Another central issue was the question of fee schedules. Witnesses at the hearings testified in support of fees at a level which eligible families could afford to pay. However, the final plan included a fee schedule which left some families paying as much as $26 a week for Title XX child care. Child advocates mounted an immediate protest, in the form of communications to state agencies and the Governor, particularly by parents, and through the press. At least one member of Congress joined in that effort. In response to the overwhelming public pressure, the state amended its final plan to set a maximum fee of $11 a week for a family, regardless of the number of children in care.

Presently, the Council is working to simplify the eligibility forms which the state is requiring applicants to complete, to protect the confidentiality of the information collected for Title XX purposes, and to keep it out of the state's computerized welfare information system. The Council has developed its own eligibility form which it is pressuring the state to adopt, and it has real hope of success.

For further information, contact:

The Day Care Crisis Council
201 North Wells, Room 642
Chicago, Illinois 60606
312/332-1721

APPENDIX A

TITLE XX FEDERAL ALLOCATIONS, USE, AND MEDIAN INCOME – BY STATE

		FY76 ALLOCATION (in millions)	ESTIMATED FY76 USE (in millions)[1]	FY77 ALLOCATION (in millions)	FY77 MEDIAN INCOME (for family of four)
*	Alabama	$ 42.25	$ 42.25	$ 42.30	$ 12,805
	Alaska	4.00	3.90	3.975	19,368
*	Arizona	24.50	9.55	25.45	15,230
	Arkansas	24.25	19.76	24.375	11,890
	California	245.50	245.50	247.25	15,931
	Colorado	29.00	29.00	29.525	15,629
	Connecticut	36.75	36.75	36.525	16,476
	Delaware	6.75	6.75	6.775	15,231
*	District of Columbia	9.00	9.00	8.55	15,093
	Florida	91.50	91.50	95.675	14,788
*	Georgia	57.00	57.00	57.725	13,666
#	Hawaii	10.00	10.00	10.025	17.069
	Idaho	9.25	9.25	9.45	14,075
#	Illinois	133.75	133.75	131.65	16,350
#	Indiana	63.25	30.60	63.025	14,478
	Iowa	34.50	34.50	33.775	14,371
	Kansas	27.25	27.25	26.85	14,395
	Kentucky	39.75	39.75	39.70	12,514
#	Louisiana	44.75	44.75	44.525	12,600
#	Maine	12.25	12.25	12.375	12,552
	Maryland	48.50	48.50	48.425	16,650
	Massachusetts	69.25	69.25	68.60	15,630
*	Michigan	107.75	107.75	107.575	16,174
*	Minnesota	46.50	46.50	46.325	15,792
	Mississippi	27.25	12.60	27.475	11,562
	Missouri	56.75	54.05	56.50	13,770
#	Montana	8.50	8.50	8.70	13,686
	Nebraska	18.25	18.23	18.25	13,364
#	Nevada	6.50	6.30	6.775	15,357
	New Hampshire	9.50	9.22	9.55	13,986
	New Jersey	87.75	87.75	86.70	16,727
*	New Mexico	13.25	13.25	13.275	12,143
*	New York	217.50	217.50	214.20	15,169
	North Carolina	62.75	62.75	63.425	13,183
#	North Dakota	7.50	7.50	7.525	15,005
	Ohio	127.75	127.75	126.975	15,121
#	Oklahoma	31.75	31.75	32.05	12,645
#	Oregon	26.50	26.50	26.80	15,013
	Pennsylvania	141.75	141.75	139.975	14,489
	Rhode Island	11.50	11.50	11.075	14,404
	South Carolina	32.50	32.50	32.925	13,055
*	South Dakota	8.25	7.68	8.075	12,824
	Tennessee	49.25	49.25	48.825	12,788
*	Texas	140.50	140.50	142.50	13,924
	Utah	13.75	13.75	13.897	14,003
*	Vermont	5.50	5.50	5.55	13,145
	Virginia	57.25	57.25	58.05	15,130
	Washington	40.75	40.75	41.10	15,401
	West Virginia	21.50	21.50	21.175	12,569
#	Wisconsin	54.50	54.50	54.00	15,398
	Wyoming	4.25	3.71	4.25	14,833

* Program year begins October 1
\# No new program year until July 1, 1977
All other states begin program year on July 1, 1976

1/ from the states' final Comprehensive Annual Services Program Plans published October 1, 1975, as analyzed by the Office of the Assistant Secretary for Planning and Evaluation (HEW). These are estimates and do not necessarily represent actual expenditures.

APPENDIX B

CHILD DAY CARE EXPENDITURES IN FIRST PROGRAM YEAR, BY STATE

	CHILD CARE EXPENDITURES (in millions)	CHILD CARE AS % OF TOTAL PROGRAM	NUMBER OF CHILDREN SERVED	AVERAGE COST PER CHILD	ELIGIBILITY (% OF MEDIAN INCOME)	% AT WHICH FEES ARE CHARGED
* Alabama	$ 16.51	29.4%	17,848	$ 925	55%	
Alaska	.44	10.8	530	835	AFDC/SSI	
Arizona	4.03	42.2	10,825	373	61	
Arkansas	8.56	41.7	5,276	1,623	79	
California	46.90	18.3	55,440	846	84	50%
Colorado	5.74	19.9	9,660@	198	80@	33
Connecticut**	8.08	18.3	7,360	1,098	115	46
Delaware	3.72	55.2	2,350	1,585	76	48
* District of Columbia	2.90	21.3	3,175	912	80	50
Florida	14.23	8.9	12,660	1,124	60	39
* Georgia	17.84	24.3	14,704	1,213	61	
# Hawaii	7.00	29.5	4,853	1,442	60	
Idaho	.45	5.1	974	458	80	
# Illinois	95.89	30.7	179,000	536	80	52
# Indiana	10.45	14.6	4,050	2,581	50	
Iowa	3.93	11.4	18,836	209	80	
Kansas**	8.25	30.0	5,160	1,599	115	80
Kentucky	2.49	6.3	2,350	1,061	80	22
# Louisiana	22.22	23.7	43,931	506	48.4	
# Maine	4.30	15.4	3,801	1,131	80	
Maryland	12.36	24.4	6,825	1,811	105	40
Massachusetts	21.57	23.6	19,545	1,104	69	
* Michigan	41.17	28.7	44,600	923	80	22
* Minnesota	9.88	15.9	28,381	348	115	60
Mississippi**	5.99	48.0	2,439	2,457	115	80
Missouri	9.37	17.4	35,751	262	80	
# Montana	2.87	14.6	2,208	1,301	150% of AFDC	
Nebraska	3.91	32.5	2,400	@	62	44
# Nevada	.63	4.3	6,925	91	63	
New Hampshire**	3.00	32.9	2,614	1,151	80	53
New Jersey	37.82	32.7	25,984	1,455	80	
* New Mexico	5.22	30.0	3,915	1,333	49	all
* New York	158.98	52.2	75,730	2,099	80	
North Carolina	26.70	34.4	36,328	735	100	65
# North Dakota	.27	2.1	515	519	80	40
Ohio	25.46	18.8	58,871	430	80	51
# Oklahoma**	14.72	19.9	42,404	347	80	50
# Oregon	(Day Care not identified as separate service in plan)				115	80
* Pennsylvania	57.68	30.6	19,868	2,903	115	80
Rhode Island	1.57	13.2	5,644	278	54	
* South Carolina	7.55	16.0	4,500	1,678	80	
* South Dakota	1.46	12.4	2,917	1,862	60	40
Tennessee**	8.52	17.3	19,160	445	70	46
* Texas	34.16	18.4	21,757	1,570	60	
Utah	2.42	16.5	4,000	604	74	AFDC needs standard
* Vermont	2.27	31.1	1,640	1,383	80	50
Virginia	9.60	17.4	27,367	350	50	
Washington	6.55	16.2	13,051	502	32	
West Virginia	5.42	24.3	7,601	713	80	37
# Wisconsin**	10.94	8.0	9,900	1,105	100	64
Wyoming	.75	20.1	6,000	125	60	

* Figures are for a 12-month first program year
\# Figures are for a 21-month first program year
All other figures are for a 9-month first program year

@ Colorado: Number of children served and per child cost are for one quarter only

Nebraska: HEW could not establish per child estimates

** State plan does not distinguish between child day care and adult day care

Note: The figures in this chart include only what state's specifically identified as "day care for children". There may be other child care included in other services, such as "special services for handicapped children", "protective services", etc.

Source: Technical Notes #3, #4, and Appendix, prepared by Office of Assistant Secretary for Planning and Evaluation, January 1976 - based on analysis of final state plans

APPENDIX C

YOUR STATE AGENCY FOR TITLE XX

Mrs. Julia Oliver, Commissioner
State Department of Pensions and Security
64 North Union Street
Montgomery, Alabama 36104

Dr. Francis S. L. Williamson, Comm.
Dept. of Health and Social Services
Putch H
Juneau, Alaska 99801

William J. Mayo, Director
State Dept. of Economic Security
1515 West Jefferson
Phoenix, Arizona 85005

Dr. Roger B. Bost, Director
Dept. of Social and Rehabilitation Serv.
406 National Old Line Insurance Bldg.
Little Rock, Arkansas 72201

Mario Obledo, Secretary
State of California Health and
Welfare Agency
915 Capitol Mall, Room 200
Sacramento, California 95184

Henry Roley, Exec. Director
Department of Social Services
1575 Sherman Street
Denver, Colorado 80203

Edward M. Maher, Commissioner
State Welfare Department
110 Bartholomew Avenue
Hartford, Connecticut 06106

Mr. Earl McGinnes, Secretary
Dept. of Health and Social Services
Delaware State Hospital
New Castle, Delaware 19720

Mr. Joseph Yeldell, Director*
Department of Human Resources
District Building
14th and E Streets, N.W.
Washington, D.C. 20004

William J. Page, Jr., Secretary
Dept. of Health and Rehabilitative Serv.
1323 Winewood Boulevard
Tallahassee, Florida 32301

Mr. T. M. Jim Parham
Acting Commissioner
Department of Human Resources
State Office Building
Atlanta, Georgia 30334

Andrew I. T. Chang, Director
Dept. of Social Services and Housing
P. O. Box 339
Honolulu, Hawaii 96809

Dr. James A. Bax, Administrator
Department of Health and Welfare
State House
Boise, Idaho 83720

James L. Trainor, Acting Director
Department of Public Aid
222 College Street
Springfield, Illinois 62706

Wayne A. Stanton, Administrator
Dept. of Public Welfare
State Office Building, Room 701
100 North Senate Avenue
Indianapolis, Indiana 46204

Kevin Burns, Commissioner
Department of Social Services
Lucas State Office Building
Des Moines, Iowa 50319

Dr. Robert C. Harder, Secretary
Dept. of Social and Rehabilitation
Services
State Office Building
Topeka, Kansas 66612

Mr. C. Leslie Dawson, Secretary
Department for Human Resources
Capitol Building Annex - Room 201
Frankfort, Kentucky 40601

Dr. William H. Stewart, Comm.
Health and Human Resources
Administration
Post Office Box 44215
Baton Rouge, Louisiana 70804

David E. Smith, Commissioner
State Department of Health and Welfare
State House
Augusta, Maine 04330

Richard A. Batterton, Secretary
Dept. of Human Resources
1100 North Eutaw Street
Baltimore, Maryland 21201

Jerald L. Stevens, Commissioner*
Department of Public Welfare
600 Washington Street
Boston, Massachusetts 02111

Dr. John T. Dempsey, Director
Michigan Department of Social Services
Commerce Center Building
300 South Capitol Avenue
Lansing, Michigan 48936

Vera Likins, Commissioner
Minnesota Dept. of Public Welfare
Centennial Building
658 Cedar Street
St. Paul, Minnesota 55155

Max M. Cole, Commissioner
State Dept. of Public Welfare
P. O. Box 4321
Fondren Station
Jackson, Mississippi 39216

Cleighton Penwell, Director
Department of Human Resources
318 Public Service Building
Salem, Oregon 97310

Mr. Frank S. Beal, Secretary
Department of Public Welfare
Health and Welfare Building
Harrisburg, Pennsylvania 17120

John J. Affleck, Director
Dept. of Social and Rehabilitation Serv.
Aime J. Forand
State Office Building
600 New London Avenue
Cranston, Rhode Island 02920

Dr. R. Archie Ellis, Commissioner
Department of Social Services
P. O. Box 1520
Columbia, South Carolina 29202

Dr. Frijthjof O. M. Westby, Secretary
Department of Social Services
State Capitol Building
Pierre, South Dakota 57501

Horace Bass, Commissioner
State Department of Public Welfare
204 State Office Building
Nashville, Tennessee 37219

Raymond W. Vowell, Commissioner
State Department of Public Welfare
John H. Reagan Building
Austin, Texas 78701

Paul S. Rose, Executive Director
Department of Social Services
221 State Capitol
Salt Lake City, Utah 84114

Thomas Davis, Secretary
Agency of Human Services
State Office Building
Montpelier, Vermont 05602

William L. Lukhard, Commissioner
Department of Welfare
8007 Discovery Drive
Richmond, Virginia 23288

Charles R. Morris, Secretary
Department of Social and Health Services
Post Office Box 1788
Olympia, Washington 98504

Mr. Thomas R. Tinder, Commissioner
Department of Welfare
1900 Washington Street, East
Charleston, West Virginia 25305

Wilbur J. Schmidt, Secretary
Dept. of Health and Social Services
1 West Wilson Street
Madison, Wisconsin 53702

Harvey Peterson, Act. Coordinator
Dept. of Health and Social Services
State Office Building West, Rm. 317
Cheyenne, Wyoming 82001

Lawrence L. Graham, Director
Department of Social Services
Broadway State Office Building
Jefferson City, Missouri 65101

Theodore P. Carkulis, Director
Dept. of Social and Rehabilitative Serv.
Post Office Box 1723
Helena, Montana 59601

Mr. Alan Ihons, Director
Department of Public Welfare
1526 K Street, Fourth Floor
Lincoln, Nebraska 68508

Roger S. Trounday, Director
Nevada State Dept. of Human Resources
Union Federal Building
308 North Curry Street
Carson City, Nevada 89701

Frank E. Whaland, Commissioner
Department of Health and Welfare
State House Annex
Concord, New Hampshire 03301

Mrs. Ann Klein, Commissioner
Dept. of Institutions and Agencies
135 West Hanover Street
Trenton, New Jersey 08625

Richard W. Heim, Exec. Director
Health and Social Services Dept.
Post Office Box 2348
PERA Building
Santa Fe, New Mexico 87503

Steven Berger, Commissioner
Department of Social Services
1450 Western Avenue
Albany, New York 12203

David T. Flaherty, Secretary
Department of Human Resources
325 N. Salisbury Street
Raleigh, North Carolina 27611

T. N. Tangedahl, Exec. Dir.
Social Service Board of North Dakota
State Capitol Building
Bismarck, North Dakota 58501

Raymond F. McKenna, Director
Ohio Department of Public Welfare
30 East Broad Street
State Office Tower
32nd Floor
Columbus, Ohio 43215

Lloyd E. Rader, Director
Dept. of Institutions Social and Rehabilitative Services
Post Office Box 25352
Oklahoma City, Oklahoma 73125

APPENDIX D

YOUR H.E.W. REGIONAL OFFICE

Region I - (Maine, Vermont New Hampshire Massachusetts Rhode Island Connecticut)	Robert F. Ott Associate Regional Commissioner, CS John F. Kennedy Federal Building Government Center DHEW/SRS Room 1300 Boston, Massachusetts 02203 (617-223-6867)
Region II - (New York New Jersey)	Dr. Melvin Herman Associate Regional Commissioner, CS Federal Building DHEW/SRS 26 Federal Plaza, Room 3840 New York, New York 10007 (212-264-4626)
Region III - (Pennsylvania Delaware Virginia West Virginia District of Columbia)	Maurice Meyer Associate Regional Commissioner, CS Gateway Building, DHEW/SRS 36th & Market Streets Post Office Box 7760 Philadelphia, Pennsylvania 19101 (215-596-1316)
Region IV - (North Carolina South Carolina Georgia Florida Kentucky Tennessee Mississippi Alabama)	Edwin E. Schultz, Acting Associate Regional Commissioner, CS DHEW/SRS 50 Seventh Street, N.E. Room 746 Atlanta, Georgia 30323 (404-526-3476)
Region V - (Ohio Indiana Illinois Michigan Wisconsin Minnesota)	Eli Lipschultz Associate Regional Commissioner, CS DHEW/SRS 30th Floor - 300 S. Wacker Drive Chicago, Illinois 60606 (312-353-4239)
Region VI - (Texas Louisiana New Mexico Oklahoma Arkansas)	Dr. Peggy R. Wildman Title XX Coordinator DHEW/SRS 1200 Main Tower, 20th Floor Dallas, Texas 75202 (214-655-4155)

Region X - (Washington Oregon Idaho Alaska)	Richard McConnell Chief Program Representative, CS Arcade Plaza Building, DHEW/SRS 1321 Second Avenue Seattle, Washington 98101 (206-442-0526)
Region VII - (Missouri Kansas Nebraska Iowa)	Bill Weisent Associate Regional Commissioner, CS Federal Office Building DHEW/SRS 601 East 12th Street, 5th Floor Kansas City, Missouri 64106 (816-374-5975)
Region VIII - (North Dakota South Dakota Montana Wyoming Colorado Utah)	Fred Lund, Acting Regional Social Services Program Director Federal Office Building, DHEW/SRS 19th and Stout Streets, Room 11037 Denver, Colorado 70202 (303-837-2141)
Region IX - (Hawaii California Nevada Arizona)	Charles R. Hall Associate Regional Commissioner, CS Federal Office Building, DHEW/SRS 50 Fulton Street, Room 469 San Francisco, California 94102 (415-556-7800)

Title XX: Social Services in Your State: A Child Advocate's Handbook for Action (April 1976 by the Children's Defense Fund of the Washington Research Project, Inc.: Washington, D.C.)

Child development

BABY CARRIERS IN BOLIVIA AND SWEDEN

by Kamala Ditella and John Lind

In recent times there has been an increased interest in the study of newborn infants. Although there have been great improvements in the medical care of the neonate, we are learning that the emotional atmosphere into which the infant is born is of great importance, due to their sensitivity and vulnerability. In the field of psychoanalysis, Anna Freud,[3] Melanie Klein,[5] Winnicott[11] and Bolby[1] are some of the scientists who have stressed the importance of the early experiences of the infant. The work of ethologists such as Lorenz, Hinde, Harlow and Tinbergen have led to similar conclusions.[4] From the pediatric world of Marshall Klaus and John Kennell[6] and many others we see that there is a need for physical closeness between mother and child and a need for stimulation in the development of the child.[10] The long-term deleterious effects of early separation of mother and infant are of increasing concern.

Western culture has formed a barrier between infants and parents through a superstitious belief in the good of strict physical hygiene and schedule feeding.[8] We have not been enough aware of the child's need for close contact with the parents from the beginning of his or her life. We have quite a lot of contrasting childcare data from other cultures.[7,9] In Sweden, after the introduction of the Japanese baby carrier, an investigation was carried out of the mother's attitude toward using this type of baby carrier, known as a *kodomó*.[2] The use of the baby carrier in Sweden is compared in this paper to that of the *aguawo*, a Bolivian baby carrier used in the Altiplano of Bolivia.

Kamala Ditella, M.D., *is a psychiatrist and child psychotherapist who trained and worked at the Tavistock Clinic in London, specializing in infant observation and newborns. She is a Consultant in the Hospital de Niños, Buenos Aires, Argentina.*

John Lind, M.D., *is Professor of Pediatrics Emeritus and former Chairman of the Department of Pediatrics, Karolinska Hospital, Stockholm, Sweden; Visiting Professor of Pediatrics, Downstate Medical Center, New York.*

The Baby Carrier in Sweden

In some maternity hospitals in Sweden, as well as in well-baby clinics, the mothers and fathers are given a chance to try out the baby carrier and find out if they and the baby like it. They are told that they can start using it from the second week, and can have the baby in the carrier as long as it pleases them. We have found that the baby carrier helps the mother keep in touch with the baby and be aware of the infant's moods. The Swedish mother who uses the baby carrier does not have the whole spectrum of worrying due to separation from her infant. It also helps toward a better understanding of the infant's needs, which can be met at an early stage, and thus diminish crying.[12] The baby carrier further helps reciprocal stimulation which facilitates an adequate feeding schedule, more enjoyment of the baby. We have observed that the baby carrier has reduced some of the emotional difficulties in child rearing.

In Sweden the carrier has been a revolution in infant transportation, especially in the cities in subways, trams, and buses. The baby carrier permits the parents to take the baby with them to many places such as outings, picnics, hiking, nature walks and shopping, and not be burdened and restricted by the baby.

The carrier has also strongly promoted the participation of the fathers in infant caring. The mother has carried the baby for nine months inside her, and with the baby carrier the father has access to a similar satisfaciton. The father, like the mother, can keep a close contact with the infant through the baby carrier, and continue most of his activities at home such as reading the newspaper, watching television, and relaxing.

The Baby Carrier in the Bolivian Altiplano

One of our investigators went to the Altiplano of Bolivia and observed that the Indian women, both the Quechua-speaking and the Aymara-speaking, carry their infants in the *aguawo* on their backs most of the time. The *aguawo* is a specially woven strong cotton cloth in bright colors. It is folded in a special way to make a comfortable baby carrier. The Indian women carry the infant in the *aguawo* on their backs and turn it around to several positions according to the age, and according to the states of wakefulness and sleep of the infant. In Bolivia the baby carrier is used usually from the second week after the birth of the infant when the mother is strong enough to walk and go out. This custom is continued until the child is sometimes three years old, as the Indian women walk long distances over the mountains and thus prefer to carry the child even after he or she can walk.

Bolivian Indian women walk great distances each day to and from the market. The market is not only a place for buying and selling, but also a place where the mother finds much of her social interaction. Thus, these Indian mothers are occupied with other activities and interests besides that of child rearing. However, Indian women believe that to have a child is the most natural and important thing in their lives. They do not dream of separating the child from the mother and believe that the infant will get ill without the mother's presence. It was observed that some of the four month old infants were toilet trained. This was achieved by the infant making a signal and giving time for the mother to take the infant out of the *aguawo* to urinate and defecate outside. Perhaps the close contact and the instinctual interaction between the mother and child permits this easy and early toilet training. However, early toilet training was not an issue for the Indian mothers.

Also in Bolivia the babies were observed to cry very little. Feeding seemed to be mostly by the breast on demand and accomplished by turning around the *aguawo* to the front whenever and wherever the mother happened to be. It was observed that the mother did give enough attention to the infant when it was demanded, even if she was busy with some other activities. The infant in the baby carrier looks around and participates in the whole world of experiences of the mother and is further stimulated by the mother, who is often explaining and interpreting what she sees, even to a month old infant.

The Bolivian babies seem to be quite mature for their age and were given credit for being older by the observer, due to their mature facial expressions. Perhaps this is due to long close contact with the mother's body and mind, the emotional security of being constantly with her, and the stimulation received from the mother and the environment. The infants were frequently taken out of the *aguawo* and played with, face to face. Bolivian Indian infants did not seem to be afraid or shy of strangers at the usual periods of shyness seen in Western infants.

Conclusion

We have presented some preliminary observations from an on-going study that the authors are doing on mother-child interaction and on child development in different cultural settings. The use of the baby carrier in Sweden and in Bolivian Indian mothers of the Altiplano has been described.

REFERENCES

Bolby, J., "The nature of the child's tie to his mother," International Journal of Psychoanalysis, Vol. 39, pp. 350-370 (1958)

El portabebe, "Kango-Bebe" como uha ayuda en fomentar el vinculo madre-hijo. Revista de los Padres e hijos, Buenos Aires

Freud, A., "Some remarks on infant observation," Psychoanalytical Study of the Child, Vol. 8, pp. 9-19 (1953)

Klaus, Marshall, and John Kennell, Maternal-Infant Bonding (1976: C. V. Mosby Company)

Klein, Melanie, Developments in Psychoanalysis, (1952: Hogarth Press)

Lind, John, K. Junker, and others, Experiences of a Japanese Baby Carrier in the Infant Care, (Karolinska Hospital, Stockholm)

Tinbergen, N., The Study of the Instincts, (1951: Oxford University Press)

Winnicott, D.W., The Child and the Family, (1957: Tavistock Publications, London)

Editor's note: We were unable to obtain the footnotes for this article in time for publication.

"Baby Carriers in Bolivia and Sweden," by Kamala Ditella, M.A.D. and John Lind, M.D. Vol. 4: No. 3 (Fall 1977) Birth and the Family Journal, Berkeley, California.

The Kibbutz as a Social Experiment and as a Child-Rearing Laboratory

BENJAMIN BEIT-HALLAHMI *University of Haifa*
ALBERT I. RABIN *Michigan State University*

ABSTRACT: *The Israeli kibbutz has attracted the attention of social scientists, especially psychologists, as a unique social experiment that offers a laboratory for studying the effects of variations in child rearing on personality development. This article reviews (a) the history of the kibbutz movement and kibbutz child-rearing practices and (b) the results of research in kibbutz socialization. The research indicates that the "kibbutz personality" is essentially nonpathological and effective. Recent changes in child-rearing patterns in the kibbutz, in the form of a return to traditional family child rearing, are viewed as part of an overall social change pattern that is likely to continue in the future. Implications for further work are discussed.*

Martin Buber (1958) called the kibbutz "an experiment that did not fail." He did so after going over the history of Western utopian movements, all of which had as their central idea the commune, a relatively small social unit that would serve as the building block for the ideal society of the future. Since the beginning of the 19th century, various attempts have been made to found communes, but most of these, being little more than isolated groups of fervent believers even during their usually brief periods of existence, have failed. So far, the most successful attempt at building a utopian commune has been the Israeli kibbutz. In addition to being a social experiment—an experiment in utopia—the kibbutz has been regarded as a psychological experiment, that is, as a laboratory for testing hypotheses regarding child-rearing practices and their consequences (Rabin, 1957). The interest shown by social scientists in the kibbutz has been similar to that shown in other social experiments that combined changes in social institutions with new patterns of child rearing, such as those in contemporary China and Cuba. We present here a brief history of the kibbutz and the changes it has undergone, together with a survey of psychological studies of child rearing in the kibbutz, in order to make psychologists more conscious of the complexity of the current kibbutz situation and its implications for psychological research.

Historical Background

There were particular circumstances that made the kibbutz such a success. Actually, it was an ideal solution to the problem of colonizing Palestine in the years before the founding of the State of Israel. Settling the land with groups of young, vigorous, and idealistic individuals having attachments only to the collective was more practical and logical than settling through the traditional way of family homesteading. This form of settlement was also more defensible, a fact worth considering given the hostile environment into which Zionist settlements entered. The kibbutz differed from its predecessors in utopianism in being a part of a national revival movement and in growing out of larger social groups that supplied its members. The idea of a voluntary membership commune grew out of a combination of nationalist and socialist ideologies, the same combination that led the Zionist–socialist movement to the founding of the State of Israel. Agricultural work was seen as the way to changing the abnormal social structure of Jews in the Diaspora, and thus agricultural settlements became the instruments of both national and social change. Marxist egalitarianism was added to nationalist aspirations, so that the kibbutz would become not just a national solution, but also a human one.

Beyond the particularistic ideals of national revival and reconstruction, the kibbutz movement

---

This article is a revised version of a paper presented to the 34th Annual Convention of the International Council of Psychologists, Paris, July 1976.

Comments on an earlier version by Daniel A. Wagner and Roberta J. Goldberg are gratefully acknowledged.

Requests for reprints should be sent to Albert I. Rabin, Department of Psychology, Michigan State University, East Lansing, Michigan 48824.

shared in the universalistic ideals of returning to nature and creating a new human being. The movement, like others inspired by the teachings of Karl Marx, believed in the perfectibility of human nature, or at least in its possible amelioration. There was a strong belief in the changes that a revolutionary way of life would bring about in what seemed like persistent and undesirable human qualities. In a truly egalitarian commune, people would be less selfish, more secure, and more generous. The change in social structure was expected to lead to a psychological change in every individual. And if there were doubts about far-reaching changes in the first generation of kibbutz founders, who had been brought up in bourgeois society, then the aim of education for the kibbutz-born was defined as the creation of the new human being. Here, in forming a new child-rearing system, the kibbutz founders had a chance to make their children in the desired image of the collectivist, egalitarian, work-oriented person (Leon, 1969).

But what went into the creation of a new child-rearing system was more than just the positive vision of a better future generation. There was also the more negative element of rejecting what had been regarded as the traditional way of family life. One must remember that the founders of the kibbutz were in open rebellion against their own parents, a rebellion sometimes taking the form of a total rejection of the institution of the family. In the first years of the kibbutz, this attitude culminated in the absence of any formal marriages. The rebellion against traditional family patterns included a move toward equality between the sexes and the abolition of traditional sex roles, especially in the area of work. The ideal of the equality between the sexes and the breakdown of traditional sex roles has been one expression of the struggle against the traditions of an unjust and declining world. Thus, the emphasis was put on the dismantling of the traditional bourgeois family, with its close mother–child ties, which was perceived as promoting selfishness and individualism. Communal child rearing was seen, since the earliest days of the kibbutz movement, as a major task for the whole commune. Children were regarded as the source of future success and strength, and the best facilities were given to the children's houses. Since the kibbutzim in their earlier days were struggling and often barely surviving, children had to share in the hardships, but they still received the best of what the kibbutz could offer.

What should be kept in mind is that the kibbutz movement, very much like other communal movements, has always been a small minority within its own society. It has been very conscious of its minority status, despite other attributes that made it more influential than could be expected on a purely numerical basis. In its early years, the kibbutz movement regarded itself as an avant-garde destined to lead the rest of the Jewish people, or at least the rest of the Zionist movement, in its wake. When the masses did not follow, the consciousness of being a minority persisted. Today, the kibbutzim population makes up less than 3% of Israel's total population. In 1975 there were 241 kibbutzim in Israel, with a total population of over 92,000. The kibbutzim hold 33% of all cultivated land in Israel and produce about 33⅓% of the agricultural production and about 6% of the industrial production. Most kibbutzim are part of one of three distinct federations: the "rightist" (Ihud Hakibbutzim), the "moderate" (Hakibbutz Hameuhad), and the "leftist" (Hashomer Hatzair). The ideological distinctions that gave rise to the three federations, and that concerned their commitment to Marxist socialism, are much less pronounced today.

The Ideology of Kibbutz Child Rearing

Child rearing has been a subject of intense discussion since the first days of the kibbutz. Hand in hand with the new practices, a new ideology emerged that sought to create a theoretical base for the roles of both parents and teachers. In hindsight, it may be claimed that the new child-rearing patterns were a practical necessity, on which an ideology was later imposed, in keeping with the overall ideology of the kibbutz movement. Whether the practice or the ideology came first will be determined by historians, but the fact is that kibbutz child rearing has been accompanied by an ideology that sought to rationalize its practices and served as a significant force in affecting parents and educators. There were two significant principles, having considerable psychological consequences, in the kibbutz child-rearing ideology.

The first stated that communal child rearing would work against individualism and identification with the family unit. The second stated that experts in child rearing could inculcate the ideology of the kibbutz with greater ability and objectivity than the parents. Almost every person can become a parent, but not every person can become an effective socializer. The socializer had to educate the child according to an ideal that should go against contemporary social realities. This explicit ideology led to relegating the parents to second place as socializing agents. The major socializing agents became the nurses, the teachers, and the peer group. Since the parents were no longer the sole representatives of authority, children's attitudes toward them, and especially toward the father, were expected to become more positive.

We cannot go here into all the details of the classical pattern of child rearing in the kibbutz, which can be found elsewhere (Rabin, 1965; Spiro, 1958). The main characteristics of the kibbutz tradition are that (a) child rearing is a communal, not a family, task; (b) kibbutz parents spend little time with their children compared to parents in a traditional family; and (c) education emphasizes communal and not individual goals. What is most important from a psychological point of view is the presence of multiple caretakers at an early stage in the children's development. This characteristic, and especially the limited contact with the mother, has raised several questions regarding its possible effects. Should the multiple caretaking be conceived as a form of maternal deprivation, maternal substitution, or multiple mothering? On the basis of available research, which will be covered later, we may conclude that the latter formulation is correct. The psychological characteristics of child rearing in the kibbutz can be summarized as follows: The number of significant others interacting with the child is higher than in the traditional family, but the relationships with some of these figures are nonexclusive and discontinuous. The *metapelet* (caretaker) takes care of a group of children and is likely to be changed several times during childhood. In the infants' and children's group, the child is exposed to a uniform, less personal treatment, and his needs are satisfied less readily than in the traditional family. We might say that the child in the kibbutz lives in two worlds: One is the family unit, where he spends some of his time in continuous, exclusive, and personalized interaction, and the other is the children's house, where interaction with adults is discontinuous, nonexclusive, and less personal. Since the child has to divide his attachments between these two worlds and among a large number of human objects (parents, teachers, and peers), one may ask whether this spread of feelings weakens the dependency on one significant figure, reduces the intensity of feelings toward parents, reduces the ambivalence toward parents, or diffuses identification over many objects. Rabin (1957, 1965) hypothesized that these conditions of reduced attachment and dependence would lead to a diffusion in identification, a reduction in ambivalence toward parents, and a reduction in sibling rivalry. Regev (Note 1) summarized these hypotheses into two: the moderation hypothesis and the diffusion hypothesis. The moderation hypothesis states that the kibbutz child has more moderate feelings toward objects in his environment, and the diffusion hypothesis states that the kibbutz child divides his attachment among a greater number of objects. The moderation and diffusion hypotheses have been cited by kibbutz educators as an indication of the success of kibbutz child rearing in creating a personality that is better suited for kibbutz life (Golan, 1961).

Psychological Studies of Child Rearing in the Kibbutz

The kibbutz as a natural laboratory has aroused the interest of two groups of researchers: psychodynamically oriented psychologists (Rabin, 1957; Rapaport, 1958) and anthropologists of the "culture and personality" school (Spiro, 1958). The anthropological approach to the kibbutz regards it as a different culture that leads to a different personality type. In the kibbutz, several social institutions, especially economics and the family, were different enough from those of other societies to designate it as a separate culture. At the same time, the kibbutz offered the advantage of being a part of Western culture, in the normal sense of the term, and its members could be easily communicated with. The first systematic observations of child rearing in the kibbutz appeared in the literature of the early 1950s (Irvine, 1952; Spiro, 1953). Since then, the number of social science publications on the topic has grown immensely (Rabin, 1971; Sharabany, 1975), and their conclusions can not be easily summarized in one article.

Some comments on methodology in kibbutz studies are in order. Research on child rearing in the kibbutz has been of several kinds: clinical–observational (Bettelheim, 1969; Caplan, 1954), anthropological (Spiro, 1958), and psychological–systematic (Kohen-Raz, 1968; Rabin, 1965). The number of systematic studies is surprisingly low, compared to the attention given to kibbutz child rearing in the literature. Some of the most quoted publications on the kibbutz (e.g., Bettelheim, 1969) are based on extremely limited observations, and when it comes to studies of the kibbutz system, there seems to be an almost inverse relationship between the frequency of citation and methodological rigor. Since the body of reliable findings is limited, one should proceed with caution toward inferences and conclusions. Speculations and inferences from observations and clinical data have their value, but they should be recognized as such. It should also be noted that the better-controlled studies (e.g., Nevo, in press) have found few differences between kibbutz and nonkibbutz groups.

The questions that psychologists have asked about the kibbutz child-rearing system were both of a theoretical nature (e.g., Will changes in mother–child relationships support psychoanalytic predictions?) and of an "applied" nature (e.g., What can be learned from the kibbutz experience to improve other child-rearing systems?). It is interesting to note that most psychological research on the kibbutz has focused on individual personality development and has not looked at some significant aspects of kibbutz life such as orientation toward work, alienation, and self-actualization. The clearly individualistic bias of academic psychology has to be regarded as the main cause for the concentration on individual personality dynamics.

Answers to several questions regarding kibbutz-born children are briefly summarized below. These questions include the extent of psychopathology, immaturity, identification with parents, and peer relations.

PSYCHOPATHOLOGY

Since the kibbutz caretaking situation was perceived as lying somewhere between maternal deprivation on one side and normal maternal contacts in the traditional family on the other, it was assumed that the relative deprivation would have its effects in the form of a greater prevalence of psychopathology. Some of the first observations on the kibbutz attempted to estimate the prevalence of pathological symptoms. Caplan (1954) found more symptoms only for younger ages (up to the age of 7), but Kaffman (1965) found no particular prevalence of psychopathology in kibbutz children. Nevo (in press) found no differences between kibbutz-born and city-born adults on the California Psychological Inventory.

IMMATURITY AND RETARDED DEVELOPMENT AMONG CHILDREN

The evidence on this point is not clear. Some studies show retarded development in infancy (Caplan, 1954; Rabin, 1961, 1965), but the majority of studies dealing with kibbutz infants have shown no developmental retardation (Fried, 1960; Gewirtz, 1965; Kohen-Raz, 1968). Handel (1961) found less maturity among kibbutz adolescents, but Rabin (1965) found more maturity among 10-year-old children and among adolescents in the kibbutz. Some of the disagreement in findings may be due to different sampling, during different periods, while the kibbutz child-rearing system was undergoing significant changes. The more recent studies show no developmental deficits, a fact that can be explained as the result of more individualized and relaxed caretaking in infancy.

IDENTIFICATION WITH AND ATTITUDES TOWARD PARENTS

The evidence shows quite clearly that identification of kibbutz children with their parents is more diffuse (Luria, Goldwasser, & Goldwasser, 1963; Rabin, 1957, 1965; Rabin & Goldman, 1966; Spiro, 1953) but nevertheless positive. Since childhood experiences in the kibbutz are expected to reduce ambivalence toward parents, attitudes toward them are expected to be more positive. This is indeed the finding (Devereux et al., 1974; Rabin, 1965; Spiro, 1958). There is support for the claim that the father in the kibbutz has become more nurturant and less authoritarian compared to the father in the traditional family.

PEER RELATIONS

Compared with the less intense parental identifications in the kibbutz, the peer group becomes very significant psychologically, and strong feelings of solidarity and group identity are formed (Etzioni, 1957; Golan, 1961; Rettig, 1966). Devereux et al. (1974) reported that peers in the kibbutz were perceived as secondary to the parents, and there was no difference from city children in this respect, but the kibbutz peers were seen as exerting more control.

EFFECTIVENESS AS ADULTS

Only a few studies have looked at kibbutz-born adults, and follow-up studies of kibbutz children are now being carried out (Rabin & Beit-Hallahmi, Note 2); however, the available findings show the kibbutz-born young adult to be remarkably effective, productive, and well-adjusted in his overall functioning (Amir, 1969; Nevo, in press; Rabin, 1965).

CAPACITY FOR INTIMACY

The diffusion of identification and the reduced attachment to a few objects at an early age would lead to a reduced capacity for (or the need for) intimacy (Bettelheim, 1969; Spiro, 1958). Support for this hypothesis was found by Handel (1961), who used only self-reports, and by Sharabany (1974), who compared friendships among 11- and 12-year-olds in the kibbutz and in the city.

THE "KIBBUTZ PERSONALITY"

On the basis of the findings presented so far, we may conclude that the personality of the kibbutz-born is nonpathological, effective, shows only moderate but positive attachment to others, and shows a reduction in intimate rivalry and ambivalence. As noted above, the most striking general finding is that the majority of studies, and especially those complying with more rigorous methodological standards, found few differences between kibbutz and nonkibbutz groups. It is important to remember that in all cases, the control groups to whom the kibbutz groups were compared were made up of Israeli-born individuals. This means that the comparisons were made within the same basic culture, and it seems plausible that comparisons across cultures (e.g., a kibbutz group to an American group) would have produced clear differences. It has been suggested, with some supporting data, that Israeli culture as a whole is more collectivistic than most Western cultures today (Crandall & Gozali, 1969), and thus it becomes more difficult to separate the effects of kibbutz child rearing from the general effects of the culture. From a theoretical viewpoint, one may want to conclude that the case for the kibbutz as a separate culture producing a separate "personality" still has to be proven. From an "applied" viewpoint, one can point to the absence of pathology and to the presence of effectiveness and productiveness produced by multiple mothering. In any case, the limitations of our data base should be kept in mind. How newer developments in the kibbutz system may lead us to ask new questions and find better answers is discussed in the next section.

Recent Changes in Kibbutz Child-Rearing Practices

Over the past 15 years there has been a major trend toward closer parent–child contacts and toward more individual caretaking patterns in the communal child-rearing system. The changes have taken two major forms: (a) family sleeping arrangements for infants until a certain age (in some cases until adolescence) and (b) provision of more *metapelot* (caretakers) for the infants' house. Until 1950, family-based sleeping arrangements were in effect in only four kibbutzim. Since then, the new arrangement has spread over many more kibbutzim in the rightist federation and to some kibbutzim in the moderate federation, but the debate over sleeping arrangements has spread to all three kibbutz federations (Shepher, 1971). Changes from the communal sleeping arrangement to the family sleeping arrangement have been noted for some years now (Shepher, 1969).

In the family-based sleeping arrangement, the children return to their parents in the afternoon and then stay there until the next morning, when they go back to the children's house. This arrangement may begin at different ages. At some kibbutzim it starts at age 6; at others it starts at birth and extends until age 12. In this latter group, most of the crucial elements in traditional, kibbutz child rearing disappear. Under the family-based sleeping arrangement, the mother becomes the most significant figure, the parents become the main socializers, and the *metapelet* and the peer group recede in importance. The children's house may be compared to a day care center, the influence of which may be significant in some respects but cannot be compared to the influence of the "classical" children's house.

Family-based sleeping arrangements abolish the most unique aspect of kibbutz child rearing—multiple mothering at an early age. The children are transferred to communal children's houses later on, but the bond with the mother is formed at an early age. The parents not only spend more time together with their children but also become the main socializers. They no longer see the children only during recreation periods when parents and children play together, but they now have to discipline their children and train them in all areas of social behavior. Peer-group influence is reduced but not altogether abolished. The collectivist orientation in child rearing remains very much in existence, and the peer group remains very stable.

Unlike city children, kibbutz children spend most of their time, until the age of 18, with a limited number of peers. They are exposed to fewer social stimuli, and their environment is more uniform. They are led to identify strongly with their peer group, and such an identification is likely to emerge. It is rare for city children to spend their time with the same peer group from kindergarten through high school, but this is exactly what happens in the kibbutz.

The return to traditional, nonkibbutz child-rearing patterns also involves a change in relation to siblings, who assume a more significant role in early childhood. In those kibbutzim where the infants are still in the infants' house, better caretaking in infancy can prevent whatever initial deprivation kibbutz infants may have suffered from in the past. It may also create greater attachment to the *metapelet* (nurse) in this initial stage. Something else that is changing and will continue to change is child-rearing attitudes. Studies of first-generation and second-generation kibbutz mothers indicate a change in terms of putting more emphasis on individual attention to children, encouraging more affectional ties with parents, and considering motherhood as an important role for every kibbutz woman (Rabin, 1964, 1970).

Explaining the Change

The explanations for recent changes in child-rearing practices in the kibbutz may be sought in several areas. There might have been changes in the ideology of child rearing, based on the experiences over the years. There might have been wider structural changes within the kibbutz, and there might have been wider changes in the surrounding Israeli society that have influenced the kibbutz movement. We will try to examine all relevant factors, starting with possible changes in educational philosophy. Was it self-criticism by kibbutz educators and parents that led them to "mend their ways" in the more conservative direction? Has it been the development of greater psychological-mindedness and sensitivity to the shortcomings of "orthodox" methods? Has feedback from psychological studies affected the kibbutz community?

The relationship between the kibbutz movements and social science research has not always been an easy one. Initially, social scientists were critical, and kibbutz members were defensive. Psychoanalysts' preliminary interest in the kibbutz as a deviant or potentially pathological pattern of life, especially in the area of child rearing, has not endeared the researcher to the kibbutz community. Moreover, a utopian, struggling movement tends to view outside observers not sharing its ideology as potential critics and enemies. One should bear in mind that the kibbutz has always been a minority subculture, fighting against the destructive influences of the wider society that would reduce it to a smaller minority or abolish it altogether. We should remember that because of tensions with the wider society, very few utopian communes have survived as long as the kibbutz. In this context, it is easy to see why studies by outside researchers were regarded as hostile incursions, aimed at tarnishing the image of an idealistic enterprise. At the same time, there were other factors that led kibbutz movements to assume a different and more positive attitude toward social science research. The first factor was the special psychological-mindedness of the kibbutz leaders, especially in the area of education. Communal education in the kibbutz was based on theoretical foundations that included psychodynamic theory (Golan, 1961; Rabin & Hazan, 1973). Kibbutz educators have regarded themselves as an educational avant-garde, conscious of the psychological consequences of what they were planning. Psychoanalytic concepts have been in usage in the kibbutz movement since its beginning, and this prepared the ground for acceptance of psychological research as an ally (Katz & Lewin, 1973). The second factor was the feeling within the kibbutz that the results of psychological studies vindicated kibbutz child-rearing methods. Indeed, the "kibbutz personality" as it emerges from psychological studies is quite positive, and so there was little need to modify the child-rearing system that brought it about.

We chose to look at the changes in child-rearing practices in a wider context. We decided to ask whether these changes had been unique and isolated or whether there had been changes in other aspects of the kibbutz system that may have been related to the changes in patterns of child rearing. Changes in all kibbutz institutions have been observed, and they are all in the same direction of increased privatism and "familism." The changes have been economic, political, ideological, and psychological. A growing conservatism is being manifested in all of these areas, and the changes in child rearing are just one part of the general trend. In terms of the relationship between the original kibbutz ideology and later historical developments, we might say that the trend is from ideological purity to ideological compromise. Many of these changes are too recent to have been studied systematically, but they are easy to observe (Rabin, Note 3) and have been noted by all students of kibbutz life in recent years. Considerable evidence regarding the changes and the often heated discussions that accompanied them is available in the periodical literature of the kibbutz movement. There is general agreement on two points: the comprehensive nature of the changes, covering almost every aspect of kibbutz life, and the unified direction characterizing all of these changes.

One of the main aims of the kibbutzim has been settling the land, and the kibbutzim started as agricultural collectives. The past 25 years have seen a growing industrialization so successful as to turn many kibbutzim into holding companies for a variety of enterprises. The ideological change away from socialism has been correlated with the actual change in patterns of production and consumption. What was started as a deliberate attempt to create a working class is now a comfortable bourgeoisie. The second generation of the kibbutz, which is the first to be born and raised there, is now the dominant group in many kibbutzim. This generation has satisfied some, but not all, of the expectations of its parents. For this generation, and succeeding ones, the kibbutz is not a new venture into utopia but the reality into which they were born. They were not selected, much less self-selected like their parents. They are more pragmatic and less idealistic. Recent trends in the kibbutz include a "consumerist" life-style that consists of (a) aiming for higher living standards to match the life-style of the Israeli middle class, (b) greater freedom in making career choices, and (c) an emphasis on specialized higher education and individual success. All of these represent departures from the early kibbutz ideology. The importance of outside pressures on the kibbutz can not be minimized. The kibbutz, as a minority avant-garde movement, has treated the wider society with ambivalence. One of the aims of kibbutz education was to immunize and isolate youngsters from the influences of the nonkibbutz world, but the growing economic and political involvement of the kibbutz in the larger society has made isolationism impossible.

Historical changes in the wider context—the State of Israel—have brought about a different atmosphere in the kibbutz movement, which has entailed many changes in social relationships and patterns of family life. Some of the important general changes in Israeli society that the kibbutz community could not escape were the rise in living standards, the general political and ideological trends in Israel—in the direction of greater conservatism, and the decline of socialist ideals. The general ideological climate in Israel in the last 25 years has changed in the direction of a growing alliance with capitalism and the United States and a decline in adherence to socialist ideas and movements. The kibbutzim were important tools of the Zionist movement before the founding of the state. Ever since then, the kibbutzim and Zionism as a whole have been suffering the pains of success. As patterns of idealistic and militant behavior became institutionalized, the tradition of kibbutz life was seen as dysfunctional.

The success of the Zionist movement in establishing the State of Israel and the later economic success of the kibbutz movement have given the initial utopian venture the character of a successful revolution that has lost its zeal and thus failed. The feeling of mission and struggle, the stand of opposition to traditional culture, and the support of social renewal can no longer be maintained. The kibbutz may be compared to other successful revolutionary movements whose success has brought about their decline and a return to prerevolutionary behaviors. It is hard to be a successful revolution, and it may be even harder to survive as a successful utopia.

IDEOLOGY AND CHILD-REARING PRACTICES

The connection between overall ideology and child-rearing patterns becomes clear once we look at changes within the three kibbutz federations (leftist, moderate, and rightist) in regard to child rearing and in regard to other aspects of kibbutz ideology. We would predict that the more orthodox (i.e., leftist) kibbutzim would keep the communal pattern of child rearing, while reforms in the direction of the traditional (nonkibbutz) family should appear in the less orthodox (i.e., rightist) kibbutzim. This is indeed the case, with clear connections between ideological orthodoxy in child rearing and in other areas. The rightist kibbutzim are also more involved in using hired work, which is contrary to the socialist kibbutz philosophy. Today, even the leftist kibbutzim employ hired workers, but their use is still self-conscious and limited. Changes in child-rearing patterns first appeared in the rightist kibbutzim and are now becoming more prevalent in the moderate kibbutz movement. The change in each individual kibbutz is decided upon by majority vote, following a decision in principle by the particular kibbutz federation.

Our suggestion here is that changes in child-rearing patterns in the more traditional direction are positively related to changes in the economic structure of the kibbutz in a more conservative direction. That is, there will be a positive correlation between changes to family-based sleeping arrangements and the prevalence of hired work in a kibbutz. Those kibbutzim that are more "orthodox" on child-rearing issues are likely to be more "orthodox" in other areas. Today, family-based sleeping arrangements are most common in the rightist kibbutz federation and are almost unknown in the leftist federation. Shepher (1967) reported a correlation between family sleeping arrangements and a greater degree of ideological indifference on the part of kibbutz members. Within the same kibbutz federation it was found that members of kibbutzim where communal sleeping arrangements were in effect showed a greater degree of ideological involvement and readiness for public-service roles compared to members from kibbutzim where the family-based sleeping arrangement was in effect.

Given recent changes in the kibbutz, it is possible to predict that the trend from kibbutz child rearing back to the traditional family will continue in the near future. Since, as we have shown, changes in economic, social, and ideological factors have brought about changes in child rearing, the continuation of those background trends in the "bourgeoisation" of the kibbutz will lead inevitably to a reduction in the differences between kibbutz and city child-rearing patterns. One can conceivably picture a point at which communal child rearing will be limited to only a few orthodox kibbutzim. The picture today is that "classical" communal child rearing exists only in the leftist kibbutz movement (Hashomer Hatzair), with the other two kibbutz movements undergoing changes in the direction away from communal child rearing.

SEX ROLES AND CHILD-REARING PATTERNS

A case may be made for the connection between the recent changes in child-care patterns and the development of sex-role specialization in the kibbutz. Complete sexual equality and sharing of work responsibility has been one of the ideals of the kibbutz movement. The needs of the kibbutz in its earlier years were for more manpower for physical, mainly agricultural work, and women were regarded as equal partners in sharing the burden. Communal child rearing contributed to the freeing of women from the traditional tasks of mothering so that they were available as workers. The ideal of sexual equality has been far from reality even in the earlier days of the kibbutz (Rabin, 1970; Tiger & Shepher, 1975), but the present situation is similar to those found in other areas of kibbutz life. Recent developments in the kibbutz show a pattern of consistent movement toward more traditional patterns of sex roles, marriage, and family life and a clear revival of the traditional division of labor between the sexes. As Tiger and Shepher (1975) show, there is a clear polarization of work between men and women, with men predominantly in production and women predominantly in communal services. Women are involved in the same types of jobs that fit the traditional female role, except that most of these jobs serve the whole community and not just the family. Thus, women are concentrating in communal service jobs, including the kitchen, the laundry, the infants' and the children's houses, etc. Women are almost excluded from agricultural field work or industrial jobs (Tiger & Shepher, 1965).

Talmon (1974) indicates that women in the kibbutz have been in favor of greater family autonomy and a greater role for the family in child rearing. Her explanation for the apparently greater familism of women is based on the change in women's roles in the kibbutz over time. In the early days of the kibbutz movement, women were equal partners in the labor system, since the birth rate was low and the members were all young. Gradually, women's reproductive role became predominant, limiting their involvement in hard physical labor. Men dominated the productive work roles in the kibbutz, since work was becoming more specialized and demanded permanent work assignments.

The economic success of the kibbutz and the rise in living standards made the participation of women in heavy physical labor unnecessary. Manpower in the kibbutz became less of a problem, and one of the practical reasons for communal child care was thus removed. The service jobs in which women have specialized are for the most part routine, thankless jobs. Investing more in the family is one major way in which kibbutz women can find more personal satisfaction, as opposed to the frustrations and impersonality of the communal service jobs. Rabin (1970) presents data on the discontent of kibbutz women with their service jobs and on their support for familism. The growing return to family-based sleeping arrangements has been correlated with the return to the traditional division of labor among the sexes (Shepher, 1967). It is possible to conceive of the kibbutz now as a collective of families and no longer a collective of individuals. Within this collective, women are returning to their traditional roles as family caretakers and are withdrawing from the roles of collective caretakers. Since these new roles are more satisfying to women, it is understandable why women have become the main supporters of familism (Talmon, 1974). Men in the kibbutz continue to derive their satisfactions and status from their productive work jobs (Tiger & Shepher, 1975).

Conclusion

The present orientation of the kibbutz child-rearing system should be described as more individualistic than ever before. The decline of collectivistic ideology has led to this change in educational orientation, which is likely to lead to further changes in the communal education system, especially in education for the early years. The most important change is likely to be a decline in communal sleeping arrangements for infants, which will change mother–child relationships significantly.

Psychologists should now write about the "classical" or "historical" kibbutz, as opposed to the present one, which is certainly a paradox for a movement that seemed to embody a breakdown of some basic human traditions and a rebellion against all of history. One can no longer speak of the "kibbutz" in general but must be more specific. If the kibbutz is to continue as a child-rearing laboratory, experimental conditions have to be specified and monitored. The kibbutz is no longer a single, child-rearing laboratory, but it includes several different laboratories (or experimental conditions). What we observe is a general pattern of departures from the original kibbutz ideology, a pattern that encompasses all areas of life in the kibbutz. The changes in child-rearing patterns make up one component in this wider historical trend.

If a specific child-rearing pattern is assumed to lead to a certain personality pattern, then a change in child-rearing methods in any direction should lead to differences in the previously established pattern. The historical changes should lead to differences between the "baseline" personality and the present one that are important both factually and theoretically. Generalizations about the "kibbutz personality" should be kept close to empirical findings. Moreover, the changes in child-rearing practices give us an opportunity to test again our theoretical notions. Historical changes have set up a natural experimental design. Children growing up now under the communal sleeping arrangements can be compared to children growing up under the family-based sleeping arrangement in a neighboring kibbutz.

Findings regarding "orthodox" kibbutz child rearing can be compared with data based on current practices, and the first steps in this direction are being taken (Regev, Note 1). The differences we have pointed to between the "classical" and the "modern" kibbutz may come as a surprise to psychologists who have preferred the simplicity of the textbook and the easy psychological generalization to the complexity of history and living organizations. The kibbutz has its own dynamics of development that are bound up with wider historical changes. One might say that the days of the kibbutz as a simple experiment are over. Those studying it must face more complexity and variety than before, but they also have greater opportunities to answer some significant psychological questions.

REFERENCE NOTES

1. Regev, E., *Sleeping arrangements and psychological development in the kibbutz.* Unpublished research proposal, Haifa University, 1976.
2. Rabin, A. I., & Beit-Hallahmi, B. *Family and communally reared (kibbutz) children 20 years later.* Unpublished manuscript, Michigan State University, 1976.
3. Rabin, A. I. *Changing times in the kibbutz.* Unpublished manuscript, Michigan State University, 1971.

REFERENCES

Amir, Y. The effectiveness of the kibbutz-born soldier in the Israel Defense Forces. *Human Relations,* 1969, *22,* 333–344.

Bettelheim, B. *The children of the dream.* New York: Macmillan, 1969.

Buber, M. *Paths in utopia.* Boston: Beacon Press, 1958.

Caplan, G. Clinical observations on the emotional life of children in the communal settlements of Israel. In M. S. E. Senn (Ed.), *Problems of infancy and childhood.* New York: Josiah Macy, Jr., Foundation, 1954.

Crandall, V. C., & Gozali, J. The social desirability responses of children of four religious-cultural groups. *Child Development,* 1969, *40,* 751–762.

Devereux, E. C., et al. Socialization practices of parents, teachers and peers in Israel: The kibbutz versus the city. *Child Development,* 1974, *45,* 269–281.

Etzioni, A. Solidaric work groups in the kibbutz. *Human Organization,* 1957, *16,* 2–7.

Fried, Y. [Psychomotor development of kibbutz children.] *Ofakim,* 1960, *41,* 303–312.

Gewirtz, J. L. The course of infant smiling in four child rearing environments in Israel. In B. M. Foss (Ed.), *Determinants of infant behavior III.* London: Methuen, 1965.

Golan, S. *Hahinukh hameshutaf* [Communal education]. Merhavia, Israel: Sifriat Poalim, 1961.

Handel, A. [Self-concept of the kibbutz adolescent.] *Megamot,* 1961, *11,* 142–159.

Irvine, E. E. Observations on the aims and methods of child-rearing in communal settlements in Israel. *Human Relations,* 1952, *5,* 247–276.

Kaffman, M. A comparison of psychopathology: Israeli children from kibbutz and from urban surroundings. *American Journal of Orthopsychiatry,* 1965, *35,* 509–520.

Katz, F., & Lewin, G. Early childhood education. In A. I. Rabin & B. Hazan (Eds.), *Collective education in the kibbutz.* New York: Springer, 1973.

Kohen-Raz, R. Mental and motor development of kibbutz, institutionalized, and home-reared infants in Israel. *Child Development,* 1968, *39,* 489–504.

Leon, D. *The kibbutz.* New York: Pergamon, 1969.

Luria, Z., Goldwasser, M., & Goldwasser, A. Response to transgression in stories by Israeli children. *Child Development,* 1963, *34,* 271–280.

Nevo, B. Personality differences between kibbutz born and city born adults. *American Journal of Psychology,* in press.

Rabin, A. L. The Israeli kibbutz (collective settlement) as a "laboratory" for testing psychodynamic hypotheses. *Psychological Record,* 1957, *7,* 111–115.

Rabin, A. I. Kibbutz adolescents. *American Journal of Orthopsychiatry,* 1961, *31,* 493–504.

Rabin, A. I. Kibbutz mothers view "collective education." *American Journal of Orthopsychiatry,* 1964, *34,* 140–142.

Rabin, A. I. *Growing up in the kibbutz.* New York: Springer, 1965.

Rabin, A. I. The sexes: Ideology and reality in the Israeli kibbutz. In G. M. Seward & L. C. Williamson (Eds.), *Sex roles in a changing society.* New York: Random House, 1970.

Rabin, A. I. *Kibbutz studies.* East Lansing: Michigan State University Press, 1971.

Rabin, A. I., & Goldman, H. The relationship of severity of guilt to intensity of identification in kibbutz and non-kibbutz children. *Journal of Social Psychology,* 1966, *69,* 159–163.

Rabin, A. I., & Hazan, B. (Eds.). *Collective education in the kibbutz.* New York: Springer, 1973.

Rapaport, D. The study of kibbutz education and its bearing on the theory of development. *American Journal of Orthopsychiatry,* 1958, *28,* 587–597.

Rettig, K. S. Relation of social systems to intergenerational changes in moral attitudes. *Journal of Personality and Social Psychology,* 1966, *4,* 400–414.

Sharabany, R. *Intimate friendship among kibbutz and city children and its measurement.* Unpublished doctoral dissertation, Cornell University, 1974.

Sharabany, R. Socialization in the Israeli kibbutz—Bibliography. JSAS *Catalog of Selected Documents in Psychology,* 1975, *5,* 185. (Ms. No. 847)

Shepher, J. *Hishtakfut sidrei hahalana bamivneh hahaevrati shel hakibbutz.* Tel-Aviv: Ihud Hakibbutzim vehakvutzot, 1967.

Shepher, J. Familism and social structure: Case of the kibbutz. *Journal of Marriage and the Family,* 1969, *31,* 567–573.

Shepher, J. [Sleeping arrangement for children in the kibbutz.] In *Yalkut Hahinuh Hameshutaf bagil Harakh.* Merhavia, Israel: Hakibbutz Haartzi, 1971.

Spiro, M. Education in a communal village in Israel. *American Journal of Orthopsychiatry,* 1953, *23,* 120–130.

Spiro, M. *Children of the kibbutz.* Cambridge, Mass.: Harvard University Press, 1958.

Talmon, Y. *Family and community in the kibbutz.* Cambridge, Mass.: Harvard University Press, 1974.

Tiger, L., & Shepher, J. *Women in the kibbutz.* New York: Harcourt Brace Jovanovich, 1975.

Longitudinal IQ Outcomes of the Mother-Child Home Program

John Madden, Phyllis Levenstein, and Sidney Levenstein

Verbal Interaction Project

MADDEN, JOHN; LEVENSTEIN, PHYLLIS; and LEVENSTEIN, SIDNEY. *Longitudinal IQ Outcomes of the Mother-Child Home Program.* CHILD DEVELOPMENT, 1976, 47, 1015–1025. Low-income families participated in several variations of a home-based intervention program which focused on modeling verbal interaction between mother and child around selected toys and books. Long-term results from a quasi-experimental design suggested that the amount of IQ difference between groups was dependent on the amount of program intervention within the range of conditions examined. Initial short-term experimental results have not confirmed this conclusion and indicate the need for increased attention to the conduct of the program and for more informative experimental research.

The Mother-Child Home Program (MCHP) has combined child's play with mother-child dialogue to foster the cognitive and socioemotional development of low-income 2- to 4-year-olds to prevent educational disadvantage in their later years. This paper summarizes one cognitive outcome, IQ scores on standardized tests for children who entered this early childhood intervention program in 1967, 1968, and 1969, and for untreated groups compared with them, and also contains an initial report of recent experimental results for children who entered in 1973.

The MCHP was first developed by the Verbal Interaction Project as a pilot project in 1965 (Levenstein & Sunley 1968). The program's major assumption was that the principal cognitive element missing from the early experience of many children vulnerable to educational disadvantage was a sufficient amount of verbal interaction in the family, centered on perceptually rich and ordered stimuli, and embedded in the affective matrix of the child's most enduring relationships, especially that with his mother.

The program essentially consisted of home visits by "Toy Demonstrators" to model for mother-child dyads the verbal interaction features of books and toys permanently assigned to the child. The MCHP was developed by the Verbal Interaction Project from a pilot project in 1965–1966 (Levenstein & Sunley 1968). Its rationale, method, and short-term results have been described in detail elsewhere (Levenstein 1970, 1975, in press).

Preliminary results suggested that the program had a substantial short-term effect on IQ scores (Levenstein 1970) and stimulated several questions about this effect:

1. Will program "graduates" retain a satisfactory level of IQ scores into the school years?

2. Will subsequent cohorts of the program perform as well with Toy Demonstrators of lower educational and work skills than those of the social workers with masters' degrees who pioneered this role in 1967–1968?

3. What will be the long-term effects of varying the length of the program?

4. Which background variables relate to IQ score, and can posttreatment differences be plausibly attributed to preexisting group differences?

The primary focus of this report will be IQ comparisons between differently treated groups at one posttest period, referred to hereafter as "follow-up." A brief report of recently obtained short-term experimental results will also be included.

The purpose of the program is not to modify IQ scores. However, if the rationale and conduct of the program are valid, the program should have at least an indirect effect on IQ.

The research described in this report was sponsored by Family Service Association of Nassau County, Inc., and State University of New York at Stony Brook and was supported by the U.S. Department of Health, Education, and Welfare—Children's Bureau, National Institute of Mental Health, and Office of Education—by the Carnegie Corporation of New York, and by the Rockefeller Brothers Fund. Authors' address: Verbal Interaction Project, 5 Broadway, Freeport, New York 11520.

Method

Design

The research followed a "quasi-experimental" design (Campbell & Stanley 1963). The basic plan consisted of pretesting intact groups with repeated measures following pretest. There was also one "after-only" comparison group which was not pretested. The specific intervention and testing schedules for each group are provided below in the group descriptions. In 1967, when five groups were started, randomization was by location of three suburban housing projects from which dyads were recruited. In 1968 and 1969, there was no random assignment of groups to varying trreatments, as treatments did not vary. Group and family differences were controlled by their shared residence in low-income housing.

Subjects

The long-term data were gathered on 151 children (80 boys and 71 girls) 4 to 6 years old at follow-up. All lived in three suburbs (A, B, and C) of New York City and were from low-income families financially eligible for low-income housing. Almost all were American born, English speaking, and socially defined as black.

The 96 treated dyads were recruited at ages 2 and 3 years by letter, followed by door-to-door canvassing, from low-income housing projects in towns A and B in 1967 and 1968. In 1968, about half came from these sources and half were referred by social agencies and lived outside of the projects.

Of the 55 comparison dyads, 25 were similarly recruited from the town A and C housing projects in 1967. The remaining 30 comparison families (all found post hoc to be black) were recruited as an out-of-project; English-speaking, American-born after-only group on four low-SES criteria from the first grade of the town A school system in 1972. The criteria were eligibility for low-income housing, residence in rented housing, occupation less than skilled, and neither parent with an education above high school.

Procedure: Mother-Child Home Program (MCHP)

In 1967, the basic MCHP consisted of 52 semiweekly visits to the dyad over a 7-month period during which 28 toys and books were assigned to the family (Levenstein 1970). Toy Demonstrators (TDs) were master's degree social workers. Several variations of this basic program that were carried out in 1967 and 1968 are included in the group descriptions provided below.

In 1968, the MCHP was changed to its present format. The program consisted of 46 semiweekly visits to the dyad each year following the local 10-month school calendar. The visits began at age 2 (Program I) and continued throughout the following year (Program II). During these visits, the TDs demonstrated verbal interaction with the child and encouraged the mother to participate in the interaction. The interaction centered on permanently assigned play materials which the TD brought weekly, a total of 12 books and 11 toys each year. These verbal interaction stimulus materials (VISM) were selected on explicit criteria, foremost of which was their capacity to stimulate verbal interaction (Levenstein 1975).

After 1967 the TDs were unpaid women volunteers (usually with 4 years of college) and paid former mother-participants (of no more than high school education). All were trained together in an initial eight-session training workshop, in weekly group conferences, and by individual supervision throughout the program year, learning the rationale, the structured cognitive curriculum, and the less formal "affective curriculum" built around the increasingly complex sequence of books and toys presented to the child. They were taught to model for the mother (rather than teach) verbal interaction techniques focused on the toys and books and spelled out in guide sheets contained in a "Toy Demonstrator's Visit Handbook." The TD involved the mother early in the home session with the aim of fading into the background while the mother took over the main responsibility for the verbal interaction, utilizing as much of the modeled behavior as she wished.

The aim of the cognitive curriculum contained in the "Toy Demonstrator's Visit Handbook" was to help the mother to assist the child in building concepts through "instrumental conceptualism," Bruner's phrase applied to the child's conceptual development through his interchange of language with his mother around meaningful experiences in his environment (Bruner, Olver, Greenfield, et al. 1966). The general goal of the affective curriculum was to promote, without counseling or teaching, the socioemotional development of the child and to promote child-rearing behavior functional to the child's learning and the well-being of both. The two curricula have been described in detail elsewhere (Levenstein, in press). The cost of the program, without research components, was estimated to be about $400 per year for each dyad.

Treated Groups: Variations of the MCHP

The 96 treated dyads were scheduled to receive one of six 1- or 2-year variations of the MCHP and were pretested and enrolled in the program in September 1967, 1968, and 1969. Group membership in this report is based on intended treatment rather than on the treatment actually received, and families who received much less than the amount of treatment intended are included here. The ages of the children as they are specified below were defined at the time of pretest as the range from 4 months less than to 6 months greater than the stated age.

Treated Groups: 1-Year Variations

T67-I + Short II.—This group, from the town A housing project, entered in September 1967 at age 2 and received Program I plus one of two shortened versions of Program II during the following year. In the second year, the mothers were offered nine additional home sessions and seven VISM. Of the group, eight accepted the full short Program II, seven accepted only the VISM, and two declined any further intervention. Toy Demonstrators for this group were social workers. The group was posttested six times (May 1968, May 1969, December 1969, December 1971, January 1973, and January 1974).

T67-I.—This group, from the town A housing project, entered in September 1967 at age 3, received only Program I with social workers as TDs, and was posttested five times (May 1968, December 1969, December 1970, January 1973, and January 1974).

T67-C_1 + I.—This group, age 2 and 3, from the town B housing project, entered and was pretested in September 1967. The group received 1 year of placebo treatment (home visits plus non-VISM gifts) to serve as a comparison group to control for the Hawthorne effect. In the following year the MCHP was offered to all eligible families in this group's housing project. For ethical and human relations reasons, this group was also offered, and accepted, Program I with non-social-worker TDs following its year of placebo treatment with a social worker. Group T67-C_1 + I was posttested six times (May 1968, May 1969, November 1969, December 1971, January 1973, and January 1974).

Treated Groups: 2-Year Variations

T68-I + II.—This group, from the town A and town B housing projects, entered in September 1968 at age 2 and received Programs I and II (the first group to receive the full MCHP) with non-social-worker TDs. The group was posttested seven times (May 1969, May 1970, December 1970, December 1971, January 1973, January 1974, and January 1975).

T69-I + II.—This group, from the town A and town B housing projects and from nonproject residences, entered in September 1969 at age 2 and received Programs I and II with non-social-worker TDs, the same treatment received by the T68-I + II Group. The group was posttested four times (May 1970, May 1971, January 1973, and January 1974).

T69-VISM Only.—This group, from town A nonproject residences, entered and was pretested in September 1969 at age 2 and received only the VISM, delivered weekly, for Programs I and II. The group was posttested four times (May 1970, May 1971, January 1973, and January 1974).

Untreated Comparison Groups

The 55 comparison (test only) dyads entered the research project in three different groups in 2 years, 1967 and 1972.

C_2-67.—This group, from the town C housing project, entered in September 1967 at ages 2 and 3. The group was pretested in September 1967 and posttested together five times (May 1968, December 1969, January 1973, January 1974, and January 1975). The group was also tested as two subgroups, the subgroup of children age 2 at entry in December 1971 and the subgroup age 3 at entry in December 1970, making a total of six posttests for each subgroup.

C_4-67.—This group, from the town A housing project, entered in September 1967 at age 4 and was pretested in 1967 (having been recruited for a version of the program for 4-year-olds which was canceled when it was discovered that these children were going into the then new Head Start Program). This group was posttested three times (December 1971, January 1973, and January 1974).

C_5-72.—This group, from town A non-housing-project residences, entered at age 6 and was tested three times (January 1973, January 1974, and January 1975), having been recruited on low-income criteria previously described. Group C_5-72 entered the 1972–1973 follow-up study as an after-only group with no previous project contact.

IQ Tests and Test Schedules

IQ measures were the Cattell Developmental and Intelligence Scale (Cattell) for children age 2 or younger, the Stanford-Binet Intelligence Scale (S-B) for children from age 3 through kindergarten, and the Wechsler Intelligence Scale for Children (WISC) for children in and beyond first grade. A verbal IQ score was obtained from the Peabody Picture Vocabulary Test (PPVT).

The group comparison of most interest is that at follow-up. For each of the seven groups in this comparison, follow-up was defined as that test period when the mean group age was nearest to 5 and when nearly all children in the group were tested on the S-B. Also, WISC scores are reported at one later test period for those groups who reached third grade.

Although all children but one were pretested, no clear adjustment can be made for pretest IQ because pretest IQs were composed of both Cattell and S-B scores mixed both within and between groups. The Cattell was intended as a downward extension in age of the 1937 S-B, but the standardization data do not provide a basis for conversion of Cattell to S-B scores (Cattell 1940).

After the bulk of these data were gathered, the S-B (1960) and the WISC (1949) were revised. Because the S-B test items have not essentially changed in the new standardizations, it is possible to convert old into new scores. To give a rough idea of the effect of such a conversion on the data reported here, at age 61 months, the score of a child who received the same score as the mean of the untreated C_2-67 group would be reduced from 97.8 points to 89, and the score of a child who received the same score as the mean score of the treated T68-I + II group at age 65 months would be reduced from 106.2 to 99 (Terman & Merrill 1973). No such conversion can be made from WISC to WISC-R scores at this time.

Demographic Data

The demographic data reported here were systematically collected in two interviews. The

TABLE 1

DEMOGRAPHIC CHARACTERISTICS OF TREATED AND COMPARISON GROUPS AT ENTRY

	SUBJECT GROUP[a]										
	Child			Father			Mother		Family		
										Residence	
ENTRY YEAR AND PROGRAM DESIGNATION	N	Age	% Male	Years of School	% Occupation 6 or 7[b]	% Always Present	Years of School	% Receiving Welfare	Size	Project	Non-project
					Treated						
1967, T67-I	14	3	35.7	9.6	85.7	57.1	10.7	28.6	4.9	x	...
1967, T67-I + Short II	17	2	58.8	10.1	100.0	76.5	11.2	17.6	6.2	x	...
1967, T67-C_1 + I	8	2 & 3	75.0	9.8	85.7	62.5	10.2	12.5	6.1	x	...
1968, T68-I + II	24	2	41.7	10.5	71.4	60.9	10.5	37.5	5.5	x	...
1969, T69-I + II	27	2	55.6	11.3	59.1	65.4	10.6	38.5	5.0	x	x
1969, T69-VISM Only	6	2	50.0	10.5	100.0	33.3	10.5	66.7	4.7	...	x
					Comparison						
1967, C_2-67	15	2 & 3	73.3	10.5	80.0	93.3	11.3	6.7	5.3	x	...
1967, C_4-67	10	4	50.0	10.3	71.5	20.0	10.6	60.0	5.9	x	...
1972, C_5-72[c]	30	6	50.0	9.6	100.0	23.3	9.8	82.1	5.8	...	x

[a] Subjects defined by inclusion in follow-up test.
[b] Hollingshead scales 6 or 7 (unemployed, unskilled, semiskilled).
[c] Entry in 1972–1973 as after-only group.

first occurred just before pretesting in a home interview with the child's mother conducted by the program supervisor responsible for supervising the dyad's TD throughout the program. The second was conducted at follow-up.

Results

Demographic Characteristics of Sample

Table 1 presents demographic data for the nine treated and control groups in areas usually considered associated with low-income status of the family: education of both parents, occupation of father, frequency of the father's presence in the home, family size, and proportion of mothers receiving welfare aid.

Most of the group means and proportions of table 1 items are as expected for a low-income sample. The average level of father's education was below high school graduation, from mid-ninth to mid-eleventh grades, but higher than that sometimes reported for poverty groups (e.g., Klaus & Gray 1968). Most fathers in the sample were in low-status occupations: unemployed, unskilled, or semiskilled. This was the pattern for all groups, but it was less true for the T68-I + II and T69-I + II groups than for the others, which raises

TABLE 2

PERCENTAGE OF SUBJECTS COMPLETING ASSIGNED PROGRAMS AND PERCENTAGE AVAILABLE AT FOLLOW-UP

		TIME PERIOD		
SUBJECT GROUP	N AT ENTRY	% Completing First Program Year	% Completing Second Program Year	% Available for Testing at Follow-up
T67-I	16	100	...	88
T67-I + Short II	17	100	88	100
T67-C_1 + I	10	90	...	80
T68-I + II	29	90	70	86
T69-I + II	33	94	76	85
T69-VISM Only	12	100	75	50
C_2-67	19	...	...	84
C_4-67	10	...	...	100
C_5-72	30	...	...	...

a question of group equivalence on this variable. Two-thirds of the fathers in the total sample were living in the home, but here there was wide variation among the groups, with two comparison groups showing the greatest extremes, from 20% present for the C_4-67 group to 93% present for the C_2-67 group.

The average level of mother's education was a little higher than that of fathers and ranged from ninth to eleventh grade. About one-third of the mothers in the total sample were receiving welfare aid, but there was great variation among the groups, from 6.7% mothers on welfare for the C_2-67 group to 82% on welfare for the C_5-72 group. The proportion of mothers receiving welfare in every group was roughly similar to the proportion of fathers absent from home.

Family size (total number of home residents) varied among the groups, from means of 4.7 (T69-VISM Only) to 6.2 (T67-I + Short II), with an average of 5.5 for the total sample.

Apart from the C_5-72 group, which was consistently lower than the other groups on SES indicators, SES variations did not clearly favor one level of treatment over another.

Retention Rates

The number of children in each group at program entry completing designated programs and available for testing is reported in table 2. These rates are of concern not only as they affect the data but as an indicator of the feasibility of the program.

In follow-up, 84% of the children originally enrolled were available for testing, excluding the C_4-67 and C_5-72 groups, which had no opportunity for attrition. This number includes those who did not complete their assigned program but who were tested at follow-up. Maternal acceptance of the programs appeared to be high. Of all treated dyads, 95% completed the first year and 80% completed the second year of intended treatment. The T68-I + II and T69-I + II dyads completed about 85% of the planned number of home sessions, and nearly all anonymous evaluations mailed by program mothers reported a highly favorable opinion of the program. The rate of return of the anonymous questionnaires was 46%. In untreated groups, acceptance of the testing seemed equally high. All mothers appeared to view it as a service from which they received information about impending developmental disabilities, and they gave good cooperation. Of course, such evaluations by "happy consumers" must be treated with caution.

IQ Status

Tables 3 and 4 summarize IQ test scores for all nine groups. Pretest Cattell and S-B scores give an indication of pretest group equivalence, even though it may not be assumed that the two tests are equivalent. The follow-up test period was defined separately for each group as the period when: (*a*) nearly all subjects were tested on the S-B and (*b*) the group mean age was nearest 5. Third-grade WISC scores are also reported for groups entering in 1967 and 1968. Test scores obtained at the other time intervals indicated in the group descriptions are not reported here because they do not permit clear comparisons between groups.

IQ status of treated groups.—The mean WISC score for the T68-I + II group is well above the national norm of 97.7 for 6–11-year-old children with fathers completing 9–11 years of schooling (Roberts 1971, p. 55). The S-B scores of the other group receiving 2 full years of treatment predict similar WISC scores for that group as well.

The other treated groups present a more variable picture. There is relatively little difference between the larger two groups (T67-I and T67-I + Short II), both obtaining WISC scores below the 97.7 norm. The performances of the T67-C_1 + I and the T69-VISM Only groups were better than those of the larger 1-year treated groups, but the small size of these groups and the 50% attrition of the T69-VISM Only group limit confidence in their mean performance as an estimate of treatment effect.

IQ status of comparison groups.—Table 4 presents a consistent picture of IQ scores for the comparison groups. All three groups obtained WISC scores below the 97.7 norm, and the available S-B scores were below those of the treated subjects.

These group summaries provide a preliminary set of answers to the first three questions raised above. The 2-year treated groups with TDs who had no formal social work training retained satisfactory levels of IQ scores into the school years. With the exception of the T67-C_1 + I and T69-VISM Only groups, groups receiving less than 2 years of treatment obtained somewhat lower scores at follow-up. The comparison groups consistently obtained scores at or below their expected level based on norms for children with fathers with 9–11 years of education.

Treatment Comparisons

The long-term effects of varying intensities of the program were examined at follow-up for seven of the nine groups. The T69-VISM Only group was excluded from these analyses because the treatment received by this group is not qualitatively comparable to other treatments, and the C_5-72 group because it was not tested at follow-up as defined above.

To test the relation between length of program treatment and follow-up IQ, the remaining groups were classified into three levels of treatment. The 2-year treated level contained the T68-I + II and T69-I + II groups; the 1-year treated level contained the T67-I, T67-I + Short II, and T67-C_1 + I groups, and the untreated level was composed of the C_2-67 and the C_4-67 groups. As above, children originally assigned to a group and available for testing were included in the analysis, regardless of treatment actually received. Distributed throughout the groups were 26 younger siblings of treated or comparison children

TABLE 3

IQ SCORES FOR TREATED GROUPS

SUBJECT GROUP AND VARIABLE	TEST PERIOD: Pretest Cattell	Pretest S-B	Follow-up S-B	Third-Grade WISC
T67-I:				
N [a]	...	14	14	12
IQ	...	89.5	102.8	94.6
SD	...	11.9	13.9	10.6
Age (grade) [b]	...	3	5½(K)	8½(3)
Months after pretest	...	...	28	64
T67-I + Short II:				
N	17	...	17	14
IQ	83.2	...	100.8	97.4
SD	6.7	...	9.9	10.5
Age (grade)	2	...	4½	8½(3)
Months after pretest	...	...	28	76
T67-C_1 + I:				
N	3	4	8	7
IQ	86.7	94.2	106.6	108.0
SD	15.0	6.1	9.4	11.2
Age (grade)	2	3	4½,5½(−K)	8½,9½(3,4)
Months after pretest	...	...	28	76
T68-I + II:				
N	13	11	24 [c]	24 [c]
IQ	88.4	91.3	106.2	103.9
SD	12.2	3.7	11.2	10.9
Age (grade)	2	2	5½(K)	8½(3)
Months after pretest	...	...	40	76
T69-I + II:				
N	25	2	27 [d]	...
IQ	86.4	117.0	111.8	...
SD	10.1	21.2	15.2	...
Age (grade)	2	2	5½(K)	...
Months after pretest	...	...	40	...
T69-VISM Only:				
N	6	...	6	...
IQ	87.0	...	103.2	...
SD	7.4	...	10.1	...
Age (grade)	2	...	5½(K)	...
Months after pretest	...	...	40	...

[a] Subjects tested on S-B at follow-up.
[b] For 50%+ of group.
[c] Excludes one subject who scored 109 on the WISC at follow-up.
[d] Excludes one subject who scored 107 on the WISC at follow-up.

TABLE 4

IQ SCORES FOR COMPARISON GROUPS

SUBJECT GROUP AND VARIABLE	TEST PERIOD: Pretest Cattell	Pretest S-B	Follow-up S-B	Third-Grade WISC
C_2-67:				
N	10	5	15 [a]	14 [a]
IQ	94.1	88.0	97.8	96.1
SD	7.8	10.3	12.8	15.0
Age (grade) [b]	...	2,3	4½,5½(−K)	8½,9½(3,4)
Months after pretest	...	...	28	76
C_4-67:				
N	...	...	10	10
IQ	...	...	91.0	96.3
SD	...	...	8.2	10.3
Age (grade)	...	...	4	8½(3)
Months after pretest	...	...	0	56
C_5-72:				
N	...	...	...	27
IQ	...	...	...	93.9
SD	...	...	...	8.6
Age (grade)	...	...	...	8½(3)
Months after pretest	...	...	...	24

[a] Excludes one who scored 40 on the Cattell in follow-up and 36 on the S-B at third grade.
[b] For 50%+ of group.

who were removed from the analysis to reduce violations of the analysis-of-variance assumption of independence of observations.

Differences between levels of treatment for the remaining subjects were tested by a hierarchical analysis of variance (Kirk 1968, p. 232). An approximate method suggested by Snedecor (1956, p. 271) was used to correct for the unequal number of subjects per group. Differences between groups receiving the same kind of treatment were not significant, $F(4,82) < 1$, allowing pooling of variance. After pooling, the difference between the three levels of treatment was significant, $F(2,86) = 4.23$, $p < .05$. The mean IQ difference between 2-year treated and untreated groups after removing siblings was 12.9 points.

These results indicate, first, that there were significant differences in follow-up IQ scores between differently treated groups and, second, that these differences were not due to group differences which occurred within treatment categories. The results are consistent with the hypothesis of a linear relation between amount of intervention and follow-up IQ scores.

Although this analysis was somewhat conservative in classifying subjects according to assigned treatment rather than treatment received, the IQ differences cannot be unequivocally attributed to the MCHP, because most groups were not randomly assigned to treatments and dyads were not randomly assigned to groups. Even though no major systematic differences between the groups in this analysis were evident at pretest, it is possible that there were relevant pretest differences that were not evident because they were imperfectly measured.

Sibling IQ Differences

One possible source of the IQ differences reported above could be differences between the kinds of families recruited for the different groups. The presence of siblings in the data allows at least a partial test of this alternative hypothesis.

From 1967 through 1974, 52 sibling pairs entered the program in which the older child was the first family member to enter the program, in which the older entered at least a year before the younger, and in which both siblings were pretested on the Cattell. The mean pretest IQ score for the older siblings was 87.1, and for the younger siblings it was 95.4. The mean "pretest differential" (Phillips, Note 1) was 8.3 points, $t(51) = 4.19$, $p < .001$.

It appears that the pretest differential does not extend to posttest. Of the 52 sibling pairs, both members of 28 pairs were tested immediately after receiving the full program. The mean posttest difference on the S-B was 2.4 points, which was not significant. The pretest differential is consistent with the hypothesis that there is some effect of the program on IQ that occurs with the home. The failure to find posttest differences between siblings indicates that the effect of the program (or other effective agents) is not to add some number of points to pretest IQ.

Of more interest here are IQ scores after completion of the program. Seven of the 10 C_4-67 children had younger siblings who completed the program and who were posttested at approximately 4 years of age. The C_4-67 children had themselves been pretested at age 4. The mean difference in S-B scores favoring program children over their older comparison siblings was 16.1 points, $t(6) = 3.70$, $p < .01$, contradicting the hypothesis that IQ differences between treated and comparison children are due to preexisting differences between families rather than the program.

In all of these comparisons, younger siblings scored higher than their older siblings had at about the same age. However, it does not appear likely that this systematic age order of differences caused the IQ differences. The birth-order literature would not predict such an effect, and our data do not indicate a general increase in local IQ scores that would account for the effects. The major weaknesses of these findings are the small number of comparisons of treated and comparison children after the program and the possibility that these families, being to some extent self-selected, are atypical.

Subject to these qualifications, the available data for siblings suggest that effects of different treatments are evident within families and thus may not be completely accounted for by preexisting differences between families.

Correlation between IQ and Other Variables

The remaining question concerned the relation of follow-up IQ to other background and outcome variables. Follow-up IQs were correlated with 50 background and outcome variables, a full list of which is available from the authors. The 50 background variables included demographic attributes of parents, grandparents, and family (e.g., education, occupation, health, family size), other characteristics of parents (e.g., father's employment and mother's style of dealing with home physical environment), and other characteristics of index children (e.g., psychosocial problems).

Table 5 lists only those Pearson r's and point-biserial coefficients significant at $p < .05$ for the combined 2-year treated groups (T68-I + II and T69-I + II), 1-year treated groups (T67-I, T67-I + Short II, and T67-C_1 + I), comparison groups (C_2-67 and C_4-67), and all of these groups combined. The T69-VISM Only and C_5-72 groups are not represented for the same reasons they were not considered in the treatment comparisons above.

Eighteen of the 200 correlations with follow-up IQ were significant at or beyond the .05 level. Some chance large correlations are to be expected, but most relations are as anticipated. The correlations between S-B and PPVT are high, and there were several low and moderate correlations between IQ and SES indicators.

TABLE 5

CORRELATIONS OF BACKGROUND AND FOLLOW-UP VARIABLES WITH STANFORD-BINET IQ AT FOLLOW-UP FOR 1- AND 2-YEAR TREATED, UNTREATED, AND ALL GROUPS COMBINED (Pearson's and Point-biserial *r*)

	TOTAL 2-YEAR TREATED GROUP		TOTAL 1-YEAR TREATED GROUP		TOTAL UNTREATED GROUP		ALL GROUPS COMBINED	
	r	*N*	*r*	*N*	*r*	*N*	*r*	*N*
	Background Variables							
Entry age	−.21	51	.25	39	−.22	25	−.25*	115
Mother's education	.23	51	.35*	39	.46*	25	.24*	115
Hollingshead two-factor ISP score	−.36	49	−.21	36	−.15	25	−.28**	110
Father's father's education	.63**	27	.31	21	−.07	15	.25*	63
Father's father's occupation	.60	24	.06	24	−.06	14	.24	62
	Follow-up Variables							
Age at follow-up	−.06	51	.16	39	.23	25	.28**	115
PPVT	.57**	51	.77**	39	.75**	25	.64**	115
Home "physical environment description"	.09	46	.33*	37	.38	15	.13	98
Child's psychological-social problems	.36*	46	...	...	...	...	.36*	46
Post-MCHP contact	.09	46	.19	37	...	...	.21*	98
Mother's follow-up work hours	−.02	23	.04	21	−.60**	11	−.17	55
Moved post-MCHP	.15	46	.33	35	−.06	14	.22*	95

* $p < .05$.
** $p < .01$.

Of the SES and demographic variables in table 5, data were available for all dyads only for mother's education, which correlated positively with IQ. As table 1 indicates, the groups scoring highest in IQ are not highest in mother's education. Correlations with father's father's education and occupation were both in the expected direction and were largest in the 2-year treated group, but these data were missing for many families. There was a small positive correlation between IQ and the project-developed Physical Environment Description. This score is composed of 10 Likert scale items rating interview room features (e.g., spatial arrangement of furniture) and is intended to reflect styles of physical home management.

Correlations between entry age and IQ and between follow-up age and IQ reflect in part the fact that the comparison and 1-year treated groups were slightly older at entry and younger at follow-up than were the 2-year treated groups.

Several correlations may have resulted from artifacts or from small numbers of observations. The correlation of S-B with moving after the MCHP may have resulted from the residential stability of project dwellers, who were most heavily represented in the groups receiving less than 2 years of treatment. Two correlations are based on small numbers of observations. For 11 control children, having a mother who worked part- instead of full-time was associated with a higher S-B score. Mothers' reports that their children had psychosocial problems were associated with higher IQs, but there were only five such reports.

One variable not included in table 5 is preschool attendance. No correlation was possible for any groups except the C_5-72 group (where the correlation was −.07), because virtually all other children had some form of preschool experience in addition to the MCHP. Thus, if the program is found to be effective, it must be pointed out that the program plus some form of center-based preschool attendance was effective. That preschool attendance was not of itself effective is indicated by the performances of the C_2-67 and C_4-67 groups, who attended preschool but did not receive the program.

In general, the correlations between IQ and background and demographic variables that are based on enough cases to be stable go in the expected directions. Across all such variables, there appears little evidence that the IQ scores of one group are more influenced by such variables than those of others, or that follow-up IQ differences between treatments were caused by differences in background or concomitant variables.

Feasibility of MCHP Variations

The data suggest that the full 2-year variations of the MCHP, conducted by paid or volunteer interveners with a wide range of education and prior skills, were more effective than the 1-year versions. The 1968 changes from a shortened second year to a full 2-year program were less costly than the 1967 MCHP, and, contrary to expectation, the full 2-year program was easier to administer. The shortened 2-year variations (T67-I + Short II) took as much staff time and effort as and caused more staff frustration than did the full program. When dyads were seen less often in home sessions in the second year, the mothers tended to forget appointments and to withdraw from their involvement, requiring an unusual expenditure of effort by the TDs and their supervisors. Since personnel and administrative time absorbed the main cost of the program, the full 2-year MCHP (T68-I + II and T69-I + II) seemed the most feasible of all the 2-year variations, with the possible exception of the T69-VISM Only treatment.

Short-Term Experimental Results

In 1973, it became possible to begin a true field experiment, randomly assigning 51 dyads to treated and control conditions after the mothers had agreed to accept the outcome of such a lottery. The design was a 2 × 2 × 2 factorial with factors of treatment, sex, and high versus low number in family. At the end of the usual 2-year program, conducted as described above, there remained 19 treated and 16 untreated dyads. The treated children obtained a mean S-B score of 104.8, and the control children 100.9.

An analysis of covariance was performed on posttest S-B scores with a covariate of pretest Cattell. A least-squares correction was made for unequal numbers of scores per cell following Overall and Spiegel's (1969) experimental method. No effects in the analysis were significant except a correlation of .68 between pretest and posttest IQ. From an estimate of the power of the analysis, we can be somewhat better than 60% certain that there was not a true 10-point difference between treatments. Further, the initial data do not suggest that a substantial program effect on IQ is being masked by selective attrition or by chance difference between groups.

There are few other outcome variables on which both experimental treated and comparison groups may be compared. As these groups are followed up in long-term studies, more outcome will be accumulated, but for the present, there is no definitive explanation for the apparent contradiction between these short-term experimental results and the long-term quasi-experimental results.

Discussion and Conclusions

This report of findings from a longitudinal study of 151 dyads began with four questions about the long-term cognitive effects of the MCHP after the 1-year program had been followed by large short-term effects in 1967–1968, when conducted with social workers as interveners. The questions concerned IQ stability, the feasibility and effectiveness of utilizing volunteer and nonprofessional interveners, the amount of intervention necessary for maximum effect, the relation of these effects to other outcomes or events in the child's life, and whether the program did indeed have a significant effect on the IQs of treated children as compared with untreated subjects.

The long-term data support the first year's promise of the MCHP's effectiveness. Satisfactory IQ scores were retained by program graduates at least into first grade when the program was expanded to 2 full years instead of the original 1 year. The results for the full 2-year program have thus been demonstrated to be stable over time.

At the same time that the program was expanded to its present 2-year format, non-social-worker TDs were introduced as interveners. Because the most stable results were obtained under these conditions, we concluded as a practical matter that interveners with a range of education from less than high school completion through college were at least as effective as graduate social workers in producing long-term effects. This finding greatly increased the feasibility of the program for application in other settings outside the research project, a feasibility supported by the estimated annual unit cost of $400 in the model program and an average of $550 in 11 replications outside the model program.

The MCHP "graduates" appeared to benefit along a continuum of amount of exposure to the program, with groups in the full 2-year version superior to other treated groups and to untreated groups, an observation first made by Bronfenbrenner (1974). The full 2-year program was also found to be more feasible than abbreviated versions, with the exception of the VISM Only variation. Since results for the latter treatment could not be clearly interpreted, this treatment is being repeated with a larger, randomized sample which began in September 1974.

The long-term results have thus far been encouraging, and, insofar as IQ scores may be taken as an index of level of cognitive functioning, the children who received 2 full years of the MCHP do not appear to be laboring under the cognitive disadvantage usually associated with the demographic attributes which determined their acceptance into the program.

Confidence in the results of these original studies is limited due to their quasi-experimental design. The available data have generally indicated that no easily identifiable factor other than the program is likely to have been responsible for the effect. To use legal terminology, the effectiveness of the program appears to be supported by a preponderance of evidence but not beyond a reasonable doubt.

Our original plan was to validate these long-term studies with experimental data rather than study the quasi experiment in more detail. It now appears that both must be done. The results for cohorts entering from 1967 through 1972 are promising enough to mandate continued experimental research. The short-term experimental findings require a suspension of judgment concerning the effectiveness of the program and increased care in the conduct of the program and of its evaluation.

Reference Note

1. Phillips, J. R. Family cognitive profile study. Final report to the Foundation for Child Development, October 1973.

References

Bronfenbrenner, U. *Is early intervention effective? A report on longitudinal evaluations of preschool programs* (Vol. 2). (DHEW Publication No. [OHD] 74-25.) Washington, D.C.: Department of Health, Education, and Welfare, 1974.

Bruner, J. S., Olver, R. R.; Greenfield, P. M.; et al. *Studies in cognitive growth.* New York: Wiley, 1966.

Campbell, D. T., & Stanley, J. C. *Experimental and quasi-experimental designs for research.* New York: Rand McNally, 1963.

Cattell, P. *The measurement of intelligence of infants and young children.* New York: Psychological Corp., 1940.

Kirk, R. E. *Experimental design: procedures for the behavioral sciences.* Belmont, Calif.: Brooks/Cole, 1968.

Klaus, R. A., & Gray, S. W. The early training project for disadvantaged children: a report after five years. *Monographs of the Society for Research in Child Development*, 1968, 33(4, Serial No. 120).

Levenstein, P. Cognitive growth in preschoolers through verbal interaction with mothers. *American Journal of Orthopsychiatry*, 1970, **40**, 426–432.

Levenstein, P. A message from home: findings from a program for non-retarded low-income preschoolers. In M. J. Begab & S. A. Richardson (Eds.), *The mentally retarded and society.* Baltimore: University Park Press, 1975.

Levenstein, P. The Mother-Child Home Program. In M. C. Day & R. K. Parker (Eds.), *The preschool in action* (2d ed.). Boston: Allyn & Bacon, in press.

Levenstein, P., & Sunley, R. Stimulation of verbal interaction between disadvantaged mothers and children. *American Journal of Orthopsychiatry*, 1968, **38**, 116–121.

Overall, J. E., & Spiegel, D. E. Concerning least squares analysis of experimental data. *Psychological Bulletin*, 1969, **72**, 311–322.

Roberts, J. *Intellectual development of children by demographic and socioeconomic factors* (vital and health statistics data from the National Health Survey, Ser. 11, No. 10). (DHEW Publication No. [HSM] 72-1012.) Washington, D.C.: Department of Health, Education, and Welfare, 1971.

Snedecor, G. W. *Statistical methods applied to experiments in agriculture and biology.* Ames: Iowa State University Press, 1956.

Terman, L. M., & Merrill, M. A. *Stanford-Binet Intelligence Scale 1972 norms edition.* Boston: Houghton Mifflin, 1973.

A Pilot With a Difference

Elizabeth and Henry Urrows

A great deal of foundation support goes into funding pilot programs which, if they prove successful, are intended to go public with government or other wide-based financing. Unfortunately many pilots founder on one of two reefs. Either the project is launched with enthusiasm, reported in the professional literature, and dies unnoticed, or, what is worse, it is picked up and "copied" with insufficient understanding of intended results, criteria, methods and materials, distorting the original concept out of all recognition.

Now a unique collaboration of government, private, and foundation efforts is developing and replicating a pilot program of Parent Child Development Centers. It promises to avoid the familiar gaps between promise and performance. During, the current first wave of replications, the Federal Office of Child Development, the Lilly Endowment, and the Bank Street College of Education, in New York, pursue methods of program proliferation that other foundations should watch with interest.

In 1970, the U.S. Office of Equal Opportunity began planning a carefully researched program for parents of infants under three years old in low-income neighborhoods of Birmingham, New Orleans, and Houston. Now under the U.S. Office of Child Development, these model centers differed from previous Head Start and early childhood services in basing all activity on these principles:

1. The mother is by far the most important influence on her child's attitudes and developing abilities, and is the primary target.

2. Development of life-long character traits begins much earlier in infancy than had been thought.

3. A mother who is under the multiple stresses of poverty, ill health, and lack of education is least able to help her children grow into confident, curious, and ambitious adults.

The first determination was that the mother should be the central focus of the centers' work. A second distinction was an insistence on collecting base-line information about participating mothers and infants who took part as well as on control mother-infant pairs from the same neighborhoods, with continuing research on changes effected by the program.

The Parent Child Development Centers began by asking: What changes do we want in the mothers? What changes do we want in the infants? When do we hope to effect these changes? How can we measure them? What are the differences between participating children and controls? When do these differences emerge? At what ages? To what degree?

The PCDC's are alike in serving mothers and infants less than three years old from low-income families; in their emphasis on understanding how children grow and learn; in their using as center staffs neighborhood men and women who know the mothers' problems and speak their language, and in attention to practical needs of daily living: health, nutrition, consumer education, homemaking that must stretch limited income, and qualifying for high school equivalency certificates. All the centers employ mothers who have been in the program for two or three years as important aides who work with entering mothers.

Differences in Models and Their Methods. The Birmingham model serves an integrated group of black and white mother-infant pairs; 35 per cent are "intact families" with fathers living at home. Houston has entirely Mexican-American clients, 95 per cent of whose fathers are at home, in a bilingual and bicultural program. New Orleans serves all black families, half of whom are headed by mothers only.

New Orleans begins training mothers when their infants are as young as 2½ months old; Birmingham when they are between 3 and 4 months of age, Houston at 12 months.

All Birmingham activity takes place at the center, while Houston and New Orleans have experimented with

Henry and Elizabeth Urrows are freelance writers based in Ridgefield, Conn.

varying amounts of home intervention and center-based training. Birmingham emphasizes mothers training mothers, while New Orleans has paraprofessionals working with them.

Birmingham and New Orleans each have about 60 pairs of mothers and infants. Houston serves between 70 and 80 at one time and has English language classes and workshops for fathers as well as mothers.

The Replication Management Organization. The first wave of the replicating process started in 1975. It has paired the Birmingham model with a new Indianapolis center, New Orleans' program with one in Detroit, and Houston's bilingual model with another in San Antonio.

The Bank Street College of Education is responsible for making sure that the programs at the new centers are patterned after the models, and for documentation of their work in progress with a view toward gaining results comparable to those achieved during the first five years' operation of the models. It supervises the training of staff for and at the new centers that the model centers provide. It plans for the uses of manuals prepared by each model center on every key facet of its services.

The Lilly Endowment and U.S. Office of Child Development agree that having a single resource charged with project management should assure good use of pooled findings of research, taking advantage of what model centers learned during the evolvement of their programs. Just as results at model centers have been remarkably consistent, it is hoped that results at the first three replication sites will be as positive in mothers' learning and behavior, which are reflected in children who took part in the program as well as their other youngsters.

Results to Date. Evaluations after five years show the three model or pilot programs had unmistakably positive benefits.

In all three PCDC's, by the time children reached the age of three their mothers had developed more — and more effective — ways of interacting with them to encourage learning, ability to make themselves understood, attentiveness, and responsiveness to discipline in an atmosphere of maternal sensitivity and positive affection.

Compared with other intervention programs, the yardsticks and methods employed are considered meticulous in rigor. For example, at all three model centers there was random assignment of mother and infant pairs from the same neighborhoods to program and comparison groups; there were careful choice and development of a broad range of reliable, objective measures of program impact, including standardized as well as new instruments, with collection of base-line and follow-up data before, during, and after program participation.

Too often, other pilot programs confined evaluations to a single set or oversimplified array of yardsticks, with the result that those who attempted to carry out succeeding efforts had difficulty agreeing on whether the findings and conclusions adequately reflected program objectives or staff efforts. The PCDC's reports comparing the mothers and infants who took part with controls show markedly higher infant IQ's, with significantly higher self-confidence among both mothers and children, along with ability to relate to others, ability to cope with real needs after leaving the program, and curiosity about the world around them.

Critical in a program aimed at strengthening mothers' feelings of confidence were efforts to avoid having research seem to be mysterious, or an impingement on their lives beyond their control. Mothers received full explanations about research methods and tests, were permitted to be present when their children were tested, and testers were usually from their same ethnic and cultural backgrounds.

In many pilot programs, the first group of participants show more progress than their successors. The first wave of PCDC mothers showed positive changes in 24 months. Waves two and three, benefitting from earlier experience, showed desired results within 12 months.

Next Steps. Looking toward nine new replication sites (three of each model), the U.S. Office of Child Development is inviting state and local public authorities and private national organizations to become interested. The next group of sites is being chosen to vary kinds of sponsors and geographic regions. Further selections will vary the characteristics of users to test applicability of models to groups representing a universe of need estimated to be as large as a million families, with 1,200,000 children younger than three years old and incomes up to 150 per cent of the poverty level. Of these, 78 percent of mothers in two-parent families and 60 per cent of mothers who are heads of households are not employed.

In addition to the central core of research evaluation carried on by the Office of Child Development, three foundations — the Foundations' Fund for Research in Psychiatry, the Hogg Foundation, and the Spencer Foundation — have responded to particular aspects of needs for further investigation of questions uncovered by PCDC project work thus far.

Longitudinal or follow-up studies of original participants in the model centers will continue until the children attend school.

Because there are ever-increasing calls upon limited resources, it is important to make sure what states and communities will get for their money. Operational costs of PCDC's have been carefully recorded, including in-kind contributions from local sponsors. Nearly half of the original funding has been invested in research. Comparable information on many other programs to help poor families with very young children is not now available to facilitate clear cost comparisons. To aid public policy decisions generally, and the Office of Child Development in particular, it would be useful for the sake of arriving at cost-effective judgments to learn costs per family along with results for operational infant day care, Head Start, Follow Through, and other programs.

As further PCDC replications begin, states and citizens should be able to predict with confidence both the costs and the benefits they can expect if they adopt and adapt clearly detailed procedures for local requirements.

For More Information

For facts about particular centers, training materials, and the replication management process, write:

Susan Ginsberg, Director, Parent Child Development Center Project, Bank Street College of Education, 610 West 112th Street, New York, N.Y. 10025.

To learn what regional and community possibilities exist for new replications of Parent-Child Development Centers, write:

Maxine Brown, Program Officer, The Lilly Endowment, Inc., 2801 North Meridian Street, Indianapolis, Ind. 46208, and/or

Mary Robinson, Program Manager, Parent-Child Development Centers Project, U.S. Office of Child Development, 400 Sixth Street, S.W., Washington, D.C. 20201.

New Sites . . . and Sponsors

. . . Looking toward nine new replication sites (three of each model), the U.S. Office of Child Development is inviting state and local public authorities and private national organizations to become interested. The next wave of sites is being chosen to vary kinds of sponsors and geographic regions.

The University of Houston, University of New Orleans, and the Jefferson County Office of Economic Opportunity in Birmingham sponsor the model Parent Child Development Centers.

The Inman Christian Center, Merrill-Palmer Institute, and Marian College sponsor the San Antonio, Detroit, and Indianapolis replication PCDC's.

Breaking the Cycle

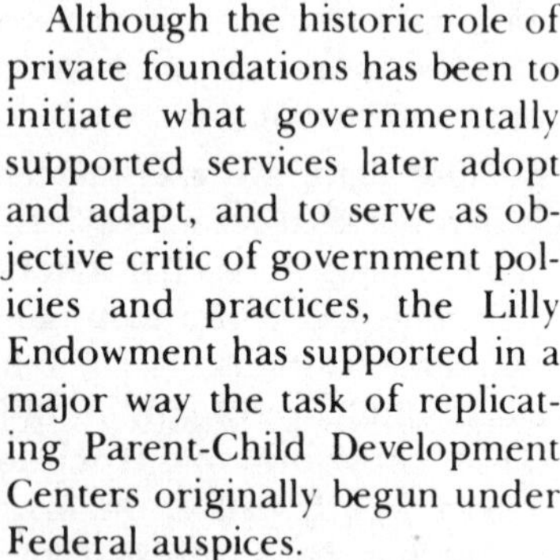

Although the historic role of private foundations has been to initiate what governmentally supported services later adopt and adapt, and to serve as objective critic of government policies and practices, the Lilly Endowment has supported in a major way the task of replicating Parent-Child Development Centers originally begun under Federal auspices.

We believe it is essential to see that the transfer process can be effective, so that states, cities, and other sponsoring entities are guided by reliable information as to what their various options can buy.

When we consider the scale of poverty, and the stubborn fact that as many as 70 per cent of Mexican-American, black, and other inner-city youth drop out of school, we need not belabor the need for new and more effective approaches to help families break the poverty cycle.

The needs for welfare reform are universally recognized. What to do that will be useful, and not risk worsening an already impossible cost situation, gets far less unanimity of judgments.

Welfare reform requires finding reliable ways to break the poverty cycle. The problems are so vast, and so complex, that no single answer can be expected to emerge. We have an obligation, however, to pursue every promising approach that works in the real world of cities, states, and communities.

The Lilly Endowment believes that private initiatives can be significant in highlighting what can be done. It believes that the good beginnings made by the model Parent-Child Development Centers can prove in time to be capable of transfer and adaptation to other local conditions, problems, and opportunities elsewhere.

Landrum R. Bolling
President
Lilly Endowment, Inc.

"A Pilot With a Difference," by Elizabeth Urrows and Henry Urrows. Foundation News, Vol. 18, No. 5, September/October 1977, pp. 38-41. Council on Foundations, Inc., New York, New York.

FATHER CARETAKING CHARACTERISTICS AND THEIR INFLUENCE ON INFANT-FATHER INTERACTION

by Milton Kotelchuck *University of Massachusetts/Boston*

Abstract

The influence of father's interactive and child-care characteristics on the infant's social behavior is explored in 5 experimental studies of infant-father interaction. Problems of methodology are discussed and father-caregiving patterns are noted. The relationship to the father was seen to be independent of the extent of his involvement in child care, although some minimal level of interaction seemed necessary. Extensive paternal caregiving was related to the preferences for the father in the laboratory and shortened duration of separation protest. The final study demonstrated that manipulation of father-infant interaction at home directly influences infant-father interaction in a laboratory setting.

Introduction

Until recently most psychologists assumed that infants related only to their mother; the father's relation to his infant was ignored. However, in the last few years researchers have demonstrated that infant-father relationships do, in fact, exist (e.g. Kotelchuck, 1972; Lewis, Weinraub, Ban, 1972; Cohen and Campos, 1974; and Lamb, 1975).

This observation logically leads to the question of whether differential paternal interaction influences the child's development. Before trying to establish any long-term effects, it must first be demonstrated that the father's interaction has an immediate influence on the child. In this paper I would like to begin to document the father's early influence on his child by examining the relationship between the father's caregiving and interactive characteristics at home and the infant's laboratory behavior.

Methodologically there are at least three ways to demonstrate a relation between home caregiving characteristics and the infant's laboratory behavior. The least sophisticated but the easiest method is *correlational.* Correlations between reported events at home and what occurs in the laboratory can be calculated without any prior manipulations in the design. The experimenter exerts no control over the distribution of data being examined. This method is probably the most commonly used one, especially where home caregiving characteristics are incidentally collected and the relation between home caregiving characteristics and laboratory behavior is secondary to the goal of the laboratory study.

Correlational studies can be used to generate hypotheses; but these must be examined cautiously. First, if the distribution of either home caregiving and interactive characteristics or laboratory behavior are markedly skewed, then no significant correlation will be found even where one might exist. This problem is almost inherent in infant-father studies, as most fathers display a very limited range of caregiving and interaction with their infants, highly skewed towards no involvement. Second, even if a significant association were found, one could always argue that it is a spurious finding. For example, if high interactive fathers predict bright children, one could argue that the brightness is really due to the mothers, who besides stimulating their children also marry interactive fathers. Hence, a high father-infant correlation would have been found, but it would not be causal.

A much more powerful variation of the correlational methodology involves prior *stratification* of fathers on the basis of their home caregiving characteristics; i.e., an examination of equal number of father types at discrete points along some continuum. This quasi-experimental method does not examine a cross-section of all fathers, as in the previous method, but only discrete stratified groups of fathers to see if there is an association with the infant's behaviors. Data from an experiment designed in this manner can be examined using analysis of variance, with the stratified father groups as an independent measure and the infant's behavior as the dependent measure. This method is appropriate only when the specific goal of the research is to directly test hypotheses about effects of home caregiving characteristics.

Compared to the correlational method, stratification is a very powerful technique. The problem of skewedness of data is rectified. If any relation exists, one should find it. However, this model is still subject to the arguments about spuriousness; something other than the chosen variable might be both influencing the father home caregiving characteristics and the infants laboratory behavior.

The third and most powerful method is *experimental.* If one really believes that father home caregiving characteristics causally and directly influence the child's laboratory behaviors, one should be able to manipulate and change the parents' behavior at home and subsequently observe a change in the child's laboratory behavior. This would be the most powerful demonstration of a direct causal relation and would eliminate arguments about possible spuriousness of the findings.

Correlational and stratification methodologies are static models that explore the relationship between what is presently the father's home caregiving characteristics and the infant's behavior. The experimental methodology is a dynamic model that allows one to explore how the child's behavior might change if the parent's behavior changes.

Method and Sample

This paper will examine the relationship between paternal home caregiving and interactional characteristics and the infant's lab behavior in five separate experiments which my colleagues and I have conducted in the past few years (Kotelchuck, 1972; Spelke, Zelazo, Kagan, Kotelchuck, 1973; Lester, Kotelchuck, Spelke, Sellers and Klein, 1974; Ross, Kagan, Zelazo, Kotelchuck, 1974; and Zelazo, Barber, Kotelchuck and David, 1976). No single study is comprehensive, but all five together make for a coherent picture.

Each experiment uses basically the same paradigm. The infant's behavioral reactions are recorded as a function of the manipulation of the presence and absence of the mother, the father, and a female stranger in a large playroom.

The experiments begin with the infant located in the center of a large playroom surrounded by toys and facing his parents, who were seated at one end of the room. The parents are instructed not to initiate interaction with the child, but to sit quietly and read. They are to respond naturally, but briefly, if the child approached them or if the child is upset. It is emphasized to the parents that the child's spontaneous reactions are of primary interest. The strangers are given similar instructions. Every three minutes, one of the adults was signaled either to enter or depart from the room, according to one of the following schedules.

Each schedule is composed of 13 episodes and lasted 39 minutes. For either schedule, a parallel set of events occurs for each of the three adults (e.g. the mother leaves the room twice, once with the father remaining and once with the stranger remaining; the father leaves twice, once with mother remaining and once with stranger remaining; the stranger left twice, once with mother remaining and once with father remaining; the mother enters twice, once with the father present and once with the stranger present, and so forth). These balanced schedules allow for equal comparison of the child's response to each of the three adults. The duration of the child's playing, crying, proximity to a person, touching a person, proximity to the door, vocalizations, smiles, fixations and interactions are coded continuously throughout the 39-minute session.

In total, about 300 families were studied, with the children ranging in age from 6 to 24 months. Most of the studies used middle class first born children from the Boston area. The new element in all of these studies was that fathers and infants were directly observed.

Order of Presence in the Experimental Room

Episode	Order 1	Order 2
1	Mother and Father	Mother and Father
2	Mother	Mother
3	Mother and Stranger	Father and Stranger
4	Stranger	Stranger
5	Stranger and Father	Stranger and Mother
6	Father	Mother
7	Father and Mother	Mother and Father
8	Father	Mother
9	Father and Stranger	Mother and Stranger
10	Stranger	Stranger
11	Stranger and Mother	Stranger and Father
12	Mother	Father
13	Mother and Father	Father and Mother

The five experiments had a variety of goals. In three experiments, the relation between home caregiving characteristics and infant lab behavior was a subsidiary question, and was analyzed using a correlational methodology. These three experiments were my doctoral thesis, the goal of which was to show the existence of father-infant ties (Kotelchuck, 1972), a cross cultural replication in Guatemala (Lester et al., 1974), and a replication in the child's own home (Ross et al., 1974). The fourth experiment, using a stratification design, directly explored the effects of high, medium and low interacting fathers on the infant's laboratory behavior at 12 months of age (Spelke et al., 1973). The last study, an experimental design, was an attempt to directly manipulate the father's interaction with his year old child in their home, in order to observe its consequences on the infant's behavior in the laboratory (Zelazo et al. 1976).

Ascertainment of Child Care Information

In all studies, data on home caregiving characteristics was obtained by a joint maternal and paternal interview following the experimental session. Information was obtained about how much time the father spent with the child, played with the child, diapered and fed the child, and so forth. Measures of interaction were very highly correlated with the measures of child care. No direct observations of child care were made.

Obviously interview data are somewhat unreliable. Unfortunately, the behavioral alternative of sitting at another person's home for days also grossly interferes with their normal activities. There is no simple solution to the problem of obtaining accurate child care information.

A small study (Kotelchuck and Shaw, 1976) was done to test the specific validity of interviews as the source of paternal child care involvement information. Each mother and father pair was asked to fill out child-care questionnaires independently evaluating the amount of time each parent spends in various child care and interactive tasks. The results show that mothers and fathers agree much more on what fathers do than on what mothers do. Intercorrelations for paternal tasks range from .5 to .9 with an average of about .7; while intercorrelations for maternal tasks average about .2. This politically interesting finding implies that mothers and fathers have different levels of awareness of each other's child care tasks. The results of this study also indicate that there is moderate validity to parental reports of father caregiving activity, although one should always be aware of their limitations.

Paternal Child Care Characteristics

Despite the supposedly changing role of the father in our society, the traditional observation that mothers take care of their young children and fathers have minimal responsibility for childrearing was confirmed in these five studies. Middle class mothers in Boston in the 1970's still overwhelmingly had the principal child care responsibilities in their families (Kotelchuck, 1972). Mothers spent more time with their children, 6 to 21 months of age, than fathers did (9.0 versus 3.2 hours, $p. < .001$) and were available essentially for the child's whole waking day. Mothers spent more time feeding their children (1.45 hours versus 0.25 hours, $p. < .001$) and cleaning their children (.92 hours versus .15 hours, $p. < .001$), than did the fathers.

Of the mothers, 64% were totally and solely responsible for the child's care; 9.1% shared child care responsibility with another person. Only 7.6% of the fathers shared infant caretaking responsibilities equally with their wives and only 25% total had any regular daily child care responsibilities. In other words, 75% of middle class fathers in Boston do not physically care for their children on a regular day-to-day basis. Even more remarkably, 43% of all the fathers report they never changed diapers at all! These data reveal that fathers were involved only in a minimal amount of the child's care, especially in those tasks of childrearing that are often viewed as routine and somewhat boring.

Mothers spent more absolute time playing with their children than did the fathers (2.3 to 1.2 hours, $p. < .01$). Duration playing showed the least mother-father difference of any home caregiving measures. Moreover, fathers spent a greater percentage of their time with their children in play activities (37.5%) than mothers did (25.8%). The exact consequence of the differences in proportion of play to total time spent with a child is unclear, but it appears reasonable to suggest that this contributes to the father's attractiveness to his child despite his restricted availability. Similarly, Lamb (1975) suggests that the different types of games mothers and fathers play with their infants also enhance the father's attractiveness.

Relation of Paternal Child-Care Involvement and Infant's Laboratory Behavior

In all the studies, infant and toddlers relate similarly to their mothers and fathers, irrespective of the vast differences in mother-infant and father-infant caretaking and interaction. Crude amount of caretaking or playing are, therefore, not the critical variables in determining who the child is comfortable with or to whom the child relates. Moreover, given the limited amount of paternal child-care activities found in most middle class families and the fact that most children relate to their fathers in the laboratory situation, it should not be surprising that virtually no significant correlations were found between these two sets of data. There is no simple 1:1 relationship between amount of paternal child-care activities at home and the infant's laboratory behavior.

Yet, there is evidence that paternal caregiving practices make a difference. First, there appears to be a minimum level of paternal caretaking necessary for a relationship to exist. In the initial study (Kotelchuck, 1972), those few children who did not relate to their fathers (operationally defined as infants who did not spend at least 15 seconds in his proximity on arrival) came overwhelmingly from families with the lowest caretaking fathers($x^2 = 7.9, p < .01$).

Also in Guatemala, where paternal caretaking and interaction is virtually nonexistent, it does make a difference in the children's behavior. Children in Guatemala related much less to their fathers than they do in the United States; e.g. they are less proximal, show less protest on paternal departures, etc. (Lester et al. 1974). Mother/father differences were more marked in Guatemala than in the U.S.; and stranger/father differences are lessened. Very very low paternal interaction seems to affect who the child relates to. Biller (1971) has noted, in a similar view, that children in families with the father absent or with very low interacting fathers seemed behaviorally similar. Perhaps some minimal level of interaction is necessary for a child to be basically comfortable with a person, but how little is yet unclear.

Second, the children's preferences and extensiveness of interaction with the father in the laboratory are partially related to paternal caregiving at home. Significant positive correlations are found between overall proximity to the father for 12 to 21 month old infants and extent of his caregiving, in the Kotelchuck (1972) laboratory study ($r = .35$, $p < .01$) and even more strongly in the Ross et al. (1974) home based study ($r = .43$, $p < .01$). A similar positive relationship was noted in Lewis, Weinraub and Ban (1972). Maternal proximity remained independent of paternal involvement. In neither Ross et al. (1974) or Kotelchuck (1972) was overall extensiveness of separation protest predicted by paternal involvement. Reported measures of caregiving activities were more predictive of the child's paternal preferences than were play or interactive measures in both studies. The highest inter-correlation noted ($r = .51$, $p < .01$) occurred between paternal proximity in the joint mother-father present episodes (1, 7, 13) (i.e., episodes in which the child has a choice of which parent to go to) and the number of diapers changed by the father per week (Ross et al., 1974).

The influence of paternal home child-care characteristics on the infant's interactive preferences with the father in experimental situations was more strongly seen in the home than in the laboratory. The laboratory is a more unfamiliar situation for the child and probably results in more unusual behaviors obscuring the association. But, paternal caregiving characteristics clearly influence the child's positive interactive behavioral preferences in experimental situations, be it in the child's home or in an unfamiliar setting.

Third, the age span of intense separation protest is shortened for the infant in families with multiple caretakers. That is to say, infants whose mothers and fathers both actively take care for them tend to show separation protest later and terminate it earlier than children with only a single mother caretaker.

The stratified study by Spelke et al. (1973), which looked at 36 12-month-old infants in three groups (12 each with high, medium and low interacting fathers) clearly demonstrated that the most separation distress (crying when left alone with a stranger) occurred in infants with the lowest paternal involvement, an intermediate amount of distress in infants with medium paternal involvement, and the least distress in the infants with highest paternal involvement ($F(4.60) = 3.32$, $p < .01$). That is to say, at 12 months of age, when protest first starts reliably occurring in laboratory situations in the United States, protest is inversely related to paternal involvement. Since protest occurs for almost all 15 and 18 month old infants (Kotelchuck, 1972) separation protest must be commenced at a later age for those children with higher paternal involvement. Stated differently, infants with high interacting fathers are less vulnerable to separation trauma at these younger ages.

These findings are generally supported by a similar finding at 12 months in the Kotelchuck (1972) study showing that the less frequently fathers bathed and dressed their infants at home, the greater amount of time the infants cried when left alone with a stranger ($r = -.40$, $p < .05$). Also consistent with these findings are the reports of earlier onset of separation protest in Guatemala (9 months of age) where there is virtually no paternal involvement (Lester et al. 1974), and an even earlier onset (6 months of age) in Ganda infants who are almost constantly carried on the mother's back (Ainsworth, 1967).

These findings imply that the age of onset of separation protest is partially a function of exclusiveness of maternal caregiving; exposure to more figures, including the father, appears to buffer the child from early separation distress. The child's familiarity or lack of familiarity with parental departures, should vary with the extent of caregiver exclusiveness. One can hypothesize that infants are exposed to more parental departures in high paternal interacting and caregiving families than in exclusive maternal caregiving families, perhaps making those infants less vulnerable to separation trauma at this very early age.

Likewise, a parallel finding occurs at the older end of the normal age range of separation protest in laboratory situations. Kotelchuck (1972) found that extensive separation protest at 21 months of age seems to occur principally in families with low caregiving fathers ($r = -.39$, $p < .05$) and hence in exclusive maternal caregiving families. Thus, overall, it appears that the age span of separation protest is shortened in high paternal interacting families.

Fourth, in none of the studies was paternal caregiving characteristics predictive of the child's ability to relate to or be friendly with an unfamiliar person. A relationship with a second familiar person does not obviously generalize to unfamiliar adults. Results from other studies show that avoidance of strangers remains high even among children "raised" in multiple caretaking contexts such as Day Care centers

(Keaisley, Zelazo, Kagan and Hartman, 1975) or Kibbutzim (Maccoby and Feldman, 1973).

Fifth, there were virtually no sex differences in any of the studies. Boys and girls responded similarly to the experimental manipulations; they did not respond differentially to their parents on the basis of their sex.

An interesting sex difference did emerge, though it was not of the infants' interaction with the fathers', but the fathers' interaction with the infants. In the Boston area, fathers of first born children report that they play about half an hour a day longer with their first born sons than with their first born daughters ($p < .001$). What the long term effect of this will be is not clear. However, at 21 months of age, the oldest age looked at in the Kotelchuck (1972) study, boys played more and interacted more with their fathers than boys played or interacted with their mothers. Early specific sex by parent interactions did not appear significant in any of the statistical analyses, although it is possible that the effects only begin to be manifested at older ages, such as 21 months of age.

The Intervention Study

Up until now, all the findings mentioned have been based on the results of the static correlational or stratification type paradigms in which the relation between the father's present care of his child and the child's present behavior is examined. Only by actively changing the father's interaction with the child and seeing if it really changes the child's behavior, can it be demonstrated that it is his caregiving and involvement alone (and not some spurious characteristic of his wife, for example) that is truly influencing the child's behavior. This would require a Type 3 experimental methodology.

Zelazo, Barber, Kotelchuck , and David (1976) tried to experimentally manipulate father-child interaction. Twenty very low interacting fathers were selected, based on their answers to a child care questionnaire. These men did little or no caretaking, almost no playing, and were hardly present while their child was awake. Hence, the investigators had no qualms about asking them to play ½ hour a day with their children for 4 weeks. All the children were first born males, 12 months of age. The fathers were given a schedule of games and toys to play: peek-a-boo, xylophones, jack-in-the-boxes, and so forth. The activities were chosen in order to guarantee that there would be some kind of structured interaction between the father and his son. A house visitor trained the father, checked on his playing and gave him a chart which he and his wife were supposed to check off each night after he played the prescribed games.

The design was a classic before-after design. All the parents and infants came to the laboratory for one pre-intervention testing. In half the cases, the intervention occurred (the experimental group) and in half nothing happened (the controls). After 6 weeks all were retested in the laboratory to look for differences. The paradigm was slightly different from the other four studies in that there was a 20 minute free play period, with both the parents in the room reading, followed by a modified series of maternal and paternal departures.

While these are still preliminary results, it is clear that this limited intervention markedly influenced the children in the experimental group. First, in the free play session, children in the experimental group increased their interaction with their fathers; they spent more time near them, initiated more interaction with them, and looked at them more. These changes occurred despite the stability in the fathers' interaction toward their children across the two testings; that is, the fathers showed no increases in their looking at their children or their initiation of interaction. This stability was probably influenced by our instructions which urged him not to initiate interactions. Second, there was a decrease in reliance on the mother for the experimental group; there was less maternal touching, vocalizations, and fixations. By contrast, infants in the control group increased interaction with their mothers. Third, there was an increase in the use of the father during the separation or stress episodes; paternal proximity, fixation, touching increased, especially after the departure of the mother, although no changes in the duration of crying or playing (the overt protest measures) were noted.

The results strongly imply that paternal interaction at home can directly influence the behavior of the infants in a laboratory situation. Father-infant interaction is not something immutable. If a father changes his behavior, it can have an immediate effect in changing his child's behavior toward him.

In summary, the five studies reviewed in this paper all demonstrate that the father's involvement with his infant directly influences the infant's early social behavior. While a relationship to the father was seen to be independent of the extent of his involvement in child care, some minimal level of interaction seemed necessary. Extensive paternal caregiving was related to the preferences for the father in the laboratory and shortened duration of separation protest. What might be the positive long-term effects of increased father-infant interaction remains to be explored. The immediate influence of the father on his infant's behavior can no longer be doubted.

BIBLIOGRAPHY

Ainsworth, M. *Infancy in Uganda: Infant Care and the Growth of Attachment.* Baltimore: John Hopkins Press, 1967.

Biller, H. The mother child relationship and the father absent boys' personality development. *Merrill Palmer Quarterly,* 1971, 17, 227-241.

Cohen, L.J., and Campos, J.J. Father, mother, and stranger as elicitors of attachment behaviors in infancy. *Developmental Psychology,* 1974, *10,* 146-154.

Keasley, R., Zelazo, P., Kagan, J. and Hartman, R. Separation protest in day care and home reared infants. *Pediatrics* 1975, in press.

Kotelchuck, M. The nature of the child's tie to his father. Unpublished doctoral dissertation, Harvard University, 1972.

Kotelchuck, M. and Shaw, L. Inter-reliabilities of maternal and paternal reports of their child care activities. In preparation 1976.

Lamb, M.E. Fathers: Forgotten contributors to child development. *Human Development,* 1975, *18,* in press.

Lester, B.M., Kotelchuck, M., Spelke, E., Sellers, J.J., and Klein, R.E. Separation protest in Guatemalan infants: Cross-cultural and cognitive findings. *Developmental Psychology,* 1974, *10,* 79-85.

Lewis, M., Weinraub, M., and Ban, P. Mothers and fathers, girls and boys: Attachment behavior in the first two years of life. *Educational Testing Services Research Bulletin* (Princeton, N.J.), 1972.

Maccoby, E., and Feldman, S. Mother-attachment and stranger-reactions in the third year of life. *Monog. Soc. for Res. in Child Devel.,* 1972, 37, 146.

Ross, G., Kagan, J., Zelazo, P., and Kotelchuck, M. Separation protest in infants in home and laboratory. *Developmental Psychology,* 1975, *11,* 256-257.

Spelke, E., Zelazo, P., Kagan, J., and Kotelchuck, M. Father interaction and separation protest. *Developmental Psychology,* 1973, *9,* 83-90.

Zelazo, P., Barber, L., Kotelchuck, M., and David J. Father and Sons: An Experimental Manipulation of Infant-Father Attachment. In preparation.

"Father Caretaking Characteristics and Their Influence on Infant-Father Interaction," by Milton Kotelchuck. Paper presented at 83rd Annual Convention of the American Psychological Association. Chicago, Illinois, September, 1975.

Television and Free Time

Marie Winn Miller

A look back at some of the common routines once enforced by parents—regular naps, solitary play, and the like—reveals that children were once faced with regular periods of time they were required to deal with on their own. Today not merely are children's lives packed with a greater number of meetings, lessons, and other structured activities than ever before, but all the possible chinks of empty time cropping up between these activities are filled in with the mortar of television. That curiously unvalued commodity called free time has been eliminated almost entirely from children's lives.

Let us look at some children's daily routines:

James Harrison is 3 years old. He wakes up in the morning at seven o'clock, gets dressed with a little help, and watches "Captain Kangaroo" until breakfast. He spends the morning at nursery school. After arriving home from school, he eats lunch, watches "Sesame Street" and "Mr. Rogers" from one to two-thirty. Then his mother takes him to the park where he rides his tricycle and swings on the swing. From the park he goes shopping with his mother. He comes home, watches cartoons or "Sesame Street" again while his mother prepares dinner. After dinner he plays a game with his father, watches "Zoom," has a bath, and goes to bed.

Margo Brown is 7. She gets up in the morning at seven-thirty, dresses, watches "Bugs Bunny," has breakfast, watches "Felix the Cat," and leaves for school. She comes home at three-thirty, changes into play clothes, and plays outside for an hour with her friends if the weather is good. If the weather is unpleasant, she and her friends watch television at one of their houses. At four o'clock on Monday afternoons she has a piano lesson. On Wednesday afternoons at four-thirty she goes to dancing class. Thursday afternoon is the Brownie meeting. On Fridays she stays after school for an arts and crafts program. She usually watches her favorite programs after her regular afternoon activities until her dinner is ready: "Batman," if she's home early enough, followed by "Superman," "The Brady Bunch," and sometimes "I Dream of Jeannie." Her older sister usually watches with her. After dinner she does her homework, practices the piano, and usually watches another television program before her bedtime at eight-thirty or nine (depending on the program)—either "Happy Days," "Little House on the Prairie," "The Waltons," or "Sanford and Son" (depending on the day).

Danny Evans is going on 14 and in the eighth grade. He gets up at seven, dresses, eats breakfast, looks at the sports page of the morning paper, and leaves for school at eight. He returns at four-thirty, grabs something to eat, and heads for the park where he plays ball with a regular group of friends every day. If it rains or if it's too

---

cold, they play in a basement playroom in Danny's apartment house. When he comes home around five-thirty or six, he collapses in front of the television set and watches whatever his younger brother is watching, usually "Star Trek." He has dinner in the kitchen with his brother and little sister while watching television, since his parents eat later. The kids usually watch the "Partridge Family" or "Mod Squad" during dinner. After dinner he does homework, usually missing one of the programs the younger children watch, but sometimes he does his homework and half-watches at the same time. He often watches one more television program with his mother and father after the younger children have gone to bed, a movie or "Masterpiece Theater." His bedtime is around ten-thirty.

There is something these three children have in common with one another and with a great number of children in America: they have no free time.

Competing with TV

In many families parents fill up their children's free time as a direct result of a competition that has been set up with the television set. If they do not "do" something, the parents fear, the children will turn to the television set. Thus they expend gargantuan amounts of energy to deflect their children's interest from the mechanical rival. When energy flags or other duties call, the parents resort to television with a desperation that reveals their underdog position in the power struggle they are waging with the mechanical rival.

"The thing I notice is that I have to spend a lot of my time and mental energy avoiding television. I have to keep thinking up things to do to keep the kids from watching TV. Their normal inclination is to watch television when they have no scheduled activity, and only if I make some sort of effort can I keep them from doing it," reports a mother of three young children.

A mother of two boys aged 7 and 5 tells an interviewer:

"I can't stand the idea of families where the kids come home from school and turn on the TV. You never get to talk to your kids. But it's complicated, you see. I don't *need* the TV as a baby-sitter at three-thirty when the kids come home from school, so I don't want them to watch then. I *do* need it between five and seven when I'm making dinner. That's when I *want* them to watch. And they *do* watch television then. It certainly makes life a lot easier for me. The trouble is they want to watch at three-thirty also. And unless I dream up something terrific for them to do then, they don't just want to play. They pester and pester me to let them watch."

A Brooklyn mother reports:

"I spend the weekends driving the children around to places just to keep them from the TV. Two weeks ago I drove from Brooklyn to Hershey, Pennsylvania, just to get the kids away from the television set. That's an eight-hour drive!"

The following story, told by a nontelevision-watching New York mother, is a good example of the competition for a child's time that the television set often establishes:

"A few weeks ago I went to a hospital to visit a little boy with a broken arm, a six-year-old boy I really like. There was a television set at the foot of his bed and he had the controls at hand. His mother had told me that he was really looking forward to my visit, and yet the whole visit was dominated by the presence of the television set. I arrived with a couple of good storybooks and I proceeded to read him a story but I quickly realized that the moment I or the story wasn't quite interesting enough, he was going to turn on that television set. And in fact every so often he *did* turn it on, just to see what was on. I went on desperately, reading stories, playing cards, and hangman and tic-tac-toe, telling jokes, because I was determined not to let that damn set win. I was definitely competing against that television set the whole hour I was there. I practically had to stand on my head, but I think I did win, but not a complete victory, only about seventy-five–twenty-five in my favor."

For some parents, competition with the television set reflects an underlying lack of trust in their children's capacity to amuse themselves. A New York mother of two children shows her understanding of the relationship between her use of the television set and her fear of unfilled time:

"I tell the kids, 'Get out of my hair and go watch television,' because I can't imagine their being on their own without something to *stimulate* them—I think that's why television is such a problem in our house."

A mother of two young children began to limit her children's television consumption to an hour a day. She tells an interviewer:

"I began to realize that the message I was giving him every time I broke down and said 'Yes you *can* watch one more program' was 'No, you're not able to do anything else with your head besides watch television.' The message was that I didn't think he had the *capacity* to do anything else with his time himself and so I was giving him an out with the television."

In many families, of course, children fill their free time themselves by turning on the television set. But even in those families that limit television watching, the competition parents engage in with the television set effectively eliminates free time in their children's lives. If either the television set or some competing activity is always available, there is never a time during the day when a child has "nothing to do."

"Nothing to Do"

What is the function of free time in a child's life? Wouldn't it be just as well if the child's life were so full of things to do that the whole question of having "nothing to do" would be eliminated?

There is a picture book by Russell Hoban called *Nothing to Do*[1] that shows the value of free time for a young child, as well as the problems parents face in regard to a child's unorganized time.

Hoban's book deals with little Walter Possum, a member of an endearing family of humanoid possums, who bothers his parents because he has "nothing to do." Father Possum tells Walter to "play with your toys." But Walter doesn't feel like it. The father assigns him a job—to rake the leaves. But Walter soon loses interest. The only activity that seems to relieve the tedium is quarreling with his sister Charlotte, a terrible pest.

When Mother Possum needs to clean the house, Father gives Walter a smooth brown stone and instructs him to rub it when he has nothing to do. It is a magic stone, Father tells him. "You have to look around and think while you're rubbing it, and then the stone gives you something to do."

Naturally, belief in the magic of the stone leads Walter to discover all manner of things to do. He finds a long-lost ball, he visits a friend, he dreams up a buried treasure game. He even devises a clever way to keep his irksome little sister from interrupting his game by presenting her with a stick that is also invested with putative magic powers. Besides having fun, he stays out of his parents' hair all afternoon.

Hoban's book, as is the case with all fine books for young children, contains guidance for parents as well as entertainment for children. The child needs help, suggests Hoban, in gaining access to his inner resources. The clever possum-parent, discovering that straightforward rejection of the "go find something to do on your own and don't bother me" variety only serves to exacerbate the child's dependent, clingy tendencies, encourages the child to find pleasure in his own inventiveness by making a game out of the very idea of thinking up things to do.

The possum-child is not really fooled—that is a crucial point (he proves it by using the same stratagem to get his sister to amuse herself). But still the magic stone works, though the child clearly understands that it contains no thoughts, that he himself is providing the good ideas.

What is that magic stone that Father Possum gave Walter? It is a necessary release, an embodiment of the idea that it is *all right* to be less dependent, that his parents are *permitting* him to act on his own, to use his time in his own way. This was what Walter required in order to be able to deal with his free time.

If Father Possum had given his son a different sort of magic device, a box, for instance, that glistened and gleamed, changed shapes and colors, and contained its own amusement, the parental purpose might have been equally served (to keep Walter out of the way). But were it the most entrancing source of entertainment, it would still have been an extension of the parent. Though fascinated by it, the child would have found in it no release from his helplessness, no source of growth or confidence in his own abilities. For that is the primary function of free time in a child's life, to provide the necessary opportunities for reducing his dependence and developing his separate self. This cannot happen in one or two or twenty grand epiphanies, but only through a gradual, day after day, year after year accumulation of free-time experiences, each providing a revelation so tiny, perhaps, that neither the child nor the parent recognizes it. Only through those free-time experiences, those self-propelled activities in which games are invented and dreams dreamed, will the child discover a self dependable enough to sustain him in place of those people and things he has been dependent on for so long. Without such experiences, the child will ultimately grow less dependent on his parents, but he may continue to remain dependent—on his peer group, on authority figures, on other experiences that allow him to remain a passive rather than an active participant in life.

Attachment and Separation

Television appears to have been instrumental in bringing about the demise of free time in children's lives. And yet, isn't television viewing itself a free-time activity?

The word "free" in the phrase "free time" is often accepted as a modifier of time, as if time were some real thing that has characteristics of its own apart from people or things, as if some kinds of time are "free," possessed of certain attributes of free-ness, while other kinds of time are not free. But time, of course, is not a corporeal thing. Its only reality is in relation to the person experiencing it. Free time, therefore, must be understood as defining the person experiencing that particular time, not the time itself; that is, free time is time when *a person is free* of certain limitations otherwise imposed upon his time, when he is able to act on his own volition, at his own pace, in his own way, free from all pressures and demands apart from those he invents.

And yet if a child's free time is defined as time when he is left to his own devices, free to fall back upon his own resources, then clearly there is a period at the beginning of life when those devices and resources must first be developed.

The infant does not differentiate between himself and his mother or the outside world. He has no "I" that is separate from others. His inner realities—hunger, fullness, pain, pleasure—merge with surrounding people and things in an overwhelming singleness of purpose: to live, to take in food, air, and a variety of visual, aural, and tactile sensory messages.

The developing child's first great task is to extricate himself from this undifferentiated mass and emerge as a *self*. A sign that this process has begun to occur comes when the infant ceases to treat his mother's comings and goings with equanimity. It is commonly observed that at about 7 or 8 months infants begin to howl and protest as if the world were coming to an end whenever their mother leaves the room. This behavior is an indication that the child has taken the first step in separating himself from his mother and the world at large. For only when the mother is perceived as a separate person can the infant grieve at her absence.[2]

The process of separation continues gradually during early childhood. Though the infant soon understands that he is physically separated from other people and things, there follows a period of time when he does not yet distinguish between his own feelings and objective reality. His understandings of the laws of physical causality, for instance, are almost totally egocentric and his own wishes and fears dominate his perceptions of reality. Those early years of life are indeed "magic years," when the child's inner world and the outside environment are still connected by primitive, irrational ties.[3]

A child's unoccupied time during those earliest years, the time not spent eating or sleeping or actively involved with a grown-up, is still governed by forces and pressures outside of his actual "self." Time cannot be free for a child for whom the events of time are so beyond control that it is only by chance that cause is ever followed by effect. The absence of a clearly defined self prevents the infant and very young child from manipulating his time in a free way;

he is still in the thrall of a primary bondage to other people and things. The ability to communicate with language, to exercise control over his own body, to operate, in short, with some degree of independence, must be developed before the child can make use of time in his own way.

Most parents operate with an instinctive understanding of their child's need for a certain kind of time-filling during the first years of life. Knowing that the baby cannot gainfully employ his waking time to his own advantage, and realizing that the child's mental development is crucially affected by the nature of his human contacts during those gradually lengthening periods of waking time, parents intervene purposefully and to good effect during the first three years of life. That is to say, they cuddle the baby, dandle him, sing little songs to him, play games with his fingers and toes, rather than leaving him to his own devices.

Parents have also come to understand that the first attachment of the child to his mother or other nurturing adult, that attachment that resists separation with loud protests, serves to set the foundations for the child's future ability to love and nourish in his own right.

These understandings serve to make a child's time less than free during his first years. For it is clear that were the child left to his own devices and resources (whatever they might be), his rudimentary abilities and his developing personality would atrophy.

But quite a different situation exists when the child approaches the age of three. Now there is a distinct decline in the intensity of his attachment. He no longer grieves loudly and passionately when his mother leaves. He no longer clings to her for security in new situations. The emotional foundations have been laid, as it were, and a new developmental stage begins in which the child starts to explore his environment with increased interest and tenacity. The drive of curiosity begins to overtake the drive for security and dependence.

Of course, the attachment behavior does not altogether disappear. The child swiftly returns to the safety of his mother when he is frightened or hurt. But the symbiotic ties are weakened; he has taken his first steps toward independence. There is an evolutionary purpose to this behavior progression from a mother-centered, passive, receptive orientation to an environment-centered, active, learning style of life: the individual's survival in society is necessarily a function of active, adaptive behavior. Yet it is at this point in a child's development, somewhere between the ages of 2 and 3, that mothers are most likely to begin turning on the television set for their young children, filling in the empty spaces in the child's day with an experience that temporarily but inexorably returns him to a state of attachment and dependence.

The consequences for the child must be seen as a developmental setback. While watching television, the young child is once again as safe, secure, and receptive as he was in his mother's arms. He need offer nothing of himself while he watches, as he must do, for instance, when he plays with another child. He runs none of the small risks that his normal exploratory behavior entails: he won't get hurt, he won't get into trouble, he won't incur parental anger. Just as he is beginning to emerge from his infant helplessness, he is lured back into passivity by the enticements of the television set.

Free Time and Filled Time

Once a child reaches a stage at which he is capable of shaping time to his own needs, in choosing television he may fill empty time in a way that impinges upon his freedom and deprives him of those opportunities for re-creation of his self that are available in the course of truly "free" time. Such time may be called "filled" time to distinguish it from free time.

The distinction between filled time and free time may best be illustrated by an example from real life:

A four-year-old boy has a regular rest period in his room after lunch. His room is equipped with toys, books, drawing materials, an easy-to-operate phonograph and records. There is a window that looks out on a street.

At one time he actually slept during his rest period—it was a true nap. Now he is likely to engage in a variety of activities he himself chooses. Today he begins with blocks, building a series of high towers. That morning at nursery school the tall and complicated rocket ship he had constructed out of blocks had been deliberately knocked down by another child. Now, in his own room, he destroys each of his own towers with a ruthless swipe, wreaking imaginary revenge on the morning's miscreant. He is in control now; he has devised a means of letting out his pent-up anger. Though he is only filling time during his rest period, he has shaped the time freely to suit his inner needs.

Next he attempts to build a bridge out of blocks. He has seen someone else construct an elaborate bridge, but his own bridge does not work—the blocks keep falling down. He can't figure out how to do it. He proceeds to form a bridge with his own body instead, arching his back in the air. His success at this activity compensates somewhat for his failure with the block-bridge. He has begun to understand and act upon a rudimentary principle: one's sense of well-being depends upon a certain amount of success; failure makes one feel bad. Had he continued to work on the bridge until he had solved the architectural problem, he might have learned a different lesson, one to do with the relation of perseverance and hard work to success. Instead he went in a different direction.

Tiring of his acrobatics, he puts on a record and lies on his bed to listen. It is a record he has heard at least a hundred times. He reaches out for a special pillow with a soft cover and sucks his thumb while stroking the pillow with his fingertip. He half-listens to the record. The other part of his mind is somewhere else, somewhere soft and hazy and comfortable. He recognizes the feeling well, having traveled to that place many times. But he is dimly aware of a change. As he strokes and sucks and listens, occasional words and images of real things begin to enter the vague nothingness—thoughts, associations, ideas. Every once in a while he removes his thumb to inspect it, plays with his other fingers, tries to suck another finger to see if the pleasure is the same.

When the record is finished he goes to turn another on, but becomes interested instead in the turntable. He puts a piece of paper on it and watches it go round and round. Soon he has devised an entire game with little bits of paper going around on the turntable. It is *his* game, having come from an idea in his head. Then his mother comes in. The rest period is over.

The child has experienced a period of time he was free to manipulate in his own way. His use of time, free from all structures and pressures, was a step in the direction of self-discovery.

Consider another child whose empty time between lunch and the afternoon outing is filled with several hours of television viewing. His time is indeed filled by the television experience, but while he is engaged with the program he is free to do nothing but watch and listen. His will is nonexistent; his personal pace and needs are irrelevant. He does not think his own thoughts while watching television as he does when devising his own games; his mind is being "thinked for" by the television program. In a sense his relationship with the television program might be described as a return to that original, undifferentiated one-ness of infancy, so thoroughly do the child and the television image fuse into a single entity. As he watches the screen, the boundaries between inside and outside grow dim and vague, not unlike his state in the not-so-distant past when his self was still merged with the world and a single other. He has little power over time as he watches television. That particular aggregate of genetic endowment and adaptive behavior that defines the child's new self comes into play far less when he watches television than when he is engaged in any other activity. Indeed, the self is frequently obliterated, temporarily but completely, as the child descends into a trancelike state of consciousness.

Of course, not all the child's time should be unstructured and unconstrained by others even after he has reached the stage when he can profit from free time. There are things to learn and skills to acquire that require him to place his time in the hands of others. But he must have *some* free time to control if he is to prosper. With television in his home, that is precisely what he does not have.

Paradise Lost

If the child's access to free time plays an important part in his development, and if the prevailing attitude toward children today is centered around fulfilling the child's own needs, why do parents insist on filling their children's time so relentlessly?

A partial explanation lies in the difficult transition the mother must make as the child moves from its first all-encompassing attachment to the next stage of development. At this juncture it is natural for mothers to fret about the child's new independent activities. Whereas the child once clung to her and followed her about like a puppy, now she must pursue the child and keep him out of trouble. Moreover, with the intense attachment period still so vivid in her mind, the mother tends to feel rejected by the child's growing involvement with the world around him. Her subliminal sense of Paradise Lost as her supreme importance diminishes makes this a difficult period for her. Since her relationship with the child is rapidly changing, she must find new ways of dealing with the child's higher activity level while coping with her own feelings of loss.

Ideally the mother will make changes in her daily procedures that will not work at cross-purposes with the child's developmental needs.

Perhaps it is partly the mother's ambivalent feelings about the child's new independence that compels her to use television to fill his time. Instead of adjusting to the child's emotional separation and craving for activity, she effectively limits her child's involvement with the outside world and prevents him from making new attachments by delivering him to the passive experience of the television set. Perhaps she feels that since she alone cannot entertain her child and make him happy, she will supply a substitute in the form of the television set. Thus she hangs on to her illusion of remaining the center of her child's universe, as indeed she so recently was. Thus she retains her supremacy in spite of the child's burgeoning independence, and in spite of his efforts to find an identity separate from hers.

The Easy Out

But the more obvious explanation of why parents of young children turn to television is that it presents the *easiest* and most reliable relief from the increasing difficulties of child care. The strategies once used by parents to survive life with small children simply seem too much trouble to parents today.

A mother notes:

"When I had Sally and we didn't have a TV set I guess I felt less pressured to do other things, because I had no choice. If she needed attention and I was making dinner I said, 'Oh, to hell with dinner —we'll just eat fifteen minutes later,' and I'd sit down and read her a story or get her started off playing with something. But when Henry was born and we had a television set, I started using it more. It offered an easy out, and it replaced some sort of effort on my part."

This easy out does not merely allow the parent to make less effort; it also provides an occupation that is quiet and unobtrusive. This is why great numbers of parents feel they couldn't survive life without Saturday morning cartoons.

A mother of three boys says:

"I practically beg them to turn on the television set on Saturday mornings so they'll be quiet and I can sleep. When they play with each other they're just too noisy. They always play Emergency and love making the siren noises—*Weeeeoweeeowee!* When they play with each other every toy is out, every hat is on, every truck is moving—I suppose that's fine, but I can't stand it! I need my sleep! The six-year-old is usually up at the crack of dawn, and if it weren't for TV, he'd be playing with all the toys, too. But now he turns on the set and watches quietly until nine, when we get up."

The immediate benefits parents gain from the instant child-pacifying powers of the television set may prove costly in the long run. A look at some of the results of parental use of television suggests that the parents' lot is ultimately made harder, not easier, because of their use of television to fill in their children's time.

The Half-Busy Syndrome

An illustration of the counterproductive consequences of relying on television to fill the empty chinks in a child's day is seen in a combination of circumstances that might be called the *half-busy syndrome.* This describes a cycle in which the mother is *half*-busy *all* the time. She goes about her various duties and occasional leisure-time activities in bits and spurts, stopping whatever she is doing to take care of this or that, answering the child's persistent questions, taking make-believe tastes of endless mud-pies, admiring drawings. She is busy, but never too busy to look up from her book or stop her work to attend to the child's needs or wishes.

She becomes hardened to the half-busy way of life and finds a certain satisfaction in the idea that she is a "good mother." But occasionally she feels she must have some relief from being constantly "on tap." The television set suddenly seems the only solution.

She feels a bit guilty about using the television set as a baby-sitter, but what else is she to do? She has tended, minded, soothed, coaxed, and displayed the patience of seven saints. She must get away somehow. After all, children are children and it is their nature to seek attention. She does not know that there is something about her state of "half-busy-ness" and perpetual availability that actually works against her own needs, making her child *more* demanding and creating the necessity of turning to the television set for relief.

Parents intuitively understand that children's behavior bears some relation to their own availability. For instance, it is universally observed that children are particularly troublesome when their mothers are on the telephone. But this is assumed to be an isolated phenomenon. Mothers who devote great *quantities* of attention to a child in the course of each day do not generally understand that the *quality* of that attention is a crucial factor.

Research findings suggest that the quality of a parent's attention matters considerably. In one experiment a selected group of preschool children was left for a period of time with a consistently available and attentive adult, while a second group spent a similar period of time with an adult who pretended to be busy with his own work. The children in the "low availability" condition proved to be considerably more demanding of the researcher's attention than the group whose caretaker was consistently available. The quality of the available caretaker's attention seemed to allow the children to play more independently and make fewer demands on him. The caretaker who seemed to be busy was far more beleaguered.[4]

A later research study observed nursery-age children with their mothers, some of whom were instructed to be busy and some to be wholly attentive. The results showed that many more bids for maternal attention were made when the mother was busy than when she was completely available to the playing child.[5]

Thus it appears that a reduction of free time in the child's life leads to an increase in dependence. For clearly the child whose mother is half-busy all the time is never more than half-free himself. He is never presented with the real necessity of confronting time in his own way. Whatever the reasons the mother feels compelled to be involved in *all* the child's time, if only in a partial way, the result of this behavior for her is disastrous: she is deprived of any truly free time for herself. And a reverse process may very well operate here: a mother deprived of free time grows dependent upon her child for emotional gratification that might better come from other sources.

The experiences of mothers who have changed the quality of their attentiveness confirm the likelihood that being half-busy throughout the day makes children more demanding and dependent. When periods of complete attention are alternated with periods of nonavailability to the child, both mother and child begin to enjoy truly free time.

A mother of two preschool children reports:

"One day I realized that I had fallen into the habit of caring for the children in a halfway sort of manner all the time. I'd get half a letter written and then have to stop because a child needed something. It went on that way most of the day and I'd never get away completely except when I plopped them in front of the television. I hated doing that, but I just couldn't help it. I needed to get away. Then I began to realize that I was in a sort of vicious circle, not really doing my own things, and not really enjoying the children very much either. Meanwhile I had a sinking feeling that time was passing, that there were only so many years when the children would be small, and that somehow I was never really completely committed to them, nor was I ever completely free of them.

"I was late coming to this realization and I actually had to work hard to make a change. It might have been easier if I had started right from the start. But of course when they were babies they needed a different sort of attention, didn't they? What I wanted to do now was *to really be with them* when I was with them, not just give them half of my attention. I'd drop everything for a while and really play with them, *down on the floor* much of the time. I wouldn't keep trying to get back to my letter or doing something else.

"But the other part of it was that I worked on getting away just as completely, without plugging them into the TV. It seemed somehow fair that if I gave them my time completely, they could also give me some time completely to myself. I didn't even think then that they would profit from having time entirely to themselves. But in fact I began to realize that often that was the case. I'd tell them that I was going to do something for a while and they could not interrupt me, and that when I was finished I'd do something with them. And then *I stuck to my guns!*

"I started out little by little, because they wouldn't let go at first. I'd say, 'I'm going to sit here and read to the bottom of the page.' And then I'd persist, no matter what they did, even though it meant ignoring things like falling down or a fight. It never got to a life-or-death situation—I suppose I would have intervened then. Gradually I increased the time I was unavailable to them, slowly, page by page.

"It worked. In fact, it was pretty easy. Now they will really give me time, without demanding attention or getting attention in devious ways—by getting hurt, for instance, or by making a horrible mess. Somehow, my giving them honest-to-goodness attention really seems to make a difference. It seems to fill them up, in a way, almost as if they've had enough to eat. They become calmer, less clingy. They seem to be more capable of being on their own for longer periods of time."

Waiting on Children

When television is used to fill in children's free time, parents are often led to compensate for lost opportunities to become close to their children by waiting on them more than they might ordinarily do. It might surprise a great number of parents to learn that the many little services they provide children who could easily help themselves are debilitating to the children. They might be even more surprised to realize that their compulsion to wait on their children is related to the role television plays in their family life.

There have always been parents who like to "baby" their children unnecessarily. Literature is full of horrendous models of such parents who perform ridiculous services for their perfectly capable (and usually ungrateful) offspring and openly struggle to hold on to their children by keeping them mentally and physically dependent.

But the mothers who fetch drinks and snacks for their television-watching children, who release them from their chores so that they may watch their favorite programs, are not all Mrs. Portnoys. While the infantilizing effects on their children's development may be similar, their motives for waiting on their children are frequently related to their use of television as a surrogate parent.

An illustration of the relationship between children's television watching and parents' waiting on children is given by Caroline L., a musician and the mother of two school age children:

"I've scheduled my life and my work in such a way that I can be there when the children come home from school. I want to be of some help to them, to greet them, to make them feel good in some way. Well . . . [she laughs with embarrassment] I regret to say that they plunk themselves in front of the television as soon as they come home, and sometimes I can barely get two sentences out of them before they're involved in their program. Then I can't get another word out of them. And so I bring them some carrot sticks or Triscuits and cheese for a snack, feeling a little ridiculous about it, because they're certainly old enough to peel their own carrots and make their own snacks. But somehow I allow myself to do it. I mean, if they love those television programs so much . . ."

Caroline L. brings her children snacks because she can think of no other way to maintain communication with them as they watch television. She feels rejected, cut off from normal human contact with her children. Moreover, she feels guilty that she set up this situation herself, by using the television regularly for her own convenience when the children were smaller.

She is aware of her dependence on the television set when she notes her alternatives, as she sees them:

"The funny thing is, when they come home from school I really have a desire to sit down and talk to them about what they're doing in school. I'd love to hear about that. But they don't want to talk about it. I'm sure if I were willing to do something with them in the afternoon, something they really like, at least there would be a chance they'd be willing to do that instead of watch TV. Maybe not. But I'd have to completely devote my time to entertaining them, even to the extent of not answering the phone. And that's really hard for me. I've tried."

In this way countless parents whose normal communications with their children have been damaged by the television set, who are regularly "turned off" by their children in favor of the television set (just as they "plugged in" their children when they were younger), now perform unnecessary little services to manifest their love and devotion, to show their children in deed rather than word that they care for them and want them to be happy. That is the only possibility left to them, they feel, since their words have been preempted by television's electronic words.

A child psychotherapist and consultant for a New York private school comments on the effects of waiting on children:

"It's a very infantilizing thing for mothers to wait on children, clear away their dishes, bring them drinks and little snacks while the children sit there watching television. Long after children reach an age when they ought to begin to develop self-reliance, they can't help but continue to regard their parents as servicing people. Of course, babies don't see their parents as servicing people—they *need* to be taken care of. But when seven- or eight-year-old children habitually ask their parents to fetch them a glass of water because they're watching a television program, and the parents meekly comply, then there's something unwholesome going on.

"The parents rarely bring this up as an issue, however," notes the therapist. "I just pick it up as they're talking. They'll be describing a certain situation and they'll mention that so-and-so called them to bring him a sandwich—that he's watching TV—and so-and-so is ten years old!" There is a certain amount of wonder in the therapist's voice as she relates this incident.

"The parents feel guilty about allowing their children to watch so much television," she continues, "and so they try to compensate by waiting on their children. It's not that they are trying to keep them dependent, as parents sometimes do. But these parents just don't seem to know what else to offer. Somehow they have come to think that *they* have to do all the offering. That's what astonishes me."

Drifting

If one were to seek the effects of the large-scale reduction of free time among a generation of children growing up with television, an understanding of the importance of free time in children's lives would lead one to look for signs of increased dependence. A few experienced observers of children have, indeed, begun to observe such signs.

For example, the founder and director of an excellent children's camp in Vermont began to observe a curious increase in homesickness in the early sixties. There had always been a small number of campers afflicted with homesickness, but now an epidemic seemed to have struck. The camp had devised a number of successful strategies for combating homesickness, and these were now applied with equal success. Nevertheless the increased incidence of homesickness continued to be a problem year after year. When the director checked with counselors from other camps, he learned that they had not encountered a similar problem. It was a mystery. Perhaps the answer would be found in some aspect of life at his camp that differed from other camps.

There was indeed one great difference: while other camps filled every minute of the campers' day with programmed activities, rests, and meals, this particular camp interspersed its programmed activities with four half-hours during which the children were free to pursue their own interests. These were called "drifting" periods. The camp director had deliberately structured a program that combined planned activities with free periods, believing that the opportunities provided by the free-time periods were as important for the children as those planned for them. Whatever growth took place during the camp months, he felt, depended as much on the child's deployment of the drifting periods as on his success at the programmed activities. However, he and his staff could not fail to observe that homesickness was most acute during those free-time periods.

The camp had been running in very much the same way, with the same sort of staff and the same population of middle- and upper-middle-class children, for over twenty years. Why now, starting in the mid-sixties, were the free-time periods making numbers of children sufficiently uncomfortable to feel homesick?

Since the youngest children at the camp were aged nine, the first television-bred children would have arrived in camp in the mid-sixties. These were children who had far less experience of free time in their lives than previous generations. When suddenly confronted with regular doses of free time, they reacted with anxiety and homesickness.

For homesickness is always a cry against a surfeit of independence, a cry to return to a more dependent situation in which the child need not function as a separate self. It represents a longing to return to that cozy family group of which the child was once an actual physical appendage, and from which he must, someday, extricate himself emotionally if he is to grow up successfully.

When a child's opportunities to experience free time are limited, he is more likely to remain in a state of inner dependence. While his life is completely filled with adult-devised programs on television, his dependence will not be apparent, for he is spared the need to act independently. But when he is forced to confront unstructured time, as the campers were, he will find himself resourceless. His dependence will be exposed.

A New Gresham's Law of Child Activity

It is all very well to sing the apotheosis of free time for children and exhort parents to turn off their television sets. It is the *reality* of free time that makes it so difficult for parents to stick to their resolve to limit their children's television consumption.

The situation modern parents face upon turning off the television set frequently proves to be discouraging. After expecting their offspring to suddenly metamorphose into Victorian children who pursue hobbies and wholesome adventures, it is depressing to see them hanging around doing nothing. In a variety of rude ways the children reject those fine, creative activities with which they are supposed to fill the vacuum, challenging the parents to either amuse them themselves or relent and let them watch television.

Is it partly or wholly because of their early television experiences that children today are less capable of dealing with free time? Do they have greater difficulties in combating boredom than children did in the pre-television era?

A sort of Gresham's Law of Child Activity seems to operate here:

passive amusements will drive out active amusements. Since passive amusements require less effort than active ones, human nature dictates that, all other things being equal, doing something easier is preferable to doing something harder.

Observe a child playing with a simple wooden truck who is presented with a complicated mechanical locomotive. Whereas he had been obliged to amuse himself by pushing the symbolic vehicle around the floor, devising an imaginary route in and out and under furniture (providing his own sound effects), now he watches the new toy with fascination, amazed by the smoke spouting from the stack, charmed by the rhythmic toot-toot of the engine, delighted by its ability to propel itself backward and forward.

But after a while the child's pleasure in the new toy begins to diminish. The fascinating toy, after all, has a limited repertory of actions: it moves, blows smoke, and goes toot-toot. The child wrings a terminal bit of amusement from the toy by taking it apart to see how it works. And it is finished.

The child's play with the simple wooden truck does not lead to a similar habituation because its range of activities is limited only by his own imagination.

But now the troublesome aspect of Gresham's Law of Child Activity becomes apparent: for though the attractiveness of the mechanical plaything is brief, there is something so compelling about the passive pleasure it affords the child that the appeal of another toy requiring active participation is diminished. When the mechanical toy breaks down, the child is not likely to go back to his wooden truck. That sort of play seems a bit dull and tame, a bit *difficult* now. How silly it seems to push a truck around the house and pretend that it's real when a painted truck that moves on its own is so much *realer!*

Not only will the child choose this particular mechanical toy over the more effort-demanding symbolic toy it was meant to replace, but in the future he will tend to choose a passive occupation over an active one. Passive play experiences inevitably make active play less appealing, and therefore less likely to occur spontaneously.

The television set is the one mechanical toy that does not lead easily to habituation and boredom, though the child's involvement with it is as passive as with any other mechanical toy. It chugs and toots and produces movements, while the child watches with wonder. But its actions and sounds are far less repetitive than the toy train's, so the watching child can maintain wonder and fascination almost indefinitely.

But just as the ordinary mechanical toy changes a child's relationship to symbolic toys, so do the passive pleasures of television watching transform his relationship to his own time. The strong pleasures of that safe, effortless, ever-amusing experience make the pleasures afforded by active entertainments seem too much like *work*.

This is not to say that normal children will stay huddled before the television all day in preference to playing baseball or going to a game with their father or baking a chocolate cake or engaging in some other appealing activity. Certain activities will always confound Gresham's Law of Child Activity by dint of their special attractions: special trips and activities, particularly with parents, beloved sports and games, activities that dovetail with the child's special interests. But those activities have got to be *pretty good.* Otherwise there's always television.

"TV is a killer of time for my children," reports a mother. "I think they'd almost rather do *anything* than watch TV. If I find them something they like to do and do it with them, they're perfectly happy. They'd prefer that to watching TV. It's just so much less effort to watch TV than to have to think of something to do. So if they don't have something *special* to do, like getting a Halloween costume ready or even going to a friend's house, their first thought is to watch TV."

Another mother says:

"What I find with my seven-year-old is that it's the *excuse* of television, the very *presence* of the television set when he doesn't know what to do with himself, or when he has a day when another child isn't coming over to play, that keeps him from looking to himself for something to do. Instead, he'll want to sit in front of the television set just to let something come out at him. That's been the hardest thing about television for me. If the television were not there, if it didn't exist, he wouldn't have that problem."

A mother of a five-year-old boy observes:

"My child is not the kind of child who will make a scene or have a temper tantrum. He'll just mope around and be bored. And I find it very hard to take that. It bothers me to think that he can't do anything with his time. The presence of the television is the excuse. He knows in the back of his mind that when he really hits rock bottom he can go to that television set."

An educator and authority on early childhood with forty years of experience as teacher and principal has noted a change in children's behavior since the advent of television:

"Young children today have a sophistication that comes from all their contacts with the outside world via television, but sophistication and maturity are not the same thing.

"Children today are often *less* mature in their ability to endure small frustrations, or to realize that something takes a longer time to do, that it isn't *instant.* They're less tolerant of letting themselves become absorbed in something that seems a little hard at first, or in something that is not immediately interesting. I spend a lot of time at school telling children that they have to participate in activities and try things even if something doesn't seem all that interesting right at the start."

Other teachers observe that young children today find it harder to work by themselves than children did in the pretelevision era, that there is a constant need for adult supervision or entertainment.

Whether children are so used to immediate gratification via the television set that their abilities to amuse themselves have atrophied, or whether a simple lack of experience with free time has left them with undeveloped abilities, it nevertheless seems clear that children today have greater difficulty dealing with free time than children of past eras.

For when those favorite, special activities are not available (as often is the case, which is what makes them so special), then children today are not likely to enlarge their interests by trying something new. They will not take the same desperate measures to combat boredom that children of the past had need to resort to:

inventing games, playing make-believe, reading, rereading, writing to pen pals, pursuing hobbies—activities that grow on a child and make him grow. With the presence of a source of passive amusement in every home, readily available to the child at the first sign of boredom, a child's time becomes more and more dominated by this single time-suspending activity.

Sickness As a Special Event

Before television there were occasions in almost every child's life when he was faced with a great deal of unexpected free time: those inevitable days when he was removed from his normal schedule of activities by sickness.

Most adults today who grew up before television have strong memories of their childhood illnesses.

A mother thinks back:

"My mother worked when I was a child, but when I was sick she stayed home for at least a few days. So I remember those times very well. I remember the endless card games, and playing Hangman hundreds of times, and cutting out pictures from magazines with her. I remember lying in bed and calling her to come and bring me this or that, again and again and again. And I remember how wonderful it felt, that she always came! I suppose I ran her ragged, but that's a very important memory for me, to this day."

Another parent relates:

"I remember being excruciatingly bored when I was sick. But that boredom sometimes led to odd activities. I'd make up stories and illustrate them, out of sheer desperation. Or I'd decide to learn French by reading the French dictionary. (I only got to page three.) Or I'd look through old photograph albums and daydream about life in the old days."

It is remarkable how often the actual physical discomforts of sickness are absent from these childhood memories, although a child's sickness is in reality dominated by symptoms and the mental changes that accompany them: fever, nausea, weakness, coughing, itching, pain, accompanied by restlessness, insecurity, depression, and other aberrations or exaggerations of the child's normal mental state.

But while the adult's memory may linger upon the romantic aspects of his childhood illnesses—the confirmation it afforded of parental devotion, the creative ferment it often inspired—at the time it was a tedious reality for his parents. Parents have always dreaded the days when their children were sick. It is distressing enough for parents to suffer the natural anxiety that a child's sickness provokes, the sharp reminder of his vulnerability and mortality; the child's sudden reversion to dependency and his need for steady services compound the unpleasantness. The parents' pity and sympathy for the child's discomfort are invariably tempered with impatience and weariness at his temporarily more difficult behavior.

Television has transformed the experience of sickness for parents and children in America. It is a more effective drug than aspirin in ameliorating the symptoms of disease. Television makes the time pass more quickly, and the child concentrates less on the stomachache, the general malaise, the itching, or whatever wretchedness the particular infliction has visited upon him. The relief is felt equally strongly by the parent, who formerly bore the burden of helping the child pass time and keeping his mind off his physical discomforts. Gone are the onerous requirements of time and patience on the parent's part—the endless story readings, the tedious card games ("I thought I'd go mad if I had to play one more game of War"), the listening to whiny complaints, the steady need to restrain impatience, to maintain sympathy, to act more lovingly than ever.

But however tiresome and unpleasant sickness may have been all around, being sick was undoubtedly a special event in pre-television days. Then a child did special things, had special relationships with his parents and siblings. And in a curious way the specialness of sickness helped define the normalities of life for children. The elongation of time in the sick bed changed the child's concept of normal time and helped him to develop a rudimentary understanding of the relationship between time and activity. The opportunities that sickness afforded a child for a more contemplative relationship with his parents frequently exposed both to new aspects of the other's personality. Best of all, from the child's viewpoint, the usual sibling battle was suspended when he was sick. Parents no longer had to take pains to be "fair" about their allocation of time or affection: sickness was special, and parents were able to bestow on the sick child giant doses of time and affection without fear of provoking mutinous jealousy among his siblings (in fact, their jealousy was merely repressed, something not lost on the sick child and treasured in later memory).

Since the advent of television, the times a child is sick are special only inasmuch as he is allowed to watch more television than ever.

"When the children are sick I'm likely to let them watch all they want," says a mother who normally limits her children's television viewing. "Otherwise I'd have to read to them all day. Also, it's slightly making up to them for the miserable time they're having."

"When the kids are sick it's permissive time so far as the television is concerned," another mother observes. "Usually we're pretty strict about television, but when they're sick I feel they ought to have a special treat, somehow. Although," she adds thoughtfully, "it's a little odd to make a treat of something I normally disapprove of. But it's too tempting not to let them watch."

It is almost cruel to suggest that a parent faced with the mental and physical rigors of coping with a sick child not take advantage of a mechanical aid to ease the task. But the parent ought to reflect on the consequences for the child: a "special event" of childhood made ordinary and forgettable, an opportunity lost for strengthening family relations. Moreover, the strangeness and unreality of illness is exaggerated by hours of television fantasy. Though the mother's lot is made easier, there is no question but that those stories read, those card games played, those quiet times together, enrich the child's life, and are an especial loss for today's child whose television viewing has already cut down on shared experiences with his parents.

The Disappearance of "Real Life"

In the not too distant past children were expected to be passive participants in their school experiences. The idea used to be that the teacher had a body of material to teach that children were to soak in as part of a process called "learning." In this one-way process any activity on the children's part other than that specifically directed by the teacher was considered inappropriate.

Much of the success of this educational system depended on the personality of the teacher. If he was wise and kindly and graced with that indefinable charisma characterizing gifted teachers and performers, then children, like the audience at a good play, would try to conform to his rigorous behavior requirements and thus manage to soak in the required information. If the teacher possessed none of these gifts, very little learning occurred.

When school let out in the old days, children ran amok. Outside the boundaries of the schoolroom they ran, played games, dreamed, plotted, planned, yelled like Indians, skipped stones, started fires, made fences, baked cookies, rolled in the mud—played freely. Once school was over, children took charge of their own activity.

Within the last decade a change has been taking place in the classroom. Children are being encouraged to initiate, to explore, to manipulate, and the one-way process of education has been shifting to an interactive situation between the teacher and the child. Children are no longer bound by rigid codes of behavior, but are allowed to move freely, to talk naturally to each other and to the teacher in the course of their school activities. The success of this new style of education depends less on the teacher's charismatic personality and more on his intelligence and intuition, as well as on the equipment available in the classroom for the children's manipulations and explorations. As in the past, some children learn and some children resist. But in either case the children spend their school day in a more natural state of activity.

The atmosphere at three o'clock is calmer today. When school lets out, kids no longer behave like creatures let out of cages. In their child-centered classrooms they seem to have released an adequate amount of energy. But for many of these children activity is just about over for the day. They head for home to settle down in front of their television sets. They watch the screen and passively soak in images, words, and sounds hour after hour, as if in a dream.

It might seem to even out. If school has become an active experience, then why shouldn't the child spend a few passive hours watching television? The answer is that no matter how child-centered and "free" a school situation may be, it is still organized and goal-centered. The child hasn't the freedom of choice and freedom to control his own time that he has after school, when he can play a game or not, throw stones or not, daydream or not. Though the hours in a modern classroom may be more active, more amusing, less punitive and repressive than in the old-fashioned classroom, the child is still being manipulated in certain directions, by the teacher, by the equipment in the classroom, by the time organization of the day. If he spends his nonschool time watching television, *that* time is also being effectively organized and programmed for him. When, then, is he going to live his *real life?*

NOTES

1. Russell Hoban, *Nothing to Do* (New York: Harper and Row, 1964).
2. See John Bowlby, *Attachment and Loss* (New York: Basic Books, 1969).

3. See Selma Fraiberg, *The Magic Years* (New York: Charles Scribner's Sons, 1959).
4. J. Gewirtz, "A Factor Analysis of Some Attention-Seeking Behaviors of Young Children," *Child Development*, Vol. 27, 1956.
5. R. R. Sears, L. Rau, and R. Alpert, *Identification and Child Rearing* (Stanford, Cal.: Stanford University Press, 1965).

Day care

Day Care: Serving Preschool Children

DONALD J. COHEN, M.D. IN COLLABORATION WITH ADA S. BRANDEGEE, M.A.

As a society, we believe that all children deserve care that encourages their social, emotional, physical, and intellectual growth. Our nation has a long history of commitment to children and the institutions that serve their growth. We have established public education, promoted medical services, and created many other resources for children. But we have always recognized that parents are the primary influence on the development of their children and have the fundamental right to guide their children's experiences.

Today, American life places increasing pressures on parents and families. More and more American parents are unable to care for their preschool children all day, 7 days a week. There are growing numbers of single-parent families and families in which both parents work outside the home. Other parents, present during the day, either lack needed resources or face problems that affect the quality of the care they give their children. In the past, these families might have turned to trusted relatives or to lifelong friends and neighbors. Now, however, increased mobility and the disruption of the extended family have eliminated these alternatives for most Americans.

In recent years, day care has emerged as a natural response to these and other changes in American family life; it has become a valuable and often vital resource for a broad range of American families.

Types of Child Care Arrangements

There are different types of child care programs besides day care. And there are different types of day care ranging from makeshift babysitting by an older child to comprehensive programs designed to meet broad community needs. These different child care arrangements must be distinguished in order to understand what we mean by quality day care.

Custodial Day Care

Custodial day care amounts to babysitting, either for individual children or groups. Only the immediate needs of the child are considered: health and safety, something to eat, and some sort of activity to pass the time. There is no planning to meet developmental needs, either immediate or long range. There is no attempt to plan for the child's need for personal, responsive human relationships; for intellectual stimulation; for health or nutrition beyond immediate needs; or for parent involvement in the care being provided.

Nursery Schools

Nursery schools are educational programs available only part time—usually half a day, from 2 to 5 days a week. They do not attempt to provide comprehensive care as a service to absent parents. They concentrate on the child's social, emotional, and cognitive development, with the assumption that the parents will be able to provide for his health, nutrition, and all other needs. A nursery school is not developmental day care, but developmental day care includes the essential elements of a nursery school.

Developmental Day Care

Developmental day care, which is also called *quality day care,* provides security and warmth, together with a range of developmental opportunities that parents normally provide when they have the necessary time and resources. These opportunities include the chance to be with other children; individual attention to each child's strengths and needs; and activities designed to promote physical, social, emotional, and intellectual development. To insure that these opportunities are provided, quality day care employs trained caregivers; follows a carefully planned curriculum; uses the services of consultants in health, education, nutrition, and other fields; and encourages parent interest and involvement in all aspects of the program.

Two other forms of child care which are sometimes confused with quality day care are comprehensive child development programs and compensatory education.

Comprehensive Child Development Programs

Comprehensive child development programs provide many varied curricular activities, services, and opportunities to children and their families. Their purpose is to support family life in the broadest sense and to facilitate the development of the children in the family. A comprehensive child development program may include quality day care for those who need and want it. In addition, it may include such services as family counseling, genetic counseling, health and nutritional services, home visiting programs, programs for adolescent mothers, vocational training for parents, homemaker services, and other programs designed to meet the needs of the families who take part.

Compensatory Education

Compensatory education, by definition, is a special program for children with special needs. The term, "compensatory," does not necessarily imply a deficiency in the child or his background; needs regarded as special may be only the result of a cultural or economic *difference* from the surrounding community. The essential idea of compensatory education is that it should make up for some special disadvantage, providing disadvantaged children with the basic attitudes and skills most other children acquire naturally during the preschool years. Although compensatory education may be offered as part of quality day care, the two are not the same. Day care is care of the whole child, in all his aspects. Compensatory education has certain clearly defined goals and objectives chosen to prepare the child for what society will expect of him.

The Function of Day Care

Quality day care has three major functions: it serves as an extension of the family; it aids children's development; and it is a way for society to intervene constructively when families and children need help.

Day Care as an Extension of the Family

Quality day care provides the positive experiences that most families try to give their children. It extends and supplements the parents' care in a way consistent with the values and goals of the child's family and culture. Quality day care strengthens the child's basic attachment to his parents and sustains them as the major force in his personal development.

Day care programs are more successful when parents are deeply involved in them. In fact, parent involvement is vital for a quality program. A full-day program with no involvement of the parents can actually tend to separate some families by subjecting the children to a second, conflicting set of rules, values, and expectations.

For many parents and probably for most programs, parent involvement in day care might better be seen as a right than an obligation. Whatever is expected of parents in the program must be sensibly weighed against the other demands on their time and energy. However, when a day care program is open to parent involvement in a free and easy manner and when parents are invited to participate as much as they are able, even overworked mothers and fathers are often eager to share in the work and responsibility of starting and operating a day care program. When they do, not only their own children but the entire program will benefit.

In many communities, day care as an extension of the family will encounter problems of ethnic relevance. Children achieve dignity and self-respect with the help of positive images of themselves, their parents, and their communities. To ignore or slight a child's background is to defeat the basic goals of the program by damaging his self-image; impeding his social development; weakening the family; and encouraging division between the child, his ethnic group, and the rest of society. A mixture of ethnic backgrounds in one group requires careful planning to encourage each child to retain pride in his own culture, display it to other children, accept and appreciate their differences from him, and yet remain a member of the group.

Day Care as an Aid to Child Development

The years from 3 to 6 are an optimal period for mastering certain developmental tasks. Preschool developmental day care presents many opportunities to help a child master such tasks as:

- developing a sense of self and a sense of autonomy
- developing a healthy personal identity
- developing concepts of morals and personal rights
- dealing with certain psychological impulses and with guilt, anxiety, and shame
- learning how to get along with others
- mastering language and using it to produce desired results
- learning more about the symbols and concepts of culture (for example, numbers and letters, drawing "realistically")
- acquiring concepts of space, time, and objects.

Day Care as Intervention

Anna Freud commented that "any child's normal development is based on the fulfillment not of a single need but of a whole series and hierarchy of needs, stemming from all sides of his personality. * * * A normal and happy family can, with luck, fulfill all these conditions, but most families fail to do so for one reason or another."[1] She goes on to say that no institution can fully meet all the child's requirements, but that families in trouble can find the help they need by taking elements from a variety of institutions, including family care, foster care, residential care, and day care. "Even destitute families would function better if day care came to their permanent help, and if residential care could be asked for in short-term emergencies."[2] Day care, then, can function as one component of a system of supports to the family, together with such components as social service programs, health programs, and programs to increase employment.

The intervention function of day care is particularly important for three groups of children: children who are vulnerable, those who are handicapped or disabled, and those from families who live in poverty.

Vulnerable children are those whose development is at risk. Through special circumstances of birth, physical endowment, or difficult life experiences, some children are particularly unable to measure up to developmental tasks and problems. They have special needs for the continuity of care, stimulation, affection, stability, and thoughtfulness of a quality day care program.

Handicapped or disabled children include those who suffer from such afflictions as severe mental retardation, physical handicaps, or a childhood psychosis. The care of these children can be too much for even the most affluent family. Parents who must care for such a child 24 hours a day, 7 days a week, will be overloaded with responsibility. It will be a strain for the whole family, and the child's development will suffer. Day care can relieve such parents of a portion of their caregiving burden.

Children from families in poverty are the third and by far the largest group for whom intervention may be important. Not all poor families need day care, but many of their children lack the healthy and developmentally sound environment that day care can provide.

A quality day care program can identify the children of a community and assess their needs, can help make services available to them, and can involve the parents and help to strengthen the family. But there are limits to what even the best program can accomplish. Day care can be only one of many important influences. The child lives in the context of a family and a community, and what happens to him in those spheres will in the long run be more important than what happens in day care. What day care can accomplish is to help the child's developmental

[1] Anna Freud, *The Writings of Anna Freud, Vol. 5, Research at the Hampstead Child Therapy Clinic and Other Papers.* (New York: International Universities Press, 1969), p. 80.

[2] Ibid., p. 81.

progress and to help him and his family find ways to cope with the circumstances of their lives.

Dangers of Day Care

Any responsible person involved in day care must recognize the danger that it may hold for children and families. Enthusiasm for the many potential benefits should be tempered by the realization that day care can be a source of harm, and that a good program requires a commitment to constant thoughtfulness and careful monitoring.

The most obvious danger is that the child may be neglected, abused physically or emotionally, or exposed to unsafe or unhealthy conditions. But there are also more subtle possibilities for damage. Some unusually sensitive or immature children have difficulty separating from their parents; some have trouble accommodating to group activities and noise; and some with developmental difficulties may find it even harder to progress in the relatively hurried, tense atmosphere of many day care programs. Other conditions may also put stress on any child: subjection to a routine; exposure to other, more aggressive children; exposure to different backgrounds and different languages; and perhaps the most difficult, the breaks in continuity that occur more or less frequently when caregivers change. Children may thus have to deal with a series of emotional attachments and separations. They may withhold their emotions and become suspicious of adults, or they may learn to make only superficial attachments.

Day Care Settings

The setting of a program—its size and degree of organization and formality, as well as the physical surroundings—has an effect on the type of care provided. Four different types of settings are usually distinguished.

- In-home day care is care for the children of one family by someone who is not a family member, in either the children's home or the caregiver's home. (The caregiver's children may also be included.)
- Family day care is provided in the caregiver's home for the children of more than one family. The number of children is usually limited to six, including those of the caregiver. The home is rarely extensively altered.
- Family group day care is provided in the caregiver's home for 7 to 12 children, including those of the caregiver. More than one caregiver is involved, and the home usually requires alterations such as additional rooms, bathrooms, exits, etc.
- Center-based day care is for 13 or more children in a building which is usually not a home. The day care center has a staff of two or more.

Of the four, day care centers serve approximately 10 percent of the children in day care; in-home care and family care each serve 40 to 50 percent; and family group care serves a relatively small number.

In-Home Day Care

In-home day care is the simplest and most convenient for the parents. It is also most natural for the children, since all the children of one family can stay together, often in their accustomed surroundings. The caregiver may be a relative or family friend with whom the children are familiar and who may also do housework or cook for the family. All arrangements are centered on the needs of the children of one family. However, in-home care also has disadvantages. It is difficult or impossible to provide in one home all the services that could be provided in a center; the children have less opportunity for socializing and group interaction; and play space, materials, and equipment may be very limited. Since few trained people are willing to work in a single home, the caregiver likely sees himself or herself more as household help than as a child care professional. In-home care is not licensed, and it is more difficult to monitor the quality of care given in one home than in a larger, more organized setting.

Family Day Care

Family day care also has the advantage of keeping the children of each family together. The setting is a private home, which is a more natural setting for younger children than a center, yet it is possible to get trained workers to operate a family care program. The setting is particularly good for handicapped children who may need a very close relationship with the caregiver, extending over several years, without interruption. Children who are sick (but not seriously ill) can still be accommodated in a family care program. Hours and other procedural arrangements are not as flexible as in-home care but can be far more flexible than those of a day care center. On the other hand, family day care requires an adequate facility and the homes of those who are prepared to offer care may not meet the requirements. It is usually necessary to redecorate and rearrange, and for family group day care it is often necessary to add more rooms to the house. Even then, play space is likely to be more restricted than in a day care center. The quality of the care can be monitored more easily than that of in-home care, since family day care programs can be licensed more easily, and the arrangement is more professional than that for in-home care.

Family Group Day Care

Family group day care is offered in a homelike setting and shares many advantages of family care. While it is less flexible and informal than family day care, it may be more flexible than center-based care.

Center-Based Day Care

Center-based day care is provided in facilities devoted to, and sometimes designed for, the care of young children. The setting can be planned entirely for the needs of the program, rather than having to double for family living. In particular, it is easier in a center to plan a schoollike setting for the educational component of the program. It is easier to find highly trained personnel to work in centers, easier and more economical to use the services of specialists such as physicians, psychologists, and social workers. The relatively formal character of the day care center makes it easier to involve parents in planning, organization, and volunteer work of all sorts. But center-based day care also has drawbacks. Since it does not resemble a home environment, transition may be difficult for young children. The number of people involved requires a relatively high degree of organization, and the rules and procedures usually needed for efficiency can make center-based care the least flexible type of day care.

This handbook focuses on family day care and center-based care. Relatively little is known about in-home care—statistically important as it is—or about family group care. For most practical purposes, a family group setting is closely similar to a small day care center and most of the same considerations apply, while in-home care is closely similar to family day care.

When parents can choose among the different types of day care settings, their choice should depend on the developmental levels and needs of the individual child. As a loose generalization, center-based care tends to offer a better-trained staff, more interaction among children the same age, a more structured curriculum, and a bigger and better selection of space and equipment. Family care, on the other hand, usually has the advantages of more cross-age contact; a warmer, more natural style of caregiving; a closer, less formal relationship with the child's family; and a more flexible schedule, which can be important for young children who spend long hours in day care. On the whole, family day care might well be recommended for younger, less mature children, while more advanced children will be better able to take advantage of the learning opportunities in a day care center.

A Day Care Network or System

A day care network or system is not a different setting but a systematic combination of programs in various settings under a central administration. A system makes it possible to minimize the disadvantages and maximize the advantages of the different types of settings. In one system, the intimacy and flexibility of the family setting can be combined with the resources and capabilities of the large day care center, and the center can become a focal point from which services are extended to all the other settings. Central administration makes it possible to provide professional consultation and other resources to the community's day care programs; counseling and consultation to families; expert curriculum planning; professional training for day care staff; a pool of substitute workers; a communitywide screening system; and the economies of mass purchasing of supplies, food, and equipment.

Such a system allows families to choose family care if they wish, without having to sacrifice the benefits of trained personnel, curriculum, and special consultation available at a center. They have the option of starting a child in a small family setting and advancing him to a center when he is ready. Children in an in-home or family setting could be taken to another setting for short periods, perhaps a few times a week, as a gradual introduction to a more formal program. Children and parents alike could use the center for such services as consultations and counseling. The system, in short, makes it possible to combine the advantages of all types of day care.

Starting Day Care Programs

When a community lacks developmental day care, those who want to create a program often tend to think first of a day care center. Most of the day care literature focuses on centers, and a center may seem the most natural form because of the models provided by the public schools and by programs, such as Head Start, which have emphasized center-based activities.

However, family day care has important advantages for an organized community effort. Frequently, the greater part of the job can be done by locating and organizing the family day care programs that already exist, rather than by a massive campaign to set up a big new program. In addition to the real advantages of a family setting, the difficulties and delays involved in organizing, equipping, and staffing a center should commend family day care as an attractive way for a community to acquire the elements of day care service.

References

General

American Joint Distribution Committee. *Guide for Day Care Centers.* Geneva, Switzerland: AJDC, 1962.

Appalachian Regional Commission. *Child Development Manuals: Vol. I, Federal Programs for Young Children; Vol. II, Programs for Infants and Young Children* (Part I, Education and Day Care; Part II, Nutrition Programs; Part III, Health Programs; Part IV, Equipment and Facilities). Washington, D.C.: Appalachian Regional Commission, 1970.

Beer, E.S. *Working Mothers and the Day Nursery.* Mystic, Conn.: Lawrence Verry, 1970.

Boguslawski, D.B. *Guide for Establishing and Operating Day Care Centers for Young Children.* New York: Child Welfare League of America, 1968.

Chandler, C.A.; Lourie, R.A.; and Peters, A. *Early Child Care: The New Perspectives.* Edited by L. Dittmann. New York: Atherton Press, 1968.

Child Welfare League of America. *CWLA Standards for Day Care Service.* New York: Child Welfare League of America, 1969.

Day Care and Child Development Council of America. *Planning a Day Care Center.* Washington, D.C.: Day Care and Child Development Council of America, 1971.

Day Care: A Statement of Principles. Child Development. Office of Child Development. U.S. Department of Health, Education, and Welfare. Publication No. (OCD) 73–2. Washington, D.C.: Government Printing Office.

Evans, E.B.; Shub, B.; and Weinstein, M. *Day Care: How to Plan, Develop, and Operate a Day Care Center.* Boston: Beacon Press, 1971.

Fein, G.G. and Clarke-Stewart, A. *Day Care in Context.* New York: John Wiley & Sons, 1973.

Freud, A. "Nursery School Education: Its Uses and Dangers." In *The Writings of Anna Freud,* Vol. 4. New York: International Universities Press, 1968.

Grotberg, E.H., ed. *Day Care: Resources for Decisions.* Washington, D.C.: Office of Economic Opportunity, 1971.

Howard, N.K. *Day Care: An Annotated Bibliography.* Urbana, Ill.: ERIC Clearinghouse on Early Childhood Education, University of Illinois, 1971.

Howell, Mary C. "Employed Mothers and Their Families. Part I." *Pediatrics* 52, No. 2 (1973): 252-263.

Howell, Mary C. "Effects of Maternal Employment on the Child. Part II." *Pediatrics* 52, No. 3 (1973): 327-343.

Keyserling, M.D. *Windows on Day Care: A Report Based on Findings of the National Council of Jewish Women on Day Care Needs and Services in Their Communities.* New York: National Council of Jewish Women, 1972.

Murphy, L. *Caring for Children Series.* A series of booklets on children in day care. Office of Child Development. U.S. Department of Health, Education, and Welfare. Publication No. (OCD) 73–1026, 1027, 1028, 1029, 1030. Washington, D.C.: Government Printing Office, 1970.

Parker, R., ed. *The Preschool in Action: Exploring Early Childhood Programs.* Boston: Allyn and Bacon, 1972.

Prescott, E.; Millich, C.; and Jones, E. *The "Politics" of Day Care. Day Care: Vol. 1.* Washington, D.C.: National Association for the Education of Young Children, 1972.

Prescott, E.; Jones, E.; and Kritchevsky, S. *Day Care as a Child-Rearing Environment. Day Care: Vol. 2.* Washington, D.C.: National Association for the Education of Young Children, 1972.

Read, K.H. *The Nursery School: A Human Relationships Laboratory.* 5th ed. Philadelphia: W.B. Saunders Co., 1971.

Ryan Jones Associates. *How to Operate Your Day Care Program.* Wyomissing, Pa.: Ryan Jones Associates, 1970.

Some Organizations Which Publish Materials Relevant to Day Care

American Library Association
Children's Service Division
50 East Huron Street
Chicago, Ill. 60611

Association for Childhood Education International
3615 Wisconsin Avenue, NW.
Washington D.C. 20016

Bank Street College of Education
69 Bank Street
New York, N.Y. 10014

Black Child Development Institute
1028 Connecticut Avenue, NW.
Washington, D.C. 20036

Child Study Association of America
9 East 89th Street
New York, N.Y. 10028

Child Welfare League of America
67 Irving Place
New York, N.Y. 10003

Consortium on Early Childbearing and Childrearing
Suite 618
1145 19th Street, NW.
Washington, D.C. 20036

Day Care and Child Development Council of America
Suite 1100
1401 K Street, NW.
Washington, D.C. 20005

Educational Resources Information Center (ERIC)
Clearinghouse on Early Childhood Education
805 West Pennsylvania Avenue
University of Illinois
Urbana, Ill. 61801

ERIC Document Reproduction Service
The National Cash Register Co.
4931 Fairmont Avenue
Bethesda, Md. 20014

Family Service Association of America
44 East 23d Street
New York, N.Y. 10010

Government Printing Office
Washington, D.C. 20402
(Many documents published by various Government agencies and departments can be obtained directly from the GPO.)

National Association for the Education of Young Children (NAEYC)
1834 Connecticut Avenue, NW.
Washington, D.C. 20009

National Federation of Settlements and Neighborhood Centers
232 Madison Avenue
New York, N.Y. 10016

Office of Child Development
U.S. Department of Health, Education, and Welfare
Box 1182
Washington, D.C. 20013

Journals Related to Child Care

American Journal of Orthopsychiatry. Published by the American Orthopsychiatric Association, 1775 Broadway, New York, N.Y. 10019.

Child Development. Published by the Society for Research in Child Development, University of Chicago Press, 5750 Ellis Avenue, Chicago, Ill. 60637.

Child Welfare. Journal of the Child Welfare League of America, Inc., 44 East 23d Street, New York, N.Y. 10010.

Childhood Education. Published by the Association for Childhood Education International, 3615 Wisconsin Avenue, NW., Washington, D.C., 20016

Children Today. Published by the Office of Child Development, U.S. Department of Health, Education, and Welfare. Washington, D.C.: Government Printing Office, Washington, D.C. 20402.

Exceptional Children. Published by the Council for Exceptional Children, 1201 16th Street, NW., Washington, D.C.

Journal of the American Academy of Child Psychiatry. Publication of the American Academy of Child Psychiatry, 100 Memorial Drive, Cambridge, Mass. 02142.

Young Children. Published by the National Association for the Education of Young Children, 1834 Connecticut Avenue. NW., Washington, D.C., 20009.

Development of the Preschool Child

Most parents provide a child with extraordinary opportunities for learning and growth. Through their daily care and concern, they know how to respond to their child in most any situation: they know when to step in to provide him or her with encouragement or protection; when to stay at a distance and allow their child to test her capacities and to develop new skills; when to shield him from something sad or worrisome and when to give him the chance to deal with new anxieties.

Most parents know much that would be hard for them to put into words. From a slight hesitancy or sideward glance they know their child is frightened. From a brightness in her eyes they know that she is eager for something. From a faint holding back and lack of pep invisible to anyone else, they suspect that their little boy will soon have a fever.

A child's parents are his best teachers. Just by talking with their child, explaining things, and doing things while he watches, parents can instruct their child about uncountable objects, duties, and social expectations. By observing his parents, the child learns a style of speech, a way of solving problems, and a sense of knowing what to do when there's nothing much to do. As his parents perform all the routines of daily living—as they figure out bills, cook, dial the phone, read the paper, write notes, count change, and handle crises—the child will watch and will learn to imitate their actions and attitudes.

The kinds of things that go on between most parents and their 3- to 6-year-old children are not usually detailed in child psychology books. Scientists generally study in laboratories, not homes. They know more about how children deal with pleasant strangers who test them than about how children love, fear, or adore their parents, brothers, and sisters and how they interact with their different family members. Yet how the child acts at home and what he needs from home are central to our thinking about quality day care. In planning and delivering day care, we should ask: is the child in this day care setting receiving the kind of love, care, attention, stimulation, and example that is available in a healthy home?

The home provides a model of developmental care that is not in the least mysterious. Here, development takes place gradually. Most mothers and fathers can tell when their child is doing well and when he has a problem. In the same way, anyone who consistently cares for a child can tell when things are going well for him. There is a natural continuity between what a child requires at home and in day care, and between what lets us know things are going well or badly in either setting. Formal considerations about standards necessary for day care should not cloud the fact that *quality day care means caring for a child.*

While it is relatively easy to decide which kinds of experiences are necessary in day care to best stimulate development in a child, it is difficult to provide these experiences. What most parents do by instinct and out of their sense of responsibility may not emerge naturally in a day care situation. A mother caring for her own child can rely on intuition and learned good judgments; a caregiver working with several children needs greater planning and procedures. Day care planners must always be aware of the child's needs, of the caregiver's capacity to meet those needs, and of the kinds of supports, resources, and structures that both the child and the caregiver require.

The study of day care must begin with the children to be served. This chapter will introduce these children, who can change as much in 3 years as adults do in 3 decades. Our major concern is to portray how children develop "when things go well"—a phrase that we use often—and how day care can support both the child and his family when there are problems in the child's development.

We have two basic assumptions. The first is our belief that in most essential ways, children are very much more alike than they are different. In thinking about development, important differences in culture, life style, and community needs and wishes must not be obscured; however, we believe it is even more important to remember that there is a natural biological and evolutionary similarity in children's bodies and minds—a similarity in their drives, feelings, wishes, and ideas that cuts across social, ethnic, racial, and sexual distinctions.

Our second underlying assumption is that each child is also a unique and precious individual. Each child has a specific endowment, as well as his own history and experiences, all of which allow children to differ in their sensitivities and their ways of understanding, reacting, and coping.

This chapter outlines the implications of these two assumptions for day care and indicates how day care can respect the needs of all children for certain kinds of care while being able to meet each child's individual needs.

Preconditions of Development

No one can force a child to develop and move toward maturity. The way we talk about development indicates this; we say that a certain kind of care facilitates, or supports, or enhances, or encourages development. There are, however, many necessary *preconditions* for a healthy development to be possible. Some of these have to be met even before the child is born. Some deal with factors that affect the child's physical growth; others relate to his mental and emotional well-being. For a child to have the chance of developing to his fullest potential, these preconditions must be met.

Healthy Genetic Endowment

Everyone appreciates the importance of a child's natural endowment, which can set limits on what the child can achieve even with the best opportunities. Though all parents would like to endow their children with the most positive abilities and characteristics, some families have a history of conditions which could pass serious mental or physical problems onto their children. For such families, the medical science of genetics can provide counseling and testing during pregnancy. Through genetic counseling, couples can be advised about their chances for having a healthy baby. After a child is conceived, tests on samples of the amniotic fluid that surrounds the fetus can detect any of over 100 problem conditions present in the unborn child. The use of both these relatively recent medical services can help lower the frequency of genetic disease.

Prenatal Care

Even before a woman conceives, she should be medically well, adequately nourished, physically mature, and psychologically prepared to have a child. To help insure the healthy development of her unborn child, the mother must eat properly and should receive medical attention aimed at preventing anemia, infections, high blood pressure, and excessive weight gain. She should eliminate heavy smoking and exposure to unnecessary medication and X-rays, and she should try to control any other factors that could seriously affect the fetus.

One of the major goals of prenatal care is to maintain pregnancy to full term. Prematurity is one of the main causes of infant mortality during the first days of life, yet it is often preventable through early medical care. Unfortunately, prematurity most often occurs among poverty-level families who cannot afford the special medical care, attention, and nutrition the infant needs during his first months.

Although pregnancy, labor, and delivery are far less dangerous for both mother and child today than several decades ago, medical advances cannot fully benefit a woman who comes for them late in pregnancy. Nor can obstetric care completely remove the potential dangers which arise when a woman has too many babies too closely spaced, when she conceives at too young or too old an age, when she has been exposed to infections during her pregnancy, or when she suffers from excessive strain and tension at this time. By the time of delivery or even during the last months of pregnancy, it may be too late to prevent the harm done by the use of over-the-counter or unsafe-during-pregnancy medications, or the lack of adequate genetic counseling which led to the conception of a child with high genetic risk.

Physical Care, Love, and Attention

Another essential precondition to development is the physical well-being of each child. Physical care includes adequate nutrition, immunizations, regular pediatric checkups in addition to medical attention for illnesses, and regular dental care. It also involves preventing exposure to such dangers as lead paint and avoiding serious accidents.

In the process of receiving such continuous, attentive care during the first months of life, a child also receives affection, intellectual stimulation, and the opportunity to form secure social attachments—all essential for further development. Children need attention, yet the kind of attention they receive is most important. When adult reactions are active and responsive to the child's own behavior, the child learns about the value of his own actions and about the responses he can expect from other people. Such experiences, repeated with people who love him, help the child gain a sense of identity and develop as a social being.

The child must also have the opportunity to learn about limits and structure: to know what responses he can reasonably expect from adults, what standards he is expected to uphold, and what consequences he can predict for both his acceptable and unacceptable behavior. At the same time, he needs flexibility and diversity to stimulate his curiosity. As the child matures, limits and rules have to change, and new and more complex expectations have to be introduced. An individual balance between the child's need for variety and stimulation and his need for stability and predictability will encourage healthy intellectual and social development.

Models

As children move from infancy into the preschool years, they begin to identify with and to imitate the actions and attitudes of adults important to them. These adults, whether they are aware of it or not, serve as models for the child. For a child to develop socially acceptable behavior, he needs the presence of respected adults who themselves act in accepted ways and who will reward the child for behavior that they feel is good and worthwhile.

All these factors are only preconditions for development. Their fulfillment cannot guarantee intelligence nor any other quality or ability. When these preconditions are not met, the effects on the child's development are often painfully clear by the age of 3. Unfortunately, by this age, they may not be completely reversible.

There is no single, critical period of development. Each day of a child's life is important. For development to proceed normally, these preconditions continue to be important throughout childhood. When the conditions for development are met, most children are able to move to maturity through successive stages of understanding and behavior.

Major Aspects of Development

There have been many attempts to define development: some definitions stress the increasing complexity of a child's behavior and feelings as he grows older; others focus on the ways children become more realistic about the world; others emphasize the child's widening social horizons; still others are concerned with the acquisition of intellectual abilities such as solving problems, using abstract symbols, and learning a large vocabulary. While we need not be overly concerned with theory, it is useful to understand the major aspects of a child's development from ages 3 to 6—the changes that take place in his ability to use language; his sense of identity, competence, and morality; his learning and cognitive abilities; and his general social and emotional functioning.

Growth in each of these areas tends to proceed together. Functioning in one area cannot really be understood without considering the functioning of each of the others. Thus, poor language development may be linked to a child's feeling of incompetence and to his inability to function socially; while a healthy social and emotional development will likely be a positive influence on a child's ability to learn.

Language

There are dramatic differences in the language of the 3-year-old, the 4- or 5-year-old, and the 6-year-old child. The 3-year-old is like a student mastering a musical instrument—while there may be moments of musical excellence, more often the instrument, rather than the musician, is in control. In a child of this age, such variability and continuing experimentation with language can be charming. If the child can't remember the words of a song, any words will do if they sound right. The feeling is the message. "Old MacDonald had a farm, Eh, I, I, I, you. And on farm, Ey, I, I, I, oh had a horse. Ho-ho-ho—cow and horse."

The 4- or 5-year-old still invents new words, such as "to screwdriver" a screw or "to bow" a shoe. A confusing situation can be "calamacious"; an unpleasant child can be "fugzy." Favorite words can be great fun to pronounce, and language can be a never-ending game.

By contrast, the 6-year-old is a master speaker. He may search for the correct word or not understand many that he hears, but he no longer plays with words nor invents them so readily.

Using language is, of course, central to any form of intellectual growth. Most important in shaping a child's use of language is what he hears, and how he is responded to, in his home. Different families respond differently to children's comments. In some families, conversation between parents and children is spontaneous and natural, while in others this kind of verbal attention to children is more difficult to achieve or is less highly valued.

Yet it is outside the home where a child's language ability is really tested. There has been much discussion about the richness, adequacy, utility, and grammatical structure of the language of different social classes and ethnic groups. Certainly, nonstandard English should not be considered deficient. Children in Northern ghettos, for example, can express the most complicated thoughts and the broadest range of feelings using nonstandard "black" English. Their vocabulary is well-adapted to their environment with words and expressions which capture the tone of their daily experiences. The issue about linguistic inferiority is not raised in relation to children whose native language is not English. Rather, there is a general concern felt by parents and educators about appropriate ways of introducing these children to English while preserving the child's ability to use and value his first language.

The major concern in either case should be what type of language competence does the child need to be able to succeed in terms of his parents' expectations and his own. For the great majority of children, this question comes down to what degree of language competence they need in order to succeed in schools which require fluent use of standard English.

Day care can offer children the opportunity of speaking freely and being spoken to, and of feeling a sense of competence in language. Generally, parents with a non-English or nonstandard-English background very much want their children to learn standard English. But this must be approached gradually, after the child feels respected for what he is and after he has had the opportunity of expressing himself in his own language or language style.

Identity

A child's self-concept has roots in his earliest experiences. The sense of who he is, what he wishes to do, and what is expected of him emerges from daily encounters with parents, neighbors, and friends. During the preschool years, the child begins to collect these raw materials for the ultimate shaping of his mature identity.

There are many facets of identity. In the preschool and early school-age years these partial identities have not yet developed into a coherent personal sense of wholeness. It is only during adolescence that the individual may begin to ask of himself, "These are the various things people have told me about myself; this is what they have expected me to be and do; here is the way I thought I had to act. But who am I really, and what do I want to become?"

Physical Identity. Knowledge of how the body looks and works is not innate. The child acquires a sense of physical identity by using his body; he learns how his body looks and works, what his body needs, the position and function of different parts and their associated feelings. Through bumps, bruises, scratches, and caresses, by grasping, falling, eating, touching, and being touched—through every type of stimulus the infant and young child receives, he develops a sense of physical individuality.

Parents also help the child learn how his body works—by feeding him when he is hungry, keeping him warm and his diapers dry, and thus teaching him to recognize his own needs. They help to focus the child's attention on his inner body. Through toilet training, for example, the child learns how to cope with and control urges and feelings that occur within himself.

During the preschool years, four important aspects of physical identity emerge: the sense of size, strength, gender, and race or racial awareness.

No child can ignore being smaller than his parents or being unable to reach a high shelf or see above a counter. Yet children generally do not feel small. When the child's experiences have been good—when he hasn't been repeatedly hospitalized, severely humiliated, or physically abused—he may see himself as a person who is physically big. His sense of physical stature is reinforced when people pay "big" attention to him and when he is capable of doing "big" things by himself. Similarly, when things have gone well, the child feels strong—even though at times he must ask for help when doing something that requires an adult's strength.

In developing a sense of physical identity, the child brings together his various experiences: being smaller and weaker than adults, being responded to in different ways by adults and peers, feeling a sense of accomplishment in difficult tasks. Ask a preschooler who feels good about himself to draw a picture of a child and his father; the child may equal the father's size or be only slightly smaller, out of courtesy.

The child's perception of gender is another important aspect of physical identity. Although many of the stereotyped social roles determined by sexual identity are in the process of change in our culture, the basic physical differences between males and females are unchanging. By age 3, a child clearly knows that he or she is a boy or a girl. Children at this age can quickly identify themselves in photos, can point out children that resemble them, and know that they are more like either their mother or father. Once perceived, the child's sense of his or her sexual identity becomes, with rare exceptions, permanent.

Awareness of social expectations, both implicit and explicit, develops along with the child's sexual identification. Are boys more active, aggressive, and rough because of society's demands? Are girls more thoughtful, obedient, and gentle because these qualities are essential to their assigned social role? This certainly seems, at least in large part, to be true. It will take years to determine the impact of changing social conditions—particularly the questioning of sexual stereotypes—on children's emerging gender identities. We still do not really understand the various biological and social causes of behavior patterns that are typical of one sex or the other. Meanwhile, children will continue to learn from both the mirror and the people in their lives that they are either boys or girls. This knowledge will help set some enduring patterns of expectations and behavior which affect not only the child's own self-concept but what he or she expects of the opposite sex as well.

Racial identity is somewhat similar to gender identity. The 4-year-old child knows that his skin is black, brown, white, yellow, or red; that he resembles one group of people more than another; and that he looks similar to, or different from, other children. At this age, children are curious in a healthy, open way about the differences in appearance between individuals.

Yet, as the sense of racial identity develops, it may affect the child's values of himself in relation to others. Children's racial attitudes reflect the attitudes of the people who surround them. A preschool child who has lived only among people of his own race or ethnic group may be curious and a bit frightened by a person with a different color skin. Differences often lead to discomfort in the 3- or 4-year-old. Depending on the cues he receives from family and friends, this discomfort either can lead to knowledge and empathy or it can produce prejudice and intolerance. If given the opportunity, a child will quickly work through his concern and form natural relationships despite physical differences.

On the basis of daily experiences during his first years, the child of age 4 or 5 has a variety of ways in which he sees himself. His physical identity is a collection of characteristics and expectations concerning size, strength, gender, and race. The child of this age seldom understands or sees these aspects of himself as parts of a whole person. He does not yet have a clear picture of how these different aspects hold together to make him the unique individual that he is.

Personal Identity. For the young child, there is no sharp separation between the developing sense of physical identity and the developing personal or social identity. Personal identity is an individual's perception of himself as a person with desires, wishes, beliefs, ideas, and feelings, and with a history and a future of his own. For the preschool child, the past and future are much less real than for the adolescent and adult, and the child's developing personal identity is thus very responsive to current situations.

The personal identity of a 3- to 6-year-old evolves from two major types of experiences: (1) how the child is treated by the people close to him, and (2) what he observes about the adults he admires. If the child is treated with respect and love, he will perceive himself as worthwhile and lovable. If he receives meaningful responses, he will grow to feel that his actions and opinions are strong and valuable. If he can effect a change in his world through purposeful action—such as a protest about his room which leads to a new sleeping arrangement—he will begin to learn that he can be effective.

In countless social situations, the child learns how others respond to him, and thus develops a sense of himself. "I am the child who gets into trouble." "I'm the sweet little girl, no brains, all heart." "I am really clever." "I am the kind of child you can't resist loving." "I am a big nobody."

The preschool child is extremely sensitive to the way his mother and father, and other adults whom he loves, behave toward others and are treated by others. Through identification with these adults, the child's personal identity develops. If his parents treat each other with respect, the child will imitate them and will be likely to become a kind, understanding person. In the same way, a child can learn alienation and humiliation after seeing his big, strong father cower before an employer, or after eating with his mother in the kitchen while the "nice folks" for whom she works eat at the dining room table. And a very young girl can be conditioned to believe that women have an inferior role, if she feels that her mother is bored and frustrated by housework while Daddy returns each evening with exciting stories about his working day.

The preschooler's personal identity consists of bits and pieces of social interactions, observations, and fantasies; it is a quiltwork of partial identifications, imitations, and pretendings. He can see himself as one type of person in one setting and an entirely different person in another setting. The devil at home can immediately become an angel at grandmother's, depending upon what he feels is expected of him.

In adolescence, this sense of changeable identity can lead to anxiety; in the preschool child, it is natural and healthy. It is, in fact, unhealthy when a child's sense of identity is too early closed: when a 6-year-old is made to feel that he is "hyperactive, uncontrollable, unpredictable"; that he is "just plain dumb"; or that he is "just another migrant—no use fussing with him." In an environment which is stressful, a preschool child can identify himself with the unhealthy aspects of some adult or can increasingly show the undesirable qualities that people attribute to him. These characteristics may become a permanent part of his identity. Such children must be shown, with honesty, that they have other more positive potentialities that can be developed.

Preschool children develop pictures of themselves and of their different identities in different situations on the basis of routine, daily, and unnotable experiences which occasionally may be heightened by truly powerful moments of human interaction. When all is going well, these identities are flexible. Indeed, it is the ability of children to change their self-perceptions that causes real optimism about the possible benefits for personality development to be gained from preschool programs. By school age, some of this flexibility and openness may be lost.

Competence

"I *know* I'm a good woodworker," Timmy, age 6, told a grownup friend, as he displayed a small boat he had made from scrap lumber. "It's really kind of easy, once you know how. But it took me 2 whole years to learn how to use the big hammer."

"Everybody likes my paintings," Marla, age 5, told an admirer. "That's because I plan. I think about what I do before I do it. * * * Maybe I'll give one to Uncle Howie for his birthday."

"I do it, I do it. Don't help me. I write my own name," 3-year-old Lisa told her father who wanted to print her name on her scribble-drawing of "a house, a bird, and here's the playground."

From the many experiences of learning, doing, and achieving, from every "I do it" and "don't help me," the child derives a sense of competence—a feeling that he can, indeed, "do it." Preschool children want to do things. Their need to achieve and accomplish is an inborn drive as important as their need for affection. Only in the most adverse situations is this motivation stifled.

The concept of competence relates to the *motivation* to do things well, the actual *ability* of the individual to accomplish both what he wants and what is expected of him, as well as the *sense* of personal ability. A child develops real competence and feels like a competent person if certain conditions are present: specifically, physical and mental health and a supportive environment.

The physically healthy child learns, plays, and acquires skills at a relatively predictable pace. The importance of good health is best understood by observing children handicapped with even minor difficulties: impaired vision, excessive clumsiness, or mild retardation. In working to overcome their disabilities, these children can develop important skills, as well as a sense of competence. But, for them, achievement requires greater efforts. The handicapped child's struggle to achieve shows both the strength of the natural drive for competence and the importance of good health in making this an easily reachable goal.

A supportive environment is as important to the child as good health. The child's surroundings—both human and inanimate—have to stimulate and support an emerging sense of competence. The preschooler needs opportunities to work with various materials, to finish what he starts, and to be rewarded for success. A child at this age makes use of a world of inanimate objects, of playthings and puzzles and useful junk, that he can shape to his own ends and for his own, personal reward. "Doing" also involves children in social situations with adults, where work can be encouraged, praised, and respected. A child's drawing, an arrangement of doll house furniture, a building-block construction, a few nails hammered into a board—all may be important expressions of a child's originality and competence. But whether he develops and feels a sense of competence depends largely on how his work is valued by the people he loves and respects.

Cognition

Cognition refers to mental growth and activity. It defines most of the processes of thinking and knowing that most children employ daily: from planning what to do in the morning, to learning the rules of a game or making up an excuse for a messy room. Cognition includes thinking, remembering, problem solving, planning, imagining, judging, and deciding. These processes develop along with the use of language, although they are not entirely dependent on it. Even infants are "cognitively" very active: when a baby smiles upon hearing his mother's voice or cries as a stranger approaches, that baby shows that his mental processes are functioning.

Parents and observers of children are usually charmed by youthful "errors" in understanding. When preschoolers try to understand causality in nature, for example, they often assume that things can think and act as people do. They may imagine that thunder is made by an angry giant in the sky, that dreams are sent by pillows, that rain falls because it knows that flowers are dry.

Testing situations have been devised in psychology laboratories to increase our understanding of how children think. In one situation, a child watches an adult pour water from a very thin, tall container, where the water column is high, into a very wide container. The child is then asked, "Which glass has more water?" To the adult, the answer is obvious: the same amount is in each. But to the preschooler, the thin glass holds more water: "Look how high up it comes." Even if the water is poured back and forth between the two glasses, the child will center his attention on the height of the column. He cannot generalize his observations to understand that the containers only shape the water column; they do not add to or substract from it.

For the preschooler, the problem of "same object, different perspective" may be almost impossible to solve. Things are different if one sees them differently. For example, a 4-year-old walking through a field noticed a full moon slightly above a row of distant buildings. When he later saw the moon high overhead, he became confused and asked, "Is this the same moon that we saw before?"

The concept of time can be just as perplexing to young children. Adults can generally keep a sequence of events and periods of time clearly in mind. The child, however, understands time in relation to present events. A boring and uneventful day will be longer for a 3-year-old than 2 exciting days. With similar logic, a 5-year-old, unhappy during his sister's birthday party, says, "She was 3 yesterday and now she's 4. I don't want her to catch up with me."

While some children can be quite sophisticated and know that babies come from inside their mothers, it may be difficult for them to think of themselves as having been babies and particularly hard to realize a time when they were not yet born. At best, they were "inside Mommy's tummy" a long time ago. "I've just been here for 4 years? I can't believe that. What was I doing before that?"

Children's errors in logic and understanding reflect natural stages in the development of cognition. During the preschool years, children slowly develop their ideas of causality, space, velocity, objectivity, and time. They gradually learn that events and objects have a permanence and reality of their own, regardless of a viewer's changing perspective.

While children of different socioeconomic backgrounds may exhibit great differences in the use of language, they usually think about things in a similar fashion. After reaching a certain stage of maturity, most children know that the quantity of water in the two different-shaped containers is the same. Language sophistication mainly determines the child's ability to describe the perception; it has much less effect upon his ability to use logic for solving problems or making correct judgments.

Many preschool programs, especially those designed for children from low-income families, emphasize "cognitive" development: the use of language, basic concepts such as the correct use of "above" and "below" and similar abstract terms, and preacademic skills such as counting and learning the alphabet. It is important to distinguish the acquisition of this type of knowledge from a child's general intelligence. An inarticulate child often can think and understand as well as a verbally gifted child and may excel in some areas, such as originality and motor maturity.

Of course, programs which stress cognitive skills may be quite valuable for children with limited experience in language usage and formal learning. They can prepare a child for classroom instruction and give him a sense of academic competence. However, the potential gains from a highly structured, academically oriented program for preschoolers must be weighed—for each individual child and for groups of children—against the potential harm. A child's natural curiosity and desire to learn can be stifled if he is pressured to learn too much too soon. For each child, the educator must ask: "Is this child's own creative, novel way of thinking being dulled by my demands that he learn what I want him to learn *now?* Am I inattentive to his strengths and possible creativity by encouraging only standardized, rote, and stereotyped skills?"

Social and Emotional Growth

Between ages 3 and 6, the child makes a giant leap from the small world of the family with limited outside contacts, to a world of many different friends, teachers, and influences. Parents are likely to know what their 2-year-old is doing at all times, but they take for granted that their 5-year-old has a social world of his own. "Hey, Mom, Jeremy Frank has a football sweat shirt just like that." "Who is Jeremy Frank?" she asks. "Oh, my best friend at camp."

When the child feels comfortable and secure in both his home and his expanding community and when people important to him think well of him, the child develops a sense of value and self-esteem. He appreciates himself. And when his attempts at achievement are successful, when he experiences accomplishment and reward, the child feels that he can do new things and make changes in his world. He thus gains a feeling of personal control.

Much of the child's development, especially his social development and behavior, between ages 3 and 6 is determined by two factors: his senses of self-esteem and personal control. If a child thinks he is important and good and able to control his actions, he will achieve and perform both for his own satisfaction and for those around him and will grow socially, emotionally, and mentally. If, however, a child has little experience with success and reward or is insecure, he may feel that events occur because of other, more powerful people. The sense of his own potential ability and worth may never fully develop.

In a child's social and emotional development, periods of tranquility or stability are normally mixed with periods of emotional upheaval. Children cannot be isolated from worries and anxieties related to the family and community. Nor can a child be kept from having periods of emotional upset which are related to his own psychological development, to new feelings, and to increasing awareness. Trying to completely protect a child from worry and anxiety is an impossible as well as an undesirable goal. Emotional stress can provide opportunities for emotional growth in which old routines are disturbed and new ways of coping appear.

If the child is supported through periods of stress and helped to face uncomfortable situations, he can develop the skills needed to deal with worries, anxieties, and tensions. Through such experiences, he may acquire a deeper sense of identity and competence. No child, however, should be purposefully stressed or have too much expected of him. Children left to face emotional crises without support may later be vulnerable to developmental disturbance and emotional problems.

For a 3- or 4-year-old child, the introduction to full-time day care can be a challenging or difficult transition. Mother is lost; new children appear; the physical environment is changed; and new routines are introduced. The adjustment can lead to either new social and emotional skills or to a repression of feelings and a sense of resentment. The outcome depends largely on whether the child's parents and caregivers respond to his worries with supportive concern.

Preschool programs usually focus on fostering social and emotional skills. Both in nursery schools and in developmental day care programs, the child is helped to deal with feelings in constructive ways, to find means for expressing his energy and creativity, and to work with other children in mutually satisfying activities.

For many preschool children—especially those whose lifelong environments have been insecure—a day care program that emphasizes social and emotional development may be the first place they receive needed care, attention, and individualized concern. In such a program, the child can acquire a new sense of self and learn new ways of coping with loneliness, anger, and the need for personal expression. His emerging sense of value will influence his social growth and his sense of competence. Oftentimes, children's IQ scores increase during the time they are in quality day care programs. These gains are related not to changes in innate intelligence but to the child's unfolding motivation to achieve and become involved with people, to his new trust, and his increased self-esteem.

Personal Styles

Confronted with a broken toy car, the child studied it for several moments, realized the problem, and fixed it. In the same situation another child might have knocked on it and thrown it to the floor, asked his mother to fix it, ignored it for another toy, or simply cried.

Practically any situation presents the individual with a variety of alternative responses; there are lots of ways to fix a toy, to cross a street, or to avoid frustration. And all may even lead to the same end. These different approaches or *personal styles* are mainly determined by three factors—endowment, personal experiences, and parental influences—though nobody knows why each child develops his own particular style.

From birth, children differ: some are quiet, others noisy; some calm, others jittery; some require little attention, others are terribly demanding. Each child has his own unique history: illnesses, accidents, separations, human interactions, observations, and experiences that differ from those of every other person. And finally, each child receives distinct parental influences. Each is encouraged towards certain behaviors by a series of rewards and punishments and subtle reactions; furthermore, every child imitates the actions, attitudes, and opinions of his parents.

Three types of personal styles are particularly evident and important: how a child mentally perceives a situation (cognitive style); how he physically reacts to a situation (behavioral style); and how he avoids psychological pain (defensive style).

A *cognitive style* is a way of organizing and dealing with the facts at hand. A complicated barnyard picture is shown to two children, and they are asked to describe it: one immediately names individual items—the animals, trees, tools, the people at work—while the second begins to describe the picture as a whole—the farm with the animals scattered about on a sunny day.

Children with different cognitive styles have different ways of perceiving a situation: some children tend to notice details and may ignore the similarities between different objects and events; other children tend to concentrate on the situation as a whole and may not bother with details. These perceptual differences reveal *aspects of cognitive style, not intelligence.* Two children can have different mental approaches to a situation, even though they are equally bright. The distinctionmaker can clearly know that apples and oranges and pears are all fruits; the child who generalizes can probably tell you, if asked, the differences between two apples in shape, size, and color.

Just as there are styles of cognition, so there are uniquely different styles of behavior. A child's *behavioral style* is the way he does, or does not, get things done. Included are such aspects of behavior as the child's promptness in starting an activity, his speed in working, the degree of concentration and interest he shows, and the number of unnecessary actions he uses. Children with different behavioral styles may all produce a final product. There is no "right" way to get dressed or to draw a picture; any number of alternative methods can be used, even though some styles can be more effective than others in certain situations.

Behavioral extremes range from children who are impulsive to those who are inhibited. An *impulsive* child reacts too quickly, especially in potentially dangerous situations, where good judgment would indicate a slower pace; the *inhibited* child may react too slowly and fearfully, especially in situations not generally dangerous or frightening. Between these two extremes is a wide range.

The third type of personal style, *defensive style,* relates to feelings and to the avoidance of emotional pain. There are no children untouched by some sadness or loss. Every child must learn early in life to deal with fears, worries, and upsets, whether it be the first separation from his parents, watching a scary television program, hearing or seeing his parents argue, or waiting for a newborn brother to be brought home from the hospital.

When things go well for the child and his family, these feelings become an accepted part of life, just like feelings of hunger or pleasure. However, the child usually learns to avoid those situations he has found too frightening or anxiety-producing in the past. Placed in situations that do make him afraid, he develops ways to protect himself against the full impact of anxiety. These acquired ways of coping with or managing strong, unpleasant feelings constitute the individual's defensive style.

All children try to keep their fears, worries, and anxieties to manageable size—they joke about things that worry them, whistle in the dark, play games about murder and death, and devise little stories that explain the unknown. Each child's defensive style is personal and unique, even though each leads to the same end by reducing emotional pain. To avoid being frightened by a scary movie, one child may turn his head or his thoughts from the screen; another may try to convince himself that it isn't real but "just pretend" or "crazy"; another may imitate the frightening action by pretending to shoot a gun to escape feeling shot at; while still another may simply leave the room.

From the never-quite-the-same circumstances that determine individual characteristics, children develop the styles of thinking, acting, and feeling (cognition, behavior, and defenses) that constitute their own, unique personalities. The hallmark of quality day care is its ability to recognize each child's distinctive personality and to adapt its program to respect each child's right to be treated as a unique person.

Morals

Consider three mothers, each alone at home with an infant and a 4-year-old son. The first is young, unwed, and lonely. The second, a more mature housewife, has several school-age children, as well as many friends and interests. The third has a successful, part-time career and a husband who cares for the children when she is working. In each case, the 4-year-old has just spilled his juice for the second time and is now disturbing the baby's sleep by noisily playing trains with the kitchen chairs. Each of these women will react differently to her son; each will define his actions differently. Is he naughty, aggressive, or healthily assertive? The way each reacts will reinforce in the child her definition of the behavior and will help shape the way the child labels his actions as good or bad.

Confronted with the actions of their children parents respond in terms of both their own upbringing and their experiences as adult members of the community. They remember how as children they were shown, or not shown, love, and how they were disciplined. In every family, parents set limits and rules and show some form of disapproval. What these are and how they are expressed depend very much on the particular child, family, and community. What kind of child do the parents really want to have? What kind of a community are they preparing the child to live in? What will the community tolerate now from a child?

It is in the give-and-take between parent and child that children learn empathy and what is morally acceptable: which impulses they can express openly and which they must suppress, where their individual rights begin and where they infringe upon others, and how to handle disagreements. The child's moral development is determined by his recognition of his own behavior as good or bad and his desire to conform to accepted standards.

Children pass through stages of moral development. Though they at first perceive an action as "bad" because of the punishment connected with it, they may later feel it is "bad" because it disregards the rights of others. In the process of moral growth, children develop new perceptions of themselves, of their rights, and of their parents and community.

By age 3, children are expected to behave in a socially acceptable way in many situations: to start responding to the "don'ts"—in regard to playing with food, biting or pinching, taking another's toy; as well as the "do's"—to help clean up, to say "thank you," and to show interest in cooperating with others. At this age, children easily lapse from these moral do's and don'ts. They do what they're told, but mostly when somebody is around to encourage or guide their actions.

By age 6, the child has usually adopted and modifed these rules and expectations as his own. He has a new moral feeling, an inner sense of what is right and wrong, what is fair, and what is acceptable. He may feel guilty if he messes his room and anxious if he takes another child's toy. He feels proud when he acts fairly or does his share. Yet, even at this age, children often behave in ways they know to be wrong.

Children, parents, and communities may differ in what they consider acceptable behavior, though many of the differences tend to be surface ones. By age 6, children know the difference between being given an apple by the grocery store owner, paying for one, and stealing one. Taking an apple is stealing in a rich or a poor community, and the child who does it usually feels a sense of unpleasant concern. However, this doesn't mean that there may not be more apple stealing in one neighborhood, where the children might be more hungry, than in another; it doesn't mean that children won't steal apples "just for the fun of it"; nor does it mean that every time a child takes an apple he will feel he has stolen. Still, by this age, children in all types of communities will generally be more content when they behave according to their own inner values and concept of fairness—which they have learned from their past experiences and observations.

Another place children learn moral definitions is TV, possibly the most important new educator of community standards. There are now perhaps only one or two national television programs for children which show adults as always respectful of children's rights and feelings and which present acceptable role-models to the young viewer. Too much TV aimed at children shows violence and disrespect; condones hitting, beating, and murder; and portrays the tough, brutal, and insensitive person as someone to be admired. Television also teaches children about deception. By age 5, every child knows that commercials deceive—that the toys are never as big or exciting as they look on TV; that no toy will bring scores of new friends to his door; that no cereal or vitamin can talk or turn him into a giant or a hero. Television's message to children is clear: deception is a widely practiced way of trying to achieve a goal.

Parents and others concerned with a child's welfare usually try to counteract television's harmful effects. Competent caregivers can and do limit a child's exposure to television, as well as help him understand and evaluate the programs he watches. Caregivers also can become additional models for the child, demonstrating rightness and fairness and ways to deal with situations related to moral judgments. There is no more sensitive interface between parents and caregivers than the area of morals and discipline. Caregivers are professionals and must not act contrary to their principles and beliefs; still, it is their duty to strengthen the child's respect for parental attitudes and customs. They may oftentimes be caught between these two obligations, when they feel that what a parent has done or told a child, either directly or by example, is wrong. Such conflicts must be handled on an individual basis and often benefit from the intervention of a professional third party. The primary concern of all involved should be the welfare of the child.

Playing and Reality

When is a preschool child not playing? He makes a game out of washing and eating, out of taking a bath, walking upstairs, going shopping, and falling asleep. He's always playing at something—except when he's very sad, distracted (by the television, for example), or asleep. Parents know their child is becoming ill when he stops playing and that he's recovering when his playfulness resumes. Playing is a sign of health.

Play begins with the infant in his mother's lap—she tickles the baby's foot, the baby grabs out to touch, they both smile and laugh. Through play, the young child learns to use different objects—toys, rattles, puzzles, his own body.

There are no sharp lines in the child's world between play and work, between the world of dreams and the world of hard reality. Does the 3-year-old who is learning the alphabet song consider this work or play? Does the 4-year-old who is busy managing her make-believe store feel she is playing or working? Does the 5-year-old who is tensely up at bat think he is simply playing a game?

Children at play are able to explore and practice new roles and skills; they can learn about new materials, acquire social abilities, and learn to cope with trying experiences. Through play the child learns to identify and distinguish the different spheres or levels of being: levels of activity and inactivity, of winning and losing, of loving and hating, of being unimaginative and creative, social and businesslike.

Children at play can become tough generals who boss "little soldiers." They can become parents who firmly put children to sleep. They can build bridges, bake cakes, and fly to Mars. They can learn how and when to exercise their fantasies. In short, their play enables them to be active in depicting what they feel and think about all parts of their lives. Their play can also become a part of everything they do.

Adults can provide opportunities for rich and worthwhile play in several ways. They can help a child feel secure. They can assure him that his play will be respected and not too rigidly supervised or arbitrarily disturbed. And they can provide a few necessary props such as blocks, balls, and creative materials. Such an environment is especially important in day care. When adults provide the necessary opportunities, most healthy children will quickly demonstrate their capacity for elaborate and imaginative play. Only in the totally engrossing play experience does the 3- to 6-year-old bring together all his or her social, emotional, and intellectual capabilities.

Learning

Learning is a many-sided concept. This chapter has already touched on many of the different kinds of things that children learn—the *content of their knowledge*. And it has described important factors that facilitate learning—the *preconditions of learning* such as good health, high self-esteem, responsive adults, and opportunities to explore. A look at some of the theories concerning a more technical aspect of learning—how children learn or the *process of learning*—follows. These various theories assign quite different explanations of how an individual learns. All have some usefulness but, since each theory tends to concentrate on one aspect of personality, no one alone can define the entire process.

Reinforcement Theory. When a child behaves well, it is natural for an adult to show pleasure. And if a child performs an especially commendable task, such as cleaning his room or raking leaves, he is often told how well he has done and given candy or some other treat. The candy and praise are *positive reinforcement* or *rewards* for the child's behavior. Similarly, when a child breaks the rules, an adult is likely to scold or show displeasure in some other way. The scolding and displeasure are *negative reinforcements* or *punishments.*

Children learn to pattern their behavior so that they receive approval or rewards and avoid punishment. Children who have been rewarded will learn ways to maintain their rewards and, having been punished, they will learn ways to end or avoid that punishment.

Most 4-year-old children do not expect to be rewarded for every good action or to be punished each time they do something wrong. They know that punishments and rewards are given only once in a while. This way of timing and arranging rewards and punishments is called an *intermittent schedule* and is a concept basic to reinforcement theory.

A 4-year-old also knows that a specific behavior may be rewarded or punished in one situation, yet not in another. Throwing a ball, for example, may be forbidden inside the house, although very much encouraged on the ballfield. So the child must learn those situations or *stimulus conditions* in which a particular behavior is appropriate.

Reinforcement theory sharpens our concern for knowing precisely what we want children to learn and it helps us understand how we shape children's behavior through our use of rewards and punishments, sometimes without being aware of it. Programs based on this theory carefully define appropriate and inappropriate behavior, select types of reinforcement, define the schedule of reinforcement, and monitor changes in the child's behavior to determine the success of the program.

Association Theory. Almost everyone is familiar with Pavlov's dogs. At first, they salivated only when they saw food; later, after receiving food on many occasions when a bell was rung, they salivated at the sound of the bell. On a picnic, people seeing a charcoal fire may have the same reaction: they may have learned to associate the charcoal burner with hamburgers, just as the dogs associated the bell with food.

According to this theory, a child's mental growth is an ever-increasing collection of associations, and each child learns to respond to new situations, or *stimuli* (such as the food and the bell), with new behavior, or *responses* (such as the salivation). While this is a useful explanation of how children learn some things, association theory is weak in explaining complex or imaginative behavior. Advocates of association theory have tried to explain this kind of behavior with concepts such as *verbal mediation.* As a child acquires the use of language, it becomes a middle link, or *mediator,* between a stimulus and the response. The stimulus, rather than setting off an immediate behavioral response, triggers a series of complex associations in language within the child's mind, and these associations then lead to the response.

For example, association theory might explain why a child crosses the street to avoid a mean-looking stranger. When the child sees the stranger, it sets off memories about hearing that a child was once beaten by a stranger and about warnings that his parents have offered. These associations lead to different ideas about what to do—"Should I throw a stone?" "Should I run away?" "Should I carry a big stick?"—and then to the final idea, to cross the street. This final idea leads to the decision to cross.

Association theory is most helpful in explaining how children learn very simple behaviors—like smiling at the sound of a voice that has been associated with pleasant experiences. This theory, in conjunction with reinforcement theory, may also help caregivers understand how their actions and reactions to children can influence or lead to certain behavior in a child. However, in comparison to the reinforcement and cognitive theories, pure association theory has limited application for caregivers.

Cognitive Theory. Cognitive theory, which is most widely known because of the work of Piaget, is more concerned with the child's mental ability than with his behavior. It emphasizes that changes in the way a child thinks determine the changes in the way he acts. According to cognitive theory, a child learns by using his available mental capacities for understanding as much as he is able and then developing new concepts and ideas to help him in new and more complex situations.

Studies based on this theory concern the ways children interpret their observations and experiences. How does a child learn a rule? How does he apply a rule to a particular situation? How does he develop an abstract concept? Does the way he understands one concept determine the way he understands others?

The explanations of how a child learns which are offered by cognitive theory are far more complicated than those of reinforcement theory. While reinforcement theory states that a reward influences a change in a child's behavior, cognitive theory states that the reward indicates to the child that his thinking or mental operations are correct. Another way of looking at the difference in the theories is in relation to how active the child is considered to be. Reinforcement theory views the child as very responsive to his environment and particularly affected by the rewards and punishments he is given. Cognitive theory, on the other hand, views the child as a very active organizer of his own experience.

Unlike reinforcement theory which sees learning as the same process at all ages, cognitive theory is quite sensitive to the different ways children understand and organize their experiences at *different stages of development.* It explains how children's errors in logic and amusing distortions of their perceptions are related to particular stages of their mental growth—for example, how children, depending on their intellectual maturity, perceive a quantity of water as determined by the shape of its container. However, while cognitive theory can clearly detail the development of a child's way of thinking, it offers little explanation for what motivates a child to pass through the various stages of mental growth (a central concern of psychoanalytic theory to be discussed later).

The use of cognitive theory involves specifying (1) what mental processes the child is capable of, (2) what types of experiences are beyond the child's capacity to understand, and (3) what internal (maturational) and external (social) forces are operating on the child to enable him to acquire more complex and abstract mental abilities. Preschool programs based on cognitive theory usually begin by assessing a child's current mental abilities and then helping him either to fully use his ability or to acquire new ways of perceiving and understanding. For example, a child may be found to have difficulty in following directions because he cannot fully use the concepts of "bigger than" and "smaller than." Instruction is then aimed at helping him with these concepts. As he learns, his ability to follow directions should improve.

Much learning during the preschool and early school years involves acquiring new concepts and ways of organizing ideas. Cognitive development and learning must be distinguished from mere rote learning, which is the acquisition of behavior based on reinforcement techniques.

Psychoanalytic Theory. In psychoanalysis, as in the other learning theories discussed, the child is seen as having motivating drives and the capacity to adapt and learn. More than the other theories, however, psychoanalysis stresses that how and what a child learns is related to the impact that the adults who care for the child have upon him from the time of his birth, and to the impact of his current level of human relationships and general personality development as well. Psychoanalytic theory helps us understand why a child wants to learn and why some children, with normal intelligence and good health, do not learn. According to this theory, learning depends on more than rewards or intellectual functions.

Learning how to ride a bike, for example, may mean more to a child than simply being able to coordinate muscles. It may be a way of pleasing his parents or himself, of showing his power, or of indicating that he can now go places without depending on his parents. A child ready physically, but not emotionally, to assert himself in this way may not learn to ride a bike in spite of rewards. Similarly, for some children, learning to read brings new feelings of mastery, independence, pride in acting like a grownup, or a delightful sense that a new world of secrets can now be revealed. For others, who may be equally intelligent, learning to read may be uninteresting, frightening, or confusing because they are less prepared to venture into an adult role by reading rather than by being read to.

Psychoanalytic theory focuses attention on the meanings that underlie a child's behavior. A caregiver may wonder why a 5-year-old constantly dresses and acts like Superman. Realizing that this activity gives the child a way of denying that he is frightened, the caregiver can help the child express his feelings and can try to help him become more comfortable in the day care program.

Probably the most important contribution of psychoanalysis as a learning theory useful to day care is its emphasis on the importance of human relations in the lives of children. During the first years of life, children form very special relationships with their parents and their caregivers, and these color their attitudes and feelings throughout life. Sensitive caregivers become aware of how important they are in the lives of the children they care for. They recognize that children will learn new things because of them and that a child will feel emotional upset and pain if he is transferred from their care. In terms of a child's potential ability to learn and to take pleasure in learning, it is likely to be more beneficial for the child to have a single, affectionate, and dependable caregiver for several years than to have a series of changing caregivers who may be better trained professionally.

Relations Between Theories. Each of these theories has a contribution; each has been used in some way in designing curricula; and each focuses on different features of the learning process. Depending on the particular situation and the particular child's needs, one theory may be more useful, for the moment, than another. For example, a caregiver might react in several different ways to a child's drawing of a tall boy standing next to a smaller building. If the caregiver knows the child has trouble understanding the difference between "big" and "small," she might use the drawing to explain these concepts of size. If, instead, she knows that the child has a poor self-image, she may see the drawing as an expression of his improving self-esteem and may comment about how pleased he must be with the many new things he has learned. However, if drawing a picture is this child's way of avoiding some activity which he has trouble doing, the caregiver may politely praise the child for the picture but may then more strongly reward him for attempting the other activity. Of course, no caregiver will think about what theory of learning she or he may be using at these different times, but rather will act naturally. The purpose of the learning theories is to help caregivers understand how to plan and to know what to do when acting naturally doesn't seem to work.

There are general features of learning and development which cut across all of the theories. For example, certain features of the learning process clearly relate to the developmental level of the child. Very young children are likely to repeat a behavior that has been reinforced, while older children are more likely to go on to something else. Young children tend to learn faster when they receive a direct, personally meaningful reward, such as candy. Older children are more eager to please adults by learning; for them, material rewards may become less powerful than social ones. As children develop, they try different approaches to solving problems and become more independent of the immediate situation. They also become increasingly able to make use of language or verbal instructions to think or to learn a new task.

From 3 to 6 years of age, children show marked improvements in two spheres, attention and discrimination. The 6-year-old is far more able than the 3-year-old to pay attention to critical features and to distinguish details. He is also better able to relate what he has learned in the past to a similar situation in the present.

All of these changes in learning are very much related to a child's sense of personal value, his experience with success, and other factors that we commonly associate with personality development. If a child has positive feelings about the people around him and has previously been rewarded for imitating their behavior, he is likely to use these people as models for his future behavior, to identify with their attitudes and values.

A child who has had profitable social and personal experiences will become increasingly able, between the ages of 3 and 6, to learn how to learn. The process of learning involves the ability to pay attention to appropriate features of a situation, to avoid being distracted by irrelevant details and events, to organize perceptions, to use appropriate mental operations, to monitor one's success—especially in terms of rewards and punishments—and to maintain an internal sense of direction.

In quality day care, this normal process of learning can be strongly supported. Acquiring the skills necessary for learning is far more important for the preschooler than acquiring any particular kind of knowledge of numbers, the alphabet, or what we usually call "formal" education. In fact, overemphasis on formal, rote learning may inhibit the child from the kind of involvement and exploration that is essential to learning.

Problems in Development

"When things go well for a child" is a phrase which covers a multitude of conditions, from good continuing health and a stable home with loving parents to progressive emotional, intellectual, and social development. Even when things do go well, however, every child between the ages of 3 and 6 still faces the normal aches and pains and crises of growing up. Both parents and caregivers must be able to sense such problems. They should know when help is needed and when to let the child work through things alone. Both should also know when and where to ask for help should a major problem arise.

Every child experiences some difficulties with his feelings which create concern in those who care for him. Sometimes these periods can be traced to a specific event—such as moving to a new house, entering day care, arguments between parents, or the birth of a sibling—but often there may be no apparent cause.

During times of emotional upset, children generally show their stress by relatively obvious personality changes. Some children react with *immaturity*; they may, for example, revert to bed-wetting or demand increased physical attention such as sitting on a parent's lap or tagging on mother's arm. Other children show *changes in feelings* by withdrawing or becoming sad, fearful, or tense. Children can also show marked *changes in conduct,* acting aggressively and with unusual nastiness. Or they may experience *bodily changes*—such as loss of appetite, stomachaches, or even vomiting. Since these conditions are all closely related, one child may exhibit a combination of changes in personality and bodily functions during periods of emotional upset.

Every stage of development has its related problems. To understand a child's problems, one must view them in the context of (1) the stage of development the child has reached, (2) the developmental tasks which the child is facing, and (3) the normal ranges and patterns of behavior found in children at that particular stage of development. In meeting children's problems, there are also many ways of discussing them: by *symptoms* (such as bed-wetting or destructiveness); by underlying *cause* (such as insecurity or family upheaval); by the *system of functioning* which has been affected (such as disturbances of language functioning or emotional control); by *syndrome* or *constellation* of symptoms and signs (such as a perfectionistic personality); or by very broad *categories* (such as disturbances in the normal rate or progress of development). Of course, these different approaches to discussing developmental problems do overlap. For convenience, the following sections move among these different ways of describing the developmental difficulties most likely to be of concern to caregivers. These include problems in developmental progress, attention problems, language problems, social problems, physical problems, and fears and habits.

It should be clear, however, that no aspect of a child's functioning can be understood in isolation. The child's general social, emotional, and intellectual functioning has to be viewed in the context of his family life, his community, and his current child care situation.

It should also be clear that there is no simple cookbook approach to a particular problem in development. There are many different ways in which a caregiver may respond to a child's difficulty. At times she may simply continue to provide affectionate care and allow the child to deal with his anxiety or difficulties by himself. Every experienced parent and caregiver knows that by tolerating and helping a child understand the reasons for bed-wetting during a period of stress, for example, she helps the child regain control quickly and that an angry, critical reaction will only add to the child's problem. Day care should provide a flexible setting where minor problems and their symptoms can be tolerated long enough for the child to help himself.

In other situations, the caregiver may help the child turn a passive experience, such as having a bad case of the chicken pox, into an active one, by encouraging him to play doctor to dolls who need bandages. In still other cases, the caregiver may help the child learn new ways to express feelings or find substitutes for difficult behavior. She or he may, for example, help a child who throws blocks during a temper tantrum learn to talk about his anger or may encourage a game in which dolls get angry with each other and then settle their argument. The choice between waiting, turning passivity into activity, substituting, verbalizing, and other approaches as responses to a child's problem will depend on the child, the parents, the caregiver, and the resources available to the program.

Disturbances in Developmental Progress

Children develop at their own rates, and there are broad ranges of what can be considered normal or typical behavior for any given age. In any group, there are children with more mature speech, personality, and general behavior than that of most children their age, and there are others whose development lags behind. Among a group of 4-year-olds, for example, there will usually be only one or two children who can tie their shoelaces, but most of these children will be able to put on their coats or draw a picture of a person.

The concept of *developmental lag,* or *developmental retardation,* covers those situations in which a child, for any reason, is significantly lacking what can be expected of typical children of the same age. It usually applies to a child who is quite clearly slow in developing intellectual abilities and social and motor skills. Such a child can be recognized by his need for more assistance than other children of the same age, by his bewilderment or uncooperativeness in situations that most children master easily, or because he does not engage in the typical activities expected of children his age. The parents of a developmentally lagging child often recognize the child's slowness or inability to keep up with other children. Yet, perhaps equally often, parents may not be aware of the child's difficulties, especially if they have had little experience in caring for other children.

There are many causes for developmental lag or retardation. Three prime causes are sensory problems, mental retardation, and environmental deprivation. Only careful assessment by trained professionals can lead to an accurate diagnosis, and sometimes even professionals will be unsure of the cause without observing the child over many months. Day care programs can serve a vital role for parents and communities by identifying children with developmental difficulties as early as possible.

Sensory Problems. A child who appears slow may, upon careful examination by physicians, psychologists, or other professionals, be found to have specific perceptual, visual, or hearing problems. Poor vision or hearing in children is frequently not discovered until the child reaches preschool or even school age, by which time he may have major problems with language, general cognitive skills, and social relations.

Mental Retardation. Although there are hundreds of causes for mental retardation, all are usually grouped into two main types: those organic or physical in nature and those without apparent organic origins.

Children whose mental retardation is organic in nature—caused, for example, by Down's syndrome or phenylketonuria (PKU)—usually have very severe developmental disabilities which are recognized and usually brought to a physician's attention during the child's first years. Among the organic causes of mental retardation are abnormal structure of the child's brain, prenatal or birth-related damage to the brain, severe brain infections or injury after birth, metabolic problems that injure or affect the brain, and diseases and disturbances of the central nervous system that negatively affect the child's ability to develop and to learn. Children with this type of retardation typically have disabilities in all spheres of their development.

Of all mentally retarded children, those with organically caused problems and severe retardation are only a very small percentage. They are unlikely to enter a day care program without already having their conditions detected and diagnosed. But there are children whose milder disabilities related to organic damage may be detected and treated only after the child has entered day care, kindergarten, or elementary school.

Those children whose mental retardation is from nonorganic causes also have low intelligence by standard intelligence tests—but usually not as low as in organic retardation—and have significant difficulties in behaving according to the norms for their age. The diagnosis of this type of retardation must be reserved for only those children whose performance, under the best of circumstances, is consistently below normal. A 4-year-old who scores very poorly on his first IQ test only because he is frightened or the tester inexperienced is obviously not retarded.

Some mentally retarded children whose disabilities are not organically caused are said to have *familial cultural retardation* because it is frequently found in entire families who may have trouble functioning in society. This type of retardation is less severe than organic retardation and interferes less with general functioning. Any label such as "familial cultural retardation" must be applied with great caution and only after the child has been carefully evaluated by competent professionals.

A great deal can be done for children whose retardation is either organic or nonorganic in nature, but it is probably those children with familial cultural retardation who can be helped most dramatically. Intensive intervention programs during the preschool years have brought remarkable advances in the general functioning and the tested intelligence of these children.

Environmental Deprivation. Poor performance in preschool day care commonly results when a child's family and community environment have limited his opportunities for growth. Many children from stressed, overworked families living below the poverty level arrive in preschool programs lacking critical intellectual and social skills. Upon formal testing, these children may show moderate or even severe impairment, particularly in their ability to use language. With sensitive evaluation, the cause will usually be found to be neither an organic nor an intellectual deficit, but rather the stresses and restrictions of the child's earlier experiences.

Sometimes the only way to determine whether a child suffers from the real intellectual deficits of mild retardation or from the effects of environmental deprivation is to see how he responds to a change of environment such as that provided by quality day care. There clearly are children who, even in the best homes and programs, still show the effects of mild mental retardation. It is equally clear, however, that there are children who will be unable to express their real potential and intelligence until they are given the opportunities and support available in a quality day care program. With quality care, these children can blossom into assertive and competent individuals. Without such care, or with only inadequate or custodial day care, their potential may be further inhibited.

The Role of Day Care. For the benefit of children with developmental retardation, no matter what the cause, day care should provide three major services. First, the caregiver should assess the general level of functioning of all the children to detect those whose development is *significantly* below normal. Second, the caregiver should convey his or her impressions to the parents and assist them in obtaining adequate evaluation for the child. And, finally, the day care program should adapt to accommodate, if possible, the needs of those children whose functioning is not so severely impaired that they require special programs.

The evaluation and diagnosis of developmentally retarded children often require the services of special consultants. No single test is conclusive, and information about the child's functioning, background, and experiences must all be weighed together with what is found from examination and laboratory testing. In the process of evaluation, a caregiver's observations and his or her ability to report them accurately may be crucial to a correct diagnosis of the child's condition. The treatment program for the child will often involve similar collaboration between specialists, the parents, and the caregiver.

Attention Problems

In every nursery school, day care center, and elementary classroom, there is probably at least one child, usually a boy, who is always physically active and unable to pay attention. Such a child may be hyperkinetic, which means that he is very active and has a short attention span. He can't concentrate long enough to listen to a story or to watch a half-hour television program. He may jump in and out of games and, when upset, may punch or scratch. At mealtimes, he may move about between mouthfuls and fiddle incessantly with the silverware. While other children are napping, he may walk about the room and create disturbances. These characteristics of the *hyperkinetic behavioral disturbance*—poor attention, easy distractability, seemingly continual movement, and difficulties in planning and carrying out tasks that require concentration—present problems and irritation to parents, caregivers, and peers alike.

There are some children who show all the signs of the hyperkinetic behavioral disturbance except for the continual physical movement. Rather than being constantly in motion, these children may show decreased activity, or *hypoactivity,* and often appear to be daydreaming. Though their bodies may be still, their thoughts are perpetually active. Children with this form of attention disturbance may not seem as troublesome as those who are hyperactive, but they can create a great deal of tension in a household where they need constant prodding to get dressed, finish tasks, or keep up with the rest of the family.

To control these difficult kinds of behavior, parents and caregivers often resort to threats or punishment, but to no avail. Punishment may make the child even more upset and less able to pay attention. Rewards may be somewhat more helpful, but these too are usually limited in their effectiveness.

Both hyperactive and hypoactive children have major learning difficulties. Often, their conditions are not diagnosed until the children are problems in kindergarten or fail in first grade. It is important in day care to identify children with attention and behavior problems and to help the parents obtain adequate medical evaluation.

No clear cause can be found for the attention difficulties of many children. Some children, upon careful professional evaluation, are found to have signs of minimal cerebral dysfunction or mild brain damage, including: clumsiness, twitching when hands are held straight forward, difficulty in walking a straight line, trouble in tapping to rhythm, and other indications of impairment of fine motor coordination and of the ability to organize behavior.

Sometimes hyperactivity and hypoactivity are related to major emotional problems and difficulties in the child's family life. The early history of children with attention problems often reveals prematurity or some difficulty at birth. Yet troubles in paying attention similar to those found in hyperkinetic behavioral disturbance can be caused by many factors that are immediately affecting the child's performance—such as hunger, sleep deprivation, family stress, difficulties in hearing or seeing, tensions in the school or day care program, or care which does not fulfill the child's individual needs for affection, stimulation, and stable human relations. Before a child can be diagnosed as suffering from hyperkinetic behavioral disturbance, it must be certain that his behavior is not the result of adverse conditions such as these.

For the child found to be hyperkinetic, treatment always involves a careful ordering of his experiences both at home and in day care. In such treatment, the child's individual needs are recognized and met, and appropriate stimulation and reasonable structure are carefully balanced. A comprehensive treatment program may involve the use of stimulant medication, which is prescribed and carefully monitored by a physician. This medication may increase the child's ability to pay attention and to concentrate. Of course, the day care program should never coerce a family into accepting any particular type of treatment and should never—under any circumstances—label a child. With carefully planned care, many children with these problems show profound changes in their behavior.

Language Problems

Many, perhaps most, children between ages 2½ and 4 experience two kinds of language difficulty—cluttering and speech "immaturity." For some, these difficulties continue through their first few years in school.

Cluttering is shown by many children when they become excited. "I want, I want, I want an ice cream cone." "Do you know, know, do you know what I saw?" At certain stages of development, 25 percent or more of a child's speech may be cluttered. Even a 6-year-old will clutter his speech with repetitions when he is excited, tired, or not concentrating on what he is trying to say—when, for example, his mother asks what he's done at school and he wants to run out to play.

Cluttering is relatively emotionally painless for the child and usually arouses no anxiety. Cluttering is not stuttering—the repetition of the same syllable of a word: "th, th, th, th, thanks for the help," or, "Read me the st, st, st, story that I, I, I, I like." When a child stutters, he is obviously uncomfortable about his speech. He may try to avoid certain sounds and adopt rituals to stop the stuttering, such as putting a finger to his lips when he starts a repetition. Stuttering usually begins shortly before school age when cluttering is coming to an end.

No one really knows whether children with cluttered speech become stutterers. There may be some truth to the idea that a child becomes a stutterer the day he is labeled as one. The child whose parents treat cluttering or other early speech difficulties as abnormal is probably more likely to develop a serious and enduring speech problem. If a child who clutters is constantly interrupted and corrected, he is unlikely to develop pleasure or confidence in his speech fluency.

Speech immaturity is the other common childhood difficulty. A 3-year-old girl has a favorite candy—"wife avers," her way of saying Life Savers. A 6-year-old who is quite good at chess still calls her rook a "wook," and another talks about his trip to the science "zeum," the museum. These forms of speech immaturity are sometimes thought to be cute, and amused parents may encourage the child to continue to mispronounce "w" for "r," "th" for "s," or "hoe-see" for "horse." But speech immaturities usually represent a phase, a passing stage in the child's acquisition of mature pronunciation.

Cluttering and speech immaturities are problems in talking, not in understanding or using language for communication or thought. If ignored, they correct naturally as the child develops.

There are, however, several serious language problems that will not correct without treatment. The most worrisome is a child's total inability to learn to use language. Symptoms range from total absence of speech (muteness) in a 3-year-old, to very garbled or peculiar language. Children with severe speech difficulties require expert evaluation since causes can include deafness, mental retardation, severe developmental disturbances (such as childhood autism), aphasia, and other significant disabilities.

It is important to distinguish the child who cannot learn to speak or who uses unusual language from the quiet, inhibited child who speaks seldom. Many children are quite bashful outside their homes, though talkative with their parents. For some of these children, the term *elective mutism* has been used. Children from bilingual homes or from families with limited verbal interaction may be silent or soft-spoken when they first enter day care or any other new situation. The child whose limited speech is the result of fear and insecurity usually shows that he can understand what is said to him and when placed in a secure setting eventually begins to speak readily and clearly.

Social Problems

Children are socialized by their parents and immediate culture to become certain kinds of adults. What one family may consider normal preschool behavior, another family may consider abnormal, and behavior that is adaptive and healthy in one subgroup may, in another, seem strange. Before considering a child's actions as normal or abnormal, one must understand the kinds of experiences, social expectations, and general environment which have shaped the child's life.

Even when seen in the context of family and community, however, some children clearly have difficulty relating to adults and peers. In the preschool years, there are three main types of social disability: over-inhibition, over-excitability, and disorganization.

Overly inhibited children range from those who are simply shy to those who are fearful of strangers and new situations, uncommunicative, and not playful. In a supportive day care setting which allows children to respond at their own pace, the shy child can gradually begin to relate first with his caregiver and then with children of his age.

The child who is truly afraid of strangers may pose more serious problems. A 3-year-old entering day care for the first time may have major difficulties leaving his parents and may show signs of real panic if this separation is handled roughly. Most parents are aware of the way their children react to separations and, by informing the caregiver of possible problems, can make the situation easier for both the child and the caregiver.

The fearful child should enter day care slowly. There might be several visits with a parent to the day care setting and then a visit or two in which the parent leaves for a short time. When a child realizes that his parents trust him there and that they will return, his initial fears of separation are usually reduced. It may sometimes be inconvenient for either parent to stay with the child during the first days of day care. However, for the child who has problems in separation, there is no substitute for this gradual introduction and for the kind of support and security that comes with the parent being near.

There are situations when a child's anxiety may be increased by allowing the parent to stay too long. Some children are really not frightened about separation but have a psychological need to be bossy or to control their parents and other adults. And others quickly reflect the anxiety of their mothers when they are near, yet do quite well alone as soon as they feel a measure of security and encouragement.

For the child, especially the younger child, who does have trouble with separation and must be in day care, a family day care setting may offer more security and reassurance than a center setting. More similar to home, with fewer children, and with the possibility of closer attachment to the caregiver, family day care requires a less strenuous adaptation for a child.

In general, the more sympathetic and warm the caregiver can be with the frightened, inhibited child and the more the day care situation resembles the child's home, the less anxiety the child will experience. If, however, the caregiver is stern or angry with the child or his parents and if the setting greatly differs from the child's usual surroundings, the transition to day care will be more difficult.

Some degree of anxiety and fear in the child entering day care is perfectly normal. These feelings indicate that he has a warm, healthy attachment to his parents and that he is free enough to express his concern when placed in a situation that is new and untested.

There are some children who can enter day care with a total lack of concern. They seem to have no trouble at all separating from their parents or later changing from one caregiver or program to another. This lack of anxiety is not necessarily a sign that the child is independent and secure; on the contrary, it may indicate that he is holding back the expression of his fears or even that he is unable to feel any closeness to people. Such children have most likely undergone many difficult separations and stressful experiences which have left them too insecure to show how worried they really are when left in a strange situation. They can neither form close relationships nor express their full potential in areas that require liveliness and imagination. A sign of emotional progress for such a child may be his developing a possessive attachment to a caregiver, whereby he could begin to feel free to express his true feelings about someone for whom he cares.

The social difficulties of the *overly excitable* child are quite different from those of the inhibited child. Excitable children often exhibit characteristics similar to those of hyperkinetic behavioral disturbance. For these children, quiet play may be difficult, and any change or stimulation may lead to a stream of wild, joyless activity. Their excitability may be associated with excessive and inappropriate responses, such as laughing too much at a joke or becoming too angry over a disagreement. It is important to distinguish the excitable child from one who is normally lively, vigorous, and enthusiastic. Being with an overly excitable child is like walking a tightrope: even when the child is quiet, he may at any time explode and release his pent-up energy.

The proper choice of a day care setting is as important for the excitable child as it is for the inhibited one; in each case, the child's general welfare must be the prime concern. For example, in a sedate day care home, an excitable child might be seen as a troublemaker and impossible to manage. If the caregiver is uncomfortable with such a child, his excitability is likely to increase. The excitable, vigorous, physically oriented child would find a quiet setting maddening, though he might really thrive in a day care center with plenty of space, a generous outdoor area, and caregivers who tolerate and enjoy occasional rough-and-tumble.

There are impulsive and destructive children whose excitability may present real problems in day care. By age 3, such children may already be a difficulty to both caregivers and themselves; by 5, they can be dangerous to other children as well.

One type of impulsive-destructive child exhibits "episodic" or "periodic" aggression; he is easy to get along with most of the time but without warning may viciously attack another person. This usually occurs when the child is angry about not getting his way, or when he is expected to perform more maturely than he is able. It is also more likely to occur when he is overly tired or pressured. In periodic aggression, the child is clearly conscious of his actions and is attuned to others' behavior; however, the attack differs from the normal anger of a child in its intensity and the physical harm it can cause.

A caregiver can try to prevent the child who exhibits episodic anger from becoming too frustrated or upset by helping him choose activities that he can perform successfully. On a day when the child is tired or tense he should be helped into activities that are less difficult than usual or which do not require that he work up to his full abilities. For the child whose aggression is triggered by losing in a competitive game or situation, the caregiver can help find activities that do not involve winners and losers. However, even when a caregiver is thoughtful about a child's needs, some episodes of aggression probably will occur. When an episode does take place, the caregiver should quickly act to stop the child before he hurts someone, breaks something of value, or does something else that will make him ashamed and others angry. After the episode is controlled, by holding the child if necessary, the caregiver should try to explain to the child what happened, and what else he could have done. "You got really angry with Benjamin because he played with the truck you like. You know, you could have *told* him you wanted it. * * * I won't let you hit anybody because then you'd feel really bad about that too."

Some children show generally aggressive and impulsive behavior, often as a result of totally unstructured homes where they have had little opportunity to learn socially acceptable behavior. With quality care, these children not only can learn how to deal with other children and adults but can also develop a new sense of self-control and pleasure in being with people.

The child whose behavior is *disorganized* may exhibit features of both the inhibited and the overly excitable child. What most characterizes behaviorally disorganized children is their lack of systematic play and pleasant, satisfying social relations. Such a child may move quickly from one activity to another, show little capacity for long, thematic kinds of play—such as playing store or house—and may never form attachments to other children or adults. His behavior may be grossly immature in some ways and odd in others: for example, he may speak poorly or wet his pants, have unusual mannerisms or gestures, or may continually repeat the same word or phrase.

For these children, day care must be supervised by professionals capable of providing therapy as well as education and care. The average caregiver must learn to recognize the difference between a young child's normal silliness and immaturities and those that characterize development that has gone awry.

Physical Problems

Every child will most likely suffer some physical problem, whether it be a cold, a case of measles, or a serious physical handicap. Although a caregiver should be aware of and responsive to the difficulties of any child, he or she is in a particularly good position—because of long-term proximity to a number of children—to recognize and help those whose physical troubles are related to problems in development or in their emotional well-being.

Most children between ages 3 and 6 will have some problems or "odd" episodes in eating, sleeping, and toileting. Every experienced caregiver knows there is nothing wrong with the child who will eat only peanut butter and jelly sandwiches for lunch, or who has "an accident" and wets himself during sleep or while too busily involved in play, or who is too tired to play yet too alert to nap. Even though such problems are normal, the caregiver should be alert to their nature and to any additional troubles which could indicate a more serious problem. For example, it is fairly typical for a child to bed-wet occasionally; however, one who suddenly reverts to regular bed-wetting and who exhibits other unusual behaviors may be undergoing a period of stress or reacting to some other emotional or developmental problem. If the condition continues, the caregiver should speak to the child's parents and consider with them a possible professional evaluation.

The caregiver should also be aware of certain physical problems which are directly associated with the emotions. Some of these conditions—asthma and eczema, for example—are not actually caused by the child's state of mind; others, such as frequent vomiting, may result directly from the child's inability to cope with his feelings and anxiety. Asthma, eczema, chronic diarrhea, clogged ears, nose stuffiness, migraine headaches, and recurrent vomiting all have one thing in common: when the afflicted child is upset, worried, unhappy, or disturbed, his physical condition worsens. Such illnesses are often part of a stress cycle: the greater the child's upset, the worse the affliction gets; the less the upset, the milder the affliction.

For example, at times of stress, family upset, or disturbance in his living situation, a child suffering with eczema may be covered from head to toe with an itchy, oozing, and crusty rash. At such times, the one and only thing he wants to do is scratch. Appropriate care includes helping the child find alternatives to scratching—ways to keep his hands busy and his mind off his body. It also includes helping him find more useful ways of coping with stress and emotional pressures. With sensitive care, children with eczema can become perfectly clear of any rash, and this is true of any of the stress-accelerated conditions.

The proper functioning of a child's body is related to how he feels about himself and to how he is valued and treated by others. For the child in day care, the caregiver will be the most important person in his life for many hours a day, so to some children, care and thoughtful attention can literally make the difference between sickness and health.

Fears and Habits

Certain fears are not only normal, but also necessary. Children learn to fear crossing a busy street, playing with matches, and talking to strangers alone. When fears become so strong that they affect regular behavior, especially when they have no rational basis, they are called *phobias.*

Similarly, part of normal learning during the preschool years involves the development of habits, such as washing, cleaning up, and desiring to eat meals at regularly scheduled intervals. When habits become excessive and constrict the individual's general activity, they are called either *obsessions* which are persistent and irrational thoughts, or *compulsions,* which are persistent and irrational actions.

Preschool children may go through periods when their fears are overly strong and dramatically interfere with daily activities. For example, a child may fear being bitten by a dog. Perhaps he fears the dog's wildness, has heard of another child being bitten, or has been nipped at himself—although he may have had no particularly bad experience with dogs. But, because of his fears, he may resist going outside alone and may even become upset at the sight of a dog through the window.

The reason for such fears is simple and understandable: the preschool child is concerned about his body and general health. The object of the child's fear—an elevator or a horse, for example—may not be an actual danger, yet may be used as a symbol of some profound and serious threat. For the child, as for an adult, the symbol can be more real than reality.

During the preschool years, children's rituals and habits are related to the normal tasks of development. Young children are often very concerned with schedule and regulation; they feel more secure if they know what is going to happen and are able to expect it. The preschooler may be uncomfortable with changes in routine—"first we go to the grocery store and *then* to the bakery." The natural desire for regularity, however, can get out of control. Some children develop patterns of thinking and behavior that may serve no useful purpose but that can upset daily family life.

Rituals involving eating, urinating, and washing are quite common and show the close link between childhood phobias and obsessions. Rituals and habits are often performed so as to avoid frightening ideas and events. A child who is afraid of the dark may develop a ritual before bedtime: he may wash his hands, clean his room, wash his hands again, urinate, wash his hands, and on and on. He will perform all sorts of seemingly meaningless actions to keep busy. The ritual serves to avoid a worrisome thought or event, but since the idea or impulse eventually returns, the child only becomes more engrossed in his ritual.

The fact that a preschool child can develop phobias and obsessions indicates that he has reached a certain level of intellectual and emotional maturity. These problems indicate that the child has formed an early understanding of causality, realizes that dangers exist, is concerned about his body, takes responsibility for protecting himself, and has developed particular cognitive, behavioral, and defensive styles that move him towards this kind of action.

Even the most habit-prone and fearful child can benefit from quality day care programs if the staff is able to appreciate his general needs. Involved in programs that increase positive social experiences and opportunities for developing a sense of competence, the timid and frightened child is often able to outgrow his inhibition and fearfulness.

Understanding Developmental Problems

Problems in development can be understood as expressions of the same developmental processes that were discussed in relation to the healthy growth of children. Each child's behavior reflects what he is as a whole person—a person with a mind, a body, a family, a culture, a history, and a current life situation. Awareness of problems in a child's development must cut across labels, so that his specific needs can be identified and met.

Understanding how a child's social, emotional, intellectual, and physical growth are so closely related allows us to see the importance of day care programs which deal with the whole child. With the problem child in day care, there is little distinction between good education, good care, and therapy. All three depend on the caregiver's own commitment, competence, and concern. Quality day care depends on quality caregivers more than on anything else.

How Day Care Supports Development

All children who are born healthy have the innate capacity for emotional, intellectual, and social growth. For this capacity to develop, certain conditions must be met. Day care can support development during the preschool years by providing a child with the kind of care he receives from his own parents. When day care aims at continuing the positive support to development that a child normally experiences at home, it meets four essential conditions.

- It promotes the child's physical health by identifying problems, helping the family to obtain medical help, and working to prevent the occurrence of new disease.
- It provides the child meaningful social experiences with competent and concerned caregivers and with children of the same age.
- It creates opportunities for learning by making materials and situations available in an organized, thoughtful manner.
- It supports the child's family life by involving parents in the care of their children, keeping them informed about their children when they are in day care, making parenthood a pleasant and rewarding opportunity rather than an extra burden, and helping parents feel secure that their children are receiving quality care. All parents want their children to become certain kinds of adults. Day care must support their values and goals, while helping parents to find the best ways to reach the goals they have for their children and for themselves as parents.

References

Billingsley, A. *Black Families in White America*. Englewood Cliffs, N.J.: Prentice-Hall, 1968.

Birch, G. and Gussow, J.D. *The Disadvantaged Child. Health, Nutrition, and School Failure*. New York: Grune & Stratton, 1970.

Buxbaum, E. *Troubled Children in a Troubled World*. New York: International Universities Press, 1970.

Chess, S., et al. *Your Child is a Person: A Psychological Approach to Parenthood Without Guilt*. New York: Viking Press, 1972.

Coles, R. *Migrants, Sharecroppers, Mountaineers*. Boston: Little, Brown & Co., 1972.

Coles, R. *The South Goes North*. Boston: Little, Brown & Co., 1972.

Comer, J.P. *Beyond Black and White*. New York: Quadrangle, 1971.

Deutsch, M. *The Disadvantaged Child*. New York: Basic Books, 1967.

Erikson, E.H. *Childhood and Society*. New York: W.W. Norton & Co., 1950.

Erikson, E.H. "Identity and the Life Cycle." *Psychological Issues* 1, No. 1 (1959), Monograph 1.

Flavell, J. *The Developmental Psychology of Jean Piaget*. New York: Van Nostrand, 1965.

Fraiberg, S.H. *The Magic Years*. New York: Charles Scribner's Sons, 1959.

Freud, A. *Normality and Pathology in Childhood: Assessments of Development*. New York: International Universities Press, 1966.

Freud, A. *The Writings of Anna Freud: Indications for Child Analysis and Other Papers*. Vol. 4 (1945–56). New York: International Universities Press, 1968.

Freud, A. *The Writings of Anna Freud: Research at the Hampstead Child-Therapy Clinic and Other Papers.* Vol. 5 (1956–65). New York: International Universities Press, 1969.

Galambos, J.W. *A Guide to Discipline.* Washington, D.C.: National Association for the Education of Young Children, 1969.

Gardner, G.E. *The Emerging Personality: Infancy Through Adolescence.* New York: Delacorte Press, 1970.

Gould, R. *Child Studies Through Fantasy. Cognitive-Affective Patterns in Development.* New York: Quadrangle Books, 1972.

Grotberg, E., ed. *Critical Issues in Research Related to Disadvantaged Children.* Princeton, N.J.: Educational Testing Service, 1969.

Guttentag, M., Issue ed. "The Poor: Impact on Research and Theory." Full issue of *The Journal of Social Issues* 26, No. 2 (1970).

Hellmuth, J., ed. *Disadvantaged Child.* Vol. 1. New York: Brunner/Mazel, 1967.

Hellmuth, J., ed. *Disadvantaged Child.* Vol. 2: *Head Start and Early Intervention.* New York: Brunner/Mazel, 1968.

Hellmuth, J., ed. *Disadvantaged Child.* Vol. 3: *Compensatory Education: A National Debate.* New York: Brunner/Mazel, 1970.

Hymes, J.L., Jr. *The Child Under Six.* Englewood Cliffs, N.J.: Prentice-Hall, 1963.

Ilg, F.L. and Ames, L.B. *Child Behavior.* New York: Harper & Row, 1955.

Lewis, M. *Clinical Aspects of Child Development.* Philadelphia: Lea & Febiger, 1971.

Lichtenberg, P. and Norton, D. *Cognitive and Mental Development in the First Five Years of Life.* Public Health Service Publication No. 2057. U.S. Department of Health, Education, and Welfare. Washington, D.C.: Government Printing Office, 1970.

McCandless, B.R. *Children: Behavior and Development.* New York: Holt, Rinehart & Winston, 1967.

Murphy, L.B., et al. *The Widening World of Childhood: Path Toward Mastery.* New York: Basic Books, 1962.

Mussen, P.H.; Conger, J.J.; and Kagan, J. *Child Development and Personality.* New York: Harper & Row, 1969.

Mussen, P.H., ed. *Carmichael's Manual of Child Psychology.* 2 Vols. New York: John Wiley & Sons, 1970.

Pavenstedt, E., ed. *The Drifters: Children of Disorganized Lower Class Families.* Boston: Little, Brown & Co., 1967.

Piaget, J. *Play, Dreams, and Imitation in Childhood.* New York: W.W. Norton & Co., 1962.

Quay, H.C. and Werry, J.S., eds. *Psychopathological Disorders of Childhood.* New York: John Wiley & Sons, 1972.

Report of the Conference on the Use of Stimulant Drugs in the Treatment of Behaviorally Disturbed Young School Children. Sponsored by the Office of Child Development and the Office of the Assistant Secretary for Health and Scientific Affairs, U.S. Department of Health, Education, and Welfare, Washington, D.C., Jan. 11–12, 1971.

Senn, M.J.E. and Solnit, A.J. *Problems in Child Behavior and Development.* Philadelphia: Lea & Febiger, 1968.

Stone, L.J. and Church, J. *Childhood and Adolescence: A Psychology of the Growing Person.* 3d ed. New York: Random House, 1973.

Thomas, A.; Chess, S.; and Birch, H. *Temperament and Behavior Disorders in Children.* New York: New York University Press, 1968.

Williams, F., ed. *Language and Poverty: Perspectives on a Theme.* Chicago: Markham Publishing Co., 1970.

Winnicott, D.W. *Playing and Reality.* New York: Basic Books, 1971.

Zigler, E.F. and Child, I.L. *Socialization and Personality Development.* Reading, Mass.: Addison-Wesley Publishing Co., 1973.

Excerpts from Serving Preschool Children, by Donald J. Cohen, M.D. in collaboration with Ada S. Brandegee, M.A. Number 3 in Day Care Series (U.S. Dept. of Health, Education, and Welfare. Office of Human Development, Office of Child Development. 1974) DHEW Publ. No. (OHD) 74-1057

Family Day Care:

An Education and Support System Model Developed by Cooperative Extension of New York State

by Natalie D. Crowe and Barbara A. Pine

PREFACE

This publication describes a multifaceted community based educational and support program for family day care. The program components include a community based resource center for family day care providers, a meeting place where they can share ideas and experiences daily. Weekly informal educational programs for the adults and activities planned for the children, as well as an eight week certificate course take place at the Resource Center. Teen Aides receive training which enables them to work with children in family day care homes. Supports to family day care include an equipment loan service, a "matchmaking" referral service, linkage to the community human services network, and a monthly newsletter. A community based advisory committee determines program direction.

Developed over the past three years with family day care providers, this pilot effort has been supported primarily by special needs funds from Extension Service-USDA. Other support came from the New York State College of Human Ecology, New York State Cooperative Extension, Cornell University, Cornell Institute for Career Education, the State of New York, New York State Department of Social Services, Nassau County Cooperative Extension Association, Nassau County Senior Community Services Project, Nassau County Department of Social Services, Day Care Council of Nassau County, Nassau County Neighborhood Youth Corps, USDA Summer lunch program in the Town of Hempstead. Primary support for years four and five is from the Carnegie Corporation of New York.

This publication is addressed to people interested in developing an educational and support program in family day care. They may include:

- Cooperative Extension specialists and agents with human resources programming responsibilities for adults and youth
- social workers and community outreach workers in human services and child caring agencies
- child care and staff development training officers in social services/welfare departments
- child care councils concerned with family day care as a viable child care option for families
- family day care providers associations
- community colleges, colleges and universities whose faculties guide students preparing for the child caring and human services professions.

The publication's purpose is to help generate ideas and stimulate support for family day care in communities and to provide some practical information learned in the pilot program. It is also a resource to people who have made requests for information about the program. The last section is a workbook to aid people when they assess needs and determine resources needed to develop a family day care program similar to that described in this publication, either in whole or in part.

The program is designed for anyone who cares for children in a home situation, whether the care givers have received a license or their homes have received certification; whether the children are

---

Editor's note: A table titled "Day Care Arrangements of Children 3 to 13 Years Old" can be found in the Statistics section at the end of this chapter on Children.

publically subsidized, or whether their families have made private arrangements with a family day care provider.

Throughout this report the following terms are used interchangeably:

family day care provider
care giver
family day care parent
family day care mother

A slide/script/cassette program, *Learning With Love: Family Day Care,* is a visual presentation of the program, available from Visual Communications Office, 412 Roberts Hall, Cornell University, Ithaca, New York 14853. A comprehensive report, *Family Day Care, A Cooperative Extension Pilot Program,* has been distributed nationwide to libraries in the Land Grant College system and to Cooperative Extension Family Life Specialists in each state.

Natalie D. Crowe, Associate Professor and Program Coordinator, New York State Cooperative Extension

Barbara A. Pine, Cooperative Extension Specialist: Family Day Care and Program Director

DEFINITIONS*

Family Day Care - day care of a child in the home of another family including before and after school care.

Family Day Care Parent - someone who takes care of other people's children. That care is provided in the day care parent's own home for fewer than 24 hours a day. Family day care parents are sometimes called family day care providers, day care mothers, teacher mothers or, less frequently, babysitters.

Licensed Family Day Care Home - a private enterprise offering family day care with a permit or license to do so from New York State Department of Social Services. A license is necessary by law when "day care is provided for 3 or more children away from their own homes for less than 24 hours per day in a family home which is operated for such purpose, for compensation or otherwise, for more than 5 hours per week."*

In New York State, there may be no more than six children, including the care giver's own, in the home and fewer if infants and toddlers are cared for.

The family day care parent works independently recruiting children for care, setting fees, etc.

Authorized Child Care Agency - This is any social agency, private or public which operates a child care program and is authorized to do so by the New York State Department of Social Services. This includes local county Departments of Social Services who provide child care services. Authorized agencies are required to adhere to State rules and regulations.

Certified Family Day Care Home - a family day care home which is affiliated with an authorized child care agency and is certified or approved to provide family day care by that agency which also provides supervision and referrals of children. Thus, the license to operate is granted by the local agency.

"Illegal" Family Day Care Home - when care is provided for 3 or more children and the home is not licensed, or where more than 6 children under 14 years old are cared for. Note that a family day care parent caring for only two children including her own would *not* be considered illegal.

Subsidized Family Day Care - when an authorized child care agency such as a local Department of Social Services places children in a family day care home, the agency usually pays for all or part of that care.

Private Family Day Care - a parent whose income is too high to qualify for financial help in paying for day care, makes private arrangements to pay a family day care parent. Parents who have to pay the full cost of family day care are often given no assistance in finding family day care homes and are sometimes excluded from using certified family day care homes.

*Definitions are based on the rules and regulations of the New York State Department of Social Services for Family Day Care.

INTRODUCTION

There is increasing evidence that very early experiences have an important effect on the growth and development of human beings. Beginning in infancy, children are heavily influenced by their environment.

The critical period in child development, according to Burton White, Director of the Harvard Laboratory for Human Development, begins at about the age of seven or eight months. By the age of three, children should have acquired the ability to understand most of the language they will use in ordinary conversation throughout their lives. They also have adopted their social styles, including the way they will relate to other children and to adults. By age three, the basic shaping of the child is usually accomplished. When both parents work outside the home and with increasing numbers of single parent families, more parents are sharing the very important early years in their children's lives with surrogate parents. Sometimes the surrogate parents are professionals in child care centers, but more frequently they are family day care providers. A 1973 publication of the U.S. Department of Health, Education and Welfare states, "It is estimated that over 91 percent of all day care services in the United States takes place in private home settings commonly referred to as family day care homes." Family day care is the oldest form of non-parental out-of-home child care in our society. It is the most widespread and it is growing as the demand for child care grows.

Some of the reasons parents give for their preference for family day care are that it is most like the care the parent would give at home and it offers more personal attention. The day care home is usually located in the parent's neighborhood. There is flexibility in hours to accommodate shift workers, commuters' hours, before and after care of school-aged children. Several small children in one family including infants, toddlers and school-aged children can be cared for in one home. Frequently care is available for the slightly ill child.

Over six million children under six years of age are in need of child care. There is little data on the number of school-aged children who need before and after school care; one estimate is 14 million. Just over one million children are cared for in day care centers and family day care homes that are licensed or approved. Where are the rest of the children? Many, of school age, come home to empty houses or are just "out" after school. Many are in family day care homes that have not been licensed or approved and where care givers have no educational or support system.

Quality child care in a family day care home means a care-giving environment that ensures that the child's physical needs are met, that the child's sense of belonging to the family of origin is not weakened by the family day care experience, that the child has opportunities to develop relationships of trust and attachment to a small number of familiar adults responsible for his or her own care, that suitable opportunities are available for spontaneous pleasurable learning experiences fostering the growth of the child's developing competencies. The best family day care setting approximates a good natural home. The qualities most parents like to see nurtured in their children are the same whether the child is at home or in a family day care setting.

Care givers try to care for children the way parents want them cared for. Days are long. In suburban communities, most workers commute for at least an hour to and from work. This means that some children are brought to the care giver's home as early as six in the morning — right out of bed. In fact, some children complete their night's sleep at the care giver's home. Then, it's breakfast for the care giver's family and the day care children who may arrive over a period of two hours. Some school-aged children may come for a while before the school bus picks them up and return after school. Children are in the day care home until parents come for them — sometimes on time, sometimes late. Holidays are usually workdays in family day care. Most family day care providers do not have the benefit of paid holidays, vacations, sick days.

Usually there is a play area in the home where independent play can take place under the supervision of the care giver while she tends to meal preparation and household necessities. The entire home can be an environment for learning as the child "helps." Concepts of size, shape and color can be learned as pots and pans are stacked and disassembled. Empty, clean, food containers with no sharp edges can be nested. Concepts of hot, cold, turning on and off, cleanliness, wet and dry can be learned from hand washing before eating. Language develops as the care giver talks with the child.

Some children may be served two or three meals and two snacks during the time they are at the care giver's home. Depending on the age and need of the child, one or two naps are taken. Some care givers prefer to have children near in age, while others find that with a wider age range, children learn from each other. Usually children play outdoors part of the time.

Most family day care providers have some toys and play equipment for the children, but they must purchase these items themselves. Some ask parents to provide equipment or to provide food for snacks or meals. There is no allowance for play equipment, consumable supplies or food.* The average range of payment to family day care providers is twenty to twenty-five dollars a week in New York State.

The pilot program described in this report was prompted by a conviction that family day care providers are very important people in the lives of young children and their families. It attempts to build on the strengths of family day care.

The role of Cooperative Extension in this pilot program is that of a friend, ally and supporter of family day care providers; an educator, a resource, a linker of isolated care givers to each other and to the community human services network; a broker between care givers and families seeking child care; a parent educator.

The basic concept upon which the program was developed is the Extension philosophy of starting with the people where they are and involving them in determining their needs and program goals. Cooperative Extension is a facilitator of learning as well as a teacher and resource. The focus of the program is the family day care provider as a learner, as a person who has much to share with other care givers and from whom there is much to learn.

*New York City rates may differ; a food and equipment allowance may be provided.

THE PILOT PROGRAM

The Storefront Resource Center—Its Beginning

The program is located in Nassau County, a large suburban county on Long Island, adjacent to New York City. Nearly 1,500,000 people live within its 274 square mile area. Because the county is large, a target area was chosen which included the villages of Roosevelt, Freeport, and Uniondale. There are 7000 children five years of age or under and an additional 20 thousand children aged 6-18 in these three communities. A high percentage of the population receives public assistance, mostly aid to dependent children. The number of working mothers exceeds the national average.

When the program began in 1972, approximately 450 children in the target area were being cared for in a variety of group settings. There were 141 county family day care homes certified by the county Department of Social Services, 34 of which were in the target area. Many children were being cared for through private arrangements with neighbors, friends and relatives.

In order to reach these care givers, a storefront was rented on the main street in Roosevelt. With the help of the Nassau County Cooperative Extension staff and friends, the storefront was scrubbed, curtains were made and toys, books, furniture and equipment were collected. The program director recruited a program aide and a senior citizen aide from the community to help staff the resource center each day from 10-3:30 p.m. As the program expanded, another aide was added.

Except for the relatively few certified care givers in the community, no one seemed to know who was taking care of children. Therefore invitations to visit the center were sent home with kindergarten, first and second grade children. The program staff posted the invitation on community bulletin boards, provided stuffers for supermarket grocery bags, supplied Expanded Food and Nutrition Education Program aides and other Cooperative Extension personnel with invitations to extend to their contacts in the neighborhood. And people came.

A Visit To The Storefront

The storefront resource center gives visibility to the program; it is one way of reaching out to unknown care givers. A sign in the window invites ANYONE who takes care of children to stop in with the children.

The cheery playroom immediately attracts the children. It is lined with shelves of toys, books, plants, sprouting seeds, sea snails edging along the side of their glass house. There is a staff member to read a story or invite participation in an activity appropriate to the children's interests. There is a senior aide to hold, cuddle and rock a baby or guide a toddler safely to balls or blocks. This frees the care givers to talk with the program staff, other family day care providers or to attend an educational program in the meeting room at the rear of the storefront.

A log is kept of who comes to the storefront resource center, with whom, and the reason for their visit. This log is a valuable record in evaluating the program.

When family day care mothers visit the resource center, they are happy to talk with each other and to talk with someone who is interested in them and in the children they are caring for. They are often alone with up to six children for ten to twelve hours a day. They need and want to interact with other adults, to find out what they do, what they feed the children, how they handle problems, how they manage their time and the demands of their own families as well as the children they care for, how they relate to parents — all sorts of questions are asked and common concerns shared.

Weekly Educational Programs

Workshops are held every Wednesday at the storefront. For the first few months handwritten invitations to the workshops were sent to people who had visited the resource center. They were encouraged to bring other care givers with them. As family day care providers came to know the staff and program, the mailing list grew. The monthly calendar and announcements of the program were sent in penalty privilege envelopes.

Workshops and Meetings

The weekly educational program is a two-hour training session that may be led by staff, a family day care parent, or community resource persons from various divisions in the health department, police and fire departments, American Red Cross, consumer agencies, day care center directors and early childhood education specialists, from Cornell and nearby colleges and universities.

Monthly calendars of activities are planned four times a year by the advisory committee to insure that the educational program meets the needs of family day care providers as they perceive them. The informal curriculum is planned to respond to concerns, issues and needs, and to increase knowledge and skills. Subjects cover a wide range of child development and human relations topics; those identified recently have shown a growing sophistication and professionalism. Most sessions are planned as separate entities, although topics are often expanded in later sessions. Much collateral learning takes place during the weekly educational sessions.

Experiential learning is preferred by family day care providers: workshops, discussions, short audiovisual presentations to spark interaction, teaching each other skills, role playing. Many of the weekly programs help to link care givers to the community human services network. Workshop leaders representing the broad spectrum of educational and service agencies teach in their area of expertise, learn about family day care and share information with the family day care parents about how the resources of their organization can serve family day care.

The focus is on the family day care provider as a learner who is involved in identifying, planning, and implementing the learning experience. The program director and staff are resource people who provide the environment for and facilitate learning. They may themselves teach, bring other teachers or resource people to the group, or facilitate sharing of the wealth of knowledge that exists among family day care providers themselves.

Trips

Organized trips are an important part of an informal educational program. Places to visit include the firehouse, library, farm, the local park, or a museum. Many free parks offer a variety of facilities: bicycle paths, swimming pools, creative playgrounds, demonstration gardens, children's theater and miniature train rides.

In addition to the learning experiences that these trips provide, everyone has a good time. A family day care parent who had been reluctant to attempt a trip on her own with six children gets a willing, helping hand from another care giver or a member of the program staff. Admission rates are reduced or free for school groups. In the friendly, relaxed environment that is characteristic of all program activities, friendships are formed, good feelings are fostered. And the care givers will often get together with each other and return to places visited or they will explore new places of interest and share their discoveries with each other and the staff.

In Nassau County the police bus is sometimes available free of charge; sometimes a school bus is rented. For local trips, family day care parents are helped to organize car pools. Longer trips are usually planned for school holidays or during the summer to include the school-aged children. Sometimes family day care fathers or parents of children in family day care go along. When bus transportation is provided for a trip, day care parents call a week prior to the date of the trip and reserve space for themselves and their children. Reservations are made on a first-come, first-serve basis and on that day the phone usually begins to ring as we are unlocking the resource center door! Parents of day care children must sign permission slips, which the care giver brings to the center on the day of the trip.

Summer Programs

In the summer, school-aged children are in family day care full-time. Care givers often have six children in their homes. Limited size and lack of an adequate cooling system at the pilot program resource center make the use of outdoor facilities necessary. Resource people are invited to lead workshops at the parks. These include sessions on music, nature activities, and parent-made learning materials.

The pilot program has participated in the USDA Free Summer Lunch Program for three years. For eight weeks during the summer, 264 lunches are delivered daily to the resource center. Day care parents, on rotating schedules, help the program staff assemble and distribute the lunches to 40 care givers participating in the program. On the day of a picnic, lunches are distributed at the park rather than at the resource center. Care givers not participating in the lunch program pack their own lunches; snacks and beverages are planned for all the picnickers.

Loan Closet

It is difficult for family day care providers to afford the equipment necessary for a day care home. Strollers, high chairs, playpens and even cribs are essential in the care of infants and toddlers. The loan closet at the resource center helps meet some of these needs. Day care parents can borrow games, books and small toys that have been donated or purchased at garage sales and thrift shops. The items are loaned at no cost, the care giver is only asked to return them as soon as they are no longer needed.

When something is borrowed, a card is attached to the family day care provider's card in the program participant file. If an item is not returned after three months, staff calls the care giver to see if it is still in use. Often, equipment travels directly to another care provider without returning to the loan closet.

Caseworkers from the Department of Social Services frequently use the loan closet to assist newly certified family day care parents or those who are unable to travel to the resource center.

Outreach Efforts

Teen-Aide Program

The Teen-Aide Program is an effort to reach family day care givers who cannot attend weekly programs on a regular basis. Recruited from the local community, three teen-aides work as program staff members after school and during summers. They have a combined experience of training in child development and working directly with children in day care homes. Using resources available at the storefront, teen-aides plan activities for a variety of ages. Their home visits are scheduled at the family day care parents' request.

Although conceived of as a relief for day care mothers, the mothers want to participate. The teen-aide visits are a source of new ideas for day care mothers and are a reinforcement of the regular educational program. In addition to the obvious value of this aspect of the program, the teen-aides provide a model for teens in the family day care homes and the community in working with young children.

The teen-aides report in writing and evaluate each experience as they attempt to improve the quality of their program and increase their knowledge of children. Their reports are discussed at their training sessions with the program staff. Because the function of program staff is defined as educational and support to family day care, rather than regulation or service, the staff visit homes only when invited by the family day care provider. Thus, they will not be confused with a caseworker.

Newsletter

Most of the regular program participants live within fifteen miles of the resource center, though care givers who live at a great distance visit the program occasionally. To reach these care givers and to provide a vehicle for communication among family day care providers and some parents, the staff prepares a monthly newsletter.

The newsletter is published monthly and is one way of keeping in touch with over 500 care givers in the county. Day care parents and parents are encouraged to contribute articles or ideas to the newsletter. Format includes a report, usually with pictures, on a special family day care event or program at the resource center, an article on some aspect of child development, a section on tested recipes to help in planning meals for family day care children or ideas for cooking with children and an idea for learning activities.

Department of Social Services Involvement in Certificate Course

In cooperation with the Nassau County Department of Social Services, a 16-hour certificate training course is offered. Planned by a committee of family day care mothers and staff from the Department of Social Services and the Cooperative Extension Family Day Care program staff, the course is modeled on the approach to educational programs developed at the resource center. The 8-week course is open to anyone caring for children in a home situation and is offered at two sites, including the resource center. One hundred twenty-five care givers have completed the course and received their certificates at special ceremonies.

Working with Parents

The resource center provides a referral service to parents who want a home setting for child care. Staff explain how the program works and our role in the referral. Information about needs in the care arrangement, details about the children needing care, and other essential information is noted on a referral form.

During the interview, staff assists the parent in determining his or her needs as well as those of the children. Families eligible for subsidized child care are referred to the Department of Social Services. An attempt is made to match the parent with at least two care givers who have requested referrals. The care givers are notified of the parent's interest and if they agree, the parent is given names and phone numbers. The fee is determined by the parent and the care provider based upon the number of hours care will be provided.

Program Advisory Committee

The program advisory committee is one way of insuring that the program meets the need of participants and promotes community support and understanding.

At first the pilot program's program adivsory committee was composed of seven interested family day care mothers, a parent using family day care and a community resident employed as an assistant to the director in the New York City Family Day Care Careers Program who had had experience working with advisory groups. The committee helped with program planning, interviewing, and selecting the program aide and choosing representatives to accompany the program specialist when there was an invitation to present the program to various groups.

A formal Board of Directors, with 20 members, is being formed to replace the original committee. Its members will represent a wider range of interests in the community and will include those presently on the advisory committee. A set of guidelines for operation of the board, membership and functions will be developed.

Staff Training

Regular inservice training for staff is prepared by the program director. Much of the staff training is planned around developmental activities and ways of relating to children. When working with children visiting the Resource Center with care givers, the staff models and thus teaches ways of coping with behaviors and activities that may be helpful as care givers plan for children of different ages. Other staff inservice instruction relates to community organization, the formal human and child care services networks and developing social service skills.

Student Involvement

The pilot program was designed to permit involvement of college students who want experience in the field.

Field experience is planned jointly by the student, faculty and pilot program director to meet the objectives of all participants. Day-to-day supervision and professional feedback are provided by the pilot program director. Students report progress against the objectives planned.

Two students worked in the exploratory phase before the pilot program was funded; three students have participated during the first three years. A student in Human Development and Family Studies was teamed with a teen-aide in the first teen-aide visits to family day care homes. A Communication Arts student helped design a leaflet explaining the program and assisted with the newsletter. A student in Community Service Education spent the summer and a fall semester studying the delivery of social services to family day care. She developed a comprehensive calendar of summer recreation programs offered in the county.

Attracting Program Participants

New program participants are attracted in several ways. Because the program is so visible in the community, many people find *us*. This is especially true of unlicensed care providers who are not in contact with any type of child care agency. Care givers tell each other about the program, often inviting to a workshop a friend who then becomes involved in the program.

When Department of Social Services caseworkers certify new homes in the community, they describe the pilot program and urge the care giver to visit the resource center. The Department also sends a list of newly certified homes to the program staff so that these care givers can be added to our mailing list. All receive the monthly newsletters, and those care givers in the communities directly served by the storefront receive a monthly calendar of events and weekly flyers as well.

Fxcepts from Family Day Care: An Education and Support System Model Developed by Cooperative Extension, New York State, by Natalie D. Crowe and Barbara A. Pine. A 1975 extension publication of the New York State College of Human Ecology. (A Statutory College of the State University: Cornell University, Ithaca, New York). Reprinted with permission.

National Summary of Type of Day Care

This table shows the type of day care received by children, the various types of day care delivered by each State, and the costs.

Table is based on State submissions of SSRR Form 5 - Day Care Services Provided to Children.

The counts of children reflect all child recipients of day care under Titles IV and XX rather than only primary recipients.

Table Highlights

- Approximately 565,000 children received day care services under Titles XX and IV during the April-June quarter (660 fewer children than during the previous quarter).

- The types of day care services and the percentages of children who received them were:

Type of Day Care	Percent of Children Served
Day Care Center Services	55
Family Day Care Home Services	23
In-Home Day Care Services	19
Group Day Care Home Services	2

- Of the total number of children receiving day care services, 72 percent received full-time day care services (a decrease of 4 percentage points over the second quarter), and 28 percent received part-time day care services (an increase of 4 percentage points).

Annotations to Tables

1. North Carolina submitted substantial revisions too late for inclusion.
2. New Jersey and Rhode Island did not submit cost data in time for this report.
3. Due to reporting difficulties, Michigan's count of children reflects one month of data rather than one quarter while expenditures are for the quarter. Michigan was unable to provide day care data by category of recipient for this report (Tables 10 and F only).

- The total number of children receiving day care, by type of day care, full time and part time, follows:

Type of Day Care	Number of Children			Percent	
	Total	Full time	Part time	Full time	Part time
Group Day Care Home Services	12,992	10,464	2,528	81	19
Day Care Center Services	313,529	242,390	71,139	77	23
In-Home Day Care Services	109,167	65,383	43,784	60	40
Family Day Care Home Services	129,637	86,882	42,755	33	67
TOTAL	565,325	405,119	160,206	72	28

- Full time center care was the type of care received by the greatest number of chldren.

- Approximately $158 million were spent during the third quarter on day care services; this represents 23 percent of the expenditures for social services for this period.

- The total cost of day care by type of day care, full time and part time, follows:

Type of Day Care	Cost of Day Care			Percent of Cost	
	Total	Full time	Part time	Full time	Part time
Group Day Care Home Services	$ 2,225,050	$ 1,852,764	$ 372,286	83	17
Day Care Center Services	$112,289,224	$ 96,170,278	$16,118,946	86	14
In-Home Day Care Services	$ 18,633,211	$ 12,879,854	$ 5,753,357	69	31
Family Day Care Home Services	$ 24,690,442	$ 20,054,906	$ 4,635,536	81	19
TOTALS	$157,837,927	$130,957,802	$26,880,125	83	17

- Distribution of day care expenditures by type of day care:

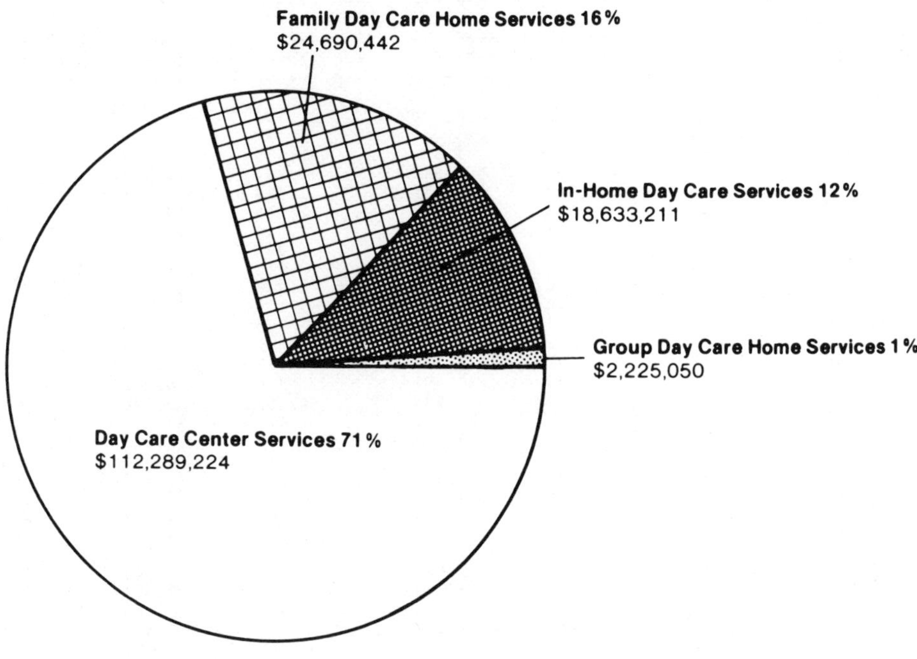

- Percentage of Day Care Cost, by Category:

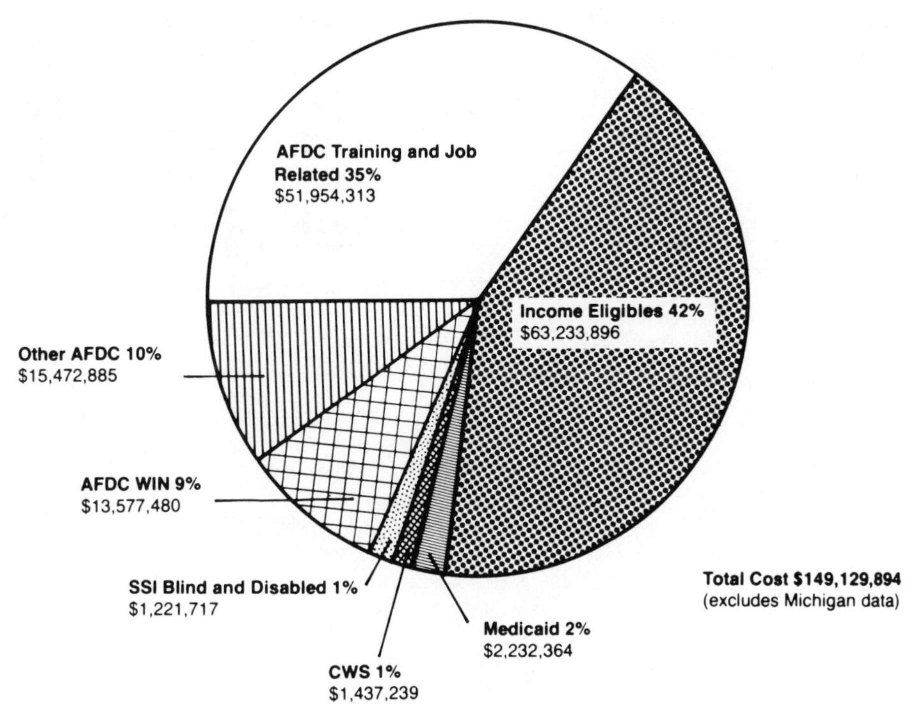

NATIONAL SUMMARY OF TYPE OF DAY CARE BY STATE

Quarter Ending: JUN. 1976

STATES	IN-HOME DAY CARE				FAMILY DAY CARE HOME			
	FULL-TIME		PART-TIME		FULL-TIME		PART-TIME	
	# Children	Total Cost	# Children	Total Cost	# Children	Total Cost	# Children	Total Cost
Alabama	396	44,318	82	6,508	1,131	403,300	143	30,058
Alaska	0	0	0	0	97	35,476	23	8,391
Arizona	86	13,546	44	7,636	1,555	296,793	1,041	116,557
Arkansas	145	13,595	53	2,348	254	27,785	71	2,686
California	4,359	1,954,813	3,147	455,315	2,997	1,557,548	1,354	278,866
Colorado	3,378	420,719	1,553	106,321	2,248	479,659	485	53,461
Connecticut	3,178	359,121	3,704	256,168	3,013	341,788	2,231	175,799
Delaware	3	500	0	0	281	112,930	22	4,534
Dist of Columbia	126	107,310	280	172,140	142	73,500	19	3,908
Florida	0	0	0	0	1,538	594,703	0	0
Georgia	1,675	510,364	1,226	240,177	196	128,245	82	61,516
Hawaii	420	92,270	673	68,436	205	136,346	183	71,981
Idaho	3	865	2	22,545	91	11,827	9	851
Illinois	6,358	1,336,650	5,801	1,224,338	1,737	360,577	917	189,865
Indiana	189	16,743	82	10,401	326	28,879	94	12,069
Iowa	135	17,266	130	7,538	1,454	195,870	612	40,296
Kansas	0	0	0	0	3,424	388,703	599	47,957
Kentucky	102	19,606	42	5,139	360	55,825	130	17,517
Louisiana	0	0	0	0	630	40,320	451	14,400
Maine	257	14,800	60	3,471	187	71,593	7	1,298
Maryland	1,110	38,792	439	15,070	2,790	58,613	1,415	16,751
Massachusetts	4,475	1,306,583	0	0	595	178,918	0	0
Michigan	10,543	2,040,960	10,543	2,040,960	3,239	564,718	3,238	564,718
Minnesota	596	213,009	602	83,438	1,314	369,368	766	112,483
Mississippi	1,575	14,387	1,777	16,666	999	3,343	1,077	3,693
Missouri	1,409	84,341	806	15,762	7,063	597,634	2,462	62,913
Montana	0	0	0	0	2,397	184,146	595	25,071
Nebraska	643	416,889	240	117,540	3,528	505,468	950	122,115
Nevada	37	5,621	32	4,427	3	667	41	6,504
New Hampshire	475	61,922	460	61,919	802	100,350	334	21,541
New Jersey	729		120		957		1,044	
New Mexico	320	30,131	223	13,920	469	75,921	330	35,075
New York	2,582	355,535	4,395	19,130	12,983	3,919,957	10,470	905,433
North Carolina	462	0	236	0	257	0	144	0
North Dakota	36	4,662	51	6,911	182	18,880	229	15,198
Ohio	1,137	877,430	116	103,868	3,866	2,974,138	318	262,988
Oklahoma	789	50,738	1,178	46,040	1,846	246,081	390	28,397
Oregon	102	32,663	179	27,996	1,462	501,260	1,430	240,745
Pennsylvania	3,121	852,688	772	210,918	1,274	348,069	112	30,600
Rhode Island								
South Carolina	384	0	294	0	365	0	230	0
South Dakota	176	36,189	107	14,757	1,086	261,146	520	75,639
Tennessee	648	47,810	490	33,066	1,507	379,984	114	12,093
Texas	7,571	587,384	1,216	40,685	788	551,799	39	1,773
Utah	0	0	0	0	1,348	298,415	1,260	147,705
Vermont	79	17,188	127	21,223	594	134,325	308	52,221
Virginia	1,919	300,587	1,144	121,773	3,089	560,932	2,393	255,529
Washington	915	304,598	677	132,068	1,999	764,447	1,376	311,957
West Virginia	869	174,496	142	0	3,309	781,187	415	0
Wisconsin	1,871	102,765	539	16,739	3,642	197,388	696	22,254
Wyoming	0	0	0	0	1,263	136,085	1,586	170,130
TOTAL	65,383	12,879,854	43,784	5,753,357	86,882	20,054,906	42,755	4,635,536

See the annotations on the first page of this article.

(CONT.)

NATIONAL SUMMARY OF TYPE OF DAY CARE BY STATE

Quarter Ending: JUN. 1976

STATES	GROUP DAY CARE HOME				DAY CARE CENTER			
	FULL-TIME		PART-TIME		FULL-TIME		PART-TIME	
	# Children	Total Cost	# Children	Total Cost	# Children	Total Cost	# Children	Total Cost
Alabama	0	0	0	0	4,544	2,334,737	135	29,203
Alaska	0	0	0	0	114	41,637	57	20,712
Arizona	0	0	0	0	5,290	1,166,771	3,572	412,507
Arkansas	2	330	2	63	2,625	976,332	217	38,276
California	758	400,177	807	212,743	24,117	17,065,781	13,033	4,703,292
Colorado	0	0	0	0	2,747	324,494	592	65,341
Connecticut	0	0	0	0	4,410	1,299,984	117	9,208
Delaware	20	8,003	18	1,813	1,485	891,666	152	43,665
Dist of Columbia	0	0	0	0	558	262,138	65	19,321
Florida	0	0	0	0	8,154	3,152,929	922	356,511
Georgia	50	24,396	17	10,995	10,861	4,797,381	1,360	870,385
Hawaii	0	0	0	0	1,334	587,178	480	77,428
Idaho	0	2,894	1	2,029	21	6,143	9	1,125
Illinois	0	0	0	0	2,138	460,343	348	72,185
Indiana	0	0	0	0	2,704	775,905	36	6,788
Iowa	0	0	0	0	5,972	798,742	958	78,753
Kansas	7,176	1,005,024	966	82,327	1,531	206,294	1,882	142,436
Kentucky	12	2,420	0	0	1,768	384,130	377	40,943
Louisiana	0	0	0	0	5,656	622,160	664	36,575
Maine	91	5,193	10	577	916	491,826	108	27,260
Maryland	0	0	0	0	2,463	92,020	1,316	919
Massachusetts	4	120	0	0	8,970	4,153,769	3,295	738,035
Michigan	3	397	3	396	4,258	1,747,942	4,257	1,747,942
Minnesota	73	24,297	77	14,667	4,095	1,593,479	295	76,867
Mississippi	38	133	23	66	2,546	1,280,368	90	34,680
Missouri	1,270	113,245	238	5,522	8,291	742,545	2,739	67,492
Montana	0	0	0	0	1,112	100,480	366	21,660
Nebraska	18	2,863	6	611	2,051	745,603	131	43,293
Nevada	37	6,816	14	2,207	0	0	8	1,027
New Hampshire	0	0	0	0	1,583	472,935	521	48,155
New Jersey	0		0		871		421	
New Mexico	17	4,212	12	1,946	1,057	573,869	741	265,120
New York	104	47,045	35	2,967	34,119	22,052,448	13,144	2,172,713
North Carolina	62	0	60	0	3,601	0	402	0
North Dakota	1	111	5	877	336	95,212	165	33,851
Ohio	0	0	0	0	3,679	2,994,355	136	121,726
Oklahoma	0	0	0	0	15,139	3,093,132	1,865	197,353
Oregon	28	10,307	14	2,437	2,506	930,458	2,253	412,868
Pennsylvania	39	10,655	19	5,191	24,621	6,726,703	8,192	2,238,137
Rhode Island								
South Carolina	61	0	5	0	5,428	0	476	0
South Dakota	24	6,227	5	599	235	61,063	108	20,347
Tennessee	299	101,072	41	5,871	4,374	2,234,159	692	129,892
Texas	5	17,813	1	0	12,043	6,993,637	1,314	162,582
Utah	0	0	0	0	1,242	347,648	803	102,253
Vermont	49	12,620	20	3,915	768	264,551	449	116,698
Virginia	165	30,612	91	7,621	1,925	635,702	335	57,875
Washington	58	15,782	38	6,846	2,147	703,266	635	177,915
West Virginia	0	0	0	0	694	181,819	44	0
Wisconsin	0	0	0	0	4,729	645,680	307	17,683
Wyoming	0	0	0	0	562	60,864	555	59,949
TOTAL	10,464	1,852,764	2,528	372,286	242,390	96,170,278	71,139	16,118,946

See the annotations on the first page of this article.

NATIONAL SUMMARY OF DAY CARE

This table indicates the number of children who received day care, by type and duration of day care (full time or part time) for each category of recipient.

Table is based on State submissions of SSRR Form 5 - Day Care Services Provided to Children.1/

Table Highlights

- Of children receiving day care services, AFDC remained by far the largest category during the third quarter. The percents for the categories were:

Category	Percent of Children Served
AFDC Training & Job-Related	31
AFDC - Other	17
IE	30
AFDC-WIN	19
Medicaid	1
CWS	1
SSI Blind & Disabled	1

1/Data by category of recipient was not available for Michigan.

Summary of Day Care, by Category,
Quarter Ending June, 1976

	Number of children in care	Percent of total for full time	Percent of total for part time	Cost ($)	Percent of cost full time	Percent of cost part time
AFDC Training & Job Related						
In-home Day Care	37,705	63	37	7,333,933	69	31
Family Day Care Home	45,229	72	28	11,039,402	84	16
Group Day Care Home	2,541	70	30	614,234	77	23
Day Care Center	77,758	80	20	32,966,744	88	12
Other AFDC						
In-home Day Care	9,081	73	27	1,769,252	85	15
Family Day Care Home	14,760	69	31	1,281,538	81	19
Group Day Care Home	4,527	88	12	346,715	91	9
Day Care Center	60,784	79	21	12,075,380	89	11
Income Eligible						
In-home Day Care	7,156	85	15	1,608,373	91	9
Family Day Care Home	25,926	78	22	7,236,570	85	15
Group Day Care Home	3,484	83	17	951,615	84	16
Day Care Center	124,693	78	22	53,437,338	86	14
Medicaid						
In-home Day Care	745	88	12	132,865	92	8
Family Day Care Home	1,107	83	17	425,557	87	13
Group Day Care Home	154	94	6	57,293	95	5
Day Care Center	3,955	72	28	1,616,649	84	16
SSI Blind & Disabled						
In-home Day Care	138	78	22	35,915	90	10
Family Day Care Home	111	83	17	20,685	77	23
Group Day Care Home	57	93	7	22,211	89	11
Day Care Center	2,778	76	24	1,142,906	86	14
AFDC - WIN						
In-home Day Care	33,097	53	47	3,593,932	71	29
Family Day Care Home	34,354	54	46	2,991,280	75	25
Group Day Care Home	2,208	73	27	223,962	83	17
Day Care Center	32,910	73	27	6,768,306	80	20
CWS						
In-home Day Care	159	58	42	77,021	87	13
Family Day Care Home	1,673	66	34	565,974	76	24
Group Day Care Home	15	60	40	8,227	89	11
Day Care Center	2,136	75	25	786,017	89	11

See the annotations on the first page of this article.

NATIONAL SUMMARY OF DAY CARE

Quarter Ending: JUN. 1976

TYPE OF DAY CARE	CATEGORIES OF CHILDREN					
	AFDC TRAINING & JOB RELATED			OTHER AFDC		
	No. Children	Total Cost	% of Total $	No. Children	Total Cost	% of Total $
In-Home Day Care						
Full Time	23,616	5,091,197	46.97	6,643	1,503,335	13.87
Part Time	14,089	2,242,736	60.41	2,438	265,917	7.16
Family Day Care Home						
Full Time	32,767	9,269,431	47.56	10,174	1,034,234	5.31
Part Time	12,462	1,769,971	43.48	4,586	247,304	6.08
Group Day Care Home						
Full Time	1,787	472,948	25.53	3,975	314,106	16.96
Part Time	754	141,286	37.99	552	32,609	8.77
Day Care Center						
Full Time	61,851	29,025,926	30.74	48,198	10,735,993	11.37
Part Time	15,907	3,940,818	27.42	12,586	1,339,387	9.32

NATIONAL SUMMARY OF DAY CARE

Quarter Ending: JUN. 1976

TYPE OF DAY CARE	CATEGORIES OF CHILDREN					
	INCOME ELIGIBLES			MEDICAID		
	No. Children	Total Cost	% of Total $	No. Children	Total Cost	% of Total $
In-Home Day Care						
Full Time	6,057	1,457,440	13.45	658	122,755	1.13
Part Time	1,099	150,933	4.07	87	10,110	.27
Family Day Care Home						
Full Time	20,112	6,123,808	31.42	923	370,108	1.90
Part Time	5,814	1,112,762	27.34	184	55,449	1.36
Group Day Care Home						
Full Time	2,887	797,956	43.08	144	54,310	2.93
Part Time	597	153,659	41.32	10	2,983	.80
Day Care Center						
Full Time	97,595	46,173,414	48.90	2,833	1,356,255	1.44
Part Time	27,098	7,263,924	50.55	1,122	260,394	1.81

NATIONAL SUMMARY OF DAY CARE

Quarter Ending: JUN. 1976

	CATEGORIES OF CHILDREN					
	SSI BLIND & DISABLED			AFDC WIN		
TYPE OF DAY CARE	No. Children	Total Cost	% of Total $	No. Children	Total Cost	% of Total $
In-Home Day Care						
Full Time	108	32,176	.30	17,665	2,564,700	23.66
Part Time	30	3,739	.10	15,432	1,029,232	27.72
Family Day Care Home						
Full Time	92	15,827	.08	18,468	2,248,583	11.54
Part Time	19	4,858	.12	15,886	742,697	18.24
Group Day Care Home						
Full Time	53	19,818	1.07	1,606	185,889	10.04
Part Time	4	2,393	.64	602	38,073	10.24
Day Care Center						
Full Time	2,103	980,281	1.04	23,957	5,447,863	5.77
Part Time	675	162,625	1.13	8,953	1,320,443	9.19

NATIONAL SUMMARY OF DAY CARE

Quarter Ending: JUN. 1976

	CATEGORIES OF CHILDREN					
	CWS					
TYPE OF DAY CARE	No. Children	Total Cost	% of Total $			
In-Home Day Care						
Full Time	93	67,291	.62			
Part Time	66	9,730	.26			
Family Day Care Home						
Full Time	1,107	428,197	2.20			
Part Time	566	137,777	3.38			
Group Day Care Home						
Full Time	9	7,340	.40			
Part Time	6	887	.24			
Day Care Center						
Full Time	1,595	702,604	.74			
Part Time	541	83,413	.58			

Editor's note: For additional figures on day care, see Appendix B, "Child Day Care Expenditures in First Program Year, by State" (part of Title XX: Social Services in Your State, which is the third item in this CHILDREN section).

Social Services U.S.A. April-June 1976. U.S. Dept. of Health, Education and Welfare, Office of Human Development Services. Publ. No. (OHDS) 77-03300

Child abuse

The Diagnostic Process and Treatment Programs

Ray E. Helfer, M.D.

Foreword

On January 31, 1974, the Child Abuse Prevention and Treatment Act (P.L. 93-247) was signed into law. The Act established for the first time within the Federal Government a National Center on Child Abuse and Neglect. Responsibility for the activities of the Center was assigned to the U.S. Department of Health, Education, and Welfare which, in turn, placed the Center within the Children's Bureau of the Office of Child Development.

The Center will provide national leadership by conducting studies on abuse and neglect, awarding demonstration and research grants to seek new ways of identifying, diagnosing and preventing this nationwide problem, and by giving grants to States to enable them to increase and improve their child protective services.

One of the key elements of any successful program is public awareness and understanding, as well as the provision of clear and practical guidance and counsel to those working in the field. It is for this reason that the National Center on Child Abuse and Neglect is publishing a series of six booklets—three comprehensive and related volumes describing the roles and responsibilities of professionals, and the community team approach among a wide range of other subjects; three shorter booklets will deal with the diagnosis of child abuse and neglect from a medical perspective, working with abusing parents from a psychiatric viewpoint, and setting up a central registry.

While some material in all these publications deals with studies of specific local programs as opposed to generalized approaches, they are not intended to represent categorical *models* upon which other programs should be based in order to be effective. Rather, they are intended to provoke thinking and consideration, offer suggestions and to stimulate ideas. Similarly, the views of the authors do not necessarily reflect the views of HEW.

We are deeply indebted to the six individuals who reviewed all these publications: Dr. Vincent DeFrancis, Mr. Phillip Dolinger, Ms. Elizabeth Elmer, Dr. Frederick Green, Dr. C. Henry Kempe and Dr. Eli Newberger. Their expertise and advice have been invaluable in putting this series together.

We hope that everyone concerned with detection, prevention and treatment of child abuse and neglect will find some, if not all, of these publications of use in the vital work in which they are engaged.

We hope, too, that they will be of use to those individuals and organizations wishing to become involved.

Dr. Helfer is a Professor in the Department of Human Development, College of Human Medicine at Michigan State University.

Introduction

The purpose of this manual is to provide all physicians and nurses with the necessary background to understand the basic process in developing the diagnosis and the concept of treatment programs for abused and neglected children and their families. This material is not intended to be a "textbook" for the specialists in this vast area, be they physicians, social workers, judges, lawyers, law enforcement officers, school teachers, nurses or others.

While the author feels most strongly that these specialists *must* exist in every community or area with 150,000 or more population and that they must have a thorough understanding of this field, in excess of the information in this manual, those thousands of physicians and nurses who are not specialists in the area of child abuse and neglect but still work with family members (adults and children alike) need a basic understanding of this serious problem and what they and others can do about it.

This manual is put together in a manner that will allow the reader to understand the material at a rapid pace, with easy access to the information provided when a quick review is desired.

Beginning on page 6 the left hand page contains written material which is necessary for understanding the descriptive outline given in the display on the right hand page of the manual.

Some of the written material presented in this manual was originally published by Gerber in Pediatric Basics, Nos. 10 and 11, 1974 and is reprinted here with their permission.

The Long-Term Treatment Phase

Even though most physicians may not be involved with the day-to-day aspect of the long-term (6 months to years) treatment phase, they must have a basic understanding of what can be accomplished during this period. The role of the general pediatrician or family physician during this phase is to support the total treatment plan and to provide follow through. Without an understanding of what is to be expected and how those helping the family go about this task, the physician can be of little help and support; he even may be counter productive.

The treatment programs that are effective in helping families who are abusive or neglectful of their children are based on our current understanding of the psycho-dynamics and "patho-physiology" of this problem. Most of the last decade was spent identifying the basic causes of child abuse and neglect. We are now in the period of initiating treatment programs developed from this theoretical framework. The next step of course, will be the initiating of early identification and preventive programs which are beginning to become feasible.

This discussion of the specific therapeutic programs which are helpful for the abused and/or neglected child and his family requires a review of some of the material that was covered at the beginning of this manual.

This material is presented in a different format to emphasize how the never-ending cycle of child abuse and neglect can be interrupted.

World of Abnormal Rearing (W.A.R.). Children who are abused and neglected find themselves reared in an unusual atmosphere, which we call the "World of Abnormal Rearing" (W.A.R.). W.A.R. children have experienced some very negative and detrimental happenings during their childhood, affecting them in many ways resulting in a variety of presentations to professionals, child abuse and/or neglect being only two of the many "spin-offs" from this abnormal rearing cycle. This point is discussed in more detail later.

The World of Abnormal Rearing will be reviewed in five separate sections moving counterclockwise around the W.A.R. cycle in the following order:

A. Conception—Pregnancy—Child
B. Unrealistic Expectations—Role Reversal—Compliance
C. Lack of Trust—Isolation—"I'm no Damn Good"
D. Selection of "friends" and mates
E. Childhood missed

Display #11

World of Abnormal Rearing

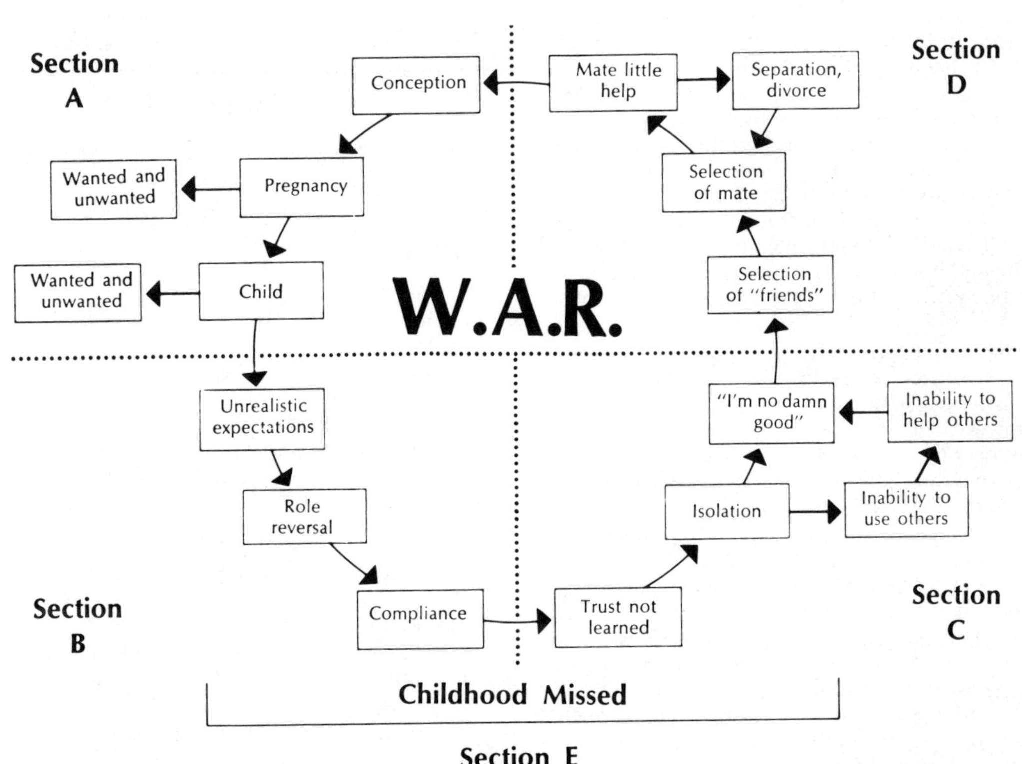

The W.A.R. Cycle, Section A

Conception—Pregnancy—Child

Most, but not all, conceptions lead to an on-going pregnancy. Although the advent of abortion interrupts a large number of pregnancies, it seems to interrupt less pregnancies of W.A.R. children. Girls who are reared in this unusual atmosphere have a strong desire to become pregnant. They often refuse the use of birth control and dismiss any thought of abortion. It is likely, therefore, that the decrease in number of children as a result of improved birth control methods and abortion will result in a *proportional increase* in the number of babies being born to girls reared in this World of Abnormal Rearing.

Conception, therefore, often leads to a wanted pregnancy in W.A.R. children, especially in the young age group. Unfortunately, the pregnancy is wanted for very selfish reasons, i.e., to resolve some special problem for the mother. The new baby is supposed to get her away from an unhappy experience in her home, or will keep her company or even take care of her and comfort her in her loneliness.

As the pregnancy comes to completion, the child may or may not have the capability of meeting the expectations that the parent(s) have developed throughout the W.A.R. years. Many young mothers who had every desire to get pregnant, with great expectations that the baby would resolve one of their many problems, find themselves even worse off than before. Their baby does not—or is not able to meet these needs.

Display #12

Treatment Programs For Section A Of The W.A.R. Cycle

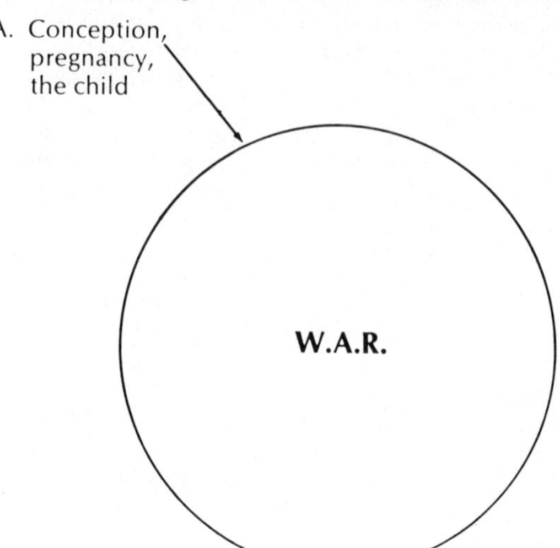

Family planning and birth control measures must be pursued, even though frequently resisted by those reared in the W.A.R. A referral to family planning is *not* enough. Special counseling is necessary.

Abortion is rarely considered a viable alternative in many W.A.R. mothers since they *often* want to be pregnant.

The W.A.R. Cycle, Section B

Unrealistic Expectations, Role Reversal and Compliance

The World of Abnormal Rearing continues on in its never-ending cycle producing a child upon whom is placed very unrealistic expectations. These parents truly expect that the baby will resolve one or more of their many problems. When the baby is fortunate and doesn't have colic, sleeps at the same time as do the parents, doesn't make too many demands, reminds the parent of someone whom they like, has other very positive traits, is the right sex, etc., then things may go "reasonably well." On the other hand, when some or all of these factors or behaviors are reversed and the baby is not able to meet the expectations of the parents, then the child may well be in trouble. The stresses of caring for a small child are great enough for parents who are reared positively, but are almost impossible for the parents who have been brought up in the World of Abnormal Rearing.

There are some families who have such high expectations of children that there is no child who can meet them. These children are abused just because they are children. They find themselves in situations that are impossible to cope with, they become scapegoats and they can never do the right thing. They are constantly being chastised, belittled, neglected, and, often physically injured.

Children who are born into the World of Abnormal Rearing strive desperately to comply. Professionals often become very confused by this compliance since complying children may look like "good children" in that they are taking care of mother or dad and often may even try to care for the doctor or nurse. When one reflects on normal child developmental patterns, it becomes clear that the child in question is not acting his or her age, rather acting much older than one might expect. Although compliance is certainly something that all children and parents strive for to some degree, the extent of the compliance demanded by parents bringing their children up in the W.A.R. far exceeds the normal expectations.

One of our parents told a public health nurse not long ago, "sometimes I think my baby's my mother." This is a very common feeling on the part of W.A.R. parents. They really expect the child to do for them that which they wished their mother had done when they were small. Another mother, who was having great difficulty in accepting her child as a child, said "I don't hit my child anymore since I joined Parents Anonymous, but I don't like the little bastard any better." She was very pleased that she was able to stop hitting, but someone had to help her see the child as a child and see him as someone she truly could like.

Display #13

Treatment Programs For Section B Of The W.A.R. Cycle

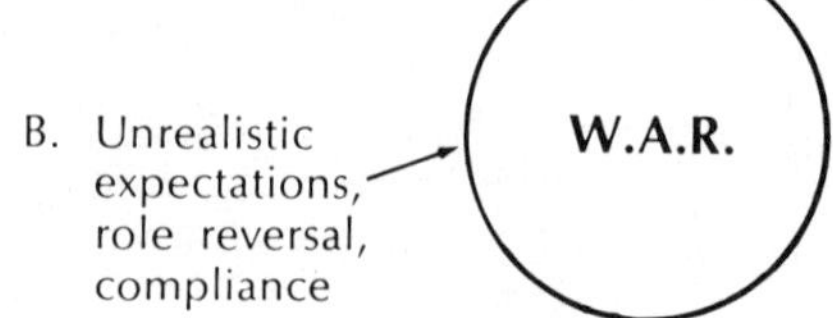

W.A.R. Parents must learn:

1. About normal child development
2. How to react to normal child behavior
3. What to expect of children
4. How to play with their children
5. General rearing and parenting skills

This can be done through:

1. Parenting courses—in schools, churches, doctors' offices, mental health centers, etc.
2. Group discussion sessions
3. Nursery school and grade school cooperatives
4. Some form of modeling of parenting

Many W.A.R. parents truly expect the child to take on the role of the parents and not act like a child. When a child must assume these roles then "Role Reversal" is painfully clear as you observe the child's behavior in the presence of the parent.

W.A.R.

The W.A.R. Cycle, Section C

Lack of Trust, Isolation, and "I'm No Damn Good"

One of the basic skills that is not learned by children reared in this unusual manner is the ability to trust. Consider how a child learns to trust people; it stems from some very early life experiences. A little two year old runs to his mommy and cries, "I'm hurt. Up." Instead of being picked up and comforted, the mother says, "Oh, you stupid kid, you fell again," or "Don't bother me, I've got my own problems." The child learns very quickly that people are not around to help him when he has a problem. On the contrary, he learns that he must role reverse and take care of mother or father when *they* have a problem. If every time a child comes to someone for help he gets chastised, hit, or criticized, he will soon learn that people are not around to be helpful, rather, they hurt you. He best not depend on people if he has a problem.

One 8-year-old girl had been abused most of her life. When asked, "What do you do when you have a problem, any kind of a problem?," she immediately answered by saying, "It's best if I deal with those myself." The concepts of distrust and lack of confidence in other people are learned quickly by W.A.R. children. They grow up to believe that they "damn well better deal with their own problems." One mother has yet to trust me enough to give me her phone number. To my knowledge, she has never given anybody her phone number.

Distrust on the part of the W.A.R. children leads to isolation. They find that they better handle their own problems and are not able to rely on people when a problem arises. In talking to these women and men about whom they relied on when they were in school, it is clear that they had no one. As our World of Abnormal Rearing cycle depicts, lack of trust and isolation leads to an inability to use other people positively, an inability to help other people and finally, a conviction that they are truly "no damn good." The self-image gradually but definitely degenerates. One 28-year-old mother was asked, "When was the last time you were helpful to someone?" After a great hesitation, she said, "I think when I was fourteen."

The W.A.R. Cycle, Section D

Selecting "Friends" and Mates

W.A.R. children, as they reach adolescence, find that their home and school experiences with friends and parents have been, for the most part, a disaster. They have major personal needs, but have never developed the skills to have these needs completely fulfilled. Selecting friends is not one of their special talents, which places their ability to select a mate in equal jeopardy. W.A.R. children find it most difficult to find someone with whom they can set up a close

Display #14

Treatment Programs For Section C Of The W.A.R. Cycle

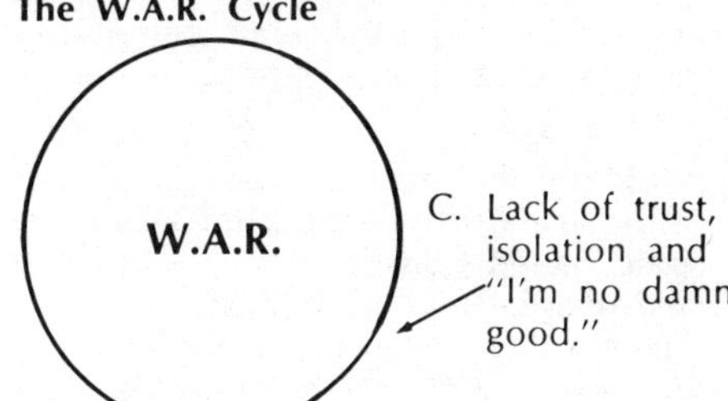

W.A.R. parents must:

1. Have the wall of isolation broken down
2. Learn how to trust others
3. Develop a better self image
4. Learn how to help others
5. Have access to others

This can be done through:

1. Providing them with a parent aide—a non-professional to establish a friendship
2. Joining a "lay" group—e.g., Parents Anonymous
3. Helping them get telephones and transportation
4. Finding suitable babysitters
5. Group therapy with professional guidance

THIS IS THE MOST SIGNIFICANT ASPECT OF THERAPY: TEACHING TRUST AND IMPROVING THE SELF-IMAGE WILL OFTEN TAKE MONTHS, BUT IT CAN BE DONE IN MOST CASES.

Display #15

Treatment Programs For Section D Of The W.A.R. Cycle

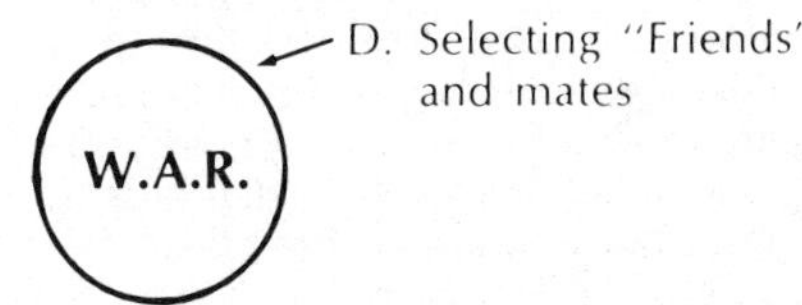

Major needs:

1. Strengthen inter-spouse relationship.
2. Teach spouse how to recognize when wife or husband is up tight.
3. Once recognized, what to do about it.
4. Skills on how to select friends and where they can be found.

This can be done by:

1. Marriage counselor, if counselor understands dynamics of the W.A.R.
2. Involving husband in **all** phases of treatment plan, especially in areas A, B, C and E.
3. Encourage maintaining marriage where possible, separation and/or divorce only if no other alternative.*

* This recommendation is made because the partners, particularly the mother, during the crisis need someone; if not their spouse, they often find one very similar to the mate they just left. One mother said, "Isn't it interesting that my boyfriend beats me just like my husband did?" (and so did her father).

relationship, much less a marriage or living arrangement with someone who can meet many of their needs. A desire to leave the home and find someone who can help them supersedes their selectivity. The mates who are selected are soon found to be unhelpful and unsupporting. Shortly, the new marriage or living arrangment is often seen as unsatisfactory.

One of the major goals of this type of mate relationship is to have a baby. A baby, unlike a pregnancy of more normally reared individuals, is most often conceived for bizarre and unusual reasons. Almost invariably children who have been brought up in the W.A.R. get the impression that the baby is going to resolve one of their problems. As indicated earlier, the pregnancy is supposed to free them from their unhappy home, prove to their parents and themselves they can indeed be good parents, provide them with someone to keep them company, or to role reverse and begin to parent the parents. Once a baby is produced for these reasons, he is placed into an almost impossible situation. The cycle of the World of Abnormal Rearing now begins again with the new baby having to meet the same demands and expectations as did the parents when they were young. As one mother so sadly related, "I wanted all this time to have my baby, and when he was born he didn't do anything for me."

The W.A.R. Cycle, Section E

Childhood Missed

Referring back to Display #11 (The W.A.R.), the phrase under this figure indicates that there is a significant gap in the developmental processes of W.A.R. children. They spend so much time trying to meet the needs of their parents that large segments of normal childhood must be relinguished. In not being allowed to experience many normal developmental happenings and required to spend much more time role reversing and complying, these children miss much of the most helpful learning processes necessary in becoming a parent, i.e., childhood. Having experienced childhood is a major pre-requisite to parenting. This includes, among other things, being treated as a child, the ability to develop a trusting relationship with others, learning the skills of establishing friendships, and feeling good about oneself. Many, if not all of these traits, are jeopardized in W.A.R. children.

W.A.R. children, when they become parents, truly expect their children to role reverse. For example, when mother's upset they need to be responsive. They relinguish the right to act like a child and experience normal child development, replacing it with those skills that they learn to help them meet the unrealistic expectations of their parents. The better they are at this, the more likely they will be accepted into the family. The more the child acts like a child, i.e., acts his age, the less likely he is to be accepted into this family. A 4 year old has trouble getting "permission" to have an occasional tantrum, explore the cupboards, scribble, say he's angry, etc.

Very frequently we find *siblings* of abused children who have learned the roles that they must play and they do it very well. On the other hand, we often find the *abused* child as someone who just cannot meet the expectations of the parents, and consequently finds himself verbally or physically attacked. One abusive mother, when asked "how did it go when you were little" said, "Just great. I got along very well with my parents." Confused, I finally asked, "How was it with your sister?" She immediately replied, "Oh, my father beat her severely."

The physician and others aware of child developmental sequences can pick up these developmental gaps as he observes children who are reared in this world. They often act more mature than their chronological age even though the parents may see the child as being especially difficult. On the other hand, there are some W.A.R. children who give every appearance of being very difficult children to handle. Their rearing experiences have indicated to them that they are truly "bad kids" and if this continues unabated they will soon take on the life style that their parents have fostered.

Display #16

Treatment Programs For Section E Of The W.A.R. Cycle

E. CHILDHOOD MISSED

A. The abused and/or neglected child plus his/her siblings must be involved in treatment plan.
   1. Important to recall siblings also reared in W.A.R.
   2. Even though they may fare better physically.

B. The basic premise of children's treatment program is to teach children IT IS O.K. TO BE A CHILD.*
   1. Will need out of home experiences—nursery school, day care, grade school, special groups, play therapy, and even foster care at times.
   2. School personnel must understand the W.A.R. if they are to be helpful.

C. One of basic tenets of parents' therapy is to teach them IT IS O.K. TO HAVE A CHILD BE A CHILD.*

* Sometimes these achievements take significant time. In the judgment of those working with the parents, if the home is not safe for the child(ren), then the courts must be involved for temporary foster home placement.

Additional Points About Therapeutic Approaches

A few additional points should be made about therapeutic approaches for families who are abusive and/or neglectful.

Handling Crises

The crisis often precipitates, but is *not* the basic causative factor of the abusive act. Although treating the crisis is a major component of therapy, it is not an end in itself. Crisises fall into two major areas: Personal and Logistical. Every attempt must be made to assist the family in handling both aspects of these problems.

Personal counseling and advice needs to be readily available to the family at all hours of the day and night. Assessment as to their ability to handle personal crises must be made, and all those involved in the treatment program should be fully aware of potential problems.

Logistical crises must also be handled quickly. These include finding transportation, food, money, housing, clothing, etc. There is no point in trying to deal with many of the issues mentioned earlier if you have a hungry, ill and cold family. These crises are best handled by someone who knows community services very well.

As those involved with the family learn more about their needs, crises can be anticipated and thereby prevented. When this can occur, great progress has been made.

Handicraft Skills of Baby Care

Very frequently, parents who are abusive and/or neglectful find it extremely difficult to physically handle their babies. Some of these difficulties lie directly in the area of "handicraft." Things such as diapering, feeding, picking up, walking and playing with the child are skills not readily available to parents who have experienced the W.A.R. If, added to this, one or more of the parents is mentally retarded, additional difficulty develops.

Use of school and hospital training programs for parents with retardation and/or other problems in handling small children is of utmost importance. The Public Health Nurse can also be most helpful. She can serve in many of the other therapeutic roles discussed earlier as she begins to help the mother and father deal with small children.

Relatives

Inasmuch as the great majority of parents who are abusive and/or neglectful of their children are W.A.R. children themselves, there is little advantage to be gained by using the relatives as caretakers of the child in the long term treatment program. More often than not, the relatives have a negative influence on the parents and their incorporation in the treatment program should be very carefully planned if at all possible. Having a maternal grandmother care for the baby while the mother is learning some of the skills that she missed as a child may well be detrimental, since it is this very same grandmother who had difficulty in rearing the child's mother when she was small.

On occasion one can find a relative who is seen positively and can be incorporated into the treatment program. When one of the two parents has had more positive childhood experiences than the other, relatives on this side of the family might be useful. Every caution must be taken when relatives are considered as part of long-term treatment.

The Hard-Core or Incurable Family

It is estimated that about 10 percent of the families who are abusive to their children are psychotic or otherwise seriously ill psychiatrically. In addition to this, there is another 10 percent who, for a variety of reasons, cannot be reached. Even after extensive attempts to work with the family for a year, the result may yield little benefit.

Some of those who are hardest to reach, in addition to the severely psychiatrically ill, are those who believe that "God told me that it was alright to beat my baby." They produce biblical references with which they justify their interpretation of child rearing. Some States have, unfortunately, seen fit to give more legal rights to parents who use religious grounds to abuse or neglect their children than to parents who do not. This of course is an intolerable situation and must be changed.

Another group that is very difficult to deal with is the group with racial and/or cultural reasons that interfere with being helped. When these variables are added to the adverse affects of the W.A.R., occasionally the two are sufficient to prevent significant improvement by therapeutic efforts.

Like all diseases, there is a small group of individuals who are not helped with our current understanding of therapeutic approaches. When the point of no return has been reached, every effort must be made to continue to protect the child, and to suggest permanent removal by the courts. Unfortunately, State laws give very low priority to the rights of children when permanent removal is indicated.

Most parents, on the other hand, can be helped. Our goal at this point in our understanding should be to see a significant amount of improvement in approximately 70-75 percent of the families who have the problem of child abuse and/or neglect within 6-9 months after treatment begins.

Display #17

Additional Suggestions About Treatment

A. Crises must be handled:
   1. W.A.R. parents rarely have learned the skills of solving their own crises.
   2. It is hard to work on areas A through E if major crises still exist, e.g., no food, no transportation, husband without work, etc.
   3. We must anticipate crises where possible, and prevent.
   4. Crises are not the cause of abuse, rather the participating factor.

B. Handicraft skills for baby care are needed:
   1. Many W.A.R. parents have never learned how to physically handle a baby.
   2. Some abusive and neglectful parents are mentally retarded.
   3. The skill of playing with children needs to be taught.*

* One W.A.R. mother said, "I can't wait till my baby is 2 years old so I can play with her."

Display #18

Use of relative in treatment plan:

1. Rarely are relatives helpful—after all, this is where the W.A.R. began.
2. Use great caution if someone suggests using grandmother as a foster mother for child.
3. Occasionally, parents or siblings of a "more positively reared" spouse may be useful.

Some families cannot be helped:

1. Although the psychotic or otherwise seriously psychiatrically ill parents may be helped personally, making them into reasonable parents is *often* most difficult.
2. Fanatics are very hard to help.
3. Some families just don't respond.
4. We should be able to help 70-75 percent with our present understanding and treatment programs.
5. As seen in many diseases, there is certain percentage of patients who are resistent to present therapeutic regimens.

The Problem of Responsibility

Coordination of Services

Physicians should be readily aware that the social service system, i.e., Protective Services, has as its major function the coordination of *acute* care services. This may go on for two to four months, possibly six, but rarely any longer.* When one defines the roles of various individuals involved in treatment, it is clear that no group or agency sees as its responsibility the *long-term* coordination of services to families who have been abusive and/or neglectful. This is a serious gap in the services available to these ill families and is one that must be rectified in the very near future.

Little is gained by getting angry at departments of social services for not accepting the task of long-term coordination since it is not part of their current job description. Every attempt must be made to change this in every community throughout the country.

The Role of the Physician

The fact that our existing community services do not provide long-term therapy and follow-through is both surprising and alarming to physicians when they first realize the existence of the problem. And yet, we are used to this. It is not unusual for the physician to find that the implementation of treatment programs for any disease lags behind the understanding of how to treat a given illness. Consider the attempts to develop community and public health programs for tuberculosis, venereal disease, drug abuse, preventive immunizations for polio, etc. This problem is certainly present in the area of child abuse and neglect. Although the understanding as to how to provide treatment to large numbers of families is available, the actual implementation of these treatment programs has not occurred in most communities. Physicians must, as they have in other instances, be the advocates and prime movers for the development of such programs. We can no longer sit back and assume that these will occur. One of the most disastrous effects of the child abuse reporting law, although there have been many positive effects, is that it essentially says to the physician, "if you just report you have no further responsibility." This is unalterably false and physicians cannot assume that treatment will take place once a report has been made. Every effort must be generated to develop multidisciplinary child abuse and neglect programs within the community in which the physician resides.

* We recently completed a study of six protective service programs. Ninety percent of their interaction with the family was completed in one month.

Display #19

The Physician As An Agent For Change

The cause of a very serious, life threatening disease is known and treatment programs which can be effective for some 70-75 percent of these families are available.

And Yet,

Our "Delivery of Services" system is not implementing what can be done.

* * * *

Physicians have the capability of influencing this system and making it move from single disciplines working in isolation to a trusting multidisciplinary community program.

And Yet,

Around the country the cry is, "Physicians just won't get involved!"

* * * *

All physicians who work with any family member need to know the basic causes and present therapeutic concepts.

And Yet,

It only takes *one* physician in a community to exhibit concern and commit himself or herself to seeing that change does occur.*

* The major reason the American Academy of Pediatrics initiated the development of the six self-instructional units for their members and others is to help professionals to become knowledgeable in the area of child abuse and neglect and serve as prime movers in developing community programs. Information about the self-instructional units should be addressed to the author.

Display #20

The most challenging task that remains is the early identification of W.A.R. children so that they can be provided the training they need. There is sufficient understanding to begin *preventive* service programs now, long before child abuse and neglect starts in the next generation. *Those children who will be helped the most are as yet unborn.*

Speculations

Call it fantasy, dreaming, knowledge of the field or what you will, the next ten years must see:

1. Child Protection diagnostic and consultation teams developed for every 300,000 population area.
2. Every hospital with 50 or more children's beds have an identifiable team which works closely with the community child abuse program.
3. Physicians (mostly pediatricians and/or family physicians) actively involved.
4. Long-term treatment and coordination programs a part of each community program.
5. Protective Services must become a multidisciplinary group rather than solely a short term, social work group as it is currently.
6. Early recognition and preventive programs developed.
7. These prevention programs must, for the most part, begin in the hospital during the perinatal period.
8. Schools becoming much more actively involved with parenting programs both for the students and their parents.
9. Family Courts expanding their services and be seen as helpful at a much earlier point in time.
10. Our knowledge about the W.A.R. broadened and this lead directly to a better understanding of Early Child Development, thereby helping families develop the skills necessary to begin wiping out the W.A.R.

Excerpts from The Diagnostic Process and Treatment Programs. U.S. Dept. of Health, Education, and Welfare. National Center on Child Abuse and Neglect. DHEW Publ. No. (OHD) 77-30069

American Humane Association Publishes Highlights of National Study of Child Neglect and Abuse Reporting for 1975

by Vincent De Francis, J.D.
Director, Children's Division
American Humane Association

In 1973, to test the feasibility of a system for determining the number of child abuse and neglect cases officially reported across the country, the Children's Bureau awarded a grant to the Children's Division of the American Humane Association to conduct a National Study of Child Neglect and Abuse Reporting. As part of this study, AHA has gathered data provided by participating and non-participating States. Below are highlights drawn from data collected for calendar year 1975, the second year of the study.

It is important to note that the complete accuracy of the data on which these highlights are based is subject to question. The National Study was not intended at the outset to provide complete, accurate nationwide data on child abuse and neglect. The project was primarily planned to demonstrate the feasibility of creating a voluntary system for collecting uniform data about cases of child abuse and neglect officially reported to protective service agencies in all the States. At this early stage of the study, emphasis has been on encouraging States to participate and to set up uniform systems for gathering and storing data. In this phase, it has not been possible to insist that participating States supply complete and fully accurate data.

By the end of 1975, 29 States and Territories were cooperating in the National Study system and were supplying more or less detailed and reliable information. Additional, less complete and less specific data was provided by non-participating States. The highlights below are a composite of information drawn from both groups of States for the year 1975.

Although the limitations described must be kept in mind, this 1975 report provides the best available information on the reporting of child abuse and neglect cases across the nation and on the characteristics of abuse and neglect. If anything, the data below may err on the side of understating the extent of the problem.

i. Reporting: Child Neglect and Abuse

Total number of reports of neglect and abuse	289,837	
Number of cases investigated	228,899	(79.0%)
Status undetermined	60,938	(21.0%)
Of investigated cases of neglect and abuse (228,899):		
Found to be valid	136,504	(59.6%)
Found not valid	92,395	(40.4%)

Thus, the validation rate for neglect and abuse cases was found to be a ratio of 60-40.

ii. Neglect versus Abuse

Number of neglect cases reported	69,408	(63.0%)
Number of abuse cases reported	40,718	(37.0%)

Ratio of neglect to abuse reporting was found to be about 2 neglect to 1 abuse case.

Number of neglect/abuse cases reported (i.e., undifferentiated neglect and abuse)	179,711
TOTAL	289,837

Comment:
The near 2-1 ratio of neglect over abuse reporting shows a lower than true ratio because:

(1) Seven States reported only abuse cases and made no count of neglect reports;

(2) No State reported neglect cases only;

(3) All reporting laws make reporting of abuse mandatory but not all make neglect reporting mandatory;

(4) Eleven States reported abuse and neglect together, with no differentiation.

iii. Involved Children in Reported Cases

A total of 304,329 children were reported as being involved in reported cases during the year. There was no significant difference between the sexes of the children involved.

iv. Sources of Reports

Neglect and abuse reports were made to the mandated authorities by many agencies and individuals in the communities. Data on this aspect of the study was grouped as follows:

Sources	Percentage of all Reports
Agency Sources Public and private social agencies, schools and school personnel, law enforcement, courts, hotlines	39.4
Individuals Neighbors, friends, relatives, siblings, self-referrals	40.6
Medical Sources Hospitals, physicians, nurses, coroners, medical examiners	9.7
Other, Not Specified	8.5

v. Who Were Alleged Abusers-Neglecters?

Findings identified natural parents as the persons principally responsible for neglect and abuse, with a scattering of other caretakers:

Relationship (by percentage)		Percentage of Total
Natural Parents		83.8
Mothers	57.70	
Fathers	26.10	
Stepparents		6.08
Stepfathers	4.95	
Stepmothers	1.13	
Adoptive Parents		.10
Fathers	.06	
Mothers	.04	
Paramours		1.80
Male	1.28	
Female	.52	
Other Relatives		2.40
Siblings	.40	
Others	2.00	
Babysitters		.90

Other categories with very small percentages included foster parents, grandparents, institutional staff, and neighbors. The percentages are rounded out by "unknowns."

vi. Types of Abuse Reported*

These statistics relate to types of abuse identified in validated cases of abuse, or neglect and abuse.

		Percentage of Total
Physical Injuries, Minor (Contusions, abrasions, unspecified, no visible injuries)	30,310	50.3
Sexual Abuse	6,372	10.6
Physical Injuries Major (bone fractures, subdural hematomas, internal injuries, brain damage, skull fractures)	1,384	2.3
Burns, Scalding	1,578	2.6
Congenital and Environmental, Drug Addiction	33	.1
Physical Abuse (unspecified)	20,557	34.1
TOTAL	60,234	

vii. Types of Neglect Reported*

These statistics relate to types of neglect identified in validated cases of neglect, or neglect and abuse.

		Percentage of Total
Physical Neglect (unspecified, gross household neglect, lack of supervision, abandonment, exposure to elements, inadequate shelter, clothing, hygiene, etc.)	100,542	78.1
Medical Neglect (lack of medical diagnosis and treatment, malnutrition, etc.)	12,388	9.6
Emotional Neglect (psychological impairment, failure to thrive)	10,030	7.8
Educational Neglect	5,714	4.5

Neglect, Type Not Recorded	25,058
TOTAL	153,732

*More than one category may have been reported for each child.

Child Abuse and Neglect Reports. February 1977. National Center on Child Abuse and Neglect. U.S. Dept. of Health, Education, and Welfare. DHEW Publ. No. (OHD) 77-30086

WORKING WITH ABUSIVE PARENTS

An interview with Jolly K. by Judith Reed

What I can tell you is what you won't get from the other speakers—the guts of a person going through child abuse. Being there doesn't automatically make you an expert on child abuse but it tells what it's like . . .

"Child abusers are going through hell. We have a vision of how powerful our anger can be, a concept of where this anger will take us if we are pushed too far, and the constant dread that we will be pushed that far. For abuse is usually not a singular incident but part of a consistent pattern . . .

"We don't like being child abusers any more than society likes the problem of abuse. If a positive approach is offered abusers, they will usually respond . . .

"I'm convinced that parents are aware of their feelings and let others know. But we don't know how to listen. Too many of our parents have told society time and time again: 'Help me! I'm at my wit's end. Help me before I bring my kid there too!' How can we learn to listen and respond? Too many parents are afraid to go to agencies because they fear that their child will be taken away . . .

"Our defense mechanisms may make it difficult to read us but look to see what went into our lives to make us this way . . . It's true that we're socially alienated, most of us with good reason. Ninety percent of us were abused as children. I can remember not being loved when I was a child. But I just thought I was a rotten little kid and that's why I was being tossed from foster home to foster home. Since most of us grew up viewing others as part of negative, hurtful relationships, why should we form more relationships now? . . .

"The feeling parents most often talk about in P.A. is fear—fear of what they're doing, fear of what will happen if they don't get help and fear of what will happen if they do. And, of course, their fears are reality-based.

"Many of us in P.A. also have a constant dread that our behavior is indicative of insanity, that we are losing our minds. We think: 'I had no control over a lot of things in my life and now I have no control over even my mind!' Many times we also work in symptoms that we have read about—game-playing, attention-getting. Then comes fear that we really are that psychopathic . . .

"I've abused my child physically and emotionally. Now I can talk in retrospect. I live in bits and pieces of those feelings now, but not the hell!"

* * *

The speaker is Jolly K., graduate of 35 foster homes, former abusive parent and founder of Parents Anonymous, Inc. of Los Angeles, California, a private organization of self-help groups that now has 1,500 members in 150 chapters in the United States and Canada.

Jolly is speaking to one of the many professional and lay citizen groups she addresses across the country each year in her role as director of programs for the organization—workers in state departments of social services and other agencies involved in the problems of child abuse and neglect, delegates to child welfare conferences, researchers and advisory groups.

Jolly founded her organization, first known as Mothers Anonymous, in 1970. It happened, as she tells it, in response to her bitter complaints to her therapist that there was no place for fearful abusers—and potential abusers—to turn for services. "Well, why don't you start one?" was his answer.

In 1974 Parents Anonymous received a grant from the Children's Bureau, OCD, to help establish additional chapters—by preparing and distributing materials on the organization and by providing technical assistance to communities wishing to form such groups, including the training of regional coordinators and local group leaders.

How is a P.A. chapter formed? Who are the parents who join such groups? Who leads them and what do they do in their meetings? To find out, CHILDREN TODAY discussed the following questions with Jolly K.

CT: *How do your members learn about Parents Anonymous?*

Jolly K.: Surprisingly, over 80 percent of our members come by themselves after hearing about us on television or radio programs or through newspaper stories and other published materials. The remaining 20 percent are referred through agency contacts, the courts, mental health practitioners and friends, neighbors or relatives.

CT: *How does a new chapter get started and where may a chapter meet?*

Jolly K.: New chapters are the direct result of someone's dedicated interest coupled with his or her willingness to work in developing the chapter. Chapters may be started by a parent with an abuse problem or a professional or a service agency wishing to help such parents. More specific information on starting a chapter is contained in our new *Chapter Development Manual.**

A chapter may meet in any non-threatening environment, such as a YMCA or YWCA, church, school or community center. We definitely must not meet in a city, county, state or Federal agency such as a Department of Public Welfare, Bureau of Adoptions or police department. Because feelings like "I have to have a clean house" and "Those kids better behave" can lead to potential pressure situations, we do not recommend that chapter meetings be held in private homes.

CT: *Are most of your members parents who have abused their children or are a good proportion mothers*

Judith Reed is the editor of Children Today.

or fathers who fear they may? What percentage of members have had a child removed from their home?

Jolly K.: The majority of P.A. parents have already experienced the anguish of having an active problem, but we are beginning to see more and more parents become involved prior to actual abusive behavior. By the end of 1976 we expect to have more concrete information on this. We also will be gathering data on the percentage of parents who have children in placement.

CT: *Who, besides parents, are involved in the chapters?*

Jolly K.: All chapters have a Sponsor and Chairperson. The sponsor should be a professional who has a profound respect for the self-help concept and understands group dynamics. Our sponsors include psychiatrists, psychologists, marriage and family counselors, social workers, ministers and others. If a sponsor is already employed by an agency that has an authoritative position in regard to parents with abuse problems, such as a protective service agency, he or she must work with P.A. autonomously, not as a representative of the agency.

The chairperson is always a parent. He or she may be the parent who helped start the group, or one of several who worked to form the chapter and who was later chosen informally to serve as chairperson by the other parents.

Many of our chapters also have various volunteers working with and for the chapter. Babysitters who care for the children during meeting times constitute the largest number of volunteers. We also have volunteers who help by providing transportation, hanging P.A. posters, circulating P.A. literature, making public contacts on our behalf and raising funds.

CT: *What is the relationship between a P.A. chapter and the national organization?*

Jolly K.: The National Office is committed to provide chapters with the support necessary to start and maintain a P.A. chapter. This is accomplished primarily by providing literature, public exposure, technical assistance and consultation. An individual chapter is autonomous in most things; however, each is part of an overall national movement and receives support from the National Office. The main benefit, of course, is that there is strength, encouragement and unity in numbers, so that no one chapter is left with the overwhelming sense of responsibility, of "having to do it all by themselves."

CT: *Can you tell us something about what happens at a meeting?*

Jolly K.: Meetings begin and take shape in many different ways. Sometimes they start by someone saying, in response to the body language of a member, "Hey, what's happening?" Other times it begins by picking up on a problem a member was discussing at the last meeting or by asking for follow-up on a phone crisis call.

If I were at a meeting of a new group I might say, "Look, we're meeting here for a purpose—we're here to talk about what's churning inside us. Let's do something now to stop this behavior." We'd exchange telephone numbers and addresses and begin to form a lot of support contact.

I remember one meeting when a member, Lenny, was sitting on the couch, sharing with us how "down" she felt. Questioned many times as to the whys and wherefores, Lenny answered by saying, "I don't know," "I'm so confused" and "Stop badgering me." All the while she was quietly crying. She appeared so vulnerable, so young at that moment and most of all, so very needy.

I reached out, put my arms around her, practically putting her into my lap as if she were a lonely, lost child. At this, Lenny cried openly, much in the same way that a hurt, pained child cries. We as a group then knew, and verbally discussed the fact, that there are times when our need for nurturing exceeds our need to know the whys and wherefores. We also found out that when this overwhelming need is fulfilled—for Lenny it was within a half an hour's time—we can then turn our attention and response to the realities of our daily situations. Most of all, we learned that we can ask for inner fulfillment, that some others will respond with positive methods to help, and that we are not bad, unloveable people.

Another typical moment came at a meeting when Joel told other members: "I did it! Last week," she said, "I got so teed off at my son!" (He is five). "But instead of abusing him I squashed the milk carton I was holding until the milk went all over the place . . . I released my anger in a more positive way and it worked. Now I know I can do other things besides being abusive when I'm uptight."

Sure, the members laughed, but most important, we learned. Joel had shown us that a potential abusive situation can be averted, that we can be non-abusive regardless of how uptight we are! Call these heavy times or light times in a meeting. More than anything else, we in P.A. call the meetings "our time." The times with Lenny and Joel were very real moments in Parents Anonymous.

CT: *How do members support one another between meetings and in emergencies?*

Jolly K.: My last answer illustrated support but also a lot of caring. Suppose Joel had not squashed the milk carton. Alternate ways to release angry feelings include calling another member and releasing the feelings over the phone. Joel could also have asked another member to care for her boy until she "pulled it together," or she could have asked to have someone care for her (meaning stay with her) for a while.

CT: *Is P.A. the sole source of help for most of the parents involved, or are some also receiving treatment or therapy through another source? And is therapy suggested and/or provided with the guidance of P.A.? For example, do some chapters use the services of professionals, such as psychiatrists, etc?*

Jolly K.: Many of our members are receiving services other than P.A. and, yes, P.A. supports and suggests other therapy alternatives. On an as-needed basis we utilize the advice and input of professionals other than our chapter sponsor.

CT: *Do many parents drop out of the program? And if so, for what reasons?*

Jolly K.: Some members drop out after realizing that a group situation isn't their cup of tea. Others find P.A. uncomfortable for them. Also, some drop out by choosing to use other treatment resources.

CT: *Have you found that there are certain kinds of parents with whom P.A. cannot work successfully? Are you able to guide them to other help?*

Jolly K.: We've not found "certain kinds" of parents that we're not able to work with. We have found that some people find our program to be less successful for them. Again, we're not the "cup of tea" that they find comforting. When we are made aware of this, yes, we usually are able to guide them to other helping resources.

We have also found that persons who are acutely mentally ill and who come to a P.A. meeting may find that the group can't offer them the comprehensive services they need. It may also be that the group feels it is not prepared to deal with the behavior that may arise from their illness. In such cases the group, with the assistance of the sponsor, is able to refer the person to a more appropriate source.

CT: *What is the rate of recidivism for those who attend meetings? Do you follow up former members?*

Jolly K.: Recidivism has been very, very low. In the five years of the program's existence, we know of only two incidents which resulted in a child's hospitalization. That's not to say all is sweetness and roses and that our members have become "instant Pollyannas." It is to say that life- or limb-threatening abuse has been vastly reduced.

No, we do not do a formal follow-up on former members.

CT: *Do you feel that members of P.A., who have voluntarily sought help, are typical of most abusive parents?*

Jolly K.: Yes . . . emphatically, yes. We are seeing much the same, and then some, of the parents so often described in the available literature and research studies. We are seeing the very withdrawn, the very aggressive, the isolationist, the uptight, the psychotic . . . in short, we are seeing human beings displaying a lot of different "typical human traits."

CT: *How many members meet in an average group and how long do most parents remain members?*

Jolly K.: Average group size is between six to 10 members, with most members staying in for one or more years.

CT: *What is the percentage of men to women in your groups?*

Jolly K.: Too small a percentage. The average among the groups would probably be 25 to 30 percent men. Confirmed percentages are not currently available.

CT: *Do both parents in an abusive family usually attend meetings? And what have you found the role of the non-abusing (passive) parent to be?*

Jolly K.: No. Again, this is not one of our most successfully realized objectives. Incidentally, we've found the passive parent to be not so darn passive as people think. We know that a whole lot of "behind the scenes setting of the stage" is going on and contributing to the activeness of the active abusing parent.

CT: *Is dependency on the P.A. group a problem for members who must leave for one or another reason? Is any follow-up provided for those who do move away?*

Jolly K.: Dependency can be and is a problem when a member leaves the group. But then the P.A. program is based on the premise that we, as members, will work towards resolving our problems, including how to handle relationships that are broken. The only follow-up provided is whatever is asked for or through the suggestion that a departing parent get involved with a chapter in the city he or she is moving to. If none exists, parents are encouraged to start one.

CT: *What action is taken if the group learns that a member has committed an abusive act or fears that he will?*

Jolly K.: Group peer pressure, group commitment to work extra hard with the parent and, as an extreme last resort, if P.A. doesn't work and the parent doesn't stop, then with or without the parent's agreement other people will be asked to intervene and provide services that will guarantee the safety of the child or children and the parent. ■

---

* A copy of *Chapter Development Manual* and other material produced by Parents Anonymous, including a general information flyer on child abuse, are available from Parents Anonymous, 2930 W. Imperial Highway, Suite 332, Inglewood, California 90303.

Children Today, Vol. 4, No. 3 (May-June1975), pp. 6-9. Published by the Children's Bureau, Office of Child Development, Office of Human Development, U.S. Dept. of Health, Education, and Welfare. Washington, D.C.

HEW News, Monday, January 7, 1977

Arabella Martinez, HEW's Assistant Secretary for Human Development Services, announced on November 7, 1977, the award of a $375,000 grant to expand Parents Anonymous, the national organization of self-help groups for parents who have abused their children.

The one-year grant was made by the National Center on Child Abuse and Neglect in the Children's Bureau of the Administration for Children, Youth and Families. ACYF is located within the Office of Human Development Services.

Federal funds, to be matched equally by State and local contributions, will be used to create State offices for the Parents Anonymous program. These offices will assist in the development of a network of self-help groups for parents within each State.

"The award is designed to generate greater State and local support for Parents Anonymous, which is the only self-help organization combatting the child abuse problem," Assistant Secretary Martinez said.

The Assistant Secretary also noted: "A recent survey showed that 94 percent of a group of State social service officials polled had a positive attitude toward the self-help treatment approach."

Since 1974, when Parents Anonymous first received HEW funding, the organization has grown from 65 chapters to more than 600 chapters across the U.S., with a total of 6,000 members. The national headquarters of Parents Anonymous is located in Redondo Beach, California.

An evaluation conducted last year found that participation in the self-help groups results in a sharp decrease in physical and verbal abuse toward children.

Parents responding to a questionnaire who said they had physically or verbally abused their children reported an immediate reduction in abusive incidents--in many cases to "almost never" --after only one month of membership in a Parents Anonymous group.

The evaluation, conducted by Behavior Associates of Tucson, Arizona, was based on questionnaires completed by 613 Parents Anonymous members throughout the country.

The study also reported significant increases in members' feelings of self-esteem, social contacts, knowledge of child development, and ability to deal with stress--all considered important factors in helping parents to stop abusive behavior.

Members were generally very satisfied with their participation in Parents Anonymous groups, which create a supportive atmosphere where parents can vent angry feelings, learn alternative ways to cope with child and family problems and help themselves while helping others.

Most of the parents said they themselves had been verbally or physically abused as children--a finding, the study noted, which substantiates research showing that abused children tend to become abusive parents.

Also supporting current research was the finding that 92 percent of the parents interviewed tended to focus abuse on only one of their children--often the child with special problems or the child considered to be most like themselves.

Each all-volunteer Parents Anonymous group is led by a chairperson, who is a parent with an abuse problem, and by a sponsor, generally a social worker, psychologist, or professional counselor.

The National Center on Child Abuse and Neglect was created by the Child Abuse Prevention and Treatment Act of 1974 to provide Federal leadership for efforts to prevent, identify and treat child abuse and neglect.

Hew News. Monday, January 7, 1977. Administration for Children, Youth and Families.

CHILD ABUSE AND NEGLECT: The Alcohol Connection

Margaret Hindman

Last year, public agencies across the nation received over 300,000 reports of suspected child abuse. Each year 2,000 children die in circumstances in which abuse or maltreatment is suspected (Besharov 1976). No one knows for sure how many more children suffer abuse which isn't reported to the authorities.

For many years, child abuse was virtually ignored. Publicity generated by the more sensational cases has increased public awareness of the problem and highlighted the tremendous need for prevention and remediation. Only since the 1960s have researchers and service agencies begun to look at the reasons behind child abuse and the people who are the abusers. And it is only very recently that researchers have begun to look at the relationship between alcoholism and child abuse and neglect.

Child abuse is a term which varies widely in meaning. The Child Abuse Prevention and Treatment Act of 1974 defines child abuse and neglect together as "the physical or mental injury, sexual abuse, negligent treatment, or maltreatment of a child under the age of 18 by a person who is responsible for the child's welfare under circumstances which indicate that the child's health or welfare is harmed or threatened thereby." This definition does not distinguish between abuse and neglect although other definitions do focus on whether the act is one of commission or omission. However, either neglect or abuse can lead to fatal results.

The Alcohol Connection

Studies reveal that parents with alcohol problems have a high potential for exhibiting neglect of their children, especially through erratic and inconsistent parenting.

Margaret Cork (1969), in interviews with 115 children of alcoholic parents, observed that many of the youngsters said they felt rejected, not only by the alcoholic parent, but also by the nonalcoholic spouse. Older children in these families are often forced to assume the parent role, caring for younger siblings and parents as well. These children seem to run a high risk of developing not only emotional and behavioral problems, but alcohol problems too, later in life (Cork 1969, Fox 1972,

Margaret Hindman, a former staff writer with the National Clearinghouse for Alcohol Information, is now director of public information at Hood College in Frederick, Maryland. She is also a free lance writer on alcohol issues and a member of the Task Force on Children of Alcoholic Parents of the Alcoholism Council of Maryland Citizens of Montgomery County, Inc.

Miller 1975). A connection between alcoholism and physical abuse of children appears repeatedly in reports by protective service and social workers, as well as in research reports on abused children.

Dr. Henry Kempe (1972), first to describe the "battered child syndrome," maintains that alcohol plays a part in approximately one-third of child abuse cases. In many more cases, he adds, alcohol can be related in some way to the family problem that led to the child abuse.

Some researchers suggest that alcohol may play a major role in specific types of child abuse. In a study of incest victims, Y.M. Tormes (undated) reports that alcohol frequently seems to be a factor in father-daughter incest occurrences.

In general, however, these studies and reports are based on subjective impressions rather than hard data. Surprisingly, although alcoholism has been singled out as a factor in child abuse, parents are rarely questioned directly about drinking practices in investigations of child abuse cases. Traditionally, the attention of social agencies and researchers who are involved with child abuse cases has been focused mainly on the protection of the child, resulting in a paucity of data about the abusers.

More recently, researchers have begun efforts to isolate the factors involved in child abuse in order to pinpoint pathways to prevention, early intervention, and family rehabilitation. Attention has been focused on situational factors, personality factors, and characteristics of the homes of abused children.

Child Abuse Factors

In examining situations in which child abuse and neglect are most likely to occur, recent research has consistently pointed to families which are socially isolated, have a parental history of abuse as a child, have youthful and inexperienced parents, and greater than average complications with pregnancies (Smith, Hanson and Noble 1974; Kent 1975). It is interesting to note that social isolation and, in many cases, childhood abuse experienced by parents are both factors common in alcoholic families.

Personality characteristics associated with child abusers are also strikingly similar in some respects to personality characteristics which describe alcoholic persons. Child abusers are most often described as having a low frustration tolerance, low self-esteem, impulsivity, dependency, immaturity, severe depression, problems with role reversals, difficulty in experiencing pleasure, and lack of understanding of the needs and abilities of infants and children (Spinetta and Rigler 1972).

Low self-esteem and low frustration tolerance are also mentioned often in connection with alcoholic people, as are most of the other characteristics cited above for child abusers. Role reversals, too, are not uncommon in alcoholic families, in which children often are expected to function as adults while the parents are engaged in an almost childlike preoccupation with self (Cork 1969, Fox 1972).

Researchers in the child abuse field have also identified characteristics which are common to children who have been abused. Whether these factors precipitated the abuse or emerged as a consequence is unknown. These factors include: retardation, deformity, illness, behavioral problems including hyperactivity, disobedience, and delinquency; and emotional problems (Caffey 1972). Certainly, such characteristics as behavioral problems, disobedience, and emotional problems are common among children of alcoholic parents as well (Bosma 1975, Chafetz, et al. 1971, Kammeier 1971, Fox 1972).

In addition, a link has been suggested between the "fetal alcohol syndrome" and child abuse. The birth defects and growth deficiencies said to occur in some children of women who drink alcoholically during pregnancy may well make the child more susceptible to abuse and neglect by a parent, researchers suggest (Mayer and Black 1976).

The similarity in situational as well as in personality factors between child abusers and alcohol abusers provides substance to the inference that there is a connection between the two problems. Still, there has been virtually no research directly addressing the relationship.

New Studies Underway

Two studies, funded recently by the Office of Child Development, Department of Health, Education, and Welfare, are currently underway aimed at determining whether the relationship exists. Although neither of the projects has produced enough data on which to base firm conclusions, both seem to offer evidence to support the connection between alcoholism and child abuse and neglect.

In Boston, the Washingtonian Center for Addictions (a private multi-modality treatment center for drug addiction and alcoholism) is engaged in a study of the child care practices of 100 alcoholic persons and 100 drug addicts. The subjects are persons in treatment at the Center.

In a preliminary report of the study findings, researchers Drs. Joseph Mayer and Rebecca Black note that "not all alcoholics seriously abuse or neglect their children, although the majority have difficulties in child rearing." As might be expected, many of the alcoholic persons are themselves children of alcoholic parents. In addition, the researchers found that many alcoholic males report they were physically punished by their parents and several reported they were abused as children.

The researchers suggest that "a substantial proportion of those families in which children are either abused or neglected are families in which there is an alcoholic parent . . . although the proportion of child abuse cases in which alcoholism may play a role varies widely depending on as yet unknown factors."

Alcoholism "may be somewhat more frequently associated with neglect than abuse," they say.

In many situations alcoholic fathers recognize that drinking creates the potential for physical abuse of their children, and some have developed conscious ways of avoiding this potential physical abuse, report Drs. Mayer and Black. "These fathers report making a deliberate decision not to discipline their children while they are drinking," the researchers have discovered. They point out that these fathers, while drinking, are considerably more likely to abuse their wives than their children.

On the other hand, there are cases of child abuse by alcoholic parents who fail to recognize the risk of abuse while drinking and who have not devised ways of protecting their children. "Interestingly, none of the alcoholics who were reported as abusing a child were in treatment at the time the abuse occurred," Drs. Mayer and Black point out.

"This suggests that recognition of the drinking problem and of problems likely to be associated with the drinking problem may help to reduce abuse of children during drinking," they suggest. Such a finding has obvious implications for child abuse prevention, adding to the reasons for providing treatment for drinking problems in families.

In looking at the question of child neglect in families with an alcoholism problem, the Boston researchers have found "considerable evidence of the occurrence of emotional neglect and inconsistency in care." Fathers who are alcoholic report total withdrawal from the children when they are drinking, and inconsistency in the amount of attention they give even when not drinking. Often, discipline is inconsistent and communication is poor.

Significantly, Drs. Mayer and Black report that their clients are eager to accept help in dealing with their child rearing problems. Alcoholic parents "welcome the opportunity to discuss their children and their relationships with their children."

In another research project in San Antonio, Texas, the Mexican American Neighborhood Civic Organization is looking at relationships between alcohol and drug abuse and child abuse/neglect with an eye to developing cooperative relationships among various agencies working with young people. The study's target area is densely populated, with a very high percentage of young people and a high proportion of low income families. The majority of the area's residents are Spanish surnamed.

Although no information from the study will be available until Spring 1977, project director Bario Chapa points out that parents who have abused their children appear to be very open in discussing their drinking behavior.

The San Antonio researchers will question 1,200 persons including a control group, a group of child abusers, and a group of substance abusers.

Treatment Gaps

The idea of cooperative arrangements between agencies dealing with child abuse cases and alcoholism treatment centers is a new concept. The bulk of treatment services for problems associated with alcohol are often focused solely on the alcoholic client. Few alcoholism treatment programs take into consideration the problems alcohol has caused for the nonalcoholic spouse and the children, although there is a growing trend toward family treatment (Hindman 1976). Child abuse, particularly, is a possibility rarely mentioned even by those providing services to children of alcoholic parents.

In the field of child abuse treatment, services designed to protect children from abuse and neglect are provided through a network of State and local agencies including hospitals, courts, the police, and public and private social welfare agencies. Often services are directly exclusively at helping the child rather than being aimed at the entire family.

Despite the association between child abuse/neglect and alcoholism that has been made by researchers in the child abuse field, there is seldom an effort to address the alcohol problem specifically in dealing with child abuse, even when the focus is on rehabilitation of the family.

Dr. Douglas J. Besharov, director of the Office of Child Development's National Center on Child Abuse and Neglect, advocates a new focus on parents, directing efforts toward rehabilitation of the family rather than relying on the tactic of removing children from the home to foster care or institutions. As an integral part of this focus, attention must be given to the factors, such as alcoholism, which may be associated with the abuse.

Most people react to seeing an abused child with "utter disbelief, denial, and avoidance," Dr. Besharov observes. "Finding the cruel and tragic conditions of the child beyond their capacity to understand, they deny the injury was deliberate." However, because child abuse is receiving more publicity, people are not likely to continue denying that it takes place, he says, warning that "now there is a danger that denial will turn to outrage and overreaction.

"But such reactions must be tempered if any progress is to be made," Dr. Besharov says. "Only with the application of objective and enlightened policies can treatment, research, prevention, and education be successfully performed. We must come to realize that there are two victims of child abuse—the child and the parent."

Well-known pediatrician Vincent J. Fontana agrees. Dr. Fontana, who is associated with the New York University College of Medicine and the New York Foundling Hospital for Parent and Child Development, says, "Few parents would willfully injure their children. However, during stressful situations some parents lose control and lash out—physically and verbally—at their children. With the many stresses all of us experience these days, there is more adult frustration and anger that can trigger child abuse." Such maltreatment can be stopped, he believes. "First, society must recognize that child abusers are not criminals but rather people badly in need of help."

Treatment Alternatives

One mode of response to this perception of parents as victims of child abuse is the voluntary self-help group, Parents Anonymous, founded in California in 1970. Patterned after Alcoholics Anonymous, the organization works through groups that provide child abusing parents with an opportunity to talk over their common problems.

Unlike AA, Parents Anonymous groups have as a sponsor a social worker or another professional concerned with child abuse. Sessions are led by members and focus on group discussions. The sponsor suggests possible resources for persons who voice a need for counseling or other assistance outside the group sessions.

A spokesperson for the nationwide organization said that many members of the 500 chapters are also members of Alcoholics Anonymous. "Alcoholism seems to be a pretty common problem among our members," she commented, although no statistics are available to support this observation. She noted that many child abusers are reluctant to seek treatment for problems such as alcoholism because of a fear of social agencies. "Many of them have had previous contact with agencies and are afraid of legal repercussions if they talk about child abuse," she observed.

In its literature, Parents Anonymous stresses the need for a family focus in preventing and treating child abuse. The organization points out that many parents who abuse their children also can and do relate to their children in healthy, loving ways. "Abuse is often only a small part of the parent-child relationship, but a part that a parent must have help in resolving if it is not to become overwhelming," the group notes.

The National Institute on Alcohol Abuse and Alcoholism supports efforts to coordinate alcoholism and child abuse treatment services more closely. "We are acutely aware of the problems faced by children of alcoholic parents and recognize that child abuse in this population is an issue that deserves more attention," comments Dr. Ernest Noble, NIAAA Director.

"Child abuse and maltreatment are family and community problems," Dr. Besharov agrees. "If we are to prevent and treat these problems, we must have a community commitment to foster the emotional and behavioral hygiene of the individual, the family, and the community. Child abuse must be understood as a function of controlled or uncontrollable personal, familial, and social stress."

Often it is a symptom of "deep personal, psychological, and social dysfunction," Dr. Besharov continues. "Similarly, alcoholism can be characterized by the same sorts of dysfunction. While there is no hard evidence, it seems clear that the person who is debilitated by alcoholism will have difficulties in caring for his or her children.

"We must teach parents that when they are under stress, their children can be in danger. We must offer help in an understanding atmosphere, even though further abuse or maltreatment cannot be condoned. Often these parents are difficult to reach, for they are usually isolated people, fearful of the possible community response to their behavior."

The social isolation of families in which both alcoholism and child abuse are present results in a double stigma, presenting special problems in early intervention and requiring the development of carefully coordinated strategies by community agencies, Dr. Besharov says.

It is clear that alcoholism treatment facilities must increase their awareness of the potential for child abuse by alcoholic parents and work to develop a similar awareness among agencies working with abused children.

As more is learned about the relationship between alcoholism and child abuse and neglect, alcoholism workers must direct greater attention to the need for:

- Incorporation of children's services into the alcoholism treatment setting, emphasizing family involvement in the treatment process, and paying special attention to the possibility of child abuse and neglect.
- Education of social agencies which deal with child abuse and neglect to the need for comprehensive family services and treatment of alcoholism and alcohol abuse problems when they are detected in abusing parents.
- Education of alcoholism workers to recognize the potential for child abuse by alcoholic parents and training to deal with the reality of child abuse in a manner which focuses on rehabilitation of the family. Professionals who come in contact with these children must be trained to recognize the early signs of potential child abuse.
- Continuation of research about the dynamics of the association between alcohol abuse and child abuse/neglect in order to develop effective and timely strategies for prevention, intervention, and rehabilitation.

References

Besharov, D.J. Building a community response to child abuse and maltreatment. *Caring*, 2(2), 1976.

Bosma, W.G.A. Alcoholism and teenagers. *Md. State Med. J.*, 24(6): 62-68, 1975.

Caffey, J. Significance of history in diagnosis of traumatic injury to children. *J. of Pediatrics*, 67, 1965.

Chafetz, M.E., Blane, H.T., and Hill, M.J. Children of alcoholics: Observations in a child guidance clinic. *Q J Stud Alc*, 32: 687-689, 1971.

Cork, M.R. *The Forgotten Children*. Toronto: Paperjacks, in association with Addiction Research Foundation, 1969.

Elmer, E. Failure to thrive: Role of the mother. *Pediatrics*, 25: 717-725, 1960.

Elmer, E. *Children in Jeopardy*. Pittsburgh: U. of Pittsburgh Press, 1967.

Fontana, V.J. We must stop the vicious cycle of child abuse. *Caring*, 2(1), 1976.

Fox, R. Treating the alcoholic's family. In: Catanzaro, R.J. (ed) *Alcoholism*. Springfield, Ill.: Charles C. Thomas, 1968 (pp. 105-115).

Hindman, M.H. Family therapy in alcoholism. *AH & RW*, 1(1): 2-9 (1976).

Kammeier, M.L. Adolescents from families with and without alcohol problems. *Q J Stud Alc*, 32: 364-372, 1971.

Kempe, C.H. and Helfer, R.E. *Helping the Battered Child and His Family*. New York: Lippincott, 1972.

Kempe, C.H., Silverman, F.N., Steele, B.F., Droegemuelle, W. and Silver, H.K. The battered child syndrome. *J. Am Med Assoc*, 181: 17-24, 1962.

Kent, J.T. What is known about child abusers? In: Harris, S.B. (ed.) *Child Abuse Present and Future*. Chicago: National Committee for Prevention of Child Abuse, 1975.

MacClennan, A. Incest—A causitive factor. *The Journal*, 4(5), 1975.

Mayer, J. and Black, R. "The Relationshipo Between Alcoholism and Child Abuse/Neglect." Paper presented at the 7th Annual Medical-Scientific Session of the National Council on Alcoholism Forum, Washington, D.C., May, 1976.

Miller, D. "Family Problems, Social Adaptation, and Sources of Help for Children of Alcoholic and Non-Alcoholic Parents." Unpublished report, 1976.

Smith, S.M., Hanson, R., and Noble, S. Social aspects of the battered baby syndrome. *Brit. J of Psychiatry*, 125: 568-582, 1974.

Spinetta, J.J. and Rigler, D. The child abusing parent: A psychological review. *Psychological Bulletin*, 77: 296-304, 1972.

DOES CHILD ABUSE CAUSE ALCOHOL ABUSE?

An interesting, but disturbing, sidelight which has received little attention in the literature is the contention by some that children who are physically abused by their parents are at high risk for turning to alcohol and drug abuse as they grow older. A New York psychiatrist, Dr. Arthur Green, testified before the New York State legislature that abused and neglected children are characterized by "self-destructive thought, anxiety, and impairment of self-concept," and that these youngsters are more likely to engage in self-destructive actions.

A recent study of female alcohol and drug abusers in residential treatment communities indicated that 44 percent had been sexually assaulted, often by a father or relative, before the age of 15. In reporting the study results, Dr. Judianne Jensen-Gerber noted, "We never look at it (sexual assault and incest) as a very important factor that brings women to alcoholism, drug abuse, acting out, running away, prostitution, illegitimacy, venereal disease. We never see trends" (MacClennan 1975).

Alcohol Health and Research World, Vol. 1, No. 3 (Spring 1977)
National Institute on Alcohol Abuse and Alcoholism. Dept. of Health, Education, and Welfare. DHEW Publ. No. (ADM) 77-157

Adolescents

EARLY ADOLESCENTS:
Neglected, Misunderstood, Miseducated

by Karl N. Stauber

MR. STAUBER IS ASSISTANT DIRECTOR OF THE MARY REYNOLDS BABCOCK FOUNDATION

This article has drawn heavily on the writings of Dr. Joan Lipsitz of the Learning Institute of North Carolina. In particular, it has used material from her recently published report to the Ford Foundation entitled "Growing Up Forgotten: A Review of Research and Programs Concerning Early Adolescence." Lexington, Massachusetts: Lexington Books, D. C. Heath and Company.

1) ***Early adolescence, from 10 to 15 years old, is a time of tremendous upheaval. Almost all children during this period are difficult, obstreperous, disruptive, and almost impossible to deal with. The best thing we can do with children during this period is to isolate them and wait for them to grow up.***
   True______ False______

2) ***Junior high students are children or, at most, in a transition stage between childhood and adolescence.***
   True______ False______

3) ***Junior high school age youth are all basically similar in their growth rate, developmental state, and social and intellectual maturity.***
   True______ False______

If you look at the social institutions in America today, you will see that they function on the premise that all three of these statements are true. We keep 10- to 15-year-olds out of the workplace, out of a vital homelife, and in the junior high/middle school or juvenile correction facility. We allow our media to portray them as typically dangerous or undesirable.

We treat them as children. We tell them to have fun with their friends, stay out of trouble, and make good grades in school. We tell them that when they grow up we will give them responsibilities.

We put them in school situations where they are grouped primarily by chronological age. We expect a sexually active 13-year-old girl to have the same basic interests and skills as a 13-year-old boy who is three years away from puberty.

If you stop to consider these statements, you will see how absurd and potentially harmful they are. Research shows that the period between 10 and 15 years of age is one of stability rather than turmoil for most adolescents. Almost all of us know a number of young people who have gone or are going through this period of life with relative ease. And yet, we continue to allow the media to portray the stereotypical teenager as a troublemaker. We continue to allow our schools, courts, and other social institutions to deny this age group an active and responsible role in our society.

We continue to ignore the fact that the onset of puberty has come four months earlier every decade. While most of us know 12-year-olds who are physiologically capable of reproduction, we continue to think of 12-year-olds as children. By continuing to ignore the present potential of these human beings, we run the risk of diminishing their own self-worth and increasing their dependence on peers for reinforcement and esteem.

In the alternative school and open school movements, we have acknowledged the fact that high school and elementary school students need optional learning experiences. Yet, during the period of life when variability of development is at its great-

Mr. Stauber is assistant director of the Mary Reynolds Babcock Foundation, in Winston-Salem, N.C., which has as one of its two major program interests the field of early adolescence.

est, during early adolescence, we stick primarily to a single educational model — the junior high school.

It is possible to quantify some of our neglect of this age group. Out of all the programs that prepare teachers in this country, only twelve programs focus on the junior high or middle school. Each year this country spends millions of dollars on juvenile delinquency yet, in fiscal year 1971, the National Institute for Child Health and Human Development spent less than 1 percent of its grants and contracts budget for research with a primary emphasis on adolescence. Out of all of the residencies and internships that exist for medical doctors, only a handful focus on the young adolescent. The major reports published during the last few years on youth (Coleman, Martin, and Brown) almost totally ignore the young adolescent. In almost every state, junior high school teachers see more students than do elementary or high school teachers. According to a September 1975 report in *Newsweek* magazine, more crimes are committed by children under 15 than by adults over 25. Out of all the doctors in the United States, only 500 are members of the Society of Adolescent Medicine. Only 5 percent of the generalists practicing family medicine, internal medicine, or pediatrics have received training in adolescent health care. The majority of runaways in this country are 15 or younger. Except for the 4-H Clubs, almost all national voluntary organizations and clubs have had declining memberships from among young adolescents over the last few years. This list could go on, but let us stop.

If you are shocked by the things we know about this age group, then you should be even more shocked by what we do not know. We do not know as a society what schooling for this age group should be. The following gaps in schooling for young adolescents must be addressed. First, there is no relationship between the junior high school as an institution and the young people whom we know from research, personal and theoretical knowledge. The major tasks of this period of life include separation, individuation, and commitment. Yet there are few aspects of schooling that currently accommodate these tasks.

Second, schools fail to recognize the differential growth rate of young adolescents. As stated earlier, schools continue to maintain age segregation and grade structures based on chronological age rather than on the developmental needs of the student.

Third, there is very little interaction between other service agencies and the schools. The schools cannot fulfill all the needs of young adolescents, and yet, some would try and hold the schools solely responsible for the health and well-being of this age group.

Fourth, there has been no recent national review of the difference between our ideology and our schooling for this age group. A growing host of conflicting demands have been placed upon the schools for this age group: end school earlier, expand dropout prevention programs, teach more of the basics, and expand career education. Given these conflicting signals, it is not surprising that the junior highs have continued to do what they have been doing for the past 60 years — make do.

In the juvenile justice area, it is clear that there is a steady climb in the arrest rate from age 10 until it peaks at 16. And yet, our current policies do little to address this fact. We know that the onset of delinquency for chronic offenders occurs at around age 12 and yet we do not know what changes need to be made in family, school, and community resources to address this early onset of criminal behavior.

In the medical and health care delivery areas, our knowledge gaps are immense. We know that our health facilities to serve this age group are limited and we know that they are bursting at the seams. We know that there are only a few medical doctors who are willing or able to specialize in serving the special needs of this age group. We know that our mental health system has failed to serve this age group at almost every level. And yet, we do not know what constitutes adequate delivery of medical or mental health care to young adolescents or how such services can be made more widely available.

In respect to families and young adolescents, what we do not know far outweighs what we do know. Many of us think we know how to be a good parent for young children, but what is the best parenting for young adolescents? Many of us think we know what we expect of the families of young children, but what do we expect of the families of young adolescents? What should we expect? What are the responsibilities of social programs to families of young adolescents?

Again, the list could go on, but even astonishment has its limits. One hopes it is clear that the myths are damaging, our neglect is appalling, and our ignorance is mighty. One could point a finger at foundations and say that they have largely ignored this age group, but so has almost everyone else. Foundations are no more responsible for this neglect than society in general. This period of life, however, is an ideal target for the types of actions in which foundations take pride.

One need is creation of a national dialogue about this age group. Foundations have already assisted in bringing this about in the areas of drug abuse, aging, and community development. By contributing to the development of such a dialogue on early adolescence, foundations can help legitimate the future involvement of all levels of government.

Identification and support of leaders and advocates for this age group is still another need. Foundations have supported these activities for minorities, and for the fields of child development, medicine, poverty and higher education. By providing such aid, foundations can assist the underrepresented and help provide society with a "passing gear" by speeding up the development of new leadership.

Foundations can also help early adolescents and those who are concerned about them by supporting research that focusses on the massive knowledge gaps surrounding this age group. Information is needed about the interrelationships among cognitive, social, and biological growth variables; or the suitability of various types of intervention programs for juvenile offenders; or the relationship between cognitive development and social groups. Interested foundations have an opportunity to help decide the research agenda relating to this age group just as they have in the areas of prenatal development, nutrition, and food production.

Foundations can help early adolescents by funding the development of networks so that those working with this age group can share their knowledge and experiences. Foundations have helped to do this in the arts, sciences, and environmental field. This type of activity supports the wider utilization of knowledge and the distribution of power.

Foundations can also support individual projects that show how services can be improved for this age group. These types of projects, which may only directly affect a few young adolescents, will provide new models for service delivery and thus increase the options available to all of us.

The Ford Foundation and the Mary Reynolds Babcock Foundation have already begun to work and grant funds in the area of early adolescence. The needs and opportunities, however, are much greater than the funds available from either or both foundations. Perhaps, however, other foundations will begin to develop an interest in this most overlooked age group among minors in America. ●

For further information, please contact: Dr. Terry Saario, the Ford Foundation, 320 East 43rd Street, New York, N.Y. 10017; or Karl Stauber, Mary Reynolds Babcock Foundation, 102 Reynolda Village, Winston-Salem, N.C. 27106.

"Early Adolescents: Neglected, Misunderstood, Miseducated," by Karl N. Stauber. Foundation News, Vol. 18, No. 5 (September/October 1977) Council on Foundations, Inc.; 888 7th Ave., New York, New York

Programs for Adolescents

Programs to prepare adolescents for their roles as parents seem to fall naturally into the public school program, although such programs may also be sponsored by civic organizations such as the Boy Scouts, Boy's Clubs of America, 4-H, Girl Scouts and neighborhood and community centers. Since schools are the major institution serving all children, they have the opportunity to design programs to bring teenagers together with young children for the mutual benefit of both.

Consideration should be given to the age level at which such experiences are provided. In light of high dropout rates at the senior high school level, as well as increasing rates of pregnancy among senior high school girls, such offerings might best be made available at the junior high level. Programs that serve this age group can provide concomitant benefits to the students at a critical point in their own development. By studying the behavior of young children, adolescents can gain insights into their own behavior at the point of their own "identity crisis."

There are also advantages in providing courses at the senior high level, however. As students progress from adolescents to young adults—as they enter those years in which family life is typically established—such courses can have a very high degree of relevance to individual students and can also serve to minimize or reduce dropout rates as students achieve a better understanding of the responsibilities associated with parenthood and the demands that may soon be made upon them.

1. *Integration with school curricula.*
If such programs are to attract a wide range of students and provide them with effective child care experiences, careful consideration must be given to their design and placement in the curricular structure. Those programs that currently exist are generally considered to be the domain of the home economics department, because of the specialized training of their staff in child development. Present programs, however, reach only a small fraction of those who will eventually need parenthood education.

Most of these programs fail to provide students any actual experience with the young children they are ostensibly learning about. The programs usually are confined to one instructional department within the high school, rather than reaching out to the resources of the entire school system.

This is not to say that there are no home economics departments operating excellent programs. For example, the Texas Department of Education offers a broad-based, three-part program in homemaking education, comprised of classroom courses in family living and child development, work-study opportunities as child-care aides and pre-employment laboratory training in child development. All three aspects provide experiences working with young children; all three (but especially the work-study program) attract relatively large numbers of boys—about one-third of the total homemaking enrollment. Although based in an existing instructional department, the Texas homemaking program reaches out to other departments and to the community as resources.

Not all departments are so flexible, however. The assignment of parenting programs to any single professional domain needs careful examination. Possibly more effective programs could be afforded through the combined efforts of a number of departments. Many disciplines have a contribution to make to the clear understanding of the changing nature of the family and the impact of the modern world on child-rearing practices.

Cooperation is required not only among departments within the high school but also among the various age divisions as well. Secondary school efforts should be articulated with elementary education and adult education, thus at least partially relieving the age segregation that so restricts young people's lives. The contributions of community agencies and individuals with particular professional competence should be incorporated into a team effort. Pediatricians, dentists, mental health nurses and parents could be extensively involved in the planning and implementation of such programs.

It is this kind of broad-based cooperation that the U.S. Office of Education and the Office of Child Development are hoping to encourage through their joint effort in developing programs across the country in "Education for Parenthood." Three major projects make up this program: (1) development and dissemination of a model curriculum for secondary school students, called "Exploring Childhood"; (2) a survey and report on other parenthood education curriculums and materials now being used in schools; and (3) grants to several national voluntary youth-serving organizations to promote parenthood education programs among young people in communities throughout the nation.

"Exploring Childhood" is designed as a one-year elective course for teenage boys and girls, adaptable to the needs of adolescents of varied cultural backgrounds. The curriculum combines classroom study with field-site experience in child care settings. Teachers guides, teacher training materials and a manual for school administrators interested in starting an "Exploring Childhood" program in their districts will be made available.

2. *Suggested approaches.*
No single approach to parenthood education can suit the concerns or resources of every community. However, states wishing to revise the home economics or family living curriculum at the junior high and high school levels should consider the usefulness of the following approaches to providing students with preparation for parenthood:

a. *Providing field experience with young children.* This must be considered a central factor in any program seeking to move beyond the traditional homemaking or family living classroom course. Some high schools have established and operated child development laboratories within their own buildings. Others have joined forces with nearby kindergartens or formed cooperative agreements with child care centers. The students can participate in the laboratory or center two or three days a week. On other days, they attend courses in child development, parenting or family living and learn to integrate their classroom learning with their actual experiences with young children.

The Montgomery County public school system in Maryland has instituted a year-long course at the senior high level that provides for student involvement in child development laboratories located in each of the system's high schools. Lab experience includes planning, observation, research and interaction with very young children. In addition to providing training for parenthood, students receive occupational training in child care. This type of laboratory learning is provided, on a rotating basis, to several thousand students each year.

Child centers, located within or near the high school, can provide opportunities for students in a variety of classes. Cooking classes may take responsibility for planning nutritive meals and get practical experience in the preparation and serving of food. Business students might participate in the center's administrative operation. Much of the basic center equipment, from furniture to blocks, might be made in the shop courses. The drama, music and arts departments could each offer their particular talents.

b. *Using films and other media.* Films, film strips and audio cassettes enable the instructor to bring case studies into the classroom that might be difficult to observe in their natural setting. Videotapes of the students working in the center can provide an important dimension to the classroom critique.

c. *Providing work-study programs,* in which junior and senior high school students work part-time in Head Start, day care centers and other programs for children are now quite common. States that wish to encourage school programs that contribute to preparation for parenthood should first ascertain what is already being done at the local school level. Once information becomes available, a state might well bring together the educators who have already been involved in order to make plans for wider utilization of effective curriculum related to field experience.

d. *Providing career preparation.* These programs require more intensive and more supervised on-the-job training, with related classroom instruction. The aim is to provide students with marketable skills in addition to the general training in child development, child care and parenting.

While the above listing does provide examples of possible options for the consideration of state departments of education, it cannot be emphasized strongly enough that any approach or combination of approaches must be coordinated with the programs of other departments and agencies. An incoherent "layering on" of new programs, in addition to being needlessly expensive, cannot result in the targeting of scarce resources to meet the most urgent unmet needs of children and families.

Two other excerpts from The Role of the Family in Child Development: Implications for State Policies and Programs can be found in this book. One is the second item in this CHILDREN section and one is Item 10 in the ADULTS section.

Excerpted from The Role of the Family in Child Development: Implications for State Policies and Programs; The fifteenth report of The Education Commission of the States Early Childhood Project (December 1975). Denver, Colorado. Reprinted with permission.

Group Foster Homes

Dodie Butler, Runaway House and Group Foster Home Counselor with Joe Reiner, New Education Project Coordinator and Bill Treanor, SAJA Coordinator

Annie came to the Runaway House in the spring of the year. A 15-year-old with raggedy red hair, she arrived with a suitcase and a fantastic story about having been a runaway for several months, just stopping in D.C. on the way north from Florida. A couple of days later, we discovered that she was from an extremely abusive home in suburban Virginia. After some pressure from the RH counselors, Annie agreed to call her parents to assure them that she was alive and well. Much to her surprise, she discovered that her parents had disappeared! They had split from Virginia the day after Annie did, taking their other five kids with them, and could not be found.

We learned from Annie that her parents often moved abruptly, without telling the kids in advance and that she had attended twelve different public and parochial schools. Later we learned that Annie's father was a petty criminal—something the kids in the family did not know. The police were after him for forgery. To keep their location a secret, the parents often kept their kids out of school for months after moving to a new town.

We had a devil of a time finding a jurisdiction which would claim Annie. D.C. would not recognize her as its problem and the suburban city she ran from was not willing to take her into custody because her parents were no longer residents of the town! We finally badgered the Virginia jurisdiction into taking Annie into the custody of its child welfare department, but the entire process took nearly 6 weeks.

About five percent of the kids coming through the Runaway House (four or five a month) are kids like Annie, society's throwaways. These are kids with no alternatives—nowhere to go, no one who wants them. They come from hostile or indifferent environments and are at a loss as to where to turn. Because of the shortage of foster homes for teenagers, there is great likelihood that they will be institutionalized if arrested for being on the streets.

During the first year and a half that Runaway House was open, we ran into many of these throwaways. Several of them spent extended periods of time at the house; some lived there for 6 months to a year. The transient nature of RH wasn't particularly good for these people, but there were no alternatives.

With this population in mind, we decided to establish an alternative ourselves: a group foster home. The idea was that the house would be a full-time residence—a home—for these "throwaway" kids. Annie was eventually placed in this home by a juvenile court judge. We thought that most of the kids would live there for a fairly short time (2 or 3 months), until a suitable situation, perhaps a foster family, was found. We found that those "suitable situations" were scarce, and the length of stay was extended to 6 months and finally extended to the 18th birthday, or to the time when the young person could take care of himself.

We were planning to house a population similar to that which came through Runaway House—black and white, male and female, young people between the ages of 13 and 18. We felt that this mixture would provide the greatest opportunity for service and would lead to a positive living/learning experience for the kids. We did not want a "Boys' Home" or a "Girls' Home," but a real family experience. In accepting both sexes into one group foster home, we've given the young people the opportunity to develop friendships other than the narrow dating relationships that often prevail during adolescence. We've had few problems with the kids exploiting this living arrangement. On the contrary, they seem to need and enjoy the brother/sister relationships that have grown among them.

In planning the "Second House" (RH is obviously the first), we decided to have two staff members, one male and one female, as full-time residential counselors. Running a paraprofessional project the way we do means cutting expenses to the bare minimum, i.e., hiring live-in counselors rather than paying three, 8-hour shifts.

Even more important than the financial necessity for live-in staff is the necessity for a "homelike" situation. Male and female staff members living in the house contribute to a natural, rather than an institutional environment. The two counselors are male and female models for the kids. This home environment provides much security and stability that these young people's lives have lacked. People are living in the house together—it is their home.

Our feeling is that most of the kids who are removed from the community, "sent up", are removed at a detriment to themselves, to the community, and to the people who actually do need to be institutionalized. These kids can live in the community, they can live with people. They need love, families, and the experience of living with others. More programs housing "throwaway" kids would alleviate the incredible overcrowding in detention facilities and in public residential treatment facilities, and would allow these institutions to better serve the people who really do need to be removed from the community. Kids can be cared for in group foster homes at a much lower cost than in institutions. The money saved can be used by the community for other purposes.

Establishing a House

When organizing a paraprofessional, low-budget group foster home, three things must be done simultaneously: you must assemble a staff, find the actual building to house the project, and track down financing to cover the initial months of operation. You can't open for business until they fall together, yet there is no chronological order.

Many people organizing youth service projects try to get funding before staff, or house, or kids. We feel strongly that lack of financing does not have to halt the project. You can start the house with almost no money and ask financial sources to donate money to keep it going. You'll probably need about $5,000 to cover the first 3 or 4 months. We creamed seed money for Second House from foundation grants to Runaway House. Anyway, you can pull together staff and real estate while looking around for seed money.

When searching for project housing, it helps if you make a friend who is a real estate agent to tip you off to listings, and housing and zoning codes. He can help you to understand the ins and outs of renting and buying property.

The Origins of Second House

In November of 1969, we hired Judy Tobin, 24. Judy had a year's experience as a child welfare worker in Cincinnati, and a year's work as a D.C. Youth Division policewoman. She was tired of established social welfare work and agreed to be the woman counselor at Second House. Judy spent November familiarizing herself with the counseling situation and the kids at Runaway House. We tentatively hired a seminary student to be the second counselor. November was spent tracking down a house and financial backing.

We searched for a house for a long time and could find nothing in the Dupont Circle neighborhood, where RH is located. Judy happened to be going with an SAE (Sigma Alpha Epsilon) fraternity member who knew that the SAE house in the neighborhood (1856 19th St.) was failing and that the fraternity was looking for someone to take the house off its hands. We were able to rent the four story, 10-bedroom house for only $225 a month, which covered the owner's taxes and insurance. This is a perfect example of how personal contacts, luck, and just talking to everyone you know pays off.

The staff, money, and building for the project all fell together about the first of the year. Judy and the seminary student moved into the house around the first of December. One thing that slowed progress was the extensive remodeling and repair work required on the 19th Street house. This took a lot of staff time and energy, and slowed the process of filling the house with kids. The building had been a party house for the fraternity and was in a shambles. It took time and even more effort to make the house liveable to meet the D.C. requirements for rooming and boarding house licenses . . . which we had to have to house and feed the kids legally. When we opened our second group foster home, Third House (we've never been very creative in naming projects) in 1971, we were very careful to obtain a house that did not require extensive repair.

Jay Berlin, 22, a Georgetown University Foreign Service School graduate, was hired to replace the seminary student as the second counselor during the first part of January.

At that time we were operating under a minimum number of assumptions: We knew that we wanted to serve the population of "throwaways." We were planning to have a male and a female counselor and about 10 kids. We felt that we would need a psychiatrist. We were not sure how he would fit in and left that decision to the future. Bill Treanor had previously contacted the National Institute of Mental Health. A psychiatrist in their adolescent program, working with runaways, was very interested in working with Runaway House. When Bill discussed the idea of a group foster home, the psychiatrist agreed to work with us.

Having run into so many throwaway kids at Runaway House, we knew there was a great need for this group foster home, and felt that it would be easy to fill the house. We still thought that the length of stay would be from a few weeks to a few months. We had worked well with throwaways at RH and expected a high rate of success.

These assumptions were tested as Second House evolved. In some ways, as you will see, they were very naive, but we were correct in assuming that there was a need for a group foster home, and that we could make it work.

Filling the House

Bill Treanor took a 4-month leave of absence and traveled to Mexico in January. So it was up to the counselors to make Second House work. The house had been established to take care of throwaways who showed up at Runaway House, yet we had to find a way to cover expenses. We also wanted Second House to be legitimate, i.e., legal. Therefore, it was decided that kids who came through the Runaway House, who were to be placed at Second House, would have to be placed there legally. The Runaway House counselors, with the consent of the individual involved, would take the kid to court, have him placed in the custody of his local welfare department and then placed in our group foster home. This is not as difficult as it sounds. There are few alternatives for kids of this type. Judges are usually happy that we have everything set up in advance and are willing to take these kids off their hands. In this way we are able to receive child support stipends from welfare departments for kids referred by Runaway House.

In cases where the parents were closely involved, and recognized a need for foster placement for their child, the RH counselors arranged for child support from the parents.

The most certain way to make sure that the house was self-supporting was to take not only kids who came through Runaway House, but also kids on referral from other agencies such as public and private social welfare agencies, psychiatric facilities and juvenile courts . . . and from parents. We decided to do this for monetary reasons more than anything else. We also wanted to have the house filled to capacity as quickly as possible because we wanted to work with the maximum number of people that we could help at one time. We knew that welfare departments in D.C. and the surrounding counties would be able to pay to place their kids on their caseloads with us. These kids are throwaways who would normally be placed in mental hospitals or overcrowded detention facilities.

We typed letters of introduction announcing our presence as a new resource for teenage placement and sent them to all the appropriate agencies (public and private, religious and nonreligious social welfare agencies, counseling services, mental health and psychiatric facilities). We found these in a directory published for our area. We tried to cover the five jurisdictions that most of the Runaway House population comes from, the four counties surrounding the District (Arlington and Fairfax in Virginia, Montgomery and Prince Georges in Maryland), and the District of Columbia itself. We followed up these letters with phone calls asking for personal appointments so that we could describe more fully what we were trying to do and what services we offered. We asked for suggestions and found out what the agencies' needs were.

In the process of these interviews, we actually trained ourselves in making contacts and working with agencies. As our awareness of the needs of the established agencies grew, we were able to incorporate this information in our proposed program. In this way we acquainted the community with our project while acquiring referrals.

In making agency contacts for referrals, the best people to deal with are the actual caseworkers who have kids needing placement. Try to arrange a monthly meeting with caseworkers and supervisors. You'll find these caseworkers on the staffs of juvenile courts, welfare departments, and private agencies. Also make yourselves known to public defenders and other lawyers who handle juvenile court cases. It is important to have the supervisors present at these meetings so that you can answer their questions and meet any objections or doubts in their minds. But the real source of referrals, and access to the system, is the workers.

Most caseworkers, especially those working for public agencies, have unbearable caseloads. Yet they really want to find good placements for all their kids—placements which are not readily available. If you are offering something that makes sense, is within their financial reach, and is good for the kids, the caseworker will try to use your house and may even buck his superiors if necessary.

This is the process that we followed to build up the group at the Second House. It took us too long to fill the house to capacity (nearly nine months) because we had to feel our way along. However, if you make a point of sending out letters and following them up with personal appointments with supervisors, and if you address meetings of caseworkers, and pursue every lead you get, you should be able to fill a house with six to eight kids, once you have a staff, etc., in a couple of months. We were able to do this when we opened Third House, a year later.

When we applied for Government funding, we had to have letters of endorsement from the agencies placing kids at Second House. We found that these letters were very helpful in getting other agencies and influential people to back us. It added greatly to our credibility. You can do the same thing—get letters of endorsement for your project from mental health facilities, psychiatrists, judges, and public welfare departments. Each letter you receive can be used to support your request for the next one.

Dealing With the System

It is important to note that we did not ask anyone for permission to open Second House. We decided, at the very inception of the project, that we would comply with the laws and regulations necessary for the maintenance of the house, but would find ways to get around those laws and regulations that were totally unreasonable or detrimental to the kids.

It is almost always possible to get around anything. These are our organizing rules of thumb: 1) never ask permission; and 2) learn to get around obstacles. We establish a project, start working with kids, and leave the burden of responsibility for enforcing regulations on the bureaucrat. We deal with laws and regulations when we run into them—but do not go looking for trouble by seeking permission. In this situation the contradictions in the system can work to your advantage. You can juxtapose the judges and caseworkers placing kids with you (as their only alternative to institutionalization) against the bureaucrat hassling you about the triple kitchen sink required for a boarding house license. The District is somewhat unique in that there is no specific licensing procedure for group foster homes or halfway houses. It is not clear how much our experience can help people in other parts of the country.

In seeking referrals from the District of Columbia Welfare Department, we discovered that they referred kids on a contract basis negotiated between the private agency and the welfare department. Child care stipend, type of case referred, services rendered, and maximum number of cases to be referred, are enumerated in the contract. After 9 months of negotiation, inspection, and attempts to meet the welfare department's varied requirements for the boarding and rooming house licenses (we could not afford a dishwasher or heavy metal fire doors) we were accepted by the welfare department under license pending status.

Perhaps other paraprofessionals starting group foster homes or halfway houses in jurisdictions which have specific licensing procedures for this type of service project can get around requirements for professional degrees, supervision, etc., by becoming "boarding houses for youth" instead.

We went to all the trouble of obtaining the contract with the D.C. Welfare Department for several reasons. We wanted Second House to serve not only the white population of the suburbs but the black population of the community around us as well. We wanted D.C. kids who come through the Runaway House to have the option of Second House—which was available through D.C. court placement via welfare department custody.

We also sought a D.C. contract to gain legitimacy with the surrounding suburban jurisdictions and with private agencies. The suburban jurisdictions have no means of licensing a facility that is not within their territories and, therefore, use the existence of our D.C. contract as a quasi-license. Consequently, we became a placement facility with the D.C. Welfare Department, even though the stipend that the welfare department was willing to pay per child per month was inadequate and even though this stipend was less than what we were charging. It was vital that Second House be recognized by the District as a foster care service.

It is important to arrive at the proper monthly stipend as soon as possible. We originally charged $200 per month per child, but that figure was more arbitrary than realistic. There are two criteria for determining monthly rates. The first, of course, is a determination of actual operating expenses, prorated over the number of kids to be housed. Before you send out letters stating your costs, do some research and find out what similar projects in your area are charging in order to determine what the traffic will bear.

Two-hundred dollars a month was inadequate to cover our expenses and we presently charged $350 a month per person. We don't get that from everyone—the District doesn't pay us that much, although we are attempting to revise the District rate. When we take kids on private contract from their parents, we negotiate a contract with the individual parents, arriving at an amount based on what we need and what they can afford to pay.

Three hundred and fifty dollars per month is an institutional rate, which we qualify for because of the services and supervision we offer and because we have professional (volunteer) consultants. This is much higher than the monthly rate that families receive when taking a foster child.

Our two group foster homes just about support themselves. At full capacity they each post about a $350 surplus, which evens out over the long run during the weeks that the houses operate under full capacity. This also covers the discrepancy in payments for D.C. kids and people on private placement.

Building Up the Group

We built up a group slowly. The first Second House resident was placed there by her parents, a 15-year-old girl who came through Runaway House in January, 1970. The girl needed to be out of the home while her parents went through a painful divorce. This private referral gave us credibility in seeking public referrals.

The second person we took was also a girl, aged 14, referred by a psychiatric facility. She had been in residential treatment for over a year and her living at Second House was seen as a way to ease her back into the community.

We then took in a boy on referral from a suburban public welfare agency. The welfare caseworker, whom we had met during our initial meetings, referred the 17-year-old to us. The next boy, age 16, came through the same suburban welfare department.

Two girls, ages 18 and 15, came to us in the summertime via the Runaway House. RH counselors handled the job of tracking down financial resources. One of these girls was taken into suburban court custody and then placed with us. We were able to take the other girl when a private individual agreed to provide $100 per month for her support. Both girls were the throwaway kids that Second House was established for.

During this time, January through August of 1970, we were trying to solicit outside funds as much as possible, but the money from referrals was keeping us alive. We were not actually self-supporting until the contract with the D.C. Welfare Department went through in September. At that time, three black kids from D.C. were placed with us, two boys, both 14, and a 17-year-old girl. This filled the house. Second House operated at a deficit of $8,000 during the first year. This was covered by extra money raised for Runaway House.

In September 1970, Dodie Butler, 21, moved into Second House to replace Judy Tobin who had enrolled in Catholic University's School of Social Work. Dodie had worked for Runaway House for the past 7 months and therefore, as a member of SAJA's extended family, knew the kids and the Second House routine. The transition period evolved naturally, as Judy became involved in her class work and gradually moved out of the house.

Developing Intake Procedures

Not long after we opened Second House, we decided that we needed some way of screening the kids who would live there. It was at that time that we began to work with our psychiatric consultant. After some discussion with him, we decided that it would be wise for him to interview the candidates for the house. We discovered that most referring agencies have tested and evaluated the kids on their caseloads and that, as a placement agency, we had a right to see the tests. So we asked for a written social history and a psychiatric evaluation of each person referred to Second House. When kids are referred by Runaway House, the RH counselors arrange for evaluations by volunteer psychiatrists or the local mental health clinic.

This step is used to screen out people who are inappropriate for the program—for example, kids with a history of violent criminal behavior, addiction to hard drugs or girls who are pregnant or with dependent children. These are kids we cannot help due to the open nature of the house and our own limited skills as counselors.

Unless this written material shows that the case is totally inappropriate for Second House, we arrange an interview conducted by the consulting psychiatrist with the counselors present. The purpose of this interview is to meet the young person, to find out how he feels about himself, how he handles problems, and to determine his needs. It also serves to acquaint him with what Second House is and what we have to offer him.

We decided at the very outset of the project that we would only take kids who wanted to live in our group foster home. No one can be placed with us against his wishes.

By the time we make a decision on admitting a young person, we have received four sets of information: the social worker's initial contact with the runaway which usually includes a description of the young person from the worker's subjective point of view, a written psychological evaluation, a written social history, and a personal interview with the psychiatrist present. After the interview the counselors meet with the psychiatrist to discuss what they saw, what they thought the kid was into, and what they felt about living and working with the individual. Then in consultation with the psychiatrist, we set initial expectations for each individual entering the house.

The admittance decision determines the composition and the focus of the foster home. It also influences, to a large extent, the eventual structure of the house. If the counselors accept young people who are into acting-out or whose behavior is self-destructive, their relationship with the kids will involve giving permission, physical controls, and other restricting measures. If the kids entering the foster home have few needs for external controls, the staff's role can be more flexible. The counselors must assess themselves and their own capabilities in dealing with these kids and must decide what relationship they want with the people in the house.

This admissions procedure is critical from the young person's point of view. Kids want to make it in the group foster home. Admitting someone we could not cope with would be tantamount to setting him up for failure. We can't promise that we'll be able to handle every kid we accept into the house, but evaluating our abilities accurately can prevent our causing more damage to the individual. Usually we can win a young person's affection and admiration rapidly.

Each new resident has a 10-day trial period in the house. This gives him a chance to see how he feels about the group living situation, and we can get an idea of how he will fit into the house. If it were to become evident during this trial period that the situation was unworkable, we would make other living arrangements for the new person.

At various times there have been suggestions that the kids in the house have a voice in the selection of new members—none of which have really stuck. We leave the admission decision to the house counselors and psychiatrist who, hopefully, have a more long-range view of the situation.

Actually Running the House

By October 1970, things were finally together! We had everything we needed, including kids, and then all we had to do was to run a group foster home. But it was not as easy as all that.

Second House was established because of a need we found in the Runaway House. Several throwaway kids had lived at RH for extended periods of time—two girls for nearly a year. We felt that it was inappropriate for kids to live at RH for so long. Although we had had a few behavior problems at RH, we did not anticipate the behavior problems that we eventually ran into as kids were placed in Second House.

Runaway House is a very transient place and the environment is, for the most part unstructured. Kids who live at RH for extended periods of time have to fend for their own food and obey house rules, but few demands and little responsibility are placed on them. There must be a survival mechanism within the chaos of Runaway House to hold intact those kids who have been abused so much of their lives. At Second House, where there is a higher level of demand and responsibility placed upon them—plus a much higher level of security—that mechanism disappears and the kids often act out their emotional problems. This acting out involves running away, sometimes severe drug abuse, outbursts of violence directed at the counselors and at each other, and destructive sexual relationships.

Our original assumption had been that taking a kid from an unhealthy home and transplanting him in a healthy, supportive environment would solve his problems. We soon revised that assumption!

We soon learned that most kids go through a behavioral "cycle" after they move into the safety of a group foster home. During his early days at the house, a person will be very "good" while he feels out the people and environment around him. Then as trust and security build up, there is more testing of limits and acting out against real or imagined threatening situations. Many kids, having been starved for trust and affection for so long, are extremely frightened by the warmth and intimacy of the group foster home. After months of trial and error, testing and acting out, a more open, healthy person emerges, a person who has learned to confront and deal with his personal problems and who no longer sees the world around him as a hostile place to live.

When we started Second House, we tried to simulate a family, the counselors assuming parental roles. It was apparent that the kids tended to regard the counselors as substitute parents, and as authority figures.

In these parental roles we took responsibility for the kids' behavior, made many decisions for them, and "mothered" them a lot. We assumed these roles in response to the needs we perceived in the young people and as a result, set up a confusing situation, obviously we're not their parents. We were too young and the living situation was too temporary for us to be able to be "good parents" to them. We compounded the confusion by telling the kids we were not their parents, all the while fulfilling parental functions. They responded with the same defenses that had served to insulate them from their real parents.

We are continually reevaluating our roles as workers in the group foster homes. This process has at times been painful as we have had to reject many of the working assumptions that each of us has brought to the project. The counselor must respond to the ages and needs of the kids involved. His role depends on the amount of control and structure that the individuals in the house need and on the personalities and abilities of the workers involved.

Rules and structures can quickly take on a meaning of their own. It is important to be aware of this and to continually review the effectiveness of any rules and structures you come up with. Remember the goal of the rule or structure and check out whether or not it facilitates arrival at that goal. For example, if your goal is that kids take responsibility for helping keep the house clean, do not take that responsibility from them by forcing them to do work. Instead come up with something that will encourage them to take the initiative. Heavy rules can stifle kids' taking initiative to act responsibly.

We were each raised within the American single family unit. Therefore it is a continual struggle to develop new ways of group living in the foster homes. We do not want to be into a parental control trip and are learning to relate to the kids in the group foster homes as people, not as "SAJA kids." Much of the demand for this evolution of our ideas has come from the kids. We have a lot more to learn from them.

As the group takes more power and responsibility for decisionmaking within the houses and within SAJA staff, people are breaking out of their counselor roles. In doing so we are more able to be real, fallible human beings. And we're breathing a sigh of relief!

As a paraprofessional project, a counter-cultural organization, and as an organization operating on the brink of financial disaster, we are opposed to employing housekeepers, cooks, etc. All tasks to be done in the house are assumed by the people living in the house.

Everyone is responsible for doing dishes and for cooking dinners on a rotating schedule. Indeed, we feel it is almost a political issue. Everyone has to cook dinner—male and female, kids and staff—or wash floors, or take out the garbage. Our group foster homes are homes, not institutions, and cooks and housekeepers do not fit that image. We feel that it is important for kids to learn to cook, clean, and work together as part of learning to take care of themselves.

Our experience in the group foster home has a long and often unsuccessful history with regard to getting chores done. The best method seems to be sitting down with the kids, deciding what work needs to be done, and splitting it up among all the people in the house. Then decide who will see that the jobs get done, what penalties there should be (if any) for jobs allowed to slide, and how to get occasional big jobs done. Good luck at coming up with a working system for getting the mundane work done. Our experience has been that we have a meeting, set up a system which works for a while, and when enthusiasm for that system winds down and the mess becomes unbearable, we have another meeting and try again.

Initially we required that all of the kids in the house go to school. In time, however, we found that a mandatory school policy was detrimental for many reasons. The absentee rate at the high school was approaching 40 percent. There was an amazing proliferation of drugs. The racial discrimination, instability, insecurity, and fear operating in the school were all the things we were trying to alleviate in the lives of our kids. Several of the young people at Second House had learning difficulties, stemming from inadequate elementary school backgrounds. This made it extremely difficult for them to keep up in class. The remedial programs at the school were totally inadequate. It turned out that society's and the welfare department's demands that the kids go to school were actually very destructive.

School attendance is no longer a requirement at SAJA's group foster homes. We do believe, however, that a young person's time should be structured. Now our kids do not have to go to public school. They can have full time jobs, when appropriate, or can go to vocational or trade schools. Also, SAJA's eventual solution to the lack of individual attention and the impossible learning situation in the public schools was to start its own school, a free school, in the fall of 1971. But that is another story.

Structuring the Summer

The first summer (1970) at Second House, there were five kids in the house and we did not structure any summer activities. The kids did not have jobs, nor did they go to school, and the summer stretched into a long period of boredom. The kids were around the house most of the time and had very little to do. There was also a much higher potential for them to get into trouble, since their time was not structured. Contact with each other 24 hours a day made everyone irritable in the hot summer weather.

The next summer we decided to offer diversified activities and to require that the kids' time be structured somehow. We borrowed a farm in Maryland, about an hour and a half from D.C. so that the kids could spend time out of the city. We also created jobs for the kids in the houses through Neighborhood Youth Corps program that we set up. In this way the kids were able to make some money, meet new people, and feel that they had accomplished something.

Structuring time so that the kids are out of the house during part of each day is important during the winter as well as during the summer. This offers them diversified contacts, and experiences and takes a great load off the counselors. This can be done several ways. The organization can offer programs, as we did, that give the kids positive ways to fill their time. Volunteers may be able to take individual kids camping or traveling, which offers new experiences and much needed personal attention. Or the kids can get jobs on their own, which gives them a certain feeling of independence.

In October of 1971 we finally hired a support person who would work in both houses and take some of the load off the counselors. He is George Allen, 26, a graduate of the University of Kentucky Law School. The need for more staff in the group homes was apparent for a long time but we were unable to afford another staff person until the fall of 1971. This need became especially clear when we hired a couple to staff Third House. For the first 3 months of their work at Third House they were unable to take time off together because there was no one to cover the house for them.

The swing counselor, who does not live in either house, can gain an overview of the situation in the houses. He is a more detached person than the counselors living in the houses, which makes his decisions valuable. Since his role is different than that of the house counselors, he is another kind of person for the kids to relate to. His role is still evolving as his job is defined according to the needs of the separate houses, taking into consideration his personality and abilities.

People often ask if we have regular counseling sessions scheduled in the houses. We do not. Counseling is a 24-hour-a-day process. The young person's time is spent as nearly as possible like any other teenager's. A Second House kid lives at "home" with his "family"—a circle of people who care about him deeply. He does not live in an institution. His friends come over for dinner. He spends the daytime in school or at a job. He comes home and does his chores or cooks dinner, and spends evenings at home or out with friends.

One thing that differentiates our house from regular family homes is the weekly group meeting attended by all members of the house. During the time we were planning Second House, we discussed the possibility of weekly groups with our consulting psychiatrist who agreed to be present at those meetings. However, he never conducted the groups, and attended as a non-participating observer.

Weekly group meetings have been used in a number of ways. Sometimes they were used as business sessions, sometimes as legislative sessions establishing house rules and schedules; sometimes they were heavy, emotional sessions involving group confrontation of an individual's behavior. Eventually we decided to hold separate business meetings so that regular groups could be counted on as a vehicle for dealing with emotional situations.

Group sessions have always been useful in alleviating tension in the house because they provide a situation in which it is O.K. to let down defenses, cry, or shout at each other. This can be very important, but how well the group is handled depends on the training and skill of the people involved.

We still need time and money to better train our staff in group techniques. When organizing a group home, find a volunteer psychiatrist or psychologist who will train and advise the staff in group work so they will know what to look for and understand how the group and individuals within the group react.

It was partially for this reason—our inexperience and inability to cope with some of the kids in the group—that we decided to get another psychological consultant. This person was to advise us in working with groups and in specific, difficult cases. We also wanted someone who could help us with interpersonal problems among the staff.

We're talking about counselors working under almost impossible demands, 24 hours a day in an atmosphere where crises often arise. Terrific pressure can build up due to the time factor and demands from the kids. This pressure and any interpersonal staff conflicts must be alleviated somehow. We found it extremely helpful, if not vital, to have a safety valve structured into the work week. This took the form of therapy sessions, or talk sessions, for the staff members with a trained person to whom the staff members could relate easily.

Counseling in one of our group foster homes is sort of an asexual marriage. The personal consultant helps the male and female counselors sort out the problems they are having in living, working, and holding down responsibility together. It is easy to fall into games with the people with whom one is living. It is vital to keep this from obstructing the goal of the house: working with kids. It is also important that the two people working together be able to support one another and honestly give each other feedback. Having a personal consultant aids this process.

As time went on and problems presented themselves, we found that we were able to deal with or get around most of the obstacles to the continuing operation of Second House—i.e., financial and legal problems, interpersonal conflicts, and problems with the kids. In the process we built up a backup group of people who could be termed consultants but might be more properly called resource people. These were lawyers, doctors, dentists, judges, plumbers, caseworkers, and friends in general on whom we could draw when we needed them. If it is ever useful, when you are applying for funds, you might designate people as "consultants" who volunteer time as resource persons. (But be sure to check with each one before including him in your total number of consultants.) We have often done this.

Most of the kids who come to us from welfare are on Medicaid and can get free medical care from a Medicaid registered doctor. It is a good idea to find a family doctor, a professional you can trust, and talk him into doing the paper work involved in registering for Medicaid. Don't just go to any Medicaid doctor. If your project is exciting, you should be able to attract people for this purpose. Having a doctor you can rely on and call at any time is extremely important.

When we started the Second House, in the 10-bedroom barn on 19th Street, we were planning to have two counselors and 10 kids. After several chaotic months with two counselors and eight or nine kids, it became obvious that the kids were unable to receive the kind of individual attention they needed because of sheer numbers. In February of 1971, three kids we could not cope with left Second House. We decided then to maintain the house at a capacity of six. This policy was held to in our second group foster home, the Third House.

Paraprofessionals operating youth service projects, for which there are few models, are often unsure of themselves—we were, in organizing Second House, unsure young adults caring for juveniles adjudicated "delinquent." They may grope toward a person, or a set of theories, willing to provide "answers." Acceptance of one consultant's point of view, or a rigid theory for dealing with adolescents can severely limit the scope and effectiveness of the program.

For a while we almost forgot that we were paraprofessionals. This state of mind evolved while we were consulting with a psychiatric social worker, who was heavily into Transactional Analysis (T.A.) (re. Eric Berne, *Games People Play*), from February 1970 to September 1970. She had developed a very demanding, highly structured, parental method of working with schizophrenics. Due to our own insecurities, we accepted her suggestions on how to structure the houses and how to work with groups and how to deal with individuals within the houses.

This was destructive for us, for the kids, and for the projects. In both Runaway House and Second House, we got into "therapizing" the kids. We spent hours rapping with kids about their problems, the historical origins of these problems, etc., rather than actively doing things with them. At Second House we assumed heavy parenting roles with the kids. Yet the counselors, who were in their early 20's, were obviously not parents. This brought about destructive dependency relationships, as well as confusion and hostility among the kids.

Due to this side trip into therapy, we also felt that we could handle kids with whom we could not actually cope. Some of the kids we took into Second House at that time required a more structured environment and more controls on their behavior than the counselors were competent to supply. This drained the energies of the counselors and also caused the kids, who did not act out violently, to be overlooked in the chaos of the house.

Most of our training in counseling, structuring the environment within the houses, and running groups, during that period of time, came from this one consultant. Although we finally recognized the dangers of the course we were on, it still took months of questioning and relearning to "debrief" ourselves from this tightly structured way of relating to kids.

To avoid becoming trapped in a narrow theory of adolescent behavior, it is important to maintain a kind of check-and-balance among professional consultants and the theories of behavior that they are into. Make sure that you find therapists for kids who need therapy—you can't supply it as an untrained para-professional. Know your limitations. Take only those kids who have a chance of success in your program. These kids need no more failures in their lives.

There are no pat answers when you are living and working with kids. There are lots of questions, and there are ideas that grow and change with experience. Although it may be uncomfortable, it is necessary to operate without "answers" to respond and change as the needs and problems of the project evolve.

Using Volunteers in the Group Foster Homes

When you come right down to it, we are pretty skeptical of volunteers. It is very difficult to shift responsibility onto a part-time volunteer who has little information about what has been happening among the people in the house on a day-to-day basis. We are very protective of the houses and do not want the effectiveness of the project to become diluted through the presence of several volunteers.

Because of the 24-hour nature of the counseling job at the group foster home, we maintain very close contact with all the kids. Therefore the need for volunteer support in actually running the house is minimal.

We select volunteers almost as carefully as we select staff members. We check out motives, personality, and the kinds and amount of commitment volunteers can make.

We refuse to live in a fish bowl. Psych students who want to volunteer time to scrutinize and question "nomadic minors" are told to look elsewhere for subject matter for their term papers.

Most volunteers in the group foster homes have specific skills to teach or they volunteer for specific tasks. At different times we have had dance/yoga classes, art classes, and old-time movies in the evenings. Other people have volunteered to take the kids on camping trips, to museums, etc. One girl offered to cook dinner and answer phones at Second House to cut down on interruptions during Tuesday night group meetings. We have people on tap to act as tutors and sometimes as "big brothers" to individual kids.

We feel a lot of volunteers would be confusing to the kids. Many volunteers wandering through the house also intrude on the home-like atmosphere of the place. The kids in the houses need a few, firm trusting relationships rather than dozens of interested acquaintances.

We have always had a problem with people who want to "help" not showing up when there is actually work to do. Therefore, we test a volunteer at first by giving him low level responsibilities such as answering phones and the door during group. If he shows up on time, handles the task responsibly, and relates well with the kids, we give him more to do. These decisions rest mainly on the gut-level feelings of the people in the house about the volunteer. Some volunteers have become close friends of the house, and as they have become more skillful, have been given more responsibility.

Volunteers turn up from all kinds of places. We get an influx of volunteers (and staff applications) after each TV special or news articles on SAJA. Seminary students especially, but all students, are a source of volunteers. Some students can get university credit for this type of work.

Our personal friends are our best source of help, particularly in covering the group homes during weekend staff retreats. They spend a lot of time in the group foster homes (our homes) and become involved with the kids and the house routine. The kids like and trust them. The kids are happier when our/their friends help out at the house. It has happened the other way—regular volunteers have become our/their friends.

Maintaining Contact With Referral Agencies

During the first several months of group foster home operation we were lax in maintaining contact with agency caseworkers referring kids to our houses. We kept irregular contact by phone and occasionally invited caseworkers to dinner, but we did not submit regular reports on the individual kids to the sponsoring agencies. We were finally confronted on this by a caseworker from D.C. and quickly got it together. We developed forms which were fairly easy to fill out and gave a clear bimonthly report on the progress of individuals in the group foster homes.

It is vital to keep in touch regularly with the kids' caseworkers. Several caseworkers complained to us that they only heard from us during crises or when the kids need health or clothing allotments. We eventually learned to keep the caseworkers informed of the kids' successes as well as their crises and established much better relations with the agencies referring people to us.

Coping With the Reality of Drugs

Most of the people referred to SAJA's group foster homes have had extensive experience with soft drugs—marijuana, hashish, LSD, and mescaline. Many have used drugs self-destructively. It would be absurd for us to believe that we could get kids to stop using drugs if we came down with a lot of moralistic claptrap. Nor do punishments or restrictions stop self-destructive drug use. We learned this from our "parent" stage.

We do have a flat prohibition against drug possession or use on the premises. Drugs in the house threaten the entire project and endanger the welfare of all people in the house. A person caught with drugs in the house is in danger of being thrown out on his ear. This is made clear during the initial interview with each individual. None of us (and the kids agree on this one) will allow such irresponsibility by one person to close down the entire project.

Drug use outside the house is a different story. We are unable and unwilling to police the movements of the kids or to regulate their contacts when they are out of the house. The more responsible a kid is, the more freedom he is allowed. We have learned to recognize some forms of drug use as self-destructive behavior and therefore we tend to supervise the kids who are into drugs a little more closely.

In concerning ourselves with excessive drug use, we have found that helping each individual learn that he is a valuable, important human being is the most effective way to deal with the problem. A kid who feels O.K. about himself is not going to destroy himself by burning his mind out on drugs.

Again, we are trying to help these kids learn to take care of themselves. Therefore, instilling a sense of self-value is much more productive than a strict set of rules. Rules do not protect an individual once he is living on his own.

Establishing a Second Group Foster Home

After about a year, the number of referrals that we received at the Second House Indicated a need for another group foster home and therefore we put together Third House. Third House was to serve the same throwaway population, to have six kids and two counselors, and to operate in much the same way as Second House.

Organizing Third House was very different from setting up Second House. We knew what we were doing and had an established reputation as a child care agency. We had also made and corrected a lot of mistakes through our experience with Second House.

We applied for and received a $10,000 grant from a local foundation as seed money for the Third House's first few months of operation. We hired two ex-RH counselors to staff the house, Melinda Bird, 22, and John McCann, 22. Both had been around during the first painful, learning year of Second House and had many new ideas of their own. Our doctor found us a fine house in the neighborhood which had once been a rooming house. Four kids who had been through Runaway House, and had been taken into court custody, were waiting to move into Third House. SAJA's second group foster home opened its doors in January 1971. With a couple of additional referrals from community agencies, Third House was self-supporting in just 2 months.

Again, difficult procedures. The District required a separate contract with Third House, a development we had not expected. John did much of the required renovation himself. However, this cut down on the amount of time he could initially spend with the kids. We've learned that as much of the licensing and repair work as possible should be done before people move in. (Yet the whole project should not be held up for this reason.) At least the second time around, when you have become established and won't be stopped by bureaucrats, try to get this work done ahead of time. If you can't get the work done ahead of time, contract it out to some freaks who will work for little money. Try to arrange things so that counselors can spend the first, formative weeks of the house with the kids.

Before the house opened, the Third House counselors made several decisions about what kind of work they were planning to do and what atmosphere they wanted in the house. Their conclusions evolved from contact with Second House and from discussions with the RH kids who were moving into Third House.

John and Melinda decided to be sure to take their alloted 2 days off each week. Therefore they had to structure the house so that one person could cover it while the other staff member was off duty. The Second House counselors often went weeks without taking time off and were nearly burnt out before they started taking care of their personal needs.

They decided to try to keep things in the house as well-planned and scheduled as possible. This included taking allotted time off, splitting up responsibilities without regard to male/female roles, keeping track of the kids, etc.

The Third House counselors decided to do a "house thing" with the kids once a week—going swimming, skating, or to a movie. At first this activity was compulsory—which caused huge fights. So instead of putting energy into fighting they worked at creating exciting things for the group to do together.

Again, having learned from the Second House experience, the people starting Third House decided to look for three consultants. They wanted a consultant on group technique, a personal consultant, and a "technical" house consultant.

The Third House counselors wanted a technical consultant, which Second House did not have, who could look at the structures in the house. They were interested in an academically oriented professional to provide a dialogue about models for setting up structures and working with kids. Technical consultants can constantly call the structure and the climate of the house into question.

It is very easy to get caught up in details. "We're out of milk. Joey is late getting home from school. I have to call the plumber tomorrow." You can lose sight of what is actually evolving in the house, how it feels to the people living there, and what visitors pick up while in the house. (That is probably what happens to many parents.) A semidetached observer, who can pick up vibes and can maintain an overview of the situation, is a great help in maintaining the climate that you want in the house. This could be a consultant, another member of the staff, or both.

The house counselors must be aware of their own feelings and not become defensive when told that the atmosphere is tense, or that the kids seem disenchanted with the place. We had this difficulty at Second House. Staff members were very defensive about "their" house, and it took a long time to convince them to relax and let the house evolve more naturally. It is important to stay open to criticism and to step back once in a while to see what needs to be changed.

Third House has helped to stabilize Second House. The counselors in the two houses are able to provide support and insight into problems for each other. Soon after Third House got going, the counselors began meeting once a week, with one of the administrators, to discuss problems specific to the group foster homes. This weekly meeting eventually evolved into the group foster home collective; a natural staff grouping which makes all operating, hiring, and intake decisions for the group foster homes. Since Third House came into being, we have been able to provide more appropriate placements for the kids referred to us. We can offer a choice of two, interdependent group foster homes which differ in the personality of the group, age of the kids, personalities of counselors, etc.

A case in point is Fred, 14, who was placed temporarily with our summer farm program. Fred needed a permanent placement and we had openings in both our group foster homes. Fred had been in reform school for several months and had lived a pretty rough life before that. He was loud, lied a lot, and got into all kinds of scrapes. He spent a few days at Second House and obviously would not make it there. The Second House kids were older, more hip, and more verbal than Fred and would not put up with his noise or his shenanigans. So Fred moved to Third House. The kids in Third House are slightly younger than those at Second House, noisier as a group themselves, and less into "rapping." They saw Fred as a sort of younger brother, a pain in the neck perhaps, but a nice kid. Fred is working out well at Third House. He's acting more responsibly and cutting down on the lying. He fits into the group at Third House and might not have made it with the kids in Second House.

The group foster homes, as a part of SAJA, have quite an extended family. All of our projects are in the same neighborhood and therefore the workers in the SAJA projects live nearby. The kids in Second and Third House have over 25 staff members and ex-staff members living in the urban village around Dupont Circle to whom they can relate in a wide variety of ways. These people also provide a pool of individuals to help out in the house when counselors need time off.

Second and Third House are related families. About 10 of the kids from the group foster homes attend the SAJA—New Education Project free school. There they have another group of people to relate to.

Learning Limitations

One of the biggest lessons we have learned is that our own limitations mean we cannot help everyone. The past 2 years have tempered the idealism that originally founded Second House. At first we took kids into Second House who were quite emotionally disturbed.

However, we found we did not have the skills, or the energy, to provide a sufficiently structured environment that would protect them from their own self-destructive behavior.

Annie, whose story leads this chapter, had to leave Second House after 7 months. She cut school one day and wandered to one of the most dangerous sections of D.C. She was then "raped" in an abandoned office building. She told us afterward that she had also been "raped" the night before by a "friend" whom she had invited to her babysitting job. Annie was obviously looking for it. She could not handle the responsibility of her freedom at Second House.

Our predominantly white, middle-class staff is also questioning its ability to meet the needs of deprived black street youth. The dilemma is how to foster a healthy black consciousness without black role-models. We receive few counseling applications from black people. This may be due to their unwillingness to work for a white organization. Black people also can make more money doing similar work in government or community sponsored projects that work with black kids.

We haven't had much success with black kids who were really street kids. No matter what kind of trust or warmth was built up, a confrontation came down to black and white. This was caused by fear, lack of communication, and perceptions of the world—but it closed off all hopes of communication.

However, hundreds of black kids in the D.C. area need placements so we've reevaluated our abilities. We will now accept young blacks if they are fairly verbal, have some experience relating to whites on an intimate basis, and do not need physical controls on their behavior. In one instance we worked out a "big brother" arrangement with a black school counselor so that one of the black kids in Second House would have someone as a model.

We are not willing to take a person we can't handle, because he is the one who is hurt by this largesse. Housing someone for a couple of months and then asking him to leave, largely due to our own limitations, is not a favor.

Counselor Transition

We try to make staff turnover as smooth as possible. The new staff member moves into the house at least two weeks before the old counselor leaves. In this way he can receive on-the-job training from his predecessor and he has a chance to build up friendships with the kids which helps him to support them during the difficult time when the old counselor moves out.

The entire staff of both houses changed in the months from April to July of 1971. In early April, Chuck White, 29, an ex-seminary student, was hired to temporarily act as a third counselor at Second House, eventually replacing Jay Berlin. Later that month Sally Rodes Wood, 23, moved into Second House to replace Dodie Butler who left the first of May. Jay left in the middle of June. His departure coincided with the actual moving of Second House, from the barn on 19th Street to a smaller but nicer home at 1748 S Street a block and a half away.

Melinda and John, at Third House, had both made 6 month commitments to the house, commitments that were up around the end of June. During June, we hired David and Alfhild Lindsun to be the counselors at Third House. They are the first couple to work together within a SAJA project. They moved into Third House in late June. Melinda left the house in the first part of July and John moved out about a month later.

Counselor changeovers were rough at both houses. The kids were extremely threatened by the idea that the counselors whom they had grown to love and trust were leaving them. Some of the kids had come into the houses fearing the warmth and imtimacy there because they had been abandoned in the past by people they had trusted. Some of the kids saw this happening again when the counselors moved out of the group foster homes. A couple of them acted out this fear and danger physically—one boy ran away several times.

We tried to explain our leaving in terms of our moving on to another stage in our lives. Each kid at Second and Third House would be doing the same thing eventually, when he left the group foster home. We also made it clear that we wanted to maintain the relationships we had with the kids in the houses, and that they could build similar relationships with the new counselors. The kids understood, yet were still afraid. As the new counselors moved into their positions, and the old counselors were phased out, the kids were able to see that things were working out well, and the turmoil gradually disappeared.

We doubt if there is any way to get around the few weeks of uncertainty when old counselors leave and new staff moves in. However, we are trying to cut down on the number of times this happens to each individual in the group foster homes by asking for a year's commitment from new staff, rather than the former 6-month commitment. We also plan to hire new staff members far enough in advance so that the kids can build trust with the new people before the previous counselors move on.

Changes in the Houses

The group homes have continued to grow and evolve

over the past few months. Having survived our parental stage, Second House is now working toward a collective, communal spirit. The approach is more egalitarian; the house is much less structured. The kids are taking a more active role in running the house and send a voting delegate to foster home collective meetings. While the kids in the house are demanding more participation in determining policy, there is still a discrepancy between this desire for participation and the actual acceptance of the accompanying responsibilities.

The staff members do not cop out behind counselor roles. Their approach is nondirective and nonconfrontation oriented. The counselors accept each kid in the house as an important person and expect responsible behavior to evolve from this acceptance. We feel it is important not to hinge personal acceptance on responsible actions. Second House is attempting to reach the point where all conflicts and all decisions are resolved by the house group, with counselors having no extra group power. We are still in the groping stage.

When determining the type of atmosphere you want in the group foster home and the approach staff members will employ, there are several things to keep in mind. You must determine what mode *you* feel comfortable with. (The new counselors at Second House were not willing to put on a parent act.) You must figure out the needs of the kids in the house. Several of the kids at Second House have been around for a while and are pretty together. They can handle the responsibilities of collectively running the house. Be careful not to sell short the abilities of the kids to act responsibly. A 16- or 17-year-old who will be moving out to live on his own must learn to think for himself. He does not have the time to get into and then naturally grow out of a parent/child relationship. A 13-year-old may want and need a more structured environment and will have 3 or 4 years to grow to independence.

At Second House chores are still divided up among everyone, but the counselors no longer take responsibility upon themselves to see that kids do their work. This responsibility is shared by everyone in the house. As the counselors have become less directive, weekly group sessions have become the property of all the members of the house, with little counselor/kid distinction. Second House has a new consultant sitting in on group who participates much more than did the previous psychiatrist. He comments on the dynamics of the group and facilitates open communication.

Third House is moving in the same general direction as Second House although more slowly—the kids' interest in direct participation is not as strong as that in Second House. The workers in the house are definitely inclined toward collective operation within the house, but feel that some of the initiative for this participation must come from the kids.

The counselors rely on personal relationships and talking in dealing with problems with individual kids. They are not into laying down rules "for the kid's own good." While structures for individual kids are looser than in the past, Third House has decided to set up stronger measures around things that affect everyone—mainly house maintenance. A reward system for daily chores has been worked out. Each member of the house draws a daily chore, to which is assigned the value of his weekly allowance. If a person doesn't do his chores on a particular day—maybe he just does not feel like it—someone else in the house can complete the task and will receive one day's percentage of the allowance of the person responsible for the job. (The kids receive $3.00 per week regular allowance and $15.00 per month for clothing.) So far this has worked well. This is another way of sharing responsibility for getting work done.

The group at Third House is beginning to take responsibility for more house decisions. The collective meetings are nondirective and definitely a forum for everyone equally.

The two houses have developed very different cultures or atmospheres. This is primarily due to the types of kids who have moved in. Second House kids are hip and verbal; the house has a definite freak culture. Third House has a younger feeling and is noisier. The kids in the house, black and white, are into more of a black street culture than a hippie trip. The animal population at Third House includes two kittens, a half-grown dog, one monkey, one gerbil, and two love birds. So far, Second House is content with a dog and a cat.

SAJA's group foster home program has changed considerably in the past 2 years. What began as a temporary placement for the throwaway kids living at Runaway House, has grown into two group homes, available to the people living in them as long as they need to live there. Second and Third House now serve 12 kids. There are four resident staff people and one swing counselor. Each house has psychiatric consultants providing criticism and support for the staff. The kids are beginning to take more power over their own lives through the medium of the group. One representative from each house belongs to the foster home decisionmaking collective.

This evolution is operating continually. During the week that this chapter was being written, the kids and staff in the group foster homes tentatively changed the intake procedure for new residents so that the kids in the houses could participate in the decision. It was proposed that a representative of the kids be included in the initial interview—formerly made up of the person on referral, the consulting psychiatrist, and the two staff members. After the intake interview the person on referral would stay at the house for dinner, and afterward would meet in a group with the kids in the house. This would be followed by a meeting of the whole house, staff, and kids, to decide on the person's admission into the house.

There have been five "graduates" of our group foster homes; kids who completed their stay in the house and moved on. Two returned to their parents as planned. Three are living on their own and are still closely involved with SAJA people. Two of these kids attend the SAJA New Education Project Free School. They live in the neighborhood and are an important part of the peer group in the houses. Three more people are preparing to move out. They, too, will be living in the neighborhood and will continue going to the free school. All of these kids were candidates for reform school when we met them. Our group foster homes were their only alternatives to institutionalization. Now they can take care of themselves, and with the support of the SAJA extended family, can live productively in the community.

OTHER NICE THINGS TO DO—GROUP FOSTER HOMES

1. Check into buying food wholesale. If you have adequate storage facilities, time and money can be saved this way.
2. Have an open house for teachers and administrators if your kids go to public school. The teachers are thrilled to find someone interested in the school. It is good to know several of the teachers—especially if one of your kids gets kicked out of school and you're trying to pull strings to get him back in.
3. Have a house dog. He'll be a good watchdog and good for the kids. Our house cat had kittens which was a real treat, but we had a hard time getting rid of them. Remember that hamsters, gerbils, and white mice have a tendency to procreate profusely.
4. Set up a schedule so that everyone (male and female, counselor and kid) gets involved in cooking meals, doing dishes, and cleaning house. This quickly cuts down on role differentiation!
5. Check about free tickets to movies, circuses, concerts, etc.
6. If you get to know people in the city recreation department you may be able to use city pools, etc. for free.
7. Many organizations do service projects for underprivileged kids. Get your name on *that* list. Then only accept projects that will help you out—furniture and clothing drives, money, food, etc. will be more helpful than a party thrown for the kids by a fraternity or sorority.
8. Planning a trip? You might get the use of a car from a car rental agency or dealership if you plan far enough in advance. Or see if someone outside the organization will rent one for you. Again, planning ahead for the trip, you may be able to find somebody who knows somebody (ad infinitum) to house you and perhaps a social service organization so enamored with you that they'll provide money for you to take the kids out to dinner. (We did this in Akron, Ohio, on our way to Michigan with the Second House kids at Christmas.)
9. Furniture stores will donate rug ends and perhaps furniture to you if you contact them and then write a letter on organization stationery—probably tax deductible for them.
10. Know what to do if one of your kids gets busted. Do you need papers identifying you as legal custodian? If so, have these for all your kids. Also, know a good lawyer—and it is nice to have a friend in the juvenile division of the police force.
11. Area mental health clinics may be willing to define your kids as area residents (there may be a hassle if kids come from another jurisdiction) for therapy if that is called for.
12. Social service agencies often have monthly meetings when supervisors and caseworkers get together. Find out when these are and see if you can speak to them about your project. You can often reach 20 to 30 people this way.
13. Figure out a satisfactory phone arrangement. Perhaps have two phones, one for the kids' incoming and outgoing calls and one for "business" calls. Agree on a method for taking messages. A bulletin board or notebook near the phone may be helpful.

14. Sometimes it is helpful to make "contracts" with individual kids—verbal or written agreements outlining what he wants to get out of his experience at the house and what the people in the house are willing to do to help him. A discussion, soon after he arrives, about why he is in the group foster home and establishing goals for his stay in the house helps clarify the house expectations for him, and his expectations for the house. These contracts, or goals, may grow and change during his stay at the house.
15. For a while, we had a "fairy godmother" for Second House—a wealthy woman who did nice things for the kids.
16. Check into commodity foods from the Agriculture Department, State surplus food programs, and try to qualify for food stamps.

Excerpts from runaway house: A Youth-Run Service Project. A Report Prepared for the National Institute of Mental Health. 1974. DHEW Publ. No. (ADM) 74-44

Statistics

DAY CARE ARRANGEMENTS OF CHILDREN 3 TO 13 YEARS OLD, BY SELECTED CHARACTERISTICS: 1974 AND 1975

[**In thousands, except percent.** Civilian noninstitutional population. Includes children with no mother present, not shown separately. Data for children 3 to 6 years old and for children 7 to 13 years old obtained, respectively, from **February 1975** and **October 1974** Current Population Survey; see text, p. 1]

CHARACTERISTIC	Total	CARE IN OWN HOME			CARE IN OTHER'S HOME		Day care center	Other and not reported
		Child's parent	Child's self-care	Other	Relative	Nonrelative		
Children, ages 3 to 13	**40,765**	**32,810**	**1,828**	**2,644**	**1,174**	**1,276**	**326**	**707**
Mother in labor force	17,555	11,168	1,620	1,994	965	1,187	284	336
Employed	16,046	9,797	1,595	1,962	932	1,165	279	319
Full-time	10,323	5,168	1,331	1,642	756	940	247	239
Mother not in labor force	22,498	21,214	159	522	171	53	26	350
Marital status of mother:								
Married, husband present	33,467	27,909	1,315	1,735	835	948	211	515
Separated, divorced, widowed	5,960	4,036	441	702	253	277	103	148
Never married	625	435	24	78	49	16	8	13
PERCENT DISTRIBUTION								
Total	100.0	80.5	4.5	6.5	2.9	3.1	.8	1.7
Mother in labor force	100.0	63.6	9.2	11.4	5.5	6.8	1.6	1.9
Employed	100.0	61.1	9.9	12.3	5.8	7.3	1.7	1.9
Full-time	100.0	50.1	12.9	15.9	7.3	9.1	2.4	2.3
Mother not in labor force	100.0	94.3	.7	2.3	.8	.2	.1	1.5
Marital status of mother:								
Married, husband present	100.0	83.4	3.9	5.2	2.5	2.8	.6	1.6
Separated, divorced, widowed	100.0	67.7	7.4	11.8	4.2	4.6	1.7	2.5
Never married	100.0	69.6	3.8	12.5	7.8	2.6	1.3	2.1
Children, ages 3 to 6	**13,758**	**11,136**	**20**	**666**	**695**	**838**	**219**	**184**
PERCENT DISTRIBUTION								
Total	100.0	80.9	.1	4.8	5.1	6.1	1.6	1.3
White	100.0	82.5	.1	4.1	4.2	6.3	1.6	1.2
Enrolled in school	100.0	84.1	.2	4.5	3.4	5.0	2.1	.7
Mother in labor force	100.0	59.0	.3	9.2	9.7	16.2	3.9	1.8
Employed full-time	100.0	40.3	.6	13.2	13.5	23.3	6.6	2.5
Employed part-time	100.0	76.9	–	5.4	6.2	9.7	.7	1.1
Unemployed	100.0	89.6	–	2.2	3.1	3.7	1.0	.4
Mother not in labor force	100.0	96.9	–	.9	.8	.4	.2	.8
Black	100.0	72.4	.1	8.8	9.7	5.3	1.4	2.4
Enrolled in school	100.0	76.4	.3	8.5	8.8	3.5	1.5	1.1
Mother in labor force	100.0	54.0	.3	11.5	17.2	10.9	2.6	3.6
Employed full-time	100.0	44.5	.5	12.7	20.3	15.2	2.8	4.0
Employed part-time	100.0	63.2	–	13.2	15.0	5.9	2.7	–
Unemployed	100.0	78.7	–	4.5	7.7	1.3	.6	8.4
Mother not in labor force	100.0	90.4	–	5.8	2.6	.2	.3	1.2
Children, ages 7 to 13	**27,007**	**21,674**	**1,808**	**1,978**	**479**	**438**	**107**	**523**
PERCENT DISTRIBUTION								
Total	100.0	80.3	6.7	7.4	1.8	1.6	.4	2.0
White	100.0	81.4	6.3	6.6	1.7	1.7	.4	2.0
Mother in labor force	100.0	67.6	12.5	10.9	2.8	3.5	.8	1.9
Employed	100.0	65.7	13.2	11.6	3.0	3.7	.8	2.0
Unemployed	100.0	95.7	2.4	1.2	.2	.3	–	.2
Mother not in labor force	100.0	93.6	1.0	2.5	.6	.2	.1	2.0
Black	100.0	74.5	7.9	11.8	2.6	1.0	.3	1.9
Mother in labor force	100.0	59.4	13.7	18.0	4.3	2.0	.5	2.0
Employed	100.0	55.9	14.9	19.9	4.6	2.2	.6	2.0
Unemployed	100.0	88.8	4.4	2.5	2.1	–	–	2.2
Mother not in labor force	100.0	91.1	1.7	4.8	.6	.1	.1	1.7
By family income:								
Less than $5,000	100.0	80.4	4.5	9.3	2.6	1.0	.2	2.0
$5,000–$6,999	100.0	76.7	7.5	8.4	1.9	2.7	.5	2.2
$7,000–$9,999	100.0	81.5	6.1	7.0	2.1	1.4	.3	1.7
$10,000–$14,999	100.0	82.0	6.5	5.9	1.9	2.0	.3	1.5
$15,000–$19,999	100.0	80.0	7.6	7.3	1.1	1.7	.6	1.7
$20,000 and more	100.0	81.0	7.3	6.6	.8	1.2	.8	2.3

– Represents zero.

Source: U.S. Bureau of the Census, *Current Population Reports*, series P–20, No. 298, and unpublished data.

Persons Under 18 Years Old, by Presence of Parents and Whether Living With Mother Only, by Marital Status of Mother: 1968 to 1976

[As of March. Excludes persons under 18 years old who were heads and wives of heads of families and subfamilies]

Year and race	Persons under 18 years old (1,000)	Percent living with— Both parents	Mother only who is— Married, but separated [1]	Widowed	Divorced	Single	Father only	Neither parent
1968: Total [2]	70,617	85.0	4.9	2.3	2.9	.7	1.1	3.2
White	59,953	89.4	3.1	1.8	2.7	.2	.9	2.0
Black	9,775	58.3	15.5	5.6	4.1	3.8	2.1	10.4
1970: Total [2]	69,458	84.9	4.7	2.0	3.3	.8	1.1	3.3
White	59,026	89.2	2.8	1.7	3.1	.2	.9	2.2
Black	9,483	58.1	16.2	4.2	4.6	4.4	2.2	10.4
1975: Total [2]	66,087	80.3	5.8	2.4	5.5	1.8	1.5	2.7
White	55,500	85.4	3.8	1.9	5.1	.5	1.5	1.7
Black	9,472	49.4	18.7	5.1	8.1	9.1	1.8	7.9
1976: Total [2]	65,129	80.0	5.8	2.1	6.2	1.7	1.2	3.0
White	54,411	85.2	3.8	1.6	5.9	.5	1.2	1.9
Black	9,461	49.6	17.8	5.1	8.3	8.8	1.5	8.8

[1] Includes married but husband absent. [2] Includes races not shown separately.

Source: U.S. Bureau of the Census, *Current Population Reports*, series P-20, No. 306, and earlier issues.

Percent Distribution of Families, by Number of Own Children Under 18 Years Old: 1950 to 1976

[As of **March**, except **1955** as of **April**. Prior to 1960, excludes Alaska and Hawaii. See headnote, table 63. See also *Historical Statistics, Colonial Times to 1970*, series A 353-358]

Item	1950	1955	1960	1965	1970	1972	1973	1974	1975	1976
Families 1,000	**39,303**	**41,951**	**45,111**	**47,956**	**51,586**	**53,296**	**54,373**	**55,053**	**55,712**	**56,245**
Percent distribution	**100.0**	**100.0**	**100.0**	**100.0**	**100.0**	**100.0**	**100.0**	**100.0**	**100.0**	**100.0**
No children	48.3	44.7	43.0	43.4	44.1	44.8	45.6	46.0	46.0	46.3
1 child	21.1	19.1	18.5	17.7	18.2	18.9	19.3	19.2	19.7	19.7
2 children	16.5	18.7	18.0	16.8	17.4	17.6	17.4	17.9	18.0	18.3
3 children	7.8	9.9	11.1	11.0	10.6	10.2	9.7	9.5	9.3	9.3
4 or more children	6.3	7.6	9.4	11.1	9.8	8.6	7.9	7.4	6.9	6.3

Source: U.S. Bureau of the Census, *Current Population Reports*, series P-20, forthcoming report, and earlier issues.

Child Adoptions—Selected States and Puerto Rico: 1970 and 1975

[Represents voluntary reports by State welfare departments covering children under age 21 for whom adoption petitions were granted. States shown are those which filed complete data on total adoptions in 1975 or as noted. For additional details for individual States with varying degrees of coverage, see source. U.S. estimated total, 1970=175,000]

State	1970, total	1975 Total	1975 By relatives [1] (percent)	State	1970, total	1975 Total	1975 By relatives [1] (percent)	State	1970, total	1975 Total	1975 By relatives [1] (percent)
Ala	1,414	2,675	81	La	2,921	2,847	74	Pa	7,621	5,983	62
Ark	924	769	68	Maine	1,431	1,042	72	S. Dak	575	517	61
Conn	1,875	[2] 722	[2] 31	Mass	(NA)	1,034	3	Tenn	2,154	[4] 2,107	[4] 73
Del	382	314	71	Mich	8,879	8,912	53	Tex	12,378	6,316	66
D.C	[3] 800	293	30	Minn	3,944	[2] 3,135	[2] 50	Vt	477	502	69
Fla	7,271	6,523	67	Nev	787	388	71	Va	3,742	3,866	69
Ga	2,803	2,047	68	N.H	677	648	67	Wash	4,382	2,885	65
Hawaii	1,124	742	81	N.J	3,923	2,626	52	W. Va	1,429	1,219	83
Ind	4,800	5,379	70	N. Mex	1,173	997	70	Wis	3,721	2,573	53
Iowa	3,087	2,521	68	N.C	3,116	3,701	71	Wyo	585	543	(NA)
Ky	1,870	1,560	47	Ohio	9,373	7,588	63	P.R	271	224	65

NA Not available. [1] Relationship not reported for 24 percent in Kentucky, 11 percent in Michigan, 7 percent in Florida, and 0-4 percent in other States. [2] For fiscal year 1976. [3] For 1969. [4] For fiscal year 1975.

Source: U.S. National Center for Social Statistics, *Adoptions in 1970* and *Adoptions in 1975*, NCSS Report E-10.

Child Adoptions, by Type: 1952 to 1971

[In thousands. Includes Puerto Rico and Virgin Islands. Based on reports from State departments of public welfare with estimates added for nonreporting States, number of which varied from year to year. Prior to 1960, represents number of adoption petitions filed; thereafter, number of petitions granted]

TYPE OF ADOPTION	1952	1955	1960	1965	1966	1967	1968	1969	1970	1971
Total	**85**	**93**	**107**	**142**	**152**	**158**	**166**	**171**	**175**	**169**
By relatives	43	45	49	65	71	74	80	82	86	86
By nonrelatives	42	48	58	77	81	84	86	89	89	83
Placed by social agencies	24	27	33	53	57	62	64	67	69	66

Source: U.S. Social and Rehabilitation Service, 1952–1960, *Child Welfare Statistics*; thereafter, *Supplement to Child Welfare Statistics*.

Orphans, by Type: 1955 to 1976

[Beginning 1960, includes Puerto Rico and Virgin Islands; beginning 1972, also includes American Samoa, Guam, and citizens (including Armed Forces) overseas. Covers children under age 18 who have been orphaned at any time. Paternal orphan refers to loss of father, maternal orphan to loss of mother, full orphan to loss of both parents. Percent of child population based on Bureau of the Census estimated population of children under 18, as of July 1. Data not exactly comparable for all years because of changes in methodology]

YEAR	NUMBER (1,000)				PERCENT OF CHILD POPULATION			
	Total	Paternal	Maternal	Full	Total	Paternal	Maternal	Full
1955, July	2,710	1,830	820	60	4.8	3.2	1.5	.1
1960, January	2,955	2,055	840	60	4.5	3.1	1.3	.1
1965, January	3,290	2,330	890	70	4.7	3.3	1.3	.1
1970, July	3,260	2,300	890	70	4.6	3.2	1.3	.1
1972, July	3,074	2,166	838	70	4.4	3.1	1.2	.1
1976, July	3,507	2,445	1,008	54	5.2	3.6	1.5	.1

Source: U.S. Social Security Administration. Irregularly in *Social Security Bulletin*.

Juveniles Held in Custody, by Type of Facility—Summary: 1974 and 1975

[As of June 30, except expenditures for years ending June 30. Data based on private and State and local public juvenile detention and correctional facilities in operation when censuses were initiated (November 1974 and February 1976); also must have been in existence for at least a month before census reference date of June 30, and with a resident population at least 50 percent juvenile. However, a facility was included if it was considered a juvenile facility, even though the youthful offenders outnumbered juveniles at the time of the census. Further, at least 10 percent of a private facility's population had to have been adjudicated delinquent, in need of supervision, voluntarily admitted or awaiting court disposition. Excludes juvenile detention centers operated as part of a jail and without a separate staff or budget, nonresidential facilities, facilities exclusively for drug abusers, facilities exclusively for dependent and neglected children, foster homes, and Federal juvenile correctional facilities. For definition of terms, see source]

ITEM	PUBLIC		PRIVATE	
	1974	1975	1974	1975
Facilities, total	**829**	**874**	**1,337**	**1,277**
State-government administered	396	423	(NA)	(NA)
Local-government administered	433	451	(NA)	(NA)
Training schools	185	189	61	65
Detention centers	331	347	4	66
Reception centers [1]	19	17	5	
Ranches [2]	107	103	395	295
Halfway houses [3]	166	195	805	851
Shelters	21	23	67	(4)
Expenditures...mil. dol	**508**	**594**	**294**	**274**
Operating...mil. dol	483	560	268	254
Per person held [5]...1,000	10.3	11.5	8.5	9.5
Capital...mil. dol	25	35	26	19
Full-time staff [6]...1,000	39.4	41.2	20.6	27.7
Part-time staff [6]...1,000	6.9	11.4	8.0	

ITEM	PUBLIC		PRIVATE	
	1974	1975	1974	1975
Juveniles held	**44,922**	**46,980**	**31,749**	**27,290**
Male	34,783	37,926	22,104	19,152
Female	10,139	9,054	9,645	8,138
Type of facility:				
Training schools	25,397	26,748	4,078	3,660
Detention centers	11,010	11,089	163	830
Reception centers [1]	1,376	1,436		
Ranches [2]	5,232	5,385	16,955	13,094
Halfway houses [3]	1,727	2,122	9,919	9,706
Shelters	180	200	634	(4)
Detention status:				
Adjudicated delinquent [7]	31,270	34,107	9,874	9,809
Declared in need of supervision	4,644	4,494	4,969	4,316
Court disposition pending	7,373	7,011	481	529
Awaiting transfer [8]	458	392	63	
Voluntary admission	679	516	7,635	5,879
Dependent and neglected	498	451	7,104	4,844
Other [9]	–	9	1,623	1,913

– Represents zero. NA Not available. [1] Includes diagnostic centers. [2] Includes forestry camps and farms. [3] Includes group homes. [4] Included with detention and reception centers. [5] Based on the average daily population of the facilities. [6] Includes payroll and nonpayroll staff. [7] See headnote, table 314. [8] To another jurisdiction. [9] The emotionally disturbed, the mentally retarded, and other.

Source: U.S. Law Enforcement Administration, *Children in Custody, Advance Report on the Juvenile Detention and Correctional Facility Census of 1974*, February 1977; and 1975, October 1977.

Children's Cases Disposed of by Juvenile Courts: 1960 to 1974

[Delinquency cases are all cases of youths referred to a juvenile court for violation of a law or ordinance or for seriously antisocial conduct. This broad definition includes conduct which violates the law only when committed by children. Excludes ordinary traffic cases handled by juvenile courts, except where traffic cases are adjudicated as "juvenile delinquency" cases. Dependency and neglect cases are all cases referred to the court for some form of neglect or inadequate care on the part of parents or guardians. See also *Historical Statistics, Colonial Times to 1970*, series H 1119–1124]

ITEM	1960	1965	1969	1970	1971	1972	1973	1974
Population 10–17 years old [1] ....1,000..	25,368	29,536	32,157	32,614	32,969	33,120	33,377	33,365
Delinquency cases excluding traffic [2] ..1,000..	510	697	989	1,052	1,125	1,112	1,143	1,252
Per 1,000 population 10–17 years old......	20.1	23.6	30.7	32.3	34.1	33.6	34.2	37.5
Population under 18 years old [1] ....1,000..	64,516	69,699	69,694	69,669	69,576	69,060	68,196	67,241
Dependency and neglect cases [2] ....1,000..	131	157	127	133	131	141	158	151
Per 1,000 population under 18 years old....	2.0	2.3	1.8	1.9	1.9	2.0	2.3	2.2

[1] U.S. Bureau of the Census estimates of civilian population as of July 1, except 1960 and 1970, as of April 1.

[2] Delinquency cases based on data from a national sample of juvenile courts. Since 1970, based on all courts reporting, whose jurisdiction includes about two-thirds of the Nation's population; dependency and neglect cases based on reports from courts serving about one-half of the child population under 18 years of age. See text for detail.

Source: 1960–1973, U.S. Office of Human Development and U.S. Office of Youth Development, *Juvenile Court Statistics*, annual. Beginning 1974, The National Center for Juvenile Justice, Pittsburgh, Pa.

U.S. Bureau of the Census, Statistical Abstract of the United States: 1977 (98th edition) Washington, D.C., 1977.

Series H 1119–1124. Juvenile Court—Cases Handled: 1940 to 1970

[In thousands, except rate]

Year	Population under 18 years old: Total [1]	Dependency and neglect cases: Total	Dependency and neglect cases: Rate per 1,000 population	Population, 10–17 years old: Total [1]	Delinquency cases: Total [2]	Delinquency cases: Rate per 1,000 population	Year	Population under 18 years old: Total [1]	Dependency and neglect cases: Total	Dependency and neglect cases: Rate per 1,000 population	Population, 10–17 years old: Total [1]	Delinquency cases: Total [2]	Delinquency cases: Rate per 1,000 population
	1119	1120	1121	1122	1123	1124		1119	1120	1121	1122	1123	1124
1970	69,669	133	1.9	32,614	1,052	32.3	1955	55,568	106	1.9	20,111	431	21.4
1969	69,694	127	1.8	32,157	989	30.7	1954	53,737	103	1.9	19,551	395	20.2
1968	69,831	141	2.0	31,566	900	28.5	1953	51,987	103	2.0	18,980	374	19.7
1967	69,878	154	2.2	30,837	811	26.3	1952	50,296	98	1.9	18,201	332	18.2
1966	69,851	161	2.3	30,124	745	24.7	1951	48,598	97	2.0	17,705	298	16.8
1965	69,699	157	2.3	29,536	697	23.6	1950	47,017	93	2.0	17,397	280	16.1
1964	69,625	150	2.2	29,244	686	23.5	1949	45,775	98	2.1	17,365	272	15.6
1963	68,371	146	2.1	28,056	601	21.4	1948	44,512	103	2.3	17,314	254	14.9
1962	67,092	141	2.1	26,989	555	20.6	1947	43,301	104	2.4	17,344	262	15.1
1961	65,789	140	2.1	26,056	503	19.3	1946	41,759	101	2.4	17,419	295	16.9
1960	64,516	131	2.0	25,368	510	20.1	1945	41,313	----	----	17,512	344	19.6
1959	63,038	128	2.0	24,607	483	19.6	1944	(NA)	----	----	17,738	330	18.6
1958	61,238	124	2.0	23,443	470	20.0	1943	(NA)	----	----	18,309	344	18.7
1957	59,336	114	1.9	22,173	440	19.8	1942	(NA)	----	----	18,648	250	13.4
1956	57,377	105	1.8	20,623	520	25.2	1941	(NA)	----	----	18,916	224	11.8
							1940	40,365	----	----	19,138	200	10.5

NA Not available.

[1] U.S. Bureau of the Census estimates of civilian population as of July 1, except 1940, 1950, 1960, and 1970, as of April 1.

[2] For 1940–1956, includes traffic cases.

Series H 1125–1134. Persons in Custody in Training Schools for Juvenile Delinquents and in Detention Homes: 1950, 1960, and 1970

[1970 based on 20-percent sample, 1960 on 25-percent sample, and 1950 on complete count. Comparability of figures is affected by differences in classification]

Series No.	Characteristic	1970: Training schools for juvenile delinquents: Total	1970: Public	1970: Private	1970: Detention homes	1960: Training schools for juvenile delinquents: Total	1960: Public	1960: Private	1960: Detention homes	1950: Training schools for juvenile delinquents: Total	1950: Public	1950: Private	1950: Detention homes
1125	Total	66,457	57,691	8,766	10,272	45,695	38,359	7,336	10,821	36,986	29,042	7,944	3,894
1126	Male	52,769	46,867	5,902	6,590	33,765	29,681	4,084	7,680	23,968	21,679	2,289	3,018
1127	Female	13,688	10,824	2,864	3,682	11,930	8,678	3,252	3,141	13,018	7,363	5,655	876
1128	White	39,757	33,428	6,329	6,754	31,294	24,900	6,394	7,342	28,578	21,342	7,236	2,847
1129	Negro and other	26,700	24,263	2,437	3,518	14,401	13,459	942	3,479	8,408	7,700	708	1,047
1130	Under 10 years	1,006	647	359	481	476	327	149	785	735	507	228	334
1131	10–13 years	7,291	5,581	1,710	1,986	6,131	4,858	1,273	2,468	5,170	3,908	1,262	527
1132	14 years	8,272	6,873	1,399	1,656	6,078	5,067	1,011	1,625	4,859	3,825	1,034	342
1133	15–19 years	42,767	37,929	4,838	5,937	31,316	26,676	4,640	4,988	23,978	19,360	4,618	1,244
1134	20 years and over	7,121	6,661	460	212	1,694	1,431	263	955	2,244	1,442	802	1,447

U.S. Bureau of the Census, Historical Statistics of the United States, Colonial Times to 1970, Bicentennial Edition, Part 1. Washington, D.C., 1975

Part four : Health

Health (general)

The Population Now

Persons with a usual place of medical care, according to age, sex, color, and family income: United States, 1974
(Data are based on household interviews of a sample of the civilian noninstitutionalized population)

Sex, color, and family income	All ages	Under 15 years	15-44 years	45-64 years	65 years and over
	Percent of population with a usual place of medical care				
Total	80.5	89.8	74.1	79.7	85.0
Sex					
Male	75.6	90.1	65.7	74.1	82.3
Female	85.0	89.5	81.9	84.8	86.9
Color					
White	81.2	91.2	75.0	80.0	85.1
All other	75.2	82.4	67.7	76.9	84.2
Family income[1]					
Less than $5,000	77.9	82.9	68.2	79.0	85.3
$5,000-$9,999	79.8	87.1	72.6	80.1	88.6
$10,000-$14,999	81.7	92.1	75.2	80.4	85.3
$15,000 or more	83.2	93.7	77.8	82.1	82.7

[1] Excludes unknown family income.

SOURCE: Division of Health Interview Statistics, National Center for Health Statistics: Data from the Health Interview Survey.

Editor's note: For material on the special nutritional requirements of the human fetus, the pregnant woman, the newborn baby and the lactating mother; the nutritional deficiencies discovered among adolescents; and the eating patterns and special needs of the elderly, see Part IV: Nutrition and the Life Cycle in SOURCEBOOK ON FOOD AND NUTRITION (1978: Marquis Academic Media).

Usual place of medical care, according to age, sex, color, and family income: United States, 1974

(Data are based on household interviews of a sample of the civilian noninstitutionalized population)

Age, sex, color, and family income	Population in thousands	Usual place of medical care										
		All places	Private doctor's office or doctors' clinic	Group practice	Hospital outpatient clinic	Hospital emergency room	Company or industry clinic	Home	Other place of care	Usual place unknown	No regular place of care	Unknown whether regular source of care
		Percent distribution										
ALL AGES												
Total	207,334	100.0	50.5	21.9	3.8	0.4	0.3	0.2	2.2	1.2	14.9	4.7
Sex												
Male	100,024	100.0	47.2	20.4	3.6	0.4	0.3	0.2	2.2	1.2	17.7	6.7
Female	107,309	100.0	53.6	23.2	4.0	0.3	0.2	0.2	2.2	1.2	12.2	2.8
Color												
White	180,725	100.0	52.2	22.7	2.6	0.3	0.3	0.2	1.9	1.2	14.3	4.5
All other	26,608	100.0	39.4	16.4	12.4	1.1	0.4	*	4.3	1.1	18.8	6.0
Family income [1]												
Less than $5,000	32,316	100.0	47.0	17.3	7.2	0.6	0.2	0.3	4.1	1.1	19.1	2.9
$5,000-$9,999	47,398	100.0	50.1	19.9	4.8	0.6	0.3	0.2	2.8	1.2	16.6	3.6
$10,000-$14,999	51,666	100.0	51.9	23.3	3.0	0.3	0.3	0.1	1.6	1.2	14.1	4.2
$15,000 or more	63,265	100.0	52.4	25.4	2.1	0.1	0.3	0.2	1.4	1.3	11.6	5.2
UNDER 15 YEARS												
Total	54,588	100.0	52.5	27.1	5.2	0.5	0.2	0.1	2.8	1.5	8.7	1.5
Sex												
Male	27,827	100.0	52.0	27.8	5.3	0.5	0.1	*	2.8	1.5	8.5	1.4
Female	26,761	100.0	52.9	26.4	5.2	0.5	0.2	*	2.7	1.6	8.9	1.6
Color												
White	45,831	100.0	55.4	28.3	3.1	0.3	0.1	0.1	2.2	1.6	7.5	1.3
All other	8,758	100.0	36.9	20.7	16.4	1.3	*	*	5.7	1.3	15.0	2.6
Family income [1]												
Less than $5,000	6,746	100.0	43.0	20.3	11.3	1.0	*	*	5.8	1.1	15.4	1.6
$5,000-$9,999	12,853	100.0	50.2	23.7	7.0	0.8	*	*	3.8	1.3	11.3	1.6
$10,000-$14,999	15,394	100.0	55.7	27.7	4.0	0.4	*	*	2.3	1.8	6.5	1.4
$15,000 or more	16,685	100.0	55.4	32.7	2.5	*	*	*	1.2	1.5	5.2	1.0

See footnote at end of table.

Usual place of medical care, according to age, sex, color, and family income: United States, 1974—Continued

(Data are based on household interviews of a sample of the civilian noninstitutionalized population)

Age, sex, color, and family income	Population in thousands	Usual place of medical care										
		All places	Private doctor's office or doctors' clinic	Group practice	Hospital outpatient clinic	Hospital emergency room	Company or industry clinic	Home	Other place of care	Usual place unknown	No regular place of care	Unknown whether regular source of care
		Percent distribution										
15-44 YEARS												
Total	89,143	100.0	46.2	20.1	3.4	0.4	0.3	0.1	2.5	1.0	19.6	6.3
Sex												
Male	43,201	100.0	41.7	17.1	2.7	0.5	0.4	0.2	2.2	1.0	24.8	9.5
Female	45,942	100.0	50.5	22.9	4.1	0.4	0.2	0.1	2.9	1.0	14.7	3.4
Color												
White	77,506	100.0	47.5	21.1	2.4	0.3	0.2	0.1	2.4	1.0	18.9	6.0
All other	11,637	100.0	37.7	13.2	10.0	1.3	0.5	*	3.8	1.0	23.8	8.5
Family income [1]												
Less than $5,000	10,746	100.0	37.5	14.6	7.1	1.0	*	*	6.7	0.9	26.9	4.9
$5,000-$9,999	20,041	100.0	45.0	18.1	4.4	0.6	0.3	0.2	3.0	1.0	22.4	5.0
$10,000-$14,999	24,194	100.0	47.2	22.1	2.7	0.4	0.3	*	1.6	0.9	19.3	5.5
$15,000 or more	29,541	100.0	49.9	22.5	2.0	0.1	0.3	0.2	1.6	1.1	15.2	7.0
45-64 YEARS												
Total	42,862	100.0	52.7	20.2	3.4	0.1	0.4	0.1	1.5	1.1	14.4	6.0
Sex												
Male	20,419	100.0	48.2	18.5	3.5	0.2	0.5	*	1.9	1.1	16.8	9.1
Female	22,443	100.0	56.8	21.8	3.4	*	0.4	*	1.0	1.2	12.2	3.1
Color												
White	38,514	100.0	53.8	20.7	2.6	0.1	0.4	0.1	1.2	1.1	14.2	5.9
All other	4,348	100.0	43.4	16.3	11.1	*	*	*	3.9	1.4	16.3	6.8
Family income [1]												
Less than $5,000	6,001	100.0	49.8	17.4	8.1	*	*	*	2.1	1.0	18.3	2.7
$5,000-$9,999	9,016	100.0	52.9	19.1	4.1	*	0.4	*	2.1	1.0	15.3	4.5
$10,000-$14,999	9,957	100.0	55.4	20.0	2.5	*	0.5	*	1.0	1.0	14.0	5.6
$15,000 or more	14,807	100.0	53.3	23.5	2.0	*	0.5	*	1.3	1.4	11.7	6.2

See footnote at end of table.

Usual place of medical care, according to age, sex, color, and family income: United States, 1974—Continued
(Data are based on household interviews of a sample of the civilian noninstitutionalized population)

Age, sex, color, and family income	Population in thousands	Usual place of medical care										
		All places	Private doctor's office or doctors' clinic	Group practice	Hospital outpatient clinic	Hospital emergency room	Company or industry clinic	Home	Other place of care	Usual place unknown	No regular place of care	Unknown whether regular source of care
65 YEARS AND OVER		Percent distribution										
Total	20,740	100.0	59.5	19.2	2.8	0.2	0.2	0.8	0.7	1.5	12.0	3.0
Sex												
Male	8,578	100.0	57.8	18.3	3.4	*	0.4	*	0.6	1.5	14.1	3.6
Female	12,163	100.0	60.8	19.8	2.4	*	*	1.2	0.8	1.6	10.5	2.6
Color												
White	18,875	100.0	60.2	19.5	1.8	*	0.2	0.8	0.6	1.6	12.0	2.9
All other	1,866	100.0	52.7	16.0	12.3	*	*	*	*	*	11.5	4.3
Family income [1]												
Less than $5,000	8,823	100.0	59.7	18.2	3.7	*	*	0.6	1.1	1.6	13.1	1.6
$5,000-$9,999	5,488	100.0	63.9	18.9	2.1	*	*	0.7	*	2.0	9.5	2.0
$10,000-$14,999	2,122	100.0	61.0	20.2	2.2	*	*	*	*	*	10.4	4.3
$15,000 or more	2,231	100.0	56.5	21.5	1.7	*	*	*	*	*	11.6	5.7

[1] Excludes unknown family income.

SOURCE: Division of Health Interview Statistics, National Center for Health Statistics: Data from the Health Interview Survey.

Persons with barriers to medical care, according to type of barrier, age, sex, color, and family income: United States, 1974

(Data are based on household interviews of a sample of the civilian noninstitutionalized population)

Age, sex, color, and family income	Type of barrier to care						
	Doctor not available when needed	Cost too much	Did not know where to go	No way to get to doctor	Office hours not convenient	Trouble getting ap-pointment	Other[1]
	Percent of population with specified barrier to care						
ALL AGES							
Total	2.7	2.5	1.0	1.2	1.7	5.0	0.6
Sex							
Male	2.3	2.1	0.7	0.8	1.6	3.8	0.5
Female	3.1	3.0	1.2	1.6	1.7	6.0	0.6
Color							
White	2.8	2.4	1.0	1.1	1.7	5.1	0.6
All other	2.1	3.3	1.1	2.1	1.7	3.9	0.5
Family income[2]							
Less than $5,000	3.2	5.1	1.3	3.6	1.7	5.1	0.8
$5,000-$9,999	2.9	3.8	1.3	1.4	1.9	5.2	0.5
$10,000-$14,999	2.6	1.8	0.9	0.6	1.7	4.9	0.5
$15,000 or more	2.6	0.8	0.6	0.3	1.6	5.2	0.5
UNDER 15 YEARS							
Total	2.3	1.8	0.6	1.1	1.5	3.3	0.4
Sex							
Male	2.2	1.7	0.8	1.0	1.7	3.3	0.5
Female	2.3	2.0	0.5	1.2	1.2	3.4	0.3
Color							
White	2.5	1.9	0.6	0.9	1.3	3.5	0.4
All other	1.1	1.7	*	2.1	2.1	2.6	*
Family income[2]							
Less than $5,000	2.5	3.7	1.2	3.7	1.5	3.9	*
$5,000-$9,999	2.6	2.9	0.9	1.3	2.0	3.6	*
$10,000-$14,999	2.4	1.2	0.5	0.7	1.6	3.1	*
$15,000 or more	1.9	0.6	*	*	1.0	3.4	*
15-44 YEARS							
Total	3.1	2.9	1.3	1.0	2.3	6.8	0.5
Sex							
Male	2.4	2.3	0.8	0.4	1.9	4.6	0.4
Female	3.8	3.4	1.8	1.6	2.6	8.8	0.8
Color							
White	3.2	2.8	1.3	0.9	2.3	6.9	0.6
All other	2.5	3.9	1.3	1.9	1.9	5.6	*

See footnotes at end of table.

Persons with barriers to medical care, according to type of barrier, age, sex, color, and family income: United States, 1974—Continued

(Data are based on household interviews of a sample of the civilian noninstitutionalized population)

Age, sex, color, and family income	Type of barrier to care						
	Doctor not available when needed	Cost too much	Did not know where to go	No way to get to doctor	Office hours not convenient	Trouble getting appointment	Other[1]
	Percent of population with specified barrier to care						
15-44 YEARS—Continued							
Family income[2]							
Less than $5,000	4.6	6.0	1.9	3.6	2.9	8.8	0.7
$5,000-$9,999	3.4	5.0	1.6	1.3	2.4	7.1	0.7
$10,000-$14,999	2.7	2.3	1.3	0.6	2.1	6.5	0.5
$15,000 or more	3.0	0.9	0.9	0.3	2.2	6.5	0.5
45-64 YEARS							
Total	2.7	3.0	0.7	0.9	1.2	4.4	0.7
Sex							
Male	2.3	2.0	0.5	0.5	1.1	3.5	0.7
Female	3.0	3.8	0.9	1.2	1.2	5.2	0.7
Color							
White	2.6	2.8	0.6	0.8	1.2	4.6	0.7
All other	3.0	4.7	*	1.6	*	2.8	*
Family income[2]							
Less than $5,000	3.3	8.6	1.3	3.1	*	3.3	1.5
$5,000-$9,999	2.7	3.7	1.0	1.2	1.4	4.3	*
$10,000-$14,999	2.6	1.7	*	*	1.3	4.3	*
$15,000 or more	2.7	0.9	0.5	*	1.2	5.1	0.6
65 YEARS AND OVER							
Total	2.2	2.0	1.0	2.8	0.8	2.7	0.7
Sex							
Male	2.2	2.1	1.0	2.1	0.8	2.5	*
Female	2.1	2.0	1.0	3.2	0.8	2.8	0.9
Color							
White	2.1	1.9	1.0	2.7	0.8	2.8	0.8
All other	2.7	*	*	3.9	*	*	*
Family income[2]							
Less than $5,000	1.8	2.6	0.9	3.7	1.0	2.8	*
$5,000-$9,999	2.3	2.0	1.7	2.2	*	3.0	*
$10,000-$14,999	2.4	*	*	*	*	*	*
$15,000 or more	3.0	*	*	*	*	3.4	*

[1] Includes both "other specified" and "other unspecified" responses.
[2] Excludes unknown family income.

NOTE: A person can report more than one barrier to care.

SOURCE: Division of Health Interview Statistics, National Center for Health Statistics: Data from the Health Interview Survey.

Contraceptive use by currently married women 15-44 years of age, according to method of contraception, race, and age: United States, 1965, 1970, and 1973

(Data based on household interviews of samples of women in the childbearing ages)

Race, age, and year of survey	Number of currently married women in thousands	Percent using contra-ception	Method of contraception							
			Total	Wife steri-lized	Hus-band steri-lized	Pill	IUD	Dia-phragm	Condom	All other
			Percent distribution of women using contraception							
All races 15-44 years[1]										
1965	24,710	63.9	100.0	7.0	5.1	23.9	1.2	9.9	21.9	30.9
1970	25,577	65.0	100.0	8.5	7.8	34.2	7.4	5.7	14.2	22.4
1973	26,646	69.7	100.0	12.4	11.1	36.0	9.6	3.4	13.5	13.8
15-24 years:										
1965	5,324	59.8	100.0	1.3	1.5	48.7	1.9	4.4	15.7	26.5
1970	6,212	63.4	100.0	1.0	1.3	58.5	8.8	2.5	9.0	19.0
1973	5,977	68.8	100.0	3.7	2.2	65.2	10.5	1.6	8.3	8.7
25-34 years:										
1965	9,316	68.3	100.0	6.8	5.4	25.2	1.3	8.9	23.3	29.2
1970	10,484	68.6	100.0	7.9	7.3	34.7	9.7	5.6	13.4	21.4
1973	11,311	73.0	100.0	11.4	11.2	35.3	12.4	3.2	13.3	13.3
35-44 years:										
1965	10,070	61.9	100.0	10.2	6.6	9.8	0.7	13.9	23.8	35.0
1970	8,881	61.9	100.0	14.7	13.1	16.1	3.6	8.0	18.9	25.7
1973	9,358	66.4	100.0	19.4	17.0	17.7	5.3	5.1	17.4	18.0
White 15-44 years										
1965	22,382	64.9	100.0	6.3	5.4	24.0	1.0	10.4	22.4	30.3
1970	23,220	65.7	100.0	7.5	8.3	34.0	7.3	5.7	14.8	22.3
1973	24,249	70.7	100.0	11.6	11.8	35.5	9.4	3.6	14.1	13.9
15-24 years:										
1965	4,724	59.6	100.0	1.1	1.7	51.4	1.5	4.4	15.4	24.6
1970	5,595	63.8	100.0	0.7	1.3	58.9	8.2	2.6	9.3	19.1
1973	5,384	69.2	100.0	3.5	2.4	64.4	10.4	1.7	8.8	8.7
25-34 years:										
1965	8,387	69.4	100.0	6.2	5.7	25.0	1.1	9.4	23.6	29.1
1970	9,578	69.0	100.0	7.1	7.8	34.4	9.6	5.6	14.0	21.5
1973	10,347	73.7	100.0	11.1	11.7	34.9	12.1	3.2	13.8	13.2
35-44 years:										
1965	9,271	63.2	100.0	8.9	7.0	9.9	0.7	14.4	24.6	34.4
1970	8,047	63.5	100.0	12.9	14.0	16.1	3.6	8.1	19.5	25.8
1973	8,518	67.9	100.0	17.5	18.1	17.7	5.2	5.3	18.1	18.2

See footnote at end of table.

Contraceptive use by currently married women 15-44 years of age, according to method of contraception, race, and age: United States, 1965, 1970, and 1973—Continued

(Data based on household interviews of samples of women in the childbearing ages)

Race, age, and year of survey	Number of currently married women in thousands	Percent using contra-ception	Method of contraception							
			Total	Wife steri-lized	Hus-band steri-lized	Pill	IUD	Dia-phragm	Condom	All other
Black 15-44 years			Percent distribution of women using contraception							
1965	2,091	57.2	100.0	14.4	0.5	21.7	2.9	5.1	17.0	38.5
1970	2,031	59.2	100.0	19.3	1.1	37.4	7.6	5.2	6.7	22.7
1973	2,081	60.3	100.0	23.1	1.7	43.5	12.7	2.0	5.3	11.5
15-24 years:										
1965	555	61.5	100.0	3.2	0.6	27.8	5.7	3.2	17.7	41.7
1970	506	60.5	100.0	1.7	0.0	59.3	10.2	2.5	6.8	19.4
1973	547	66.2	100.0	6.5	0.1	73.5	11.9	0.1	2.1	5.8
25-34 years:										
1965	794	62.8	100.0	12.6	0.4	27.3	3.0	4.3	20.3	32.1
1970	787	67.3	100.0	16.7	1.0	39.2	8.3	5.4	5.4	24.1
1973	819	63.8	100.0	17.9	2.8	42.5	16.8	2.9	4.9	12.3
35-44 years:										
1965	742	47.9	100.0	27.9	0.6	7.9	0.0	7.9	11.5	44.1
1970	738	49.4	100.0	37.9	2.1	16.4	4.3	7.1	8.6	23.5
1973	715	51.9	100.0	46.8	1.6	15.9	7.7	2.7	9.1	16.3

[1] Includes all other races not shown separately.

NOTE: Data from 1965 and 1970 National Fertility Survey and 1973 National Survey of Family Growth.

SOURCE: Westoff, C. F.: Trends in contraceptive practice: 1965-1973. Fam. Plann. Perspect. 8(2):54-57, Mar./Apr. 1976. (Copyright: reprinted with permission.)

Life expectancy at specified ages, according to color and sex: United States, selected years 1900-75
(Data are based on the National Vital Registration System)

Specified age and year	Total	Color			
		White		All other	
		Male	Female	Male	Female
	Remaining life expectancy in years				
Birth					
1900 [1]	47.3	46.6	48.7	32.5	33.5
1960	69.7	67.4	74.1	61.1	66.3
1970	70.9	68.0	75.6	61.3	69.4
1971	71.1	68.3	75.8	61.6	69.7
1972	71.1	68.3	75.9	61.5	69.9
1973	71.3	68.4	76.1	61.9	70.1
1974	71.9	68.9	76.6	62.9	71.2
1975	72.5	69.4	77.2	63.6	72.3
Age 20					
1900-1902 [1]	42.8	42.2	43.8	35.1	36.9
1960	52.4	50.1	56.2	45.5	49.9
1970	53.1	50.3	57.4	44.7	52.2
1971	53.3	50.5	57.5	44.9	52.3
1972	53.3	50.4	57.5	44.6	52.5
1973	53.4	50.5	57.7	44.9	52.6
1974	53.9	51.0	58.1	45.7	53.6
1975	54.4	51.4	58.6	46.3	54.7
Age 65					
1900-1902 [1]	11.9	11.5	12.2	10.4	11.4
1960	14.3	12.9	15.9	12.7	15.2
1970	15.2	13.1	17.1	13.3	16.4
1971	15.2	13.2	17.2	13.2	16.3
1972	15.2	13.1	17.1	13.1	16.3
1973	15.3	13.2	17.3	13.1	16.2
1974	15.2	13.4	17.6	13.4	16.8
1975	16.0	13.7	18.1	13.7	17.5

[1] Death registration areas only. The death registration areas increased in number from 10 States and the District of Columbia in 1900 to the entire coterminous United States in 1933.

SOURCES: National Center for Health Statistics: Vital Statistics of the United States, Vol. II, for data years 1900-72, Washington, U.S. Government Printing Office; for 1973 and 1974, Health Resources Administration, DHEW, Rockville, Md., in preparation; and for 1975, Health Resources Administration, DHEW, Rockville, Md., to be published.

Death rates, according to color, sex, and age: United States, 1975
(Data are based on the National Vital Registration System)

Age	Color								
	Total			White			All other		
	Both sexes	Male	Female	Both sexes	Male	Female	Both sexes	Male	Female
	Number of deaths per 100,000 resident population								
All ages[1]	888.5	1,013.2	770.3	896.8	1,015.3	783.8	833.6	999.1	682.5
Under 1 year	1,641.0	1,829.3	1,443.7	1,413.0	1,594.4	1,222.3	2,765.3	3,001.1	2,523.0
1-4 years	70.8	77.8	63.5	64.4	71.3	57.1	101.0	108.8	93.0
5-9 years	35.7	42.1	29.1	33.6	39.4	27.5	46.3	55.9	36.8
10-14 years	35.7	45.5	25.6	34.1	43.3	24.4	44.6	57.4	31.6
15-19 years	101.5	147.4	54.4	99.1	144.5	52.4	114.8	164.3	65.4
20-24 years	138.2	209.6	67.2	124.9	189.5	59.8	220.2	340.7	110.7
25-29 years	136.7	200.0	74.5	116.5	168.9	64.1	277.2	435.8	141.7
30-34 years	151.0	205.9	97.8	126.7	169.5	84.3	318.0	477.1	183.4
35-39 years	209.6	276.7	146.2	176.2	230.2	124.0	442.4	630.8	288.9
40-44 years	326.1	419.4	237.2	284.1	363.5	206.9	621.0	844.7	434.7
45-49 years	512.4	667.2	366.1	463.1	606.0	326.6	893.6	1,166.4	657.8
50-54 years	784.6	1,044.1	544.2	727.4	971.3	499.7	1,276.7	1,690.0	914.1
55-59 years	1,199.8	1,615.1	821.3	1,131.3	1,534.6	761.6	1,843.7	2,392.8	1,367.4
60-64 years	1,832.7	2,522.8	1,226.8	1,755.4	2,443.7	1,149.5	2,553.7	3,280.8	1,939.0
65-69 years	2,574.7	3,636.3	1,731.4	2,516.5	3,590.9	1,662.7	3,082.0	4,036.7	2,331.0
70-74 years	4,050.5	5,555.6	2,945.1	3,917.9	5,462.2	2,798.8	5,505.6	6,534.9	4,667.0
75-79 years	6,205.1	8,253.7	4,878.6	6,146.7	8,253.6	4,801.8	6,879.9	8,254.3	5,832.0
80-84 years	9,102.6	11,593.3	7,686.9	9,257.7	11,832.0	7,813.5	7,364.5	9,167.4	6,180.9
85 years and over	15,187.9	17,572.6	14,031.4	15,707.5	18,257.9	14,494.1	10,102.9	11,693.8	9,177.3

[1] Includes unknown age.

NOTE: Excludes deaths to nonresidents of the United States.

SOURCE: Division of Vital Statistics, National Center for Health Statistics.

Persons exercising regularly and type of exercise, according to sex and age: United States, 1975
(Data are based on household interviews of a sample of the civilian noninstitutionalized population)

Sex and age	Civilian noninstitutionalized population in thousands	Percent exercising regularly[1]	Type of exercise						
			Ride bicycle	Do calisthenics	Jog	Lift weights	Swim	Walk	All other
Both sexes			Percent of population engaging in specific type of exercise						
All ages 20 years and over	135,655	48.6	10.9	13.5	4.8	3.4	11.8	33.8	6.8
20-44 years	71,084	53.7	16.1	17.3	7.3	5.4	16.9	33.8	6.9
45-64 years	43,145	43.4	6.5	10.8	2.7	1.5	8.0	32.9	6.5
65 years and over	21,426	42.3	2.9	6.1	1.2	*	2.8	35.7	6.9
Male									
All ages 20 years and over	63,665	48.5	10.8	13.5	7.2	6.3	13.3	32.5	6.4
20-44 years	34,268	52.7	14.9	17.5	10.6	10.1	18.8	31.4	6.2
45-64 years	20,567	42.0	6.7	10.1	3.8	2.6	8.1	31.4	5.9
65 years and over	8,830	47.3	4.3	5.9	2.1	*	4.1	39.4	8.1
Female									
All ages 20 years and over	71,990	48.7	11.1	13.5	2.7	0.8	10.5	35.0	7.1
20-44 years	36,816	54.6	17.2	17.1	4.1	1.1	15.0	36.0	7.5
45-64 years	22,579	44.6	6.4	11.4	1.6	*	7.8	34.2	7.1
65 years and over	12,595	38.7	1.8	6.3	*	*	1.9	33.0	6.0

[1] Regular exercise is defined as any exercise on a weekly basis.

NOTE: More than one type of exercise can be reported per person.

SOURCE: Division of Health Interview Statistics, National Center for Health Statistics: Provisional data from the Health Interview Survey.

Obesity among persons aged 20-74 years based on triceps skinfold measurements, according to sex and age: United States, 1971-74
(Data are based on physical examinations of a sample of the civilian noninstitutionalized population)

Sex and age	Percent of population classified as obese[1]
Male	
All ages 20-74 years	13.0
20-44 years	14.0
45-74 years	11.8
Female	
All ages 20-74 years	22.7
20-44 years	19.1
45-74 years	26.9

[1] Obesity is defined as falling above the sex-specific 85th-percentile measurements for ages 20-29 years.

SOURCE: Division of Health Examination Statistics, National Center for Health Statistics: Data from the Health and Nutrition Examination Survey.

Venereal disease cases, according to type of venereal disease: United States, 1941-75

(Data are based on reporting by State health departments)

Year	Type of venereal disease								
	Syphilis					Gonorrhea	Chancroid	Granuloma inguinale	Lympho-granuloma venereum
	All stages [1]	Primary and secondary	Early latent	Late and late latent	Congenital				
	Number of cases								
1941	485,560	68,231	109,018	202,984	17,600	193,468	3,384	639	1,381
1942	479,601	75,312	116,245	202,064	16,918	212,403	5,477	1,278	1,888
1943	575,593	82,204	149,390	251,958	16,164	275,070	8,354	1,748	2,593
1944	467,755	78,443	123,038	202,848	13,578	300,676	7,878	1,759	2,858
1945	359,114	77,007	101,719	142,187	12,339	287,181	5,515	1,857	2,631
1946	363,647	94,957	107,924	125,248	12,106	368,020	7,091	2,232	2,603
1947	372,963	106,539	107,767	121,980	12,271	400,639	9,039	2,403	2,688
1948	338,141	80,528	97,745	123,972	13,309	363,014	8,631	2,315	2,494
1949	288,736	54,248	84,331	121,931	14,295	331,661	7,218	2,611	2,170
1950	229,723	32,148	64,786	112,424	13,446	303,992	5,796	2,017	1,635
1951	198,640	18,211	52,309	107,133	12,836	270,459	5,707	1,637	1,332
1952	168,734	11,991	38,365	101,920	9,240	245,633	3,837	1,069	1,235
1953	156,099	9,551	32,287	100,195	8,021	243,857	3,490	785	1,103
1954	137,876	7,688	24,999	93,601	7,234	239,661	3,294	607	917
1955	122,075	6,516	21,553	84,741	5,515	239,787	2,863	584	875
1956	126,219	6,757	20,014	89,851	5,535	233,333	2,322	419	602
1957	130,552	6,251	19,046	96,856	5,452	216,476	1,860	348	449
1958	116,630	6,661	16,698	85,974	4,839	220,191	1,574	332	436
1959	119,981	8,178	17,592	86,776	5,215	237,318	1,604	282	485
1960	120,249	12,471	16,829	84,195	4,593	246,697	1,555	273	800
1961	125,262	18,781	19,146	80,942	4,388	265,665	1,595	296	842
1962	124,188	20,084	19,924	78,264	4,085	260,468	1,401	203	635
1963	128,450	22,045	18,683	81,736	4,140	270,076	1,242	196	589
1964	118,247	22,733	18,104	72,184	3,737	290,603	1,260	145	543
1965	113,018	23,250	17,315	67,636	3,505	310,155	1,083	144	873

See footnote at end of table.

Venereal disease cases, according to type of venereal disease: United States, 1941-75—Continued

(Data are based on reporting by State health departments)

Year	Type of venereal disease								
	Syphilis					Gonorrhea	Chancroid	Granuloma inguinale	Lympho-granuloma venereum
	All stages [1]	Primary and secondary	Early latent	Late and late latent	Congenital				
	Number of cases								
1966	110,128	22,473	16,974	66,149	3,464	334,949	950	164	625
1967	103,546	21,090	15,618	62,653	3,050	375,606	777	127	372
1968	98,195	20,182	15,379	58,905	2,596	431,380	827	174	349
1969	96,679	18,679	15,399	59,262	2,223	494,227	959	126	525
1970	87,934	20,186	15,425	49,537	1,903	573,200	1,189	168	587
1971	94,383	23,336	17,843	50,429	2,047	624,371	1,507	103	615
1972	95,076	24,000	20,354	48,056	1,951	718,401	1,298	88	828
1973	90,609	25,080	22,293	40,931	1,650	809,681	1,338	73	556
1974	84,164	24,728	24,290	33,465	1,334	874,161	1,064	51	374
1975	82,397	25,746	26,166	29,264	1,024	945,945	811	54	386

[1] Includes stage of syphilis not stated.

SOURCE: Center for Disease Control: VD Fact Sheet, 1975, 32d ed. DHEW Pub. No. (CDC) 76-8195. Public Health Service. Atlanta, Ga.

Consumption of alcohol by persons 18 years of age and over, according to selected characteristics: United States, January 1975

(Data are based on household interviews of a sample of the civilian noninstitutionalized population)

Characteristic	Drinking level						
	All levels	Abstainers or less than 1 drink per year	Infrequent drinkers (1-6 drinks per year)	Drinkers, average daily consumption of absolute alcohol: 0.100 oz. or less	0.101-0.200 oz.	0.201-0.550 oz.	0.551 oz. or more
	Percent distribution						
Total	100	34	10	21	7	11	16
Sex							
Male	100	25	8	18	7	14	25
Female	100	43	11	25	6	8	7
Race							
White	100	33	10	22	7	11	16
Black	100	47	10	19	3	7	9
Family income							
Less than $5,000	100	53	10	16	3	5	11
$5,000-$9,999	100	39	11	15	4	11	16
$10,000-$14,999	100	28	10	25	9	12	15
$15,000 or more	100	16	8	27	10	16	21
Marital status							
Single	100	19	11	22	8	13	28
Married	100	33	9	22	8	11	15
Separated, divorced, or widowed	100	51	11	19	2	6	9
Education							
Less than high school graduate	100	50	9	16	3	6	13
High school graduate	100	27	10	23	8	13	18
Some college	100	22	13	26	8	12	18
College graduate	100	21	6	28	11	16	16

SOURCE: Calculated from tables in: Rappeport, M., Labaw, P., and Williams, J.: The Public Evaluates the NIAAA Public Education Campaign; A Study for the U.S. Department of Health, Education, and Welfare, Vols. I and II. Princeton. Opinion Research Corporation, July 1975.

Smoking status of persons 21 years of age and over, according to sex and age: United States, 1975
(Data are based on telephone interviews of a sample of the noninstitutionalized population resident in private households)

Sex and age	Smoking status			
	All statuses	Never	Former	Current
Male	Percent distribution			
All ages 21 years and over	100.0	31.5	29.2	39.3
21-24 years	100.0	42.7	16.0	41.3
25-34 years	100.0	33.6	22.5	43.9
35-44 years	100.0	27.0	25.8	47.1
45-54 years	100.0	22.9	36.0	41.1
55-64 years	100.0	27.6	38.8	33.7
65 years and over	100.0	39.6	36.2	24.2
Female				
All ages 21 years and over	100.0	56.6	14.5	28.9
21-24 years	100.0	56.1	9.9	34.0
25-34 years	100.0	48.1	16.5	35.4
35-44 years	100.0	45.9	17.7	36.4
45-54 years	100.0	51.8	15.5	32.8
55-64 years	100.0	59.0	15.0	25.9
65 years and over	100.0	79.1	10.7	10.2

NOTE: Smoking status is defined as: Never—never having smoked as many as 100 cigarettes; former—having smoked at least 100 cigarettes but not smoking cigarettes now; current—having smoked at least 100 cigarettes and smoking cigarettes now.

SOURCE: Center for Disease Control and National Institutes of Health: Adult Use of Tobacco, 1975. Public Health Service. Atlanta, Ga., June 1976.

Consumer products with the highest product hazard index scores[1] listed in rank order, according to age of person injured: Contiguous United States, July 1, 1975-June 30, 1976

(Data are based on reporting by a sample of hospital emergency rooms)

Rank	All ages	Under 15 years	15 years and over
		Product category[2]	
1	Bicycles and bicycle equipment, including add-on features (baskets, horns, nonstandard seats, handlebars)	Bicycles and bicycle equipment, including add-on features (baskets, horns, nonstandard seats, handlebars)	Stairs (including folding stairs), steps, ramps, landings
2	Stairs (including folding stairs), steps, ramps, landings	Stairs (including folding stairs), steps, ramps, landings	Football, activity, related equipment and apparel
3	Football, activity, related equipment and apparel	Swings, slides, seesaws, and playground equipment	Baseball, activity, related equipment and apparel
4	Baseball, activity, related equipment and apparel	Nonglass tables and unspecified tables	Bicycles and bicycle equipment, including add-on features (baskets, horns, nonstandard seats, handlebars)
5	Swings, slides, seesaws, and playground equipment	Football, activity, related equipment and apparel	Basketball, activity, and related equipment
6	Nonglass tables and unspecified tables	Swimming, swimming pools, and related equipment	Cooking ranges, ovens, and related equipment
7	Swimming, swimming pools, and related equipment	Baseball, activity, related equipment and apparel	Liquid fuels, kindling, illuminating (including gasoline, kerosene, lighter fluid, fuel for chafing dishes and fondue pots, charcoal starter, etc.)
8	Beds, including springs, frames, bunk beds, and unspecified beds (excluding mattresses or box springs, water beds, sofa beds, infant beds, and special beds)	Beds, including springs, frames, bunk beds, and unspecified beds (excluding mattresses or box springs, water beds, sofa beds, infant beds, and special beds)	Home workshop powersaws and unspecified saws
9	Liquid fuels, kindling, illuminating (including gasoline, kerosene, lighter fluid, fuel for chafing dishes and fondue pots, charcoal starter, etc.)	Liquid fuels, kindling, illuminating (including gasoline, kerosene, lighter fluid, fuel for chafing dishes and fondue pots, charcoal starter, etc.)	Floors and flooring materials
10	Nails, carpet tacks and screws, thumbtacks	Nails, carpet tacks and screws, thumbtacks	Ladders and stools (excluding chain ladders)
11	Basketball, activity, and related equipment	Chairs, sofas, and sofa beds	Power lawnmowers and unspecified lawnmowers
12	Chairs, sofas, and sofa beds	Architectural glass, including glass doors	Nails, carpet tacks and screws, thumbtacks
13	Bleaches and dyes, cleaning agents, and caustic compounds	Skates, skateboards, and scooters	Bleaches and dyes, cleaning agents, and caustic compounds
14	Architectural glass, including glass doors	Bleaches and dyes, cleaning agents, and caustic compounds	Batteries, all kinds
15	Floors and flooring materials	Furnaces and floor furnaces	Chairs, sofas, and sofa beds
16	Cooking ranges, ovens, and related equipment	Charcoal	Architectural glass, including glass doors
17	Power lawnmowers and unspecified lawnmowers	Desks, storage cabinets, bookshelves, and magazine racks	Bathtubs, nonglass shower enclosures, and shower structures other than doors and panels

See footnotes at end of table.

Consumer products with the highest product hazard index scores[1] listed in rank order, according to age of person injured: Contiguous United States, July 1, 1975-June 30, 1976—Continued

(Data are based on reporting by a sample of hospital emergency rooms)

Rank	All ages	Under 15 years	15 years and over
	Product category[2]		
18	Skates, skateboards, and scooters	Nonelectric fences and unspecified fences	Household chemical products other than bleaches and dyes, cleaning agents, caustic compounds, paints, solvents and lubricants, waxes, and polishes (e.g., fumigants, adhesives, photographic chemicals, carbon tetrachloride, acid, chemical deodorizer)
19	Furnaces and floor furnaces	Basketball, activity, and related equipment	Beds, including springs, frames, bunk beds, and unspecified beds (excluding mattresses or box springs, water beds, sofa beds, infant beds, and special beds)
20	Bathtubs, nonglass shower enclosures and shower structures other than doors and panels	Floors and flooring materials	Matches

[1] Based on a frequency severity index (FSI) computed by the Consumer Product Safety Commission. The FSI is derived from the estimated number of injuries treated in emergency rooms for a product category and the mean severity of those injuries.

[2] Excluded are products either not under Consumer Product Safety Commission jurisdiction or under questionable or shared jurisdiction, and products lacking in sufficient specificity to be meaningful.

NOTE: Data obtained through the National Electronic Injury Surveillance System.

SOURCE: U.S. Consumer Product Safety Commission: Annual Report, Fiscal Year 1976. Washington. U.S. Government Printing Office, Oct. 1976.

Health, United States, 1976-1977, U.S. Dept. of Health, Education, and Welfare, Public Health Service, Health Resources Administration, DHEW Publ. No. (HRA) 77-1232 Stock No. 017-022-00553-1

Helping People at Home

in Sweden and the Netherlands

Alfred J. Kahn and Sheila B. Kamerman

MRS. M. has been hospitalized suddenly. Her husband is unable to take time off from work to take care of the children, and there is no relative or neighbor to care for the baby or help with cooking, cleaning, shopping, and other household chores.

Johnny is home from first grade because of a sore throat. His mother works and has no one to stay with him.

The old man in the apartment upstairs feels helpless after the sudden death of his wife. He cannot cope with the housework and needs someone to help him bathe and take him for a walk.

Seventy-three-year-old Mrs. L. is frightened about living alone after having had a heart attack. She worries about carrying heavy packages from the supermarket, and she cannot do the laundry or the heavy cleaning.

In Sweden, home helps—publicly employed and paid and specially trained—can provide assistance in such cases. All that is needed is a telephone call to the local municipal Home Help Service, where the "organizer" in charge of social services for the neighborhood will obtain the facts, assess the need for help, and make appropriate arrangements. Services are available, on request, to people of all classes and income levels. Although wealthy people may purchase such services elsewhere, middle-class, working-class, and poor people make regular and frequent use of a range of services provided under this program. Services are free to the poor and are paid for by others according to a sliding scale of fees related to the income of the recipient. "Light" medical or nursing care is provided free to all.

The Netherlands, another high-coverage country, follows a somewhat different administrative pattern. Public funds are channeled through many private nonprofit groups, which actually deliver this service. Here, too, home helps are valued highly and are considered essential to a modern society.

Home Help in Sweden

Observing a home help organizer at work on an average day and asking her questions give some idea of the services; what home help workers are like; how they are selected and trained; whom they help and what they do; how extensive the service is and what some of the problems are.

Mrs. O. is a typical home help organizer. Trained as a social worker (some are trained as nurses), she is currently employed by the Stockholm Municipal Home Help Service Agency in a branch office located in a large suburban housing development. She is one of a staff of twelve who are responsible for the supervision of 467 home helps, working from two to twenty-five hours per week (although more and more home helps are working a full forty-hour week), servicing 1,069 old people.

This concentration on older people is quite routine in Sweden today; about three-quarters of the services provided go to either the elderly or the handicapped, while only about one-quarter are directed toward families with young children.

Mrs. O. supervises and organizes the work of thirty-seven home helps, who in turn provide a range of services and care to the 137 elderly people composing her caseload. The morning we visited began, as she explained, like every other morning, with a three-hour "telephone time" from 8:00 to 11:00 A.M. People call with requests for service, for information, to change appointments, to complain. Home help staff call to obtain their instructions for the day, to offer information based on the previous day's experiences, or to notify the organizer of their illness and the need for a replacement to be sent out. Some staff come directly to the office, but most report by telephone because the community is large and spread out and traveling to the office is time-consuming.

During these hours Mrs. O. also has to schedule future jobs as requests for service arise, arrange substitutes for part-time staff unable to work that day, and respond to questions and complaints. She called one elderly man to notify him of a change in schedule. She called another to prepare him for the fact that his regular worker was ill, and a "stranger" would come that day to bathe him and cook him a meal. Following a call from another "customer," she phoned a woman's regular home help to ask her to accompany the woman to a doctor's appointment, wait for her, and then take her home.

A staff member called in sick and Mrs. O. phoned each of her clients to ask if they could manage without help for a day or two. She explained to us that if they can take care of themselves and just need help for cleaning or occasional chores, they will wait until their "regular" is back. But older people who need personal care and cooking services cannot wait and Mrs. O. arranged for substitute helpers to be sent them. In cases such as these, or other emergencies where a client becomes ill and suddenly requires help, it may be necessary to reschedule a worker's time, temporarily eliminating service to a more independent older person in order to provide care for the more needy; but no such change is made without notifying the client.

An eighty-two-year-old man called to request thorough cleaning for his apartment. Mrs. O. tried to arrange for this from the municipal service patrol—a specially equipped truck with trained personnel who do heavy cleaning for the elderly and/or handicapped—but their schedule was very busy and they could not service him for several months. She called him back and suggested waiting for the service, but he was insistent, becoming increasingly upset at the idea of a delay. His daughter was coming to visit him for the first time in a long while, and he wanted his home to be spotless when she saw it. Mrs. O. tried again, unsuccessfully, to obtain service from a private cleaning firm. Finally, she remembered that a home help in one of the other districts "specializes" in heavy cleaning, because she enjoys it. Mrs. O. called the organizer in that district, and they worked out an arrangement for an exchange of services.

Later on in the morning Mrs. O. was faced with the unpleasant task of having to discharge one of her staff. The woman had been late, repeatedly, in arriving for her scheduled appointments and on several occasions had neither shown up nor telephoned. Even worse, she had been indiscreet, repeating a confidence given by one of her elderly pensioners. Mrs. O. explained to us that working with the elderly requires patience, sensitivity, warmth, and tact. Indeed, her manner on the telephone, with both her own staff and her clients, is a remarkable illustration of all these qualities.

After lunch, we accompanied Mrs. O. as she made home visits. Every "customer" is visited at least once during the time service is provided, and more often if there is regular, ongoing care involved. In addition, special visits are made if there are problems, or if the case is a "difficult" one. Our first visit was to the home of Mrs. T., a seventy-eight-year-old woman who had been living alone since her husband died a few months before. She was afraid to open her door when we arrived, and only after several minutes of reassurance by Mrs. O. did she unbolt it, first checking our appearance through the half-open chained door. Mrs. O. talked with her briefly, asking her if she was satisfied with her helper. Had the marketing been done properly? Was the house cleaned well? Was everything all right? Mrs. T. complained about the service, but was so vague that it was hard to tell what the problem was. After some probing by Mrs. O., it appeared that Mrs. T. was becoming increasingly frightened about going out alone in the street, and even about being home alone. She has no relatives or friends, and what she fears most is becoming ill with no one knowing. Mrs. O. tried to reassure her, suggesting that she schedule a helper to come in three times weekly, for slightly shorter periods of time, instead of the twice-a-week service Mrs. T. was then receiving. As we left, Mrs. O. mentioned to us the need for a more extensive telephone visiting service for the isolated elderly like Mrs. T.

Our second visit was to seventy-three-year-old Mr. Z., living alone since his wife died. He immediately initiated a discussion of his finances, explaining that his wife had always handled household expenses and he was having difficulty managing food purchases because prices were so high. Mrs. O. spent some time helping him prepare a weekly budget. Apart from having someone come in once a week to clean and do laundry, Mr. Z. is totally independent.

We stopped next at Mrs. Q.'s because she had been to the doctor's the day before and her helper had reported to Mrs. O. that she thinks more regular service is needed. Mrs. O. wanted to see how Mrs. Q. felt, suggest more extensive service, but review first with Mrs. Q. what additional kinds of help she thought she needed and how best to schedule service.

Our fourth visit was to a seventy-six-year-old woman who was entering the hospital shortly for an operation. Her eighty-year-old husband is severely arthritic and she was concerned about leaving him alone. Our visit here was extensive, as Mrs. O. reviewed with the woman her husband's needs and wants, and what the best plan might be for helping him while she was hospitalized—and helping both of them on her return home, while she convalesced.

Our last visit of the day was to Mrs. R., also to discuss her financial situation. She is a mildly senile woman, very absent-minded and forgetful. She could not remember where she put her bank books, and had no money for food. The helper had called Mrs. O. earlier, to report the loss. Apparently this is a frequent occurrence and after searching in several places—in a drawer among her underclothes, in back of the sugar bowl, on a top shelf in the closet—Mrs. O. wearily promised to call Mrs. R.'s daughter and ask her to try to locate the bank books or have them replaced. Mrs. O. told us that this happens several times a month, but usually Mrs. R. remembers in a day or so where she put them, only to forget again later. Mrs. R. is so forgetful that she sometimes fails to eat the meal prepared for her by the home help and on other occasions eats the meal but insists she hasn't and says none was ever prepared. Mrs. O. and the helper, in case of emergency, keep in touch with the daughter, who lives some distance away. They have all agreed that as long as it is possible they will help Mrs. R. stay in her own home, since she becomes distraught at any suggestion of leaving it. Mrs. O.'s last action before starting for her own home was to make a note to call Mrs. R.'s daughter during her telephone time the next morning. And so her day ends.

Although almost all the western European countries have much more extensive home help service than we do in the United States, Sweden's publicly funded, organized, and delivered system of services for the elderly, the handicapped, or families with children in need of temporary help is particularly well developed. In fact, more than 1 percent (87,000) of Sweden's eight million inhabitants work as home helps, employed full time or part time, by the hour or by the day, providing different types of care and exposed to different levels of training. Granted that less than four thousand of these are full-time workers, and another eighteen thousand are part of Sweden's unique program whereby relatives may be paid for caring for family members under special circumstances, this still represents the equivalent of approximately one full-time worker for every 260 people.

There are three major categories of home help service in Sweden:

Domestic helpers are homemakers or "housewife substitutes," specially trained women who serve as housekeepers or surrogate mothers, assisting families with children when the mother is not able to manage her home because of a serious illness or hospitalization. This type of assistance can also be given to a housewife in need of help to prevent illness or overstrain. It is essentially temporary or short-term emergency help.

Home care attendants are women who provide regular and continuing assistance to the aged and handicapped. This service usually involves light nursing care, personal care, and a range of household and chore services, and is expected to be ongoing and long term.

Child care attendants provide temporary child care when a child in a day nursery or primary school is ill or in need of someone to care for him at home.

Modeled after a similar program in Britain, home help service was first introduced in Sweden by the Swedish Red Cross during the 1920s. The program continued under the auspices of this and other voluntary organizations until the 1940s, when the government began to assume responsibility for service provision. Initially, the program was directed primarily toward provision of emergency services to families with small children when the mother was ill or unable for some other reason to cope with household responsibilities and child care. At first, these consisted of routine housekeeping chores in addition to some personal care (e.g., bathing a sick person). Gradually, the service was expanded to include shopping, escort, information, and referral services. Coverage has increased enormously during the last decade and since 1965 has been provided by the local municipalities and funded by the central government on a 35/65 matching basis. (It is anticipated that this will soon be changed to a 50/50 basis.)

At the beginning, the service was provided solely by middle-aged women whose children were grown and whose household responsibilities had decreased, leaving them with spare time (but limited skills) to do some kind of work. Part-time employment in managing other households seemed a natural and convenient form of work for people already experienced in running a house. Usually working only a few hours a week, these women received little or no training and had no trade union affiliation and no social security rights. The first qualified, regular home helps underwent special training programs for eight months at first and then for up to eighteen months, including child-care practice, domestic work, and training in light medical or nursing care. As the service expanded, training became more formalized and consistent, but also shorter and more specialized, related directly to the type of service to be provided. Even today, some inconsistency persists between, for example, Stockholm and the rest of the country. Most home helps outside Stockholm are required to undergo a 160-hour training program that includes courses in psychology, child development, nutrition and home economics, labor market questions, sociology, and health care. Practical experience is also required in traditional household chores. In contrast, home helps in Stockholm go through an intensive one-week training program only, providing general information on services for the elderly, food suitable for the elderly, light medical and personal care, shopping, and the like. In addition, for workers who will be caring for the more "difficult" cases (handicapped or mentally ill), there are additional required courses, among them special courses for care of the sick (24 hours), for care of the mentally ill (24 hours), for care of those with impaired hearing (20 hours), for care of the blind (20 hours), and on nutrition (12 hours). Workers receive their regular salary while they are being trained. For home care attendants providing "night-watching" in homes of the sick or frail elderly, two special courses of forty-two lessons each are provided under the auspices of the Red Cross. (All other training is done under governmental auspices.) These courses are compulsory for all doing this type of work unless they have had previous nursing training or extensive experience, and workers do not receive salaries while in this program. Throughout the service, in Stockholm and the rest of Sweden, the home help service organizers have much more training than the workers themselves; they generally are either social workers or nurses, and one current complaint by staff is the built-in dichotomy between supervisors and the home helps.

Although the service was initiated primarily for families with children, by the late 1950s, as a result of declining birth rates and increased longevity, the quantity of care had increased and the focus of the program changed to include greater stress on service for the elderly and the handicapped. At the same time two other types of service emerged: home-care attendants, specially trained and more experienced workers, akin to social workers, who work with the more complicated and demanding cases (usually the mentally ill or more severely handicapped); and child-care attendants, who take care of children of working or studying parents when the child is ill and cannot attend his usual day-care center or school. Currently, these workers are also used to substitute for family day-care mothers in case of their illness, or temporarily to replace staff in day-care centers or nursery schools when needed.

As demand for service grew, various innovative approaches to provision were developed. For example, in sparsely populated areas where home helps are scarce, mobile service teams operate. In addition, where there is extensive demand for specialized services such as heavy cleaning for elderly or handicapped people living alone, similar mobile services have been developed. Stockholm initiated "service vans" in the mid-1960s—two-member working teams who carry with them special equipment and specialize in miscellaneous heavy cleaning jobs such as washing windows and floors, waxing floors, and so forth. In the countryside, such special mobile teams may also have equipment for hairdressing, meals-on-wheels, home delivery of frozen and other foods, arrangements for carrying books back and forth from the public library to the isolated and homebound.

The newest "home help" is the rural mailman (or woman). By an agreement between the postal service and the local social welfare organizations, the rural mailman is subsidized for taking over some social services—for instance, to check up on the condition of an elderly person living alone, help him or her to chop wood, bring in water, or clear snow, contact a doctor or social worker, shop, bring food and medicine, or just visit and provide a little companionship. The postal service charges 88¢ for each errand. The recipient pays half the cost of this service if he can afford it; otherwise, it is free, paid for by local government.

As noted earlier, home help services are available to all people (and used by almost all) regardless of income level. Light medical or nursing care (chiropodist services; bathing the elderly or ill person; helping a patient take medication; treating bed sores; taking temperature and pulse) is provided free of charge to all. However, other services are paid for according to income, on a sliding scale. Thus, an old person who pays for domestic help is charged a maximum of $2.64 per hour (a fee that does not cover the actual cost of service) and about one-fifth of those receiving services pay this fee; most pay nothing. One of the most important aspects of the service for the elderly is that help can be obtained as it is needed, for only one or two hours a day, once or twice a week. (Of course, more extensive service is available if needed and wanted.) This means that old people do not have to commit themselves to a whole day of service, when what they really need is several brief periods of care each week. At present, the government is spending about $60.5 million for home help services, and planned expenditures for 1974–75 are $66 million. About the same amount is spent by local government. And about 10 percent of the central government expenditures is for experimental programs for providing care for the elderly and handicapped in sparsely populated areas.

Of the 8,000,000 people living in Sweden, more than 1,300,000 are over sixty-seven (the retirement age in Sweden), and more than one-tenth of these receive some form of home help service. In general, more services are provided in the large cities such as Stockholm or Göteborg, because more old people live there and, for a variety of reasons, they tend to stay out of institutions until they are well into their eighties. If one looks at the overall volume of home help service, most goes for the care of the elderly and handicapped. Yet of the approximately 1,000,000 Swedes who are members of families with young children, 10 percent also received some form of home help service (as of the late 1960s); more than one-half of these received domestic help (the emergency, short-term home help service) while the remainder utilized the temporary child-care service.

A few of the homemakers still work for voluntary organizations but the overwhelming percentage of service is provided by the government directly under local public auspices. Fully trained personnel employed by municipalities are paid $550 a month for a full-time job (about 37.5 hours per week, but the exact amount may vary from week to week). If they remain overnight in a home (but are not working as "night watchers"), they receive a small additional supplement. Home-care attendants and child-care attendants are usually employed on a part-time basis and are paid about $3.00 an hour, the equivalent of what an unskilled industrial worker earns. Supplementary wages are paid to those who work odd shifts (evenings or weekends). Only a small percentage of these workers are unionized although by now all are covered by social security benefits. This lack of unionization and of organization tends to underscore the low status of the job and the weakness of the bargaining position of these women.

As the demand for service continues to grow at an increasingly rapid rate, there is great concern in Sweden that the quality of service has not kept pace with expanded quantity. *Women in Municipal Service*, a recent report of a special Task Force for Women appointed by the municipal (city) council of Stockholm, is very critical of the home help program in Stockholm. The report concludes that the service is provided almost exclusively by women, the work is clearly of low status, workers have little job security (since most are part-time), and working conditions are unsatisfactory (for example, an elderly client may see no need to have a good reading lamp available for a "night watcher"). Many are employed and paid by the hour and cannot plan how extensively they will work from week to week. They receive little training (only one-fifth have taken the longer 160-hour training program required elsewhere in Sweden), work without contact with other colleagues, and have few opportunities for promotion or career advancement. The Task Force made certain recommendations to the Stockholm social welfare administration. Among these are the following: (1) the number of home-care attendants (those serving the handicapped and the elderly) should be substantially increased; (2) special efforts should be made to recruit men for the service, beginning with a few pilot programs in one or two districts; (3) basic training should be extended to cover the standard 160-hour program instituted elsewhere in Sweden; (4) additional, more specialized and advanced training programs should be developed (and workers paid salaries while in these programs); (5) training programs and career ladders should be developed whereby home helps might be able to become home help organizers; and (6) efforts should be made to institute group meetings among the home helps as well as other approaches to increase their contact with one another. In addition, home helps should be encouraged to participate more actively in the organization and management of their work.

One home help commenting about the need for more and improved training said, "Although most home helps are experienced housewives—women over forty who have been married and raised families of their own—it is important for young girls to come into the service too. What is really needed is a good, basic introductory training course for girls who have never managed their own homes. They don't need courses in cleaning with complicated machines, the way they teach the course now. An old person often has only one room and a tiny kitchen and you don't need any special equipment to clean that. And they don't need to learn so much theory. What these girls really need to learn is how to listen patiently to old people. Ninety percent of our job consists of just listening. And another piece is getting the old ones to go outside for a walk, even if just for a little while. The cleaning part is the least important; often it's the company and a little attention that makes the real difference."

Home Help in the Netherlands

The Netherlands warrants discussion both because of its substantial coverage and because of its use of private, charity-based agencies to deliver home help service. In this sense—public reimbursement but decentralized, voluntary agency–based administration—the Dutch pattern will be familiar to Americans.

The Netherlands is working actively to decrease its institutionalized population of the aged and to cut the future ratio of institutionalized care. Another motive for expanding the home help service, although of lesser importance, is the desire to avoid family breakup in emergencies. It is estimated that in 1973 the Netherlands had a staff of some 55,000 women carrying out home help activities. About 14,000–15,000 actually work at the job full time and tend to be assigned to family situations in which the mother cannot fulfill her responsibilities because of a family emergency or a personal disability. These full-time workers tend to include the 7,000 formally trained home helps. The others, some 45,000 older women, work about one-third time, at hours which both suit their own situations and meet the needs for service. These are married people or widows who want to do part-time work. Life experience, rather than school, prepares them. In addition, there are administrative and "support" personnel.

As is true of many social services in Europe, the home help expansion occurred after World War II. Budgetary appropriations by government for this purpose have increased dramatically, and by 1972 total expenditures were $123.5 million, with the government paying $98.8 million. Thus, government meets more than four-fifths of the total cost, and the difference is made up by user fees and private charitable contributions.

The Netherlands Homemaker Service was developed and is administered by several hundred voluntary independent agencies which are subsidized by the central government. In recent years, public policy has encouraged agencies to merge their operations through consolidation or affiliation in order to effect economies of scale. Larger agencies are able to support a more extensive range of services and to provide professional supervision. Closer ties with social work practice and connection with other social services are also facilitated.

Americans may find this pattern interesting, given our limited development thus far and our considerable commitment to the voluntary sector. The Dutch have been proud of their ability to use administrative and financial incentives to reduce the agencies rendering service from about one thousand to under five hundred. Their recent administrative research documents as an achievement the gradual growth since 1968 in agency case loads and staffs and the modest tendency to move from a completely sectarian voluntary pattern of organization to a system with more nonsectarian services. There are still six major national voluntary organizations in the field, but they are coordinated by a national central agency. Increased centralization is being sought even as government increases its own leadership role.

But how does the service operate? Application for service may be made directly to the agency either by telephone (as in Amsterdam) or in person at the agency offices (as in Arnhem). As in the Swedish program, after basic particulars are taken regarding the family situation, a home visit is arranged to round out the information necessary for assessment of the client's need for service and to determine the kind of help that should be offered, the amount of time required of the worker, and so forth. Two to four hours one to three times a week is common for the aged. Family emergencies require full-time coverage. The fee—approximately $29 a week at the time of our visits, well beyond the ability of the average person to pay completely—is met in part by government subsidy and in part by an income-related weekly payment. If the applicant cannot meet his part of the agency's fees, an application for subsidy is made in his behalf to the local public assistance authorities which provide social aid to those in need. In Amsterdam the local authority, by gentlemen's agreement, accepts the agency's determination of financial ability to pay, making it unnecessary for the client to approach the local authority himself, a procedure designed to minimize embarrassment. Thus we find an approach similar to that used in Sweden: a universal service with a sliding fee scale based on financial ability as assessed by the agency in discussion with the client, and coverage on a "means test" basis for those who can pay no fee at all. Assignment of the case to a home help worker for service is made through the "leader" or "guide," as first-level supervisors are called; these may or may not be social workers. Supervisory direction of the leaders is exercised by a chief social worker. Such a three-tier organizational structure also accommodates specialist workers and, in the case of broad-purpose agencies, provides for liaison with other service sectors of the agency.

The government controls expenditures by means of subsidy regulations and a budget. Each voluntary agency is given a ceiling quota for reimbursement upon which it draws (at an agreed rate per service unit) as it renders services. A computer program produces a monthly balance for each agency. A small reserve fund and a shifting of funds at the year's end take care of overspending. (This approach to management is part of the force behind the effort to consolidate small programs.)

Line personnel in the homemaker service consist of on-the-job or briefly trained part-time home helps; full-time home helps, who may receive training of up to a year; and professionally trained homemakers. The latter are graduates of a training school. Although they are described as "professionals," we would not consider them such; European usage of the word "professional" seems to correspond to our use of "occupational" or "vocational." Although staff are almost exclusively women, the Netherlands, like Sweden and Britain, is attempting to recruit men into the service, so far with very limited success.

The geriatric service is staffed by the part-time workers, recruited from the ranks of lower-middle-class and working-class housewives who provide well-defined domiciliary help that enables old people to live in their own homes, thereby postponing or avoiding institutionalization. Services include cleaning, food preparation, shopping, personal help, bathing, and dressing. This is not a medical care service; if a nurse is needed, one is called. However, help with dressing, and what the Swedish term "light medical care," is in order.

Home helps in geriatric service are minimally trained on the job; as experienced housewives, they are seen as ready for the household demands of the job, although they receive some guidance through their leaders (supervisors) to enable them to spot cases which should be referred for additional attention or for special help or more frequent visits. They are expected to watch for changes in health status, nutritional practice, physical activity. Sometimes volunteers are available for household repair work, for taking clients for walks, for errands, or for sewing. A large home help agency would not ordinarily organize such voluntary services, leaving that task to other community organizations (churches, for example), but when such help for the aged is available it is used by the home help agency as an additional resource that supplements or substitutes for the basic service. One agency regarded such volunteer work as a useful supplement, but another expressed some reservations about its regular reliability. As noted, part-time workers are employed to provide home help to old people, and for the foreseeable future, recruitment of personnel is expected to be adequate.

The general family service is staffed by professionally trained home helps who, as their title suggests, perform substitute household-management and child-care tasks for a housewife in the event of her illness, absence, incapacity, or incompetence. The service is based on the belief that providing a substitute for the housewife is often necessary, but it is emphasized that the home help is not a member of the family and that maintaining "professional distance" is appropriate. Although she may help out over a prolonged period, round-the-clock services, for example, are not provided, and only in an extreme emergency may she stay with a family overnight, and then only with the supervisor's permission and with provision made for appropriate overtime payment, time off, and so forth. This policy is intended in part to prevent the possibility of exploitation and in the interest of regularizing hours of work and other aspects of the job.

The services of professionally trained home helps, or school graduates, are ordinarily reserved for difficult cases such as may be presented by a family which is large, has several young children, or includes a handicapped member. Some school graduates with experience may take additional training to become specialists, working with problem families, overburdened mothers, the chronically ill, the mentally disturbed, the retarded, and so forth. The home help's task is to perform a working, helping, or teaching role as required by the family after assessment of circumstances and need. In general, emphasis is placed on the concrete nature of the service and on meeting the specific needs of the client. When assigned to a case, the worker receives instructions from the leader regarding management of the case. After supervisory discussion of an ongoing case, the worker may be given special tasks related to a treatment objective—for example, to teach a mother how to play with a child, to encourage independence, or to avoid overdependence.

Professional home help is time-limited. A six-month assignment to a case would be the outside limit and exceptional. It is agency policy to help the family make alternative arrangements to meet continuing requirements through relatives, through reorganization of household management, or through the market. Responsibility to help the family work out such arrangements would lie with the leader or possibly, in a large agency, with another staff member.

Something of the flavor of the service is suggested by looking at the training program for homemakers. The training school we visited in Arnhem, like the others (about twenty-five in all), is privately run and directed. Curriculum is influenced by government policy as expressed through the Education Ministry and through the family affairs division of the Ministry of Culture, Recreation, and Social Work. Also involved, of course, is the national organization, the Central Board of Home Help Service in the Netherlands. The students, a young, lively, attractive group, look much like American high school seniors or college freshmen. Living quarters are in an old mansion of some elegance, set in a garden. Most of the ground floor is taken up by a spacious living or common room, very tastefully furnished and decorated. The bedrooms, upstairs, were somewhat simpler in decor but pleasant and also furnished in good taste, with two, three, or four students to a room, depending on its size.

The school currently draws most of its students from young women who have been employed by home help agencies for six months and who have been selected to be sent for training, with expenses paid by the agency in return for a commitment to return to employment after graduation. Applications for admission must also be supported by recommendations from the home-town school and from other sources, as well as a home visit with the applicant's family. The training course has a duration of one-and-a-half years; the first six months are spent in residence, since this is predominantly the period of classroom and theoretical studies although supervised fieldwork is also gradually introduced. The curriculum is organized in units, emphasizing such areas as religious and cultural influences on family life and development; primary social units and social structures; the housewife's role and child rearing; and the homemaker function. Practical laboratory work starts in the school, accompanied in the first eight weeks of the course by a half-day per week spent in the field under the supervision of "a good housewife" who functions as a field instructor. Thereafter, the student moves to somewhat longer and more difficult field placements with regular normal-client families assigned through the home help agency, and eventually to some experience with more complex problems (for example, a family with a member with a mild handicap). Case experiences are written up by the student and used for class discussion.

Across the road from the school's residential quarters is another building housing "laboratories" and ordinary classrooms. Here are laundry rooms with various washing and pressing machines, kitchens with a range of appliances and cookers, cleaning aids of different types, all apparently designed to familiarize students with the types of equipment that they may expect to encounter in practice. Indeed, the equipment is so varied, shiny, and elegant that one is prompted to wonder if the girls would be ready to adapt to and cope with households that are less generously equipped.

At the beginning of the course the student is introduced to social structures by being sent out to interview a variety of people—police and post office officials, staffs of social and welfare agencies, old people at home. Educational experiences are faithfully recorded in a log—an educational scrapbook, or record—together with special essays, observations, newspaper clippings, and photographs to illustrate ranges of human emotions, evaluations, recommendations. The book provides a complete record of the student's educational experience.

After six months of residence, marked by continuous evaluation by everyone with whom the student is educationally involved, there is a final examination to conclude the first phase of the course, with examination questions covering materials studied on family structure, social agencies, social insurance, and homemaker theory, and including a case analysis. Among materials submitted for final evaluation is the student's profile of a family, with attention to strengths and problems.

After she completes the six months of academic work in residence, the student returns to the agency for a "block placement"—a year's supervised work, starting with simple case assignments and moving to work with families of large size, problem situations, and the like. Again, records are kept for fortnightly supervisory evaluation. During the practice year students return to the school for five study days—discussion, special lectures, and so forth.

This is an occupation, not a "profession" in the usual sense of the term. As in Sweden, administration and supervision are usually assigned to social workers, nurses, public administration personnel—not to experienced home help graduates.

The home help service is widely used, predominantly by working- and middle-class families; the well-to-do tend to make private arrangements. Informants expressed some amusement when asked if any attempt is made to publicize the service, and then suggested that recruitment publicity serves to make the service known. In any case, the emergence of large professionally staffed agencies providing other social services as well (see below) brings home help resources into direct contact with potential clients. Despite widespread knowledge of the service, however, some doctors apparently are not familiar with it. And there are also some misconceptions; sometimes households will seek home helps for the "spring cleaning."

An Underdeveloped Service in the United States

In the United States the home help is referred to by a number of names— "homemaker," "home health aide," "home aide"—but the description officially adopted by the national standard-setting organization and increasingly used by local agencies is "homemaker–home health aide." Whatever the names—or the reasons—this is a service field in which we lag.[1] According to a 1972 report to a U.S. Senate subcommittee on aging, the international association in the homemaker field suggested that there is reasonable coverage when a country has one homemaker per 1,500 population. The American rate is one per 7,000, with a heavy clustering on the eastern seaboard. France has one per 2,000; Denmark one per 760; the United Kingdom one per 667; and the Netherlands one per 380. In general most of these personnel serve the elderly. In Britain, the rate is 5.5 home helps per 1,000 elderly, and the government sees the need for a twofold or threefold expansion.[2]

Norms are not firmly established in this field but experience suggests that at least 15 percent of the elderly can make good use of the service. The demand for family services will vary with many social factors in a given place. If the United States were to match the Dutch coverage rate we would have 400,000 to 500,000. If we were to meet the recommendation of the International Association our total would be about 150,000. The White House Conference on Aging saw need for 300,000. Our current total is closer to 40,000.

The service in the United States, like that in Sweden, began as a way of allowing children to stay in their own homes during emergency absences of their parents, but has increasingly been used for the elderly and handicapped. The homemaker–home health aide service is positively regarded, by those who understand it, as a preventive child welfare service.

It is widely believed and has been occasionally shown that in-home services can be provided with less cost, in both money and human stress, than out-of-home care. It has been repeatedly shown that "emergency" use of out-of-home care is likely to lead to long-term care or permanent family breakup.

Strangely, despite this, the need for homemaker service as a family and child welfare preventive measure has led to only modest provision everywhere—few metropolitan areas in the United States have significant coverage. Despite the relative frequency of family emergencies and the needs of families who are often far from relatives and friends who might help out, the burden remains on the individual family. People find their own resources and pay for the service out of their own pockets. The homemaker working in families with children becomes a symbol of dependency, neglect, poverty, disorganization—and her assistance is not seen as a necessity similar to medical and nursing care. And as is often the case, because average people do not identify with such needs, provision remains inadequate. After all, it is for "those others."

On the other hand, the obvious need of older people for help to make it possible for them to continue an independent life in the com-

1. For recent U.S. data write to the National Council for Homemaker–Home Health Aide Services, 67 Irving Place, New York City, 10003.

2. In 1972 there were 2,600 full-time homemakers or home helps in the U.K. and 72,000 part-timers. The full-time equivalent total was 35,185. The coverage was 15 per 10,000 population, while the Dutch rate was over 26.

munity, instead of having to rely on institutional care, has apparently spurred a substantial expansion in services in the United States, as in much of Europe. The expansion continues as the aged constitute increasingly significant percentages of the total population—not that we in the United States have followed this to any logical conclusion. Home health aides in the United States are available for up to one hundred days of service through Medicare, but only by referral of a physician, after at least three days of hospitalization or nursing home care, not as a preventive service. Little service is available; and for what there is available, on a fee-for-service basis, costs are prohibitive to most individuals—about $4.50 per hour—far beyond what the average older person can afford.[3] Homemaker services also have been funded out of the Older Americans Act, but only on a project basis and on a declining scale. Most of the remainder of the public funding is as a public welfare social service, requiring a diagnostic assessment and the economic status designated as the eligibility level in each state. Government has concentrated on payment, not on service delivery, and our development is on quite a small scale compared with that of European leaders. Voluntary philanthropy seems to favor homemaker–home health aides, but the resources from this source are limited. Expansion of in-home services was urged by the most recent White House Conference on Aging.

In short, we should recognize the need for two types of service: homemaker–home health aide service in conjunction with professional therapy and a more routine service to meet common, widely shared needs for supplementary household service and help. The latter category justifies large-scale coverage lest old people in particular find that they cannot remain in the community. Both the Netherlands and Sweden, as well as Britain, Denmark, France, and West Germany among other European countries, recognize the need for large-scale staffing. The United States does not; or at least our performance suggests that we do not, despite rhetorical statements to the contrary.

There are, of course, issues and debates among the Europeans. The development of the service away from a narrowly "domestic work" function (housework, not individualized help and training) has stimulated some criticism, and this has been reinforced by government concern about costs. Pressures for economy and rationalization of service would seem to be reinforced by personnel shortages.

Even in the Netherlands we heard some doubts expressed, for example, about the wisdom of extending the training program to two years and gathered that the Ministry of Culture, Recreation, and Social Work does not quite share the conviction of the Education Ministry that this is a good move. The new policy would bring students into the training program at the age of sixteen, immediately after graduation from a domestic science high school program. In view of the high rate of attrition (about 25 percent per year, since these young women will soon be starting their own families), extension of the program may raise costs unrealistically. On the other hand, the view was expressed that perhaps there would be fewer losses to competing occupations if the students were attracted at an earlier age. It was also suggested that the extra educational time might be better used through extension of the general education.

One question about the home help or the homemaker–home health aide service that strikes the observer rather forcibly concerns its con-

3. This is approximately what the fee in Sweden would be, if all the costs of service provision were included. However, no one there is expected to pay a full fee for this service.

tinuing viability in its present form, given its underlying theory, namely, replacement of the "good housewife." Large families are less common, family relations are changing, outside employment of mothers is increasing, technological reorganization of household management through greater use of convenience foods and new cleaning and food-processing methods may be combining to make the all-purpose "good housewife" obsolete. In the face of such tendencies, one should expect mounting pressures to rationalize the service in order to cut costs and economize the use of scarce labor. After all, there are relatively fewer middle-class families with personal cleaning and maid service than there were a decade ago, and the coverage is declining rapidly. The change is most marked in the United States, but is under way in all industrialized countries where domestic work is often defined as low-status or dirty work. In a normal home, someone must still take the role of "woman of the house," or there must be husband-wife sharing; but home care is less often a chosen form of employment. (The Netherlands has not yet felt this problem. Compared with most of industrialized Europe, relatively few of its women work, and home help employment is regarded as a good work opportunity.) In any case, the work pays relatively poorly and may suffer in fringe benefits as well. In the face of this it seems rather strange to attempt expansion of something like domestic service for the old or for the family in crisis.

Recognizing that home helps supply a universally needed service, but that the service should be rationalized and that there eventually may be a problem in recruiting people to the work in its more traditional forms, the Dutch have been experimenting with alternative arrangements. One is to send children as "guests" to another family if illness or emergency takes a parent away for a brief period. (This system corresponds to American neighborhood emergency standby foster home arrangements or small neighborhood shelters. Provision is limited and accountability difficult.) Another alternative is to use group all-day-care arrangements for the children while one parent is away, thus permitting the employed parent to continue to work. A third alternative is to arrange for a home help worker to cover several homes in an area with minimal service, performing essential chores while the children are cared for elsewhere, but not moving in.

These approaches deal with situations involving families with children. In situations involving the aged and the handicapped, where the service is part time, for a few days a week, there have been other experimental approaches. For example, a team arrives with truck and cleaning equipment, takes care of the apartment, and moves on, much as do commercial cleaning services which work on an hourly basis in the United States and whose higher fees and task-oriented, rather than personal-service–oriented, approach to the job seems to decrease the stigma, if any, of the work. Such service, of course, does not take care of the "friendly visiting," shopping, and case-finding functions of the home helps. Presumably, these would be covered by other aspects of the community service system, including volunteer visitors. Or, as in Sweden, the home help would continue to provide this part of the service, but some of the more onerous aspects such as heavy cleaning would be implemented by such specialized teams. Similarly, in the United States, Meals-on-Wheels might provide a supplement to or partial substitute for homemaker–home health aide service.

Our observations on the service in Sweden and the Netherlands, the international dialogue in this field, and national experimentation all seem to indicate that what we are really dealing with are three different service situations, even though they face similar tasks in meeting personal and environmental needs. One provides services for the aged, often needed only once or twice a week, for several hours at a time, but on a long-term basis. The second provides coverage for a mother (or father), often on an intensive but short-term basis, to keep the family together and avoid placement of the children. The third represents one of a "package" of home health services to hasten the return home from a hospital or institution, or to prevent such placement in the first place. In the United States these three services are most often provided through multiservice agencies, such as social service agencies, welfare departments, or family agencies, or through health agencies, community nursing agencies, or hospital outpatient clinics. Increasingly, however, the service is provided through free-standing homemaker–home health aide service agencies. Approximately 26 percent of the more than 1,700 agencies in the United States and Canada responding to a 1973 survey by the National Council for Homemaker–Home Health Aide Services were such homemaker—home health aide agencies, and slightly over one-half of these were under public auspices.

Our best child welfare programs have demonstrated ingenuity in offering family coverage with homemakers, standby foster homes, day homes, and the like. But all of it is on a small scale. Medicaid-Medicare took a step forward in helping some people meet the cost of service but did not cope with service availability and delivery. Indeed, Medicare set up a self-defeating rule under which the service is reimbursable only as a postinstitutional measure.

In short, provision in this country has not yet absorbed the realities—that family emergencies are normal, occurring at predictable rates in all social strata, that senior citizens can be sustained in the community with specified services, and that a homemaker–home health aide program is a basic social utility which can be developed and administered on a scale and in a fashion to suit the American scene. Perhaps the time for major movement has arrived.

Family Therapy In Alcoholism

by Margaret Hindman
Staff Writer, National
Institute on Alcohol Abuse
and Alcoholism

"Alcohol is not a problem for the alcoholic—it's a solution. Everyone around the alcoholic has the problem." (From The Neglected Majority by Joan Sauer)

Family therapy, although it has been an accepted treatment modality in the mental health field for more than two decades, is relatively new to alcoholism treatment. However, it has already elicited enthusiastic endorsement from a growing number of prevention, treatment, and research professionals and was recognized as "the most notable current advance in the area of psychotherapy" in a review of alcoholism treatment trends in the *Second Special Report to the U.S. Congress on Alcohol and Health from the Secretary of Health, Education, and Welfare* (1974).

The modality has been hailed by some therapists as the treatment of choice for alcoholic persons whose families are intact, and has been found to provide some success even in cases where family disintegration has already begun. In addition, family therapy appears to facilitate early intervention.

Family therapy is based on a social-systems model of alcoholism which differs from the traditional, individually oriented medical model in several respects. Most notably, the family system, rather than the "sick alcoholic," becomes the focus of therapy, and the goal of treatment is an improvement in family functioning rather than simply the achievement of sobriety for the alcoholic person.

"People who have worked with alcoholics have known in a very pragmatic way for a long time that the alcoholic cannot be steered toward a newer, more useful, productive, and satisfying life without considering the interpersonal surrounding environment," comments Dr. Shirley Smoyak (1973), of the psychiatric nursing graduate program at Rutgers University. She calls family therapy "the growing edge of theoretical and therapeutic developments" in treating alcoholism.

Indeed, it has frequently been reported in the literature and observed by alcoholism counselors that hospitalized patients often grow worse after visits from family members, as though family interaction has a direct bearing on symptoms. Similarly, other family members sometimes get worse as the patient gets better, as though sickness in one of its members were essential to the family's way of operating. It has been observations such as these that have led many alcoholism counselors to an interest in family therapy, according to Toronto researchers Donald Meeks and Polly Kelly (1970).

By changing to a family systems orientation, many therapists are finding that "through the involvement of the entire family in treatment, family interactions can be employed therapeutically," they say. "Moreover, when changes in one of its members are not accompanied by corresponding changes in the family as a whole, the others may find it difficult to adjust to the one who has changed."

Traditionally, alcoholism has been viewed by therapists and researchers solely as a destructive force in the life of the family. New research, however, indicates that in some families alcoholism—despite its ultimate destructiveness—actually serves a positive function. One striking example, cited by George Washington University researcher Peter Steinglass, is a couple who were capable of physical closeness only when one or both were drunk. "Clinical evidence suggests that alcohol use plays a significant role in the interactional life of a family, perhaps most clearly in the manner in which the family negotiates socially with the outside environment, but also as an adjunct to intrafamily patterns of behavior," Dr. Steinglass reports. "In fact, some recent theoretical notions suggest that alcohol use may have significant adaptive consequences regarding family behavior" (Steinglass, forthcoming).

Of course, the role of alcoholism in families varies widely—since families differ by reason of education, geography, and social class, to name just a few variables, University of Pittsburgh researcher Vincent Foley points out (1976). Therefore, a single treatment approach appropriate for all alcoholic families does not exist; likewise, what is appropriate for a family at one stage in the development of alcoholism will not be appropriate for the same family at a different point. Like other proponents of family therapy, Dr. Foley is convinced that because of its flexibility this approach can be useful in treating nearly all cases in which the family of the alcoholic person remains intact.

The Theory

Family therapy encompasses a range of approaches. In fact, family systems therapy is not a treatment method in the usual sense, according to a report by the Group for the Advancement of Psychiatry (1970). The report points out that "there is no generally agreed on set of procedures followed by practitioners who consider themselves family therapists," although they are all convinced that there is a relationship between individual and family psychopathology, and they believe in the therapeutic benefits of seeing the family together.

Family systems theory in its most often applied form derives in large part from the work of Georgetown University psychiatrist Murray Bowen (1975). The theory, he explains, focuses on functional factors of relationships—*what, how, when,* and *where.* It avoids a preoccupation with *why,* thereby avoiding the placing of blame.

Dr. Bowen regards alcoholism as "one of the common human dysfunctions, existing in the context of an imbalance in functioning of the total family system." Excessive drinking occurs when family anxiety is high, he says. Then the drinking stirs even higher anxiety in those dependent on the one who drinks; the higher the anxiety, the more the other family members react by unconsciously doing more of what they were already doing. This self-feeding process can spiral into a functional collapse, and the process can become a chronic pattern, Dr. Bowen says.

Therapy, then, must be directed initially at the family member or members who have the most resourcefulness, and the most potential for modifying their own functioning, he says. According to Dr. Bowen, when family relationship systems are modified through family therapy, the alcoholic dysfunction decreases, even though the dysfunctional partner may not have been part of the therapy. In fact, Dr. Bowen reports having successful clinical results without ever having seen the alcoholic family member in a therapy session. Even though "cures" have occurred without any involvement on the part of the alcoholic, he stresses "family therapy with two spouses is one of the high roads to successful results."

Key Concepts

Dr. Bowen's theories have been modified in practice by some alcoholism counselors who have been influenced by his work but who believe that special emphasis must be given to achieving abstinence. In an extensive review of the literature describing family therapy in the alcoholism field, Dr. Steinglass (forthcoming) reports that while family therapists differ in their interpretation and application of family therapy, several widely accepted key concepts which form the foundation of the modality can be identified:

- The family is viewed as an operational system, and pathology is defined as a structural or functional imbalance in the family.
- Families are seen as tending to establish a sense of balance or stability, and have built-in mechanisms to resist any change from that level of stability (the concept of homeostasis).
- Psychopathology is redefined in family terms.
- The focus is on communication patterns within the family, and communications, both verbal and nonverbal, are seen as reflecting the basic structural and interactional patterns governing the family's behavior, frequently becoming the primary focus of attention during therapy sessions.
- There is a focus on "behavioral context." The therapist is interested not only in internal processes, but also in the relationships between individual behavior and the interactional field within which the behavior is expressed.
- There is a concern with the boundaries separating individual members of the family as well as with the relationship of the nuclear family to the outside world. Alcoholic families have been described as having very rigid boundaries, leading to a characteristic sense of isolation within the community.

Dr. Steinglass emphasizes that the goals of family therapists in treating alcoholism center around improvement in function, flexibility, and growth potential of the family system as a whole—rather than the more limited focus on reducing the alcoholic member's drinking. In fact, in some situations, sobriety for the alcoholic member may not be a priority, he suggests, particularly in cases where the drinking arose in response to a specific stress situation. While a number of therapists agree that moderation in drinking may be an acceptable goal for the alcoholic family member during the early stages of the alcoholism, most insist on abstinence in families in which the alcoholism is an established part of the family interaction system (Berenson 1976, Hinkle 1974).

Application of the Theory

However, the idea that treatment goals must encompass more than sobriety is basic to all family therapists. True recovery involves a new lifestyle and the creation of support for new patterns of behavior, says Celia Dulfano, family therapist and director of a social work training program in alçoholism for the New York State Department of Mental Health.

Ms. Dulfano works with alcoholic families using a conjoint model of family therapy in which members of a single family are seen together by the therapist. This model appears to be the one most commonly used by family therapists.

She strongly advocates therapist contact with the entire family before beginning work with the alcoholic. "It must be understood that the whole family will be seen in therapy, and the drinking problem will be dealt with," she says. "If work with the individual alcoholic begins before a family contract has been set, it will be extremely difficult to get the family into therapy later," she comments. "The family members are happy to relinquish their problem member into expert hands, and not at all anxious to explore their own limitations and the parts they play in the drinking problem. And the alcoholic, who is necessarily receiving support from the therapist, is reluctant to let the therapist see him in a context where he is scapegoated."

Similarly, the therapist who initially sees the spouse alone may find a like pattern of resistance, in which the spouse claims the alcoholic partner will not come for therapy but in fact does not want the spouse included at the risk of losing the therapist's support, Ms. Dulfano warns.

It is not unusual, however, for individual family members to be involved in individual or group counselling with other therapists as an adjunct to the family therapy sessions. Participation in Alcoholics Anonymous and Al-Anon is also encouraged by many therapists.

Teaching the family about alcoholism is an important part of family therapy, Ms. Dulfano notes. She voices concern, however, that, in some instances, family therapists may concentrate on family interaction without ever openly confronting the alcoholism. On the other hand it is important that the family learn not to blame the alcoholism for all problems which arise. "The interpersonal relationships which prevent the family from functioning as a healthy unit must be corrected, and family members must learn to grow as individuals," she states.

A major focus of therapy, she believes, is to improve communication and build trust between a couple affected by many years of mutual hurt and dissatisfaction, by helping them to talk directly. Other important tasks include the re-establishment of a satisfactory sexual relationship as well as a realignment of parenting responsibilities as the alcoholic family member becomes sober and participates more fully in family life.

Family therapists take an active role in teaching, contracting with family members for changes in behavior, and analyzing transactions. Family members are encouraged to talk directly to each other, to become aware of verbal and nonverbal interactions, and to try out new ways of relating in the family system. Often, such techniques as role reversal and videotaping of sessions are employed to help family members look more objectively at the patterns of their interactions. In addition, the therapist, in his or her interaction with family members, can provide them with a model of rational adult behavior.

The frame of reference of therapy sessions always remains transactional. For example, attention is not directed to what one family member is doing to another, but rather to how these people are participating together in this behavior (Press 1975).

Although conjoint family therapy is the model most commonly used, family therapy has been adapted successfully to other formats and settings. Virtually every therapeutic setting can be adapted to incorporate family issues, Dr. Steinglass points out.

Multiple-couples group therapy is a form of family treatment which appears to be increasing in popularity among alcoholism therapists, he notes. The technique retains the format of group therapy—the traditional treatment of choice for alcoholism—while acknowledging the importance of family factors. In addition to the other advantages offered by the family focus, it furnishes a unique setting in which to work on problems of social isolation and interaction with the outside world—very often major issues for alcoholic families.

Researchers have found that the multiple family group setting helps members tolerate better the anxiety generated by an individual with a drinking problem. In addition, the similarity of their problems allows group members to break down other members' rationalizations as well as to encourage fellow members to stay in treatment (Berman 1968; Gallant et al 1970). Peer group assistance in the working-through process offers the advantages of traditional group therapy, while the inclusion of family members broadens the benefits of treatment, notes Kenneth K. Berman, head of a multiple-couples therapy program at the VA Hospital in East Orange, N.J.

Dr. Steinglass, in his work with multiple-couples groups in an inpatient setting, found that the couples responded very positively to his treatment approach, a fact "particularly impressive to the therapists in light of the fact that all couples had failed repeatedly in previously therapeutic efforts" (Steinglass, Davis and Berenson 1975).

Dr. Steinglass points to several major implications of the family therapy approach for alcoholism treatment. Because the modality encourages work with family members and facilitates entry into the family through concerned nonalcoholic members, the likelihood of early intervention is increased, he believes. In addition, he visualizes an increasingly important role for family treatment agencies in working with the alcoholic family which may come for help with other problems but may need help also in recognizing an alcoholism problem. It is estimated that 15 to 20 percent of all applications to family service agencies involve a drinking problem (Meeks and Kelly 1970).

Treatment Programs

In fact, the experience of alcoholism treatment programs with an emphasis on family treatment bears out the prediction that the modality is effective in reaching the alcoholic at an early stage.

One such program in Montgomery County, Ohio, gears outreach efforts to family members rather than to the alcoholic person. The approach of the Family Alcoholism Care and Treatment (FACT) program is based on a recognition that family members generally seek help before the alcoholic member does. By hooking these people into a treatment program, staff members can become involved before the total collapse of the family occurs, according to education specialist Paul Lubben. Even if the alcoholic member is reluctant to become involved in treatment, positive and constructive assistance and guidance can be made available to the emotionally distraught family, he points out.

The experience of the FACT staff, in its first 2 years of operation, apparently bears out the hypothesis that a family approach leads to earlier intervention. In comparison with the alcoholic persons treated in the county's acute care alcoholism program, FACT clients were found to average about 10 years younger. "This is of extreme importance because in many cases, that 10-year difference is the difference between repairable pathological damage and irreparable pathological damage" said an evaluation report prepared by officials of the program, whose offices are in Dayton.

Baltimore Program

In Baltimore, Md., the Families and Children's Center of the University of Maryland Hospital takes a somewhat different tack in using the family approach to get the alcoholic client into early treatment. The center operates a demonstration program, funded by the National Institute on Alcohol Abuse and Alcoholism (NIAAA), which performs a dual function: to help children of alcoholic parents overcome behavior problems, such as truancy from school; and to draw alcoholic parents into treatment at a relatively early stage of the illness.

Dr. Marvin Kamback, director of the center, explains that the child's symptoms (like alcoholism of the parent) are considered an indicator of a malfunction in the family. Through therapy which focuses on the family system, the family can be helped to develop more functional ways of interacting and the symptoms generally disappear, he says.

Families are referred to the program mostly by the hospital's general pediatrics clinic or by private physicians when a behavior problem is detected. If it is determined that one or both parents are alcoholic, the family is invited to participate in the center's therapy program. Families in which no alcoholism exists are referred elsewhere for treatment. The program "seems to be reaching these families before the alcoholism problem has become too acute and while the chances of successful recovery are very good," Dr. Kamback notes.

An attempt is made to involve all family members in the therapy sessions. If one parent misses a session, the counselor makes contact by telephone or letter to inform the absent member of what happened at the session and to urge continued participation. Changes in communication patterns, as well as changes in the symptoms exhibited by the children and parents, are the goals of treatment.

In addition to the treatment function, the Baltimore project also contains a prevention aspect, aimed at the children. One basic intent of the program is to use family therapy to "break the cyclic pattern of alcoholism," Dr. Kamback says. Children of alcoholic parents are more likely than their peers to suffer from alcoholism in later years, and are also more likely to suffer from a variety of social, developmental, and personality problems. Staff members believe that the generational cycle of alcoholism can be broken if intervention in the alcoholic family occurs at an early stage and these symptomatic children are helped before they develop severe problems. This help involves teaching the children new ways to interact as family members and new patterns of behavior which, it is hoped, will not include alcoholism in later life.

A similar prevention principle is being tested by a demonstration program in New Rochelle, N.Y., at the Center for Family Learning. An NIAAA-funded community prevention grant finances the project which seeks to develop techniques for preventing alcoholism in targeted populations of families—those in which there is a concern either about the development of a drinking problem in a spouse or about present or future drinking problems in one of the children.

The program staff recruits families, through a broad community-outreach effort, to participate in a 10-week training program. Families are exposed to information about alcoholism and participate in a series of multiple family group sessions to discuss family and alcoholism issues in greater depth. The focus of the project is educational rather than therapeutic. The program has been in operation too short a time to determine its effect on the participants, but the first group of families involved in the venture were "enthusiastically positive" about their experience, staff members report. Plans have been made to evaluate measures of effectiveness of different recruitment techniques, participant satisfaction, attitude and knowledge change about alcoholism and family system functioning, and behavioral changes.

Prevention Models

Authorities agree that approaches which focus on promoting positive family development as a way of decreasing the likelihood of alcohol abuse show promise as prevention devices. "Given parents' powerful effects on children's development, [it is important to] help parents understand their own verbal, subverbal, and behavioral messages to their children and help them to deliberately send those messages they mean to be sending," suggests Dr. Judith Frankel D'Augelli, of the Addictions Prevention Laboratory at Pennsylvania State University (1976). She describes a primary prevention model aimed at a general audience of parents, rather than focusing specifically on a high risk target population, as one approach incorporating family influence in prevention. The "family communication and parenting model" she describes places a major emphasis on experiential learning, through role play and similar techniques. Couples are encouraged to participate together in the 6-session series of workshops.

A broad application of similar principles is contained in a U.S. Jaycees alcohol abuse prevention model for parents called "All in the Family." A booklet used in the program outlines the family influences in shaping drinking behavior; it is designed to be used in informal group discussion settings by parents. The program, underwritten by the NIAAA, stresses the importance of dealing with children in the context of family life development, taking advantage of "teachable moments"—those times when children ask questions about parental behavior. Drawing from family systems theory, the program booklet states: "If prevention efforts are to succeed, and if alcohol misuse is to be brought under control, heavy reliance must be placed on the concept of responsibility in the family setting. The family is the place to begin because through it, we shape, mold, guide, and influence our children the most for the rest of their lives."

Research Initiatives

Although family-centered programs are increasing, many questions remain about the roles families play in alcoholism. In an attempt to more clearly define family issues in alcoholism, several research initiatives are underway examining such questions as how family rituals might contribute to the transmission of alcoholism from parent to child, the role of the nonalcoholic spouse, ways by which family interaction might perpetuate drinking, and the effect of drunkenness on the way the family functions.

Dr. Steinglass and his colleagues at George Washington University are examining factors which contribute to the maintenance of pathological drinking patterns in alcoholic families. If these factors can be isolated, he says, the information will help in planning successful psychotherapeutic interventions. The 3-year study is funded by the NIAAA.

Based on data gathered in a previous study of inhospital treatment of couples in which one member was alcoholic, the researchers hypothesize that drinking may sometimes stabilize family interactions by helping the family to deal with its problems. If this is the case, therapists would have to aim treatment for these families at the underlying concerns of the family to avoid its breakup when the alcoholism can no longer be used as the excuse for all other troubles, Dr. Steinglass suggests. In addition, the research by his group may provide information with predictive value regarding prognosis, treatment of choice, motivation for therapy, and degree of flexibility versus degree of resistance to change over time in families with an alcoholic member.

Family Observations

Dr. Steinglass' research group is gathering much of its data from observations of alcoholic families in their homes. In addition, the researchers monitor multiple-family discussion groups involving middle class families with chronic cases of alcoholism and a history of unsuccessful treatment. Discussion groups are held in the homes of volunteer participants, and members of the research team attend as observers.

Another NIAAA-funded research project which focuses on alcoholic couples is underway at the University of Vermont under the direction of Dr. Sheldon Weiner. The 3-year research project looks at interactions between spouses during sobriety and during drinking. Three types of couples were compared: those in which one member is alcoholic, those with psychiatrically defined problems, and those defined as "normal." By comparing alcoholic couples with control groups, the researchers are attempting to more clearly identify patterns of maladaptive behavior which have relevance to the planning of treatment intervention, Dr. Weiner says.

Dr. Steven J. Wolin, another researcher at George Washington University, is studying family interactions in an attempt to learn why alcoholism is transmitted from parent to child in some families but not in others. The 3-year project compares families in which alcoholism becomes a central focus of family life with families in which the alcoholic member does not significantly interfere with the normal functioning of other family members.

Dr. Wolin believes his research findings may help in identifying factors which make some families more treatable than others, as well as providing data which can aid in determining treatments of choice.

The research attention being given to family factors in alcoholism represents a promising new thrust in a field where the emphasis has traditionally been the "sick alcoholic person," comments Dr. Albert Pawlowski, chief of the NIAAA Extramural Research Branch.

In an extensive review of the literature dealing with family influences in alcoholism, California social work professor Joan Ablon (1976) also strongly advocates further research into family factors. "A chief goal of future research must be the charting of an eclectic, comprehensive approach that views alcohol-related problems as not totally unique to the class phenomenon of family crisis," she comments. "Furthermore, the details of alcohol-related problems must be explored holistically and in depth, taking into account all potentially significant psychological, social, and cultural characteristics of all family members. Only such a comprehensive approach can give appropriate cognizance to the reality that alcoholism is a multifaceted affliction which crucially affects the family as a total unit and each member as an interacting individual of the collectivity," Dr. Ablon concludes.

"The bulk of treatment services which are available are designed to respond to late stage alcoholism and do not meet the needs of people whose alcoholism is identified at earlier stages of the illness," notes the *Second Special Report on Alcohol and Health.* Family treatment offers a new alternative in the alcoholism field by providing therapists with a different and often dramatically successful approach in reaching the alcoholic person at an early stage when chances for recovery are higher. In addition, the focus on the family unit helps to insure that recovery will be lasting, since the home environment and family structure are changing as the alcoholic family member achieves a healthy level of functioning.

As family therapist Murray Bowen comments, "Family therapy offers no magic for the total problem. But the theory provides a different way for concep-

Al-Anon—for Families of Alcoholic People

Al-Anon is a well established and proven source of "self-help" treatment for the families of alcoholic people.

Al-Anon members generally maintain that alcoholism is an illness and consequently advocate a medical model of treatment, focusing on the alcoholic person as the 'patient'—the antithesis of the family systems approach which identifies alcoholism as a family dysfunction and directs treatment at the entire family. In practice, however, many of the principles of Al-Anon reflect steps basic to family systems therapy.

"Recovery from alcoholism involves the healing of the emotional illness of all members of the family. If the alcoholic recovers emotionally and family members do not, there may be a serious breach in the family structure. . . . To begin in the usual manner of attempting to force the alcoholic to stop drinking without first learning and changing one's own self will simply make the matter worse," according to the Rev. Joseph Kellerman in an Al-Anon publication (1969). The words sound very much like some of the basic tenets of family systems theory.

Many family therapists consider participation in Al-Anon a valuable adjunct to their work with alcoholic families. "Although for the most part they fly in the face of the theoretical notions that underlie the family therapy movement, several of the operational principles bear a remarkable resemblance to principles advocated by many family therapists," comments Dr. Peter Steinglass (1976), of the George Washington University Center for Family Research. For instance, the Al-Anon principle of "loving detachment" is quite similar to a principle advocated by many family therapists who suggest that families will achieve growth only when individual members concentrate on changing their own behavior rather than attempting to manipulate or change others in the family, he points out.

There is empirical evidence that the involvement of a spouse in some form of treatment is beneficial to the recovery of the alcoholic, even if the focus remains on the alcoholic as the identified patient and family members are simply regarded as collaterals (Finlay 1974). In addition, studies show that male members of Alcoholics Anonymous have been found to have an easier time maintaining sobriety if their wives were simultaneously attending Al-Anon, Dr. Steinglass notes.

tualizing the problem, and the therapy provides a number of different approaches to resolving the problem not available with conventional theory and therapy."

As more information about family factors in alcoholism becomes known, through continuing research as well as through evaluation of programs now testing various family oriented models of treatment and prevention, the family systems approach is likely to find even wider application to the problems of alcoholism. A focus on family interactions should become part of all treatment programs, NIAAA officials recommend. The family approach provides therapists and alcoholism programs with another effective tool for helping alcoholic people and their families to deal with the problems facing them.

References

Ablon, Joan. Family structure and behavior in alcoholism: A review of the literature. In: Kissin, B. and Begleiter, H., eds. *The Biology of Alcoholism, Vol. IV.* New York: Plenum Press, 1976.

Alcoholism: A Family Illness. New York: Christopher D. Smithers Foundation, Inc., 1972.

Berenson, David. Techniques of treating the alcoholic family. In: Newman, J., ed. *Family Treatment Methods in Alcohol Abuse and Alcoholism—Proceedings of a Workshop.* University of Pittsburgh Publications, 1976, pp. 77-98.

Berman, Kenneth K. Multiple conjoint family groups in the treatment of alcoholism. *Journal of the Medical Society of New Jersey,* 65 (1) : 6-8, 1968.

Bowen, Murray. Alcoholism as viewed through family systems theory and family psychotherapy. In: Seixas, F. A. ; Cadoret, R.; and Eggleston, S., eds. *The Person with Alcoholism (Annals of the New York Academy of Science,* Vol. 233), 1974, pp. 115-122.

D'Augelli, Judith Frankel. Parenting skills for alcohol abuse prevention: A programmatic approach. In: O'Gorman, P., and Wick, eds. *Proceedings of the Lancaster Conference on Adolescent Alcohol Education.* New York: National Council on Alcoholism, 1976.

Dulfano, Celia. Alcoholism in the family system. In: *Proceedings of Family Therapy Conference,* Fordham University School of Social Work Publication, forthcoming.

"The Field of Family Therapy." *Group for the Advancement of Psychiatry Reports.* Vol. VIII, No. 78, 1970. Published by the Group for the Advancement of Psychiatry, 419 Park Ave., New York, N.Y. 10016.

Finlay, Donald G. Alcoholism: Illness or problem in interaction? *Social Work,* 19 (4) : 398-405, 1974.

Foley, Vincent D. Structural family therapy: One approach to the treatment of the alcoholic family. In: Newman, J., ed. *Family Treatment Methods in Alcohol Abuse* and *Alcoholism—Proceedings of a Workshop.* University of Pittsburgh Publication, 1976. pp. 53-76.

Gallant, D.M.; Rich, A.; Bey, E.; and Terranova, L. Group psychotherapy with married couples: A successful technique in New Orleans alcoholism clinic patients. *Journal of Louisiana State Medical Society,* 122 (2) : 41-44, 1970.

Hinkle, Lorraine M. "Treatment of the Family System with a Recovering Alcoholic." Paper presented at the National Conference on Social Welfare, 101st Forum, Cincinnati, Ohio, 1974.

Kellerman, J.L. *A Guide for the Family of the Alcoholic.* New York: Al-Anon Family Group Publications, 1969.

Meeks, Donald E. and Kelly, Colleen. Family therapy with the families of recovering alcoholics. *Quarterly Journal of Studies on Alcohol,* 31 (2) : 399-413, 1970.

Press, Leonard. Treating the family. *Maryland State Medical Journal,* 24 (1) : 32-36, 1975.

Sauer, Joan. *The Neglected Majority.* Milwaukee: DePaul Publications, 1976.

Second Special Report to the U.S. Congress on Alcohol and Health from the Secretary of Health, Education, and Welfare. Washington, D.C.: Superintendent of Documents, U.S. Government Printing Office, 1974.

Smoyak, Shirley A. Therapeutic approaches to alcoholism based on systems theories. *Occupational Health Nursing,* 21 (4) : 27-30, 1973.

Steinglass, Peter. Family therapy in alcoholism. In: Kissin, B. and Begleiter, H., eds. *The Biology of Alcoholism, Vol. V: Rehabilitation.* New York: Plenum Press (forthcoming).

Steinglass, Peter; Davis D.; and Berenson, D. "In-Hospital Treatment of Alcoholic Couples." Paper presented at the American Psychiatric Association 128th Annual Meeting, Anaheim, Calif., May 1975.

"Child Abuse and Neglect: The Alcohol Connection," also by Ms. Hindman, is included in the CHILDREN section of this FAMILY FACTBOOK.

Alcohol Health and Research World, Fall 1976 (National Institute on Alcohol Abuse and Alcoholism, Department of Health, Education, and Welfare)

Childbirth

BIRTHS TO DATE AND LIFETIME BIRTHS EXPECTED PER 1,000 WOMEN BY RACE AND MARITAL STATUS: JUNE 1976

(Civilian noninstitutional population. Data limited to women reporting on birth expectations. For meaning of symbols, see page II)

Race and age	All women		Currently married (except separated)		Widowed, divorced, and separated		Single	
	Births to date	Lifetime births expected	Births to date	Lifetime births expected	Births to date	Lifetime births expected	Births to date	Lifetime births expected
ALL RACES								
18 to 24 years....	528	2,031	818	2,141	1,136	1,942	161	1,931
25 to 29 years....	1,442	2,099	1,569	2,202	1,725	2,161	424	1,424
30 to 34 years....	2,266	2,445	2,362	2,535	2,458	2,575	535	939
35 to 39 years....	(NA)	(NA)	2,956	2,994	(NA)	(NA)	(NA)	(NA)
WHITE								
18 to 24 years....	468	2,038	776	2,127	998	1,878	60	1,960
25 to 29 years....	1,392	2,062	1,540	2,175	1,606	2,053	138	1,262
30 to 34 years....	2,218	2,391	2,347	2,514	2,166	2,265	203	632
35 to 39 years....	(NA)	(NA)	2,910	2,949	(NA)	(NA)	(NA)	(NA)
BLACK								
18 to 24 years....	946	1,974	1,309	2,304	1,760	2,230	667	1,787
25 to 29 years....	1,914	2,422	1,969	2,508	2,187	2,567	1,516	2,081
30 to 34 years....	2,770	2,994	2,697	2,923	3,249	3,419	1,654	2,013
35 to 39 years....	(NA)	(NA)	3,555	3,579	(NA)	(NA)	(NA)	(NA)

Source: U.S. Bureau of the Census, Current Population Reports, Series P-20, No. 300, and unpublished Current Population Survey data.

This table and the one on the following page are from:
U.S. Bureau of the Census, Current Population Reports, Series P-20, No. 307, "Population Profile of the United States: 1976." U.S. Government Printing Office, Washington, D.C., 1977.

CHILDREN EVER BORN PER 1,000 WOMEN BY RACE AND MARITAL STATUS, AND PERCENT CHILDLESS FOR WOMEN EVER MARRIED: 1960 TO 1976

(Data are for resident population in 1960 and 1970 and for civilian noninstitutional population in 1976. For meaning of symbols, see page II)

Subject	All races			White			Black		
	1976	1970	1960	1976	1970	1960	1976	1970	1960
CHILDREN EVER BORN PER 1,000 WOMEN									
All Women (Rates exclude births to single women)									
15 to 44 years	1,389	1,616	1,746	1,377	1,584	1,712	1,492	1,851	2,016
18 to 44 years	1,595	[2]1,869	1,969	1,576	1,828	1,929	1,753	2,184	[3]2,268
15 to 19 years	59	75	127	58	69	117	67	118	208
18 and 19 years	126	[2]152	265	122	139	245	146	242	[3]406
20 to 24 years	508	678	1,030	492	648	993	618	918	1,320
25 to 29 years	1,304	1,738	2,007	1,297	1,709	1,960	1,415	1,996	2,383
30 to 34 years	2,121	2,596	2,452	2,106	2,551	2,398	2,321	2,956	2,882
35 to 39 years	2,766	2,980	2,518	2,710	2,920	2,471	3,229	3,450	2,905
40 to 44 years	3,062	2,927	2,407	3,003	2,852	2,362	3,518	3,520	2,758
45 to 49 years	3,069	2,688	2,247	3,009	2,633	2,200	3,493	3,162	2,603
All Women (Rates include births to single women)									
18 to 44 years	1,645	1,918	(NA)	1,593	1,848	(NA)	2,051	2,415	(NA)
18 and 19 years	181	206	(NA)	143	163	(NA)	401	477	(NA)
20 to 24 years	582	736	(NA)	519	674	(NA)	1,005	1,205	(NA)
25 to 29 years	1,359	1,790	(NA)	1,311	1,732	(NA)	1,769	2,274	(NA)
30 to 34 years	2,158	2,640	(NA)	2,116	2,569	(NA)	2,572	3,196	(NA)
35 to 39 years	2,807	3,015	(NA)	2,722	2,934	(NA)	3,492	3,639	(NA)
40 to 44 years	3,091	2,952	(NA)	3,013	2,864	(NA)	3,694	3,649	(NA)
45 to 49 years	3,085	2,707	(NA)	3,014	2,643	(NA)	3,596	3,256	(NA)
WOMEN EVER MARRIED									
15 to 44 years	2,082	2,357	2,314	2,017	2,281	2,253	2,676	2,974	2,808
18 to 44 years	2,094	[2]2,372	2,331	2,029	2,297	2,270	2,690	3,001	[3]2,816
15 to 19 years	548	633	792	500	574	729	1,021	1,029	1,258
18 and 19 years	588	[2]648	824	535	588	757	(B)	1,088	[3]1,320
20 to 24 years	897	1,064	1,441	835	998	1,370	1,444	1,627	2,030
25 to 29 years	1,539	1,978	2,241	1,498	1,918	2,171	1,946	2,536	2,835
30 to 34 years	2,291	2,804	2,627	2,248	2,733	2,559	2,753	3,390	3,190
35 to 39 years	2,931	3,167	2,686	2,853	3,086	2,629	3,600	3,822	3,139
40 to 44 years	3,190	3,096	2,564	3,110	3,077	2,516	3,858	3,817	2,949
45 to 49 years	3,206	2,840	2,402	3,135	2,777	2,354	3,740	3,393	2,761
SINGLE WOMEN									
18 to 44 years	212	211	(NA)	73	98	(NA)	856	850	(NA)
18 and 19 years	69	67	(NA)	27	32	(NA)	296	302	(NA)
20 to 24 years	171	159	(NA)	64	77	(NA)	675	658	(NA)
25 to 29 years	358	428	(NA)	109	208	(NA)	1,296	1,306	(NA)
30 to 34 years	504	595	(NA)	151	263	(NA)	1,600	1,871	(NA)
35 to 39 years	725	593	(NA)	255	271	(NA)	(B)	1,939	(NA)
40 to 44 years	724	460	(NA)	284	236	(NA)	(B)	1,659	(NA)
45 to 49 years	361	352	(NA)	138	203	(NA)	(B)	1,379	(NA)
PERCENT CHILDLESS FOR WOMEN EVER MARRIED									
15 to 44 years old	18.8	16.4	15.0	19.7	16.8	14.6	11.6	13.7	18.7
15 to 19 years	55.1	50.7	43.6	57.8	53.7	46.4	26.6	31.0	25.3
20 to 24 years	41.7	35.9	24.2	44.2	37.7	25.0	19.8	20.8	17.0
25 to 29 years	21.7	15.8	12.6	22.4	16.1	12.3	15.2	12.3	14.2
30 to 34 years	10.5	8.3	10.4	10.8	8.1	9.6	6.5	9.1	15.8
35 to 39 years	6.6	7.4	11.1	6.4	7.0	10.2	7.1	9.8	20.0
40 to 44 years	7.5	8.6	14.1	7.2	8.1	13.0	8.0	13.0	24.7
45 to 49 years	7.8	10.8	18.1	7.4	10.1	17.1	11.4	17.5	27.9

[1]Since single women are counted as childless, these rates are comparable to those shown for women of all marital statuses combined in previously published Census Bureau reports on fertility.
[2]Rate is for White and Black women combined.
[3]Rate is for Black and other races.

Source: U.S. Bureau of the Census; for 1976, Current Population Reports, Series P-20, No. 300, and unpublished Current Population Survey data; for 1970, 1970 Census of Population, Vol. II, 3A, Women by Number of Children Ever Born; for 1960, U.S. Census of Population: Vol. II, 3A, Women by Number of Children Ever Born.

VITAL STATISTICS AND HEALTH AND MEDICAL CARE

Fertility Rate and Birth Rate, by Age of Mother, by Race: 1940 to 1970

[Total fertility rates are the sums of birth rates, by age of mother, multiplied by 5. Birth rates are live births per 1,000 women in specified group. Prior to 1959, births adjusted for underregistration; thereafter, registered live births. Based on 50-percent sample of births for 1951–1954, 1956–1966, and 1968–1970; on 20- to 50-percent sample for 1967]

Year and race	Total fertility rate	Birth rate, by age of mother							
		10–14 years	15–19 years	20–24 years	25–29 years	30–34 years	35–39 years	40–44 years	45–49 years
	11	12	13	14	15	16	17	18	19
TOTAL									
1970	2,480	1.2	68.3	167.8	145.1	73.3	31.7	8.1	0.5
1969	2,465	1.0	66.1	166.0	143.0	74.1	33.4	8.8	.5
1968	2,477	1.0	66.1	167.4	140.3	74.9	35.6	9.6	.6
1967	2,573	.9	67.9	174.0	142.6	79.3	38.5	10.6	.7
1966	2,736	.9	70.6	185.9	149.4	85.9	42.2	11.7	.7
1965	2,928	.8	70.4	196.8	162.5	95.0	46.4	12.8	.8
1964	3,208	.9	72.8	219.9	179.4	103.9	50.0	13.8	.8
1963	3,333	.9	76.4	231.2	185.8	106.2	51.3	14.2	.9
1962	3,474	.8	81.2	243.7	191.7	108.9	52.7	14.8	.9
1961	3,629	.9	88.0	253.7	197.9	113.3	55.6	15.6	.9
1960	3,654	.8	89.1	258.1	197.4	112.7	56.2	15.5	.9
1959	3,670	.9	89.1	257.5	198.6	114.4	57.3	15.3	.9
1958	3,701	.9	91.4	258.2	198.3	116.2	58.3	15.7	.9
1957	3,767	1.0	96.3	260.6	199.4	118.9	59.9	16.3	1.1
1956	3,689	1.0	94.6	253.7	194.7	117.3	59.3	16.3	1.0
1955	3,580	.9	90.5	242.0	190.5	116.2	58.7	16.1	1.0
1954	3,543	.9	90.6	236.2	188.4	116.9	57.9	16.2	1.0
1953	3,424	1.0	88.2	224.6	184.1	113.4	56.6	15.8	1.0
1952	3,358	.9	86.1	217.6	182.0	112.6	55.8	15.5	1.3
1951	3,269	.9	87.6	211.6	175.3	107.9	54.1	15.4	1.1
1950	3,091	1.0	81.6	196.6	166.1	103.7	52.9	15.1	1.2
1949	3,110	1.0	83.4	200.1	165.4	102.1	53.5	15.3	1.3
1948	3,109	1.0	81.8	200.3	163.4	103.7	54.5	15.7	1.3
1947	3,274	.9	79.3	209.7	176.0	111.9	58.9	16.6	1.4
1946	2,943	.7	59.3	181.8	161.2	108.9	58.7	16.5	1.5
1945	2,491	.8	51.1	138.9	132.2	100.2	56.9	16.6	1.6
1944	2,568	.8	54.3	151.8	136.5	98.1	54.6	16.1	1.4
1943	2,718	.8	61.7	164.0	147.8	99.5	52.8	15.7	1.5
1942	2,628	.7	61.1	165.1	142.7	91.8	47.9	14.7	1.6
1941	2,399	.7	56.9	145.4	128.7	85.3	46.1	15.0	1.7
1940	2,301	.7	54.1	135.6	122.8	83.4	46.3	15.6	1.9
WHITE									
1970	2,385	.5	57.4	163.4	145.9	71.9	30.0	7.5	.4
1969	2,360	.4	55.2	161.4	142.8	72.0	31.6	8.1	.5
1968	2,368	.4	55.3	162.6	139.7	72.5	33.8	8.9	.5
1967	2,453	.3	57.3	168.8	140.7	76.5	36.6	9.8	.6
1966	2,609	.3	60.8	179.9	146.6	82.7	40.0	10.8	.7
1965	2,790	.3	60.7	189.8	158.8	91.7	44.1	12.0	.7
1964	3,074	.3	63.2	213.1	176.2	100.5	47.7	13.0	.7
1963 [1]	3,201	.3	68.1	224.7	181.5	102.6	48.9	13.4	.8
1962 [1]	3,348	.4	73.1	238.0	187.7	105.2	50.2	14.1	.8
1961	3,502	.4	78.8	247.9	194.4	110.1	53.2	14.8	.9
1960	3,533	.4	79.4	252.8	194.9	109.6	54.0	14.7	.8
1959	3,544	.4	79.2	251.7	195.5	111.3	55.1	14.7	.9
1958	3,560	.5	81.0	251.4	194.8	113.0	55.8	14.8	.8
1957	3,625	.5	85.2	253.8	195.8	115.9	57.4	15.4	.8
1956	3,546	.3	83.2	247.1	190.6	114.4	57.0	15.4	.8
1955	3,446	.3	79.2	236.0	186.8	114.1	56.7	15.4	.9
1954	3,415	.4	79.0	230.7	185.0	115.1	56.2	15.4	.9
1953	3,306	.4	77.2	219.6	181.5	111.9	55.1	15.0	.9
1952	3,250	.4	75.0	212.5	180.5	111.4	54.4	14.8	.9
1951	3,157	.4	75.9	206.0	174.2	106.5	52.6	14.6	1.0
1950	2,977	.4	70.0	190.4	165.1	102.6	51.4	14.5	1.0
1949	3,009	.4	72.1	194.6	165.2	101.5	52.2	14.6	1.1
1948	3,022	.4	71.1	195.5	163.9	103.6	53.5	15.2	1.1
1947	3,230	.4	69.8	207.9	179.1	113.0	58.4	16.1	1.2
1946	2,901	.3	50.6	179.8	164.0	110.0	58.4	15.9	1.3
1945	2,421	.3	42.1	134.7	133.1	100.5	56.3	16.0	1.4
1944	2,501	.3	45.3	147.9	137.7	98.2	54.1	15.5	1.2
1943	2,664	.3	52.1	161.1	150.7	100.2	52.2	15.0	1.3
1942	2,577	.3	51.8	162.9	145.6	92.3	47.2	14.1	1.3
1941	2,328	.2	47.6	141.6	130.1	85.2	45.1	14.3	1.4
1940	2,229	.2	45.3	131.4	123.6	83.4	45.3	15.0	1.6
NEGRO AND OTHER									
1970	3,067	4.8	133.4	196.8	140.1	82.5	42.2	12.6	.9
1969	3,148	4.6	133.3	197.8	144.2	88.9	45.9	13.9	1.0
1968	3,197	4.4	133.3	200.8	144.8	91.2	48.6	15.0	1.2
1967	3,385	4.1	135.2	212.1	155.9	99.1	52.4	16.8	1.2
1966	3,615	4.0	135.5	228.9	169.3	107.9	57.7	18.4	1.4
1965	3,891	4.0	136.1	247.3	188.1	118.3	63.8	19.2	1.5
1964	4,153	4.0	138.7	268.6	202.0	127.5	67.5	20.9	1.5
1963 [1]	4,269	4.0	139.9	277.3	211.8	129.3	68.9	21.0	1.5
1962 [1]	4,396	3.9	144.6	285.7	217.4	132.4	72.0	21.7	1.5
1961	4,533	4.0	152.8	292.9	221.9	136.2	74.9	22.3	1.5

[1] Excludes New Jersey; State did not require reporting of race.

VITAL STATISTICS

Fertility Rate and Birth Rate, by Age of Mother, by Race: 1940 to 1970—Con.

Year and race	Total fertility rate	Birth rate, by age of mother							
		10–14 years	15–19 years	20–24 years	25–29 years	30–34 years	35–39 years	40–44 years	45–49 years
	11	12	13	14	15	16	17	18	19
NEGRO AND OTHER—Con.									
1960	4,522	4.0	158.2	294.2	214.6	135.6	74.2	22.0	1.7
1959	4,595	4.2	160.5	297.9	220.2	138.1	75.0	21.2	1.8
1958	4,727	4.3	167.3	305.2	224.2	142.3	78.4	21.8	1.9
1957	4,798	5.6	172.8	307.0	228.1	143.5	78.7	23.5	2.0
1956	4,730	4.7	172.5	299.1	225.9	139.4	78.8	23.6	2.0
1955	4,550	4.8	168.3	283.4	219.6	133.5	75.4	22.1	2.1
1954	4,474	4.9	170.3	274.7	215.7	131.3	72.9	22.5	2.1
1953	4,283	5.1	165.4	261.4	206.4	125.7	70.0	23.0	2.2
1952	4,147	5.2	162.9	254.0	194.2	122.0	66.6	21.9	2.2
1951	4,091	5.4	166.7	252.5	184.2	117.9	66.5	22.6	2.2
1950	3,928	5.1	163.5	242.6	173.8	112.6	64.3	21.2	2.6
1949	3,855	5.1	162.8	241.3	167.0	107.3	63.9	21.1	2.5
1948	3,742	4.9	157.3	237.0	159.6	104.1	62.5	20.4	2.8
1947	3,575	4.6	146.6	223.7	150.6	102.4	62.7	21.4	3.1
1946	3,238	3.7	121.9	197.3	139.2	99.3	61.0	21.8	3.5
1945	3,017	3.9	117.5	172.1	125.4	97.1	61.3	22.3	3.7
1944	3,075	3.9	121.5	182.4	126.8	97.3	58.4	21.5	3.2
1943	3,128	4.0	133.4	187.2	125.1	93.9	56.9	21.5	3.7
1942	3,022	3.9	131.8	182.3	119.6	88.1	54.0	20.8	4.0
1941	2,956	4.0	128.3	175.0	118.1	86.2	54.1	21.5	4.1
1940	2,870	3.7	121.7	168.5	116.3	83.5	53.7	21.5	5.2

Birth Rate, by Race, by Live-Birth Order: 1940 to 1970

[Rates are live births per 1,000 women aged 15–44 years in specified race group. Live-birth order refers to number of children born alive to mother. Prior to 1959, births adjusted for underregistration; thereafter, registered live births. Figures for not stated birth order have been distributed. Based on 50-percent sample of births for 1951–1954, 1956–1966, and 1968–1970; on 20- to 50-percent sample for 1967]

Year and race	Total	Birth rate, by live-birth order						
		1st	2d	3d	4th	5th	6th and 7th	8th and over
	20	21	22	23	24	25	26	27
TOTAL								
1970	87.9	34.1	24.2	13.7	7.2	3.8	3.2	1.8
1969	86.5	32.8	23.4	13.4	7.4	4.0	3.5	2.0
1968	85.7	32.1	22.5	13.2	7.5	4.2	3.9	2.3
1967	87.6	30.8	22.6	13.9	8.3	4.8	4.5	2.7
1966	91.3	31.0	22.5	14.8	9.2	5.4	5.2	3.2
1965	96.6	29.8	23.4	16.6	10.7	6.4	6.0	3.7
1964	105.0	30.4	25.1	18.8	12.3	7.3	6.9	4.1
1963	108.5	29.9	26.1	19.9	13.1	7.8	7.3	4.3
1962	112.2	30.1	27.0	21.1	13.8	8.2	7.5	4.4
1961	117.2	31.1	28.4	22.4	14.6	8.5	7.8	4.5
1960 *	118.0	31.1	29.2	22.8	14.6	8.3	7.6	4.3
1959	118.8	31.5	29.9	23.0	14.5	8.2	7.4	4.2
1958	120.2	32.2	30.6	23.3	14.4	8.1	7.3	4.2
1957	122.9	33.7	31.7	23.9	14.4	7.9	7.1	4.2
1956	121.2	33.5	31.9	23.6	13.9	7.6	6.8	4.0
1955	118.5	32.9	31.9	23.1	13.3	7.2	6.4	3.8
1954	118.1	33.6	32.4	22.7	12.8	6.8	6.0	3.8
1953	115.2	33.4	32.5	21.9	12.0	6.3	5.5	3.6
1952	113.9	34.0	32.7	21.3	11.3	5.8	5.2	3.6
1951	111.5	34.9	32.6	20.0	10.2	5.3	5.0	3.6
1950	106.2	33.3	32.1	18.4	9.2	4.8	4.7	3.6
1949	107.1	36.2	32.1	17.1	8.6	4.7	4.7	3.7
1948	107.3	39.6	30.9	16.1	8.0	4.5	4.6	3.6
1947	113.3	46.7	30.3	15.6	7.9	4.5	4.6	3.7
1946	101.9	38.5	27.9	14.5	7.8	4.5	4.7	3.8
1945	85.9	28.9	22.9	13.4	7.5	4.5	4.8	4.0
1944	88.8	30.2	23.8	13.8	7.6	4.5	4.9	4.0
1943	94.3	34.7	25.5	13.5	7.4	4.4	4.8	4.0
1942	91.5	37.5	22.9	11.9	6.6	4.1	4.6	3.9
1941	83.4	32.2	20.7	11.2	6.4	4.1	4.7	4.1
1940	79.9	29.3	20.0	10.9	6.4	4.1	4.8	4.3

Year and race	Total	Birth rate, by live-birth order						
		1st	2d	3d	4th	5th	6th and 7th	8th and over
	20	21	22	23	24	25	26	27
WHITE								
1970	84.1	32.8	23.7	13.3	6.8	3.4	2.7	1.2
1969	82.4	31.5	22.9	13.1	7.0	3.6	2.9	1.4
1968	81.5	30.9	22.1	12.8	7.1	3.8	3.2	1.6
1967	83.1	29.7	22.1	13.5	7.9	4.3	3.7	1.8
1966	86.4	30.1	22.0	14.4	8.7	4.9	4.3	2.1
1965	91.4	28.9	23.0	16.2	10.2	5.8	5.0	2.4
1964	99.9	29.8	24.8	18.5	11.7	6.7	5.7	2.7
1963 [1]	103.7	29.4	25.9	19.6	12.6	7.1	6.1	2.9
1962 [1]	107.5	29.8	26.9	20.9	13.3	7.5	6.2	2.9
1961	112.2	30.7	28.3	22.2	14.0	7.7	6.4	2.9
1960 *	113.2	30.8	29.2	22.7	14.1	7.5	6.1	2.8
1959	113.9	31.2	29.9	22.9	13.9	7.3	5.9	2.8
1958	114.9	31.9	30.6	23.1	13.8	7.2	5.7	2.7
1957	117.7	33.4	31.7	23.7	13.7	7.0	5.6	2.7
1956	116.0	33.2	31.9	23.4	13.1	6.6	5.2	2.6
1955	113.8	32.6	32.0	22.9	12.6	6.2	4.9	2.5
1954	113.6	33.3	32.8	22.6	12.0	5.9	4.6	2.5
1953	111.0	33.3	32.9	21.6	11.1	5.4	4.3	2.5
1952	110.0	34.1	33.1	21.0	10.4	5.0	4.0	2.5
1951	107.7	35.0	32.9	19.5	9.4	4.5	3.9	2.5
1950	102.3	33.3	32.3	17.9	8.4	4.1	3.7	2.5
1949	103.6	36.3	32.2	16.6	7.9	4.0	3.8	2.7
1948	104.3	39.9	31.1	15.7	7.4	3.9	3.7	2.6
1947	111.8	47.8	30.8	15.3	7.4	4.0	3.8	2.7
1946	100.4	39.5	28.5	14.4	7.3	4.0	3.9	2.8
1945	83.4	29.0	23.3	13.2	7.0	3.9	4.0	3.0
1944	86.3	30.4	24.2	13.6	7.1	4.0	4.1	3.1
1943	92.3	35.2	25.9	13.2	6.9	3.9	4.0	3.1
1942	89.5	38.3	23.1	11.5	6.1	3.6	3.8	3.1
1941	80.7	32.5	20.7	10.7	5.9	3.6	3.9	3.2
1940	77.1	29.4	20.0	10.5	5.9	3.6	4.1	3.5

See footnotes at end of table.

VITAL STATISTICS AND HEALTH AND MEDICAL CARE

Birth Rate, by Race, by Live-Birth Order: 1940 to 1970—Con.

Year and race	Total	Birth rate, by live-birth order						
		1st	2d	3d	4th	5th	6th and 7th	8th and over
	20	21	22	23	24	25	26	27
NEGRO AND OTHER								
1970	113.0	42.4	26.9	15.9	9.7	6.2	6.7	5.3
1969	114.8	42.2	26.4	15.9	10.1	6.6	7.4	6.3
1968	114.9	40.6	25.3	15.7	10.4	7.0	8.5	7.4
1967	119.8	38.4	25.9	16.8	11.5	8.1	10.1	9.0
1966	125.9	37.4	26.0	18.0	12.8	9.4	11.6	10.7
1965	133.9	35.8	26.6	19.6	14.6	10.8	13.8	12.6
1964	141.7	34.8	27.4	21.1	16.0	12.1	15.8	14.4
1963 [1]	144.9	33.8	27.6	21.8	16.9	13.1	16.6	15.1
1962 [1]	148.8	33.1	28.0	22.8	17.8	13.7	17.6	15.7
1961	153.5	33.6	28.8	23.7	18.8	14.1	18.4	16.0
1960 *	153.6	33.6	29.3	24.0	18.6	14.1	18.4	15.6
1959	156.0	33.9	29.8	24.4	19.1	14.5	18.7	15.6
1958	160.5	34.7	31.0	25.4	19.5	14.9	19.1	15.9
1957	163.0	36.1	31.6	25.7	19.8	15.3	19.0	15.6
1956	160.9	35.9	31.7	25.2	19.7	15.0	18.7	15.0
NEGRO AND OTHER—Con.								
1955	155.3	35.0	30.7	24.4	19.1	14.6	17.4	14.1
1954	153.2	35.6	29.7	24.4	19.1	14.2	16.5	13.5
1953	147.2	34.1	29.5	23.8	18.4	13.3	15.4	12.8
1952	143.3	33.1	29.2	24.0	18.1	12.4	14.2	12.4
1951	142.1	34.1	29.9	23.9	16.9	11.2	13.5	12.2
1950	137.3	33.8	30.3	22.9	15.3	10.4	12.6	12.0
1949	135.1	35.4	30.8	21.2	14.0	9.8	12.2	11.8
1948	131.6	37.3	29.5	19.4	12.9	9.2	11.7	11.6
1947	125.9	38.4	26.2	17.3	12.1	8.8	11.4	11.6
1946	113.9	31.1	23.4	16.0	11.8	8.7	11.3	11.7
1945	106.0	27.9	20.1	14.7	11.3	8.7	11.3	11.9
1944	108.5	28.7	21.1	15.6	11.7	8.6	11.3	11.6
1943	111.0	31.0	22.2	15.5	11.4	8.4	11.0	11.6
1942	107.6	31.0	21.1	14.9	10.8	8.1	10.5	11.1
1941	105.4	29.8	20.6	14.5	10.6	8.0	10.6	11.3
1940	102.4	28.6	19.6	14.1	10.5	7.8	10.4	11.3

* Denotes first year for which figures includes Alaska and Hawaii.

[1] Excludes New Jersey; State did not require reporting of race.

VITAL STATISTICS **B 99–115**

Median Interval Between Births, by Race: 1930 to 1969

[**In months.** Excludes Alaska and Hawaii. Excludes institutional population. Based on sample]

Series No.	Race and interval	Year of birth of child							
		1965–1969	1960–1964	1955–1959	1950–1954	1945–1949	1940–1944	1935–1939	1930–1934
	WHITE								
	Median interval in months from—								
99	First marriage of mother to birth of first child	15.5	14.5	16.2	17.7	18.4	20.2	20.1	20.3
100	Birth of first child to birth of second child	29.3	25.9	28.2	30.7	32.9	32.8	32.0	32.2
101	Birth of second child to birth of third child	33.1	31.6	33.0	31.3	33.1	34.0	34.2	31.8
102	Birth of third child to birth of fourth child	35.0	31.2	30.4	30.0	32.5	34.4	32.8	33.1
	NEGRO AND OTHER								
	Median interval in months from—								
103	First marriage of mother to birth of first child		9.0	11.9	12.7	11.1	10.7	12.9	11.9
104	Birth of first child to birth of second child		23.3	23.4	23.3	24.9	27.3	22.8	27.6
105	Birth of second child to birth of third child		23.8	23.3	23.4	24.6	24.1	22.6	(B)
106	Birth of third child to birth of fourth child		22.1	22.9	22.4	23.8	24.0	(B)	(B)

B Not shown; base for estimate is too small (number of children reported by women surviving to 1969 is less than 150,000).

U.S. Bureau of the Census, Historical Statistics of the United States, Colonial Times to 1970, Bicentennial Edition, Part 1. Washington, D.C., 1975

Choices in Childbirth — The Nurse-Midwifery Service at San Francisco General Hospital

Judith Goldschmidt, C.N.M.
Rosemary Mann, C.N.M.

Two years ago when the California State Department of Maternal Child Health granted H.E.W. funds to the University of California for establishment of a nurse-midwifery service, San Francisco General looked like an unlikely site for a successful service and eventual school of nurse-midwifery. The hospital had a physical plant that was known to be inadequate. All laboring women shared a five-bed common labor room, and a new hospital under construction had been bogged down in city construction politics for a number of years. In the community the reputation for obstetrical care at San Francisco General had deteriorated to the point where fewer than thirty women a month delivered there. Like most county hospitals, it also served a designated high-risk population. As an affiliate of the University of California San Francisco Medical Center, it shared that institution's reputation for "aggressive obstetrical management."

However, a reality which worked in the favor of the establishment of a nurse-midwifery service at San Francisco General, was the growing home birth movement and the proliferation of groups and literature advocating alternatives in childbirth. Against this background, Dr. Richard Sweet, Director of Obstetrics and Gynecology at San Francisco General Hospital, became project director of the nurse-midwifery service. In partnership with nurse-midwives Peggy Emery, Rosemary Mann, and Susan Leibel, they created a model nurse-midwifery service which was receptive to innovation and open to alternatives in birth. The nurse-midwifery program aimed at providing personalized care on a woman-to-woman basis, individualized teaching during prenatal care, supportive continuous attendance during labor and delivery, and a recognition of the mothers' and infants' need for each other in the immediate postpartum period. An Alternative Birth Center was established, initially in a room which was down the hall from the common labor room. It was small, without its own bath, but it nevertheless offered families the space to define their own birth experience, whether it be to have their other children with them, friends present, giving the baby a Leboyer bath, or taking movies and making tapes. It also gave the midwives experience with bed deliveries, and provided a precedent for doing away with many of the routines associated with hospital care, including intravenous fluids, enemas, preps, and electronic monitoring.

Word quickly spread about the presence of the nurse-midwifery service. San Francisco General found itself reclaiming some of its traditional clientele. Women from the Philippines, from Mexico, and El Salvador were choosing San Francisco General because midwifery care was what they were used to in their own countries. Responding to innovations such as the Alternative Birth Center, young professionals, physicians' wives, and others who were hitherto unfound at county hospitals, started to seek out midwifery care. Then the San Francisco Foundation recognized the innovations at San Francisco General by sponsoring the Alternative Birth Center, paying a coordinator's salary and providing funds for the decoration of a room. The Foundation also sponsored the establishment of a branch of the San Francisco Women's Center at the hospital and paid for a media expert to develop tapes and movies for the various ethnic groups served by the county hospital. One year after the nurse-midwifery service opened, San Francisco General moved to its new hospital and the coordinator of the Alternative Birth Center, who is also a nurse-midwife, was able to open two rooms on the postpartum unit, and develop classes specifically to aid families that wished to assume more responsibility for their care.

Although a separate entity, the Alternative Birth Center has been inexorably bound in the public mind with the nurse-midwifery service, partly because the ABC is coordinated by a midwife and also because the standards of normal care as described in the protocols are very much midwifery standards. Until recently, the Alternative Birth Center was largely used by the nurse-midwives and not used regularly by the resident physicians. This was partly because the ABC was not an officially accepted responsibility of either labor and delivery or postpartum. There was no regular nursing staff or housekeeping staff for the two rooms. What this meant in practice was that the midwife on duty assumed responsibility for the women in labor who were using the Alternative Birth Center. She attended their deliveries and was responsible for nursing care of the infant and mother for the first two hours postpartum, whether the labor was twenty-four or five hours long. The midwife then restocked supplies, washed and made the bed, and washed the bathroom and floor. The willingness of the midwives to provide this kind of service was largely an expression of their desire to see an Alternative Birth Center in a county hospital. We are happy to report that the Alternative Birth Center rooms *are* now an official part of the hospital and are staffed by delivery and postpartum nurses and served by housekeeping.

That the midwifery service is not synonymous with the Alternative Birth Center is obvious when we look at the families who register for care. About 50% select the service because they come from a country where midwives are the usual birth attendants, or because they want a female attendant during prenatal and intrapartum care. They are generally not interested in alternative styles of birthing, to the extent that an occasional woman will even request a delivery room or an episiotomy. However, they are very receptive to prenatal teaching and prepared childbirth. Of the other 50% who are interested in the Alternative Birth Center, about half either change their mind or develop some complicating factor that warrants the added support available in the labor area. However, labor in the traditional labor and delivery area does not mean traditional care. Offering choices to the woman in the labor and delivery area and individualization of her care is still the hallmark of nurse-midwifery. The use of honeyed teas, constant support, varied activity and multiple positions during labor, no episiotomy whenever possible, presence of loved ones and children, and delivery in the labor bed are all part of this care, whether the delivery takes place in the labor room or the Alternative Birth Center. Indeed, 66% of all the patients deliver in the Alternative Birth Center or in the labor room. Use of the delivery area is dictated only when the delivery itself is complicated. Patients at a county hospital are usually the last to be offered genuine choices or encouraged to assume responsibility for their own care. To be able to create choices for this population is one of the pleasures of running a nurse-midwifery service at a county hospital.

The nurse-midwifery service has now completed its second year. In the last year, the number of families selecting the service has increased 50%. The nurse-midwives now conduct an average of eight to ten new patient visits per week, sixty to seventy prenatal visits and ten to fifteen postpartum family planning visits per week. The nurse-midwifery service has now cared for 462 women and has registered another 240 families for birth in the upcoming year. This gives a projected birth rate of thirty per month. This rate is 30-35% of the total obstetrical load of the hospital. There are currently four full-time positions for nurse-midwives on the service, with three full-time and two half-time nurse-midwives providing twenty-four hour maternity care to normal pregnant women and their families.

The nurse-midwifery service has become a powerful change agent for those currently training to be obstetricians and family health physicians. The reaction of the families to the personalized care, the success of different midwifery techniques, the use of different postures during labor, and the need for little medication when active support is available, have all been noticed by the resident physicians, and are becoming incorporated by them in their own practice. It is not at all unusual to see women being encouraged to squat or otherwise change position if labor has arrested during the second stage instead of immediate recourse to instrumentation.

The good relationship that the nurse-midwifery service enjoys with the resident staff is due not only to the quality of care but also to the collegial status that was built in when the service was started. The nurse-midwives have clinical appointments in the School of Medicine, attend faculty and staff meetings, and share responsibility for education of the medical students and teaching rounds. Those women being cared for by the nurse-midwives who develop special problems during pregnancy or labor are followed jointly by the obstetrical and midwifery services until the problem is resolved or delivery has been completed.

The nurse-midwifery service also serves as an educational setting for the preparation of nurse-midwives. The second class of refresher students is under way. These students are nurse-midwives trained in other countries or those who have been out of practice and in need of taking the American College of Nurse-Midwives examination. By January, 1978, a basic midwifery program will be launched.

Conclusion

Three challenges are now facing the nurse-midwifery service at San Francisco General. The most pressing challenge is that of freeing ourselves from the medical model of obstetrical care. The kind of care that the nurse-midwives give is different in that it demands different energies. For example, the number of deliveries per month is not reflective of the time we spend since we provide constant attendance all throughout labor. Our time is increasingly taken with demonstrations, as interested doctors and others from the community come to see the service. Physicians increasingly ask to do internships with us and our teaching time has increased as a result. The safety of a nurse-midwifery service is no longer an issue. It has been established. The issue now is to build into our service the kind of time off and support needed by the midwives so as not to burn out.

A second problem for the nurse-midwifery program is that of arranging third-party payment for nurse-midwifery care. At the present time, support for the program is extended by grants on a time-limited basis rather than on fee for service.

The third challenge facing the midwives at San Francisco General is how to better prepare families and women to assume responsibility for their labors and deliveries. We are in the surprising position of having changed an institution so that it offers more choices than some women are able to make.

"Choices in Childbirth—The Nurse-Midwifery Service at San Francisco General Hospital," by Judith Goldschmidt, C.N.M. and Rosemary Mann, C.N.M. Vol. 4, No. 3 (Fall 1977) Birth and the Family Journal, Berkeley, California.

Children

Height of children and youths at selected percentiles, according to sex and age: United States
(Data are based on physical examinations of samples of the civilian noninstitutionalized population)

Age [1]	Male			Female		
	10th	50th	90th	10th	50th	90th
	Standing height in inches at percentile shown					
2 years	32.9	34.2	36.2	32.3	34.2	36.2
3 years	35.6	37.4	39.4	35.2	37.0	39.0
4 years	38.3	40.5	42.6	38.0	40.0	42.0
5 years	40.8	43.3	45.4	40.4	42.7	44.8
6 years	43.1	45.7	48.0	42.7	45.1	47.6
7 years	45.3	47.9	50.4	44.7	47.5	50.2
8 years	47.3	50.0	52.6	46.7	49.8	52.8
9 years	49.3	52.0	54.9	48.8	52.0	55.4
10 years	51.2	54.1	57.3	51.0	54.4	58.0
11 years	53.2	56.4	59.9	53.4	57.0	60.5
12 years	55.2	58.9	62.8	56.0	59.6	63.0
13 years	57.4	61.6	65.7	58.3	61.8	65.1
14 years	59.8	64.2	68.4	59.6	63.1	66.4
15 years	62.3	66.5	70.4	60.3	63.7	67.1
16 years	64.5	68.3	71.8	60.7	63.9	67.4
17 years	66.0	69.4	72.6	61.1	64.2	67.4
18 years	66.4	69.6	73.0	61.4	64.4	67.3

[1] Includes ONLY children with birthday age plus or minus 3 months; all other children excluded from table.

NOTE: Figures are smoothed values of standing height. Data from the Health Examination Survey, Cycles II and III, 1963-65 and 1966-68, and the Health and Nutrition Examination Survey, Cycle I, 1971-74.

SOURCE: National Center for Health Statistics: Vital and Health Statistics. Series 11. Health Resources Administration, DHEW, Rockville, Md. To be published.

Weight of children and youths at selected percentiles, according to sex and age: United States
(Data are based on physical examinations of samples of the civilian noninstitutionalized population)

Age [1]	Male			Female		
	10th	50th	90th	10th	50th	90th
	Weight in pounds at percentile shown					
2 years	24.16	27.20	31.70	22.75	26.01	29.94
3 years	27.73	32.23	37.36	27.03	31.08	36.46
4 years	31.39	36.80	42.59	30.51	35.18	41.73
5 years	35.18	41.16	47.84	33.64	38.93	46.80
6 years	39.06	45.61	53.59	36.86	43.03	52.67
7 years	43.05	50.38	60.32	40.54	48.15	60.38
8 years	47.16	55.78	68.48	45.08	54.76	70.64
9 years	51.43	62.02	78.42	50.53	62.74	82.89
10 years	56.26	69.31	89.95	56.79	71.76	96.34
11 years	62.10	77.82	102.67	63.87	81.46	110.14
12 years	69.36	87.70	116.25	71.72	91.56	123.44
13 years	78.48	99.10	130.34	80.14	101.63	135.47
14 years	89.60	111.93	144.56	88.43	110.85	145.59
15 years	101.54	125.02	158.53	95.64	118.34	153.31
16 years	112.79	136.91	171.89	100.93	123.22	158.03
17 years	121.87	146.19	184.26	103.70	124.98	159.57
18 years	127.62	151.85	194.91	104.65	124.82	159.28

[1] Includes ONLY children with birthday age plus or minus 3 months; all other children excluded from table.

NOTE: Figures are smoothed weight values. Data from the Health Examination Survey, Cycles II and III, 1963-65 and 1966-68, and the Health and Nutrition Examination Survey, Cycle I, 1971-74.

SOURCE: National Center for Health Statistics: Vital and Health Statistics. Series 11. Health Resources Administration, DHEW, Rockville, Md. To be published.

Self-assessed drinking levels of junior and senior high school students, according to marijuana use, use of hard drugs, and school grades: United States, spring 1974

(Data are based on questionnaires administered in a sample of classrooms)

Kind of drug use and school grades	Percent distribution for each category	Drinking level: All levels	Abstainer	Infre-quent	Light	Moderate	Moderate/heavy	Heavy
		Percent distribution						
Total	100.0	100.0	27.3	16.3	16.6	15.5	13.7	10.6
DRUG USE IN PAST 6 MONTHS								
Marijuana								
None	71.0	100.0	37.7	19.5	17.2	13.4	7.7	4.6
1 or 2 times	6.9	100.0	8.4	9.7	19.7	24.1	22.0	16.0
3 or more times	22.1	100.0	3.2	3.7	11.8	21.2	29.7	30.5
Hard drugs								
None	96.4	100.0	28.8	15.7	16.6	15.9	13.1	9.9
1 or 2 times	1.6	100.0	3.0	3.6	7.1	15.2	32.5	38.6
3 or more times	2.0	100.0	5.3	4.1	6.1	13.5	23.8	47.1
SCHOOL GRADES								
A's	10.2	100.0	37.3	20.5	19.1	11.8	7.7	3.6
A's and B's	24.6	100.0	29.5	19.9	17.1	16.2	11.6	5.7
B's	16.3	100.0	25.9	15.6	20.2	16.1	12.8	9.5
B's and C's	28.5	100.0	25.8	15.5	15.8	16.8	14.3	11.8
C's	11.3	100.0	23.4	13.0	13.0	14.3	19.0	17.4
C's and D's	7.6	100.0	22.9	11.8	16.0	13.2	17.7	18.5
D's and F's	1.6	100.0	24.5	8.6	8.0	17.5	20.5	20.9

NOTE: Drinking level is defined by the frequency and amount of alcohol consumed. Abstainers do not drink or drink less than once a year. Heavy drinkers drink at least once a week and consume 5 or more drinks per typical drinking occasion. The intermediate categories are defined by a combination of frequency of drinking and amount of alcohol consumed per typical drinking occasion.

SOURCE: Rachal, J. V., et al.: A National Study of Adolescent Drinking Behavior, Attitudes and Correlates. Research Triangle Park, N.C. Research Triangle Institute, Apr. 1975.

Current cigarette smoking among persons 12-18 years of age, according to sex and age: United States, selected years 1968-74

(Data are based on telephone interviews of samples of the noninstitutionalized population resident in private households with telephones)

Sex and age	1968	1970	1972	1974
Male	Percent in age group who are current cigarette smokers			
All ages 12-18 years	14.7	18.5	15.7	15.8
12-14 years	2.9	5.7	4.6	4.2
15-16 years	17.0	19.5	17.8	18.1
17-18 years	30.2	37.3	30.2	31.0
Female				
All ages 12-18 years	8.4	11.9	13.3	15.3
12-14 years	0.6	3.0	2.8	4.9
15-16 years	9.6	14.4	16.3	20.2
17-18 years	18.6	22.8	25.3	25.9

NOTE: A current smoker is a person who has smoked at least 100 cigarettes and who now smokes cigarettes on a regular basis at least weekly.

SOURCES: Regional Medical Programs Services, National Clearinghouse for Smoking and Health: Teenage Smoking, National Patterns of Cigarette Smoking Ages 12 Through 18, in 1968 and 1970, DHEW Pub. No. (HSM) 72-7508, Health Services and Mental Health Administration, Rockville, Md.; National Institutes of Health: Teenage Smoking, National Patterns of Cigarette Smoking, Ages 12 Through 18, in 1972 and 1974, DHEW Pub. No. (NIH) 76-931, Public Health Service, Bethesda, Md.

Health, United States, 1976-1977. U.S. Dept. of Health, Education, and Welfare, Public Health Service, Health Resources Administration. DHEW Publ. No. (HRA) 77-1232. Stock No. 017-022-00553-1

What Difference Does Health Care Make in the Lives of Children?

We know a lot about child health, yet American children are nowhere near as healthy as they could be. Good health is not distributed equitably among the nation's children.

> A child's destiny in Sweet Water [Alabama], if he is black and poor *or* white and poor, is to be born to a mother who had received no prenatal care, to be born outside a hospital, in a rural cabin, attended either by a midwife (with various degrees of experience and training) or simply by a relative. Then the newborn infant gets no pediatric examination, no injections or 'shots' to prevent this or that disease, no vitamin supplements, no evaluation, no treatment of any kind. The heart is not heard, nor the lungs, abnormalities are not noticed, nor are attempts made at correction. Advice is not given, nor reassurance. Worst of all, accidents and injuries and illnesses are part of life, and either "take" the child or "spare" him or her. Fractures heal or they don't, often without the benefit of splints or casts. Infections go away or they don't. Burns and lacerations and cuts and sores and rashes either "clear up" or "stop themselves" or "leave the child" or they don't, with obvious results: Worse and worse pain, more and more incapacity and disability—and always those complications, which themselves get no more care and attention and treatment than whatever kind of "pathology" caused the "sequelae" in the first place.[1]

There are hard numbers to show that every year, inadequate and unequal provision of health care services to children and pregnant women in this country results in the unnecessary deaths of thousands of children. Many thousands more are disabled or suffer chronic conditions which, if untreated, rob them of years of their lives, impair their productivity, and cost the rest of us millions of dollars for remedial services and support. The statistics are a national scandal.

—The international statistics on infant deaths show that the infant mortality rate in the United States is worse than in 14 other countries.[2] And within the United States there are startling variations, ranging from 23 deaths in Mississippi to 12.2 deaths in Utah per 1,000 live births[3] and from 26.2 for nonwhites, nationwide, to 15.2 for whites.[4]

—After infancy, contrasts in mortality figures remain. Among children aged 1 to 4, minority children die at a rate 70 percent higher than whites. And in the 5 to 9 age group, minority children die at a rate 40 percent higher than white children.[5]

—Figures on how many American mothers die in childbirth show that three times as many nonwhite as white mothers die.[6]

—Every year, thousands of children suffer from lead paint poisoning. In the course of a year, 300 to 400 children die from it and 6,000 more suffer irreversible brain damage.[7]

—One indicator of malnutrition is a low hemoglobin level. Of all children ages 1 to 5, 30 to

---

[1] Robert Coles, *Children in Crisis*, Vol. III, "The South Goes North"(Boston: Little Brown, 1967), p. 611.

[2] Provisional figures from a report of the United Nations, *Demographic Yearbook of the United Nations* (New York, 1973).

[3] National Center for Health Statistics, U.S. Department of Health, Education and Welfare, *Vital Statistics of the United States, 1974, Vol. 2, Part A* (Washington, D.C.: U.S. Government Printing Office, 1974).

[4] National Center for Health Statistics, U.S. Department of Health, Education and Welfare, *Monthly Vital Statistics Report, Summary Report, Final Mortality Statistics, 1973, Vol. 23, No. 11* (Washington, D.C.: U.S. Government Printing Office, 1975).

[5] *Monthly Vital Statistics Report, Summary Report, Final Mortality Statistics, 1973, Vol. 23, No. 11,* Table 3.

[6] *Monthly Vital Statistics Report, Summary Report. Final Mortality Statistics, 1973, Vol. 23, No. 11.*

[7] Frederick Green, M.D., "Getting Ready for National Health Insurance: Shortchanging Children," Statement before the Subcommittee on Oversight and Investigations of the United States House Committee on Interstate and Foreign Commerce, 7 October 1975.

40 percent are below standard.[8] Low hemoglobin levels or other nutritional deficiencies are found twice as often among black Americans as among white Americans,[9] affecting one out of every three black children.

—The Watts area of Los Angeles contained only 17 percent of the city's population, but in category after category it harbored nearly 50 percent of the city's ills. It had 48.5 percent of amoebic infections, 42 percent of food poisoning, 44.8 percent of whooping cough, 39 percent of epilepsy, 42.8 percent of rheumatic fever, 44.6 percent of dysentery, 46 percent of venereal disease, 36 percent of meningitis and 65 percent of reported tuberculin reactors. The death rate in Watts was 22.3 percent higher than for the remainder of the city.[10] The incidence of tuberculosis was four times higher in Watts than in the rest of Los Angeles County.[11]

—Native American children die from heart disease, influenza, and pneumonia twice as frequently as other children.[12]

—In a Chicano community in California, children display a whole range of vivid contrasts with national averages: four times as much amoebic dysentery, twice as much measles, mumps, and tuberculosis, and 1.4 times as much hepatitis.[13]

—Pregnancy in young teenagers is on the rise. Both the number and rate of births to 14- to 16-year-old girls rose steadily between 1965 and 1973.[14] Mothers under 15 years old are twice as likely as those between ages 20 to 34 to have babies of low birth weight[15]—a condition disproportionately associated with infant deaths, birth defects, mental retardation, and a variety of other tragic outcomes.[16]

Like good health, good health care is also inequitably distributed among the nation's children.

—Many children receive no care at all. Experts estimate that in 1971 at least ten million U.S. children under age 16 received no medical care whatsoever.[17]

—According to a nationwide survey conducted in 1974, 22 percent of American children ages 6 to 16 had not seen a dentist in the past two years. Among children in families earning less than $7,000, 37 percent had not been to a dentist in the past two years and 21 percent had never been to a dentist.[18]

—When U.S. children reach school age, they have an average of three decayed teeth; about half of all school-age children suffer from gum disease.[19]

—Immunizing children is clearly effective in preventing childhood diseases. Yet in 1974 nearly 5 million children ages one through four—or 37 percent—were not adequately immunized against polio. Forty percent were not vaccinated against rubella.[20]

—In a 1972 study conducted by Meharry Medical College of 1,266 poor families in Nashville, Tennessee, physicians and dentists interviewed and examined family members to identify health needs. They found that:
(a) among families with already diagnosed medical problems, only 13 percent were receiving proper medical attention;
(b) 97 percent of the people in the study had health problems. For example, of every 100 persons, 51 needed a regular physical examination, 45 needed one or more

[8] Unpublished data from the National Center for Health Statistics, U.S. Department of Health, Education and Welfare, as described and summarized in a report of the National Council of Organizations for Children and Youth, *America's Children, 1976, A Bicentennial Assessment* (Washington, D.C., 1976), p. 36.

[9] Unpublished data from the Office of Planning and Evaluation, National Institutes of Health, U.S. Department of Health, Education and Welfare, as described and summarized in a report of the American Public Health Association for the 102nd Annual Meeting, *Minority Health Chart Book* (New Orleans: 1974) p. 49.

[10] Rodger Hurley, *Poverty and Mental Retardation: A Causal Relationship* (New York: Random House, 1969), p. 134.

[11] Herbert G. Birch and Joan Dye Gussow, *Disadvantaged Children and School Failure* (New York: Harcourt, Brace and World, 1970), p. 243.

[12] Unpublished data from the Indian Health Service, U.S. Department of Health, Education and Welfare, as described and summarized in *America's Children, 1976, A Bicentennial Assessment.*

[13] Report of the East Los Angeles Health System, Inc., California Chicano Urban Health Study, December, 1973, cited in *Minority Health Chart Book*, p. 58.

[14] Jack Hood Vaughn, President, Planned Parenthood Federation of America, "The National School-Age Mother and Child Health Act of 1975," Testimony on Senate Bill 2358 before the Subcommittee on Health, Senate Committee on Labor and Public Welfare, 4 November 1975, p. 7.

[15] H. Chase, "Trends in 'Prematurity': United States, 1950-1967," *American Journal of Public Health*, Vol. 60 (1970), Table 8, p. 1978.

[16] *America's Children, 1976, A Bicentennial Assessment*, p. 34; Testimony of Jack Hood Vaughn, p. 2.

[17] Charles U. Lowe and Duane F. Alexander, "Health Care of Poor Children" in *Children and Decent People*, Alvin Schorr, ed. (New York: Basic Books, 1974), p. 81.

[18] Unpublished data from the "Health Interview Survey, 1974," on file with the National Center for Health Statistics, Health Resources Administration, Public Health Service, U.S. Department of Health, Education and Welfare, Washington, D.C.

[19] American Dental Association, *Dentistry and National Health Programs* (1971), cited in *America's Children, 1976, A Bicentennial Assessment*, p. 36.

[20] U.S. Center for Disease Control, Public Health Service, U.S. Department of Health, Education and Welfare, *United States Immunization Survey, 1974* (Atlanta, 1975).

immunizations, and 94 had inadequate diets;

(c) 95 percent of the persons examined by the dentist had unmet needs for dental services and more than 90 percent of diagnosed dental problems were receiving no care at all.[21]

These numbers quantify a great deal of needless pain and suffering. But the question remains: Would health care make a difference?

The answer is yes.

The elimination of poverty in this country would also make a difference in these statistics, and a very substantial one. But we should not let ourselves be put in a position of having to choose between improving employment opportunities and family income on the one hand or improving health services on the other. Suspending action in the field of health until changes occur in other infinitely more immovable fields like income redistribution is foolish. If we wait to provide equal health care for the poor until they are no longer too poor to pay for it, generations of children will suffer. The same can be said about housing, education and jobs. Action needs to be taken on all these issues, simultaneously, not one to the exclusion of the others.

Furthermore, trying to improve children's health solely by reducing poverty overlooks the unique contribution health care can make. It is not a token gesture. It can have real consequences for real people. The relationship between health care and children's health is perhaps most clearly demonstrated in studies of the effect of prenatal care on the outcome of pregnancy.

—Mothers who have had no prenatal care are three times more likely to give birth to infants with low birth weights,[22] which is associated with almost half of all infant deaths,[23] and substantially increases the likelihood of birth defects.[24]

—A landmark study of all births in New York City in 1968 showed that death rates of infants born to mothers in each of four categories of risk were lowest among infants whose mothers had adequate care, slightly higher if their mothers had intermediate care and the highest if the mothers had inadequate care. Mothers who began their prenatal care in the first eleven weeks of preganancy and had at least nine visits had an infant mortality rate of 6.0 per 1,000, compared to a rate more than three times as high (19.0 per 1,000) for women who delayed their first visit until the twenty-eighth week or later and had fewer than five visits. The researchers concluded that "Generally, adequacy of care . . . is strongly and consistently associated with infant birth weight and survival, an association that is pronounced throughout the entire first year of life."[25]

1,125 infants died in New York City in 1968, for reasons related primarily to inadequate prenatal care.[26] As Robert Coles observed in his foreword to the report of that study, these children "were not the victims of a profession's intellectual or scientific inadequacies. They were not boys and girls born too soon—because certain fatal diseases have yet to be understood and made responsive to medical treatment. They were boys and girls who, with their mothers, of course, needed only what millions of others received: adequate medical attention. Their deaths were, by and large, utterly avoidable."[27]

There are other specific conditions where the effects of medical care can be isolated and measured. Experts agree that if strep throat were detected and treated adequately, rheumatic fever and chronic rheumatic heart disease would be almost nonexistent.[28] Yet in 1972, approximately 68,000 children under age 17 suffered from these two conditions.[29] Where organized health services have been made readily available to families, their impact is striking. In Baltimore, Maryland, where four comprehensive care programs were established in the most underserved areas of the city, the incidence of

[21] Meharry Medical College, Center for Health Care Research, "Study of Unmet Needs for Health and Welfare Services: Phase I, The 1972-3 Study." Invitational Presentation at the President-Elect's Session, American Public Health Association, 102nd Annual Meeting, New Orleans, La., 21 October 1974.

[22] National Center for Health Statistics, U.S. Department of Health, Education and Welfare, *Monthly Vital Statistics Report, Summary Report, Final Natality Statistics* (Washington, D.C.: U.S. Government Printing Office, 1973), p. 8.

[23] National Foundation, *Annual Report 1974*, p. 9. Cited in *America's Children, 1976, A Bicentennial Assessment*, p. 34.

[24] National Foundation, *Facts: 1976*, p. 7. Cited in *America's Children, 1976, A Bicentennial Assessment*.

[25] David M. Kessner, *Infant Death: An Analysis by Maternal Risk and Health Care* (Washington, D.C.: Institute of Medicine, National Academy of Sciences, 1973), p. 1.

[26] *Infant Death: An Analysis by Maternal Risk and Health Care*, p. 13 ff.

[27] *Infant Death: An Analysis by Maternal Risk and Health Care*, p. viii.

[28] The Boston Children's Medical Center and Richard I. Feinbloom, *Child Health Encyclopedia: The Complete Guide for Parents* (Boston: Delacorte Press, 1975), p. 479.

[29] National Center for Health Statistics, U.S. Department of Health, Education and Welfare, *Prevalance of Chronic Circulatory Conditions, United States, 1972,* U.S. Department of Health, Education and Welfare Publication No. (HRA) 75-1521 (Washington, D.C.: U.S. Government Printing Office, 1974), p. 21.

rheumatic fever was reduced by 60 percent among children in the census tracts eligible for any of the programs, while in the surrounding areas its incidence increased by 20 percent.[30]

We have learned a great deal about the effects on children's health when communities take specific steps to organize and provide comprehensive health care services to families.[31]

—Comparing infant mortality rates by income and race in nineteen cities, the spread among cities ranged from 22.3 in Pittsburgh to 2.8 in Denver. Denver had not only the lowest differentials between white and nonwhite and between low-income and other areas, it also had the lowest absolute rate in its low-income areas for both whites and nonwhites of the nineteen cities surveyed.[32] Denver has probably come closer than any city in the country to making comprehensive health services available to all its residents through an integrated network of neighborhood health centers and Children and Youth projects.

—Evaluations of many maternal and child health programs taking active steps to enroll pregnant women, monitor their health carefully and provide regular infant care have shown remarkable reductions in mortality, prematurity and illness.[33] In Providence, Rhode Island, for instance, the part of the city served by the Maternal and Infant Care Project at St. Joseph's Hospital showed a reduction in infant mortality from 47.4 per 1,000 live births in 1966 to 25.2 per 1,000 in 1970, while in more affluent census tracts the rate increased from 20.1 per 1,000 live births in 1966 to 21.4 in 1970.[34]

—Neighborhood health centers have been notably successful at extending health services in poor communities. Until recently there was a neighborhood health center in Lowndes County, Alabama, and the infant mortality rate was reduced from 46.9 per 1,000 live births in 1967 to 28.3 in 1971. Over that same period of time, infant mortality rates in neighboring counties changed little. Similarly, in Bolivar County, Mississippi, the infant mortality rate decreased from 48.5 to 31.0 deaths per 1,000 live births during the first four years a neighborhood health center was located there. Among Blacks, who comprised nearly all the patients served at the Bolivar center, the rate was reduced from 57.2 to 35.7, while the rate for whites increased slightly from 13.5 to 13.7.[35]

—In virtually every community where access to comprehensive care was improved, there was a substantial reduction in hospital admissions and in the inappropriate use of hospital emergency rooms.[36]

---

[30] Leon Gordis, "Effectiveness of Comprehensive Care Programs in Preventing Rheumatic Fever," *The New England Journal of Medicine*, Vol. 289 (August 1973).

[31] There have been a number of evaluations of the demonstration programs that have reorganized the delivery of care. Of the studies that have focused on the effect on health outcome of improved organization and comprehensiveness of care, only two have failed to demonstrate a clear relationship. One compared two groups of infants and found no discernible difference in their health status after a year during which half of them received care in an organized setting while the other half received sporadic care. (Leon Gordis and Milton Markowitz, "Evaluation of the Effectiveness of Comprehensive and Continuous Care," *Pediatrics*, Vol. 42, November 1971.) Another study measured three specific kinds of illnesses in children and found that the incidence of these illnesses or their detection and treatment was not related to the children's source of care. (David Kessner, *Assessment of Medical Care for Children*, Vol. III, "Contrasts in Health Status," Washington, D.C.: Institute of Medicine, National Academy of Sciences, 1971.) The failure of these two studies to show positive correlations between type of care and health status is by no means conclusive. The variables chosen because they are measurable are narrow, and often do not represent the array of qualities one would like to know about in evaluating program effectiveness. Had other characteristics been measured, or had the measures themselves been more sensitive, different conclusions may well have been reached.

[32] National Center for Health Statistics, Health Resources Administration, U.S. Department of Health, Education and Welfare, *Selected Vital and Health Statistics on Poverty and Non-Poverty Areas of 19 Large Cities, United States, 1969-71*, DHEW Publication No. (HRA) 76-1904 (Rockville, Ind.: U.S. Government Printing Office, 1975), Table E, p. 16. The differentials included a high of 22.3 in Pittsburgh (39.4 in nonwhite low-income areas and 17.1 for whites in the remainder of the city), and a spread of 19 in Indianapolis, 19.4 in Philadelphia, and 18.8 in Chicago. In only three cities was the spread less than 10: 7.5 in San Francisco, 5.8 in Minneapolis, and 2.8 in Denver.

[33] Maternal and Child Health Service, U.S. Department of Health, Education and Welfare, *Promoting the Health of Mothers and Children, Fiscal Year, 1972*, Federal Stock No. 1730-00029 (Washington, D.C.: U.S. Government Printing Office, 1972).

[34] *Promoting the Health of Mothers and Children*, p. 6.

[35] Karen Davis, "A Decade of Policy Developments in Providing Health Care for Low Income Families," in Robert H. Haveman, ed., *A Decade of Federal Anti-Poverty Policy: Achievements, Failures and Lessons*, pp. 47-48. (In press.)

[36] Louis I. Hochheister, Kenneth Woodward, Evan Charney, "Effect of the Neighborhood Health Center on the Use of the Pediatric Emergency Departments in Rochester, N.Y.," *New England Journal of Medicine*, Vol. 285 (July 1971). Robert M. Hollister, Bernard M. Kramer, Seymour S. Bellin, eds., *Neighborhood Health Centers* (Lexington, Mass.: Lexington Books, D.C. Heath and Co., 1974). Mile Square Health Center, "Mile Square Health Center, Inc., 1973: Year of Transition," Chicago, 1974.

—In Boston, Massachusetts, among families randomly assigned to a comprehensive care program, there was a significant increase in receipt of preventive services and a significant reduction in laboratory costs, prescription medications, hospitalizations, operations and illness visits.[37]

Health services make a difference in the incidence of death and disease, but they also make a difference in the quality of life we lead—a difference much more difficult to measure. Any parent who has sat up for a night with a feverish child or a child in pain knows that, although the illness may not be critical, and although it may go away by itself 80 percent of the time, if medical intervention can reduce that child's discomfort from five days to one, that is indeed a significant accomplishment. Any citizen who is concerned about the kind of society we live in must recognize that a full range of child health services should be available to all, rather than available to some on the basis of income or race.

---

[37] L.S. Robertson, J. Kosa, M.C. Heaggerty, R.J. Haggerty and J.J. Alpert, "Toward Changing the Medical Care System: Report of An Experiment," in Robert Haggerty, M.D., *The Boundaries of Health Care*. Reprinted from Alpha Omega Honor Society, *Pharos of Alpha Omega Alpha*, Vol. 35, pp. 106-11 (1972).

Ch. 1, "What Difference Does Health Care Make in the Lives of Children?" and Appendix C, "Major Federal Programs Which Finance or Provide Health Services for Children and Expectant Mothers," from Doctors and Dollars are not Enough: How to Improve Health Services for Children and their Families. Report by the Children's Defense Fund of the Washington Research Project, Inc. © 1976 by the Washington Research Project, Inc.)

APPENDIX C

Major Federal Programs Which Finance or Provide Health Services for Children and Expectant Mothers

Program and Authorizing Legislation	Purpose	Population eligibile for services	Activities	Financing	State Contact	Federal Agency*
Maternal and Child Health Services (MCH) Social Security Act, Title V, Sections 501, 503	To reduce infant mortality and improve the health of mothers and children by providing financial support to states to extend and improve related health services, especially in rural and low-income areas.	Determined by states. In general any mother or child who comes to the clinic may receive services.	Grants to states to support maternity clinics, public health nurse home visits, well-child clinics, pediatric clinics, school health and vision-hearing screening, dental care for children and pregnant women, immunizations, mental retardation clinics and screening programs.	Federal/State matched Formula Grants	Division of Maternal and Child Health in the State Health Department	Office of Maternal and Child Health (in the Bureau of Community Health Services, Health Services Administration, Public Health Service, U.S. Department of Health, Education and Welfare) 5600 Fishers Lane, Rockville, Md. 20852 Tel. 301-443-6600
Maternal and Child Health: Program of Projects Social Security Act, Title V Maternal and Infant Care (MIC)	To reduce the incidence of mental retardation and other handicaps caused by complications associated with childbearing, and to reduce infant and maternal mortality.	Diagnostic and preventive services to all women and infants within the target area. Treatment to women and infants who would not otherwise receive services because they are from low-income families or other circumstances beyond their control.	Grants to specific projects serving particular target populations (or areas) to identify high-risk mothers and provide full prenatal care, including hospitalization as needed, care for delivery, post-natal care and infant care	Federal/State matched Formula Grants	Division of Maternal and Child Health in the State Health Department	Office of Maternal and Child Health (in the Bureau of Community Health Services, Health Services Administration, Public Health Service, U.S. Department of Health, Education and Welfare) 5600 Fishers Lane, Rockville, Md. 20852 Tel. 301-443-6600
Children and Youth (C & Y)	To provide comprehensive health services to children living in areas with high concentrations of low income families.	Screening, diagnostic and preventive services available to all children and youth within the target area. Treatment, correction of defects, aftercare available only to children and youth who otherwise would not receive such services because of low income or circumstances beyond their control.	Grants to specific projects serving particular target populations (or areas) to provide comprehensive health care services to children and youth.	same as above	same as above	same as above
Intensive Infant Care	To provide necessary health care to infants during their first year of life when they have conditions or are in circumstances which increase the hazards to their health, in order to help reduce the incidence of mental retardation and other handicapping conditions caused by complications associated with childbearing, to help reduce infant mortality.	Available only to infants in the area served by the program who would otherwise not receive such services because they are from low-income families or for other reasons beyond their control.	Grants to specific projects serving particular target populations (or areas) to provide appropriate services for intensive care of infants, including surgical and specialized consultative services, and for follow-up care of the infant during the first year of life.	same as above	same as above	same as above
Dental Care	To promote the dental health of children and youth of school and pre-school age, particularly in areas with concentrations of low-income families.	Diagnostic, screening and preventive services to all children in the area served by the program. Treatment, correction and aftercare to children in the area who would not otherwise receive services because of low income or some other reasons beyond their control.	Grants to specific projects serving particular target populations (or areas) to provide preventive services, treatment and correction of dental problems with aftercare as well.	Federal/State matched formula grants	Division of Maternal and Child Health in the State Health Department.	Office of Maternal and Child Health (in the Bureau of Community Health Services, Health Services Administration, Public Health Service, U.S. Department of Health, Education and Welfare) 5600 Fishers Lane, Rockville, Md. 20852 Tel. 301-443-6600
Family Planning	To develop projects with special attention to family planning services for mothers in needy areas and among groups with special needs.	Primarily for low-income women living within the area served by the program. Treatment only for women who would not otherwise receive such services because of low-income or for other reasons beyond their control.	Grants to specific projects among particular target populations (or areas) to provide comprehensive family planning services including those medical, educational and social services related to family planning and contraception.	same as above	same as above	same as above

Program and Authorizing Legislation	Purpose	Population eligible for services	Activities	Financing	State Contact	Federal Agency*
Crippled Children's Services (CCS) Social Security Act, Title V, Sections 501, 504	To assist states, especially in rural areas, in locating children with crippling conditions or suffering from conditions leading to crippling and providing a full range of diagnostic and corrective services.	All children under age 21 with a handicapping condition, as defined by the state, are eligible for diagnostic services. Flexible income standards applied for treatment services.	Grants to state crippled children's agencies to pay cost of medical, hospital, diagnostic and convalescent care, to locate children and see that the child gets needed care and follow-up.	Federal/State matched formula grants	Division of Maternal and Child Health or Division of Crippled Children in the State Health Department	Office of Maternal and Child Health (in the Bureau of Community Health Services, Health Services Administration, Public Health Service, U.S. Department of Health, Education and Welfare) 5600 Fishers Lane, Rockville, Md. 20852 Tel. 301-443-6600
Family Planning Services Public Health Service Act, Title X, Section 314(e)	To provide families full opportunity to exercise freedom of choice to determine the number and spacing of their children through access to information and medical services-particularly for low-income families and to those who would not receive such help for other reasons beyond their control.	Available to all persons desiring such services, with payment requested from individuals able to pay for all or part of their services.	Comprehensive family planning services including those medical, educational and social services related to family planning and contraception.	Federal/State matched formula grants	State Health Department	Office for Family Planning (in the Bureau of Community Health Services, Health Services Administration, Public Health Service, U.S. Dept. of Health, Education and Welfare) 5600 Fishers Lane, Rockville, Md. 20852 Tel. 301-443-2430
Indian Health Service Snyder Act of 1924 Indian Health Transfer Act of 1954	To improve the health of all Indians and Alaskan natives on or near reservations.	All Indians and Alaskan natives living on or near reservations.	Funds to provide a full range of comprehensive health care programs, including dental and nutrition care, psychiatric care, sanitation, health education.	Federal funding of direct services.	Eleven area offices throughout the U.S.	Indian Health Service (in the Health Services Administration, Public Health Service, U.S. Department of Health, Education and Welfare) 5600 Fishers Lane, Rockville, Md. 20852 Tel. 301-443-1083
Migrant Health Public Health Service Act, Title IV, Section 319, as amended.	To increase the availability of high-quality comprehensive health services to migrant and seasonal farmworkers and their families through the establishment of family health services and payment for the cost of other necessary care.	Migrant and seasonal agricultural workers and their families.	Funds to provide acute and preventive medical care, maternity care, hospitalization, dental care and rehabilitation through family clinics and purchase-of-care arrangements.	Federal grants to public and non-profit agencies.	State Health Department	Office for Migrant Health (in the Bureau of Community Health Services, Health Services Administration, Public Health Service, U.S. Dept. of Health, Education and Welfare) 5600 Fishers Lane, Rockville, Md. 20852 Tel. 301-443-1153
Community Health Centers Comprehensive Health Planning and Public Health Service Act, Section 314(e)	To provide comprehensive services to urban or rural areas where there is a shortage of medical personnel and services, through neighborhood health centers, family health centers and community health networks.	Anyone residing in the target area.	A broad range of out-patient, medical care referral and environmental health services.	Federal grants to non-profit private or public organizations or agencies.	State Health Department	Office for Community Health Centers (in the Bureau of Community Health Services, Health Services Administration, Public Health Service, U.S. Dept. of Health, Education and Welfare) 5600 Fishers Lane, Rockville, Md. 20852 Tel. 301-443-2270
Health Maintenance Organizations Health Maintenance Organization Act of 1973	To provide encouragement for the establishment and expansion of health maintenance organizations.	Anyone enrolled in the HMO.	Provision of comprehensive health services on a prepaid capitation basis with emphasis on primary care and preventive services.	Federal grants for feasibility studies, planning and initial development. Once established, loans or loan guarantees to meet operational deficits for the first three years.	State Health Department	Office for Health Maintenance Organizations (in the Bureau of Community Health Services, Health Services Administration, Public Health Service, U.S. Dept. of Health, Education and Welfare) 5600 Fishers Lane, Rockville, Md. 20852 Tel. 301-443-4106
Community Mental Health Centers Community Mental Health Centers Amendments of 1975	To continue and expand community mental health services.	Anyone residing in the catchment area.	Provision of comprehensive mental health services.	Federal grants to non-profit private or public organizations or agencies.	State Health Department, State Mental Health Department or State Department of Human Resources.	Community Mental Health Support Branch, National Institute of Mental Health (in the Alcohol, Drug Abuse and Mental Health Administration, Public Health Service, U.S. Dept. of Health, Education and Welfare) 5600 Fishers Lane, Rockville, Md. 20852 Tel. 301-443-3623
Comprehensive Health Service Grants Comprehensive Health Planning and Public Health Service Act, Section 314(d)	To assist states in establishing and maintaining adequate public health services in accordance with priorities and goals established by states.	Varies with service.	Provision of communicable disease programs, environmental health services, chronic disease programs, laboratory services, home health, public health nursing services and community mental health services.	Formula grants to states.	State Health Department or State Mental Health Department.	Bureau of Community Health Services (in the Health Services Administration, Public Health Service, U.S. Dept. of Health, Education and Welfare) 5600 Fishers Lane, Rockville, Md., 20852 Tel. 301-443-6350
Medicaid Social Security Act, Title XIX	To provide financial assistance for medical services to families certified as eligible by state welfare or Medicaid agency.	Those certified eligible by the state Welfare or Medicaid Agency including families with dependent children (AFDC), and in some states other medically needy individuals.	Varies with the state. Includes payment for inpatient hospital care, outpatient hospital care, nursing home care, physicians care, laboratory and x-ray services, home health services, family planning, Early and Periodic Screening, Diagnosis and Treatment, and other services at the option of the state.	Federal-state matched reimbursement for services provided.	State Medicaid Agency (Usually State Department of Health or Welfare)	Medical Services Administration (in the Social and Rehabilitation Service, U.S. Dept. of Health, Education and Welfare) Room 5118, Switzer Bldg., 330 C Street, S.W., Washington, D.C. 20201 Tel. 202-245-0377

Program and Authorizing Legislation	Purpose	Population eligible for services	Activities	Financing	State Contact	Federal Agency*
Early and Periodic Screening, Diagnosis and Treatment (EPSDT) (A specific part of the Medicaid program) Social Security Act, Title XIX, Section 1905(a)(4)(B)	To provide preventive health care to children in low-income families by identifying, diagnosing and treating medical, dental and developmental problems.	Varies state to state-Medicaid eligible population.	Varies with the state. Assessment of an individual's physical and mental health, diagnostic services for those found to need them, treatment within the amount, duration and scope of the State plan but always including eyeglasses, hearing aids, other treatment for visual and hearing defects and dental services.	Federal-state matched reimbursement for services provided.	State Medicaid Agency (Usually State Department of Health or Welfare)	Early and Periodic Screening, Diagnosis and Treatment (in the Medical Services Administration, Social and Rehabilitation Service, U.S. Dept. of Health, Education and Welfare) Switzer Bldg., 330 C St., S.W., Washington, D.C. 20201 Tel. 202-245-0055
Social Services, Title XX Social Security Act, Title XX (Social Service Amendments of 1974) (replaces IV-A)	To furnish services to families directed at: achieving or maintaining self-support and/or self-sufficiency; preventing or remedying neglect, abuse or exploitation of children and adults unable to protect their own interests of preserving, rehabilitating or re-uniting families; preventing or reducing inappropriate institutional care by providing for community-based care or other forms of less intensive care; securing referral or admission for institutional care when appropriate.	Determined by states (only limitation is on income level).	Grants to states to support services which include but are not limited to child care services, protective services for children and adults, family planning services for all AFDC recipients, services related to the management and maintenance of the home, transportation services, information, referral, and counseling services. May include medical care if it is an integral but subordinate part of a service, provided funds are not available to the individual under Title XIX (Medicaid).	State matched federal reimbursement, possibly supplemented by fees	Varies by state. Usually State Department of Welfare or State Human Services Agency	Community Services Administration (in the Social and Rehabilitation Services, U.S. Dept. of Health, Education and Welfare) Room 5129, Switzer Building, 330 C Street, S.W., Washington, D.C. 20201 Tel. 202-245-8717
Headstart Economic Opportunity and Community Partnership Act, 1974	To find and remedy health defects of each child enrolled in a Headstart Program by introducing the child and family to continuing sources of health care, nutritious meals, and health education.	Children enrolled in Headstart	Funds to facilitate and sometimes provide medical, dental and developmental assessment, referral, treatment for children enrolled in Head Start, and health education for staff, parents and children enrolled in Headstart.	Federal project grants with some local matching funds.	Varies by state	Office of Child Development (in the Office of the Secretary, U.S. Dept. of Health, Education and Welfare) P.O. Box 1182, Washington, D.C. 20013 Tel. 202-755-7782
Special Supplemental Food Program for Women, Infants and Children (WIC) National School Lunch Act of 1966, as amended	To provide special nutritious food supplements to pregnant and lactating women, and to children up to 4 years old at nutritional risk because of inadequate nutrition and income.	Pregnant or lactating mothers, and non-nursing mothers to 6 months after delivery, and children up to 5 years who reside in approved project area if they are eligible for care at free or reduced cost from local agency serving project area, if they have nutritional needs.	Provision of specific supplemental foods.	Federal grants to states	WIC Coordinator, State Department of Health, or comparable state agency, Indian tribes, bands or groups	Food and Nutrition Service (in the Dept. of Agriculture) 500 12th St., N.W., Washington, D.C. 20250 Tel. 202-447-4370
Child Nutrition Programs National School Lunch Act and Child Nutrition Act of 1966, as amended						
National School Lunch Program	To provide nutritious lunches in schools to children, particularly needy children.	All children in a participating school. Reduced price or free lunches to those who have need as determined by local school officials in accordance with national income standards.	Provision of food and cash assistance.	Federal funds and federally donated foods to participating schools.	State Department of Education	Food and Nutrition Service (in the U.S. Dept. of Agriculture) 500 12th St., N.W., Washington, D.C. 20250 Tel. 202-447-9065
School Breakfast Program	To provide nutritious breakfasts in schools to children, particularly needy children or children who travel long distances to school.	All children in participating school. Reduced price or free breakfasts to those who have need as determined by local school officials in accordance with national income standards.	Provision of food and cash assistance.	Federal funds and federally donated foods to participating schools.	State Department of Education	same as above
Child Care Food Program	To provide nutritious meals for preschool and school-age children in public and private nonprofit institutions (day-care centers, camps, settlement houses), particularly needy children.	All children in participating institutions. Reduced price or free meals to those who have need.	Provision of food and cash assistance.	Federal funds and federally donated foods to participating institutions.	State Department of Education	same as above Tel. 202-447-9072

*For many programs more detailed information is available through Regional Offices than through the Central/Washington office.

Region I (Connecticut, Maine, Massachusetts, New Hampshire, Rhode Island, Vermont)
John F. Kennedy Federal Bldg.
Government Center
Boston, Mass. 02203
617-223-7291

Region II (New York, New Jersey, Puerto Rico, Virgin Islands)
Federal Building
26 Federal Plaza
New York, N.Y. 10007
212-264-3620

Region III (Delaware, Maryland, Pennsylvania, Virginia, West Virginia, District of Columbia)
3535 Market Street
Philadelphia, Pa. 19101
215-597-6482

Region IV (Alabama, Florida, Georgia, Kentucky, Mississippi, North Carolina, South Carolina, Tennessee)
50 Seventh Street, NE
Atlanta, Georgia 30323
404-526-5001

Region V (Illinois, Indiana, Michigan, Minnesota, Ohio, Wisconsin)
300 South Wacker Drive
Chicago, Illinois 60606
312-353-5122

Region VI (Arkansas, Louisiana, New Mexico, Oklahoma, Texas)
1114 Commerce Street
Dallas, Texas 75202
214-749-2436

Region VII (Iowa, Kansas, Missouri, Nebraska)
601 East 12th Street
Kansas City, Missouri 64106
816-374-3438

Region VIII (Colorado, Montana, North Dakota, South Dakota, Utah, Wyoming)
1961 Stout Street
Denver, Colorado 80202
303-837-2694

Region IX (Arizona, California, Hawaii, Nevada, Guam, Trust Territory of Pacific Island, American Samoa)
Federal Office Building
50 Fulton Street
San Francisco, Cal. 94102
415-556-2246

Region X (Alaska, Idaho, Oregon, Washington)
Arcade Plaza
1321 Second Avenue
Seattle, Washington 98101
206-442-0486

Part five :
Work and income

Work and income

THE WORKING FAMILY IN CRISIS

by Nancy Seifer

Introduction

I'm delighted to have this opportunity to share with you some new thoughts I've had about the problems of working class women and their families as they face the crises of the mid-1970's. The first question people generally ask is, "Who are working class women?" So let me begin with a broad definition. In brief, they are women who generally have a high school education or less, who if they work hold blue collar or lower level white collar jobs, and whose total annual income for a family of four falls somewhere between $9 and $13 or $14,000, the range which for northern cities the labor department describes as between "low" and "moderate" standards of living, but which nowadays anyone would call dangerously inadequate.

For the past 5 years or so, much of my work has focused on working class women and their concerns. I first became involved with working class communities as an aide to the former Mayor of New York City, John Lindsay, where I set up an Office of Ethnic Affairs within City Hall. This was in 1970 when tensions between minority groups and lower income or working class whites were flaring. And most white ethnic communities, feeling the economic pinch of inflation in the late 60's, cut off from city programs and services, angered by what they perceived as growing numbers of programs for minority groups that their tax dollars were paying for but they were not entitled to, began to raise their voices in protest. In an attempt to depolarize group tensions and reduce alienation between those communities and blacks and other minorities, I helped to create some new community organizations and spur the city agencies to respond to their needs.

I found myself working with the women in those working class white ethnic communities far more than the men. It seemed that as unaccustomed as they all were to working with city agencies, it was the women more often than the men who were willing to put themselves on the line and organize to bring day care centers, senior citizens centers and other new programs into their communities.

When I left City Hall, I went to work for the American Jewish Committee's National Project on Ethnic America, now called the Institute on Pluralism and Group Identity. My first major project there culminated in the publication of a pamphlet entitled, Absent From the Majority: Working Class Women in America. And this past summer I spent several months travelling around the country and interviewing 10 working class women of different ethnic backgrounds, regions, and ages about change in their lives for a book which I'm tentatively calling Voices Rising. The book will consist primarily of oral histories, with each of the women recounting the story of her life and the major issues which she is concerned with.

All of that is a form of an introduction, and also a statement of my concern for working class women having their own voice. I am here today not to speak for working class women but to hopefully shed some light on what some of their problems are as they have been expressed to me, in relationship to American society.

One of the major problems of working class families today in my view is a problem which relates to class, education and status in America. It is rooted in the gap in values and communications between professionals and non-professionals in our society.

In more affluent or comfortable times, that gap is perhaps less troublesome. But when growing numbers of less well-educated lower income people badly need services and programs designed and delivered for the most part by more highly educated and higher paid professionals, the gap becomes a major problem. At present, millions of working class people are in need of various kinds of assistance. But one wonders if their message is ever clearly heard.

Before I tackle the specific theme of my talk, I'd like to briefly discuss the women's movement and its relationship to working class women. First, because the changing role of women often creates problems in and of itself in working class families. And second, because that relationship helps to illustrate the broader problem I'd like to discuss.

"The Problem" In The Context of Changing Women's Roles

As we all know, the movement, unlike Venus, did not rise from the sea. As some have said, if there were no Betty Friedan and no Gloria Steinem, there would have been others, such was the climate of society in the sixties. But Betty Friedan's book, often viewed as the occasion of birth of the second feminist movement, and Gloria Steinem's ideas, articulation, and imagery helped to conceptualize a fairly new state of affairs in American society that was out of synchronization with women's traditional roles. Women had little to do with creating this new state of affairs, yet their lives were most profoundly touched by them.

By 1960 it was already clear that women were going to live longer and have fewer children. Even those with large families had less physical work to do in the home which took fewer hours, thanks to technology. In short, women as a group would be performing "women's functions" for a shorter period of time. Then, economic factors played an important role. As inflation began to spiral in the second half of the sixties, growing numbers of housewives were forced into the labor market to help make ends meet. Their husbands' salaries alone became inadequate. At the same time, the divorce rate began to rise dramatically and since in 9 cases out of 10 women don't receive regular alimony payments, or any payments at all, the number of working female heads of household increased dramatically.

While those factors and many others created a climate in which a movement for equality for women could take root, there was another important one which triggered the birth of the movement. That is education, and in particular higher education. College-educated women were increasingly aware of the fact that they were educated for careers or professions to which they were then denied entry. Some, already in the work force, were angered and frustrated at being refused promotions to "men's jobs." Others, housewives with considerable education, were frustrated with their lives yet didn't relish the idea of going to work as secretaries after being at home for 10 or 20 years. Regardless of their degree, that was often the only kind of job they could get.

Finally, the movements of the sixties gave the needed impetus for the spawning of a new women's movement. It became clear to the millions of college students and college-educated people involved in the student movement, the anti-war movement, the Civil Rights movement, that if they were women, they were not around when decision-making time came. Most likely, they were still in the back room making coffee and licking envelopes. Those years of fighting for what was right and fighting for the rights of others culminated in an awareness of the extent to which their own rights were being denied. It suddenly became clear that for no reason other than their sex, power and influence were beyond their reach. Clearly, especially when it came to college students and recent college graduates involved in those movements there was no difference between women and men in terms of education and experience.

I think that in looking at the lives of working class women vis-à-vis the women's movement, we can't forget that context. The movement burst onto the scene with the natural bias of its original spokeswomen. One of the messages which came across most loud and strong was a demand for access to men's jobs and equal entry into the professions. Obviously, that message was not going to arouse a great following among women whose husbands may be truck drivers or assembly line workers. Women who if they had to go out to work might themselves find a job on an assembly line, or perhaps in a typing pool.

If their husband's salary was adequate to keep the family in food and shelter, the majority of working class housewives would undoubtedly choose not to work outside the home, given the jobs they are likely to find. For the most part, they are not the challenging, stimulating, thought-provoking kinds of jobs that middle class feminists were encouraging their sisters to leave home for. The anti-housewife message that came across was both a threat and an insult to them. But it was quite obviously unintentional. The women sending out the message in the early days were in effect sending out a call, a challenge to their sisters to do something more interesting and gratifying with their lives. The assumption, of course, was that they had the skills and knowledge and would find the opportunity. There seemed to be little awareness in those early days that the vast majority of women in America have a high school education or less.

Then of course several other of the movement's messages, distorted as they were by the media, ran into head-on conflict with the values of working class women. The importance of the roles of wife and mother; the concept of institutionalized day care centers run by outside professionals; the notion of casual, free, legalized abortion; the positive portrayal of lesbianism; and several other issues.

The result was something that I have labelled for lack of a better descriptive term the "class culture clash" in America. Interestingly, according to almost all the recent public opinion polls and surveys on women, there is much greater agreement on many of the movement's issues between poor black and other minority women and middle class women, than there is between either of those groups and working class women. For the poor and the affluent, change is often much more appealing than it is to groups that are economically and socially marginal.

But over the past few years, a great deal has changed in America and there seems to be much less hostility towards the women's movement on the part of working class women. There seems to be a greater sense of appreciation of the movement's accomplishments, to be more precise, though there remains a great deal of hesitancy about identifying with or giving approval to the movement itself.

The Communications Gap

Most working class women still don't seem to identify with the movement's more visible leaders or what they perceive the message to be as it comes through the t.v. screen. But they do acknowledge the real accomplishments that the movement has made through law, through the courts, in new public policy and in programs.

As I travelled around the country this summer I heard the phrase "I'm no women's libber but..." repeatedly. And the "but" has to do with a lot of things that are meaningful to the lives of growing numbers of women, especially those in the work force. Equal pay is always mentioned as the most important accomplishment of the movement. And then equal access to higher-paying jobs that blue collar or lower-level white collar working women have been denied in the past. Then as the need for day care centers grows, there seems to be greater awareness of what the movement's pressure has accomplished in that area. Equal educational opportunity, decent health care, an end to discrimination in the areas of credit and insurance are all issues around which there is a growing broad-based concensus. And they are all issues which have something to do with the impact of the economy on the change in women's roles.

Ironically, if we look back now to the 60's and the climate which produced the movement, it was those very issues which caused a significant shift in women's roles. Now that the dust is settling and the flames of the early days of rhetoric and controversy have died down, it is clear that it is around those very issues that women in America seem to find most common ground.

As I see it, the problem that remains vis-à-vis working class women and the women's movement, as undefinable as it has become, is one of communications, values and perceptions. The same communications gap exists perhaps between all lower income and upper income women in America, but poor minority women with forums like the National Welfare Rights Organization have been far more successful at articulating their own agendas over the past decade or two than have working class women. It is, in many ways a far more urgent agenda and yet differs dramatically from that of lower middle income women who as one writer put it, "are not secure enough to gamble what little they barely have for indulgence in utopian hopes."

For the most part, working class people in America are in the position of reacting or responding to new ideas and programs put forth by middle class professionals. Rarely, except through organized labor, do they have the opportunity to initiate and articulate their own agendas. It is now an old cliche that they have bought the American dream with growing aspirations for upward mobility. But despite the current economic catastrophes, that is still probably more true than it is untrue. If it is true, that means that large scale social change is threatening to both their values and their aspirations.

In terms of the women's movement, that seems to mean "Yes, we want justice in the workplace if we do work, and in the market place, and in the schools, but we don't want the intrinsic role of woman -- that of mother and wife -- to be tampered with or downgraded. And what's more, what choices do we have? Even if we want to have experiences that would be self-fulfilling out of the home, what are our chances of getting a college degree? Or a glamorous job? Or some interesting work? Or travelling? Or even having a vacation away from home? To us, there is nothing more important than being a good mother and wife and the emotional satisfaction that comes from that."

So in my view, much of the negative reaction to the women's movement, especially in the early days, had much to do with a clash in values and in vastly differing basic life experiences.

A movement that basically espoused new choices and options for women at its core, made the lack of options for the majority of women in America even more glaring. And the values of highly educated, articulate women were visible in the way they communicated the message, which often served to further divide, quite unintentionally.

An Illustration of "The Problem"

I am currently involved in designing a project which will attempt to get a handle on the communications barriers between working and middle class women in America. And an experience I had last weekend made me even more aware of the degree of the problem and of how unconscious most people are that it exists. The communications gap stood out in bold relief at a meeting I attended in Washington with a group of about 15 middle class professional women, all of whom were apparently feminists.

We were there as members of a national advisory council for a new project set up to implement Title IX of the Education Amendments of 1972, which is addressed to ending sex discrimination in the schools. The project was specifically set up to monitor the implementation of Title IX, whose regulations are expected to be released shortly by H.E.W.

As I sat in the room, I was struck by the middle class professional bias of many of the women, in both the underlying assumptions that were made about the task at hand and the language used. It was totally unintentional and unconscious, but it was there. And despite all of the best intentions, that kind of a biased perspective would prevent the message from reaching some crucial audiences.

It was assumed, for example, that most women in America are fully aware of the fact that sex discrimination exists in our schools and that they are alert to the forms that it takes. It was also assumed that a sizeable number of women know that there is such a thing as Title IX, and that there will be regulations forthcoming on the basis of which complaints can be filed.

It was further assumed that a good number of women know what filing a complaint means. I didn't. The term has such a legalistic tone, that it brings to mind the notion of filing a suit and I assumed that some bureaucratic process or at least the filling out of forms was involved. None of that is true. Filing a complaint simply means writing a letter to the appropriate government agencies informing them that incidents of sex discrimination exist and have not been corrected. So why not talk about writing letters instead of filing complaints?

The whole project in fact is based on several assumptions that do not mesh with the realities of most women in America. It is set up to monitor complaints initiated by individuals only, to see that the government does take action, and since the budget is rather small that is all the staff can reasonably handle. But without a large scale public education campaign as to what all of that means and how the lives of young girls are affected by sex discrimination in the schools, the women who can be counted on to file complaints will most likely be middle class feminists and what's more, activists. That, after all, is not a very sizeable group of the population.

Ironically, being a white middle class feminist myself, I found myself involved in a chorus throughout the day-long meeting with a Chicana woman and a black woman repeating the same message over and over again: if the project is going to reach anyone beyond feminists who already subscribe to all the newsletters, and are a part of the information network, there has to be a different style of communicating, a different presentation of the issues, and a different use of language. Having undergone a process of sensitization over the past few years to the way in which working class women perceive our society, and knowing something about the additional burdens of the poor, that experience made me realize how far we have to go, as American women, in learning how to communicate with one another.

"The Problem" As it Affects Working Class Families

That same division or gap in values, needs and perceptions which I referred to earlier as a "class culture clash" is perhaps at the root of some of the major problems faced by working class -- many of them white ethnic --families today. It may not yet be a crisis to most families, but it is surely growing to critical proportions as economic and social problems skyrocket.

First, the economy. There was an interesting article in last Friday's New York Times which brought the values question to mind. It was an attempt to analyze whether or not we are now in a recession or a depression. Our Secretary of the Treasury, Mr. Simon, offhandedly tossed in the old saw about calling it a recession when you are out of work, and a depression when I am. The article got nowhere in telling us what it is that we are now in, since there is no agreement among economists, government officials, and clearly none among Democrats and Republicans.

But in comparing the Great Depression to whatever it is that we are now living through, it made mention of the fact that we now have such "safeguards and stabilizers" like unemployment insurance, public service employment, bank deposit insurance, food stamps and welfare payments which we did not have then.

That point was interesting for a number of reasons, not the least of which is that the day before the Labor Department reported that 5 states have already run out of unemployment insurance funds and had to appeal to the federal government for help, and it is expected that as many as 30 states may run out by 1976 and will have to apply to a federal fund set up to keep the nationwide unemployment compensation system afloat.

Totally apart from the realities of the situation, and the fact that the unemployed are indeed luckier, if you will allow such an irony, than they were in the Great Depression in that fewer will be without food and shelter and have to sell apples on street corners, the psychological and emotional damage is devastating.

As we all know from the flood of statistics covering the pages of our newspapers, when unemployment statistics are broken down, the number of professional and technical employees out of work is minimal compared to the numbers of semi-skilled and unskilled workers. And it is to this very group of workers, the men in particular, that having a job is perhaps essential to having a sense of oneself, or to having pride in one's existence, and one's role as breadwinner.

Last week in New York City thousands of unemployed construction workers marched on City Hall and blocked traffic on the Brooklyn Bridge for hours. They tied up a good part of lower Manhattan. Some of them carried signs that said, "We want jobs or some heads are gonna roll," and "We want to put food on our tables, we demand jobs."

They were not saying that they were starving, and they were probably all receiving some form of unemployment benefits. But that isn't the point. These are the same people who vocalized their low regard for welfare hand-outs in the sixties. At that time, they were viewed as racists. But as we saw last week, when it came to the point that they themselves were in a similar situation, they were not only angry, they were near-violent.

The American ethic of "making it on your own," not taking anything from anyone, certainly not government, is one of the most important values to many white ethnic working class people in America. Once they reach the point where they can't make it on their own, even though it is through no fault of their own, there seems to be an overwhelming sense of failure. (For the best description of how the inability to succeed in the workplace is turned into a personal sense of failure, I suggest a reading of The Hidden Injuries of Class by Richard Sennett and Jonathan Cobb.)

But it seems that what's happening now, during this post-Watergate period with seemingly endless revelations about corruption in government and big business, is that the loss of a job may be seen less as a personal failure. There is a growing sense of anger at the system, which certainly won't solve anyone's immediate problems, but which may well lead to new forms of public policy in the long-run.

While I am focusing my remarks today chiefly on the working class family, that is the traditional two-parent family, I feel compelled to mention the fact that there has been a tremendous increase in the divorce rate among these families in the past decade and that at the rate we are going now, many of the single mothers losing their jobs now will surely end up on the welfare rolls. Until we get new and enforceable laws on the books dealing with equitable layoffs systems, they will continue to be the first fired and the last re-hired.

While I don't find it surprising at all, a male reporter for the Chicago-Sun Times wrote this week that a "surprising 37 per cent" of the people now getting unemployment insurance in Illinois are women. That makes more than a lot of sense, since women now constitute 40 per cent of the work force. And chances are, given the positions of most women in the labor force, that figure will rise to well over 40 per cent if the economy continues to decline.

The Emotional Crisis

In two-parent families where both husband and wife work, and statistics show that that is now the majority at any given time in working class families, the loss of the wife's job is surely a severe blow. There have been countless reports in recent days of companies reclaiming boats, cars, t.v. sets, where people could not keep up with the payments. And many of these are the families I described earlier, who bought the American dream, and who had steadily rising aspirations and expectations during the fifties and sixties when the economy was expanding. They are people who can afford few luxuries in life, and who must often pay for those they have on credit. People who were not in any way prepared either financially or emotionally for the situation they now find themselves in.

But perhaps the most emotionally devastating situation for men in working class families is to lose their own jobs and have their wives go out to work. Women can often find typing jobs when their husbands are knocked off the factory line or a construction site closes down. But when women become the breadwinners, totally apart from women's lib, the shift in roles makes a deep impact. The wife may gain a new sense of her own worth, but the husband loses his and she must cope with the tensions that undoubtedly arise.

Perhaps the most startling statistics to come down the pike in recent days came from the newest Louis Harris Poll. Fifty-two per cent of the nation's families have been directly affected by rising unemployment out of a sample of 1,543 families. About 30 per cent had at least one member laid off. Nine per cent had lost overtime, and 13 per cent had their work week cut back. But even more revealing of the stress that families are living under is the fact that 74 per cent of those polled said they saw unemployment in their own communities growing, compared to 58 per cent who said so last November, only 4 months ago.

The tension and fear reflected in those figures is also reflected in the growing waiting family lists of family service agencies and other counselling, therapeutic and treatment facilities. One major New York agency reported that for the first time more cases were initiated by men than by women. And at the same time, mental health budgets are being cut back in cities and states across the nation, and individual agencies are being forced to cut back on their own budgets.

No one knows exactly how many of the individuals or families seeking counselling are working class, nor do we know how many are seeking help for problems related to the economy. But it is a good guess that many more working class families than ever before are seeking help and that the reasons have something to do with fears about the present and the future: about making it, surviving, and all the tensions that naturally arise between husband and wife, or between parents and children in times of stress.

That brings us back to the notion of the "class culture clash," and the gap between professionals and non-professionals in America. A number of parallels could be drawn between the way the women's movement first came across, and the way in which social services are currently provided. There is in this area as well what we might call a lack of snychronization between the senders of the message and the recipients, based on different educational and cultural backgrounds, different life experiences, different values and different perceptions.

To illustrate the point, say for example, a man comes into a family service agency for counselling. He's just been laid off from his job, he's on unemployment and his wife is out looking for a job. After years of steady income, he can't pay his bills or meet his mortgage payments and he fears that he may lose his house. He feels like a total failure, and can't bear the thought that his wife might have to support the family.

Then, say he arrives at the agency and is assigned to a feminist social worker. First, he may have never revealed his feelings about himself as a failure to anyone before, so he may be there only out of pure desperation, feeling extremely vulnerable. But he's there because he wants practical help if possible and a sympathetic ear. How, for example, can he deal with his feelings about his wife? For purely hypothetical purposes, let's say the feminist social worker has never actually felt what it's like to be economically marginal, let alone poor. And she doesn't fully comprehend why the man feels so devastated about having lost his job, since after all, isn't everybody these days? And she thinks that it's fine that his wife is going out to work. In fact she thinks it's great, the wife won't be so dependent anymore.

Without exaggerating too much, I think you understand the point I'm trying to make. The experiences and values of "professional America" are most often not those of working class America. Even when professionals come from working class backgrounds, they are most often taught to unlearn the values that they were brought up with and to adopt new ones. The value gap or the culture clash becomes increasingly important at times of enormous stress like the present, when people who never before would seek any kind of help related to psychological or emotional disturbance, are now in great need of that kind of help.

Beyond the question of values, there are often class and ethnic differences in both verbal and non-verbal communications styles and emotional expressiveness that most professionals are still not being trained to look for, but which are still often readily apparent in first, second and even third generation Americans. So that even if all the working class families who needed help sought it, and even if mental health or counselling agencies could possibly handle all the cases that came to them, the quality of treatment offered would most likely suffer due to the lack of awareness of class and cultural differences.

The Importance of Family

It is difficult at a time like this to discuss the ways in which I've found working class women to be changing in terms of their roles as women, apart from the economic crisis. The crisis is so overwhelming in its impact that it seems to dwarf virtually everything else. But I would like to mention some of the changes that I became aware of and a few thoughts related to public policy.

When I began my travels early last summer to interview working class women about change in their lives, I really set out to explore the issue. I had very few preconceived notions apart from the fact that they were less likely to change their roles as women because of a movement, and that if there was a change in roles it probably had more to do with their life circumstances. In other words, working class women are far less likely than middle class women to pick up a book or some articles, go to a few meetings, and suddenly become what some have called "overnight feminists," eager to change their life styles and their relationships with their husbands, if they are married.

What I found, if I can generalize based on the ten women whom I got to know in depth, plus others I had worked with and met in New York, Chicago and other cities where I spent some time, was that the women's movement had little direct impact on them, although I did sense an indirect impact. What did happen most often was that these women were confronted with a problem or a situation in their lives to which they felt compelled to react. Many of them found themselves becoming activists, were often surprised at themselves, and ended up with a very different perception of themselves and of the power they could have over their lives.

But few of those who became activists identified themselves as feminists. There are a number of factors involved here but I will focus on only one right now. The word "feminist" and the term "women's lib" have come to have, in the minds of many women, an anti-male or "man-hating" tinge. And virtually all of the working class women I've come into contact with, even those who are unhappy with their own marriages or relationships, do not want to hate men. In fact their husbands play essential roles in their lives and in no way do they see them as being part of "the problem."

Interestingly, in cases where women have had more direct and personal contact with middle class feminists working through organizations to bring about change, there seems to be a greater acceptance of and identification with the terms. Obviously, where they have not had to depend on distorted media images but have met movement activists in person, there is a greater understanding that being a feminist and not liking men are not necessarily synonymous.

Anita Cupps of Sumiton, Alabama, right outside Birmingham, was what she herself calls a typical housewife. Her husband is a coal miner and she has two kids, 6 and 3. It was when her second child was born with a severe birth defect and rare blood disease that she found herself becoming an activist. All that Anita and her husband Johnny had to save that child's life was the hospital card that all miners have, which covers all medical expenses for the family. Without that card, they never could have afforded the kind of major surgery needed to save their child's life.

Anita and Johnny, like all other mining families, knew quite a bit about what was happening at the United Mine Workers' headquarters in Washington under Tony Boyle. Apart from the Yablonski murders, what disturbed them the most was the fact that their union dues were being, as they put it, "pissed away" by Boyle with his limousines and chauffeurs and other outrageous expenditures. And they feared that the union was dangerously close to bankruptcy.

So, in the last United Mine Workers elections, Anita suddenly found herself out campaigning for the local pro-Miller slate in Alabama. She and a handful of other women ran a campaign the likes of which had never before been run in that part of the State. Women appeared at the miner's health clinics and other locations handing out leaflets and flyers, and they participated in political rallies which had been men-only territory in the past. For their labors, they were rewarded with not only derision and disdain from many of the miners and their wives, they also received some wicked telephone calls warning them to stay out of things and some slashed tires. The rest is history -- Boyle was defeated as you know, Arnold Miller won, and one of their three local candidates made it.

Anita probably always had whatever it takes to be an activist within her. It was a matter of having the circumstances bring out that part of her personality. She's geared up for the next election now and she's going to fight like hell. But in the meantime she's happy and busy as a housewife, she's involved in a new statewide coalition of black and white lower income women called Alabama Women for Human Rights, and with women's church groups in her area. But Anita Cupps does not in any way consider herself a feminist.

A contrasting example, although one which I think represents the minority, is Bonnie Halascsak from an area near Gary, Indiana. Bonnie worked at U.S. Steel for many years as a secretary for the plant's fire department. She reached the top of her promotional scale after some time and the next job up on the promotion ladder was that of plant security guard.

Neither the company nor the union really liked the idea. There had never been a woman plant security guard before, but Bonnie wanted it and she fought for it. Through the laws and eventually through union pressure, she overcame the company's resistance and they unwillingly took her into Chicago to buy her a police woman's uniform, since they had no proper uniform for a woman at U.S. Steel.

Bonnie's husband, by the way, works for the management of U.S. Steel. And she has 3 young kids. But he supported her all the way even though her new job meant working all 3 shifts and that they'd have to have a baby-sitter for much of the time.

Then, U.S. Steel was hit with a back pay suit by minority employees and the suit was broadened to include women. At that point, one of the union leaders contacted some women from NOW in Chicago, who then volunteered to help with the suit and provided legal aid. Bonnie was one of the 3 women at U.S. Steel who was willing to stick her neck out and become publicly involved. She suddenly found herself working with middle class feminists with whom she discovered she had a lot more in common than she did with many of the women she lives near and works with.

To make a very long story short, she now considers herself a feminist and is an active one. For a short time, there existed a group called Steelworkers NOW. It disbanded after the suit was settled, largely for political reasons. But Bonnie is determined to set up a local Indiana NOW chapter. Her concerns have gone way beyond equal rights in the workplace and now span the gamut of women's concerns.

Still, Bonnie is now embroiled in an ongoing personal dilemma. Her inclination is to spend even more time out of the home to pursue her interests, but her husband still comes first. They have an excellent marriage, and he's encouraged her all the way, but he has now begun to feel that enough is enough and she is likely to make a lot of compromises in the interest of family.

All this leads me to my final point. When it comes to public policy and programs relating to working class women, from my own experience I have found that in many ways it is preferable to deal with changing roles of women in the context of family. Given the values and the life experiences of lower income people, a change in the wife's role often has a much greater impact on the family than in higher income families. It is therefore not only less threatening for both men and women, but also much more logical to view the reverberations of changing women's roles not in isolation, but in the context of family -- the husbands and children who are first to feel the impact.

It should never be assumed that programs that work well for middle class women will work equally well for all other groups of women. In fact, they can not work at all unless people's values are fully understood. In planning such programs, it should be understood that family is still of paramount importance to working class women. They do not see themselves as independent entities with a variety of options in life including exciting, rewarding careers. For the most part, they do not choose to live in orbits separate from their husbands. They may want to exert greater independence in the home as well as in the workplace, but family is still of paramount importance.

In closing, therefore, it is my view that if the working class family is in crisis, it is a crisis created primarily by the economy, and secondarily by social change, particularly the change in women's roles. That change entails a change in men's roles, and in the structure of the family, yet the working class women I know want desperately to keep that family intact.

Editor's note: The reader is also referred to "The Work-Family Role System" by Joseph Pleck, in the ADULTS part of this FAMILY FACTBOOK.

"The Working Family in Crisis: Who is Listening?" by Nancy Seifer. This speech was presented to the Wayne State University Conference on March 9, 1975.

MONEY INCOME AND POVERTY STATUS OF FAMILIES AND PERSONS IN THE U.S.: 1975 AND 1974 REVISIONS (Advance Report)

NOTE

In processing the data collected in the March 1976 Current Population Survey, the Bureau of the Census utilized a new computer processing system designed to take maximum advantage of the Bureau's expanded computer capabilities. The revised system also incorporates many improvements in the procedures used to process the data. A detailed discussion of these improvements and the subsequent revisions to the 1974 income and poverty data (for comparability with 1975 data) is provided in a later section, entitled "Revised 1974 Money Income and Poverty Statistics."

INTRODUCTION

The median income of all families in the United States was $13,720 in 1975 and there were about 25.9 million persons below the poverty level, according to results of the Current Population Survey (CPS) conducted in March 1976 by the Bureau of the Census. Median family income in 1975 increased about 6 percent over the revised 1974 median. However, after adjusting for the 9 percent increase in prices between 1974 and 1975,[1] the 1975 median in terms of constant dollars decreased by $360 or about 3 percent. The 25.9 million persons below the poverty level in 1975 ($5,500 for a nonfarm family of four) comprised 12 percent of the U.S. population. Overall, the poverty population was 2.5 million or 10.7 percent higher than the revised 1974 figure.

MONEY INCOME IN 1975

The decline in real median family income reflected the continued sluggishness in the economy during 1975, as evidenced by a decline of 2 percent in the real Gross National Product between 1974 and 1975.[3] During the same period, the average annual unemployment rate for the nation increased from 5.6 percent in 1974 to 8.5 percent in 1975.[4] The rise in the unemployment rate was accompanied by an increase in the number of persons who exhausted their unemployment benefits, from about 2.0 million in 1974 to 4.3 million in 1975.[5]

[1] The percentage increase in prices between 1974 and 1975 is computed by dividing the annual average Consumer Price Index (CPI) for 1975 by the annual average value of the CPI for 1974.

[3] U.S. Department of Commerce, Bureau of Economic Analysis, **Survey of Current Business,** Volume 56, Number 7, July 1976, p. 1.

[4] U.S. Department of Labor, Bureau of Labor Statistics, **Employment and Earnings,** Volume 23, Number 1, July 1976, p. 19.

[5] Data were obtained from the U.S. Department of Labor, Employment and Training Administration, Office of Administration and Management.

Although real median income for all families declined between 1974 and 1975, it did not show uniform movement by race and ethnic origin. White families had a median income of $14,270 in 1975, which represented a constant dollar decline of 3 percent below their 1974 median. The median income of Black families ($8,780 in 1975) showed no statistically significant change in real terms. (See table 1.) In addition, sampling variability was too large to reliably determine whether there was an actual difference between the percentage changes in median income for Black and White families. Families with a head of Spanish origin had a median income of $9,550 in 1975, a decline in real terms of 8 percent below their 1974 median.

The 1975 median incomes of families in the Northeast ($14,480) and North Central ($14,540) regions represented decreases in real terms of 5 percent and 3 percent, respectively. Median income in 1975 of families in the South ($12,240) and West ($14,320) regions did not represent statistically significant changes in real terms.[6]

Of the 56.2 million families in the United States in March 1976, 7.9 million or 14.1 percent received incomes of $25,000 or more in 1975. There were 17.1 million families (30.3 percent) with incomes between $15,000 and $25,000; 12.6 million families (22.3 percent) with incomes between $10,000 and $15,000; 11.9 million families (21.1 percent) with incomes between $5,000 and $10,000; and 6.8 million families (12.0 percent) with incomes below $5,000.

Men and women who were income recipients in 1975 had median incomes of $8,850 and $3,390, respectively.

[6] The apparent regional variation in the percentage changes in real median family income (see table 1) cannot be confirmed because of the large sampling variability associated with these estimates.

The 1975 median income for men, expressed in real terms, showed a decline of about 4 percent below the 1974 median. In contrast, the real median income for women did not show a statistically significant change between 1974 and 1975.

Although the median earnings of both male and female year-round full-time workers increased substantially between 1974 and 1975, the high rate of inflation during this period caused a slight decline in their real earnings. (See table 12.) Men working year round full time had a median earnings of $12,760 in 1975 while comparable women had a median earnings of $7,500.

Table A. Families and Unrelated Individuals by Total Money Income in 1975

(Families and unrelated individuals as of March 1976)

Total money income	Families	Unrelated individuals
Number............thousands..	56,245	20,234
Percent....................	100.0	100.0
Under $2,000.......................	2.1	14.1
$2,000 to $2,999...................	2.4	15.6
$3,000 to $3,999...................	3.4	12.4
$4,000 to $4,999...................	4.1	8.9
$5,000 to $5,999...................	4.1	7.3
$6,000 to $6,999...................	4.2	5.8
$7,000 to $7,999...................	4.3	5.7
$8,000 to $8,999...................	4.4	4.9
$9,000 to $9,999...................	4.1	4.2
$10,000 to $10,999.................	4.6	3.8
$11,000 to $11,999.................	4.3	2.6
$12,000 to $12,999.................	4.8	2.8
$13,000 to $13,999.................	4.2	2.0
$14,000 to $14,999.................	4.4	1.8
$15,000 to $15,999.................	4.4	1.7
$16,000 to $16,999.................	4.0	1.1
$17,000 to $17,999.................	3.6	0.9
$18,000 to $19,999.................	6.7	1.3
$20,000 to $24,999.................	11.6	1.6
$25,000 to $49,999.................	12.7	1.3
$50,000 and over...................	1.4	0.2
Median income......................	$13,719	$4,882
Mean income........................	15,546	6,623

Table 1. SELECTED CHARACTERISTICS OF ALL FAMILIES—NUMBER OF FAMILIES, MEDIAN INCOME, MEAN INCOME, AND STANDARD ERRORS, BY RACE OF HEAD AND SPANISH ORIGIN OF HEAD: 1975, 1974 (Revised), and 1974

(Families as of March of the following year. An asterisk (*) preceding percent change indicates statistically significant change at the 95 percent confidence level)

Selected characteristics	1975					1974[r]			Percent change (median income)		1974			Difference (1974[r]-1974)		
	Number (thou-sands)	Median income: Value	Median income: Stand-ard error	Mean income: Value	Mean income: Stand-ard error	Number (thou-sands)	Median income	Mean income	Current dollars	In 1975 dollars	Number (thou-sands)	Median income	Mean income	Number (thou-sands)	Median income	Mean income
ALL RACES																
All families	56,245	$13,719	$52	$15,546	$50	55,698	$12,902	$14,711	*6.3	*-2.6	55,712	$12,836	$14,502	-14	$66	$209
Type of Residence																
Nonfarm	54,045	13,829	52	15,640	51	53,306	12,991	14,782	*6.5	*-2.5	53,314	12,934	14,568	-8	57	214
Farm	2,200	10,845	383	13,251	337	2,392	10,612	13,131	2.2	-6.4	2,398	10,431	13,020	-6	181	111
Inside metropolitan areas	37,801	14,909	60	16,685	63	37,716	13,921	15,708	*7.1	*-1.9	37,741	13,771	15,458	-25	150	250
1,000,000 or more	21,446	15,550	79	17,422	87	21,317	14,648	16,440	*6.2	*-2.7	21,351	14,475	16,169	-34	173	271
Inside central cities	8,225	12,957	133	14,930	129	8,416	12,341	14,115	*5.0	*-3.8	8,459	12,025	13,825	-43	316	290
Outside central cities	13,221	17,156	99	18,973	115	12,901	16,206	17,957	*5.9	*-3.0	12,893	16,315	17,707	8	-109	250
Under 1,000,000	16,356	14,139	83	15,717	90	16,399	13,083	14,758	*8.1	-1.0	16,390	12,940	14,531	9	143	227
Inside central cities	7,588	13,031	139	14,958	133	7,575	12,202	14,136	*6.8	-2.1	7,553	12,013	13,918	22	189	218
Outside central cities	8,768	14,859	105	16,374	122	8,824	13,839	15,292	*7.4	-1.6	8,837	13,622	15,055	-13	217	237
Outside metropolitan areas	18,443	11,600	79	13,214	78	17,982	11,057	12,620	*4.9	*-3.9	17,971	11,045	12,494	11	12	126
Region																
Northeast	12,670	14,481	148	16,381	149	12,562	13,950	15,618	*3.8	*-4.9	12,588	13,796	15,400	-26	154	218
North Central	15,023	14,541	150	16,128	158	15,030	13,732	15,390	*5.9	*-3.0	15,019	13,736	15,215	11	-4	175
South	18,440	12,236	127	14,153	148	18,101	11,322	13,277	*8.1	-1.0	18,099	11,230	13,072	2	92	205
West	10,111	14,316	243	16,177	251	10,006	13,235	15,148	*8.2	-0.9	10,006	13,160	14,887	-	75	261
Type of Family																
Male head	48,763	14,816	51	16,633	55	48,468	13,863	15,697	*6.9	*-2.1	48,470	13,788	15,464	-2	75	233
Married, wife present	47,318	14,867	51	16,693	56	47,069	13,923	15,767	*6.8	*-2.2	46,971	13,847	15,532	98	76	235
Wife in paid labor force	20,833	17,237	78	18,633	72	20,404	16,221	17,538	*6.3	*-2.6	20,273	16,461	17,492	131	-240	46
Wife not in paid labor force	26,486	12,752	60	15,166	80	26,665	12,231	14,411	*4.3	*-4.5	26,698	12,082	14,044	-33	149	367
Other marital status	1,444	12,995	291	14,686	296	1,399	11,658	13,343	*11.5	2.1	1,499	11,737	13,325	-100	-79	18
Female head	7,482	6,844	85	8,463	81	7,230	6,488	8,106	*5.5	*-3.3	7,242	6,413	8,059	-12	75	47
Number of Earners[1]																
No earners	6,788	5,232	52	6,559	73	6,170	4,925	6,109	*6.2	*-2.7	6,181	4,835	5,912	(X)	(X)	(X)
1 earner	19,466	11,568	72	13,592	85	18,930	11,000	12,690	*5.2	*-3.6	19,584	10,955	12,340	(X)	(X)	(X)
2 earners	21,377	16,058	65	17,434	73	21,637	14,866	16,328	*8.0	-1.0	21,968	14,746	16,150	(X)	(X)	(X)
3 earners	5,348	20,531	169	22,146	162	5,284	19,173	20,660	*7.1	-1.9	5,278	19,348	20,701	(X)	(X)	(X)
4 earners or more	2,455	23,785	253	25,830	266	2,717	22,886	24,505	*3.9	*-4.8	2,701	22,784	24,311	(X)	(X)	(X)
Size of Family																
2 persons	21,280	11,040	78	13,130	72	20,837	10,406	12,411	*6.1	*-2.8	20,823	10,238	12,203	14	168	208
3 persons	12,252	14,025	100	15,580	99	12,103	13,030	14,661	*7.6	-1.4	12,137	12,938	14,552	-34	92	109
4 persons	11,276	15,848	93	17,513	118	11,003	14,969	16,598	*5.9	*-3.0	11,002	14,747	16,251	1	222	347
5 persons	6,171	16,466	137	18,496	165	6,320	15,552	17,168	*5.9	*-3.0	6,313	15,412	17,008	7	140	160
6 persons	2,969	16,134	227	18,121	275	2,992	15,290	17,151	*5.5	-3.3	3,005	15,002	16,767	-13	288	384
7 persons or more	2,296	14,529	269	16,853	260	2,443	14,600	16,739	-0.5	*-8.8	2,432	14,960	16,713	11	-360	26
Employment Status and Occupation of Head[2]																
Head in labor force	43,456	15,560	49	17,372	58	43,215	14,643	16,433	*6.3	*-2.6	43,216	14,483	16,164	-1	160	269
Head employed	41,078	15,886	49	17,750	60	40,425	14,966	16,786	*6.1	*-2.7	40,419	14,776	16,497	6	190	289
White-collar workers	18,900	18,782	89	21,400	108	18,515	17,858	20,338	*5.2	*-3.6	18,518	18,019	19,742	-3	-161	596
Professional, technical, and kindred workers	6,589	20,498	178	23,237	177	6,313	19,229	21,930	*6.6	*-2.3	6,312	19,441	21,069	1	-212	861
Salaried	5,904	20,004	158	22,129	161	5,643	18,800	20,818	*6.4	*-2.5	5,632	19,202	20,287	11	-402	531
Self-employed	685	[3]27,766	686	32,786	909	670	[3]26,362	31,289	5.3	-3.5	681	23,553	27,541	-11	2,809	3,748
Managers and administrators, except farm	6,455	20,612	176	23,443	213	6,372	19,724	22,541	*4.5	*-4.2	6,364	19,707	21,876	8	17	665
Salaried	5,222	21,626	180	24,655	235	5,152	20,491	23,481	*5.5	*-3.3	5,146	20,506	22,878	6	-15	603
Self-employed	1,233	15,378	306	18,312	479	1,220	15,979	18,571	-3.8	*-11.8	1,218	15,278	17,641	2	701	930
Sales workers	2,463	17,720	200	20,196	268	2,469	16,848	18,769	*5.2	-3.6	2,481	16,593	18,340	-12	255	429
Clerical and kindred wkrs	3,393	13,959	154	14,815	140	3,361	13,406	14,322	*4.1	*-4.6	3,361	13,325	14,242	-	81	80
Blue-collar workers	17,178	14,560	66	15,251	58	16,858	13,593	14,393	*7.1	*-1.9	16,858	13,674	14,366	-	-81	27
Craft and kindred workers	8,458	15,783	83	16,459	84	8,347	14,890	15,532	*6.0	*-2.9	8,336	14,838	15,497	11	52	35
Operatives, incl. transport	6,825	13,666	105	14,418	88	6,687	12,772	13,653	*7.0	-2.0	6,691	12,894	13,628	-4	-122	25
Operatives, exc. transport	4,530	13,346	130	14,056	106	4,400	12,551	13,278	*6.3	*-2.6	(NA)	(NA)	(NA)	(X)	(X)	(X)
Transport equip. operatives	2,295	14,300	190	15,135	156	2,287	13,315	14,375	*7.4	-1.6	(NA)	(NA)	(NA)	(X)	(X)	(X)
Laborers, except farm	1,895	12,325	132	12,857	158	1,823	10,952	11,897	*12.5	3.1	1,831	10,979	11,912	-8	-27	-15
Service workers	3,405	11,392	194	12,676	134	3,396	10,848	11,896	*5.0	-3.8	3,390	10,727	11,806	6	121	90
Private household workers	140	4,664	425	6,181	466	167	4,307	5,722	8.3	-0.8	166	4,166	5,263	1	141	459
Service workers, exc. private household	3,265	11,739	198	12,955	136	3,229	11,196	12,215	*4.8	-3.9	3,224	11,098	12,143	5	98	72
Farm workers	1,595	9,116	224	12,270	320	1,656	8,802	11,450	3.6	-5.1	1,652	8,571	11,507	4	231	-57
Farmers and farm managers	1,169	9,802	299	13,402	415	1,255	9,653	12,170	1.5	-7.0	1,254	9,498	12,278	1	155	-108
Farm laborers and supervisors	426	7,855	307	9,164	322	401	7,354	9,193	6.8	-2.1	398	7,164	9,077	3	190	116
Head unemployed	2,378	9,676	186	10,830	150	2,790	10,220	11,324	*-5.3	*-13.3	2,797	10,202	11,358	-7	18	-34
Head not in labor force	12,788	7,168	63	9,344	53	12,483	6,749	8,751	*6.2	*-2.7	12,497	6,736	8,750	-14	13	1

- Represents zero. NA Not available. [r]Based on revised methodology X Not applicable.

[1]For the years 1975 and 1974[r], excludes families with members who are in the Armed Forces. Therefore the difference in the number, median income, and mean income between 1974[r] and 1974 are not directly comparable.

[2]Employment status and occupation of head as of March of the following year.

[3]Based on Pareto estimate.

Table 1. SELECTED CHARACTERISTICS OF ALL FAMILIES—NUMBER OF FAMILIES, MEDIAN INCOME, MEAN INCOME, AND STANDARD ERRORS, BY RACE OF HEAD AND SPANISH ORIGIN OF HEAD: 1975, 1974 (Revised), AND 1974—Con.

(Families as of March of the following year. An asterisk (*) preceding percent change indicates statistically significant change at the 95 percent confidence level)

Selected characteristics	1975					1974[r]			Percent change (median income)		1974			Difference 1974[r]-1974		
	Number (thousands)	Median income: Value	Median income: Standard error	Mean income: Value	Mean income: Standard error	Number (thousands)	Median income	Mean income	Current dollars	In 1975 dollars	Number (thousands)	Median income	Mean income	Number (thousands)	Median income	Mean income
ALL RACES--Continued																
Educational Attainment of Head																
Total, 25 years and over	52,202	$14,258	$51	$16,027	$53	51,456	$13,404	$15,186	*6.4	*-2.5	51,488	$13,326	$14,962	-32	$78	$224
Elementary: Total	10,758	8,472	86	10,209	71	11,209	8,143	9,729	*4.0	*-4.7	11,219	8,241	9,867	-10	-98	-138
Less than 8 years	5,784	7,427	107	9,221	91	5,970	7,134	8,748	4.1	*-4.6	5,977	7,073	8,840	-7	61	-92
8 years	4,975	9,927	143	11,359	108	5,240	9,495	10,847	*4.5	*-4.2	5,242	9,728	11,037	-2	-233	-190
High school: Total	25,514	13,750	67	14,891	63	25,146	13,182	14,320	*4.3	*-4.4	25,154	13,190	14,260	-8	-8	60
1 to 3 years	7,964	11,451	116	12,782	97	7,926	11,246	12,383	1.8	*-6.7	7,940	11,384	12,517	-14	-138	-134
4 years	17,550	14,729	72	15,849	79	17,220	14,013	15,212	*5.1	*-3.7	17,214	13,941	15,063	6	72	149
College: Total	15,930	19,262	98	21,774	117	15,101	18,257	20,678	*5.5	*-3.3	15,114	18,265	19,913	-13	-8	765
1 to 3 years	7,090	16,579	116	18,083	139	6,681	15,956	17,438	*3.9	*-4.8	6,700	15,892	17,187	-19	64	251
4 years or more	8,840	21,961	148	24,735	171	8,420	20,561	23,248	*6.8	*-2.1	8,415	20,124	22,084	5	437	1,164
WHITE																
All families	49,873	14,268	52	16,111	54	49,440	13,408	15,252	*6.4	*-2.5	49,451	13,356	15,047	-11	52	205
Type of Residence																
Nonfarm	47,768	14,391	53	16,225	55	47,160	13,517	15,344	*6.5	*-2.5	47,166	13,466	15,134	-6	51	210
Farm	2,105	11,237	420	13,531	347	2,279	10,906	13,355	3.0	-5.6	2,284	10,750	13,246	-5	156	109
Inside metropolitan areas	32,848	15,548	61	17,408	69	32,829	14,566	16,386	*6.7	*-2.2	32,850	14,377	16,136	-21	189	250
1,000,000 or more	18,251	16,356	97	18,310	97	18,215	15,412	17,236	*6.1	*-2.8	18,241	15,261	16,960	-26	151	276
Inside central cities	5,861	14,286	149	16,196	163	6,082	13,394	15,289	*6.7	-2.3	6,122	13,076	14,955	-40	318	334
Outside central cities	12,390	17,436	105	19,309	119	12,133	16,383	18,211	*6.4	*-2.5	12,120	16,565	17,973	13	-182	238
Under 1,000,000	14,597	14,644	88	16,282	97	14,613	13,633	15,327	*7.4	-1.6	14,608	13,486	15,107	5	147	220
Inside central cities	6,307	14,063	151	15,887	151	6,281	13,047	15,082	*7.8	-1.2	6,266	12,970	14,857	15	77	225
Outside central cities	8,290	15,009	114	16,581	126	8,333	14,027	15,511	*7.0	-2.0	8,342	13,830	15,294	-9	197	217
Outside metropolitan areas	17,025	12,020	74	13,608	82	16,611	11,446	13,011	*5.0	*-3.8	16,601	11,429	12,893	10	17	118
Region																
Northeast	11,505	14,853	155	16,797	157	11,421	14,324	16,037	*3.7	*-5.0	11,447	14,164	15,831	-26	160	206
North Central	13,816	14,849	152	16,465	166	13,842	14,014	15,732	*6.0	*-2.9	13,827	14,017	15,561	15	-3	171
South	15,435	13,078	155	15,085	168	15,154	12,165	14,201	*7.5	-1.5	15,147	12,050	13,985	7	115	216
West	9,117	14,499	255	16,445	270	9,023	13,375	15,285	*8.4	-0.7	9,029	13,339	15,048	-6	36	237
Type of Family																
Male head	44,493	15,094	51	16,949	58	44,232	14,134	15,997	*6.8	*-2.2	44,238	14,055	15,772	-6	79	225
Married, wife present	43,311	15,125	52	16,992	59	43,049	14,183	16,050	*6.6	*-2.3	42,969	14,099	15,823	80	84	227
Wife in paid labor force	18,609	17,550	82	18,963	77	18,283	16,488	17,827	*6.4	*-2.5	18,176	16,825	17,813	107	-337	14
Wife not in paid labor force	24,702	13,042	71	15,508	85	24,766	12,480	14,739	*4.5	*-4.2	24,793	12,381	14,365	-27	99	374
Other marital status	1,182	13,793	346	15,350	320	1,182	12,431	14,055	*11.0	1.7	1,270	12,438	14,047	-88	-7	8
Female head	5,380	7,651	92	9,183	101	5,208	7,405	8,923	3.3	*-5.3	5,212	7,363	8,893	-4	42	30
Number of Earners[1]																
No earners	5,753	5,645	53	7,038	83	5,205	5,329	6,568	*5.9	*-2.9	5,217	5,197	6,343	(X)	(X)	(X)
1 earner	17,245	12,198	66	14,230	93	16,823	11,579	13,268	*5.3	*-3.5	17,369	11,482	12,908	(X)	(X)	(X)
2 earners	19,146	16,360	67	17,803	79	19,376	15,166	16,688	*7.9	-1.2	19,702	15,055	16,501	(X)	(X)	(X)
3 earners	4,835	21,005	172	22,672	173	4,755	19,655	21,216	*6.9	-2.1	4,740	19,912	21,319	(X)	(X)	(X)
4 earners or more	2,183	24,203	260	26,391	286	2,435	23,467	25,165	*3.1	*-5.5	2,422	23,401	25,040	(X)	(X)	(X)
BLACK																
All families	5,586	8,779	126	10,401	97	5,491	8,006	9,647	*9.7	0.5	5,498	7,808	9,515	-7	198	132
Type of Residence																
Nonfarm	5,497	8,871	127	10,453	97	5,390	8,070	9,683	*9.9	0.7	5,396	7,862	9,549	-6	208	134
Farm	89	4,942	764	7,164	1,094	101	5,223	7,720	-5.4	-13.3	102	5,170	7,681	-1	53	39
Inside metropolitan areas	4,281	9,494	145	11,084	115	4,235	8,759	10,262	*8.4	-0.7	4,240	8,489	10,115	-5	270	147
1,000,000 or more	2,770	10,105	193	11,710	149	2,725	9,619	11,051	5.1	-3.7	2,733	9,463	10,960	-8	156	91
Inside central cities	2,115	9,874	195	11,399	166	2,132	9,255	10,630	*6.7	-2.2	2,134	9,062	10,523	-2	193	107
Outside central cities	655	11,276	310	12,713	330	593	10,797	12,563	4.4	-4.3	600	10,975	12,514	-7	-178	49
Under 1,000,000	1,511	8,323	242	9,938	176	1,510	7,376	8,837	*12.8	3.4	1,507	7,120	8,582	3	256	255
Inside central cities	1,157	7,884	286	9,634	201	1,140	7,025	8,422	*12.2	2.8	1,137	6,775	8,214	3	250	208
Outside central cities	354	9,757	628	10,933	357	369	8,643	10,118	12.9	3.4	370	8,418	9,714	-1	225	404
Outside metropolitan areas	1,305	6,684	222	8,160	152	1,256	6,132	7,575	9.0	-0.1	1,258	6,136	7,491	-2	-4	84
Region																
Northeast	1,039	9,992	457	11,550	365	1,023	9,191	10,965	8.7	-0.4	1,021	8,788	10,678	2	403	287
North Central	1,138	10,505	453	11,990	440	1,134	10,170	11,258	3.3	-5.4	1,135	9,846	11,144	-1	324	114
South	2,896	7,696	305	9,181	216	2,823	6,834	8,312	*12.6	3.2	2,829	6,730	8,228	-6	104	84
West	513	9,731	866	11,442	688	511	9,035	10,809	7.7	-1.3	513	8,585	10,687	-2	450	122
Type of Family																
Male head	3,581	11,389	145	12,617	123	3,557	10,527	11,717	*8.2	-0.9	3,558	10,365	11,564	-1	162	153
Married, wife present	3,352	11,526	150	12,769	129	3,357	10,697	11,841	*7.7	-1.3	3,346	10,530	11,700	11	167	141
Wife in paid labor force	1,903	14,355	179	15,275	173	1,809	13,179	14,228	*8.9	-0.2	1,791	12,982	14,119	18	197	109
Wife not in paid labor force	1,449	8,543	190	9,479	158	1,548	7,957	9,052	*7.4	-1.6	1,555	7,773	8,913	-7	184	139
Other marital status	230	8,955	533	10,396	405	200	7,943	9,645	12.7	3.3	212	7,942	9,413	-12	1	232
Female head	2,004	4,898	82	6,442	112	1,934	4,542	5,839	*7.8	-1.2	1,940	4,465	5,756	-6	77	83

[r] Based on revised methodology X Not applicable.

[1] For the years 1975 and 1974[r], excludes families with members who are in the Armed Forces. Therefore the difference in the number, median income, and mean income between 1974[r] and 1974 are not directly comparable.

Table 1. SELECTED CHARACTERISTICS OF ALL FAMILIES—NUMBER OF FAMILIES, MEDIAN INCOME, MEAN INCOME, AND STANDARD ERRORS, BY RACE OF HEAD AND SPANISH ORIGIN OF HEAD: 1975, 1974 (Revised), AND 1974—Con.

(Families as of March of the following year. An asterisk (*) preceding percent change indicates statistically significant change at the 95 percent confidence level)

Selected characteristics	1975					1974r			Percent change (median income)		1974			Difference (1974r-1974)		
	Number (thousands)	Median income		Mean income		Number (thousands)	Median income	Mean income	Current dollars	In 1975 dollars	Number (thousands)	Median income	Mean income	Number (thousands)	Median income	Mean income
		Value	Standard error	Value	Standard error											
BLACK--Continued																
Number of Earners[1]																
No earners	978	$3,511	$66	$3,839	$68	918	$3,364	$3,602	4.4	-4.4	914	$3,324	$3,579	(X)	(X)	(X)
1 earner	1,958	7,086	137	7,836	107	1,844	6,501	7,305	*9.0	-0.1	1,935	6,360	7,191	(X)	(X)	(X)
2 earners	1,918	12,914	189	13,659	150	1,970	11,929	12,534	*8.3	-0.8	1,968	11,820	12,551	(X)	(X)	(X)
3 earners	434	15,808	401	16,912	394	444	12,880	14,487	*22.7	*12.5	456	12,862	14,194	(X)	(X)	(X)
4 earners or more	225	18,147	725	20,095	620	227	16,722	17,781	8.5	-0.6	226	16,648	17,568	(X)	(X)	(X)
SPANISH ORIGIN OF HEAD																
All families	2,499	9,551	229	11,096	206	2,475	9,540	10,853	0.1	*-8.3	2,477	9,559	10,908	-2	$-19	$-55
Type of Residence																
Nonfarm	2,470	9,590	231	11,129	208	2,451	9,550	10,848	0.4	*-8.0	2,453	9,555	10,907	-2	-5	-59
Farm	30	(B)	(B)	(B)	(B)	25	(B)	(B)	(B)	(B)	25	(B)	(B)	-	(B)	(B)
Inside metropolitan areas	2,096	9,857	239	11,405	231	2,057	9,882	11,204	-0.3	*-8.6	2,059	9,857	11,220	-2	25	-16
1,000,000 or more	1,432	9,977	282	11,558	291	1,385	9,981	11,456	(Z)	*-8.4	1,387	9,977	11,441	-2	4	15
Inside central cities	857	8,861	373	10,637	370	832	8,993	10,208	-1.5	-9.7	833	8,968	10,216	-1	25	-8
Outside central cities	575	11,185	570	12,931	462	553	11,615	13,333	-3.7	*-11.8	554	11,726	13,282	-1	-111	51
Under 1,000,000	665	9,642	387	11,075	374	673	9,641	10,686	(Z)	-8.4	672	9,596	10,766	1	45	-80
Inside central cities	435	9,461	443	10,731	455	423	9,319	10,517	1.5	-7.0	423	9,395	10,650	-	-76	-133
Outside central cities	230	10,085	942	11,726	654	249	10,160	10,973	-0.7	-9.1	249	9,935	10,962	-	225	11
Outside metropolitan areas	403	8,209	405	9,490	415	418	7,961	9,122	3.1	-5.5	418	7,957	9,373	-	4	-251
Region																
Northeast	551	8,170	469	9,809	427	520	8,425	10,168	-3.0	-11.1	523	8,530	10,412	-3	-105	-244
North Central	187	11,707	1,359	12,934	1,270	190	12,059	13,153	-2.9	-11.0	190	12,299	13,570	-	-240	-417
South	735	8,757	671	10,881	664	765	9,004	10,389	-2.7	-10.9	764	8,980	10,272	1	24	117
West	1,026	10,292	493	11,606	511	1,000	10,213	11,125	0.8	-7.7	1,001	10,234	11,147	-1	-21	-22
Type of Family																
Male head	1,978	10,925	226	12,433	240	2,013	10,718	11,952	1.9	*-6.6	2,013	10,832	12,039	-	-114	-87
Married, wife present	1,896	10,950	239	12,397	239	1,926	10,803	12,038	1.4	*-7.1	1,921	10,896	12,120	5	-93	-82
Wife in paid labor force	790	13,821	344	14,781	336	783	13,083	14,197	5.6	-3.2	770	13,311	14,481	13	-228	-284
Wife not in paid labor force	1,107	9,191	283	10,696	320	1,143	9,130	10,560	0.7	-7.8	1,152	9,184	10,542	-9	-54	18
Other marital status	82	10,415	1,231	13,262	1,681	87	9,245	10,055	12.7	3.2	91	9,721	10,342	-4	-476	-287
Female head	522	4,785	196	6,025	241	462	4,854	6,062	-1.4	-9.7	465	4,800	6,010	-3	54	52
Number of Earners[1]																
No earners	349	3,544	142	3,864	168	305	3,719	4,122	-4.7	*-12.7	304	3,692	4,116	(X)	(X)	(X)
1 earner	944	7,952	224	9,179	269	917	7,777	8,896	2.3	-6.3	937	7,754	8,811	(X)	(X)	(X)
2 earners	865	12,640	303	13,653	370	874	11,979	12,931	5.5	-3.3	897	11,995	12,984	(X)	(X)	(X)
3 earners	206	15,716	495	16,501	662	228	14,958	16,184	5.1	-3.7	228	15,752	16,434	(X)	(X)	(X)
4 earners or more	100	19,877	1,326	20,644	1,103	118	17,948	18,582	10.7	1.5	111	18,969	19,091	(X)	(X)	(X)

- Represents zero. B Base less than 75,000. r Based on revised methodology X Not applicable. Z Less than 0.05 percent.

[1]For the years 1975 and 1974r, excludes families with members who are in the Armed Forces. Therefore the difference in the number, median income, and mean income between 1974r and 1974 are not directly comparable.

Table 2. SELECTED CHARACTERISTICS FOR FAMILIES WITH HEADS WORKING YEAR ROUND FULL TIME—NUMBER OF FAMILIES, MEDIAN INCOME, MEAN INCOME, AND STANDARD ERRORS, BY RACE OF HEAD AND SPANISH ORIGIN OF HEAD: 1975, 1974 (Revised), AND 1974

(Families as of March of the following year. An asterisk (*) preceding percent change indicates statistically significant change at the 95 percent confidence level)

Selected characteristics	1975					1974r			Percent change (median income)		1974			Difference (1974r-1974)		
	Number (thousands)	Median income		Mean income		Number (thousands)	Median income	Mean income	Current dollars	In 1975 dollars	Number (thousands)	Median income	Mean income	Number (thousands)	Median income	Mean income
		Value	Standard error	Value	Standard error											
ALL RACES																
All families	32,876	$17,163	$60	$19,209	$68	33,446	$16,001	$17,968	*7.3	*-1.7	34,195	$16,072	$17,618	-749	$-71	$350
Type of Residence																
Nonfarm	31,364	17,330	60	19,415	70	31,779	16,130	18,138	*7.4	*-1.6	32,478	16,271	17,779	-699	-141	359
Farm	1,513	12,871	362	14,922	434	1,667	12,295	14,723	4.7	-4.1	1,717	12,006	14,575	-50	289	148
Inside metropolitan areas	22,663	18,316	72	20,416	83	23,189	16,956	19,040	*8.0	-1.0	23,702	17,235	18,654	-513	-279	386
1,000,000 or more	12,910	19,113	96	21,328	114	13,182	17,795	19,925	*7.4	*-1.6	13,459	18,197	19,545	-277	-402	380
Inside central cities	4,338	17,082	162	19,207	185	4,564	16,075	17,958	*6.3	*-2.6	4,677	15,980	17,567	-113	95	391
Outside central cities	8,572	20,115	138	22,401	142	8,618	18,843	20,966	*6.8	*-2.2	8,782	19,229	20,599	-164	-386	367
Under 1,000,000	9,752	17,314	103	19,209	120	10,007	15,936	17,874	*8.6	*-0.5	10,243	15,879	17,483	-236	57	391
Inside central cities	4,243	16,800	148	18,816	183	4,326	15,575	17,689	*7.9	-1.2	4,452	15,382	17,344	-126	193	345
Outside central cities	5,509	17,729	139	19,511	158	5,681	16,194	18,015	*9.5	0.3	5,791	16,244	17,590	-110	-50	425
Outside metropolitan areas	10,214	14,871	89	16,529	115	10,257	13,809	15,545	*7.7	-1.3	10,493	13,816	15,276	-236	-7	269
Region																
Northeast	7,469	17,866	173	19,994	194	7,713	16,839	18,805	*6.1	*-2.8	7,855	17,199	18,520	-142	-360	285
North Central	9,180	17,659	174	19,466	204	9,524	16,355	18,283	*8.0	-1.1	9,784	16,610	17,956	-260	-255	327
South	10,511	15,773	148	17,876	214	10,471	14,460	16,586	*9.1	-0.1	10,711	14,225	16,174	-240	235	412
West	5,716	18,138	298	20,218	353	5,738	16,962	18,839	*6.9	-2.0	5,846	17,247	18,484	-108	-285	355
Type of Family																
Male head	30,538	17,673	61	19,763	72	31,222	16,407	18,426	*7.7	*-1.3	31,836	16,647	18,079	-614	-240	347
Married, wife present	29,794	17,723	62	19,806	73	30,487	16,453	18,490	*7.7	*-1.3	31,008	16,701	18,139	-521	-248	351
Wife in paid labor force	14,468	19,288	81	20,821	85	14,539	17,924	19,477	*7.6	*-1.4	14,665	18,497	19,396	-126	-573	81
Wife not in paid labor force	15,326	16,122	83	18,847	116	15,948	15,039	17,591	*7.2	*-1.8	16,344	14,732	17,010	-396	307	581
Other marital status	745	15,977	263	18,039	417	735	14,553	15,745	*9.8	0.6	828	14,583	15,828	-93	-30	-83
Female head	2,338	10,684	151	11,973	134	2,224	10,143	11,541	*5.3	-3.5	2,359	9,868	11,399	-135	275	142
Number of Earners[1]																
No earners	1	(B)	(B)	(B)	(B)	2	(B)	(B)	(B)	(B)	3	(B)	(B)	(X)	(X)	(X)
1 earner	11,559	14,156	81	16,329	122	11,456	13,004	14,967	*8.9	-0.3	11,949	12,935	14,428	(X)	(X)	(X)
2 earners	15,241	17,606	74	19,150	87	15,633	16,408	17,979	*7.3	*-1.7	15,919	16,722	17,760	(X)	(X)	(X)
3 earners	4,091	21,937	179	23,666	189	4,099	20,435	22,046	*7.4	-1.6	4,118	20,328	22,078	(X)	(X)	(X)
4 earners or more	1,969	25,219	507	27,271	290	2,235	23,962	25,791	*5.2	-3.6	2,206	23,829	25,563	(X)	(X)	(X)
Size of Family																
2 persons	9,415	16,066	109	17,891	116	9,514	14,980	16,803	*7.2	-1.7	(NA)	(NA)	(NA)	(X)	(X)	(X)
3 persons	7,597	16,542	120	18,398	127	7,549	15,264	17,227	*8.4	-0.7	(NA)	(NA)	(NA)	(X)	(X)	(X)
4 persons	7,960	17,598	102	19,861	146	8,012	16,519	18,508	*6.5	*-2.4	(NA)	(NA)	(NA)	(X)	(X)	(X)
5 persons	4,456	18,508	170	20,921	198	4,691	17,326	19,224	*6.8	-2.1	(NA)	(NA)	(NA)	(X)	(X)	(X)
6 persons	2,013	18,793	216	21,163	354	2,071	17,397	19,743	*8.0	-1.0	(NA)	(NA)	(NA)	(X)	(X)	(X)
7 persons or more	1,435	18,356	481	20,471	336	1,609	17,623	19,691	4.2	-4.6	(NA)	(NA)	(NA)	(X)	(X)	(X)
Employment Status and Occupation of Head[2]																
Head in labor force	32,552	17,185	61	19,219	68	33,125	16,027	18,000	*7.2	*-1.8	33,538	16,146	17,681	-413	-119	319
Head employed	32,146	17,239	61	19,282	69	32,332	16,092	18,078	*7.1	*-1.8	32,624	16,259	17,766	-292	-167	312
White-collar workers	16,072	19,805	90	22,571	116	15,842	18,755	21,380	*5.6	*-3.2	15,881	19,082	20,843	-39	-327	537
Professional, technical, and kindred workers	5,632	21,450	179	24,122	184	5,409	20,080	22,919	*6.8	-2.1	5,442	20,361	22,162	-33	-281	757
Salaried	5,113	20,924	178	23,006	165	4,898	19,590	21,689	*6.8	-2.1	4,932	20,035	21,288	-34	-445	401
Self-employed	519	[3]29,352	828	35,120	1,029	511	[3]28,568	34,720	2.7	-5.9	511	[3]26,290	30,600	-	2,278	4,120
Managers and administrators, except farm	5,810	21,395	176	24,294	227	5,753	20,307	23,230	*5.4	*-3.5	5,737	20,396	22,657	16	-89	573
Salaried	4,799	22,204	181	25,295	246	4,725	21,008	24,041	*5.7	*-3.2	4,718	21,057	23,498	7	-49	543
Self-employed	1,012	16,355	415	19,543	552	1,028	16,723	19,502	-2.2	*-10.4	1,019	16,521	18,764	9	202	738
Sales workers	1,985	18,945	257	21,501	296	2,032	17,685	19,623	*7.1	-1.8	2,030	17,761	19,311	2	-76	312
Clerical and kindred workers	2,645	15,187	155	16,286	151	2,647	14,495	15,566	*4.8	*-4.0	2,672	14,407	15,424	-25	88	142
Blue-collar workers	12,502	15,679	70	16,473	66	12,830	14,546	15,388	*7.8	-1.2	13,092	14,507	15,310	-262	39	78
Craft and kindred workers	6,484	16,672	101	17,479	94	6,621	15,621	16,320	*6.7	*-2.2	6,718	15,798	16,267	-97	-177	53
Operatives, incl. transport	4,810	14,814	99	15,675	101	4,993	13,730	14,692	*7.9	-1.1	5,118	13,775	14,574	-125	-45	118
Operatives, exc. transport	3,141	14,526	117	15,321	123	3,264	13,394	14,331	*8.5	-0.6	(NA)	(NA)	(NA)	(X)	(X)	(X)
Transport equipment operatives	1,669	15,574	243	16,340	176	1,729	14,470	15,374	*7.6	-1.4	(NA)	(NA)	(NA)	(X)	(X)	(X)
Laborers, exc. farm	1,208	13,420	231	14,249	196	1,217	12,006	13,167	*11.8	2.4	1,256	11,952	13,192	-39	54	-25
Service workers	2,348	13,664	203	14,738	161	2,370	12,803	13,777	*6.7	-2.2	2,361	12,725	13,698	9	78	79
Private household workers	25	(B)	(B)	(B)	(B)	25	(B)	(B)	(B)	(B)	41	(B)	(B)	(B)	(B)	(B)
Service workers, exc. pvt. household	2,323	13,736	202	14,818	161	2,346	12,877	13,849	*6.7	-2.3	2,320	12,842	13,825	26	35	24
Farm workers	1,225	10,191	254	13,507	396	1,290	9,552	12,186	6.7	-2.2	1,290	9,339	12,263	-	213	-77
Farmers and farm managers	944	10,708	357	14,454	494	1,024	10,280	12,722	4.2	-4.6	1,011	10,234	12,875	13	46	-153
Farm laborers and supervisors	281	8,984	378	10,328	418	266	7,782	10,123	*15.4	5.8	279	7,717	10,044	-13	65	79
Head unemployed	406	12,991	365	14,199	362	793	13,501	14,813	-3.8	*-11.8	914	13,165	14,655	-121	336	158
Head not in labor force	324	14,944	486	18,211	964	321	13,141	14,655	*13.7	4.2	657	12,458	14,356	-336	683	299

- Represents zero. B Base less than 75,000. NA Not available. r Based on revised methodology X Not applicable.

[1] For the years 1975 and 1974r, excludes families with members who are in the Armed Forces. Therefore the difference in the number, median income, and mean income between 1974r and 1974 are not directly comparable.

[2] Employment status and occupation of head as of March of the following year.

[3] Based on Pareto estimate.

Table 2. SELECTED CHARACTERISTICS FOR FAMILIES WITH HEADS WORKING YEAR ROUND FULL TIME—NUMBER OF FAMILIES, MEDIAN INCOME, MEAN INCOME, AND STANDARD ERRORS, BY RACE OF HEAD AND SPANISH ORIGIN OF HEAD: 1975, 1974 (Revised), AND 1974—Continued

(Families as of March of the following year. An asterisk (*) preceding percent change indicates statistically significant change at the 95 percent confidence level)

Selected characteristics	1975					1974^r			Percent change (median income)		1974			Difference (1974^r-1974)		
	Number (thousands)	Median income: Value	Median income: Standard error	Mean income: Value	Mean income: Standard error	Number (thousands)	Median income	Mean income	Current dollars	In 1975 dollars	Number (thousands)	Median income	Mean income	Number (thousands)	Median income	Mean income
ALL RACES--Continued																
Educational Attainment of Head																
Total, 25 years and over	31,043	$17,573	$61	$19,613	$71	31,420	$16,409	$18,400	*7.1	*-1.9	32,078	$16,628	$18,056	-658	$-219	$344
Elementary: Total	3,696	13,194	150	14,091	129	4,052	12,193	13,292	*8.2	-0.9	4,234	12,198	13,382	-182	-5	-90
Less than 8 years	1,777	12,132	208	13,212	180	1,890	11,174	12,300	*8.6	-0.5	1,984	11,182	12,440	-94	-8	-140
8 years	1,918	14,148	146	14,905	182	2,163	13,127	14,159	*7.8	-1.2	2,250	13,187	14,213	-87	-60	-54
High school: Total	15,529	16,333	73	17,584	83	16,082	15,341	16,635	*6.5	*-2.4	16,468	15,362	16,562	-386	-21	73
1 to 3 years	3,960	14,892	144	16,010	135	4,270	14,158	15,301	*5.2	*-3.6	4,433	14,320	15,424	-163	-162	-123
4 years	11,570	16,790	80	18,123	101	11,812	15,760	17,117	*6.5	*-2.4	12,035	15,878	16,981	-223	-118	136
College: Total	11,818	21,269	121	24,005	135	11,286	20,044	22,750	*6.1	*-2.8	11,376	20,097	21,958	-90	-53	792
1 to 3 years	4,932	18,638	131	20,461	171	4,791	17,557	19,454	*6.2	*-2.7	4,842	18,069	19,162	-51	-512	292
4 years or more	6,886	23,512	156	26,544	190	6,495	22,382	25,181	*5.0	*-3.7	6,534	21,698	24,030	-39	684	1,151
WHITE																
All families	29,941	17,486	63	19,582	73	30,512	16,262	18,302	*7.5	*-1.5	31,174	16,467	17,959	-662	-205	343
Type of Residence																
Nonfarm	28,469	17,669	63	19,815	75	28,894	16,401	18,499	*7.7	*-1.3	29,511	16,681	18,146	-617	-280	353
Farm	1,472	13,014	363	15,070	441	1,618	12,429	14,774	4.7	-4.1	1,663	12,195	14,637	-45	234	137
Inside metropolitan areas	20,281	18,735	74	20,921	90	20,778	17,313	19,489	*8.2	-0.8	21,218	17,686	19,100	-440	-373	389
1,000,000 or more	11,336	19,672	100	21,969	125	11,570	18,304	20,537	*7.5	*-1.5	11,819	18,754	20,145	-249	-450	392
Inside central cities	3,226	17,992	194	20,211	230	3,405	16,913	19,059	*6.4	-2.5	3,508	17,136	18,568	-103	-223	491
Outside central cities	8,110	20,385	140	22,668	147	8,165	18,987	21,154	*7.4	-1.6	8,311	19,383	20,810	-146	-396	344
Under 1,000,000	8,945	17,597	105	19,594	127	9,208	16,193	18,171	*8.7	-0.4	9,399	16,240	17,786	-191	-47	385
Inside central cities	3,684	17,278	152	19,466	202	3,788	16,057	18,186	*7.6	-1.4	3,879	16,032	17,869	-91	25	317
Outside central cities	5,260	17,850	144	19,684	163	5,419	16,286	18,161	*9.6	0.4	5,521	16,384	17,729	-102	-98	432
Outside metropolitan areas	9,660	15,085	90	16,768	119	9,735	13,993	15,769	*7.8	-1.2	9,956	14,044	15,527	-221	-51	242
Region																
Northeast	6,908	18,087	185	20,254	205	7,145	17,034	19,096	*6.2	-2.7	7,287	17,470	18,807	-142	-436	289
North Central	8,660	17,754	181	19,580	212	8,969	16,467	18,450	*7.8	-1.2	9,211	16,794	18,121	-242	-327	329
South	9,177	16,323	165	18,556	237	9,172	15,028	17,217	*8.6	-0.5	9,364	14,744	16,800	-192	284	417
West	5,195	18,331	313	20,503	379	5,227	16,988	18,865	*7.9	-1.1	5,312	17,340	18,559	-85	-352	306
Type of Family																
Male head	28,163	17,905	64	20,035	76	28,806	16,587	18,675	*7.9	*-1.1	29,387	16,916	18,326	-581	-329	349
Married, wife present	27,532	17,945	65	20,065	77	28,170	16,627	18,731	*7.9	*-1.1	28,668	16,958	18,375	-498	-331	356
Wife in paid labor force	13,078	19,500	84	21,092	91	13,157	18,097	19,724	*7.8	-1.3	13,286	18,753	19,674	-129	-656	50
Wife not in paid labor force	14,454	16,372	86	19,135	121	15,013	15,248	17,860	*7.4	*-1.6	15,382	14,919	17,254	-369	329	606
Other marital status	630	16,332	330	18,714	475	636	14,885	16,204	*9.7	0.5	719	15,082	16,351	-83	-197	-147
Female head	1,778	11,210	177	12,406	156	1,706	10,629	12,000	*5.5	-3.4	1,787	10,465	11,928	-81	164	72
Numbers of Earners[1]																
No earners	1	(B)	(B)	(B)	(B)	2	(B)	(B)	(B)	(B)	3	(B)	(B)	(X)	(X)	(X)
1 earner	10,578	14,531	83	16,790	131	10,489	13,364	15,369	*8.7	-0.4	10,924	13,270	14,818	(X)	(X)	(X)
2 earners	13,804	17,842	79	19,452	94	14,211	16,589	18,239	*7.6	*-1.5	14,473	16,986	18,015	(X)	(X)	(X)
3 earners	3,764	22,207	184	24,028	200	3,741	20,782	22,439	*6.9	-2.1	3,747	20,740	22,563	(X)	(X)	(X)
4 earners or more	1,781	25,907	638	27,753	308	2,049	24,383	26,207	*6.3	-2.6	2,026	24,234	25,999	(X)	(X)	(X)
BLACK																
All families	2,496	13,445	188	14,597	143	2,480	12,425	13,432	*8.2	-0.9	2,558	12,137	13,197	-78	288	235
Type of Residence																
Nonfarm	2,459	13,532	186	14,670	144	2,437	12,495	13,466	*8.3	-0.8	2,513	12,228	13,230	-76	267	236
Farm	37	(B)	(B)	(B)	(B)	43	(B)	(B)	(B)	(B)	45	(B)	(B)	-2	(B)	(B)
Inside metropolitan areas	1,983	14,153	182	15,295	165	2,001	12,962	14,052	*9.2	(Z)	2,060	12,882	13,888	-59	80	164
1,000,000 or more	1,317	14,816	219	16,080	206	1,355	13,472	14,754	*10.0	0.8	1,381	13,585	14,747	-26	-113	7
Inside central cities	967	14,711	233	15,998	234	1,032	13,099	14,320	*12.3	2.9	1,036	13,197	14,316	-4	-98	4
Outside central cities	350	15,206	523	16,305	427	323	16,011	16,136	-5.0	*-13.0	344	15,419	16,044	-21	592	92
Under 1,000,000	666	12,381	291	13,742	267	645	11,830	12,579	4.7	-4.1	679	11,208	12,143	-34	622	436
Inside central cities	490	12,374	314	13,751	314	460	11,824	12,379	4.7	-4.1	488	11,212	11,904	-28	612	475
Outside central cities	175	12,406	719	13,719	505	186	11,845	13,073	4.7	-4.0	192	11,193	12,753	-6	652	320
Outside metropolitan areas	513	11,354	277	11,900	248	480	9,463	10,846	*20.0	*9.9	498	9,054	10,335	-18	409	511
Region																
Northeast	490	14,998	517	16,226	507	496	13,397	14,784	12.0	2.6	487	13,506	14,580	9	-109	204
North Central	481	15,896	900	17,117	647	524	13,827	15,388	15.0	5.3	544	13,987	15,226	-20	-160	162
South	1,282	11,991	353	12,862	326	1,238	10,564	11,724	*13.5	4.0	1,291	10,260	11,522	-53	304	202
West	243	14,836	1,278	15,479	955	222	15,885	15,321	-6.6	-14.4	237	14,639	14,827	-15	1,246	494

B Base less than 75,000. r Based on revised methodology X Not applicable. Z Less than 0.05 percent.

[1] For the years 1975 and 1974^r, excludes families with members who are in the Armed Forces. Therefore the difference in the number, median income, and mean income between 1974^r and 1974 are not directly comparable.

Table 2. SELECTED CHARACTERISTICS FOR FAMILIES WITH HEADS WORKING YEAR ROUND FULL TIME—NUMBER OF FAMILIES, MEDIAN INCOME, MEAN INCOME, AND STANDARD ERRORS, BY RACE OF HEAD AND SPANISH ORIGIN OF HEAD: 1975, 1974 (Revised), AND 1974—Continued

(Families as of March of the following year. An asterisk (*) preceding percent change indicates statistically significant change at the 95 percent confidence level)

Selected characteristics	1975					1974r			Percent change (median income)		1974			Difference (1974r-1974)		
	Number (thousands)	Median income: Value	Median income: Standard error	Mean income: Value	Mean income: Standard error	Number (thousands)	Median income	Mean income	Current dollars	In 1975 dollars	Number (thousands)	Median income	Mean income	Number (thousands)	Median income	Mean income
BLACK--Continued																
Type of Family																
Male head	1,963	$14,635	$173	$15,733	$162	1,992	$13,380	$14,366	*9.4	0.2	2,020	$13,236	$14,214	-28	$144	$152
Married, wife present	1,862	14,738	179	15,829	167	1,897	13,426	14,442	*9.8	0.6	1,917	13,311	14,318	-20	115	124
Wife in paid labor force	1,191	16,771	328	17,549	210	1,172	15,205	16,115	*10.3	1.1	1,175	14,877	16,008	-3	328	107
Wife not in paid labor force	672	11,933	212	12,780	238	724	11,113	11,736	7.4	-1.6	742	11,257	11,644	-18	-144	92
Other marital status	100	13,072	658	13,943	614	95	11,897	12,851	9.9	0.7	103	11,582	12,273	-8	315	578
Female head	533	9,306	167	10,417	236	489	8,607	9,625	*8.1	-0.9	538	8,123	9,377	-49	484	248
Number of Earners[1]																
No earners	-	(B)	(B)	(B)	(B)	-	(B)	(B)	(B)	(B)	-	(B)	(B)	(X)	(X)	(X)
1 earner	828	9,760	146	10,379	162	808	9,031	9,532	*8.1	-1.0	858	8,708	9,260	(X)	(X)	(X)
2 earners	1,230	14,902	217	15,511	184	1,226	13,753	14,433	*8.4	-0.7	1,247	13,777	14,417	(X)	(X)	(X)
3 earners	282	18,110	601	19,398	477	287	15,326	16,740	*18.2	8.3	298	14,563	15,988	(X)	(X)	(X)
4 earners or more	152	18,995	1,083	20,859	718	159	19,146	19,567	-0.8	-9.1	155	18,838	19,779	(X)	(X)	(X)
SPANISH ORIGIN OF HEAD																
All families	1,327	12,944	280	14,249	305	1,345	12,212	13,628	6.0	-2.9	1,401	12,184	13,544	-56	28	84
Type of Residence																
Nonfarm	1,304	13,024	279	14,333	309	1,329	12,230	13,642	*6.5	-2.4	1,385	12,196	13,560	-56	34	82
Farm	22	(B)	(B)	(B)	(B)	16	(B)	(B)	(B)	(B)	16	(B)	(B)	-	(B)	(B)
Inside metropolitan areas	1,115	13,289	301	14,629	341	1,129	12,643	14,067	5.1	-3.7	1,173	12,622	13,961	-44	21	106
1,000,000 or more	759	13,156	362	14,795	433	757	12,860	14,338	2.3	-6.3	778	12,885	14,238	-21	-25	100
Inside central cities	443	12,390	467	14,080	603	425	11,851	12,942	4.5	-4.2	435	11,966	12,991	-10	-115	-49
Outside central cities	316	14,259	733	15,797	601	332	14,592	16,123	-2.3	-10.5	342	14,365	15,826	-10	227	297
Under 1,000,000	356	13,568	515	14,274	540	372	12,192	13,517	11.3	2.0	395	12,095	13,414	-23	97	103
Inside central cities	236	13,026	724	13,760	652	231	11,916	13,468	9.3	0.2	244	12,008	13,584	-13	-92	-116
Outside central cities	120	14,477	683	15,291	950	141	12,666	13,597	14.3	4.7	151	12,226	13,139	-10	440	458
Outside metropolitan areas	211	11,167	534	12,246	614	216	10,410	11,334	7.3	-1.7	228	10,346	11,401	-12	64	-67
Region																
Northeast	257	12,378	692	13,602	655	265	11,936	13,505	3.7	-5.0	279	12,007	13,689	-14	-71	-184
North Central	105	14,463	1,013	15,616	1,377	113	13,980	15,977	3.5	-5.2	116	14,668	16,449	-3	-688	-472
South	423	11,851	759	13,743	1,015	436	11,049	12,905	7.3	-1.7	452	10,990	12,540	-16	58	365
West	542	13,658	791	14,686	710	532	12,802	13,784	6.7	-2.2	555	12,697	13,684	-23	105	100
Type of Family																
Male head	1,207	13,453	268	14,730	325	1,239	12,580	13,976	*6.9	-2.0	1,288	12,565	13,885	-49	15	91
Married, wife present	1,166	13,446	272	14,583	321	1,200	12,614	14,016	*6.6	-2.3	1,242	12,589	13,905	-42	25	111
Wife in paid labor force	512	15,845	327	16,812	413	521	14,532	15,725	*9.0	-0.1	520	14,588	15,988	1	-56	-263
Wife not in paid labor force	654	11,144	361	12,837	456	679	11,313	12,702	-1.5	*-9.7	722	11,216	12,407	-43	97	295
Other marital status	42	(B)	(B)	(B)	(B)	38	(B)	(B)	(B)	(B)	46	(B)	(B)	-8	(B)	(B)
Female head	119	8,224	594	9,378	561	107	8,378	9,585	-1.8	-10.1	113	8,174	9,654	-6	204	-69
Number of Earners[1]																
No earners	-	(B)	(B)	(B)	(B)	1	(B)	(B)	(B)	(B)	1	(B)	(B)	(X)	(X)	(X)
1 earner	534	9,323	331	10,726	372	521	9,505	10,700	-1.9	*-10.1	553	9,258	10,448	(X)	(X)	(X)
2 earners	575	14,438	352	15,502	500	585	13,030	14,232	*10.8	1.5	609	13,044	14,256	(X)	(X)	(X)
3 earners	140	16,647	541	18,044	784	152	16,431	17,929	1.3	-7.2	156	17,611	18,158	(X)	(X)	(X)
4 earners or more	77	21,657	1,479	22,323	1,202	87	18,906	19,683	14.6	5.0	82	19,996	20,521	(X)	(X)	(X)

- Represents zero. B Base less than 75,000. r Based on revised methodology X Not applicable.

[1] For the years 1975 and 1974r, excludes families with members who are in the Armed Forces. Therefore the difference in the number, median income, and mean income between 1974r and 1974 are not directly comparable.

Table 3. FAMILY INCOME IN 1947, 1950, 1955, 1960, 1965, AND 1967 TO 1975–FAMILIES BY TOTAL MONEY INCOME, BY RACE OF HEAD

(In current dollars. Families as of March of the following year)

Total money income	1975	1974[r]	1974	1973	1972	1971	1970	1969	1968	1967	1965	1960	1955	1950	1947
ALL RACES															
Number...............thousands..	56,245	55,698	55,712	55,053	54,373	53,296	52,227	51,586	50,823	50,111	48,509	45,539	42,889	39,929	37,237
Percent....................	100.0	100.0	100.0	100.0	100.0	100.0	100.0	100.0	100.0	100.0	100.0	100.0	100.0	100.0	100.0
Under $1,000.....................	2.1	2.4	1.3	1.1	1.3	1.5	1.6	1.6	1.8	2.1	2.9	5.0	7.7	11.5	10.7
$1,000 to $1,999................			1.4	1.8	2.2	2.5	3.0	3.1	3.4	4.4	6.0	8.0	9.8	13.2	16.6
$2,000 to $2,999................	2.4	2.6	2.7	3.2	3.7	4.2	4.3	4.6	5.1	6.0	7.2	8.7	11.0	17.8	22.0
$3,000 to $3,999................	3.4	3.6	3.7	4.1	4.6	4.8	5.0	5.3	6.1	6.4	7.7	9.8	14.5	20.7	19.7
$4,000 to $4,999................	4.1	4.1	4.1	4.5	4.9	5.4	5.3	5.4	6.0	6.6	7.9	10.5	15.5	13.6	11.7
$5,000 to $5,999................	4.1	4.4	4.4	4.6	5.0	5.7	5.8	5.9	6.9	7.8	9.3	12.9	12.7	9.0	7.7
$6,000 to $6,999................	4.2	4.4	4.4	4.8	5.2	5.5	6.0	6.4	7.6	8.4	9.5	10.8	9.5	5.2	4.1
$7,000 to $7,999................	4.3	4.4	4.5	4.9	5.6	6.2	6.3	7.3	8.2	8.9	9.7	8.7	6.6	2.9	2.4
$8,000 to $9,999................	8.5	9.4	9.3	10.0	11.2	12.3	13.6	14.4	15.2	15.5	14.6	11.3	6.3	2.9	2.4
$10,000 to $14,999..............	22.3	24.2	24.4	25.5	26.1	26.9	26.8	26.7	25.0	22.6	17.7	10.6	4.8		
$15,000 to $24,999..............	30.3	28.6	28.3	26.2	23.0	19.5	17.7	15.6	12.1	9.3	6.2	2.8	0.9	3.2	2.7
$25,000 and over................	14.1	11.9	11.5	9.3	7.3	5.3	4.6	3.7	2.6	2.1	1.4	0.9	0.5		
Median income[1]........dollars...	13,719	12,902	12,836	12,051	11,116	10,285	9,867	9,433	8,632	7,933	6,956	5,620	4,418	3,319	3,031
WHITE															
Number...............thousands..	49,873	49,440	49,451	48,919	48,477	47,641	46,535	46,022	45,437	44,814	43,497	41,123	38,982	(NA)	34,120
Percent....................	100.0	100.0	100.0	100.0	100.0	100.0	100.0	100.0	100.0	100.0	100.0	100.0	100.0	100.0	100.0
Under $1,000.....................	1.8	2.0	1.1	1.0	1.1	1.3	1.4	1.4	1.5	1.8	2.4	4.1	6.6	10.0	9.0
$1,000 to $1,999................			1.0	1.3	1.7	2.0	2.4	2.5	2.9	3.9	5.1	6.8	8.7	12.1	14.9
$2,000 to $2,999................	1.9	2.0	2.1	2.6	3.1	3.5	3.8	4.2	4.5	5.2	6.4	8.1	10.4	17.3	22.3
$3,000 to $3,999................	2.9	3.0	3.1	3.5	4.0	4.4	4.6	4.8	5.4	5.8	6.9	9.3	14.3	21.3	20.8
$4,000 to $4,999................	3.6	3.6	3.7	4.1	4.5	5.0	4.9	4.9	5.6	6.2	7.6	10.5	16.0	14.5	12.4
$5,000 to $5,999................	3.9	4.2	4.2	4.3	4.7	5.4	5.5	5.6	6.7	7.6	9.3	13.3	13.4	9.6	8.1
$6,000 to $6,999................	4.0	4.2	4.2	4.5	5.0	5.4	5.8	6.2	7.6	8.4	9.8	11.2	9.9	5.5	4.4
$7,000 to $7,999................	4.2	4.3	4.3	4.7	5.4	6.1	6.3	7.2	8.3	9.1	10.1	9.2	7.1	3.0	2.5
$8,000 to $9,999................	8.4	9.2	9.2	10.0	11.3	12.5	13.8	14.7	15.7	16.1	15.4	12.1	6.9	3.1	2.6
$10,000 to $14,999..............	22.7	24.8	25.1	26.3	27.1	28.0	27.9	28.0	26.2	23.8	18.8	11.2	5.3		
$15,000 to $24,999..............	31.7	29.9	29.7	27.6	24.2	20.6	18.7	16.6	12.9	10.0	6.7	3.1	1.0	3.5	3.0
$25,000 and over................	15.1	12.8	12.4	10.0	7.9	5.8	5.0	4.0	2.8	2.2	1.6	1.0	0.5		
Median income[1]........dollars...	14,268	13,408	13,356	12,595	11,549	10,672	10,236	9,794	8,937	8,234	7,251	5,835	4,613	3,445	3,157
BLACK AND OTHER RACES															
Number...............thousands..	6,373	6,258	6,262	6,134	5,896	5,655	5,413	5,215	5,074	5,020	4,782	4,333	3,907	(NA)	3,117
Percent....................	100.0	100.0	100.0	100.0	100.0	100.0	100.0	100.0	100.0	100.0	100.0	100.0	100.0	100.0	100.0
Under $1,000.....................	5.0	6.0	2.2	2.5	2.7	2.9	3.4	3.4	4.1	4.9	7.2	13.4	19.0	28.1	28.8
$1,000 to $1,999................			4.4	5.3	6.3	6.5	7.7	8.3	8.6	9.5	13.6	18.3	20.8	25.3	33.6
$2,000 to $2,999................	6.4	6.9	6.9	7.6	8.7	9.8	9.0	8.6	10.2	13.0	14.6	14.8	17.6	23.4	18.7
$3,000 to $3,999................	7.3	8.1	8.2	8.4	9.1	8.7	8.8	9.9	11.9	11.5	14.8	14.0	17.2	13.4	8.4
$4,000 to $4,999................	7.6	7.6	7.8	8.3	8.5	8.9	8.2	9.4	10.0	10.1	10.8	10.4	11.1	4.4	4.3
$5,000 to $5,999................	6.0	6.4	6.3	7.2	7.5	8.1	9.0	8.8	8.8	9.8	9.5	8.7	5.8	1.9	3.1
$6,000 to $6,999................	5.8	6.5	6.7	6.8	6.5	7.1	7.4	8.2	7.7	8.0	6.8	6.7	4.8	1.5	2.0
$7,000 to $7,999................	5.3	5.6	6.1	6.5	6.9	7.3	6.9	7.5	7.0	7.0	6.5	4.5	1.8	1.0	0.7
$8,000 to $9,999................	10.1	10.2	10.1	10.4	10.2	10.6	11.3	12.0	10.7	10.0	7.2	4.2	1.3	0.7	0.4
$10,000 to $14,999..............	20.2	19.5	19.0	19.1	18.0	17.9	17.3	15.6	14.7	11.9	7.6	4.4	0.6		
$15,000 to $24,999..............	20.1	18.6	17.9	14.4	13.2	10.5	9.4	7.3	5.5	3.6	1.3	0.6	-	0.3	0.1
$25,000 and over................	6.4	4.6	4.4	3.5	2.4	1.7	1.5	1.0	0.8	0.6	0.1	-	-		
Median income[1]........dollars...	9,321	8,578	8,265	7,596	7,106	6,714	6,516	6,191	5,590	5,094	3,993	3,230	2,544	1,869	1,614
BLACK															
Number...............thousands..	5,586	5,491	5,498	5,440	5,265	5,157	4,928	4,774	4,646	4,589	(NA)	(NA)	(NA)	(NA)	(NA)
Percent....................	100.0	100.0	100.0	100.0	100.0	100.0	100.0	100.0	100.0	100.0	(NA)	(NA)	(NA)	(NA)	(NA)
Under $1,000.....................	5.2	6.4	2.3	2.5	2.8	2.9	3.5	3.4	3.9	5.1	(NA)	(NA)	(NA)	(NA)	(NA)
$1,000 to $1,999................			4.8	5.7	6.6	6.6	8.2	8.7	9.1	10.1	(NA)	(NA)	(NA)	(NA)	(NA)
$2,000 to $2,999................	7.0	7.4	7.4	8.3	9.2	10.6	9.5	9.2	10.9	13.7	(NA)	(NA)	(NA)	(NA)	(NA)
$3,000 to $3,999................	7.9	8.8	8.9	9.1	9.4	9.0	9.2	10.2	12.3	11.9	(NA)	(NA)	(NA)	(NA)	(NA)
$4,000 to $4,999................	8.3	8.0	8.2	8.5	8.7	9.4	8.2	9.6	10.6	10.4	(NA)	(NA)	(NA)	(NA)	(NA)
$5,000 to $5,999................	6.3	6.3	6.3	7.4	7.6	8.3	9.3	8.9	8.8	10.3	(NA)	(NA)	(NA)	(NA)	(NA)
$6,000 to $6,999................	5.9	7.1	7.2	6.7	6.5	7.1	7.7	8.5	7.6	8.0	(NA)	(NA)	(NA)	(NA)	(NA)
$7,000 to $7,999................	5.4	5.8	6.1	6.8	7.0	7.4	6.9	7.6	7.2	6.9	(NA)	(NA)	(NA)	(NA)	(NA)
$8,000 to $9,999................	10.1	10.5	10.3	10.3	10.4	10.9	11.2	12.0	10.5	9.4	(NA)	(NA)	(NA)	(NA)	(NA)
$10,000 to $14,999..............	20.6	19.7	19.1	19.0	17.5	17.2	16.9	14.8	14.0	11.0	(NA)	(NA)	(NA)	(NA)	(NA)
$15,000 to $24,999..............	18.3	16.7	16.2	13.0	12.2	9.5	8.5	6.5	4.7	2.9	(NA)	(NA)	(NA)	(NA)	(NA)
$25,000 and over................	5.0	3.0	3.2	2.7	2.1	1.1	1.0	0.6	0.4	0.3	(NA)	(NA)	(NA)	(NA)	(NA)
Median income[1]........dollars...	8,779	8,006	7,808	7,269	6,864	6,440	6,279	5,999	5,360	4,875	(NA)	(NA)	(NA)	(NA)	(NA)

- Represents zero. NA Not available. [r]Based on revised methodology

[1]Since medians were calculated using more detailed intervals than those shown above, they will not be the same as those calculated using the above intervals.

Note: For the years 1960 to 1970, the number of White and Black and Other Races families will not add to All Races because the numbers for All Races were adjusted to population controls based on the 1970 census. These controls are not available by race.

Table 4. FAMILY INCOME IN 1947, 1950, 1955, 1960, 1965, AND 1967 TO 1975—FAMILIES BY TOTAL MONEY INCOME IN CONSTANT DOLLARS, BY RACE OF HEAD

(In 1975 dollars. Families as of March of the following year)

Total money income	1975	1974[r]	1974	1973	1972	1971	1970	1969	1968	1967	1965	1960	1955	1950	1947
ALL RACES															
Number...............thousands..	56,245	55,698	55,712	55,053	54,373	53,296	52,227	51,586	50,823	50,111	48,509	45,539	42,889	39,929	37,237
Percent...................	100.0	100.0	100.0	100.0	100.0	100.0	100.0	100.0	100.0	100.0	100.0	100.0	100.0	100.0	100.0
Under $3,000....................	4.5	4.5	4.6	4.3	4.6	5.1	5.3	4.9	5.0	5.9	7.4	10.2	12.6	16.1	15.0
$3,000 to $4,999................	7.5	6.6	6.9	6.5	6.6	6.8	6.7	6.5	6.8	7.4	8.2	9.5	10.3	13.3	14.3
$5,000 to $6,999................	8.3	7.9	8.0	7.6	7.8	8.1	7.5	7.4	7.9	8.1	9.1	10.4	12.8	16.7	21.8
$7,000 to $9,999................	12.8	12.3	12.4	12.0	12.3	13.0	13.0	12.3	13.3	13.8	15.1	19.0	22.6	24.7	20.2
$10,000 to $11,999..............	8.9	9.1	9.4	8.2	8.6	9.0	9.6	9.8	10.2	10.8	11.0	14.8	14.8		
$12,000 to $14,999..............	13.4	13.6	13.8	13.5	13.6	14.8	14.8	14.8	15.0	15.4	16.0	12.4	11.2	29.2	28.6
$15,000 to $24,999..............	30.3	30.7	30.7	32.5	31.8	30.5	30.5	31.4	30.3	28.5	25.0	18.6	12.9		
$25,000 and over................	14.1	15.3	14.2	15.3	14.8	12.6	12.6	12.8	11.5	10.2	8.2	5.0	2.8		
Median income[1].........dollars..	13,719	14,082	14,009	14,595	14,301	13,668	13,676	13,849	13,354	12,788	11,867	10,214	8,881	7,422	7,303
WHITE															
Number...............thousands..	49,873	49,440	49,451	48,919	48,477	47,641	46,535	46,022	45,437	44,814	43,497	41,123	38,982	(NA)	34,120
Percent...................	100.0	100.0	100.0	100.0	100.0	100.0	100.0	100.0	100.0	100.0	100.0	100.0	100.0	100.0	100.0
Under $3,000....................	3.7	3.6	3.7	3.4	3.8	4.3	4.4	4.1	4.2	5.1	6.3	8.5	10.8	14.1	12.8
$3,000 to $4,999................	6.5	5.6	5.9	5.7	5.7	6.0	5.9	5.8	6.0	6.5	7.2	8.7	9.5	12.4	13.2
$5,000 to $6,999................	7.9	7.4	7.5	6.9	7.1	7.6	7.0	6.8	7.2	7.5	8.2	9.9	12.3	16.4	22.4
$7,000 to $9,999................	12.6	11.9	12.0	11.5	11.8	12.6	12.5	11.8	12.9	13.4	14.8	19.2	23.0	25.7	21.2
$10,000 to $11,999..............	8.9	9.1	9.6	8.2	8.6	9.0	9.6	9.8	10.3	10.9	11.3	15.5	15.6		
$12,000 to $14,999..............	13.8	14.0	14.2	13.8	13.9	15.3	15.2	15.1	15.4	15.9	16.7	13.0	11.9	31.3	30.4
$15,000 to $24,999..............	31.7	32.0	32.0	34.1	33.2	31.9	31.9	33.0	31.7	30.0	26.5	19.8	13.9		
$25,000 and over................	15.1	16.4	15.2	16.5	15.8	13.4	13.5	13.7	12.2	10.9	8.9	5.4	3.0		
Median income[1].........dollars..	14,268	14,633	14,577	15,254	14,858	14,182	14,188	14,379	13,826	13,273	12,370	10,604	9,271	7,702	7,608
BLACK AND OTHER RACES															
Number...............thousands..	6,373	6,258	6,262	6,134	5,896	5,655	5,413	5,215	5,074	5,020	4,782	4,333	3,907	(NA)	3,117
Percent...................	100.0	100.0	100.0	100.0	100.0	100.0	100.0	100.0	100.0	100.0	100.0	100.0	100.0	100.0	100.0
Under $3,000....................	11.4	11.4	11.9	11.5	11.8	12.2	12.8	12.1	12.1	13.2	17.6	26.4	30.7	37.3	38.9
$3,000 to $4,999................	14.9	14.3	14.7	13.6	14.3	13.9	13.2	12.9	13.9	15.7	16.9	17.0	18.4	23.1	25.4
$5,000 to $6,999................	11.8	12.1	12.3	12.8	12.9	13.1	11.8	12.7	14.5	14.0	17.0	15.4	18.2	19.3	15.7
$7,000 to $9,999................	15.4	15.3	15.8	16.3	15.8	16.9	17.5	17.5	16.9	17.9	17.9	17.1	18.2	13.3	10.4
$10,000 to $11,999..............	9.3	8.8	8.6	8.5	8.0	9.2	9.4	10.0	9.3	9.6	8.2	9.1	7.7		
$12,000 to $14,999..............	10.9	10.8	10.7	11.2	11.0	10.8	11.5	12.0	10.9	10.8	9.6	6.6	4.1	6.9	9.7
$15,000 to $24,999..............	20.1	20.7	20.2	19.7	20.3	18.7	18.6	17.9	17.7	15.1	11.3	7.5	2.6		
$25,000 and over................	6.4	6.6	5.9	6.4	6.0	5.1	5.3	4.9	4.7	3.7	1.6	0.9	0.1		
Median income[1].........dollars..	9,321	9,361	9,020	9,200	9,142	8,923	9,032	9,089	8,648	8,212	6,812	5,871	5,113	4,178	3,888
BLACK															
Number...............thousands..	5,586	5,491	5,498	5,440	5,265	5,157	4,928	4,774	4,646	4,589	(NA)	(NA)	(NA)	(NA)	(NA)
Percent...................	100.0	100.0	100.0	100.0	100.0	100.0	100.0	100.0	100.0	100.0	(NA)	(NA)	(NA)	(NA)	(NA)
Under $3,000....................	12.2	12.3	12.8	12.2	12.4	12.6	13.4	12.6	12.5	14.0	(NA)	(NA)	(NA)	(NA)	(NA)
$3,000 to $4,999................	16.2	15.3	15.7	14.6	14.8	14.7	13.8	13.5	14.7	16.5	(NA)	(NA)	(NA)	(NA)	(NA)
$5,000 to $6,999................	12.2	12.6	12.6	13.2	13.2	13.8	11.9	13.1	15.1	14.5	(NA)	(NA)	(NA)	(NA)	(NA)
$7,000 to $9,999................	15.5	16.1	16.3	16.6	16.0	17.1	18.0	17.9	17.1	18.5	(NA)	(NA)	(NA)	(NA)	(NA)
$10,000 to $11,999..............	9.8	8.9	8.7	8.4	8.1	9.5	9.4	10.1	9.4	9.5	(NA)	(NA)	(NA)	(NA)	(NA)
$12,000 to $14,999..............	10.8	10.9	10.8	11.2	10.8	10.9	11.3	11.9	10.8	10.3	(NA)	(NA)	(NA)	(NA)	(NA)
$15,000 to $24,999..............	18.3	19.2	18.7	18.7	19.2	17.7	18.0	16.9	16.8	14.0	(NA)	(NA)	(NA)	(NA)	(NA)
$25,000 and over................	5.0	4.7	4.3	5.2	5.4	3.8	4.2	3.9	3.6	2.8	(NA)	(NA)	(NA)	(NA)	(NA)
Median income[1].........dollars..	8,779	8,737	8,522	8,804	8,831	8,558	8,703	8,807	8,292	7,859	(NA)	(NA)	(NA)	(NA)	(NA)

NA Not available. [r]Based on revised methodology
[1]Since medians were calculated using more detailed intervals than those shown above, they will not be the same as those calculated using the above intervals.

Note: For the years 1960 to 1970, the number of White and Black and Other Races families will not add to All Races because the numbers for All Races were adjusted to population controls based on the 1970 census. These controls are not available by race.

Table 7. AGE OF HEAD—FAMILIES AND UNRELATED INDIVIDUALS BY TOTAL MONEY INCOME: 1975 AND 1974 (Revised)

(Numbers in thousands. Families and unrelated individuals as of March of the following year)

Total money income	1975								1974[r]							
	Total	Age of head							Total	Age of head						
		14 to 24 years		25 to 34 years	35 to 44 years	45 to 54 years	55 to 64 years	65 years and over		14 to 24 years		25 to 34 years	35 to 44 years	45 to 54 years	55 to 64 years	65 years and over
		Total	18 to 24 years							Total	18 to 24 years					
FAMILIES																
Total																
Total	56,245	4,042	4,021	12,885	11,107	11,125	8,923	8,163	55,698	4,242	4,210	12,681	10,865	11,230	8,645	8,035
Under $2,000	1,209	236	221	333	197	157	182	104	1,364	297	276	306	200	215	204	143
$2,000 to $2,999	1,356	238	233	222	180	160	201	356	1,432	207	206	267	148	168	192	450
$3,000 to $3,999	1,908	262	262	315	258	183	231	660	1,991	250	250	368	223	188	262	700
$4,000 to $4,999	2,293	299	298	395	260	243	299	797	2,261	237	234	386	276	223	277	862
$5,000 to $5,999	2,310	239	239	394	291	255	330	800	2,452	310	306	398	304	259	342	840
$6,000 to $6,999	2,351	255	254	480	326	278	326	686	2,466	309	309	470	314	315	341	717
$7,000 to $7,999	2,444	285	285	477	357	324	353	648	2,456	308	305	507	343	327	365	606
$8,000 to $8,999	2,495	276	276	616	379	328	373	522	2,556	314	314	566	407	373	367	530
$9,000 to $9,999	2,320	271	271	599	367	319	341	423	2,656	355	355	725	427	366	375	408
$10,000 to $10,999	2,597	268	268	709	483	392	362	383	2,879	278	278	783	522	481	461	354
$11,000 to $11,999	2,415	235	235	637	404	413	365	362	2,756	282	282	782	440	462	450	340
$12,000 to $12,999	2,716	233	233	802	524	445	389	323	2,859	234	234	829	598	479	432	287
$13,000 to $13,999	2,373	192	192	703	482	388	356	252	2,596	169	169	761	526	492	411	237
$14,000 to $14,999	2,460	129	129	689	552	472	406	212	2,389	154	154	687	512	425	403	208
$15,000 to $15,999	2,490	118	118	711	535	493	425	209	2,415	125	125	683	567	546	335	160
$16,000 to $16,999	2,224	119	119	682	545	450	285	143	2,233	108	108	617	504	533	330	140
$17,000 to $17,999	2,041	83	83	603	450	463	295	147	2,009	94	94	581	465	457	294	119
$18,000 to $19,999	3,793	128	128	1,009	869	900	643	243	3,441	96	96	897	864	851	517	215
$20,000 to $24,999	6,518	130	130	1,443	1,693	1,730	1,135	387	5,844	90	90	1,232	1,665	1,616	947	294
$25,000 to $49,999	7,148	46	46	1,017	1,746	2,466	1,443	431	5,961	26	26	800	1,396	2,221	1,153	366
$50,000 and over	783	2	2	49	208	267	182	74	682	-	-	38	164	233	188	58
Median income....dollars..	13,719	8,752	8,791	13,659	15,921	17,569	14,869	8,057	12,902	8,646	8,698	12,946	15,339	16,557	13,619	7,505
Standard error....dollars..	52	119	119	83	101	117	120	86	43	107	107	71	95	102	117	76
Mean income....dollars..	15,546	9,344	9,386	14,321	17,464	19,550	17,114	10,771	14,711	8,956	9,008	13,641	16,614	18,513	16,121	10,037
Standard error....dollars..	50	97	97	74	113	136	142	106	47	82	82	71	102	118	143	106
Head Year-Round Full-Time Worker																
Percent of total excl. Armed Forces	59.3	48.0	48.3	69.6	74.0	73.1	59.2	10.3	61.1	51.0	51.3	71.1	76.5	75.3	61.1	10.4
Median income....dollars..	17,163	11,793	11,793	15,664	18,005	19,646	18,294	15,962	16,001	10,840	10,853	14,644	16,963	18,464	16,572	13,529
Standard error....dollars..	60	147	147	82	123	123	158	425	52	127	127	88	111	135	149	288
Mean income....dollars..	19,209	12,367	12,367	16,494	19,945	21,974	20,643	19,553	17,968	11,258	11,271	15,528	18,498	20,757	19,375	17,623
Standard error....dollars..	68	148	148	87	134	162	195	509	62	107	107	82	116	137	198	556
UNRELATED INDIVIDUALS																
Total																
Total	20,234	3,392	3,237	3,537	1,420	2,036	2,998	6,851	18,926	2,954	2,810	3,120	1,392	1,967	2,980	6,512
Under $1,000	1,155	420	292	121	64	157	224	167	984	364	255	103	89	144	166	119
$1,000 to $1,499	646	154	148	61	31	72	111	217	746	150	141	55	33	77	128	302
$1,500 to $1,999	1,062	173	163	56	40	85	185	523	1,373	163	158	67	26	112	213	792
$2,000 to $2,499	1,744	188	182	86	45	129	199	1,096	1,734	175	172	82	53	89	259	1,077
$2,500 to $2,999	1,408	162	162	86	30	62	201	866	1,517	167	162	66	34	72	180	998
$3,000 to $3,499	1,518	185	183	94	39	85	223	893	1,349	195	192	105	39	88	176	745
$3,500 to $3,999	1,000	168	167	101	30	69	135	497	834	143	139	88	54	48	133	368
$4,000 to $4,999	1,796	391	391	199	78	171	241	716	1,533	301	300	187	68	158	239	580
$5,000 to $5,999	1,468	337	336	201	61	138	194	537	1,381	319	319	249	77	150	244	343
$6,000 to $6,999	1,173	292	292	191	85	131	185	290	1,300	290	288	238	70	156	231	315
$7,000 to $7,999	1,159	242	242	298	76	128	172	242	1,013	185	183	260	78	149	168	174
$8,000 to $8,999	994	202	202	278	99	94	134	187	908	142	142	264	99	87	173	143
$9,000 to $9,999	844	148	148	263	62	98	146	128	734	109	109	255	70	64	129	107
$10,000 to $11,999	1,296	168	168	482	126	154	204	162	1,233	139	139	384	150	179	200	181
$12,000 to $14,999	1,355	120	120	521	202	182	186	146	1,073	75	75	367	180	167	161	123
$15,000 to $19,999	1,004	32	32	357	203	157	153	101	721	25	25	241	137	128	107	84
$20,000 to $24,999	314	5	5	86	80	57	49	37	256	5	5	63	65	54	43	26
$25,000 and over	298	5	5	56	69	68	55	45	235	7	7	45	72	46	30	36
Median income....dollars..	4,882	4,629	4,824	8,985	9,502	6,385	4,915	3,311	4,603	4,395	4,621	8,227	8,764	6,295	4,984	2,984
Standard error....dollars..	41	77	75	113	314	178	121	24	46	93	91	109	195	147	117	22
Mean income....dollars..	6,623	5,016	5,234	9,433	10,850	8,295	6,759	4,536	6,240	4,853	5,061	8,861	10,169	7,779	6,298	4,283
Standard error....dollars..	45	65	66	108	246	194	125	50	47	83	85	124	240	176	124	57
Year-Round Full-Time Worker																
Percent of total excl. Armed Forces	32.8	33.0	34.6	59.5	64.1	50.9	39.7	4.1	34.1	34.9	36.4	62.4	65.7	56.7	40.0	4.2
Median income....dollars..	9,799	7,587	7,587	11,219	12,177	9,896	8,853	7,793	8,892	7,056	7,075	9,803	11,041	8,823	8,218	7,684
Standard error....dollars..	79	116	116	129	269	232	196	409	72	116	119	105	255	260	157	437
Mean income....dollars..	10,936	7,919	7,919	11,853	13,224	11,627	10,283	8,774	10,136	7,554	7,579	10,781	12,570	10,422	9,479	8,693
Standard error....dollars..	92	104	104	130	311	298	228	395	94	136	137	163	304	219	248	344

- Represents zero. [r]Based on revised methodology

Table 8. SELECTED CHARACTERISTICS OF ALL PERSONS 14 YEARS OLD AND OVER—NUMBER WITH INCOME, MEDIAN INCOME, MEAN INCOME, AND STANDARD ERRORS, BY SEX: 1975, 1974 (Revised), AND 1974

(Persons as of March of the following year. An asterisk (*) preceding percent change indicates statistically significant change at the 95 percent confidence level)

Selected characteristics	1975					1974[r]			Percent change (median income)		1974			Difference (1974[r]-1974)		
	Number with income (thousands)	Median income		Mean income		Number with income (thousands)	Median income	Mean income	Current dollars	In 1975 dollars	Number with income (thousands)	Median income	Mean income	Number with income (thousands)	Median income	Mean income
		Value	Standard error	Value	Standard error											
MALE																
All males	71,234	$8,853	$46	$10,429	$46	70,863	$8,452	$9,861	*4.7	*-4.0	70,627	$8,379	$9,717	236	$73	$144
Race and Spanish Origin																
White	63,629	9,300	54	10,832	50	63,388	8,854	10,223	*5.0	*-3.8	63,207	8,794	10,083	181	60	140
Black	6,485	5,560	106	6,633	77	6,409	5,486	6,318	1.3	*-7.1	6,364	5,370	6,210	45	116	108
Spanish origin[1]	2,945	6,777	176	7,680	194	3,052	6,443	7,251	5.2	-3.6	3,030	6,481	7,300	22	-38	-49
Region, Race, and Spanish Origin																
Northeast: All races	16,084	9,511	147	10,888	135	16,141	9,188	10,291	3.5	*-5.2	16,105	8,986	10,106	36	202	185
White	14,809	9,755	157	11,121	144	14,899	9,436	10,489	3.4	*-5.3	14,876	9,235	10,326	23	201	163
Black	1,098	7,181	442	7,863	300	1,095	6,807	7,602	5.5	-3.3	1,079	6,482	7,153	16	325	449
Spanish origin[1]	516	7,023	369	7,572	401	530	7,020	7,549	(Z)	-8.3	528	7,033	7,659	2	-13	-110
North Central: All races	19,220	9,504	171	10,665	145	19,393	9,144	10,243	3.9	*-4.8	19,298	9,149	10,124	95	-5	119
White	17,850	9,672	177	10,860	153	18,074	9,280	10,411	4.2	-4.5	17,992	9,295	10,290	82	-15	121
Black	1,262	7,408	556	7,910	356	1,237	7,655	7,892	-3.2	-11.3	1,222	7,568	7,824	15	87	68
Spanish origin[1]	224	7,803	1,031	8,964	1,165	271	7,719	8,554	1.1	-7.4	269	7,582	8,736	2	137	-182
South: All races	22,722	7,762	118	9,625	139	22,346	7,323	9,002	*6.0	-2.9	22,273	7,262	8,874	73	61	128
White	19,072	8,546	139	10,356	160	18,705	8,042	9,716	*6.3	-2.6	18,658	7,988	9,570	47	54	146
Black	3,493	4,737	176	5,658	163	3,457	4,373	5,165	8.3	-0.7	3,434	4,306	5,154	23	67	11
Spanish origin[1]	948	6,118	405	7,298	578	960	5,729	6,842	6.8	-2.2	957	5,669	6,696	3	60	146
West: All races	13,208	9,321	256	10,911	228	12,983	8,742	10,234	6.6	-2.3	12,951	8,619	10,080	32	123	154
White	11,897	9,587	284	11,194	248	11,710	8,933	10,406	7.3	-1.7	11,681	8,846	10,275	29	87	131
Black	632	7,110	1,115	7,330	530	620	6,255	7,339	13.7	4.1	629	6,139	7,219	-9	116	120
Spanish origin[1]	1,256	6,997	546	7,784	441	1,291	6,556	7,160	6.7	-2.2	1,276	6,696	7,302	15	-140	-142
Relationship to Family Head																
In families	62,975	9,204	54	10,691	50	63,065	8,775	10,102	*4.9	*-3.9	62,890	8,707	9,962	175	68	140
Head	48,535	11,270	49	12,750	59	48,295	10,773	12,124	*4.6	*-4.1	48,249	10,715	11,924	46	58	200
Married, wife present	47,114	11,333	50	12,818	60	46,907	10,837	12,208	*4.6	*-4.2	46,765	10,790	12,002	142	47	206
Other marital status	1,421	8,682	288	10,476	299	1,387	8,197	9,297	5.9	-3.0	1,484	8,227	9,465	-97	-30	-168
Relative of head	14,440	2,281	36	3,772	45	14,771	2,133	3,490	*6.9	-2.0	14,641	2,095	3,496	130	38	-6
Unrelated individuals	8,259	6,732	110	8,433	105	7,797	6,244	7,912	*7.8	-1.2	7,737	6,147	7,733	60	97	179
Age																
14 to 19 years	7,127	974	14	1,743	33	7,633	966	1,650	0.8	*-7.6	7,623	962	1,679	10	4	-29
20 to 24 years	8,687	5,484	73	5,913	57	8,604	5,441	5,748	0.8	*-7.7	8,464	5,343	5,639	140	98	109
25 to 34 years	15,103	11,037	72	11,498	70	14,641	10,581	10,985	*4.3	*-4.4	14,623	10,661	10,933	18	-80	52
35 to 44 years	11,026	13,331	101	14,731	126	10,913	12,767	14,023	*4.4	*-4.3	10,903	12,582	13,682	10	185	341
45 to 54 years	11,192	13,207	104	14,762	150	11,288	12,369	13,947	*6.8	-2.2	11,265	12,381	13,722	23	-12	225
55 to 64 years	9,219	10,640	123	12,556	149	9,091	9,973	11,786	*6.7	-2.2	9,080	9,924	11,686	11	49	100
65 years and over	8,880	4,959	55	6,991	97	8,692	4,638	6,706	*6.9	-2.0	8,669	4,535	6,466	23	103	240
Occupation Group of Longest Job[2]																
Total with earnings	59,268	9,674	52	10,579	49	59,866	9,121	9,982	*6.1	*-2.8	59,752	9,064	9,853	114	57	129
White-collar workers	23,103	13,081	81	14,455	98	22,640	12,490	13,840	*4.7	*-4.0	22,450	12,329	13,533	190	161	307
Professional, technical, and kindred workers	8,292	14,311	135	15,848	169	7,961	13,689	15,148	*4.5	*-4.2	7,944	13,391	14,609	17	298	539
Salaried	7,508	14,070	134	14,995	150	7,213	13,480	14,271	*4.4	*-4.4	7,242	13,267	13,975	-29	213	296
Self-employed	784	21,182	986	24,010	998	748	19,522	23,603	8.5	-0.6	702	16,970	21,152	46	2,552	2,451
Managers and administrators, except farm	7,608	14,807	145	16,548	183	7,434	14,548	16,313	1.8	*-6.7	7,331	14,354	16,105	103	194	208
Salaried	6,185	15,720	176	17,709	200	6,070	14,959	17,063	*5.1	*-3.7	5,988	14,817	16,892	82	142	171
Self-employed	1,423	9,885	482	11,505	400	1,365	11,728	12,978	*-15.7	*-22.8	1,343	11,636	12,593	22	92	385
Sales workers	3,589	10,291	242	11,665	237	3,549	9,427	10,810	*9.2	(Z)	3,454	9,401	10,648	95	26	162
Clerical and kindred workers	3,613	10,040	171	9,625	136	3,696	9,288	8,961	*8.1	-1.0	3,721	9,209	8,844	-25	79	117
Blue-collar workers	27,450	8,812	63	8,870	45	28,411	8,427	8,374	*4.6	*-4.2	28,380	8,408	8,379	31	19	-5
Craft and kindred workers	11,998	10,870	83	10,690	69	11,953	10,560	10,293	*2.9	*-5.7	12,001	10,552	10,287	-48	8	6
Operatives, incl. transport wkrs.	10,179	8,577	97	8,656	67	10,763	8,224	8,185	*4.3	*-4.4	10,670	8,218	8,163	93	6	22
Operatives, exc. transport wkrs	6,798	8,312	126	8,372	79	7,291	8,084	7,920	2.8	*-5.8	(NA)	(NA)	(NA)	(X)	(X)	(X)
Transport equip. operatives	3,381	9,032	159	9,225	125	3,472	8,524	8,739	*6.0	-2.9	(NA)	(NA)	(NA)	(X)	(X)	(X)
Laborers, except farm	5,274	3,991	157	5,141	81	5,695	3,401	4,706	*17.3	7.5	5,709	3,591	4,770	-14	-190	-64
Service workers	5,768	4,503	143	5,887	92	5,733	4,202	5,426	7.2	-1.8	5,765	4,414	5,524	-32	-212	-98
Private household workers	50	(B)	(B)	(B)	(B)	75	605	553	(B)	(B)	91	395	944	-16	210	-391
Service workers, except private household	5,718	4,580	142	5,937	92	5,658	4,321	5,491	6.0	-2.9	5,674	4,540	5,597	-16	-219	-106
Farm workers	2,948	2,469	124	5,292	212	3,081	2,400	4,934	2.9	-5.7	3,157	2,286	4,839	-76	114	95
Farmers and farm managers	1,446	4,803	317	7,856	398	1,578	4,908	7,220	-2.1	-10.3	1,627	4,597	6,930	-49	311	290
Farm laborers and supervisors	1,502	1,517	117	2,822	121	1,503	1,247	2,534	21.7	11.5	1,530	1,280	2,616	-27	-33	-82
Educational Attainment																
Total, 25 years and over	55,420	10,878	49	12,254	54	54,626	10,404	11,656	*4.6	*-4.2	54,540	10,307	11,474	86	97	182
Elementary: Total	11,655	5,473	64	6,722	59	12,187	5,315	6,449	3.0	*-5.7	12,165	5,398	6,632	22	-83	-183
Less than 8 years	6,381	4,665	67	5,845	71	6,617	4,509	5,566	3.5	*-5.2	6,623	4,551	5,758	-6	-42	-192
8 years	5,273	6,642	109	7,785	95	5,570	6,511	7,499	2.0	*-6.5	5,542	6,621	7,676	28	-110	-177
High school: Total	25,773	10,942	59	11,496	64	25,594	10,622	11,137	*3.0	*-5.6	25,535	10,602	11,108	59	20	29
1 to 3 years	7,842	8,825	103	9,534	92	7,883	8,919	9,458	-1.1	*-9.3	7,887	9,017	9,626	-4	-98	-168
4 years	17,931	11,834	71	12,354	81	17,711	11,338	11,884	*4.4	*-4.4	17,648	11,290	11,770	63	48	114
College: Total	17,992	14,782	91	16,925	121	16,845	14,118	16,213	*4.7	*-4.1	16,840	13,662	15,527	5	456	686
1 to 3 years	7,655	13,060	115	13,972	144	7,221	12,412	13,477	*5.2	*-3.6	7,221	12,322	13,275	-	90	202
4 years or more	10,337	16,682	148	19,111	177	9,624	16,001	18,265	*4.3	*-4.5	9,619	15,067	17,218	5	934	1,047

- Represents zero. B Base less than 75,000. NA Not available. [r]Based on revised methodology X Not applicable. Z Less than 0.05 percent.

[1]Spanish origin may be of any race, but the vast majority are white.

[2]Amounts shown are median and mean earnings.

Table 8. SELECTED CHARACTERISTICS OF ALL PERSONS 14 YEARS OLD AND OVER—NUMBER WITH INCOME, MEDIAN INCOME, MEAN INCOME, AND STANDARD ERRORS, BY SEX: 1975, 1974 (Revised), AND 1974—Continued

(Persons as of March of the following year. An asterisk (*) preceding percent change indicates statistically significant change at the 95 percent confidence level)

Selected characteristics	1975					1974r			Percent change (median income)		1974			Difference (1974r–1974)		
	Number with income (thousands)	Median income		Mean income		Number with income (thousands)	Median income	Mean income	Current dollars	In 1975 dollars	Number with income (thousands)	Median income	Mean income	Number with income (thousands)	Median income	Mean income
		Value	Standard error	Value	Standard error											
FEMALE																
All females	60,807	$3,385	$21	$4,513	$21	59,642	$3,082	$4,161	*9.8	0.6	59,213	$3,079	$4,142	429	$3	$19
Race and Spanish Origin																
White	52,936	3,420	22	4,550	23	52,038	3,117	4,203	*9.7	0.5	51,689	3,114	4,184	349	3	19
Black	6,969	3,107	55	4,134	49	6,779	2,814	3,759	*10.4	1.2	6,720	2,806	3,738	59	8	21
Spanish origin[1]	2,380	3,202	111	3,798	95	2,353	3,008	3,577	6.4	-2.5	2,341	3,065	3,639	12	-57	-62
Region, Race, and Spanish Origin																
Northeast: All races	13,815	3,652	81	4,794	65	13,934	3,362	4,457	*8.6	-0.5	13,838	3,442	4,456	96	-80	1
White	12,395	3,591	85	4,744	69	12,569	3,271	4,404	*9.8	0.6	12,493	3,336	4,400	76	-65	4
Black	1,282	4,051	250	4,945	179	1,260	4,134	4,697	-2.0	-10.2	1,245	4,060	4,710	15	74	-13
Spanish origin[1]	537	4,074	259	4,448	221	490	4,127	4,333	-1.3	-9.6	489	4,172	4,430	1	-45	-97
North Central: All races	16,281	3,386	71	4,489	70	16,034	3,057	4,097	*10.8	1.5	15,860	3,106	4,105	174	-49	-8
White	14,797	3,341	75	4,448	74	14,598	3,034	4,079	*10.1	0.9	14,456	3,080	4,088	142	-46	-9
Black	1,402	3,850	248	4,920	220	1,389	3,251	4,288	18.4	8.5	1,356	3,343	4,282	33	-92	6
Spanish origin[1]	169	3,678	580	4,155	513	163	3,115	3,774	18.1	8.2	162	3,404	4,057	1	-289	-283
South: All races	19,595	3,118	69	4,172	58	18,912	2,799	3,843	*11.4	2.1	18,800	2,761	3,798	112	38	45
White	15,762	3,317	77	4,342	67	15,239	3,003	4,019	*10.5	1.2	15,145	2,952	3,965	94	51	54
Black	3,722	2,427	77	3,466	105	3,563	2,197	3,118	10.5	1.2	3,548	2,193	3,107	15	4	11
Spanish origin[1]	689	2,258	304	3,130	219	729	2,332	3,053	-3.2	-11.3	724	2,382	3,110	5	-50	-57
West: All races	11,116	3,497	116	4,802	109	10,762	3,211	4,429	8.9	-0.2	10,716	3,228	4,396	46	-17	33
White	9,982	3,480	120	4,789	116	9,632	3,195	4,421	8.9	-0.2	9,594	3,222	4,393	38	-27	28
Black	564	3,530	419	4,744	392	567	3,384	4,410	4.3	-4.4	571	3,337	4,245	-4	47	165
Spanish origin[1]	984	3,123	282	3,852	268	972	2,887	3,557	8.2	-0.9	966	2,895	3,565	6	-8	-8
Relationship to Family Head																
In families	49,213	3,187	27	4,269	23	48,837	2,880	3,926	*10.7	1.4	48,494	2,905	3,934	343	-25	-8
Head	7,297	4,690	64	5,791	64	7,019	4,412	5,532	*6.3	-2.6	7,021	4,430	5,545	-2	-18	-13
Wife of head	30,062	3,608	44	4,536	30	29,739	3,262	4,147	*10.6	1.3	29,496	3,315	4,148	243	-53	-1
Other relative of head	11,854	1,684	31	2,653	36	12,079	1,541	2,449	*9.3	0.1	11,976	1,524	2,461	103	17	-12
Unrelated individuals	11,595	4,092	62	5,551	52	10,805	3,755	5,221	*9.0	-0.2	10,720	3,724	5,084	85	31	137
Age																
14 to 19 years	6,499	867	13	1,299	24	6,612	844	1,230	2.7	*-5.9	6,609	771	1,274	3	73	-44
20 to 24 years	7,777	3,526	66	3,981	45	7,719	3,297	3,713	*6.9	-2.0	7,608	3,282	3,678	111	15	35
25 to 34 years	11,212	5,052	73	5,592	50	10,674	4,514	5,012	*11.9	2.5	10,612	4,532	4,984	62	-18	28
35 to 44 years	8,188	4,705	71	5,541	63	7,878	4,451	5,175	*5.7	-3.1	7,792	4,520	5,197	86	-69	-22
45 to 54 years	8,191	5,066	79	5,855	68	8,334	4,719	5,496	*7.4	-1.6	8,270	4,738	5,487	64	-19	9
55 to 64 years	7,508	3,900	71	5,075	67	7,328	3,623	4,768	*7.6	-1.4	7,289	3,637	4,723	39	-14	45
65 years and over	11,432	2,642	26	3,579	38	11,096	2,387	3,276	*10.7	1.4	11,033	2,375	3,233	63	12	43
Occupation Group of Longest Job[2]																
Total with earnings[3]	42,926	3,953	42	4,717	25	42,854	3,563	4,297	*10.9	1.7	42,650	3,631	4,306	204	-68	-9
White-collar workers	25,854	5,382	48	5,781	36	25,254	4,908	5,285	*9.7	0.5	25,028	4,881	5,278	226	27	7
Professional, technical, and kindred workers	6,388	7,862	117	7,654	83	6,159	7,402	7,080	*6.2	-2.7	6,097	7,405	7,101	62	-3	-21
Managers and administrators, except farm	2,164	6,860	166	7,507	166	1,885	6,690	7,093	2.5	-6.0	1,908	6,754	7,068	-23	-64	25
Sales workers	3,056	1,984	68	2,869	72	3,067	1,850	2,808	7.2	-1.7	2,981	1,963	2,934	86	-113	-126
Clerical and kindred workers	14,246	5,322	51	5,303	38	14,143	4,806	4,798	*10.7	1.5	14,042	4,699	4,740	101	107	58
Blue-collar workers	6,382	4,157	57	4,285	48	6,742	3,865	4,015	*7.6	-1.5	6,700	3,889	4,032	42	-24	-17
Craft and kindred workers	601	4,847	222	5,132	206	607	4,906	5,054	-1.2	-9.5	597	4,885	5,007	10	21	47
Operatives, including transport workers	5,265	4,177	61	4,260	50	5,620	3,869	3,970	*8.0	-1.1	5,607	3,880	3,987	13	-11	-17
Laborers, except farm	517	2,645	343	3,558	188	515	2,330	3,285	13.5	4.0	496	2,436	3,363	19	-106	-78
Service workers	10,118	1,646	45	2,483	32	10,258	1,463	2,249	*12.5	3.1	10,194	1,478	2,305	64	-15	-56
Private household workers	1,926	712	20	857	33	2,076	680	827	4.7	-4.1	2,052	464	985	24	216	-158
Service workers, except private household	8,192	2,164	45	2,865	37	8,182	1,963	2,610	*10.2	1.0	8,142	1,978	2,638	40	-15	-28
Educational Attainment																
Total, 25 years and over	46,531	3,913	31	5,051	25	45,311	3,519	4,665	*11.2	1.9	44,996	3,605	4,642	315	-86	23
Elementary: Total	9,795	2,396	21	2,992	29	10,138	2,240	2,806	*7.0	-2.0	10,064	2,257	2,859	74	-17	-53
Less than 8 years	5,133	2,252	25	2,709	34	5,275	2,132	2,592	*5.6	-3.2	5,259	2,132	2,625	16	-	-33
8 years	4,663	2,641	47	3,303	47	4,864	2,372	3,039	*11.3	2.0	4,805	2,417	3,114	59	-45	75
High school: Total	24,997	4,085	40	4,797	30	24,348	3,773	4,495	*8.3	-0.8	24,229	3,837	4,510	119	-64	-15
1 to 3 years	7,418	3,308	42	3,950	46	7,218	3,129	3,741	*5.7	-3.1	7,239	3,210	3,883	-21	-81	-142
4 years	17,579	4,549	51	5,155	37	17,131	4,203	4,813	*8.2	-0.8	16,990	4,209	4,777	141	-6	36
College: Total	11,739	6,724	96	7,311	66	10,825	6,158	6,787	*9.2	(Z)	10,704	5,974	6,617	121	184	170
1 to 3 years	5,815	5,403	105	6,060	76	5,414	4,969	5,641	*8.7	-0.4	5,367	4,912	5,576	47	57	65
4 years or more	5,924	8,327	127	8,539	104	5,411	7,713	7,933	*8.0	-1.1	5,337	7,395	7,665	74	318	268

- Represents zero.
r Based on revised methodology
Z Less than 0.05 percent.
[1]Spanish origin may be of any race, but the vast majority are white.
[2]Amounts shown are median and mean earnings.
[3]Includes other occupational groupings not shown separately.

Table 9. SELECTED CHARACTERISTICS OF PERSONS 14 YEARS OLD AND OVER WORKING YEAR ROUND FULL TIME—NUMBER WITH INCOME, MEDIAN INCOME, MEAN INCOME, AND STANDARD ERRORS, BY SEX: 1975, 1974 (Revised), AND 1974

(Persons as of March of the following year. An asterisk (*) preceding percent change indicates statistically significant change at the 95 percent confidence level)

Selected characteristics	1975					1974[r]			Percent change (median income)		1974			Difference (1974[r]-1974)		
	Number with income (thousands)	Median income: Value	Median income: Standard error	Mean income: Value	Mean income: Standard error	Number with income (thousands)	Median income	Mean income	Current dollars	In 1975 dollars	Number with income (thousands)	Median income	Mean income	Number with income (thousands)	Median income	Mean income
MALE																
All males	37,278	$13,144	$51	$14,714	$69	37,931	$12,222	$13,757	*7.5	*-1.5	38,915	$12,152	$13,364	-984	$70	$393
Race and Spanish Origin																
White	33,960	13,459	53	15,090	74	34,559	12,527	14,097	*7.4	*-1.6	35,455	12,434	13,708	-896	93	389
Black	2,770	9,848	134	10,203	108	2,852	8,883	9,461	*10.9	1.6	2,927	8,705	9,146	-75	178	315
Spanish origin[1]	1,511	9,588	199	10,741	292	1,565	8,978	10,075	6.8	-2.1	1,642	9,007	9,824	-77	-29	251
Region, Race, and Spanish Origin																
Northeast: All races	8,668	13,468	146	15,116	190	9,036	12,630	14,088	*6.6	-2.3	9,208	12,539	13,693	-172	91	395
White	8,056	13,627	151	15,339	202	8,399	12,777	14,300	*6.7	-2.3	8,575	12,705	13,928	-176	72	372
Black	517	11,504	408	11,896	364	548	10,818	10,891	6.3	-2.6	538	10,305	10,128	10	513	763
Spanish origin[1]	281	9,156	532	10,290	525	304	8,514	9,915	7.5	-1.5	322	8,635	9,726	-18	-121	189
North Central: All races	10,366	13,590	155	14,883	202	10,758	12,705	14,071	*7.0	-2.0	11,059	12,623	13,721	-301	82	350
White	9,791	13,695	160	14,997	211	10,134	12,806	14,227	*6.9	-2.0	10,423	12,738	13,876	-289	68	351
Black	524	11,937	493	12,360	459	592	11,249	11,344	6.1	-2.8	606	10,737	11,026	-14	512	318
Spanish origin[1]	117	11,188	1,199	11,784	1,166	144	10,548	11,640	6.1	-2.8	153	10,383	11,499	-9	165	141
South: All races	11,719	11,864	148	13,710	221	11,648	10,961	12,712	*8.2	-0.8	11,947	10,863	12,322	-299	98	390
White	10,190	12,536	176	14,427	247	10,123	11,559	13,382	*8.5	-0.6	10,377	11,508	12,978	-254	51	404
Black	1,466	7,978	275	8,612	234	1,441	7,634	7,909	4.5	-4.2	1,489	7,411	7,744	-48	223	165
Spanish origin[1]	497	8,780	604	10,452	958	499	8,012	9,578	9.6	0.4	514	7,836	9,127	-15	176	451
West: All races	6,525	14,018	244	15,718	353	6,490	13,121	14,650	*6.8	-2.1	6,700	12,837	14,184	-210	284	466
White	5,923	14,274	258	16,048	382	5,903	13,283	14,809	*7.5	-1.5	6,080	12,979	14,358	-177	304	451
Black	263	11,167	794	11,452	704	271	10,622	10,706	5.1	-3.7	294	10,227	10,576	-23	395	130
Spanish origin[1]	616	10,054	564	10,983	633	618	9,779	10,190	2.8	-5.8	653	9,691	10,028	-35	88	162
Relationship to Family Head																
In families	33,833	13,335	54	14,937	73	34,558	12,440	13,967	*7.2	*-1.8	35,404	12,369	13,609	-846	71	358
Head	30,534	13,891	54	15,596	79	31,222	12,995	14,597	*6.9	*-2.1	31,835	12,896	14,292	-613	99	305
Married, wife present	29,789	13,923	55	15,637	80	30,487	13,039	14,658	*6.8	*-2.2	31,007	12,935	14,347	-520	104	311
Other marital status	745	12,691	330	13,971	454	735	11,324	12,035	*12.1	2.7	828	11,292	12,226	-93	32	-191
Relative of head	3,299	8,229	138	8,843	108	3,336	7,647	8,078	*7.6	-1.4	3,569	7,091	7,514	-233	556	564
Unrelated individuals	3,446	11,297	157	12,524	180	3,373	10,280	11,599	*9.9	0.7	3,511	9,686	10,901	-138	594	698
Age																
14 to 19 years	572	5,657	141	5,810	148	584	5,243	5,352	*7.9	-1.1	696	4,492	4,517	-112	751	835
20 to 24 years	3,303	8,521	95	8,855	94	3,361	8,081	8,309	*5.4	*-3.4	3,567	7,709	7,759	-206	372	550
25 to 34 years	10,256	12,777	81	13,408	83	10,243	11,948	12,539	*6.9	*-2.0	10,492	12,037	12,361	-249	-89	178
35 to 44 years	8,382	14,730	105	16,542	148	8,511	13,855	15,357	*6.3	*-2.6	8,617	13,586	15,002	-106	269	355
45 to 54 years	8,331	14,808	107	16,796	179	8,737	13,778	15,671	*7.5	-1.5	8,758	13,641	15,423	-21	137	248
55 to 64 years	5,518	13,518	145	15,723	210	5,552	12,454	14,786	*8.5	-0.5	5,776	12,454	14,409	-224	-	377
65 years and over	917	11,501	381	14,290	514	942	9,734	13,372	*18.2	8.3	1,009	8,670	11,870	-67	1,064	1,502
Occupation Group of Longest Job[2]																
Total with earnings	37,267	12,758	50	14,029	61	37,916	11,889	13,145	*7.3	*-1.7	38,898	11,835	12,762	-982	54	383
White-collar workers	17,643	14,924	77	17,025	109	17,377	14,253	16,209	*4.7	*-4.1	17,414	13,997	15,796	-37	256	413
Professional, technical, and kindred workers	6,415	16,133	154	18,159	184	6,199	15,296	17,416	*5.5	*-3.4	6,277	14,873	16,679	-78	423	737
Salaried	5,857	15,773	152	17,220	161	5,681	14,921	16,312	*5.7	*-3.1	5,775	14,661	15,908	-94	260	404
Self-employed	558	24,763	1,370	28,018	1,159	518	24,816	29,536	-0.2	-8.6	502	21,501	25,537	16	3,315	3,999
Managers and administrators, except farm	6,477	16,093	169	18,072	198	6,433	15,572	17,447	*3.3	*-5.3	6,371	15,425	17,280	62	147	167
Salaried	5,379	16,814	174	19,108	214	5,287	16,017	18,207	*5.0	*-3.8	5,236	16,079	18,062	51	-62	145
Self-employed	1,097	11,283	355	12,997	468	1,146	12,935	13,940	*-12.8	*-20.1	1,135	12,795	13,674	11	140	266
Sales workers	2,297	14,025	235	15,866	291	2,326	12,591	14,210	*11.4	2.1	2,280	12,523	13,942	46	68	268
Clerical and kindred workers	2,453	12,152	135	12,379	140	2,419	11,661	11,747	*4.2	*-4.5	2,486	11,514	11,397	-67	147	350
Blue-collar workers	15,418	11,686	59	11,830	51	16,246	10,916	11,050	*7.1	*-1.9	16,938	10,868	10,829	-692	48	221
Craft and kindred workers	7,780	12,789	88	12,899	74	8,014	11,966	12,121	*6.9	*-2.1	8,295	12,028	11,995	-281	-62	126
Operatives, incl. transport wkrs.	5,827	11,142	87	11,191	74	6,339	10,310	10,419	*8.1	-1.0	6,567	10,176	10,153	-228	134	266
Operatives, exc. transport wkrs.	3,793	11,034	99	11,024	88	4,187	10,204	10,221	*8.1	-0.9	(NA)	(NA)	(NA)	(X)	(X)	(X)
Transport equip. operatives	2,034	11,406	178	11,501	132	2,152	10,567	10,804	*7.9	-1.1	(NA)	(NA)	(NA)	(X)	(X)	(X)
Laborers, except farm	1,812	9,057	162	9,296	128	1,893	8,499	8,633	*6.6	-2.4	2,076	8,145	8,312	-183	354	321
Service workers	2,636	9,488	120	10,199	124	2,650	8,888	9,399	*6.8	-2.2	2,811	8,612	9,108	-161	276	291
Private household workers	-	(B)	(B)	(B)	(B)	-	(B)	(B)	(B)	(B)	13	(B)	(B)	-13	(B)	(B)
Service workers, except private household	2,636	9,488	120	10,199	124	2,650	8,888	9,399	*6.8	-2.2	2,798	8,638	9,136	-148	250	263
Farm workers	1,570	5,935	229	8,397	361	1,643	5,477	7,495	8.4	-0.7	1,735	5,298	7,201	-92	179	294
Farmers and farm managers	1,128	6,630	372	9,334	485	1,227	5,779	8,133	14.7	5.1	1,266	5,459	7,809	-39	320	324
Farm laborers and supervisors	442	5,292	214	6,004	292	416	5,093	5,614	3.9	-4.8	469	5,097	5,559	-53	-4	55
Educational Attainment																
Total, 25 years and over	33,404	13,821	51	15,446	74	33,986	12,897	14,440	*7.2	*-1.8	34,652	12,786	14,119	-666	111	321
Elementary: Total	4,071	9,628	133	10,062	110	4,573	8,888	9,412	*8.3	-0.7	4,755	8,968	9,611	-182	-80	-199
Less than 8 years	1,979	8,647	164	9,225	146	2,168	7,990	8,540	*8.2	-0.8	2,283	7,912	8,829	-115	78	-289
8 years	2,092	10,600	167	10,853	160	2,405	9,888	10,199	*7.2	-1.8	2,471	9,891	10,334	-66	-3	-135
High school: Total	16,202	13,029	64	13,667	84	16,878	12,239	12,951	*6.5	*-2.5	17,280	12,274	12,876	-402	-35	75
1 to 3 years	4,132	11,511	113	11,960	118	4,533	11,024	11,602	*4.4	*-4.3	4,723	11,225	11,751	-190	-201	-149
4 years	12,070	13,542	72	14,251	104	12,346	12,728	13,447	*6.4	*-2.5	12,557	12,642	13,299	-211	86	148
College: Total	13,131	16,906	108	19,311	144	12,534	15,865	18,279	*6.6	*-2.4	12,618	15,227	17,519	-84	638	760
1 to 3 years	5,297	14,989	134	16,369	179	5,171	13,940	15,403	*7.5	-1.5	5,213	13,718	15,134	-42	222	269
4 years or more	7,834	18,450	150	21,301	204	7,363	17,716	20,299	*4.1	*-4.6	7,405	17,188	19,198	-42	528	1,101

\- Represents zero. B Base less than 75,000. NA Not available. [r]Based on revised methodology X Not applicable.
[1]Spanish origin may be of any race, but the vast majority are white.
[2]Amounts shown are median and mean earnings.

Table 9. SELECTED CHARACTERISTICS OF PERSONS 14 YEARS OLD AND OVER WORKING YEAR ROUND FULL TIME—NUMBER WITH INCOME, MEDIAN INCOME, MEAN INCOME, AND STANDARD ERRORS, BY SEX: 1975, 1974 (Revised), AND 1974—Continued

(Persons as of March of the following year. An asterisk (*) preceding percent change indicates statistically significant change at the 95 percent confidence level)

Selected characteristics	1975					1974r			Percent change (median income)		1974			Difference (1974r-1974)		
	Number with income (thousands)	Median income		Mean income		Number with income (thousands)	Median income	Mean income	Current dollars	In 1975 dollars	Number with income (thousands)	Median income	Mean income	Number with income (thousands)	Median income	Mean income
		Value	Standard error	Value	Standard error											
FEMALE																
All females	17,479	$7,719	$39	$8,262	$41	16,974	$7,174	$7,684	*7.6	-1.4	18,017	$6,957	$7,411	-1,043	$217	$273
Race and Spanish Origin																
White	15,126	7,737	42	8,332	44	14,751	7,235	7,747	*6.9	*-2.0	15,658	7,021	7,482	-907	214	265
Black	2,036	7,392	111	7,549	91	1,913	6,677	7,031	*10.7	1.4	2,042	6,371	6,699	-129	306	332
Spanish origin[1]	629	6,577	211	6,926	189	668	6,043	6,399	8.8	-0.3	732	5,957	6,261	-64	86	138
Region, Race, and Spanish Origin																
Northeast: All races	4,002	8,006	116	8,662	122	3,995	7,614	8,177	*5.1	-3.7	4,249	7,467	7,954	-254	147	223
White	3,513	7,936	120	8,622	131	3,524	7,590	8,192	*4.6	*-4.2	3,753	7,434	7,968	-229	156	224
Black	420	8,269	373	8,511	273	414	7,700	7,761	7.4	-1.6	436	7,627	7,522	-22	73	239
Spanish origin[1]	150	6,920	430	7,297	409	138	6,697	7,223	3.3	-5.3	145	6,588	7,157	-7	109	66
North Central: All races	4,573	7,829	127	8,336	137	4,528	7,300	7,708	*7.2	-1.7	4,788	7,085	7,425	-260	215	283
White	4,139	7,753	134	8,307	146	4,112	7,273	7,707	*6.6	-2.3	4,358	7,058	7,416	-246	215	291
Black	415	8,355	359	8,528	385	401	7,481	7,704	11.7	2.3	416	7,244	7,486	-15	237	218
Spanish origin[1]	41	(B)	(B)	(B)	(B)	(B)	(B)	(B)	(B)	(B)	61	(B)	(B)	-9	(B)	(B)
South: All races	5,837	7,067	116	7,596	109	5,492	6,444	6,974	*9.7	0.5	5,865	6,210	6,689	-373	234	285
White	4,775	7,234	128	7,803	124	4,546	6,610	7,119	*9.4	0.3	4,825	6,393	6,855	-279	217	264
Black	1,035	6,279	280	6,641	208	919	5,777	6,265	8.7	-0.4	1,013	5,440	5,889	-94	337	376
Spanish origin[1]	186	5,793	436	6,098	425	211	5,282	5,718	9.7	0.5	236	5,222	5,606	-25	60	112
West: All races	3,067	8,359	207	8,899	210	2,958	7,811	8,297	7.0	-1.9	3,114	7,594	8,009	-156	217	288
White	2,698	8,370	233	8,931	228	2,569	7,860	8,312	6.5	-2.4	2,722	7,635	8,028	-153	225	284
Black	167	8,350	729	8,329	748	179	7,380	7,766	13.1	3.7	178	7,168	7,451	1	212	315
Spanish origin[1]	251	6,929	630	7,218	561	268	6,254	6,506	10.8	1.5	291	6,162	6,315	-23	92	191
Relationship to Family Head																
In families	14,333	7,555	41	8,055	43	13,927	7,041	7,502	*7.3	*-1.7	14,900	6,835	7,239	-973	206	263
Head	2,338	8,477	117	9,127	109	2,224	7,915	8,573	*7.1	-1.9	2,359	7,608	8,427	-135	307	146
Wife of head	9,909	7,574	50	8,020	52	9,644	7,063	7,430	*7.2	-1.7	10,323	6,900	7,207	-679	163	223
Other relative of head	2,086	6,652	90	7,018	100	2,059	6,283	6,682	*5.9	-3.0	2,217	5,837	6,124	-158	446	558
Unrelated individuals	3,147	8,608	103	9,208	109	3,047	7,812	8,516	*10.2	1.0	3,117	7,612	8,234	-70	200	282
Age																
14 to 19 years	431	4,568	131	4,581	131	381	4,545	4,543	0.5	*-7.9	467	3,875	3,696	-86	670	847
20 to 24 years	2,496	6,598	66	6,735	83	2,548	6,140	6,233	*7.5	-1.5	2,704	5,849	5,827	-156	291	406
25 to 34 years	4,579	8,401	68	8,720	70	4,197	7,742	7,971	*8.5	-0.6	4,411	7,604	7,794	-214	138	177
35 to 44 years	3,336	8,084	114	8,711	97	3,270	7,552	8,082	*7.0	-1.9	3,410	7,418	7,936	-140	134	146
45 to 54 years	3,711	7,980	100	8,646	95	3,751	7,442	8,096	*7.2	-1.8	3,943	7,359	7,894	-192	83	202
55 to 64 years	2,585	7,785	111	8,438	115	2,509	7,374	8,010	*5.6	-3.3	2,716	7,044	7,705	-207	330	305
65 years and over	341	7,250	359	8,047	351	319	7,091	7,757	2.2	-6.3	365	6,085	6,965	-46	1,006	792
Occupation Group of Longest Job[2]																
Total with earnings[3]	17,452	7,504	38	7,930	38	16,945	6,970	7,383	*7.7	-1.4	17,977	6,772	7,108	-1,032	198	275
White-collar workers	12,530	8,288	49	8,712	46	11,949	7,711	8,087	*7.5	-1.5	12,384	7,581	7,872	-435	130	215
Professional, technical, and kindred workers	3,316	10,639	99	10,797	97	3,230	9,747	10,020	*9.2	(Z)	3,390	9,570	9,739	-160	177	281
Managers and administrators, except farm	1,397	9,125	52	9,749	207	1,227	8,698	9,061	4.9	-3.9	1,287	8,603	8,843	-60	95	218
Sales workers	751	5,460	167	6,252	165	714	5,330	6,249	2.4	-6.1	753	5,168	6,158	-39	162	91
Clerical and kindred workers	7,065	7,562	49	7,790	41	6,778	6,946	7,183	*8.9	-0.2	6,954	6,827	6,968	-176	119	215
Blue-collar workers	2,395	6,368	77	6,680	72	2,636	6,028	6,275	*5.6	*-3.2	2,824	5,838	6,024	-188	190	251
Craft and kindred workers	258	7,268	328	7,866	310	327	6,783	7,173	7.2	-1.8	328	6,492	6,824	-1	291	349
Operatives, including transport workers	1,979	6,251	81	6,490	71	2,163	5,940	6,116	*5.2	*-3.6	2,333	5,766	5,892	-170	174	224
Laborers, except farm	158	6,937	370	7,114	336	146	6,132	6,617	13.1	3.7	163	5,891	6,295	-17	241	322
Service workers	2,454	5,204	81	5,328	65	2,281	5,101	5,136	2.0	*-6.5	2,644	5,824	4,861	-363	-723	275
Private household workers	193	2,413	226	2,658	153	174	2,722	2,953	-11.4	-18.8	282	2,676	3,017	-108	46	-64
Service workers, except private household	2,261	5,414	80	5,556	67	2,107	5,249	5,316	3.1	*-5.5	2,362	5,046	5,081	-255	203	235
Educational Attainment																
Total, 25 years and over	14,552	8,117	48	8,633	45	14,045	7,553	8,032	*7.5	-1.5	14,846	7,370	7,816	-801	183	216
Elementary: Total	1,163	5,460	85	5,718	102	1,315	5,378	5,586	1.5	*-7.0	1,455	5,304	5,506	-140	74	80
Less than 8 years	519	5,109	141	5,316	144	616	5,091	5,081	0.4	*-8.1	687	5,022	5,048	-71	69	33
8 years	644	5,691	105	6,042	142	698	5,708	6,032	-0.3	*-8.6	768	5,606	5,915	-70	102	117
High school: Total	8,406	7,444	50	7,785	49	8,234	7,004	7,324	*6.3	*-2.6	8,696	6,881	7,166	-462	123	158
1 to 3 years	1,807	6,355	98	6,728	118	1,831	5,933	6,329	*7.1	-1.9	1,977	5,919	6,373	-146	14	-44
4 years	6,599	7,777	57	8,074	53	6,403	7,320	7,609	*6.2	*-2.7	6,720	7,150	7,399	-317	170	210
College: Total	4,983	10,369	90	10,744	88	4,496	9,488	10,044	*9.3	0.1	4,695	9,271	9,738	-199	217	306
1 to 3 years	2,235	9,126	131	9,344	104	2,032	8,247	8,694	*10.7	1.4	2,116	8,072	8,460	-84	175	234
4 years or more	2,748	11,359	118	11,884	129	2,464	10,525	11,157	*7.9	-1.1	2,579	10,357	10,787	-115	168	370

- Represents zero.
B Base less than 75,000.
NA Not available.
r Based on revised methodology
Z Less than 0.05 percent.
[1] Spanish origin may be of any race, but the vast majority are white.
[2] Amounts shown are median and mean earnings.
[3] Includes other occupational groupings not shown separately.

Table 12. WORK EXPERIENCE AND TOTAL MONEY EARNINGS—CIVILIANS 14 YEARS OLD AND OVER, BY SEX: 1975, 1974 (Revised), AND 1974

(Numbers in thousands. Persons 14 years old and over as of March of the following year)

Total money earnings	Male									Female								
	Total	Worked last year								Total	Worked last year							
		Worked at full-time jobs				Worked at part-time jobs					Worked at full-time jobs				Worked at part-time jobs			
		Total	50 to 52 weeks	27 to 49 weeks	26 weeks or less	Total	50 to 52 weeks	27 to 49 weeks	26 weeks or less		Total	50 to 52 weeks	27 to 49 weeks	26 weeks or less	Total	50 to 52 weeks	27 to 49 weeks	26 weeks or less
1975																		
Total	59,509	51,261	37,316	7,806	6,140	8,247	2,802	1,822	3,623	43,725	28,853	17,738	5,225	5,889	14,872	5,170	3,671	6,030
Without earnings	240	92	50	7	36	148	88	17	42	799	395	285	36	74	404	255	49	99
With earnings	59,268	51,169	37,267	7,799	6,104	8,099	2,714	1,804	3,580	42,926	28,458	17,452	5,189	5,815	14,468	4,914	3,622	5,931
$1 to $999 or loss	6,005	2,286	482	106	1,697	3,719	580	436	2,703	9,084	2,723	261	123	2,339	6,360	762	873	4,725
$1,000 to $1,499	1,712	900	109	113	679	812	245	230	337	2,847	1,256	130	149	977	1,592	429	571	591
$1,500 to $1,999	1,489	863	139	139	586	626	237	234	155	2,090	949	104	206	639	1,141	400	500	241
$2,000 to $2,499	1,762	1,064	215	214	635	698	327	246	126	2,330	1,027	169	283	575	1,303	614	520	169
$2,500 to $2,999	1,191	767	154	173	440	424	255	117	53	1,606	825	166	342	316	781	423	292	66
$3,000 to $3,499	1,334	942	275	298	369	392	242	94	55	2,136	1,249	389	540	320	887	540	285	61
$3,500 to $3,999	947	758	218	305	235	189	114	52	23	1,513	1,044	461	461	123	469	320	131	18
$4,000 to $4,999	2,352	2,027	863	720	445	324	159	117	48	3,417	2,758	1,662	893	203	659	430	205	25
$5,000 to $5,999	2,507	2,296	1,269	710	316	212	142	56	13	3,314	2,813	2,075	604	133	501	381	106	13
$6,000 to $6,999	2,536	2,387	1,529	682	176	149	88	40	20	3,081	2,778	2,224	490	65	303	245	53	4
$7,000 to $7,999	2,934	2,817	2,013	660	144	116	67	37	13	2,681	2,552	2,156	354	43	129	98	27	3
$8,000 to $8,999	2,910	2,843	2,101	638	103	67	38	23	6	2,163	2,059	1,795	240	24	105	85	19	2
$9,000 to $9,999	2,902	2,847	2,295	473	79	56	21	23	11	1,626	1,564	1,393	158	13	62	50	7	4
$10,000 to $11,999	6,149	6,075	5,170	837	68	74	43	23	7	2,330	2,251	2,061	169	21	79	69	10	-
$12,000 to $14,999	8,128	8,058	7,127	859	73	69	40	23	6	1,699	1,646	1,530	100	15	54	44	5	4
$15,000 to $19,999	8,024	7,935	7,304	601	31	89	50	38	2	775	747	674	65	8	28	18	9	2
$20,000 to $24,999	3,162	3,142	3,006	123	14	20	9	9	2	141	137	128	9	-	5	3	-	2
$25,000 and over	3,224	3,161	2,998	149	14	63	56	7	-	93	82	75	6	1	11	3	8	-
Median earnings.......dollars	9,674	10,918	12,758	7,667	2,071	1,204	2,451	2,005	662	3,953	5,853	7,504	4,551	1,291	1,274	2,799	1,867	628
Standard error......dollars	52	46	50	83	39	34	49	57	13	42	37	38	53	24	23	51	36	7
Mean earnings.........dollars	10,579	11,880	14,029	8,701	2,823	2,355	3,838	3,130	841	4,717	6,139	7,930	5,047	1,739	1,920	3,237	2,219	645
Standard error......dollars	49	52	61	93	46	63	143	149	31	25	31	38	51	27	24	47	47	15
1974[r]																		
Total	60,094	51,520	37,996	7,973	5,552	8,575	2,801	1,964	3,811	43,637	28,613	17,237	5,490	5,887	15,024	4,696	3,763	6,565
Without earnings	229	101	80	5	16	128	95	11	23	783	381	292	40	50	402	257	50	94
With earnings	59,866	51,419	37,916	7,967	5,536	8,447	2,706	1,953	3,787	42,854	28,232	16,945	5,450	5,837	14,621	4,439	3,712	6,471
$1 to $999 or loss	6,264	2,281	523	117	1,641	3,983	606	434	2,942	9,940	2,876	179	156	2,542	7,063	841	973	5,250
$1,000 to $1,499	1,856	1,008	159	97	752	848	276	276	296	2,867	1,286	124	186	975	1,582	403	596	582
$1,500 to $1,999	1,543	862	126	166	570	681	230	255	195	2,112	950	105	181	664	1,162	403	517	241
$2,000 to $2,499	1,851	1,071	279	214	578	780	335	297	148	2,480	1,214	214	436	564	1,266	553	534	180
$2,500 to $2,999	1,085	704	149	249	305	381	200	131	51	1,692	904	187	445	272	788	406	315	67
$3,000 to $3,499	1,365	981	297	353	331	383	224	117	44	2,134	1,419	491	643	285	715	425	242	48
$3,500 to $3,999	1,034	837	302	319	216	198	110	62	26	1,596	1,154	543	506	105	442	265	150	28
$4,000 to $4,999	2,330	2,008	998	694	317	322	176	124	21	3,709	3,006	1,851	954	202	703	466	204	32
$5,000 to $5,999	2,813	2,578	1,518	838	221	236	133	78	25	3,610	3,253	2,467	677	109	356	262	85	9
$6,000 to $6,999	2,893	2,791	1,865	751	175	101	64	29	8	3,036	2,855	2,382	424	50	181	134	42	5
$7,000 to $7,999	3,226	3,125	2,343	673	109	101	62	33	5	2,463	2,358	2,038	289	31	105	89	13	3
$8,000 to $8,999	3,306	3,246	2,530	618	98	60	33	23	3	2,022	1,947	1,768	169	11	76	56	20	-
$9,000 to $9,999	3,031	2,990	2,459	487	43	41	22	16	3	1,514	1,449	1,307	131	11	65	53	3	9
$10,000 to $11,999	6,793	6,713	5,726	906	82	80	46	29	4	1,878	1,838	1,682	145	10	40	31	6	3
$12,000 to $14,999	8,071	7,992	7,162	778	50	79	56	22	1	1,122	1,092	1,015	72	4	30	17	7	6
$15,000 to $19,999	6,855	6,787	6,300	458	30	68	44	17	7	536	507	477	27	4	29	20	8	2
$20,000 to $24,999	2,771	2,735	2,606	122	8	36	31	2	4	94	83	79	5	-	10	9	-	1
$25,000 and over	2,779	2,709	2,574	126	9	70	57	10	4	48	40	37	3	-	8	5	-	4
Median earnings.......dollars	9,121	10,366	11,889	7,275	1,829	1,142	2,360	2,021	645	3,563	5,402	6,970	4,180	1,194	1,078	2,523	1,779	617
Standard error......dollars	50	42	42	82	40	34	48	48	13	40	32	34	49	24	24	47	37	10
Mean earnings.........dollars	9,982	11,248	13,145	8,197	2,644	2,278	3,955	2,832	794	4,297	5,638	7,383	4,584	1,556	1,709	2,964	2,026	665
Standard error......dollars	45	48	56	80	49	60	153	103	32	23	29	34	44	22	24	52	34	28

- Represents zero.
[r] Based on revised methodology

Table 12. WORK EXPERIENCE AND TOTAL MONEY EARNINGS—CIVILIANS 14 YEARS OLD AND OVER, BY SEX: 1975, 1974 (Revised), AND 1974—Continued

(Numbers in thousands. Persons 14 years old and over as of March of the following year)

Total money earnings	Male									Female								
	Total	Worked last year								Total	Worked last year							
		Worked at full-time jobs				Worked at part-time jobs					Worked at full-time jobs				Worked at part-time jobs			
		Total	50 to 52 weeks	27 to 49 weeks	26 weeks or less	Total	50 to 52 weeks	27 to 49 weeks	26 weeks or less		Total	50 to 52 weeks	27 to 49 weeks	26 weeks or less	Total	50 to 52 weeks	27 to 49 weeks	26 weeks or less
1974																		
Total	60,102	51,514	38,970	7,382	5,162	8,588	3,079	1,852	3,658	43,694	29,129	18,283	5,343	5,502	14,565	5,048	3,414	6,103
Without earnings	350	123	72	10	41	227	137	14	76	1,044	424	306	37	81	620	403	65	152
With earnings	59,752	51,392	38,898	7,372	5,121	8,361	2,942	1,836	3,582	42,650	28,705	17,977	5,307	5,421	13,945	4,645	3,349	5,951
$1 to $999 or loss	6,313	2,517	749	155	1,611	3,796	773	417	2,606	9,778	3,111	443	261	2,407	6,666	1,125	901	4,638
$1,000 to $1,499	1,846	986	229	110	647	860	314	248	298	2,902	1,335	251	200	884	1,567	477	546	545
$1,500 to $1,999	1,554	882	236	158	488	673	243	236	193	2,115	995	191	217	586	1,120	431	431	259
$2,000 to $2,499	1,833	1,077	358	228	490	757	348	270	138	2,508	1,266	337	432	496	1,242	593	472	178
$2,500 to $2,999	1,134	751	239	234	279	383	181	131	71	1,672	937	284	425	228	735	398	267	70
$3,000 to $3,999	2,423	1,835	753	622	460	589	335	181	72	3,716	2,662	1,188	1,095	379	1,055	635	318	101
$4,000 to $4,999	2,325	1,998	1,105	606	288	326	191	100	35	3,705	3,042	1,983	877	183	662	406	187	68
$5,000 to $5,999	2,839	2,584	1,582	780	223	255	149	77	29	3,590	3,220	2,494	618	108	371	242	105	24
$6,000 to $6,999	2,885	2,749	1,900	700	150	136	67	30	40	3,014	2,831	2,351	419	61	183	126	44	13
$7,000 to $7,999	3,287	3,149	2,406	628	116	138	87	31	20	2,425	2,318	2,049	249	21	107	72	21	13
$8,000 to $9,999	6,448	6,323	5,133	1,036	153	125	71	32	23	3,581	3,448	3,130	288	31	132	81	32	19
$10,000 to $14,999	14,799	14,608	12,958	1,487	164	191	89	69	32	2,940	2,865	2,642	195	29	75	45	18	13
$15,000 to $24,999	9,372	9,281	8,714	519	49	91	66	11	14	655	629	594	28	7	26	13	6	7
$25,000 and over	2,692	2,651	2,535	109	6	41	29	4	9	49	44	41	3	-	5	2	-	3
Median earnings.......dollars	9,064	10,288	11,835	7,148	1,810	1,222	2,203	2,031	687	3,631	5,311	6,772	4,027	1,172	1,097	2,243	1,763	642
Mean earnings.........dollars	9,853	11,081	12,762	7,994	2,758	2,300	3,389	2,743	1,180	4,306	5,570	7,108	4,416	1,603	1,703	2,590	2,082	797

- Represents zero.

Table 14. RESIDENCE, RACE, SEX, AGE, AND EDUCATIONAL ATTAINMENT OF HEAD—HOUSEHOLDS BY TOTAL MONEY INCOME: 1975, 1974 (Revised), AND 1974

(Numbers in thousands. Households as of March of the following year)

Selected characteristics	All house-holds	Under $1,000	$1,000 to $1,999	$2,000 to $2,999	$3,000 to $3,999	$4,000 to $4,999	$5,000 to $5,999	$6,000 to $6,999	$7,000 to $7,999	$8,000 to $8,999	$9,000 to $9,999	$10,000 to $11,999	$12,000 to $14,999	$15,000 to $24,999	$25,000 to $49,999	$50,000 and over	Median income: Value (dollars)	Median income: Standard error (dollars)	Mean income: Value (dollars)	Mean income: Standard error (dollars)
RESIDENCE																				
1975																				
Total	72,867	1,133	1,846	3,923	3,956	3,654	3,461	3,284	3,302	3,253	3,044	6,159	8,779	18,584	7,653	837	11,800	48	13,779	43
Nonfarm	70,365	1,031	1,755	3,778	3,804	3,503	3,329	3,166	3,159	3,124	2,929	5,980	8,499	18,082	7,415	811	11,867	48	13,827	44
Farm	2,503	102	91	145	152	151	132	119	143	129	114	179	280	503	238	26	9,767	319	12,408	313
1974[r]																				
Total	71,163	1,087	2,297	4,068	3,697	3,499	3,461	3,441	3,286	3,280	3,296	6,764	8,863	17,074	6,309	740	11,197	43	13,094	41
Nonfarm	68,432	950	2,186	3,905	3,561	3,347	3,254	3,317	3,156	3,141	3,169	6,536	8,588	16,536	6,080	704	11,264	43	13,131	41
Farm	2,731	136	110	163	136	152	208	124	130	139	127	227	275	538	229	36	9,532	294	12,159	335
1974																				
Total	71,120	1,248	2,397	4,091	3,742	3,547	3,491	3,390	3,348	3,295	3,275	6,785	8,910	16,843	6,088	670	11,101	(1)	12,893	(1)
Nonfarm	68,382	1,110	2,281	3,924	3,600	3,391	3,281	3,276	3,206	3,144	3,153	6,555	8,635	16,312	5,883	630	11,167	(1)	12,928	(1)
Farm	2,738	138	115	167	141	155	210	114	142	151	123	231	274	532	205	40	9,287	(1)	12,041	(1)
RACE OF HEAD																				
1975																				
Total	72,867	1,133	1,846	3,923	3,956	3,654	3,461	3,284	3,302	3,253	3,044	6,159	8,779	18,584	7,653	837	11,800	48	13,779	43
White	64,392	897	1,382	3,075	3,266	3,003	2,971	2,818	2,881	2,849	2,639	5,435	7,964	17,166	7,230	817	12,340	45	14,288	47
Black	7,489	215	449	799	643	623	445	415	381	354	357	658	703	1,143	302	3	7,408	109	9,247	82
Spanish origin[2]	2,948	57	127	181	198	194	200	197	174	169	147	286	345	540	120	14	8,865	196	10,524	187
1974[r]																				
Total	71,163	1,087	2,297	4,068	3,697	3,499	3,461	3,441	3,286	3,280	3,296	6,764	8,863	17,074	6,309	740	11,197	43	13,094	41
White	62,984	861	1,713	3,304	3,007	2,906	2,960	2,901	2,830	2,865	2,899	6,096	8,068	15,833	6,027	713	11,710	44	13,579	44
Black	7,263	214	565	714	640	549	450	519	418	380	357	589	697	988	176	7	6,964	84	8,661	77
Spanish origin[2]	2,897	50	102	180	194	209	204	183	177	164	166	301	359	484	112	10	8,906	195	10,317	168
1974																				
Total	71,120	1,248	2,397	4,091	3,742	3,547	3,491	3,390	3,348	3,295	3,275	6,785	8,910	16,843	6,088	670	11,101	(1)	12,893	(1)
White	62,945	1,001	1,767	3,309	3,045	2,941	2,988	2,853	2,861	2,895	2,889	6,139	8,146	15,651	5,813	646	11,604	(1)	13,384	(1)
Black	7,262	238	603	723	653	560	450	507	426	364	349	577	670	951	181	9	6,795	(1)	8,509	(1)
Spanish origin[2]	2,896	57	107	180	191	206	199	181	177	163	167	287	357	492	122	10	8,920	(1)	10,358	(1)
SEX OF HEAD																				
1975																				
Total	72,867	1,133	1,846	3,923	3,956	3,654	3,461	3,284	3,302	3,253	3,044	6,159	8,779	18,584	7,653	837	11,800	48	13,779	43
Male	55,269	530	579	1,323	1,694	2,063	2,138	2,182	2,267	2,334	2,246	4,939	7,639	17,185	7,336	815	14,023	51	15,873	51
Female	17,598	603	1,267	2,600	2,261	1,591	1,323	1,103	1,035	920	797	1,220	1,140	1,398	317	23	5,361	52	7,201	49
1974[r]																				
Total	71,163	1,087	2,297	4,068	3,697	3,499	3,461	3,441	3,286	3,280	3,296	6,764	8,863	17,074	6,309	740	11,197	43	13,094	41
Male	54,377	514	714	1,398	1,724	1,988	2,269	2,264	2,296	2,463	2,549	5,629	7,879	15,897	6,072	719	13,163	41	15,034	48
Female	16,787	572	1,583	2,670	1,973	1,511	1,193	1,177	991	816	747	1,135	984	1,177	237	21	5,070	56	6,809	50
1974																				
Total	71,120	1,248	2,397	4,091	3,742	3,547	3,491	3,390	3,348	3,295	3,275	6,785	8,910	16,843	6,088	670	11,101	(1)	12,893	(1)
Male	54,348	575	721	1,453	1,762	2,032	2,298	2,243	2,376	2,475	2,572	5,666	7,926	15,731	5,873	644	13,135	(1)	14,810	(1)
Female	16,772	673	1,676	2,638	1,980	1,514	1,193	1,146	972	820	704	1,119	983	1,113	216	26	4,937	(1)	6,683	(1)

[r] Based on revised methodology

[1] Standard errors for mean and median incomes in 1974 are not shown because the differences between the 1974 and 1974[r] estimates are not due to sampling variability but to the revised methodology for processing the income data. In addition, the 1974 and 1975 estimates are not strictly comparable because of the revised methodology.

[2] Spanish origin may be of any race, but the vast majority are white.

Table 14. RESIDENCE, RACE, SEX, AGE, AND EDUCATIONAL ATTAINMENT OF HEAD—HOUSEHOLDS BY TOTAL MONEY INCOME: 1975, 1974 (Revised), AND 1974—Continued

(Numbers in thousands. Households as of March of the following year)

Selected characteristics	All households	Under $1,000	$1,000 to $1,999	$2,000 to $2,999	$3,000 to $3,999	$4,000 to $4,999	$5,000 to $5,999	$6,000 to $6,999	$7,000 to $7,999	$8,000 to $8,999	$9,000 to $9,999	$10,000 to $11,999	$12,000 to $14,999	$15,000 to $24,999	$25,000 to $49,999	$50,000 and over	Median income: Value (dollars)	Median income: Standard error (dollars)	Mean income: Value (dollars)	Mean income: Standard error (dollars)
AGE OF HEAD																				
1975																				
Total	72,867	1,133	1,846	3,923	3,956	3,654	3,461	3,284	3,302	3,253	3,044	6,159	8,779	18,584	7,653	837	11,800	48	13,779	43
14 to 24 years	5,877	170	197	352	415	476	420	420	433	413	375	704	676	740	85	3	8,138	96	8,989	81
25 to 34 years	15,510	191	240	300	407	507	518	586	643	795	799	1,685	2,643	4,936	1,200	60	13,127	67	13,959	68
35 to 44 years	'12,227	135	147	210	303	312	328	391	401	435	421	985	1,732	4,363	1,840	225	15,542	99	17,091	108
45 to 54 years	12,820	203	162	308	297	362	363	390	432	412	418	936	1,456	4,258	2,540	285	16,322	115	18,233	127
55 to 64 years	11,631	264	327	539	536	524	509	508	497	494	476	920	1,341	3,004	1,503	188	12,485	122	14,841	121
65 years and over	14,802	169	773	2,214	1,999	1,473	1,322	990	896	704	553	930	931	1,285	486	76	5,585	47	8,063	69
1974[r]																				
Total	71,163	1,087	2,297	4,068	3,697	3,499	3,461	3,441	3,286	3,280	3,296	6,764	8,863	17,074	6,309	740	11,197	43	13,094	41
14 to 24 years	5,866	173	265	324	383	395	466	436	442	429	460	714	681	647	47	3	8,112	92	8,701	82
25 to 34 years	14,949	178	239	320	438	496	528	617	686	736	910	1,864	2,592	4,394	894	57	12,472	64	13,300	66
35 to 44 years	11,886	171	114	193	272	322	342	363	390	473	485	1,083	1,791	4,230	1,480	177	14,897	107	16,244	99
45 to 54 years	12,901	228	221	291	302	347	391	444	450	442	430	1,117	1,542	4,170	2,282	244	15,438	104	17,244	111
55 to 64 years	11,299	199	374	566	542	505	563	550	526	521	489	1,101	1,397	2,576	1,198	192	11,470	101	13,941	121
65 years and over	14,263	137	1,083	2,375	1,760	1,435	1,172	1,032	792	679	522	886	861	1,056	407	66	5,292	53	7,634	70
1974																				
Total	71,120	1,248	2,397	4,091	3,742	3,547	3,491	3,390	3,348	3,295	3,275	6,785	8,910	16,843	6,088	670	11,101	(1)	12,893	(1)
14 to 24 years	5,834	191	268	322	397	399	446	420	444	445	449	730	662	615	46	1	8,070	(1)	8,554	(1)
25 to 34 years	14,947	210	242	314	468	505	545	605	691	733	889	1,859	2,564	4,393	880	48	12,481	(1)	13,165	(1)
35 to 44 years	11,861	187	128	205	276	337	374	391	400	472	483	1,107	1,790	4,116	1,419	177	14,633	(1)	15,945	(1)
45 to 54 years	12,916	222	232	321	306	343	362	433	496	448	474	1,164	1,583	4,133	2,167	230	15,174	(1)	16,977	(1)
55 to 64 years	11,301	224	359	585	523	530	572	529	513	522	479	1,092	1,444	2,555	1,225	148	11,490	(1)	13,802	(1)
65 years and over	14,260	214	1,168	2,344	1,771	1,432	1,191	1,011	804	674	501	833	867	1,032	352	66	5,168	(1)	7,427	(1)
EDUCATIONAL ATTAINMENT OF HEAD																				
1975																				
Total	72,867	1,133	1,846	3,923	3,956	3,654	3,461	3,284	3,302	3,253	3,044	6,159	8,779	18,584	7,653	837	11,800	48	13,779	43
Elementary: Less than 8 years	8,354	209	613	1,222	980	820	649	542	440	386	339	537	607	823	181	5	5,513	73	7,565	73
8 years	7,102	128	330	732	650	546	537	475	402	331	290	587	720	1,099	265	9	7,378	108	9,394	89
High school: 1 to 3 years	11,146	251	383	814	846	740	625	659	643	547	511	1,011	1,308	2,240	535	32	9,125	106	10,799	80
4 years	24,101	325	322	779	962	950	1,020	1,032	1,174	1,210	1,154	2,299	3,484	7,040	2,224	127	12,647	63	13,905	66
College: 1 to 3 years	10,206	114	119	248	336	358	383	357	358	443	429	960	1,393	3,307	1,296	105	14,049	125	15,550	112
4 years or more	11,959	106	80	127	182	239	245	219	285	337	321	765	1,266	4,077	3,151	560	19,040	135	21,734	145
Total, head 25 years old and over	66,990	963	1,650	3,571	3,541	3,178	3,041	2,865	2,869	2,840	2,669	5,455	8,103	17,844	7,568	834	12,296	46	14,199	46
Elementary: Less than 8 years	8,266	204	603	1,214	972	808	642	539	430	380	336	532	604	814	181	5	5,518	73	7,576	73
8 years	6,947	113	313	716	635	525	531	467	395	319	279	577	711	1,094	263	9	7,440	109	9,470	91
High school: 1 to 3 years	10,178	187	326	705	729	641	555	591	594	490	463	924	1,236	2,178	526	32	9,582	112	11,175	85
4 years	21,441	274	265	655	803	755	837	834	947	1,016	968	1,952	3,137	6,683	2,188	127	13,256	67	14,463	71
College: 1 to 3 years	8,882	98	77	179	250	255	276	264	273	357	336	795	1,230	3,111	1,276	105	15,125	119	16,464	123
4 years or more	11,276	86	66	102	152	194	199	169	230	279	287	674	1,186	3,963	3,131	556	19,721	136	22,410	150
1974[r]																				
Total	71,163	1,087	2,297	4,068	3,697	3,499	3,461	3,441	3,286	3,280	3,296	6,764	8,863	17,074	6,309	740	11,197	43	13,094	41
Elementary: Less than 8 years	8,569	221	811	1,242	947	782	696	582	462	442	327	594	590	743	119	11	5,404	69	7,186	69
8 years	7,324	140	395	799	669	561	542	472	404	367	333	672	693	1,051	222	5	7,211	109	9,003	85
High school: 1 to 3 years	10,903	215	419	815	755	729	651	630	555	578	540	1,100	1,325	2,099	461	31	9,193	100	10,578	79
4 years	23,538	322	441	781	852	903	980	1,058	1,148	1,153	1,270	2,576	3,648	6,511	1,758	134	12,207	58	13,354	60
College: 1 to 3 years	9,680	103	158	298	289	304	366	397	425	422	480	1,008	1,337	2,927	1,056	111	13,207	104	14,903	108
4 years or more	11,150	95	72	133	185	220	226	303	292	318	347	812	1,269	3,744	2,694	449	17,996	135	20,662	145

[r] Based on revised methodology

[1] Standard errors for mean and median incomes in 1974 are not shown because the differences between the 1974 and 1974[r] estimates are not due to sampling variability but to the revised methodology for processing the income data. In addition, the 1974 and 1975 estimates are not strictly comparable because of the revised methodology.

Table 14. RESIDENCE, RACE, SEX, AGE, AND EDUCATIONAL ATTAINMENT OF HEAD—HOUSEHOLDS BY TOTAL MONEY INCOME: 1975, 1974 (Revised), AND 1974—Continued

(Numbers in thousands. Households as of March of the following year)

Selected characteristics	All households	Under $1,000	$1,000 to $1,999	$2,000 to $2,999	$3,000 to $3,999	$4,000 to $4,999	$5,000 to $5,999	$6,000 to $6,999	$7,000 to $7,999	$8,000 to $8,999	$9,000 to $9,999	$10,000 to $11,999	$12,000 to $14,999	$15,000 to $24,999	$25,000 to $49,999	$50,000 and over	Median income: Value (dollars)	Median income: Standard error (dollars)	Mean income: Value (dollars)	Mean income: Standard error (dollars)
EDUCATIONAL ATTAINMENT OF HEAD--Continued																				
1974r--Continued																				
Total, head 25 years old and over	65,298	913	2,031	3,745	3,314	3,105	2,995	3,005	2,844	2,851	2,836	6,049	8,182	16,428	6,262	737	11,639	46	13,488	43
Elementary: Less than 8 years	8,447	212	797	1,229	931	774	682	571	448	439	320	589	588	739	119	11	5,411	69	7,210	69
8 years	7,186	127	381	789	647	545	535	458	398	359	324	666	685	1,046	222	5	7,278	110	9,066	87
High school: 1 to 3 years	9,984	171	348	709	667	641	570	564	499	498	491	1,011	1,276	2,051	458	31	9,663	105	10,943	84
4 years	20,838	249	338	669	711	753	766	847	941	961	1,039	2,213	3,273	6,204	1,741	132	12,761	61	13,919	65
College: 1 to 3 years	8,385	81	113	243	222	218	267	311	317	319	372	853	1,176	2,745	1,035	111	14,162	132	15,725	120
4 years or more	10,457	73	54	106	135	174	174	254	243	274	290	717	1,184	3,643	2,687	447	18,734	134	21,379	150
1974																				
Total	71,120	1,248	2,397	4,091	3,742	3,547	3,491	3,390	3,348	3,295	3,275	6,785	8,910	16,843	6,088	670	11,101	([1])	12,893	([1])
Elementary: Less than 8 years	8,591	248	821	1,249	939	789	700	556	445	441	307	566	605	759	152	14	5,356	([1])	7,278	([1])
8 years	7,321	158	373	779	671	541	504	474	396	381	327	690	724	1,069	225	9	7,407	([1])	9,169	([1])
High school: 1 to 3 years	10,912	230	440	801	715	761	648	585	571	539	546	1,105	1,305	2,149	476	40	9,302	([1])	10,705	([1])
4 years	23,486	374	489	782	904	919	1,007	1,059	1,147	1,160	1,267	2,590	3,591	6,336	1,728	131	12,036	([1])	13,206	([1])
College: 1 to 3 years	9,678	127	171	305	289	316	393	384	462	436	439	961	1,386	2,860	1,050	100	13,205	([1])	14,716	([1])
4 years or more	11,133	112	103	175	222	221	239	332	327	338	388	874	1,299	3,671	2,457	376	17,554	([1])	19,577	([1])
Total, head 25 years old and over	65,286	1,057	2,130	3,769	3,345	3,148	3,045	2,970	2,904	2,849	2,826	6,055	8,248	16,228	6,042	669	11,519	([1])	13,281	([1])
Elementary: Less than 8 years	8,473	238	807	1,234	924	783	684	547	429	437	302	561	604	756	152	14	5,364	([1])	7,307	([1])
8 years	7,184	145	360	768	650	522	500	460	390	373	319	681	719	1,065	223	9	7,477	([1])	9,233	([1])
High school: 1 to 3 years	9,999	174	362	710	628	669	577	518	518	463	492	1,011	1,257	2,105	473	40	9,770	([1])	11,087	([1])
4 years	20,804	299	388	660	756	767	802	852	944	960	1,041	2,218	3,224	6,048	1,714	130	12,664	([1])	13,763	([1])
College: 1 to 3 years	8,389	103	125	251	216	229	293	307	345	327	345	802	1,231	2,684	1,030	100	14,073	([1])	15,521	([1])
4 years or more	10,438	97	86	145	169	178	188	285	279	290	328	782	1,213	3,571	2,450	376	18,300	([1])	20,259	([1])

[r]Based on revised methodology; for details see page 4.

[1]Standard errors for mean and median incomes in 1974 are not shown because the differences between the 1974 and 1974[r] estimates are not due to sampling variability but to the revised methodology for processing the income data. In addition, the 1974 and 1975 estimates are not strictly comparable because of the revised methodology.

Table 17. PERSONS BELOW THE POVERTY LEVEL BY FAMILY STATUS, SEX OF HEAD, RACE, AND SPANISH ORIGIN: 1966, 1969, 1971 AND 1973 TO 1975

(Numbers in thousands. Persons as of March of the following year)

Family status	Number below poverty level							Poverty rate						
	1975	1974r	1974	1973	1971	1969	1966	1975	1974r	1974	1973	1971	1969	1966
ALL PERSONS														
All Races														
Total	25,877	23,370	24,260	22,973	25,559	24,147	28,510	12.3	11.2	11.6	11.1	12.5	12.1	14.7
65 years and over	3,317	3,085	3,308	3,354	4,273	4,895	5,114	15.3	14.6	15.7	16.3	21.6	25.7	28.5
In families	20,789	18,817	19,440	18,299	20,405	19,175	23,809	10.9	9.9	10.2	9.7	10.8	10.4	13.1
Head	5,450	4,922	5,109	4,828	5,303	5,008	5,784	9.7	8.8	9.2	8.8	10.0	9.7	11.8
Related children under 18 years	10,882	9,967	10,196	9,453	10,344	9,501	12,146	16.8	15.1	15.5	14.2	15.1	13.8	17.4
Related children 5 to 17 years	8,034	7,358	7,526	6,880	7,440	6,966	8,646	16.3	14.8	15.1	13.7	14.5	13.5	17.1
Other family members	4,457	3,928	4,135	4,018	4,757	4,667	5,879	6.4	5.7	6.0	5.9	7.2	7.2	9.5
Unrelated individuals	5,088	4,553	4,820	4,674	5,154	4,972	4,701	25.1	24.1	25.5	25.6	31.6	34.0	38.3
65 years and over	2,125	1,975	2,065	2,014	2,566	2,709	2,607	31.0	30.3	31.8	32.0	42.4	47.4	53.8
White														
Total	17,770	15,736	16,290	15,142	17,780	16,659	19,290	9.7	8.6	8.9	8.4	9.9	9.5	11.3
65 years and over	2,634	2,460	2,642	2,698	3,605	4,125	4,357	13.4	12.8	13.8	14.4	19.9	23.7	26.4
In families	13,799	12,181	12,517	11,412	13,566	12,623	15,430	8.3	7.3	7.5	6.9	8.2	7.8	9.7
Head	3,838	3,352	3,482	3,219	3,751	3,575	4,106	7.7	6.8	7.0	6.6	7.9	7.7	9.3
Related children under 18 years	6,748	6,079	6,180	5,462	6,341	5,667	7,204	12.5	11.0	11.2	9.7	10.9	9.7	12.1
Related children 5 to 17 years	4,916	4,408	4,483	3,958	4,544	4,143	5,154	11.9	10.5	10.7	9.3	10.4	9.4	11.9
Other family members	3,213	2,750	2,855	2,731	3,474	3,381	4,120	5.2	4.5	4.7	4.5	5.8	5.8	7.4
Unrelated individuals	3,972	3,555	3,773	3,730	4,214	4,036	3,860	22.7	21.8	23.2	23.7	29.6	32.1	36.1
65 years and over	1,736	1,624	1,697	1,711	2,223	2,328	2,307	28.0	27.6	28.9	29.7	40.3	45.0	51.7
Black and Other Races														
Total	8,107	7,634	7,970	7,831	7,780	7,488	9,220	29.3	28.3	29.5	29.6	30.9	31.0	39.8
65 years and over	683	625	666	656	668	770	757	34.0	32.5	34.7	35.5	38.4	47.4	53.4
In families	6,990	6,636	6,923	6,887	6,839	6,552	8,379	28.0	27.2	28.4	28.8	29.7	29.6	38.9
Head	1,612	1,570	1,627	1,609	1,552	1,433	1,678	25.3	25.1	26.0	26.2	27.4	26.9	33.9
Related children under 18 years	4,134	3,888	4,016	3,991	4,003	3,834	4,942	38.9	37.1	38.4	38.3	38.7	37.7	48.2
Related children 5 to 17 years	3,119	2,949	3,043	2,922	2,896	2,823	3,492	39.4	37.8	39.0	37.9	37.9	37.2	48.6
Other family members	1,244	1,179	1,280	1,287	1,283	1,286	1,759	15.6	15.5	16.7	17.4	18.2	19.4	27.7
Unrelated individuals	1,116	999	1,047	944	941	936	841	40.9	38.0	40.0	37.8	44.9	45.5	53.1
65 years and over	390	351	368	303	343	381	300	59.9	55.9	58.6	57.1	63.6	70.2	77.3
Black														
Total	7,545	7,182	7,467	7,388	7,396	7,095	8,867	31.3	30.3	31.4	31.4	32.5	32.2	41.8
65 years and over	652	591	626	620	623	723	722	36.3	34.3	36.4	37.1	39.3	49.2	55.1
In families	6,533	6,255	6,506	6,560	6,530	6,245	8,090	30.1	29.3	30.3	30.8	31.2	30.9	40.9
Head	1,513	1,479	1,530	1,527	1,484	1,366	1,620	27.1	26.9	27.8	28.1	28.8	27.9	35.5
Related children under 18 years	3,884	3,713	3,819	3,822	3,836	3,677	4,774	41.4	39.6	40.7	40.6	40.7	39.6	50.6
Related children 5 to 17 years	2,924	2,820	2,901	2,793	2,789	2,699	3,369	41.6	40.3	41.4	39.9	40.2	38.9	51.1
Other family members	1,136	1,063	1,157	1,211	1,210	1,202	1,696	16.9	16.4	17.6	18.7	19.1	20.0	29.4
Unrelated individuals	1,011	927	961	828	866	850	777	42.1	39.3	41.0	37.9	46.0	46.7	54.4
65 years and over	366	335	349	289	318	355	286	61.1	58.0	60.5	59.2	64.4	73.2	79.9
Spanish Origin														
Total	2,991	2,575	2,601	2,366	(NA)	(NA)	(NA)	26.9	23.0	23.2	21.9	(NA)	(NA)	(NA)
65 years and over	137	117	116	95	(NA)	(NA)	(NA)	32.7	28.8	28.5	24.9	(NA)	(NA)	(NA)
In families	2,755	2,374	2,394	2,209	(NA)	(NA)	(NA)	26.3	22.4	22.6	26.5	(NA)	(NA)	(NA)
Head	627	526	527	468	(NA)	(NA)	(NA)	25.1	21.2	21.3	19.8	(NA)	(NA)	(NA)
Related children under 18 years	1,619	1,414	1,433	1,364	(NA)	(NA)	(NA)	33.1	28.6	29.0	27.8	(NA)	(NA)	(NA)
Related children 5 to 17 years	(NA)	(NA)	(NA)	(NA)	(NA)	(NA)	(NA)	(NA)	(NA)	(NA)	(NA)	(NA)	(NA)	(NA)
Other family members	508	435	434	377	(NA)	(NA)	(NA)	16.5	13.7	13.7	12.6	(NA)	(NA)	(NA)
Unrelated individuals	236	201	207	157	(NA)	(NA)	(NA)	36.6	32.6	33.7	29.9	(NA)	(NA)	(NA)
65 years and over	56	47	48	42	(NA)	(NA)	(NA)	52.5	52.8	53.2	51.0	(NA)	(NA)	(NA)
PERSONS IN FAMILIES WITH MALE HEAD AND MALE UNRELATED INDIVIDUALS														
All Races														
Total	13,609	11,901	12,484	11,616	14,151	13,735	18,260	7.8	6.8	7.1	6.6	8.1	8.0	10.8
65 years and over	1,411	1,290	1,425	1,462	1,828	2,373	2,710	9.8	9.0	10.0	10.5	13.6	18.3	21.7
In families	11,943	10,355	10,877	10,121	12,608	12,296	16,948	7.1	6.2	6.5	6.0	7.5	7.4	10.3
Head	3,020	2,598	2,757	2,635	3,203	3,181	4,063	6.2	5.4	5.7	5.5	6.8	6.9	9.3
Related children under 18 years	5,284	4,605	4,809	4,282	5,494	5,253	7,884	9.8	8.3	8.7	7.6	9.3	8.6	12.6
Related children 5 to 17 years	3,844	3,396	3,546	3,126	3,928	3,823	5,504	9.4	8.2	8.5	7.4	8.9	8.4	12.3
Other family members	3,638	3,151	3,310	3,204	3,910	3,862	5,001	5.7	5.0	5.2	5.1	6.3	6.4	8.7
Unrelated individuals	1,667	1,547	1,607	1,495	1,543	1,439	1,312	19.9	19.5	20.4	19.8	23.9	26.2	29.3
65 years and over	410	378	390	391	445	575	563	27.7	25.8	26.8	27.1	32.6	40.0	44.5
White														
Total	10,446	9,063	9,437	8,500	10,635	10,128	12,779	6.6	5.8	6.0	5.4	6.8	6.5	8.5
65 years and over	1,106	1,025	1,133	1,134	1,494	1,980	2,258	8.4	7.8	8.6	8.9	12.1	16.6	19.6
In families	9,221	7,902	8,238	7,409	9,468	9,046	11,784	6.1	5.2	5.5	4.9	6.2	6.0	8.0
Head	2,444	2,063	2,185	2,029	2,560	2,506	3,070	5.5	4.7	4.9	4.6	5.9	6.0	7.7
Related children under 18 years	3,934	3,396	3,500	3,001	3,889	3,598	5,092	8.2	6.9	7.1	6.0	7.4	6.7	9.2
Related children 5 to 17 years	2,816	2,475	2,549	2,171	2,750	2,624	3,550	7.8	6.7	6.9	5.7	7.0	6.5	8.9
Other family members	2,843	2,444	2,553	2,379	3,019	2,941	3,622	4.9	4.3	4.5	4.2	5.4	5.4	7.0
Unrelated individuals	1,225	1,161	1,200	1,091	1,167	1,083	995	17.4	17.7	18.3	17.5	21.5	24.1	26.6
65 years and over	299	294	292	287	338	449	460	23.8	23.7	23.7	22.9	28.8	36.4	41.3

Note: Data for years 1966 to 1974 are shown for persons by race of head, while data for 1974r and 1975 are shown for persons by their own race.

NA Not available. r Based on revised methodology

Table 17. PERSONS BELOW THE POVERTY LEVEL BY FAMILY STATUS, SEX OF HEAD, RACE, AND SPANISH ORIGIN: 1966, 1969, 1971 AND 1973 TO 1975–Continued

(Numbers in thousands. Persons as of March of the following year)

Family status	Number below poverty level							Poverty rate						
	1975	1974[r]	1974	1973	1971	1969	1966	1975	1974[r]	1974	1973	1971	1969	1966
PERSONS IN FAMILIES WITH MALE HEAD AND MALE UNRELATED INDIVIDUALS--Continued														
Black														
Total	2,761	2,477	2,671	2,824	3,267	3,328	5,210	18.2	16.5	17.7	18.5	21.2	21.5	33.4
65 years and over	292	241	261	299	296	366	420	27.6	23.6	25.7	29.6	30.0	40.2	49.7
In families	2,365	2,140	2,320	2,496	2,943	3,020	4,930	16.9	15.4	16.6	17.7	20.3	20.6	33.0
Head	509	470	506	553	605	629	946	14.2	13.2	14.2	15.4	17.2	17.9	27.6
Related children under 18 years	1,161	1,062	1,151	1,188	1,507	1,539	2,667	22.1	20.0	21.7	21.7	25.5	25.0	39.9
Related children 5 to 17 years	887	814	885	895	1,107	1,109	1,861	22.6	20.8	22.7	22.0	25.3	24.4	40.7
Other family members	694	608	663	756	831	852	1,317	13.4	12.2	13.0	14.9	16.4	17.1	27.3
Unrelated individuals	396	338	351	328	324	308	280	34.0	28.5	29.9	29.1	36.5	36.5	43.2
65 years and over	103	75	86	97	88	112	93	51.7	38.4	44.1	56.8	54.7	68.1	72.7
PERSONS IN FAMILIES WITH FEMALE HEAD AND FEMALE UNRELATED INDIVIDUALS														
All Races														
Total	12,268	11,469	11,775	11,357	11,409	10,412	10,250	34.6	33.6	34.4	34.9	38.0	38.4	41.0
65 years and over	1,905	1,795	1,883	1,893	2,449	2,522	2,404	26.4	26.3	27.6	28.4	38.4	41.4	44.2
In families	8,846	8,462	8,563	8,178	7,797	6,879	6,861	37.5	36.5	36.8	37.5	38.7	38.2	39.8
Head	2,430	2,324	2,351	2,193	2,100	1,827	1,721	32.5	32.1	32.5	32.2	33.9	32.7	33.1
Related children under 18 years	5,597	5,361	5,387	5,171	4,850	4,247	4,262	52.7	51.5	51.5	52.1	53.1	54.4	58.2
Related children 5 to 17 years	4,190	3,962	3,980	3,754	3,513	3,143	3,142	50.0	48.7	48.6	48.2	49.7	51.2	55.1
Other family members	819	777	825	814	847	805	878	15.0	14.1	14.9	16.0	17.5	17.5	18.6
Unrelated individuals	3,422	3,007	3,212	3,179	3,611	3,532	3,389	28.9	27.3	29.3	29.7	36.6	38.7	43.5
65 years and over	1,716	1,597	1,675	1,624	2,122	2,134	2,044	31.9	31.7	33.2	33.5	45.2	49.9	57.0
White														
Total	7,324	6,673	6,852	6,642	7,146	6,531	6,511	28.1	26.5	27.2	27.9	32.1	32.1	33.9
65 years and over	1,527	1,435	1,508	1,564	2,112	2,144	2,099	23.7	23.6	24.8	26.3	36.8	38.9	42.3
In families	4,577	4,278	4,279	4,003	4,099	3,577	3,646	29.4	27.7	27.6	28.0	30.4	29.1	29.7
Head	1,394	1,289	1,297	1,190	1,191	1,069	1,036	25.9	24.8	24.9	24.5	26.5	25.7	25.7
Related children under 18 years	2,813	2,683	2,680	2,461	2,452	2,068	2,112	44.2	42.9	42.6	42.1	44.6	45.2	46.9
Related children 5 to 17 years	2,100	1,933	1,934	1,787	1,794	1,519	1,604	40.5	38.8	38.5	37.8	40.6	41.2	44.2
Other family members	370	306	302	352	456	440	498	9.7	7.7	7.6	9.8	13.0	12.4	13.4
Unrelated individuals	2,747	2,394	2,573	2,639	3,047	2,953	2,865	26.3	24.6	26.5	27.7	34.7	36.6	41.2
65 years and over	1,437	1,330	1,405	1,423	1,885	1,878	1,847	29.1	28.7	30.3	31.6	43.4	47.7	55.2
Black														
Total	4,784	4,705	4,796	4,564	4,129	3,766	3,657	53.6	54.3	55.4	55.4	55.8	57.8	65.1
65 years and over	360	350	365	321	328	358	302	48.7	50.0	51.7	48.4	54.7	64.0	64.8
In families	4,168	4,116	4,186	4,064	3,587	3,225	3,160	54.3	55.0	55.9	56.5	56.1	58.2	65.3
Head	1,004	1,010	1,024	974	879	737	674	50.1	52.2	52.8	52.7	53.5	53.3	59.2
Related children under 18 years	2,724	2,651	2,668	2,635	2,329	2,137	2,107	66.0	65.0	65.7	67.2	65.5	68.2	76.6
Related children 5 to 17 years	2,036	2,006	2,016	1,898	1,881	1,592	1,508	65.8	65.0	65.2	64.8	66.6	66.7	74.7
Other family members	441	455	494	455	379	350	379	28.5	31.0	33.3	32.2	30.2	34.4	39.9
Unrelated individuals	616	589	611	500	542	541	497	49.7	50.1	51.9	47.3	54.4	55.5	63.7
65 years and over	263	260	262	193	230	243	193	65.7	68.1	68.8	60.5	68.9	75.7	83.9

Note: Data for years 1966 to 1974 are shown for persons by race of head, while data for 1974[r] and 1975 are shown for persons by their own race.

[r] Based on revised methodology

TABLE 19. SELECTED CHARACTERISTICS OF FAMILES BELOW THE POVERTY LEVEL BY SEX AND RACE OF HEAD: 1975, 1974 (REVISED), AND 1974

(Numbers in thousands. Families as of March of the following year)

Selected characteristics	All races			White			Black		
	1975	1974[r]	1974	1975	1974[r]	1974	1975	1974[r]	1974
All Families									
Total	5,450	4,922	5,109	3,838	3,352	3,482	1,513	1,479	1,530
Age of Head									
14 to 24 years	850	724	733	577	463	470	264	256	255
25 to 44 years	2,466	2,249	2,333	1,693	1,492	1,547	721	711	741
45 to 64 years	1,406	1,264	1,282	1,041	896	898	330	344	357
65 years and over	728	686	760	528	502	567	197	168	177
Size of Family									
2 persons	1,784	1,622	1,705	1,367	1,228	1,315	393	374	373
3 persons	1,074	936	971	801	650	672	257	271	281
4 persons	939	819	844	636	557	562	290	240	258
5 persons	614	605	616	442	386	391	154	201	207
6 persons	451	394	412	271	224	234	169	163	168
7 persons or more	589	545	560	321	307	308	250	231	243
Number of Related Children Under 18 Years									
No children	1,278	1,134	1,234	1,061	922	1,015	199	186	198
1 and 2 children	2,263	2,019	2,064	1,612	1,364	1,383	620	622	640
3 and 4 children	1,309	1,208	1,246	863	765	792	413	418	426
5 children or more	599	561	565	302	300	292	282	254	266
Educational Attainment of Head									
Total, 25 years old and over	4,600	4,198	4,376	3,261	2,889	3,012	1,249	1,223	1,275
Elementary: Total	1,922	1,837	1,873	1,365	1,283	1,294	530	523	547
Less than 8 years	1,293	1,232	1,275	877	801	817	397	415	441
8 years	629	605	598	488	482	477	133	108	106
High school: Total	2,208	1,970	2,036	1,495	1,286	1,330	669	651	668
1 to 3 years	1,118	990	1,011	708	578	585	393	397	411
4 years	1,090	980	1,026	787	708	745	276	254	257
College: Total	470	392	466	401	320	388	49	49	59
Number of Workers[1]									
No workers	2,174	1,904	1,937	1,456	1,242	1,288	688	637	618
1 worker	2,069	1,893	2,127	1,472	1,308	1,470	567	555	622
2 workers	883	841	814	673	614	590	180	203	202
3 workers or more	295	257	230	209	166	133	77	81	88
Employment Status of Head									
Employed	2,154	1,900	2,048	1,628	1,412	1,508	474	446	502
Unemployed	505	443	449	361	308	305	135	127	137
Not in labor force	2,761	2,553	2,584	1,821	1,610	1,646	902	903	888
In Armed Forces	30	27	27	28	22	23	2	3	3
Work Experience of Head									
Head worked last year	2,745	2,553	2,691	2,051	1,850	1,935	634	654	712
Worked 50 to 52 weeks	1,070	996	1,180	826	764	896	225	218	271
Full time	866	812	980	693	655	772	155	146	196
Worked 1 to 49 weeks	1,675	1,557	1,511	1,225	1,085	1,040	409	436	440
Reason for working part year:									
Unemployed	785	627	643	588	448	452	176	172	177
Other	890	931	868	637	638	587	234	263	263
Head did not work last year	2,675	2,343	2,390	1,760	1,480	1,524	877	823	815
Head in Armed Forces	30	27	27	28	22	23	2	3	3
Occupation of Longest Job of Head									
Head worked last year	2,745	2,553	2,691	2,051	1,850	1,935	634	654	712
Professional and managerial workers	303	237	254	263	202	221	30	21	24
Clerical and sales workers	297	261	290	235	193	214	60	64	73
Craft and kindred workers	384	327	320	329	266	255	48	53	59
Operatives, including transport workers	513	502	523	382	345	363	121	145	148
Service workers, including private household	617	574	611	344	311	321	254	256	282
Laborers, except farm	244	231	244	182	172	178	58	56	63
Farmers and farm laborers	386	423	450	316	361	382	62	57	63
Families With A Male Head									
Total	3,020	2,598	2,757	2,444	2,063	2,185	509	470	506
Age of Head									
14 to 24 years	387	272	287	319	216	229	64	53	55
25 to 44 years	1,093	957	1,021	889	756	801	166	166	189
45 to 64 years	956	822	833	776	660	661	156	146	154
65 years and over	585	548	616	460	431	493	122	104	108

[r]Based on revised methodology

[1]Includes families with civilian heads only for 1974[r] and 1975. In addition, figures for 1974 are not strictly comparable to figures for 1974[r] and 1975 because unpaid family workers are not classified as workers in the 1974 figures but are classified as workers in the 1974[r] and 1975 figures.

TABLE 19. SELECTED CHARACTERISTICS OF FAMILIES BELOW THE POVERTY LEVEL BY SEX AND RACE OF HEAD: 1975, 1974 (REVISED), AND 1974—Continued

(Numbers in thousands. Families as of March of the following year)

Selected characteristics	All races			White			Black		
	1975	1974[r]	1974	1975	1974[r]	1974	1975	1974[r]	1974
Families With A Male Head--Continued									
Size of Family									
2 persons	1,025	881	957	884	748	829	127	121	121
3 persons	457	407	425	365	330	338	84	67	74
4 persons	478	398	421	399	313	323	73	71	85
5 persons	402	324	339	330	258	263	55	52	61
6 persons	278	228	245	211	167	181	58	53	55
7 persons or more	380	361	370	253	246	251	113	105	111
Number of Related Children Under 18 Years									
No children	1,100	957	1,041	940	814	895	144	125	133
1 and 2 children	950	801	833	767	626	640	168	154	169
3 and 4 children	671	554	594	538	427	456	107	109	115
5 children or more	300	286	290	199	196	194	90	83	89
Educational Attainment of Head									
Total, 25 years old and over	2,633	2,327	2,471	2,125	1,847	1,956	445	416	451
Elementary: Total	1,284	1,218	1,226	994	917	912	274	272	288
Less than 8 years	891	820	844	652	571	580	227	232	250
8 years	393	398	382	342	346	332	47	40	38
High school: Total	1,013	861	933	831	719	773	151	123	139
1 to 3 years	497	405	423	410	313	321	80	81	91
4 years	516	456	511	421	406	452	71	42	48
College: Total	336	248	311	301	210	271	20	21	23
Number of Workers[1]									
No workers	893	716	765	717	566	611	164	133	131
1 worker	1,150	991	1,174	946	805	949	181	162	201
2 workers	715	669	646	575	537	516	115	114	116
3 workers or more	232	196	173	179	132	108	49	57	57
Employment Status of Head									
Employed	1,526	1,319	1,416	1,256	1,078	1,145	221	209	242
Unemployed	289	234	240	244	185	188	41	42	45
Not in labor force	1,176	1,019	1,074	917	777	828	246	216	217
In Armed Forces	30	27	27	28	22	23	2	3	3
Work Experience of Head									
Head worked last year	1,857	1,645	1,745	1,533	1,339	1,409	272	268	303
Worked 50 to 52 weeks	847	777	884	716	654	743	113	113	131
Full time	731	687	785	618	581	663	95	98	113
Worked 1 to 49 weeks	1,010	868	861	817	685	666	159	155	173
Reason for working part year:									
Unemployed	570	444	446	473	363	357	79	75	78
Other	439	423	414	344	323	308	80	80	95
Head did not work last year	1,133	927	986	884	701	753	236	198	200
Head in Armed Forces	30	27	27	28	22	23	2	3	3
Occupation of Longest Job of Head									
Head worked last year	1,857	1,645	1,745	1,533	1,339	1,409	272	268	304
Professional and managerial workers	264	184	205	232	163	184	22	10	12
Clerical and sales workers	104	82	96	98	75	82	3	6	14
Craft and kindred workers	377	319	312	328	261	250	42	50	56
Operatives, including transport workers	346	313	326	284	237	246	54	66	70
Service workers, including private household	174	130	149	117	92	104	44	37	43
Laborers, except farm	219	221	236	168	169	176	48	50	57
Farmers and farm laborers	373	397	423	307	342	366	57	49	51
Families With A Female Head									
Total	2,430	2,324	2,351	1,394	1,289	1,297	1,004	1,010	1,024
Age of Head									
14 to 24 years	463	452	446	257	247	241	200	203	200
25 to 44 years	1,373	1,291	1,312	803	735	746	556	545	553
45 to 64 years	450	443	449	265	236	237	173	197	202
65 years and over	143	137	144	68	72	74	75	65	69
Size of Family									
2 persons	759	742	748	482	480	486	266	253	252
3 persons	617	529	546	435	320	334	173	205	207
4 persons	461	421	423	237	244	239	217	169	173
5 persons	212	281	277	112	128	128	99	149	146
6 persons	173	166	167	59	56	53	111	110	113
7 persons or more	208	185	190	68	60	57	137	124	132

[r]Based on revised methodology

[1]Includes families with civilian heads only for 1974[r] and 1975. In addition, figures for 1974 are not strictly comparable to figures for 1974[r] and 1975 because unpaid family workers are not classified as workers in the 1974 figures but are classified as workers in the 1974[r] and 1975 figures.

TABLE 19. SELECTED CHARACTERISTICS OF FAMILIES BELOW THE POVERTY LEVEL BY SEX AND RACE OF HEAD: 1975, 1974 (REVISED), AND 1974—Continued

(Numbers in thousands. Families as of March of the following year)

Selected characteristics	All races			White			Black		
	1975	1974[r]	1974	1975	1974[r]	1974	1975	1974[r]	1974
Families With A Female Head--Continued									
Number of Related Children Under 18 Years									
No children	178	177	193	122	109	120	55	61	65
1 and 2 children	1,315	1,218	1,231	844	738	743	451	468	471
3 and 4 children	637	653	652	325	338	336	305	309	311
5 children or more	300	276	275	103	103	98	193	171	177
Educational Attainment of Head									
Total, 25 years old and over	1,967	1,872	1,905	1,136	1,043	1,056	804	807	824
Elementary: Total	638	619	647	371	364	382	256	251	259
Less than 8 years	402	412	431	225	229	237	170	183	191
8 years	236	207	216	146	135	145	86	68	68
High school: Total	1,196	1,109	1,103	665	568	557	518	527	529
1 to 3 years	621	585	588	298	265	264	313	316	320
4 years	575	524	515	367	303	293	205	211	209
College: Total	134	144	155	101	110	117	29	29	36
Number of Workers[1]									
No workers	1,281	1,188	1,172	738	676	677	524	504	486
1 worker	919	902	953	526	503	521	386	393	421
2 workers	168	172	168	99	76	74	66	89	86
3 workers or more	62	61	58	30	34	25	28	24	30
Employment Status of Head									
Employed	629	581	632	372	334	363	253	236	260
Unemployed	216	208	209	117	123	117	95	86	92
Not in labor force	1,585	1,534	1,510	905	832	818	656	688	671
Work Experience of Head									
Head worked last year	887	908	947	518	510	526	362	385	408
Worked 50 to 52 weeks	223	219	296	110	110	152	112	105	141
Full time	135	124	195	75	74	109	60	48	83
Worked 1 to 49 weeks	664	689	650	408	400	374	250	281	267
Reason for working part year:									
Unemployed	214	182	196	115	85	95	97	97	99
Other	449	507	454	294	315	279	154	184	169
Head did not work last year	1,543	1,416	1,405	876	779	772	641	624	615
Occupation of Longest Job of Head									
Head worked last year	887	908	947	518	510	526	362	385	408
Professional and managerial workers	39	53	49	31	39	37	8	11	12
Clerical and sales workers	194	180	194	136	118	132	57	57	59
Craft and kindred workers	7	8	8	1	5	5	5	3	3
Operatives, including transport workers	167	189	197	98	107	117	67	80	78
Service workers, including private household	443	443	462	228	220	217	210	221	239
Laborers, except farm	25	9	8	15	3	2	10	6	6
Farmers and farm laborers	14	26	27	9	18	16	4	8	12
PERCENT BELOW POVERTY LEVEL									
All Families									
Total	9.7	8.8	9.2	7.7	6.8	7.0	27.1	26.9	27.8
Age of Head									
14 to 24 years	21.0	17.1	17.3	16.9	12.9	13.2	45.7	42.0	41.8
25 to 44 years	10.3	9.6	9.9	8.1	7.2	7.5	27.6	27.8	28.9
45 to 64 years	7.0	6.4	6.4	5.8	5.0	5.0	19.1	20.5	21.2
65 years and over	8.9	8.5	9.5	7.1	6.9	7.7	29.3	26.1	27.7
Size of Family									
2 persons	8.4	7.8	8.2	7.1	6.5	6.9	22.6	23.1	23.0
3 persons	8.8	7.7	8.0	7.4	6.1	6.3	20.9	21.8	22.5
4 persons	8.3	7.4	7.7	6.3	5.7	5.7	27.9	24.6	26.4
5 persons	9.9	9.6	9.8	8.1	6.9	7.0	26.7	31.1	31.9
6 persons	15.2	13.2	13.7	10.9	9.0	9.4	39.8	35.6	37.4
7 persons or more	25.6	22.3	23.0	19.3	16.6	16.8	43.8	41.9	43.6

[r]Based on revised methodology

[1]Includes families with civilian heads only for 1974[r] and 1975. In addition, figures for 1974 are not strictly comparable to figures for 1974[r] and 1975 because unpaid family workers are not classified as workers in the 1974 figures but are classified as workers in the 1974[r] and 1975 figures.

TABLE 19. SELECTED CHARACTERISTICS OF FAMILIES BELOW THE POVERTY LEVEL BY SEX AND RACE OF HEAD: 1975, 1974 (REVISED), AND 1974—Continued

(Numbers in thousands. Families as of March of the following year)

Selected characteristics	All races			White			Black		
	1975	1974[r]	1974	1975	1974[r]	1974	1975	1974[r]	1974
PERCENT BELOW POVERTY LEVEL--Continued									
All Families--Continued									
Number of Related Children Under 18 Years									
No children	5.1	4.6	5.1	4.6	4.1	4.5	11.7	11.8	12.5
1 and 2 children	10.2	9.3	9.5	8.3	7.2	7.3	25.7	26.3	27.0
3 and 4 children	17.1	15.4	15.9	13.2	11.5	11.9	41.5	39.0	39.8
5 children or more	37.8	32.2	32.7	27.9	24.3	23.9	59.7	52.9	55.2
Educational Attainment of Head									
Total, 25 years old and over	8.8	8.2	8.5	7.0	6.3	6.6	24.9	25.1	26.1
Elementary: Total	17.9	16.4	16.7	15.3	13.6	13.7	31.2	31.0	32.4
Less than 8 years	22.4	20.6	21.3	19.6	17.3	17.6	32.3	32.6	34.7
8 years	12.6	11.5	11.4	10.9	10.1	10.0	28.5	26.0	25.6
High school: Total	8.7	7.8	8.1	6.6	5.7	5.9	26.2	26.1	26.7
1 to 3 years	14.0	12.5	12.7	10.5	8.6	8.7	34.7	34.3	35.3
4 years	6.2	5.7	6.0	4.9	4.5	4.8	19.4	19.1	19.2
College: Total	3.0	2.6	3.1	2.7	2.3	2.8	6.5	7.0	8.4
Number of Workers[1]									
No workers	31.1	29.8	31.3	24.6	22.9	24.7	68.9	68.2	67.6
1 worker	10.9	10.3	10.9	8.8	8.0	8.5	29.1	30.2	32.1
2 workers	4.1	3.9	3.7	3.5	3.1	3.0	9.5	10.3	10.3
3 workers or more	3.7	3.2	2.9	2.9	2.3	1.9	11.4	12.1	12.9
Employment Status of Head									
Employed	5.2	4.7	5.1	4.4	3.9	4.1	13.9	13.5	15.1
Unemployed	21.2	15.9	16.1	18.4	13.3	13.2	35.8	28.2	30.3
Not in labor force	23.0	22.1	22.3	18.0	16.5	16.8	52.5	55.1	53.9
In Armed Forces	3.9	2.9	2.9	4.0	2.8	2.8	2.2	3.4	3.4
Work Experience of Head									
Head worked last year	6.1	5.7	6.0	5.1	4.6	4.8	16.1	16.4	17.8
Worked 50 to 52 weeks	3.1	2.9	3.3	2.7	2.4	2.8	8.4	8.1	9.8
Full time	2.6	2.4	2.9	2.3	2.1	2.5	6.2	5.9	7.7
Worked 1 to 49 weeks	15.7	15.4	15.8	13.3	12.5	12.7	32.1	33.4	35.6
Reason for working part year:									
Unemployed	14.1	14.0	14.9	12.4	11.8	12.3	24.8	28.4	30.7
Other	17.5	16.5	16.6	14.3	13.1	13.0	41.2	37.6	39.9
Head did not work last year	25.2	23.9	24.8	19.8	17.9	18.8	55.9	58.1	57.4
Head in Armed Forces	3.9	2.9	2.9	4.1	2.7	2.8	(B)	3.5	3.4
Occupation of Longest Job of Head									
Head worked last year	6.1	5.7	6.0	5.1	4.6	4.8	16.1	16.4	17.8
Professional and managerial workers	2.2	1.8	1.9	2.0	1.6	1.8	7.0	5.3	5.8
Clerical and sales workers	4.7	4.2	4.6	4.1	3.4	3.8	11.5	13.7	15.3
Craft and kindred workers	4.1	3.4	3.3	3.7	3.0	2.8	9.2	9.5	10.8
Operatives, including transport workers	6.7	6.4	6.7	5.8	5.1	5.4	12.1	13.9	14.4
Service workers, including private household	15.9	14.7	15.4	12.0	10.7	10.8	27.2	27.5	30.0
Laborers, except farm	10.7	9.9	10.3	10.0	9.4	9.5	14.3	11.9	13.7
Farmers and farm laborers	21.8	22.6	22.8	19.5	20.9	20.9	48.4	47.1	46.0
Families With A Male Head									
Total	6.2	5.4	5.7	5.5	4.7	4.9	14.2	13.2	14.2
Age of Head									
14 to 24 years	11.7	7.8	8.2	10.7	6.9	7.3	22.5	16.9	17.6
25 to 44 years	5.3	4.7	5.0	4.8	4.1	4.3	10.6	10.5	11.9
45 to 64 years	5.4	4.7	4.7	4.8	4.1	4.1	12.5	12.0	12.7
65 years and over	8.3	7.9	8.9	7.1	6.7	7.7	26.0	22.9	23.8
Size of Family									
2 persons	5.7	5.0	5.4	5.3	4.5	5.0	11.9	11.9	11.9
3 persons	4.5	4.0	4.1	3.9	3.6	3.6	10.9	8.3	9.1
4 persons	4.7	4.0	4.2	4.3	3.4	3.5	10.6	10.8	12.9
5 persons	7.0	5.6	5.9	6.3	4.9	5.0	13.0	12.0	14.0
6 persons	10.4	8.5	9.1	9.0	7.1	7.7	21.9	19.3	20.7
7 persons or more	19.1	16.8	17.3	16.2	14.1	14.5	30.7	28.8	30.2
Number of Related Children Under 18 Years									
No children	4.9	4.3	4.7	4.5	4.0	4.3	10.7	9.9	10.5
1 and 2 children	5.1	4.4	4.5	4.6	3.8	3.9	11.7	10.8	11.8
3 and 4 children	10.2	8.3	8.9	9.2	7.2	7.6	19.3	18.0	19.2
5 children or more	24.7	20.7	21.3	21.0	17.8	17.9	38.0	32.2	34.5

B Base less than 75,000.
[r] Based on revised methodology
[1] Includes families with civilian heads only for 1974[r] and 1975. In addition, figures for 1974 are not strictly comparable to figures for 1974[r] and 1975 because unpaid family workers are not classified as workers in the 1974 figures but are classified as workers in the 1974[r] and 1975 figures.

TABLE 19. SELECTED CHARACTERISTICS OF FAMILIES BELOW THE POVERTY LEVEL BY SEX AND RACE OF HEAD: 1975, 1974 (REVISED), AND 1974—Continued

(Numbers in thousands. Families as of March of the following year)

Selected characteristics	All races			White			Black		
	1975	1974[r]	1974	1975	1974[r]	1974	1975	1974[r]	1974
PERCENT BELOW POVERTY LEVEL--Continued									
Families With A Male Head--Continued									
Educational Attainment of Head									
Total, 25 years old and over	5.8	5.2	5.5	5.1	4.5	4.8	13.5	12.8	13.9
Elementary: Total	14.2	12.8	12.9	12.8	11.2	11.1	22.9	22.6	24.0
Less than 8 years	18.6	16.6	17.1	17.1	14.5	14.7	25.1	25.0	26.9
8 years	9.2	8.8	8.4	8.7	8.1	7.8	16.2	14.7	14.1
High school: Total	4.7	4.0	4.3	4.2	3.6	3.9	9.9	8.1	9.2
1 to 3 years	7.6	6.2	6.4	7.0	5.3	5.5	12.4	12.4	13.9
4 years	3.4	3.0	3.4	3.0	2.9	3.2	8.0	4.9	5.6
College: Total	2.3	1.8	2.2	2.2	1.6	2.1	3.5	4.0	4.4
Number of Workers[1]									
No workers	17.8	15.5	17.3	15.5	13.3	15.1	46.2	39.9	40.9
1 worker	7.4	6.6	7.2	6.6	5.8	6.3	17.5	16.3	18.9
2 workers	3.6	3.3	3.2	3.2	2.9	2.8	7.2	7.1	7.1
3 workers or more	3.1	2.6	2.3	2.6	1.9	1.6	9.2	10.8	10.8
Employment Status of Head									
Employed	4.1	3.6	3.8	3.7	3.2	3.4	8.8	8.5	9.8
Unemployed	14.7	9.8	10.0	14.3	9.0	9.1	17.4	13.3	14.4
Not in labor force	13.5	12.3	13.0	11.7	10.4	11.1	32.3	31.0	31.1
In Armed Forces	3.9	2.9	2.9	4.0	2.8	2.8	2.2	3.4	3.5
Work Experience of Head									
Head worked last year	4.6	4.0	4.3	4.1	3.6	3.8	9.5	9.3	10.5
Worked 50 to 52 weeks	2.7	2.4	2.7	2.5	2.2	2.4	5.6	5.5	6.2
Full time	2.4	2.2	2.5	2.2	2.0	2.3	4.8	4.9	5.6
Worked 1 to 49 weeks	11.2	10.3	10.8	10.2	9.1	9.5	19.4	18.8	21.9
Reason for working part year:									
Unemployed	11.5	11.1	11.7	10.8	10.4	10.7	15.5	17.0	18.9
Other	10.9	9.5	10.1	9.4	8.0	8.3	25.8	20.9	25.1
Head did not work last year	15.1	13.5	14.7	13.1	11.3	12.4	35.5	34.6	35.0
Head in Armed Forces	3.9	2.9	2.9	4.1	2.7	2.8	(B)	3.5	3.5
Occupation of Longest Job of Head									
Head worked last year	4.6	4.0	4.3	4.1	3.6	3.8	9.5	9.3	10.5
Professional and managerial workers	2.1	1.5	1.6	1.9	1.4	1.5	6.7	3.3	3.8
Clerical and sales workers	2.2	1.7	2.0	2.3	1.7	1.9	1.2	2.8	6.0
Craft and kindred workers	4.0	3.3	3.3	3.7	2.9	2.8	8.3	9.1	10.5
Operatives, including transport workers	5.0	4.4	4.5	4.6	3.8	3.9	6.7	7.8	8.4
Service workers, including private household	6.5	4.9	5.5	5.4	4.2	4.6	9.7	8.8	10.0
Laborers, except farm	9.9	9.7	10.2	9.4	9.4	9.5	12.4	11.0	12.9
Farmers and farm laborers	21.4	21.7	22.1	19.3	20.2	20.6	46.7	43.0	42.5
Families With A Female Head									
Total	32.5	32.1	32.5	25.9	24.8	24.9	50.1	52.2	52.8
Age of Head									
14 to 24 years	62.7	60.5	60.1	58.7	55.6	55.1	68.3	68.6	67.5
25 to 44 years	40.8	41.6	42.0	35.1	35.2	35.5	53.7	55.6	56.1
45 to 64 years	20.0	19.5	19.8	15.2	13.3	13.4	36.6	42.0	43.0
65 years and over	12.7	12.3	13.0	7.4	7.9	8.1	36.9	34.6	36.8
Size of Family									
2 persons	22.6	23.0	23.2	18.2	18.6	18.8	39.6	42.1	41.9
3 persons	30.0	28.6	29.6	27.8	23.1	24.1	37.5	46.9	47.5
4 persons	44.6	41.8	42.1	36.0	36.4	36.0	61.5	53.5	54.4
5 persons	49.8	51.2	49.9	41.7	38.6	37.9	64.3	70.6	68.9
6 persons	57.2	52.2	52.5	43.6	41.6	39.3	68.9	60.1	61.7
7 persons or more	67.1	63.6	64.8	67.3	58.8	56.4	68.2	66.7	69.5
Number of Related Children Under 18 Years									
No children	7.5	7.7	8.3	6.2	5.5	6.1	15.5	19.6	21.0
1 and 2 children	36.1	36.0	36.5	32.1	30.6	31.0	46.3	50.1	50.4
3 and 4 children	57.9	55.5	55.0	50.7	48.4	47.8	69.0	66.2	65.9
5 children or more	80.9	76.5	75.3	78.0	74.6	70.5	82.1	76.7	79.0

B Base less than 75,000.

[r]Based on revised methodology

[1]Includes families with civilian heads only for 1974[r] and 1975. In addition, figures for 1974 are not strictly comparable to figures for 1974[r] and 1975 because unpaid family workers are not classified as workers in the 1974 figures but are classified as workers in the 1974[r] and 1975 figures.

TABLE 19. SELECTED CHARACTERISTICS OF FAMILIES BELOW THE POVERTY LEVEL BY SEX AND RACE OF HEAD: 1975, 1974 (REVISED), AND 1974—Continued

(Numbers in thousands. Families as of March of the following year)

Selected characteristics	All races			White			Black		
	1975	1974[r]	1974	1975	1974[r]	1974	1975	1974[r]	1974
PERCENT BELOW POVERTY LEVEL--Continued									
Families With A Female Head--Continued									
Educational Attainment of Head									
Total, 25 years old and over	29.2	28.9	29.3	23.0	21.9	22.1	47.0	49.3	50.1
Elementary: Total	37.8	36.0	37.6	32.1	30.1	31.5	50.9	51.8	53.3
Less than 8 years	40.7	40.0	41.8	35.0	34.0	34.9	52.0	53.4	55.8
8 years	33.6	29.9	31.3	28.4	25.1	27.2	48.9	47.9	47.2
High school: Total	31.3	30.9	30.7	24.1	22.1	21.7	50.4	53.9	53.9
1 to 3 years	44.6	43.3	43.3	33.6	31.7	31.5	64.1	62.8	63.0
4 years	23.7	23.4	23.0	19.7	17.5	16.9	38.0	44.4	44.1
College: Total	10.9	12.2	13.1	9.8	11.1	11.8	16.1	16.7	20.5
Number of Workers[1]									
No workers	65.5	66.5	66.3	57.2	57.6	58.2	81.5	83.9	82.0
1 worker	26.5	27.5	28.8	20.8	20.9	21.7	42.2	46.8	48.4
2 workers	11.1	11.0	10.8	8.3	6.4	6.2	21.7	25.1	26.1
3 workers or more	11.4	10.3	9.5	7.9	7.7	5.5	19.6	17.3	20.6
Employment Status of Head									
Employed	16.7	16.5	17.9	13.2	12.7	13.7	28.0	27.8	30.5
Unemployed	52.7	52.3	53.2	45.8	47.4	46.2	65.9	61.9	66.7
Not in labor force	47.8	46.5	45.7	39.1	36.0	35.3	68.6	72.7	70.7
Work Experience of Head									
Head worked last year	20.3	21.2	21.9	16.1	16.2	16.5	33.0	35.3	37.4
Worked 50 to 52 weeks	8.2	8.4	10.9	5.4	5.6	7.5	17.4	17.2	21.9
Full time	5.8	5.6	8.3	4.2	4.4	6.1	11.3	9.9	15.4
Worked 1 to 49 weeks	40.2	41.3	40.4	34.8	34.1	32.6	54.7	58.5	60.1
Reason for working part year:									
Unemployed	36.6	38.4	39.3	30.7	27.4	28.5	48.7	59.5	60.8
Other	42.1	42.5	41.0	36.9	36.5	34.3	59.9	58.0	59.7
Head did not work last year	49.5	48.0	48.2	40.4	37.8	38.0	70.8	73.9	72.4
Occupation of Longest Job of Head									
Head worked last year	20.3	21.2	21.9	16.1	16.2	16.5	33.0	35.3	37.4
Professional and managerial workers	5.4	8.0	7.2	5.2	7.0	6.5	7.8	11.8	12.6
Clerical and sales workers	12.0	11.9	12.6	10.2	9.4	10.3	20.8	22.8	24.3
Craft and kindred workers	(B)	(B)	(B)	(B)	(B)	(B)	(B)	(B)	(B)
Operatives, including transport workers	24.9	27.4	28.8	21.1	22.2	24.4	34.0	40.0	39.8
Service workers, including private household	36.9	35.3	37.0	32.4	30.1	30.0	43.6	43.2	46.9
Laborers, except farm	(B)	(B)	(B)	(B)	(B)	(B)	(B)	(B)	(B)
Farmers and farm laborers	(B)	(B)	(B)	(B)	(B)	(B)	(B)	(B)	(B)

B Base less than 75,000.
[r]Based on revised methodology
[1]Includes families with civilian heads only for 1974[r] and 1975. In addition, figures for 1974 are not strictly comparable to figures for 1974[r] and 1975 because unpaid family workers are not classified as workers in the 1974 figures but are classified as workers in the 1974[r] and 1975 figures.

This material has not been excerpted in its entirety.

U.S. Bureau of the Census, Current Population Reports, Series P-60, No. 103, "Money Income and Poverty Status of Families and Persons in the United States: 1975 and 1974 Revisions." (Advance Report) U.S. Government Printing Office, Washington, D.C., 1976.

Employee-Benefit Plans—Summary: 1960 to 1975

[Coverage data refer to civilian wage and salary workers at end of year; contributions, to amounts subscribed by employers and employees, in total. An "employee-benefit plan" is any type of plan sponsored or initiated unilaterally or jointly by employers or employees and providing benefits that stem from the employment relationship and that are not underwritten or paid directly by government (Federal, State, or local). In general, the intent is to include plans that provide in an orderly predetermined fashion for (1) income maintenance during periods when regular earnings are cut off because of death, accident, sickness, retirement, or unemployment and (2) benefits to meet medical expenses. Excludes workmen's compensation required by statute and employer's liability. See also *Historical Statistics, Colonial Times to 1970*, series H 70–114]

ITEM	1960	1965	1970	1972	1973	1974	1975
Covered employees:							
Life insurance and death [1] ......mil..	34.2	41.9	51.8	55.2	57.8	60.6	62.4
Accidental death and dismemberment......mil..	20.9	28.4	38.7	40.7	42.7	44.3	46.5
Health benefits:							
Hospitalization [2 3] ......mil..	39.3	45.7	53.1	54.2	56.8	57.6	58.2
Surgical [2] ......mil..	37.4	43.4	51.5	52.9	55.4	56.1	56.6
Regular medical [2] ......mil..	28.2	38.2	48.0	49.4	53.7	54.9	56.1
Major medical [4] ......mil..	8.8	16.6	24.6	26.4	27.6	28.2	29.6
Coverage, private employees:							
Temporary disability [5 6] ......mil..	24.5	24.5	29.7	31.3	32.0	31.7	31.1
Long-term disability......mil..	(X)	1.9	7.0	9.5	10.6	11.1	11.5
Retirement [7] ......mil..	18.7	21.8	26.1	27.5	29.2	30.3	30.3
Contributions: [8]							
All employees, total......bil. dol..	12.5	19.9	34.9	45.4	50.5	57.7	67.3
Life insurance and death [1] ......bil. dol..	1.4	2.2	3.6	4.3	4.4	4.7	5.1
Accidental death and dismemberment.bil. dol..	.1	.1	.2	.3	.3	.3	.3
Health benefits:							
Hospitalization [3] ......bil. dol..	2.5	4.3	7.6	9.5	10.5	11.4	13.3
Surgical and regular medical......bil. dol..	1.3	2.1	4.0	5.2	5.9	7.0	8.2
Major medical [4] ......bil. dol..	.5	1.1	2.3	3.6	4.1	4.6	5.7
Private employees:							
Temporary disability [5 9] ......bil. dol..	1.2	1.6	3.1	3.7	3.9	4.4	4.7
Retirement [7] ......bil. dol..	5.5	8.4	14.0	18.5	21.1	25.0	29.9
Benefits paid: [8]							
All employees, total......bil. dol..	7.8	13.6	26.1	32.9	36.2	42.0	47.9
Life insurance and death [1] ......bil. dol..	1.0	1.6	2.5	2.9	3.2	3.4	3.6
Accidental death and dismemberment.bil. dol..	(Z)	.1	.2	.2	.2	.3	.3
Health benefits:							
Hospitalization [3] ......bil. dol..	2.4	4.2	7.3	8.9	9.6	11.1	13.1
Surgical and regular medical......bil. dol..	1.1	1.8	3.6	4.5	5.2	6.3	7.4
Major medical [4] ......bil. dol..	.4	1.0	2.4	3.2	3.4	4.0	4.5
Private employees:							
Temporary disability [5 9] ......bil. dol..	1.0	1.3	2.5	2.9	3.2	3.7	3.8
Retirement [7] ......bil. dol..	1.7	3.5	7.4	10.0	11.2	12.9	14.8
PERCENT OF WORKERS COVERED [10]							
All employees:							
Life insurance and death......	57.8	63.7	69.0	71.1	71.2	73.5	77.3
Accidental death and dismemberment......	35.3	43.1	51.5	52.4	52.7	53.7	57.6
Health benefits:							
Hospitalization......	66.5	69.4	70.7	69.8	70.0	69.9	72.2
Surgical......	63.3	65.9	68.6	68.1	68.3	68.1	70.1
Regular medical......	47.7	58.0	63.9	63.6	66.2	66.5	69.5
Major medical......	14.8	25.2	32.7	34.0	34.0	34.2	36.7
Private employees:							
Temporary disability......	48.7	44.3	47.9	49.1	47.9	46.8	47.5
Long-term disability......	(X)	3.4	11.2	12.8	15.8	16.4	17.6
Retirement......	37.2	39.5	42.1	43.1	43.7	44.0	46.2
PERCENT CONTRIBUTIONS OF TOTAL WAGES AND SALARIES [10]							
All employees:							
Life insurance and death......	.54	.64	.68	.71	.65	.63	.65
Accidental death and dismemberment......	.03	.03	.04	.05	.04	.04	.04
Health benefits......	1.63	2.15	2.64	2.98	3.02	3.11	3.45
Private employees:							
Temporary disability......	.53	.54	.71	.76	.71	.73	.75
Retirement......	2.46	2.86	3.25	3.74	3.82	4.14	4.73

X Not applicable. Z Less than $50 million.

[1] Includes group and wholesale life insurance but excludes Servicemen's Group Life Insurance program.

[2] Includes persons covered by group comprehensive major-medical insurance as well as those with basic benefits.

[3] Includes private hospital plans written in compliance with State temporary disability insurance law in California. [4] Group supplementary and comprehensive major-medical insurance written by commercial insurance companies. [5] Includes private plans written in compliance with State temporary disability insurance laws in California, Hawaii, New Jersey, and New York; and formal sick-leave plans. Excludes credit accident and health insurance. [6] Starting 1963, excludes long-term disability policies. [7] Includes pay-as-you-go and deferred profit-sharing plans, plans for non-profit organizations, union pension plans, and railroad plans supplementing the Federal railroad retirement program. Excludes plans for the self-employed and tax-sheltered annuities. Retirement coverage estimates exclude annuitants. [8] Includes data for supplemental unemployment insurance benefits, not shown separately. [9] Includes data under long-term disability policies. [10] For all employees, coverage and contributions relate to private and government full-time and part-time civilian employees and payroll; for private employees, to wage and salary full-time and part-time labor force and payroll in private industry.

Source: U.S. Social Security Administration, *Social Security Bulletin*, September 1977.

PROTECTION AGAINST SHORT-TERM SICKNESS INCOME LOSS: 1950 TO 1975

[**In millions of dollars except percent.** "Short-term sickness" refers to short-term or temporary nonwork-connected disability (lasting not more than 6 months) and the first 6 months of long-term disability. See also *Historical Statistics, Colonial Times to 1970*, series H 115–124]

ITEM	1950	1960	1965	1970	1971	1972	1973	1974	1975
Short-term sickness: Income loss	4,816	8,591	11,333	16,799	17,154	19,555	21,069	21,797	23,687
Total protection provided [1]	**942**	**2,430**	**3,349**	**5,848**	**6,072**	**6,780**	[2] **7,267**	[2] **7,970**	[2] **8,710**
Protection as percent of loss	19.6	28.3	29.6	34.8	35.4	34.7	34.5	36.6	36.8
Benefits provided by protection:									
Individual insurance	153	393	483	694	731	772	795	851	973
Group benefits to workers in private employment	474	1,211	1,602	2,952	3,030	3,390	3,650	4,145	4,337
Private cash insurance [3]	231	638	767	1,476	1,489	1,614	1,736	2,024	2,010
Publicly operated cash sickness funds [4]	63	172	269	411	411	412	446	485	538
Sick leave	180	400	566	1,066	1,130	1,364	1,469	1,636	1,789
Sick leave for govt. employees	315	826	1,264	2,202	2,311	2,618	2,711	2,844	3,240

[1] Provided by individual insurance, group benefits to workers in private employment, and sick leave for government employees. [2] Includes benefits for the sixth month of disability payable under old-age, survivors, disability, and health insurance program, not shown separately. [3] Group accident and sickness insurance and self-insurance privately written either on a voluntary basis or in compliance with State temporary disability insurance laws in Calif., N.J., and N.Y. Includes a small but undetermined amount of group disability insurance benefits paid to government workers and to self-employed persons through farm, trade, or professional associations. [4] Includes State-operated plans in Rhode Island, California, and New Jersey; State Insurance Fund and special fund for disabled unemployed in New York; and provisions of Railroad Unemployment Insurance Act.

Source: U.S. Social Security Administration, *Social Security Bulletin*, May 1977.

U.S. Bureau of the Census, Statistical Abstract of the United States: 1977 (98th edition) Washington, D.C., 1977.

The Life Work of Women *

The majority of American women want lives which combine homemaking and paid employment.

Nine out of 10 adult American women have already spent some of their lives in paid employment, although only 42 percent[1] are currently employed. Among those now employed, 31 percent hold full-time jobs and 11 percent work part time. Nearly one-half of American women think the ideal life pattern would be to stay home with young children, then combine homemaking with a job and career during the balance of their working years.

Women Working at Home

The 58 percent of women not in the paid labor force included homemakers, the retired, students —particularly among the 18-24 age group—and the unemployed. There is considerable overlapping of the homemaker, retired, and student categories for these reasons:

- The unemployed and the retired-from-the-labor-force often describe themselves as "homemakers."
- Those who work part time may consider themselves predominantly students or homemakers. The role of homemaker can obviously be full-time, part-time, or retirement work.
- Conversely, some widows who were homemakers now describe themselves as retired.

Smaller proportions of those with a post-high school education consider themselves predominantly homemakers.

Table 2-1 shows how women describe their principal occupations.

Women Working Outside the Home

Although the future may hold more options, the largest proportion of women with paid employment currently work in clerical/sales occupations. These typists, clerks, secretaries, and office machine operators comprise 13 percent of all women and 38 percent of those in the paid labor force.

Twelve percent of all women are in professional, technical, and managerial jobs, but half of this group work in education or health fields, principal-

TABLE 2-1

SELF-DESCRIBED "PRINCIPAL" OCCUPATION

Occupation	Percent
Homemakers	49%
Professional/technical	8
Managers/administrators	4
Clerical/sales	13
Craft (skilled)	[1]
Operatives (unskilled)	3
Service	5
Household workers	1
Students	5
Unemployed/laid off	3
Retired	9
	100

[1] Less than 1 percent mention.

[1] Bureau of the Census labor force participation rates show 45.7 percent of women 16 and over were in the labor force in 1974. Survey figures here are for women 18 and over actually employed *on the date of interview in 1975,* and therefore differ slightly.

*See the Introductory Notes to "Motherhood, Family Planning, and Child Care," in the ADULTS section (sub-section, "Wives and Mothers")

TABLE 2-2

PRINCIPAL OCCUPATION

	All Women	Age: 18-24	25-34	35-44	45-54	55-64	65 Plus	Education: Less than H.S.	H.S. Grad.	Post-H.S. Educ.	Race: White	Black	Spanish [1] American	Marital Status: Never Married	Now Married	Div./Sep.	Widow
Homemaker [2]	49%	29%	59%	54%	52%	53%	48%	58%	53%	39%	49%	48%	49%	7%	62%	38%	36%
Professional/technical																	
Teacher/education	4	3	6	6	5	3	([3])	([3])	([3])	11	5	4	4	8	4	5	3
Nurses/medical/health	2	3	3	3	2	2	([3])	([3])	1	5	2	2	2	2	3	2	1
Other professional/technical	2	2	3	3	2	2	([3])	([3])	1	4	2	3	4	4	2	2	1
Managers/administrators	4	1	3	5	4	6	1	2	4	3	3	3	2	2	3	4	4
Clerical/sales	13	19	14	15	11	15	1	5	19	13	14	8	16	19	12	15	9
Craft	([3])	0	([3])	([3])	([3])	([3])	0	1	([3])	0	([3])	0	2	0	([3])	([3])	1
Operatives	3	2	3	3	6	2	1	6	3	([3])	3	3	4	1	3	6	3
Service	5	5	3	5	8	4	([3])	6	5	3	4	7	4	5	3	15	3
Household workers	1	1	0	2	2	1	0	2	([3])	([3])	1	3	4	1	0	1	1
Students [2]	5	28	2	0	([3])	0	0	2	3	11	6	4	6	31	1	1	0
Unemployed/laid off	3	7	2	2	3	1	1	4	3	1	2	6	2	8	1	5	2
Retired	9	0	([3])	1	2	10	46	13	6	8	9	9	4	7	4	6	39

[1] Small sample size.
[2] Some homemakers and students are also employed but consider their "principal" occupation as homemaker or student.
[3] Less than 1 percent.

ly in teaching and nursing. Only 9 percent of women are members of labor unions.

Table 2-2 suggests no great changes have occurred in women's occupational opportunities despite recent individual and legal pressures to permit women to assume new job roles with opportunities for promotion to management and supervisory posts.

Bureau of the Census figures show the number of women managers and administrators increased about 22 percent between 1960 and 1970. According to the survey of women, most moves up to management appear to be due to seniority promotions. There is little evidence of younger workers entering managerial positions not formerly open to women (table 2-2). Manager/administrator proportions are 3 percent among those ages 25-34, and the rise in promotions has affected 6 percent among those 55-64.

Minority women show nearly the same occupational profile as white majority women do (table 2-2). This similarity does not hold true for men of different race/ethnicities.

Although white women do clerical work in somewhat greater proportions than black women, the minorities have done as well as white women in obtaining jobs as teachers and nurses. Such "helping professions" are clearly the dominant "professions" of women.

Education

Minority women lag behind in education attainment (table 2-3), but on the whole, American women are becoming increasingly well educated. At least some post-high school education is now the majority experience of women under 35 (figure 2-1).

Young women in their twenties have the most education. Numerically, this age group will continue to move through the population as a bulge; they were the post-World War II babies who are now the Nation's young adults.

Half of American women say they want more education. Those who have the most want more. The drive for education—particularly to finish college—is strongest among those who already have some post-high school education. Among this group, the desire to continue education rises to 64 percent.

What Women Are Paid

Over one-third of women have no income of their own (figure 2-2). This figure includes 38 percent of white women, 34 percent of those with Spanish heritage, and only 24 percent of black women. Six out of 10 Spanish-heritage and white women have husbands' wages to support the family, but only 35 percent of black women have such support.

In 1974, Bureau of the Census figures showed that full-time employed women made only 57 percent of what men earned. The median cash incomes for that year were $6,957 for women and $12,152 for men.

Although the median incomes of women are dramatically different from the median incomes of men, 6 out of 10 women currently employed think they are paid equally with men who hold the same type of job at their place of employment (table 2-4).

TABLE 2-3

EDUCATION	*All Women*		RACE: *White*		*Black*		*Spanish American*	
Elementary	10%	28%	8%	24%	28%	51%	20%	48%
Some high school	18		16		23		28	
Graduated high school	35		37		26		30	
Some college	22	37%	22	39%	17	23%	18	22%
Graduated college	10		11		4		2	
Post graduate	5		6		2		2	
	100		100		100		100	

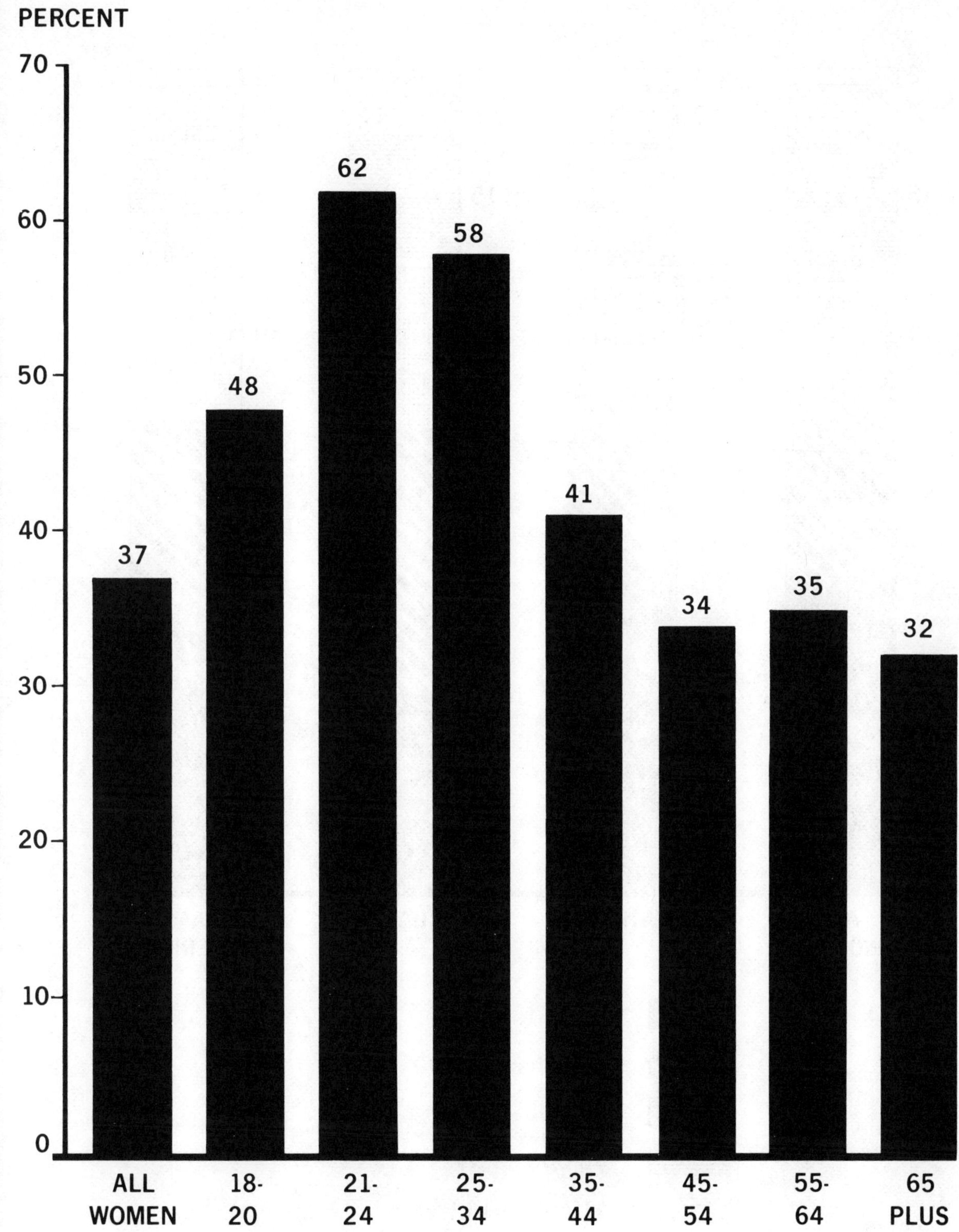

FIGURE 2-1 POST-HIGH SCHOOL EDUCATION BY AGE

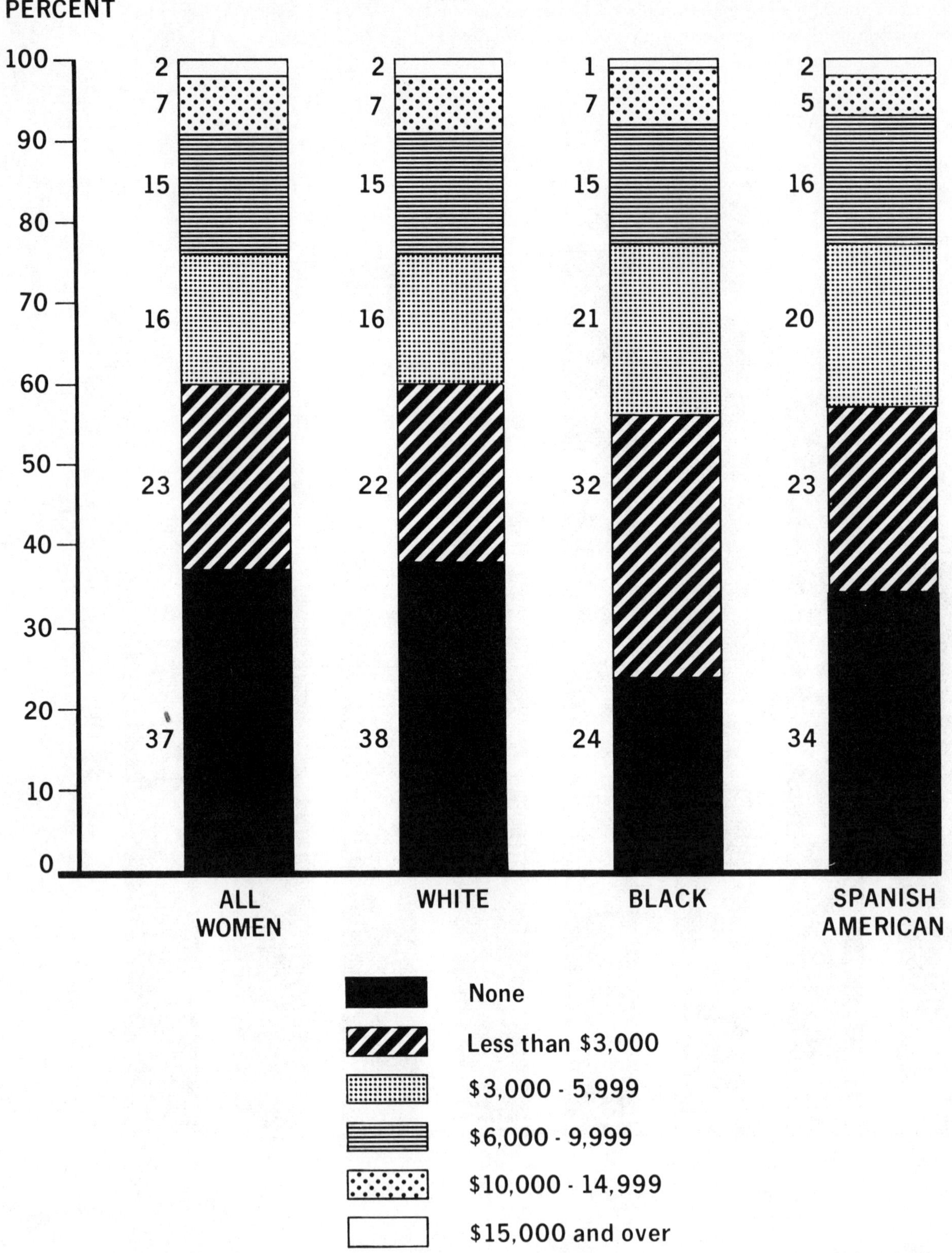

FIGURE 2-2 INDIVIDUAL INCOME (ANY SOURCE) BY RACE

As the occupational profile of women in table 2-2 shows, most women don't work in the same type jobs men do. In fact, nearly 1 in 5 employed women can't answer questions about equal pay and promotion because, as they say, "No men work in my type job."

Clerks, nurses, and teachers don't mention unequal treatment or perceive pay discrimination. In their fields, the pay is equal, since most of the jobholders are women.

Employed divorcees, for whom jobs are more important as family income, feel more than the married and single women that they've been discriminated against in pay. In fact, 39 percent of them, compared to 17 percent of all employed women, think men are paid more for the same work. Widows are also more aware of discrimination (table 2-4).

Two-thirds of black women think they are paid equally with men. Black women feel less discriminated against, regarding pay, than their white counterparts do (table 2-4).

The earnings profiles are only slightly different for white compared to minority women.

Of women with their own incomes (full- or part-time employment, alimony, child support, investments, etc.), 62 percent receive less than $6,000. Of course, those with part-time, alimony, and child support incomes pull down the overall average.

Among married couples in the labor force, most women earn less than their husbands. In only 19 percent of these dual-income homes do the woman's earnings amount to at least half of the two incomes.

TABLE 2-4

BELIEVE PAID EQUALLY WITH MEN FOR SAME JOB

	CURRENTLY EMPLOYED WOMEN	EMPLOYED BY RACE: *White*	*Black*
Yes, paid equally . . .	59%	58%	67%
No men hold similar job.	17	18	12
No, not paid equally	17	18	10
Don't know	7	6	11
	100	100	100

EMPLOYED BY MARITAL STATUS

	Single/ Never Married	*Now Married*	*Divorced/ Separated*	*Widowed*
Yes, paid equally . . .	66%	59%	49%	51%
No men hold similar job.	15	19	12	19
No, not paid equally	13	14	39	20
Don't know	6	8	. . . .	10
	100	100	100	100

Work Patterns

In-and-out work experience is always cited as one reason for women's lower incomes. Only 1 in 5 women has worked continuously throughout her adult life.

The major reason women leave their jobs is to have a baby. However, today's young mothers are more likely to return to work when their children are small than mothers did in the past. About half (48 percent) of mothers who are now employed and under 35 went back to work when their children were preschoolers, compared to 29 percent of employed mothers now over 35.

Nearly 4 out of 10 women who plan to return to the labor force after an absence say they will need additional training to do so. Sixty percent of those who have never been employed but want to enter the labor force in the future say they will need training.

Life-Work Patterns

When asked to describe the dominant work pattern of their lives, half of all women say they have either combined or alternated paid employment with homemaking (table 2-5). Table 2-6 shows five work patterns as practiced by women from each of the three attitude groups described earlier: Traditional Outlook, Balancing Outlook, or Expanding Outlook women. More Traditional Out-

TABLE 2-5

DOMINANT LIFE-WORK PATTERN

Homemaker continuously	11%
Employed, then became full-time homemaker	20
Alternated employment and being full-time homemaker	19
Combined employment and being homemaker at same time	31
Employed continuously	19
	100

TABLE 2-6

DOMINANT WORK PATTERN OF ADULT LIFE BY CONCEPT OF WOMEN'S ROLE

	All Women	*Traditional Outlook*	*Balancing Outlook*	*Expanding Outlook*
Homemaker continuously	11%	18%	9%	7%
Employed, then became full-time homemaker	20	23	23	13
Alternated employment and being full-time homemaker	19	21	18	18
Combined employment and being homemaker at same time	31	30	32	31
Employed continuously	19	8	18	31
	100	100	100	100

TABLE 2-8

EXPECTATION FOR SEEKING PAID EMPLOYMENT AMONG 58 PERCENT OF WOMEN NOT IN LABOR FORCE NOW

Employed in past and expect to return in future	19%
Never employed in past but expect to seek employment in future	2
Total expect employment	21
Employed in past and might return in future	5%
Never employed in past but might seek employment in future	1
Total might seek employment	6
Total not now employed and not expecting to seek employment (includes those retired from employment)	31%
	58

look women have been homemakers, while more Expanding Outlook women have been continuously employed.

When their employment histories are traced, 91 percent of women have worked at paid employment at some time during their adult lives (table 2-7 and figure 2-3). Of the 9 percent who have never held a paid job, 6 percent never intend to. However, 2 percent think they will work in the future, and the remaining 1 percent aren't sure. Among the 49 percent who worked in the past, 19 percent expect to return to work in the future (table 2-8).

Half of American women think the ideal life would be to combine employment and homemaking, with time at home during the years their children are young (figure 2-4 and table 2-9). This proportion is similar for Traditional, Balancing, and Expanding Outlook women. Most of the rest of the Traditional women, however, would choose to be mainly homemakers, while the majority of the rest of the Expanding Outlook women would favor employment throughout their adult lives.

The national survey found a great deal of difference in life-style choice according to age; young women are far less interested in being only homemakers than older women are. But there are no indications of a wholesale trend away from homemaking. Younger or even the Expanding Outlook women are saying they want homemaking as part —but only a part—of a full life which *combines* homemaking and career.

TABLE 2-7

EMPLOYMENT IN ADULT LIFE

Currently employed outside the home	
Those who have worked continuously	26%
Those who have been in and out of labor force and are now employed	16
	42
Not currently employed outside the home	
Those who have worked in the past full time	39
Those who have worked in the past part time	10
	49
Total employed now or ever	91

TABLE 2-9

IDEAL LIFE-STYLE CHOICE BY AGE

	18-24	*25-34*	*35-44*	*45-54*	*55-64*	*65-*
Mainly a homemaker	9%	10%	21%	28%	30%	40%
If have children, stay home when children young, combine job or career with homemaking at other times in life	51	58	44	46	47	42
Combine job or career with homemaking and child care, if have children throughout life	31	27	30	22	17	12
Mainly a job holder or career woman	9	5	5	4	6	6
	100	100	100	100	100	100

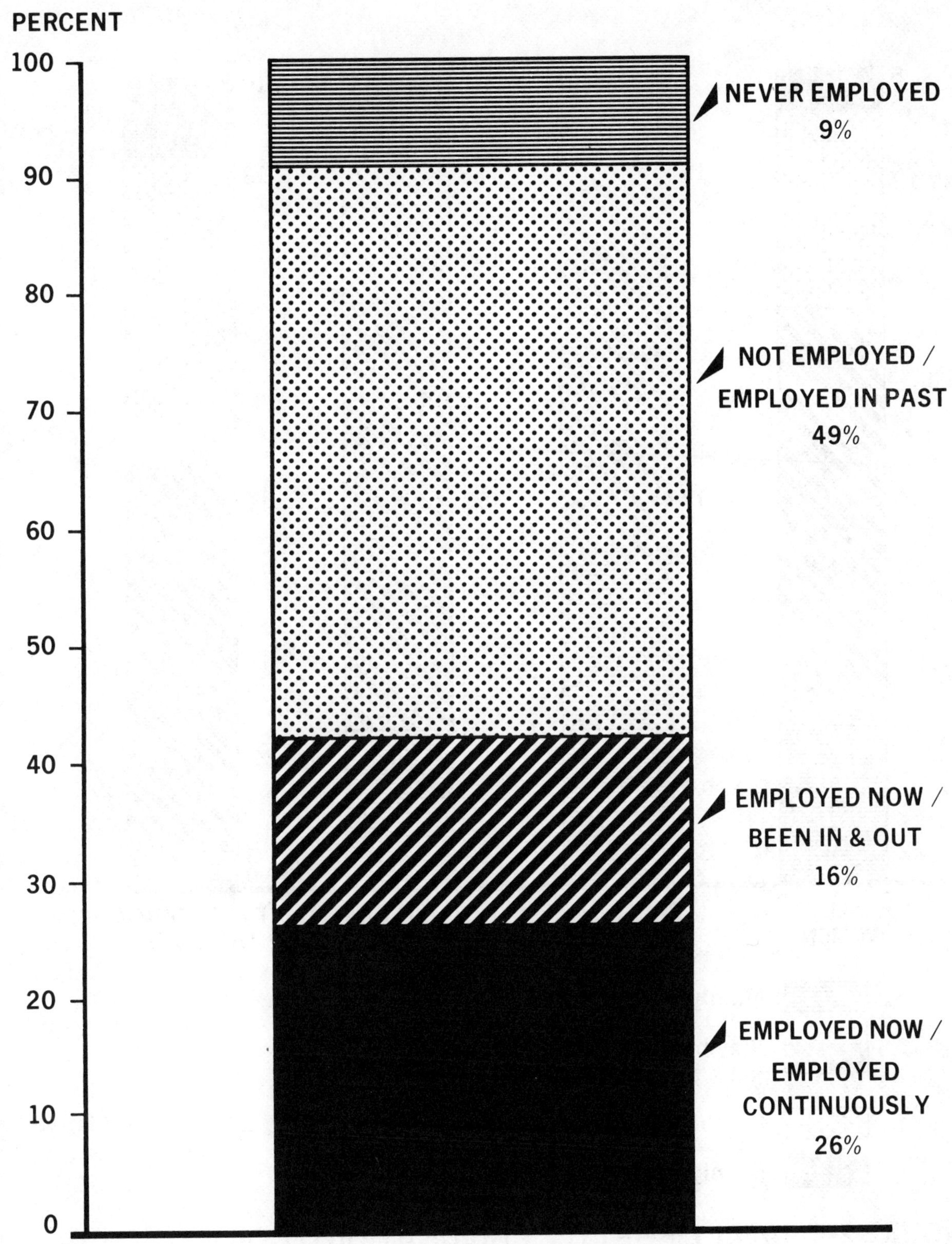

FIGURE 2-3 EMPLOYMENT HISTORY

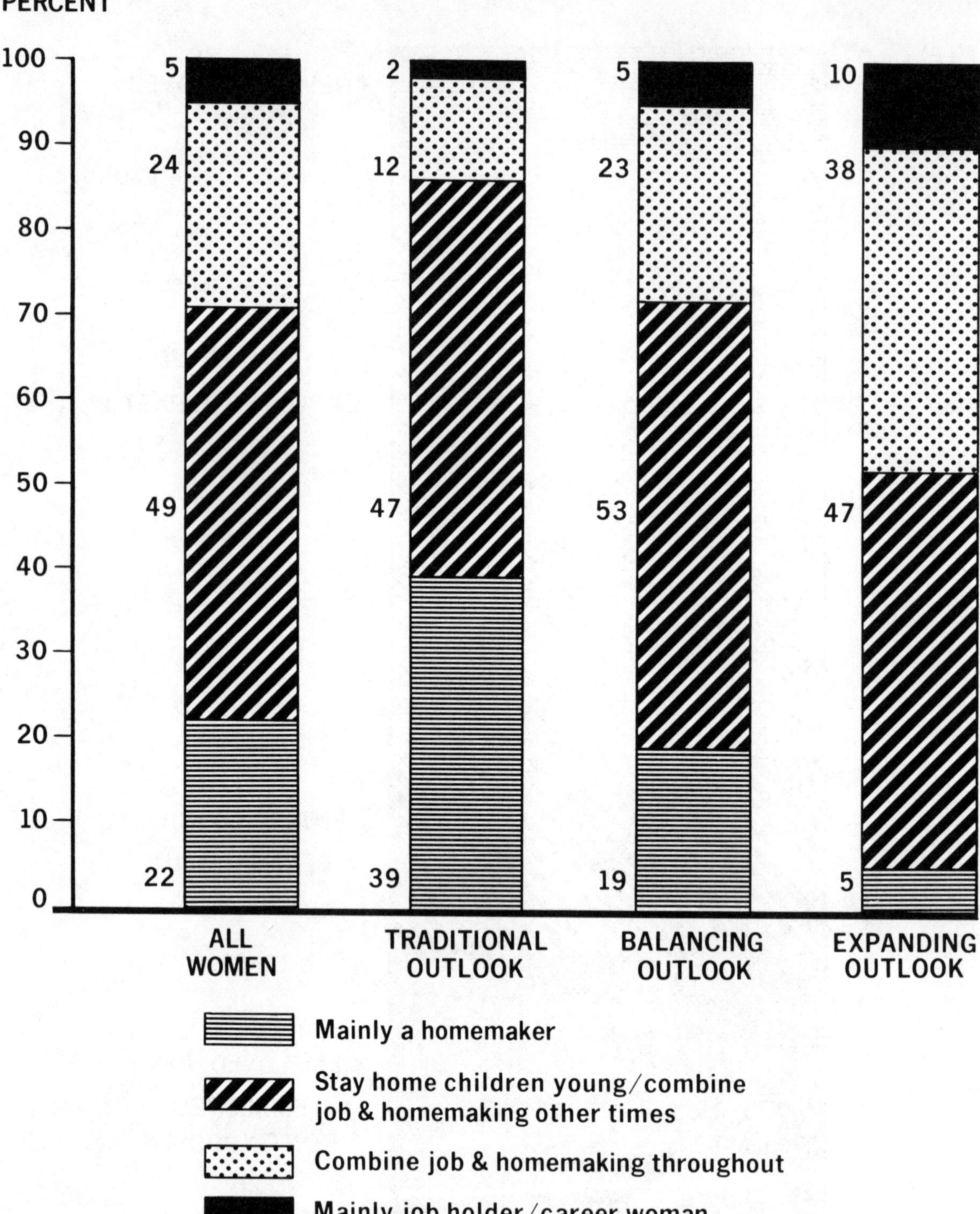

FIGURE 2-4 IDEAL LIFE-STYLE CHOICE BY OUTLOOK ON WOMEN'S ROLES

American Women Today & Tomorrow, Market Opinion Research, 1977. National Commission on the Observance of International Women's Year (GPO Stock No. 052-003-00249-3)

Women who head families: a socioeconomic analysis

Special Labor Force Report shows women who headed families were younger and more likely to work in 1975 than 1960, but the family income of almost 4 out of 10 was below $5,000

BEVERLY JOHNSON MCEADDY

Over the course of the last 35 years, families headed by women have become a significant, although still small portion of America's population. Between 1940 and 1975, families headed by women doubled in number, reaching 7.2 million, or 1 out of every 8 families. At the same time, the number of families headed by men grew to 48.5 million, only a 70-percent increase (table 1). The accelerated growth of families headed by women in recent years, especially since 1970, has been of concern in part because 1 out of every 3, as compared with 1 out of every 18 of the families headed by men, is living at or below what is generally defined as the poverty level.[1]

Age, marital status, and race

Women heading their own families are much younger today than in earlier periods. Since 1960, their median age has dropped substantially from 50.5 to 43.4 years (table 2). In March 1975, 1 of every 10 female family heads was under age 25, compared with 1 of every 25 in 1960. Even though this young age group typically experiences the greatest difficulties in the labor market, the unemployment rate of female family heads age 25 to 44 is also very high.

The younger average age of today's female heads is directly related to the changes in their marital composition. Over the past 15 years, the number of divorced women heading families tripled and the number of single (never married) women nearly doubled (table 3). On the other hand, the number of widows, who accounted for half of all women heading families in 1960, increased by only 14 percent.

Contributing to the upsurge in families broken by divorce were several long- and short-term developments that coincided in the late 1960's and early 1970's. One was a major effort to reform the divorce laws, and especially to advocate the adoption of no-fault divorce regulations. As of January 1974, 23 States had adopted some form of no-fault divorce laws; just since 1971, 16 States have adopted the no-fault concept.[2] Another development was the availability of free legal aid which enabled persons in many of the poorer families to obtain a divorce. Moreover, society's attitudes toward divorce had relaxed.[3] Increasingly, young wives were having fewer children, and were living in an economy which offered many the opportunity to get jobs paying enough for them to think of living independently of their husbands.

Black women accounted for a third of the overall increase in the number of female heads since 1960, but only one-fifth of the increase in divorced female heads. In contrast, black women accounted for four-fifths of the total growth of all single women heading families. By March 1975, 1 out of every 5 black female heads had never married, compared with 1 out of 10 in 1960. This tremendous gain may be explained by a relaxation in social attitudes regarding never-married women as mothers. Such a change may also have permitted an increasing number of black mothers who had never been married to accurately report their marital status.[4] Furthermore, in most parts of our country today, single women are allowed to adopt children, a custom that was once unheard of. Black women heading families were more than twice as likely to be single as white, and because their marital composition is so different from their white counterparts, a large gap exists between their median ages, 38.3 and 45.7 years, respectively.

Beverly Johnson McEaddy is a social science research analyst in the Office of Current Employment Analysis, Bureau of Labor Statistics.

Labor force participation

The proportion of all female family heads in the labor force has drifted slowly upward, from 49.9 percent in 1960 to 50.9 percent in 1965, and to 52.9 and 54.3 percent in 1970 and 1975. Over this same period, the labor force participation rate for wives rose at a much faster pace—from 30.5 percent in 1960 to 44.4 percent in 1975. The most recent increases in labor force participation rates occurred in the younger age groups for family heads and in both the younger and middle-age groups for wives.

Table 1. Number and proportion of families headed by women and men, selected years, 1940 to present

[Numbers in thousands]

Year	All families			
	Total	Headed by men	Headed by women	
			Total	As percent of total families
1940[1]	32,166	28,550	3,616	11.2
1947[1]	35,794	32,397	3,397	9.5
1950	39,303	35,624	3,679	9.4
1955[1]	41,951	37,717	4,234	10.1
1960	45,062	40,568	4,494	10.0
1965	47,836	42,830	5,006	10.5
1970	51,227	45,654	5,573	10.9
1971	51,947	45,997	5,950	11.5
1972	53,280	47,096	6,184	11.6
1973	54,361	47,761	6,600	12.1
1974	55,041	48,243	6,798	12.4
1975	55,700	48,462	7,238	13.0

[1] Data were collected in April of 1940, 1947, and 1955 and March of all other years.

SOURCE: Data for 1940, 1947, 1950, and 1955 are from **Households and Families by Type: March 1975 (Advance Report), Current Population Reports, Population Characteristics**, Series P-20, No. 282 (Bureau of the Census, 1975), table 5. Data for 1960 and later are from Special Labor Force Reports on Marital and Family Characteristics of Workers for the year specified, produced by the Bureau of Labor Statistics.

Despite the tremendous increase in the participation rates of wives under 45 years of age, the labor force participation rates for women who head families remain higher than those of wives, as shown below:

	Total, 16 and older	*16 to 24*	*25 to 34*	*35 to 44*	*45 to 54*	*55 to 64*	*65 and older*
1970							
Female heads	52.9	51.6	60.9	67.1	70.4	58.5	11.1
Wives	40.8	45.6	39.3	47.2	49.5	35.8	7.9
1975							
Female heads	54.3	56.8	60.9	66.7	67.0	56.0	9.7
Wives	44.4	55.2	48.3	52.1	50.3	35.8	7.2

Only among the 16- to 24-year-olds was the 1975 participation rate for women heading families not significantly higher than that for wives. This proximity of rates for women in the youngest ages is due to the spectacular increases in labor force participation made by wives age 20 to 24. From 1970 to 1975, their participation rate rose from 47.4 to 57.1 percent, while the rate for female heads under age 25 grew by less than half that amount.

The age factor is also important when comparing the higher labor force participation rates of divorced, separated, and single female heads, whose median ages are in the 30's, with the lower participation rates of widows heading families and wives, whose median ages are 60 and 41.8 years, respectively.

A higher proportion of black than white wives in the population work or look for work, but the reverse applies to black and white family heads. The labor force participation rate for black female heads was 51.1 percent in 1975, compared with 55.6 percent for white female heads (table 4). This is probably due to the higher proportion of never-married family heads among the blacks and their lower participation rate—47.2 percent—compared with 59.5 percent for the white single family heads. Another contributing factor could be the greater proportion of black women with young children in the home, 71 percent compared with 57 percent for white heads.

Widows had the lowest labor force participation rate of women heading families—38.1 percent. Over 6 out of every 10 of these women are 55 years old or over, ages when many working women retire from the labor force. A majority of widows have financial resources such as social security payments available to them on the basis of their husbands' work record. Moreover, widows with children are often discouraged by the social security earnings test from working to supplement their income.[5] Despite the receipt of social security benefits, one-third of the widowed mothers are poor, with poverty more likely if there are three children or more. Nevertheless, widows with children were better off financially than divorced and separated mothers.[6]

Work experience. The cumulative number of persons who work at some time during the year is, of course, greater than the number who work at any one time. Women who head their own families are no exception to this—although 3.9 million women heading families were working in March 1975, 4.3 million female family heads reported working at some time during 1974. They represented 60 percent of all women heading families and were more likely than wives to be working full time at year-round jobs

Table 2. Age of female family heads, by race, 1960, 1970, 1975

[Numbers in thousands]

Race and age	1960 [1]		1970		1975	
	Number	Percent	Number	Percent	Number	Percent
ALL RACES						
Total	4,494	100.0	5,573	100.0	7,238	100.0
Under 25 years	180	4.0	437	7.8	738	10.2
25 to 34 years	620	13.8	919	16.5	1,613	22.3
35 to 44 years	921	20.5	1,075	19.3	1,511	20.9
45 to 54 years	948	21.1	1,115	20.0	1,335	18.4
55 to 64 years	782	17.4	917	16.4	932	12.9
65 years and over	1,043	23.2	1,115	20.0	1,108	15.3
Median age (years)	50.5		48.2		43.4	
WHITE						
Total	3,547	100.0	4,185	100.0	5,211	100.0
Under 25 years	121	3.4	283	6.8	437	8.4
25 to 34 years	404	11.4	588	14.1	1,072	20.6
35 to 44 years	692	19.5	749	17.9	1,030	19.8
45 to 54 years	770	21.7	870	20.8	999	19.2
55 to 64 years	649	18.3	744	17.8	765	14.7
65 years and over	912	25.7	951	22.7	909	17.4
Median age (years)	52.2		50.4		45.7	
BLACK						
Total	947	100.0	1,349	100.0	1,937	100.0
Under 25 years	59	6.2	150	11.1	293	15.1
25 to 34 years	214	22.6	325	24.1	526	27.2
35 to 44 years	230	24.3	319	23.6	460	23.7
45 to 54 years	180	19.0	237	17.6	315	16.3
55 to 64 years	134	14.2	164	12.2	155	8.0
65 years and over	131	13.8	155	11.5	187	9.7
Median age (years)	43.8		41.3		38.3	

[1] Data for blacks in 1960 include all races other than white. The racial distribution for 1960 is based on data from the **Census Population, 1960, Subjects Reports,** PC(2)-4A and 4B (Bureau of the Census, 1963).

—55 percent compared with 43 percent of wives. Part of the explanation for this difference may lie in the heavier financial burdens shouldered by the women who head their own families, especially if children are present. However, even when working full time all year, earnings of female heads were relatively low: in 1974, their median family income was $7,610.[7]

Unemployment. Since 1970, the overall unemployment rate for women who head families has been 3 to 4 percentage points higher than the rate for male heads and has been somewhat higher than the rate for wives. As shown below, the difference between the unemployment rates of women heading families and wives is almost entirely because of the higher jobless rate of black women heading families:

	1970			*1975*		
	Total	*White*	*Black*	*Total*	*White*	*Black*
Female family heads	5.6	4.7	7.5	10.0	8.7	14.0
Married women, husband present	4.8	4.6	6.6	8.5	8.3	11.0
Married men, wife present	2.6	2.5	3.8	6.0	5.7	11.4

Table 3. Marital status of female family heads, by race, 1960, 1970, 1975

Marital status and race	Number (in thousands)			Percent distribution		
	1960 [1]	1970	1975	1960	1970	1975
ALL RACES						
Total	4,494	5,573	7,238	100.0	100.0	100.0
Never married	521	610	922	11.6	10.9	12.7
Married, husband absent	980	1,324	1,645	21.8	23.7	22.7
Divorced	750	1,258	2,109	16.7	22.5	29.1
Widowed	2,243	2,389	2,558	49.9	42.8	35.3
WHITE						
Total	3,547	4,185	5,211	100.0	100.0	100.0
Never married	419	385	491	11.8	9.2	9.4
Married, husband absent	624	776	952	17.6	18.5	18.3
Divorced	642	1,058	1,714	18.1	25.3	32.9
Widowed	1,862	1,966	2,052	52.5	47.0	39.4
BLACK						
Total	947	1,349	1,937	100.0	100.0	100.0
Never married	102	218	417	10.8	16.2	21.5
Married, husband absent	354	535	674	37.4	39.7	34.8
Divorced	110	192	367	11.6	14.2	19.0
Widowed	381	403	476	40.2	29.9	24.6

[1] Data for blacks in 1960, includes all races other than white. The racial distribution for 1960 is based on data from the **Census of Population, 1960, Subjects Reports,** PC(2)-4A and 4B (Bureau of the Census, 1963).

The economic recession at mid-decade had a greater impact on the unemployment rate of the husbands—which rose 130 percent from 1970—than on the rate for women family heads, which rose by some 80 percent.

Occupations

The number of employed women heading families increased by 30 percent between March 1970 and March 1975, but their occupational pattern did not change significantly. As is the case for women in general, employed female family heads were more concentrated in lower skilled, lower paid occupations than employed male heads, and their occupational pattern was altered substantially by their marital status and race (table 5). Those who had never married were considerably younger and thus had more formal schooling than other women heading families. White single heads were more likely to hold professional-technical jobs than divorced, separated, and widowed white women. Black single heads were more likely to hold clerical jobs than other black women heading families.

The educational levels of female heads by age and race in table 6 show, in part, why the young heads were several rungs up the occupational ladder from the older female heads. Professional-technical jobs frequently require education beyond high school, and most clerical employees must have a high school diploma. Yet, 1 out of every 4 female heads has not even attended high school, and for those age 45 or over, the situation is worse, particularly if they are black women.

Children

The unprecedented growth in the number of single and divorced women heading families has been accompanied by a phenomenal increase in the number of children living in such families. In March 1975, 1 out of 7 children under age 18 were in families without fathers, up from 1 out of 10 in March 1970.[8] More than 9 million children were members of such families; about one-fourth of them were under age 6. In the last few years, the proportion of female-headed families with preschoolers has not shown as much increase as that of families with school age children, a reflection of the substantial decline in fertility rates among American women.

About 54 percent of the 9 million children had working mothers in 1975. For these mothers, the greater the number of children, the smaller the chance of being in the work force, as indicated by their labor force participation rates. They ranged from 67.4 percent for mothers with one child under age 18; 62.0 percent for two children; 54.1 percent for three children; 48.4 percent for four children; and 34.6 percent for five children.

Table 4. Labor force status of female family heads, by marital status and race, March 1975

[Numbers in thousands]

Labor force status and race	All female family heads	Never married	Married, husband absent	Divorced	Widowed
ALL RACES					
Population	7,238	922	1,645	2,109	2,558
Labor force	3,932	499	892	1,563	974
Labor force participation rate	54.3	54.1	54.2	74.1	38.1
Employed	3,540	454	753	1,419	912
Unemployed	392	45	139	144	62
Unemployment rate	10.0	9.0	15.6	9.2	6.4
WHITE					
Population	5,211	491	952	1,714	2,052
Labor force	2,895	292	535	1,288	778
Labor force participation rate	55.6	59.5	56.2	75.1	37.9
Employed	2,643	283	449	1,175	735
Unemployed	252	9	86	113	43
Unemployment rate	8.7	3.1	16.1	8.8	5.5
BLACK					
Population	1,937	417	674	367	476
Labor force	989	197	346	256	185
Participation rate	51.1	47.2	51.3	69.8	38.9
Employed	851	161	294	227	167
Unemployed	138	36	52	29	18
Unemployment rate	14.0	18.3	15.0	11.3	9.7

Unemployment increased with the number of children in the home: In March 1975, female heads with one or two children had an unemployment rate of 8.6 percent, compared to a rate of 17.1 percent for women with three children or more. Several other factors are involved in this relationship.

The higher the educational level of a mother heading her own family, the lower the average number of children per family: 1.8 for those women with 4 years of college or more, compared with 2.9 for women heads with less than 8 years education.[9]

Black mothers heading families were twice as likely as white mothers to have three children or more, 30 out of 100, compared with 15 out of 100. These black mothers also had lower participation rates, higher unemployment rates, lower educational levels, and higher rates of poverty.

Income

In 1974, the median income for all female family heads was $6,400, less than half that of husband-wife families—$13,800. About 2.8 million female heads had a total family income of less than $5,000 and almost 3 out of 4 of these women had children under 18 in the home (table 7). The labor force participation rate for these mothers was 41.8 percent and their unemployment rate was a staggering 24.2 percent. At the upper end of the income scale, 2.1 million women heading families had a total family income of $10,000 or more. Their labor force participation rate was 83.6 percent; their unemployment rate was 4.6 percent; and only 4 out of 10 of the women in this income bracket had children under 18.

A larger proportion of black than of white women heading families had less than $5,000 total family income—6 out of 10 compared with 3 out of 10. Nevertheless, for both races, labor force participation was highest and unemployment lowest for women in the highest income group.

As noted earlier, a common characteristic of families headed by women is poverty. In 1974, for nonfarm families headed by women, the poverty cutoff was $5,014 for a four-person family (11 percent higher than in 1973 because of inflation), $3,822 for a three-person family and $3,167 for a two-person family.[10] By these standards, about 2.2 million families headed by women were living in poverty. As might be expected, black families were more likely to be poor—over 1 out of 2 were below the poverty level. Typical traits of these families included having a family head who was unlikely to have graduated from high school, had little or no work experience during the previous year, or worked in a low paying occupation. Also, many of these families had no earners.[11]

A disproportionate share of all children under 18 in families headed by women lived in poor families. In 1974, 9 out of 10 of the women living below the poverty level had children under 18 in the home. These children comprised over 50 percent of all children in female-headed families compared with only 8 percent for male-headed families.[12] For blacks, these proportions were 2 out of 3 for female heads and 1 out of 5 for male heads. Hence, children in families headed by women commonly grow up in an environment affected not only by the psychological strains resulting from a single parent—the mother—having the sole responsibility for their discipline, training, health, and guidance, but also the physical problems related to poverty.[13]

The 5 million women who had family incomes above the poverty line were not by any means well off. As shown below, less than 30 percent of families headed by women reported 1974 incomes as high as $10,000 or more, compared with 70 percent of families headed by men living with their wives:

	Family headed by husband	*Family headed by woman*
Total	100.0	100.0
Under $5,000	9.1	38.8
$5,000 to $6,999	7.8	15.8
$7,000 to $9,999	13.3	16.9
$10,000 and over	69.8	28.5

Table 5. Major occupation group of employed female family heads, by marital status and race, March 1975

[Percent distribution]

Major occupation group	All races				White				Black			
	Total	Never married	Divorced or separated	Widowed	Total	Never married	Divorced or separated	Widowed	Total	Never married	Divorced or separated	Widowed
Total employed:												
Number (thousands)	3,541	454	2,173	913	2,644	284	1,624	736	852	161	523	168
Percent	100.0	100.0	100.0	100.0	100.0	100.0	100.0	100.0	100.0	100.0	100.0	100.0
White-collar workers	55.7	58.8	57.3	50.5	62.1	61.3	64.9	56.4	35.6	52.2	34.0	25.0
Professional and technical	12.2	16.5	11.9	11.0	13.1	19.0	12.7	11.5	8.7	8.1	9.2	7.7
Managers and administrators, except farm	5.4	5.1	5.1	6.2	6.4	6.7	6.2	6.9	2.0	2.5	1.9	2.4
Salesworkers	4.2	3.1	4.0	5.1	5.0	2.5	5.0	5.8	1.9	3.7	1.3	1.8
Clerical workers	33.9	34.1	36.3	28.1	37.7	33.1	41.0	32.1	23.0	37.9	21.6	13.1
Blue-collar workers	16.6	20.3	16.3	15.4	16.2	21.8	15.2	15.8	17.5	18.0	19.1	12 5
Craft and kindred workers	1.5	2.2	1.4	1.5	1.6	2.1	1.4	1.6	1.2	1.9	1.0	1.2
Operatives, except transport	13.3	16.7	13.1	11.9	12.7	18.3	12.2	11.7	14.7	14.9	15.7	11.3
Transport equipment operatives	.6	.2	.7	.7	.8	.4	.7	.8	.4	--------	.6	--------
Nonfarm laborers	1.2	1.1	1.1	1.3	1.1	1.1	.9	1.6	1.3	1.2	1.9	--------
Service workers	27.2	20.5	26.3	32.7	21.2	16.5	19.8	26.4	46.4	28.6	46.8	61.3
Private household workers	4.4	4.4	4.0	5.1	1.8	.7	1.7	2.4	12.7	11.2	11.5	17.3
All other service workers	22.8	16.1	22.2	27.6	19.4	15.8	18.0	23.9	33.7	17.4	35.4	44.0
Farmworkers	.4	.4	.1	1.1	.5	.4	.1	1.1	.4	.6	--------	1.2

The existing income differential between families headed by women and men is explained largely by the number of earners present and their source of income. Husband-wife families were more likely to have earned income. Ninety-one percent of husband-wife families compared with 76 percent of female-headed families had at least one earner in 1974. Male-headed families were also twice as likely as female-headed families to have two earners or more —6 out of 10 compared to 3 out of 10. However, the income differential narrowed significantly when female-headed families had two earners or more. Their median income was $10,990 compared to $16,870 for a multiearner husband-wife family.

Table 6. Years of school completed by female family heads, March 1975

Years of school completed		All female family heads	Under 45 years old	45 years and older
WHITE				
Total:	Number	5,211	2,540	2,671
	Percent	100.0	100.0	100.0
Elementary:	8 years or less	24.3	14.4	33.7
High school:	1 to 3 years	18.7	21.1	16.4
	4 years	36.9	43.3	30.9
College:	1 to 3 years	12.1	13.3	11.0
	4 years or more	7.9	7.8	8.0
BLACK				
Total:	Number	1,937	1,280	658
	Percent	100.0	100.0	100.0
Elementary:	8 years or less	26.7	15.1	49.4
High school:	1 to 3 years	31.6	35.4	24.3
	4 years	31.1	38.0	17.8
College:	1 to 3 years	7.7	8.7	5.8
	4 years or more	2.8	2.8	2.7

Table 7. Family income of female family heads, by labor force status and presence of own children under 18, March 1975

[Numbers in thousands]

Family income	Population	Labor force	Labor force participation rate	Unemployed	Unemployment rate
All female family heads	7,238	3,931	54.3	391	9.9
With own children under 18	4,402	2,636	59.9	326	12.4
Family income under $3,000, total	1,373	459	33.4	141	30.7
With own children under 18	1,085	396	36.5	129	32.6
Family income $3,000–$4,999, total	1,436	597	41.6	97	16.2
With own children under 18	1,036	491	47.4	86	17.5
Family income $5,000–$6,999, total	1,144	639	55.9	53	8.3
With own children under 18	765	500	65.4	41	8.2
Family income $7,000–$9,999, total	1,225	840	68.6	53	6.3
With own children under 18	710	575	81.0	39	6.8
Family income $10,000 and over, total	2,059	1,396	67.8	47	3.4
With own children under 18	806	674	83.6	31	4.6

One out of every 8 families headed by women had an annual income of $15,000 or more. The majority of these families had two earners or more.

Most women heading families (4.4 million) have a combination of earnings and other income. As expected, their income level ($8,230 in 1974) was well above that of the 1.1 million women who either had earnings only ($6,830) or the 1.7 million women who had other income only ($3,510).

Income other than earnings includes social security payments, public assistance payments, interest, dividends, and rental income. The majority of the recipients of public assistance in the United States in 1974 were female family heads who received Aid for Families with Dependent Children (AFDC).

Conclusion

The incidence of poverty is still overwhelmingly the most important difference between the families headed by women and men. Although the social and demographic characteristics of women heading families have changed, their climb to a higher income bracket remains difficult. The number of poor families headed by women is continuously rising, while that of men is steadily falling. From 1970 to 1974, the number of poor families headed by women had risen by 21 percent, while those headed by men had declined by 17 percent. For several million of these women, the barriers impeding the climb continue to be inadequate training and education for the current job market, and, in some cases, heavy child care responsibilities. More paid employment would seem to be the solution, but in reality most of these women are at the lower end of the occupation ladder. Unless they can penetrate the more skilled occupations that pay higher salaries, they will not be able to provide their families an adequate or comfortable living. □

FOOTNOTES

[1] Family Head—The term family head as used in this article refers to the head of a primary or secondary family residing with one or more persons who are related by blood, marriage, or adoption.

Unless otherwise indicated, data in the tables and most of the text are based primarily on information from supplementary questions in the March 1975 survey of the labor force conducted for the Bureau of Labor Statistics by the Bureau of the Census through its Current Population Survey. Estimates based on a sample, such as those shown in the tables, may vary considerably from results obtained by a complete count in cases where the numbers shown are small. Therefore, differences between small numbers or percents based on them may not be significant. For more information, see Howard Hayghe, "Marital and family characteristics of workers, March 1975," *Monthly Labor Review,* November 1975, pp. 52–56, reprinted with additional tabular data and an explanatory note as Special Labor Force Report 183.

Families are classified as being above or below the low-income level according to the poverty index adopted by a Federal Interagency Committee in 1969. The poverty thresholds are updated every year to reflect changes in the Consumer Price Index (CPI). Thus, the poverty threshold for a nonfarm family of four headed by a woman was $5,014 in 1974, about 11 percent higher than the comparable 1973 cutoff of $4,521. For further details, see *Characteristics of the Population below the Poverty Level: 1974, Current Population Reports, Consumer Income,* Series P-60, No. 102 (Bureau of the Census, 1976), pp. 1, 143, and 146.

[2] See Beatrice Rosenberg and Ethel Mendelsohn, "Legal Status of Women," *The Book of States, 1974–75,* Vol. XX (Lexington, Ky., Council of State Governments, 1974).

[3] See *Female Family Heads, Current Population Reports, Special Studies,* Series P-23, No. 50 (Bureau of the Census, 1974), p. 1. Also see Paul C. Glick, *Some Recent Changes in American Families, Current Population Reports, Special Studies,* Series P-23, No. 52 (Bureau of the Cenus, 1974), p. 8.

[4] *Female Family Heads,* p. 1.

[5] See Lucy B. Mallan, "Young Widows and Their Children: A Comparative Report," *Social Security Bulletin,* May 1975, pp. 3–21.

[6] Mallan, "Young Widows and Their Children," p. 5.

[7] See *Money Income in 1974 of Families and Persons in the United States, Current Population Reports, Consumer Income,* Series P-60, No. 101 (Bureau of the Census, 1976), table 52, p. 104.

[8] *Children of Working Mothers, March 1975,* Summary/Special Labor Force Report (Bureau of Labor Statistics, August 1975), table 1.

[9] *Household and Family Characteristics: March 1975, Current Population Reports, Population Characteristics,* Series P-20, No. 291 (Bureau of the Census, 1976), table 14, p. 68.

[10] See *Characteristics of the Population below the Poverty Level: 1974,* table A-3, p. 146.

[11] *Money Income and Poverty Status of Families and Persons in the United States: 1974, Current Population Reports, Consumer Income,* Series P-60, No. 99 (Bureau of the Census, 1975), p. 22.

[12] *Characteristics of the Population below the Poverty Level: 1974,* table 29.

[13] For more detail, see Robert L. Stein, "The economic status of families headed by women," *Monthly Labor Review,* December 1970, pp. 3–10.

Special Labor Force Report 190. (Reprinted from June 1976, Monthly Labor Review) Bureau of Labor Statistics, U.S. Dept. of Labor.

Part six : Housing

Housing

Rent or Buy?

Evaluating alternatives in the shelter market

Introduction

Should I rent or buy?

At some time in your life, you are likely to face a choice between owning or renting a house or other shelter. The decision to own or rent depends on many things. These can be looked at from three aspects:

- What kind of shelter meets your preferences and needs?
- How much is it going to cost and how much can you spend each month for shelter?
- How can you make the best investment of your money while obtaining shelter that meets your needs?

The personal preference aspect. Looking at it from the first aspect, you will want to consider such factors as your age and family status, the stability of employment of the various members of the family, and the likelihood of your moving from one location to another.

Beyond these, the choice has some highly subjective elements. Do you like to "putter around" the house and yard on do-it-yourself projects, or do you dislike having to be responsible for maintenance, small repairs, lawn tending? Is the idea of "putting down roots" and gaining homeowner status in the community important to you?

Because shelter requirements and wants vary widely from individual to individual, from family to family, and from one time to another, it is

---

This pamphlet was prepared by Raymond W. Gieseman of the Division of Living Conditions Studies in the Office of Prices and Living Conditions, with the collaboration of Georgena Potts and Rosalie Epstein of the Bureau's Office of Publications.

not possible to make any blanket statement about the kind of shelter that is "best." It is not likely that anyone else can give you much guidance about the weight to be given to all the different subjective considerations which enter into the decision.

The cost aspect. A second aspect of the shelter decision concerns the costs you will incur and how much you can afford to spend for the kind of shelter you want and need. How different are costs of ownership and rental? Is there any way to compare them? What can you afford to spend?

The amount you spend for shelter is influenced by personal considerations and by your income, both your present income and what you expect it to be in the future. Information on what others spend for shelter is given on page 3. Costs when owning are analyzed in Part II, and Part III provides you with a basis for comparing the costs of owning and renting shelter.

The investment aspect. The third aspect of shelter decisions concerns the prudent investment of your money. Would you be better off investing your money in homeownership over a period of time, or saving your downpayment money and setting aside an amount each month, putting these funds into savings accounts or stocks and bonds, and so on?

This pamphlet is designed to help you analyze these investment factors and apply them to your own situation, so that you can make a judicious decision as to the better course for you to follow. The pamphlet describes and illustrates a technique for estimating the various costs and returns of being a homeowner or renter and then takes you step by step through the decision process with examples and worksheets so you can determine what the alternatives are for you, on the basis of choices and market conditions in your own area. The appendix gives additional details which you will need in working out your examples.

Part I. Differences between owning and renting

Can you afford to own?

If you are thinking of buying a home, you will need enough money to make a downpayment on the purchase. This can be an important barrier to homeownership for families and individuals who do not have adequate savings. On the other hand, when savings are sufficient to allow a choice between buying or renting, there is need to weigh the advantages of investing savings in shelter compared with other investment forms.

Unlike buying, there is no shelter investment requirement when you rent. In addition to saving the downpayment required to buy shelter, renters also do not have the settlement costs that are involved in buying and selling a house.

Renters do not have the long-term commitment to save regularly that homeowners have taken on through long-term financing of their home purchase. However, when the monthly cost to rent is less than to own, renters also have this same opportunity to save regularly. When these savings can be invested along with the savings from initial costs of ownership, returns while renting can be attractive.

How much should you spend for shelter?

Whether you buy or rent, you must consider the proportion of your income you want to spend for shelter. Many elements enter into the decision, varying with individuals, locations, and life styles. There are no hard and fast rules.

Commonly heard rules of thumb suggest that the average family or individual should spend about one-quarter of income for shelter (sometimes stated as "one week's pay out of every month"), and that a buyer ordinarily looks for a house within a market price 2½ times his annual income. But none of the data available from studies of actual spending support these conventional rules of thumb, or the suitability of any generalization that would be applicable to all families.

The rules cited above do not include outlays for utilities. However, when comparing homeownership costs with rental rate quotations, it is desirable to use a concept which includes these outlays. Therefore, the term "shelter" as used in this pamphlet has been broadened to include utilities—heat, electricity, water and sewerage, but excluding telephone.

Information on actual shelter expenditures obtained by the Bureau of Labor Statistics in a national survey of families and individuals in 1960 and 1961 indicates that, on the average, owners and renters spent 16 percent of their annual income after taxes on shelter, including utilities. For homeowner families, shelter expenditures included outlays for mortgage interest, property insurance, property taxes, maintenance and repairs, and utilities, and averaged 15 percent of income after taxes in 1960-61. This figure would have been about 20 percent if cash outlays including mortgage principal payments made by homeowners were included. For renter families, shelter outlays, including utilities, averaged 18 percent.

Results of the survey also indicate that well-to-do families spend a smaller proportion of income on shelter than families with smaller incomes. This applies both to homeowners and renters.

How do tax benefits affect shelter costs?

If you decide to buy shelter, you may benefit by being able to deduct a part of your ownership costs when filing your income tax returns. Amounts spent for interest and taxes are deductible items in Federal and many State and local returns. The amount you save will depend on your income and the amount of other expenses you have to itemize. These savings tend to lower the cost of owning. Renters do not have similar tax benefits for any portion of their shelter outlays.

How do price changes affect monthly costs of owning or renting?

Over time, costs of shelter change in response to price change. Home purchase prices and mortgage interest rates have moved upward in recent years, as have property taxes, property insurance rates, and prices of maintenance and repair items and services. In 1973, prices for these elements of shelter, as measured in the Consumer Price Index, were 64 percent higher than in 1965.

The price change measure cited above includes current-year home buyers. However, the vast majority of homeowners own homes or are paying for homes that were purchased in earlier years. Costs for these owners are not affected by changes in home purchase prices and mortgage interest rates. For these owners, shelter costs increased 25 percent over the 8-year period due to increases in taxes, insurance, and prices for repair and maintenance items and services.

For renters, increases in costs were similar to those experienced by those who owned their homes, as landlords passed on increased costs resulting from higher taxes, insurance rates, and prices for repairs and maintenance. Available information suggests that, on average, contract rent levels rose about 27 percent between 1965 and 1973. Table 1 summarizes these changes in shelter costs for the period 1965-73.

Table 1. Effects of price change on shelter costs, 1965-73
(Index: 1965 = 100)

Year	Homeownership costs [1]		Contract rent
	Including changes in purchase prices and mortgage interest rates	Purchase prices and mortgage interest rates held constant	
1965	100.0	100.0	100.0
1966	105.0	101.8	101.6
1967	108.6	104.0	103.7
1968	116.9	106.8	106.6
1969	128.8	110.5	110.6
1970	142.1	114.6	115.6
1971	145.9	118.7	120.0
1972	151.8	122.3	124.3
1973	163.5	125.4	126.9

[1] Includes home purchase and financing costs, property taxes, home ownership insurance premiums, and outlays for maintenance and repairs.

Note: Data are for December of each year.

Source: Based on data from the Consumer Price Index of the Bureau of Labor Statistics.

Over time, costs for existing homeowners and rental rates for occupants of the same unit tend to respond similarly to price change, although changes in housing needs and responsiveness of local housing markets to these needs may affect the relationship in particular places at particular times. The exception comes, of course, when a particular rental unit is sold. The decision to sell is a factor over which the owner has control; the renter does not.

How does the type of shelter affect the comparison?

The type of shelter you are interested in is an important factor affecting costs and, therefore, the decision to buy or rent. Recent trends in the shelter market have increased the variety of shelter types available for owning or renting. As a result, the comparison of costs and returns between buying and renting can involve similar or widely divergent shelter types.

Between 1960 and 1970, many apartment units were constructed to accommodate large numbers of young people who were entering the job market for the first time, and young couples who were setting up housekeeping but lacked the resources to buy. Many of these have since acquired some savings and have started families, which make them likely candidates for homeownership. But rising construction costs and higher prices for homesites have made it more costly for them to buy. During the same period the numbers of older individuals and couples whose families were grown also increased. These factors encouraged a wider variety of shelter types. Typical is the trend toward combining the features of apartment-style living with homeownership.

Ownership of condominium and cooperative apartments, which until recently was centered in a few metropolitan areas, is growing. Many of these units are attached townhouses or in multi-unit structures (garden style "walk-up" apartments or elevator high-rises). In the condominium form of ownership, the owner-occupier owns a single unit within a structure and shares in the ownership of the grounds and common areas. Under the cooperative ownership plan, each owner-occupant owns a prorated share of the total project. Mobile homes offer still another option of ownership to the prospective home buyer.

Because shelter units for sale and for rent differ widely in type, size, age, location, underlying financing, and so forth, you may seldom have the opportunity or the need to determine whether, *for the same quality or quantity of shelter*, it is cheaper to own or rent. But there is need for some method of comparing costs and returns for types of shelter that meet your requirements. Parts II and III provide a basis for such a comparison.

Part II. Analyzing shelter costs and returns

The amount you can spend for rent and be as well off—from the viewpoint of investment—as if you owned your home, over a specified number of years, depends upon a number of factors. These include (1) the terms of purchase for shelter that meets your needs; (2) the monthly outlays required to retain and maintain your home; (3) the tax savings you experience as a homeowner; (4) your estimate of net proceeds from the sale of your home after a given number of years; and (5) the plans you make for alternative use of your money. The following sections provide background information on each of these factors and several examples to illustrate the analysis.

Terms of purchase

Few home buyers can buy a house outright. They have to borrow, arranging for the purchase in one of the following ways: (1) conventional financing; (2) financing guaranteed by the Veterans Administration (VA)—available only to veterans; and (3) financing insured by the Federal Housing Administration (FHA). Conventional loans are made by private lending institutions (primarily banks and savings and loan companies), according to terms agreed to by the borrower and the lender. VA and FHA loans are also financed by private lenders, but are subject to Government regulation, and the lender is insured against possible default in payment.

Downpayment. The downpayment depends on the appraised value of the property and the amount the lender agrees to finance. There are no minimum downpayment requirements for conventional loans, but the amount commonly runs between 10 and 25 percent of the appraised value. The downpayment for government-backed loans is also determined by agreement between the borrower and the lender, but minimum requirements have been established by law. Under recently approved legislation governing FHA loans, the buyer must pay at least 3 percent down on the first $25,000, 10 percent on the next $10,000, and 20 percent on the excess over $35,000. The mortgage must not exceed $45,000. There is no minimum downpayment required for VA loans unless the asking price exceeds the appraised value of the property.

Settlement costs. Another item of cost in buying a house is settlement. These costs occur when property is exchanged. They include closing costs, loan discounts, prepaid items, and sales commissions. *Closing costs* are charges for obtaining the mortgage loan and transferring the real estate title. A *loan discount* is a charge assessed by a lender to improve his return (these are sometimes called *mortgage points*). *Prepaid items* are amounts required for advance payment of real estate taxes, insurance premiums, and other assessments such as fees paid for improvements to sidewalks, roads, and sewers.

For buyers, settlement costs include closing costs and amounts required for prepaid items. The settlement costs for sellers are loan discount payments and sales commissions.

Settlement costs vary from locality to locality and with the purchase price of the house. In a study of applications received for Government-backed loans during March 1971, settlement costs (including loan discount payment, if any) averaged $1,937 or about 10 percent of the contract sale price.[1] The report states: "It is apparent that the two most expensive settlement cost items were loan discount payments, or points, and sales commission. Neither of these costs, however, was paid by the buyer at closing. Therefore, buyer settlement costs represented only about 23 percent of total settlement costs. The seller absorbed more than three-quarters of total settlement costs and probably attempted to recapture some or all of this expense through an increased sale price." Thus, settlement costs amount to about 2 percent of the market price for the buyer and 8 percent for the seller. Comparable data were not available for homes with conventional loans.

Mortgage term. Most mortgages commonly run between 20 and 30 years in length. The term of the mortgage may differ with the three types of loan programs. For example, in 1971, mortgage terms for conventional loans averaged 26.2 years for new houses and 24.2 years for existing houses while 99 percent of the VA-guaranteed loans on new houses and 87 percent of the loans on existing houses had mortgage terms of 26 to 30 years. The average length of the full term for FHA loans on homes purchased in 1971 was 29.9 years and 28.9 years, respectively, for new and existing homes.

The average mortgage term on all three types of loan programs has been increasing in recent years. Differences in length of term among the programs have, however, been diminishing.

[1] *Report on Mortgage Settlement Costs* (Washington, U.S. Department of Housing and Urban Development and Veterans Administration, January 1972).

Mortgage interest rates. In recent years mortgage interest rates have fluctuated considerably for all types of loans. Rates are usually different for government-guaranteed loans and conventional loans. Ceiling rates for FHA- and VA-guaranteed loans are established jointly by the respective agencies and are announced by the Secretary of Housing and Urban Development. Rates on conventional loans are regulated by State governments. Ceiling and contract interest rates for loans on existing houses since 1970 are shown in table 2.

When the going interest rate is above the State or Federal ceiling rate, it is sometimes necessary to pay a loan discount, or "mortgage points", in order to obtain a loan. The additional charges for mortgage points are normally assessed at the time of settlement and are included in settlement costs, discussed earlier.

FHA-backed loans are subject to an annual insurance premium of one-half of 1 percent of the mortgage balance owed. Some lenders may also require private mortgage insurance on conventional loans. Premiums will vary with the individual insurer.

Effects of terms on cost of financing. The price and amount paid down on a home determine the size of loan required. The mortgage term and the rate of interest determine the cost of financing such a loan. The following example illustrates how the cost of financing is affected by the mortgage term and the interest rate.

Suppose a $30,000 home is purchased with a $3,000 downpayment and the balance is financed for 20 years at 7 percent interest. The monthly mortgage payment will be $210 and the total cost of the loan is $50,300. Increasing the mortgage term from 20 to 30 years lowers monthly payments to $180, but increases the amount paid in interest by $14,500, making the total cost of the loan $64,800. Similarly, in-

Table 2. Rates for FHA, VA, and conventional loans, 1970-74

FHA		VA		Conventional	
Date set	Ceiling rate	Date set	Ceiling rate	Year	Contract interest rate
January 1970	8½	January 1970	8½	1970	8.20
December 1970	8	December 1970	8		
January 1971	7½	January 1971	7½	1971	7.54
February 1971	7	February 1971	7	1972	7.38
August 10, 1973	7¾	July 1973	7¾	1973	7.86
August 25, 1973	8½	August 1973	8½		
January 1974	8¼	January 1974	8¼		
April 1974	8½	April 1974	8½		
May 1974	8¾	May 1974	8¾	1974[1]	8.51
July 1974	9	July 1974	9		
August 1974	9½	August 1974	9½		

[1] January-June.

Sources: U.S. Department of Housing and Urban Development and Veterans Administration. Contract interest rates for conventional loans were tabulated from monthly rates for existing homes published in *Federal Home Loan Bank Board News* and were not adjusted for differences in loan volume between months.

creasing or decreasing the mortgage interest rate affects both the monthly payment and the total cost of the loan.

For additional information to help evaluate the cost of financing home loans, see table A-1 in the appendix.

Gross monthly outlays of homeowners

In addition to the monthly mortgage payment, other shelter outlays incurred on a regular basis are those for real estate taxes, property insurance premiums, costs of maintenance and repairs, and allowances for fuel and utilities. Excluded from this discussion are major improvements to house and grounds.

Estimates for some types of costs—taxes, insurance, and utilities—usually can be obtained from the seller or the real estate agent. (Also, tax payments are public records and can be verified in the appropriate office of local government). Maintenance and repair costs are more difficult to estimate for a particular house. In a 1968 study, annual maintenance and repair costs were estimated to run from ¾ to 1 percent of the value of the property.[2]

Monthly mortgage payments for principal and interest established at the time of purchase do not change during the life of the mortgage unless the loan is refinanced. Property taxes, however, as well as insurance rates and prices of maintenance and repair items and services, are not fixed. Table 3 shows year-to-year changes over the last decade for these items and for fuel and utilities.

Effects of tax savings on shelter costs of homeowners

One of the potential benefits of homeownership is a reduction in the amount of personal income tax that must be paid. Interest paid on the mortgage and the real estate taxes assessed against the property are tax deductible under Federal and most State and local income tax regulations, if deductions are itemized.

The effect of these tax savings when prorated monthly is to lower the homeowner's gross monthly outlay for shelter. The amount of such savings depends on the amount of income that would be taxed if deductions were not itemized and on the rate of taxation on this income.

Table 3. Changes in Consumer Price Index for all items, selected shelter components, and fuel and utilities, 1964-73

Consumer Price Index item	Percent change from preceding year									Percent change, 1964-73
	1965	1966	1967	1968	1969	1970	1971	1972	1973	
All items	1.9	3.4	3.0	4.7	6.1	5.5	3.4	3.4	8.8	48.0
Shelter item:										
Property taxes	4.4	3.7	6.7	6.1	5.5	10.1	9.1	9.4	.7	71.1
Insurance	6.9	4.9	5.8	4.8	5.2	2.5	6.1	2.1	−1.0	43.7
Maintenance and repairs	3.0	5.4	4.6	7.0	9.2	7.6	7.2	4.9	8.8	74.5
Fuel and utilities	.2	.2	.9	2.0	2.7	5.9	5.7	3.7	11.5	37.3

Note: Changes calculated from published indexes for December of each year.
Source: Bureau of Labor Statistics.

[2] John P. Shelton, "The Cost of Renting Versus Owning a Home", *Land Economics*, February 1968, pp. 59-72.

Typically, the amount of interest paid on home loans is highest in the first year and declines over time as the loan balance declines. On the other hand, property taxes tend to rise, due to higher property values and changes in tax rates. Having more property taxes to deduct tends to offset the smaller amounts of interest that can be deducted each year a house is owned.

Estimating net proceeds from sale of house

The decision to purchase a house should include an estimate of what the net proceeds would be if the house were sold at some future date. Buying a house usually requires investing some savings at the time of purchase. Further, additional money is regularly invested through the monthly principal payments—sometimes referred to as "forced savings."

The value of a homeowner's savings in the house depends on the market price of the house at the time of sale, selling costs, and any debts or liens against it. If a house is sold at the original purchase price, net proceeds will be amounts initially invested in downpayment and settlement, *plus* whatever portion of mortgage payments has been applied to reducing the principal, and *minus* selling costs and any taxes owed. However, if the value of the house has risen, the net proceeds from its sale may amount to more than the owner's purchased equity.

For example, assume a $25,000 house is purchased with a downpayment of $2,000, and the remaining $23,000 is financed at 7 percent for 30 years. Settlement costs are $500. After 10 years, the house is sold for $34,000 and selling costs are $2,700 (8 percent of market value). The net proceeds and gain from the sale of the house might look like this:

Sale price of house	$34,000
Less amounts owed at time of sale:	
Selling costs	2,700
Mortgage balance owed	19,800
Net proceeds from sale of house	$11,500
Less amounts invested:	
Downpayment and settlement costs	2,500
Reduction in mortgage balance (principal payments)	3,200
Gain from appreciation	$ 5,800

Rate of change in market value of owned home. The future market value of a house depends on its location, its age and structural condition, its adaptability to the needs of buyers, the overall need for housing, and general economic conditions. Neighborhood and community characteristics also have an effect on its future market value. In some localities, houses on an average may appreciate as much as 5 or 6 percent a year, or more; in others, they may bring less than the amount originally paid. In the example above, the house increased in value from $25,000 to $34,000 in 10 years, or an average of approximately 3 percent a year.

Two factors that tend to make homes appreciate in value are (1) rising costs of building new houses and (2) the higher cost of land suitable for housing. When the total cost of new houses goes up, home buyers tend to bid up the prices of existing houses.

The cost of construction for residential structures increased sharply between 1960 and 1972, rising nearly 80 percent during the period—an average annual increase of 5 percent a year This means that a house built for $10,000 in 1960 would have cost about $18,000 to build in 1972.

Another reason for rising home prices is the rise in the value of the land on which the house is situated. In recent years, the scarcity of suitable sites for building in major metropolitan areas has caused land values to increase. Prices for new homesites under FHA-insured loans doubled between 1960 and 1972, and market value of sites occupied by existing homes increased by more than 80 percent.

Rising construction costs and site costs are reflected in the prices of new and existing one-family homes purchased with FHA-backed loans. Between 1960 and 1972, the average sale price for new homes increased nearly 70 percent, or an average of about 4½ percent a year. Prices for existing homes sold in 1972 were almost 50 percent higher than prices for existing homes purchased in 1960, which represented almost a 3½ percent annual rate of increase. These rates compare with an average annual increase of about 3 percent in the price of all consumer goods and services over the same 12-year period.

The long-term trend is thus for houses to appreciate in value, but of course there is no guarantee that a particular house will do so, particularly during periods of recession. For example, one-family houses in 22 cities declined almost 29 percent in market value between 1925 and 1933.

Selling costs. Amounts that have to be paid at the time a house is sold are called selling costs. These usually include a brokerage fee paid to the real estate agent and may include a loan discount payment to enable the buyer to obtain a loan, if the house is sold to a buyer who finances his purchase through a government-backed loan.

The cost of selling a house can reduce the advantage of home purchase. How the buyer fares depends on the length of stay in the house and the rate of appreciation. For instance, if the selling costs amounted to 8 percent of the market price, the owner would have to realize an increase of 8 percent or more in the price of the house in order to recover his investment. If the rate of appreciation was approximately 3 percent a year, the owner would have to keep the house for 3 years or more in order to get back enough to balance out his initial down-payment and settlement costs.

Mortgage balance owed. A final deduction, before net proceeds from the sale of the house can be estimated, is the amount owed on the mortgage.

In most home financing, loans are amortized, or paid off, by a sequence of equal payments over a number of years. Since the loan balance is highest when the loan is first obtained, the amount applied to interest consumes a major portion of the regular monthly payments in the first few years, and only a small amount of the monthly payments goes to the purchase of additional equity. Thus, if a house is sold within 5 or 10 years of purchase, a substantial portion of the proceeds may be needed to retire the balance of the mortgage.

For example, on a 30-year, 7-percent loan, 94 percent of the initial loan amount would still be owed after 5 years of ownership. Even after

10 years of ownership, 86 percent of the principal would remain to be paid. The percent of the loan balance still owed on this loan at different times is shown below:

	Percent of mortgage balance still owed
After 5 years	94
After 10 years	86
After 15 years	74
After 20 years	57
After 25 years	33
After 30 years	0

Appendix table A-2 shows similar percentages for 20-, 25-, and 30-year loans at different interest rates.

Alternative investment opportunities

Some may prefer to put their money to work in other forms of investment, rather than buy a house. Other types of investment generally make it easier to respond to a change in circumstances or to take advantage of changing rates of return.

Downpayment and settlement costs. Invested in a savings account, funds (the equivalent of which the homeowner uses for downpayment and settlement costs) may earn 4, 5, or 6 percent a year, or more. The value of an investment of $2,500, compounded annually, is shown in table 4 for selected periods and rates of return. For further details on how these amounts were determined, see appendix table A-4.

Table 4.
Value of $2,500 compounded annually at selected rates of return

Period	4 percent	5 percent	6 percent
1 year	$2,600	$ 2,625	$ 2,650
5 years	3,042	3,190	3,345
10 years	3;700	4,072	4,477
20 years	5,477	6,632	8,017
30 years	8,107	10,805	13,357

Thus, at the end of a year, $2,500 invested at 5 percent would have returned $125 in interest. To gain this same amount in one year, the purchaser who used the $2,500 to buy a $25,000 house would have to sell it for enough to recover his investment (downpayment and principal payments, and selling costs), plus the $125 he could have earned by investing the money at 5 percent.

Regular monthly saving. When renting, additional savings may be needed to offset benefits homeowners have in being "forced" to save regularly through monthly mortgage principal payments and having houses that appreciate in value over a period of years. These savings are possible when the total cost to rent per month is lower than the monthly shelter outlay to own.

A regular savings program for renters may require more self-discipline than for those who buy. However, the cumulative effect of savings —often overlooked—might provide an incentive for such self-discipline. Regular savings of as little as $25 a month ($300 a year) could earn the amounts shown in table 5 if invested for the periods and at the rates of return illustrated. These values are based on information provided in appendix table A-5.

Table 5.
Value of savings of $25 per month at selected rates of return

Period	4 percent	5 percent	6 percent
5 years	$ 1,650	$ 1,700	$ 1,725
10 years	3,675	3,850	4,050
20 years	9,100	10,150	11,325
30 years	17,125	20,375	24,375

The combined value of the $2,500 investment and of savings of $25 a month over a 10-year period at 5 percent interest is $7,922 ($4,072 plus $3,850). This amount would accrue to the renter and could partially or fully offset net proceeds from owning and then selling a home. If it were possible to save as much as $50 per month by renting, the investment amount would total $11,772 ($4,072 plus $7,700) after 10 years, and would compare favorably with the net proceeds from owning illustrated in the example on page 10. Average annual yields for selected types of investments are shown in appendix table A-6.

Part III. Comparing investment returns from owning and renting

The following section outlines procedures which can be used to estimate how much you could spend for rented shelter and be as well off, from the viewpoint of investment, as if you bought a house. Over time, as your income and shelter needs change, or if your job requires that you move, you may wish to reconsider your shelter requirements. At that time, regardless of whether you are an owner or a renter, these procedures can be applied to evaluate your new alternatives.

There are six steps in the procedure:

1. Determine the purchase price and terms of financing for a house you would consider buying;
2. Estimate your gross monthly shelter outlay as a homeowner;
3. Estimate your net monthly shelter outlay as a homeowner;
4. Estimate your net proceeds if you were to sell the house at a specified price after a given period;
5. Estimate the amount of monthly savings required to offset net proceeds from owning, if you decide to rent;
6. Estimate the rent level which, in combination with a savings program, would equal your net monthly shelter outlay as a homeowner.

The first three steps help you establish the costs of owning a specific shelter unit that meets your needs and circumstances. Step 4 helps you determine the expected return from owning and then selling the unit after a period of time. Step 5 develops an alternative plan for saving the equivalent of these returns. In Step 6, you determine a rental rate that is comparable with the monthly cost of owning after allowing for the savings plan. Examples are given to illustrate the procedures. Space is provided to assist you in working through the steps for your own situation.

Step 1. Determine the purchase price and terms of financing for a house you would consider buying.

In Example A, page 14, the price of the house is the average price for new homes purchased in 1971 with FHA-insured loans. The terms of financing—loan ratio, interest rate, and mortgage term—were typical of FHA-insured loans in that year.

Example B shows a house with the same purchase price and terms of financing as in Example A, but with a larger downpayment. The lower cost for debt service in Example B ($128.80 compared with $156.10) is due entirely to the larger downpayment.

For your example, you will need to determine the price of the house or condominium apartment to be analyzed and the amount of downpayment required (or that you plan to make). After you subtract the downpayment, the balance of the sale price remaining is the amount to be borrowed. Sometimes part of the settlement costs are also financed; if this is true in your case, this sum should be included in the amount to be borrowed.

To determine the monthly payment you need to know the rate of interest on home loans and the number of years over which you plan to finance the balance. Then, using the rates in appendix table A-1 and the example illustrating its use, you can determine the amount of the monthly payment.

For your example, you may have an actual estimate of settlement costs received from a realtor or other source. If this is not available, you may want to use an estimate based on a percent of the sale price of the house, such as the 2-percent estimate discussed on page 7.

Step 2. Estimate your gross monthly shelter outlay as a homeowner.

In addition to regular monthly payments to service the home mortgage, your expenses will include property taxes, insurance, and maintenance and repair bills. You may not be billed each month for these costs, but they can be prorated on a monthly basis. You should also estimate average monthly outlays for utilities that would be included in the monthly rent check if you were renting.

In the table on page 15 the "other monthly costs" are 1971 average costs estimated by FHA for a house with an average price of $23,835.

You will find suggestions to help you estimate monthly amounts for property taxes, insurance, and maintenance and repairs for your example on page 8.

Step 3. Estimate your net monthly shelter outlay as a homeowner.

Both mortgage interest and property taxes paid are tax deductible. This frequently makes it worthwhile for homeowners to itemize rather

Terms of purchase and financing

	Example A	Example B	Your example
Sale price of unit	$23,835	$23,835	$______
Terms of financing:			
Downpayment:			
Amount	1,535	5,435	______
Percent of sale price	6.4	22.8	______
Characteristics of the mortgage:			
Amount borrowed	22,300	18,400	______
Interest rate (percent)	7½	7½	______
Mortgage term (years to maturity)	30	30	______
Monthly cost of debt service:			
Payment to principal and interest	156.10	128.80	______
Mortgage insurance premium (if any)	—	—	______
Total to debt service per month	156.10	128.80	______
Initial outlay required to purchase:			
Downpayment	1,535	5,435	______
Settlement costs	532	532	______
Total initial outlay required	2,067	5,967	______

Gross monthly shelter outlay to own

	Example A	Example B	Your example
Monthly debt service:			
Mortgage payment	$156.10	$128.80	$______
Mortgage insurance premium (if any)	—	—	______
Total to debt service each month	156.10	128.80	______
Other monthly costs:			
Real estate taxes	34.79	34.79	______
Property insurance	10.16	10.16	______
Maintenance and repairs[1]	13.29	13.29	______
Utilities	26.87	26.87	______
Total other costs each month	85.11	85.11	______
Estimated shelter outlay per month:			
Debt service (principal and interest)	156.10	128.80	______
Other costs	85.11	85.11	______
Gross monthly shelter outlay	$241.21	$213.91	______

[1] Include monthly fees if the unit is a condominium or cooperative.

than to use the standard deduction when figuring their income taxes. Examples on page 17 illustrate the potential savings in Federal income taxes for homeowners at different levels of income, if they itemize their expenses for mortgage interest and real estate taxes. Not shown here are additional savings which may accrue to homeowners from similar deductions when filing State and local income tax returns.

In the table on page 16 taxes are figured when there are no deductions for homeownership expenses. The calculations use 1972 rates applicable for married persons filing jointly and claiming four personal exemptions ($750 each). The standard deduction amounts to 15 percent of adjusted gross income, or a maximum of $2,000.

In the table on page 17 the tax liabilities with deductions for homeownership expenses are based on the monthly amounts for real estate taxes and mortgage interest shown in Step 2 for Examples A and B. The $417 deduction for real estate taxes is the $34.79 shown in Step 2, converted to an annual basis. The $1,667 deduction for mortgage interest in Example A was obtained by annualizing the mortgage payment shown in Step 2 ($156.10 × 12 = $1,873.20) and calculating the amount for mortgage interest as a percent of the annual mortgage payment. (According to appendix table A-3, 89 percent of the first year's payment goes to interest. Thus, $1,873.20 × .89 = $1,667.15. By the same process, mortgage interest for Example B was $1,375.58.

Tax liability without deductions for mortgage interest and real estate taxes

				Your example
Income before taxes	$10,000	$15,000	$25,000	
Less deductions:				
Standard or "other"[1]	1,500	2,000	2,000	
Less personal exemptions	2,000	3,000	3,000	
Equals taxable income	$ 5,500	$10,000	$20,000	
Tax liability:				
Annual	$ 905	$ 1,820	$ 4,380	
Monthly	$ 75	$ 152	$ 365	

[1] Examples assume the standard deduction equals or exceeds amounts for "other" deductions which can be itemized, excluding all mortgage interest and property taxes. Based on 1972 rates.

Amounts for "other" itemized deductions in Examples A and B—charitable contributions, medical and dental expenses, other deductible interest and taxes, and other losses or expenses that can be itemized—were assumed to total 80 percent of the standard deduction ($1,200 and $1,600, respectively, of the $10,000 and $15,000 income levels), and 100 percent ($2,000) when income is $25,000.

The monthly saving by itemizing mortgage interest and taxes shown for Examples A and B was obtained by comparing the tax liabilities with and without allowable deductions for homeownership expenses.

Tax liability with deductions for mortgage interest and real estate taxes

				Your example
For Example A (larger monthly mortgage payments):				
Income before taxes	$10,000	$15,000	$25,000	______
Less deductions:				
Real estate taxes	417	417	417	______
Mortgage interest	1,667	1,667	1,667	______
Other	1,200	1,600	2,000	______
Less personal exemptions	3,000	3,000	3,000	______
Equals taxable income	$ 3,716	$ 8,316	$17,916	______
Tax liability:				
Annual	$ 572	$ 1,450	$ 3,796	______
Monthly	$ 48	$ 121	$ 316	______
Monthly tax saving by itemizing mortgage interest and taxes[1]	$ 27	$ 31	$ 49	______
For Example B (smaller monthly mortgage payments):				
Income before taxes	$10,000	$15,000	$25,000	______
Less deductions:				
Real estate taxes	417	417	417	______
Mortgage interest	1,376	1,376	1,376	______
Other	1,200	1,600	2,000	______
Less personal exemptions	3,000	3,000	3,000	______
Equals taxable income	$ 4,007	$ 8,607	$18,207	______
Táx liability:				
Annual	$ 621	$ 1,514	$ 3,878	______
Monthly	$ 52	$ 126	$ 323	______
Monthly tax saving by itemizing mortgage interest and taxes[1]	$ 23	$ 26	$ 42	______

[1] Tax saving equals the difference between monthly tax liability without homeownership deductions (p. 16) and monthly liability with deductions. Based on 1972 rates.

Net monthly shelter outlay can then be figured by subtracting the estimated tax saving from the gross monthly outlay estimated in Step 2. The results for Examples A and B are shown below.

Net monthly shelter outlay to own

	Income before taxes			Your example
	$10,000	$15,000	$25,000	$______
Example A:				
Gross monthly shelter outlay (p. 15)	$241	$241	$241	$______
Less tax saving (from p. 17) ..	27	31	49	______
Net monthly shelter outlay ..	$214	$210	$192	$______
Example B:				
Gross monthly shelter outlay (p. 15)	$214	$214	$214	$______
Less tax saving (from p. 17) ..	23	26	42	______
Net monthly shelter outlay ..	$191	$188	$172	$______

In your example, you can estimate your potential tax savings by refiguring your last year's tax return, using the mortgage interest and property tax rates for your situation. If you used the standard deduction last year, you will need to compile a list of other deductions you could have used and their amounts. When the amount for "other items" you have to deduct equals or exceeds the standard deduction, you benefit from every dollar paid out for mortgage interest and property taxes by itemizing.

Estimated tax savings shown above are based on amounts of mortgage interest and property taxes paid in the first year of purchase. This gives maximum write-off allowance to homeowners, since the amount of mortgage interest paid will decrease as the loan balance declines. It is likely, however, that part of this loss of mortgage interest write-off will be offset by higher property taxes, as the assessment rate and the value of the house change with time.

Step 4. Estimate your net proceeds if you were to sell the house at a specific price after a given period.

Before you proceed with this step and the steps that follow, it is necessary to determine the length of time over which you want to compare your alternatives when owning and renting. The time span you select becomes your "planning period." In the examples that follow, values for planning periods of 5, 10, and 20 years are shown. Information has been provided to help you work through your own example for a 5-, 10-, 20-, or 30-year period.

Net proceeds represent the amount received from sale of the house, less the costs of selling and less the balance owed on the mortgage. Any proceeds in excess of these expenses represent 1) the return of your equity and 2) gain from appreciation.

It may seem unrealistic to attempt to estimate proceeds from the sale of a house you have not yet purchased, but this step is necessary if you wish to evaluate your likely returns as well as your costs. It requires an estimate of the future market value of the house at the probable time of sale.

Future market value of dwelling unit and selling costs

Several different rates of appreciation are used below to illustrate the future market value of a house priced at $23,835 in 1971, after 5, 10, and 20 years. Your estimate of the rate of appreciation for the house you are considering should be based on local market conditions, present and expected, and should allow for changes in general economic conditions. The data in appendix table A-4 will assist you with your example.

Estimated future market value of house

Appreciation per year	After 5 years	After 10 years	After 20 years
0 percent	$23,835	$23,835	$23,835
2 percent	26,300	29,100	35,400
4 percent	29,000	35,300	52,200
6 percent	31,900	42,700	76,400
__ percent, your example	____	____	____

For the future market prices shown above, the selling costs (at 8 percent of the market value of the house) would be:

Estimated costs of selling house

Appreciation per year	After 5 years	After 10 years	After 20 years
0 percent	$1,907	$1,907	$1,907
2 percent	2,104	2,328	2,832
4 percent	2,320	2,824	4,176
6 percent	2,552	3,416	6,112
__ percent, your example	____	____	____

Amount still owed on house

A mortgage loan is paid off at a very slow rate in the early years, but the rate accelerates as the year of final payment approaches. In Example A, page 20, after 10 years the balance remaining to be paid off on the $22,300 loan is approximately $19,400. After 20 years, the balance owed is $13,150, all of which would be retired in the last 10 years of the mortgage. Appendix table A-2 will help you to determine the amount that would still be owed on your mortgage after different periods of time.

Estimated balance owed on mortgage

	Example A	Example B	Your example
Mortgage term (in years) (from p. 14)	30	30	______
Rate of interest (percent) (from p. 14)	7½	7½	______
Mortgage balance owed:			
Initial balance	$22,300	$18,400	______
After 5 years	21,200	17,500	______
After 10 years	19,400	16,000	______
After 20 years	13,150	10,850	______

Net proceeds from sale of house

The calculations shown here are for a $23,835 house with a $22,300 loan (see Step 1, Example A) and a hypothetical 4-percent annual rate of appreciation. The net proceeds follow from estimates made above.

Net proceeds from owning

	After 5 years	After 10 years	After 20 years
Net proceeds for Example A:			
Market value of house (from p. 19)	$29,000	$35,300	$52,200
Less selling costs (from p. 19)	2,320	2,824	4,176
Less mortgage balance owed (from p. 20)	21,200	19,400	13,150
Net proceeds	$ 5,480	$13,076	$34,874
Net proceeds for Example B:			
Market value of house	$29,000	$35,300	$52,200
Less selling costs	2,320	2,824	4,176
Less mortgage balance owed	17,500	16,000	10,850
Net proceeds	$ 9,180	$16,476	$37,174
Your example:			
Market value of house	______	______	______
Less selling costs	______	______	______
Less mortgage balance owed	______	______	______
Net proceeds	______	______	______

The net proceeds shown in the examples do not take into account the possibility that you may have to pay capital gains taxes on part of your gain. The gain you realize by selling is *not* taxed if, within one year of the date of sale, you buy and occupy another house whose market price equals or exceeds the price you received for your old house, less selling costs and allowable expenses for improvements.

Step 5. Estimate the amount of monthly savings required to offset net proceeds from owning, if you decide to rent.

If you do not buy a house, you presumably have available the amount of money you would have spent on downpayment and settlement costs. This amount has potential for growth in other types of investment.

In the example below, a $2,067 investment—the amount of downpayment and settlement costs in Example A, Step 1—grows to $2,637 in 5 years and to $5,483 in 20 years, at 5 percent interest a year. A $5,967 investment (from Example B) grows to $7,613 in 5 years and to $15,830 in 20 years.

You can determine this growth potential, at the rate of return you specify, by using the table of compound interest (see appendix table A-4), applied to the amount of the downpayment and settlement costs you specified in Step 1. Appendix table A-6 shows the average annual returns on selected types of investment.

Interest and dividends received during the year are subject to taxation as personal income. You may want to allow for this by specifying a rate of return that is roughly net after taxes. For example, if you anticipate a 5-percent return per year on your money, you may want to use 4 percent when working through your example.

Value of savings not used for downpayment and settlement

Initial investment and rate of return per year	Value of initial investment		
	After 5 years	After 10 years	After 20 years
Example A, investment of $2,067:			
4 percent	$2,515	$ 3,059	$ 4,528
5 percent	2,637	3,367	5,483
6 percent	2,765	3,702	6,628
Example B, investment of $5,967:			
4 percent	$7,261	$ 8,831	$13,073
5 percent	7,613	9,720	15,830
6 percent	7,983	10,686	19,136
Your example, investment of $____:			
____ percent	$____	$____	$____

Advantage (or disadvantage) of investing in a house

The value of money not invested in a house (downpayment and settlement costs) plus the interest earned thereon for an appropriate number of years is deducted from net proceeds from owning a house, as estimated in Step 4, to determine the additional savings, if any, needed to balance the investment gain from owning. The examples below are based on net proceeds shown in Step 4 and on initial investments of $2,067 (Example A) and $5,967 (Example B), compounded at 5-percent net return per year.

Additional savings needed when renting

	5 years	10 years	20 years
Example A, initial investment of $2,067:			
Net proceeds from sale of house (p. 20)	$5,480	$13,076	$34,874
Less alternative investment, at 5 percent (p. 21)	2,637	3,367	5,483
Net advantage from investment in house	$2,843	$ 9,709	$29,391
Additional saving required each month (at 5 percent interest) to offset net advantage of owning[1]	$ 42	$ 63	$ 72
Example B, initial investment of $5,967:			
Net proceeds from sale of house	$9,180	$16,476	$37,174
Less alternative investment, at 5 percent	7,613	9,720	15,830
Net advantage from investment in house	1,567	6,756	21,344
Additional saving required each month (at 5 percent interest) to offset net advantage of owning[1]	$ 23	$ 44	$ 53
Your example, with initial investment of $____:			
Net proceeds from sale of house	____	____	____
Less alternative investment, at____ percent	____	____	____
Net advantage from investment in house	____	____	____
Additional saving required each month (at ____ percent interest) to offset net advantage of owning[1]	____	____	____

[1] Obtained by dividing the net advantage from investment in house by factors given and explained in appendix table A-5.

For short periods of ownership of 1 to 3 years, the costs of buying and selling a house can use up much or all of the equity acquired. Savings not used for downpayment and settlement costs by renting, plus the investment return on these savings, in many cases will equal or exceed the net proceeds from buying and then selling a house.

For longer periods of time, as in the 5-, 10-, and 20-year periods in the illustration on page 22, the renter may need to supplement his initial saving from downpayment and settlement costs with a regular monthly amount to maintain parity with the owner.

In 10 years, the net proceeds from sale of the house, when purchased with an initial investment of $2,067 (Example A), exceed the alternative investment of the same amount invested over the 10-year period by $9,709. However, the advantage can be offset, while renting, by saving an additional $63 a month. These savings, when regularly invested, plus the alternative investment, balance the returns when renting with those from homeownership over the 10-year period. The monthly savings requirement in Example B over the 10-year period ($44) is lower than for Example A, due to the larger initial investment and interest earned ($9,720 compared with $3,367).

Step 6. Estimate the rent level which, in combination with a savings program, would equal your net monthly shelter outlay as a homeowner.

The difference between net monthly shelter outlay as a homeowner (Step 3) and the amount of monthly savings required to offset the gain (or loss) from investing in a house (Step 5) is the monthly outlay for rent which would leave the renter as well off, from an investment viewpoint, as if he had bought a house. In other words, to come out even with the homeowner over a period of time, the renter can spend for shelter only an amount equal to the difference between his investment program and the homeowner's shelter outlay. Of course, there is no assurance that rental shelter will be available in any given locality at a rate which makes this possible.

Results for Examples A and B are given on page 24, when the net shelter outlay per month is based on tax savings for a family of four persons with $15,000 annual income. In each case, the monthly saving and the balance available for monthly rent equal the net outlay per month to own.

The results indicate that the anticipated time interval is crucial. Thus, a renter who wanted to break even with an owner over a 20-year period would have to save more per month and spend less for rent than a renter who wanted to break even with an owner over a 5- or 10-year period.

In Example B, the lower net monthly outlay to own is due to the larger initial downpayment, which reduces the size of loan required and thereby reduces monthly payments. Alternatively, a renter investing an equivalent larger initial amount has to save less each month to break even with owning, so the monthly rental rate is nearly the same in the two examples.

Note that, in both examples, calculations are based on 4-percent appreciation for the house and 5-percent net return on alternative investments. Changing the expected rate of appreciation, as for example to 5 percent, would have increased the need for regular savings when renting and lowered the balance available for monthly rent. On the other hand, increasing the rate of return on alternative investments tends to lower the need for regular savings and to increase the balance available for monthly rent.

Balance available for monthly rent

	Planning period		
	5 years	10 years	20 years
From Example A, with income of $15,000:			
Net monthly shelter outlay per month to own (p. 18)	$210	$210	$210
Less monthly saving for alternative investment if renting (p. 22)	42	63	72
Balance available for monthly rent	$168	$147	$138
From Example B, with income of $15,000:			
Net monthly shelter outlay per month to own (p. 18)	$188	$188	$188
Less monthly saving for alternative investment if renting (p. 22)	23	44	53
Balance available for monthly rent	$165	$144	$135
Your example, with income of $______:			
Net monthly shelter outlay per month to own (p. 18)	____	____	____
Less monthly saving for alternative investment if renting (p. 22)	____	____	____
Balance available for monthly rent	____	____	____

The results of these calculations as shown in Steps 1 through 6 will not, of course, in themselves determine your shelter decision, but they may help you, along with other considerations, to decide among your alternatives.

One closing note. It is important to remember that

- Over time, the personal factors involved in your shelter decision change.
- Over time, the cost factors involved in your shelter decision change.
- Over time, the investment factors involved in your shelter decision change.
- Over time, general economic conditions and the options available in the shelter market change.

If you keep these factors in mind, you will be far more likely to choose wisely when you come to decide whether you will be better off financially to

RENT OR BUY.

Appendix. Supplementary tables for analyzing shelter costs and returns.

Cost of financing home loans

Data in table A-1 can be used to estimate the amount of the monthly mortgage payment for any size of home loan. The following example illustrates its use.

EXAMPLE: John Jones needs a $24,500 home purchase loan, which he can obtain at 8 percent per year, for 30 years. What are his monthly mortgage payments?

ANSWER: $7.34 × 24.5 = $179.83.

Table A-1. Cost to finance $1,000, selected years and rates of interest

Rate of interest	Years financed					
	20 years		25 years		30 years	
	Monthly cost	Total cost	Monthly cost	Total cost	Monthly cost	Total cost
5½	$6.88	$1,651	$6.15	$1,845	$5.68	$2,045
6	7.17	1,721	6.45	1,935	6.00	2,160
6½	7.46	1,790	6.76	2,028	6.33	2,279
7	7.76	1,862	7.07	2,121	6.66	2,398
7½	8.06	1,934	7.39	2,217	7.00	2,520
8	8.37	2,009	7.72	2,316	7.34	2,642
8½	8.68	2,083	8.06	2,418	7.69	2,768
9	9.00	2,160	8.40	2,520	8.05	2,898
10	9.66	2,318	9.09	2,727	8.78	3,161

Source: Based on rates published in such sources as *Payment Table for Monthly Mortgage Loans* and *Comprehensive Mortgage Payment Tables*, publications Nos. 292 and 392, respectively (Boston, Financial Publishing Co.).

Mortgage payments

The tables presented here help determine the rate at which home loans are retired and the percent of mortgage payments used to pay interest in selected years.

The following example shows how table A-2 can be used:

1. *To estimate the amount still owed on a mortgage after mortgage payments have been made regularly for a specified number of years.*

EXAMPLE: John Jones just financed $20,000 through a 30-year home loan at 7 percent. How much will he still owe on the mortgage after 10 years?

ANSWER: $20,000 x .86 = $17,200.

Table A-2. Percent of original loan amount still owed after specified number of years, selected mortgage terms, at different rates of interest

Interest rate	After 5 years	After 10 years	After 15 years	After 20 years	After 25 years	After 30 years
	Life of mortgage—30 years					
5	92	81	68	51	28	0
5½	92	83	69	52	30	0
6	93	84	71	54	31	0
6½	94	85	72	55	32	0
7	94	86	74	57	33	0
7½[1]	95	87	75	59	34	0
8	95	88	77	60	36	0
9	96	89	79	63	39	0
10	97	91	82	66	41	0
	Life of mortgage—25 years					
5	89	74	55	31	0	
5½	89	75	56	32	0	
6	90	76	58	33	0	
6½	91	77	59	34	0	
7	91	79	61	36	0	
7½	92	80	62	37	0	
8	92	81	64	38	0	
9	93	83	66	40	0	
10	94	85	69	43	0	
	Life of mortgage—20 years					
5	83	62	35	0		
5½	84	63	36	0		
6	85	64	37	0		
6½	86	66	38	0		
7	86	67	39	0		
7½	87	68	40	0		
8	87	69	41	0		
9	89	71	43	0		
10	90	73	45	0		

[1] Percentages at this rate of interest are used to determine the mortgage balance owed on 30-year loans in Examples A and B, discussed on p. 20.

Source: See table A-1.

The following example shows how table A-3 can be used:

1. *To estimate the amount of mortgage interest paid in a given year.*

EXAMPLE: John Jones has a 30-year, 7-percent loan. His mortgage payments are $150 a month ($1,800 a year). How much of the $1,800 was used to pay interest in the first year?

ANSWER: $1,800 x .87 = $1,566.

Table A-3. Mortgage interest as a percent of annual mortgage payments in selected years, selected mortgage terms, at different rates of interest

Interest rate	1st year [1]	5th year	10th year	15th year	20th year	25th year	30th year
	Life of mortgage—30 years						
5	77	72	64	54	40	24	3
5½	81	75	68	57	43	26	3
6	83	78	71	60	47	28	3
6½	85	80	73	63	49	30	3
7	87	83	76	66	52	32	4
7½	89	86	79	68	55	34	4
8	91	88	81	71	57	36	4
9	93	90	84	75	61	39	5
10	95	92	87	79	65	42	5
	Life of mortgage—25 years						
5	71	64	54	40	24	3	
5½	74	68	57	43	26	3	
6	77	71	60	47	28	3	
6½	79	73	63	49	30	3	
7	82	76	66	52	32	4	
7½	84	79	68	55	34	4	
8	86	81	71	57	36	4	
9	89	84	75	61	39	5	
10	92	87	79	65	42	5	
	Life of mortgage—20 years						
5	62	54	40	24	3		
5½	66	57	43	26	3		
6	69	60	47	28	3		
6½	72	63	49	30	3		
7	74	66	52	32	4		
7½	77	68	55	34	4		
8	79	71	57	36	4		
9	82	75	61	39	5		
10	85	79	65	42	5		

[1] Only the first-year percentages shown here are used to compare the investment advantages of owning and renting.

Source: See table A-1.

Future value of an investment

Table A-4 can be used to determine the future value of an initial investment of any given sum, at different rates of return and over different time periods. The table may also be used to determine the future cost of an item (or group of items) whose price is changing by a certain percentage each year. The following examples show how table A-4 can be used:

1. To estimate the future market value of any house or property.

EXAMPLE: The current market value of a house is $25,000, and it is expected to appreciate 4 percent a year over the next 10 years. What would be its value in 10 years?

Answer: $25,000 x 1.480 = $37,000.

2. To estimate future value of a fixed sum of money invested at different rates of return for a given number of years.

EXAMPLE: The sum of $2,000 is invested for 20 years at 5½ percent return per year. What is the value of the $2,000 in 20 years?

ANSWER: $2,000 x 2.918 = $5,836.

3. To estimate the future cost of any items of expenditure or expenditures for groups of items whose prices are subject to an expected percentage change (increase) each year.

EXAMPLE: John Jones spends $30 a month ($360 a year) for utilities, and he expects this outlay to increase 1 percent a year due to price change. What would his monthly utility bill be in 5 years, due to this price change?

ANSWER: $30 x 1.051 = $31.53.

Table A-4. Factors for compounding returns and costs, selected interest rates and time periods

Interest rate	5 years	10 years	20 years	30 years
1	1.051	1.105	1.220	1.348
2	1.104	1.219	1.486	1.811
3	1.159	1.344	1.806	2.427
4	1.217	1.480	2.191	3.243
4½	1.246	1.553	2.412	3.745
5	1.276	1.629	2.653	4.322
5½	1.307	1.708	2.918	4.984
6	1.338	1.791	3.207	5.743
7	1.403	1.967	3.870	7.612
8	1.469	2.159	4.661	10.063

Source: Derived from compound interest tables. For example, see *C.R.C. Standard Mathematical Tables*, (Cleveland, Chemical Rubber Publishing Co.).

Accumulated savings

Table A-5 presents the factors to be used in estimating the total amount of savings accumulated, over varying periods of time, by investing a fixed amount of money each month at one of three different rates of return. The examples below show how the table can be used:

1. To estimate the worth of a regular program for saving money.

EXAMPLE: John Jones saves $50 each month which he invests in a program which he estimates will yield a 5 percent return compounded annually. If he does this each month for 20 years what will be the approximate value of his savings?

ANSWER: $50 × $406 = $20,300.

Of this, $50 × 240 months = $12,000 savings
$20,300 – $12,000 = $8,300 interest earned.

2. *To estimate the monthly savings needed to accumulate a specified sum of money over a period of years.*

EXAMPLE: Edna Smith wants to accumulate $5,000 in savings by setting aside a fixed amount each month for 10 years. If her savings earn 5 percent compounded annually, how much does she set aside each month to acquire the $5,000?

ANSWER: $5,000 ÷ $154 = $32.47.

Table A-5. Factors for use in estimating accumulated savings, selected interest rates and time periods

Interest	Value of savings of $1 per month in number of years			
	5 years	10 years	20 years	30 years
4	$66	$147	$364	$ 685
5	68	154	406	815
6	69	162	453	975
7	71	171	508	1,169
8	73	180	569	1,409

Source: See Paul M. Hummel and Charles L. Seebeck, Jr., *Mathematics of Finance* (New York, McGraw-Hill Publishing Co., 1956), pp. 77-88.

Yield on selected types of investment

Table A-6 can be useful in comparing alternative ways of investing a given sum of money.

Table A-6. Average annual yield on selected types of investments, 1960-73
(Percent)

Year	Aaa corporate bonds [1] (Moody's)	High-grade municipal bonds [1] (Standard & Poor's)	U.S. Government bonds [1]	Savings accounts in savings associations [2]
1960	4.41	3.73	4.01	3.86
1961	4.35	3.46	3.90	3.90
1962	4.33	3.18	3.95	4.08
1963	4.26	3.23	4.00	4.17
1964	4.40	3.22	4.15	4.19
1965	4.49	3.27	4.21	4.23
1966	5.13	3.82	4.66	4.45
1967	5.51	3.98	4.85	4.67
1968	6.18	4.51	5.25	4.68
1969	7.03	5.81	6.10	4.80
1970	8.04	6.51	6.59	5.06
1971	7.39	5.70	5.74	5.33
1972	7.21	5.27	5.63	5.39
1973	7.44	5.18	6.30	p5.55

[1] *Economic Report of the President*, February 1974, p. 317.

[2] *Savings and Loan Fact Book, 1974* (Chicago, U.S. Savings and Loan League, 1974), p. 17

P = Preliminary.

U.S. GOVERNMENT PRINTING OFFICE : 1977 O—249-927

How homeownership trends have changed

During the first half of the 20th century, more Americans rented than owned their homes, as shown in the accompanying chart. Large downpayment requirements and the lack of long-term financing, where buyers could pay for the rest of their home out of regular monthly savings, discouraged homeownership. Federal legislation enacted during the 1930's was the first step toward changing this pattern.

In 1932, the Federal Home Loan Bank Act established a nationwide system to provide a credit reserve for savings and loan associations. This was followed in 1933 by the establishment of the Home Owners Loan Corporation to finance long-term loans at low interest rates for homeowners unable to refinance delinquent loans through normal channels. Further legislation in 1934 established the Federal Housing Administration and the system of mutual mortgage insurance.

As a result of the mortgage insurance system, residential loan practices were substantially changed. The long-term amortized loan quickly became almost universal for both insured and noninsured loans. Economic conditions of the 1930's and the war years of the early 1940's delayed public response to these changes. By 1946, however, a backlog of housing needs, coupled with savings accumulated by families and individuals during the war years, touched off a boom in residential housing construction. This trend was further accelerated by the institution of VA-guaranteed loans under the Servicemen's Readjustment Act of 1944. Further increases in purchasing power during the 1950's helped to bring homeownership within reach of many more families.

During the latter half of the 1960's the movement toward homeownership leveled off. Rising home purchase prices coupled with higher financing costs were important factors influencing this change in trend.

Percent of housing units occupied by owners, 1920-1970

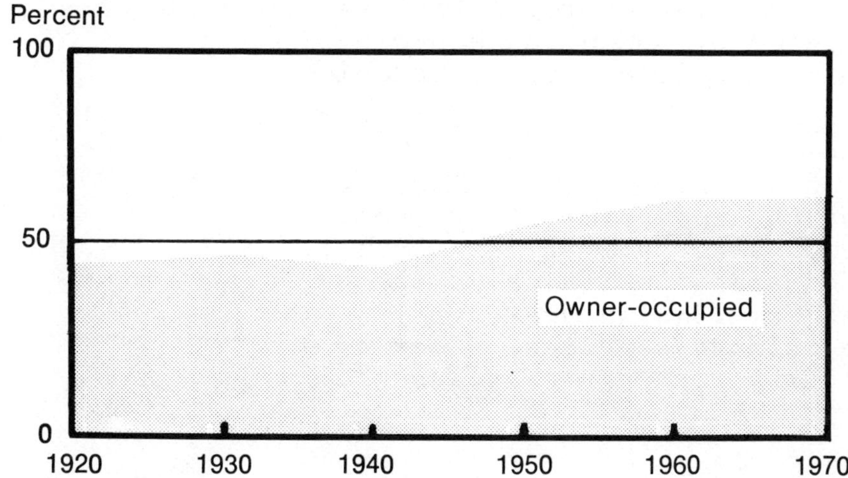

Source: Decennial census data, Bureau of the Census.

U.S. Department of Labor, Bureau of Labor Statistics, Bulletin 1823, (1974) Stock No. 029-001-01341-8/
Catalog No. L2.3:1823.

Women and Housing

A Report on Sex Discrimination in Five American Cities *

Findings and Recommendations

> It [sex bias in housing] is alive and well. The chronicle of instances of discrimination showed that from all points of view, women are having problems. It is clear that local agencies have been active on race discrimination, but have not recognized sex discrimination.
>
> -- *Panel Member, Atlanta Hearing*

Women are having problems. These four words perhaps best summarize our findings which, taken together, yield a bleak portrayal of the inequities women face in our cities' housing markets. Whether as consumers of the *product* or as a participant in the shelter *process*, the American woman is a second class citizen. Some inequities are the consequence of *individual* male prejudices. Others are entrenched in *institutional* practices, underpinned by sexual stereotypes, which result in women being detrimentally viewed as statistical abstractions rather than as individuals.

Our investigations focused on five metropolitan areas.* Yet the common barriers faced by women in each city compel our conclusion that this is a national problem.

Our chief findings are:

1. *Women in the cities studied have faced, in the past, discrimination on account of their sex on a variety of fronts in their search for shelter. Much of this discrimination continues to the present and includes sex bias in marketing, lending and shelter-related services. Lack of equal rental opportunity represents an especially pressing problem.*

2. *Discrimination against women, historically, has been overt; today it is increasingly subtle, disguised by ruses or hidden behind superficially*

This pamphlet was prepared by Raymond W. Gieseman of the Division of Living Conditions Studies in the Office of Prices and Living Conditions, with the collaboration of Georgena Potts and Rosalie Epstein of the Bureau's Office of Publications.

*Atlanta, St. Louis, San Antonio, San Francisco, New York

neutral criteria, such as marital status, which in practice have a discriminatory impact.

3. *Women, generally, are not aware of the nature or extent of sex discrimination. Nor have they been informed of existing legal remedies applicable to such conduct.*

4. *Myths and stereotypes about women are the underpinning of prejudicial attitudes shared by many persons in the housing system. These myths and stereotypes have deep roots in the nation's history and have played key roles in the socialization or conditioning of women and men in this country. Many are not now, nor have been, factually accurate.*

5. *Neither public agencies nor private organizations maintain and compile statistics pertinent to women's access to shelter or housing-related services and facilities. This absence of "hard data" represents an impediment to fashioning sure-footed solutions as well as raising the level of public awareness to the problem.*

6. *Women outside a male-headed household represent a sharply growing demographic trend in the cities studied. They are disproportionately adversely affected by a shortage of decent housing, moderately priced, in the cities studied, and by the marketing practices of those who control this shelter.*

7. *Discrimination on account of sex frequently is "layered" with discrimination on account of some other characteristic of a woman, e.g., her race, source of income or marital status.*

8. *Lending institutions have "discounted", partially or totally, a woman's income in making decisions on applications for mortgage credit. Some lending institutions will condition a mortgage loan on sundry devices which discourage child bearing by the mortgagors. We found conflicting evidence on the extent to which these practices of lenders continue.*

9. *Sex-based discrimination in the law, especially in laws relating to property, to family and to domicile, further reinforce sex discrimination in housing. Similarly, sex discrimination in other areas of American life, e.g., in employment, are interwoven with and reinforce such sex discrimination.*

10. *Women are virtually excluded from key policy-making jobs in the Nation's shelter system. This appears to be equally true in the public and private sectors.*

We have laced this Report with more than 20 recommendations in an attempt to encourage solutions to the problems delineated by these findings. Like the problem, which has many facets, its solution hardly lends itself to a simple recipe. Mindful of this, we recommend an attack on many fronts, including

- *public education efforts to inform women of problems and remedies as they relate to sex bias in housing, as well as to explode myths about women which underpin institutionalized sex discrimination;*
- *vigorous and persistent government compliance efforts;*
- *data collection to facilitate monitoring of industry and government practices, to pinpoint problem areas, and to measure progress;*
- *imaginative and affirmative administration of housing-related government programs in order to expand equal housing choice for women;*
- *coalitions of women working for reform at the local level; and finally*
- *expanding opportunities for women to participate in policy-making decisions which shape the growth and operation of the shelter system.*

While these recommendations outline important tasks for HUD, we do not believe that any single agency can or should be expected to shoulder this responsibility alone. Thus our recommendations are made through HUD to others as well -- the American public, the Congress, the State and local governments, industry, and most importantly, to the nation's women.

THE WOMAN APARTMENT SEEKER
AND
LANDLORD BIAS

Single women -- unmarried, widowed, separated or divorced -- represent a major share of the market for the Nation's rental units. [1]

Shunned frequently by the seller of single family dwellings, grudgingly accommodated by the mortgage creditors (often on discriminatory terms), reluctant to assume the responsibilities of home ownership, and generally lower on the economic scale, the single woman in the urban metropolitan areas probes the shelter market for the medium-priced unit, with basic amenities, in a safe neighborhood and strategically-located relative to public commuter transportation and shopping.

Two harsh realities often emerge from her quest for this shelter: (a) these units are in increasingly short supply relative to the demand, and (b) landlord bias.

In cities covered by this Project the single woman faced in 1974-1975 a tight rental market.

These market conditions are far from even-handed in their impact on men and women because of woman's greater dependence on rental units (especially moderately-priced apartments). In New York, for example, while 75 percent of the households are rental, 84 percent of those headed by women rent as do 87 percent of single women.

This greater dependence on the rental market for shelter is the product of various factors. Women earn less than men.

Even where a woman can afford a home purchase, she encounters (as we shall see) sex-based discrimination that tends to keep her in an apartment. And where she is awarded the house as a part of the property settlement, the divorced woman frequently is forced into more modest rental quarters because of the unreliability of support payments and problems of job market re-entry. [9]

Particularly disadvantaged by the tight conditions is the woman heading a household. Far more likely to have child custody than the man, the divorced woman parent is often in search of the rare find -- the moderately-priced 3-4 bedroom apartment in a decent neighborhood.

The woman fortunate enough to find a vacant apartment or house for rent, suitable to her needs and pocket-book, must overcome still another hurdle: landlord sex bias. In some cases we found this discrimination to be bold and blatant. More frequently, however, it is subtle and disguised, a step removed from "No women wanted" but in impact just as real -- and just as wrong.

OVERT SEX BIAS: ONE FACE OF DISCRIMINATION

Discrimination has many faces. Today where its basis is race it rarely shows itself as outright bigotry. Sexism, however, is not so shy, as we listened to women detail their experiences in seeking access to rental units in 5 American cities.

In several cities, single women seeking rental units reported that they were required to get a male to co-sign the lease, and without regard to either her or his financial status. [15]

Three facially neutral criteria surfaced during the Hearings and Workshops as prevalent practices in the rental industry for refusing to rent to women:

(1) Children are not allowed.

(2) Prefer married couples.

(3) Sorry -- no single roommates.

Each, either because it is a ruse or because it has a discriminatory impact on women, may violate Federal or State laws or both prohibiting sex discrimination in housing.

NO CHILDREN, PLEASE

In our society, women far outnumber men in functioning as a single parent with custody of one or more children. Far more than men, the woman's shelter needs are influenced by her responsibility for rearing children of marriages broken by abandonment, voluntary separation, divorce or death. Thus, a landlord policy of "no children admitted" tends to have greater exclusionary consequences for women than for men. This is clearly so if the prohibition is on single parents with children. As a New York attorney, Janice Goodman, suggested to the Panel:

> Denying housing to people with children is really discrimination against women, since we all know the parent with custody of the child is usually the mother. So making this blanket rule that we don't want children or unmarried parents is really direct discrimination against women. [18]

Sex discrimination may manifest itself in other than the outright denial of access. In New York one witness told the Panel that while <u>two-bedroom</u> apartments will be rented to a single parent with one male child; if the child is female, the woman parent is rented only a <u>one-bedroom</u>

apartment which parent and child share "no matter what the age is". [27]

In screening applicants, some New York landlords refuse to count alimony payments, child care "or even public assistance". [28]

The growth of households headed by women is one of the most dramatic demographic phenomenon of the past decade. "Of the net increment of 2.3 million households between the March 1971 and 1972 Current Population Survey dates, fewer than half were headed by a husband-wife couple".[29]

And the fastest growing household, by far, is the woman-headed family with children. [30] Any policy to expand decent shelter opportunities for these households must take into account the discriminatory market behavior which these households confront in major metropolitan areas.

Another dimension of the problem, the Panels were told, is the absence of child care facilities. In New York City where 83 percent of the female-headed households rent, one witness warned the Panel:

> ... very little attention has been paid to the specific needs of female heads of households with young children, and this goes beyond the question of shelter, but it goes to the related issues of ability to get employment, whereever the female head of the household is employable, and also to the prerequisite provision for care for the children, because you will find one kind of discrimination frequently encountered by the working head of a household who has young children is the unwillingness of the management agent to accept her as a tenant because of the non-supervision of younger children in large numbers in a development which tends to be used as a discriminatory measure against the female, when in fact there are no facilities available for the care of those children.
>
> So the alternative is to work and leave them unsupervised or not to work and be on welfare and then you encounter other ramifications that are involved with being a non-working head of the household on welfare.
>
> So that some attention should be paid to the necessity for developing housing specifically geared to provide child care facilities or communal living, something in this direction that begins to provide supervisory aspects for the children of the female heads of the household, therefore, freeing them both to work and to qualify as legitimate members of society. [31]

Many others have called attention to this need, and there appears to be no single solution to it. [32] Local communities should be encouraged, we believe, to use Title I funds under the 1974 Housing and Community Development Act for the provision of strategically-located child care centers. Local coalitions of women's organizations (see Chapter 6, infra.) could assess the problems in their own cities, and depending upon their sense of priorities, attempt to get local government to request Title I funds for this purpose.

Even when she has no children in tow, the separated or divorced woman finds that her marital status is a badge of unacceptability for many landlords. Since women are three times as likely to be separated or divorced than men, marital status bias has a discriminatory impact on women.

NO VACANCY: SEPARATED OR DIVORCED WOMEN

Various reasons are offered for excluding the single woman: unstable incomes; women will bring men into the house; women overuse the facilities; will get pregnant and lose their jobs.

Economics, security and companionship -- separately or in combination -- encourage many women to seek shelter which they can share. Although we were not able to secure statistical data there is reason to believe that women more than men in this country share rental space with their own sex.

VACANCY: EXCEPT FEMALE ROOMMATES

Yet many women find that landlords will not rent to them if they have another woman as a roommate even though two men roommates would not be excluded.

Excluding female roommates has a direct discriminatory impact on women who are, in fact, lesbians. According to one witness, there were "roughly 7,000,000 lesbians in the United States in 1948". [45]

Representatives from homosexual organizations called the Panel's attention in New York to the discrimination encountered by the lesbian. It includes not only exclusion by landlords, but discriminatory evictions.

Because of the stigma associated with being identified as homosexual in this country, lesbians face a special reluctance to complain of landlord bias against them. Moreover, there is a question of the applicability of fair housing laws to such discrimination. But such prejudices founded on sexual preference have no place in a truly open housing market.

* * * *

From the testimony offered at the Hearings, the denial of equal rental opportunities deserves priority attention in any strategy to expand housing choice for women. It manifests itself in both disparate treatment accorded women by landlords, as well as in facially neutral practices which have a discriminatory impact. Additionally, although no evidence was offered at the Hearings, it is apparent from our examination of real estate newspaper advertising that some rental ads express a sex preference in violation of the laws described in Chapter 6, infra.

We recommend, then, that HUD

1. *Issue Guidelines pursuant to the Federal Fair Housing Act which clarify the law's application to landlord practices which, although facially neutral, have a discriminatory impact on women. These would include criteria excluding from occupancy single persons on account of their marital status, single parents, and roommates, where no economic basis for the criteria exists, and if it does, no other less restrictive method is available.*

2. *Accelerate the processing, on a priority basis, of complaints alleging rental sex discrimination.*

3. *Convene newspaper publishers to clarify their responsibilities under the Federal Fair Housing Act as it relates to sexist advertising.*

Notes

1. There are no published census data which clarify the tenant population by sex. This conclusion, though we believe "stands to reason", would need verification.

9. Testimony of Mr. Miller, op.cit., p.176.

15. Testimony of Judy Sweeney, National Organization for Women, St. Louis Chapter, St. Louis Hearing, 224.

18. Testimony of Emily Goodman, attorney, New York Hearing, p.67.

27. Testimony of Ms. DeSaram, op.cit., p.165.

28. Testimony of Ms. Norton, op.cit., p.200.

29. Ross and MacIntosh, The Emergence of the Female-Headed Household (Urban Institute, 1973) p.7.

30. Ibid., p.12.

31. Testimony of Leila Long, op.cit., pp.99-100.

32. See, e.g., Karen Hapgood and Judith Getzels, Planning, Women and Change (A.S.P.O., 1974) pp.18-19.

45. Testimony of Jane O'Leary, Lesbian Feminist Liberation, New York Hearing, 224.

HOMEOWNERSHIP: MARKETING, CREDIT AND OTHER BARS

> In 1970, ... 68 percent of all families headed by men owned their homes contrasted to 48 percent of all families headed by women. [6]

While the reasons for this disparity are varied, we have found an important contributing factor to be sex bias of brokers, lenders and, to some extent, developers.

Additionally, the woman who is able to secure a home has often had to pay a sex tariff and, in some cases, is refused essential housing-related services and protections, e.g., insurance, on account of her sex.

To these sexist practices in the housing market, we now turn.

1. Discriminatory Marketing

> *It shall be unlawful (a) to refuse to sell ... after the making of a bona fide offer, or to refuse to negotiate for the sale ... or otherwise make unavailable or deny a dwelling to any person because ... of sex.*
>
> -- Federal Fair Housing Act, 1974, sec.804(a)

For an estimated 90 percent of the homeownership of existing houses, brokers and their sales persons are the "gatekeepers", influencing the choice of the prospect, as well as controlling actual access to the house itself.

> I think you have to recognize that the bulk of the properties that go for sale on the market are listed with brokers. The brokers have the authority, or they have the influence, at least, to direct the buyer to a specific property or to direct him [sic] away from the property. [7]

The broker, in addition to working with both seller and buyer, has direct relationships with lenders. In this role the broker "qualifies" the buyer for the kind of financing the buyer will require. Sometimes the broker pursues secondary loan possibilities; in short, anything to arrange expeditious financing to assure a closing on the transaction.

In these pivotal institutional roles, the broker has played, studies and court cases have shown, a leading role in creating and maintaining segregated neighborhoods. [8]

Testimony before the Hearing Panels in the five cities, revealed that

- some brokers cling to prejudicial attitudes toward women, inhibiting their ability to offer services to them on an equal basis;
- brokers with years of experience rarely are involved in the sale of homes to single women or women heads of households;
- developers and owners, without the services of a broker, discriminate against women in the marketing of their units;
- brokers steer women to and away from certain available units, and

- brokers employ discriminatory 'credit criteria' in qualifying the woman prospect.

BROKER PREJUDICES

Brokers interact with the woman client in a variety of contexts. Even in the context typically most favorable to the woman -- membership in a male headed household -- the woman does not get equal treatment in the "provision of services or facilities in connection" with the transaction.

A San Antonio real estate broker, with 15 years of experience and a former President of the local real estate board, could not recall ever selling a house to a single woman.

SINGLE WOMEN ACCOUNT FOR FEW SALES

> Q. Do you sell to many women, single women, I mean?
>
> A. Not in my own personal experience. I would like to but I just can't think right off hand of a number of single women I have sold to. [12]

In San Francisco, the head of a realtor firm which has a reputation for equal treatment in the community, told the Panel that only 2 to 3 percent of its sales in a recent year were to single women or women heads of households.[13] This in a city where women form 43 percent of the workforce and in an area with the nation's highest per capita income.

With respect to the marketing of residential properties, the Panel was told in St. Louis that:

DEVELOPER BIAS

> There are several communities that are developing properties around lakes, and the package deal is that you are allowed -- invited, in fact, to come and stay overnight at this lake development and then tour the property. Well she received an invitation, but when they found out she was single, they told her it didn't apply to her and she wouldn't be welcome to take that. [20]

From this statement, as elsewhere in some of the testimony before the Panels, it is difficult to assess whether the discrimination is rooted in sex or in marital status.

If the criterion creates greater "head winds" for women than for men, a refusal to show based on marital status should violate applicable Federal and State laws. [21] Single women, and this includes widows and divorcees, who are not heads of households, far exceed the number of single males. The burden of a refusal to sell based on marital status weighs much more heavily, therefore, and much more unequally on the female population. [22]

Moreover, the courts have held that the law is broken if one of the reasons for the developer's action is forbidden by the statute. [23]

At the other end of the economic spectrum, the Panel learned in Atlanta that male heads of households would be preferred in the marketing by the Atlanta Public Housing Authority of Turnkey III Housing. [24] Given the growth of families with a female head and their disproportionate reliance on public housing, such a policy has an especially adverse impact on women and should be reconsidered.

STEERING BY BROKERS

Brokers employ a variety of tactics to channel customers to units for sale based upon the brokers' own biases and their perception of the biases of the sellers or those in the community where the property is located. Such conduct has been labelled "steering" in situations where race or ethnic bias is involved. Its impact is to maintain racially segregated neighborhoods in many American cities. It is against the law -- whether its basis is race or sex.

Adverse impact on property values is generally offered as an explanation for racial steering by brokers. We learned in Atlanta that brokers would tend to equate the entry of single women into a neighborhood with declining property values. [29]

BROKER'S DISCRIMINATORY CREDIT SCREENING

The single woman has been shunned by the broker because of the likelihood she would be refused a loan by the mortgage lender. "It was understood that she could not buy, period," one broker with 12 years of experience admitted to the Panel in Atlanta, "unless she had cash to assume a loan." The result was:

> ... very few of us ever make the attempt to get loans. Anyone that came to us, we made no attempts to get them loans. We always looked for a loan assumption for that divorcee, for that single woman, whatever. [30]

There was considerable evidence offered that brokers continue to treat the woman prospect differently by screening them against their perception of the lenders' loan criteria -- even when these criteria may have changed.

> In the case of a woman, in order to have a hedge against the discriminatory lending practices, the realtor may say that you might have to have 30 percent down [even though the prevailing requirement in a conventional loan is 20 percent down] [31]

One broker described how it was common to prefer, in the case of identical offers for a house, the offer from a married couple to that of a single woman because the former poses, in the brokers' view, fewer problems to make the transaction work.

> We've had cases of this type more times than I would like to remember, where two sets of people are trying to buy the same property in this tight housing market. They will, in both cases, offer identical offers, that is, the owner-price cash and their contingency. And at that point the realtor will normally advise the seller to take an offer from other than a single woman ... the reason for this is that the realtor from past experience knows that it is more difficult to qualify a single woman for a loan than it will be probably for a married couple. [32]

Our conclusions do not stand alone. In its study of the mortgage credit industry in Hartford, Connecticut, the U.S. Commission on Civil Rights described how the brokers' marketing practices were influenced by their acting as a part of the lenders' screening process. And Senator William Brock, in testifying on behalf of a federal law against sex bias in housing, remarked:

> A real estate agent knowing that a credit worthy woman will face difficulty in obtaining a mortgage on account of her sex will tend not to view women as viable potential customers and will discourage an active search for home purchase. [33]

In refusing to deal with the woman home buyer, the broker points the finger at the lender as the one to blame. There is considerable merit in that accusation as we shall see in the next section.

2. Credit Discrimination

> *Have you had an incident which occurred to you from which you believed you were discriminated against on account of sex in the area of housing ...?*

Yes, Ma'am ... The first time was approximately the last part of 1970. I decided that I was tired of paying rent. I preferred to live in a house and build some equity. I found a house that a friend of my family had offered to sell me ... I called a savings and loan institution in Decatur that my family had had their house mortgaged for years. When I called to ask for an appointment to make a loan application, they flatly told me that it was not the policy of their organization to take an application for a mortgage by a woman.

-- Atlanta Hearing, November 8, 1974

* * * *

The President of the New York Bankers Association, Howard Cross, conceded yesterday that banks might discriminate against women in making loans, but he said, that men at the top were not responsible.

-- New York Times, October 12, 1973

Credit discrimination is a spearpoint in women's efforts to eliminate sexism in the nation's economic institutions. The guarded admission of the New York banking official and the testimony of the young, white female professional from Decatur, Georgia, tell us why. Discrimination on account of sex by mortgage lenders in this country has been bold, overt, and deliberate. It reaches deep in the nation's credit system.. It has recognized neither class nor race bounds. The married woman and the unmarried, although in different ways, have been its victims. So, too, have the young and the aged.

> The [Federal Reserve] Board favors the elimination of discrimination in credit extensions ... The denial of credit based upon group identification, rather than upon factors specifically related to an individual's creditworthiness, works to the economic disadvantage of applicants and creditors alike. [34]
>
> -- *Jeffrey Bucher, Member Board of Governors, Federal Reserve System*

Without a mortgage, most Americans would never own a home. If you fail to "qualify" for a loan, you don't qualify for a house. However, the processes governing the distributing of mortgages in this country are far from well understood. At best they might be characterized as a mystic blend of subjectively weighing objective criteria. Credit worthiness of the borrower and the security

LENDER BIAS: WOMEN OUTSIDE HUSBAND/WIFE HOUSEHOLD

value of the property are the subject of elaborate underwriting formulas designed to minimize the incidence of default and narrow the lender's loss in the event of foreclosure.

Yet in the five cities we visited, we discovered that there is ample opportunity for the lender to apply them unequally to women and to men, inserting subjective judgment and even personal bias into the process of deciding whether to extend the credit. All women, however, do not receive the same unequal treatment. In this section we are concerned with those living outside a husband-wife household.

Most adult women in America, at one time during their lives, live outside a husband-wife household. In San Francisco today, 55 percent of the women are either single, separated, widowed or divorced. In the Atlanta metropolitan area, in 1970, of the 246,364 women employed

- 50,737 were single
- 16,463 were married women with absent husbands and
- 20,675 were divorced.

Looking at national figures, we find that of the 33 million women who work, 37 percent are either single, widowed or divorced. And of the 63 percent who are married, some will be separated and, hence, living outside a husband-wife household.

The fastest growing family-type in this country, as we noted earlier, is the female-headed family. Reporting on the changing role of women, Hapgood and Getzels found that the economic and sexual liberation of women has signalled new options for young women.

> Increasing numbers are choosing to remain single. They want independent life styles to be as legitimate for them as for men. Young women are assuming serious careers, not biding their time until marriage. Growing numbers of young women want to be considered full-fledged permanent residents, serious participants in community life. [36]

In the five metropolitan areas we examined, women living outside a husband/wife household represent nearly 48 percent of the female population. [37] In each metropolitan area we heard testimony that they are at a disadvantage in seeking to obtain a mortgage.

In *St. Louis*, a broker from one of the reputable agencies testified to the obstacles manufactured by savings and loan associations in 1973 to avoid extending credit to women home buyers she had screened and found qualified. One obstacle was to require that women applicants secure mortgage insurance as a prerequisite for getting a loan commitment.

Even with a good salary, the single woman often has to overcome special requirements to get the loan. One such case concerned a white woman who was an assistant treasurer of a hardware corporation in California. She owned a home with $20,000 in equity in it.

> Among the requirements made of her were that she pay off a $450 debt, a department store $300 debt, that she supply a copy of her divorce, written verification of divorce papers, $104 worth of information, despite the fact that she has worked for thirteen years for this establishment. [41]

Nor is the discrimination limited to permanent financing. The single woman wishing to build on the lot she owns has difficulty finding construction money. As one single female in *San Francisco* recalled:

> I had a good job and I had already bought the lot and I could not get my bank to grant me money for a construction loan ... They took the application but nothing would happen. I must have gone to fifteen different places but I couldn't get a loan because I was single. I needed a co-signer, who had to be a man, and I doubt whether that's changed very much. [42]

The lenders' bias against the single woman stems, in part, from the U.S. Federal Housing Administration's (FHA) preference -- a preference which persists -- for the traditional nuclear family.

> The mortgagor who is married and has a family generally evidences more stability than a mortgagor who is single because, among other things, <u>he</u> has responsibilities holding <u>him</u> to <u>his</u> obligations. [emphasis added] [50]

While the lenders' preference for the nuclear family affects all unmarrieds, there is evidence that the bias creates a heavier burden for women than for men.

> The women with the greatest difficulty in gaining access to mortgage finance are single women -- unmarried, widowed, separated or divorced women. Each is treated somewhat differently by mortgage lending institutions but for all it is their status as women who are not part of a male-headed household that is of greatest significance to mortgage lenders. [51]

HUD figures show that married couples and unmarried males account for nearly all the mortgages on new houses insured under the Section 203(b) Program. (See Appendix G) This preference results, as we earlier pointed out, in "waves" for the single female in other parts of the housing delivery system. Brokers possessing identical offers for the same property will advise the seller to sell to other than the single woman. [52]

In other situations, the broker, in order to hedge against the lender's discrimination, will inform the single female buyer that she must have a 30 percent down payment, even though the prevailing practice for conventional loans is to require only 20 percent. [53]

There are three times as many divorced women in America as there are divorced men. [55] Thus, a preference accorded the married person tends to discriminate against women more than it does men. A 1972 survey by the Federal Home Loan Bank revealed that "in most cases the association didn't loan to women or single women, they always dealt with family units". [56]

CREDIT AND THE DIVORCED WOMAN

From a variety of sources we heard testimony that the divorced woman is no better off than the single girl seeking a mortgage loan. Indeed, frequently, the divorced woman's problems start with marriage.

> The credit basis that a woman builds up when she is single is usually dissolved when she marries, because her credit file -- her past credit file -- is put into the credit file of her husband, and it becomes one. Only if the woman goes to the credit bureau and asks that she have a separate file in her own name does she get one. And this has only come about in the last few months. The credit bureau has changed its policies and will do this. [57]

> Widowed and divorced women fit into one category in that they have no credit in their own name and possibly poor credit from their ex-husband's name. They find it difficult, if not impossible, to buy a home. [58]

Following the break-up of the marriage, the lender invokes the subjective notion of "emotional instability" to characterize the divorced woman applicant as unqualified for a mortgage.

> Divorcees are really considered as unstable, emotionally unstable ... by insurance companies, credit card issuers, numerous groups, corporations ... a divorced woman is considered emotionally unstable, and we cannot find anything that exists that says the divorced man is unstable. [59]

The divorced woman's standing in the eyes of the mortgage lender is weakened by her complicated financial circumstances. As observed by the Director of the Atlanta's Women's Information Center:

> In cases of divorcees, alimony and child care, child support, do not count as income to lenders. [61]

In its recent study of lending practices in Hartford, Connecticut, the U.S. Civil Rights Commission also reached the conclusion that "the divorced woman ... has considerable difficulty in obtaining a mortgage, both because of the alleged probability of an unstable economic situation and because of her social position." [62]

The results of a 1973 questionnaire distributed by the D.C. Commission on Status of Women to 107 mortgage lending institutions revealed that:

(1) sex and marital status frequently determine whether or not mortgage applications will be acted upon formally;

(2) alimony and child support are often discounted as valid sources of income, regardless of their reliability;

(3) working wives' salaries are often not fully counted as part of a family income; and

(4) some institutions ask applicants about their parental plans and birth control practices. [65]

THE WORKING WIFE'S INCOME

For years mortgage lenders in this country have considered a dollar in a woman's hand worth about half as much, or less, than a dollar in the hand of her husband. This sexist criterion has had the effect of denying home-ownership to thousands of families unable to meet the lender's qualifying formula because that portion of the income stream, which represented the woman's salary, was "discounted".

> One of the most prevalent discriminatory practices in mortgage lending has been the practice of routinely discounting or totally ignoring the income of working wives in computing family income. Such practices have prevented many families from achieving homeownership or compelled them to accept housing that does not suit their needs and incomes. [72]

This discriminatory treatment of incomes has persisted in the face of substantial and stable participation by women in the Nation's labor force. Thirty-five million women were in the labor force in 1973; 42 percent worked full-time year round; the expectancy for women now entering the labor force is employment for an average of 25 years. Three out of every 5 women workers are married. [73] Yet, in 1971 a Federal Home Loan Bank survey of savings and loan associations showed:

- that 25 percent would not count <u>any</u> of the income of a wife, age 25, with two school children, who held a full-time secretarial position;
- that more than 50 percent would limit credit to 50 percent or less of her salary; and
- that only 22 percent would count it all

Other studies have corroborated these findings. [74]

In a major way, conventional lenders' policies regarding the working wife's income have been influenced by the underwriting criteria of FHA, a federal agency, not to count any of the wife's income. [75] The policy of the Veterans Administration was similarly influential. [76]

FHA's policy was changed in the middle sixties to permit counting the wife's income under "circumstances indicating that such income may normally be expected to continue through the early period of the mortgage risk".[77]

The Veterans Administration however, retained a policy of discounting the wife's income until July 18, 1973.[78] On that day a new circular was approved, stating: "In consideration of present-day social and economic patterns, the Veterans Administration will hereafter recognize in full both the income and expenses of the veteran and spouse in determining the ability to repay a loan." [79]

While pressures by public interest groups and perhaps other factors have prodded Federal agencies into a more equitable treatment of the working wife's income, we found evidence that many mortgage lenders still refuse to credit fully the income of the working wife.

Since a higher proportion of minority families rely on the wife's salary for part of the family's income, the impact of policies discounting the wife's income has been much harsher on the non-white. Arthur Flemming, Chairman of the Civil Rights Commission, described their findings in this regard to the House Subcommittee on Consumer Affairs at its hearings in June 1974 on credit discrimination legislation:

> The system of mortgage finance in the Nation, under which women are inequitably treated, reflects a reluctance by many in the lending community to alter traditional policies and standards, even though many are unrealistic and others facilitate illegal acts. Sex discrimination in credit is totally at odds with the reality of modern-day America in which more than 33 million women work and make up more than 40 percent of the labor force. Yet lending institutions in many instances cling to images of women as unstable, unreliable, and in need of male protection.
>
> * * *
>
> We conclude that "for minorities and women, the mortgage finance system is a stacked deck -- stacked sometimes inadvertently, often unthinkingly, but stacked, nonetheless." After interviews with over 75 real estate brokers, lenders, home buyers, public interest groups, and Federal and city housing specialists, the Commission was able to discern a pattern of discriminatory practices. [84]

* * * * *

For all too many lenders, it would appear, it is "business as usual" in their practices relating to women. But there is ample reason for hope that things are changing. The four federal financial regulatory agencies, so key to determining the pace and direction of industry reform, are recognizing that civil rights is also *their* responsibility. New federal legislation described in Chapter 5 should assure that "sex discrimination" share in this recognition.

Even within the industry, men like Eugene H. Adams, Chairman of the Governing Council of the American Bankers Association, are urging their peers to re-examine old practices and question past assumptions about women. [86] Again, new federal legislation will encourage, hopefully, others to listen.

Finally, HUD has the responsibility to see that gains made are in fact consolidated, that sex bias in lending does not simply go underground, but goes -- period. Thus, we recommend that HUD:

1. *Expand the pilot data collection and analysis Project with the federal financial regulatory agencies to a nationwide effort, and make this information available to public interest organizations and others.*

2. *Encourage the federal financial regulatory agencies to make civil rights an integral part of their regular examinations.*

3. *Administer all new and existing federal programs designed to increase the availability of residential mortgage credit in such a way that favoritism to the nuclear (husband-wife) family is ended and homeownership opportunities are expanded without regard to sex or marital status.*

4. *Assist -- through seminars, technical assistance, and other resources -- local women's organizations and others in conducting local surveys of practices of lending institutions.*

3. Discrimination in the Provisions of Services or Facilities in Connection with Housing

> *It shall be unlawful to discriminate against any person ... in the provision of services or facilities in connection (with the sale or rental of a dwelling) on account of ... sex.*
> -- Federal Fair Housing Law, 1974, sec.804(b)

Barriers to access, however important, emerge as but one dimension in the mosaic of sex discrimination in housing in this country. Indisputably, shelter is more than a roof with supporting walls. With the physical structure there must be related services and facilities for even modest enjoyment to be possible. A tenement without a door that locks or with landlord harassment is hardly a bargain. It's not enough to acquire a home if you can't get insurance, or anyone to assist with its maintenance without unconscionable gouging.

Yet in the cities we visited, these complaints were heard from women. Moreover, the complainants believe that they suffer these grievances because they are women.

Notes

6. U.S. Commission on Civil Rights, Mortgage Money: Who Gets It? A Case Study in Mortgage Lending Discrimination in Hartford, Connecticut (June, 1974), p.3. [hereafter Hartford Report]

7. Hearing before the U.S. Commission on Civil Rights, Baltimore, Maryland, 138 (1970).

8. Rose Halper, Racial Policies and Practices of Real Estate Brokers (Minneapolis: Univ. of Minnesota Press, 1969); U.S. Commission on Civil Rights, Equal Opportunity in Suburbia (July 1974) pp.16 et.seq.; United States v Alexander and Cloutier Realty Co. (DC. ND.Ga 1970); United States v Mintzes (DC.Md)304F. Supp.1305; United States v West Suburban Board of Realtors,P-H Equal Housing Opportunity Reporter, parag. 13,641.

12. Testimony of Mazie Hill, San Antonio Hearing, 157.

13. Testimony of Irv Wiener, San Francisco Hearing, 192-3.

20. Testimony of Ms. Sweeney, St. Louis Hearing, 224-5.

21. A practice need not be intended to discriminate in order to be a violation of law and regulation. If the effect of the practice is discriminatory and it has no economic basis, a practice may violate the law. See, Federal Home Loan Bank Guideline, 12 C.F.R. sec.531.8(b); Griggs v. Duke Power Co., 401 U.S. 424(1971).

22. Testimony of Leila Long, Assistant Administrator for Equal Opportunity, New York City Housing and Development Administration, New York Hearing, 93.

23. Simth v. Sol D. Adler Realty Co., 436 F 2nd 344(7th Cir.,1970).

24. Testimony of Lester Percells, Executive Director of Atlanta Housing Authority, Atlanta Hearing, 101 (II).

29. Testimony of Ms. Hlass, op.cit., 131.

30. Testimony of Ms. Nelson, op.cit., 114 (II).

31. Testimony of Ms. Slaughter, op.cit., 111.

32. Ibid., 109-110.

33. U.S. Senate, Hearings Before Subcommittee on Housing and Urban Affairs of Committee on Banking, Housing and Urban Affairs, Proposed Housing and Community Development for 1973, 93d Cong., 1st Sess., July 27, 1973, p.1228.

34. House of Representatives, Hearings Before Subcommittee on Consumer Affairs of Committee on Banking and Currency on HR 14856 and 14908, 93d Cong., 2d Sess., June 20, 1974, p.31.

36. Karen Hapgood and Judith Getzels, Planning, Women and Change, (American Society of Planning Officials, Rept. No.301, April 1974) p.13.

37. See Appendix

41. Testimony of Maxine Brown, Housing Planner, Association of Bay Area Governments, San Francisco Hearing, 64.

42. Testimony of Ms. Wright, President UNITE, San Francisco Hearing, 158-9.

50. U.S. Department of Housing and Urban Development, Mortgage Credit Analysis Handbook for Mortgage Insurance on One to Four-Family Properties (1972) sec. 2-7a.

51. Hartford Report, p.26.

52. Testimony of Ms. Slaughter, op.cit., p.109-110.

53. Ibid., p.11.

55. Hapgood and Getzels, op.cit., p.20.

56. Testimony of Robert Hoilien, Vice President, Home Federal Savings and Loan Association, San Francisco Hearing, 217.

57. Testimony of Maxine Robinson, Director, Women's Information Center, YWCA, Atlanta Hearing, 68 (I); see also Testimony of Mr. Hoilien, op.cit., p.217.

58. Testimony of Mary Hartmen, op.cit., p.84 (I).

59. Testimony of Maxine Robinson, op.cit., p.60.

61. Testimony of Maxine Robinson, op.cit., p.58.

62. Hartford Report, p.28.

65. District of Columbia, Commission on Status of Women, Sixth Annual Report, 1973.

72. Steven Rhode, "Ending Sexism in the Mortgage Market", Remarks at National Presidents' Meeting sponsored by National Council of Negro Women, September 14, 1974, pp.1-2.

73. U. S. Department of Labor, Women's Bureau, "Highlights of Women's Employment and Education", June 1974; "Twenty Facts on Women Workers", June 1974.

74. Survey released by the United States Savings and Loan League, involving more than 400 large Savings and Loan Associations, showed that only 28 percent of these S and Ls would give full credit to a working wife's income. See also D.C. Commission on Status of Women Report, 1973, which documented discrimination by lenders in Washington, D.C. area.

75. Testimony of Robert A. Drolich, Executive Director, Greater St. Louis Savings and Loan League, St. Louis Hearing, 54; Testimony of

C. L. Hunnicutt, President. San Antonio Chapter of Mortgage Bankers Association, op.cit., pp.129-150; Testimony of Ed Hiles, Executive Vice President, Gerogia Savings and Loan League, Atlanta Hearing, 134 (II).

76. Ibid., especially testimony of Mr. Hiles, Atlanta Hearing.

77. U.S. Department of Housing and Urban Development, Mortgage Credit Analysis Handbook for Mortgage Insurance on One to Four-Family Properties (1972), sec.1-22.

78. Washington Post, February 24, 1973; see also Hartford Report, pp.25-26.

79. U.S. Veterans Administration, Dept. of Veterans Benefits Circular No. 26-73-24, July 18, 1973.

84. House Hearings, op.cit., p.133.

86. Remarks by Eugene H. Adams before Florida Bankers Association, Bal Harbour, Florida, June 23, 1973; Indiana Bankers Association, French Lick, Indiana, June 13, 1974, reprinted in House Hearings, op.cit., p.310-4. See also Richard McConnell, "Take a New Look at Women Borrowers", BANKING: Journal of American Bankers Association, August 1973; "Loans to Women: A Case for Questioning Lending Criteria", Savings and Loan News, January 1974.

Appendix

MARITAL STATUS OF WOMEN IN FIVE METROPOLITAN AREAS (1970)

SMSA	Not-Married Female* %	Not-Married Male* %
Atlanta	43.1	35.6
St. Louis	44.1	35.2
San Antonio	45.2	41.4
San Francisco	45.9	42.3
New York	48.1	39.6

* Includes Single, Divorced, Separated and Widows or Widowers

Source: U.S. Department of Commerce, Bureau of the Census, 1970

This material has not been excerpted in its entirety.

U.S. Dept. of HUD, Office of the Assistant Secretary for Fair Housing and Equal Opportunity (1975). Prepared by the National Council of Negro Women, Inc. Stock No. 023-000-00316-3

Equal Opportunity in Housing: A Manual for Corporate Employers

OBLIGATIONS OF FEDERAL CONTRACTORS TO GIVE HOUSING ASSISTANCE TO MINORITY EMPLOYEES

> ". . . in accordance with obligations imposed under its contracts with the government of the United States of America, plaintiff CATERPILLAR TRACTOR CO. affirmatively recruits persons of the Negro race for employment in technical and professional capacities . . .
>
> "[Because of defendant apartment house owner's refusal to rent to black management employee] CATERPILLAR TRACTOR CO. has suffered and will continue to suffer damages for the reason that such racial discrimination as heretofore alleged makes it more difficult for plaintiff CATERPILLAR TRACTOR CO. to recruit competent and skilled black employees. Such racial discrimination casts doubt upon the good faith of plaintiff CATERPILLAR TRACTOR CO.'s representations to [black employees that they would obtain suitable housing without discrimination]."
>
> —*Caterpillar Tractor Co. v. Hansen (Complaint)*
> *U.S. District Court, So. Dist. Ill., 1971.*

Pursuant to Executive Order 11246 (as amended) and its implementing regulations, corporations holding major Federal contracts have an obligation to affirmatively hire and promote minority group members and, where appropriate, to develop goals and timetables for that purpose which meet the approval of the Government. They have no obligation under the Order, however, to deal with minority housing problems, segregation and discrimination except to the extent that these factors have or are likely to have a negative impact on their equal employment opportunity progress.

The basic documents outlining the Government's requirements in the EEO field are Executive Order 11246 and the Department of Labor regulations known as Revised Order No. 4.[1] Section 60-2.23 of Revised Order No. 4 requires Federal contractors to make an "in-depth analysis" of a variety of factors, including housing availability. If the company finds that *"lack of access to suitable housing inhibits recruitment efforts and employment of qualified minorities"*, then "special corrective action should be appropriate."

Original Order Number 4[2] required that corrective action might be appropriate only where inadequate housing opportunity inhibited minority employment in professional and management positions. Revised Order No.

4 extends this requirement to technicians, sales workers, office and clerical, skilled craftsmen and trainees—the full range of occupations covered by the Order.[3]

According to a spokesman in the Office of Federal Contract Compliance (OFCC), Department of Labor, which coordinates compliance activities of the Government, access to housing continues to remain a significant problem, with its importance increasing as more blacks reach manager/transferee status. It is felt at the Department of Labor that an employer cannot excuse a bad hiring and promotion record solely on the basis that discrimination exists in the housing market; this is not always outside the control of the employer and where feasible can and should be changed by affirmative employer actions.[4]

Revised Order No. 4 requires contractors to see if lack of access to housing is hurting minority employment efforts. The U.S. Civil Rights Commission has strongly urged OFCC to go one step further. Under the Commission proposal, each contractor, as part of compliance requirements, would have to demonstrate that housing within reasonable access is available on a non-discriminatory basis and available to meet all employee income ranges of current and potential employees.[5]

The outlook would thus seem to be for continuing government interest in the linkage between jobs and housing.

HOW CORPORATIONS HAVE AIDED MINORITY EMPLOYEES TO FIND HOUSING

A substantial number of major corporate employers have taken steps to assist minority employees locate decent housing, either on a "one-time" basis as the result of a complaint by a black employee, or as a formal program, ready for use as the need arises.

Corporations have contracted with non-profit open housing centers to relocate minority employees, or have contributed funds or services to these centers; have pressured landlords and real estate brokers to provide non-discriminatory service; have signed fair housing pledges; or have taken other action. These company initiatives will be discussed in turn.

A. Relocation of Minorities by Open Housing Centers

A number of corporations have developed relationships with fair housing centers under which minority employees are assisted to find housing.

Typically under these arrangements, the open housing centers advise minority employees of their rights under the law; help them determine whether they are financially able to buy a home, and in what price range; provide information on neighborhood characteristics; refer employees to landlords and real estate brokers, often providing escorts; provide legal anti-discrimination back-up where necessary; and arrange mortgage financing for homebuyers.

These services, if duplicated on an "in-house" basis, would be very costly. And, the specialized knowledge and techniques needed to adequately assist minorities in a basically hostile housing environment may not be worth developing in-house until the flow of minorities increases substantially.

With respect to transferred employees, the open housing centers are able to save the company dollars by speeding up the process of home-buying. Every week not spent in a motel, not eating meals and renting a car at company expense, and not house-hunting on company time constitutes a significant saving. The impact on employee morale that the company "cares" cannot be calculated in monetary terms, but is nonetheless real. Also, the company, as an aid in recruiting, can point out to potential employees the existence of its special housing program.

The company-open housing center arrangements take varying forms, based on company preference. Some are contracts providing for annual consultation/availability fees plus individual referral fees for each employee assisted by the center. There are also contracts or memoranda of understanding which contain an annual flat fee for all employees. Some agreements provide a flat fee for a stated number of employees; if the number of referrals during the year exceeds the maximum, then additional payments are made or the agreement is renegotiated for the following year. Finally, in some instances, the company merely makes a contribution to the open housing center based on past or prospective services to its employees.

The annual cost to companies of such arrangments varies from several hundred to several thousand dollars, depending on the movement of minorities into and within the companies, and on usage of the open housing center's services by on-board employees.

In the New York Metropolitan Area, the Open Housing Center of the New York Urban League provides housing services in New York City while the Urban League of Westchester County provides services in the northern suburbs.

Among the corporations which have relocation agreements with both these Urban Leagues are General Electric Company, American Standard Company, Continental Can Company, Consolidated Edison, and the accounting firms of Arthur Anderson & Company; Haskins & Sells; Lybrand, Ross Bros. & Montgomery; Price, Waterhouse & Company; and Arthur Young & Company. IBM Corporation has made contributions to both organizations based on services rendered.

The Open Housing Center has relationships also with General Motors Corporation, the American Stock Exchange, General Telephone and Electronics, Celanese Corporation, Equitable Life Assurance Society, Bankers Trust Company, Chemical Bank, and First National City Bank. The Westchester Urban League relocates minorities for General Foods Corporation, Bristol-Myers Company, Ciba-Geigy Corporation, The Nestle Company, Philip Morris, Standard Oil Company of New Jersey, Union Carbide Corporation and several other companies.

In Cincinnati, General Electric Company and Procter and Gamble Company have for about five years utilized Housing Opportunities Made Equal (HOME) as a relocation resource. Agreements provide for an annual retainer to cover a specified number of referrals. GE's corporate equal opportunity office reports that HOME "can use pressure to obtain housing because they are authorized to tell owners of large numbers of apartments for rent, that these companies sponsor fair housing. A legal fund has been established recently to bring suit against those realtors or owners who discriminate."[6]

In the midpeninsula suburbs below San Francisco, companies including Hewlett-Packard Company, Syntex Corporation, Alza Corporation and Varian Associates, have along with Stanford University and several cities contracted for an Employer Subscription Service provided by Midpeninsula Citizens for Fair Housing (MCFH). MCFH services cost the subscribing employers from $25 to $100 per month.

In Denver, the Metro Housing Center has on a fee basis provided housing-related services to Western Electric Company (assisting minority employees with housing discrimination cases), United Bank of Denver and Martin Marietta Corporation, Denver Division (preparation of pamphlets on housing opportunities and conducting seminars on housing for employees), and Honeywell in Littleton, Colorado (finding homes close to plant for "hard-core unemployed" people being trained for electronics work).

In White Plains, N.Y., Westchester Residential Opportunities, Inc. (WRO) has entered into contracts with IBM Corporation, General Foods Corporation, New York Telephone Company and Consolidated Edison Company to relocate minority employees into homes and to consult on equal opportunity in housing matters. AT&T Long Lines has made a contribution to WRO in exchange for such services. WRO keeps the companies informed on new housing developments locally and nationally (relating to site selection problems, for example) discusses the housing situation with prospective new hires or transferees, and assists employees, black and white, transferring and on-board, to find homes. Employees are assisted to arrange mortgage financing, and WRO sometimes makes second mortgage loans from its own funds to homebuying employees. (A sample contract is appended as Exhibit A, page 29).

IBM has summed up its relationships with WRO and two local Urban Leagues as follows:

> "They provide a comprehensive service, including financial counseling, housing selection, mortgage placement, assistance (where necessary) in investigating possible discrimination, and (where necessary) second mortgage programs. They also provide general consulting services to IBM on trends and developments in the local housing market. . . This program has proved so successful that IBM is exploring ways to implement it in other large metropolitan areas."[7]

B. Direct Pressure on Real Estate Brokers and Apartment House Owners

> ". . . our top management lowers a pretty hefty economic persuader on the heads of those builders, owners or agents who refuse to sell or rent to our relocating minority group employees. I am a case-in-point and although the company was not forced to take any formal action when a major builder here refused to sell me the new home we selected, it took him only a few hours to confirm the fact that he would lose considerable sales to my colleagues by the single act of discrimination. So, we got the house!"[8]
>
> —*Black Executive, Eastern Air Lines*

The most common company reaction to discrimination in housing perpetrated on a minority group employee is to exert muscle against the discriminator. In many cases a simple letter or telephone call has been enough, while in a few instances a suit has been brought or threatened. A real estate broker or landlord, when confronted by the threat to his livelihood which corporate removal of business would entail, is likely to conclude that crime doesn't pay.

Beyond interceding in individual instances of discrimination, some companies have attempted to gain across-the-board real estate industry cooperation in obtaining housing for minority group employees.

Intervention by Management. When a black employee of GTE Sylvania, Inc. got the run-around at a large apartment complex near its Danvers, Massachusetts facility, the personnel manager went over to the complex, demanded to see the owner and told him that Sylvania would not tolerate discriminatory treatment of its employees. The apartment was made available.

A black MBA candidate landed a 1971 summer job with Minnesota Mining and Manufacturing Company in Saint Paul. He went to an apartment house and asked for a three-month rental; although these were generally available, he was told "one year minimum". His manager called the apartment owner, told him he was sending his employee back to rent the apartment and hung up. The apartment was rented to the summer employee.

In 1968, IBM Corporation personnel in Lexington, Kentucky became concerned that minority employees assigned to the plant were encountering difficulty in obtaining access to suitable broker listings, despite recent passage of a State fair housing law. As a result, IBM's local management advised the bank administering its Home Guarantee Plan that IBM would do business only with those brokers who would provide service to prospective purchasers on a non-discriminatory basis. This policy was transmitted to the local realty board and its member real estate brokers. There was an immediate and dramatic improvement of brokers' services to IBM's minority employees.

A minority group employee relations assistant working for PPG Industries in Greensburg, Pennsylvania was able to fill out an application and place a deposit on a suitable apartment—but then could get no answer from the apartment house owner. He complained to the plant manager who called the landlord for an explanation. The apartment was made available.

A real estate broker hesitated to sell a house in a Chicago suburb to a black employee of Allstate Insurance Company, saying that "you wouldn't be happy there". The employee alerted the assistant vice president—personnel who brought in company counsel who proceeded to contact the broker and threaten an injunction lawsuit. The employee got the house.

In Columbus, Ohio in 1970, a black executive of American Urban Corporation was slated to move into a single-family house in a development built by American Urban. Some neighbors began passing out handbills decrying the fact that the developer was selling to a black family. The company's president personally intervened. He told the agitators that his company was going to obey the open housing law and that was that. The neighborhood quieted down and the executive moved in without incident.

Complaints and Lawsuits. Caterpillar Tractor Co. is the only company known to have sued a discriminator in the name of the company. As the quotation from the Federal court complaint indicates (see page 3 above), Caterpillar based its action on the fact that the landlord's discrimination intensified its difficulties in recruiting and promoting minorities. Caterpillar, according to a company spokesman, was "not afraid to become involved in a social problem which we knew would create reactions in the total community".[9]

The company issued press releases both at the time of instituting suit and upon settling the case out-of-court. The employee plaintiff was offered the apartment and was paid $1,500 in compensation. The same spokesman concluded, "It opened up the eyes of a lot of apartment owners as to what could happen . . . We're convinced that now they know that legally they are in trouble if they discriminate".[10]

Another company, Physics International in San Leandro, California brought a complaint to the California Fair Employment Practices Commission on behalf of a group of black Atlanta University students who were to be trainees over the summer and who were given the run-around by a realty firm. Unfortunately, the processing of the complaint dragged on, the students could not obtain housing and were sent back to Atlanta.

A black plant supervisor of Michigan Bell Telephone wanted to move into a predominantly white subdivision in Ann Arbor, Michigan. The neighborhood association tried to prevent it by putting pressure on the realtor. The employee and the company's local public relations manager went to the city human relations commission to complain, and as a result the employee was able to effect the purchase.

The Buddy System. Some companies relate that a satisfactory method of relocating minority employees is to assign them locally-knowledgeable "buddies". At Goodyear Tire and Rubber, a black employee who went to the same college or is originally from the same part of the country as the newcomer assists him in house-hunting. GTE Sylvania reports that "the presence of a business-attired white man accompanying a black looking for housing can have a very positive effect on the attitude of landlords".[11]

Requiring Fair Housing Pledges. Reacting to a series of instances where transferring employees were discriminated against by real estate brokers in the Cleveland area, 15 companies with facilities in Cleveland (including General Electric Company, General Motors Corporation, Standard Oil Company, Republic Steel Corporation and Ford Motor Company) jointly decided in April, 1971 to utilize only those realtors whose policy was to show homes on an open occupancy basis.

Under an agreement worked out by the Businessmen's Interracial Committee and the Cleveland Real Estate Board, with the aid of the director of Operation Equality, Cleveland Urban League, real estate brokers were required to sign a non-discrimination pledge as a precondition to obtaining client referrals from the companies, and were expected to live up to the pledge in practice. The companies furnish to employees interested in home-buying or home-selling — either as a result of a company-initiated transfer or otherwise—the names only of cooperating real estate brokers, and indicate that only these brokers are to be used.

The announcement of this program to the public is appended as Exhibit B, page 31, and a General Electric Company directive relating to it is reproduced in part as Exhibit C, page 33.

Another major effort to use corporate influence to open up the real estate market for minorities has been tried in Southern California. There, the Autonetics and Rocketdyne divisions of North American Rockwell Corporation, the Data Systems and Guidance and Control Systems divisions of Litton Systems, and the Hughes Missile Systems Division of Hughes Aircraft Company have made separate mailings to a large number of apartment owners and real estate brokers requesting that they sign a non-discrimination pledge if they wished to do business with new and transferred employees of the company. Litton's Data Systems Division sent approximately 7,000 letters to apartment owners and 1,000 letters to realtors in the San Fernando Valley; it received 113 positive responses from apartment owners and 205 from realtors, a 4% response. Autonetics' letter and accompanying pledge are appended as Exhibits D and E, pages 35 and 36 respectively.

McDonnell Douglas Corporation in St. Louis County similarly requires that brokers and owners sign fair housing pledges before their names or housing accommodations will be listed by the company's housing office. The registrant is informed that "As a condition of listing your property in our housing office, it is necessary that we receive from you a signed statement agreeing to equal treatment of any employee referred to you, regardless of race, color, religion, sex or national origin" Corporate counsel reports that the company has nevertheless had to "black ball" a number of owners and brokers it caught discriminating.

Other companies have adopted a similar tack. Monsanto Company in St. Louis requires a written non-discrimination pledge, as does the Sperry Gyroscope Division of Sperry Rand Corporation on Long Island, New York. General Electric Company in San Jose, California has put together an approved EEO realtor listing. Polaroid Corporation in the Boston area has sent letters to realtors, asking cooperation in placing blacks. A Litton Systems spokesman in Pascagoula, Mississippi reports "pretty good results" from talking with realtors and apartment owners about treating whites and blacks the same way.[12]

An NCR executive in Dayton, Ohio reports that since NCR is the largest employer there the company's informal message to the real estate industry not to give them problems has been heeded. American Telephone and Telegraph in Piscataway, New Jersey has compiled a list of apartments; some landlords said they "want to see a person's face" before renting, and were not included on the list. Procter and Gamble, when transferring a black employee to Jackson, Tennessee, contacted the Chamber of Commerce which recommended a real estate broker who sold the employee a suitable house and arranged a mortgage. Prior to passage of the Federal Fair Housing Act, DuPont in 1966 went directly to about 30 apartment owners in Wilmington, Delaware and asked their cooperation in eliminating discrimination. Many apartments were opened up in this fashion.

American Telephone and Telegraph Company (New York City), Illinois Bell Telephone Company, and Control Data Corporation (Minneapolis) all report that they require the companies who relocate their executives to utilize only non-discriminatory brokers. This requirement is sometimes included in the contract retaining the relocation company.

Gaining assurances of non-discrimination is especially important when a substantial number of employees are moved to a new or enlarged facility. Shell Oil Company reports that, at the time of its 1970 move to Houston, personnel from their relocation office met with realtors and apartment owners groups to inform them that some relocating employees would be minorities and that the Company expected they would receive equal treatment. Although some smaller real estate operators and homeowners did discriminate, the Company expressed satisfaction with the treatment that minorities received in general. When moving 450 headquarters personnel to Los Angeles recently, Atlantic Richfield Company retained a relocation company which orally informed all realtors it dealt with that they had to act non-discriminatorily. According to the Company, there were no problems related to racial discrimination.

It is also interesting to note that in response to a questionnaire circulated to commercial banks by the American Bankers Association (ABA), 139 banks indicated that they attempted to use their contacts within the real estate community to foster open housing policies by the real estate brokers and homebuilders financed by them.[13]

C. Rental of Apartments; Policy Statements; Contributions to Open Housing Centers.

Apartment Rentals. In Hendersonville, North Carolina, General Electric Company has leased an apartment building with six 2-bedroom units in an all-white neighborhood. The tenants, who are on the average evenly divided between whites and blacks, are Company trainees on 6-months to 1-year assignments at that location. GE subsidizes the rentals.

In the summer of 1969, Polaroid Corporation in the Boston area rented apartments which it made available to minority employees who were newly hired or transferred at Company request.

Fairchild-Hiller brought in a number of engineers, including blacks, to Hagerstown, Maryland 5 years ago. It signed renewable 1-year leases on an apartment in each of three major apartment complexes in town, with the option of renting more. It was made clear to the rental agents that refusal to rent to the Company, specifically for blacks, could lead to pulling other employees out of the complexes. Since the apartments were rented to the Company and not to individual blacks, this insulated apartment owners from backlash to some extent. (This occurred, of course, prior to passage of the Federal Fair Housing Act).

Policy Statements. After some minority employees encountered discrimination, 27 corporations with facilities in Northern New Jersey adopted and publicized a fair housing statement which endorsed "the principle of fair housing for all Americans" and stated that "we do not knowingly cooperate with any individual, firm or agency which discriminates against any of our employees with respect to housing". The statement was coordinated by Esso Research and Engineering Company; full text of the statement with the corporate signatories appears as Exhibit F, page 37.

Minority Housing Council. At its Lynn plant, General Electric Company established a Minority Housing Council in early 1970 to assist new professional minority employees in locating suitable housing. The Council utilizes fair housing organizations and the scattering of real estate brokers who have committed themselves to the program. More recently, it has been broadened to cover housing problems of all minority employees, which has meant focusing on apartment rentals in Lynn.

Contributions to Open Housing Centers. Recognizing the important role that non-profit open housing centers play both in dealing with a community problem and in assisting corporate employees to overcome discrimination, many corporations have given financial assistance to such centers.

In at least two cases, companies have loaned employees to run fair housing centers. The Safety Razor Division of the Gillette Company lent a young black employee, Carl Freeman,.to Association for Better Housing to open up an office in suburban Newton, Massachusetts. Paid full salary by the company, he was expected to remain six months, until December, 1972.

The Ran Tec Division of Emerson Electric Company released Kenneth C. Kelly, a black engineer, to direct the Fair Housing Council of the San Fernando Valley (California) for a year in 1969-70. Responding to the initiative of Mr. Kelly, who was president of the Council at the time, the company permitted him to work three days per week at the Council and paid him a high percentage of his regular salary.

The Operation Equality fair housing program of Seattle Urban League lists as "major contributors" the following: Boeing Company, Fisher Flouring Mills, General Telephone Company, Leckenby Steel Company, Lockheed Company, Kampe Construction, Pacific Car & Foundry, Pacific Northwest Bell, Rainier Brewing Company, Retail Merchants Association, Seattle Times, Scott Paper, Simpson Timber Company, Washington Mutual Savings Bank, Washington Natural Gas and Western International Hotels.

Connecticut Housing Investment Fund has received contributions from General Electric, Xerox, Peoples Bank, Pitney Bowes, Northeast Utilities, J.M. Ney, Remington Arms, Remington Electric, Timex, Scovill, Southern New England Telephone, United Illuminating, and Warnaco. County Trust Company and National Bank of Westchester have supported Westchester Residential Opportunities, Inc.

The Morris County (New Jersey) Fair Housing Council has received contributions from Warner-Lambert Corporation and IBM Corporation, and the Fair Housing Council of Bergen County has been supported by CPC International, Western Union and IBM. Royal Olivetti Corporation and Sussman & Blumenthal have contributed to Housing Now (Hartford). Gillette Research Institute has made a donation to Suburban Maryland Fair Housing Council.

Baltimore Neighborhoods Inc., one of the oldest of the fair housing centers, received almost $19,000 in 1972 from Operation Push, funded by the Baltimore business community, and has received annual contributions of $250 and over from Sears Roebuck & Company, the Rouse Company, Baltimore Federal Savings and Loan, Baltimore Gas & Electric Company, Baltimore Life Insurance Company, Chesapeake & Potomac Telephone Company, Commercial Credit Corporation, Fidelity Deposit Company, Monumental Properties, Noxell Corporation, Weaver Brothers and Union Trust Company.

In California, the Fair Housing Council of Orange County has received corporate support from The Equal Opportunity Employers Association of Orange County ($1,500), and from Hunt-Wesson Foods, Glass Containers Corporation, Aeronutronic Division of Philco Ford, Autonetics Division of North American Rockwell, Ground Systems Division of Hughes Aircraft, Northrup Corporation, Collier Chemical and McDonnell Douglas. Westside Fair Housing Council in Los Angeles has benefited from gifts from General Telephone Company and Ring Brothers Developers.

The ABA survey of commercial banks ascertained that 59 banks contribute to "fair access" housing organizations and that in 1970 44 banks gave $143,775 to them, an average of over $3,000 per contributing bank.[13]

A few open housing centers have had capital needs as well as operating needs, and these have also been responded to by business. Connecticut

Housing Investment Fund, which is active on a large scale in integrating white neighborhoods throughout Connecticut, has borrowed $1 million each from Aetna Life Insurance Company, Connecticut General Life Insurance Company, and Travelers Insurance Companies to fund the making of second mortgages to black families integrating the suburbs who lack enough cash for a full downpayment (and to occasional whites whose moves promote racial integration). The companies are partially protected by a Ford Foundation guarantee.

In Chicago, Home Investments Fund, a similar group, has sold 4% and other low interest debentures in 4-figure and 5-figure amounts to Carson, Pirie Scott Foundation, Inland Steel-Ryerson Foundation, Hospital Service Corporation, CNA Foundation, the De Soto Foundation and Quaker Oats Foundation. HIF also has received contributions from the Jewel Foundation and Illinois Bell Telephone Company. Most of the foundations supporting HIF are company-affiliated or related.

Finally, Aetna Life has loaned funds to Housing Now (Hartford) to assist that organization to make downpayment money available to low income homebuyers under Federal assistance programs.

Other Activities. United Nuclear Corporation, Southern New England Telephone Company and Olin Corporation have included in their in-house newsletters articles which describe the fair housing services of Connecticut Housing Investment Fund. See Exhibit G, page 39. The four major rubber companies in Akron have agreed to publicize the fair housing services of Fair Housing Contact Service (Akron) by distributing its literature to minority employees, displaying posters on bulletin boards and referring minority group employees for aid in securing housing in white neighborhoods.

Pitney-Bowes, Inc. in Stamford, Connecticut has assisted employees in filing applications for apartments in the newly-built Stamford Towers development and other middle-income developments. Cummins Engine Company in Columbus, Indiana, provided information to its employees concerning a new 100-unit single-family development built for moderate income families under section 235 of the National Housing Act.

FOOTNOTES

1. Published in the Federal Register on December 4, 1971. (36 Fed. Reg. 23152, 41 C.F.R. Sec. 60-2 (Supp. 1972). Emphasis in section 60-2.23 quotation is added.
2. February 5, 1970 (35 Fed. Reg., Vol. 25, 1970).
3. 41 C.F.R. Sec. 60-2.23 (Supp. 1972).
4. Interview with William J. Kilberg, Associate Solicitor, U.S. Department of Labor, August 29, 1972.
5. Interview with Martin E. Sloane, Assistant Staff Director for Civil Rights Program and Policy, U.S. Commission on Civil Rights, August 28, 1972.

6. Memorandum entitled "General Electric Company: Special Housing Programs" dated July 27, 1972, prepared by Joyce A. Lawson, Consultant—EO/MR, General Electric Company, on file at WRO.

7. Letter of Edward T. Buhl, then Managing Attorney, IBM Corporation, to Leonard Schramm, HUD, dated January 14, 1972, on file at WRO.

8. Letter of J.O. Plimpton, Jr., Division Vice President, Eastern Air Lines Incorporated, dated November 10, 1971, to Roger N. Beilenson, on file at WRO.

9. Letter of Jim Folck, Community Affairs Manager, Caterpillar Tractor Co., to Ms. Hedy Epstein, Greater St. Louis Committee for Freedom of Residence, dated June 15, 1972, on file at WRO.

10. Telephone interview with Mr. Folck, August 15, 1972.

11. Letter of Paul K. Alexander, Personnel Development Manager, Lighting Products Group, GTE Sylvania, Inc., to Roger N. Beilenson, dated November, 1972, on file at WRO.

12. Telephone interview with Claude A. Culpepper, Manager, Community Services, Litton Ship Systems, July, 21, 1972.

13. "Urban and Community Affairs; A Banking Survey" (The American Bankers Association, undated).

This material has not been excerpted in its entirety.

Prepared by Westchester Residential Opportunities, Inc. under contract with the U.S. Dept. of HUD. (1973)

HOME MORTGAGE LENDING AND SOLAR ENERGY

Regional and Urban Planning Implementation Inc.
Cambridge, Massachusetts

David Barrett
Peter Epstein
Charles M. Haar

I. The Importance of Financing

Solar energy heating and hot water systems are operating in hundreds of American homes today. They hold the promise of supplying much of the energy used in the home, which today accounts for one-fifth of total national energy consumption. But this will only come to pass if hundreds, thousands, and finally millions of individuals decide to buy or build solar-equipped housing.

Many factors will affect this process, including the price and availability of competing energy sources, improvements in the design of solar energy systems, and similar issues that will determine how soon such systems make economic as well as environmental sense. **One of the most important of these factors may be the willingness of lenders to provide mortgage loans for solar housing, and in particular the terms on which financing is available. This is not so much because of what makes solar energy systems different and unusual, but rather because of what they have in common with many other aspects of housing: a large capital cost that must be financed and paid for over time.**

IMPACT OF FINANCING TERMS

It has long been recognized that the market for housing is extremely sensitive to financing terms. First, the availability of mortgage financing is essential for the vast majority of housing transactions that take place. Few home buyers can pay cash, and few will be able to manage the substantial additional costs of solar heating unless these can be financed in whole or in part.

Second, most families have a relatively limited amount of money available to use as a down payment, and thus the strength of the housing market is strongly affected by how much of the purchase price is covered by financing. Many people want to own a solar home today, and many more will wish to as available systems become more cost effective. Nevertheless, the number actually in a position to buy such a home will be greatly affected by the proportion of the costs that can be financed.

Third, loan terms—interest rate, length of payment period, and amount financed—directly determine the monthly payment that housing owners will make to finance solar energy installations. The size of this monthly payment (and the downpayment) will significantly affect the economics of solar energy systems from the owner's perspective.

SOME ILLUSTRATIONS

A general idea of the range of financing possibilities and their impact on costs, can be found in Table 1. This table illustrates the differences among the size of the downpayment and monthly loan payments for an $8,000 solar energy system financed under different loan types prevalent in single family home financing. As can be seen in the bottom line of this table, the type of financing used has a substantial effect on the size of the monthly payment—and therefore, on the amount of monthly energy cost savings needed to make such a system "pay for itself" on a current basis.

For example, a conventional home mortgage for 70% of the total system cost of $8,000 (as shown in the first vertical column on the left of the chart) would provide $5,600 towards the cost of the system at an interest rate of 8.5% to be paid off over 27 years. The purchaser would need to make a $2,400 downpayment, and then make monthly payments for principal and interest on the loan of $44.15 for the remainder of the 27 years. If an FHA-insured loan was obtainable for 93% of the system cost, the downpayment would be reduced to $560, and the monthly payments would be $58.53 for the 30-year term of that loan. On the other hand, if the system could only be financed through a short-term home improvement loan (as in the last column on the right), the full cost might be borrowed, eliminating the downpayment entirely—but increasing the monthly payment to $179.98 a month for the five-year term of the loan. Thus the financing terms have a direct and critical effect on the costs of such a system to the homeowner.

Table 1

HOW FINANCING AFFECTS SOLAR COSTS

ILLUSTRATIVE LOAN TERMS AND MONTHLY DEBT SERVICE UNDER PRIVATE LENDER FINANCING ALTERNATIVES

	LOAN TYPE							
	FIRST MORTGAGE					SECOND MORTGAGE	HOME IMPROVEMENT	
	Conventional			FHA	VA	Conventional	Title 1	Conventional
Loan/Value Ratio	70%	80%	90%	93%	100%	75%	100%	100%
Interest Rate	8.5%	8.75%	9.0%	8.25%	9.0%	13.5%	11.5%	12.5%
Maturity (years)	27	27	27	30	30	10	12	5
Mortgage Insurance	-	15%	25%	5%	-	-	5%	-
Monthly Cost per $1,000 of Loan	$7.88	$8.16	$8.41	$8.06	$8.23	$15.23	$13.13	$22.50
DOWNPAYMENT FOR AN $8,000 SOLAR ENERGY SYSTEM	$2,400	$1,600	$800	$560	0	$2,000	0	0
MONTHLY COST FOR AN $8,000 SOLAR ENERGY SYSTEM	$44.15	$52.23	$60.53	$58.53	$64.37	$91.36	$105.07	$179.98

Figure 1

DISTRIBUTION OF LOAN ORIGINATIONS FOR NEWLY BUILT RESIDENCES, BY LOAN TYPES AND LENDER GROUPS, 1974

SINGLE FAMILY
Total Volume $24.132 Billion

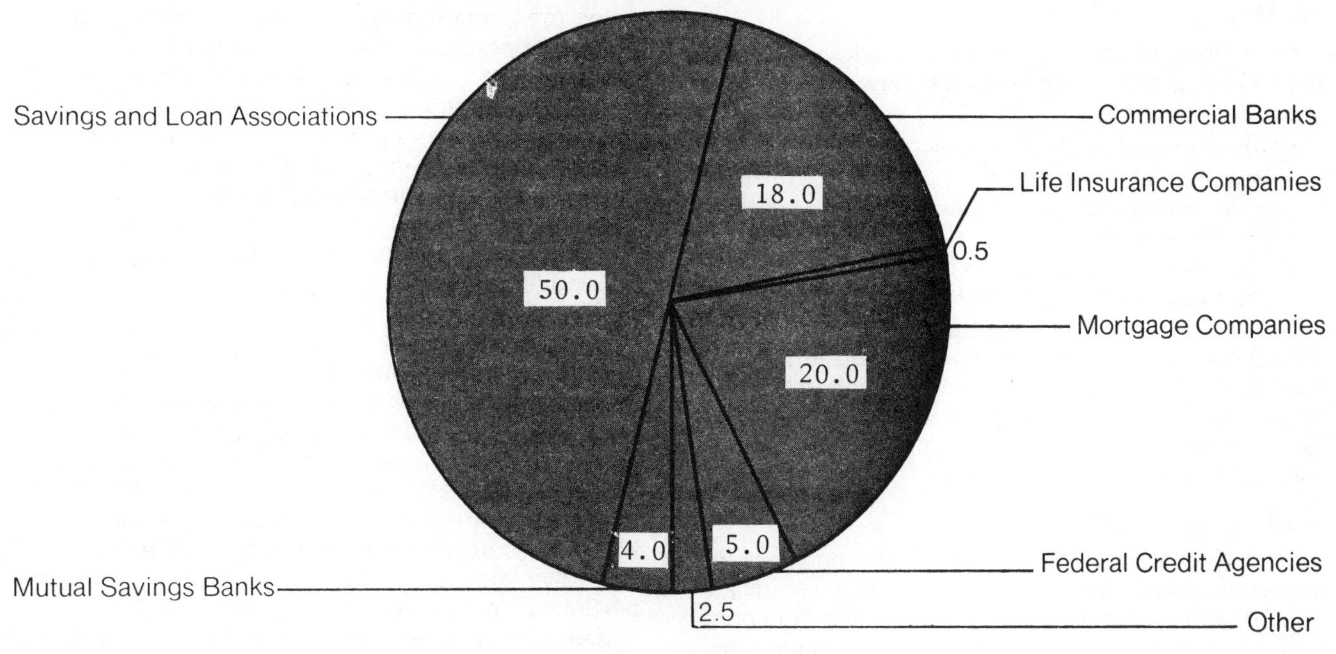

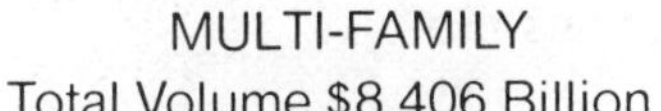
MULTI-FAMILY
Total Volume $8.406 Billion

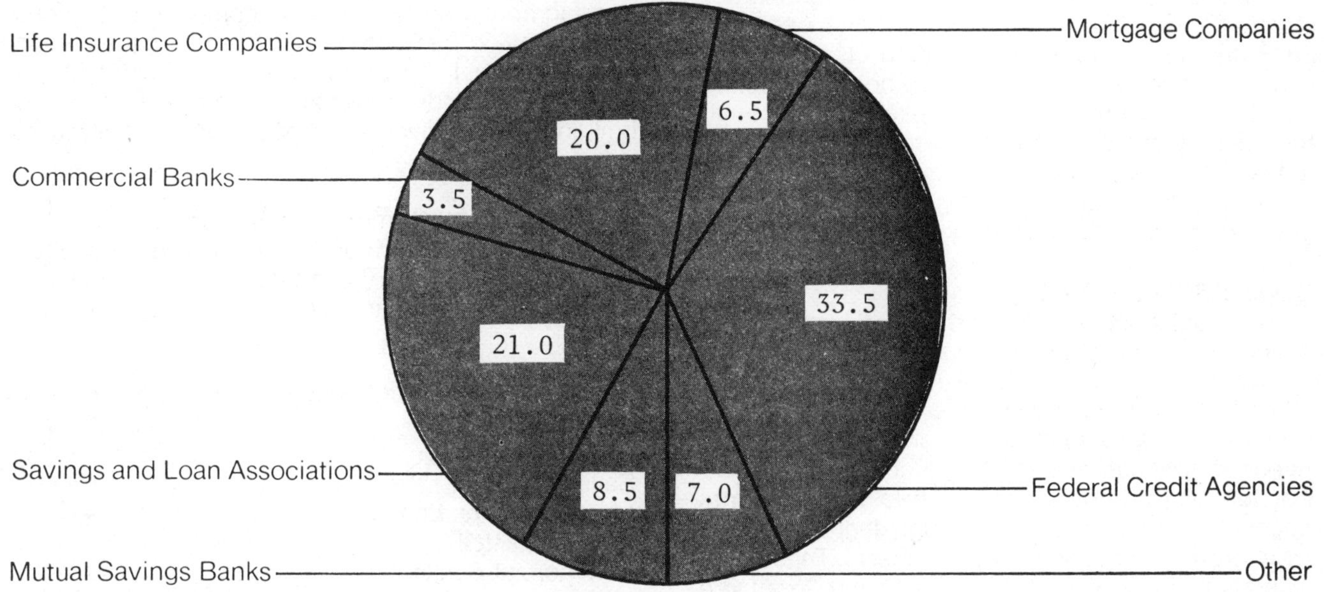

Source: U.S. Department of Housing and Urban Development

II. An Overview of Residential Finance

WHO'S WHO IN THE PRIMARY MORTGAGE MARKET

Four types of institutional lenders originate more than 90% of the mortgage on new homes written each year:

- "thrift institutions" (as savings and loan associations, mutual savings banks, and similar institutions are commonly designated)
- commercial banks
- life insurance companies
- mortgage companies or bankers.

These primary lenders deal directly with the borrower, and provide him with construction funds and mortgage credit. And their policies and practices largely determine the reception accorded any new type of housing innovation on its first being introduced into the primary mortgage market.

THRIFT INSTITUTIONS

Thrift institutions have been in the business of channeling personal savings into residential loans for more than one hundred years, and are the dominant private institutions in the residential mortgage market today. More than 5,500 of these institutions provide over half of all permanent loans for single family homes and nearly one third of those for multi-family structures. Since savings deposits have generally been less subject to withdrawal than other kinds of banking accounts, the "thrifts" have been well suited for making long term mortgage investments. Although they also represent the major source of construction funds for single family homes, their primary motive for making short-term credit available is to be in a position to write the permanent mortgage later.

COMMERCIAL BANKS

The residential lending and general investment policies of commercial banks vary greatly with institutional size, the nature of local economic activity and other factors. In most instances, however, they are oriented primarily towards the short-term financial needs of local businesses. Moreover, the sizable proportion of their deposits in checking accounts necessitates their maintaining a high degree of liquidity in order to meet withdrawal requests. These considerations generally preclude their tying up a large proportion of their assets in permanent mortgages, and explain their preeminence as a supplier of construction funds for both single and multi-family buildings. Nevertheless, in total volume, commercial banks are still among the major sources of permanent residential loans.

LIFE INSURANCE COMPANIES

Real estate mortgages have historically been an attractive investment for life insurance companies, given the long term nature of their liabilities and the general importance attached to certainty and stability of income in calculating premiums. Until the mid-sixties, life insurers ranked second to savings and loans as a source of permanent mortgage funds for individual homes. Since that time, however, life insurance companies have steadily shifted their portfolios from single family residences to multi-family and commercial properties, and in most instances, withdrawn altogether from mortgage lending on individual residences.

MORTGAGE COMPANIES

Mortgage companies (or mortgage bankers) began appearing in the postwar era to act as independent middlemen who would make loans to borrowers on behalf of out-of-state lending institutions such as life insurance companies and mutual savings banks. Mortgage companies generally have little capital of their own, and rarely maintain permanent mortgage portfolios. In recent years, as life insurance companies have phased out their single family lending activity, mortgage companies have reoriented their operations toward the Federally supported secondary market in which mortgage loans are bought and sold. In geographic terms, mortgage company operations concentrate in the Southern and Western states which have traditionally been net importers of capital from other regions and where population growth and new building activity have been proceeding at a rapid pace.

The table below summarizes the number of individual institutions for each of the lender types described above. Figure 1 shows their respective shares of loans made on new homes in 1974.

Primary Sources of Residential Mortgage Loans

Type	Number of Institutions
Savings & Loan	5,039
Mutual Savings Banks	478
Total THRIFTS	5,517
Commercial Banks	14,457
Life Insurance Companies	1,833
Mortgage Companies	1,450

Source: U.S. Department of Housing and Urban Development

FEDERAL SUPPORT AND REGULATION

The mortgage market would be far smaller in size and considerably different in structure and functioning than it is today in the absence of the public support for home mortgage financing that has evolved over the past forty years. **At the present time, a diverse array of Federal mortgage insurance programs, interest subsidies, secondary market support operations, and banking and income tax regulations combine to establish the context within which institutions provide residential mortgage loans.** In particular, two classes of public institutions—Federal credit agencies and secondary market entities—may have a marked influence on the availability of financing for solar homes.

FEDERAL CREDIT AGENCIES

The Federal Housing Administration (FHA), now part of HUD, was established to insure conventional mortgage loans made by private lenders. Its early successes were instrumental in demonstrating the soundness of the long-term, self-amortizing mortgage—today the commonly accepted credit instrument used to finance home purchases. Insurance programs modeled on FHA's were subsequently established for ex-servicemen and rural families under the auspices of the Veteran's Administration (VA) and Farmer's Home Administration (FmHA), respectively. In recent years, FHA's mortgage insurance programs have experienced increased competition from private mortgage insurers (PMI's). Learning from FHA's experience, the PMI's have been able to offer lenders faster service without the limits on interest rates and loan amounts inherent in government insurance programs.

SECONDARY MARKET ENTITIES

Originally the secondary market consisted primarily of institutional investors who sought to purchase mortgages as investments, but were not organized to make residential loans directly to borrowers. On occasion, primary lenders also act as secondary purchasers; when their supply of funds exceeds the local demand for mortgage loans, they may choose to acquire mortgages from banks or mortgage companies located in other housing markets.

In recent years the secondary market has increasingly come to be identified with three government-supported agencies whose function is to join the primary mortgage market to the nation's larger capital markets in order to provide local banks with liquidity and assure a steadier supply of credit for the home-building industry. These three entities are: (1) the Government National Mortgage Association (GNMA), organized primarily to provide a secondary market for loans written under the Federal government's subsidized interest rate programs; (2) the Federal National Mortgage Association (FNMA), whose mortgage purchase programs feed money into local housing markets when capital is in short supply; and (3) the Federal Home Loan Mortgage Corporation (FHLMC), organized to enable savings institutions participating in the Federal Home Loan Bank system to maintain their mortgage loan portfolios on a more liquid footing.

GNMA is Federally owned, and operates within the Department of Housing and Urban Development. FNMA (since it was spun off from HUD in 1968) and FHLMC are privately owned, but Federally regulated and supported stock corporations.

III. The Lender's Perspective on Solar Homes

AWARENESS AND RECEPTIVITY

The fourfold increase in crude oil prices following the 1973-1974 oil embargo led to price increases in all energy sources and set the stage for the growing interest in solar and other alternative energy systems. Lenders are no less aware of these critical changes than the rest of us. More than three fourths of lenders responding said that energy costs have increased as a factor in their own residential financing decisions since energy costs began to rise in 1973. Virtually all believed that the impact of energy costs would continue, and the majority believed it would increase in the next five years.

This growing sensitivity of lenders to energy costs is paralleled by an increasing awareness of the solar alternative, and accompanied by a surprising optimism as to the rate at which it will become a reality.

Most lenders interviewed knew of the existence of residential solar energy heating systems, and some had a good idea of how such systems work. About one-fourth had already seen estimates of energy savings, cost-benefit analyses, or specific plans, models or installed systems. Several commercial banks had among their business customers small solar equipment manufacturers or architectural firms involved in solar projects. One savings bank surveyed was in the process of developing a new solar-heated branch office, and several other institutions are already utilizing solar energy for space heating or hot water purposes.

As should be expected, the most informed lenders tend to be those who have dealt with actual loan requests. Even here, however, the amount of information gathered on technical and even economic aspects of solar heating frequently reflects a personal interest bank officers have in the subject, rather than any analytic requirements of the loan decision. In fact, there are many issues that may weigh more heavily in the balance than detailed analyses of this sort—such as lenders' assessment of when and if such systems will be commercially available in their own areas as an option for the average homeowner.

Lenders appear to have a very positive outlook on the future of residential solar energy in this context. Of the lenders surveyed who were prepared to express an opinion, more than one-fourth thought that systems would be commercially available in their own areas within five years, and half thought this would happen within five to ten years.

Lender optimism on the prospects for the solar alternative is accompanied by a widespread belief that it is in the public interest and warrants public support. In fact, more than three-fourths of lenders questioned believed that there was a "high priority" need for the development of solar or other alternative energy sources. An even larger proportion supported an active government role in the development and dissemination of solar energy systems. And, nearly three-fourths were in favor of financial subsidies, at least in the short run, if they proved necessary.

LENDER CONCERNS: AN INTRODUCTION

This positive lender attitude towards solar energy systems will undoubtedly be welcomed by the growing ranks of solar advocates. And it should be equally heartening for them to learn that lenders have already proven themselves receptive to financing requests to some degree. In fact, virtually all lenders surveyed believed that they would seriously consider financing requests today. More than a dozen New England lenders had already been approached, and loans had been made in half of these cases. And Florida lenders surveyed had been making loans on homes with solar hot water systems for over thirty years.

At the same time, it should be recognized that lender support for the development of solar in the national interest, and even optimism as to its probable rate of development, is not synonymous with the unrestricted availability of financing for solar homes today. **Whatever lenders attitudes on public issues may be, they must make loan decisions in a manner that accords with their day to day standards of business operations, and the standards of the numerous public regulatory agencies concerned with a sound banking system and protection of depositors' interests. Those who favor residential uses of solar energy will have to understand and respond to the legitimate concerns involved if the inclination of lenders to support solar is to result in the actual availability of financing.** In this context, three areas of current uncertainty deserve the greatest attention: the impact on property values; technical performance of the systems; and estimates of future savings in energy costs.

LENDER CONCERNS: THE FOCUS ON VALUE

The focus on value is inherent in the position of a lender in relation to any property on which he makes a loan and should be understood by those seeking financing for solar homes. Lenders in fact have a number of concrete and reasonably predictable concerns regarding the performance and economics of residential solar energy systems that must be addressed in any effort to obtain financing (see Figure 2). **However, regardless of the specific uncertainty** (be it the energy output of the system itself, the availability of trained maintenance personnel, the unfamiliar physical appearance), **it interests the lender primarily insofar as it affects the value of the property involved and the ease with which the home can be disposed of under foreclosure conditions.**

The controlling factors here are that mortgage loans are made in relation to the value of the property offered as collateral, rather than its costs—and that **there is considerable uncertainty right now as to how much value a solar energy system adds to housing.** As pithily expressed by one bank executive, the underwriting of a solar home will center on the same question posed when evaluating a loan request for any property, namely: "What is its 'drop dead' value? . . . What's it worth under the hammer?"

THE PROBLEM OF VALUATION AND "OVERIMPROVEMENTS"

Over time, of course, the market place will serve as the definitive arbiter of value, with the knowns, unknowns, virtues and liabilities of solar systems reflected in the price consumers are willing to pay for new and used homes that incorporate solar energy devices. But right now, and for the next few years, this information will be lacking in most markets, and lenders will have to proceed in the absence of any significant volume of experience in the sale of "comparable" homes.

What they will necessarily consider—and what those

promoting solar must consider—is the possibility that the market value of a solar installation (in terms of resale of the property) may be less than the costs associated with it, and that loans offered will therefore be a proportionally smaller part of the additional sales price.

Such a disparity between costs and value would not be unique to solar energy systems, and is in fact a familiar part of housing market experience. There are many examples of what lenders in New England often call "overimprovements": housing features with costs greater than market values. The type of feature involved can range from better-than-average construction techniques (such as studs centered 12" instead of 16", or above-standard insulation), unique architectural features (such as marble floors, copper flashing or interior balconies, and three-car garages) to such familiar luxury items as tennis courts, horse barns, and docks. Whether or not a particular feature is an "overimprovement" will vary among areas: in some neighborhoods a swimming pool may add as much to value as it costs, while in others it would be an overimprovement. There are similar variations on a regional basis: central air conditioning is considered an overimprovement in most New England areas but a necessity fully reflected in market value in many parts of the South. Overimprovements tend to be concentrated in custom-built and more expensive homes rather than in speculatively-built sale housing.

INNOVATIONS AS "OVERIMPROVEMENTS"

The question at issue here for those concerned with marketing solar housing is, of course, the extent to which lenders will treat the additional costs involved in solar as such an "overimprovement" and thus exclude it from property valuation in determining the maximum amount they will lend. In this connection, it is instructive to examine how lenders have approached other "housing innovations" in the past.

Lenders interviewed in the present study often took issue with the allegation that they were intrinsically resistant to new housing technologies. They noted examples of unusual or innovative housing proposals which they had financed, including houses with new types of energy systems, and a small number of radical design changes (such as domes and foam houses). They more frequently cited such past innovations in materials as the introduction of drywall (to replace plastering) and the introduction of plastic pipe (to replace iron and copper piping), and past advances in energy systems (for example, the introduction of gas and electric heated homes, and so called "total energy systems"). And they noted the efforts to introduce "pre fab" and "modular" housing, and the advent of central air-conditioning systems, as further illustrations of technical changes confronted in the relatively recent past. **Unlike solar energy systems, most of these advances involved either comparable or—more often—lower first costs than the materials or equipment replaced.** The lenders thus faced two questions at the outset: the "technical" assessment of whether the equipment or materials would perform as claimed; and the appraisal judgment of whether the market would impose an even greater reduction in value of such homes—initially or over time—than the achieved reduction in cost or proposed reduction (if any) in selling price.

In many cases (for example, with early designs of electric heating), lenders did answer this latter question by placing values lower than costs on these "innovative" features. **What is also important is that the first of these concerns—the uncertainty of performance—was essentially a particular form of lender concern over value (and related to it, of the likelihood of default).** In other words, performance failure was seen as a contingency that might require expenditures for repair or replacement by the owner-borrower, potentially jeopardizing his financial reliability and reducing the market value of the property unless and until such action was taken. In some cases the likelihood of technological or economic obsolence—that is, the development of better or cheaper systems—is an equal or greater concern in the valuation decision than the possibility of performance failure.

LENDER VIEWS ON THE IMPACT OF SOLAR ON HOUSING VALUE TODAY

With these considerations in mind, it should not be surprising to learn that some lenders tend to believe solar installations at present may be "overimprovements" in whole or in part. This is not to say that there is no optimism for the longer run. **Lenders observed that when and if (or where today) such systems are demonstrably reliable and economically desirable for a home buyer, the impact on value may be felt not only as a rise in the value of homes that have such systems, but also as a fall in value of conventional homes that lack them.** And they noted the probability that there would be a similar impact on the market value of developable land to reflect its suitability as a site for solar installations. But it is their perceptions of the impact on home value today that are most critical to solar manufacturers, builders and buyers.

Less than half of lenders responding in the present survey believed that such systems would add appreciably to home value at this time. They often cautioned that they could not say to what extent the increase in value would match the increase in costs, and frequently noted that the increase in value would occur and be maintained only so long as the system performed satisfactorily. Lenders fear that such properties will sell more slowly than conventionally heated homes, adding a hard to quantify but nonetheless tangible impediment to increasing the value as far as the costs. **If, as some lenders observed, it would add to value "in the right market," or "for some people but not for all," a proper appraisal will reflect a discount of the full amount.**

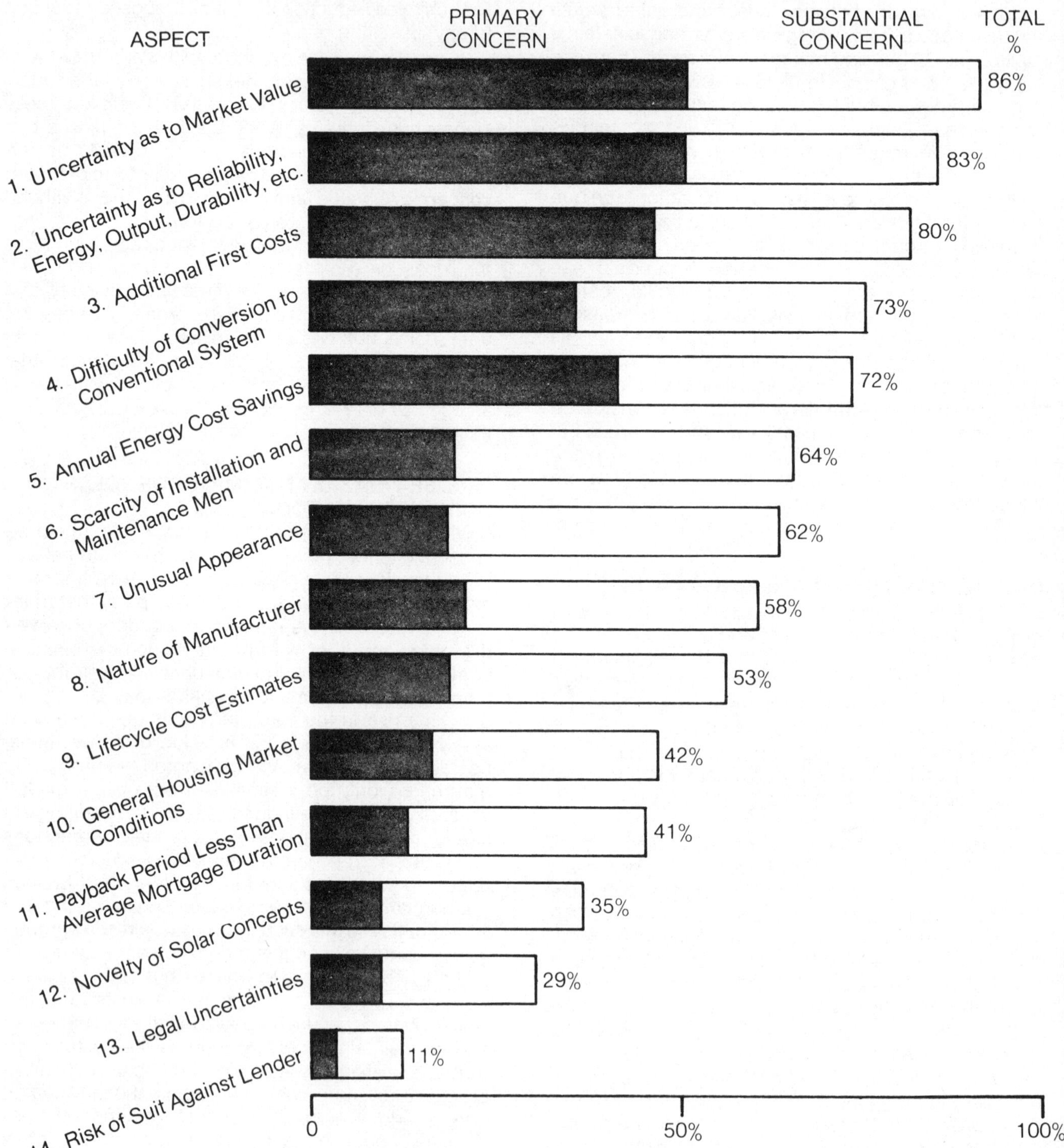
ISSUES OF CONCERN TO LENDERS IN MAKING LOANS
PERCENTAGE OF LENDERS IDENTIFYING SELECTED ASPECTS OF SOLAR ENERGY HEATING SYSTEMS AS PRIMARY OR SUBSTANTIAL CONCERNS IN FUTURE LENDING DECISIONS
ASPECT
PRIMARY CONCERN
SUBSTANTIAL CONCERN
TOTAL %
1. Uncertainty as to Market Value
86%
2. Uncertainty as to Reliability, Energy, Output, Durability, etc.
83%
3. Additional First Costs
80%
4. Difficulty of Conversion to Conventional System
73%
5. Annual Energy Cost Savings
72%
6. Scarcity of Installation and Maintenance Men
64%
7. Unusual Appearance
62%
8. Nature of Manufacturer
58%
9. Lifecycle Cost Estimates
53%
10. General Housing Market Conditions
42%
11. Payback Period Less Than Average Mortgage Duration
41%
12. Novelty of Solar Concepts
35%
13. Legal Uncertainties
29%
14. Risk of Suit Against Lender
11%
0
50%
100%

Figure 2

The sense of uncertainty exemplified by the qualifications noted here was echoed by the nearly one-third of lenders questioned who preferred not to express an opinion because there was insufficient evidence available or they simply didn't know. Some thought there would be no reflection of the system's costs in property value—or that the inclusion of the system would in fact reduce the value of the home. Among lenders in this last group, one lender attributed his expectation of a net loss in value to his belief that the costs involved could not be fully recaptured in the sales price and that developers, aware of this, would "remove" an equivalent amount of cost (and value) somewhere else in the house. Others viewed the problem as based on the uncertainties surrounding the physical and economic performance of currently available systems. As one lender put it, "No one is convinced there is a workable product." In the same vein, another saw proof of the risks involved in the large number of small firms "with fundamentally different ideas" in various stages of development; since "they can't all be right," he would wait for the inevitable shake-out to occur and discount property values, or not loan at all, in the meantime.

DIVERSITY OF RESPONSE

Not all lenders take such a wait-and-see stance. In fact, one of the most striking findings of the study was the diversity of attitudes and opinions among lenders on many aspects of financing solar homes (and the possibility for "shopping the market" to obtain adequate financing). This was well illustrated by the different opinions as to whether or not solar energy systems represent a housing "innovation" that will cause problems in financing. There was a clear division between those who perceived solar systems as something radically new and difficult to assess (in the words of one commercial banker, "the biggest potential change in years in housing design"), and those who saw it as merely "another type of heating system" —or at least as relatively straightforward to evaluate for lending purposes.

But even with this range of attitudes, **the question of valuation is obviously a crucial one. Although lenders emphasize that it is the market that establishes value, their judgments and educated guesses as to what market value is will be unusually important until there is the "body of experience" that they (and most everyone else) is waiting for.** Some lenders place far more emphasis on the borrower's ability to pay than on property value. ("We lend to people, not to things," as one put it.) But, regardless of ability to pay, lenders are—by statute, regulation and business practice—loaning against value. **The extent to which they judge solar system costs to be reflected by increased home values will in large part define the extent to which financing will be available on workable terms for the majority of homebuyers.**

LENDER CONCERNS: TECHNICAL PERFORMANCE

It has been suggested here that lender's concerns over technical and performance aspects of solar energy systems will be resolved primarily in the context of property valuations. But some of these concerns will raise other issues as well, including the problem of technical review, and of the presence or ease of conversion to a standard heating system.

TECHNICAL APPRAISAL OF SOLAR SYSTEMS

Financial institutions generally lack the motivation, and in many instances the skills, to examine the technical details of construction—including basic mechanical systems—with the same care they devote to assessing the marketability, value and overall livability of homes proposed for mortgage financing. As one lender summarized the review priorities: "We're far more likely to reject [a property] because there s no second bath or we don't like the layout [than over the heating and air conditioning.] " Except for some of the insurance companies and the very largest banks, the financial organizations interviewed generally had no in-house staff with mechanical engineering or architectural credentials.

Where special needs arise, a detailed engineering review will be undertaken using an outside consultant if necessary. **Such a review is generally the rule in large, complex multi-family projects, but a rare exception in a single-family house and smaller rental developments. The need simply does not arise.** In fact, none of the lenders on single-family homes could recall cases where building plans called for use of equipment by unknown manufacturers or unusual system configurations. Nor were problems of unreliability with mechanical systems a contributing cause to default or a factor in a bank's failure to recoup its investment in a home in the case of foreclosure.

However, when lenders receive their first loan requests on solar heated homes, they are confronted by a situation where uncertainties regarding the mechanical reliability of the heating system itself do, in fact, have a direct bearing on the value of property as security for the mortgage. In many cases, before a lender will consider financing a significant part of this solar first cost as part of the total mortgage, our interviews suggest that he will require a thorough engineering appraisal of the system proposed for installation—possibly at the borrower's expense. Where the lender can't make such an evaluation, or sees it as too much trouble to obtain for a single loan request, he may be even more conservative in respect to the terms on which financing will be provided, if it is provided at all.

WARRANTIES—A MINOR CONCERN

One possible solution to concern over performance failures that has been suggested is the provision of "warranties" by solar manufacturers, installers or home builders. But the lenders interviewed attached little if any importance to the availability of a warranty for solar products. They tended to believe that if the manufacturer was a small company with limited economic resources, the warranty would prove of little or no value (even if the firm was still in business when the problem arose). Conversely, if the producer is large and reputable, the warranty is viewed as largely superfluous since the firm will, in most cases, feel obligated to stand behind its components—particularly in light of the stiffening legal context of implied fitness and warranty of products.

On the other hand, the entry of major companies with national reputations into the field might help make the difference in many cases. A substantial number of lenders noted they they would obviously feel more comfortable with a name manufacturer of established reputation, who was certain to remain in business over the life of the system. But only a few felt that the production of systems and/or major components by a well known supplier might be an absolute prerequisite for their making financing available. And a fourth of those interviewed expressed "little or no" concern with the manufacturer's identity. **This diversity of attitudes again suggests that a refusal by any one lender should not deter a home builder or buyer from continuing to seek a lender who will make a loan.**

LENDER CONCERNS: ESTIMATING ENERGY SAVINGS

There is one further "technical" issue of central concern to borrowers and lenders in the financing of solar housing: the manner in which projected utility cost savings are taken into account in financing decisions. **The expectation of operating cost savings is of course the very aspect of solar energy systems that holds the promise of their widespread adoption in housing. But at least at the outset, there are likely to be some real problems raised by lenders' treatments of these projections in the evaluation of multifamily rental properties, and in their use for gauging the value of single-family installations and underwriting applicants for home mortgages.**

RECOGNITION OF ENERGY COSTS IN MULTI-FAMILY INCOME PROPERTIES

In most instances, lenders employ the "economic" or "income" valuation approach to assessing mortgage loan requests for income-producing properties such as rental housing developments. No matter what precise valuation technique is employed, solar heating's impact on the attractiveness of a project for mortgage financing will be reflected in a straightforward manner, since the estimated solar costs and savings enter directly into the net cash flow equation (income less operating expenses and mortgage debt service).

As part of his loan application, the developer will have submitted a detailed *pro forma* for the proposed development—that is, a statement itemizing the major constituents of gross income and expenses. A large part of the first costs for the solar energy system will be reflected in the line item for annual debt service (amortization of loan principal plus interest). Other components of total expenses—particularly the allocations for repairs and maintenance, utility costs, real estate taxes, insurance, and any reserves for replacement or other contingencies—might also be affected to some extent by the inclusion of solar heating. By the time serious developer interest in using solar heat for rental units materializes, these estimates may prove relatively easy to verify based on actual operating experience with specific systems in single-family homes, other types of commercial properties, and government demonstration programs. However, as lenders noted, at the present time, it would be difficult to devise a credible financial projection for a solar heated development. Since economic feasibility is based entirely on cash flow, the income stream would have to be determined "within reasonable probability." Otherwise the cash flow projections would have to be discounted heavily in the appraisal process—or the project rejected altogether.

Most lenders indicated they would in fact ask for (or prepare themselves) income statements comparing the project's economics both with and without the solar system. In situations where the solar heated project failed to show a more attractive net income stream than the same project when conventionally heated, most lenders indicated that they would be responsive to a developer's contention that the solar system was desirable as a hedge against future increases in fuel prices. **Nevertheless, almost all insisted that, for valuation purposes, net operating income under both solar and conventional alternatives would be examined solely on the basis of current utility prices, with no allowance for fuel price inflation over time. This is consistent with general practice for quantifying other components of cash flow which may well vary unpredictably from year to year, such as real estate taxes, wages for security and maintenance personnel and the basic rent schedule for the units themselves.**

ENERGY COST SAVINGS AS A MEANS OF VALUATION IN SALES HOUSING

While the valuation of income properties automatically reflects energy costs savings in property appraisal, this is not generally the case where single family and other "sales" housing is concerned. In appraising the value of such housing, lenders normally look to information on the sale of "comparable homes." However, in the case of solar homes, this information will be lacking for several years, and lenders will be reluctant to use "replacement costs" (that is, the price of the solar installation) as an alternative indicator of value. **Given the inapplicability of these usual appraisal measures, some lenders will turn to consideration of energy costs savings as a partial if not wholly satisfactory surrogate.** But they will necessarily encounter many of the same problems involved in the valuation of income properties—and can be expected to handle them in a similar manner.

Solar first costs can be determined with some reliability, but in reviewing estimates of fuel savings with solar heat, the lender must contend with the claims of manufacturers and developers which he suspects may be inflated and self-serving, or else obtain "educated guesses" from more disinterested experts. Lenders will tend to discount the estimates to some degree, and to resist the use of projected increases in alternative fuel costs.

The approach to valuation will vary considerably, from payback period and lifecycle cost analyses to the "capitalizing" of estimated savings and discounted cash flow approximations of present value. **None of these types of analysis was viewed as determining the decision on whether to loan or not, but rather as partial guides in appraising value.**

CREDIT REVIEW PROCEDURES: A BIAS AGAINST SOLAR

The skepticism of lenders regarding the reflection of solar costs and savings in property value will surely be the primary problem for "average" home buyers who want to go solar. But there is another problem as well which has to do with the way lenders evaluate a borrower's capacity to pay off a mortgage loan.

Most lenders use a comparison of projected housing costs to loan applicant income as a guide to determining the maximum size loan for which a given individual can qualify. The widely followed standard is that housing costs should not exceed 25% of income. **But in most cases, this calculation of housing costs does not include energy costs, and is limited to Principal and Interest payments on the loan, property Taxes, and frequently, hazard Insurance premiums (thus often referred to by the acronym "PITI"). The resulting problem for solar homes is that savings in utility bills will not improve the borrower's financial capacity as evaluated by the lender. At the same time, the higher first costs of the property, as reflected in a higher mortgage request (and higher principal and interest payments), and higher insurance premiums and property taxes, do raise the income requirement as established by the PITI test.**

This will not be true in all cases. More than half of lenders questioned indicated they will make some allowance for projected energy cost savings. But this will tend to be a qualitative rather than a quantitative adjustment. Many lenders, and particularly mortgage companies who plan to sell their loans to other institutions, adhere to the PITI standards of purchasing institutions to assure the widespread marketability of those loans. Others—such as thrift institutions loaning for their own accounts—are not yet willing to rely on projections of energy cost savings from relatively untried solar energy systems.

A LEAD ROLE FOR BUILDERS AND DEVELOPERS

The questions considered in this chapter are only part of the many problems confronting solar users and solar proponents as they strive to make this energy source a practical alternative today. **In terms of the specific issues related to the financing of solar housing, however, it is important to note that lenders believe that the impetus for change will come from builders and developers, if it comes at all.** They already view them as the lead actors in the advent of energy conserving initiatives generally, and have reason to believe that this will be the case in solar as well.

WHO TAKES THE INITIATIVE?

There was an important division of attitude as to the proper role for lenders in the process of increasing energy conservation in housing. With respect to whether they as lenders would try to induce a builder to provide energy conservation features, more than half said that they either had already done so or would do so in the future. Some even went so far as to explicitly condition a loan on builder adherence to an energy-related recommendation. On the other hand, a sizeable percentage emphasized that their role "was either to lend or not to lend"—not to interfere in design questions that fell within the responsibility of builders and developers.

While lenders often take the initiative to encourage single-family home buyers to consider energy costs in their housing decisions, there is, again, a division of opinion among lenders as to the nature of their role. Some feel they have a responsibility to advise and even "protect" the individual borrower, and will try to convince loan applicants of the desirability of making current expenditures (as on improved insulation) that will yield benefits over time. Others take a "lower profile" position, responding only to direct questions from loan applicants on the issue, or even refusing to express an opinion.

But whatever the individual attitude, there was a consensus that the overall impact of lender actions on this issue was small compared to the play of forces between home builders and home buyers. If a more "energy conscious" buying public is seeking fuel-saving features and willing to pay the higher first costs involved, builders will respond accordingly. And if builders find that energy conservation in design is in their own interest, lenders expect that "they will sell it to home buyers" (and to lenders, too).

DEVELOPERS AS A LENDER INFORMATIONAL SOURCE

On the balance, the lenders with whom we spoke seemed to feel that developers, whose success depends to a large degree on their constantly seeking a marketing edge over their competitors, had a stronger incentive than did financial institutions to keep abreast of new housing technologies. Several of those interviewed presumed that any experienced homebuilder would have thoroughly investigated solar systems from a technical viewpoint and convinced himself of their marketability, before ever having decided to build solar heated homes or approach a bank for financing. When commercial interest does materialize, the lender would expect the developer to make a complete presentation of his grounds for believing solar systems are feasible, and to supply much of the technical data needed to make a property appraisal and arrive at a final lending decision.

The builders and developers of single-family housing may thus be the wedge that opens the mortgage market for the wider development of solar homes. But solar manufacturers and designers will have to convince builders of the reliability and saleability of their systems, and show them how solar homes will be better for them—as housing entrepreneurs, not as public minded energy conservationists.

THE ADVENT OF ELECTRIC HEATING: A LESSON FROM THE PAST

In regard to this key issue, an important question is raised by lenders' perspective on the manner in which electric-heated homes first entered their areas. Some of the problems faced at the outset were analogous to those facing the solar alternative today: uncertainty as to how well a particular system would perform; concern that a "better" system would be rapidly developed and reduce the market value of earlier systems already installed; and the question of the marketability and value of the homes involved.

Some lenders recall considerable hesitance in financing all-electric homes for these reasons, and remember initial uncertainties as to which of various radiant heating designs—floor, ceiling, wall, baseboard—would prove to be most effective and best received. Once again, the typical strategy was to reflect the risk directly in the loan structure by offering an amount that was a lower than average proportion of costs.

But perhaps significantly, lenders generally believe that their reservations in regard to electric heated homes, and any reduced availability of "normal" financing that resulted, had little if any impact on the rate at which such homes were built. Aside from any competitive attractiveness that such housing offered to potential buyers, **lenders frequently attributed the rapid market penetration of electric heated and "all-electric" homes primarily to the financial incentives provided to home builders by electric utilities with an interest in increasing their own markets. In this, as in other housing innovations, they identified the builder as the key figure in determining the rate of market acceptance.** As one lender observed, electric utility companies had made it "in the builders interest" to build electric-heated homes, and builders had constructed such homes and "sold" lenders and buyers on them. Similarly, natural gas suppliers in his area had made it "in the builder's interest" to build gas-heated homes, and builders constructed such homes and "sold" lenders and buyers on them. He was now waiting to see who—if anyone—would make it "in the builder's interest" to build solar heated homes, and expected a convincing presentation in loan requests from local builders when and if this occurred.

IV. Open Doors, Cautious Lenders: The Availability of Mortgage Credit

SOLAR SYSTEM, HOUSING TYPE, AND EASE OF FINANCING

Lenders appear generally receptive to mortgage requests on solar homes. Few will reject such a request outright without at least having first considered the specifics of the proposal. But the terms on which financing will be offered will vary considerably, depending on the type of project, the specifics of the proposal, and the attitudes and experiences of the particular lending institution involved.

Solar hot water systems, given their lower first cost, are likely to be easier to finance in full in the private market today than space heating systems. In respect to solar heated residences, most bankers prefer and expect that mortgages will initially be written on custom-built, single family homes for relatively affluent borrowers. While some lenders would rather deal at first with an experienced developer, most doubted that solar use would prove appropriate at the present time in either rental projects or non-luxury homes built for sale. As one lender put it: "There should be an economic and reliable product before the average person gets involved."

SOLAR HOT WATER: A MORE MANAGEABLE FIRST COST

Solar domestic hot water systems have a number of well-established advantages over solar heating. They operate year round; they require far less collector area, and are therefore easier to integrate into house design in many cases; and their total costs are a much smaller proportion of total housing costs. Although the present study focused on issues related to solar space heating, lenders were also questioned about hot water systems. Not surprisingly, they viewed this as a far easier housing feature to finance for the reasons just noted. As with space heating, the same unanswered questions remain as to the relationship between actual costs and market value and the recognition of energy cost savings.

HIGH PRICED, SINGLE FAMILY HOMES: THE LEADING EDGE

For many reasons, custom-built family homes will be the easiest type of solar-heated property to finance privately. The upper-income borrower is often seeking (or at least is able to accept) a mortgage with a low enough loan-to-value ratio to provide a comfortable margin of safety for the lender. And banks would rather loan at first to those who are financially able to absorb any unexpected costs that might be occasioned by system failure and who are more likely to repay the mortgage irrespective of problems with the system or loss in the property's value. As one lender described it, he hoped his first applicant would be "an affluent engineer, sophisticated about the technology, looking for 40 percent financing on an $80,000 home that he plans to live in for a long time."

Many lenders surveyed believe that this preference for upper income borrowers in an "experimental" situation is not only sound business practice but socially desirable as well, placing the financial risks associated with solar systems on "those who can best afford them." Conversely, in the lender's view, an "unproven innovation" is not suitable for the average "entry level" buyer "who is already putting his last dollar together to buy the house," and lacks a "financial cushion." And finally a small but viable market clearly exists for solar systems, regardless of their current economics, among upper income buyers motivated by factors other than cost savings: energy conservation, environmental consciousness, a "pioneering spirit," and even a special type of status seeking.

THE TYPICAL SUBDIVISION: ONE HOME AT A TIME

Where a permanent mortgage has been requested, the loan officer has an absolute assurance that the cost of a solar system is worth the going price to at least one consumer—namely, the purchaser himself. Speculative sales housing raises different issues, with some lenders feeling that the absence of "an actual buyer in hand" makes the situation too risky. The construction lender may question the ability of the developer to successfully market solar-heated homes on a speculative basis in other than luxury markets—regardless of how attractive solar heat may or may not be from an investment point of view (payback periods, etc.).

Some loan officers indicated, however, that at first they will be even more likely to finance a developer than a home buyer. In their view, the developer will have already applied his considerable professional expertise to evaluating both the technical performance of the system he has selected and the marketability of the resulting product. One lender said that the "question is an academic one," since "a credible developer won't come until the thing makes market sense". When that "credible developer" arrives, banks surveyed will have no trouble lending to him—but they don't generally expect him to appear tomorrow.

Lenders will be even more inclined than usual to make financing available only to those developers with whom they already have a working relationship, or who have a sound and established reputation, and to those who have financial resources of their own sufficient to handle any serious difficulties that might arise in the installation or operation of the solar energy system. **And in those few cases where lenders do decide to finance speculative homes with solar heat, they will most likely restrict the builder to only one or two units at a time.** (In New England, most lenders do not finance very far ahead of sales in any case.) As one lender put it, "we would probably swallow hard on one or two houses," and then see "how those units sold before financing any more." One or two houses "would probably be no problem" particularly with "a developer who always sold what he built."

SOLAR APARTMENTS: HARDER TO QUALIFY

From the lender's perspective, the larger scale of multi-family development makes them a more risky setting to try out solar energy technologies for the first time. Nevertheless, more than two-thirds of those interviewed indicated that if a mortgage application for a solar heated multi-family development met their lending criteria in other respects (e.g., rent levels, location, net operating income), they would be receptive to making the loan. A big "if," for here, too, there was a strong presumption that credible proposals will not be forthcoming until such time as the economics of solar heat are fully competitive with conventional alternatives. (This skepticism, it should be noted, partly reflects the fact that few of the New England loan officers surveyed had seen workable figures for new rental housing of any description over the past two years.)

In addition to the considerations noted above in regard to financing developers of speculative sale housing, lenders will also be looking for developers who believe sufficiently in the concept and system being used to commit themselves to stay with the property and handle any unforseen problems. A few lenders indicated that they might impose limitations on the resale of multi-family projects to assure such a commitment.

However, as the economics of solar use become more favorable, system adoptions may spread even faster in the multi-family than in the single family sector. The developers of multi-family housing and the lenders who finance them are highly sensitive to energy costs and eager to adopt any innovation that will convert their costs to fixed rather than variable expenses. Thus, whenever the economics of solar installation begin to become truly competitive with conventional heating, one can anticipate a relatively rapid rate of acceptance of solar heat on the part of those who underwrite income properties.

HEDGING AGAINST UNCERTAINTY

Until more market experience accumulates on solar homes, most first mortgage loans will be made in amounts that leave out part of the additional costs attributable to the solar system.

Financial institutions, as we have seen, will in many situations be prepared to lend on solar heated homes. However, for as long as the data remains shallow on system performance and market value, lenders proceeding with such loans will find some way to hedge their risks in the specific terms and conditions on which financing is extended. Loan officers emphasize that the mortgage "is a very flexible instrument." Above all, this flexibility resides in the ability of the lender to limit his exposure by reducing the loan amount as a proportion of actual costs. This can be accomplished in several ways: (1) by appraising the property at a value lower than its cost or selling price; (2) by offering the borrower a lower than normal loan-to-value ratio, or (3) by both methods combined. **The net effect of these methods of risk reduction when applied to financing requests for solar homes will be to impose higher down payment requirements on prospective homeowners and necessitate larger contributions of equity from developers and housing investors.**

In respect to the appraisal of single family homes, it seems clear that many lenders will treat solar systems as analogous to "overimprovements". In other words, their appraisal of value will exclude whatever portion of solar first cost they feel to be in excess of the system's contribution to market value. In the case of multi-family income properties, a comparable reduction in appraised value will be achieved in large part by insisting on higher allowances for expense items such as maintenance and repair and utility costs for use in the auxiliary or "back-up" heating system, compared to the figures shown by the developer in his loan application.

OTHER TERMS AND CONDITIONS

Loans on solar homes are unlikely to differ in interest rates or loan duration from loans on conventional homes. Unlike some loan transactions, where interest rates are negotiated and adjusted to reflect risk, standard single family mortgage loans are simply "made or not made". When made, they reflect the current interest rate and loan term for the class of property (new or used), and a small spread for loan-to-value ratios. "Banks don't horsetrade on interest rates," as one lender put it. In fact, any other practice would be illogical: higher interest rates or a shorter loan term, by increasing the monthly debt service, would not only fail to compensate for a higher risk, but make a poor risk into a worse one. "If we don't like the property, we don't make the loan; 12 percent of nothing is nothing."

Other aspects of the loan may leave room for negotiation. The borrower might agree to personal recourse on the note where this was not customary; the loan might be strengthened by adding a cosigner or by making an offsetting deposit of money in the bank. Second mortgage financing might be available, though at a higher interest rate. But these are not conditions that will be initiated by lenders in any substantial proportion of cases, nor will they fit the needs and capabilities of most prospective borrowers.

In a very few instances, loan officers described additional measures that might be taken to further reduce the lender's risk exposure on multi-family properties using solar systems. These included withholding some portion of the loan until the performance of the installed system had been demonstrated; requiring a bonded warranty of performance; and actively enforcing requirements for the funding of contingency reserves. The flexibility suggested by these approaches to hedging risks should not obscure the more fundamental conclusion: namely, that financing institutions will be reluctant to underwrite solar apartments until such time as they can feel comfortable financing them on essentially the same terms as any conventionally heated property.

SOME RECENT EXPERIENCE

In light of the relatively minute amount of development underway nationwide, the high proportion of lenders (nearly one-fourth of fifty-five surveyed in New England) that had been approached with at least initial requests to consider lending on solar-heated home development was unexpected. Full comparisons are not possible since in some cases the lender preferred not to discuss all the details of the loan. It should also be kept in mind that the number of cases involved is small and the circumstances of each loan tended to be idiosyncratic. Nonetheless, it is clear that—consistent with the findings presented above—**the loans tended to represent a lower than average proportion of the total house cost; the homes tended to be considerably more expensive than average new homes; and either the home builder or home purchaser often had an established relationship with the lender involved.**

LEAD BANKS AND INITIAL LENDING REQUESTS

Lenders often differed in respect to their general willingness to lend on solar homes, the type of requests they felt most comfortable in handling at first, and the specific terms and conditions they would impose. However, the reader should bear in mind that **it takes only one institution to finance a solar home. If ten percent of the nation's mortgage lenders were prepared to do so on reasonable terms, they could easily accommodate the probable volume of solar home development within the next few years.**

In this connection, it should also be emphasized that there is a general recognition within the lending community of the variety of responses likely to any new technology such as solar and a belief that there are, in fact, "lead" banks that are more likely to provide financing and set an example which others will follow later on. While it is often the largest institutions that take this lead role, size itself is not the only determinant. A borrower seeking financing to build or buy a solar home is well advised to seek out the bankers within his own area who have a reputation for innovative lending policies.

Differences among lender types are almost as important as these distinctions within lender types. The clearest example is that of mortgage companies which are dependent on the saleability of their loans. They appear far less likely to meet solar financing needs than do thrift institutions, which are lending for their own account in whole or in part. The relative scarcity of thrift institutions in some areas may make financing more difficult to obtain. **But the fundamental finding is still that a variety of attitudes prevail—and a persistent effort to find a lender who will make a loan on acceptable terms will prove worthwhile.**

This material has not been excerpted in its entirety.

Prepared for the Division of Energy, Building Technology and Standards, Office of Policy Development and Research, U.S. Dept. of HUD in cooperation with the U.S. Energy Research and Development Administration. (1977)

Construction Materials—Indexes of Wholesale Prices: 1970 to 1976

[**1967=100.** For discussion of wholesale price index, see text, p. 469. See also *Historical Statistics, Colonial Times to 1970*, series N 140–155]

COMMODITY	1970	1973	1974	1975	1976
All materials [1]	**112.5**	**138.5**	**160.9**	**174.0**	**187.7**
Softwood lumber:					
Douglas fir	108.7	209.6	213.7	212.0	250.8
Southern pine	114.7	187.9	184.5	175.3	217.3
Other	115.0	226.6	220.8	205.3	257.8
Hardwood lumber	114.6	169.0	189.5	160.3	176.0
Millwork	116.0	144.2	157.1	160.4	176.8
Plywood	108.4	155.2	161.1	161.2	186.9
Softwood	113.6	194.0	186.8	200.6	247.4
Hardwood	102.5	112.7	130.2	119.5	122.5
Building paper and board	101.0	112.8	123.5	127.1	138.7
Prepared paint	112.4	122.2	145.7	166.9	174.2
Finished steel prod.:					
Structural shapes	115.3	140.7	179.0	216.3	227.1
Reinforcing bars	110.3	124.1	201.5	199.2	182.4
Black pipe, carbon	113.3	137.8	178.7	204.6	219.1
Wire nails [2]	114.8	140.4	207.1	241.4	243.6
Nonferrous metal products	124.7	135.0	187.1	171.6	181.5
Copper water tubing	122.9	133.3	174.7	134.2	147.7
Building wire	123.2	108.2	169.7	125.8	118.4

COMMODITY	1970	1973	1974	1975	1976
Plumbing fixtures [3]	111.2	125.8	149.1	162.3	174.1
Enameled iron	107.2	129.6	158.1	188.4	201.2
Vitreous china	106.3	120.8	134.2	146.6	159.0
Brass fittings	115.7	128.8	155.7	162.2	174.1
Heating equipment	110.6	120.4	135.0	150.7	158.1
Steam and hot water	110.8	122.7	139.0	153.9	162.4
Metal doors, sash, trim	113.0	124.5	147.3	162.5	171.5
Plate glass	(NA)	115.0	115.0	120.4	126.4
Concrete ingredients	112.6	131.2	148.7	172.3	186.2
Concrete products	112.2	131.7	151.7	170.5	179.6
Pipe	103.8	118.6	143.6	169.4	169.1
Structural clay products [4]	109.9	123.3	135.2	151.2	163.4
Gypsum products	99.7	120.9	137.6	144.0	154.2
Asphalt roofing	102.7	135.5	196.0	225.9	238.1
Insulation materials	123.2	137.4	156.5	196.2	212.3
Vinyl covering	96.3	103.2	117.9	135.4	144.5

NA Not available. [1] See footnote 2, table 1324. [2] 8d common.
[3] Includes brass fittings. [4] Excludes refractories.

Source: U.S. Bureau of Labor Statistics, *Wholesale Prices and Price Indexes*, monthly and annual.

Percent of New Privately-Owned One-Family Houses with Various Characteristics: 1970 to 1976

[**Percent distribution, except total houses.** Data beginning 1973 show percent distribution of characteristics for all houses completed (includes new houses completed, houses built for sale completed, contractor-built and owner-built houses completed, and houses completed for rent). Data for 1970 cover contractor-built, owner-built, and houses for rent for year construction started and houses sold for year of sale. Percents exclude houses for which characteristics specified were not reported. See also headnote, table 1352]

CHARACTERISTIC	1970	1973	1974	1975	1976
Total houses......1,000	793	1,174	932	866	1,026
Financing	**100**	**100**	**100**	**100**	**100**
Mortgage	84	85	83	82	85
FHA-insured	30	8	7	9	6
VA-guaranteed	7	8	8	8	8
Conventional	47	69	69	58	67
Farmers Home Admin				7	5
Cash or equivalent	16	15	17	18	15
Floor area (sq. feet)	**100**	**100**	**100**	**100**	**100**
Under 1,200	36	25	24	25	22
1,200–1,599	28	31	29	30	29
1,600–1,999	16	33	34	34	37
2,000–2,399	21				
2,400 and over		12	13	11	12
Number of stories	**100**	**100**	**100**	**100**	**100**
1	74	67	65	65	63
2 or more	17	23	25	23	25
Split level	10	10	10	12	12
Number of bedrooms	**100**	**100**	**100**	**100**	**100**
2 or less	13	12	13	14	12
3	63	64	64	65	65
4 or more	24	23	23	21	23

CHARACTERISTIC	1970	1973	1974	1975	1976
Number of bathrooms	**100**	**100**	**100**	**100**	**100**
1 or less	32	21	22	24	20
1½	20	19	18	17	13
2	32	41	40	40	45
2½ or more	16	19	21	20	22
Foundation	**100**	**100**	**100**	**100**	**100**
Full or partial basement	37	41	45	45	45
Slab	36	38	36	35	36
Crawl space	27	21	19	20	19
Heating fuel	**100**	**100**	**100**	**100**	**100**
Electricity	28	42	49	49	48
Gas	62	47	41	40	39
Oil	8	10	9	9	11
Other	1	1	1	2	2
Central air conditioning	**100**	**100**	**100**	**100**	**100**
With	34	49	48	46	49
Without	66	51	52	54	51
Parking facilities	**100**	**100**	**100**	**100**	**100**
Garage	58	65	68	67	72
Carport	17	13	10	9	8
No garage or carport	25	22	22	24	20

Source: U.S. Bureau of the Census and U.S. Dept. of Housing and Urban Development, *Construction Reports*, series C25, *Characteristics of New One Family Homes* (a joint publication).

U.S. Bureau of the Census, Statistical Abstract of the United States: 1977 (98th edition) Washington, D.C., 1977.

General Housing Characteristics

GENERAL

This report presents statistics on general housing characteristics from the 1975 Annual Housing Survey for the United States by inside and outside standard metropolitan statistical areas (SMSA's) and each of the four geographic regions. The Annual Housing Survey was designed to provide a current series of information on the size and composition of the housing inventory, the characteristics of its occupants, the changes in the inventory resulting from new construction and from losses, the indicators of housing and neighborhood quality, the characteristics of recent movers, and the characteristics of urban and rural housing units. The survey, performed for the Department of Housing and Urban Development, is authorized under sections 501 and 502(d), 502(e), and 502(f) of the Housing and Urban Development Act of 1970, Title 12, United States Code 1701z-1 and 1701z-2. The Bureau of the Census is authorized under Title 31, United States Code 686, to perform special work or services for Federal agencies.

The statistics presented in this report are based on information from a sample of housing units. The information for the survey was collected by personal interview from October to December 1975.

Sample size.—The statistics presented in this report are based on a sample of housing units and are, therefore, subject to sampling variability. The designated sample consisted of approximately 79,900 housing units located throughout the United States. The sample was selected from units enumerated in the 1970 census and updated to include units constructed since 1970. Detailed information on the sample design, size of sample, estimation procedure, and sampling variability associated with these data is given in appendix B.

Derived figures (medians, etc.)—Shown in this report are medians and percents. The median, which is a type of average, is the middle value in a distribution; i.e., the median divides the distribution into two equal parts—one-half the cases fall below the median and one-half the cases exceed the median. Derived figures are not presented (but indicated by three dots "...") if there are less than 25 sample cases in the distribution or the base.

Medians for rooms, persons, and years of school completed by head are rounded to the nearest tenth; selected monthly housing costs as percentage of income to the nearest percent. Travel time is rounded to the nearest minute and distance from home to work is rounded to the nearest mile. Medians for value, income, and purchase price of mobile homes and trailers are rounded to the nearest hundred dollars; rent, real estate taxes last year, and selected monthly housing costs are rounded to the nearest dollar.

In computing medians for rooms and persons per housing unit, the whole number is used as the midpoint of the interval so that, for example, the category "4 rooms" is treated as an interval ranging from 3.5 up to 4.5 rooms. When computing medians for distance and travel time to work, household heads reporting "no fixed place of work" are excluded; for median purchase price of mobile homes and trailers, the category "not purchased" is excluded. Units reporting "no cash rent" are excluded from the computation of median rent; for selected monthly housing costs as percentage of income, units in the category "not computed" are excluded. "Not reported" categories are excluded from the computation of medians.

The median number of school years completed by the head of the household was computed after the statistics on years of school completed had been converted to a continuous series of numbers (e.g., completion of the first year of high school was treated as completion of the 9th year and completion of the first year of college as completion of the 13th year). Heads completing a given school year were assumed to be distributed evenly within the interval from 0.0 to 0.9 of the year. Because of the inexact assumption as to the distribution within an interval, the median school years completed is more appropriately used for comparing different groups and the same group at different dates than as an absolute measure of educational attainment.

The medians presented for 1975 are generally computed on the basis of the distributions as shown in this report. The medians presented for 1970 are computed on the basis of the distributions as tabulated in 1970, which are sometimes more detailed than the distributions shown in this report.

When the median falls in the lower terminal category of an open-ended distribution, the method of presentation is to show the initial value of the next category followed by a minus sign; thus, for example, if the median falls in the category "Less than $5,000," it is shown as "$5,000–." When the median falls in the upper terminal category of an open-ended distribution, the method of presentation is to show the initial value of the terminal category followed by a plus sign; thus, for example, if the median falls in the category "$60,000 or more," it is shown as "$60,000+."

Standard Metropolitan Statistical Areas: 1970

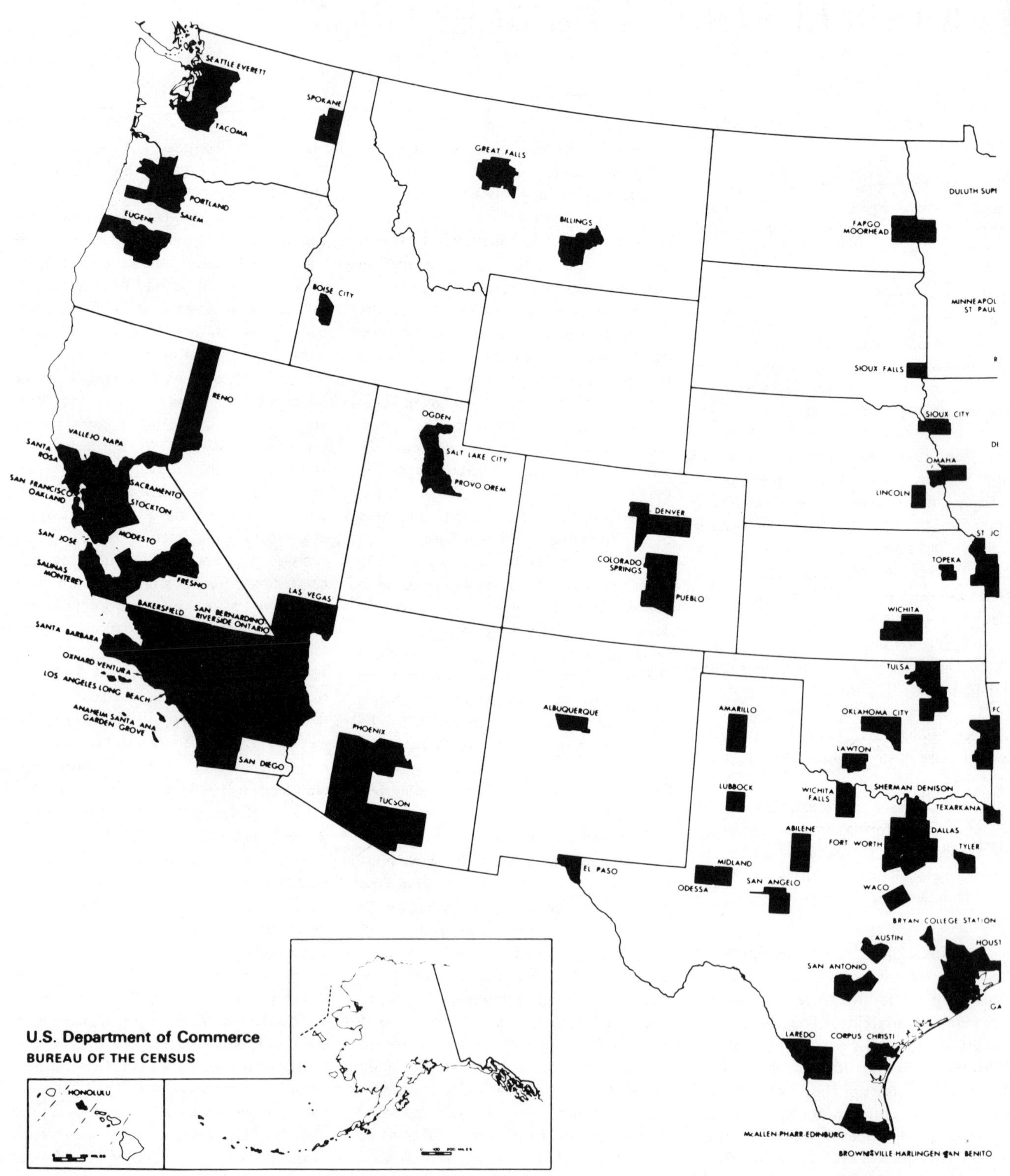

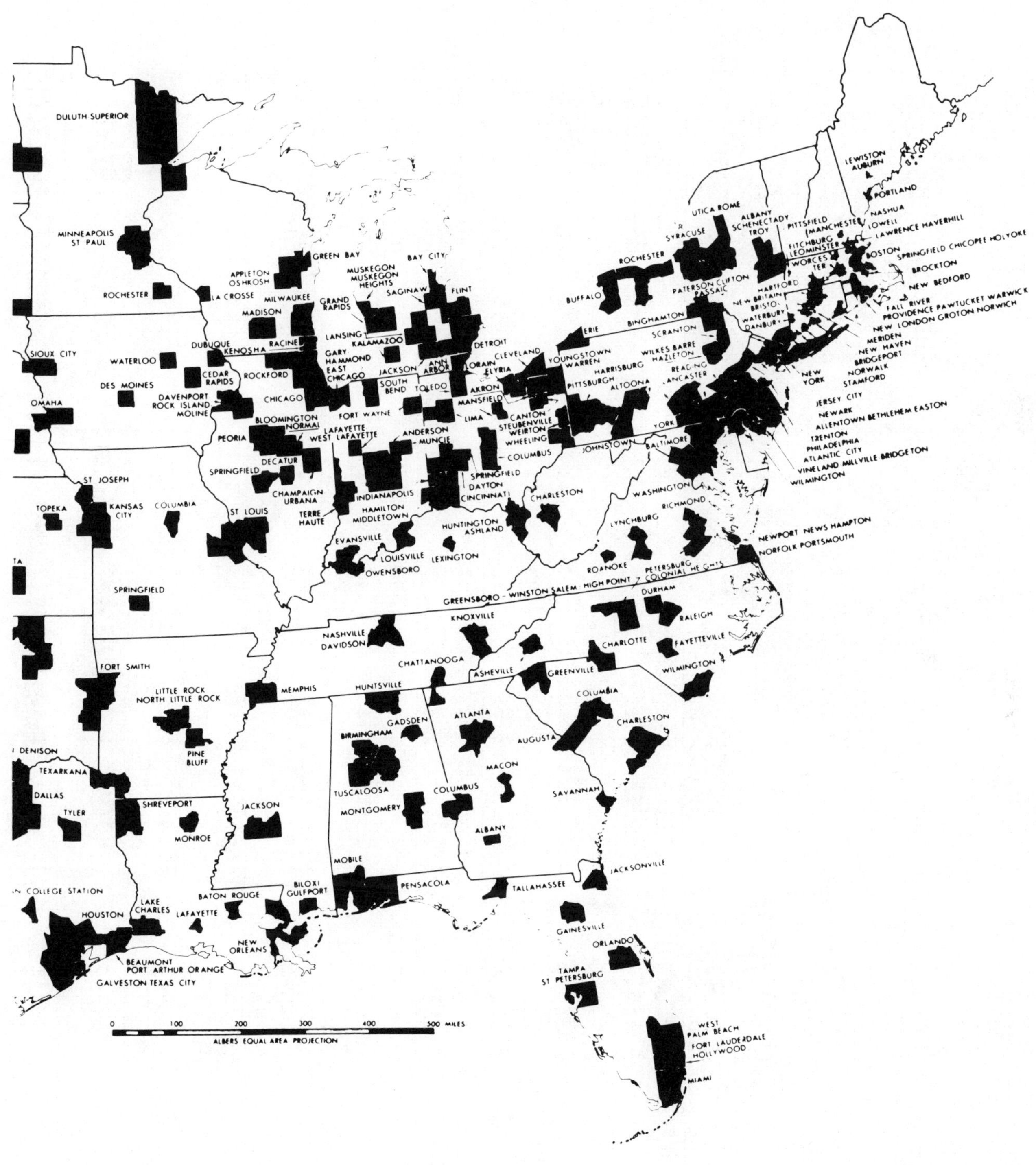
DULUTH SUPERIOR
MINNEAPOLIS ST PAUL
ROCHESTER
LA CROSSE
APPLETON OSHKOSH
GREEN BAY
MILWAUKEE
MADISON
RACINE
KENOSHA
DUBUQUE
SIOUX CITY
WATERLOO
CEDAR RAPIDS
DES MOINES
ROCKFORD
DAVENPORT ROCK ISLAND MOLINE
OMAHA
CHICAGO
GARY HAMMOND EAST CHICAGO
BLOOMINGTON NORMAL
PEORIA
LAFAYETTE WEST LAFAYETTE
DECATUR
SPRINGFIELD
CHAMPAIGN URBANA
ST JOSEPH
TOPEKA
KANSAS CITY
COLUMBIA
ST LOUIS
TERRE HAUTE
SPRINGFIELD
MUSKEGON MUSKEGON HEIGHTS
BAY CITY
SAGINAW
FLINT
GRAND RAPIDS
LANSING
KALAMAZOO
JACKSON
ANN ARBOR
DETROIT
SOUTH BEND
TOLEDO
FORT WAYNE
ANDERSON
MUNCIE
INDIANAPOLIS
LIMA
HAMILTON MIDDLETOWN
EVANSVILLE
OWENSBORO
LOUISVILLE
LEXINGTON
HUNTINGTON ASHLAND
SPRINGFIELD
DAYTON
CINCINNATI
COLUMBUS
LORAIN ELYRIA
CLEVELAND
AKRON
MANSFIELD
CANTON
STEUBENVILLE WEIRTON
WHEELING
YOUNGSTOWN WARREN
ERIE
PITTSBURGH
JOHNSTOWN
ALTOONA
CHARLESTON
BUFFALO
ROCHESTER
SYRACUSE
UTICA ROME
ALBANY SCHENECTADY TROY
BINGHAMTON
SCRANTON
WILKES BARRE HAZLETON
HARRISBURG
READING
LANCASTER
YORK
BALTIMORE
WASHINGTON
PITTSFIELD
MANCHESTER
FITCHBURG LEOMINSTER
WORCESTER
LEWISTON AUBURN
PORTLAND
NASHUA
LOWELL
LAWRENCE HAVERHILL
BOSTON
SPRINGFIELD CHICOPEE HOLYOKE
BROCKTON
NEW BEDFORD
FALL RIVER
PROVIDENCE PAWTUCKET WARWICK
NEW LONDON GROTON NORWICH
PATERSON CLIFTON PASSAIC
NEW HARTFORD
NEW BRITAIN
BRISTOL
WATERBURY
DANBURY
MERIDEN
NEW HAVEN
BRIDGEPORT
NORWALK
STAMFORD
NEW YORK
JERSEY CITY
NEWARK
ALLENTOWN BETHLEHEM EASTON
TRENTON
PHILADELPHIA
ATLANTIC CITY
VINELAND MILLVILLE BRIDGETON
WILMINGTON
RICHMOND
LYNCHBURG
ROANOKE
PETERSBURG COLONIAL HEIGHTS
NEWPORT NEWS HAMPTON
NORFOLK PORTSMOUTH
GREENSBORO – WINSTON SALEM HIGH POINT
DURHAM
RALEIGH
FAYETTEVILLE
CHARLOTTE
WILMINGTON
GREENVILLE
ASHEVILLE
KNOXVILLE
NASHVILLE DAVIDSON
CHATTANOOGA
FORT SMITH
LITTLE ROCK NORTH LITTLE ROCK
PINE BLUFF
MEMPHIS
HUNTSVILLE
GADSDEN
BIRMINGHAM
ATLANTA
AUGUSTA
COLUMBIA
CHARLESTON
MACON
TUSCALOOSA
COLUMBUS
MONTGOMERY
SAVANNAH
ALBANY
DENISON
TEXARKANA
DALLAS
TYLER
SHREVEPORT
MONROE
JACKSON
MOBILE
PENSACOLA
TALLAHASSEE
JACKSONVILLE
COLLEGE STATION
HOUSTON
LAKE CHARLES
LAFAYETTE
BATON ROUGE
BILOXI GULFPORT
NEW ORLEANS
BEAUMONT PORT ARTHUR ORANGE
GALVESTON TEXAS CITY
GAINESVILLE
ORLANDO
TAMPA ST PETERSBURG
WEST PALM BEACH
FORT LAUDERDALE HOLLYWOOD
MIAMI
0 100 200 300 400 500 MILES
ALBERS EQUAL AREA PROJECTION

CHARACTERISTICS OF THE HOUSING INVENTORY: 1975 AND 1970

(NUMBERS IN THOUSANDS. DATA BASED ON SAMPLE, SEE TEXT. FOR MINIMUM BASE FOR DERIVED FIGURES (PERCENT, MEDIAN, ETC.) AND MEANING OF SYMBOLS, SEE TEXT)

UNITED STATES	TOTAL		INSIDE SMSA'S						OUTSIDE SMSA'S	
			TOTAL		IN CENTRAL CITIES		NOT IN CENTRAL CITIES			
	1975	1970	1975	1970	1975	1970	1975	1970	1975	1970
ALL HOUSING UNITS	79 087	68 672	53 031	46 289	24 245	22 608	28 785	23 681	26 057	22 383
VACANT--SEASONAL AND MIGRATORY	1 534	973	341	206	41	24	300	183	1 193	766
TENURE, RACE, AND VACANCY STATUS										
ALL YEAR-ROUND HOUSING UNITS	77 553	67 699	52 690	46 083	24 205	22 584	28 485	23 498	24 864	21 616
OCCUPIED UNITS	72 523	63 445	49 666	43 859	22 749	21 395	26 918	22 464	22 857	19 586
OWNER OCCUPIED	46 867	39 886	30 383	26 090	11 280	10 300	19 104	15 790	16 484	13 796
PERCENT OF ALL OCCUPIED	64.6	62.9	61.2	59.5	49.6	48.1	71.0	70.3	72.1	70.4
WHITE	43 072	37 005	27 613	24 041	9 369	8 850	18 244	15 191	15 459	12 964
BLACK	3 309	2 568	2 382	1 825	1 714	1 335	668	490	927	742
RENTER OCCUPIED	25 656	23 560	19 283	17 769	11 469	11 095	7 814	6 674	6 373	5 790
WHITE	20 788	19 601	15 251	14 574	8 177	8 392	7 074	6 182	5 537	5 027
BLACK	4 252	3 607	3 490	2 913	2 893	2 498	597	416	762	693
VACANT YEAR-ROUND UNITS	5 030	4 254	3 023	2 224	1 456	1 189	1 567	1 035	2 007	2 030
FOR SALE ONLY	577	501	373	298	155	130	218	168	204	203
HOMEOWNER VACANCY RATE	1.2	1.2	1.2	1.1	1.3	1.2	1.1	1.1	1.2	1.5
FOR RENT	1 489	1 666	1 168	1 142	717	745	451	397	321	524
RENTAL VACANCY RATE	5.4	6.6	5.7	6.0	5.8	6.3	5.4	5.6	4.7	8.3
RENTED OR SOLD, NOT OCCUPIED	667	345	443	190	166	86	277	104	225	155
HELD FOR OCCASIONAL USE	1 050	998	395	281	122	65	274	216	655	717
OTHER VACANT	1 246	744	645	313	297	163	348	150	602	431
COOPERATIVES AND CONDOMINIUMS										
OWNER OCCUPIED	869	NA	815	NA	332	NA	482	NA	54	NA
COOPERATIVE OWNERSHIP	361	NA	338	NA	203	NA	135	NA	24	NA
CONDOMINIUM OWNERSHIP	507	NA	477	NA	129	NA	348	NA	30	NA
VACANT FOR SALE ONLY	119	NA	103	NA	34	NA	69	NA	16	NA
COOPERATIVE OWNERSHIP	5	NA	4	NA	2	NA	2	NA	1	NA
CONDOMINIUM OWNERSHIP	114	NA	99	NA	32	NA	67	NA	15	NA
UNITS IN STRUCTURE										
ALL YEAR-ROUND HOUSING UNITS	77 553	67 699	52 690	46 083	24 205	22 584	28 485	23 498	24 864	21 616
1, DETACHED	49 489	44 801	30 161	27 219	10 707	11 430	19 454	17 603	19 328	17 582
1, ATTACHED	3 129	1 990	2 637	1 814	1 507		1 130		492	176
2 TO 4	9 802	9 007	7 928	7 184	5 086	4 753	2 842	2 430	1 874	1 823
5 OR MORE	11 792	9 829	10 651	8 934	6 730	6 225	3 921	2 709	1 141	895
MOBILE HOME OR TRAILER	3 342	2 073	1 313	933	174	176	1 138	757	2 029	1 140
OWNER OCCUPIED	46 867	39 886	30 383	26 090	11 280	10 300	19 104	15 790	16 484	13 796
1, DETACHED	39 787	34 397	25 451	22 088	8 782	7 978	16 668	14 110	14 337	12 309
1, ATTACHED	1 534	1 113	1 430	1 046	868	755	562	291	104	67
2 TO 4	2 138	2 161	1 812	1 750	1 169	1 147	643	603	326	411
5 OR MORE	585	464	553	412	307	277	246	135	32	52
MOBILE HOME OR TRAILER	2 822	1 752	1 137	794	154	144	984	650	1 685	958
RENTER OCCUPIED	25 656	23 560	19 283	17 769	11 469	11 095	7 814	6 674	6 373	5 790
1, DETACHED	7 082	7 736	3 656	4 163	1 585	1 851	2 071	2 312	3 426	3 573
1, ATTACHED	1 350	794	1 027	702	553	463	474	238	323	93
2 TO 4	6 772	6 218	5 426	4 988	3 494	3 294	1 932	1 694	1 346	1 229
5 TO 9	3 028	2 284	2 627	1 970	1 619	1 319	1 008	652	401	313
10 TO 19	2 514	2 219	2 252	2 003	1 293	1 272	959	731	262	216
20 TO 49	2 058	1 873	1 918	1 761	1 236	1 277	682	484	140	112
50 OR MORE	2 332	2 115	2 201	2 044	1 667	1 587	533	456	131	71
MOBILE HOME OR TRAILER	519	321	176	139	21	32	155	107	344	183
YEAR STRUCTURE BUILT										
ALL YEAR-ROUND HOUSING UNITS	77 553	67 699	52 690	46 083	24 205	22 584	28 485	23 498	24 864	21 616
APRIL 1970 OR LATER	11 212	NA	7 450	NA	2 404	NA	5 046	NA	3 762	NA
1965 TO MARCH 1970	9 831	8 874	6 619	6 043	2 270	4 172	4 349	7 677	3 212	2 831
1960 TO 1964	8 060	8 082	5 892	5 806	2 274		3 618		2 168	2 275
1950 TO 1959	13 600	14 499	9 892	10 708	3 894	4 304	5 998	6 404	3 708	3 791
1940 TO 1949	7 974	8 786	5 461	6 147	2 659	14 108	2 801	9 417	2 514	2 639
1939 OR EARLIER	26 877	27 458	17 377	17 378	10 704		6 673		9 500	10 080

CHARACTERISTICS OF THE HOUSING INVENTORY: 1975 AND 1970--CONTINUED

(NUMBERS IN THOUSANDS. DATA BASED ON SAMPLE, SEE TEXT. FOR MINIMUM BASE FOR DERIVED FIGURES (PERCENT, MEDIAN, ETC.) AND MEANING OF SYMBOLS, SEE TEXT)

UNITED STATES	TOTAL		INSIDE SMSA'S						OUTSIDE SMSA'S	
			TOTAL		IN CENTRAL CITIES		NOT IN CENTRAL CITIES			
	1975	1970	1975	1970	1975	1970	1975	1970	1975	1970
YEAR STRUCTURE BUILT--CONTINUED										
OWNER OCCUPIED	46 867	39 886	30 383	26 090	11 280	10 300	19 104	15 790	16 484	13 796
APRIL 1970 OR LATER	6 527	NA	3 671	NA	812	NA	2 859	NA	2 856	NA
1965 TO MARCH 1970	6 205	5 264	3 920	3 284	981	773	2 938	2 511	2 285	1 980
1960 TO 1964	5 462	5 213	3 830	3 571	1 226	1 051	2 604	2 520	1 632	1 642
1950 TO 1959	9 958	10 220	7 274	7 545	2 502	2 616	4 772	4 929	2 684	2 675
1940 TO 1949	4 984	4 953	3 438	3 370	1 456	1 505	1 981	1 865	1 546	1 582
1939 OR EARLIER	13 731	14 235	8 251	8 319	4 302	4 354	3 949	3 965	5 480	5 916
RENTER OCCUPIED	25 656	23 560	19 283	17 769	11 469	11 095	7 814	6 674	6 373	5 790
APRIL 1970 OR LATER	3 653	NA	2 993	NA	1 341	NA	1 652	NA	660	NA
1965 TO MARCH 1970	3 091	2 813	2 387	2 268	1 185	1 065	1 201	1 203	704	545
1960 TO 1964	2 247	2 476	1 841	2 026	958	1 019	883	1 007	406	450
1950 TO 1959	3 091	3 647	2 298	2 829	1 249	1 539	1 049	1 290	793	818
1940 TO 1949	2 551	3 264	1 795	2 484	1 085	1 574	710	910	756	780
1939 OR EARLIER	11 023	11 361	7 970	8 163	5 651	5 899	2 319	2 264	3 053	3 198
PLUMBING FACILITIES										
ALL YEAR-ROUND HOUSING UNITS	77 553	67 699	52 690	46 083	24 205	22 584	28 485	23 498	24 864	21 616
WITH ALL PLUMBING FACILITIES	74 847	63 301	51 740	44 589	23 711	21 869	28 029	22 721	23 107	18 712
LACKING SOME OR ALL PLUMBING FACILITIES	2 706	4 398	950	1 494	493	716	456	778	1 756	2 904
OWNER OCCUPIED	46 867	39 886	30 383	26 090	11 280	10 300	19 104	15 790	16 484	13 796
WITH ALL PLUMBING FACILITIES	46 025	38 224	30 158	25 622	11 221	10 177	18 937	15 445	15 867	12 602
LACKING SOME OR ALL PLUMBING FACILITIES	842	1 662	225	468	59	123	166	345	617	1 194
RENTER OCCUPIED	25 656	23 560	19 283	17 769	11 469	11 095	7 814	6 674	6 373	5 790
WITH ALL PLUMBING FACILITIES	24 422	21 711	18 762	16 968	11 137	10 601	7 625	6 367	5 659	4 743
LACKING SOME OR ALL PLUMBING FACILITIES	1 234	1 849	520	801	331	494	189	307	714	1 047
COMPLETE BATHROOMS										
ALL YEAR-ROUND HOUSING UNITS	77 553	67 699	52 690	46 083	24 205	22 584	28 485	23 498	24 864	21 616
1	48 459	51 885	32 471	35 850	16 986	18 502	15 485	17 348	15 988	16 035
1 AND ONE-HALF	10 383		7 400		2 613		4 788		2 983	
2 OR MORE	15 736	10 723	11 677	8 305	3 991	3 099	7 686	5 206	4 059	2 417
ALSO USED BY ANOTHER HOUSEHOLD	589	5 086	422	1 923	335	982	87	941	167	3 163
NONE	2 386		719		280		439		1 667	
OWNER OCCUPIED	46 867	39 886	30 383	26 090	11 280	10 300	19 104	15 790	16 484	13 796
1	24 184	28 923	14 422	18 508	6 047	7 656	8 376	10 852	9 762	10 415
1 AND ONE-HALF	8 490		5 963		1 993		3 970		2 527	
2 OR MORE	13 256	9 039	9 717	6 986	3 150	2 467	6 566	4 519	3 540	2 053
ALSO USED BY ANOTHER HOUSEHOLD	31	1 923	22	596	18	177	4	418	9	1 328
NONE	906		259		72		187		647	
RENTER OCCUPIED	25 656	23 560	19 283	17 769	11 469	11 095	7 814	6 674	6 373	5 790
1	20 957	20 072	16 001	15 650	9 829	9 877	6 173	5 772	4 956	4 422
1 AND ONE-HALF	1 526		1 193		529		665		333	
2 OR MORE	1 793	1 312	1 453	1 061	702	536	751	525	341	251
ALSO USED BY ANOTHER HOUSEHOLD	439	2 176	312	1 059	253	681	59	377	127	1 117
NONE	939		323		157		167		616	
COMPLETE KITCHEN FACILITIES										
ALL YEAR-ROUND HOUSING UNITS	77 553	67 699	52 690	46 083	24 205	22 584	28 485	23 498	24 864	21 616
FOR EXCLUSIVE USE OF HOUSEHOLD	75 309	64 727	51 764	45 069	23 677	22 040	28 087	23 029	23 546	19 658
ALSO USED BY ANOTHER HOUSEHOLD	160	2 972	112	1 013	85	544	27	469	47	1 959
NO COMPLETE KITCHEN FACILITIES	2 084		814		443		371		1 271	
OWNER OCCUPIED	46 867	39 886	30 383	26 090	11 280	10 300	19 104	15 790	16 484	13 796
FOR EXCLUSIVE USE OF HOUSEHOLD	46 435	39 094	30 290	25 914	11 272	10 261	19 019	15 653	16 144	13 180
ALSO USED BY ANOTHER HOUSEHOLD	4	791	3	176	3	39	-	136	1	616
NO COMPLETE KITCHEN FACILITIES	429		90		5		85		339	
RENTER OCCUPIED	25 656	23 560	19 283	17 769	11 469	11 095	7 814	6 674	6 373	5 790
FOR EXCLUSIVE USE OF HOUSEHOLD	24 661	22 327	18 776	17 207	11 118	10 728	7 658	6 480	5 885	5 120
ALSO USED BY ANOTHER HOUSEHOLD	117	1 232	76	562	59	367	17	195	41	671
NO COMPLETE KITCHEN FACILITIES	878		431		293		139		447	

CHARACTERISTICS OF THE HOUSING INVENTORY: 1975 AND 1970--CONTINUED

(NUMBERS IN THOUSANDS. DATA BASED ON SAMPLE, SEE TEXT. FOR MINIMUM BASE FOR DERIVED FIGURES (PERCENT, MEDIAN, ETC.) AND MEANING OF SYMBOLS, SEE TEXT)

UNITED STATES	TOTAL		INSIDE SMSA'S						OUTSIDE SMSA'S	
			TOTAL		IN CENTRAL CITIES		NOT IN CENTRAL CITIES			
	1975	1970	1975	1970	1975	1970	1975	1970	1975	1970
ROOMS										
ALL YEAR-ROUND HOUSING UNITS	77 553	67 699	52 690	46 083	24 205	22 584	28 485	23 498	24 864	21 616
1 ROOM	1 291	1 226	1 025	957	760	716	265	241	266	270
2 ROOMS	2 182	2 357	1 619	1 770	1 071	1 220	549	550	563	587
3 ROOMS	8 165	7 445	6 162	5 578	3 661	3 525	2 502	2 053	2 003	1 868
4 ROOMS	15 954	14 113	10 642	9 230	5 255	4 904	5 387	4 326	5 312	4 883
5 ROOMS	19 126	16 998	12 473	11 233	5 499	5 286	6 974	5 947	6 653	5 765
6 ROOMS	15 645	13 609	10 541	9 271	4 554	4 078	5 987	5 194	5 104	4 338
7 ROOMS OR MORE	15 190	11 950	10 227	8 044	3 405	2 856	6 822	5 187	4 963	3 906
MEDIAN	5.1	5.0	5.0	5.0	4.7	4.7	5.3	5.3	5.1	5.1
OWNER OCCUPIED	46 867	39 886	30 383	26 090	11 280	10 300	19 104	15 790	16 484	13 796
1 ROOM	33	90	19	44	5	18	14	25	14	46
2 ROOMS	192	279	101	151	31	63	70	88	91	127
3 ROOMS	1 154	1 275	651	728	264	326	387	402	503	548
4 ROOMS	6 300	5 876	3 527	3 296	1 363	1 382	2 164	1 914	2 773	2 581
5 ROOMS	13 115	11 394	8 257	7 376	3 190	3 062	5 067	4 315	4 858	4 018
6 ROOMS	12 666	10 720	8 596	7 405	3 463	3 034	5 132	4 371	4 070	3 315
7 ROOMS OR MORE	13 407	10 251	9 233	7 090	2 963	2 416	6 269	4 674	4 174	3 161
MEDIAN	5.7	5.6	5.8	5.7	5.7	5.6	5.9	5.8	5.5	5.4
RENTER OCCUPIED	25 656	23 560	19 283	17 769	11 469	11 095	7 814	6 674	6 373	5 790
1 ROOM	995	944	812	793	636	616	177	177	182	151
2 ROOMS	1 629	1 763	1 296	1 444	908	1 043	387	400	334	319
3 ROOMS	6 092	5 381	4 916	4 386	3 073	2 919	1 842	1 467	1 176	995
4 ROOMS	8 292	7 088	6 285	5 347	3 519	3 213	2 765	2 135	2 008	1 741
5 ROOMS	4 985	4 705	3 620	3 416	2 042	2 004	1 578	1 412	1 365	1 289
6 ROOMS	2 367	2 385	1 632	1 622	946	931	686	691	735	763
7 ROOMS OR MORE	1 295	1 294	722	762	345	369	378	393	572	532
MEDIAN	4.0	4.0	3.9	3.9	3.8	3.8	4.0	4.1	4.2	4.3
BEDROOMS										
ALL YEAR-ROUND HOUSING UNITS	77 553	67 699	52 690	46 083	24 205	22 584	28 485	23 498	24 864	21 616
NONE	1 671	1 630	1 357	1 312	990	984	367	328	314	319
1	11 273	10 681	8 720	8 163	5 237	5 214	3 483	2 949	2 553	2 517
2	26 259	22 929	17 276	15 008	8 425	7 822	8 852	7 186	8 983	7 921
3	28 551	23 945	18 792	16 058	7 364	6 591	11 429	9 467	9 758	7 888
4 OR MORE	9 799	8 526	6 544	5 557	2 190	1 986	4 354	3 570	3 255	2 970
OWNER OCCUPIED	46 867	39 886	30 383	26 090	11 280	10 300	19 104	15 790	16 484	13 796
NONE AND 1	1 807	2 059	1 148	1 274	485	605	663	669	659	784
2	13 657	11 973	8 275	7 299	3 518	3 298	4 757	4 002	5 382	4 674
3	23 001	18 810	15 237	12 795	5 475	4 822	9 762	7 973	7 764	6 015
4 OR MORE	8 403	7 040	5 724	4 723	1 801	1 581	3 923	3 142	2 680	2 317
RENTER OCCUPIED	25 656	23 560	19 283	17 769	11 469	11 095	7 814	6 674	6 373	5 790
NONE	1 278	1 280	1 067	1 101	819	855	248	246	211	179
1	8 249	7 599	6 773	6 257	4 291	4 205	2 482	2 052	1 476	1 342
2	10 651	9 300	7 852	6 900	4 387	4 107	3 464	2 793	2 799	2 399
3	4 440	4 269	2 971	2 858	1 655	1 591	1 316	1 267	1 470	1 411
4 OR MORE	1 037	1 117	620	658	316	341	304	317	417	459
ALL OCCUPIED HOUSING UNITS	72 523	63 445	49 666	43 859	22 749	21 395	26 918	22 464	22 857	19 586
PERSONS										
OWNER OCCUPIED	46 867	39 886	30 383	26 090	11 280	10 300	19 104	15 790	16 484	13 796
1 PERSON	6 101	4 762	3 696	2 813	1 729	1 372	1 968	1 441	2 404	1 949
2 PERSONS	14 767	12 010	9 188	7 455	3 582	3 152	5 605	4 302	5 579	4 555
3 PERSONS	8 396	6 985	5 534	4 660	2 044	1 832	3 490	2 828	2 862	2 325
4 PERSONS	8 542	6 925	5 806	4 813	1 834	1 699	3 972	3 114	2 736	2 112
5 PERSONS	4 914	4 554	3 380	3 181	1 096	1 085	2 284	2 096	1 533	1 373
6 PERSONS	2 370	2 468	1 606	1 709	562	594	1 045	1 115	764	759
7 PERSONS OR MORE	1 778	2 182	1 173	1 459	433	566	741	893	605	724
MEDIAN	2.8	3.0	2.9	3.1	2.7	2.8	3.1	3.3	2.6	2.7
RENTER OCCUPIED	25 656	23 560	19 283	17 769	11 469	11 095	7 814	6 674	6 373	5 790
1 PERSON	8 262	6 389	6 430	5 120	4 183	3 544	2 247	1 576	1 831	1 268
2 PERSONS	7 733	6 773	5 956	5 271	3 360	3 229	2 596	2 042	1 777	1 502
3 PERSONS	4 187	3 923	3 092	2 924	1 723	1 716	1 369	1 208	1 094	999
4 PERSONS	2 719	2 875	1 925	2 058	1 063	1 180	862	878	794	817
5 PERSONS	1 392	1 643	974	1 133	590	655	384	478	418	510
6 PERSONS	687	915	453	610	257	361	196	250	234	304
7 PERSONS OR MORE	677	1 043	453	653	293	411	160	242	224	390
MEDIAN	2.1	2.3	2.0	2.2	2.0	2.1	2.1	2.4	2.3	2.6

CHARACTERISTICS OF THE HOUSING INVENTORY: 1975 AND 1970--CONTINUED

(NUMBERS IN THOUSANDS. DATA BASED ON SAMPLE, SEE TEXT. FOR MINIMUM BASE FOR DERIVED FIGURES (PERCENT, MEDIAN, ETC.) AND MEANING OF SYMBOLS, SEE TEXT)

UNITED STATES	TOTAL		INSIDE SMSA'S						OUTSIDE SMSA'S	
			TOTAL		IN CENTRAL CITIES		NOT IN CENTRAL CITIES			
	1975	1970	1975	1970	1975	1970	1975	1970	1975	1970
ALL OCCUPIED HOUSING UNITS--CON.										
PERSONS PER ROOM										
OWNER OCCUPIED	46 867	39 886	30 383	26 090	11 280	10 300	19 104	15 790	16 484	13 796
0.50 OR LESS	26 827	21 130	17 187	13 480	6 764	5 650	10 423	7 829	9 640	7 651
0.51 TO 1.00	18 161	16 188	12 057	11 028	4 087	4 015	7 970	7 013	6 104	5 160
1.01 TO 1.50	1 585	2 068	995	1 313	373	518	622	794	590	756
1.51 OR MORE	294	499	144	270	56	117	88	153	149	229
RENTER OCCUPIED	25 656	23 560	19 283	17 769	11 469	11 095	7 814	6 674	6 373	5 790
0.50 OR LESS	13 450	10 599	10 158	8 109	6 007	5 119	4 151	2 990	3 292	2 490
0.51 TO 1.00	10 484	10 467	7 941	7 942	4 680	4 849	3 261	3 093	2 544	2 525
1.01 TO 1.50	1 305	1 714	916	1 213	594	785	322	428	389	501
1.51 OR MORE	416	780	268	505	188	342	80	163	148	275
WITH ALL PLUMBING FACILITIES	70 447	59 934	48 920	42 589	22 358	20 777	26 562	21 812	21 527	17 345
OWNER OCCUPIED	46 025	38 224	30 158	25 622	11 221	10 177	18 937	15 445	15 867	12 602
1.00 OR LESS	44 248	35 940	29 041	24 109	10 791	9 557	18 250	14 552	15 207	11 831
1.01 TO 1.50	1 521	1 910	979	1 274	373	511	606	763	542	636
1.51 OR MORE	256	374	138	239	56	109	82	129	118	135
RENTER OCCUPIED	24 422	21 711	18 762	16 968	11 137	10 601	7 625	6 367	5 659	4 743
1.00 OR LESS	22 918	19 634	17 642	15 373	10 388	9 530	7 254	5 843	5 275	4 261
1.01 TO 1.50	1 193	1 520	890	1 160	588	764	302	396	303	361
1.51 OR MORE	311	556	230	435	162	307	68	128	81	121
HOUSEHOLD COMPOSITION BY AGE OF HEAD										
OWNER OCCUPIED	46 867	39 886	30 383	26 090	11 280	10 300	19 104	15 790	16 484	13 796
2-OR-MORE-PERSON HOUSEHOLDS	40 767	35 124	26 687	23 276	9 551	8 928	17 136	14 348	14 080	11 847
MALE HEAD, WIFE PRESENT, NO NONRELATIVES	35 427	30 806	23 038	20 418	7 849	7 543	15 189	12 876	12 389	10 388
UNDER 25 YEARS	1 063	800	554	457	161	164	393	293	509	343
25 TO 29 YEARS	3 089	2 252	1 965	1 501	653	490	1 312	1 011	1 123	751
30 TO 34 YEARS	3 818	2 938	2 536	2 018	712	643	1 824	1 375	1 282	919
35 TO 44 YEARS	7 510	7 097	5 163	4 956	1 573	1 641	3 590	3 315	2 347	2 141
45 TO 64 YEARS	14 650	13 230	9 758	8 879	3 464	3 430	6 294	5 448	4 892	4 351
65 YEARS AND OVER	5 298	4 490	3 062	2 607	1 286	1 173	1 776	1 434	2 236	1 882
OTHER MALE HEAD	1 563	1 298	1 066	828	469	376	596	452	497	471
UNDER 65 YEARS	1 207	974	859	638	365	282	494	356	348	336
65 YEARS AND OVER	356	324	206	190	104	94	102	96	150	134
FEMALE HEAD	3 776	3 019	2 583	2 030	1 233	1 010	1 350	1 020	1 193	989
UNDER 65 YEARS	2 830	2 159	1 952	1 498	898	718	1 054	780	878	661
65 YEARS AND OVER	946	860	631	532	334	292	297	241	315	328
1-PERSON HOUSEHOLDS	6 101	4 762	3 696	2 813	1 729	1 372	1 968	1 441	2 404	1 949
UNDER 65 YEARS	2 621	2 075	1 691	1 320	771	633	919	688	930	754
65 YEARS AND OVER	3 480	2 688	2 005	1 493	957	740	1 048	754	1 474	1 194
RENTER OCCUPIED	25 656	23 560	19 283	17 769	11 469	11 095	7 814	6 674	6 373	5 790
2-OR-MORE-PERSON HOUSEHOLDS	17 394	17 171	12 852	12 649	7 285	7 551	5 567	5 098	4 542	4 522
MALE HEAD, WIFE PRESENT, NO NONRELATIVES	11 517	12 759	8 162	9 179	4 280	5 161	3 882	4 019	3 355	3 579
UNDER 25 YEARS	2 299	2 282	1 561	1 613	720	846	842	767	737	669
25 TO 29 YEARS	2 555	2 408	1 862	1 759	915	910	947	849	693	649
30 TO 34 YEARS	1 416	1 531	975	1 088	504	588	470	500	441	443
35 TO 44 YEARS	1 741	2 154	1 235	1 516	651	847	584	669	506	638
45 TO 64 YEARS	2 398	3 148	1 706	2 285	976	1 376	731	909	692	863
65 YEARS AND OVER	1 109	1 236	823	918	515	594	309	324	285	318
OTHER MALE HEAD	1 578	1 143	1 238	883	715	583	523	301	340	259
UNDER 65 YEARS	1 469	1 010	1 149	786	661	514	488	272	320	224
65 YEARS AND OVER	109	132	89	97	54	68	35	29	20	35
FEMALE HEAD	4 299	3 270	3 452	2 586	2 290	1 807	1 162	779	847	683
UNDER 65 YEARS	3 918	2 899	3 173	2 312	2 095	1 613	1 078	699	745	588
65 YEARS AND OVER	381	370	279	274	195	195	84	80	102	96
1-PERSON HOUSEHOLDS	8 262	6 389	6 430	5 120	4 183	3 544	2 247	1 576	1 831	1 268
UNDER 65 YEARS	5 559	4 109	4 447	3 408	2 868	2 358	1 579	1 050	1 111	701
65 YEARS AND OVER	2 703	2 279	1 983	1 712	1 316	1 186	668	526	720	567
PERSONS 65 YEARS OLD AND OVER										
OWNER OCCUPIED	46 867	39 886	30 383	26 090	11 280	10 300	19 104	15 790	16 484	13 796
NONE	35 247	29 752	23 385	20 029	8 168	7 476	15 217	12 552	11 862	9 724
1 PERSON	7 722	6 822	4 673	4 115	2 094	1 923	2 580	2 192	3 049	2 707
2 PERSONS OR MORE	3 899	3 311	2 325	1 946	1 018	900	1 307	1 045	1 574	1 365
RENTER OCCUPIED	25 656	23 560	19 283	17 769	11 469	11 095	7 814	6 674	6 373	5 790
NONE	20 987	19 005	15 838	14 359	9 225	8 783	6 612	5 575	5 150	4 646
1 PERSON	3 808	3 599	2 783	2 684	1 841	1 836	942	848	1 025	915
2 PERSONS OR MORE	861	956	663	726	403	475	260	251	198	229

CHARACTERISTICS OF THE HOUSING INVENTORY: 1975 AND 1970--CONTINUED

(NUMBERS IN THOUSANDS. DATA BASED ON SAMPLE, SEE TEXT. FOR MINIMUM BASE FOR DERIVED FIGURES (PERCENT, MEDIAN, ETC.) AND MEANING OF SYMBOLS, SEE TEXT)

UNITED STATES	TOTAL		INSIDE SMSA'S: TOTAL		INSIDE SMSA'S: IN CENTRAL CITIES		INSIDE SMSA'S: NOT IN CENTRAL CITIES		OUTSIDE SMSA'S	
	1975	1970	1975	1970	1975	1970	1975	1970	1975	1970
ALL OCCUPIED HOUSING UNITS--CON.										
OWN CHILDREN UNDER 18 YEARS OLD BY AGE GROUP										
OWNER OCCUPIED	46 867	39 886	30 383	26 090	11 280	10 300	19 104	15 790	16 484	13 796
NO OWN CHILDREN UNDER 18 YEARS	25 987	21 088	16 477	13 226	6 793	5 838	9 685	7 388	9 510	7 863
WITH OWN CHILDREN UNDER 18 YEARS	20 880	18 797	13 906	12 864	4 487	4 462	9 419	8 402	6 974	5 933
UNDER 6 YEARS ONLY	3 672	2 959	2 378	2 016	765	670	1 613	1 346	1 294	943
1	2 092	1 491	1 353	990	435	342	919	648	739	500
2	1 370	1 182	894	824	281	262	613	562	476	358
3 OR MORE	210	287	131	202	49	65	82	137	79	85
6 TO 17 YEARS ONLY	12 901	11 188	8 692	7 674	2 798	2 740	5 894	4 934	4 209	3 515
1	4 983	4 267	3 295	2 890	1 112	1 092	2 183	1 798	1 688	1 377
2	4 408	3 630	3 017	2 522	900	873	2 117	1 649	1 391	1 109
3 OR MORE	3 509	3 291	2 379	2 262	786	774	1 593	1 487	1 130	1 030
BOTH AGE GROUPS	4 307	4 650	2 837	3 174	924	1 053	1 912	2 121	1 471	1 475
2	1 612	1 186	1 059	815	338	271	721	544	553	370
3 OR MORE	2 695	3 464	1 778	2 359	587	782	1 191	1 578	917	1 105
RENTER OCCUPIED	25 656	23 560	19 283	17 769	11 469	11 095	7 814	6 674	6 373	5 790
NO OWN CHILDREN UNDER 18 YEARS	16 648	14 246	12 817	11 189	7 838	7 309	4 980	3 880	3 831	3 057
WITH OWN CHILDREN UNDER 18 YEARS	9 008	9 313	6 466	6 580	3 631	3 786	2 835	2 794	2 542	2 733
UNDER 6 YEARS ONLY	3 389	3 379	2 443	2 453	1 270	1 354	1 173	1 099	946	926
1	2 239	2 051	1 605	1 510	840	826	765	684	634	540
2	964	1 041	701	742	348	406	354	336	263	299
3 OR MORE	185	287	137	200	82	121	54	79	49	87
6 TO 17 YEARS ONLY	3 684	3 654	2 648	2 587	1 545	1 533	1 103	1 054	1 037	1 067
1	1 539	1 455	1 183	1 074	679	651	504	423	357	381
2	1 151	1 081	809	768	476	442	333	326	342	313
3 OR MORE	994	1 119	656	745	391	440	265	306	338	373
BOTH AGE GROUPS	1 934	2 280	1 375	1 540	816	899	559	641	559	740
2	687	565	505	403	266	225	239	178	182	162
3 OR MORE	1 248	1 715	870	1 137	550	674	320	463	378	578
PRESENCE OF SUBFAMILIES										
OWNER OCCUPIED	46 867	NA	30 383	NA	11 280	NA	19 104	NA	16 484	NA
NO SUBFAMILIES	46 066	NA	29 850	NA	11 058	NA	18 792	NA	16 216	NA
WITH 1 SUBFAMILY	788	NA	524	NA	217	NA	307	NA	264	NA
SUBFAMILY HEAD UNDER 30 YEARS	407	NA	254	NA	97	NA	157	NA	153	NA
SUBFAMILY HEAD 30 TO 64 YEARS	312	NA	221	NA	101	NA	121	NA	90	NA
SUBFAMILY HEAD 65 YEARS AND OVER	70	NA	49	NA	20	NA	30	NA	21	NA
WITH 2 SUBFAMILIES OR MORE	13	NA	10	NA	5	NA	5	NA	4	NA
RENTER OCCUPIED	25 656	NA	19 283	NA	11 469	NA	7 814	NA	6 373	NA
NO SUBFAMILIES	25 444	NA	19 136	NA	11 379	NA	7 757	NA	6 307	NA
WITH 1 SUBFAMILY	211	NA	145	NA	90	NA	56	NA	66	NA
SUBFAMILY HEAD UNDER 30 YEARS	142	NA	94	NA	57	NA	37	NA	47	NA
SUBFAMILY HEAD 30 TO 64 YEARS	55	NA	38	NA	27	NA	11	NA	17	NA
SUBFAMILY HEAD 65 YEARS AND OVER	14	NA	13	NA	6	NA	7	NA	1	NA
WITH 2 SUBFAMILIES OR MORE	1	NA	1	NA	-	NA	1	NA	-	NA
PRESENCE OF OTHER RELATIVES OR NONRELATIVES										
OWNER OCCUPIED	46 867	NA	30 383	NA	11 280	NA	19 104	NA	16 484	NA
NO OTHER RELATIVES OR NONRELATIVES	41 497	NA	26 690	NA	9 607	NA	17 083	NA	14 807	NA
WITH OTHER RELATIVES AND NONRELATIVES	87	NA	65	NA	30	NA	34	NA	22	NA
WITH OTHER RELATIVES, NO NONRELATIVES	4 400	NA	2 977	NA	1 332	NA	1 645	NA	1 422	NA
WITH NONRELATIVES, NO OTHER RELATIVES	884	NA	652	NA	311	NA	341	NA	232	NA
RENTER OCCUPIED	25 656	NA	19 283	NA	11 469	NA	7 814	NA	6 373	NA
NO OTHER RELATIVES OR NONRELATIVES	21 999	NA	16 466	NA	9 704	NA	6 762	NA	5 533	NA
WITH OTHER RELATIVES AND NONRELATIVES	78	NA	67	NA	39	NA	28	NA	10	NA
WITH OTHER RELATIVES, NO NONRELATIVES	1 950	NA	1 444	NA	939	NA	505	NA	507	NA
WITH NONRELATIVES, NO OTHER RELATIVES	1 628	NA	1 306	NA	786	NA	519	NA	323	NA
YEARS OF SCHOOL COMPLETED BY HEAD										
OWNER OCCUPIED	46 867	NA	30 383	NA	11 280	NA	19 104	NA	16 484	NA
NO SCHOOL YEARS COMPLETED	239	NA	136	NA	61	NA	75	NA	103	NA
ELEMENTARY: LESS THAN 8 YEARS	4 307	NA	2 248	NA	1 095	NA	1 153	NA	2 059	NA
8 YEARS	4 943	NA	2 625	NA	1 030	NA	1 594	NA	2 318	NA
HIGH SCHOOL: 1 TO 3 YEARS	6 935	NA	4 240	NA	1 633	NA	2 607	NA	2 695	NA
4 YEARS	15 873	NA	10 278	NA	3 699	NA	6 579	NA	5 595	NA
COLLEGE: 1 TO 3 YEARS	6 630	NA	4 839	NA	1 809	NA	3 030	NA	1 791	NA
4 YEARS OR MORE	7 940	NA	6 018	NA	1 951	NA	4 066	NA	1 923	NA
MEDIAN	12.4	NA	12.6	NA	12.5	NA	12.6	NA	12.2	NA

CHARACTERISTICS OF THE HOUSING INVENTORY: 1975 AND 1970--CONTINUED

(NUMBERS IN THOUSANDS. DATA BASED ON SAMPLE, SEE TEXT. FOR MINIMUM BASE FOR DERIVED FIGURES (PERCENT, MEDIAN, ETC.) AND MEANING OF SYMBOLS, SEE TEXT)

UNITED STATES	TOTAL		INSIDE SMSA'S						OUTSIDE SMSA'S	
			TOTAL		IN CENTRAL CITIES		NOT IN CENTRAL CITIES			
	1975	1970	1975	1970	1975	1970	1975	1970	1975	1970
ALL OCCUPIED HOUSING UNITS--CON.										
YEARS OF SCHOOL COMPLETED BY HEAD--CON.										
RENTER OCCUPIED	25 656	NA	19 283	NA	11 469	NA	7 814	NA	6 373	NA
NO SCHOOL YEARS COMPLETED	260	NA	186	NA	124	NA	62	NA	74	NA
ELEMENTARY: LESS THAN 8 YEARS	2 858	NA	1 885	NA	1 308	NA	576	NA	974	NA
8 YEARS	2 184	NA	1 479	NA	997	NA	482	NA	705	NA
HIGH SCHOOL: 1 TO 3 YEARS	4 240	NA	3 127	NA	2 005	NA	1 121	NA	1 114	NA
4 YEARS	8 062	NA	6 189	NA	3 488	NA	2 701	NA	1 872	NA
COLLEGE: 1 TO 3 YEARS	4 051	NA	3 203	NA	1 798	NA	1 405	NA	848	NA
4 YEARS OR MORE	4 000	NA	3 214	NA	1 748	NA	1 466	NA	786	NA
MEDIAN	12.4	NA	12.5	NA	12.4	NA	12.6	NA	12.2	NA
YEAR HEAD MOVED INTO UNIT										
OWNER OCCUPIED	46 867	39 886	30 383	26 090	11 280	10 300	19 104	15 790	16 484	13 796
1974 OR LATER	7 448	NA	4 677	NA	1 574	NA	3 103	NA	2 771	NA
MOVED IN WITHIN PAST 12 MONTHS	3 999	NA	2 509	NA	843	NA	1 666	NA	1 489	NA
APRIL 1970 TO 1973	10 309	NA	6 592	NA	2 155	NA	4 436	NA	3 718	NA
1965 TO MARCH 1970	9 002	14 387	6 027	9 582	2 195	3 402	3 832	6 180	2 975	4 805
1960 TO 1964	6 097	7 729	4 128	5 245	1 581	1 984	2 547	3 262	1 969	2 484
1950 TO 1959	7 837	9 675	5 387	6 634	2 155	2 694	3 232	3 940	2 450	3 041
1949 OR EARLIER	6 175	8 094	3 573	4 628	1 619	2 221	1 954	2 407	2 602	3 466
RENTER OCCUPIED	25 656	23 560	19 283	17 769	11 469	11 095	7 814	6 674	6 373	5 790
1974 OR LATER	13 837	NA	10 344	NA	5 743	NA	4 601	NA	3 493	NA
MOVED IN WITHIN PAST 12 MONTHS	9 698	NA	7 199	NA	3 976	NA	3 223	NA	2 499	NA
APRIL 1970 TO 1973	5 782	NA	4 419	NA	2 640	NA	1 778	NA	1 363	NA
1965 TO MARCH 1970	3 225	17 482	2 478	13 210	1 657	7 890	821	5 320	747	4 272
1960 TO 1964	1 310	2 845	982	2 182	668	1 507	314	676	328	663
1950 TO 1959	861	1 854	637	1 389	464	985	172	404	224	465
1949 OR EARLIER	641	1 379	424	989	297	714	127	275	217	390
HEAD'S PRINCIPAL MEANS OF TRANSPORTATION TO WORK[1]										
OWNER OCCUPIED	32 755	NA	21 969	NA	7 561	NA	14 408	NA	10 786	NA
DRIVES SELF	23 654	NA	16 299	NA	5 546	NA	10 753	NA	7 355	NA
CARPOOL	5 591	NA	3 523	NA	1 108	NA	2 416	NA	2 068	NA
MASS TRANSPORTATION	1 103	NA	1 046	NA	505	NA	541	NA	58	NA
BICYCLE OR MOTORCYCLE	211	NA	145	NA	42	NA	103	NA	67	NA
TAXICAB	22	NA	12	NA	9	NA	3	NA	10	NA
WALKS ONLY	734	NA	384	NA	175	NA	209	NA	350	NA
OTHER MEANS	126	NA	72	NA	24	NA	49	NA	54	NA
WORKS AT HOME	1 164	NA	374	NA	106	NA	268	NA	790	NA
NOT REPORTED	149	NA	114	NA	47	NA	67	NA	35	NA
RENTER OCCUPIED	16 496	NA	12 382	NA	6 775	NA	5 607	NA	4 114	NA
DRIVES SELF	10 108	NA	7 611	NA	3 683	NA	3 927	NA	2 497	NA
CARPOOL	2 787	NA	1 920	NA	997	NA	922	NA	868	NA
MASS TRANSPORTATION	1 597	NA	1 572	NA	1 297	NA	275	NA	24	NA
BICYCLE OR MOTORCYCLE	181	NA	131	NA	68	NA	63	NA	51	NA
TAXICAB	59	NA	48	NA	44	NA	4	NA	10	NA
WALKS ONLY	1 166	NA	775	NA	511	NA	264	NA	391	NA
OTHER MEANS	80	NA	60	NA	35	NA	25	NA	20	NA
WORKS AT HOME	433	NA	195	NA	87	NA	108	NA	239	NA
NOT REPORTED	85	NA	71	NA	52	NA	19	NA	14	NA
DISTANCE FROM HOME TO WORK[1]										
OWNER OCCUPIED	32 755	NA	21 969	NA	7 561	NA	14 408	NA	10 786	NA
LESS THAN 1 MILE	2 374	NA	1 058	NA	379	NA	678	NA	1 317	NA
1 TO 4 MILES	8 063	NA	5 190	NA	2 350	NA	2 840	NA	2 873	NA
5 TO 9 MILES	5 768	NA	4 438	NA	1 778	NA	2 660	NA	1 331	NA
10 TO 29 MILES	9 346	NA	7 075	NA	1 891	NA	5 184	NA	2 270	NA
30 TO 49 MILES	1 559	NA	947	NA	162	NA	784	NA	613	NA
50 MILES OR MORE	486	NA	213	NA	56	NA	157	NA	274	NA
WORKS AT HOME	1 164	NA	374	NA	106	NA	268	NA	790	NA
NO FIXED PLACE OF WORK	3 648	NA	2 405	NA	720	NA	1 685	NA	1 243	NA
NOT REPORTED	346	NA	270	NA	119	NA	152	NA	76	NA
MEDIAN	7.9	NA	8.6	NA	6.6	NA	9.9	NA	5.6	NA

[1]LIMITED TO HEADS WHO REPORTED HAVING A JOB THE WEEK PRIOR TO ENUMERATION.

CHARACTERISTICS OF THE HOUSING INVENTORY: 1975 AND 1970--CONTINUED

(NUMBERS IN THOUSANDS. DATA BASED ON SAMPLE, SEE TEXT. FOR MINIMUM BASE FOR DERIVED FIGURES (PERCENT, MEDIAN, ETC.) AND MEANING OF SYMBOLS, SEE TEXT)

UNITED STATES	TOTAL		INSIDE SMSA'S						OUTSIDE SMSA'S	
			TOTAL		IN CENTRAL CITIES		NOT IN CENTRAL CITIES			
	1975	1970	1975	1970	1975	1970	1975	1970	1975	1970
ALL OCCUPIED HOUSING UNITS--CON.										
DISTANCE FROM HOME TO WORK[1]--CON.										
RENTER OCCUPIED	16 496	NA	12 382	NA	6 775	NA	5 607	NA	4 114	NA
LESS THAN 1 MILE	2 111	NA	1 305	NA	766	NA	538	NA	807	NA
1 TO 4 MILES	5 214	NA	3 973	NA	2 437	NA	1 536	NA	1 241	NA
5 TO 9 MILES	2 901	NA	2 384	NA	1 311	NA	1 072	NA	517	NA
10 TO 29 MILES	3 635	NA	2 968	NA	1 362	NA	1 606	NA	668	NA
30 TO 49 MILES	424	NA	282	NA	96	NA	186	NA	142	NA
50 MILES OR MORE	130	NA	80	NA	39	NA	41	NA	51	NA
WORKS AT HOME	433	NA	195	NA	87	NA	108	NA	239	NA
NO FIXED PLACE OF WORK	1 451	NA	1 025	NA	543	NA	481	NA	426	NA
NOT REPORTED	195	NA	171	NA	133	NA	37	NA	25	NA
MEDIAN	4.9	NA	5.4	NA	4.7	NA	6.9	NA	3.9	NA
TRAVEL TIME FROM HOME TO WORK[1]										
OWNER OCCUPIED	32 755	NA	21 969	NA	7 561	NA	14 408	NA	10 786	NA
LESS THAN 15 MINUTES	9 690	NA	5 608	NA	2 173	NA	3 435	NA	4 081	NA
15 TO 29 MINUTES	9 756	NA	7 318	NA	2 785	NA	4 532	NA	2 438	NA
30 TO 44 MINUTES	4 936	NA	3 792	NA	1 096	NA	2 696	NA	1 145	NA
45 TO 59 MINUTES	1 702	NA	1 218	NA	310	NA	908	NA	484	NA
1 HOUR TO 1 HOUR AND 29 MINUTES	1 220	NA	842	NA	224	NA	618	NA	378	NA
1 HOUR 30 MINUTES OR MORE	375	NA	225	NA	62	NA	163	NA	150	NA
WORKS AT HOME	1 164	NA	374	NA	106	NA	268	NA	790	NA
NO FIXED PLACE OF WORK	3 648	NA	2 405	NA	720	NA	1 685	NA	1 243	NA
NOT REPORTED	264	NA	187	NA	84	NA	103	NA	77	NA
MEDIAN	21	NA	23	NA	21	NA	24	NA	17	NA
RENTER OCCUPIED	16 496	NA	12 382	NA	6 775	NA	5 607	NA	4 114	NA
LESS THAN 15 MINUTES	5 772	NA	3 853	NA	2 009	NA	1 844	NA	1 920	NA
15 TO 29 MINUTES	5 061	NA	4 120	NA	2 323	NA	1 797	NA	941	NA
30 TO 44 MINUTES	2 165	NA	1 818	NA	976	NA	842	NA	346	NA
45 TO 59 MINUTES	811	NA	698	NA	394	NA	303	NA	113	NA
1 HOUR TO 1 HOUR AND 29 MINUTES	539	NA	468	NA	299	NA	168	NA	71	NA
1 HOUR 30 MINUTES OR MORE	141	NA	102	NA	63	NA	39	NA	39	NA
WORKS AT HOME	433	NA	195	NA	87	NA	108	NA	239	NA
NO FIXED PLACE OF WORK	1 451	NA	1 025	NA	543	NA	481	NA	426	NA
NOT REPORTED	124	NA	104	NA	79	NA	25	NA	20	NA
MEDIAN	19	NA	21	NA	22	NA	20	NA	15-	NA
HEATING EQUIPMENT										
ALL YEAR-ROUND HOUSING UNITS	77 553	67 699	52 690	46 083	24 205	22 584	28 485	23 498	24 864	21 616
WARM-AIR FURNACE	38 964	28 772	27 284	20 502	10 870	8 644	16 415	11 857	11 680	8 270
STEAM OR HOT WATER	14 554	13 820	12 152	11 647	6 813	6 817	5 340	4 830	2 402	2 174
BUILT-IN ELECTRIC UNITS	5 061	3 520	3 019	2 224	1 228	938	1 791	1 285	2 042	1 296
FLOOR, WALL, OR PIPELESS FURNACE	6 994	5 878	4 837	4 154	2 463	2 062	2 373	2 093	2 158	1 723
ROOM HEATERS WITH FLUE	5 255	7 910	2 496	4 176	1 343	2 306	1 153	1 870	2 759	3 733
ROOM HEATERS WITHOUT FLUE	3 689	3 949	1 577	1 782	968	1 033	609	749	2 112	2 167
FIREPLACES, STOVES, OR PORTABLE HEATERS	2 341	3 269	808	1 212	275	571	534	641	1 533	2 058
NONE	695	581	516	387	245	214	271	173	178	194
OWNER OCCUPIED	46 867	39 886	30 383	26 090	11 280	10 300	19 104	15 790	16 484	13 796
WARM-AIR FURNACE	28 143	20 885	19 240	14 693	6 776	5 516	12 464	9 177	8 903	6 192
STEAM OR HOT WATER	6 894	6 401	5 407	5 047	2 097	2 001	3 309	3 045	1 488	1 354
BUILT-IN ELECTRIC UNITS	2 555	1 797	1 208	918	349	283	859	634	1 347	880
FLOOR, WALL, OR PIPELESS FURNACE	3 675	3 410	2 326	2 295	1 132	1 086	1 194	1 208	1 350	1 115
ROOM HEATERS WITH FLUE	2 360	3 782	937	1 731	364	787	572	945	1 423	2 050
ROOM HEATERS WITHOUT FLUE	1 910	1 955	725	755	391	363	334	393	1 185	1 200
FIREPLACES, STOVES, OR PORTABLE HEATERS	1 159	1 510	386	539	111	210	276	329	773	970
NONE	171	145	155	112	59	54	95	58	17	34
RENTER OCCUPIED	25 656	23 560	19 283	17 769	11 469	11 095	7 814	6 674	6 373	5 790
WARM-AIR FURNACE	8 856	6 630	6 679	5 014	3 509	2 737	3 170	2 276	2 176	1 616
STEAM OR HOT WATER	6 898	6 810	6 143	6 121	4 315	4 480	1 829	1 641	755	689
BUILT-IN ELECTRIC UNITS	2 070	1 439	1 553	1 142	787	589	765	553	518	297
FLOOR, WALL, OR PIPELESS FURNACE	2 905	2 142	2 237	1 663	1 208	876	1 028	787	668	478
ROOM HEATERS WITH FLUE	2 387	3 428	1 373	2 180	868	1 370	505	810	1 015	1 248
ROOM HEATERS WITHOUT FLUE	1 420	1 603	712	877	489	585	223	292	708	726
FIREPLACES, STOVES, OR PORTABLE HEATERS	823	1 257	326	557	146	320	180	237	497	700
NONE	297	252	261	216	147	138	114	78	36	37

[1]LIMITED TO HEADS WHO REPORTED HAVING A JOB THE WEEK PRIOR TO ENUMERATION.

CHARACTERISTICS OF THE HOUSING INVENTORY: 1975 AND 1970--CONTINUED

(NUMBERS IN THOUSANDS. DATA BASED ON SAMPLE, SEE TEXT. FOR MINIMUM BASE FOR DERIVED FIGURES (PERCENT, MEDIAN, ETC.) AND MEANING OF SYMBOLS, SEE TEXT)

UNITED STATES	TOTAL		INSIDE SMSA'S						OUTSIDE SMSA'S	
			TOTAL		IN CENTRAL CITIES		NOT IN CENTRAL CITIES			
	1975	1970	1975	1970	1975	1970	1975	1970	1975	1970
ALL YEAR-ROUND HOUSING UNITS.	77 553	67 699	52 690	46 083	24 205	22 584	28 485	23 498	24 864	21 616
AIR CONDITIONING										
ROOM UNIT(S).	22 781	16 939	15 782	12 402	7 260	6 143	8 522	6 258	6 999	4 537
CENTRAL SYSTEM.	15 536	7 263	11 626	5 650	4 464	2 489	7 161	3 161	3 911	1 613
NONE.	39 236	43 492	25 282	28 027	12 480	13 951	12 802	14 076	13 954	15 465
ELEVATOR IN STRUCTURE										
4 FLOORS OR MORE.	3 585	3 295	3 435	3 229	2 776	2 770	659	459	151	66
WITH ELEVATOR	2 727	2 342	2 616	2 295	2 042	1 936	574	359	111	47
WALK-UP	858	953	818	934	733	834	85	100	40	19
1 TO 3 FLOORS	73 968	64 404	49 255	42 854	21 429	19 814	27 826	23 040	24 713	21 550
BASEMENT										
WITH BASEMENT	37 123	34 467	27 442	25 592	13 453	13 163	13 989	12 429	9 681	8 876
NO BASEMENT	40 430	28 978	25 248	18 267	10 752	8 232	14 496	10 035	15 182	10 711
SOURCE OF WATER										
PUBLIC SYSTEM OR PRIVATE COMPANY.	64 485	55 294	48 431	41 948	24 023	22 348	24 407	19 600	16 055	13 345
INDIVIDUAL WELL	11 607	11 102	3 887	3 851	164	220	3 723	3 631	7 721	7 251
DRILLED	9 698	NA	3 366	NA	153	NA	3 213	NA	6 332	NA
DUG	1 652	NA	412	NA	6	NA	406	NA	1 239	NA
NOT REPORTED.	257	NA	108	NA	5	NA	103	NA	149	NA
OTHER	1 461	1 298	372	279	18	15	355	265	1 088	1 019
SEWAGE DISPOSAL										
PUBLIC SEWER.	56 484	48 188	44 293	37 834	23 489	21 722	20 804	16 112	12 191	10 354
SEPTIC TANK OR CESSPOOL	19 694	16 602	8 146	7 693	695	784	7 451	6 909	11 548	8 909
OTHER	1 375	2 904	250	552	20	77	230	475	1 124	2 352
ALL OCCUPIED HOUSING UNITS.	72 523	63 445	49 666	43 859	22 749	21 395	26 918	22 464	22 857	19 586
TELEPHONE AVAILABLE										
YES	65 289	55 412	45 364	39 239	20 126	18 514	25 238	20 724	19 925	16 173
NO.	7 234	8 034	4 302	4 620	2 623	2 881	1 679	1 739	2 932	3 414
AUTOMOBILES AND TRUCKS AVAILABLE										
AUTOMOBILES:										
1	34 898	30 268	22 729	20 070	10 312	9 715	12 417	10 355	12 169	10 198
2	20 537	18 600	14 709	13 144	5 211	4 738	9 499	8 406	5 827	5 456
3 OR MORE	5 073	3 495	3 618	2 498	1 123	870	2 495	1 628	1 455	997
NONE.	12 016	11 081	8 610	8 146	6 103	6 071	2 507	2 074	3 406	2 936
TRUCKS:										
1	13 647	NA	6 815	NA	2 105	NA	4 710	NA	6 832	NA
2 OR MORE	1 357	NA	549	NA	153	NA	396	NA	808	NA
NONE.	57 518	NA	42 302	NA	20 491	NA	21 811	NA	15 217	NA
OWNED SECOND HOME										
YES	3 033	2 890	2 100	1 965	823	890	1 277	1 075	934	925
NO.	69 490	60 557	47 567	41 902	21 926	20 515	25 641	21 387	21 923	18 655
HOUSE HEATING FUEL										
UTILITY GAS	40 933	35 014	30 941	27 021	15 193	13 931	15 748	13 091	9 992	7 992
BOTTLED, TANK, OR LP GAS.	4 146	3 807	978	1 188	100	300	878	889	3 168	2 619
FUEL OIL, KEROSENE, ETC..	16 299	16 473	11 024	10 943	4 681	4 939	6 343	6 005	5 276	5 530
ELECTRICITY	9 173	4 876	5 863	3 172	2 393	1 372	3 470	1 800	3 310	1 704
COAL OR COKE.	573	1 821	248	874	107	493	140	381	325	947
WOOD.	852	794	138	119	18	19	121	101	714	675
OTHER FUEL.	78	266	58	223	51	160	8	62	20	44
NONE.	468	395	415	326	206	192	209	134	52	70

CHARACTERISTICS OF THE HOUSING INVENTORY: 1975 AND 1970--CONTINUED

(NUMBERS IN THOUSANDS. DATA BASED ON SAMPLE, SEE TEXT. FOR MINIMUM BASE FOR DERIVED FIGURES (PERCENT, MEDIAN, ETC.) AND MEANING OF SYMBOLS, SEE TEXT)

UNITED STATES	TOTAL		INSIDE SMSA'S						OUTSIDE SMSA'S	
			TOTAL		IN CENTRAL CITIES		NOT IN CENTRAL CITIES			
	1975	1970	1975	1970	1975	1970	1975	1970	1975	1970
ALL OCCUPIED HOUSING UNITS--CON.										
COOKING FUEL										
UTILITY GAS	32 493	31 244	26 199	25 530	14 718	14 945	11 481	10 585	6 293	5 714
BOTTLED, TANK, OR LP GAS	5 440	5 314	1 672	1 873	188	393	1 484	1 480	3 768	3 441
ELECTRICITY	33 944	25 768	21 484	15 975	7 644	5 781	13 840	10 193	12 460	9 793
FUEL OIL, KEROSENE, ETC.	76	303	35	180	15	107	20	73	41	123
COAL OR COKE	23	157	7	58	3	28	4	30	16	99
WOOD	230	405	36	65	3	14	33	51	194	340
OTHER FUEL	3	43	1	30	-	19	1	12	3	12
NONE	315	213	232	155	177	117	55	38	82	58
ALL OCCUPIED 1-FAMILY HOMES	53 096	NA	32 876	NA	11 963	NA	20 913	NA	20 219	NA
STORM WINDOWS OR OTHER PROTECTIVE WINDOW COVERING										
ALL WINDOWS COVERED	24 444	NA	15 137	NA	4 729	NA	10 408	NA	9 307	NA
SOME WINDOWS COVERED	5 284	NA	3 015	NA	1 105	NA	1 910	NA	2 269	NA
NO WINDOWS COVERED	22 770	NA	14 303	NA	5 932	NA	8 371	NA	8 467	NA
NOT REPORTED	597	NA	421	NA	197	NA	224	NA	175	NA
STORM DOORS										
ALL DOORS COVERED	25 364	NA	15 747	NA	5 103	NA	10 644	NA	9 616	NA
SOME DOORS COVERED	6 188	NA	3 597	NA	1 363	NA	2 234	NA	2 590	NA
NO DOORS COVERED	20 915	NA	13 092	NA	5 287	NA	7 806	NA	7 823	NA
NOT REPORTED	629	NA	440	NA	210	NA	229	NA	190	NA
ATTIC OR ROOF INSULATION										
YES	39 290	NA	24 837	NA	8 308	NA	16 529	NA	14 453	NA
NO	8 762	NA	4 733	NA	2 106	NA	2 628	NA	4 029	NA
DON'T KNOW	4 137	NA	2 678	NA	1 260	NA	1 417	NA	1 459	NA
NOT REPORTED	907	NA	628	NA	289	NA	339	NA	278	NA

FINANCIAL CHARACTERISTICS OF THE HOUSING INVENTORY: 1975 AND 1970

(NUMBERS IN THOUSANDS. DATA BASED ON SAMPLE, SEE TEXT. FOR MINIMUM BASE FOR DERIVED FIGURES (PERCENT, MEDIAN, ETC.) AND MEANING OF SYMBOLS, SEE TEXT)

UNITED STATES	TOTAL		INSIDE SMSA'S						OUTSIDE SMSA'S	
			TOTAL		IN CENTRAL CITIES		NOT IN CENTRAL CITIES			
	1975	1970	1975	1970	1975	1970	1975	1970	1975	1970
ALL OCCUPIED HOUSING UNITS	72 523	63 445	49 666	43 859	22 749	21 395	26 918	22 464	22 857	19 586
INCOME[1]										
OWNER OCCUPIED	46 867	39 886	30 383	26 090	11 280	10 300	19 104	15 790	16 484	13 796
LESS THAN $2,000	1 557	3 775	775	1 818	347	864	428	954	782	1 956
$2,000 TO $2,999	1 846	1 949	911	977	471	463	441	514	935	972
$3,000 TO $3,999	1 992	1 835	1 063	950	488	445	575	505	928	885
$4,000 TO $4,999	1 870	1 771	1 017	950	496	443	521	507	853	821
$5,000 TO $5,999	1 882	1 921	1 037	1 038	457	473	580	565	845	883
$6,000 TO $6,999	1 774	2 057	962	1 161	387	520	575	641	812	895
$7,000 TO $7,999	1 820	7 330	1 041	4 605	408	1 889	633	2 716	780	2 725
$8,000 TO $9,999	3 524		2 035		884		1 151		1 489	
$10,000 TO $12,499	5 278	10 404	3 202	7 478	1 250	2 758	1 952	4 720	2 076	2 926
$12,500 TO $14,999	4 542		2 966		1 148		1 817		1 576	
$15,000 TO $24,999	13 338	6 762	9 547	5 390	3 131	1 864	6 416	3 525	3 791	1 373
$25,000 TO $34,999	4 556	2 083	3 551	1 722	1 107	580	2 444	1 142	1 005	361
$35,000 OR MORE	2 889		2 276		704		1 572		613	
MEDIAN	13500	9700	15200	11000	13500	10100	16400	11600	11000	7500
RENTER OCCUPIED	25 656	23 560	19 283	17 769	11 469	11 095	7 814	6 674	6 373	5 790
LESS THAN $2,000	2 044	3 892	1 399	2 679	1 033	1 898	365	780	646	1 214
$2,000 TO $2,999	2 230	1 877	1 557	1 336	1 117	927	440	409	672	541
$3,000 TO $3,999	2 189	1 815	1 637	1 294	1 114	882	523	412	552	522
$4,000 TO $4,999	1 830	1 750	1 321	1 267	865	843	456	424	509	484
$5,000 TO $5,999	1 655	1 847	1 198	1 354	760	875	438	479	458	493
$6,000 TO $6,999	1 644	1 814	1 208	1 356	720	845	488	511	436	459
$7,000 TO $7,999	1 552	4 620	1 171	3 554	725	2 095	445	1 459	382	1 066
$8,000 TO $9,999	2 622		1 962		1 131		831		660	
$10,000 TO $12,499	3 214	3 928	2 462	3 186	1 338	1 760	1 124	1 426	752	742
$12,500 TO $14,999	1 983		1 552		781		771		430	
$15,000 TO $24,999	3 673	1 634	2 975	1 406	1 457	768	1 517	638	698	228
$25,000 TO $34,999	671	381	547	339	266	202	280	137	125	43
$35,000 OR MORE	347		294		161		133		53	
MEDIAN	7800	6300	8200	6700	7200	6100	9800	7700	6800	5300
SPECIFIED OWNER OCCUPIED[2]	37 329	31 726	25 692	22 059	9 498	8 543	16 193	13 516	11 638	9 667
VALUE										
LESS THAN $5,000	533	1 824	168	551	84	239	83	312	365	1 273
$5,000 TO $7,499	843	2 253	287	987	154	528	133	459	556	1 267
$7,500 TO $9,999	1 096	2 654	519	1 459	333	822	186	638	577	1 195
$10,000 TO $12,499	1 621	3 303	815	2 050	475	1 074	340	976	806	1 253
$12,500 TO $14,999	1 484	3 089	863	2 121	481	1 028	382	1 093	621	968
$15,000 TO $17,499	2 238	3 317	1 204	2 391	686	1 015	518	1 376	1 035	927
$17,500 TO $19,999	2 120	3 116	1 293	2 404	698	902	595	1 502	827	711
$20,000 TO $24,999	4 406	4 680	2 898	3 740	1 334	1 214	1 564	2 526	1 508	940
$25,000 TO $29,999	4 804	4 444	3 369	3 709	1 302	1 044	2 067	2 665	1 435	736
$30,000 TO $34,999	4 318		3 228		1 118		2 110		1 090	
$35,000 TO $39,999	3 750	2 050	2 814	1 760	862	444	1 953	1 316	936	289
$40,000 TO $49,999	4 663		3 671		950		2 721		993	
$50,000 TO $59,999	2 345		1 903		420		1 483		441	
$60,000 TO $74,999	1 623	997	1 368	887	308	234	1 060	653	255	110
$75,000 OR MORE	1 484		1 292		293		999		192	
MEDIAN	29500	17100	32200	19000	26900	16400	35300	20800	23400	12200
VALUE-INCOME RATIO										
LESS THAN 1.5	10 158	12 083	6 705	8 028	2 968	3 489	3 737	4 538	3 453	4 055
1.5 TO 1.9	7 187	6 237	5 120	4 624	1 836	1 643	3 283	2 981	2 067	1 613
2.0 TO 2.4	5 468	4 056	3 910	3 026	1 280	995	2 630	2 030	1 558	1 030
2.5 TO 2.9	3 773	2 401	2 653	1 748	815	577	1 838	1 170	1 121	654
3.0 TO 3.9	4 182	2 434	2 925	1 695	934	602	1 991	1 093	1 256	739
4.0 OR MORE	6 420	4 215	4 290	2 747	1 623	1 147	2 668	1 600	2 129	1 469
NOT COMPUTED	142	300	88	192	43	89	46	103	54	108
MEDIAN	2.1	1.8	2.1	1.8	2.0	1.7	2.2	1.9	2.1	1.7
MORTGAGE STATUS										
WITH MORTGAGE, DEED OF TRUST, OR LAND CONTRACT	23 501	NA	17 294	NA	6 033	NA	11 261	NA	6 206	NA
OWNED FREE AND CLEAR	13 829	NA	8 398	NA	3 465	NA	4 932	NA	5 431	NA

[1]INCOME OF FAMILIES AND PRIMARY INDIVIDUALS IN 12 MONTHS PRECEDING DATE OF ENUMERATION; SEE TEXT.
[2]LIMITED TO 1-FAMILY HOMES ON LESS THAN 10 ACRES AND NO BUSINESS ON PROPERTY.

FINANCIAL CHARACTERISTICS OF THE HOUSING INVENTORY: 1975 AND 1970--CONTINUED

(NUMBERS IN THOUSANDS. DATA BASED ON SAMPLE, SEE TEXT. FOR MINIMUM BASE FOR DERIVED FIGURES (PERCENT, MEDIAN, ETC.) AND MEANING OF SYMBOLS, SEE TEXT)

UNITED STATES	TOTAL		INSIDE SMSA'S						OUTSIDE SMSA'S	
			TOTAL		IN CENTRAL CITIES		NOT IN CENTRAL CITIES			
	1975	1970	1975	1970	1975	1970	1975	1970	1975	1970
SPECIFIED OWNER OCCUPIED[1]--CON.										
MORTGAGE INSURANCE										
UNITS WITH MORTGAGE OR SIMILAR DEBT	23 501	NA	17 294	NA	6 033	NA	11 261	NA	6 206	NA
INSURED BY FHA, VA, OR FARMERS HOME ADMIN	7 833	NA	6 159	NA	2 602	NA	3 556	NA	1 675	NA
NOT INSURED OR INSURED BY PRIVATE MORTGAGE INSURANCE[2]	11 464	NA	8 113	NA	2 439	NA	5 674	NA	3 352	NA
DON'T KNOW	2 425	NA	1 776	NA	561	NA	1 215	NA	650	NA
NOT REPORTED	1 778	NA	1 247	NA	432	NA	815	NA	530	NA
UNITS OWNED FREE AND CLEAR	13 829	NA	8 398	NA	3 465	NA	4 932	NA	5 431	NA
REAL ESTATE TAXES LAST YEAR										
LESS THAN $100	4 905	NA	1 920	NA	823	NA	1 097	NA	2 985	NA
$100 TO $199	3 877	NA	1 962	NA	915	NA	1 047	NA	1 915	NA
$200 TO $299	3 551	NA	2 271	NA	1 058	NA	1 212	NA	1 280	NA
$300 TO $349	1 903	NA	1 277	NA	524	NA	754	NA	625	NA
$350 TO $399	1 516	NA	1 121	NA	466	NA	655	NA	394	NA
$400 TO $499	3 080	NA	2 408	NA	922	NA	1 485	NA	672	NA
$500 TO $599	2 361	NA	1 898	NA	667	NA	1 231	NA	462	NA
$600 TO $699	2 161	NA	1 825	NA	598	NA	1 226	NA	336	NA
$700 TO $799	1 513	NA	1 341	NA	413	NA	928	NA	172	NA
$800 TO $999	2 198	NA	1 888	NA	521	NA	1 367	NA	310	NA
$1,000 OR MORE	3 279	NA	2 907	NA	549	NA	2 358	NA	372	NA
NOT REPORTED	6 988	NA	4 874	NA	2 043	NA	2 831	NA	2 114	NA
MEDIAN	380	NA	476	NA	393	NA	535	NA	192	NA
SELECTED MONTHLY HOUSING COSTS[3]										
UNITS WITH A MORTGAGE	23 501	NA	17 294	NA	6 033	NA	11 261	NA	6 206	NA
LESS THAN $100	390	NA	174	NA	97	NA	77	NA	217	NA
$100 TO $119	706	NA	392	NA	239	NA	153	NA	314	NA
$120 TO $149	1 912	NA	1 151	NA	578	NA	573	NA	762	NA
$150 TO $174	2 087	NA	1 389	NA	636	NA	754	NA	698	NA
$175 TO $199	2 531	NA	1 828	NA	773	NA	1 055	NA	703	NA
$200 TO $224	2 407	NA	1 840	NA	681	NA	1 159	NA	567	NA
$225 TO $249	2 052	NA	1 608	NA	579	NA	1 030	NA	443	NA
$250 TO $274	1 694	NA	1 316	NA	422	NA	894	NA	378	NA
$275 TO $299	1 404	NA	1 113	NA	321	NA	792	NA	291	NA
$300 TO $349	2 178	NA	1 739	NA	469	NA	1 270	NA	439	NA
$350 TO $399	1 367	NA	1 151	NA	280	NA	871	NA	216	NA
$400 TO $499	1 381	NA	1 167	NA	278	NA	889	NA	214	NA
$500 OR MORE	729	NA	653	NA	131	NA	522	NA	76	NA
NOT REPORTED	2 662	NA	1 774	NA	551	NA	1 223	NA	888	NA
MEDIAN	230	NA	240	NA	215	NA	256	NA	198	NA
UNITS OWNED FREE AND CLEAR	13 829	NA	8 398	NA	3 465	NA	4 932	NA	5 431	NA
LESS THAN $50	1 966	NA	766	NA	388	NA	379	NA	1 200	NA
$50 TO $69	2 593	NA	1 330	NA	661	NA	669	NA	1 263	NA
$70 TO $79	1 251	NA	713	NA	364	NA	349	NA	538	NA
$80 TO $89	1 229	NA	771	NA	327	NA	443	NA	459	NA
$90 TO $99	1 008	NA	705	NA	289	NA	416	NA	303	NA
$100 TO $119	1 515	NA	1 105	NA	413	NA	692	NA	410	NA
$120 TO $149	1 239	NA	977	NA	326	NA	651	NA	262	NA
$150 TO $199	866	NA	718	NA	187	NA	531	NA	148	NA
$200 OR MORE	409	NA	362	NA	87	NA	275	NA	47	NA
NOT REPORTED	1 751	NA	950	NA	423	NA	527	NA	800	NA
MEDIAN	82	NA	92	NA	83	NA	98	NA	67	NA
SELECTED MONTHLY HOUSING COSTS AS PERCENTAGE OF INCOME[3]										
UNITS WITH A MORTGAGE	23 501	NA	17 294	NA	6 033	NA	11 261	NA	6 206	NA
LESS THAN 5 PERCENT	123	NA	97	NA	46	NA	51	NA	26	NA
5 TO 9 PERCENT	2 139	NA	1 581	NA	651	NA	930	NA	558	NA
10 TO 14 PERCENT	5 141	NA	3 842	NA	1 373	NA	2 469	NA	1 299	NA
15 TO 19 PERCENT	5 041	NA	3 800	NA	1 277	NA	2 523	NA	1 242	NA
20 TO 24 PERCENT	3 305	NA	2 462	NA	790	NA	1 672	NA	842	NA
25 TO 29 PERCENT	1 887	NA	1 352	NA	428	NA	924	NA	536	NA
30 TO 34 PERCENT	1 042	NA	789	NA	246	NA	544	NA	253	NA
35 TO 39 PERCENT	570	NA	409	NA	160	NA	249	NA	161	NA
40 TO 49 PERCENT	602	NA	427	NA	189	NA	238	NA	175	NA
50 PERCENT OR MORE	925	NA	714	NA	304	NA	411	NA	211	NA
NOT COMPUTED	62	NA	46	NA	17	NA	29	NA	16	NA
NOT REPORTED	2 662	NA	1 774	NA	551	NA	1 223	NA	888	NA
MEDIAN	18	NA	18	NA	18	NA	18	NA	18	NA

[1]LIMITED TO 1-FAMILY HOMES ON LESS THAN 10 ACRES AND NO BUSINESS ON PROPERTY.
[2]DATA ARE NOT SEPARABLE.
[3]SUM OF PAYMENTS FOR REAL ESTATE TAXES, PROPERTY INSURANCE, UTILITIES, FUEL, WATER, GARBAGE AND TRASH COLLECTION, AND MORTGAGE AT TIME OF ENUMERATION.

FINANCIAL CHARACTERISTICS OF THE HOUSING INVENTORY: 1975 AND 1970--CONTINUED

(NUMBERS IN THOUSANDS. DATA BASED ON SAMPLE, SEE TEXT. FOR MINIMUM BASE FOR DERIVED FIGURES (PERCENT, MEDIAN, ETC.) AND MEANING OF SYMBOLS, SEE TEXT)

UNITED STATES	TOTAL		INSIDE SMSA'S						OUTSIDE SMSA'S	
			TOTAL		IN CENTRAL CITIES		NOT IN CENTRAL CITIES			
	1975	1970	1975	1970	1975	1970	1975	1970	1975	1970
SPECIFIED OWNER OCCUPIED[1]--CON.										
SELECTED MONTHLY HOUSING COSTS AS PERCENTAGE OF INCOME[2]--CON.										
UNITS OWNED FREE AND CLEAR	13 829	NA	8 398	NA	3 465	NA	4 932	NA	5 431	NA
LESS THAN 5 PERCENT	1 274	NA	757	NA	342	NA	415	NA	516	NA
5 TO 9 PERCENT	4 124	NA	2 599	NA	1 053	NA	1 546	NA	1 525	NA
10 TO 14 PERCENT	2 503	NA	1 511	NA	560	NA	951	NA	992	NA
15 TO 19 PERCENT	1 512	NA	908	NA	365	NA	544	NA	604	NA
20 TO 24 PERCENT	902	NA	555	NA	248	NA	307	NA	348	NA
25 TO 29 PERCENT	529	NA	324	NA	133	NA	191	NA	205	NA
30 TO 34 PERCENT	328	NA	210	NA	87	NA	123	NA	118	NA
35 TO 39 PERCENT	228	NA	148	NA	59	NA	89	NA	80	NA
40 TO 49 PERCENT	265	NA	173	NA	81	NA	92	NA	91	NA
50 PERCENT OR MORE	377	NA	246	NA	103	NA	143	NA	131	NA
NOT COMPUTED	37	NA	16	NA	12	NA	4	NA	20	NA
NOT REPORTED	1 751	NA	950	NA	423	NA	527	NA	800	NA
MEDIAN	11	NA	11	NA	11	NA	11	NA	11	NA
ACQUISITION OF PROPERTY										
PLACED OR ASSUMED A MORTGAGE	31 361	NA	22 710	NA	8 361	NA	14 348	NA	8 651	NA
ACQUIRED THROUGH INHERITANCE OR GIFT	888	NA	453	NA	184	NA	269	NA	436	NA
PAID ALL CASH	3 861	NA	1 832	NA	686	NA	1 146	NA	2 029	NA
ACQUIRED IN OTHER MANNER	398	NA	222	NA	86	NA	136	NA	176	NA
NOT REPORTED	821	NA	476	NA	182	NA	294	NA	345	NA
ALTERATIONS AND REPAIRS DURING LAST 12 MONTHS										
NO ALTERATIONS OR REPAIRS	13 270	NA	8 714	NA	3 471	NA	5 243	NA	4 556	NA
ALTERATIONS AND REPAIRS COSTING LESS THAN $100[3]	10 894	NA	7 611	NA	2 622	NA	4 990	NA	3 283	NA
ADDITIONS	170	NA	96	NA	32	NA	64	NA	73	NA
ALTERATIONS	2 207	NA	1 499	NA	515	NA	984	NA	708	NA
REPLACEMENTS	1 845	NA	1 209	NA	446	NA	762	NA	636	NA
REPAIRS	8 424	NA	5 992	NA	2 061	NA	3 931	NA	2 432	NA
ALTERATIONS AND REPAIRS COSTING $100 OR MORE[3]	16 404	NA	11 761	NA	4 212	NA	7 549	NA	4 643	NA
ADDITIONS	2 245	NA	1 406	NA	406	NA	1 000	NA	838	NA
ALTERATIONS	6 210	NA	4 434	NA	1 533	NA	2 901	NA	1 776	NA
REPLACEMENTS	6 290	NA	4 493	NA	1 734	NA	2 759	NA	1 797	NA
REPAIRS	8 973	NA	6 641	NA	2 437	NA	4 204	NA	2 332	NA
NOT REPORTED	597	NA	339	NA	106	NA	233	NA	257	NA
PLANS FOR IMPROVEMENTS DURING NEXT 12 MONTHS										
NONE PLANNED	18 734	NA	12 617	NA	4 768	NA	7 849	NA	6 117	NA
SOME PLANNED	15 382	NA	10 914	NA	3 919	NA	6 995	NA	4 468	NA
COSTING LESS THAN $100	2 908	NA	2 074	NA	722	NA	1 353	NA	834	NA
COSTING $100 OR MORE	11 945	NA	8 477	NA	3 065	NA	5 412	NA	3 468	NA
DON'T KNOW	451	NA	306	NA	110	NA	195	NA	145	NA
NOT REPORTED	78	NA	57	NA	22	NA	35	NA	21	NA
DON'T KNOW	2 692	NA	1 882	NA	726	NA	1 156	NA	811	NA
NOT REPORTED	521	NA	279	NA	86	NA	193	NA	242	NA
SPECIFIED RENTER OCCUPIED[4]	24 959	22 334	19 164	17 433	11 468	11 033	7 696	6 401	5 795	4 900
GROSS RENT										
LESS THAN $50	871	1 422	548	730	456	536	92	194	323	692
$50 TO $59	505	986	290	610	213	456	78	154	214	376
$60 TO $69	715	1 409	418	962	320	726	98	236	297	447
$70 TO $79	764	1 649	461	1 197	325	901	136	295	303	453
$80 TO $99	1 889	3 701	1 197	2 879	868	2 099	329	779	693	822
$100 TO $119	2 371	3 332	1 673	2 739	1 220	1 845	453	894	697	592
$120 TO $149	3 936	3 772	2 989	3 283	2 058	1 967	931	1 316	946	489
$150 TO $174	3 368	3 304	2 717	2 986	1 627	1 525	1 090	1 461	650	318
$175 TO $199	3 013		2 623		1 465		1 158		390	
$200 TO $224	2 100		1 877		966		911		223	
$225 TO $249	1 378	1 194	1 235	1 110	566	547	670	563	143	84
$250 TO $274	999		894		378		516		105	
$275 TO $299	547		508		206		302		39	
$300 TO $349	628	265	559	254	267	145	292	108	69	12
$350 OR MORE	610		547		249		298		63	
NO CASH RENT	1 267	1 300	625	685	282	284	343	400	642	615
MEDIAN	156	108	165	114	152	107	185	130	122	84

[1]LIMITED TO 1-FAMILY HOMES ON LESS THAN 10 ACRES AND NO BUSINESS ON PROPERTY.
[2]SUM OF PAYMENTS FOR REAL ESTATE TAXES, PROPERTY INSURANCE, UTILITIES, FUEL, WATER, GARBAGE AND TRASH COLLECTION, AND MORTGAGE AT TIME OF ENUMERATION.
[3]COMPONENTS MAY NOT ADD TO TOTAL BECAUSE MORE THAN ONE IMPROVEMENT WAS MADE.
[4]EXCLUDES 1-FAMILY HOMES ON 10 ACRES OR MORE.

FINANCIAL CHARACTERISTICS OF THE HOUSING INVENTORY: 1975 AND 1970--CONTINUED

(NUMBERS IN THOUSANDS. DATA BASED ON SAMPLE, SEE TEXT. FOR MINIMUM BASE FOR DERIVED FIGURES (PERCENT, MEDIAN, ETC.) AND MEANING OF SYMBOLS, SEE TEXT)

UNITED STATES	TOTAL		INSIDE SMSA'S: TOTAL		INSIDE SMSA'S: IN CENTRAL CITIES		INSIDE SMSA'S: NOT IN CENTRAL CITIES		OUTSIDE SMSA'S	
	1975	1970	1975	1970	1975	1970	1975	1970	1975	1970
SPECIFIED RENTER OCCUPIED[1]--CON.										
GROSS RENT--CON.										
NONSUBSIDIZED RENTER OCCUPIED[2]	22 074	NA	17 134	NA	10 053	NA	7 081	NA	4 940	NA
LESS THAN $50	376	NA	156	NA	100	NA	56	NA	220	NA
$50 TO $59	303	NA	141	NA	99	NA	42	NA	162	NA
$60 TO $69	485	NA	266	NA	205	NA	61	NA	218	NA
$70 TO $79	605	NA	356	NA	250	NA	106	NA	249	NA
$80 TO $99	1 611	NA	1 005	NA	716	NA	289	NA	606	NA
$100 TO $119	2 101	NA	1 478	NA	1 074	NA	405	NA	623	NA
$120 TO $149	3 469	NA	2 655	NA	1 835	NA	820	NA	814	NA
$150 TO $174	3 045	NA	2 511	NA	1 539	NA	972	NA	534	NA
$175 TO $199	2 857	NA	2 507	NA	1 406	NA	1 100	NA	350	NA
$200 TO $224	2 022	NA	1 810	NA	932	NA	878	NA	212	NA
$225 TO $249	1 345	NA	1 209	NA	552	NA	657	NA	136	NA
$250 TO $274	975	NA	879	NA	372	NA	506	NA	97	NA
$275 TO $299	538	NA	499	NA	200	NA	299	NA	39	NA
$300 TO $349	620	NA	553	NA	264	NA	289	NA	67	NA
$350 OR MORE	603	NA	541	NA	248	NA	293	NA	62	NA
NO CASH RENT	1 118	NA	567	NA	261	NA	307	NA	551	NA
MEDIAN	162	NA	171	NA	160	NA	189	NA	124	NA
GROSS RENT AS PERCENTAGE OF INCOME										
SPECIFIED RENTER OCCUPIED[1]	24 959	22 334	19 164	17 433	11 468	11 033	7 696	6 401	5 795	4 900
LESS THAN 10 PERCENT	1 710	2 012	1 154	1 465	696	977	458	488	557	546
10 TO 14 PERCENT	3 599	3 979	2 722	3 095	1 606	1 939	1 116	1 156	877	884
15 TO 19 PERCENT	4 095	3 786	3 195	3 043	1 846	1 848	1 349	1 195	900	742
20 TO 24 PERCENT	3 572	2 657	2 837	2 169	1 613	1 333	1 224	836	735	487
25 TO 34 PERCENT	3 990	2 936	3 192	2 387	1 911	1 520	1 282	866	798	549
35 TO 49 PERCENT	2 878	5 209	2 276	4 213	1 431	2 854	844	1 359	602	996
50 PERCENT OR MORE	3 678		3 015		1 971		1 044		662	
NOT COMPUTED	1 437	1 756	773	1 061	394	561	379	500	664	695
MEDIAN	23	20	24	21	24	21	23	20	22	19
NONSUBSIDIZED RENTER OCCUPIED[2]	22 074	NA	17 134	NA	10 053	NA	7 081	NA	4 940	NA
LESS THAN 10 PERCENT	1 525	NA	1 042	NA	611	NA	430	NA	483	NA
10 TO 14 PERCENT	3 277	NA	2 477	NA	1 432	NA	1 045	NA	800	NA
15 TO 19 PERCENT	3 595	NA	2 838	NA	1 592	NA	1 246	NA	758	NA
20 TO 24 PERCENT	2 971	NA	2 386	NA	1 295	NA	1 091	NA	586	NA
25 TO 34 PERCENT	3 473	NA	2 821	NA	1 637	NA	1 184	NA	652	NA
35 TO 49 PERCENT	2 620	NA	2 083	NA	1 307	NA	775	NA	537	NA
50 PERCENT OR MORE	3 339	NA	2 786	NA	1 817	NA	969	NA	553	NA
NOT COMPUTED	1 273	NA	703	NA	362	NA	341	NA	570	NA
MEDIAN	23	NA	24	NA	25	NA	23	NA	21	NA
CONTRACT RENT										
SPECIFIED RENTER OCCUPIED[1]	24 959	22 334	19 164	17 433	11 468	11 033	7 696	6 401	5 795	4 900
LESS THAN $50	1 810	2 969	902	1 529	658	1 065	244	463	909	1 441
$50 TO $59	968	1 651	540	1 119	391	818	149	302	428	532
$60 TO $69	1 201	2 128	755	1 580	538	1 174	217	406	446	549
$70 TO $79	1 250	2 007	831	1 598	571	1 176	260	422	419	409
$80 TO $99	2 232	3 332	1 620	2 823	1 210	1 988	410	835	613	509
$100 TO $119	2 360	2 571	1 815	2 234	1 256	1 409	559	824	545	337
$120 TO $149	4 026	3 070	3 277	2 770	2 128	1 546	1 149	1 224	748	300
$150 TO $174	3 301	2 293	2 825	2 135	1 615	1 053	1 210	1 082	476	158
$175 TO $199	2 370		2 126		1 079		1 047		244	
$200 TO $249	2 338	806	2 156	762	982	396	1 173	366	182	44
$250 TO $299	1 045		979		416		563		66	
$300 OR MORE	791	207	713	200	342	124	371	76	78	7
NO CASH RENT	1 267	1 300	625	685	282	284	343	400	642	615
MEDIAN	135	90	145	98	133	91	164	113	92	63

[1]EXCLUDES 1-FAMILY HOMES ON 10 ACRES OR MORE.
[2]EXCLUDES 1-FAMILY HOMES ON 10 ACRES OR MORE, MOBILE HOMES AND TRAILERS, HOUSING UNITS IN PUBLIC HOUSING PROJECTS, AND HOUSING UNITS WITH GOVERNMENT RENT SUBSIDIES.

SELECTED HOUSING CHARACTERISTICS FOR MOBILE HOMES AND TRAILERS: 1975

(NUMBERS IN THOUSANDS. DATA BASED ON SAMPLE, SEE TEXT. FOR MINIMUM BASE FOR DERIVED FIGURES (PERCENT, MEDIAN, ETC.) AND MEANING OF SYMBOLS, SEE TEXT)

UNITED STATES	TOTAL	INSIDE SMSA'S			OUTSIDE SMSA'S
		TOTAL	IN CENTRAL CITIES	NOT IN CENTRAL CITIES	
ALL OCCUPIED MOBILE HOMES AND TRAILERS	3 342	1 313	174	1 138	2 029
ANCHORED WITH TIEDOWNS OR OTHER MEANS					
YES	1 497	572	89	483	925
NO	1 671	675	70	605	996
DON'T KNOW	113	44	10	34	69
NOT REPORTED	60	21	5	17	39
IN GROUP OF 6 OR MORE					
YES	1 591	894	157	737	697
6 TO 99	1 044	496	103	393	548
100 OR MORE	547	398	54	344	149
NO	1 751	419	18	401	1 332
NOT REPORTED	-	-	-	-	-
SITE TENURE					
OWNER OCCUPIED[1]	2 588	1 084	151	933	1 504
SITE OWNED	826	209	6	203	617
SITE RENTED	1 645	837	141	696	808
NOT REPORTED	117	38	3	34	80
RENTER OCCUPIED	519	176	21	155	344
SITE OWNED	11	1	-	1	10
SITE RENTED	480	169	21	148	311
NOT REPORTED	29	6	-	6	23
INCOME[2]					
OWNER OCCUPIED	2 822	1 137	154	984	1 685
LESS THAN $2,000	129	43	3	40	86
$2,000 TO $2,999	165	81	21	60	84
$3,000 TO $3,999	167	76	14	62	91
$4,000 TO $4,999	185	70	3	67	115
$5,000 TO $5,999	166	64	6	58	102
$6,000 TO $6,999	169	72	9	63	97
$7,000 TO $9,999	516	203	27	176	314
$10,000 TO $14,999	698	262	42	220	436
$15,000 TO $24,999	505	214	24	190	291
$25,000 OR MORE	121	52	5	47	70
MEDIAN	9500	9400	9300	9400	9600
RENTER OCCUPIED	519	176	21	155	344
LESS THAN $2,000	64	16	4	12	48
$2,000 TO $2,999	40	15	3	12	26
$3,000 TO $3,999	44	18	2	17	26
$4,000 TO $4,999	48	14	3	11	33
$5,000 TO $5,999	37	12	2	10	25
$6,000 TO $6,999	55	21	2	20	34
$7,000 TO $9,999	103	29	2	28	74
$10,000 TO $14,999	88	34	2	32	54
$15,000 TO $24,999	30	14	2	12	16
$25,000 OR MORE	9	1	-	1	8
MEDIAN	6500	6600	...	6800	6400
OWNER OCCUPIED[1]	2 588	1 084	151	933	1 504
PURCHASE PRICE					
MOBILE HOME OR TRAILER PURCHASED	2 323	987	127	860	1 336
LESS THAN $2,500	194	107	22	86	87
$2,500 TO $4,999	540	232	38	194	308
$5,000 TO $7,499	701	240	37	203	461
$7,500 TO $9,999	454	224	19	205	231
$10,000 TO $12,499	209	92	7	85	117
$12,500 TO $14,999	106	42	5	37	64
$15,000 TO $19,999	87	35	-	35	52
$20,000 OR MORE	31	15	-	15	16
MEDIAN	6500	6600	5300	6800	6500
MOBILE HOME OR TRAILER NOT PURCHASED	32	13	5	8	18
NOT REPORTED	234	84	19	65	150
YEAR ACQUIRED					
1974 OR LATER	819	318	49	269	500
1970 TO 1973	1 218	486	55	431	733
1965 TO 1969	397	184	26	158	213
1960 TO 1964	97	65	16	49	31
1950 TO 1959	39	25	3	22	14
1949 OR EARLIER	18	5	2	4	13

[1]LIMITED TO MOBILE HOMES AND TRAILERS ON LESS THAN 10 ACRES.
[2]INCOME OF FAMILIES AND PRIMARY INDIVIDUALS IN 12 MONTHS PRECEDING DATE OF ENUMERATION; SEE TEXT.

SELECTED HOUSING CHARACTERISTICS FOR MOBILE HOMES AND TRAILERS: 1975--CONTINUED

(NUMBERS IN THOUSANDS. DATA BASED ON SAMPLE, SEE TEXT. FOR MINIMUM BASE FOR DERIVED FIGURES (PERCENT, MEDIAN, ETC.) AND MEANING OF SYMBOLS, SEE TEXT)

UNITED STATES	TOTAL	INSIDE SMSA'S			OUTSIDE SMSA'S
		TOTAL	IN CENTRAL CITIES	NOT IN CENTRAL CITIES	
OWNER OCCUPIED[1]--CONTINUED					
ACQUIRED NEW					
YES	1 600	630	63	567	970
NO	954	439	84	354	515
NOT REPORTED	35	15	4	11	20
DEBT STATUS					
INSTALLMENT LOAN OR CONTRACT	1 465	535	74	461	930
OWNED FREE AND CLEAR	1 123	549	77	472	574
SELECTED MONTHLY HOUSING COSTS[2]					
MOBILE HOMES AND TRAILERS WITH INSTALLMENT LOAN OR CONTRACT	1 465	535	74	461	930
LESS THAN $100	35	7	-	7	28
$100 TO $119	62	13	3	10	49
$120 TO $149	180	44	7	37	137
$150 TO $199	513	186	29	158	326
$200 TO $249	282	132	15	117	150
$250 TO $299	109	48	8	40	61
$300 OR MORE	46	20	-	20	26
NOT REPORTED	237	85	12	73	152
MEDIAN	182	192	185	194	176
OWNED FREE AND CLEAR	1 123	549	77	472	574
LESS THAN $50	210	67	5	62	143
$50 TO $59	110	39	4	35	70
$60 TO $79	234	95	20	75	139
$80 TO $99	167	101	20	81	66
$100 TO $149	259	184	25	160	75
$150 OR MORE	25	16	-	16	9
NOT REPORTED	119	47	3	44	72
MEDIAN	75	89	87	90	65
SELECTED MONTHLY HOUSING COSTS AS PERCENTAGE OF INCOME[2]					
MOBILE HOMES AND TRAILERS WITH INSTALLMENT LOAN OR CONTRACT	1 465	535	74	461	930
LESS THAN 10 PERCENT	55	20	3	16	36
10 TO 14 PERCENT	209	70	13	57	139
15 TO 19 PERCENT	285	106	15	91	180
20 TO 24 PERCENT	222	86	9	77	136
25 TO 34 PERCENT	251	90	13	76	161
35 TO 49 PERCENT	111	38	2	37	72
50 PERCENT OR MORE	87	38	7	31	48
NOT COMPUTED	7	2	-	2	5
NOT REPORTED	237	85	12	73	152
MEDIAN	21	22	20	22	21
OWNED FREE AND CLEAR	1 123	549	77	472	574
LESS THAN 10 PERCENT	369	166	24	143	203
10 TO 14 PERCENT	193	83	15	68	110
15 TO 19 PERCENT	133	71	5	66	63
20 TO 24 PERCENT	88	54	6	48	33
25 TO 34 PERCENT	91	49	9	40	42
35 TO 49 PERCENT	60	34	7	28	26
50 PERCENT OR MORE	69	44	9	35	25
NOT COMPUTED	1	1	-	1	-
NOT REPORTED	119	47	3	44	72
MEDIAN	13	15	14	15	12
RENTER OCCUPIED	519	176	21	155	344
GROSS RENT					
LESS THAN $60	10	3	2	1	7
$60 TO $79	24	9	-	9	15
$80 TO $99	29	8	1	6	22
$100 TO $119	53	14	1	12	39
$120 TO $149	114	37	8	29	77
$150 TO $174	96	32	1	30	64
$175 TO $199	50	25	2	24	25
$200 TO $249	27	16	-	16	11
$250 TO $299	5	1	-	1	4
$300 OR MORE	1	1	-	1	1
NO CASH RENT	109	30	5	25	79
MEDIAN	142	152	...	156	138

[1]LIMITED TO MOBILE HOMES AND TRAILERS ON LESS THAN 10 ACRES.
[2]MAY INCLUDE REAL ESTATE TAXES IF SITE IS OWNED, SITE RENTAL, PROPERTY INSURANCE, UTILITIES, FUEL, WATER, GARBAGE AND TRASH COLLECTION, AND PAYMENT ON LOAN AT TIME OF ENUMERATION.

SELECTED HOUSING CHARACTERISTICS FOR MOBILE HOMES AND TRAILERS: 1975--CONTINUED

(NUMBERS IN THOUSANDS. DATA BASED ON SAMPLE, SEE TEXT. FOR MINIMUM BASE FOR DERIVED FIGURES (PERCENT, MEDIAN, ETC.) AND MEANING OF SYMBOLS, SEE TEXT)

UNITED STATES	TOTAL	INSIDE SMSA'S			OUTSIDE SMSA'S
		TOTAL	IN CENTRAL CITIES	NOT IN CENTRAL CITIES	
RENTER OCCUPIED--CONTINUED					
GROSS RENT AS PERCENTAGE OF INCOME					
LESS THAN 10 PERCENT	30	8	2	7	22
10 TO 14 PERCENT	41	17	2	15	24
15 TO 19 PERCENT	66	21	2	19	45
20 TO 24 PERCENT	59	19	-	19	40
25 TO 34 PERCENT	80	24	2	22	56
35 TO 49 PERCENT	55	28	6	22	27
50 PERCENT OR MORE	77	27	3	24	50
NOT COMPUTED	111	31	5	26	80
MEDIAN	26	28	...	27	25
CONTRACT RENT					
CASH RENT	411	146	16	130	265
NO CASH RENT	109	30	5	25	79
MEDIAN	118	125	...	127	116
ALL OCCUPIED MOBILE HOMES AND TRAILERS	3 342	1 313	174	1 138	2 029
COMPLETE BATHROOMS					
OWNER OCCUPIED	2 822	1 137	154	984	1 685
1	1 924	793	120	673	1 131
1 AND ONE-HALF	405	160	17	143	245
2 OR MORE	453	175	16	159	278
NONE	40	9	-	9	31
RENTER OCCUPIED	519	176	21	155	344
1	443	152	21	131	291
1 AND ONE-HALF	37	9	-	9	28
2 OR MORE	31	10	-	10	21
NONE	9	5	-	5	4
ROOMS					
OWNER OCCUPIED	2 822	1 137	154	984	1 685
1 ROOM	11	6	2	5	5
2 ROOMS	94	53	10	43	41
3 ROOMS	393	196	31	165	197
4 ROOMS	1 338	549	73	475	789
5 ROOMS	769	271	30	241	498
6 ROOMS	158	48	5	42	110
7 ROOMS OR MORE	59	15	2	12	44
MEDIAN	4.2	4.1	4.0	4.1	4.3
RENTER OCCUPIED	519	176	21	155	344
1 ROOM	3	1	-	1	2
2 ROOMS	29	10	4	6	18
3 ROOMS	138	45	6	39	93
4 ROOMS	250	83	11	72	167
5 ROOMS	91	36	-	36	55
6 ROOMS	4	2	-	2	3
7 ROOMS OR MORE	4	-	-	-	4
MEDIAN	3.9	3.9	...	3.9	3.8
BEDROOMS					
OWNER OCCUPIED	2 822	1 137	154	984	1 685
NONE AND 1	307	181	30	151	126
2	1 770	748	93	654	1 023
3 OR MORE	746	209	30	179	537
RENTER OCCUPIED	519	176	21	155	344
NONE	3	1	-	1	2
1	87	34	9	25	53
2	335	109	12	97	226
3 OR MORE	95	32	-	32	63

SELECTED HOUSING CHARACTERISTICS FOR MOBILE HOMES AND TRAILERS: 1975--CONTINUED

(NUMBERS IN THOUSANDS. DATA BASED ON SAMPLE, SEE TEXT. FOR MINIMUM BASE FOR DERIVED FIGURES (PERCENT, MEDIAN, ETC.) AND MEANING OF SYMBOLS, SEE TEXT)

UNITED STATES	TOTAL	INSIDE SMSA'S			OUTSIDE SMSA'S
		TOTAL	IN CENTRAL CITIES	NOT IN CENTRAL CITIES	
ALL OCCUPIED MOBILE HOMES AND TRAILERS--CONTINUED					
PERSONS					
OWNER OCCUPIED	2 822	1 137	154	984	1 685
1 PERSON	541	274	58	216	267
2 PERSONS	1 129	494	68	427	635
3 PERSONS	507	167	16	151	340
4 PERSONS	394	127	8	119	267
5 PERSONS	163	50	3	46	113
6 PERSONS	41	12	-	12	28
7 PERSONS OR MORE	48	13	1	12	35
MEDIAN	2.3	2.1	1.8	2.1	2.4
RENTER OCCUPIED	519	176	21	155	344
1 PERSON	145	49	11	38	96
2 PERSONS	153	47	4	43	106
3 PERSONS	106	37	2	35	69
4 PERSONS	75	29	1	27	47
5 PERSONS	25	8	-	8	16
6 PERSONS	13	5	3	2	8
7 PERSONS OR MORE	3	1	-	1	2
MEDIAN	2.3	2.3	...	2.4	2.2
PERSONS PER ROOM					
OWNER OCCUPIED	2 822	1 137	154	984	1 685
0.50 OR LESS	1 481	667	114	553	815
0.51 TO 1.00	1 192	420	36	384	772
1.01 TO 1.50	115	34	2	33	80
1.51 OR MORE	34	16	2	14	18
RENTER OCCUPIED	519	176	21	155	344
0.50 OR LESS	246	77	13	64	169
0.51 TO 1.00	231	84	5	79	147
1.01 TO 1.50	36	11	3	8	25
1.51 OR MORE	6	3	-	3	3
HOUSEHOLD COMPOSITION BY AGE OF HEAD					
OWNER OCCUPIED	2 822	1 137	154	984	1 685
2-OR-MORE-PERSON HOUSEHOLDS	2 281	863	95	768	1 418
MALE HEAD, WIFE PRESENT, NO NONRELATIVES	1 997	769	80	689	1 227
UNDER 25 YEARS	348	112	15	97	236
25 TO 29 YEARS	355	104	11	93	251
30 TO 34 YEARS	248	96	9	88	151
35 TO 44 YEARS	277	101	2	98	176
45 TO 64 YEARS	494	218	29	189	276
65 YEARS AND OVER	274	138	14	124	136
OTHER MALE HEAD	81	29	9	20	51
UNDER 65 YEARS	72	26	9	17	46
65 YEARS AND OVER	8	3	-	3	5
FEMALE HEAD	204	65	5	60	139
UNDER 65 YEARS	183	58	4	55	125
65 YEARS AND OVER	21	7	2	5	14
1-PERSON HOUSEHOLDS	541	274	58	216	267
UNDER 65 YEARS	337	163	43	120	174
65 YEARS AND OVER	204	111	16	96	93
RENTER OCCUPIED	519	176	21	155	344
2-OR-MORE-PERSON HOUSEHOLDS	375	127	10	117	248
MALE HEAD, WIFE PRESENT, NO NONRELATIVES	260	84	5	79	177
UNDER 25 YEARS	97	24	-	24	72
25 TO 29 YEARS	65	28	-	28	37
30 TO 34 YEARS	35	12	3	9	23
35 TO 44 YEARS	29	7	-	7	21
45 TO 64 YEARS	32	11	2	10	21
65 YEARS AND OVER	4	1	-	1	3
OTHER MALE HEAD	45	15	-	15	30
UNDER 65 YEARS	45	15	-	15	30
65 YEARS AND OVER	-	-	-	-	-
FEMALE HEAD	70	29	5	24	41
UNDER 65 YEARS	68	28	5	23	40
65 YEARS AND OVER	2	1	-	1	1
1-PERSON HOUSEHOLDS	145	49	11	38	96
UNDER 65 YEARS	106	38	10	28	68
65 YEARS AND OVER	38	11	2	9	27

SELECTED HOUSING CHARACTERISTICS FOR MOBILE HOMES AND TRAILERS: 1975--CONTINUED

(NUMBERS IN THOUSANDS. DATA BASED ON SAMPLE, SEE TEXT. FOR MINIMUM BASE FOR DERIVED FIGURES (PERCENT, MEDIAN, ETC.) AND MEANING OF SYMBOLS, SEE TEXT)

UNITED STATES	TOTAL	INSIDE SMSA'S			OUTSIDE SMSA'S
		TOTAL	IN CENTRAL CITIES	NOT IN CENTRAL CITIES	
ALL OCCUPIED MOBILE HOMES AND TRAILERS--CONTINUED					
OWN CHILDREN UNDER 18 YEARS OLD BY AGE GROUP					
OWNER OCCUPIED	2 822	1 137	154	984	1 685
NO OWN CHILDREN UNDER 18 YEARS	1 707	782	123	660	924
WITH OWN CHILDREN UNDER 18 YEARS	1 116	355	31	324	761
UNDER 6 YEARS ONLY	434	139	8	130	296
1	294	99	8	91	195
2	128	38	1	37	90
3 OR MORE	12	1	-	1	11
6 TO 17 YEARS ONLY	471	149	18	131	322
1	221	78	14	64	142
2	152	45	4	41	107
3 OR MORE	98	25	-	25	73
BOTH AGE GROUPS	210	67	4	63	143
2	99	31	2	30	68
3 OR MORE	111	36	3	34	75
RENTER OCCUPIED	519	176	21	155	344
NO OWN CHILDREN UNDER 18 YEARS	297	94	14	79	203
WITH OWN CHILDREN UNDER 18 YEARS	222	82	7	75	141
UNDER 6 YEARS ONLY	115	42	2	40	73
1	74	23	2	21	51
2	39	19	-	19	20
3 OR MORE	2	-	-	-	2
6 TO 17 YEARS ONLY	68	23	1	22	45
1	30	10	-	10	20
2	23	11	-	11	12
3 OR MORE	16	3	1	1	13
BOTH AGE GROUPS	39	17	3	14	22
2	16	5	-	5	11
3 OR MORE	23	12	3	9	11
YEARS OF SCHOOL COMPLETED BY HEAD					
OWNER OCCUPIED	2 822	1 137	154	984	1 685
NO SCHOOL YEARS COMPLETED	7	1	-	1	6
ELEMENTARY: LESS THAN 8 YEARS	248	84	6	79	163
8 YEARS	368	167	24	143	201
HIGH SCHOOL: 1 TO 3 YEARS	569	226	34	192	344
4 YEARS	1 090	421	54	367	669
COLLEGE: 1 TO 3 YEARS	327	138	27	111	189
4 YEARS OR MORE	213	100	10	90	113
MEDIAN	12.2	12.2	12.3	12.2	12.2
RENTER OCCUPIED	519	176	21	155	344
NO SCHOOL YEARS COMPLETED	1	1	-	1	-
ELEMENTARY: LESS THAN 8 YEARS	47	14	4	10	33
8 YEARS	58	12	3	9	47
HIGH SCHOOL: 1 TO 3 YEARS	117	38	4	35	78
4 YEARS	206	78	7	72	128
COLLEGE: 1 TO 3 YEARS	61	20	1	19	40
4 YEARS OR MORE	30	12	2	11	18
MEDIAN	12.2	12.3	...	12.3	12.1
STORM WINDOWS OR OTHER PROTECTIVE WINDOW COVERING					
ALL WINDOWS COVERED	1 518	514	70	444	1 004
SOME WINDOWS COVERED	171	63	8	55	108
NO WINDOWS COVERED	1 649	736	97	639	913
NOT REPORTED	4	-	-	-	4
STORM DOORS					
ALL DOORS COVERED	1 007	315	44	271	693
SOME DOORS COVERED	480	166	20	146	314
NO DOORS COVERED	1 852	832	110	721	1 020
NOT REPORTED	3	1	-	1	2
ATTIC OR ROOF INSULATION					
YES	2 805	1 058	129	929	1 747
NO	219	96	22	74	123
DON'T KNOW	296	149	22	127	147
NOT REPORTED	22	10	2	8	12

SELECTED HOUSING CHARACTERISTICS FOR NEW CONSTRUCTION UNITS: 1975

(NUMBERS IN THOUSANDS. DATA BASED ON SAMPLE, SEE TEXT. RESTRICTED TO UNITS BUILT APRIL 1970 OR LATER. FOR MINIMUM BASE FOR DERIVED FIGURES (PERCENT, MEDIAN, ETC.) AND MEANING OF SYMBOLS, SEE TEXT)

UNITED STATES	TOTAL	INSIDE SMSA'S			OUTSIDE SMSA'S
		TOTAL	IN CENTRAL CITIES	NOT IN CENTRAL CITIES	
ALL HOUSING UNITS	11 334	7 481	2 406	5 075	3 853
VACANT--SEASONAL AND MIGRATORY	122	31	2	29	91
TENURE, RACE, AND VACANCY STATUS					
ALL YEAR-ROUND HOUSING UNITS	11 212	7 450	2 404	5 046	3 762
OCCUPIED UNITS	10 180	6 664	2 153	4 511	3 516
OWNER OCCUPIED	6 527	3 671	812	2 859	2 856
PERCENT OF ALL OCCUPIED	64.1	55.1	37.7	63.4	81.2
WHITE	6 079	3 425	706	2 720	2 654
BLACK	342	173	83	91	169
RENTER OCCUPIED	3 653	2 993	1 341	1 652	660
WHITE	3 201	2 606	1 108	1 497	595
BLACK	371	322	203	119	49
VACANT YEAR-ROUND UNITS	1 031	786	251	535	246
FOR SALE ONLY	249	186	54	132	63
FOR RENT	345	301	133	168	44
OTHER VACANT	437	299	64	235	139
COOPERATIVES AND CONDOMINIUMS					
OWNER OCCUPIED	392	363	92	271	30
COOPERATIVE OWNERSHIP	53	44	19	25	9
CONDOMINIUM OWNERSHIP	340	319	73	246	21
VACANT FOR SALE ONLY	109	93	27	66	16
COOPERATIVE OWNERSHIP	2	1	-	1	1
CONDOMINIUM OWNERSHIP	107	92	27	65	15
UNITS IN STRUCTURE					
ALL YEAR-ROUND HOUSING UNITS	11 212	7 450	2 404	5 046	3 762
1	5 530	3 386	802	2 584	2 144
2 TO 4	900	705	318	387	195
5 OR MORE	3 161	2 829	1 246	1 584	332
MOBILE HOME OR TRAILER	1 621	530	39	491	1 091
OWNER OCCUPIED	6 527	3 671	812	2 859	2 856
1	4 670	2 856	671	2 185	1 814
2 TO 4	197	162	60	102	35
5 OR MORE	167	158	44	115	9
MOBILE HOME OR TRAILER	1 492	495	37	458	997
RENTER OCCUPIED	3 653	2 993	1 341	1 652	660
1	434	272	82	190	162
2 TO 4	597	457	228	229	140
5 TO 19	1 429	1 247	548	699	182
20 TO 49	527	482	179	303	46
50 OR MORE	536	499	302	198	37
MOBILE HOME OR TRAILER	129	35	2	33	94
PLUMBING FACILITIES					
ALL YEAR-ROUND HOUSING UNITS	11 212	7 450	2 404	5 046	3 762
WITH ALL PLUMBING FACILITIES	11 152	7 436	2 401	5 035	3 716
LACKING SOME OR ALL PLUMBING FACILITIES	59	14	4	10	46
OWNER OCCUPIED	6 527	3 671	812	2 859	2 856
WITH ALL PLUMBING FACILITIES	6 492	3 666	812	2 853	2 827
LACKING SOME OR ALL PLUMBING FACILITIES	35	6	-	6	29
RENTER OCCUPIED	3 653	2 993	1 341	1 652	660
WITH ALL PLUMBING FACILITIES	3 639	2 986	1 338	1 648	654
LACKING SOME OR ALL PLUMBING FACILITIES	14	7	4	3	7

SELECTED HOUSING CHARACTERISTICS FOR NEW CONSTRUCTION UNITS: 1975--CONTINUED

(NUMBERS IN THOUSANDS. DATA BASED ON SAMPLE, SEE TEXT. RESTRICTED TO UNITS BUILT APRIL 1970 OR LATER. FOR MINIMUM BASE FOR DERIVED FIGURES (PERCENT, MEDIAN, ETC.) AND MEANING OF SYMBOLS, SEE TEXT)

UNITED STATES	TOTAL	INSIDE SMSA'S			OUTSIDE SMSA'S
		TOTAL	IN CENTRAL CITIES	NOT IN CENTRAL CITIES	
COMPLETE BATHROOMS					
ALL YEAR-ROUND HOUSING UNITS	11 212	7 450	2 404	5 046	3 762
1	5 112	3 318	1 320	1 998	1 794
1 AND ONE-HALF	1 906	1 230	333	897	676
2 OR MORE	4 116	2 873	739	2 133	1 243
ALSO USED BY ANOTHER HOUSEHOLD	2	-	-	-	2
NONE	76	29	12	18	47
OWNER OCCUPIED	6 527	3 671	812	2 859	2 856
1	2 024	839	164	675	1 185
1 AND ONE-HALF	1 252	709	161	547	543
2 OR MORE	3 214	2 118	487	1 631	1 096
ALSO USED BY ANOTHER HOUSEHOLD	-	-	-	-	-
NONE	37	6	-	6	31
RENTER OCCUPIED	3 653	2 993	1 341	1 652	660
1	2 611	2 122	1 005	1 117	489
1 AND ONE-HALF	474	385	130	255	89
2 OR MORE	539	464	194	270	75
ALSO USED BY ANOTHER HOUSEHOLD	2	-	-	-	2
NONE	27	21	12	9	6
ROOMS					
ALL YEAR-ROUND HOUSING UNITS	11 212	7 450	2 404	5 046	3 762
1 ROOM	118	94	53	41	24
2 ROOMS	271	203	106	98	68
3 ROOMS	1 413	1 134	521	613	279
4 ROOMS	2 828	1 892	622	1 270	935
5 ROOMS	2 780	1 625	495	1 130	1 155
6 ROOMS	1 771	1 087	306	781	684
7 ROOMS OR MORE	2 030	1 413	301	1 113	617
MEDIAN	4.8	4.7	4.3	4.9	5.0
OWNER OCCUPIED	6 527	3 671	812	2 859	2 856
1 ROOM	9	3	-	3	6
2 ROOMS	27	11	2	9	15
3 ROOMS	210	104	16	88	106
4 ROOMS	1 130	515	83	432	614
5 ROOMS	1 883	917	219	698	967
6 ROOMS	1 418	847	222	626	571
7 ROOMS OR MORE	1 850	1 275	270	1 004	576
MEDIAN	5.5	5.8	5.9	5.8	5.2
RENTER OCCUPIED	3 653	2 993	1 341	1 652	660
1 ROOM	89	77	44	33	12
2 ROOMS	198	155	83	72	43
3 ROOMS	1 041	900	461	439	141
4 ROOMS	1 394	1 129	452	676	266
5 ROOMS	653	523	219	304	130
6 ROOMS	213	160	71	89	52
7 ROOMS OR MORE	66	49	12	37	17
MEDIAN	3.8	3.8	3.7	3.9	4.0
BEDROOMS					
ALL YEAR-ROUND HOUSING UNITS	11 212	7 450	2 404	5 046	3 762
NONE	138	112	65	47	26
1	1 644	1 399	639	760	245
2	3 810	2 515	824	1 691	1 296
3	4 282	2 437	627	1 810	1 845
4 OR MORE	1 338	988	250	738	350
OWNER OCCUPIED	6 527	3 671	812	2 859	2 856
NONE AND 1	178	108	24	85	70
2	1 671	804	139	665	868
3	3 499	1 897	446	1 451	1 602
4 OR MORE	1 178	862	204	659	316
RENTER OCCUPIED	3 653	2 993	1 341	1 652	660
NONE	99	87	49	37	12
1	1 271	1 123	548	575	149
2	1 707	1 366	566	800	341
3	493	354	145	209	139
4 OR MORE	83	64	33	31	19

SELECTED HOUSING CHARACTERISTICS FOR NEW CONSTRUCTION UNITS: 1975--CONTINUED

(NUMBERS IN THOUSANDS. DATA BASED ON SAMPLE, SEE TEXT. RESTRICTED TO UNITS BUILT APRIL 1970 OR LATER. FOR MINIMUM BASE FOR DERIVED FIGURES (PERCENT, MEDIAN, ETC.) AND MEANING OF SYMBOLS, SEE TEXT)

UNITED STATES	TOTAL	INSIDE SMSA'S			OUTSIDE SMSA'S
		TOTAL	IN CENTRAL CITIES	NOT IN CENTRAL CITIES	
ALL OCCUPIED HOUSING UNITS. . .	10 180	6 664	2 153	4 511	3 516
PERSONS					
OWNER OCCUPIED.	6 527	3 671	812	2 859	2 856
1 PERSON.	491	286	82	204	205
2 PERSONS	1 772	947	177	770	825
3 PERSONS	1 338	749	166	583	589
4 PERSONS	1 562	907	202	705	655
5 PERSONS	805	469	113	356	337
6 PERSONS	312	189	46	143	123
7 PERSONS OR MORE	246	124	26	98	122
MEDIAN.	3.2	3.3	3.4	3.3	3.2
RENTER OCCUPIED	3 653	2 993	1 341	1 652	660
1 PERSON.	1 100	923	461	462	177
2 PERSONS	1 302	1 108	474	634	193
3 PERSONS	662	509	211	299	152
4 PERSONS	326	257	99	158	69
5 PERSONS	146	107	50	57	39
6 PERSONS	61	44	21	23	16
7 PERSONS OR MORE	57	43	25	19	14
MEDIAN.	2.0	2.0	1.9	2.1	2.3
PERSONS PER ROOM					
OWNER OCCUPIED.	6 527	3 671	812	2 859	2 856
0.50 OR LESS.	3 137	1 871	400	1 471	1 265
0.51 TO 1.00.	3 098	1 673	386	1 287	1 426
1.01 TO 1.50.	244	112	22	90	131
1.51 OR MORE.	49	15	4	11	34
RENTER OCCUPIED	3 653	2 993	1 341	1 652	660
0.50 OR LESS.	1 918	1 601	716	885	317
0.51 TO 1.00.	1 594	1 294	574	720	300
1.01 TO 1.50.	123	83	45	38	40
1.51 OR MORE.	18	14	6	8	4
HOUSEHOLD COMPOSITION BY AGE OF HEAD					
OWNER OCCUPIED.	6 527	3 671	812	2 859	2 856
2-OR-MORE-PERSON HOUSEHOLDS	6 036	3 385	730	2 655	2 650
MALE HEAD, WIFE PRESENT, NO NONRELATIVES.	5 479	3 089	642	2 448	2 390
UNDER 25 YEARS.	427	181	30	150	247
25 TO 29 YEARS.	1 009	563	131	432	446
30 TO 34 YEARS.	1 021	606	96	509	416
35 TO 44 YEARS.	1 344	831	181	650	513
45 TO 64 YEARS.	1 348	748	181	568	600
65 YEARS AND OVER	330	161	22	139	169
OTHER MALE HEAD	154	84	20	64	70
UNDER 65 YEARS.	141	79	20	58	63
65 YEARS AND OVER	13	5	-	5	8
FEMALE HEAD	402	212	68	144	190
UNDER 65 YEARS.	370	199	64	135	172
65 YEARS AND OVER	32	13	4	9	18
1-PERSON HOUSEHOLDS	491	286	82	204	205
UNDER 65 YEARS.	366	224	65	159	142
65 YEARS AND OVER	125	62	17	45	63
RENTER OCCUPIED	3 653	2 993	1 341	1 652	660
2-OR-MORE-PERSON HOUSEHOLDS	2 553	2 070	880	1 190	483
MALE HEAD, WIFE PRESENT, NO NONRELATIVES.	1 720	1 381	533	848	340
UNDER 25 YEARS.	458	364	145	218	94
25 TO 29 YEARS.	471	384	145	238	88
30 TO 34 YEARS.	224	177	72	105	48
35 TO 44 YEARS.	186	152	47	105	34
45 TO 64 YEARS.	260	204	75	128	56
65 YEARS AND OVER	121	101	49	52	20
OTHER MALE HEAD	258	225	102	123	33
UNDER 65 YEARS.	254	221	98	122	33
65 YEARS AND OVER	5	5	4	1	-
FEMALE HEAD	574	463	245	218	111
UNDER 65 YEARS.	543	439	227	212	104
65 YEARS AND OVER	31	24	18	6	7
1-PERSON HOUSEHOLDS	1 100	923	461	462	177
UNDER 65 YEARS.	814	712	334	377	103
65 YEARS AND OVER	286	211	127	85	74

SELECTED HOUSING CHARACTERISTICS FOR NEW CONSTRUCTION UNITS: 1975--CONTINUED

(NUMBERS IN THOUSANDS. DATA BASED ON SAMPLE, SEE TEXT. RESTRICTED TO UNITS BUILT APRIL 1970 OR LATER. FOR MINIMUM BASE FOR DERIVED FIGURES (PERCENT, MEDIAN, ETC.) AND MEANING OF SYMBOLS, SEE TEXT)

UNITED STATES	TOTAL	INSIDE SMSA'S			OUTSIDE SMSA'S
		TOTAL	IN CENTRAL CITIES	NOT IN CENTRAL CITIES	
ALL OCCUPIED HOUSING UNITS--CON.					
OWN CHILDREN UNDER 18 YEARS OLD BY AGE GROUP					
OWNER OCCUPIED	6 527	3 671	812	2 859	2 856
NO OWN CHILDREN UNDER 18 YEARS	2 574	1 421	309	1 112	1 153
WITH OWN CHILDREN UNDER 18 YEARS	3 953	2 250	503	1 747	1 703
UNDER 6 YEARS ONLY	1 150	644	137	507	506
1	683	373	77	296	310
2	414	250	60	189	164
3 OR MORE	54	22	-	22	32
6 TO 17 YEARS ONLY	1 838	1 053	229	825	785
1	632	356	77	278	277
2	693	402	91	311	290
3 OR MORE	513	296	61	235	218
BOTH AGE GROUPS	964	552	137	415	412
2	418	242	59	183	176
3 OR MORE	547	311	79	232	236
RENTER OCCUPIED	3 653	2 993	1 341	1 652	660
NO OWN CHILDREN UNDER 18 YEARS	2 432	2 040	938	1 103	391
WITH OWN CHILDREN UNDER 18 YEARS	1 221	952	403	549	269
UNDER 6 YEARS ONLY	519	409	160	249	110
1	378	300	131	169	78
2	126	97	24	73	29
3 OR MORE	15	12	5	7	3
6 TO 17 YEARS ONLY	471	363	155	209	107
1	223	174	67	107	49
2	140	117	52	65	23
3 OR MORE	107	73	36	37	34
BOTH AGE GROUPS	232	180	89	91	52
2	98	82	36	46	16
3 OR MORE	134	98	53	45	36
YEARS OF SCHOOL COMPLETED BY HEAD					
OWNER OCCUPIED	6 527	3 671	812	2 859	2 856
NO SCHOOL YEARS COMPLETED	16	8	2	6	8
ELEMENTARY: LESS THAN 8 YEARS	338	127	28	99	211
8 YEARS	413	173	27	146	240
HIGH SCHOOL: 1 TO 3 YEARS	801	363	66	297	439
4 YEARS	2 270	1 156	236	920	1 114
COLLEGE: 1 TO 3 YEARS	1 162	748	199	550	414
4 YEARS OR MORE	1 527	1 097	254	842	430
MEDIAN	12.7	13.0	13.8	12.9	12.5
RENTER OCCUPIED	3 653	2 993	1 341	1 652	660
NO SCHOOL YEARS COMPLETED	8	7	1	6	1
ELEMENTARY: LESS THAN 8 YEARS	178	125	70	55	53
8 YEARS	152	97	62	35	55
HIGH SCHOOL: 1 TO 3 YEARS	378	283	126	157	95
4 YEARS	1 205	992	406	586	213
COLLEGE: 1 TO 3 YEARS	845	728	326	402	117
4 YEARS OR MORE	887	761	349	412	126
MEDIAN	12.9	13.0	13.0	13.0	12.6
INCOME[1]					
OWNER OCCUPIED	6 527	3 671	812	2 859	2 856
LESS THAN $2,000	134	53	10	42	82
$2,000 TO $2,999	130	55	11	44	75
$3,000 TO $3,999	145	51	10	40	94
$4,000 TO $4,999	163	56	8	48	107
$5,000 TO $5,999	210	76	19	56	134
$6,000 TO $6,999	222	86	17	69	136
$7,000 TO $7,999	254	101	21	80	152
$8,000 TO $9,999	505	223	60	163	282
$10,000 TO $12,499	740	355	81	274	385
$12,500 TO $14,999	671	358	78	280	313
$15,000 TO $24,999	2 192	1 407	298	1 108	785
$25,000 TO $34,999	714	516	118	398	198
$35,000 OR MORE	446	335	80	255	111
MEDIAN	15400	18000	18000	18000	12400

[1]INCOME OF FAMILIES AND PRIMARY INDIVIDUALS IN 12 MONTHS PRECEDING DATE OF ENUMERATION; SEE TEXT.

SELECTED HOUSING CHARACTERISTICS FOR NEW CONSTRUCTION UNITS: 1975--CONTINUED

(NUMBERS IN THOUSANDS. DATA BASED ON SAMPLE, SEE TEXT. RESTRICTED TO UNITS BUILT APRIL 1970 OR LATER. FOR MINIMUM BASE FOR DERIVED FIGURES (PERCENT, MEDIAN, ETC.) AND MEANING OF SYMBOLS, SEE TEXT)

UNITED STATES	TOTAL	INSIDE SMSA'S			OUTSIDE SMSA'S
		TOTAL	IN CENTRAL CITIES	NOT IN CENTRAL CITIES	
ALL OCCUPIED HOUSING UNITS--CON.					
INCOME[1]--CON.					
RENTER OCCUPIED	3 653	2 993	1 341	1 652	660
LESS THAN $2,000	179	128	84	44	51
$2,000 TO $2,999	199	128	87	41	71
$3,000 TO $3,999	228	176	94	82	52
$4,000 TO $4,999	174	143	82	62	30
$5,000 TO $5,999	192	146	80	66	45
$6,000 TO $6,999	254	210	109	101	44
$7,000 TO $7,999	184	155	69	86	30
$8,000 TO $9,999	414	330	134	196	84
$10,000 TO $12,499	457	374	150	224	83
$12,500 TO $14,999	383	331	129	202	52
$15,000 TO $24,999	751	665	245	420	86
$25,000 TO $34,999	142	119	38	81	24
$35,000 OR MORE	95	87	41	46	8
MEDIAN	10000	10500	9000	11600	8200
SPECIFIED OWNER OCCUPIED[2]	4 206	2 639	641	1 998	1 567
VALUE					
LESS THAN $5,000	12	3	-	3	10
$5,000 TO $7,499	27	3	1	1	24
$7,500 TO $9,999	17	4	3	1	12
$10,000 TO $12,499	37	11	6	4	27
$12,500 TO $14,999	35	7	-	7	28
$15,000 TO $17,499	83	18	6	12	65
$17,500 TO $19,999	131	54	21	33	77
$20,000 TO $24,999	359	179	61	117	180
$25,000 TO $29,999	454	244	60	184	209
$30,000 TO $34,999	508	307	92	215	202
$35,000 TO $39,999	570	362	93	269	208
$40,000 TO $49,999	871	607	152	455	264
$50,000 TO $59,999	452	319	55	264	132
$60,000 TO $74,999	346	270	47	223	76
$75,000 OR MORE	303	250	41	209	53
MEDIAN	38900	42100	38600	43400	33700
VALUE-INCOME RATIO					
LESS THAN 1.5	595	352	98	253	243
1.5 TO 1.9	881	605	168	437	276
2.0 TO 2.4	827	545	133	412	282
2.5 TO 2.9	654	432	96	336	222
3.0 TO 3.9	656	401	85	316	255
4.0 OR MORE	577	299	59	239	279
NOT COMPUTED	15	5	2	4	10
MEDIAN	2.4	2.3	2.2	2.4	2.4
MORTGAGE INSURANCE					
UNITS WITH MORTGAGE OR SIMILAR DEBT	3 707	2 423	589	1 834	1 284
INSURED BY FHA, VA, OR FARMERS HOME ADMIN	1 216	795	258	537	421
NOT INSURED OR INSURED BY PRIVATE MORTGAGE INSURANCE[3]	1 797	1 174	228	946	622
DON'T KNOW	426	278	58	220	147
NOT REPORTED	269	175	44	131	94
UNITS OWNED FREE AND CLEAR	498	216	52	164	282

[1]INCOME OF FAMILIES AND PRIMARY INDIVIDUALS IN 12 MONTHS PRECEDING DATE OF ENUMERATION; SEE TEXT.
[2]LIMITED TO 1-FAMILY HOMES ON LESS THAN 10 ACRES AND NO BUSINESS ON PROPERTY.
[3]DATA ARE NOT SEPARABLE.

SELECTED HOUSING CHARACTERISTICS FOR NEW CONSTRUCTION UNITS: 1975--CONTINUED

(NUMBERS IN THOUSANDS. DATA BASED ON SAMPLE, SEE TEXT. RESTRICTED TO UNITS BUILT APRIL 1970 OR LATER. FOR MINIMUM BASE FOR DERIVED FIGURES (PERCENT, MEDIAN, ETC.) AND MEANING OF SYMBOLS, SEE TEXT)

UNITED STATES	TOTAL	INSIDE SMSA'S			OUTSIDE SMSA'S
		TOTAL	IN CENTRAL CITIES	NOT IN CENTRAL CITIES	
SPECIFIED OWNER OCCUPIED[1] --CON.					
REAL ESTATE TAXES LAST YEAR					
LESS THAN $100	400	152	32	120	248
$100 TO $199	288	85	24	62	202
$200 TO $299	324	148	31	117	176
$300 TO $349	194	107	18	89	87
$350 TO $399	141	86	18	68	55
$400 TO $499	310	208	53	155	101
$500 TO $599	251	164	38	126	87
$600 TO $699	254	190	46	144	64
$700 TO $799	194	167	49	118	26
$800 TO $999	264	225	62	163	39
$1,000 OR MORE	467	406	61	345	61
NOT REPORTED	1 118	699	208	491	419
MEDIAN	463	610	604	611	269
SELECTED MONTHLY HOUSING COSTS[2]					
UNITS WITH A MORTGAGE	3 707	2 423	589	1 834	1 284
LESS THAN $100	32	7	3	4	25
$100 TO $119	35	10	1	9	25
$120 TO $149	112	33	8	25	80
$150 TO $174	126	45	13	33	81
$175 TO $199	178	84	21	63	94
$200 TO $224	250	141	50	91	108
$225 TO $249	256	159	42	117	98
$250 TO $274	278	187	63	124	91
$275 TO $299	297	201	52	149	96
$300 TO $349	545	389	88	302	156
$350 TO $399	437	345	83	262	92
$400 TO $499	446	352	77	275	94
$500 OR MORE	237	207	39	168	30
NOT REPORTED	476	262	50	213	214
MEDIAN	304	327	309	332	256
UNITS OWNED FREE AND CLEAR	498	216	52	164	282
SELECTED MONTHLY HOUSING COSTS AS PERCENTAGE OF INCOME[2]					
UNITS WITH A MORTGAGE	3 707	2 423	589	1 834	1 284
LESS THAN 5 PERCENT	6	2	2	1	4
5 TO 9 PERCENT	102	56	9	46	46
10 TO 14 PERCENT	405	263	65	198	142
15 TO 19 PERCENT	853	602	159	443	251
20 TO 24 PERCENT	789	539	130	409	250
25 TO 29 PERCENT	511	341	77	264	170
30 TO 34 PERCENT	242	161	45	117	81
35 TO 39 PERCENT	99	64	16	48	35
40 TO 49 PERCENT	90	54	16	38	36
50 PERCENT OR MORE	127	74	21	54	53
NOT COMPUTED	7	4	-	4	4
NOT REPORTED	476	262	50	213	214
MEDIAN	22	21	21	21	22
UNITS OWNED FREE AND CLEAR	498	216	52	164	282
SPECIFIED RENTER OCCUPIED[3]	3 627	2 989	1 341	1 648	638
GROSS RENT					
LESS THAN $50	90	65	55	10	25
$50 TO $59	77	54	35	19	23
$60 TO $69	79	53	32	21	26
$70 TO $79	44	31	19	12	13
$80 TO $99	59	30	26	4	29
$100 TO $119	81	46	28	18	35
$120 TO $149	285	194	118	76	92
$150 TO $174	495	384	193	191	111
$175 TO $199	579	503	260	243	76
$200 TO $224	490	450	189	262	39
$225 TO $249	392	363	123	240	29
$250 TO $274	301	268	68	200	33
$275 TO $299	178	168	57	111	11
$300 TO $349	192	172	70	102	19
$350 OR MORE	184	165	60	105	20
NO CASH RENT	101	44	11	34	57
MEDIAN	198	206	190	220	160

[1]LIMITED TO 1-FAMILY HOMES ON LESS THAN 10 ACRES AND NO BUSINESS ON PROPERTY.
[2]SUM OF PAYMENTS FOR REAL ESTATE TAXES, PROPERTY INSURANCE, UTILITIES, FUEL, WATER, GARBAGE AND TRASH COLLECTION, AND MORTGAGE AT TIME OF ENUMERATION.
[3]EXCLUDES 1-FAMILY HOMES ON 10 ACRES OR MORE.

SELECTED HOUSING CHARACTERISTICS FOR NEW CONSTRUCTION UNITS: 1975--CONTINUED

(NUMBERS IN THOUSANDS. DATA BASED ON SAMPLE, SEE TEXT. RESTRICTED TO UNITS BUILT APRIL 1970 OR LATER. FOR MINIMUM BASE FOR DERIVED FIGURES (PERCENT, MEDIAN, ETC.) AND MEANING OF SYMBOLS, SEE TEXT)

UNITED STATES	TOTAL	INSIDE SMSA'S			OUTSIDE SMSA'S
		TOTAL	IN CENTRAL CITIES	NOT IN CENTRAL CITIES	
SPECIFIED RENTER OCCUPIED[1]--CON.					
GROSS RENT AS PERCENTAGE OF INCOME					
LESS THAN 10 PERCENT	143	114	55	59	29
10 TO 14 PERCENT	492	413	175	238	79
15 TO 19 PERCENT	651	528	225	303	123
20 TO 24 PERCENT	698	598	246	352	100
25 TO 34 PERCENT	699	588	270	318	111
35 TO 49 PERCENT	391	337	169	169	54
50 PERCENT OR MORE	443	360	186	174	83
NOT COMPUTED	110	51	14	36	59
MEDIAN	23	23	24	23	23
CONTRACT RENT					
CASH RENT	3 526	2 945	1 331	1 614	581
NO CASH RENT	101	44	11	34	57
MEDIAN	179	186	172	196	141
HEATING EQUIPMENT					
ALL YEAR-ROUND HOUSING UNITS	11 212	7 450	2 404	5 046	3 762
WARM-AIR FURNACE	8 076	5 488	1 754	3 734	2 589
STEAM OR HOT WATER	833	631	210	421	202
BUILT-IN ELECTRIC UNITS	1 704	1 017	341	676	688
FLOOR, WALL, OR PIPELESS FURNACE	269	178	76	102	91
OTHER MEANS	275	87	23	64	188
NONE	54	49	-	49	5
OWNER OCCUPIED	6 527	3 671	812	2 859	2 856
WARM-AIR FURNACE	5 163	3 067	692	2 375	2 096
STEAM OR HOT WATER	311	177	29	148	133
BUILT-IN ELECTRIC UNITS	746	308	62	246	437
FLOOR, WALL, OR PIPELESS FURNACE	101	43	16	27	58
OTHER MEANS	184	55	13	42	129
NONE	23	20	-	20	2
RENTER OCCUPIED	3 653	2 993	1 341	1 652	660
WARM-AIR FURNACE	2 219	1 858	882	976	360
STEAM OR HOT WATER	456	399	167	232	57
BUILT-IN ELECTRIC UNITS	752	571	228	343	180
FLOOR, WALL, OR PIPELESS FURNACE	150	120	55	65	30
OTHER MEANS	54	23	9	14	31
NONE	24	22	-	22	2
SELECTED EQUIPMENT					
ALL YEAR-ROUND HOUSING UNITS	11 212	7 450	2 404	5 046	3 762
WITH AIR CONDITIONING	7 578	5 412	1 800	3 612	2 166
ROOM UNIT(S)	1 953	1 224	378	845	729
CENTRAL SYSTEM	5 625	4 188	1 421	2 767	1 437
4 FLOORS OR MORE	564	529	292	237	35
WITH ELEVATOR IN STRUCTURE	544	510	284	225	35
WITH BASEMENT	2 834	2 029	592	1 436	805
WITH PUBLIC OR PRIVATE WATER SUPPLY	9 151	6 798	2 386	4 412	2 353
WITH SEWAGE DISPOSAL	11 173	7 445	2 404	5 041	3 729
PUBLIC SEWER	7 794	6 246	2 347	3 899	1 548
SEPTIC TANK OR CESSPOOL	3 379	1 199	57	1 142	2 180
ALL OCCUPIED HOUSING UNITS	10 180	6 664	2 153	4 511	3 516
AUTOMOBILES AND TRUCKS AVAILABLE					
AUTOMOBILES:					
1	5 161	3 223	1 099	2 124	1 939
2	3 564	2 523	674	1 849	1 041
3 OR MORE	617	412	105	308	205
NONE	838	506	276	230	332
TRUCKS:					
1	2 210	1 008	241	766	1 202
2 OR MORE	179	61	20	41	118
NONE	7 791	5 595	1 892	3 703	2 196

[1]EXCLUDES 1-FAMILY HOMES ON 10 ACRES OR MORE.

SELECTED HOUSING CHARACTERISTICS FOR NEW CONSTRUCTION UNITS: 1975--CONTINUED

(NUMBERS IN THOUSANDS. DATA BASED ON SAMPLE, SEE TEXT. RESTRICTED TO UNITS BUILT APRIL 1970 OR LATER. FOR MINIMUM BASE FOR DERIVED FIGURES (PERCENT, MEDIAN, ETC.) AND MEANING OF SYMBOLS, SEE TEXT)

UNITED STATES	TOTAL	INSIDE SMSA'S			OUTSIDE SMSA'S
		TOTAL	IN CENTRAL CITIES	NOT IN CENTRAL CITIES	
ALL OCCUPIED HOUSING UNITS--CON.					
OWNED SECOND HOME					
YES	394	260	83	176	134
NO.	9 786	6 405	2 070	4 334	3 382
HOUSE HEATING FUEL					
UTILITY GAS	4 552	3 465	1 106	2 359	1 087
BOTTLED, TANK, OR LP GAS.	747	167	10	157	580
FUEL OIL, KEROSENE, ETC.	955	515	115	399	441
ELECTRICITY	3 824	2 464	920	1 544	1 360
COAL OR COKE.	4	-	-	-	4
WOOD.	47	8	-	8	39
OTHER FUEL.	5	4	2	2	1
NONE.	47	42	-	42	4
COOKING FUEL					
UTILITY GAS	2 590	1 916	604	1 312	674
BOTTLED, TANK, OR LP GAS.	866	217	9	208	649
ELECTRICITY	6 707	4 526	1 538	2 988	2 181
FUEL OIL, KEROSENE, ETC.	6	3	-	3	3
COAL OR COKE.	1	-	-	-	1
WOOD.	7	-	-	-	7
OTHER FUEL.	1	-	-	-	1
NONE.	3	2	2	-	1
ALL OCCUPIED 1-FAMILY HOMES	6 726	3 658	792	2 866	3 068
STORM WINDOWS OR OTHER PROTECTIVE WINDOW COVERING					
ALL WINDOWS COVERED	3 026	1 476	221	1 255	1 550
SOME WINDOWS COVERED.	256	130	27	103	126
NO WINDOWS COVERED.	3 327	1 961	512	1 449	1 366
NOT REPORTED.	117	92	32	60	25
STORM DOORS					
ALL DOORS COVERED	2 359	1 100	169	931	1 258
SOME DOORS COVERED.	927	472	87	385	455
NO DOORS COVERED.	3 321	1 994	503	1 491	1 327
NOT REPORTED.	120	93	33	59	27
ATTIC OR ROOF INSULATION					
YES	6 065	3 246	687	2 559	2 819
NO.	257	138	38	99	120
DON'T KNOW.	261	167	31	136	93
NOT REPORTED.	143	107	35	72	35

CHARACTERISTICS OF HOUSING UNITS WITH BLACK HOUSEHOLD HEAD: 1975 AND 1970

(NUMBERS IN THOUSANDS. DATA BASED ON SAMPLE, SEE TEXT. FOR MINIMUM BASE FOR DERIVED FIGURES (PERCENT, MEDIAN, ETC.) AND MEANING OF SYMBOLS, SEE TEXT)

UNITED STATES	TOTAL		INSIDE SMSA'S						OUTSIDE SMSA'S	
			TOTAL		IN CENTRAL CITIES		NOT IN CENTRAL CITIES			
	1975	1970	1975	1970	1975	1970	1975	1970	1975	1970
ALL OCCUPIED HOUSING UNITS	7 561	6 174	5 872	4 739	4 607	3 833	1 265	906	1 689	1 436
TENURE										
OWNER OCCUPIED	3 309	2 568	2 382	1 825	1 714	1 335	668	490	927	742
PERCENT OF ALL OCCUPIED	43.8	41.6	40.6	38.5	37.2	34.8	52.8	54.1	54.9	51.7
RENTER OCCUPIED	4 252	3 607	3 490	2 913	2 893	2 498	597	416	762	693
COOPERATIVES AND CONDOMINIUMS										
OWNER OCCUPIED	51	NA	47	NA	38	NA	9	NA	4	NA
COOPERATIVE OWNERSHIP	40	NA	38	NA	32	NA	6	NA	2	NA
CONDOMINIUM OWNERSHIP	11	NA	10	NA	6	NA	4	NA	2	NA
UNITS IN STRUCTURE										
OWNER OCCUPIED	3 309	2 568	2 382	1 825	1 714	1 335	668	490	927	742
1, DETACHED	2 680	2 065	1 857	1 365	1 260	933	597	432	823	700
1, ATTACHED	248	202	246	200	216	179	30	22	2	2
2 TO 4	223	221	215	209	196	184	19	25	8	11
5 OR MORE	46	41	46	40	41	37	4	3	-	2
MOBILE HOME OR TRAILER	113	38	18	11	-	3	18	8	94	27
RENTER OCCUPIED	4 252	3 607	3 490	2 913	2 893	2 498	597	416	762	693
1, DETACHED	1 098	1 119	602	586	444	418	158	168	496	534
1, ATTACHED	329	251	278	238	240	207	38	30	52	13
2 TO 4	1 164	974	1 041	874	905	769	136	105	123	99
5 TO 9	514	388	480	366	395	327	86	39	34	22
10 TO 19	412	349	397	337	305	300	92	38	15	11
20 TO 49	264	250	261	246	221	228	40	18	3	4
50 OR MORE	436	265	421	261	384	247	37	14	15	3
MOBILE HOME OR TRAILER	34	10	10	4	-	2	10	3	24	6
YEAR STRUCTURE BUILT										
OWNER OCCUPIED	3 309	2 568	2 382	1 825	1 714	1 335	668	490	927	742
APRIL 1970 OR LATER	342	NA	173	NA	83	NA	91	NA	169	NA
1965 TO MARCH 1970	315	222	166	118	94	61	72	57	149	104
1960 TO 1964	359	254	251	165	150	95	101	70	107	89
1950 TO 1959	598	524	463	382	322	249	141	133	135	141
1940 TO 1949	510	471	363	335	257	251	106	84	147	136
1939 OR EARLIER	1 185	1 097	966	825	808	679	158	146	220	272
RENTER OCCUPIED	4 252	3 607	3 490	2 913	2 893	2 498	597	416	762	693
APRIL 1970 OR LATER	371	NA	322	NA	203	NA	119	NA	49	NA
1965 TO MARCH 1970	409	243	331	195	244	152	87	43	78	48
1960 TO 1964	338	254	286	209	215	162	71	48	51	45
1950 TO 1959	571	554	448	451	366	362	82	89	123	103
1940 TO 1949	533	649	407	523	340	446	67	77	125	126
1939 OR EARLIER	2 031	1 906	1 695	1 534	1 525	1 376	170	159	336	372
PLUMBING FACILITIES										
OWNER OCCUPIED	3 309	2 568	2 382	1 825	1 714	1 335	668	490	927	742
WITH ALL PLUMBING FACILITIES	3 076	2 198	2 316	1 727	1 695	1 305	622	422	760	471
LACKING SOME OR ALL PLUMBING FACILITIES	233	369	66	98	19	30	46	68	167	271
RENTER OCCUPIED	4 252	3 607	3 490	2 913	2 893	2 498	597	416	762	693
WITH ALL PLUMBING FACILITIES	3 827	2 973	3 355	2 695	2 800	2 362	555	333	472	278
LACKING SOME OR ALL PLUMBING FACILITIES	425	634	135	218	93	136	42	82	290	416
COMPLETE BATHROOMS										
OWNER OCCUPIED	3 309	2 568	2 382	1 825	1 714	1 335	668	490	927	742
1	2 001	1 902	1 395	1 468	1 053	1 115	342	354	606	434
1 AND ONE-HALF	543		462		334		128		81	
2 OR MORE	527	272	456	246	305	183	151	64	71	26
ALSO USED BY ANOTHER HOUSEHOLD	6	394	6	111	6	38	1	73	-	283
NONE	232		63		17		46		169	
RENTER OCCUPIED	4 252	3 607	3 490	2 913	2 893	2 498	597	416	762	693
1	3 410	2 836	2 983	2 572	2 524	2 258	459	314	426	263
1 AND ONE-HALF	207		184		130		54		23	
2 OR MORE	178	78	161	72	123	60	38	12	16	6
ALSO USED BY ANOTHER HOUSEHOLD	79	693	69	269	61	180	8	89	10	424
NONE	379		92		54		37		287	

CHARACTERISTICS OF HOUSING UNITS WITH BLACK HOUSEHOLD HEAD: 1975 AND 1970--CONTINUED

(NUMBERS IN THOUSANDS. DATA BASED ON SAMPLE, SEE TEXT. FOR MINIMUM BASE FOR DERIVED FIGURES (PERCENT, MEDIAN, ETC.) AND MEANING OF SYMBOLS, SEE TEXT)

UNITED STATES	TOTAL		INSIDE SMSA'S						OUTSIDE SMSA'S	
			TOTAL		IN CENTRAL CITIES		NOT IN CENTRAL CITIES			
	1975	1970	1975	1970	1975	1970	1975	1970	1975	1970
ALL OCCUPIED HOUSING UNITS--CON.										
COMPLETE KITCHEN FACILITIES										
OWNER OCCUPIED	3 309	2 568	2 382	1 825	1 714	1 335	668	490	927	742
FOR EXCLUSIVE USE OF HOUSEHOLD	3 161	2 316	2 352	1 768	1 713	1 322	640	446	809	549
ALSO USED BY ANOTHER HOUSEHOLD	1	251	1	58	1	13	-	45	-	193
NO COMPLETE KITCHEN FACILITIES	146		28		-		28		118	
RENTER OCCUPIED	4 252	3 607	3 490	2 913	2 893	2 498	597	416	762	693
FOR EXCLUSIVE USE OF HOUSEHOLD	3 905	3 161	3 364	2 778	2 803	2 421	561	358	541	382
ALSO USED BY ANOTHER HOUSEHOLD	36	446	31	135	27	77	4	58	5	311
NO COMPLETE KITCHEN FACILITIES	311		95		63		32		216	
ROOMS										
OWNER OCCUPIED	3 309	2 568	2 382	1 825	1 714	1 335	668	490	927	742
1 ROOM	-	5	-	4	-	3	-	1	-	2
2 ROOMS	9	24	6	14	3	9	3	5	3	10
3 ROOMS	86	115	41	68	27	48	14	21	45	47
4 ROOMS	453	424	258	248	179	168	79	80	194	175
5 ROOMS	1 011	748	687	526	485	381	202	145	324	222
6 ROOMS	1 013	734	763	550	562	414	201	136	250	184
7 ROOMS OR MORE	738	518	628	415	459	312	169	103	111	103
MEDIAN	5.6	5.5	5.8	5.6	5.8	5.6	5.7	5.5	5.2	5.1
RENTER OCCUPIED	4 252	3 607	3 490	2 913	2 893	2 498	597	416	762	693
1 ROOM	151	112	127	99	115	88	12	11	24	13
2 ROOMS	214	253	172	207	144	181	28	27	42	46
3 ROOMS	999	861	800	704	661	613	139	91	199	157
4 ROOMS	1 404	1 151	1 185	909	967	771	218	138	219	242
5 ROOMS	839	721	677	587	548	497	129	89	162	135
6 ROOMS	455	361	372	287	323	246	50	41	83	74
7 ROOMS OR MORE	190	146	156	119	136	102	21	18	34	27
MEDIAN	4.0	4.0	4.0	4.0	4.0	4.0	4.0	4.1	4.0	4.0
BEDROOMS										
OWNER OCCUPIED	3 309	2 568	2 382	1 825	1 714	1 335	668	490	927	742
NONE AND 1	98	157	67	109	52	81	15	28	31	48
2	1 030	874	718	590	522	433	197	157	312	285
3	1 642	1 154	1 165	832	845	601	320	231	476	322
4 OR MORE	539	383	432	294	295	220	136	74	108	89
RENTER OCCUPIED	4 252	3 607	3 490	2 913	2 893	2 498	597	416	762	693
NONE AND 1	1 355	1 219	1 177	1 059	998	932	179	127	178	160
2	1 779	1 505	1 445	1 181	1 158	999	287	181	334	324
3	902	697	690	527	580	442	110	85	212	169
4 OR MORE	216	189	178	149	157	127	21	21	38	40
PERSONS										
OWNER OCCUPIED	3 309	2 568	2 382	1 825	1 714	1 335	668	490	927	742
1 PERSON	471	335	314	213	246	159	67	54	157	122
2 PERSONS	745	625	515	436	363	327	151	109	230	189
3 PERSONS	619	430	479	316	358	234	121	83	141	113
4 PERSONS	527	364	383	276	260	201	123	75	145	87
5 PERSONS	375	271	292	204	192	147	100	57	83	67
6 PERSONS	244	198	181	147	134	106	47	41	63	51
7 PERSONS OR MORE	328	345	219	232	161	161	58	71	109	112
MEDIAN	3.2	3.3	3.3	3.3	3.2	3.3	3.4	3.5	3.0	3.0
RENTER OCCUPIED	4 252	3 607	3 490	2 913	2 893	2 498	597	416	762	693
1 PERSON	1 201	847	1 002	713	854	630	149	83	198	134
2 PERSONS	1 020	799	847	666	701	577	147	89	173	133
3 PERSONS	747	578	642	483	502	412	139	71	105	95
4 PERSONS	483	450	388	371	315	315	73	55	95	79
5 PERSONS	345	315	286	251	244	211	42	40	59	64
6 PERSONS	191	222	142	169	122	141	20	28	50	53
7 PERSONS OR MORE	265	396	183	260	155	211	28	49	83	136
MEDIAN	2.4	2.8	2.4	2.7	2.3	2.6	2.5	3.0	2.6	3.3
PERSONS PER ROOM										
OWNER OCCUPIED	3 309	2 568	2 382	1 825	1 714	1 335	668	490	927	742
0.50 OR LESS	1 613	1 172	1 172	826	864	621	307	205	441	346
0.51 TO 1.00	1 335	997	993	748	706	546	287	202	342	250
1.01 TO 1.50	276	280	181	187	120	129	60	58	95	92
1.51 OR MORE	85	119	36	64	23	39	13	25	48	55

CHARACTERISTICS OF HOUSING UNITS WITH BLACK HOUSEHOLD HEAD: 1975 AND 1970--CONTINUED

(NUMBERS IN THOUSANDS. DATA BASED ON SAMPLE, SEE TEXT. FOR MINIMUM BASE FOR DERIVED FIGURES (PERCENT, MEDIAN, ETC.) AND MEANING OF SYMBOLS, SEE TEXT)

UNITED STATES	TOTAL		INSIDE SMSA'S						OUTSIDE SMSA'S	
			TOTAL		IN CENTRAL CITIES		NOT IN CENTRAL CITIES			
	1975	1970	1975	1970	1975	1970	1975	1970	1975	1970
ALL OCCUPIED HOUSING UNITS--CON.										
PERSONS PER ROOM--CON.										
RENTER OCCUPIED	4 252	3 607	3 490	2 913	2 893	2 498	597	416	762	693
0.50 OR LESS	1 837	1 306	1 538	1 086	1 295	948	243	138	299	220
0.51 TO 1.00	1 855	1 501	1 556	1 262	1 259	1 084	297	179	299	239
1.01 TO 1.50	404	492	310	380	263	320	47	59	94	112
1.51 OR MORE	155	309	86	186	76	146	10	40	70	123
WITH ALL PLUMBING FACILITIES	6 903	5 171	5 671	4 422	4 495	3 667	1 177	755	1 231	749
OWNER OCCUPIED	3 076	2 198	2 316	1 727	1 695	1 305	622	422	760	471
1.00 OR LESS	2 759	1 893	2 113	1 499	1 551	1 142	562	357	646	394
1.01 TO 1.50	249	228	170	175	120	127	50	48	79	54
1.51 OR MORE	68	77	34	54	23	36	10	17	34	23
RENTER OCCUPIED	3 827	2 973	3 355	2 695	2 800	2 362	555	333	472	278
1.00 OR LESS	3 375	2 389	2 979	2 184	2 470	1 921	509	263	396	205
1.01 TO 1.50	353	401	302	357	262	310	41	47	51	44
1.51 OR MORE	99	182	74	154	68	131	6	23	25	28
HOUSEHOLD COMPOSITION BY AGE OF HEAD										
OWNER OCCUPIED	3 309	2 568	2 382	1 825	1 714	1 335	668	490	927	742
2-OR-MORE-PERSON HOUSEHOLDS	2 838	2 232	2 068	1 613	1 468	1 176	601	437	770	620
MALE HEAD, WIFE PRESENT, NO NONRELATIVES	1 991	1 669	1 453	1 221	1 020	881	433	341	538	447
UNDER 25 YEARS	47	46	30	31	18	22	13	9	17	14
25 TO 29 YEARS	180	107	140	81	89	57	51	24	39	26
30 TO 34 YEARS	203	152	157	119	108	82	48	37	46	32
35 TO 44 YEARS	460	393	356	311	249	223	107	88	104	82
45 TO 64 YEARS	800	723	587	529	427	389	160	140	213	194
65 YEARS AND OVER	301	248	182	150	128	108	54	42	119	99
OTHER MALE HEAD	200	132	156	92	113	68	43	24	44	40
UNDER 65 YEARS	153	100	124	73	88	54	36	19	29	27
65 YEARS AND OVER	47	32	32	19	26	14	7	5	15	13
FEMALE HEAD	647	432	459	299	334	227	125	72	188	133
UNDER 65 YEARS	508	330	367	239	276	183	91	56	141	91
65 YEARS AND OVER	139	102	92	60	59	44	34	16	47	42
1-PERSON HOUSEHOLDS	471	335	314	213	246	159	67	54	157	122
UNDER 65 YEARS	234	181	171	128	141	98	30	30	63	53
65 YEARS AND OVER	237	154	143	85	105	61	38	24	94	69
RENTER OCCUPIED	4 252	3 607	3 490	2 913	2 893	2 498	597	416	762	693
2-OR-MORE-PERSON HOUSEHOLDS	3 051	2 759	2 488	2 200	2 039	1 868	448	332	564	559
MALE HEAD, WIFE PRESENT, NO NONRELATIVES	1 369	1 554	1 052	1 206	819	1 003	233	203	317	348
UNDER 25 YEARS	188	206	143	167	98	138	45	29	45	39
25 TO 29 YEARS	275	259	229	213	166	174	63	39	46	46
30 TO 34 YEARS	197	212	157	171	130	140	27	31	40	41
35 TO 44 YEARS	249	326	207	255	167	212	40	43	43	70
45 TO 64 YEARS	312	417	218	307	181	259	36	48	95	111
65 YEARS AND OVER	147	134	98	93	77	79	21	14	49	41
OTHER MALE HEAD	249	200	211	160	171	137	40	22	38	40
UNDER 65 YEARS	227	172	193	140	156	120	37	20	34	32
65 YEARS AND OVER	22	28	18	20	15	17	3	3	4	8
FEMALE HEAD	1 434	1 006	1 225	834	1 049	727	176	107	209	172
UNDER 65 YEARS	1 345	927	1 163	778	997	679	166	99	182	149
65 YEARS AND OVER	89	79	62	56	52	48	9	8	27	23
1-PERSON HOUSEHOLDS	1 201	847	1 002	713	854	630	149	83	198	134
UNDER 65 YEARS	908	616	789	537	669	476	121	61	119	79
65 YEARS AND OVER	292	231	213	176	185	154	28	22	79	55
PERSONS 65 YEARS OLD AND OVER										
OWNER OCCUPIED	3 309	2 568	2 382	1 825	1 714	1 335	668	490	927	742
NONE	2 446	1 898	1 833	1 414	1 314	1 033	519	382	613	484
1 PERSON	640	492	419	303	299	223	120	80	221	189
2 PERSONS OR MORE	223	178	130	108	101	80	29	29	94	70
RENTER OCCUPIED	4 252	3 607	3 490	2 913	2 893	2 498	597	416	762	693
NONE	3 637	3 041	3 058	2 498	2 524	2 138	534	360	578	543
1 PERSON	519	468	365	344	312	298	53	46	154	123
2 PERSONS OR MORE	96	98	67	71	57	61	10	10	29	27

CHARACTERISTICS OF HOUSING UNITS WITH BLACK HOUSEHOLD HEAD: 1975 AND 1970--CONTINUED

(NUMBERS IN THOUSANDS. DATA BASED ON SAMPLE, SEE TEXT. FOR MINIMUM BASE FOR DERIVED FIGURES (PERCENT, MEDIAN, ETC.) AND MEANING OF SYMBOLS, SEE TEXT)

UNITED STATES	TOTAL		INSIDE SMSA'S						OUTSIDE SMSA'S	
			TOTAL		IN CENTRAL CITIES		NOT IN CENTRAL CITIES			
	1975	1970	1975	1970	1975	1970	1975	1970	1975	1970
ALL OCCUPIED HOUSING UNITS--CON.										
OWN CHILDREN UNDER 18 YEARS OLD BY AGE GROUP										
OWNER OCCUPIED	3 309	2 568	2 382	1 825	1 714	1 335	668	490	927	742
NO OWN CHILDREN UNDER 18 YEARS	1 773	1 387	1 245	945	916	706	328	239	529	443
WITH OWN CHILDREN UNDER 18 YEARS	1 536	1 181	1 137	881	798	629	340	252	398	300
UNDER 6 YEARS ONLY	200	150	149	114	95	80	54	34	51	36
1	118	85	94	65	66	46	28	19	24	20
2	70	48	48	36	24	26	24	11	22	11
3 OR MORE	12	17	7	12	5	8	2	4	5	5
6 TO 17 YEARS ONLY	952	703	694	526	489	380	205	146	258	177
1	365	265	267	199	185	146	83	53	98	66
2	239	184	183	141	130	103	53	39	56	43
3 OR MORE	347	254	244	186	174	131	69	54	103	68
BOTH AGE GROUPS	384	327	294	241	214	169	80	72	90	86
2	115	62	95	50	67	36	29	14	20	12
3 OR MORE	269	266	199	191	148	133	51	58	70	74
RENTER OCCUPIED	4 252	3 607	3 490	2 913	2 893	2 498	597	416	762	693
NO OWN CHILDREN UNDER 18 YEARS	2 316	1 860	1 893	1 522	1 592	1 327	301	195	423	338
WITH OWN CHILDREN UNDER 18 YEARS	1 936	1 747	1 597	1 391	1 301	1 171	296	220	339	356
UNDER 6 YEARS ONLY	557	466	479	393	364	329	116	63	78	74
1	353	250	305	215	230	181	75	35	48	35
2	156	148	134	124	100	104	34	20	22	24
3 OR MORE	48	68	40	53	33	44	7	9	8	15
6 TO 17 YEARS ONLY	871	740	700	587	582	499	119	89	171	153
1	313	265	260	218	211	186	49	31	53	48
2	249	188	207	153	175	131	32	22	42	35
3 OR MORE	309	287	233	217	196	181	37	35	76	70
BOTH AGE GROUPS	508	540	418	411	356	343	62	69	90	129
2	134	90	119	77	98	65	21	11	15	13
3 OR MORE	374	450	299	335	258	277	40	57	75	116
PRESENCE OF SUBFAMILIES										
OWNER OCCUPIED	3 309	NA	2 382	NA	1 714	NA	668	NA	927	NA
NO SUBFAMILIES	3 190	NA	2 299	NA	1 660	NA	639	NA	891	NA
WITH 1 SUBFAMILY	116	NA	81	NA	54	NA	27	NA	35	NA
SUBFAMILY HEAD UNDER 30 YEARS	73	NA	49	NA	30	NA	19	NA	25	NA
SUBFAMILY HEAD 30 TO 64 YEARS	35	NA	28	NA	20	NA	8	NA	7	NA
SUBFAMILY HEAD 65 YEARS AND OVER	8	NA	4	NA	4	NA	-	NA	3	NA
WITH 2 SUBFAMILIES OR MORE	2	NA	2	NA	-	NA	2	NA	1	NA
RENTER OCCUPIED	4 252	NA	3 490	NA	2 893	NA	597	NA	762	NA
NO SUBFAMILIES	4 203	NA	3 456	NA	2 861	NA	596	NA	746	NA
WITH 1 SUBFAMILY	49	NA	34	NA	32	NA	1	NA	16	NA
SUBFAMILY HEAD UNDER 30 YEARS	35	NA	22	NA	22	NA	-	NA	13	NA
SUBFAMILY HEAD 30 TO 64 YEARS	14	NA	12	NA	11	NA	1	NA	2	NA
SUBFAMILY HEAD 65 YEARS AND OVER	-	NA	-	NA	-	NA	-	NA	-	NA
WITH 2 SUBFAMILIES OR MORE	-	NA	-	NA	-	NA	-	NA	-	NA
PRESENCE OF OTHER RELATIVES OR NONRELATIVES										
OWNER OCCUPIED	3 309	NA	2 382	NA	1 714	NA	668	NA	927	NA
NO OTHER RELATIVES OR NONRELATIVES	2 378	NA	1 710	NA	1 217	NA	493	NA	668	NA
WITH OTHER RELATIVES AND NONRELATIVES	31	NA	28	NA	15	NA	13	NA	3	NA
WITH OTHER RELATIVES, NO NONRELATIVES	767	NA	534	NA	393	NA	141	NA	233	NA
WITH NONRELATIVES, NO OTHER RELATIVES	134	NA	110	NA	89	NA	21	NA	23	NA
RENTER OCCUPIED	4 252	NA	3 490	NA	2 893	NA	597	NA	762	NA
NO OTHER RELATIVES OR NONRELATIVES	3 404	NA	2 815	NA	2 317	NA	498	NA	588	NA
WITH OTHER RELATIVES AND NONRELATIVES	24	NA	22	NA	20	NA	3	NA	1	NA
WITH OTHER RELATIVES, NO NONRELATIVES	609	NA	458	NA	391	NA	66	NA	151	NA
WITH NONRELATIVES, NO OTHER RELATIVES	216	NA	195	NA	165	NA	30	NA	21	NA
YEARS OF SCHOOL COMPLETED BY HEAD										
OWNER OCCUPIED	3 309	NA	2 382	NA	1 714	NA	668	NA	927	NA
NO SCHOOL YEARS COMPLETED	35	NA	18	NA	7	NA	11	NA	16	NA
ELEMENTARY: LESS THAN 8 YEARS	828	NA	441	NA	311	NA	130	NA	387	NA
8 YEARS	294	NA	200	NA	150	NA	51	NA	94	NA
HIGH SCHOOL: 1 TO 3 YEARS	661	NA	475	NA	352	NA	123	NA	186	NA
4 YEARS	866	NA	708	NA	525	NA	182	NA	159	NA
COLLEGE: 1 TO 3 YEARS	360	NA	319	NA	217	NA	103	NA	41	NA
4 YEARS OR MORE	264	NA	220	NA	152	NA	68	NA	43	NA
MEDIAN	11.3	NA	12.1	NA	12.1	NA	12.1	NA	8.6	NA

CHARACTERISTICS OF HOUSING UNITS WITH BLACK HOUSEHOLD HEAD: 1975 AND 1970--CONTINUED

(NUMBERS IN THOUSANDS. DATA BASED ON SAMPLE, SEE TEXT. FOR MINIMUM BASE FOR DERIVED FIGURES (PERCENT, MEDIAN, ETC.) AND MEANING OF SYMBOLS, SEE TEXT)

UNITED STATES	TOTAL		INSIDE SMSA'S						OUTSIDE SMSA'S	
			TOTAL		IN CENTRAL CITIES		NOT IN CENTRAL CITIES			
	1975	1970	1975	1970	1975	1970	1975	1970	1975	1970
ALL OCCUPIED HOUSING UNITS--CON.										
YEARS OF SCHOOL COMPLETED BY HEAD--CON.										
RENTER OCCUPIED	4 252	NA	3 490	NA	2 893	NA	597	NA	762	NA
NO SCHOOL YEARS COMPLETED	75	NA	45	NA	34	NA	11	NA	30	NA
ELEMENTARY: LESS THAN 8 YEARS	852	NA	555	NA	457	NA	98	NA	297	NA
8 YEARS	294	NA	232	NA	199	NA	33	NA	62	NA
HIGH SCHOOL: 1 TO 3 YEARS	1 050	NA	882	NA	771	NA	111	NA	168	NA
4 YEARS	1 320	NA	1 172	NA	968	NA	205	NA	148	NA
COLLEGE: 1 TO 3 YEARS	437	NA	410	NA	326	NA	84	NA	27	NA
4 YEARS OR MORE	224	NA	194	NA	137	NA	57	NA	30	NA
MEDIAN	11.6	NA	12.0	NA	11.9	NA	12.2	NA	8.9	NA
YEAR HEAD MOVED INTO UNIT										
OWNER OCCUPIED	3 309	2 568	2 382	1 825	1 714	1 335	668	490	927	742
1974 OR LATER	425	NA	331	NA	217	NA	114	NA	94	NA
MOVED IN WITHIN PAST 12 MONTHS	228	NA	179	NA	118	NA	61	NA	49	NA
APRIL 1970 TO 1973	736	NA	536	NA	376	NA	160	NA	200	NA
1965 TO MARCH 1970	696	897	521	691	414	506	107	185	175	206
1960 TO 1964	478	510	356	379	252	280	104	99	121	131
1950 TO 1959	531	607	393	441	295	331	98	111	138	166
1949 OR EARLIER	443	554	244	314	159	219	85	95	199	240
RENTER OCCUPIED	4 252	3 607	3 490	2 913	2 893	2 498	597	416	762	693
1974 OR LATER	1 894	NA	1 636	NA	1 281	NA	355	NA	258	NA
MOVED IN WITHIN PAST 12 MONTHS	1 269	NA	1 104	NA	853	NA	250	NA	166	NA
APRIL 1970 TO 1973	1 037	NA	843	NA	735	NA	108	NA	194	NA
1965 TO MARCH 1970	765	2 448	606	2 034	518	1 733	87	301	159	414
1960 TO 1964	293	584	227	466	207	408	19	58	66	118
1950 TO 1959	173	350	128	264	110	230	18	33	45	86
1949 OR EARLIER	91	224	51	150	42	127	9	23	40	74
HEAD'S PRINCIPAL MEANS OF TRANSPORTATION TO WORK[1]										
OWNER OCCUPIED	2 145	NA	1 621	NA	1 154	NA	466	NA	524	NA
DRIVES SELF	1 405	NA	1 118	NA	793	NA	325	NA	287	NA
CARPOOL	460	NA	272	NA	171	NA	101	NA	187	NA
MASS TRANSPORTATION	151	NA	143	NA	121	NA	22	NA	8	NA
BICYCLE OR MOTORCYCLE	3	NA	3	NA	-	NA	3	NA	-	NA
TAXICAB	7	NA	7	NA	4	NA	3	NA	-	NA
WALKS ONLY	57	NA	32	NA	28	NA	4	NA	25	NA
OTHER MEANS	14	NA	6	NA	6	NA	-	NA	8	NA
WORKS AT HOME	28	NA	22	NA	17	NA	5	NA	6	NA
NOT REPORTED	18	NA	16	NA	14	NA	1	NA	3	NA
RENTER OCCUPIED	2 302	NA	1 908	NA	1 537	NA	371	NA	394	NA
DRIVES SELF	1 078	NA	912	NA	705	NA	207	NA	165	NA
CARPOOL	489	NA	351	NA	258	NA	93	NA	138	NA
MASS TRANSPORTATION	480	NA	475	NA	437	NA	38	NA	5	NA
BICYCLE OR MOTORCYCLE	10	NA	6	NA	3	NA	3	NA	4	NA
TAXICAB	18	NA	15	NA	14	NA	1	NA	3	NA
WALKS ONLY	174	NA	108	NA	84	NA	24	NA	67	NA
OTHER MEANS	10	NA	8	NA	6	NA	3	NA	2	NA
WORKS AT HOME	27	NA	18	NA	16	NA	2	NA	9	NA
NOT REPORTED	16	NA	15	NA	15	NA	-	NA	1	NA
DISTANCE FROM HOME TO WORK[1]										
OWNER OCCUPIED	2 145	NA	1 621	NA	1 154	NA	466	NA	524	NA
LESS THAN 1 MILE	171	NA	102	NA	76	NA	26	NA	69	NA
1 TO 4 MILES	534	NA	386	NA	309	NA	77	NA	148	NA
5 TO 9 MILES	436	NA	383	NA	279	NA	103	NA	53	NA
10 TO 29 MILES	630	NA	493	NA	303	NA	190	NA	137	NA
30 TO 49 MILES	96	NA	66	NA	44	NA	22	NA	30	NA
50 MILES OR MORE	20	NA	10	NA	6	NA	4	NA	10	NA
WORKS AT HOME	28	NA	22	NA	17	NA	5	NA	6	NA
NO FIXED PLACE OF WORK	183	NA	118	NA	85	NA	33	NA	64	NA
NOT REPORTED	47	NA	40	NA	34	NA	6	NA	7	NA
MEDIAN	7.7	NA	8.0	NA	7.2	NA	10.5	NA	5.6	NA

[1]LIMITED TO HEADS WHO REPORTED HAVING A JOB THE WEEK PRIOR TO ENUMERATION.

CHARACTERISTICS OF HOUSING UNITS WITH BLACK HOUSEHOLD HEAD: 1975 AND 1970--CONTINUED

(NUMBERS IN THOUSANDS. DATA BASED ON SAMPLE, SEE TEXT. FOR MINIMUM BASE FOR DERIVED FIGURES (PERCENT, MEDIAN, ETC.) AND MEANING OF SYMBOLS, SEE TEXT)

UNITED STATES	TOTAL		INSIDE SMSA'S						OUTSIDE SMSA'S	
			TOTAL		IN CENTRAL CITIES		NOT IN CENTRAL CITIES			
	1975	1970	1975	1970	1975	1970	1975	1970	1975	1970
ALL OCCUPIED HOUSING UNITS--CON.										
DISTANCE FROM HOME TO WORK[1]--CON.										
RENTER OCCUPIED	2 302	NA	1 908	NA	1 537	NA	371	NA	394	NA
LESS THAN 1 MILE	272	NA	168	NA	131	NA	38	NA	104	NA
1 TO 4 MILES	802	NA	664	NA	564	NA	101	NA	138	NA
5 TO 9 MILES	402	NA	355	NA	281	NA	74	NA	46	NA
10 TO 29 MILES	531	NA	485	NA	364	NA	122	NA	45	NA
30 TO 49 MILES	45	NA	34	NA	20	NA	14	NA	12	NA
50 MILES OR MORE	18	NA	9	NA	6	NA	3	NA	9	NA
WORKS AT HOME	27	NA	18	NA	16	NA	2	NA	9	NA
NO FIXED PLACE OF WORK	159	NA	130	NA	114	NA	16	NA	29	NA
NOT REPORTED	47	NA	44	NA	42	NA	1	NA	3	NA
MEDIAN	4.8	NA	5.3	NA	4.9	NA	7.5	NA	3.1	NA
TRAVEL TIME FROM HOME TO WORK[1]										
OWNER OCCUPIED	2 145	NA	1 621	NA	1 154	NA	466	NA	524	NA
LESS THAN 15 MINUTES	493	NA	319	NA	244	NA	75	NA	174	NA
15 TO 29 MINUTES	721	NA	585	NA	415	NA	170	NA	136	NA
30 TO 44 MINUTES	423	NA	341	NA	223	NA	117	NA	82	NA
45 TO 59 MINUTES	124	NA	100	NA	66	NA	34	NA	24	NA
1 HOUR TO 1 HOUR AND 29 MINUTES	106	NA	87	NA	60	NA	27	NA	19	NA
1 HOUR 30 MINUTES OR MORE	26	NA	18	NA	16	NA	3	NA	8	NA
WORKS AT HOME	28	NA	22	NA	17	NA	5	NA	6	NA
NO FIXED PLACE OF WORK	183	NA	118	NA	85	NA	33	NA	64	NA
NOT REPORTED	41	NA	30	NA	28	NA	2	NA	10	NA
MEDIAN	24	NA	25	NA	25	NA	27	NA	20	NA
RENTER OCCUPIED	2 302	NA	1 908	NA	1 537	NA	371	NA	394	NA
LESS THAN 15 MINUTES	597	NA	413	NA	316	NA	96	NA	184	NA
15 TO 29 MINUTES	770	NA	661	NA	535	NA	126	NA	110	NA
30 TO 44 MINUTES	395	NA	357	NA	281	NA	76	NA	37	NA
45 TO 59 MINUTES	180	NA	173	NA	141	NA	32	NA	7	NA
1 HOUR TO 1 HOUR AND 29 MINUTES	114	NA	105	NA	84	NA	20	NA	9	NA
1 HOUR 30 MINUTES OR MORE	30	NA	24	NA	21	NA	3	NA	7	NA
WORKS AT HOME	27	NA	18	NA	16	NA	2	NA	9	NA
NO FIXED PLACE OF WORK	159	NA	130	NA	114	NA	16	NA	29	NA
NOT REPORTED	31	NA	28	NA	28	NA	-	NA	3	NA
MEDIAN	24	NA	25	NA	25	NA	25	NA	15-	NA
HEATING EQUIPMENT										
OWNER OCCUPIED	3 309	2 568	2 382	1 825	1 714	1 335	668	490	927	742
WARM-AIR FURNACE	1 451	806	1 198	698	867	525	331	173	253	108
STEAM OR HOT WATER	463	356	444	342	351	281	93	62	20	14
BUILT-IN ELECTRIC UNITS	89	73	46	53	29	35	17	18	44	20
FLOOR, WALL, OR PIPELESS FURNACE	369	228	302	191	225	141	77	50	67	37
ROOM HEATERS WITH FLUE	249	456	132	273	77	190	55	82	117	183
ROOM HEATERS WITHOUT FLUE	515	419	184	180	121	116	63	64	331	238
FIREPLACES, STOVES, OR PORTABLE HEATERS	162	223	67	83	43	44	24	39	95	140
NONE	11	7	9	5	1	2	8	3	2	2
RENTER OCCUPIED	4 252	3 607	3 490	2 913	2 893	2 498	597	416	762	693
WARM-AIR FURNACE	1 102	629	1 002	582	773	487	229	94	100	47
STEAM OR HOT WATER	1 289	1 103	1 250	1 084	1 138	1 005	112	79	39	19
BUILT-IN ELECTRIC UNITS	201	140	166	127	122	103	44	23	35	14
FLOOR, WALL, OR PIPELESS FURNACE	399	227	362	205	292	166	70	39	37	22
ROOM HEATERS WITH FLUE	429	634	306	470	261	395	44	74	124	164
ROOM HEATERS WITHOUT FLUE	524	452	280	266	228	218	52	48	244	186
FIREPLACES, STOVES, OR PORTABLE HEATERS	258	389	86	152	51	104	35	48	172	237
NONE	50	33	38	28	27	19	12	9	12	5
ALL OCCUPIED HOUSING UNITS	7 561	6 174	5 872	4 739	4 607	3 833	1 265	906	1 689	1 436
AIR CONDITIONING										
ROOM UNIT(S)	1 754	899	1 450	762	1 138	622	312	140	304	137
CENTRAL SYSTEM	792	215	706	189	436	138	270	51	86	26
NONE	5 014	5 060	3 716	3 788	3 033	3 074	683	714	1 298	1 272
ELEVATOR IN STRUCTURE										
4 FLOORS OR MORE	665	539	658	537	600	516	58	21	7	2
WITH ELEVATOR	464	322	458	321	421	307	37	13	6	2
WALK-UP	201	217	200	217	179	209	21	8	2	1
1 TO 3 FLOORS	6 896	5 635	5 214	4 201	4 007	3 317	1 207	885	1 682	1 434

[1]LIMITED TO HEADS WHO REPORTED HAVING A JOB THE WEEK PRIOR TO ENUMERATION

CHARACTERISTICS OF HOUSING UNITS WITH BLACK HOUSEHOLD HEAD: 1975 AND 1970--CONTINUED

(NUMBERS IN THOUSANDS. DATA BASED ON SAMPLE, SEE TEXT. FOR MINIMUM BASE FOR DERIVED FIGURES (PERCENT, MEDIAN, ETC.) AND MEANING OF SYMBOLS, SEE TEXT)

UNITED STATES	TOTAL		INSIDE SMSA'S						OUTSIDE SMSA'S	
			TOTAL		IN CENTRAL CITIES		NOT IN CENTRAL CITIES			
	1975	1970	1975	1970	1975	1970	1975	1970	1975	1970
ALL OCCUPIED HOUSING UNITS--CON.										
BASEMENT										
WITH BASEMENT	3 250	2 847	3 085	2 712	2 600	2 368	485	344	165	136
NO BASEMENT	4 311	3 327	2 787	2 027	2 007	1 465	780	562	1 524	1 300
SOURCE OF WATER										
PUBLIC SYSTEM OR PRIVATE COMPANY	6 862	5 393	5 724	4 553	4 593	3 814	1 131	739	1 138	840
INDIVIDUAL WELL	581	641	124	157	8	15	116	142	456	483
DRILLED	440	NA	97	NA	8	NA	89	NA	343	NA
DUG	138	NA	26	NA	-	NA	26	NA	112	NA
NOT REPORTED	3	NA	1	NA	-	NA	1	NA	1	NA
OTHER	119	141	23	29	5	4	18	24	95	112
SEWAGE DISPOSAL										
PUBLIC SEWER	6 327	4 981	5 546	4 362	4 556	3 749	990	614	782	618
SEPTIC TANK OR CESSPOOL	843	533	265	242	42	56	223	186	578	290
OTHER	390	661	61	134	9	29	52	105	329	527
TELEPHONE AVAILABLE										
YES	5 951	4 315	4 823	3 547	3 777	2 866	1 046	682	1 127	768
NO	1 610	1 860	1 049	1 192	830	967	219	224	562	668
AUTOMOBILES AND TRUCKS AVAILABLE										
AUTOMOBILES:										
1	3 229	2 551	2 455	1 923	1 867	1 506	588	417	774	628
2	1 283	850	1 047	664	705	462	342	202	236	186
3 OR MORE	245	114	194	88	135	58	59	30	51	26
NONE	2 804	2 658	2 176	2 063	1 900	1 807	276	256	628	595
TRUCKS:										
1	609	NA	332	NA	214	NA	118	NA	277	NA
2 OR MORE	38	NA	19	NA	13	NA	6	NA	19	NA
NONE	6 914	NA	5 521	NA	4 380	NA	1 141	NA	1 393	NA
OWNED SECOND HOME										
YES	127	138	101	108	79	84	22	24	26	30
NO	7 434	6 039	5 771	4 631	4 528	3 751	1 243	881	1 663	1 407
HOUSE HEATING FUEL										
UTILITY GAS	4 569	3 452	3 880	2 935	3 173	2 454	706	481	689	517
BOTTLED, TANK, OR LP GAS	462	420	86	162	18	86	68	76	376	258
FUEL OIL, KEROSENE, ETC.	1 545	1 344	1 286	1 066	1 016	858	269	208	259	278
ELECTRICITY	617	300	485	247	318	184	167	63	132	53
COAL OR COKE	98	296	54	212	44	181	10	31	44	84
WOOD	204	278	31	39	6	9	25	30	173	239
OTHER FUEL	5	47	3	45	3	42	-	4	2	2
NONE	61	39	47	33	28	21	19	12	13	6
COOKING FUEL										
UTILITY GAS	5 041	4 253	4 453	3 765	3 740	3 224	713	542	588	488
BOTTLED, TANK, OR LP GAS	645	609	159	233	53	116	106	117	485	376
ELECTRICITY	1 711	1 012	1 199	620	771	413	428	207	512	392
FUEL OIL, KEROSENE, ETC.	17	59	8	41	7	33	1	9	9	18
COAL OR COKE	7	32	3	19	3	14	-	5	4	13
WOOD	94	174	18	31	3	10	15	21	76	142
OTHER FUEL	-	11	-	9	-	8	-	2	-	2
NONE	46	28	31	21	29	17	2	4	14	7

CHARACTERISTICS OF HOUSING UNITS WITH BLACK HOUSEHOLD HEAD: 1975 AND 1970--CONTINUED

(NUMBERS IN THOUSANDS. DATA BASED ON SAMPLE, SEE TEXT. FOR MINIMUM BASE FOR DERIVED FIGURES (PERCENT, MEDIAN, ETC.) AND MEANING OF SYMBOLS, SEE TEXT)

UNITED STATES	TOTAL		INSIDE SMSA'S						OUTSIDE SMSA'S	
			TOTAL		IN CENTRAL CITIES		NOT IN CENTRAL CITIES			
	1975	1970	1975	1970	1975	1970	1975	1970	1975	1970
ALL OCCUPIED 1-FAMILY HOMES	4 502	NA	3 012	NA	2 160	NA	851	NA	1 491	NA
STORM WINDOWS OR OTHER PROTECTIVE WINDOW COVERING										
ALL WINDOWS COVERED	1 177	NA	980	NA	714	NA	266	NA	197	NA
SOME WINDOWS COVERED	385	NA	313	NA	245	NA	68	NA	72	NA
NO WINDOWS COVERED	2 832	NA	1 633	NA	1 135	NA	498	NA	1 199	NA
NOT REPORTED	108	NA	85	NA	66	NA	19	NA	22	NA
STORM DOORS										
ALL DOORS COVERED	1 285	NA	1 071	NA	792	NA	279	NA	213	NA
SOME DOORS COVERED	490	NA	373	NA	290	NA	83	NA	117	NA
NO DOORS COVERED	2 619	NA	1 480	NA	1 008	NA	472	NA	1 139	NA
NOT REPORTED	109	NA	87	NA	71	NA	17	NA	21	NA
ATTIC OR ROOF INSULATION										
YES	1 975	NA	1 512	NA	1 057	NA	455	NA	463	NA
NO	1 775	NA	952	NA	675	NA	277	NA	823	NA
DON'T KNOW	612	NA	435	NA	338	NA	96	NA	178	NA
NOT REPORTED	140	NA	113	NA	89	NA	23	NA	28	NA

FINANCIAL CHARACTERISTICS OF HOUSING UNITS WITH BLACK HOUSEHOLD HEAD: 1975 AND 1970

(NUMBERS IN THOUSANDS. DATA BASED ON SAMPLE, SEE TEXT. FOR MINIMUM BASE FOR DERIVED FIGURES (PERCENT, MEDIAN, ETC.) AND MEANING OF SYMBOLS, SEE TEXT)

UNITED STATES	TOTAL		INSIDE SMSA'S: TOTAL		INSIDE SMSA'S: IN CENTRAL CITIES		INSIDE SMSA'S: NOT IN CENTRAL CITIES		OUTSIDE SMSA'S	
	1975	1970	1975	1970	1975	1970	1975	1970	1975	1970
ALL OCCUPIED HOUSING UNITS	7 561	6 174	5 872	4 739	4 607	3 833	1 265	906	1 689	1 436
INCOME[1]										
OWNER OCCUPIED	3 309	2 568	2 382	1 825	1 714	1 335	668	490	927	742
LESS THAN $2,000	232	457	129	241	105	168	24	73	103	216
$2,000 TO $2,999	248	194	130	108	89	76	41	31	117	86
$3,000 TO $3,999	201	184	101	108	69	77	33	31	100	76
$4,000 TO $4,999	227	175	142	110	107	79	35	30	85	66
$5,000 TO $5,999	199	177	124	118	87	86	37	33	75	59
$6,000 TO $6,999	175	176	110	125	76	92	35	33	65	50
$7,000 TO $7,999	147	474	93	372	62	276	31	95	54	103
$8,000 TO $9,999	309		218		162		56		91	
$10,000 TO $12,499	375	461	290	398	228	298	62	100	85	63
$12,500 TO $14,999	294		241		183		58		53	
$15,000 TO $24,999	646	234	564	214	392	159	172	55	82	20
$25,000 TO $34,999	186	35	174	33	111	24	63	9	13	3
$35,000 OR MORE	69		65		44		21		4	
MEDIAN	9500	6600	11200	7800	11100	8000	11700	7400	5800	3900
RENTER OCCUPIED	4 252	3 607	3 490	2 913	2 893	2 498	597	416	762	693
LESS THAN $2,000	595	926	444	669	394	575	50	94	150	257
$2,000 TO $2,999	533	403	400	302	341	260	59	42	133	100
$3,000 TO $3,999	527	378	423	289	361	248	62	41	104	89
$4,000 TO $4,999	382	328	311	262	261	225	49	37	71	66
$5,000 TO $5,999	327	305	263	255	216	218	47	36	63	50
$6,000 TO $6,999	224	266	184	229	144	196	39	33	40	37
$7,000 TO $7,999	248	541	211	481	183	412	28	69	37	60
$8,000 TO $9,999	369		313		250		63		56	
$10,000 TO $12,499	424	345	374	318	304	270	71	48	50	27
$12,500 TO $14,999	213		188		149		39		25	
$15,000 TO $24,999	346	101	315	95	237	81	78	14	30	6
$25,000 TO $34,999	55	15	54	13	43	11	10	2	1	1
$35,000 OR MORE	10		9		8		1		1	
MEDIAN	5300	4300	5600	4700	5400	4700	6800	4800	3900	2900
SPECIFIED OWNER OCCUPIED[2]	2 796	2 079	2 065	1 492	1 463	1 070	603	423	731	587
VALUE										
LESS THAN $5,000	162	334	67	120	38	66	29	54	95	214
$5,000 TO $7,499	188	320	89	183	63	134	26	50	99	137
$7,500 TO $9,999	219	310	143	228	116	181	27	47	76	82
$10,000 TO $12,499	237	289	150	229	120	179	30	50	87	60
$12,500 TO $14,999	189	206	148	177	125	136	23	41	42	30
$15,000 TO $17,499	267	191	194	166	153	119	41	46	74	25
$17,500 TO $19,999	245	148	191	135	151	94	40	41	54	14
$20,000 TO $24,999	405	149	333	135	245	91	88	44	72	14
$25,000 TO $29,999	345	96	284	87	195	53	89	35	61	8
$30,000 TO $34,999	160		134		82		53		25	
$35,000 TO $39,999	134	28	111	26	57	14	54	12	23	3
$40,000 TO $49,999	143		129		81		49		13	
$50,000 TO $59,999	62		54		22		32		8	
$60,000 TO $74,999	29	8	28	7	13	4	15	3	1	1
$75,000 OR MORE	10		10		3		7		-	
MEDIAN	18900	10700	20800	12300	19400	12200	24900	13100	13000	6500
VALUE-INCOME RATIO										
LESS THAN 1.5	988	865	763	626	568	466	195	159	225	240
1.5 TO 1.9	477	325	360	247	258	174	102	73	117	78
2.0 TO 2.4	308	204	233	153	155	105	78	48	75	51
2.5 TO 2.9	222	137	156	97	105	67	51	30	66	40
3.0 TO 3.9	249	161	178	109	118	75	60	35	71	51
4.0 OR MORE	529	346	362	232	247	163	115	69	167	115
NOT COMPUTED	24	40	15	28	13	20	2	8	9	12
MEDIAN	1.9	1.7	1.9	1.7	1.8	1.7	2.0	1.8	2.1	1.8
MORTGAGE STATUS										
WITH MORTGAGE, DEED OF TRUST, OR LAND CONTRACT	1 893	NA	1 533	NA	1 104	NA	429	NA	360	NA
OWNED FREE AND CLEAR	904	NA	532	NA	359	NA	173	NA	371	NA

[1]INCOME OF FAMILIES AND PRIMARY INDIVIDUALS IN 12 MONTHS PRECEDING DATE OF ENUMERATION; SEE TEXT.
[2]LIMITED TO 1-FAMILY HOMES ON LESS THAN 10 ACRES AND NO BUSINESS ON PROPERTY.

FINANCIAL CHARACTERISTICS OF HOUSING UNITS WITH BLACK HOUSEHOLD HEAD: 1975 AND 1970--CONTINUED

(NUMBERS IN THOUSANDS. DATA BASED ON SAMPLE, SEE TEXT. FOR MINIMUM BASE FOR DERIVED FIGURES (PERCENT, MEDIAN, ETC.) AND MEANING OF SYMBOLS, SEE TEXT)

UNITED STATES	TOTAL		INSIDE SMSA'S						OUTSIDE SMSA'S	
			TOTAL		IN CENTRAL CITIES		NOT IN CENTRAL CITIES			
	1975	1970	1975	1970	1975	1970	1975	1970	1975	1970
SPECIFIED OWNER OCCUPIED[1]--CON.										
MORTGAGE INSURANCE										
UNITS WITH MORTGAGE OR SIMILAR DEBT	1 893	NA	1 533	NA	1 104	NA	429	NA	360	NA
INSURED BY FHA, VA, OR FARMERS HOME ADMIN.	1 009	NA	859	NA	626	NA	233	NA	151	NA
NOT INSURED OR INSURED BY PRIVATE MORTGAGE INSURANCE[2]	591	NA	454	NA	319	NA	135	NA	138	NA
DON'T KNOW	165	NA	119	NA	86	NA	34	NA	46	NA
NOT REPORTED	127	NA	102	NA	73	NA	28	NA	25	NA
UNITS OWNED FREE AND CLEAR	904	NA	532	NA	359	NA	173	NA	371	NA
REAL ESTATE TAXES LAST YEAR										
LESS THAN $100	833	NA	387	NA	264	NA	123	NA	447	NA
$100 TO $199	312	NA	235	NA	173	NA	62	NA	77	NA
$200 TO $299	219	NA	199	NA	157	NA	42	NA	20	NA
$300 TO $349	96	NA	90	NA	70	NA	21	NA	6	NA
$350 TO $399	82	NA	78	NA	57	NA	22	NA	4	NA
$400 TO $499	146	NA	135	NA	96	NA	39	NA	10	NA
$500 TO $599	99	NA	94	NA	64	NA	29	NA	5	NA
$600 TO $699	75	NA	75	NA	43	NA	32	NA	-	NA
$700 TO $799	48	NA	41	NA	24	NA	16	NA	7	NA
$800 TO $999	70	NA	65	NA	37	NA	28	NA	5	NA
$1,000 OR MORE	70	NA	66	NA	27	NA	39	NA	4	NA
NOT REPORTED	747	NA	602	NA	452	NA	149	NA	145	NA
MEDIAN	161	NA	255	NA	243	NA	298	NA	100-	NA
SELECTED MONTHLY HOUSING COSTS[3]										
UNITS WITH A MORTGAGE	1 893	NA	1 533	NA	1 104	NA	429	NA	360	NA
LESS THAN $100	103	NA	53	NA	42	NA	11	NA	50	NA
$100 TO $119	130	NA	91	NA	78	NA	13	NA	39	NA
$120 TO $149	264	NA	185	NA	149	NA	35	NA	79	NA
$150 TO $174	221	NA	169	NA	129	NA	40	NA	53	NA
$175 TO $199	227	NA	196	NA	152	NA	44	NA	30	NA
$200 TO $224	162	NA	145	NA	105	NA	40	NA	18	NA
$225 TO $249	176	NA	161	NA	105	NA	56	NA	14	NA
$250 TO $274	136	NA	127	NA	85	NA	42	NA	8	NA
$275 TO $299	69	NA	65	NA	49	NA	16	NA	5	NA
$300 TO $349	109	NA	102	NA	66	NA	36	NA	7	NA
$350 TO $399	41	NA	38	NA	17	NA	21	NA	3	NA
$400 TO $499	40	NA	37	NA	19	NA	18	NA	2	NA
$500 OR MORE	22	NA	20	NA	7	NA	14	NA	1	NA
NOT REPORTED	194	NA	145	NA	101	NA	43	NA	49	NA
MEDIAN	189	NA	200	NA	191	NA	229	NA	144	NA
UNITS OWNED FREE AND CLEAR	904	NA	532	NA	359	NA	173	NA	371	NA
LESS THAN $50	291	NA	126	NA	83	NA	42	NA	165	NA
$50 TO $69	210	NA	119	NA	84	NA	35	NA	92	NA
$70 TO $79	84	NA	65	NA	49	NA	15	NA	20	NA
$80 TO $89	64	NA	41	NA	26	NA	15	NA	23	NA
$90 TO $99	35	NA	27	NA	19	NA	8	NA	8	NA
$100 TO $119	55	NA	48	NA	40	NA	7	NA	8	NA
$120 TO $149	36	NA	29	NA	13	NA	16	NA	7	NA
$150 TO $199	14	NA	13	NA	8	NA	5	NA	2	NA
$200 OR MORE	8	NA	7	NA	-	NA	7	NA	1	NA
NOT REPORTED	106	NA	59	NA	37	NA	22	NA	48	NA
MEDIAN	60	NA	68	NA	68	NA	68	NA	50-	NA
SELECTED MONTHLY HOUSING COSTS AS PERCENTAGE OF INCOME[3]										
UNITS WITH A MORTGAGE	1 893	NA	1 533	NA	1 104	NA	429	NA	360	NA
LESS THAN 5 PERCENT	9	NA	9	NA	9	NA	-	NA	-	NA
5 TO 9 PERCENT	114	NA	98	NA	82	NA	16	NA	16	NA
10 TO 14 PERCENT	366	NA	320	NA	218	NA	102	NA	46	NA
15 TO 19 PERCENT	351	NA	293	NA	224	NA	69	NA	58	NA
20 TO 24 PERCENT	227	NA	178	NA	126	NA	52	NA	49	NA
25 TO 29 PERCENT	168	NA	121	NA	73	NA	47	NA	47	NA
30 TO 34 PERCENT	114	NA	93	NA	67	NA	25	NA	21	NA
35 TO 39 PERCENT	85	NA	69	NA	53	NA	16	NA	16	NA
40 TO 49 PERCENT	102	NA	78	NA	53	NA	25	NA	23	NA
50 PERCENT OR MORE	154	NA	121	NA	88	NA	33	NA	33	NA
NOT COMPUTED	8	NA	7	NA	7	NA	-	NA	1	NA
NOT REPORTED	194	NA	145	NA	101	NA	43	NA	49	NA
MEDIAN	20	NA	19	NA	19	NA	21	NA	24	NA

[1]LIMITED TO 1-FAMILY HOMES ON LESS THAN 10 ACRES AND NO BUSINESS ON PROPERTY.
[2]DATA ARE NOT SEPARABLE.
[3]SUM OF PAYMENTS FOR REAL ESTATE TAXES, PROPERTY INSURANCE, UTILITIES, FUEL, WATER, GARBAGE AND TRASH COLLECTION, AND MORTGAGE AT TIME OF ENUMERATION.

FINANCIAL CHARACTERISTICS OF HOUSING UNITS WITH BLACK HOUSEHOLD HEAD: 1975 AND 1970--CONTINUED

(NUMBERS IN THOUSANDS. DATA BASED ON SAMPLE, SEE TEXT. FOR MINIMUM BASE FOR DERIVED FIGURES (PERCENT, MEDIAN, ETC.) AND MEANING OF SYMBOLS, SEE TEXT)

UNITED STATES	TOTAL		INSIDE SMSA'S						OUTSIDE SMSA'S	
			TOTAL		IN CENTRAL CITIES		NOT IN CENTRAL CITIES			
	1975	1970	1975	1970	1975	1970	1975	1970	1975	1970
SPECIFIED OWNER OCCUPIED[1]--CON.										
SELECTED MONTHLY HOUSING COSTS AS PERCENTAGE OF INCOME[2]--CON.										
UNITS OWNED FREE AND CLEAR	904	NA	532	NA	359	NA	173	NA	371	NA
LESS THAN 5 PERCENT	67	NA	44	NA	35	NA	9	NA	23	NA
5 TO 9 PERCENT	210	NA	139	NA	98	NA	41	NA	72	NA
10 TO 14 PERCENT	168	NA	98	NA	66	NA	32	NA	70	NA
15 TO 19 PERCENT	118	NA	67	NA	45	NA	22	NA	51	NA
20 TO 24 PERCENT	70	NA	35	NA	22	NA	13	NA	35	NA
25 TO 29 PERCENT	39	NA	19	NA	11	NA	8	NA	20	NA
30 TO 34 PERCENT	27	NA	13	NA	12	NA	1	NA	14	NA
35 TO 39 PERCENT	21	NA	10	NA	6	NA	4	NA	10	NA
40 TO 49 PERCENT	31	NA	17	NA	9	NA	8	NA	14	NA
50 PERCENT OR MORE	41	NA	31	NA	17	NA	14	NA	10	NA
NOT COMPUTED	7	NA	1	NA	1	NA	-	NA	5	NA
NOT REPORTED	106	NA	59	NA	37	NA	22	NA	48	NA
MEDIAN	14	NA	13	NA	12	NA	14	NA	15	NA
ACQUISITION OF PROPERTY										
PLACED OR ASSUMED A MORTGAGE	2 409	NA	1 890	NA	1 365	NA	525	NA	519	NA
ACQUIRED THROUGH INHERITANCE OR GIFT	112	NA	39	NA	14	NA	25	NA	73	NA
PAID ALL CASH	204	NA	103	NA	62	NA	41	NA	102	NA
ACQUIRED IN OTHER MANNER	23	NA	12	NA	8	NA	4	NA	11	NA
NOT REPORTED	48	NA	21	NA	15	NA	6	NA	27	NA
ALTERATIONS AND REPAIRS DURING LAST 12 MONTHS										
NO ALTERATIONS OR REPAIRS	1 199	NA	815	NA	562	NA	253	NA	384	NA
ALTERATIONS AND REPAIRS COSTING LESS THAN $100[3]	713	NA	539	NA	374	NA	165	NA	174	NA
ADDITIONS	16	NA	6	NA	5	NA	1	NA	10	NA
ALTERATIONS	108	NA	88	NA	61	NA	26	NA	20	NA
REPLACEMENTS	134	NA	99	NA	72	NA	27	NA	35	NA
REPAIRS	558	NA	424	NA	292	NA	133	NA	133	NA
ALTERATIONS AND REPAIRS COSTING $100 OR MORE[3]	1 064	NA	855	NA	636	NA	219	NA	209	NA
ADDITIONS	131	NA	86	NA	64	NA	23	NA	44	NA
ALTERATIONS	370	NA	309	NA	238	NA	72	NA	61	NA
REPLACEMENTS	427	NA	362	NA	281	NA	81	NA	65	NA
REPAIRS	576	NA	476	NA	358	NA	117	NA	101	NA
NOT REPORTED	40	NA	25	NA	15	NA	10	NA	15	NA
PLANS FOR IMPROVEMENTS DURING NEXT 12 MONTHS										
NONE PLANNED	1 235	NA	881	NA	599	NA	282	NA	354	NA
SOME PLANNED	1 274	NA	960	NA	710	NA	251	NA	313	NA
COSTING LESS THAN $100	172	NA	125	NA	94	NA	31	NA	47	NA
COSTING $100 OR MORE	1 055	NA	799	NA	595	NA	204	NA	255	NA
DON'T KNOW	44	NA	33	NA	19	NA	15	NA	11	NA
NOT REPORTED	2	NA	2	NA	1	NA	1	NA	-	NA
DON'T KNOW	251	NA	200	NA	140	NA	60	NA	51	NA
NOT REPORTED	36	NA	23	NA	14	NA	10	NA	13	NA
SPECIFIED RENTER OCCUPIED[4]	4 163	3 413	3 483	2 860	2 893	2 468	590	392	680	553
GROSS RENT										
LESS THAN $50	333	438	220	223	203	180	17	42	112	215
$50 TO $59	159	232	100	168	84	146	16	21	58	65
$60 TO $69	215	301	142	249	122	223	20	27	73	52
$70 TO $79	215	331	152	292	123	264	29	28	63	38
$80 TO $99	465	678	352	632	316	569	37	63	112	46
$100 TO $119	475	529	427	505	386	445	41	60	48	24
$120 TO $149	692	462	639	447	567	385	72	62	53	15
$150 TO $174	488	242	458	234	355	188	103	46	30	8
$175 TO $199	347		339		267		73		7	
$200 TO $224	216		207		170		38		8	
$225 TO $249	165	45	165	43	116	32	49	12	-	2
$250 TO $274	92		87		64		23		5	
$275 TO $299	48		48		25		22		1	
$300 TO $349	49	5	48	4	36	3	12	1	1	-
$350 OR MORE	40		37		22		15		2	
NO CASH RENT	167	152	61	63	37	34	24	29	106	89
MEDIAN	126	89	134	94	130	94	162	100	76	52

[1]LIMITED TO 1-FAMILY HOMES ON LESS THAN 10 ACRES AND NO BUSINESS ON PROPERTY.
[2]SUM OF PAYMENTS FOR REAL ESTATE TAXES, PROPERTY INSURANCE, UTILITIES, FUEL, WATER, GARBAGE AND TRASH COLLECTION, AND MORTGAGE AT TIME OF ENUMERATION.
[3]COMPONENTS MAY NOT ADD TO TOTAL BECAUSE MORE THAN ONE IMPROVEMENT WAS MADE.
[4]EXCLUDES 1-FAMILY HOMES ON 10 ACRES OR MORE.

FINANCIAL CHARACTERISTICS OF HOUSING UNITS WITH BLACK HOUSEHOLD HEAD: 1975 AND 1970--CONTINUED

(NUMBERS IN THOUSANDS. DATA BASED ON SAMPLE, SEE TEXT. FOR MINIMUM BASE FOR DERIVED FIGURES (PERCENT, MEDIAN, ETC.) AND MEANING OF SYMBOLS, SEE TEXT)

UNITED STATES	TOTAL		INSIDE SMSA'S						OUTSIDE SMSA'S	
			TOTAL		IN CENTRAL CITIES		NOT IN CENTRAL CITIES			
	1975	1970	1975	1970	1975	1970	1975	1970	1975	1970
SPECIFIED RENTER OCCUPIED[1]--CON.										
GROSS RENT--CON.										
NONSUBSIDIZED RENTER OCCUPIED[2]	3 295	NA	2 746	NA	2 251	NA	495	NA	549	NA
LESS THAN $50	135	NA	46	NA	35	NA	12	NA	89	NA
$50 TO $59	87	NA	39	NA	31	NA	8	NA	48	NA
$60 TO $69	136	NA	80	NA	70	NA	11	NA	55	NA
$70 TO $79	153	NA	104	NA	85	NA	20	NA	49	NA
$80 TO $99	361	NA	270	NA	237	NA	33	NA	91	NA
$100 TO $119	379	NA	339	NA	309	NA	30	NA	40	NA
$120 TO $149	567	NA	528	NA	472	NA	56	NA	40	NA
$150 TO $174	434	NA	413	NA	328	NA	84	NA	21	NA
$175 TO $199	321	NA	316	NA	247	NA	69	NA	6	NA
$200 TO $224	192	NA	186	NA	152	NA	33	NA	6	NA
$225 TO $249	158	NA	158	NA	111	NA	47	NA	-	NA
$250 TO $274	87	NA	82	NA	61	NA	21	NA	5	NA
$275 TO $299	45	NA	45	NA	24	NA	21	NA	1	NA
$300 TO $349	47	NA	46	NA	34	NA	12	NA	1	NA
$350 OR MORE	40	NA	37	NA	22	NA	15	NA	2	NA
NO CASH RENT	152	NA	56	NA	33	NA	24	NA	96	NA
MEDIAN	136	NA	146	NA	141	NA	169	NA	76	NA
GROSS RENT AS PERCENTAGE OF INCOME										
SPECIFIED RENTER OCCUPIED[1]	4 163	3 413	3 483	2 860	2 893	2 468	590	392	680	553
LESS THAN 10 PERCENT	280	268	203	200	164	173	38	28	77	67
10 TO 14 PERCENT	528	520	433	441	372	386	62	55	94	79
15 TO 19 PERCENT	631	506	544	441	461	382	83	58	87	66
20 TO 24 PERCENT	516	385	453	336	373	292	80	44	63	49
25 TO 34 PERCENT	648	480	555	416	454	361	101	55	93	64
35 TO 49 PERCENT	576	984	501	857	411	747	90	110	75	127
50 PERCENT OR MORE	765		685		576		109		80	
NOT COMPUTED	219	269	110	168	82	127	28	41	109	101
MEDIAN	25	23	26	23	26	23	27	23	22	21
NONSUBSIDIZED RENTER OCCUPIED[2]	3 295	NA	2 746	NA	2 251	NA	495	NA	549	NA
LESS THAN 10 PERCENT	216	NA	157	NA	125	NA	31	NA	59	NA
10 TO 14 PERCENT	427	NA	347	NA	288	NA	59	NA	79	NA
15 TO 19 PERCENT	449	NA	377	NA	317	NA	61	NA	72	NA
20 TO 24 PERCENT	362	NA	319	NA	254	NA	65	NA	43	NA
25 TO 34 PERCENT	485	NA	414	NA	329	NA	85	NA	71	NA
35 TO 49 PERCENT	504	NA	438	NA	365	NA	73	NA	66	NA
50 PERCENT OR MORE	652	NA	592	NA	499	NA	93	NA	60	NA
NOT COMPUTED	201	NA	102	NA	74	NA	28	NA	99	NA
MEDIAN	27	NA	28	NA	28	NA	27	NA	22	NA
CONTRACT RENT										
SPECIFIED RENTER OCCUPIED	4 163	3 413	3 483	2 860	2 893	2 468	590	392	680	553
LESS THAN $50	643	824	347	472	301	386	46	86	296	352
$50 TO $59	267	316	200	281	172	252	27	29	68	35
$60 TO $69	322	425	267	398	222	360	45	38	54	27
$70 TO $79	271	378	230	365	195	332	36	33	40	14
$80 TO $99	468	561	435	546	408	489	28	57	33	15
$100 TO $119	399	336	376	325	346	283	30	42	22	11
$120 TO $149	615	289	585	282	479	236	106	45	30	7
$150 TO $174	404	110	387	107	306	82	81	26	18	3
$175 TO $199	253		245		187		58		8	
$200 TO $249	211	19	209	18	153	13	56	5	2	1
$250 TO $299	88		87		47		40		1	
$300 OR MORE	55	3	53	3	39	2	15	1	2	-
NO CASH RENT	167	152	61	63	37	34	24	29	106	89
MEDIAN	101	71	112	76	107	76	140	78	50-	50-

[1]EXCLUDES 1-FAMILY HOMES ON 10 ACRES OR MORE.
[2]EXCLUDES 1-FAMILY HOMES ON 10 ACRES OR MORE, MOBILE HOMES AND TRAILERS, HOUSING UNITS IN PUBLIC HOUSING PROJECTS, AND HOUSING UNITS WITH GOVERNMENT RENT SUBSIDIES.

CHARACTERISTICS OF HOUSING UNITS WITH HOUSEHOLD HEAD OF SPANISH ORIGIN: 1975 AND 1970

(NUMBERS IN THOUSANDS. DATA BASED ON SAMPLE, SEE TEXT. FOR MINIMUM BASE FOR DERIVED FIGURES (PERCENT, MEDIAN, ETC.) AND MEANING OF SYMBOLS, SEE TEXT)

UNITED STATES	TOTAL		INSIDE SMSA'S						OUTSIDE SMSA'S	
			TOTAL		IN CENTRAL CITIES		NOT IN CENTRAL CITIES			
	1975	1970	1975	1970	1975	1970	1975	1970	1975	1970
ALL OCCUPIED HOUSING UNITS	3 091	2 253	2 564	1 893	1 574	1 229	990	664	527	360
TENURE										
OWNER OCCUPIED	1 330	979	1 016	767	543	406	473	361	314	213
PERCENT OF ALL OCCUPIED	43.0	43.5	39.6	40.5	34.5	33.0	47.8	54.4	59.6	59.2
RENTER OCCUPIED	1 761	1 273	1 548	1 126	1 031	823	517	303	213	147
COOPERATIVES AND CONDOMINIUMS										
OWNER OCCUPIED	22	NA	22	NA	14	NA	8	NA	-	NA
COOPERATIVE OWNERSHIP	8	NA	8	NA	8	NA	-	NA	-	NA
CONDOMINIUM OWNERSHIP	14	NA	14	NA	6	NA	8	NA	-	NA
UNITS IN STRUCTURE										
OWNER OCCUPIED	1 330	979	1 016	767	543	406	473	361	314	213
1, DETACHED	1 155	859	873	665	450	334	423	332	282	194
1, ATTACHED	31	24	30	23	14	17	16	6	1	1
2 TO 4	80	58	75	53	61	42	14	11	5	5
5 OR MORE	17	14	16	13	12	10	3	3	1	1
MOBILE HOME OR TRAILER	47	25	22	13	5	3	17	10	24	12
RENTER OCCUPIED	1 761	1 273	1 548	1 126	1 031	823	517	303	213	147
1, DETACHED	474	400	346	299	157	159	189	140	128	101
1, ATTACHED	99	51	84	48	39	32	45	16	15	3
2 TO 4	414	277	383	253	270	189	113	64	32	24
5 TO 9	274	141	254	134	186	106	69	28	19	7
10 TO 19	137	132	132	127	102	101	30	26	5	5
20 TO 49	193	158	189	156	141	140	47	16	4	2
50 OR MORE	148	105	148	104	133	95	15	10	-	1
MOBILE HOME OR TRAILER	22	9	12	4	3	1	9	3	9	4
YEAR STRUCTURE BUILT										
OWNER OCCUPIED	1 330	979	1 016	767	543	406	473	361	314	213
APRIL 1970 OR LATER	196	NA	137	NA	53	NA	84	NA	60	NA
1965 TO MARCH 1970	160	113	119	85	55	31	65	54	40	28
1960 TO 1964	144	129	117	102	60	42	57	60	26	27
1950 TO 1959	345	300	278	254	137	123	141	131	67	46
1940 TO 1949	181	161	148	127	86	74	62	53	32	34
1939 OR EARLIER	305	277	216	199	152	136	64	63	89	78
RENTER OCCUPIED	1 761	1 273	1 548	1 126	1 031	823	517	303	213	147
APRIL 1970 OR LATER	172	NA	151	NA	72	NA	79	NA	20	NA
1965 TO MARCH 1970	156	90	134	78	81	46	53	32	22	12
1960 TO 1964	122	105	111	94	62	53	49	41	10	11
1950 TO 1959	271	208	233	182	134	112	98	70	39	26
1940 TO 1949	220	227	174	198	111	140	63	58	46	29
1939 OR EARLIER	820	643	744	574	570	471	174	102	76	69
PLUMBING FACILITIES										
OWNER OCCUPIED	1 330	979	1 016	767	543	406	473	361	314	213
WITH ALL PLUMBING FACILITIES	1 301	917	1 000	735	536	392	464	343	300	182
LACKING SOME OR ALL PLUMBING FACILITIES	30	62	16	31	6	14	9	18	14	31
RENTER OCCUPIED	1 761	1 273	1 548	1 126	1 031	823	517	303	213	147
WITH ALL PLUMBING FACILITIES	1 693	1 187	1 495	1 066	1 003	781	493	285	197	121
LACKING SOME OR ALL PLUMBING FACILITIES	68	86	52	60	28	42	24	18	16	26
COMPLETE BATHROOMS										
OWNER OCCUPIED	1 330	NA	1 016	NA	543	NA	473	NA	314	NA
1	753	NA	565	NA	334	NA	231	NA	188	NA
1 AND ONE-HALF	161	NA	128	NA	51	NA	77	NA	32	NA
2 OR MORE	381	NA	302	NA	148	NA	155	NA	78	NA
ALSO USED BY ANOTHER HOUSEHOLD	1	NA	1	NA	1	NA	-	NA	-	NA
NONE	34	NA	19	NA	8	NA	11	NA	16	NA
RENTER OCCUPIED	1 761	NA	1 548	NA	1 031	NA	517	NA	213	NA
1	1 534	NA	1 353	NA	922	NA	432	NA	181	NA
1 AND ONE-HALF	67	NA	63	NA	31	NA	31	NA	4	NA
2 OR MORE	77	NA	65	NA	38	NA	27	NA	12	NA
ALSO USED BY ANOTHER HOUSEHOLD	21	NA	21	NA	15	NA	6	NA	-	NA
NONE	62	NA	46	NA	25	NA	21	NA	16	NA

CHARACTERISTICS OF HOUSING UNITS WITH HOUSEHOLD HEAD OF SPANISH ORIGIN: 1975 AND 1970--CONTINUED

(NUMBERS IN THOUSANDS. DATA BASED ON SAMPLE, SEE TEXT. FOR MINIMUM BASE FOR DERIVED FIGURES (PERCENT, MEDIAN, ETC.) AND MEANING OF SYMBOLS, SEE TEXT)

UNITED STATES	TOTAL		INSIDE SMSA'S						OUTSIDE SMSA'S	
			TOTAL		IN CENTRAL CITIES		NOT IN CENTRAL CITIES			
	1975	1970	1975	1970	1975	1970	1975	1970	1975	1970
ALL OCCUPIED HOUSING UNITS--CON.										
COMPLETE KITCHEN FACILITIES										
OWNER OCCUPIED	1 330	NA	1 016	NA	543	NA	473	NA	314	NA
FOR EXCLUSIVE USE OF HOUSEHOLD	1 321	NA	1 012	NA	543	NA	470	NA	309	NA
ALSO USED BY ANOTHER HOUSEHOLD	-	NA	-	NA	-	NA	-	NA	-	NA
NO COMPLETE KITCHEN FACILITIES	9	NA	4	NA	-	NA	4	NA	6	NA
RENTER OCCUPIED	1 761	NA	1 548	NA	1 031	NA	517	NA	213	NA
FOR EXCLUSIVE USE OF HOUSEHOLD	1 709	NA	1 507	NA	1 002	NA	506	NA	201	NA
ALSO USED BY ANOTHER HOUSEHOLD	2	NA	2	NA	2	NA	-	NA	-	NA
NO COMPLETE KITCHEN FACILITIES	50	NA	39	NA	27	NA	11	NA	11	NA
ROOMS										
OWNER OCCUPIED	1 330	979	1 016	767	543	406	473	361	314	213
1 ROOM	-	4	-	3	-	1	-	1	-	1
2 ROOMS	12	18	8	14	5	8	3	6	4	5
3 ROOMS	41	60	28	43	15	24	13	19	13	17
4 ROOMS	233	192	155	139	88	79	66	61	79	53
5 ROOMS	461	318	355	253	179	134	176	119	106	66
6 ROOMS	350	234	289	192	160	99	129	92	61	42
7 ROOMS OR MORE	233	153	181	124	95	62	86	62	51	29
MEDIAN	5.3	5.2	5.4	5.2	5.4	5.2	5.4	5.3	5.1	5.0
RENTER OCCUPIED	1 761	1 273	1 548	1 126	1 031	823	517	303	213	147
1 ROOM	55	55	51	49	41	38	10	11	4	5
2 ROOMS	137	119	119	105	82	78	37	28	18	13
3 ROOMS	427	304	391	273	254	201	137	72	36	31
4 ROOMS	647	421	565	373	370	271	195	102	81	48
5 ROOMS	335	242	284	211	191	153	93	58	50	30
6 ROOMS	109	98	92	84	63	60	29	24	17	13
7 ROOMS OR MORE	52	36	45	30	29	20	16	9	6	6
MEDIAN	3.9	3.9	3.9	3.9	3.9	3.8	3.9	3.9	4.1	4.0
BEDROOMS										
OWNER OCCUPIED	1 330	979	1 016	767	543	406	473	361	314	213
NONE AND 1	62	81	45	60	25	35	19	25	18	21
2	402	318	289	239	178	139	112	100	113	79
3	666	450	528	361	275	182	253	180	139	88
4 OR MORE	200	131	155	106	65	51	90	56	45	25
RENTER OCCUPIED	1 761	1 273	1 548	1 126	1 031	823	517	303	213	147
NONE AND 1	631	496	576	450	397	338	179	111	55	47
2	758	514	660	450	433	321	227	129	98	64
3	310	216	256	187	170	134	86	52	54	29
4 OR MORE	62	46	56	40	31	29	24	10	6	7
PERSONS										
OWNER OCCUPIED	1 330	979	1 016	767	543	406	473	361	314	213
1 PERSON	85	66	58	45	41	26	17	19	26	21
2 PERSONS	250	179	193	132	99	73	94	59	57	46
3 PERSONS	211	158	161	125	87	67	74	58	50	33
4 PERSONS	283	181	224	147	122	74	102	72	59	34
5 PERSONS	219	144	161	118	84	60	77	58	59	26
6 PERSONS	118	102	100	83	58	43	42	40	18	20
7 PERSONS OR MORE	164	150	119	117	52	62	68	55	45	33
MEDIAN	3.9	4.0	3.9	4.1	3.9	4.0	4.0	4.1	3.9	3.7
RENTER OCCUPIED	1 761	1 273	1 548	1 126	1 031	823	517	303	213	147
1 PERSON	304	185	279	166	202	129	76	37	25	19
2 PERSONS	409	262	363	235	240	173	123	61	46	27
3 PERSONS	390	249	337	224	218	162	119	63	54	24
4 PERSONS	264	217	238	193	162	141	77	52	25	24
5 PERSONS	180	145	154	127	100	92	54	35	26	18
6 PERSONS	92	91	75	79	45	57	30	22	16	12
7 PERSONS OR MORE	123	124	102	102	64	69	38	33	21	22
MEDIAN	2.9	3.3	2.9	3.2	2.8	3.2	3.0	3.3	3.1	3.6
PERSONS PER ROOM										
OWNER OCCUPIED	1 330	979	1 016	767	543	406	473	361	314	213
0.50 OR LESS	408	291	313	218	173	119	139	99	95	73
0.51 TO 1.00	704	465	546	376	298	194	248	182	158	89
1.01 TO 1.50	169	149	124	117	58	64	66	54	45	31
1.51 OR MORE	49	75	34	56	14	29	19	27	16	19

CHARACTERISTICS OF HOUSING UNITS WITH HOUSEHOLD HEAD OF SPANISH ORIGIN: 1975 AND 1970--CONTINUED

(NUMBERS IN THOUSANDS. DATA BASED ON SAMPLE, SEE TEXT. FOR MINIMUM BASE FOR DERIVED FIGURES (PERCENT, MEDIAN, ETC.) AND MEANING OF SYMBOLS, SEE TEXT)

UNITED STATES	TOTAL		INSIDE SMSA'S						OUTSIDE SMSA'S	
			TOTAL		IN CENTRAL CITIES		NOT IN CENTRAL CITIES			
	1975	1970	1975	1970	1975	1970	1975	1970	1975	1970
ALL OCCUPIED HOUSING UNITS--CON.										
PERSONS PER ROOM--CON.										
RENTER OCCUPIED	1 761	1 273	1 548	1 126	1 031	823	517	303	213	147
0.50 OR LESS	499	292	441	258	301	193	141	66	58	34
0.51 TO 1.00	900	626	803	562	551	415	252	148	96	64
1.01 TO 1.50	266	216	225	191	134	139	92	52	40	25
1.51 OR MORE	96	139	78	114	45	77	33	37	19	25
WITH ALL PLUMBING FACILITIES	2 993	2 104	2 496	1 801	1 539	1 173	957	628	498	303
OWNER OCCUPIED	1 301	917	1 000	735	536	392	464	343	300	182
1.00 OR LESS	1 086	717	845	575	465	304	380	271	241	142
1.01 TO 1.50	167	139	122	112	58	62	64	50	45	26
1.51 OR MORE	48	61	34	48	14	26	19	22	14	13
RENTER OCCUPIED	1 693	1 187	1 495	1 066	1 003	781	493	285	197	121
1.00 OR LESS	1 355	865	1 207	782	831	578	376	204	149	83
1.01 TO 1.50	256	205	220	184	131	134	89	49	36	21
1.51 OR MORE	82	117	69	100	41	69	28	31	13	17
HOUSEHOLD COMPOSITION BY AGE OF HEAD										
OWNER OCCUPIED	1 330	979	1 016	767	543	406	473	361	314	213
2-OR-MORE-PERSON HOUSEHOLDS	1 246	913	958	722	501	379	456	342	288	192
MALE HEAD, WIFE PRESENT, NO NONRELATIVES	1 066	781	823	618	427	317	396	301	243	163
UNDER 25 YEARS	48	27	38	20	18	10	19	10	11	7
25 TO 29 YEARS	115	69	78	55	35	25	43	29	37	14
30 TO 34 YEARS	158	98	119	81	68	39	51	41	39	18
35 TO 44 YEARS	268	231	220	190	100	94	120	96	48	41
45 TO 64 YEARS	383	280	305	220	170	118	135	102	78	60
65 YEARS AND OVER	94	76	64	53	35	30	29	22	30	23
OTHER MALE HEAD	58	41	43	33	23	19	20	13	14	9
UNDER 65 YEARS	46	33	36	26	17	15	20	11	9	6
65 YEARS AND OVER	12	9	7	6	6	4	1	3	5	3
FEMALE HEAD	122	91	91	71	51	43	40	28	31	20
UNDER 65 YEARS	98	74	74	59	41	35	33	24	23	15
65 YEARS AND OVER	24	16	17	12	10	8	7	4	8	5
1-PERSON HOUSEHOLDS	85	66	58	45	41	26	17	19	26	21
UNDER 65 YEARS	40	34	29	25	22	14	7	10	11	9
65 YEARS AND OVER	45	32	29	20	20	12	10	8	15	12
RENTER OCCUPIED	1 761	1 273	1 548	1 126	1 031	823	517	303	213	147
2-OR-MORE-PERSON HOUSEHOLDS	1 457	1 088	1 269	960	829	694	441	266	188	128
MALE HEAD, WIFE PRESENT, NO NONRELATIVES	979	784	835	683	522	474	314	209	144	101
UNDER 25 YEARS	197	130	148	111	80	72	67	38	50	20
25 TO 29 YEARS	188	148	162	129	94	87	67	42	26	19
30 TO 34 YEARS	117	123	103	109	65	75	38	34	14	15
35 TO 44 YEARS	215	183	197	161	122	113	75	48	18	22
45 TO 64 YEARS	195	162	167	141	122	102	45	39	28	21
65 YEARS AND OVER	67	37	59	32	38	24	21	9	8	5
OTHER MALE HEAD	102	74	96	66	62	49	34	17	6	8
UNDER 65 YEARS	93	69	88	62	57	46	31	16	6	7
65 YEARS AND OVER	9	5	9	4	6	3	3	1	-	1
FEMALE HEAD	376	229	338	210	245	171	93	39	38	19
UNDER 65 YEARS	353	217	316	200	227	162	88	37	37	17
65 YEARS AND OVER	23	12	22	11	17	9	5	2	1	2
1-PERSON HOUSEHOLDS	304	185	279	166	202	129	76	37	25	19
UNDER 65 YEARS	250	141	229	128	170	100	59	29	21	12
65 YEARS AND OVER	54	45	49	38	32	29	17	9	4	7
PERSONS 65 YEARS OLD AND OVER										
OWNER OCCUPIED	1 330	(NA)	1 016	(NA)	543	(NA)	473	(NA)	314	(NA)
NONE	1 094	(NA)	845	(NA)	444	(NA)	402	(NA)	249	(NA)
1 PERSON	176	(NA)	128	(NA)	75	(NA)	53	(NA)	48	(NA)
2 PERSONS OR MORE	60	(NA)	42	(NA)	23	(NA)	19	(NA)	18	(NA)
RENTER OCCUPIED	1 761	(NA)	1 548	(NA)	1 031	(NA)	517	(NA)	213	(NA)
NONE	1 572	(NA)	1 379	(NA)	915	(NA)	465	(NA)	192	(NA)
1 PERSON	141	(NA)	126	(NA)	90	(NA)	36	(NA)	16	(NA)
2 PERSONS OR MORE	48	(NA)	43	(NA)	27	(NA)	16	(NA)	5	(NA)

CHARACTERISTICS OF HOUSING UNITS WITH HOUSEHOLD HEAD OF SPANISH ORIGIN: 1975 AND 1970--CONTINUED

(NUMBERS IN THOUSANDS. DATA BASED ON SAMPLE, SEE TEXT. FOR MINIMUM BASE FOR DERIVED FIGURES (PERCENT, MEDIAN, ETC.) AND MEANING OF SYMBOLS, SEE TEXT)

UNITED STATES	TOTAL		INSIDE SMSA'S						OUTSIDE SMSA'S	
			TOTAL		IN CENTRAL CITIES		NOT IN CENTRAL CITIES			
	1975	1970	1975	1970	1975	1970	1975	1970	1975	1970
ALL OCCUPIED HOUSING UNITS--CON.										
OWN CHILDREN UNDER 18 YEARS OLD BY AGE GROUP										
OWNER OCCUPIED	1 330	NA	1 016	NA	543	NA	473	NA	314	NA
NO OWN CHILDREN UNDER 18 YEARS	492	NA	361	NA	207	NA	154	NA	132	NA
WITH OWN CHILDREN UNDER 18 YEARS	838	NA	655	NA	336	NA	319	NA	183	NA
UNDER 6 YEARS ONLY	158	NA	122	NA	63	NA	59	NA	36	NA
1	72	NA	60	NA	30	NA	30	NA	13	NA
2	64	NA	48	NA	25	NA	23	NA	16	NA
3 OR MORE	21	NA	14	NA	8	NA	6	NA	7	NA
6 TO 17 YEARS ONLY	436	NA	341	NA	173	NA	167	NA	95	NA
1	150	NA	118	NA	63	NA	55	NA	31	NA
2	126	NA	104	NA	52	NA	52	NA	22	NA
3 OR MORE	160	NA	119	NA	58	NA	61	NA	41	NA
BOTH AGE GROUPS	245	NA	193	NA	100	NA	92	NA	52	NA
2	46	NA	38	NA	22	NA	16	NA	9	NA
3 OR MORE	198	NA	155	NA	78	NA	77	NA	43	NA
RENTER OCCUPIED	1 761	NA	1 548	NA	1 031	NA	517	NA	213	NA
NO OWN CHILDREN UNDER 18 YEARS	792	NA	720	NA	496	NA	224	NA	72	NA
WITH OWN CHILDREN UNDER 18 YEARS	969	NA	828	NA	535	NA	293	NA	141	NA
UNDER 6 YEARS ONLY	351	NA	283	NA	167	NA	116	NA	68	NA
1	218	NA	174	NA	101	NA	72	NA	44	NA
2	101	NA	87	NA	54	NA	33	NA	14	NA
3 OR MORE	32	NA	23	NA	12	NA	11	NA	10	NA
6 TO 17 YEARS ONLY	369	NA	321	NA	223	NA	98	NA	48	NA
1	128	NA	116	NA	78	NA	38	NA	12	NA
2	115	NA	106	NA	81	NA	25	NA	9	NA
3 OR MORE	126	NA	99	NA	64	NA	35	NA	27	NA
BOTH AGE GROUPS	249	NA	224	NA	146	NA	78	NA	25	NA
2	63	NA	60	NA	35	NA	25	NA	3	NA
3 OR MORE	186	NA	164	NA	111	NA	53	NA	22	NA
PRESENCE OF SUBFAMILIES										
OWNER OCCUPIED	1 330	NA	1 016	NA	543	NA	473	NA	314	NA
NO SUBFAMILIES	1 278	NA	976	NA	525	NA	451	NA	303	NA
WITH 1 SUBFAMILY	52	NA	40	NA	17	NA	23	NA	12	NA
SUBFAMILY HEAD UNDER 30 YEARS	28	NA	21	NA	8	NA	13	NA	8	NA
SUBFAMILY HEAD 30 TO 64 YEARS	20	NA	15	NA	8	NA	8	NA	4	NA
SUBFAMILY HEAD 65 YEARS AND OVER	4	NA	4	NA	2	NA	2	NA	-	NA
WITH 2 SUBFAMILIES OR MORE	-	NA	-	NA	-	NA	-	NA	-	NA
RENTER OCCUPIED	1 761	NA	1 548	NA	1 031	NA	517	NA	213	NA
NO SUBFAMILIES	1 713	NA	1 505	NA	1 002	NA	503	NA	209	NA
WITH 1 SUBFAMILY	46	NA	42	NA	29	NA	13	NA	4	NA
SUBFAMILY HEAD UNDER 30 YEARS	31	NA	27	NA	19	NA	8	NA	4	NA
SUBFAMILY HEAD 30 TO 64 YEARS	12	NA	12	NA	9	NA	3	NA	-	NA
SUBFAMILY HEAD 65 YEARS AND OVER	3	NA	3	NA	1	NA	1	NA	-	NA
WITH 2 SUBFAMILIES OR MORE	1	NA	1	NA	-	NA	1	NA	-	NA
PRESENCE OF OTHER RELATIVES OR NONRELATIVES										
OWNER OCCUPIED	1 330	NA	1 016	NA	543	NA	473	NA	314	NA
NO OTHER RELATIVES OR NONRELATIVES	1 093	NA	834	NA	447	NA	386	NA	259	NA
WITH OTHER RELATIVES AND NONRELATIVES	2	NA	2	NA	-	NA	2	NA	-	NA
WITH OTHER RELATIVES, NO NONRELATIVES	217	NA	166	NA	89	NA	77	NA	52	NA
WITH NONRELATIVES, NO OTHER RELATIVES	19	NA	15	NA	6	NA	9	NA	4	NA
RENTER OCCUPIED	1 761	NA	1 548	NA	1 031	NA	517	NA	213	NA
NO OTHER RELATIVES OR NONRELATIVES	1 452	NA	1 270	NA	856	NA	414	NA	182	NA
WITH OTHER RELATIVES AND NONRELATIVES	5	NA	5	NA	1	NA	3	NA	1	NA
WITH OTHER RELATIVES, NO NONRELATIVES	225	NA	199	NA	132	NA	68	NA	26	NA
WITH NONRELATIVES, NO OTHER RELATIVES	78	NA	74	NA	42	NA	32	NA	4	NA
YEARS OF SCHOOL COMPLETED BY HEAD										
OWNER OCCUPIED	1 330	NA	1 016	NA	543	NA	473	NA	314	NA
NO SCHOOL YEARS COMPLETED	58	NA	36	NA	14	NA	21	NA	22	NA
ELEMENTARY: LESS THAN 8 YEARS	299	NA	206	NA	128	NA	78	NA	94	NA
8 YEARS	137	NA	110	NA	68	NA	42	NA	28	NA
HIGH SCHOOL: 1 TO 3 YEARS	198	NA	151	NA	82	NA	69	NA	46	NA
4 YEARS	364	NA	283	NA	138	NA	146	NA	80	NA
COLLEGE: 1 TO 3 YEARS	171	NA	145	NA	77	NA	68	NA	25	NA
4 YEARS OR MORE	104	NA	86	NA	36	NA	49	NA	19	NA
MEDIAN	11.6	NA	12.0	NA	11.3	NA	12.2	NA	9.8	NA

CHARACTERISTICS OF HOUSING UNITS WITH HOUSEHOLD HEAD OF SPANISH ORIGIN: 1975 AND 1970--CONTINUED

(NUMBERS IN THOUSANDS. DATA BASED ON SAMPLE, SEE TEXT. FOR MINIMUM BASE FOR DERIVED FIGURES (PERCENT, MEDIAN, ETC.) AND MEANING OF SYMBOLS, SEE TEXT)

UNITED STATES	TOTAL		INSIDE SMSA'S						OUTSIDE SMSA'S	
			TOTAL		IN CENTRAL CITIES		NOT IN CENTRAL CITIES			
	1975	1970	1975	1970	1975	1970	1975	1970	1975	1970
ALL OCCUPIED HOUSING UNITS--CON.										
YEARS OF SCHOOL COMPLETED BY HEAD--CON.										
RENTER OCCUPIED	1 761	NA	1 548	NA	1 031	NA	517	NA	213	NA
NO SCHOOL YEARS COMPLETED	81	NA	67	NA	38	NA	30	NA	14	NA
ELEMENTARY: LESS THAN 8 YEARS	473	NA	405	NA	275	NA	129	NA	68	NA
8 YEARS	158	NA	143	NA	110	NA	32	NA	16	NA
HIGH SCHOOL: 1 TO 3 YEARS	354	NA	309	NA	223	NA	86	NA	45	NA
4 YEARS	401	NA	362	NA	225	NA	137	NA	40	NA
COLLEGE: 1 TO 3 YEARS	171	NA	156	NA	95	NA	61	NA	15	NA
4 YEARS OR MORE	122	NA	107	NA	65	NA	42	NA	15	NA
MEDIAN	10.5	NA	10.6	NA	10.3	NA	11.3	NA	9.5	NA
YEAR HEAD MOVED INTO UNIT										
OWNER OCCUPIED	1 330	NA	1 016	NA	543	NA	473	NA	314	NA
1974 OR LATER	244	NA	184	NA	86	NA	98	NA	61	NA
MOVED IN WITHIN PAST 12 MONTHS	133	NA	100	NA	43	NA	57	NA	33	NA
APRIL 1970 TO 1973	377	NA	288	NA	155	NA	132	NA	89	NA
1965 TO MARCH 1970	260	NA	213	NA	99	NA	114	NA	47	NA
1960 TO 1964	185	NA	137	NA	87	NA	50	NA	48	NA
1950 TO 1959	174	NA	140	NA	85	NA	55	NA	34	NA
1949 OR EARLIER	90	NA	55	NA	30	NA	25	NA	36	NA
RENTER OCCUPIED	1 761	NA	1 548	NA	1 031	NA	517	NA	213	NA
1974 OR LATER	1 022	NA	891	NA	574	NA	317	NA	132	NA
MOVED IN WITHIN PAST 12 MONTHS	696	NA	591	NA	366	NA	225	NA	105	NA
APRIL 1970 TO 1973	417	NA	365	NA	233	NA	133	NA	51	NA
1965 TO MARCH 1970	223	NA	207	NA	160	NA	47	NA	16	NA
1960 TO 1964	52	NA	45	NA	34	NA	11	NA	7	NA
1950 TO 1959	27	NA	24	NA	17	NA	7	NA	3	NA
1949 OR EARLIER	19	NA	15	NA	13	NA	2	NA	4	NA
HEAD'S PRINCIPAL MEANS OF TRANSPORTATION TO WORK[1]										
OWNER OCCUPIED	971	NA	757	NA	402	NA	356	NA	214	NA
DRIVES SELF	703	NA	553	NA	293	NA	260	NA	150	NA
CARPOOL	194	NA	150	NA	70	NA	80	NA	45	NA
MASS TRANSPORTATION	27	NA	24	NA	19	NA	5	NA	4	NA
BICYCLE OR MOTORCYCLE	10	NA	6	NA	3	NA	3	NA	4	NA
TAXICAB	-	NA	-	NA	-	NA	-	NA	-	NA
WALKS ONLY	17	NA	11	NA	9	NA	2	NA	6	NA
OTHER MEANS	4	NA	3	NA	2	NA	2	NA	1	NA
WORKS AT HOME	11	NA	6	NA	3	NA	3	NA	5	NA
NOT REPORTED	5	NA	5	NA	3	NA	2	NA	-	NA
RENTER OCCUPIED	1 141	NA	985	NA	607	NA	378	NA	156	NA
DRIVES SELF	572	NA	481	NA	249	NA	232	NA	91	NA
CARPOOL	222	NA	184	NA	102	NA	82	NA	38	NA
MASS TRANSPORTATION	200	NA	197	NA	171	NA	25	NA	3	NA
BICYCLE OR MOTORCYCLE	13	NA	11	NA	7	NA	4	NA	1	NA
TAXICAB	3	NA	3	NA	3	NA	-	NA	-	NA
WALKS ONLY	90	NA	75	NA	54	NA	22	NA	15	NA
OTHER MEANS	8	NA	8	NA	7	NA	1	NA	-	NA
WORKS AT HOME	26	NA	18	NA	6	NA	12	NA	8	NA
NOT REPORTED	7	NA	7	NA	7	NA	-	NA	-	NA
DISTANCE FROM HOME TO WORK[1]										
OWNER OCCUPIED	971	NA	757	NA	402	NA	356	NA	214	NA
LESS THAN 1 MILE	67	NA	34	NA	19	NA	15	NA	33	NA
1 TO 4 MILES	279	NA	213	NA	128	NA	85	NA	66	NA
5 TO 9 MILES	176	NA	152	NA	103	NA	49	NA	24	NA
10 TO 29 MILES	266	NA	222	NA	92	NA	130	NA	44	NA
30 TO 49 MILES	41	NA	29	NA	8	NA	21	NA	12	NA
50 MILES OR MORE	13	NA	7	NA	6	NA	1	NA	6	NA
WORKS AT HOME	11	NA	6	NA	3	NA	3	NA	5	NA
NO FIXED PLACE OF WORK	106	NA	82	NA	35	NA	47	NA	24	NA
NOT REPORTED	12	NA	12	NA	8	NA	4	NA	1	NA
MEDIAN	7.1	NA	7.7	NA	6.5	NA	10.2	NA	4.6	NA

[1]LIMITED TO HEADS WHO REPORTED HAVING A JOB THE WEEK PRIOR TO ENUMERATION.

CHARACTERISTICS OF HOUSING UNITS WITH HOUSEHOLD HEAD OF SPANISH ORIGIN: 1975 AND 1970--CONTINUED

(NUMBERS IN THOUSANDS. DATA BASED ON SAMPLE, SEE TEXT. FOR MINIMUM BASE FOR DERIVED FIGURES (PERCENT, MEDIAN, ETC.) AND MEANING OF SYMBOLS, SEE TEXT)

UNITED STATES	TOTAL		INSIDE SMSA'S						OUTSIDE SMSA'S	
			TOTAL		IN CENTRAL CITIES		NOT IN CENTRAL CITIES			
	1975	1970	1975	1970	1975	1970	1975	1970	1975	1970
ALL OCCUPIED HOUSING UNITS--CON.										
DISTANCE FROM HOME TO WORK[1]--CON.										
RENTER OCCUPIED	1 141	NA	985	NA	607	NA	378	NA	156	NA
LESS THAN 1 MILE	158	NA	122	NA	73	NA	49	NA	36	NA
1 TO 4 MILES	352	NA	308	NA	214	NA	94	NA	44	NA
5 TO 9 MILES	205	NA	182	NA	115	NA	66	NA	23	NA
10 TO 29 MILES	236	NA	223	NA	125	NA	98	NA	14	NA
30 TO 49 MILES	28	NA	24	NA	8	NA	16	NA	4	NA
50 MILES OR MORE	12	NA	10	NA	6	NA	4	NA	2	NA
WORKS AT HOME	26	NA	18	NA	6	NA	12	NA	8	NA
NO FIXED PLACE OF WORK	104	NA	78	NA	45	NA	32	NA	26	NA
NOT REPORTED	21	NA	21	NA	15	NA	6	NA	-	NA
MEDIAN	4.8	NA	5.1	NA	4.7	NA	6.5	NA	3.3	NA
TRAVEL TIME FROM HOME TO WORK[1]										
OWNER OCCUPIED	971	NA	757	NA	402	NA	356	NA	214	NA
LESS THAN 15 MINUTES	282	NA	192	NA	101	NA	91	NA	90	NA
15 TO 29 MINUTES	327	NA	271	NA	164	NA	108	NA	56	NA
30 TO 44 MINUTES	142	NA	125	NA	54	NA	70	NA	17	NA
45 TO 59 MINUTES	64	NA	52	NA	28	NA	24	NA	12	NA
1 HOUR TO 1 HOUR AND 29 MINUTES	24	NA	20	NA	11	NA	9	NA	4	NA
1 HOUR 30 MINUTES OR MORE	9	NA	4	NA	3	NA	1	NA	5	NA
WORKS AT HOME	11	NA	6	NA	3	NA	3	NA	5	NA
NO FIXED PLACE OF WORK	106	NA	82	NA	35	NA	47	NA	24	NA
NOT REPORTED	7	NA	5	NA	3	NA	2	NA	1	NA
MEDIAN	21	NA	23	NA	22	NA	23	NA	16	NA
RENTER OCCUPIED	1 141	NA	985	NA	607	NA	378	NA	156	NA
LESS THAN 15 MINUTES	341	NA	265	NA	156	NA	109	NA	77	NA
15 TO 29 MINUTES	350	NA	321	NA	194	NA	126	NA	30	NA
30 TO 44 MINUTES	178	NA	169	NA	102	NA	67	NA	9	NA
45 TO 59 MINUTES	62	NA	59	NA	45	NA	15	NA	2	NA
1 HOUR TO 1 HOUR AND 29 MINUTES	56	NA	55	NA	45	NA	10	NA	1	NA
1 HOUR 30 MINUTES OR MORE	10	NA	7	NA	4	NA	3	NA	3	NA
WORKS AT HOME	26	NA	18	NA	6	NA	12	NA	8	NA
NO FIXED PLACE OF WORK	104	NA	78	NA	45	NA	32	NA	26	NA
NOT REPORTED	13	NA	13	NA	10	NA	3	NA	-	NA
MEDIAN	22	NA	23	NA	24	NA	22	NA	15-	NA
HEATING EQUIPMENT										
OWNER OCCUPIED	1 330	NA	1 016	NA	543	NA	473	NA	314	NA
WARM-AIR FURNACE	542	NA	412	NA	192	NA	221	NA	130	NA
STEAM OR HOT WATER	85	NA	78	NA	59	NA	19	NA	7	NA
BUILT-IN ELECTRIC UNITS	48	NA	37	NA	22	NA	15	NA	11	NA
FLOOR, WALL, OR PIPELESS FURNACE	283	NA	237	NA	109	NA	128	NA	46	NA
ROOM HEATERS WITH FLUE	106	NA	76	NA	38	NA	38	NA	30	NA
ROOM HEATERS WITHOUT FLUE	181	NA	114	NA	98	NA	16	NA	67	NA
FIREPLACES, STOVES, OR PORTABLE HEATERS	51	NA	34	NA	16	NA	18	NA	17	NA
NONE	33	NA	27	NA	9	NA	17	NA	6	NA
RENTER OCCUPIED	1 761	NA	1 548	NA	1 031	NA	517	NA	213	NA
WARM-AIR FURNACE	296	NA	253	NA	153	NA	99	NA	43	NA
STEAM OR HOT WATER	550	NA	530	NA	454	NA	76	NA	20	NA
BUILT-IN ELECTRIC UNITS	93	NA	81	NA	37	NA	44	NA	12	NA
FLOOR, WALL, OR PIPELESS FURNACE	357	NA	315	NA	139	NA	177	NA	41	NA
ROOM HEATERS WITH FLUE	180	NA	141	NA	92	NA	49	NA	39	NA
ROOM HEATERS WITHOUT FLUE	151	NA	112	NA	81	NA	31	NA	39	NA
FIREPLACES, STOVES, OR PORTABLE HEATERS	59	NA	48	NA	24	NA	24	NA	11	NA
NONE	75	NA	67	NA	50	NA	17	NA	8	NA
ALL OCCUPIED HOUSING UNITS	3 091	2 253	2 564	1 893	1 574	1 229	990	664	527	360
AIR CONDITIONING										
ROOM UNIT(S)	742	NA	641	NA	380	NA	261	NA	101	NA
CENTRAL SYSTEM	408	NA	326	NA	155	NA	171	NA	82	NA
NONE	1 941	NA	1 597	NA	1 039	NA	558	NA	344	NA
ELEVATOR IN STRUCTURE										
4 FLOORS OR MORE	336	289	335	289	308	274	27	15	1	1
WITH ELEVATOR	199	120	197	120	177	114	20	6	1	-
WALK-UP	138	169	138	169	131	160	6	9	-	-
1 TO 3 FLOORS	2 755	1 963	2 229	1 604	1 266	955	963	649	526	359

[1]LIMITED TO HEADS WHO REPORTED HAVING A JOB THE WEEK PRIOR TO ENUMERATION

CHARACTERISTICS OF HOUSING UNITS WITH HOUSEHOLD HEAD OF SPANISH ORIGIN: 1975 AND 1970--CONTINUED

(NUMBERS IN THOUSANDS. DATA BASED ON SAMPLE, SEE TEXT. FOR MINIMUM BASE FOR DERIVED FIGURES (PERCENT, MEDIAN, ETC.) AND MEANING OF SYMBOLS, SEE TEXT)

UNITED STATES	TOTAL		INSIDE SMSA'S						OUTSIDE SMSA'S	
			TOTAL		IN CENTRAL CITIES		NOT IN CENTRAL CITIES			
	1975	1970	1975	1970	1975	1970	1975	1970	1975	1970
ALL OCCUPIED HOUSING UNITS--CON.										
BASEMENT										
WITH BASEMENT	968	NA	879	NA	676	NA	204	NA	89	NA
NO BASEMENT	2 123	NA	1 685	NA	898	NA	787	NA	439	NA
SOURCE OF WATER										
PUBLIC SYSTEM OR PRIVATE COMPANY	2 904	NA	2 487	NA	1 572	NA	915	NA	417	NA
INDIVIDUAL WELL	170	NA	67	NA	1	NA	66	NA	102	NA
DRILLED	153	NA	60	NA	1	NA	59	NA	93	NA
DUG	13	NA	5	NA	-	NA	5	NA	9	NA
NOT REPORTED	3	NA	2	NA	-	NA	2	NA	1	NA
OTHER	17	NA	9	NA	-	NA	9	NA	8	NA
SEWAGE DISPOSAL										
PUBLIC SEWER	2 687	NA	2 323	NA	1 514	NA	809	NA	363	NA
SEPTIC TANK OR CESSPOOL	370	NA	223	NA	58	NA	165	NA	148	NA
OTHER	34	NA	18	NA	1	NA	17	NA	16	NA
TELEPHONE AVAILABLE										
YES	2 400	NA	2 024	NA	1 204	NA	820	NA	376	NA
NO	691	NA	540	NA	369	NA	170	NA	151	NA
AUTOMOBILES AND TRUCKS AVAILABLE										
AUTOMOBILES:										
1	1 439	NA	1 156	NA	673	NA	483	NA	283	NA
2	660	NA	528	NA	244	NA	284	NA	133	NA
3 OR MORE	140	NA	116	NA	62	NA	55	NA	24	NA
NONE	851	NA	764	NA	595	NA	168	NA	88	NA
TRUCKS:										
1	528	NA	355	NA	169	NA	186	NA	173	NA
2 OR MORE	38	NA	24	NA	14	NA	10	NA	14	NA
NONE	2 525	NA	2 184	NA	1 390	NA	794	NA	340	NA
OWNED SECOND HOME										
YES	69	68	53	54	31	34	22	21	16	14
NO	3 022	2 184	2 511	1 838	1 542	1 195	968	644	512	346
HOUSE HEATING FUEL										
UTILITY GAS	1 971	1 458	1 645	1 247	999	789	646	457	326	211
BOTTLED, TANK, OR LP GAS	118	121	46	62	3	22	43	39	73	60
FUEL OIL, KEROSENE, ETC.	499	392	459	353	354	272	106	81	40	40
ELECTRICITY	363	150	304	128	143	69	160	59	59	22
COAL OR COKE	2	36	1	29	1	26	-	3	1	7
WOOD	21	16	6	3	4	1	2	2	15	13
OTHER FUEL	9	13	9	12	9	10	-	2	-	1
NONE	108	66	94	60	60	39	34	21	14	7
COOKING FUEL										
UTILITY GAS	2 214	1 673	1 930	1 484	1 298	1 033	632	451	284	189
BOTTLED, TANK, OR LP GAS	163	146	83	80	12	31	71	49	80	67
ELECTRICITY	682	386	531	297	251	140	280	157	151	89
FUEL OIL, KEROSENE, ETC.	4	19	3	17	-	14	3	3	1	2
COAL OR COKE	-	4	-	2	-	2	-	-	-	1
WOOD	8	11	2	2	-	1	2	1	6	9
OTHER FUEL	-	3	-	2	-	2	-	1	-	1
NONE	20	10	16	8	13	6	3	2	4	1

CHARACTERISTICS OF HOUSING UNITS WITH HOUSEHOLD HEAD OF SPANISH ORIGIN: 1975 AND 1970--CONTINUED

(NUMBERS IN THOUSANDS. DATA BASED ON SAMPLE, SEE TEXT. FOR MINIMUM BASE FOR DERIVED FIGURES (PERCENT, MEDIAN, ETC.) AND MEANING OF SYMBOLS, SEE TEXT)

UNITED STATES	TOTAL		INSIDE SMSA'S						OUTSIDE SMSA'S	
			TOTAL		IN CENTRAL CITIES		NOT IN CENTRAL CITIES			
	1975	1970	1975	1970	1975	1970	1975	1970	1975	1970
ALL OCCUPIED 1-FAMILY HOMES	1 828	NA	1 368	NA	669	NA	699	NA	460	NA
STORM WINDOWS OR OTHER PROTECTIVE WINDOW COVERING										
ALL WINDOWS COVERED	231	NA	153	NA	70	NA	83	NA	78	NA
SOME WINDOWS COVERED	105	NA	76	NA	39	NA	36	NA	29	NA
NO WINDOWS COVERED	1 463	NA	1 118	NA	553	NA	565	NA	345	NA
NOT REPORTED	30	NA	21	NA	6	NA	15	NA	9	NA
STORM DOORS										
ALL DOORS COVERED	227	NA	159	NA	88	NA	71	NA	68	NA
SOME DOORS COVERED	116	NA	67	NA	36	NA	30	NA	50	NA
NO DOORS COVERED	1 453	NA	1 120	NA	536	NA	584	NA	333	NA
NOT REPORTED	32	NA	23	NA	9	NA	14	NA	9	NA
ATTIC OR ROOF INSULATION										
YES	907	NA	661	NA	321	NA	340	NA	245	NA
NO	572	NA	430	NA	226	NA	204	NA	142	NA
DON'T KNOW	311	NA	249	NA	111	NA	138	NA	63	NA
NOT REPORTED	38	NA	28	NA	11	NA	17	NA	10	NA

FINANCIAL CHARACTERISTICS OF HOUSING UNITS WITH HOUSEHOLD HEAD OF SPANISH ORIGIN: 1975 AND 1970

(NUMBERS IN THOUSANDS. DATA BASED ON SAMPLE, SEE TEXT. FOR MINIMUM BASE FOR DERIVED FIGURES (PERCENT, MEDIAN, ETC.) AND MEANING OF SYMBOLS, SEE TEXT)

UNITED STATES	TOTAL		INSIDE SMSA'S						OUTSIDE SMSA'S	
			TOTAL		IN CENTRAL CITIES		NOT IN CENTRAL CITIES			
	1975	1970	1975	1970	1975	1970	1975	1970	1975	1970
ALL OCCUPIED HOUSING UNITS	3 091	2 253	2 564	1 893	1 574	1 229	990	664	527	360
INCOME[1]										
OWNER OCCUPIED	1 330	979	1 016	767	543	406	473	361	314	213
LESS THAN $2,000	53	91	35	57	24	33	11	24	17	33
$2,000 TO $2,999	45	49	27	31	16	18	11	13	18	18
$3,000 TO $3,999	67	53	43	35	25	20	18	15	24	18
$4,000 TO $4,999	38	55	29	38	20	24	9	15	8	17
$5,000 TO $5,999	66	62	43	44	19	27	23	17	23	18
$6,000 TO $6,999	66	68	50	51	34	30	16	21	17	17
$7,000 TO $7,999	73	220	49	176	30	97	20	79	23	43
$8,000 TO $9,999	148		105		62		43		43	
$10,000 TO $12,499	179	245	133	212	74	102	59	110	46	34
$12,500 TO $14,999	141		119		60		59		21	
$15,000 TO $24,999	327	112	273	100	126	45	147	55	54	13
$25,000 TO $34,999	89	24	74	21	37	9	37	12	15	3
$35,000 OR MORE	38		35		14		21		4	
MEDIAN	11500	8500	12400	9200	11400	8600	13600	9900	9200	6100
RENTER OCCUPIED	1 761	1 273	1 548	1 126	1 031	823	517	303	213	147
LESS THAN $2,000	131	193	113	164	88	129	25	35	18	29
$2,000 TO $2,999	128	109	116	93	83	70	33	22	11	16
$3,000 TO $3,999	149	126	131	107	102	83	29	24	18	18
$4,000 TO $4,999	155	125	134	108	99	81	35	27	21	17
$5,000 TO $5,999	175	125	146	110	101	82	45	28	28	15
$6,000 TO $6,999	141	112	119	101	78	73	41	27	22	12
$7,000 TO $7,999	145	251	124	228	83	160	42	68	20	23
$8,000 TO $9,999	214		189		122		67		26	
$10,000 TO $12,499	187	171	167	159	102	106	65	53	21	12
$12,500 TO $14,999	125		107		66		40		18	
$15,000 TO $24,999	182	52	175	48	97	32	78	17	7	3
$25,000 TO $34,999	20	10	17	9	7	6	10	2	2	1
$35,000 OR MORE	9		9		3		6		-	
MEDIAN	7000	5700	7100	5800	6500	5600	8200	6600	6400	4600
SPECIFIED OWNER OCCUPIED[2]	1 141	834	879	664	455	341	424	322	262	171
VALUE										
LESS THAN $5,000	39	94	7	45	3	24	4	21	32	48
$5,000 TO $7,499	44	90	17	58	8	39	9	19	27	32
$7,500 TO $9,999	58	93	37	71	29	51	8	20	21	23
$10,000 TO $12,499	75	99	59	79	53	52	6	27	16	21
$12,500 TO $14,999	45	85	31	72	17	41	14	31	14	12
$15,000 TO $17,499	88	86	62	74	41	35	22	40	25	11
$17,500 TO $19,999	92	81	70	73	49	30	21	43	22	8
$20,000 TO $24,999	159	100	127	92	59	35	68	57	32	8
$25,000 TO $29,999	169	74	149	69	66	24	83	44	20	6
$30,000 TO $34,999	109		91		40		51		18	
$35,000 TO $39,999	111	24	96	22	41	7	55	15	15	2
$40,000 TO $49,999	86		72		25		46		14	
$50,000 TO $59,999	33		29		16		13		4	
$60,000 TO $74,999	15	9	12	8	6	3	6	5	3	1
$75,000 OR MORE	19		19		2		18		-	
MEDIAN	24100	13700	26000	15200	22300	12800	28600	17700	17100	8100
VALUE-INCOME RATIO										
LESS THAN 1.5	336	349	242	264	140	152	103	112	94	85
1.5 TO 1.9	205	163	158	137	87	64	71	73	47	26
2.0 TO 2.4	199	101	156	86	70	39	87	47	42	15
2.5 TO 2.9	98	59	80	49	35	22	45	27	18	10
3.0 TO 3.9	146	59	114	48	60	23	54	25	32	11
4.0 OR MORE	149	93	122	73	61	37	61	35	28	20
NOT COMPUTED	8	10	6	7	3	4	3	3	1	3
MEDIAN	2.1	1.7	2.1	1.7	2.0	1.6	2.2	1.8	1.9	1.5-
MORTGAGE STATUS										
WITH MORTGAGE, DEED OF TRUST, OR LAND CONTRACT	836	NA	679	NA	335	NA	344	NA	156	NA
OWNED FREE AND CLEAR	305	NA	199	NA	120	NA	80	NA	106	NA

[1]INCOME OF FAMILIES AND PRIMARY INDIVIDUALS IN 12 MONTHS PRECEDING DATE OF ENUMERATION; SEE TEXT.
[2]LIMITED TO 1-FAMILY HOMES ON LESS THAN 10 ACRES AND NO BUSINESS ON PROPERTY.

FINANCIAL CHARACTERISTICS OF HOUSING UNITS WITH HOUSEHOLD HEAD OF SPANISH ORIGIN: 1975 AND 1970--CONTINUED

(NUMBERS IN THOUSANDS. DATA BASED ON SAMPLE, SEE TEXT. FOR MINIMUM BASE FOR DERIVED FIGURES (PERCENT, MEDIAN, ETC.) AND MEANING OF SYMBOLS, SEE TEXT)

UNITED STATES	TOTAL		INSIDE SMSA'S						OUTSIDE SMSA'S	
			TOTAL		IN CENTRAL CITIES		NOT IN CENTRAL CITIES			
	1975	1970	1975	1970	1975	1970	1975	1970	1975	1970
SPECIFIED OWNER OCCUPIED[1]--CON.										
MORTGAGE INSURANCE										
UNITS WITH MORTGAGE OR SIMILAR DEBT	836	NA	679	NA	335	NA	344	NA	156	NA
INSURED BY FHA, VA, OR FARMERS HOME ADMIN.	363	NA	298	NA	159	NA	140	NA	65	NA
NOT INSURED OR INSURED BY PRIVATE MORTGAGE INSURANCE[2]	338	NA	275	NA	120	NA	154	NA	64	NA
DON'T KNOW	71	NA	60	NA	31	NA	29	NA	11	NA
NOT REPORTED	63	NA	46	NA	25	NA	21	NA	17	NA
UNITS OWNED FREE AND CLEAR	305	NA	199	NA	120	NA	80	NA	106	NA
REAL ESTATE TAXES LAST YEAR										
LESS THAN $100	176	NA	87	NA	51	NA	36	NA	89	NA
$100 TO $199	136	NA	86	NA	55	NA	32	NA	49	NA
$200 TO $299	118	NA	83	NA	52	NA	31	NA	34	NA
$300 TO $349	61	NA	53	NA	27	NA	26	NA	8	NA
$350 TO $399	63	NA	54	NA	22	NA	32	NA	9	NA
$400 TO $499	106	NA	100	NA	50	NA	49	NA	6	NA
$500 TO $599	56	NA	49	NA	17	NA	31	NA	7	NA
$600 TO $699	46	NA	43	NA	23	NA	20	NA	4	NA
$700 TO $799	28	NA	27	NA	13	NA	15	NA	1	NA
$800 TO $999	32	NA	29	NA	11	NA	19	NA	3	NA
$1,000 OR MORE	37	NA	35	NA	8	NA	27	NA	2	NA
NOT REPORTED	282	NA	233	NA	127	NA	106	NA	49	NA
MEDIAN	300	NA	363	NA	312	NA	404	NA	136	NA
SELECTED MONTHLY HOUSING COSTS[3]										
UNITS WITH A MORTGAGE	836	NA	679	NA	335	NA	344	NA	156	NA
LESS THAN $100	36	NA	17	NA	8	NA	9	NA	19	NA
$100 TO $119	49	NA	38	NA	26	NA	13	NA	11	NA
$120 TO $149	97	NA	74	NA	39	NA	35	NA	23	NA
$150 TO $174	85	NA	63	NA	35	NA	29	NA	21	NA
$175 TO $199	106	NA	85	NA	46	NA	39	NA	21	NA
$200 TO $224	101	NA	86	NA	38	NA	48	NA	15	NA
$225 TO $249	71	NA	68	NA	30	NA	38	NA	4	NA
$250 TO $274	56	NA	48	NA	28	NA	20	NA	7	NA
$275 TO $299	51	NA	48	NA	19	NA	30	NA	3	NA
$300 TO $349	70	NA	55	NA	27	NA	28	NA	15	NA
$350 TO $399	22	NA	21	NA	8	NA	13	NA	1	NA
$400 TO $499	23	NA	22	NA	8	NA	15	NA	1	NA
$500 OR MORE	7	NA	7	NA	-	NA	7	NA	-	NA
NOT REPORTED	60	NA	45	NA	25	NA	20	NA	16	NA
MEDIAN	204	NA	211	NA	201	NA	218	NA	170	NA
UNITS OWNED FREE AND CLEAR	305	NA	199	NA	120	NA	80	NA	106	NA
LESS THAN $50	95	NA	44	NA	26	NA	19	NA	51	NA
$50 TO $69	60	NA	43	NA	33	NA	10	NA	17	NA
$70 TO $79	18	NA	12	NA	3	NA	9	NA	6	NA
$80 TO $89	21	NA	18	NA	8	NA	10	NA	4	NA
$90 TO $99	13	NA	8	NA	8	NA	-	NA	5	NA
$100 TO $119	19	NA	17	NA	5	NA	12	NA	2	NA
$120 TO $149	9	NA	9	NA	7	NA	2	NA	-	NA
$150 TO $199	4	NA	2	NA	2	NA	1	NA	1	NA
$200 OR MORE	7	NA	7	NA	2	NA	5	NA	-	NA
NOT REPORTED	58	NA	39	NA	27	NA	12	NA	19	NA
MEDIAN	59	NA	66	NA	62	NA	75	NA	50-	NA
SELECTED MONTHLY HOUSING COSTS AS PERCENTAGE OF INCOME[3]										
UNITS WITH A MORTGAGE	836	NA	679	NA	335	NA	344	NA	156	NA
LESS THAN 5 PERCENT	7	NA	6	NA	6	NA	-	NA	1	NA
5 TO 9 PERCENT	62	NA	55	NA	27	NA	28	NA	7	NA
10 TO 14 PERCENT	149	NA	109	NA	39	NA	69	NA	40	NA
15 TO 19 PERCENT	173	NA	150	NA	75	NA	75	NA	23	NA
20 TO 24 PERCENT	117	NA	97	NA	48	NA	49	NA	20	NA
25 TO 29 PERCENT	91	NA	73	NA	44	NA	30	NA	17	NA
30 TO 34 PERCENT	58	NA	44	NA	17	NA	27	NA	14	NA
35 TO 39 PERCENT	36	NA	31	NA	19	NA	12	NA	5	NA
40 TO 49 PERCENT	34	NA	29	NA	17	NA	13	NA	5	NA
50 PERCENT OR MORE	42	NA	34	NA	16	NA	18	NA	8	NA
NOT COMPUTED	8	NA	6	NA	3	NA	3	NA	1	NA
NOT REPORTED	60	NA	45	NA	25	NA	20	NA	16	NA
MEDIAN	20	NA	20	NA	21	NA	19	NA	20	NA

[1]LIMITED TO 1-FAMILY HOMES ON LESS THAN 10 ACRES AND NO BUSINESS ON PROPERTY.
[2]DATA ARE NOT SEPARABLE.
[3]SUM OF PAYMENTS FOR REAL ESTATE TAXES, PROPERTY INSURANCE, UTILITIES, FUEL, WATER, GARBAGE AND TRASH COLLECTION, AND MORTGAGE AT TIME OF ENUMERATION.

FINANCIAL CHARACTERISTICS OF HOUSING UNITS WITH HOUSEHOLD HEAD OF SPANISH ORIGIN: 1975 AND 1970--CONTINUED

(NUMBERS IN THOUSANDS. DATA BASED ON SAMPLE, SEE TEXT. FOR MINIMUM BASE FOR DERIVED FIGURES (PERCENT, MEDIAN, ETC.) AND MEANING OF SYMBOLS, SEE TEXT)

UNITED STATES	TOTAL		INSIDE SMSA'S						OUTSIDE SMSA'S	
			TOTAL		IN CENTRAL CITIES		NOT IN CENTRAL CITIES			
	1975	1970	1975	1970	1975	1970	1975	1970	1975	1970
SPECIFIED OWNER OCCUPIED[1]--CON.										
SELECTED MONTHLY HOUSING COSTS AS PERCENTAGE OF INCOME[2]--CON.										
UNITS OWNED FREE AND CLEAR	305	NA	199	NA	120	NA	80	NA	106	NA
LESS THAN 5 PERCENT	31	NA	17	NA	11	NA	6	NA	14	NA
5 TO 9 PERCENT	94	NA	62	NA	28	NA	34	NA	32	NA
10 TO 14 PERCENT	61	NA	40	NA	24	NA	16	NA	21	NA
15 TO 19 PERCENT	23	NA	15	NA	9	NA	5	NA	9	NA
20 TO 24 PERCENT	9	NA	6	NA	3	NA	3	NA	2	NA
25 TO 29 PERCENT	8	NA	6	NA	5	NA	1	NA	2	NA
30 TO 34 PERCENT	5	NA	5	NA	3	NA	2	NA	-	NA
35 TO 39 PERCENT	7	NA	6	NA	6	NA	-	NA	1	NA
40 TO 49 PERCENT	3	NA	2	NA	2	NA	1	NA	1	NA
50 PERCENT OR MORE	6	NA	2	NA	2	NA	-	NA	4	NA
NOT COMPUTED	-	NA	-	NA	-	NA	-	NA	-	NA
NOT REPORTED	58	NA	39	NA	27	NA	12	NA	19	NA
MEDIAN	10	NA	10	NA	12	NA	9	NA	10	NA
ACQUISITION OF PROPERTY										
PLACED OR ASSUMED A MORTGAGE	1 021	NA	814	NA	421	NA	393	NA	208	NA
ACQUIRED THROUGH INHERITANCE OR GIFT	16	NA	7	NA	7	NA	1	NA	9	NA
PAID ALL CASH	73	NA	39	NA	22	NA	18	NA	34	NA
ACQUIRED IN OTHER MANNER	18	NA	10	NA	5	NA	5	NA	8	NA
NOT REPORTED	13	NA	9	NA	2	NA	7	NA	4	NA
ALTERATIONS AND REPAIRS DURING LAST 12 MONTHS										
NO ALTERATIONS OR REPAIRS	452	NA	329	NA	175	NA	154	NA	123	NA
ALTERATIONS AND REPAIRS COSTING LESS THAN $100[3]	323	NA	261	NA	127	NA	134	NA	62	NA
ADDITIONS	8	NA	7	NA	3	NA	4	NA	1	NA
ALTERATIONS	76	NA	60	NA	27	NA	34	NA	16	NA
REPLACEMENTS	61	NA	45	NA	30	NA	14	NA	16	NA
REPAIRS	240	NA	198	NA	97	NA	101	NA	43	NA
ALTERATIONS AND REPAIRS COSTING $100 OR MORE[3]	448	NA	358	NA	181	NA	177	NA	90	NA
ADDITIONS	70	NA	56	NA	28	NA	28	NA	14	NA
ALTERATIONS	180	NA	146	NA	83	NA	63	NA	35	NA
REPLACEMENTS	156	NA	128	NA	59	NA	69	NA	28	NA
REPAIRS	266	NA	212	NA	113	NA	98	NA	54	NA
NOT REPORTED	14	NA	10	NA	2	NA	9	NA	4	NA
PLANS FOR IMPROVEMENTS DURING NEXT 12 MONTHS										
NONE PLANNED	552	NA	416	NA	221	NA	194	NA	137	NA
SOME PLANNED	461	NA	375	NA	192	NA	183	NA	86	NA
COSTING LESS THAN $100	67	NA	48	NA	26	NA	22	NA	19	NA
COSTING $100 OR MORE	372	NA	306	NA	151	NA	155	NA	66	NA
DON'T KNOW	20	NA	19	NA	14	NA	5	NA	2	NA
NOT REPORTED	2	NA	2	NA	-	NA	2	NA	-	NA
DON'T KNOW	117	NA	81	NA	41	NA	41	NA	35	NA
NOT REPORTED	11	NA	7	NA	2	NA	6	NA	4	NA
SPECIFIED RENTER OCCUPIED	1 737	1 232	1 541	1 105	1 031	817	510	288	196	127
GROSS RENT										
LESS THAN $50	51	80	42	59	30	47	13	12	9	21
$50 TO $59	29	58	21	46	19	37	2	9	8	12
$60 TO $69	40	95	33	80	20	64	13	16	7	15
$70 TO $79	51	118	40	105	28	87	12	18	11	13
$80 TO $99	127	266	106	245	85	197	21	49	20	21
$100 TO $119	196	216	162	204	130	153	32	51	33	12
$120 TO $149	326	192	291	183	201	125	90	58	35	9
$150 TO $174	280	120	266	115	175	71	92	44	14	5
$175 TO $199	227		213		139		74		14	
$200 TO $224	125		117		62		55		8	
$225 TO $249	68	32	64	31	35	19	29	13	4	1
$250 TO $274	46		45		27		17		1	
$275 TO $299	29		29		16		13		-	
$300 TO $349	29	5	29	4	19	3	10	2	-	-
$350 OR MORE	30		28		16		12		2	
NO CASH RENT	82	50	53	32	30	16	24	16	29	18
MEDIAN	151	98	154	100	147	96	166	112	117	75

[1]LIMITED TO 1-FAMILY HOMES ON LESS THAN 10 ACRES AND NO BUSINESS ON PROPERTY.

[2]SUM OF PAYMENTS FOR REAL ESTATE TAXES, PROPERTY INSURANCE, UTILITIES, FUEL, WATER, GARBAGE AND TRASH COLLECTION, AND MORTGAGE AT TIME OF ENUMERATION.

[3]COMPONENTS MAY NOT ADD TO TOTAL BECAUSE MORE THAN ONE IMPROVEMENT WAS MADE.

[4]EXCLUDES 1-FAMILY HOMES ON 10 ACRES OR MORE.

FINANCIAL CHARACTERISTICS OF HOUSING UNITS WITH HOUSEHOLD HEAD OF SPANISH ORIGIN: 1975 AND 1970--CONTINUED

(NUMBERS IN THOUSANDS. DATA BASED ON SAMPLE, SEE TEXT. FOR MINIMUM BASE FOR DERIVED FIGURES (PERCENT, MEDIAN, ETC.) AND MEANING OF SYMBOLS, SEE TEXT)

UNITED STATES	TOTAL		INSIDE SMSA'S: TOTAL		INSIDE SMSA'S: IN CENTRAL CITIES		INSIDE SMSA'S: NOT IN CENTRAL CITIES		OUTSIDE SMSA'S	
	1975	1970	1975	1970	1975	1970	1975	1970	1975	1970
SPECIFIED RENTER OCCUPIED[1]--CON.										
GROSS RENT--CON.										
NONSUBSIDIZED RENTER OCCUPIED[2]	1 496	NA	1 336	NA	877	NA	459	NA	159	NA
LESS THAN $50	25	NA	19	NA	12	NA	7	NA	6	NA
$50 TO $59	16	NA	14	NA	12	NA	2	NA	3	NA
$60 TO $69	28	NA	22	NA	15	NA	8	NA	6	NA
$70 TO $79	36	NA	31	NA	22	NA	9	NA	6	NA
$80 TO $99	91	NA	74	NA	56	NA	18	NA	17	NA
$100 TO $119	167	NA	141	NA	112	NA	29	NA	25	NA
$120 TO $149	277	NA	246	NA	165	NA	81	NA	31	NA
$150 TO $174	259	NA	247	NA	161	NA	86	NA	12	NA
$175 TO $199	215	NA	201	NA	131	NA	70	NA	14	NA
$200 TO $224	113	NA	106	NA	56	NA	50	NA	7	NA
$225 TO $249	65	NA	61	NA	33	NA	27	NA	4	NA
$250 TO $274	43	NA	43	NA	26	NA	17	NA	-	NA
$275 TO $299	28	NA	28	NA	14	NA	13	NA	-	NA
$300 TO $349	29	NA	29	NA	19	NA	10	NA	-	NA
$350 OR MORE	29	NA	27	NA	16	NA	11	NA	2	NA
NO CASH RENT	73	NA	47	NA	27	NA	20	NA	26	NA
MEDIAN	156	NA	159	NA	155	NA	168	NA	123	NA
GROSS RENT AS PERCENTAGE OF INCOME										
SPECIFIED RENTER OCCUPIED[1]	1 737	1 232	1 541	1 105	1 031	817	510	288	196	127
LESS THAN 10 PERCENT	85	103	75	90	44	69	31	21	10	13
10 TO 14 PERCENT	232	224	197	202	117	149	80	53	35	23
15 TO 19 PERCENT	274	220	246	201	174	144	72	56	29	19
20 TO 24 PERCENT	229	156	200	143	126	105	74	39	29	13
25 TO 34 PERCENT	315	173	290	158	190	118	00	41	24	15
35 TO 49 PERCENT	208	270	191	247	140	189	50	57	17	24
50 PERCENT OR MORE	294		271		193		78		22	
NOT COMPUTED	101	86	70	65	46	43	24	22	31	21
MEDIAN	25	20	26	20	27	21	24	20	22	19
NONSUBSIDIZED RENTER OCCUPIED[2]	1 496	NA	1 336	NA	877	NA	459	NA	159	NA
LESS THAN 10 PERCENT	79	NA	71	NA	44	NA	27	NA	9	NA
10 TO 14 PERCENT	201	NA	172	NA	101	NA	72	NA	28	NA
15 TO 19 PERCENT	225	NA	203	NA	138	NA	65	NA	22	NA
20 TO 24 PERCENT	193	NA	170	NA	105	NA	65	NA	23	NA
25 TO 34 PERCENT	268	NA	249	NA	157	NA	92	NA	18	NA
35 TO 49 PERCENT	183	NA	169	NA	127	NA	41	NA	14	NA
50 PERCENT OR MORE	260	NA	243	NA	167	NA	76	NA	17	NA
NOT COMPUTED	87	NA	59	NA	39	NA	20	NA	28	NA
MEDIAN	25	NA	26	NA	27	NA	24	NA	21	NA
CONTRACT RENT										
SPECIFIED RENTER OCCUPIED[1]	1 737	NA	1 541	NA	1 031	NA	510	NA	196	NA
LESS THAN $50	92	NA	64	NA	43	NA	21	NA	28	NA
$50 TO $59	56	NA	40	NA	29	NA	11	NA	16	NA
$60 TO $69	69	NA	59	NA	43	NA	16	NA	10	NA
$70 TO $79	74	NA	57	NA	44	NA	13	NA	18	NA
$80 TO $99	169	NA	143	NA	115	NA	28	NA	26	NA
$100 TO $119	219	NA	196	NA	138	NA	59	NA	22	NA
$120 TO $149	348	NA	330	NA	234	NA	96	NA	17	NA
$150 TO $174	262	NA	245	NA	145	NA	100	NA	17	NA
$175 TO $199	163	NA	157	NA	95	NA	62	NA	5	NA
$200 TO $249	117	NA	114	NA	63	NA	50	NA	4	NA
$250 TO $299	54	NA	53	NA	29	NA	24	NA	1	NA
$300 OR MORE	32	NA	29	NA	22	NA	7	NA	2	NA
NO CASH RENT	82	NA	53	NA	30	NA	24	NA	29	NA
MEDIAN	132	NA	136	NA	131	NA	149	NA	88	NA

[1] EXCLUDES 1-FAMILY HOMES ON 10 ACRES OR MORE.
[2] EXCLUDES 1-FAMILY HOMES ON 10 ACRES OR MORE, MOBILE HOMES AND TRAILERS, HOUSING UNITS IN PUBLIC HOUSING PROJECTS, AND HOUSING UNITS WITH GOVERNMENT RENT SUBSIDIES.

U.S. Dept. of Commerce, Bureau of the Census and U.S. Dept. of HUD (1977) Stock No. 003-024-01368-1.

Part seven :
Index

Index

A

Abortions, 103-104
Administration for Children, Youth and Families, Office of Human Development Services: *HEW News, January 7, 1977*, 381
Adolescents, 387-407: children's cases disposed of by juvenile courts, 411; early, 387-389; group foster homes for, 393-407; juvenile court-cases handled, table, 411; juveniles held in custody, by type of facility, 410; persons in custody in training schools for juvenile delinquents and in detention homes, table, 411; preparing for parenthood, 390-392; statistics on early, 388
Adoption, single-parent, 115; statistics, 409-410
Adults, mid-life transition for, 212-215. *See also* Roles
Aid to Families with Dependent Children, 74
Alcohol: consumption of, table, 428; drinking levels of junior and senior high school students, 464
Alcoholism: affect on family of, 447-448; family affect on, 451-453; family therapy as treatment for, 447-453; relationship between, and child abuse and neglect, 382-386
Al-Anon, 452
Alternative life styles, as a political act, 16
American Council of Parent Cooperatives, 128
American Humane Association: *Highlights of National Study of Child Neglect and Abuse Reporting for 1975*, 375-377

B

Baby carriers, 270
Baby carriers benefit parents too, 270-271
Bailey, Douglas B. and Robert L. Lindamood: *Parent and Family Life Education*, 122-124
Beit-Hallahmi, Benjamin and Albert I. Rabin, *The Kibbutz as a Social Experiment and as a Child-Rearing Laboratory*, 272-281
Benton, M., 106-112
Birth rate: by median interval between, by race, 1939-1969, table, 458; by race, by live-birth order, 1940-1970, table, 457-458; fertility rate and, by age of mother, by race, 1940-1970, table, 456-457. *See also* Childbirth
Births: expected in woman's lifetime, 104-105; premaritally-conceived, statistics, 102
Black head of household: characteristics of housing with, table, 646-653; family income with, tables, 491-492, 494-495, 496-497; financial characteristics of housing with, table, 654-657
Blacks: income of women, graph, 522; individual income of, table, 499-502
Blood, Robert O., Jr. and Donald M. Wolfe, 134, 136, 137, 141
Boys: encouragement of, toward independent exploration, 64; preference for, 63
Broderick, Carlfred B.: *Fathers*, 106-112
Bryant, Barbara Everitt: *Motherhood, Family Planning, and Child Care*, 94-100
Butler, Dodie, with Joe Reiner and Bill Treanor: *Group Foster Homes*, 393-407

C

Census, U.S., information on mothers but not on fathers in, 107
Child abuse and neglect, 368-386; description of child abusers, 110, 383; description of Parents Anonymous, 378-380; diagnosing and treating, 368-386; grant to Parents Anonymous, 381; incest, 383, 386; National Study of Child Neglect and Abuse Reporting, 375-377; relationship between alcoholism and, 382-386; statistics on, 375-377; World of Abnormal Rearing, 369-374. *See also* National Center on Child Abuse and Neglect
Child Abuse Prevention and Treatment Act: defines child abuse and neglect, 382; when signed into law and agency established by, 368
Child adoptions: by type, table, 410; in selected states and Puerto Rico, table, 409
Child advocacy, examples of effective, 257, 260-263
Child and family development, information clearinghouse on, 234
Child care: arrangements, 117-118, 120; father's role in, 69-70; forms of, used by working mothers, 95-96; journals related to, 327; number of children who need, 353; quality versus quantity of attention to children, 309-311; waiting on children, 311-313
Child development, 270-320, 327-350: comprehensive programs for, defined, 322; day care as an aid to, 323, 349; dependence and independence, 313-314; importance of free time, 301-320; kibbutz child-rearing practices, 272-281; Mother-Child Home Program, 282-291; need for close contact with parents, 270-271; need for program for infants, 293; preschool, 327-350; program to foster cognitive and socioemotional development of low-income 2- to 4-year-olds, 282-291; references, 349-350; separation process, 305-309; state offices of, 231; TV occupies what once was free time, 301-320; Verbal Interaction Project, 282
Child development, major aspects of, 329-341; cognition, 127, 333-334; competence, 332-333; identity, physical and personal, 330-332; language, 330; learning, 338-341; morals, 336-337; personal styles, 335; playing and reality, 338; social and emotional growth, 334-335. *See also* Learning theories
Child development, preconditions of: healthy genetic endowment, 328; models, 329; physical care, love, and attention, 329; prenatal care, 328-329
Child development, problems in: as a normal part of growing up, 341-342; developmental retardation, 342-344; fears and habits, 348-349; hyperkinetic behavioral disturbance and hypoactivity, 344-345; language, 345; physical, 347-348; social, 345-347. *See also* Retardation
Childbirth: genetic counseling before, 328; instance of, and lifetime births expected per 1,000 women by race and marital status, table, 454; instance of, per 1,000 women by race and marital status, and percent childless for women ever married, table, 455; nurse-midwifery service in, 459-461; prenatal care for, 328-329. *See also* Birth rate
Childless married women, proportion of, 101
Childlessness, 60-61
Child-rearing: in the kibbutz, 273-281; psychological studies of, in the kibbutz, 274-276; stresses of, 243-245
Children: cases disposed of by juvenile courts, table, 411; cigarette smoking among, aged 12-18, according to sex and age, table, 465; custody arrangements for, 114-115; diagnostic and educational services for preschool, 126; drinking levels of, as junior and senior high school students, 464; height of, according to sex and age, table, 462; home care assistance for families with, in the Netherlands, 438-443, in Sweden, 432-438, in the U.S., 443-446; household tasks assigned to boys and girls, 65; housing discrimination against, 570; impact on, of changes in the family roles of men and women, 65, 68-69; in low-income families, 282-291; inequality of health services for, 466-470; juvenile court—cases handled, table,

411; need for close contact with parents, 270-271; need for states to provide services for parents with young, 243-245; percent distribution of families, by number of own children under 18, table, 409; persons in custody in training schools for juvenile delinquents and in detention homes, table, 411; persons under 18, by presence of parents, table, 409; pressures for achievement on boys and girls, 65; socialization experiences of boys and girls, 62; state plans for services to, 246-269; toy libraries for, 128; weight of, according to sex and age, table, 463; White House Conference (1970) on, 244; with multiple caretakers, 273-274. *See also* Adolescents, Boys, Child abuse and neglect
Children's Defense Fund of the Washington Research Project, Inc.: *Title XX: Social Services in Your State—A Child Advocate's Handbook for Action*, 246-269; *What Difference Does Health Care Make in the Lives of Children?* and *Major Federal Programs Which Finance or Provide Health Services for Children and Expectant Mothers*, 466-473
Child's literature. *See* Sex role stereotyping
Cohen, Donald J., in collaboration with Ada S. Brandegee: *Serving Preschool Children*, 321-350
Comprehensive Annual Services Program Plan, 247-251
Conflict: and its management, 148-154; areas of, in marriage, 154-156; types of, 164-171. *See also* Marriage
Contraception: effect of widespread use of, on families, 60; use of various methods of, table, 421-422
Counselling, 484
Couple's life course, flexibility in, 6
Credit, discrimination and homeownership, 578-586
Crowe, Natalie D. and Barbara A. Pine: *Family Day Care: An Education and Support System Model Developed by Cooperative Extension of New York State*, 351-358

D

Daniels, Arlene Kaplan: *Marital Status and Family*, 73-77
Day care, 321-367; arrangements of children 3 to 13 years old, table, 408; as an aid to child development, 323; as extension of family, 322-323; as intervention, 323; as setting for parent education, 127; costs of, by state, 359-367; center-based, 325; custodial, defined, 321; dangers of, 324; developmental, defined, 322; Division made part of Children's Bureau, 234; establishing state plans for services, 254-255; expenditures in first program (Title XX) year, by state, 265; family, a community based educational and support program for, 351-358; family, defined, 324, 352; family group, 325; family, newsletter for parents, 356; family, reasons some parents choose, 353; family, resource center, 354-355; in-home, 324; network or system, 325; number and percentage of children receiving care in various settings, 359-367; nursery schools, defined, 321-322; organizations which publish materials relevant to, 326-327; quality day care, defined, 322; references on, 326; role of, for children with developmental retardation, 342-344; ways it can support development of child, 349
De Francis, Vincent: *American Humane Association Publishes Highlights of National Study of Child Neglect and Abuse Reporting for 1975*, 375-377
Ditella, Kamala and John Lind: *Baby Carriers in Bolivia and Sweden*, 270-271
Divorce: in the United States, 183; no-fault legislation, 114; points of interest on laws, by state, 78-86; rates, 188-189; research on, 75
Divorced women: credit discrimination against, 582-583; housing discrimination against, 572
Divorces, number, timing, and duration of, 201-211

E

Early childhood education, 229, 234
Early intervention programs, 233-234
Education Commission of the States: *Programs for Parents of Infants and Young Children*, 123-127; *The Need for States to Provide Services to Parents with Young Children*, 243-245; *Programs for Adolescents*, 390-392
Education, compensatory (defined), 322
Elderly, home care assistance for, in the Netherlands, 438-443, in Sweden, 432-438, in the U.S., 438-446
Equality, sex, 15. *See also* Housing, Sex discrimination, Women
Erickson, Rosemary, 106
Erikson, Eric, "eight stages" of man, 212-213
Ethnic cultures, 27-28

F

Family: characteristics of new forms of, 18-22; companionate, 12-14; definitions of, 19; effect of adverse legislation on new forms of, 22; effect on, of emphasis on economic success, 4, 7; history of the, 25-37; individuals as part of the, 25-36; life cycle for "typical" mothers, 101-105; need for coordinated services for, 245; power structure, 133; role of wife-mother and role of father in nuclear, 4-5; size decreases, 60; working class, 477-487. *See also* Child care, Child development, Children, Fathers, Housing, Income, Mothers, Parents
Family cycle, 29
Family heads, female (statistics), 130. *See also* Black head of household, Spanish origin head of household
Family life: effect on, of the Industrial Revolution, 4; more public prior to the 18th century, 4
Family Life Council, 117, 120
Family life education programs, 122-124; topics for, 123
Family patterns, rebellion against traditional, in early years of kibbutz, 273
Family planning, 95, 98, 100
Family therapy: as an alcoholism prevention model, 450-451; as treatment for alcoholism, 447-453; theory of, 448
Family transitions, timing of, 28-30
Fathers: influence on infant's social behavior of interactive and child-care characteristics, 295-300; models for, 110-111; single-parent, 113-121; step-, 108; style of interaction with their children, elements affecting, 108-111; types of, 107-108
Feminist movement, 5-6. *See also* Women's movement

G

Gieseman, Raymond W., with the collaboration of Georgena Potts and Rosalie Epstein: *Rent or Buy? Evaluating Alternatives in the Shelter Market*
Glazer, Nona: *Housework: A Review Essay*, 87-93; *Interpersonal Relationships and Changing Perspectives on the Family*, 9-24
Glick, Paul C. and Arthur J. Norton: *Family Life Cycle Events*, 101-105; *Marrying, Divorcing, and Living Together in the U.S. Today*, 188-198
Goldschmidt, Judith, and Rosemary Mann: *The Nurse- Midwifery Service at San Francisco General Hospital*, 459-461

H

Handelman, Phyllis: *Mid-Life Transition and Contextual Change*, 212-216
Handicapped, home care assistance for: in the Netherlands, 438-443; in Sweden, 432-438, in the U.S., 438-446
Hareven, Tamara K.: *Family Time and Historical Time*, 25-37
Head Start, 129, 229, 232-234, 240
Health services: children's health as it relates to quality and incidence of, 466-470; federal programs financing or providing, for children and expectant mothers, table, 471-473
Health statistics, 415-431, 454-458; abortions, 103-104; alcohol consumption, table, 428; consumer products with highest product hazard index score, table, 430-431; contraception methods used, table, 421-422; death rates, by age and sex, table, 424; exercise, by age, sex, and type of activity, table, 425; gonorrhea cases, table, 426-427; life expectancy by sex and age, table, 423; obesity according to age and sex, table, 425; smoking status by age and sex, table, 429; syphilis cases, table, 426-427; venereal disease cases reported annually by type, table, 426-427
See also Birth rate; Childbirth; Medical care
Helfer, Ray E.: *The Diagnostic Process and Treatment Programs*, 368-374
HEW (Health, Education, and Welfare) Regional Offices, 268-269
Hindman, Margaret: *Child Abuse and Neglect: The Alcohol Connection*, 382-386; *Family Therapy in Alcoholism*, 447-453
Hoffman, Lois Wladis: *Changes in Family Roles, Socialization, and Sex Differences*, 59-72
Home help: description of services rendered by, for elderly, handi-

capped, and families, 432-446; in the Netherlands, 438-443; in Sweden, 432-438; in the U.S., 443-446
Home Start, 129
Homemakers: economic disadvantages of, 184; legal status of, 78-86
Homeownership: affects of price changes on, 539, table, 540; alternative investments to, tables, 547-548; amount of income spent on, 539; credit discrimination regarding, 478-486; downpayment required for, 542; FHA, VA, and conventional loans, 1970-74, table, 543; gross monthly outlays (excluding mortgage), 544, 549-551, table, 550; market value, 545, 562, table, 554; marketing discrimination towards, 575-578; minority-group member discrimination regarding, 591-593; mortgage terms and interest rates, 542, 549, tables, 560-562; net monthly outlay, table, 553; selling costs, 546, tables, 554-555; selling proceeds, 545, 553, table, 555; settlement costs required for, 542; sex discrimination in, 574-589; solar energy aspects of, 601-615; tax benefits, 539; tax liability with deductions for mortgage interest and real estate taxes, table, 550; tax liability without deductions for mortgage interest and real estate taxes, table, 551; terms of purchase, 541, 549, table, 550; trends, 1920-1970, chart, 565. *See also* Housing, Mortgage
Household tasks: assigned to boys and girls, 65; divisions of, between husband and wife, 68; time spent on, 50-52
Housework: and the valuation of women, 136; how single parent fathers manage, 119; monetary value of, 86
Housework: A Review Essay, 87-93
Housing: assistance given minority employees by corporate employers, 591-599; characteristics of new, tables, 616, 638-645; comparative investment returns from rented vs. owned, 548-559; construction costs of, table, 616; financial characteristics of, tables, 629-632, 642-644, 654-657, 666-669; racial discrimination in, 590-600; rental vs. purchase, 537-565; taxes on, table, 630, 643, 655, 667; sex discrimination in, 566-589; statistics, 616-669; trends, 1920-1970, chart, 565; value of, table, 629, 642, 666. *See also* Black household head, Homeownership, Spanish origin household head, Rental housing
Human values replace materialistic values, 15
Husband-wife decision making, 133

I

Income statistics, 488-533: as related to housing, tables, 629-631, 633, 635, 641-642, 654-655, 666-667; family, tables, 489-498; family, by age of head, table, 498; family, by educational attainment, table, 491, 494, 499-502; family, by occupation, table, 490-493; family, by race, table, 496-497; individual, by age, table, 499-502, 506; family (1969), distribution nationally, 243-244; individual, by education, table, 506-507; individual, by occupation, table, 499-502; individual, by region, table, 599-602
Inheritance, 78-86
Insurance, employee, table, 516-517
Investment: average annual yield on selected types of, table, 564; factors for compounding returns and costs of, table, 563; factors for use in estimating accumulated savings from, table, 564; future value of, 562-564; homeownership vs. other savings methods, 548-559; solar energy as, 606-609
IQ outcomes of the Mother-Child Home Program, longitudinal, 282-291

J

Jaques, Elliott, 212-213
Jung, Carl, 212-213

K

Kahn, Alfred J., and Sheila B. Kamerman: *Helping People at Home in Sweden and the Netherlands*, 432-446
Kibbutz: child-rearing patterns in, 272-281; Israeli, 18
Kotelchuck, Milton: *Father Caretaking Characteristics and Their Influence on Infant-Father Interaction*, 295-300

L

Learning theories, 338-341; association, 339; cognitive, 339-340; psychoanalytic, 340; reinforcement, 338-339; relations between, 340-341
Le Masters, E.E., 243
Levenstein, Phyllis, Sidney Levenstein, and John Madden: *Longitudinal IQ Outcomes of the Mother-Child Home Program*, 282-291
Lind, John and Kamala Ditella: *Baby Carriers in Bolivia and Sweden*, 270-271
Lopata, Helena Znaniecki: *Results of Social Change: Social Institutions-Community-Family*, 3-8; *Widowhood: Social Norms and Social Integration*, 217-225

M

Madden, John, Phyllis Levenstein, and Sidney Levenstein: *Longitudinal IQ Outcomes of the Mother-Child Home Program*, 282-291
McEaddy, Beverly Johnson: *Women Who Head Families: A Socio-economic Analysis*, 527-533
Marital relationship, 92
Marital stability: and educational level, 192-193, 195-196; four elements involved in preserving, 109
Marital status: of the black population, 199; of the population, by sex, 199; of the population, by sex and age, 200; of the Spanish-origin population, 200
Marriage: changing structure of, in the United States, 178; expanding definition of, 75; negotiation in, 143-147; observational-experimental method of studying power in, 134; power in, dependent on resources, 131, 135, 138; power, negotiation, and conflict in, 131-176; survey method to study power in, 133-134; two-career, 180; two-person career, 179; violence in, 156-164. *See also* Conflict and its management, Couple's life course
Marriages: number, timing, and duration of, 201-211; remarriage, 197-198
Married women, rights for, 175
Marrying, Divorcing, and Living Together in the U.S. Today, 188-198
Medical care: barriers to, table, 419-420; families with a usual place of, table, 415; places of, table, 416-418. *See also* Home help
Medicare, home help provisions of, 444
Meier, John H.: *Current Status and Future Prospects for the Nation's Children and Their Families*, 229-242
Men: middle adulthood of, 213-214; role changes of, related to women's changing roles, 487; working class, 482-484. *See also* Fathers
Metropolitan areas, map of standard, 618-619
Mid-life transition, 212-215
Minority-group members: housing discrimination against, 590-600
Mobile homes, characteristics of, table, 633-637
Mortgage: balance owed on, 546, tables, 555, 561; cost to finance $1,000, selected years and rates of interest, table, 560; effects of terms on cost of financing, 543, table, 550; federal support and regulation of, 605; interest as a percent of annual mortgage payments, table, 562; interest rates, 543, for FHA, VA, and conventional loans, 1970-74, table, 543; lenders, types of, 604-605, chart, 603; sex discrimination regarding, 578-586; tax liability, tables, 551-552. *See also* Homeownership, Solar energy (mortgage financing for)
Mortgages on housing, tables, 630, 655, 666-667
Mother is primary influence on her child's attitudes and developing abilities, 292
Mother-Child Home Program, 282-291
Motherhood, 59-61, 95
Mothers: effect on family of working, 67-69; family life cycle for "typical," 101-105

N

National Commission on the Observance of International Women's Year: *American Women Today and Tomorrow*, 94-100
National Center on Child Abuse and Neglect: awarded grant to Parents Anonymous, 381; when established and function described, 368
Neighborhood Family Development Centers, 238-242
Nuclear family: role of father, 5; role of wife-mother, 4-5

O

Oakley, Ann, 87, 89-90
Open housing centers: 591-593, 597-599
Orthner, Dennis K., Terry Brown, and Dennis Ferguson: *Single-parent Fatherhood: An Emerging Family Life Style*, 113-121

P

Parent and family life education, 122-124
Parent cooperatives, 128
Parent education, 125: in day care settings, 127; on radio and TV, 129; school-related programs, 125-126; skills taught in programs, 125
Parenthood classes, 120
Parent-Child Development Centers, 235-238, 292-294
Parenting, 76-77
Parents care of children: half-busy syndrome, 309-311; quality versus quantity of attention to children, 309-311
Parents: comparison of time spent with infants by mothers and fathers in various activities, 297; government assistance for single, 117; kinship support for single, 119; modeling for, 110-111; program for, of infants under three years old, 292-294; programs for young, 127; single-parent adoption, 115; support services for, 127-128; women as single, 76. *See also* Fathers, Mothers
Parents' Club, 126-127
Parents Without Partners, 117
Parent-Teachers Associations sponsor parent education programs, 125
Pleck, Joseph H.: *The Work-Family Role System*, 49-58
Poverty: extent of, table, 508-515; health care for children related to, 466-470
Prenatal care: children's health related to, 468; federal programs providing, table, 471-473
Property laws of special interest, by state, 78-86

R

Rabin, Albert I. and Benjamin Beit-Hallahmi: *The Kibbutz as a Social Experiment and as a Child-Rearing Laboratory*, 272-281
Rape, legal definitions by states as regards married or separated couples, 78-86
Reed, Judith: *Working with Abusive Parents*, 378-380
Relationships, types of interpersonal, 10-11
Rental housing: affects of price changes on, 539; amount of income spent on, 539; amount of monthly savings required to offset net proceeds from owning housing, 556-558, tables, 556-557; child discrimination in, 570; cost of, tables, 631-632, 634, 643-644, 656-657, 668-669; minority-group member discrimination in, 593-599; sex discrimination in, 568-574; solar energy aspects of, 613-614. *See also* Housing
Retardation: developmental, 342-344; role of day care for children with, 343-344; sensory problems, mental retardation, and environmental deprivation as causes of, 342-343
Roles: men's and women's, 49-58; of individuals in the family, 25-37; parents' expectations for their children as adults, 61, 66; work and family, 51-56

S

Safilios-Rothschild, Constantina, 133, 135, 138
Scanzoni, Letha and John Scanzoni: *Process in Marriage: Power, Negotiation, and Conflict*, 131-174
Seifer, Nancy: *The Working Family in Crisis: Who is Listening?* 477-487
Separation process, 305-306: effect on mother, 308-309
Separation protest, 298
Sex differences, 59, 61-62
Sex discrimination: by brokers and developers, 575-578; by landlords, 568-573; by lenders, 578-586; in housing, 566-589; in the schools, 481. *See also* Single women, Workplaces, sex-segregated
Sex equality, 15. *See also* Housing, Sex discrimination, Women
Sex role stereotyping in children's literature, 65
Sex roles and child-rearing patterns in the kibbutz, 279-280
Siblings, 29
Single women: credit discrimination against, 578-582; housing discrimination against, 570, 572, 576-578
Smith, Dorothy E., 92
Social services programs, state, 246-269
Sociological measurements, 132
Solar energy: cost-value disparity of, 606-608; energy savings with, 610-611, investment value of, 606-608; lenders' perspective on, 605-612, chart, 608; mortgage financing terms for, 601, 612-615; mortgage financing terms' affect on solar costs, table, 602; system type, housing type, and ease of financing, 612-614; technical performance of systems of, 609-610
Spanish Americans: income of women, graph, 522; individual income of, table, 499-502
Spanish origin household head: characteristics of housing with, table, 658-665; family income with, table, 492-495; financial characteristics of housing with, table, 666-669
State agencies for Title XX, 266
Statistics: number of families, by characteristics, 42, 43, 128; female family heads, 128; households, 38-41; married couples, 43; population, 44; varied, which relate to the family , 234-235
Stauber, Karl N.: *Early Adolescents: Neglected, Misunderstood, Miseducated*, 387-389
Step-fathers, 108

T

Taxes. *See* Homeownership
Title IX of the Education Amendments of 1972, 481
Title XX of the Social Security Act, 246-269; calendar, 258-259; federal allocations, use, and median income-by state, 264; state agencies for, 266

U

Unemployment, 482-484
Uniform Marriage and Divorce Act, 184
Urrows, Elizabeth and Henry Urrows: *A Pilot with a Difference*, 292-294
U.S. Bureau of the Census: *Number, Timing, and Duration of Marriages and Divorces in the United States: June 1975*, 201-211
U.S. Dept. of HEW, Office of Human Development: *National Summary of Type of Day Care*, 359-367
U.S. Dept. of HEW, Public Health Service, Health Resources Administration. *See tables listed under* Health statistics
U.S. Office of Child Development: new name of office, 229f; Parent Child Development Centers, 292-294

V

Verbal Interaction Project, 282
Violence. *See* Child abuse, Marriage, violence in

W

White House Conference on Children (1970), 244
Widowed persons are less likely than divorced persons to remarry, 206
Widowhood, 217-225
Widows: living arrangements of, 219; support systems for, 220, 222
Widows and widowers, neighborhood networks of support for, 222-223
Wife abuse, 78-86
Winn, Marie: *Television and Free Time*, 301-320
Women: a sociology for, 92; as activists, 485; as heads of families, 527-533; balancing outlook, 94-97; educational attainment of, 520-521; employment of, 518-526, 530; equal employment opportunities for, 486-487; expanding outlook, 94-97; function in the family, 74; income of, 520, 522, 523; increased employment of, 67-68; married career, in Sweden, 177; middle-class, 74; minority, in families, 75; principal occupations of, table, 518-519; proportion of married women who are childless, 101; role changes of, effect family, 487; roles of, 88-90; single, without dependents, 76; traditional outlook, 94-97; use of leisure time by, 73; work patterns of, 523-526; working class, 477-487. *See also* Divorced women, Married women, Mothers, Property laws, Single women, Working wives
Women's movement, 17, 478-481, 486-487. *See also* Feminist movement
Women's status in the family in Eastern Europe, 176
Work for pay, effect on family, 218
Work-family role system, 49-58
Working wives, 50-54
Workplace, sex-segregated, 53-54, 58
Wright, Elizabeth: *Marriage: Focus on Change*, 175-183; *Divorce in the United States*, 183-187